T0350797

Alternative Investments

Alternative Investments

CAIA *Level I*

Fourth Edition

Donald R. Chambers
Mark J.P. Anson
Keith H. Black
Hossein B. Kazemi

WILEY

Library of Congress Cataloging-in-Publication Data:

Names: Chambers, Donald R., author. | Anson, Mark Jonathan Paul, author. |
   Black, Keith H., author. | Anson, Mark Jonathan Paul. CAIA level I. |
   CAIA Association.
Title: Alternative investments : CAIA level I / Donald R. Chambers, Mark
   J.P. Anson, Keith H. Black, Hossein B. Kazemi, CAIA Association.
Other titles: CAIA level I | CAIA level one
Description: Fourth Edition. | Hoboken : Wiley, 2020. | Series: The Wiley finance |
   Revised edition of CAIA level I, [2015]
Identifiers: LCCN 2019035282 (print) | LCCN 2019035283 (ebook) |
   ISBN 9781119604143 (hardback) | ISBN 9781119604174 (adobe pdf) |
   ISBN 9781119604150 (epub)
Subjects: LCSH: Investments. | Securities. | Portfolio management.
Classification: LCC HG4521 .C45123 2019 (print) | LCC HG4521 (ebook) |
   DDC 332.63–dc23
LC record available at https://lccn.loc.gov/2019035282
LC ebook record available at https://lccn.loc.gov/2019035283

Contents

CHAPTER 7
Measures of Risk and Performance   193

PART 2

Real Assets

CHAPTER 9

PART 3

Hedge Funds

CHAPTER 14

Structure of the Hedge Fund Industry   **415**

PART 4

Private Securities

CHAPTER 20

Private Equity Assets   **635**

PART 5

Structured Products

CHAPTER 23

Introduction to Structuring   **749**

CHAPTER 24
Credit Risk and Credit Derivatives   **775**

*A*lternative Investments is designed as the primary reading resource for the Level I exam of the Chartered Alternative Investment Analyst (CAIA) Association's Charter program, as well as a textbook for university courses and a resource for alternative investment professionals. This book began three editions ago as a revision of Mark Anson's *Handbook of Alternative Assets* and represents another milestone in our efforts to continuously improve and update the CAIA curriculum. This edition includes material from a variety of contributors to the third edition of the CAIA Level II textbook. To ensure that the material best reflects up-to-date practices in the area of alternative investments, the CAIA Association invited a group of leading industry professionals to review the series, covering core areas of alternative investments: real assets, hedge funds, private equity/credit, and structured products.

FOUNDATION

Since its inception in 2002, the CAIA Association has strived to be the leader in alternative investment education worldwide, and to be the catalyst for the best education in the field wherever it lies. The CAIA program was established with the help of a core group of faculty and industry experts who were associated with the University of Massachusetts and the Alternative Investment Management Association (AIMA). From the beginning, the Association recognized that a meaningful portion of its curriculum must be devoted to codes of conduct and ethical behavior in the investment profession. To this end, with permission and cooperation of the CFA Institute, we have incorporated its Code of Ethics and the *CFA Standards of Practice Handbook* into our curriculum. Further, we leverage the experience and contributions of our members and other alternative investment professionals who serve on our board and committees to create and update the CAIA Association program's curriculum and its associated readings.

The quality, rigor, and relevance of our curriculum readings derive from the ideals upon which the CAIA Association was based. The CAIA program offered its first Level I examination in February 2003. Our first class consisted of 43 dedicated investment professionals who passed the Level I and Level II exams and met the other requirements of membership. Many of these founding members were instrumental in establishing the CAIA designation as the global mark of excellence in alternative investment education. Through their support and with the help of the founding cosponsors, the AIMA and the Center for the International Securities and Derivatives Markets (CISDM), the CAIA Association is now firmly established as the most comprehensive and credible designation in the rapidly growing sphere of alternative investments.

The AIMA is the hedge fund industry's global, not-for-profit trade association, with over 2,000 corporate members worldwide. Members include leading hedge fund managers, fund of hedge funds managers, prime brokers, legal and accounting services, and fund administrators. They all benefit from the AIMA's active influence in policy development; its leadership in industry initiatives, including education and sound practice manuals; and its excellent reputation with regulators.

The CISDM of the Isenberg School of Management of the University of Massachusetts, Amherst seeks to enhance the understanding of the field of alternative investments through research, education, and networking opportunities for member donors, industry professionals, and academics.

The CAIA Association has experienced rapid growth in its membership over the past 17 years. It is now a truly global professional organization with over 11,000 members in over 90 countries. We strive to stay nimble in our process so that curriculum remains relevant and keeps pace with the constant changes in this dynamic industry.

BENEFITS

Although the CAIA Association's origins are largely based in the efforts of professionals in the hedge fund and managed futures space, these founders correctly identified a void in the wider understanding of alternative investments as a whole. From the beginning, the CAIA curriculum has also covered private equity, commodities, and real assets, always with an eye toward shifts in the industry. Today, several hundred CAIA members identify their main area of expertise as real estate or private equity; several hundred more members are from family offices, pension funds, endowments, and sovereign wealth funds that allocate across multiple classes within the alternative investment industry. To ensure benefit to the widest spectrum of members, we have developed curriculum subcommittees that represent each area of coverage within the curriculum. Alternative investment areas and products share some distinct features, such as the relative freedom on the part of investment managers to act in the best interests of their investors, alignment of interests between asset owners and asset managers, and relative illiquidity of investment positions of some investment products. These characteristics necessitate conceptual and actual modifications to the standard investment performance analysis and decision-making paradigms.

Our curriculum readings are designed with two goals in mind. First, to provide the readers with tools needed to solve problems they counter in performing their professional duties. Second, to provide them with a conceptual framework that is essential for investment professionals who strive to keep up with new developments in the alternative investment industry.

Readers will find the publications in our series to be beneficial, whether from the standpoint of allocating to new asset classes and strategies in order to gain broader diversification or from the standpoint of a specialist needing to understand better the competing options available to sophisticated investors globally. In both cases, readers will be better equipped to serve their clients' needs.

THE CAIA PROGRAMS AND THE CAIA ALTERNATIVE INVESTMENT ANALYST SERIES

The CAIA Level I required readings are contained in this one text, supplemented only by the CFA Institute's *Standards of Practice Handbook*. Level I candidates are assumed to have mastered some knowledge of financial markets, securities pricing, and derivatives markets in advance of commencing studies for the Level I exam.

Many resources are freely available on our website (caia.org). We will continue to update the *CAIA Level I Study Guide* every six months (each exam cycle). The study guide outlines all of the readings and corresponding learning objectives (LOs) that candidates are responsible for meeting. The guide also contains important information for candidates regarding the use of LOs, testing policies, topic weightings, where to find and report errata, and much more. The entire exam process is outlined in the *CAIA Candidate Handbook* and is available at caia.org. Candidates can also access a workbook that solves the problems presented at the end of each chapter of this book and other important study aids.

We believe you will find this series to be the most comprehensive, rigorous, and globally relevant source of educational material available within the field of alternative investments.

Donald R. Chambers, PhD, CAIA
Associate Director of Curriculum
CAIA Association
June 2019

Acknowledgments

We would like to thank the many individuals who played important roles in producing this book. In particular, we owe great thanks to William Kelly, Chief Executive Officer of the CAIA Association, and our committee members:

CAIA Allocator Advisory Board and CAIA Job Task Analysis Committee

Sean Anthonisz, CAIA, Mine Super & The University of Sydney Business School
Frank Barbarino, CAIA, Templum, Inc
James Bennett, CAIA, Maine Public Employees Retirement System
Robert Bennett-Lovesey, CAIA, Global ARC & CAIA Singapore
Jim Bethea, CAIA, University of Iowa Foundation
Ryan Bisch, CAIA, Ontario Power Generation
Cameron Black, CAIA, Bluc Cross Blue Shield of Arizona
Dominic Blais, CAIA, Canadian Medical Protective Association
Joseph Borda, CAIA
Alex Bradford, CAIA, Starwood Capital
Elizabeth Burton, CAIA, Hawaii Employees Retirement System
Nathan Butler, CAIA, Voya Financial
Jenny Chan, CAIA, Children's Hospital of Philadelphia
Gang Chen, CAIA, PIMCO
Anthony (Tony) Cowell, KPMG
Edward (Ned) Creedon, University of Illinois Foundation
Pamela Fennelly Campbell, CAIA, Washington University
Darren Foreman, CAIA, Public School Employees Retirement System of Penn
Marcus Frampton, CAIA, Alaska Permanent Fund
Chase Frei, CAIA, Ashland Partners & Company LLP
John Freihammer, CAIA, Chicago Teachers Pension Fund
Craig Grenier, CAIA, Northeastern University Endowment
Weiyu Guo, CAIA, Huajin Capital (International) Ltd
Bobby Hagedorn, CAIA, Missouri Patrol Employees' Retirement System
Sajal Heda, CAIA, DAMAC Investment Company (Dubai)
Jeremy Heer, CAIA, The University of Chicago
Katy Huang, CAIA, Deutsche Bank (Suisse) SA

Drew Lerardi, CAIA, Exelon Corporation

Jason Josephiac, CAIA, United Technologies Corporation

Panayiotis Lambropoulos, CAIA, Employees Retirement Sysyem of Texas

Julia H. Lee, CAIA, Michigan State University

Grant Leslie, CAIA Tennessee Consolidated Retirement System

Yasir Mallick, CAIA, University of Toronto Asset Management

Tom Masthay, CAIA Texas Municipal Retirement System

Jason Morrow, CAIA, Utah Retirement Systems

Courtney Ann, CAIA, InvestorSpeak

Chad Myhre, CAIA, Public School & Education Employee Retirement Systems of Missouri

Michael Nicks, CAIA, Pepperdine University Endowment

Mansco Perry, CAIA Minnesota State Board of Investment

Steven Price, CAIA, Ohio School Employees Retirement System

Lin Qu, CAIA, Independent

Brian Quinn, CAIA, Newton Investment Management

Sarah Samuels, CAIA, NEPC

Andrew Sawyer, CAIA, Maine Public Employees Retirement System

Wolfdieter Schnee, CAIA, VP Fund Solutions (Liechtenstein) AG

Jamey Sharpe, CAIA, Blue Cross Blue Shield Association

Joseph Simonian, Quantitative Research, Natixis Investment Managers

Gaurav Singh, CAIA, Kuwait International Bank

Benjamin Skrodzki, CAIA, Teachers' Retirement System of the State of Illinois

Ken Stemme, CAIA, UAW Retiree Medical Benefits Trust

Graham Tedesco, CAIA, Storage Deluxe

Ryan Tidwell, CAIA, Oklahoma State University Foundation

Hilary Wiek, CAIA, Formerly the Saint Paul & Minnesota Community Foundations

Shane Willoughby, CAIA, State Universities Retirement System of Illinois

Michael Weinberg, CIO, MOV37

Thomas Woodbury, CAIA, University of Pennsylvania Investment Office

Gerald Yahoudy, CAIA, New York State Teachers

Ernest Yeung, CAIA, Changsheng Fund Management Ltd

Jasmine Yu, CAIA, BNY Mellon

Contributing Authors

Jim Campasano

Michal E. Crowder

Satyabrota Das, CAIA

Malay K. Dey

Jaeson Dubrovay, CAIA

Urbi Garay

Kathryn Kaminski, CAIA

Jim Kyung-Soo Liew

George Martin

Pierre-Yves Mathonet

Thomas Meyer

Putri Pascualy

Jason Scharfman, CAIA

Ed Szado

Reviewers and Members of Curriculum Committee

James Bachman, CAIA

Gordon Barnes, CAIA

David Blitz

Douglas Cumming

Samuel Gallo, CAIA

Sean Gill, CAIA

James T. Gillies, CAIA

Mark Hutchinson

Georg Inderst

Tom Johnson, CAIA

Tom Kehoe, CAIA

Jeff H. Li

David McCarthy

Sanjay Nawalkha

Ludovic Phalippou

Mark Rzepczynski

Danny Santiago, CAIA

Christopher Schelling, CAIA

Richard Spurgin

Shelly Tilaye, CAIA

Evgeny Vostretsov, CAIA

Mark Wiltshire, CAIA

Special credit goes to CAIA staff for their valuable contributions in painstakingly bringing the fourth edition to completion.

CAIA Staff

Charles Alvarez Zamorano, CAIA, Associate Director of Research and Publications

Yaseen Gholizadeh, Curriculum Intern

Nelson Lacey, Director of Exams

Kristaps Licis, Senior Associate Director of Exams

Nancy E. Perry, Curriculum and Exams Associate

About the Authors

The CAIA Association is an independent, not-for-profit global organization committed to education and professionalism in the field of alternative investments. The Association was established in 2002 by industry leaders under the guidance of the Alternative Investment Management Association (AIMA) and the Center for International Securities and Derivatives Markets (CISDM) with the belief that a strong foundation of knowledge is essential for all professionals. The curriculum includes two exams (Level I and Level II) administered to professional analysts in this growing field so that, upon successful completion, the individuals are designated "Chartered Alternative Investment Analysts" (CAIA). The CAIA designation has a great deal of prestige in the global community. Members come from over 80 countries on six continents.

Dr. Donald R. Chambers, CAIA, is Associate Director of Programs at the CAIA Association; Chief Investment Officer of Biltmore Capital Advisors; and Emeritus Professor at Lafayette College in Easton, Pennsylvania. Dr. Chambers previously served as Director of Alternative Investments at Karpus Investment Management. He is a member of the editorial board of the *Journal of Alternative Investments*.

Dr. Mark J. P. Anson, CAIA, CFA, CPA, PhD, JD, is a board member of CAIA and the President and Chief Investment Officer of the Bass Family Office—winner of the Family office of the Year award for 2014–2015. Dr. Anson previously served as President and Executive Director of Investment Services at Nuveen Investments Inc., Chief Executive Officer of both the British Telecom Pension Scheme and its wholly owned asset management company in London, Hermes Pension Management Limited, and Chief Investment Officer at California Public Employees' Retirement System. He has published over 100 research articles in professional journals, has won two Best Paper Awards, is the author of six financial textbooks, and sits on the editorial boards of several financial journals.

Dr. Keith H. Black, CAIA, is Managing Director of Curriculum and Exams at the CAIA Association. He was previously an Associate at Ennis Knupp and, before that, an Assistant Professor at Illinois Institute of Technology. He is a member of the editorial board of the *Journal of Alternative Investments*.

Dr. Hossein B. Kazemi is a senior adviser to the CAIA Association. He is the Michael and Cheryl Philipp Professor of Finance at the University of Massachusetts, Amherst; Director of the Center for International Securities and Derivatives Markets; a cofounder of the CAIA Association; and Editor-in-Chief of the *Journal of Alternative Investments*—the official publication of the CAIA Association; and a member of the editorial board of the *Journal of Financial Data Science*.

One

Introduction to Alternative Investments

Part 1 begins with an introduction to alternative investments and a description of the environment of alternative investing. Chapters 3 to 6 include primers on quantitative methods, statistics, and financial economics as they relate to alternative investments, as well as a chapter on derivatives and risk-neutral valuation. The last two chapters of Part 1 discuss measures of risk and performance, as well as alpha, beta, and hypothesis testing. The material is designed to provide a foundation for Parts 2 to 5, which detail each of the four main categories of alternative investments.

CHAPTER 1

What Is an Alternative Investment?

Definitions of what constitutes an alternative investment vary considerably. One reason for these differences lies in the purposes for which the definitions are being used. But definitions also vary because alternative investing is largely a new field for which consensus has not emerged, as well as a rapidly changing field for which consensus will probably always remain elusive. Analyzing these various definitions provides a useful starting point to understanding alternative investments. So we begin this introductory chapter by examining commonly used methods of defining alternative investments.

1.1 ALTERNATIVE INVESTMENTS BY EXCLUSION

Alternative investments are sometimes viewed as including any investment that is not simply a long position in traditional investments. Typically, **traditional investments** include publicly traded equities, fixed-income securities, and cash. For example, if an investment such as private equity is not commonly covered in detail in most books on investing, then many people would view it as an alternative investment.

The alternative-investments-by-exclusion definition is overly broad for the purposes of the CAIA curriculum. First, the term *investment* covers a very broad spectrum. A good definition of an **investment** is that it is deferred consumption. Any net outlay of cash made with the prospect of receiving future benefits might be considered an investment. So investments can range from planting a tree to buying stocks to acquiring a college education. As such, a more accurate definition of alternative investments requires more specificity than simply that of being nontraditional.

This book and the overall CAIA curriculum are focused on institutional-quality alternative investments. An **institutional-quality investment** is the type of investment that financial institutions such as pension funds or endowments might include in their holdings because they are expected to deliver reasonable returns at an acceptable level of risk. For example, a pension fund would consider holding the publicly traded equities of a major corporation but may be reluctant to hold collectibles such as baseball cards or stamps. Also, investments in very small and very speculative projects are typically viewed as being inappropriate for such an institution due to its responsibility to select investments that offer suitable risk levels and financial return prospects for its clients.

Not every financial institution, or even every type of financial institution, invests in alternative investments. Some financial institutions, such as some brokerage firms, are not focused on making long-term investments; rather, they hold securities to provide services to their clients. Other financial institutions, such as deposit-taking institutions like banks (especially smaller banks) might invest in only traditional investments because of government regulations or because of lack of expertise.

Of course, institutional-quality alternative investments are also held by entities other than financial institutions. Chapter 2 of this book discusses the alternative investment environment, including the various entities that commonly hold them (e.g., endowment funds and wealthy individuals).

1.2 ALTERNATIVE INVESTMENTS BY INCLUSION

Another method of identifying alternative investments is to define explicitly which investments are considered to be alternative. In this book, we classify four types of alternative investments:

1. Real assets (including natural resources, commodities, real estate, infrastructure, and intellectual property)
2. Hedge funds (including managed futures)
3. Private equity and private credit
4. Structured products (including credit derivatives)

These four categories correspond to Parts 2 to 5 of this book. Our list is not an exhaustive list of all alternative investments, especially because the CAIA curriculum is focused on institutional-quality investments. Furthermore, some of the investments on the list can be classified as traditional investments rather than alternative investments. For example, real estate and especially real estate investment trusts are frequently viewed as being traditional institutional-quality investments. Nevertheless, this list includes most institutional-quality investments that are currently commonly viewed as alternative. Exhibit 1.1 illustrates the relative proportion of these four categories of alternative investments.

The following sections provide brief introductions to the four categories.

1.2.1 Real Assets

Real assets are investments in which the underlying assets involve direct ownership of nonfinancial assets rather than ownership through financial assets, such as the securities of manufacturing or service enterprises. Real assets tend to represent more direct claims on consumption than do common stocks, and they tend to do so with less reliance on factors that create value in a company, such as intangible assets and managerial skill. So while a corporation such as Google holds real estate and other real assets, the value to its common stock is highly reliant on perceptions of the ability of the firm's management to oversee creation and sales of its goods and services. An aspect that distinguishes types of real assets is the extent to which the ownership of the real assets involves operational aspects, such as day-to-day management decisions that have substantial impacts on the performance of the assets. For example, in many instances, direct ownership of oil reserves or stockpiles of copper involve

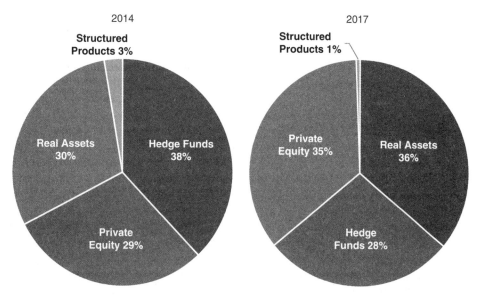

EXHIBIT 1.1 Major Alternative Asset Categories (percentages approximate), 2017
Source: Global Alternatives Survey 2017, Willis Towers Watson; CAIA Association estimates.

substantially less day-to-day managerial attention than does direct ownership of real estate, infrastructure, or intellectual property.

Natural resources focus on direct ownership of real assets that have received little or no alteration by humans, such as mineral and energy rights or reserves. Commodities are differentiated from natural resources by their emphasis on having been extracted or produced. **Commodities** are homogeneous goods available in large quantities, such as energy products, agricultural products, metals, and building materials. Most of the investments covered in the commodities section of the CAIA curriculum involve futures contracts, so understanding futures contracts is an important part of understanding commodities. Futures contracts are regulated distinctly and have well-defined economic characteristics. For example, the analysis of futures contracts typically emphasizes notional amounts rather than the amount of money posted as collateral or margin to acquire positions.

Commodities as an investment class refer to investment products with somewhat passive (i.e., buy-and-hold) exposure to commodity prices. This exposure can be obtained through futures contracts, physical commodities, natural resource companies, and exchange-traded funds.

Some real assets are operationally focused. For the purposes of the CAIA curriculum, **operationally focused real assets** include real estate, land, infrastructure, and intellectual property. The performance of these types of real assets is substantially affected by the skill and success of regular and relatively frequent managerial decision-making. Traditional common stocks are typically even more highly operationally focused.

Real estate focuses on land and improvements that are permanently affixed, like buildings. Real estate was a significant asset class long before stocks and bonds became important. Prior to the Industrial Age, land was the single most valuable asset class. Only a century ago, real estate was the most valuable asset of most individuals, because ownership of a primary residence was more common than ownership of financial investments.

Land comprises a variety of forms, including undeveloped land, timberland, and farmland. Although undeveloped land might appear to belong under the category of natural resources rather than operationally focused real assets, the option to develop land often requires substantial and ongoing managerial decision-making. **Timberland** includes both the land and the timber of forests of tree species typically used in the forest products industry. While the underlying land is a natural resource, timberland requires some level of ongoing management. Finally, **farmland** consists of land cultivated for row crops (e.g., vegetables and grains) and permanent crops (e.g., orchards and vineyards). Farmland necessitates substantial operations and managerial decisions.

Infrastructure investments are claims on the income of toll roads, regulated utilities, ports, airports, and other real assets that are traditionally held and controlled by the public sector (i.e., various levels of government). Investable infrastructure opportunities include securities generated by the privatization of existing infrastructure or by the private creation of new infrastructure via private financing.

Finally, while some descriptions of real assets limit the category to tangible assets, we define real assets to include intangible assets, such as intellectual property (e.g., patents, copyrights, and trademarks, as well as music, film, and publishing royalties). The opposite of a real asset is a financial asset, not an intangible asset. A **financial asset** is not a real asset—it is a claim on cash flows, such as a share of stock or a bond. Intangible assets, such as technology, directly facilitate production, thereby creating increased value. It can be argued that intangible assets represent a very large and rapidly increasing role in the wealth of society.

1.2.2 Hedge Funds

Hedge funds represent perhaps the most visible category of alternative investments. While hedge funds are often associated with particular fee structures or levels of risk taking, we define a **hedge fund** as a privately organized investment vehicle that uses its less regulated nature to generate investment opportunities that are substantially distinct from those offered by traditional investment vehicles, which are subject to regulations such as those restricting their use of derivatives and leverage. Hedge funds represent a wide-ranging set of vehicles that are differentiated primarily by the investment strategy or strategies implemented. Managed futures funds are included as hedge funds in Part 3.

1.2.3 Private Equity

The term **private equity** is used in the CAIA curriculum to include both equity and debt positions that, among other things, are not publicly traded. In most cases, the debt positions contain so much risk from cash flow uncertainty that their short-term return behavior is similar to that of equity positions. In other words, the value of the debt positions in a highly leveraged company, discussed within the category of private equity, behaves much like that of the equity positions in the same firm, especially in the short run. Private equity investments emerge primarily from funding new ventures, known as venture capital; from the equity of leveraged buyouts of existing businesses; from mezzanine financing of leveraged buyouts or other ventures; and from distressed debt resulting from the decline in the health of previously healthy firms.

Venture capital refers to support via equity financing to start-up companies that do not have a sufficient size, track record, or desire to attract capital from traditional sources, such as public capital markets or lending institutions. Venture capitalists fund these high-risk, illiquid, and unproven ideas by purchasing senior equity stakes while the start-up companies are still privately held. The ultimate goal is to generate large profits primarily through the business success of the companies and their development into enterprises capable of attracting public investment capital (typically through an initial public offering, or IPO) or via their sale to other companies. In the context of investment management, venture capital is sometimes treated as a separate asset class from other types of private equity.

Leveraged buyouts (LBOs) refer to those transactions in which the equity of a publicly traded company is purchased using a small amount of investor capital and a large amount of borrowed funds in order to take the firm private. The borrowed funds are secured by the assets or cash flows of the target company. The goals can include exploiting tax advantages of debt financing, improving the operating efficiency and the profitability of the company, and ultimately taking the company public again (i.e., making an IPO of its new equity). Management buyouts and management buy-ins are types of LBOs with specific managerial changes.

Mezzanine debt derives its name from its position in the capital structure of a firm: between the ceiling of senior secured debt and the floor of equity. Mezzanine debt refers to a spectrum of risky claims, including preferred stock, convertible debt, and debt that includes equity kickers (i.e., options that allow investors to benefit from any upside success in the underlying business, also called hybrid securities).

Distressed debt refers to the debt of companies that have filed or are likely to file in the near future for bankruptcy protection. Even though these securities are fixed-income securities, distressed debt is included in our discussion of private equity because the future cash flows of the securities are highly risky and highly dependent on the financial success of the distressed companies, and thus share many similarities with common stock. Private equity firms investing in distressed debt tend to take longer-term ownership positions in the companies after converting all or some portion of their debt position to equity. Some hedge funds also invest in distressed debt, but they tend to do so with a shorter-term trading orientation.

Private debt and direct lending strategies include loans made to borrowers outside of the banking system, specifically by hedge funds, private equity funds, and private credit funds. As regulations increased after the global financial crisis, banks facing stress tests and capital adequacy requirements backed away from lending, especially to non-investment-grade middle-market companies. Companies needing financing now need to approach direct lenders who are likely to make the loans easier and more quickly than banks, but at higher total interest costs.

1.2.4 Structured Products

Structured products are instruments created to exhibit particular return, risk, taxation, or other attributes. These instruments generate unique cash flows as a result of partitioning the cash flows from a traditional investment or linking the returns of the structured product to one or more market values. The simplest and most common example of a structured product is the creation of debt securities and equity securities in a traditional corporation. The cash flows and risks of the corporation's assets are structured into a lower-risk fixed cash flow stream (bonds) and a higher-risk residual cash flow stream (stock). The structuring of the financing sources of a corporation creates option-like characteristics for the resulting securities.

Collateralized debt obligations (CDOs) and similar instruments are among the best-known types of structured products. CDOs partition the actual or synthetic returns from a portfolio of assets (the collateral) into securities with varied levels of seniority (the tranches).

Credit derivatives, another popular type of structured product, facilitate the transfer of credit risk. Most commonly, credit derivatives allow an entity (the credit protection buyer) to transfer some or all of a credit risk associated with a specific exposure to the party on the other side of the derivative (the credit protection seller). The credit protection seller might be diversifying into the given credit risk, speculating on the given credit risk, or hedging a preexisting credit exposure.

Historically, the term *structured products* has referred to a very broad spectrum of products, including CDOs and credit derivatives. In recent decades, however, the term is being used to describe a narrower set of financially engineered products. These products are issued largely with the intention of meeting the preferences of investors, such as providing precisely crafted exposures to the returns of an index or a security. For example, a major bank may issue a product designed to offer downside risk protection to investors while also offering the potential for the investor to receive a portion of the upside performance in an index. Part 5 discusses these specially designed structured products along with more generic structured products, including credit derivatives and CDOs.

When the structuring process creates instruments that do not behave like traditional investments, those instruments are considered alternative investments.

1.2.5 Limits on the Categorizations

These four categories of alternative investments are the focus of the CAIA curriculum. While the categorization helps us understand the spectrum of alternative investments, the various alternative investment categories may overlap. For example, some hedge fund portfolios may contain substantial private equity or structured product exposures and may even substantially alternate the focus of their holdings through time. This being said, the four categories discussed in the previous sections represent the investment types central to the Level I curriculum of the CAIA program.

1.3 THE BLURRED LINES BETWEEN TRADITIONAL AND ALTERNATIVE INVESTMENTS

The previous sections defined the category of alternative investments by describing the investments that are or are not commonly thought of as alternative. But the question remains as to what the defining characteristics of investments are that cause them

EXHIBIT 1.2 The Blurred Lines Between Traditional and Alternative Assets

Alternative Investments	Assets Often Characterized as Traditional or Alternative	Analogous Traditional Assets
Hedge funds	Liquid alternative mutual funds	Ordinary mutual funds
Private equity	Closed-end funds with illiquid holdings	Public equities
Real assets	Public real estate and public equities of corporations with performance dominated by stable positions in real assets	Public equities with performance dominated by managerial decisions
Complex structured products	Simple structured products offering relatively stable and common risk and return characteristics	Simple derivatives used as part of a strategy with stable risk exposures

to be classified as alternative. For example, why is private equity considered an alternative investment but other equities are considered traditional investments? What is the key characteristic or attribute that differentiates these equities? The answer is that traditional equities are listed on major stock exchanges whereas private equity is not. In this case, traditional equities possess the characteristic of being publicly traded, while private equity does not.

The lines between traditional and alternative assets are not distinct and universal. **Exhibit 1.2** depicts the four categories of alternative investments (in the left column), assets that are sometimes listed as alternative and sometimes as traditional (in the middle column), and assets viewed only as traditional (in the right column). Exhibit 1.2 illustrates the lack of clear lines between alternative and traditional assets. This book will focus on those assets that are most universally described as alternative.

Note in Exhibit 1.2 that hedge fund–like returns are now available in publicly traded "liquid alternative" mutual funds. Not all hedge fund strategies are available through these public mutual funds—that is, the U.S. Investment Company Act of 1940 (the '40 Act) or Undertakings for Collective Investment in Transferable Securities (UCITS) funds—because of regulatory limits on leverage and illiquidity. So-called '40 Act (1940 Act) funds are those regulated under the U.S. Investment Company Act of 1940. Some alternative strategies are available through closed-end fund structures.

Private equity is inherently illiquid and generally is not available via '40 Act funds or other public investment pools, although several closed-end structures, such as business development corporations, hold private equity as their underlying investments. Closed-end fund structures can use modest amounts of leverage and illiquid underlying assets because the investment companies are not generally required to redeem investor shares on demand.

Among the category of real assets, real estate is most often characterized as both traditional and alternative, especially when the real estate is accessed through publicly traded investment pools, such as REITs. Some publicly traded common stocks with value primarily derived from holdings of natural resources, such as oil reserves, mineral rights, or land, are often classified as real assets. However, to the extent that a stock's value is driven by such managerial expertise as marketing, trading of assets, or technology, the returns will not be dominated by the values of underlying real assets and the stocks are more appropriately viewed as traditional operating firms.

Finally, the category of structured products varies from rather simple financial derivatives that are often classified as traditional investments (e.g., credit default swaps) to more complex derivatives, such as collateralized loan obligations, that are usually classified as alternative. Furthermore, some financial derivatives, such as futures contracts and forward contracts, can be used to replicate traditional asset exposures and thus clearly fall within the realm of traditional investing. For example, a portfolio of cash plus a long position in a forward contract on an equity index synthetically replicates a long position in the equities underlying the index. The decision of whether to classify a structured product as an alternative investment should be based on the extent to which the product offers nontraditional risk and return exposures and requires investment management methods that differ markedly from traditional investment management methods.

1.4 A HISTORY OF ALTERNATIVE INVESTING: THE U.S. CASE

Exhibit 1.3 provides a general overview of the investments typically held by institutional investors, such as banks, pension funds, endowments, and insurance companies. Throughout much of the twentieth century, each institutional-quality investment was evaluated primarily on the safety of its income and principal and tended to be evaluated on a standalone basis.

Beginning in the 1950s and 1960s, modern portfolio theory established the mechanics and advantages of diversification. Modern portfolio theory evaluates risk on a portfolio basis—formalizing the idea that much risk can be diversified away by holding a broad mix of available investments. In the 1980s and 1990s, the appropriateness of investments for institutions increasingly began to be evaluated on a portfolio basis.

The change in law and investment practices from evaluating risk on a standalone basis to a portfolio-as-a-whole basis is evidenced in Exhibit 1.3.

Beginning in the 1980s, inclusion of such assets as small-company stocks, low-quality corporate bonds, and alternative assets became more common among financial institutions, such as banks, pension funds, endowment funds, and insurance companies. Evaluated on a standalone basis, many of these assets had little or no reliable income and were at risk for loss of the original investment. But when held

EXHIBIT 1.3   Popular Institutional Quality Assets, 1890–Present

1890–1920	Government debt, real estate, mortgages, preferred stock
1920–1950	Add high-quality corporate bonds, domestic equities, agricultural debt
1950–1980	Add average-quality corporate bonds, international equities
1980–Present	Add high-yield debt, small stocks, structured products, private equity, hedge funds, real assets

in a portfolio, these relatively high-risk investments could lower the total risk of the portfolio because of their ability to provide improved diversification.

Exhibit 1.3 indicates that institutions usually did not hold common stocks prior to 1920. Most institutional-quality investments more than 100 years ago were those secured by tangible assets, such as real estate.

The underlying determinants of economic performance are changing with increasing speed. Take, for instance, the composition of the major stocks in the United States. In early 1901, the Dow Jones Industrial Average included 12 stocks: 10 common stocks and two preferred stocks. Almost every one of the 12 stocks was a commodity producer (copper, sugar, tobacco, paper, lead, coal, leather, rubber, and steel).

By 1960, the top seven Fortune 500 firms in the United States were General Motors Company, Standard Oil Company of New Jersey, Ford Motor Company, General Electric, U.S. Steel, Mobil, and Gulf Oil. The list included three oil companies and one steel company as well as two automobile manufacturers and one electrical equipment manufacturer.

Now, top firms are dominated by services and technology. The top five U.S. firms in terms of market capitalization in 2017 were Apple Inc., Alphabet Inc., Microsoft Corporation, Amazon.com Inc., and Berkshire Hathaway Inc. Facebook, Inc., was seventh in mid-2017 with a market capitalization of more than $500 billion, no inventory, and fixed assets of only about $10 billion. Clearly, it is inappropriate to view traditional assets as solid and alternative assets as speculative.

Investments closely tied to commodity prices are now viewed as alternative investments, yet they constituted most of the industrial investment opportunities in 1900. With such dramatic and increasingly rapid changes in the components of an economy, it is difficult to conclude that conservative and traditional investment principles consist of maintaining unchanging investment practices. In effect, sticking with traditional investment practices moves the risk and diversification of a portfolio through time as the economy underlying the investment opportunities shifts. It is only through a dynamic approach to asset allocation (one that adjusts to new industries, securities, and other economic changes) that a portfolio can maintain good principles of diversification.

1.5 INVESTMENTS ARE DISTINGUISHED BY RETURN CHARACTERISTICS

A popular way of distinguishing between traditional and alternative investments is by their return characteristics. Investment opportunities exhibiting returns that are substantially distinct from the returns of long only position in traditional stocks and bonds might be viewed as being alternative investments. Stock returns in this context refer to the returns of publicly traded equities; similarly, bond returns refer to the returns of publicly traded fixed-income securities.

1.5.1 Diversification

An investment opportunity with returns that are uncorrelated with or only slightly correlated with traditional investments is often viewed as an alternative investment.

An attractive aspect of this lack of correlation is that it indicates the potential to diversify risk. In this context, many alternative investments are referred to as diversifiers. A **diversifier** is an investment with a primary purpose of contributing diversification benefits to its owner. **Absolute return products** are investment products viewed as having little or no return correlation with traditional assets, and have investment performance that is often analyzed on an absolute basis rather than relative to the performance of traditional investments. The term *absolute returns* in this context should not be confused with the mathematical use of the term *absolute value* to indicate a numerical value that is always nonnegative. Diversification can lower risk without necessarily causing an offsetting reduction in expected return and is therefore generally viewed as a highly desirable method of generating improved risk-adjusted returns.

Sometimes alternative assets are viewed as synonymous with diversifiers or absolute return products. But clearly most types of investments, such as private equity, REITs, and particular styles of hedge funds, have returns that are at least modestly correlated with public equities over medium- to long-term time horizons and are still viewed as alternative investments. Accordingly, this non-correlation-based view of alternative investments does not provide a precise demarcation between alternative and traditional investments. Nevertheless, having distinct returns is often an important characteristic in differentiating alternative investments from traditional investments.

Alternative investments may be viewed as being likely to have return characteristics that are different from stocks and bonds, as demonstrated by their lack of correlation with stocks and bonds. The distinctions between traditional and alternative investments are also indicated by several common return characteristics found among alternative investments that either are not found in traditional investments or are found to a different degree. The following three sections discuss the most important potential return characteristic distinctions.

1.5.2 Illiquidity

Traditional investments have the institutional structure of tending to be frequently traded in financial markets with substantial volume and a high number of participants. Therefore, their returns tend to be based on liquid prices observed from reasonably frequent trades at reasonable levels of volume. Many alternative investments are illiquid. In this context, **illiquidity** means that the investment trades infrequently or with low volume (i.e., thinly). Illiquidity implies that returns are difficult to observe due to lack of trading, and that realized returns may be affected by the trading decisions of just a few participants. Other assets, often termed **lumpy assets**, are assets that can be bought and sold only in specific quantities, such as a large real estate project. Thin trading causes a more uncertain relationship between the most recently observed price and the likely price of the next transaction. Generally, illiquid assets tend to fall under the alternative investment classification, whereas traditional assets tend to be liquid assets. However, liquid assets can be found inside alternative investment structures such as hedge funds and structured products.

The risk of illiquid assets may be compensated for by higher returns. An illiquid asset can be difficult or expensive to sell, as thin volume or lockup provisions prevent the immediate sale of the asset at a price close to its potential sales value.

The urgent sale of an illiquid asset can therefore be at a price that is considerably lower than the value that could be obtained from a long-term comprehensive search for a buyer. Given the difficulties of selling and valuing illiquid investments, many investors demand a risk premium, or a price discount, for investing in illiquid assets. While some investors may avoid illiquid investments at all costs, others specifically increase their allocation to illiquid investments in order to earn this risk premium.

1.5.3 Inefficiency

The prices of most traditional investments are determined in markets with relatively high degrees of competition and therefore with relatively high informational efficiency. In this context, competition is described as numerous well-informed traders able to take long and short positions with relatively low transaction costs and with high speed. **Efficiency** (i.e., informational efficiency) refers to the tendency of market prices to reflect all available information.

Efficient market theory asserts that arbitrage opportunities and superior risk-adjusted returns are more likely to be identified in markets that are less competitively traded and less informationally efficient. (Market efficiency is detailed in Chapter 5.) Many alternative investments have the institutional structure of trading at inefficient prices. **Inefficiency** refers to the deviation of actual prices from valuations that would be anticipated in an efficient market. Informationally inefficient markets are less competitive, with fewer investors, higher transaction costs, and/or an inability to take both long and short positions. Accordingly, alternative investments may be more likely than traditional investments to offer returns driven by pricing inefficiencies.

1.5.4 Non-Normality

To some extent, the returns of almost all investments, especially the short-term returns on traditional investments, can be approximated as being normally distributed. The normal distribution is the commonly discussed bell-shaped distribution, with its peaked center and its symmetric and diminishing tails. The return distributions of most investment opportunities become nearer to the shape of the normal distribution as the time interval of the return computation nears zero and as the probability and magnitude of jumps or large moves over a short period of time decrease. However, over longer time intervals, the returns of many alternative investments exhibit non-normality, in that they cannot be accurately approximated using the standard bell curve. The non-normality of medium- and long-term returns is a potentially important characteristic of many alternative investments.

What structures cause non-normality of returns? First and foremost, many alternative investments are structured so that they are infrequently traded; therefore, their market returns are measured over longer periods of time. These longer time intervals combine with other aspects of alternative investment returns to make alternative investments especially prone to return distributions that are poorly approximated using the normal distribution. These irregular return distributions may arise from several sources, including (1) securities structuring, such as with a derivative product that is nonlinearly related to its underlying security or with an equity in a highly leveraged firm, and (2) trading structures, such as an active investment management strategy alternating rapidly between long and short positions.

Non-normality of returns introduces a host of complexities and lessens the effectiveness of using methods based on the assumption of normally distributed returns. Many alternative investments have especially non-normal returns compared to traditional investments; therefore, the category of alternative investments is often associated with non-normality of returns.

1.6 INVESTMENTS ARE DISTINGUISHED BY METHODS OF ANALYSIS

The previous section outlined return characteristics of alternative investments that distinguished them from traditional investments: diversifying, illiquid, inefficient, and non-normal. Alternative investments can also be distinguished from traditional investments through the methods used to analyze, measure, and manage their returns and risks. As in the previous case, the reasons for the difference lie in the underlying structures: Alternative investments have distinct regulatory, securities, trading, compensation, and institutional structures that necessitate distinct methods of analysis. Public equity returns are extensively examined using both theoretical analysis and empirical analysis. Theoretical models, such as the capital asset pricing model, and empirical models, such as the Fama-French three-factor model, detailed later in the CAIA curriculum, are examples of the extensive and highly developed methods used in public equity return analysis. Analogously, theories and empirical studies of the term structure of interest rates and credit spreads arm traditional fixed-income investors with tools for predicting returns and managing risks. But alternative investments do not tend to have an extensive history of well-established analysis, and in many cases the methods of analysis used for traditional investments are not appropriate for these investments due to their structural differences.

Alternative investing requires alternative methods of analysis. In summary, a potential definition of an alternative investment is any investment for which traditional investment methods are clearly inadequate. There are four main types of methods that form the core of alternative investment return analysis.

1.6.1 Return Computation Methods

Return analysis of publicly traded stocks and bonds is relatively straightforward, given the transparency in regularly observable market prices, dividends, and interest payments. Returns to some alternative investments, especially illiquid investments, can be problematic. One major issue is that in many cases, a reliable value of the investment can be determined only at limited points in time. In the extreme, such as in most private equity deals, there may be no reliable measure of investment value at any point in time other than at termination, when the investment's value is the amount of the final liquidating cash flow. This institutional structure of infrequent trading drives the need for different return computation methods.

Return computation methods for investments are driven by their structures and can include such concepts as internal rate of return (IRR), the computation of which over multiple time periods uses the size and timing of the intervening cash flows rather than the intervening market values. Also, return computation methods for many alternative investments may take into account the effects of leverage. While traditional investments typically require the full cash outlay of the investment's market value, many alternative contracts can be entered into with no outlay other than possibly the posting of collateral or margin or, as in the case of private equity, commitments to make a series of cash contributions over time. In the case of no investment outlay, the return computations may use alternative concepts of valuation, such as notional principal amounts. While IRR is commonly used in traditional investments, especially in the case of multiple cash contribution commitments, alternative investments such as private equity may use other methods. Chapter 3 provides details regarding return computation methods, such as IRR, that facilitate analysis of alternative investments. The chapters on private equity explain more commonly used methods, including Public Market Equivalent (PME).

1.6.2 Statistical Methods

The traditional assumption of near-normal returns for traditional investments offers numerous simplifications. First, the entire distribution of an investment with normally or near-normally distributed returns can be specified with only two parameters: (1) the mean of the distribution, and (2) the standard deviation, or variance, of the distribution. Much of traditional investment analysis is based on the representation of an investment's return distribution using only the mean and standard deviation. Further, numerous statistics, tests, tables, and software functions are readily available to facilitate the analysis of a normally distributed variable.

But as indicated previously in this chapter, many alternative investments exhibit especially non-normally distributed returns over medium- and long-term time intervals. Non-normality is usually addressed through the analysis of higher moments of the return distributions, such as skewness and kurtosis. Accordingly, the analysis of alternative investments typically requires familiarity with statistical methods designed to address this non-normality caused by institutional structures like thin trading, securities structures like tranching, and trading structures like alternating risk exposures. An example of a specialized method is in risk management: While a normal distribution is symmetrical, the distributions of some alternative investments can be highly asymmetrical and therefore require specialized risk measures that specifically focus on the downside risks. Chapter 7 introduces some of these methods.

1.6.3 Valuation Methods

Fundamental and technical methods for valuing traditional securities and potentially identifying mispriced securities constitute a moderately important part of the methods used in traditional investments. In traditional investments, fundamental equity valuation tends to focus on relatively healthy corporations engaged in manufacturing products or providing services, and tends to use methods such as financial statement analysis and ratio analysis. Many hedge fund managers use the same general fundamental and technical methods in attempting to identify mispriced stocks and bonds. However, hedge fund managers may also use methods specific to alternative investments, such as those used in highly active trading strategies and strategies based on identifying relative mispricings. For example, a quantitative equity manager might use a complex statistical model to identify a pair of relatively overpriced and underpriced stocks that respond to similar risk factors and are believed to be likely to converge in relative value over the next day or two. Additionally, alternative investing tends to focus on the evaluation of fund managers, while traditional investing tends to focus more on the valuation of securities.

Methods for valuing some types of alternative investments are quite distinct from the traditional methods used for valuing stocks and bonds. Here are several examples:

- Alternative investment management may include analyzing active and rapid trading that focuses on shorter-term price fluctuations.
- Alternative investment analysis often requires addressing challenges imposed by the inability to observe transaction-based prices on a frequent and regular basis. The challenges in illiquid markets relate to determining data for comparison (i.e., benchmarking), since reliable market values are not continuously available.
- Alternative investments such as real estate, private equity, and structured products tend to have unique cash flow forecasting challenges.
- Alternative investments such as some intellectual property and private equity funds use appraisal methods that are estimates of the current value of the asset, which may differ from the price that the asset would achieve if marketed to other investors.

These specialized pricing and valuation methods are driven by the structures that determine the characteristics of alternative investments.

1.6.4 Portfolio Management Methods

Finally, issues such as illiquidity, non-normal returns, and increased potential for inefficient pricing introduce complexities for portfolio management techniques. Most of the methods used in traditional portfolio management rely on assumptions such as the ability to transact quickly, relatively low transaction costs, and often the ability to confine an analysis to the mean and variance of the portfolio's return.

In contrast, portfolio management of alternative investments often requires the application of techniques designed to address such issues as the non-normality of returns and barriers to continuous portfolio adjustments. Non-normality techniques may involve skewness and kurtosis, as opposed to just the mean and variance. In traditional investments, the ability to transact quickly and at low cost often allows for the use of short-term time horizons, since the portfolio manager can quickly adjust positions as conditions change. The inability to trade some alternative investments, like private equity, quickly and at low cost adds complexity to the portfolio management process, such as liquidity management, and mandates understanding of specialized methods. Finally, alternative investment portfolio management tends to focus more on the potential for assets to generate superior returns.

1.7 EIGHT OTHER CHARACTERISTICS THAT DISTINGUISH ALTERNATIVE AND TRADITIONAL INVESTMENTS

Previous sections discuss differentiating alternative and traditional investments by their return characteristics and the methods by which they are analyzed. This section discusses eight additional characteristics or factors that often play a role in distinguishing alternative and traditional investments.

1. **Regulatory factors** in the context of investing refer to the role of government, including both regulation and taxation, in influencing the nature of an investment. For example, hedge funds (but not their managers) are often less regulated and typically must be formed in particular ways to avoid higher levels of regulation. Taxation is another important feature of government influence that can motivate the existence of some investment products and plays a major role in the transformation of underlying asset cash flows into investment products.

2. **Structuring** refers to the partitioning of claims to cash flows through leverage and securitization. Securitization is the process of transforming asset ownership into tradable units. Cash flows may be securitized simply on a pass-through basis (i.e., a pro rata or pari passu basis). Cash flows can also be partitioned into financial claims with different levels of risk or other characteristics, such as the timing or taxability of cash flows. The use of securities and security structuring transforms asset ownership into potentially distinct and diverse tradable investment opportunities. The nature of this transformation drives and shapes the nature of the resulting investments, the characteristics of the resulting returns, and the types of methods that are needed for investment analysis. On the other hand, lack of easily tradable ownership units can drive the selection and implementation of investment methods.

3. **Trading strategies** refer to the role of an investment vehicle's investment managers in developing and implementing trading strategies that alter the nature of an investment. A buy-and-hold management strategy will have a minor influence on underlying investment returns, while an aggressive, complex, fast-paced trading strategy can cause the ultimate cash flows from a fund to differ markedly from the cash flows of the underlying assets. The trading strategy embedded in an alternative asset such as a fixed-income arbitrage hedge fund is often the most important factor in determining the investment's characteristics.

4. **Compensation structures** refer to the ways that organizations distribute rewards. In the case of a hedge fund, compensation structures would include the financial arrangements contained in the limited partnership formed by the investors and the entity used by the fund's managers. Such arrangements usually determine the exposure of the fund's investment managers to the financial risk of the investment, the fee structures used to compensate and reward managers, and the potential conflicts of interest between parties. Compensation structures within investments, especially alternative investments, have implications for the agency costs generated by owner-manager relationships.

5. **Institutional factors** refer to the financial markets (and their policies, such as restrictions on short selling, leverage, and trading) and financial institutions related to a particular investment, such as whether the investment is publicly traded. Public trading or the listing of a security is an essential driver of an investment's nature. For example, some hotels are owned by investors as shares of publicly traded corporations, such as Hyatt and Marriott, which are usually considered to be traditional investments. Other hotels, such as those owned by investors as real estate investment trusts (e.g., Host Hotels & Resorts Inc.) and those held privately (e.g., Omni Hotels), are usually considered to be alternative investments. Other institutional structures can determine whether an investment

is regularly traded, is held by individuals at the retail level, or tends to be traded and held by large financial institutions such as pension funds and foundations.

6. **Information asymmetries** refer to the extent to which market participants possess different data and knowledge. In traditional investments, most securities are regulated and are required to disclose substantial information to the public. Many alternative investments are private placements, and therefore the potential for large information asymmetries is greater. These information asymmetries raise substantial issues for financial analysis and portfolio management.

7. **Incomplete markets** refer to markets with insufficient distinct investment opportunities. The lack of distinct investment opportunities can prevent market participants from implementing an investment strategy that satisfies their exact preferences, such as their preferences regarding risk exposures. In an ideal world, securities could be costlessly created to meet every investor need. For example, an investor may desire an insurance contract that contains a specific clause regarding payouts, but regulations may prohibit such clauses. Or perhaps a contract with regard to a potential risk may be subject to unacceptable moral hazard. **Moral hazard** is risk that the behavior of one or more parties will change after entering into a contract. As a result of this inability to contract efficiently, the investor might be unable to diversify perfectly. Trading restrictions in some alternative investments, such as large minimum investment sizes, can be viewed as exacerbating the problem of incomplete markets and the investment challenges that accompany them.

8. **Innovation** is the application of creativity. In this context, innovation has three major influences. First, especially in venture capital, innovation from nascent enterprises raises challenges regarding methods of cash flow projections, financial analysis, and portfolio management that distinguish the study of alternative investments from the study of traditional investments. Second, substantial degrees of innovation permeate the institutions surrounding alternative investments such as new structured products and derivatives. These innovations tend to inject new opportunities and challenges more in alternative investing than in traditional investing. Finally, innovation often serves as the source of superior returns in alternative assets, especially private equity.

1.8 FIVE GOALS OF ALTERNATIVE INVESTING

Having defined *what* alternative investments are from a variety of perspectives, we introduce the questions of *how* and *why* people pursue alternative investing. Understanding the goals of alternative investing is essential; the following sections provide an introduction to the most important of these goals.

1.8.1 Adding Value through Active Management

Active management refers to efforts of buying and selling securities in pursuit of superior combinations of risk and return. Alternative investment analysis typically focuses on evaluating active managers and their systems of active management, since most alternative investments are actively managed. Active management is the converse of passive investing. **Passive investing** tends to focus on buying and holding securities in an effort to match the risk and return of a target, such as a highly diversified index. An investor's risk and return target is often expressed in the form of a **benchmark,** which is a performance standard for a portfolio that reflects the preferences of an investor with regard to risk and return. For example, a global equity investment program may have the MSCI World Index as its benchmark. The returns of the fund would typically be compared to the **benchmark return,** which is the return of the benchmark index or benchmark portfolio.

Active management typically generates active risk and active return. **Active risk** is that risk that causes a portfolio's return to deviate from the return of a benchmark due to active management. **Active return** is the difference between the return of a portfolio and its benchmark that is due to active management. An important goal in alternative investing is to use active management to generate an improved combination of risk and return.

Active management is an important characteristic of almost all alternative investments. Unlike traditional investing, in which the focus is increasingly on passive portfolio management, the focus of alternative investing is often on analyzing the ability of a fund or other investment to generate attractive returns through active management.

1.8.2 Achieving Absolute and Relative Returns

The concepts of benchmark returns, absolute return products, and investment diversifiers have been briefly introduced in this chapter. Let's examine these and other concepts in more detail. In alternative investing, there are two major standards against which to evaluate returns: absolute and relative.

An **absolute return standard** means that returns are to be evaluated relative to zero, a fixed rate, or relative to the riskless rate, and therefore independently of performance in equity markets, debt markets, or any other markets. Thus, an investment program with an absolute return strategy seeks attractive absolute returns—returns unaffected by market directions. An example of an absolute return investment fund is an equity market-neutral hedge fund with equal-size long and short positions in stocks that the manager perceives as being undervalued and overvalued, respectively. The fund's goal is to hedge away the return risk related to the level of the equity market and to exploit security mispricings to generate returns in excess of the riskless rate.

A **relative return standard** means that returns are to be evaluated relative to a variable benchmark. An investment program with a relative return standard seeks attractive relative returns—returns that move in tandem with a particular market but consistently outperform that market. An example of a fund with a relative return strategy is a long-only global equity fund that diversifies across various equity sectors and uses security selection in an attempt to identify underpriced stocks. The fund's goal is to earn the benchmark return from the fund's exposure to the global equity market and to earn a consistent premium on top of that return through superior security selection.

1.8.3 Pursuing Arbitrage and Return Enhancement

The concept of arbitrage is an active absolute return strategy. **Pure arbitrage** is the attempt to earn risk-free profits through the simultaneous purchase and sale of identical positions trading at different prices in different markets. Modern finance often derives pricing relationships based on the idea that the actions of arbitrageurs will force the prices of identical assets toward being equal, such that pure arbitrage opportunities do not exist or at least do not persist. Chapter 5 provides details on arbitrage-free modeling.

The term *arbitrage* is often used to represent efforts to earn superior returns even when risk is not eliminated because the long and short positions are not in identical assets or are not held over the same time intervals. To the extent that investment professionals use the term *arbitrage* more loosely, these investment programs can be said to contain active risk and to generate relative returns.

An obvious goal of virtually any investor is to earn a superior combination of risk and return. If the primary objective of including an investment product in a portfolio is the superior average returns that it is believed to offer, then that product is often referred to as a **return enhancer**. If the primary objective of including the product is the reduction in the portfolio's risk that it is believed to offer through its lack of correlation with the portfolio's other assets, then that product is often referred to as a **return diversifier**.

1.8.4 Reduced Risk through Diversification

A primary goal of alternative investing is to reduce risk through diversification. One of the distinguishing features of most alternative investments is their lack of correlation with the major traditional asset classes of public equities and public fixed-income assets. A portfolio containing a variety of alternative assets may offer reduced risk without a proportionate reduction in expected return.

1.8.5 Avoiding Obsolescence

As evidenced by Exhibit 1.3, the asset classes viewed as appropriate for institutional investing have changed dramatically over time. Surely the asset classes used in the future for institutional investing will continue to change. Institutional investors who are the last adopters of institutional-quality asset classes will find that prices have adjusted such that the greatest opportunities have been missed. In the chapters on private equity, we will discuss the first mover advantage, whereby the first institutions to find attractive investment opportunities will derive the greatest benefits. In a similar vein, those asset allocators who are last to embrace change are likely to yield disappointing performance. In other words, those who wait to invest in alternative assets until they have become so mainstream as to be considered to be traditional may suffer from a "last-mover disadvantage."

1.9 TWO PILLARS OF ALTERNATIVE INVESTMENT MANAGEMENT

For well over a century, the set of assets deemed to be traditional institutional assets has changed dramatically. Institutional investors must decide which new asset classes to include in their portfolio and when to include those assets. Conservatism in allocating to "new" institutional investment classes runs the risk of missing out on improved diversification and perhaps missing stellar early first-mover returns (i.e., high returns resulting from institutions pouring new money into an asset class that is increasingly viewed as appropriate for them to hold). Boldly venturing into asset classes not previously included in institutional portfolios, however, also exposes institutions to the risk of underperforming their more conservative peers.

The challenge for an institutional investor is to decide, as skillfully as possible, which new types of assets to include in a portfolio and which to exclude. How does an investor make such difficult decisions? This section advocates relying on two pillars: empirical analysis and economic reasoning.

1.9.1 Empirical Analysis

Investment literature abounds with the warning that "future investment performance" should not "be inferred from or predicted based on past investment performance." This overstated warning is taken from Rule 156 of the Securities Act of 1933. In practice, much—if not most—investment analysis and decision-making is ultimately based on historical risk-adjusted performance. For example, it is primarily through historical observation that investment managers have developed opinions on the extent to which investing in equities differs from investing in bonds.

Conversely, the empirical methods used to explain the performance of alternative investments tend not to be as reliable and developed as the methods used to evaluate the performance of traditional investments. Investment professionals seek investments that can enhance the risk-adjusted performance of portfolios. But with huge numbers of potential strategies and powerful tools to backtest performance, it is risky to select opportunities based on empirical analysis alone.

1.9.2 Economic Reasoning

Historical analysis alone is insufficient for determining asset allocations. For example, in the late 1990s the performance of U.S. growth stocks was consistently and strongly positive. The outstanding performance of this sector generated historic returns with extremely attractive statistics: high mean returns, very low variances, and virtually no major drawdowns. The empirical results were so uniformly positive that they led one major investment research firm specializing in mutual funds to assign attractively low risk ratings to many U.S. equity growth funds—then came the dot-com crash of 2000, when plummeting values of growth stock funds resulted in huge losses for their investors.

Investors should be especially skeptical of empirical analyses that sound too good to be true. Economic reasoning can serve as a reliable reality check. Does solid theory support the contention that a particular asset will enhance risk-adjusted return? The addition of any new type of alternative investment into a well-diversified portfolio should be supported to the greatest extent possible by both empirics and theory.

Philosophers debate the two major approaches to the acquisition of knowledge (i.e., theory and empirics). Rationalists argue that most or all knowledge is ultimately understood through reasoning. Empiricists argue that reasoning is derived from observation. We would argue that both are needed.

The crux of the matter is that best practices in alternative investing include striving to make decisions that are supported by both sound analysis of past performance

EXHIBIT 1.4 A 2×2 Framework of Alternative Assets

		Trading Characteristics	
		Publicly Traded	Privately Traded
Primary Goal	Enhanced Returns	Hedge Funds	Private Equity/Credit
	Diversification/Risk Mgmt.	Structured Products	Real Assets

data and careful economic reasoning. This goal is executed with a balance of the two pillars: (1) evidence based on objective analysis of empirical data and (2) evidence based on an unbiased assessment of theories based on economic reasoning.

1.9.3 Viewing Alternative Assets in a 2×2 Framework

The four major categories of alternative investments (real assets, hedge funds, private equity/credit, and structured products) can be roughly viewed along two dimensions, as illustrated in Exhibit 1.4.

The distinction between publicly and privately traded assets along the horizontal dimension is rather straightforward. However, the distinction along the vertical dimension is less definitive. The top two boxes contain assets that tend to be selected more for their potential ability to deliver enhanced returns or alpha (i.e., to serve as return enhancers). In other words, superior risk-adjusted return is often the primary goal of these assets. The bottom two boxes contain assets that tend to be favored to a substantial degree by their ability to diversify a portfolio (i.e., diversifiers) or to serve as a tool to manage risk.

The distinction between the return enhancers and the diversification/risk tools is not sharp—most alternative assets are generally regarded as offering degrees of both return enhancement and risk management. Nevertheless, Exhibit 1.4 can serve as a discussion point for the crucial decision of asset allocation.

1.10 OVERVIEW OF THIS BOOK

The CAIA curriculum is organized into two levels, with Level I providing a broad introduction to alternative asset classes and the tools and techniques used to evaluate the risk-return attributes of each asset class. Level II concentrates on the skills and knowledge that a portfolio manager or an asset allocator must possess to manage an institutional-quality portfolio with both traditional and alternative assets.

Thus, Level I focuses on understanding each category of alternative investments and the methods for analyzing each. This book has been written with the expectation that readers have a moderate background in traditional investments and quantitative techniques. In some places, a Foundation Check is inserted to alert readers to particular content that is necessary background for the ensuing material. Readers may find the following sources useful in obtaining background information: *Quantitative Investment Analysis* by DeFusco, McLeavey, Pinto, and Runkle (John Wiley & Sons,

3rd edition, 2015) and *Investments* by Bodie, Kane, and Marcus (McGraw-Hill, 10th global edition, 2014).

This book is organized into five parts: Part 1 introduces foundational material for alternative investments. Parts 2–5 cover the four categories of alternative investments in the CAIA curriculum by providing extensive introductions to each:

Part 2: Real Assets

Part 3: Hedge Funds

Part 4: Private Securities

Part 5: Structured Products

REVIEW QUESTIONS

1. Define *investment*.
2. List four major types of real assets other than land and other types of real estate.
3. List the three major types of alternative investments other than real assets in the CAIA curriculum.
4. Name assets that are often characterized as traditional by some and as alternatives by others for each of the following categories: hedge funds, private equity, and real assets.
5. Approximately when did average-quality corporate bonds and international equities become commonly viewed as institutional-quality investments in the United States?
6. Name the four return characteristics that differentiate traditional and alternative investments.
7. Name four major methods of analysis that distinguish alternative investments from traditional investments.
8. Describe an incomplete market.
9. Define *active management*.
10. What distinguishes use of the term *pure arbitrage* from the more general use of the term *arbitrage*?

CHAPTER 2

The Environment of Alternative Investments

This chapter provides an introduction to the environment of alternative investing, including the participants, the financial markets, liquid alternatives, and taxation. Its focus is on explaining the purposes and functions of these components so that readers gain an understanding of why the investing environment is structured the way it is and how the different components interact.

2.1 THE PARTICIPANTS

Participants can be divided into four major categories: the buy side, the sell side, outside service providers, and regulators. This section briefly describes the primary roles of the first three categories of participants; the primary role of regulators is discussed in section 2.5.

2.1.1 The Buy Side

Buy side refers to the institutions and entities that buy large quantities of securities for the portfolios they manage. Buy side entities include asset owners and asset managers. The buy side contrasts with the sell side (detailed in section 2.1.2), which focuses on distributing securities to the public. Examples of buy-side institutions follow, with an emphasis on the perspective of alternative investing.

> PLAN SPONSORS: A **plan sponsor** is a designated party, such as a company or an employer, that establishes a health care or retirement plan (pension) for employees that has special legal or taxation status, such as a 401(k) retirement plan in the United States or a superannuation fund in Australia. Plan sponsors are companies or other collectives that establish the health care and retirement plans for the benefit of the organization's employees or members. Plan sponsors are responsible for determining membership parameters and investment choices and, in some cases, providing contribution payments in the form of cash or stock (or both). In many cases, one individual, the plan trustee, is designated with overall responsibility for managing the plan's assets, whereas the plan administrator is charged with overseeing the plan's day-to-day operations. Both the trustee and the administrator are identified

in the plan's summary plan description. As described in CAIA Level II, these funds can be designed as defined contribution plans or defined benefit plans. In defined contribution plans, employees take the investment risk, while that risk is borne by the employer in defined benefit plans.

FOUNDATIONS AND ENDOWMENTS: A **foundation** is a not-for-profit organization that donates funds and support to other organizations for its own charitable purposes. An **endowment** is a fund bestowed on an individual or institution (e.g., a museum, university, or hospital) to be used by that entity for specific purposes and with principal preservation in mind.

FAMILY OFFICE AND PRIVATE WEALTH: Family office and private wealth institutions are private management advisory firms that serve ultra-high-net-worth investors. A **family office** is a group of investors joined by familial or other ties who manage their personal investments as a single entity, usually hiring professionals to manage money for members of the office.

SOVEREIGN WEALTH FUNDS: **Sovereign wealth funds** are state-owned investment funds held for the purpose of future generations and/or to stabilize the state currency. These funds may emanate from budgetary and trade surpluses, perhaps through exportation of natural resources and raw materials such as oil, copper, or diamonds. Because of the high volatility of resource prices, unpredictability of extraction, and exhaustibility of resources, sovereign wealth funds are accumulated to help provide financial stability and future opportunities for citizens and governments. Sovereign wealth funds can also be built using the proceeds of international trade, such as countries with a large surplus in their trade balance generated by a large export sector.

PRIVATE LIMITED PARTNERSHIPS: **Private limited partnerships** are a form of business organization that potentially offers the benefit of limited liability to the organization's limited partners (similar to that enjoyed by shareholders of corporations) but not to its general partner. For tax purposes, limited partnerships tend to flow taxable revenue and expenses directly through to their partners rather than being taxed at the partnership level.

PRIVATE INVESTMENT POOLS: Hedge funds, funds of funds, private equity funds, managed futures funds, commodity trading advisers (CTAs), and the like are private investment pools that focus on serving as intermediaries between investors and alternative investments. Most U.S. funds are structured as limited partnerships and offer incentive-based compensation schemes to their managers. These limited partnerships are usually managed by the general partner, while most of the invested funds are provided by the limited partners. These structures are detailed in section 2.2.

SEPARATELY MANAGED ACCOUNTS: **Separately managed accounts** (SMAs) are individual investment accounts offered by a brokerage firm and managed by independent investment management firms. The relationship between an investment adviser and a client to whom advice is provided is typically documented by a written investment management agreement. SMAs can be thought of as being similar to pooled investment arrangements, such as mutual funds, in that a customer pays a fee to a money manager for managing the customer's investment, but SMAs tend to be differentiated from funds in five major ways:

1. A fund investor owns shares of a company (the fund) that in turn owns other investments, whereas an SMA investor actually owns the invested assets as the owner on record.
2. A fund invests for the common purposes of multiple investors, whereas an SMA may have objectives tailored to suit the specific needs of its only investor, such as tax efficiency.
3. A fund is often opaque to its investors to promote confidentiality; an SMA offers transparency to its investor.
4. Fund investors may suffer adverse consequences from other investors' redemptions (withdrawals) and subscriptions (deposits), but an SMA provides protection from these liquidity issues for its only investor.
5. Whereas the fund structure may allow investors to have limited liability, the SMA format may allow losses to be greater than the capital contribution when leverage or derivatives are used.

From an investor's perspective, the advantages of the first four distinctions typically outweigh the disadvantages of the last distinction. However, fund managers prefer the simplicity and convenience of pooled arrangements (funds).

MUTUAL FUNDS ('40 ACT FUNDS): **Mutual funds,** or **'40 Act funds,** are registered investment pools offering their shareholders pro rata claims on the fund's portfolio of assets. In the United States, mutual funds that offer their shares for sale to the public are known as '40 Act funds due to the regulations that permit their offering by registered investment advisers: the U.S. Investment Company Act of 1940. In recent years, '40 Act funds have increasingly offered alternative asset exposures through these retail fund structures. A general discussion is provided in section 2.6, along with more specific discussions throughout Parts 2 through 5.

UCITS (UNDERTAKINGS FOR COLLECTIVE INVESTMENT IN TRANSFERABLE SECURITIES): Regulation of public funds in Europe centers on the concept of UCITS. UCITS allow retail access and marketing of hedge-fund-like investment pools, somewhat akin to the retail access and marketing of '40 Act funds in the United States. UCITS conform to European regulations such that the product can be sold throughout the various members of the EU. They are subject to strict regulations, including investment restrictions, diversification requirements, minimum size requirements, an annual audit, and meeting standards involving the promoters and other parties related to the UCITS creation, distribution, and management.

MASTER LIMITED PARTNERSHIPS: **Master limited partnerships** (**MLPs**) are publicly traded investment pools that are structured as limited partnerships and that offer their owners pro rata claims. Like equities, MLP units are traded on major stock exchanges, but they have legal and tax structures similar to those of private limited partnerships.

2.1.2 The Sell Side

In contrast to buy-side institutions, **sell-side** institutions, such as large dealer banks, act as agents for investors when they trade securities. Sell-side institutions make their research available to their clients and are more focused on facilitating transactions than on managing money.

LARGE DEALER BANKS: **Large dealer banks** are major financial institutions, such as Goldman Sachs, Deutsche Bank, and the Barclays Group, that deal in securities and derivatives. Although based on the same economic principles as typical retail banks, large dealer banks are much bigger and more complex. The macroeconomic impact of a large dealer bank failure may be more widespread because of the central role this type of bank plays in the economic system at large. Generally, most large dealer banks act as intermediaries in the markets for securities, repurchase agreements, securities lending, and over-the-counter (OTC) derivatives. In addition, large dealer banks are often engaged in proprietary trading.

Large dealer banks also have large asset management divisions that cater to the investment management needs of institutional and wealthy individual clients. This involves custody of securities, cash management, brokerage, and investment in alternative investment vehicles, such as hedge funds and private equity partnerships. Some of these types of banks operate internal hedge funds and take on private equity partnerships as part of their business management service. In this role, the bank acts as a general partner with limited-partner clients.

The role of dealer banks in the primary market is to intermediate between issuers and investors, to provide liquidity, and to act as underwriters of investments. In secondary securities markets, large dealer banks trade with one another and with brokers/dealers directly over the computer or the phone, as well as play an intermediating role of facilitating trades.

Large dealer banks also engage in proprietary trading. **Proprietary trading** occurs when a firm trades securities with its own money in order to make a profit. Large dealer banks serve as counterparties to OTC derivatives such as options, forwards, and swaps that require the participation of a counterparty dealer who meets customer demand by taking the opposite side of a desired position. Dealers may accept the risk or use a matched book dealer operation, in which the dealer lays off the derivative risk by taking an offsetting position.

As part of their business management activities, large dealer banks are active as prime brokers that offer professional services specifically to hedge funds and other large institutional customers. (Prime brokers are discussed in more detail in section 2.1.3.) Several large dealer banks have ventured into off-balance-sheet financing methods, a practice that involves a form of accounting in which large expenditures are kept off the company's balance sheet through various classification methods. Companies use off-balance-sheet financing to keep their debt-to-equity and leverage ratios low.

In addition to their special role in the financial system, large dealer banks share many of the same responsibilities as conventional commercial banks, including deposit taking and lending to corporations and consumers.

BROKERS: Also on the sell side are retail brokers that receive commissions for executing transactions and that have research departments that make investment recommendations. Advantages of using brokers include their expertise in the trading process, their access to other traders and exchanges, and their ability to facilitate clearance and settlement. Because brokers play the role of middlemen in the trading process, traders can use broker services when they want to remain anonymous to other traders.

Typically, traders can manage their order exposure by breaking up large trades and distributing them to different brokers or by asking a single broker in charge of the entire trade to expose only parts of the order, so that the full size remains unknown to other traders. Brokers also often represent limit orders for clients (i.e., orders placed with a brokerage to buy or sell shares at a specified price or better). In this event, brokers monitor the markets on behalf of their clients and make decisions based on client limit and stop orders when the markets change.

The brokerage firm's proprietary trading operations involve the firm's own account, called the house account. Other sources of broker revenue include soft commissions, payments for order flow, interest on margin loans, short interest rebates (on short sales), underwriting fees when the firm helps clients sell securities, and mergers and acquisitions (M&A) fees. The major cost of running a brokerage firm is labor: the brokers and other employees who provide the firm's services to clients.

Brokerage firms and other firms with major investment activities organize their activities into three major operations: (1) front office, (2) back office, and (3) middle office. **Front office operations** involve investment decision-making and, in the case of brokerage firms, contact with clients. **Back office operations** play a supportive role in the maintenance of accounts and information systems used to transmit important market and trader information in all trading transactions, as well as in the clearance and settlement of the trades. **Middle office operations** form the interface between the front office and the back office, with a focus on risk management.

2.1.3 Outside Service Providers

Other major participants in the world of alternative investments are outside service providers, such as prime brokers, accountants, attorneys, and fund administrators. Alternative investment funds rely on outside service providers for their successful creation and operation. Their roles are briefly discussed here.

PRIME BROKERS: **Prime brokers** allow an investment manager to carry out trades in multiple financial instruments at multiple broker-dealers while keeping all cash and securities at a single firm, and have the following primary functions: clearing and financing trades for clients, providing research, arranging financing, borrowing and lending securities, and producing portfolio accounting. Prime brokers offer a range of services.

Prime brokers have a powerful tool in their ability to make margin calls. The prime broker can demand that the fund manager deposit more cash into its prime brokerage account to support its leveraged trading, and that the fund manager liquidate outstanding portfolio positions to raise cash to deposit with the prime broker. The ultimate threat is that the prime broker can seize collateral from the hedge fund manager and liquidate the collateral to raise cash.

ACCOUNTANTS AND AUDITORS: The accounting firm providing services to a hedge fund or to another alternative investment fund should include an experienced auditor and tax adviser. During the creation of the fund or investment vehicle, the accounting firm provides services largely parallel to those of an attorney: reviewing legal documents to ensure that accounting methods and allocations are appropriate and feasible, and that relevant tax issues have been addressed. The accountant helps prepare partnership returns and the necessary forms for the investors in the fund to report their shares of partnership income, deductions, gains, and losses (e.g., Schedule K-1 in the United States). The adviser also provides tax-related advice to the fund throughout the year and may be called on as a consultant on structuring and compensation issues for the principals of the general partner. The auditor performs a year-end audit of the fund, including the review of security pricing, and presents the results of this audit to the fund and its investors. Accountants usually cooperate with the prime broker and fund administrator to gather the necessary information for audits and tax returns.

ATTORNEYS: An attorney helps determine the best legal structure for a fund's unique investment strategies, objectives, and desired investors. The attorney takes care of filing any documents required by the government (federal or other levels) and creates the legal documents necessary for establishing and managing a hedge fund or another alternative investment. The attorney can offer guidance on marketing a hedge fund or another alternative investment in full compliance with all legal requirements, as well as on operational issues, such as personal trading. For example, in the United States, an attorney can provide advice regarding Securities and Exchange Commission (SEC) rules governing the use of testimonials, performance statistics, and prior performance statistics.

FUND ADMINISTRATORS: Many hedge funds and other alternative investment funds now engage a fund administrator to be responsible for bookkeeping, third-party information gathering, and securities valuation functions for all of their funds, both onshore and offshore. The **fund administrator** has ten roles: (1) maintains a general ledger account, (2) marks the fund's books, (3) maintains its records, (4) carries out monthly accounting, (5) supplies its monthly profit and loss (P&L) statements and calculates its returns, (6) verifies asset existence, (7) independently calculates fees, (8) provides an unbiased, third-party resource for price confirmation on security positions, (9) produces a monthly capital account statement for investors, and (10) apportions fund income or loss among them. The administrator takes over the duties of day-to-day accounting and bookkeeping so that managers can focus on maximizing the portfolio's returns. The administrator can also be an important source of information for the auditor and tax adviser in completing required audits and tax returns.

Hedge fund infrastructure: Hedge funds can require a complicated infrastructure and extensive technological systems. The **hedge fund infrastructure** may have three main financial components: (1) platforms, (2) software, and (3) data providers. **Financial platforms** are systems that provide access to financial markets, portfolio management systems, accounting and reporting systems, and risk management systems. **Financial software** may consist of prepackaged software programs and computer languages tailored to the needs of financial organizations. Some funds use open-source software, and others pay licensing fees for proprietary software. For a hedge fund, most of the raw material that goes into its strategy development and ongoing investment process is in the form of data. **Financial data providers** supply funds primarily with raw financial market data, including security prices, trading information, indices, and company-specific information such as income statements and balance sheets. The amount of data is dictated by the investment style. Nonetheless, most hedge fund managers are required to keep abreast of market developments and macroeconomic news.

Due to legal implications, directly marketing alternative investment vehicles can be problematic. One method of indirectly marketing private funds is to report a fund's performance to an index provider, especially if the fund's performance is attractive. Index providers compile indices of prices that assist fund managers in evaluating performance.

Consultants: Consultants may be hired by pensions, endowments, or high-net-worth individuals to provide a number of roles and services that center on advice, analysis, and investment recommendations. Clients rely on consultants to offer unbiased analysis of money managers' investment performance, as well as advice on how to best allocate funds. Clients expect their consultants to help them lay out the parameters of their investment objectives by setting out a plan for allocating assets within the framework of their objectives and risk tolerance. Consultants work closely with their clients to monitor the performance of investments while continuing to play an advisory role in a client's choice of other service providers.

Consultants are increasingly being used to serve the role of chief investment officer in small organizations. The role of an outsourced chief investment officer (OCIO) ranges from performing all of the decision-making duties of an in-house chief investment officer to a reduced role of assisting staff with a subset of decisions.

Consultants have traditionally been compensated for their services in one or more of the following ways: fees from their clients, fees from proprietary investment products, or compensation packages from the money managers for whom they generate business. **Consulting conflicts of interest** can emerge when consultants are compensated by money managers because this form of payment can detract from the ability to offer independent advice to clients and encourage the consultant to favor the money managers offering compensation. Further, the compensation that consultants receive from money managers is undisclosed and can be quite substantial. Some consultants waive their regular consulting fee, giving the impression that their services are free.

Consultants' integrity and expertise are vital parts of the consultant-client relationship because many clients rely on their consultants to set out the best investment plan for their purposes and hire the best money managers to oversee those investments. A third compensation approach has emerged in which consultants use their expertise in manager selection and risk management to serve as fund-of-funds managers to their clients. This arrangement avoids explicit fees to the investors for the consulting advice, and offers the potential that the consultants will act with substantial objectivity in the selection of managers.

DEPOSITORIES AND CUSTODIANS: **Depositories** and **custodians** are very similar entities that are responsible for holding their clients' cash and securities and settling clients' trades, both of which maintain the integrity of clients' assets while ensuring that trades are settled quickly. The **Depository Trust Company (DTC)** is the principal holding body of securities for traders all over the world and is part of the Depository Trust and Clearing Corporation (DTCC), which provides clearing, settlement, and information services. The National Securities Clearing Corporation is the DTCC's second major subsidiary in the United States. The DTCC also created the Fixed Income Clearing Corporation (FICC). The European Central Counterparty Limited (EuroCCP) is the major depository for clients in European trading markets, and offers European clients the same clearing and settlement services as those offered by the DTCC to American traders.

BANKS: A **commercial bank** focuses on the business of accepting deposits and making loans, with modest investment-related services. An **investment bank** focuses on providing sophisticated investment services, including underwriting and raising capital, as well as other activities such as brokerage services, mergers, and acquisitions.

Hedge funds may enlist the services of a commercial bank to facilitate the flow of both investment- and non-investment-related capital. In addition, hedge funds may use their commercial bank for loans, credit enhancement, and/or lines of credit. In the United States, the commercial banking and investment banking functions tend to be separated by regulation. Germany uses **universal banking**, which means that German banks can engage in both commercial and investment banking. Also unlike the United States, a large portion of German firms are privately funded and have two governance bodies: the Vorstand, or management board, and the Aufsichtsrat, or supervisory board.

Although the Japanese financial system seems superficially similar to the American system, banks are much more influential in Japan than they are in the United States, and cross-ownership is far more common. Japanese banks can hold common stock, and Japanese corporations can hold stock in other Japanese firms. A *keiretsu* is a group of firms in different industries bound together by cross-ownership of their common stock and by customer-supplier relationships. The 10 largest Japanese banks (known as city banks) are responsible for funding approximately one-third of all investments in the country. As in Germany, large banks play an active role in monitoring the decisions of the borrowing firm's management and have significant power to seize collateral, as both trustee and direct lender.

In the United Kingdom, there are two main types of banks: clearing banks, which are similar to American commercial banks, and merchant banks, similar to American investment banks. As in the United States, UK banks are not strongly involved in the firms with which they do business, and substantial stock ownership by banks is prohibited.

2.2 ALTERNATIVE INVESTMENT STRUCTURES

There are numerous legal structures used throughout investments to meet the preferences and needs of investors and managers. The names and details of these structures vary between jurisdictions. This section provides an overview of the most common aspects of these structures. The starting point is limited liability.

2.2.1 Limited Liability and Passive Investments

Limited liability is the restriction of potential loss to a fixed sum, such as the amount invested in an asset. For example, a real estate investor with limited liability may be protected from massive losses beyond the amount invested in a firm even if a jury awards massive damages to tenants who sustained damage, or a fund manager who incorporates might be protected from losses beyond the assets of the corporation. Receiving this protection in most jurisdictions requires that the investor or manager not be actively engaged in control of the firm's operations.

The issue of liability is therefore related to whether or not the investment is passive. There are two major definitions of passive investments. In the context of investment strategies, passive investments can refer to buy-and-hold strategies often designed to match the risk and return of an index. In the context of limiting liability, **passive investments** are positions in entities (such as operating firms or investment firms) over which the owner of the position does not exert substantial control and therefore may receive reduced liability exposures and/or passive investment tax treatments. For example, an investor with a small position in a corporation is usually considered to be a passive investor if the investor does not exert substantial control over the corporation's decisions. A passive investor in a corporation is not generally subject to potentially unlimited liability from damages caused by the corporation's activities. However, an investor who acquires a large stake in the company and attempts to exert a large influence on the corporation's decisions runs the risk of losing his or her protection from unlimited liability.

Limited liability is an institution found throughout the world in modern economies as a way of encouraging widespread investment. Consider the implications of an economy without limited liability for passive investors. If every investor was subject to unlimited liability from every investment, few would dare to diversify broadly, since losses in one firm (e.g., from lawsuits that awarded massive damages) could wipe out the investor's life savings. Limited liability is necessary for well-functioning capital markets, which in turn are necessary for a large, modern economy.

However, limited liability raises concerns over probity in the management of enterprises when investors and managers with limited liability are in the asymmetric position of having huge potential profits and limited losses. **Probity** is the quality of exercising strong principles such as honesty, decency, and integrity. Modern economies struggle with the potential trade-off between encouraging both probity and widespread investment. The lines between exactly what constitutes passive investing and control or significant influence differ between jurisdictions.

The following subsections provide an introduction to the investment structures that have emerged to engineer the rights and responsibilities of investors and managers.

2.2.2 Corporations and Limited Liability Companies

A **corporation** is a legal entity in which its shareholders receive distributions on a pro rata or pari passu basis and which generally provides limited liability for passive investors. A **limited liability company (LLC)** is a distinct entity: (1) designed to offer its investors ("members") protection from losses exceeding their investments absent fraud or other activities that could "pierce the veil" between the member's ownership interest in the LLC and the member's other holdings, and (2) that does not require that distributions and any other advantages of ownership be made in proportion to each member's capital contribution to the firm. Thus, unlike a corporation in which dividends are paid to owners (shareholders) based on the number of shares held, an LLC may be structured to make distributions to members with or without consideration of ownership percentages.

Throughout alternative investments, investors and managers use LLCs and other entities offering limited liability to serve as a buffer to reduce liability exposures (as well as for other purposes). For example, the largest university endowment in the world is not *directly* owned by Harvard University. It is managed by a corporation, the Harvard Management Company, Inc., and its private equity holdings have been managed by the Harvard Management Private Equity Corporation. Throughout investments, entities are created and used for various purposes such as shielding assets, reducing taxation, simplifying regulation, and avoiding entanglements in proceedings such as bankruptcy. As is demonstrated in subsequent sections, many organizational charts do not show some or all of the legal entities that exist with little function other than to serve as buffers against liability.

2.2.3 Limited Partnership Structures

Exhibit 2.1 provides a simplified view of the common form of a limited partnership as used in hedge funds, private equity funds, and other alternative investment funds. The general partner organizes the fund and manages the assets. The limited partners contribute most of the capital.

Note, however, that Exhibit 2.1 is a simplification of the typical limited partnership structure as used in practice. The general partners likely formed an LLC (let's call it the "parent LLC") that in turn formed an LLC to serve as the general partner and another LLC to serve as the investment adviser to the partnership. The personnel involved in three LLCs may be overlapping or even identical, with the primary functions being preserving liability and providing clarity with regard to control.

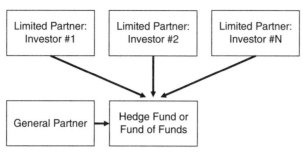

EXHIBIT 2.1 Structure of a Limited Partnership
Investment Vehicle

2.2.4 Bankruptcy-Remote Entities

The discussions of limited liability in the previous sections focused on protecting the owners of an entity from unlimited losses generated by the entity. This section discusses protecting asset owners from the potential losses and delays from bankruptcy proceedings. A bankruptcy-remote entity is often structured as a special purpose vehicle or entity. A **special purpose vehicle (SPV) or special purpose entity (SPE)** is a legal entity such as an LLC that serves a specific function (such as holding assets), often with the goal of being bankruptcy remote. A bankruptcy-remote entity is designed to provide protection from involvement in potential bankruptcy proceedings of the entities placing assets in the vehicle, and is discussed further in Chapter 25 on collateralized debt obligations. Understanding SPVs/SPEs can help clarify complex diagrams of organizational relationships.

2.2.5 Entities Facilitating Investor Taxation Differences

Another organizational complexity can be **master-feeder funds,** which are designed to provide efficient access to investors who are subject to different taxation but wish to invest in the same portfolio. Investors with U.S. tax liability would invest in onshore funds, which are structured as U.S.-domiciled vehicles subject to U.S. regulation and tax laws. Tax-exempt investors or those who owe taxes in another country may invest offshore, such as in funds domiciled in the Cayman Islands or other offshore domiciles. Offshore jurisdictions typically do not charge taxes on investment income in the country of the fund's domicile, but trust that investors will pay taxes on the investment income in their home country. Offshore vehicles should not be used to evade taxes, as they are designed to be efficient tax-neutral vehicles that investments appropriate for asset owners, with a wide array of home countries and tax regimes. Investors in offshore funds continue to be subject to taxation in their home jurisdiction.

A fund manager may manage assets, as illustrated in Exhibit 2.2. The **master trust** is the legal structure (typically offshore) used to invest the assets of both onshore investors and offshore investors in a consistent if not identical manner, so that both types of investors can share the manager's skills. Investors access the master trust through feeder funds. A **feeder fund** is a legal structure through

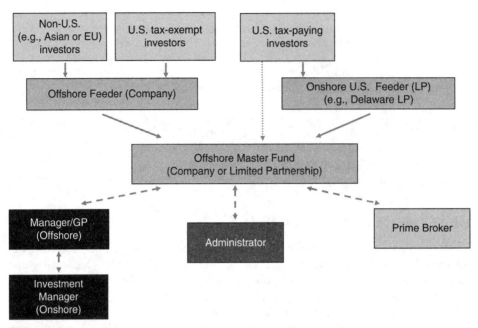

EXHIBIT 2.2 Typical Master/Feeder Hedge Fund Structure
Source: Slide 19, "Typical Master/Feeder Hedge Fund Structure," from AIMA PowerPoint presentation "Introduction to Hedge Funds and the Alternative Investment Management Industry," November 7, 2017.

which investors with common preferences with regard to taxation can have efficient access to the investment performance of the master trust. In the simplified case of two types of investors (onshore and offshore), the investors use separate feeder funds to access the master trust. Investors in both of these feeder funds benefit from the separation of funds because tax consequences flow appropriately to each investor. Together, the master trust and feeder funds are referred to as a master-feeder structure.

The purpose of the master trust is tax neutrality, not evasion. In Bermuda, for example, master trust funds pay only a corporate licensing fee, not corporate income tax. This ensures that there are no tax consequences to the fund investors at the master trust level. Instead, the tax consequences for the investors occur at their country of domicile based on the relevant feeder fund. Investors in the onshore, or U.S.-based, feeder fund are subject to the U.S. Internal Revenue Code, whereas investors in the offshore feeder fund are subject to the tax codes of their respective domiciles.

2.3 KEY FEATURES OF FUND STRUCTURES

This section reviews key features of limited partnerships that are common to various investment partnerships, including private equity funds, hedge funds, and other private placements.

2.3.1 The Four Key Partnership Documents

There are four key documents used in establishing and managing a hedge fund, private equity fund, or other private partnership: (1) **private-placement memoranda** (a.k.a. the offering memorandum), which include the formal description of an investment opportunity that complies with securities regulations; (2) a **partnership agreement** (a.k.a. a limited partnership agreement), which is a formal written contract creating a partnership; (3) a **subscription agreement**, which is an application submitted by an investor who desires to join a limited partnership; and (4) a **management company operating agreement**, which is an agreement between members related to a limited liability company and the conduct of its business as it pertains to the law.

The **limited partnership agreement (LPA)** defines its legal framework and its terms and conditions. These are the terms that the limited partners are agreeing to when making a private investment, so it is important that this document is read carefully and all of the terms are understood. In many cases, private equity managers are not fiduciaries, so limited partners should not assume that the general partner has the best interest of their investors in mind.

The LPA has two main categories of clauses: (1) investor protection clauses and (2) economic terms clauses. Investor protection clauses cover investment strategy, including possible investment restrictions, key-person provisions, termination and divorce, the investment committee, the LP advisory committee, exclusivity, and conflicts. Economic terms clauses include management fees and expenses, the GP's contribution, and the distribution of cash (i.e., the waterfall). The distribution waterfall defines how returns are split between the LP and GP and how fees are calculated. LPAs are continuously evolving, given the increasing sophistication of fund managers and investors, new regulations, and changing economic environments. In essence, the LPA lays out conditions aimed at both aligning the interests of fund managers with their investors and discouraging the GP from cheating (moral hazard), lying (adverse selection), or engaging in opportunism (holdup problem) in whatever form. Limited partners may wish to review the Private Equity Principles document from the Institutional Limited Partners Association (ILPA) to understand best practices and the important terms where the interests of LPs and GPs may diverge.

Moral hazard and adverse selection take place when there is asymmetric information between two parties (e.g., LPs and GPs). **Adverse selection** takes place before a transaction is completed, when the decisions made by one party cause less desirable parties to be attracted to the transaction. For example, if an LP decides to seek GPs that charge very low fees and offer funds with very favorable terms, the LP is likely to attract unskilled GPs that claim to be skilled.

Moral hazard, in contrast, takes place after a transaction is completed and can be defined as the changes in behavior of one or more parties as a result of incentives that come into play once a contract is in effect. For example, without proper monitoring, a GP may take excessive risk in order to increase the potential performance fee, or an unskilled manager may decide not to take substantive risk and just collect the management fee.

In economics, the holdup problem is a situation in which two parties (in this case, a GP and an LP) refrain from cooperating due to concerns that they might give the other party increased bargaining power and thereby reduce their own profits. Incentives are designed so that the fund manager's focus is on maximizing terminal wealth and performance and ensuring that contractual loopholes are not exploited (e.g., by producing overly optimistic interim results). It is through the proper alignment of the economic interests of investors and managers, not just through the LPA covenants, the advisory boards, or the committees composed of LPs, that one can eliminate many of the problems associated with the principal-agent relationship, especially in those scenarios that cannot be foreseen. To be successful, the structure must address management fees, performance-related incentives, hurdle rates, and, importantly, the fact that GPs make a substantial personal investment in each fund. Additional clauses may be required to cover reinvestments and clawbacks, as well as noneconomic terms such as key-person provisions, joint and several liability, and disclosure obligations. Together, these clauses provide LPs with moderate but sufficient control over the management of the fund. LPs are encouraged to understand all of the terms of their investment and negotiate carefully with GPs to ensure that the interests of the GP and the LP are truly aligned, as the original contract presented is likely to have terms that favor the GP. These key LPA features are described in the following sections.

2.3.2 Corporate Governance in Private Funds

The law and the LPA define and restrict the degree of control LPs have over the activities of GPs. Such controls relate, for example, to waiving or accepting investment restrictions, extending the investment period or fund duration, handling key-person-related issues, or participating in an **LP advisory committee (LPAC)**, whose responsibilities are defined in the LPA and normally relate to dealing with conflicts of interest, reviewing valuation methods, and any other consents predefined in the LPA. LPs can make decisions with either a simple majority (e.g., the decision to extend the investment period or the fund's duration) or a qualified majority (e.g., the decision to remove the GP without cause). A **qualified majority** is generally more than 75% of LPs in contrast to the over 50% required for a simple majority.

Occasionally, LPs may be offered positions on the investment committee. However, it is not clear whether LPs should actually take on this role. In limited partnership structures, an overactive LP could become reclassified as a GP, thereby losing limited liability. Generally, international industry professionals recognize that fund managers should make investment and divestment decisions without the direct involvement of investors, so as not to dilute the responsibility of the manager, create potential conflicts of interest with nonparticipating investors, or expose LPs to the risk of losing their limited liability. Also, investors do not normally have the legal rights or the required skills and experience to make such decisions.

Another important element of corporate governance is reporting to LPs. Various PE associations or industry boards have released guidelines for valuation and reporting. The obligation to disclose in compliance with these guidelines is increasingly being made part of contractual agreements. While some GPs reduce the level of detail provided to the bare minimum and share it with all LPs, others share different levels of detail depending on the specific type of investor.

2.3.3 Investment Objectives, Fund Size, and Fund Terms

In LPAs, the description of investment objectives should be specific but not too narrow. Investors should not attempt to put overly restrictive limits on a fund manager's flexibility, which could block the fund manager's ability to profit from unanticipated opportunities. Further, with uncertain investments, severe information asymmetry, and difficulties in monitoring and enforcing restrictions, fund managers may simply find ways around narrow restrictions.

The fund's size, in terms of capital committed by LPs, needs to be in line with these investment objectives. However, various factors, such as the management resources required or the number of potential opportunities, implicitly set a minimum or maximum size of the fund.

In the case of private equity, fund lives or terms are typically seven to 10 years, with possible extensions of up to three years. This represents a trade-off among better investment returns, sufficient time to invest and divest, and the degree of illiquidity still acceptable for investors.

Normally, the extension of a fund's life is approved annually by a simple majority of LPs or members of the LPAC, one year at a time versus two or more at once, during which time management fees are either reduced or eliminated altogether to stimulate quick exits.

Normally, proceeds are distributed to investors as soon as is feasible after the realization of or distribution of a fund's assets, but in some cases, LPs grant fund managers the discretion to reinvest some of the proceeds that are realized during the investment period.

2.3.4 Management Fees and Expenses

In private equity, compensation is overwhelmingly performance driven. Management fees provide a base compensation so that the fund manager can support the ongoing activities of funds, and there is a consensus that GPs should not be able to make significant profits on management fees alone. These fees need to be based on reasonable operating expenses and salaries, and be set at a level modest enough to ensure that the fund manager is motivated primarily by the carried interest, but sufficient to avoid the manager's departure to greener fields.

2.3.5 Global Regulations and Fund Structures

We present a brief overview here of global regulations and fund structures. These topics will be covered at a more comprehensive level in the CAIA Level II curriculum. The Markets in Financial Instruments Directive (MiFID) is an EU law that establishes uniform regulation for investment managers in the European Economic Area (the EU plus Iceland, Norway, and Liechtenstein). The MiFID is one of the primary pieces of European legislation dealing with regulation of investment services, including management services. The MiFID II is a revision directed toward extending the reach of MiFID to cover gaps in the 2007 document as well as addressing emerging issues, such as lack of transparency in trading occurring in dark pools.

In July 2011, the Alternative Investment Fund Managers Directive (AIFMD) came into force. This directive applies to alternative investment fund managers (AIFMs) that are located in the EU or, if located outside the EU, manage either EU funds or market funds (whether EU or non-EU) in the EU. An AIFM includes any legal or natural person whose regular business is to manage one or more alternative investment funds (AIFs). An AIF is any collective investment that invests in accordance with a specified policy, except UCITS. This captures hedge funds, private equity funds, infrastructure funds, real estate funds, and non-UCITS retail funds, whether open-ended or closed-ended and whether listed or not.

Hedge fund activity and hedge fund regulation vary tremendously outside of the United States and the EU. For example, the Australian Securities and Investment Commission (ASIC) does not regulate hedge funds differently from other managed funds.[1] Domestic hedge funds in Australia are usually organized as unit trusts, and foreign hedge funds are foreign investment funds (FIFs). Taxation is a relatively important and complex issue in Australian hedge fund ownership.

SICAVs and SICAFs are European fund structures, often domiciled in Luxembourg. Société d'Investissement à Capital Variable (SICAV) funds are publicly traded open-end funds, while Société d'Investissement à Capital Fixe (SICAF) funds are publicly traded closed-end funds. Many of these fund vehicles are organized under the UCITS framework, which includes restrictions on leverage, liquidity, and concentration of assets in the fund's portfolio. Other SICAV and SICAF funds are organized as specialized investment funds (SIFs), which give more flexibility to private equity and hedge fund managers, as the investment strategies are not as limited as under the UCITS framework.

While UCITS funds are also used in Ireland, ICAVs are also available. The Irish Collective Asset Management Vehicle (ICAV), launched by new regulations in 2015, is rapidly attracting assets. ICAVs have a goal of allowing very flexible investment vehicles and an ease of structuring new funds under simplified compliance rules.[2] This flexibility allows for both open-end and closed-end structures and may be designed to be tax compliant for U.S. investors.

In the Cayman Islands, funds may be structured in a variety of ways, including as limited companies, unit trusts, or limited partnerships. Exempted vehicles are typically managed outside of the Cayman Islands, even though they are domiciled and regulated in Cayman. Cayman vehicles tend to require a minimum investment of US$100,000, which limits the ownership to larger and hopefully sophisticated investors. The Cayman Islands Monetary Authority (CIMA) does not place restrictions on the transparency, leverage, or other investment risk features of fund vehicles.[3] Fund directors and service providers are often located in Cayman, whereas fund management activities take place in the home country of the fund manager. Master-feeder structures are one of the most common features found in Cayman funds.

2.4 FINANCIAL MARKETS

This section provides an overview of the financial markets involved in alternative investments. A **primary market** refers to the methods, institutions, and mechanisms involved in the placement of new securities to investors. A **secondary market** facilitates trading among investors of previously existing securities.

2.4.1 Primary Capital Markets

New issues are sold in primary capital markets and distributed by an underwriter, who is responsible for the organization, risk bearing (during placement), and distribution (or sale) of newly issued securities. Investment banks serve as underwriters for the placement of traditional investments. For example, investment banks place new equity issues that originate either as new and additional shares in existing securities (secondary issues) or as first-time issues of shares not previously traded (initial public offerings, or IPOs).

In the modern global economy, firms often arrange to have their shares traded in foreign markets and denominated in the currency of the foreign market. For example, a German firm could list its stock on a U.S. exchange as an American depositary receipt (ADR) or a global depositary receipt (GDR). Foreign issuers must comply with all the rules that apply to domestic firms, as well as any additional regulations that apply to foreign issuers.

Another source of securities issued in primary capital markets is securitization. **Securitization** involves bundling assets, especially unlisted assets, and issuing claims on the bundled assets. The securities are registered and sold in the public market.

Securitization can allow banks to divest loans and operating firms to divest illiquid assets such as accounts receivable to lay off risk and obtain cash. Various types of unlisted but liquid assets are also securitized, including various fixed-income securities such as mortgages. Exchange-traded funds are emerging as a major source of securitization, in which new securities are created, generally with underlying portfolios of listed securities.

Participants in alternative investments often create securities that are not subsequently listed. An example is when deal creators issue structured products, some of which are private (see Part 5). Private equity firms often use primary markets as exit strategies for their underlying investments. Large private equity firms hold substantial controlling positions in the companies. A goal of these private equity firms is to develop these companies to the point that they can be sold to the public through IPOs.

2.4.2 Secondary Capital Markets

After their initial offerings, many securities are traded in secondary capital markets, which provide greater liquidity and a continuous flow of price information. In major markets, **limit orders** can be placed by market participants to buy securities at specified maximum prices or sell securities at specified minimum prices. These limit orders tend to buy securities at bid prices and sell securities at ask prices. The price difference between the highest bid price (the best bid price) and the lowest offer (the best ask price) is the **bid-ask spread. Market making** is a practice whereby an investment bank or another market participant deals securities by regularly offering to buy securities and sell securities. The market maker seeks to receive the bid-ask spread through regularly selling at the ask price and buying at the bid price. The bid-ask spread compensates investment banks for providing liquidity to the market. Market participants that wish to have transactions executed without delay may place **market orders,** which cause immediate execution at the best available price. Participants that place market orders are **market takers,** which buy at ask prices and sell at bid prices, generally paying the bid-ask spread for taking liquidity.

The primary listing markets in the United States are the New York Stock Exchange (NYSE) and the NASDAQ. The NYSE has physically centralized trading, while the NASDAQ uses computer networks between dealers. The largest markets outside the United States include the London Stock Exchange (United Kingdom), the Tokyo Stock Exchange (Japan), the Shanghai Stock Exchange (China), the Euronext (several locations), and the Hong Kong Stock Exchange (China).

2.4.3 Third and Fourth Private Markets

Third markets are regional exchanges where stocks listed in primary secondary markets can also be traded. In the United States, third markets allow brokers and dealers to set up trades away from an exchange by listing their prices on the NASDAQ Intermarket. Third markets represent a segment of the OTC market where nonmember investment firms can make markets in and trade securities without going through the exchange.

Fourth markets are electronic exchanges that allow traders to quickly buy and sell exchange-listed stocks via the electronic communications systems offered by these markets. Because of the anonymity of traders within these electronic networks, registered broker-dealers provide sponsorship for these systems so that traders have an alternative system to physical exchanges to buy and sell stocks. These alternative trading systems are computerized trading systems that do not formally list stocks but include electronic communication networks serving retail brokers and small institutional traders, as well as electronic crossing systems that match large buy and sell orders. This system is also called the fourth market system. These private financial markets are non-regulated markets that are neither exchanges nor OTC. Much of the high-frequency trading takes place in the fourth market. The advantages of private markets may include lower transaction costs, ease of completing a transaction directly between a buyer and a seller (which may or may not involve a broker), and the ability to expedite the consummation of a transaction. Conversely, the disadvantages may include the existence of asymmetrical information (between the participants), lack of transparency, and lack of regulatory protections.

2.5 REGULATORY ENVIRONMENT

Regulation of investments is motivated by concern for the participants directly involved as well as by concern for the overall economy. Privately organized investment vehicles, such as hedge funds, have generally received reduced regulatory scrutiny because the participants involved tend to be sophisticated institutions or individuals perceived to be less in need of regulatory protection than the general public.

Especially since the financial crisis that began in 2007, regulators throughout the world have become increasingly concerned about the role of hedge funds and other investment vehicles in exacerbating systemic risk. **Systemic risk** is the potential for economy-wide losses attributable to failures or concerns over potential failures in financial markets, financial institutions, or major participants. For example, the collapse of a very large hedge fund may lead to a sequence of collapses and failures that disrupt the financial system and cause widespread economic losses, not so much from the direct asset losses of the collapse as from the inability of the other market participants to trade and manage risks due to the uncertainty that is generated. Regulators are concerned that very large investment funds, such as some hedge funds, or highly complex alternative investment products, such as collateralized debt obligations (CDOs), may increase systemic risk.

2.5.1 Five Primary Forms of Hedge Fund Regulation

Regulations of hedge funds take five primary forms:

1. Requirements regarding establishing a hedge fund, including registration, licensing, minimum capital, and waiting periods
2. Registrations or restrictions on investment advisers and hedge fund managers
3. Restrictions on distribution and marketing of hedge funds, including which marketing channels may be used (e.g., banks), whether advertising is permitted, and to whom funds may be sold
4. Restrictions on operation of a hedge fund, including leverage, liquidity, risk, reporting, and location of outside service providers
5. Requirements regarding ongoing reporting

Hedge funds may also be subject to varying levels of taxation and to special taxes, fees, or licensing costs. Understanding regulations is a crucial aspect of alternative investing. Additional information on worldwide regulations is provided in the CAIA Level II curriculum.

2.6 LIQUID ALTERNATIVE INVESTMENTS

As their name implies, **liquid alternatives** are investment vehicles that offer alternative strategies in a form that provides investors with liquidity through opportunities to sell their positions in a market. Many major alternative investments, such as private equity or hedge funds, have historically been illiquid and opaque private placements held by high-net-worth and institutional investors. Liquid alternative investments are innovative products that provide access for all investors to the same or similar strategies in an exchange-traded and transparent format.

But the nature of the liquidity offered by liquid alternatives might better be described as "offering retail access" rather than "being able to be converted into cash quickly," the reason being that many alternatives, such as managed futures funds and structured products, have offered daily liquidity for years but are not commonly viewed as liquid because the products have been predominantly accessible only to institutional and high-net-worth investors.

2.6.1 The Spectrum of Liquid Alternatives Products

Liquid alternatives span a spectrum of alternative assets and strategies, with more innovations expected to emerge. A popular investment vehicle in the United States that illustrates liquid alternatives well is real estate investment trusts (REITs). REITs hold real estate as their underlying assets. Private REITs are common. But many REITs, especially the largest, are owned through publicly traded shares. The underlying assets of many large REITs are large private real estate properties, such as office buildings, retail properties, health care facilities, and apartment complexes. Large real estate properties are often owned by institutions, directly or through limited partnerships. REITs offer retail access of similar properties to large and small investors alike. Even though the underlying real estate properties are illiquid, the shares in the REITs offer investors high levels of liquidity. Many REITs also hold liquid real estate assets, such as mortgage securities. REITs are further discussed in Chapter 13.

Real estate in general and REITs in particular have been popular in the United States for so long that some experts may not view REITs as liquid alternatives. Many discussions of liquid alternatives focus on more recent innovations that provide liquid investment vehicles for small investors to obtain exposure to classic alternative investment strategies, such as hedge fund strategies. Specifically, these new liquid alternatives include the offering of hedge fund and managed futures strategies through liquid mutual funds, such as '40 Act funds in the United States and UCITS in the EU.

Liquid alternatives tend to have substantial fee structure differences, which are discussed later in this section. Liquid alternatives differ with the extent to which their investment strategies match the investment strategies of privately placed alternative investments. In this regard, there are five distinct types of liquid alternative funds:

1. UNCONSTRAINED CLONES: These liquid funds follow virtually the same strategy as private placement products with underlying liquid assets, such as some hedge funds or managed futures funds.
2. CONSTRAINED CLONES: These liquid funds implement a similar strategy as private placement products but are limited in risk exposure by leverage, concentration, or liquidity constraints.
3. LIQUIDITY-BASED REPLICATION PRODUCTS: These liquid funds are designed to mimic illiquid private placement investments, using liquid securities as proxies.
4. SKILL-BASED REPLICATION PRODUCTS: These liquid funds are designed to mimic a highly skilled private placement strategy using a simplified and more mechanical strategy.
5. ABSOLUTE RETURN OR DIVERSIFIED PRODUCTS: These liquid funds are designed to offer absolute returns and/or diversifying returns not directly related to opportunities historically available in private placements and potentially inconsistent with alternative strategies as typically deployed.

The last category refers to products being touted as liquid alternatives that are long-only mixes of traditional investment strategies that offer returns that have exhibited relatively low correlation with the overall market. These products lack the innovation, leverage, short positions, illiquidity, and skill-based active trading that have been the hallmark of alternative investment for decades. They tend to be offered by institutions with expertise in traditional investments that are responding to investor preferences for investment products that offer diversification relative to traditional equity and bond markets.

2.6.2 Growth and Growth Factors in Liquid Alternatives

Prior to the financial crisis of 2007–09, global assets under management in liquid alternatives totaled less than $100 billion. The performance success of some alternative investment strategies during the financial crisis, such as managed futures and global macro funds, led retail investors to welcome the opportunity to diversify into those strategies and other alternative investment strategies as retail products became widely available.

By 2018, liquid alternatives had soared to over $800 billion in global AUM. Nevertheless, the proportion of assets in mutual funds that is devoted to alternative assets is only a few percentage points.

Continued growth could be driven by two primary factors. First, retail investors may continue to diversify into alternative strategies to lessen their percentage exposure to traditional stock and bond strategies. Second, the shift of retirement assets from a focus on defined benefit plans to defined contribution may mean that retail access to alternative investments will increase.

2.6.3 Three Constraints against Achieving Alternative Investment Benefits through Liquid Products

Some alternative investment strategies appear unable to be implemented through liquid retail structures, such as U.S. mutual funds or UCITS funds. There are three primary constraints.

1. Leverage: The sophisticated hedge fund strategies discussed in Part 3 often require substantial use of leverage, which is restricted within U.S. mutual funds by regulation. Specifically, there is a 300% asset coverage rule that requires a mutual fund to have assets totaling at least three times the total borrowings of the fund, thus limiting borrowing to 33% of assets. UCITS restrictions are even tighter.
2. There are regulatory constraints on concentration (i.e., lack of diversification).
3. There are illiquidity constraints (e.g., no more than 15% of a '40 Act fund or 10% of a UCITS fund can be invested in illiquid assets) that prevent substantial inclusion of private equity in open-end mutual funds.

These three regulatory issues are a primary reason why such alternative investments are organized through private placements. It should be noted that to qualify as a private placement vehicle, funds are severely limited as to the number of investors permitted. The severe limits on the number of investors lead fund managers to require large initial investment sizes, which steer the products away from small retail investors and toward large institutional investors.

Other hedge fund strategies appear quite tractable for delivery through retail products. For example, the returns of managed futures funds and hedge funds holding other liquid underlying assets can easily be delivered through retail products as long as the strategies do not require high leverage or concentration. Chapter 19 discusses the creative ways that multialternative mutual funds can be structured so as to facilitate the delivery of a large subset of hedge fund strategies through retail products.

A highly researched and debated approach to delivering hedge-fund-like strategies without necessarily using sophisticated management teams or illiquid securities is hedge fund replication. **Hedge fund replication** is the attempt to mimic the returns of an illiquid or highly sophisticated hedge fund strategy using liquid assets and simplified trading rules.

Another method of delivering alternative investment strategies through retail vehicles is the use of a closed-end mutual fund structure. **Closed-end mutual fund** structures provide investors with relatively liquid access to the returns of underlying assets even when the underlying assets are illiquid.

2.6.4 Four Factors Determining Performance of Liquid Alternatives Compared to Private Placements

Liquid alternatives are relatively new products with limited historical return data. Accordingly, there is especially high uncertainty with regard to the extent to which liquid alternatives will generate return enhancement or diversification benefits comparable to the results achieved in the past for institutional investors in private placements.

Returns from private placement vehicles and liquid alternatives may differ primarily due to four important factors, two of which relate to investment flexibility and two of which relate to fees:

1. The permissible investment strategies differ. Private placements often enjoy important flexibility with regard to leverage (including the magnitude of short positions) and concentration (lack of diversification).
2. Similarly, private placements may be able to generate higher returns due to their investment flexibility to hold more illiquid assets, thereby potentially receiving higher liquidity premiums.
3. Fees differ between liquid alternatives and private placements. Liquid alternatives tend to have lower fees because most '40 Act funds do not have incentive fees, especially asymmetric incentive fees wherein managers benefit from sharing upside profits but are limited in their exposure to downside losses. UCITS funds and Canadian investment funds do allow asymmetric incentive fees.
4. Managerial skill may differ. The higher potential fees from the asymmetric incentive fees of private placements may attract managers with greater skill. Some liquid alternative funds implement simplified trading rules rather than hiring sophisticated management teams. Note that three of the four factors favor private placement vehicles as being more likely to generate attractive returns. The only factor favoring liquid alternatives is lower fees.

2.6.5 Empirical Analysis of Liquid Alternative Investment Performance

Comparing the performance between private and public alternative funds in which the strategies match can be an effective way to estimate the risk and return differentials. A 2013 study by Cliffwater (discussed further in Chapter 19) compared funds and concluded that, on average, liquid alternative funds have lower risks and slightly to moderately lower average returns than limited partnership (or LP) funds that employ the same strategy.[4]

This brief overview of liquid alternatives lays a foundation for more detailed discussions on the underlying assets and investment strategies of the funds. Liquid alternatives are further discussed in the context of real assets in Chapters 11 and 12, hedge funds in Chapter 19, and private equity in Chapter 21.

2.7 TAXATION

Most institutional-quality alternative investments are not created or managed for the primary purpose of avoiding taxes. However, taxation can substantially affect investment returns, and therefore alternative investments are often constructed and managed to prevent additional taxation. In other words, investment pools are formed in light of taxation and with a goal of minimizing the extent to which the pooling of capital increases taxation for the investors relative to direct ownership of the underlying assets. For example, a hedge fund may be domiciled in a particular location for the purpose of preventing additional tax burdens on investors relative to the taxes that would be paid with direct investments using a separately managed and local account. Another hedge fund may be established to invest in municipal bonds for the purpose of generating tax-free income. However, the use of the hedge fund structure and its location do not make the income tax-free. Rather, it is the use of municipal bonds or other tax-free investments, whether inside or outside the hedge fund, that make the income tax-exempt.

In any case, knowledge of general global taxation is helpful in understanding the institutions and other structures involved with alternative investing. The primary objects of taxation throughout the world are income based, wealth based, and transaction based. This section summarizes taxation throughout the world primarily from the perspective of investments.

2.7.1 Income Taxation

Throughout the major economies of the world, income is taxed. Income taxation typically includes taxation on individual and corporate income. Most income taxation is progressive. **Progressive taxation** places higher-percentage taxation on individuals and corporations with higher incomes. Individual income taxation includes taxation of both wage income and investment income.

Although individual wage income and corporate earnings are often fully taxed, the primary issue for investing involves the potential for reduced income tax rates on investment income. Investment income is primarily dividend income, interest income, and capital gains. Investment income from dividends, interest, and capital gains is often either taxed at reduced rates or exempt from income taxation. Although most countries tax all of these types of investment income, the tax rules of individual countries differ primarily by the extent to which dividends, interest, and capital gains are exempted, partially taxed, or fully taxed.

Most major economies, including those of Austria, Brazil, China, Finland, France, Hong Kong, Italy, Japan, the Netherlands, Poland, Sweden, the United Kingdom, and the United States, tax investment income but offer reduced rates on some or all dividends, interest, and capital gains. In the United States, for example, state and municipal bond interest is exempt from federal taxation, and most corporate dividends are taxed at a reduced rate. However, some countries have investment income tax regimes that tax dividends, interest, or capital gains rather heavily or lightly compared to other nations. For example, Canada, Denmark, and Germany tend to have high tax rates on interest income. Australia, Belgium, New Zealand, Switzerland, and Taiwan tend to have low capital gains taxes.[5]

Other jurisdictions have no income tax or at least no income tax on particular investment pools. These jurisdictions are attractive locations for investment pools in that investors are taxed only by their home country rather than having to pay income taxes on investment income to both their home country and the domicile of the investment fund. These countries include traditional jurisdictions used by hedge funds, such as the Cayman Islands, the British Virgin Islands, Bermuda, Ireland, Luxembourg, Guernsey, and Mauritius.[6]

Some investing offers deferred taxation, in which investment income taxes are not assessed until the funds are withdrawn or distributed. For example, in the United States, qualified retirement savings are generally taxed only at withdrawal. Further, the contributions are often tax-deductible in the period in which the contribution is made. Other opportunities, such as some life insurance contracts, allow tax-deferred accrual of investment income.

Taxation of interest and dividends is generally assessed in the period in which the dividends and interest are distributed. Capital gains tend to be taxed when realized. Capital gains are realized in the period when there is a sale of a security for a price higher than the investor's cost, known as the cost basis. Investments therefore often offer a potentially valuable tax advantage of allowing wealth to be accumulated and accrued through capital appreciation that is not taxed as income until the asset is sold. Further, tax rates may be lower on capital gains, especially when an investment is held for a long time.

Taxation of investment income involves complex rules in most jurisdictions. Understanding taxation can be a very important part of investment management. For example, **Section 1256 contracts**, which include many futures and options contracts, have potentially enormous tax advantages in the United States, including having their income treated as 60% long-term capital gain and 40% short-term capital gain regardless of holding period. Proper decision-making based on this preferential tax treatment can enhance an investor's after-tax return.

2.7.2 Other Taxes and Withholding

In most jurisdictions, real estate taxation is an important form of taxation. Often, real estate taxes are assessed by local jurisdictions to fund local services such as schools and governmental services such as law enforcement. The national governments of Australia, Singapore, Belgium, Germany, and the United Kingdom tax real estate.[7] However, some jurisdictions tax wealth as a general national tax overall. For example, in Colombia, a wealth tax is assessed on all assets, including financial assets. Another important category of taxation is estate taxes that are assessed after the death of a wealthy taxpayer. For wealthy individuals, estate tax rates can be very high.

Although many countries have either drastically reduced or totally eliminated transaction taxes, several European countries continue to impose some form of tax on investment transactions. The United Kingdom uses a stamp tax of 0.5% on purchases of domestic securities, and France levies a value-added tax on commissions rather than on the transaction value. When market makers trade for their own accounts, they are usually exempted from transaction taxes. In the United States, there is a small fee assessed on securities transactions that is attributed to providing the regulatory services of the SEC.

The international convention on taxing income on foreign investments is to certify that the investor pays taxes to at least one country. Withholding taxes are therefore levied on dividend payments. Although this sometimes results in double taxation, a network of international tax treaties has been signed to prevent double taxation from occurring, so that investors receive a dividend net of withholding tax plus a tax credit from the foreign government but must pay tax on the gross dividends (minus the amount of the withholding tax credit) to the government where they reside. Although this process is potentially lengthy, it allows the investor to reclaim the withholding tax in the foreign country. Depending on the individual country's tax policies, some of the withholding can be retained by the country of origin. Some countries allow tax-free foreign investors (public pension funds) to apply for direct exemptions from tax withholding.

2.8 SHORT SELLING

Short selling financial assets is the process of borrowing securities from a securities lender, selling the securities at their market price, and eventually purchasing identical securities in the market to extinguish the loan from the securities lender. Short selling is an important part of many alternative investment strategies. Therefore, a solid understanding of short selling is vital to a complete understanding of alternative investments.

2.8.1 The Institutional Mechanics of Short Selling

Owners of stocks or other securities often leave the actual stock certificates with their brokerage firms or other financial institutions for safekeeping. Financial institutions often lend these securities to short sellers to generate income.

For example, suppose the stock of Neveright is currently selling for $50 per share. Some speculators believe that the share price of Neveright will soon fall to $40 per share and wish to take advantage of this situation. They place orders to short sell shares of Neveright through their brokerage firms. Their brokerage firms lend shares to their own customers seeking to short sell or they arrange to borrow shares from other financial institutions.

Customers of various brokerage firms hold millions of shares of Neveright in street name. **Street name** refers to the brokerage practice of having the direct legal ownership of customer securities held in the name of the brokerage firm on behalf of the customers rather than having the legal ownership of the shares reside directly with the economic owners of the securities (i.e., the customers of the brokerage firm). The brokerage firms lend shares in Neveright to the speculators that in turn get sold into the financial markets and likely deposited in other brokerage firms by the new owners of the shares.

Suppose that while the speculators maintain their short positions in Neveright, the firm pays a $1 per share dividend. Neveright distributes dividends to the current owners of record for the firm's shares, not to the previous shareholders who lent out their securities. The borrower of the securities must compensate the lender of the securities for the dividends on the securities that the corporation distributes during the holding period of the loan. **Substitute dividends** are cash flows paid by share borrowers to share lenders to compensate the lenders for the distributions paid by the corporation while the loan of stock is outstanding.

Eventually the speculators close their short positions by purchasing the stock in the open market and returning the shares to the lender. Since there is no upper limit to the price of a stock, short selling subjects the short seller to unlimited liability.

2.8.2 The Mechanics of Short Selling to the Short Seller

Consider a speculator (or hedger) that borrows 100 shares of Neveright from a broker and sells them in the market for $50. The speculator must have and post collateral to guarantee repayment of the loan. The speculator receives $5,000 (less commissions) from the sale and has a liability representing 100 shares of Neveright that must eventually be returned.

If the stock falls to $40, the speculator may buy 100 shares of Neveright for $40 a share (for a total of $4,000 less commission) and return the 100 shares to the securities lender for a profit before commission and other fees of $1,000. However, if the stock climbs to $60 and the speculator closes the position, the speculator would suffer a loss of $1,000 plus commissions. Because there is no upper limit to the price of Neveright stock, potential losses to short selling are unlimited.

The speculator is also responsible for substitute dividends (discussed earlier) and various costs, including the following:

1. The borrower of the short position posts collateral equal to the price of the assets plus margin, also known as a haircut, usually of 2%. Thus, if Fund A borrows $100,000 of stock from ABC Brokerage Firm and short sells that stock into the market, Fund A must place the proceeds of the sale (i.e., $100,000) and 2% more (i.e., $2,000) as collateral to provide protection to the lender against the risk that the borrowed stock will rise in price at the same time that Fund A becomes unable to fulfill its obligation to return the stock.

2. The lender of the securities earns interest on the collateral but typically offers the borrower of the securities a rebate. A **rebate** is a payment of interest to the securities' borrower on the collateral posted. A typical rebate is a little less than current short-term market interest rates (e.g., the general collateral rate less 0.25%). The goal of the securities lender is to receive a spread between the interest rate the lender is able to earn on the collateral and the rebate paid to the securities borrower. This compensation to the lender for their services is a cost to the borrower. Note that the securities lender takes the risk that the borrower will default and be unable to return the shares at the same time that the collateral will be insufficient to repurchase the shares in the marketplace.

3. The substitute dividend payments from the short seller (securities borrower) to the securities lender is not an economic cost to the short seller to the extent that the stock paying the dividend falls in price by an amount equal to the dividend. The short seller's gain from the stock price drop offsets the dividend to the borrower—part of the concept of dividend irrelevancy. **Dividend irrelevancy**

is the proposition that, in the absence of imperfections such as income taxation that penalized dividends, the distribution of corporate dividends does not alter shareholder wealth.

☞ APPLICATION 2.8.2A

Suppose that a short seller establishes a short position in one share of XYZ Corporation at $100 per share and that XYZ pays a dividend of $1.00 per share each year. The current rebate on XYZ shares is 1% per year and lenders require loans to be collateralized 102%. What would be the dollar profit or loss to the short seller if XYZ rose to $103 at the end of one year when the position was liquidated, and what is the effect of the dividend on that profit or loss? Assume that commission and other transaction fees totaled 5 cents per share per trade.

First, the short position loses $3 (a capital loss) when the stock rises from $100 to $103. When the stock pays dividends of $1, it is up to the short seller to make a cash payment to the securities lender in lieu of dividends, so the short seller loses another $1. Finally, an institutional short seller typically receives a short stock rebate; in this case, the rebate would be $1 (1% × $102). The total loss is $3.03 per share (−$3.00 + $1.02 − $1.00 − $0.05 commission).

Most securities lending is performed on an overnight basis, wherein securities lenders may demand return of the shares at any time and may require regular adjustment of the collateral amount to reflect the current market price of the borrowed securities. However, some short sales can be performed as term loans of perhaps six months, wherein the lender agrees not to demand return of the securities until the term has ended.

2.8.3 Special Situations Involving Short Selling

There are special risks to having short positions in equity securities, especially for stocks that are popular targets of short sellers. As the quantity of a stock's outstanding shares being lent to short sellers increases, the competition to find new stock to borrow increases. Entities that hold the stock put that stock "on special." In this context, a **special stock** is a stock for which higher net fees are demanded when it is borrowed. To the short seller, this means receiving a smaller rebate. For example, **general collateral stocks,** which are stocks not facing heavy borrowing demand, may earn a 2% rebate when risk-free rates are at 2%, whereas stocks on special may earn zero rebates or even negative rebates, wherein borrowers must pay the lenders money in addition to the interest that the lender is earning on the collateral.

When numerous speculators establish highly similar large positions, it is often referred to as a crowded trade. In the case of traders establishing large short positions, the trade is often termed a crowded short. The security being shorted can become a special stock, and in extreme cases, the security can only be made available for short sales at extraordinarily high borrowing rates as high as 20% or more.

When the inventory of stock available to borrowers becomes extremely tight, short sellers may find their position **bought in**, meaning the broker revokes the borrowing privilege for that specific stock and requires the trader to cover the short position. If shares cannot be borrowed through another lender on affordable terms, this leaves a convertible arbitrage manager without a hedge to the convertible bond position, which is likely to lead the trader to sell the bond to reduce the stock market risk of the portfolio.

Short sellers should monitor the availability of shares trading in the market to ensure that they can be purchased without substantially increasing the market price when they are needed to cover a short position. Short sellers need to be aware of the possibility of a short squeeze. A **short squeeze** occurs when holders of short positions are compelled to purchase shares at increasing prices to cover their positions due to limited liquidity. As the ratio of shares being sold short increases relative to the total number of freely floating shares, it becomes increasingly difficult to borrow additional shares, and the potential for a short squeeze increases. Several hedge fund managers being forced to buy in and cover their short positions simultaneously can put upward pressure on the price of the shorted security. The upward movement of the stock price may cause other short sellers to cover their positions, putting even more upward pressure on the stock price. As more and more hedge fund managers scramble to cover their short positions, the price of the underlying stock can rise rapidly, leaving the last few hedge fund managers squeezed out of their positions at especially elevated prices.

Another potentially huge complexity from short selling is that the lender of the security may demand that the shares be returned. Most securities are lent on a short-term basis, with the lender retaining the right to demand that the shares be returned at any moment. Usually when this happens, the broker simply arranges for another securities lender to loan shares so that the short seller maintains a seamless exposure.

But especially in times of overall market turbulence, or in times of turbulence for a particular stock, the shares become difficult to borrow. In those cases, the short seller may be forced to cover the position. This means that the short seller must purchase the shares in the market so that they can be returned to the securities lender. The short seller is therefore forced to close his position during a period of turbulence rather than at a time of his choosing. Note that an investor with a long position in a stock does not face this risk. The short seller's potential problem of being forced to liquidate a position is especially acute during a short squeeze.

REVIEW QUESTIONS

1. What is the term for a private management advisory firm that serves a group of related and ultra-high-net-worth investors?
2. In a large financial services organization, what is the name used to denote the people and processes that play a supportive role in the maintenance of accounts and information systems as well as in the clearance and settlement of trades?
3. Are dealer banks described as buy-side or sell-side market participants?
4. List several advantages of separately managed accounts (SMAs) relative to funds.
5. Which of the following participants is LEAST LIKELY to be classified as an outside service provider to a fund: arbitrageurs, accountants, auditors, or attorneys?

6. List four key legal documents necessary for establishing and managing a private fund.
7. What is a qualified majority?
8. Is the New York Stock Exchange a secondary or third market?
9. What are the three constraints against achieving alternative investment benefits through liquid products?
10. What is systemic risk?

NOTES

1. "Changing Rules: The Regulation, Taxation and Distribution of Hedge Funds around the Globe," PricewaterhouseCoopers, June 2009, http://www.pwc.com/en_US/gx/investment management-real-estate/pdf/changing-rules-0609.pdf.
2. "ICAV: Irish Collective Asset-Management Vehicle," Deloitte, 2015, https://www2.deloitte .com/content/dam/Deloitte/ie/Documents/FinancialServices/investmentmanagement/2015_ ICAV_Deloitte_Ireland.pdf.
3. "Establishing Investment Funds in the Cayman Islands," Deloitte, May 2018, http:// www2.deloitte.com/content/dam/Deloitte/ky/Documents/financial-services/Establishing% 20Investment%20Funds%20in%20the%20Cayman%20Islands%20-%20May%202018 %20DIGITAL.pdf.
4. "Performance of Private versus Liquid Alternatives: How Big a Difference?" Cliffwater, June 2013, https://www.cliffwater.com/documents/1181513.
5. Stephen M. Horan and Thomas R. Robinson, "Taxes and Private Wealth Management in a Global Context," www.cfainstitute.org/toolkit, Reading #70.
6. "Overview of U.S. Asset Management Regulation," by the Regulatory Compliance Association's Senior Fellows from Practice, who are credited as contributing authors to this chapter.
7. Horan and Robinson, "Taxes and Private Wealth Management."

CHAPTER 3

Quantitative Foundations

Quantitative tools and quantitative analysis are foundational to alternative assets. This chapter provides details regarding return computation and cash flows.

3.1 RETURN AND RATE MATHEMATICS

Returns can be computed with different compounding assumptions and, over time, with intervals of different lengths. These choices have implications for the mathematics and statistics of the returns. This section demonstrates, among other things, the usefulness of basing return computations on continuous compounding, which is tantamount to saying that the returns should be expressed as log returns.

3.1.1 The Compounding Assumption

Compounding is the recognition of interest on interest or, more generally, earnings on earnings. **Simple interest** is an interest rate computation approach that does not incorporate compounding. But returns are often compounded. For example, earning 10% over one year is equivalent to earning 9.64% per year compounded quarterly: $[1 + (.0964/4)]^4 = 1.10$.

Continuous compounding assumes that earnings can be instantaneously reinvested to generate additional earnings. **Discrete compounding** includes any compounding interval other than continuous compounding such as daily, monthly, or annual.

 FOUNDATION CHECK

In preparation for this material, understand the mathematics of simple, discretely compounded, and continuously compounded interest, including the computation of interest rates, present values, future values, or time intervals for applications involving single or multiple cash flows (including annuities). Net present value is especially important and should be understood from both a computation and interpretation perspective.

3.1.2 Logarithmic Returns

Denote R as a total (non-annualized) return or rate with no compounding. Adding 1 to R forms a wealth ratio. A **log return** is a continuously compounded return that can be formed by taking the natural logarithm of a wealth ratio:

$$R^{m=\infty} = \ln(1 + R) \tag{3.1}$$

where $\ln()$ is the natural logarithm function, $R^{m=\infty}$ is the log return, or continuously compounded return, and m is the number of compounding intervals per year.

For example, the rate of return that discounts a value of \$110 to be received in the future to a present value of \$100 expressed as a total (non-annualized) rate is 0.10. Since $R = .10$, then the log return ($R^{m=\infty}$) is 0.0953. With continuous compounding at 9.53% for one year, \$100 grows to \$110.

For very small returns, we can roughly think of $R^{m=\infty}$ and $\ln(1 + R)$ as being equal to R: as $R \to 0$ then $R \to R^{m=\infty}$ and $R \to \ln(1 + R)$.

But for larger returns, simple returns (R) and log returns can differ substantially. Generally, the use of continuous compounding and log returns provides mathematical ease and generates straightforward modeling. For example, the advantages of using log returns rather than returns based on simple interest or discrete compounding are demonstrated in the next section and involve aggregation of returns over shorter periods of time into returns over longer periods of time.

3.1.3 The Return Computation Interval and Aggregation

The **return computation interval** for a particular analysis is the smallest time interval for which returns are calculated, such as daily, monthly, or even annually. Sometimes the length of the smallest time interval for which a return is calculated is referred to as the granularity, the time resolution, or the frequency of the return measurement. While some financial studies regarding microstructure or other very short-term trading issues compute returns as often as from tick to tick (i.e., trade to trade), most studies regarding alternative investments use daily returns or returns computed over longer time intervals, such as months, quarters, or even years.

Two common tasks in return analysis involve (1) aggregating a number of returns from smaller sub-periods (e.g., days) into one larger time period (e.g., months), and (2) determining an average return (e.g., finding an average daily return based on a monthly return). Different compounding assumptions typically require different formulas for these two tasks and can introduce substantial complexities. One way to simplify many analyses is to express all rates and returns using continuous compounding (i.e., using log returns).

Let's look at an example of aggregating short-term returns into a longer-term return. The challenge is calculating multiperiod returns from single-period returns in a way that reflects compounding and therefore the true long-term growth rate. Our example begins by using simple interest for the sub-periods. We refer to the total return of an asset over the T periods from time $t = 0$ to $t = T$ as $R_{0,T}$, which can be expressed as being equal to the following product in terms of the returns of the asset over the sub-periods (R_T):

$$1 + R_{0,T} = (1 + R_1) \times (1 + R_2) \times (1 + R_3) \times \ldots \times (1 + R_T) \tag{3.2}$$

In most cases, this equation is not as easy to work with as the analogous equation using continuously compounded returns (i.e., log returns), which involves simple addition:

$$R_{0,T}^{m=\infty} = R_1^{m=\infty} + R_2^{m=\infty} + R_3^{m=\infty} + \ldots + R_T^{m=\infty} \tag{3.3}$$

Equations 3.2 and 3.3 demonstrate that whereas simple periodic returns require multiplication for aggregation, log returns require only addition when they are aggregated.

For example, an asset earns a return of 10% in the first time period and 20% in the second time period. What is the total return over both time periods assuming discrete compounding and continuous compounding? Using discrete compounding, the total return is 32%, found as $[(1.1 \times 1.2) - 1]$. If the returns had been expressed with continuously compounded returns (log returns), the process would be simplified to addition as 30%, found as $(10\% + 20\%)$. Thus, an asset growing with continuous compounding for one period at 10% and a second period at 20% grows at a total rate of 30% compounded continuously. The advantage of this additivity is useful in a variety of modeling contexts, including the computation of averages. The mean of a series of log returns has special importance:

$$\text{Arithmetic Mean Log Return} = \frac{1}{T} \sum_{t=1}^{T} R_t{}^{m=\infty} \tag{3.4}$$

When the arithmetic mean log return is converted into an equivalent simple rate, that rate is referred to as the geometric mean return. Alternatively, geometric mean returns are computed from the total (non-annualized) return over an interval as:

$$\text{Geometric Mean Return} = \sqrt[T]{1 + R_{0,T}} - 1 \tag{3.5}$$

The geometric mean return should be used with care in inferring long-term performance expectations.

3.2 RETURNS BASED ON NOTIONAL PRINCIPAL

Much investment analysis centers on the concept of the rate of return, defined as the rate at which an asset changes value (with any interim cash flows, such as dividends, considered). As a rate, a return is usually expressed as a portion or percentage of the asset's starting value. However, alternative investing often includes assets for which there is no clear starting value other than perhaps zero. Examples can include derivative contracts, such as forward contracts and swaps. This section describes some of the mathematics and modeling designed to address issues that arise when there is a zero starting value, or no clear starting value, to a contract.

3.2.1 The Challenge of Returns on Positions with Zero Value

Subsequent chapters provide an extensive discussion of forward contract prices and returns. For the purposes of this discussion, a forward contract can be simply defined as an agreement to make an exchange at some date in the future, known as the delivery date. For example, a hedge fund with an undesired exposure to receiving a payment in Japanese yen in three months and with a preference to receive that payment in euros might enter into a forward contract with a major bank. The forward contract might require the hedge fund to deliver 100 million yen in exchange for 1 million euros at a particular date, such as in three months. The hedge fund has effectively transformed its receipt of yen into a receipt of euros.

Forward contracts can usually be viewed as starting with a value of zero because the initial value of the item to be delivered is usually equal to the value of the item to be received. However, as soon as time begins to pass, it would be expected that the value of the contract would become positive to one side of the contract and negative to the other side of the contract. For example, if the value of the yen rose substantially relative to the value of the euro after the forward agreement was established, the hedge fund would perceive the commitment that it made through the forward contract as having a negative value.

Assuming the hedge fund reports its performance in euros and that the change in the yen–euro exchange rate caused a loss to the fund of 1,000 euros, the rate of return on the forward contract would need to be computed. The traditional formula for the return without any interim cash flows is:

$$\text{Return} = (\text{Ending Value} - \text{Starting Value})/\text{Starting Value}$$

The forward contract, however, has a starting value of zero, which would lead to division by zero. The next two sections discuss solutions to this challenge.

3.2.2 Notional Principal and Full Collateralization

One solution to the problem of computing return for derivatives is to base the return on notional principal. The **return on notional principal** divides economic gain or loss by the notional principal of the contract. **Notional principal** or notional value of a contract is the value of the asset underlying, or used as a reference to, the contract or derivative position. In the case of a forward contract on currency, it would be 100 million yen, 1 million euros, or even the value of either in terms of a third currency. Selecting 1 million euros as the notional principal, the change in value in the previous example could be expressed as:

$$\text{Change in Value} = -1,000\,\text{euros}/1,000,000\,\text{euros} = -0.10\%$$

However, the figure of –0.10% has little economic importance for the hedge fund, since it has not invested any capital into the contract. Usually a percentage loss is interpreted as being based on the amount of capital invested, so it has an intuitive meaning. The problem of calculating the rate of return when there is no initial investment is identical to the problem of calculating the rate of return on a fully leveraged position, such as when a position in a risky asset, like a common stock, is fully financed through borrowing.

To provide greater economic meaning, the return is often expressed on a fully collateralized basis. **Fully collateralized** means that a position (such as a forward contract) is assumed to be paired with a quantity of capital equal in value to the notional principal of the contract. Thus, the hedge fund computes the return on the combination of the forward contract and a hypothetical investment of full collateral, meaning collateral equal to the notional principal. Often a fully collateralized position has equivalent risk and return to a long position in the underlying asset using the cash or spot market.

A fully collateralized position has two components of return: (1) the change in the value of the derivative, and (2) any return on the collateral. Specifically, it is usually assumed that the investor is able to receive a short-term interest rate, such as the riskless rate on the collateral.

Defining R as the percentage change in the value of the derivative based on notional value and using continuous compounding (i.e., log returns), as discussed earlier in this chapter, the return on a fully collateralized position, R_{fcoll}, can be expressed as:

$$R_{fcoll} = \ln(1 + R) + R_f \qquad (3.6)$$

where R is the change in the derivatives price divided by its previous price or notional value.

The first term on the right-hand side of Equation 3.6 is the continuously compounded percentage change in the fully collateralized position due to changes in the value of the derivative. The second term is the percentage change in the fully collateralized position from interest on the collateral. The sum represents the total return on the fully collateralized position. All three are expressed as continuously compounded rates (log returns) and are based on one period, such as a year.

3.2.3 Partially Collateralized Rates of Return

The previous section detailed the computation of return for a fully collateralized position on a derivative contract. The concept of full collateralization is typically hypothetical; the party to the derivative has usually not actually set aside the full collateral amount in a dedicated account. However, in practice, parties to a derivative position are often required to deposit specified levels of funds to partially collateralize the position. A **partially collateralized** position has collateral lower in value than the notional value.

Suppose that the notional principal of a derivative contract is l times the quantity of collateral required (i.e., the amount of collateral required is $1/l$ times the notional principal). For example, with $l = 10$, there would be a requirement of posting one unit of cash collateral for every 10 units of notional principal (i.e., $10,000 would be the required or other collateral for a derivative position of $100,000). The formula for the log return of a partially collateralized position, R_{pcoll}, reflects the same change in the derivative contract, R, but must be adjusted to reflect the reduced denominator (starting value) due to reduced required collateral (i.e., use of leverage). The amount of interest received on the collateral declines but remains constant as a percentage of the collateral:

$$R_{pcoll} = [l \times \ln(1 + R)] + R_f \qquad (3.7)$$

The use of leverage magnifies the effect of changes in the derivative as a percentage of the money invested. This is expressed in Equation 3.7 by the use of leverage, l, to multiply the derivative's notional return, R.

☞ **APPLICATION 3.2.3**

The notional value of a derivative contract is l times the amount of collateral required to fund a position in the derivative. If R is the non-annualized return of the derivative based on its notional value and R_f is the non-annualized return on the riskless asset, what is the non-annualized log return of the collateralized position, assuming that the position is fully levered?

$$l = 3, \ R = 6\%, \text{ and } R_f = 3\%$$

3.3 INTERNAL RATE OF RETURN

The computation of traditional investment returns is not easy, but it is far easier than the computation of returns for some alternative investments. A main challenge with the analysis of some alternative investments is the lack of regularly observable market prices. Some alternative investments, such as private equity and private real estate, are analyzed using an internal rate of return approach. This approach has numerous potential complications and shortcomings. With the advantage of regular market prices, traditional investment analysis usually computes return as the change in price, net of fees, plus cash flows received (such as dividend or interest payments), divided by the initial price:

$$\text{Rate of Return} = (\text{Change in Price} + \text{Cash Flows})/\text{Initial Price} \qquad (3.8)$$

However, complications arise when prices cannot be regularly observed or when cash flows are received during the interim period, between the starting date and the ending date of the return observation. A major complexity related to these interim cash flows is that it is unclear how much return could be earned through their reinvestment. It is usually assumed that the intervening cash flows are reinvested in the same underlying investment, but this requires an interim price of that asset at the same time as the cash flows become available for reinvestment.

Since prices can be observed at least on a daily basis for most traditional investments, daily returns are easily computed from daily prices and daily cash flows. Returns over time periods in excess of one day with intervening cash flows can be computed as the accumulation of the daily returns within the time period. In other words, returns for longer time periods are formed from the daily returns of the days within the time period. Returns over time periods shorter than one day do not tend to have intervening cash flows, since dividends and interest payments are usually made on an end-of-day basis.

Despite challenges faced with various compounding assumptions and intervening cash flows, calculating the returns of most traditional investments is relatively straightforward when daily prices are available. However, return computations for investments that cannot be accurately valued each day generate challenges that are a primary topic of this chapter. For example, securities that are not publicly traded, such as private equity, do not have unambiguous daily valuations that can be used to compute daily returns. This section explains the application of the internal rate of return method to alternative investments and details the potential difficulties with interpreting and comparing internal rates of return.

3.3.1 Defining the IRR

The **internal rate of return (IRR)** can be defined as the discount rate that equates the present value of the costs (cash outflows) of an investment with the present value of the benefits (cash inflows) from the investment. Using the terminology and methods of finance, the IRR is the discount rate that makes the net present value (NPV) of an investment equal to zero.

Let CF_0 be the cash flow or a valuation related to the start of an investment (i.e., at time 0). CF_0 might be the cost of an investment in real estate, or in the case of private equity, CF_0 might be the initial investment required to obtain the investment or meet the fund's first or only capital infusion; CF_1 through CF_{T-1} are the actual or projected cash inflows if positive and cash outflows if negative, generated or required by the underlying investment. Positive cash flows are distributions from the investment to the investor, and negative cash flows are capital calls in which an additional capital contribution is required of each investor to the investment.

A CF_T may be the final cash flow when the investment terminates, the final cash flow received from selling or otherwise disposing of the investment, or a residual valuation, meaning some appraisal of the value of the remaining cash flows related to the investment. In the case of an appraised valuation of CF_T, the valuation should be designed to represent opinions with regard to the amount of cash that would be received from selling all remaining rights to the investment. The values are denoted here with the variable CF, which usually stands for cash flows, even though they may be hypothetical values or appraised values for the investments rather than actual cash flows.

Given all cash flows and/or valuations from period 0 to period T, the IRR is the interest rate that sets the left-hand side of Equation 3.9 to zero:

$$CF_0 + \frac{CF_1}{(1+\text{IRR})^1} + \frac{CF_2}{(1+\text{IRR})^2} + \frac{CF_3}{(1+\text{IRR})^3} + \dots + \frac{CF_T}{(1+\text{IRR})^T} = 0 \quad (3.9)$$

Another view of the IRR is that it is the interest rate that a bank would have to offer on an account to allow an investor to replicate the cash flows of the investment. In other words, if an investor deposited CF_t in a bank account at time t for each $CF_t < 0$ and withdrew CF_t from the bank account when $CF_t > 0$, and if the bank's interest rate on the account was IRR, then the bank account would have a zero balance after the last cash flow was deposited or withdrawn (CF_T).

3.3.2 Computing the IRR

In some simplified cases, such as investments that last only a few periods or investments in which most of the cash flows are identical (i.e., annuities), the IRR may be solved algebraically with a closed-form solution. In cases involving several different cash flows, the solution generally relies on a trial-and-error search performed by an advanced financial calculator or computer.

A simplified example to illustrate the trial-and-error method involves an investment that costs $250 million and lasts three years, generating cash inflows of $150 million, $100 million, and $80 million in years 1, 2, and 3, respectively. The IRR is found as that interest rate that solves the following equation:

$$-\$250M + \frac{\$150M}{(1 + IRR)^1} + \frac{\$100M}{(1 + IRR)^2} + \frac{\$80M}{(1 + IRR)^3} = 0 \qquad (3.10)$$

The trial-and-error process selects an initial guess for IRR, such as 10%, and then searches for the correct answer: the IRR that sets the left-hand side of Equation 3.10 to zero. Inserting IRR = 0.10 (10%) into Equation 3.10 generates a present value of inflows equal to $279.11 million and a value to the entire left-hand side of $29.11 million. The objective is to have the value of the left-hand side of the equation equal to zero. In the case of this investment, a higher discount rate will generate a lower net value. If the next guess is an interest rate of 15%, the value of the left-hand side of the equation declines to $8.65 million. The process continues with as much precision as required. The IRR of this investment is 17.33% carried to the nearest basis point.

Advanced calculators and computer spreadsheets perform the trial-and-error process automatically. This solution of 17.33% for the IRR can be found on most financial calculators by inserting the cash flows (using cash flow mode) and requesting the computation of the IRR or in a spreadsheet with a function designed to compute IRR.

In this example, the trial-and-error process for finding the IRR works well because any increase in the discount rate lowers the present value of the cash inflows, and any decrease in the discount rate raises the present value of the inflows. The solution to the IRR problem is illustrated in Exhibit 3.1. For example, on a Texas Instrument BA II Plus calculator the keystrokes can be: [on/off], CF, 2nd, [CE/C], 250, [+/-], enter ↓, ↓, 80, enter, IRR, CPT. The IRR is 17.33415.

Because the IRR is the discount rate that sets the NPV of the investment to zero, the IRR is represented by the point at where the NPV curve crosses through the horizontal axis. This occurs between 17% and 18% on the figure, which corresponds to the previous solution of 17.33%. There is only one solution, and it is quite easily

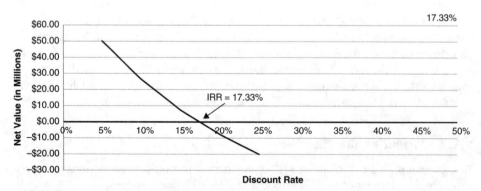

EXHIBIT 3.1 The Solution to IRR in a Simplified Investment

found. If a bank offered an interest rate of 17.33%, then an investor could deposit $250 million and withdraw $150 million, $100 million, and $80 million after one, two, and three years, respectively; and the final account balance would be $0, ignoring rounding errors.

3.3.3 IRR Measurement Intervals

The primary reason for using the IRR approach to calculate returns is that illiquidity of the underlying asset prevents observation of highly reliable and regular valuations, such as daily market prices. This section discusses types of IRRs differentiated by the time the periods over which cash flows and net asset values are estimated. Subsequent sections detail modified IRR and, in Level 2, the public equivalent IRR method.

One distinction between IRR computations is whether the cash flows are realized (observed), expected (projected), or appraised (e.g., a net asset value). Another distinction is whether the underlying investment is a single asset or a fund. Finally, IRRs are distinguished by the time interval over which the IRR is estimated relative to the inception and termination of the underlying asset. Technically, all IRR computations are point-to-point computations. Although the terms that follow are not uniformly defined in practice, they are useful for our purposes.

A **lifetime IRR** contains all of the cash flows, realized or anticipated, occurring over the investment's entire life, from its beginning to its termination. An **interim IRR** is a computation of IRR based on cash flows prior to the investment's termination. The key to an interim IRR is that generally the final cash flow at time T in the analysis would not be the termination of the investment; thus, CF_T is an estimated value rather than a realized cash flow. A **since-inception IRR** is an interim IRR that starts with the underlying investment's initial cash flow (inception date). Also, a since-inception IRR is commonly used as a measure of fund performance rather than the performance of an individual investment.

 APPLICATION 3.3.3A

Investment A is expected to cost $100 and to be followed by cash inflows of $10 after one year and then $120 after the second year, when the project terminates. The IRR is based on anticipated cash flows and is an anticipated lifetime IRR. The IRR of the investment is 14.7%.

 APPLICATION 3.3.3B

Fund B expended $200 million to purchase investments and distributed $30 million after one year. At the end of the second year, it is being appraised at $180 million. The IRR of the fund is a since-inception IRR (or interim IRR) of 2.7%.

☞ **APPLICATION 3.3.3C**

Investment C was purchased three years ago by BK Fund for $500. In the three years following the purchase, the investment distributed cash flows to the investor of $110, $120, and $130. Now in the fourth year, the investment has been appraised as being worth $400. The IRR of the investment is based on realized previous cash flows and a current appraised value. The IRR may be described as an interim IRR and is 15.0%.

3.4 PROBLEMS WITH INTERNAL RATE OF RETURN

This section begins with two major types of complications in the computation and interpretation of IRRs. In the previous section, IRR was easily computed and interpreted because of the simplified cash flow patterns used and because the investment was being viewed in isolation. The first complication arises when an investment offers a complex cash flow pattern other than the traditional pattern of a cash outflow to initiate an investment, followed only by cash inflows until the investment is terminated. The second complication occurs when investments must be compared to see which is preferred. These two complications are addressed in the first half of this section, followed by a brief discussion of other challenges.

3.4.1 Complex Cash Flow Patterns

For the purposes of this analysis of IRRs, a **complex cash flow pattern** is an investment involving either borrowing or multiple sign changes. A **borrowing type cash flow pattern** begins with one or more cash inflows and is followed only by cash outflows. An example of the borrowing pattern is when an investment such as a real estate project is sold and leased back. The divestment generates current cash at the cost of future cash outflows and may be viewed as a form of borrowing. A **multiple sign change cash flow pattern** is an investment where the cash flows switch over time from inflows to outflows, or from outflows to inflows, more than once. An example of a multiple sign change investment would be a natural resource investment involving (1) negative initial cash flows from purchasing equipment and land to set up an operation such as mining, (2) positive interim cash flows from operations, and (3) negative terminal cash flows from ceasing operation and restoration expenses. Exhibit 3.2 illustrates the complex cash flow patterns.

EXHIBIT 3.2 Complex Cash Flow Pattern Examples

Cash Flow Pattern	Time Period					
	0	1	2	3	4	5
Simplified	−	+	+	+	+	+
Complex Borrowing	+	−	−	−	−	−
Multiple sign change	−	+	−	−	−	+

EXHIBIT 3.3   Cash Flows of Hypothetical
Derivative Contract

In the case of borrowing type cash flow patterns, there is a unique solution (i.e., there is only one IRR that solves the equation), but the IRR must be interpreted differently. In borrowing type cash flow patterns, a high IRR is undesirable because the IRR is revealing the cost of borrowing rather than the return on investment. Also, when a trial-and-error search is performed to find the IRR, any increase in the discount rate lowers the present value of the cash outflows rather than lowering the present value of the cash inflows, as would be the case in a simple cash flow pattern. Thus, the trial-and-error process must operate in a reverse direction from the simplified investment cash flow pattern. In other words, if the net value with a given discount rate is positive, the next IRR in the search should be lower rather than higher, as occurs in the case of a simplified cash flow pattern.

In the case of multiple sign change cash flow patterns, the problems are more troublesome. Whenever there is more than one sign change in the cash flow stream, more than one IRR may exist. In other words, two or more answers can probably be found using the IRR formula. In fact, the maximum number of possible IRRs is equal to the number of sign changes. When more than one IRR is calculated, none of the IRRs should be used. There is no easy way for the IRR model to overcome this particular shortcoming.

Consider a derivative deal that ends poorly for Investor A. The derivative required a $5,000 outlay from Investor A to the counterparty to open. In the first period, the derivative generates an $11,500 cash inflow to Investor A from the derivative's counterparty. The derivative then generates a cash outflow of $6,550 from Investor A at the end of the second period, at which point the derivative terminates. The derivative's cash flows from the perspective of Investor A are given in Exhibit 3.3, assigning period 0 to the first nonzero cash flow.

This cash flow pattern changes signs twice, once from negative to positive and once from positive to negative. There are two IRRs: 3.82% and 26.20%. Both 3.82% and 26.20% satisfy the definition of the IRR because they set the present value of all cash inflows equal to the present value of all cash outflows. The net value of the present values of the cash inflows and outflows is illustrated in Exhibit 3.4. Note that the line crosses the horizontal axis twice, defining two different IRRs.

With the two IRR solutions 3.82% and 26.20%, there may be a temptation to think that the two IRRs can be somehow analyzed in unison to generate an intuitive feel for the derivative's attractiveness. But neither number is particularly useful, because the investment is really a combination of investing from period 0 to period 1 and borrowing from period 1 to period 2. In this particular case, the cash flow patterns have a positive net value between the two IRRs, using discount rates between 3.82% and 26.20%. But as a derivative, it is obvious that the cash flows to the other side of the derivative (the counterparty) would have the same numbers, but the signs of the cash flows would be reversed. In this case, the cash flows would be +$5,000, –$11,500, and +$6,550. From the counterparty's perspective, the IRR solutions would still be exactly the same at 3.82% and 26.20%. However, the deal's

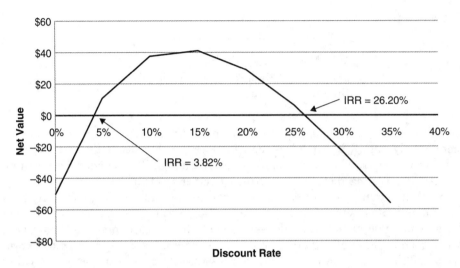

EXHIBIT 3.4   An Example of Multiple IRRs

graph would appear as a mirror image, with negative net values between the two IRRs. As we would expect with a derivative deal, gains to one side of the contract would equal losses to the other side of the contract. Both sides would view the same IRRs because they used the same cash flows, but they would be looking at opposite cash flows and opposite net values. Therefore, using only the IRRs to decide if the derivative is beneficial is not possible.

3.4.2   Comparing Investments Based on IRRs

The previous section reviewed the difficulties of computing and interpreting IRRs when an investment offers a complex cash flow stream. But even if the investments being analyzed offer simplified cash flow streams (a cash outflow followed only by cash inflows), the IRR method of measuring investment performance has serious challenges. This section details the major challenges of comparing investments based on IRR.

The major challenge with comparing IRRs across investments occurs when investments have scale differences. **Scale differences** are when investments have unequal sizes and/or timing of their cash flows. When comparing investments with different scales, an investment with a higher IRR may be inferior to an investment with a lower IRR.

The following is a simple example that illustrates the problems that occur when comparing IRRs. Assume that a bank is offering high initial yields on a limited-time basis to induce investors to open a new account. Investors are allowed to open only one account. The example includes three types of accounts, each with the following interest rates and restrictions on time and amount:

- Account Type A: Receive 100% annualized interest for the first day on the first $10,000.
- Account Type B: Receive 100% annualized interest for the first year on up to $10.
- Account Type C: Receive 20% annualized interest for the first year on up to $10,000.

The IRR of alternatives A and B is 100%, whereas the IRR of alternative C is only 20%. However, alternative A has very small scale due to a time limitation of one day (timing), and alternative B has very small scale due to a cash flow size limitation of $10 (size). If annualized market interest rates are 5%, alternative A has a net present value of less than $30, and alternative B has an NPV of less than $10. Alternative C has an NPV of about $1,500, even though its IRR is only one-fifth that of the other two alternatives. The reason for this is that although all three alternatives have favorable IRRs, alternative C has much larger scale.

In this example, it is better to receive a lower rate on a large scale. In actual investing, scale differentials can be complex and subtle. In judging when a larger scale is worth a sacrifice in return, approaches to investments using the NPV method offer substantial potential in evaluating investment opportunities of different scales. But in alternative investments, especially private equity, IRR is the standard methodology, and scale differentials represent a challenge in ranking performance.

3.4.3 IRRs Should Not Be Averaged

Another challenge to using IRRs involves aggregation. **Aggregation of IRRs** refers to the relationship between the IRRs of individual investments and the IRR of the combined cash flows of the investments. Suppose that one investment earns an IRR of 15% and another earns an IRR of 20%. What would the IRR be of a portfolio that contained both investments? In other words, if the cash flows of two investments are combined into a single cash flow pattern, how would the IRR of the combination relate to the IRRs of the individual investments? The answer is not immediately apparent, because the IRR of a portfolio of two investments is not generally equal to a value-weighted average of the IRRs of the constituent investments. If the cash flows from two investments are combined to form a portfolio, the IRR of the portfolio can vary substantially from the average of the IRRs of the two investments.

This section demonstrates the difficulty of aggregating IRRs, and the following extreme example illustrates the challenges vividly. Consider the following three investment alternatives:

Name	CF_0	CF_1	IRR
Investment A	−100	+110	10%
Investment B	+150	−150	0%
Investment C	+50	−50	0%

The IRRs of the three alternatives are easy to compute because each investment simply offers two cash flows: one at time period 0 and one at time period 1. Using Equation 3.9, the IRR for a one-period investment is found by solving the equation $0 = CF_0 + CF_1 / (1 + \text{IRR})$, which generates the equation

$$\text{IRR} = (CF_1 / -CF_0) - 1$$

Inserting the values for Investment A ($CF_0 = -100$, $CF_1 = +110$) generates the IRR of 10%, shown in the IRR column. Investments B and C both have $CF_0 = -CF_1$, so the IRRs of both Investment B and Investment C are 0%. One might expect that combining Investment A with either Investment B or Investment C would generate a portfolio with an IRR between 0% and 10% because one investment in the portfolio would have a stand-alone IRR of 10%, as with Investment A, and the other would have a stand-alone IRR of 0%, as in the case of either Investment B or C. But IRRs can generate unexpected results, as indicated by the following analysis:

Name	CF_0	CF_1	IRR
Investments A + B	+50	−40	−20%
Investments A + C	−50	+60	+20%

The computations simply sum the cash flows of two investments and compute the single-period IRR of the aggregated cash flows. The IRR of combining Investments A and B is −20%, and the IRR of combining Investments A and C is +20%. The IRRs of both combinations are well outside the range of the IRRs of the individual investments in each portfolio. What generates the unexpected result in this example is that Investments B and C begin with cash inflows and end with cash outflows (i.e., they are borrowing investments). But in practice, alternative investments, such as commodity or real estate derivatives and private equity, can have cash flow patterns sufficiently erratic to cause serious problems with aggregation of IRRs.

3.4.4   IRR and the Reinvestment Rate Assumption

Even if all the investments have simplified cash flow patterns without borrowing or multiple sign change problems, the IRR does not necessarily rank investments accurately. The use of the IRR to rank investment alternatives is often said to rely on the reinvestment rate assumption. The **reinvestment rate assumption** refers to the assumption of the rate at which any cash flows not invested in a particular investment or received during the investment's life can be reinvested during the investment's lifetime. If the assumed reinvestment rate is the same rate of return as the investment's IRR, then no ranking problem exists.

Suppose that Investment A offers an attractive IRR of 25% compared with the 20% IRR of Investment B. As previously discussed, it is possible that an investor would select Investment B over Investment A if Investment B offers a larger scale, meaning more money invested for longer periods of time. But if an investor who selects Investment A is able to invest additional funds at a 25% rate of return and is able to reinvest any cash flows from Investment A at the 25% rate, then the scale problem vanishes, and IRRs can be used to rank investments effectively. In practice, there would typically be no reason to assume that cash inflows could be reinvested at the same rate throughout the project's life, so ranking remains a problem. The reinvestment rate assumption is addressed by the modified IRR discussed in the next section.

3.4.5   Modified Internal Rate of Return

The key method (other than net present value) to address the challenges of the IRR approach is the modified IRR approach. The **modified IRR** approach addresses the challenges of multiple IRRs and the restrictiveness of the reinvestment assumption in

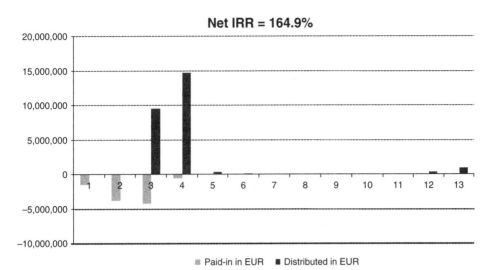

EXHIBIT 3.5 Cash Flows for Private Equity Investment

the IRR approach by discounting all project cash outflows into a present value using a financing rate, compounding all cash inflows into a future value using an assumed reinvestment rate, and calculating the modified IRR as the discount rate that sets the absolute values of that future value and that present value equal to each other. Consider a project such as one that might occur in a private equity investment that has cash flows that alternate in sign through time, as depicted in Exhibit 3.5.

Implicit in the use of IRR as a performance measure is the assumption that net distributions (such as those received in years 3 and 4 of Exhibit 3.5) can be reinvested at the IRR (164.9%!). For a project like the one illustrated, the assumption would likely be very unrealistic and would be very misleading if IRR were used to rank dissimilar projects. To address this problem, the modified IRR (MIRR) imposes user-specified rates to compound all cash inflows forward to the project's termination date and discount all cash outflows back to the project's inception date. Exhibit 3.6 illustrates the result: a single present value of the cash outflows at time 0 and a single future value of the cash inflows at time T.

The modified IRR (19%) is then very simply calculated as the discount rate that equates the future value of the cash flows to the present value of the negative cash flows (with both signs positive). Mathematically, the modified internal rate of return over the project's T years, $MIRR_T$, is found by solving the following equation:

$$MIRR_T = \left(\frac{FV \text{ of Positive Cash Flows Using the Reinvestment Rate}}{-PV \text{ of Negative Cash Flows Using the Cost of Capital}} \right)^{\frac{1}{T}} - 1$$

(3.11)

where T is the number of years between the project's first and last cash flows. Note that the negative sign in the denominator of the above Equation 3.11 is used to

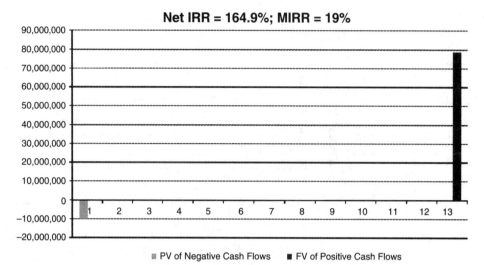

EXHIBIT 3.6   Modified IRR Example

highlight the need to use absolute values in place of negative cash flows. Equation 3.12 expands the previous equation to provide needed details.

$$\text{MIRR}_T = \left(\frac{\sum_{t=0}^{T} D_t \times (1 + RR)^{T-t}}{\left| \sum_{t=0}^{T} \frac{C_t}{(1+CC)^t} \right|} \right)^{\frac{1}{T}} - 1 \qquad (3.12)$$

where D_t is the distribution in year t, C_t is the contribution in year t, RR is the expected reinvestment rate for the period until time T, CC is the investors' cost of capital through period T, and MIRR_T is the modified IRR. Equation 3.12 can be solved for MIRR easily with most financial and nonfinancial calculators given the values of the contributions, distributions, RR, and CC.

The RR is used to find the total value that the distributions would accrue to at the end of the project's life if they were all reinvested at RR. The CC is used to find the aggregated initial cost of financing the project's contributions. To the extent that RR and CC are accurate and properly reflect implications of the various risks involved, the MIRR_T can be viewed as an indication of the return earned from the excess of the accrued distributions over the project's financing costs.

☞ **APPLICATION 3.4.5**

Assume that a private equity project has the following cash flows:

$$C_0 = -200, C_1 = 50, C_2 = -50, C_3 = 100, C_4 = 0, C_5 = 250$$

Compute the IRR and MIRR given $RR = 10\%$ and $CC = 8\%$.

> Solution: The IRR is 14.38% (which can be found iteratively or on an advanced calculator). To find the MIRR, first find the *PV* of the outflows and the *FV* of the inflows. The sum of the present values (at time 0) of $C_0 = -200$ and $C_2 = -50$ at 8% is –242.867. The sum of the future values (time $T = 5$) of $C_1 = 50$, $C_3 = 100$, and $C_5 = 250$ at 10% is 444.205. Given $PV = -242.867$, $FV = 444.205$, and $T = 5$, the MIRR is 12.83%, found by applying the lump sum time value of money formula or using a financial calculator.

3.4.6 Advantages and Disadvantages of Modified Internal Rate of Return

There is considerable debate with regard to the meaning and selection of the rates *RR* and *CC* in Equation 3.12. *RR* is usually interpreted as the firm's reinvestment rate— the expected return the firm could be expected to earn by reinvesting the distributions that it receives from the project. *CC* is often interpreted as the firm's marginal cost of capital—the expected cost of financing the project's contributions. However, different commentators and practitioners differ in their approaches, including the possibility that either or both of the rates are set equal to market rates.

The two major advantages to the MIRR approach are that it addresses two important deficiencies with IRR.

First, as illustrated in Exhibit 3.6, by imposing *RR* and *CC* for discounting the cash outflows and compounding the cash inflows, the computation of the metric (i.e., the MIRR) becomes a simple rate of return computation with no possibility of multiple solutions. Thus, the MIRR approach overcomes the multiple IRR issue that can exist when a project's cash flows have multiple sign changes through time.

Second, the MIRR approach overrides the implicit reinvestment assumption of the traditional IRR model (that cash distributions from a project can be reinvested at a rate equal to the project's IRR). When various projects are ranked by IRR, the reinvestment assumption implicit in IRR can cause the rankings to differ from those generated by the net present value rule (which is generally found to be superior). The MIRR approach addresses this problem by imposing a user-specified reinvestment rate, *RR*. In the case of private equity it makes sense that the return that is earned from reinvesting the distributions into a new project can be quite different from the return earned on the extant project.

However, the MIRR approach is viewed as having substantial disadvantages that make it a rarely used approach relative to the IRR. Note that the values of *CC* and *RR* chosen by the user *drive* the value of the resulting MIRR. For example, a high *RR* combined with a low *CC* will cause the MIRR to be high by increasing the future value of the distributions and lowering the present value of the contributions. So unlike IRR, MIRR is driven by user-selected rates (*RR* and *CC*) that conceptually are unrelated to the project.

As an example of the difficulties with the MIRR approach, consider what happens when a $1 distribution in Year 10 is added to the cash flows in Application 3.4.5. Common sense indicates that adding a single dollar to the cash inflows in year 10 should cause performance metrics to rise very slightly. In fact, the IRR rises from 11.38% to 11.42%, indicating the nearly trivial but beneficial nature of receiving a distant dollar. But the MIRR *falls* substantially from 12.83% to 11.42%—a huge decline and in the intuitively wrong direction. The extra five years added to the project's lifetime drives the MIRR closer to the *RR*. In fact, as the location of the extra dollar is moved into the future (i.e., the project's lifetime is expanded with a trivial cash flow), the MIRR approaches the *RR* because the addition of a distribution even of only $1 causes the approach to compound all of the other distributions to the project's termination. In Application 3.4.5 the assumed *RR* of 10% is less than the original project's IRR and MIRR. Therefore, stretching the project's lifetime by adding a distant dollar lowers the MIRR toward the *RR* even though the addition of an extra dollar of cash should cause a performance measure to increase.

In summary, the MIRR approach solves the problem of the IRR approach of multiple solutions and in some cases can help alleviate distortions caused by the reinvestment rate assumption. However, the results of the MIRR approach can be very sensitive to the reinvestment rate (*RR*) and financing cost (*CC*) assumed, and can generate perverse rankings relative to NPV approach.

3.4.7 Time-Weighted Returns versus Dollar-Weighted Returns

The purpose of this section is to provide details regarding time-weighted returns versus dollar-weighted returns. Briefly, **time-weighted returns** are averaged returns that assume that no cash was contributed or withdrawn during the averaging period, meaning after the initial investment. **Dollar-weighted returns** are averaged returns that are adjusted for and therefore reflect when cash has been contributed or withdrawn during the averaging period. The IRR is the primary method of computing a dollar-weighted return.

When evaluating the return of hedge funds, mutual funds, or any investment, it's important to recognize the distinction between the time-weighted return, which is similar to what is reported on performance charts in marketing literature and client letters, and the dollar-weighted return, which represents what the average investor actually earned; the two can be very different.

Suppose there is a hedge fund that in year 1 starts with $100 million of AUM (assets under management). Let's further suppose that the hedge fund generates an average annual return of 20% for each of its first three years. With such a performance history, the hedge fund attracts quite a bit of new capital. Let's assume that the hedge fund attracts $200 million in new assets for year 4, another $200 million for year 5, and nothing in year 6. Unfortunately, the new capital does not help the hedge fund manager maintain the fund's stellar performance, and the manager earns 0% in years 4, 5, and 6. If we use time-weighted returns over this six-year period, the hedge fund manager has an average annual return of 9.5%:

$$(1.2 \times 1.2 \times 1.2 \times 1.0 \times 1.0 \times 1.0)^{\frac{1}{6}} - 1 = 1.095 - 1 = 9.5\%$$

In effect, the time-weighted return assumes that a single investment (e.g., $1) was made at the beginning of the period and was allowed to grow with positive returns and decline with negative returns until the end of the measurement period, with no cash withdrawals or additional contributions. The rate that equates the initial value with the accumulated value is the time-weighted average return, and it is somewhat near the arithmetic average annual return (in this case, 10% per year). The idea is that a single sum of money invested at the start of the first year and allowed to remain in the fund until the end of the last year would accumulate to the same value as if it had been invested at a fixed return of 9.5% per year, ignoring rounding.

But in practice, investors often contribute additional cash (i.e., make additional investments) or withdraw cash (e.g., liquidate part of the investment or receive cash distributions) during the time period under analysis. Their average returns depend on whether the amount of money invested was highest during the high-performing periods or during the low-performing periods. Dollar-weighted returns adjust the average annual performance for the amount of cash invested each year. In the case of the hedge fund, an investor who had much more cash in the fund in the early years than in the later years would earn more than an investor whose money was primarily invested in the last three years, when the fund generated 0% returns.

Dollar-weighted returns can be computed for each investor using investors' cash flows into and out of the hedge fund. The total cash flows into and out of the fund for all investors can be used as an indication of the performance of an average investor. The dollar-weighted return that individual investors experience depends on their cash contributions and withdrawals.

When the timing of the aggregated cash flows for the entire hedge fund is taken into account, the bulk of the hedge fund's assets earned a 0% return in years 4, 5, and 6. The example shows that only the first $100 million earned the great rates of return of the first three years. The $400 million that flowed into the hedge fund in years 4 and 5 earned a 0% return. When the timing of the aggregated cash flows is taken into account, the dollar-weighted return (solving for the IRR with cash flows reinvested) is only 4.3%. The IRR is found in this case with $CF_0 = -100$, $CF_1 = 0$, $CF_2 = 0$, $CF_3 = -200$, $CF_4 = -200$, $CF_5 = 0$, and $CF_6 = +572.8$; that is, CF_6 is found as: $[(100 \times 1.2 \times 1.2 \times 1.2) + 200 + 200]$.

Investment managers are best evaluated on time-weighted returns, as these managers should not be held accountable for the cash flow decisions of their investors. Investors should evaluate their own investment results using dollar-weighted returns based on the cash flows from their particular investment pattern.

3.5 OTHER PERFORMANCE MEASURES

The performance measurement of illiquid investments, such as private equity, can pose substantial problems due to the limited points in time for which market values are available. In addition to IRR and MIRR, analysts often examine value ratios unadjusted for time value. This section discusses three such ratios.

3.5.1 Ratios as Performance Measures

The **distribution to paid-in (DPI) ratio,** or realized return, is the ratio of the cumulative distribution to investors to the total capital drawn from investors, and can be loosely viewed as a non-annualized measure of income (actually, distributions) in the numerator to total investment in the denominator.

$$\text{DPI}_T = \frac{\sum_{t=0}^{T} D_t}{\sum_{t=0}^{T} C_t} \qquad (3.13)$$

where D_t is the distribution in year t and C_t is the contribution in year t.

The **residual value to paid-in (RVPI) ratio,** or unrealized return, at time T is the ratio of the total value of the unrealized investments at time T to the total capital drawn from investors during the previous time periods, and can be loosely viewed as a measure of capital gain or loss, with a ratio of one indicating that, ignoring prior distributions, the investment has neither gained or lost value relative to the total contributions.

$$\text{RVPI}_T = \frac{\text{NAV}_T}{\sum_{t=0}^{T} C_t} \qquad (3.14)$$

The **total value to paid-in (TVPI) ratio,** or total return, is a measure of the cumulative distribution to investors plus the total value of the unrealized investments relative to the total capital drawn from investors, and is the sum of the income (DPI) and capital gain or loss (RVPI).

$$\text{TVPI}_T = \frac{\sum_{t=0}^{T} D_t + \text{NAV}_T}{\sum_{t=0}^{T} C_t} = \text{DPI}_T + \text{RVPI}_T \qquad (3.15)$$

Note that these ratios do not take the time value of money into account. Further, the RVPI and the TVPI depend on net asset values, which in the case of illiquid assets are usually professional estimates rather than observed market values. Their estimations are the most problematic components of return evaluation and so DPI, which is measured using only distributed capital, is seen as being the more reliable measure for mature funds.

3.5.2 The Public Market Equivalent (PME) Method

A key approach to benchmarking private equity is the PME method. The **Public Market Equivalent (PME) method** uses a publicly traded securities index that is believed to have a similar risk exposure to private equity as a return target and requires or finds the corresponding premium over public equity (e.g., 300 to 500 basis points) for a private equity investment using the investment's cash contributions (calls), distributions, and terminal value. The PME method uses the returns of a public equity market index as a base for the fund's reinvestment rate and opportunity cost of capital. Specifically, the PME method finds the added (or reduced) cash-weighted return for a private equity investment obtained by investing in the private equity investment rather than by investing in a stock market index.

For example, consider the following highly simplified example of $100 ($C_0$) invested for two years in three alternatives: PE Fund #1, PE Fund #2, and a public market equity index. At the end of two years, PE Fund #1 returns $121 ($C_2$), PE Fund #2 returns $169 ($C_2$), and an investment in the market index returns $144

EXHIBIT 3.7 Simplified PMEs for Two Funds with Two Cash Flows

Description	C_0	C_2	IRR	PME
PE Fund #1	−$100	$121	10%	−10%
Market Index	−$100	$144	20%	0%
PE Fund #2	−$100	$169	30%	+10%

(C_2). The internal rates of return (IRRs) for the three opportunities are included in Exhibit 3.7.

The rightmost column in Exhibit 3.7 is the added or subtracted performance of the PE fund relative to the public market using the PME method. For each PE fund, the PME indicates the performance (IRR) of the opportunity relative to the performance of the market index. Note that PE Fund #1 underperformed the market index by 10% per year (even though it earned 10%), whereas PE Fund #2 outperformed the market index by only 10% per year (even though it earned 30%).

This introduction provides a foundation on which to build a full understanding of the PME method. The example is extremely simple due to there being only two cash flows: one investment and one distribution. It demonstrates the essential intuition of the PME approach. Exhibit 3.7 shows that if the $100 had been invested in the public equity market, it would have grown at 20% to a value of $144. But when invested in the private equity market, it would have grown either at 10% to $121 or at 30% to $169. The public market provides a benchmark against which to evaluate both funds. It indicates that PE Fund #1 underperformed the public equity market by 10% per year and PE Fund #2 outperformed the public market by 10% per year.

Although the PME method is easy to illustrate in the simplified example of two cash flows, it becomes more technically challenging when it is applied to investments with multiple cash investments (capital calls), multiple distributions, and cash-weighted returns. It is in cases of multiple cash inflows or outflows where cash-weighted return analysis is necessary to provide valuable comparisons.

Application of the PME method involving more than two cash flows requires simulation of the performance of an investment in a public equity market index using the actual cash flows pertaining to an investment in a private fund. Part 6 of the CAIA Level II curriculum explains the application of the PME method (and other methods of evaluating investments) in detail, including variations of the method and challenges with implementing each variation. The Level II curriculum also discusses alternatives to cash-weighted returns. including multiples.

3.6 ILLIQUIDITY, ACCOUNTING CONSERVATISM, IRR, AND THE J-CURVE

As discussed in previous sections, the illiquidity of some alternative investments means that interim IRRs are often based on estimated values rather than market values. These estimated values are usually based on accounting principles that reflect the convention of conservativism. The **accounting convention of conservatism** holds that it is prudent to recognize potential expenses and liabilities as soon as possible but not to similarly anticipate potential revenues or gains, often resulting in an understatement of income and assets in the short run.

3.6.1 Accounting Conservatism and Early Fund Losses

Consider the case of a private equity fund. In the early years of the fund, the fund's management team incurs expenses while selecting investments and otherwise managing the fund. These expenditures are made to build the fund's long-run value. In an economic sense, these expenditures, if prudently made, are likely building value, not depleting value. Nevertheless, there is substantial risk that these expenditures will not create value in the long run. Therefore, accounting conservatism dictates that the expenditures should be expensed immediately rather than capitalized as an asset. The early losses due to managerial and acquisition expenses tend to generate negative interim IRRs in the early years of funds such as private equity funds.

3.6.2 Accounting Conservatism and Deferred Recognition of Gains

Another implication of accounting conservatism is to accelerate recognition of losses on investments that are likely to fail and to hold off on fully recognizing potential profits on investments that are progressing nicely. Private equity funds may be likened to gardeners who sow seeds in the knowledge that most will soon fail but those that thrive will eventually generate profits many times their cost. Consider a private equity fund experiencing a normal rate of failure in the early years. Although a few ventures thrive and might reasonably be viewed as gaining in value, the prompt recognition of potential losses will tend to generate early losses and deferred net profits. The result is that interim IRRs of successful funds may not be positive for five or more years.

Financial Accounting Standard (FAS) 157, which was introduced in 2006, seeks to require asset managers to regularly value their investments at fair value, even when the valuation is not immediately observable from market prices. Rather than holding the investment at cost until an impairment or later round of funding forces a change in valuation, the standard seeks more regular changes in value based on both changes in the fortunes of the company as well as valuations of comparable firms. Private equity firms that follow this fair value accounting will likely report company valuations that more accurately predict exit valuations, and have changes in fund NAVs that have higher volatility and higher correlation to liquid financial markets.

3.6.3 The J-Curve

The **J-curve** is a diagram popular in the analysis of private equity that plots IRR on the vertical axis and time since inception on the horizontal axis, generating the fund performance curve often likened in shape to a hockey stick and depicted in Exhibit 3.8.

The J-curve is caused by a combination of early expense recognition, early loss recognition, and deferred gain recognition. The J-curve therefore depicts an apparent decline in value during the early years of existence, the so-called valley of tears, before beginning to show the hoped-for positive returns in the later years of the fund's life. Beyond five years, the interim IRRs will give a reasonable indication of the final IRR

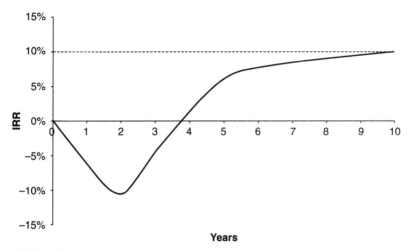

EXHIBIT 3.8 J-Curve of Interim IRRs

at the fund's maturity. Although the J-curve of interim IRRs is usually discussed in the context of funds, the J-curve can also be applied to individual ventures. Many speculative ventures possess the inherent likelihood of short-term expenses and long-term profits that generate the familiar J-curve at the venture or company level. After all, it is the aggregation of the outcomes of the individual ventures that forms the fund-level outcome.

3.7 DISTRIBUTION OF CASH WATERFALL

Limited partnerships, including private equity funds and hedge funds, have provisions for the allocation of cash inflows between general partners (GPs) and limited partners (LPs). Provisions related to the distribution waterfall are often the most complex parts of the limited partnership agreement. The **waterfall** is a provision of the limited partnership agreement that specifies how distributions from a fund will be split and how the payouts will be prioritized. Specifically, the waterfall details what amount must be distributed to the LPs before the fund manager or GPs can take a share from the fund's profits.

One important reason LPs need to understand the distribution waterfall is because of its impact on managerial incentives and, consequently, on the behavioral drivers of the fund's performance. Familiarizing themselves with the design of the waterfall's terms and conditions is one of the few opportunities LPs have to anticipate and manage risk. The waterfall's design always produces effects (sometimes unintended ones) as it drives the motivation and attitude, sense of responsibility, accountability, and priorities of fund managers.

3.7.1 Cash Waterfalls

The distribution of cash waterfalls has specialized terms, which tend to differ between private equity and hedge funds. This section introduces most of the major terms that are used in the remaining sections.

Cash inflows to a fund in excess of the costs of investment and the expenses of the fund represent the waterfall that is distributed to GPs and LPs. Excess revenue above expenses is referred to as net cash flow or profit. In calculating profit, management fees are deducted, but any fees that are based on profitability are not deducted. (Management fees are usually deducted from the fund, regardless of profitability.)

Carried interest is synonymous with an **incentive fee** or a **performance-based fee** and is the portion of the profit paid to the GPs as compensation for their services, above and beyond management fees. Carried interest is typically up to 20% of the profits of the fund and becomes payable once the LPs have achieved repayment of their original investment in the fund, plus any hurdle rate.

A **hurdle rate** specifies a return level that LPs must receive before GPs begin to receive incentive fees. When a fund has a hurdle rate, the first priority of cash profits is to distribute profits to the LPs until they have received a rate of return equal to the hurdle rate. Thus, the hurdle rate is the return threshold that a fund must return to the fund's investors, in addition to the repayment of their initial commitment, before the fund manager becomes entitled to incentive fees. The term **preferred return** is often used synonymously with hurdle rate—a return level that LPs must receive before GPs begin to receive incentive fees.

A **catch-up provision** permits the fund manager to receive a large share of profits once the hurdle rate of return has been achieved and passed. A catch-up provision gives the fund manager a chance to earn incentive fees on all profits, not just the profits in excess of the hurdle rate. A catch-up provision contains a **catch-up rate**, which is the percentage of the profits used to catch up the incentive fee once the hurdle is met. A full catch-up rate is 100%. To be effective, the catch-up rate must exceed the rate of carried interest.

Vesting is the process of granting full ownership of conferred rights, such as incentive fees. Rights that have not yet been vested may not be sold or traded by the recipient and may be subject to forfeiture. Vesting is a driver of incentives. Vesting can be pro rata over the investment period, over the entire term of the fund, or somewhere in between, such as on an annual basis.

A **clawback** clause, clawback provision, or clawback option is designed to return incentive fees to LPs when early profits are followed by subsequent losses. A clawback provision requires the GP to return cash to the LPs to the extent that the GP has received more than the agreed profit split. A GP clawback option ensures that if a fund experiences strong performance early in its life and weaker performance at the end, the LPs get back any incentive fees until their capital contributions, expenses, and any preferred return promised in the partnership agreement have been paid.

3.7.2 The Compensation Scheme

A key element of the managerial compensation structure is the nature of the incentives that align interests between fund managers and their investors. Investors and fund managers have an agency relationship in which investors are the principals and fund managers are their agents. The **compensation scheme** is the set of provisions and procedures governing management fees, general partner investment in the fund, carried-interest allocations, vesting, and distribution. As with all agency relationships, compensation schemes should be designed to align the interests of the principals (the LPs) and the agents (the GPs) to the extent that the alignment is cost-effective. It is generally cost-ineffective to try to maximize the alignment of GP and LP interests. For example, requiring huge investments into the partnership by general partners might initially appear to be an effective method of aligning LP and GP interests. However, GPs with a large proportion of their wealth invested in a single fund may manage the fund in an overly risk-averse manner.

The partnership agreement provisions, as well as other terms and conditions, such as investment limitations, transfers, withdrawals, indemnification, and the handling of conflicts of interest, tend to look quite similar across fund agreements. Surprisingly, fund terms have been relatively stable across the market cycles. The explanation for this phenomenon is that both fund managers and their investors have sufficient negotiation power to reject terms sought by the other side that differ substantially from terms widely used in the market, but not so much leverage as to move the market in one direction or the other.

Management fees are regular fees that are paid from the fund to the fund managers based on the size of the fund rather than on the profitability of the fund. The purpose of management fees is to cover the basic costs of running and administering the fund. These costs are mainly the salaries of investment managers and back-office personnel; expenses related to the development of investments; travel and entertainment expenses; and office expenses, such as rent, furnishings, utilities, and supplies. During the investment period, management fees are calculated as a percentage of the size of the LP commitment, typically between 1% and 2.5%, depending on fund size. Management fees may be charged at a lower rate or on the invested NAV of the fund after the investment period concludes or when a successor fund is formed. Although the calculation of the management fee is relatively simple and fairly objective, there are controversies surrounding the finer details.

General partners have an opportunity to earn a variety of fees from their portfolio companies. Phalippou (2017) lists a number of fees, including director fees, monitoring fees, transaction fees, restructuring fees, broken deal fees, banking fees, and advisory fees.[1] Limited partners would prefer that these fees count as **management fee offsets,** where all fees earned by general partners would reduce the management fee owed to the GP by the LPs.

The general partners' investment in the fund is the amount of capital they contribute to the fund's pool of capital. GPs typically invest a significant amount of capital in their funds, usually at least 1% of total fund capital, which is treated the same way as the capital contributed by limited partners. There are a number of reasons for this. For example, the GPs contribute a meaningful amount of capital to ensure their status as a partner of the fund for income tax reasons. More important, however, is that they contribute substantial personal wealth to the fund to help align the interests of fund managers and their investors. For all of the calculation examples that follow, the GPs' own investment in the fund is not being considered, because it has the same payoff as that of the limited partners. In other words, in this volume, the computations of the amount of cash being distributed to GPs ignore their ownership interest, since that ownership interest receives cash in the same manner as the LPs. Limited partners prefer that the GPs contribute their investment in cash at the formation of the fund, as GPs earning their commitment through forgone management fees is not an as-effective alignment of interest.

3.7.3 Incentive-Based Fees

Incentive-based or performance-based fees are a critical part of the compensation structure. Carried interest, as discussed earlier, is an incentive-based fee distributed from a fund to the fund's manager. The term *carried interest* tends to be used in private equity and real estate; the term *incentive fee* is more often used in hedge funds. Management fees are paid regardless of the fund's performance and therefore fail to provide a powerful incentive to produce exceptional investment results. Excessive and quasi-guaranteed management fees stimulate tentative and risk-averse behavior, such as following the herd. Consequently, the carried interest, meaning the percentage of the profit paid to fund managers, is the most powerful incentive to align interests and create value. The most common carried-interest split is 80%/20% (a.k.a. 80/20), which gives the fund manager a 20% share in the fund's net profits and is essential to attracting talented and motivated managers. These fees are asymmetric, as a fund manager shares in the gains of the investors, but does not compensate investors for any portion of their losses. (Note that the following examples ignore management fees for the sake of simplicity.)

☞ APPLICATION 3.7.3A

Fund A at the end of its term has risen to a total net asset value (NAV) of $300 million from its initial size of $200 million. Assuming no hurdle rate and an 80%/20% carried-interest split, the general partner is entitled to receive carried interest equal to how much? The answer is $20 million. The answer is found by multiplying the GP's share (20%) by the total profit ($100 million). The total profit is found as the difference in the NAVs. The NAVs are calculated after adding revenues and deducting expenses.

☞ APPLICATION 3.7.3B

Fund B terminates and ultimately returns $132 million to its limited partners, and the total initial size of the fund was $100 million. Assuming a carried interest rate of 20%, the general partner is entitled to receive carried interest equal to how much? The answer is $8 million. Note that if $32 million is the profit only to the LP, the total profit of the fund was higher. The answer is found by solving the following equations: LP profit = 0.8 × total profit; so $32 million = 0.8 × total profit; therefore, total profit = $40 million. The second equation is GP carried interest = 0.2 × total profit; therefore, carried interest = $8 million.

3.7.4 Aggregating Profits and Losses

In the case of multiple projects within private equity funds, two approaches are used for determining profits and distributing incentive fees. Carried interest can be

fund-as-a-whole carried interest, which is carried interest based on aggregated profits and losses across all the investments, or can be structured as deal-by-deal carried interest. **Deal-by-deal carried interest** is when incentive fees are awarded separately based on the performance of each individual investment.

☞ APPLICATION 3.7.4A

Consider a fund that makes two investments, A and B, of $10 million each. Investment A is successful and generates a $10 million profit, whereas Investment B is a complete write-off (a total loss). Assume that the fund managers are allowed to take 20% of profits as carried interest. How much carried interest will they receive if profits are calculated on a fund-as-a-whole (aggregated) basis, and how much will they receive if profits are calculated on a deal-by-deal (individual transaction) basis?

On the fund-as-a whole basis, the fund broke even, so no incentive fees will be distributed. On the deal-by-deal basis, Investment A earned $10 million, so $2 million in carried interest will be distributed to the managers.

Participating in every investment's profit, or deal-by-deal carried interest, can be problematic because the general partner can make profits on successful investments while having little exposure to unsuccessful transactions. As the limited partners take the bulk of the capital risk, this approach significantly weakens the alignment of interests. A fund-as-a-whole carried-interest approach protects the interests of the LPs but may be less effective in attracting talented managers. The fund-as-a-whole scheme may entail the risk of frustrating the fund managers, as their rewards may be deferred for years until all deals can be aggregated. Carried-interest distribution is typically one of the most intensively negotiated topics. The amount of the payment is often not as much of an issue as the timing of the payment. In practice, carried interest schemes include elements of both approaches in order to circumvent their respective limitations.

3.7.5 Clawbacks and Alternating Profits and Losses

Clawbacks are relevant to funds that calculate carried interest on a fund-as-a-whole basis. The idea of typical clawback provisions is that incentive fees distributed to managers are returned when a firm experiences losses after profits so that the total incentive fees paid, ignoring the time value of money, are equal to the incentive fees that would be due if all profits and losses had occurred simultaneously. Funds experience early profits and late losses in two primary instances. In private equity funds, it is possible that a few of the projects in which the fund has invested may successfully terminate and generate large cash inflows and profits to the fund. Other projects may fail at a later date, thereby generating large losses or write-offs. An important issue when a fund experiences large gains early in its life, followed by subsequent losses, is whether incentive fees paid on the early profits will be returned to the LPs.

Another instance in which losses follow profits is more common in the hedge fund industry, where market conditions or managerial decision-making can cause strategies to be highly successful in one time period and then highly unsuccessful in a later time period. In this case, the fund earns high profits followed by large losses. In both cases, it is possible that incentive fees, or carried interest, could be paid during the earlier profitable stage, even though subsequent losses could cause the investment to have no profit over its entire lifetime. Thus, a limited partner could end up paying incentive fees for an investment that lost money over its lifetime. Clawback provisions are designed to address this problem for limited partners.

☞ APPLICATION 3.7.5A

Consider a fund that calculates incentive fees on a fund-as-a-whole basis and makes two investments, A and B, of $10 million each. Investment A is successful and generates a $10 million profit after three years. Investment B is not revalued until it is completely written off after five years. Assume that the fund managers are allowed to take 20% of profits as carried interest calculated on an aggregated basis. How much carried interest will they receive if there is no clawback provision, and how much will they receive if there is a clawback provision?

Without a clawback provision, the fund earned $10 million after three years and distributed a $2 million carried interest to the managers. When the second investment failed, the incentive fee is not returned. In the case of a clawback provision, the fund distributed a $2 million incentive fee to the managers after three years, but when the second investment failed, the incentive fee is returned to the limited partners, since there is no combined profit.

The goal of clawback provisions is to protect the economic split agreed between the GP and LPs. The clawback provision is sometimes called a giveback or a lookback, because it requires a partnership to undergo a final accounting of all of its capital and profit distributions at the end of a fund's lifetime. Clawback provisions are the opposite of vesting. Vesting of fees is the process of making payments available such that they are not subject to being returned.

A clawback provision is a promise to repay overdistributions, but such a promise is only as good as the creditworthiness of the GP. The GP is normally organized as a limited liability vehicle with no assets other than the interest in the fund. In the partnership agreements of many funds, the clawback provision simply binds the GP and requires his or her cooperation and financial support.

The sentiment that clawbacks are worthless is not uncommon. Situations arise in which LPs are unable to receive the clawbacks they are owed. Attempting to enforce the clawback provisions may lead to years of litigation without resulting in any return of cash. The simplest and, from the viewpoint of LPs, most desirable solution is to ensure that the GP does not receive carried interest until all invested capital has been repaid to investors. With this approach, however, it can take several years before the fund's team sees any gains, and it could be unacceptable or demotivating to the fund managers. An accepted compromise for securing the clawback obligation is to place a fixed percentage of the fund manager's carried interest proceeds into an escrow account as a buffer against potential clawback liability.

Clawbacks typically refer to GP clawbacks, or corrective payments to prevent a windfall to the fund manager. However, it is also possible for LPs to receive more than their agreed percentage of carried interest. Consequently, some partnership agreements also address so-called LP clawbacks.

3.7.6 Hard Hurdle Rates

A hurdle rate, or preferred return, specifies that a fund manager cannot receive a share in the distributions until the limited partners have received aggregate distributions equal to the sum of their capital contributions as well as a specified return, known as the hurdle rate. In other words, a hurdle rate specifies a return level that LPs must receive before GPs begin to receive incentive fees. This section details hurdle rates and discusses a hard hurdle rate. A **hard hurdle rate** limits incentive fees to profits in excess of the hurdle rate.

☞ APPLICATION 3.7.6A

Consider a $10 million fund with 20% incentive fees that lasts a single year and earns a $2 million profit. Ignoring a hurdle rate, the fund manager would receive $400,000, which is 20% of $2 million. But with a hard hurdle rate of 10%, the fund manager receives the 20% incentive fees only on profits in excess of the 10% return, meaning $200,000. The first $1 million of profit goes directly to the limited partners. The fund manager collects an incentive fee only on profits in excess of the $1 million, which is the profit necessary to bring the limited partners' return up to the hurdle rate. Thus, the manager receives an incentive fee of $200,000.

The sequence of cash distributions with a hard hurdle rate is as follows:

1. Capital is returned to the limited partners until their investment has been repaid.
2. Profits are distributed only to the limited partners until the hurdle rate is reached.
3. Additional profits are split such that the fund manager receives an incentive fee only on the profits in excess of the hurdle rate.

3.7.7 Soft Hurdles and a Catch-Up Provision

A **soft hurdle rate** allows fund managers to earn an incentive fee on all profits, given that the hurdle rate has been achieved. Returning to the example of a one-year $10 million fund with a hurdle rate of 10% and profits of $2 million, a soft hurdle rate of 10% allows the fund manager to receive 20% of the entire $2 million profit, or $400,000. As long as the resulting share to the limited partners allows a return in excess of the hurdle rate, then the hurdle rate can be ignored in terms of computing the incentive fee. The limited partners receive $1.6 million, which is a 16% return.

The soft hurdle in this case allows the fund manager to receive an incentive fee on the entire profit. A soft hurdle has a catch-up provision that can be viewed as providing the fund manager with a disproportionate share of excess profits until the manager has received the incentive fee on all profits. The sequence of cash distributions with a soft hurdle rate is as follows:

1. Capital is returned to the limited partners until their investment has been repaid.
2. Profits are distributed only to the limited partners until the hurdle rate is reached.
3. Additional profits are split, with a high proportion going to the fund manager until the fund manager receives an incentive fee on all of the profits.

Once the fund manager has been paid an incentive fee on all previous profits, additional profits are split using the incentive fee. This is called a catch-up provision.

☞ APPLICATION 3.7.7A

Fund A with an initial investment of $20 million liquidates with $24 million cash after one year. The hurdle rate is 15%, and the incentive fee is 20%. What is the distribution to the fund manager if the fund uses a hard hurdle? What is the distribution to the fund manager if the fund has a soft hurdle and a 50% catch-up rate?

The first $20 million is returned to the limited partners in both cases. With a hard hurdle, the limited partners receive the first $3 million of profit, which is 15% of the $20 million investment. The fund manager receives 20% of the remaining profit of $1 million, which is $200,000. The limited partners receive 80% of the remaining $1 million, which is $800,000, for a total profit of $3.8 million. With a soft hurdle, the limited partners receive the first $3 million of profit, which is 15% of the $20 million investment. To fulfill the catch-up provision, the fund manager receives 50% of the remaining profit up to the point of being paid 20% of all profit. In this case, 50% of all of the remaining profit, or $1 million, is $500,000. Since $500,000 is less than 20% of the entire $4 million profit, the fund manager is unable to fully catch up. Had the total profits exceeded $5 million, the catch-up of the fund manager would have been completed. With $5 million of profit, the GP would receive 50% of the profits above $3 million, or $1 million (50% of the $2 million profit in excess of the profit necessary to meet the hurdle rate for the LPs). The $1 million of catch-up equals 20% of $5 million. Profits in excess of $5 million would then be split 20% to the fund manager and 80% to the limited partners.

3.7.8   Incentive Fee as an Option

Incentive fees are long call options to GPs, who receive the classic payout of a call option: If the assets of the fund rise, they receive an increasing payout, and if the assets of the fund remain constant or fall, they receive no incentive fee. The underlying asset is the fund's net asset value, and the time to expiration of the option is the time until the next incentive fee is calculated, at which time a new option is written for the next incentive fee. In the absence of a hurdle rate, the strike price of the call option is the net asset value of the fund at the start of the period or the end of the last period in which an incentive fee was paid, whichever is greater. The GPs pay for this call option by providing their management expertise.

A hurdle rate may be viewed as increasing the strike price of the incentive fee call option. A hurdle rate increases the amount by which the net asset value of the fund must rise before the fund manager receives an incentive fee. The higher the hurdle rate, the lower the value of the call option.

As a call option, incentive fees provide fund managers with a strong incentive to generate profits. The call option moves in-the-money when the net asset value of a fund rises to the point of providing a return in excess of any hurdle rate. The call option moves out-of-the-money when the net asset value of the fund falls below the point of providing a return in excess of any hurdle rate. When the option is below or near its strike price, the incentive fees provide the fund manager with an incentive to increase the risk of the fund's assets. The effect of increased risk is to increase the value of the call option. If the risks generate profits, the fund manager can benefit through high incentive fees. If the risks generate losses, the effect on the fund manager is limited to receiving no incentive fee, ignoring clawbacks.

When the incentive fee call option is deep-in-the-money, the fund manager benefits less from an increase in the risk of the underlying assets. The consequences of net asset value changes to the fund manager are more symmetrical when the option is deep-in-the-money, meaning when large incentive fees are likely. Risk aversion may motivate the fund manager to lessen the risk of the underlying assets when the incentive fee option is deep-in-the-money.

It can be argued that the multifaceted incentives generated by the optionlike character of incentive fees are perverse. The LPs prefer fund managers to take risks based on market opportunities and the risk-return preferences of the LPs. However, incentive fees can motivate fund managers to base investment decisions on the resulting risks to their personal finances. In summary, incentive fees can cause decisions involving risk to be based on the degree to which an option is in-the-money, near-the-money, or out-of-the-money.

REVIEW QUESTIONS

1. What is the general term denoting compound interest when the interest is not continuously compounded?
2. What is the primary challenge that causes difficulty in calculating the return performance of a forward contract or another position that requires no net investment? How is that challenge addressed?
3. An IRR is estimated for a fund based on an initial investment when the fund was created, several annual distributions, and an estimate of the fund's value prior to its termination. What type of IRR is this?
4. An investment has two solutions for its IRR. What can be said about the investment and the usefulness of the two solutions?
5. Two investments are being compared to ascertain which would add the most value to a portfolio. Both investments have simplified cash flow patterns of an initial cost followed by positive cash flows. Why might the IRRs of the investments provide an unreliable indication of which would add more value?
6. An analyst computes the IRR of one alternative to be 20% and another to be 30%. When the analyst combines the cash flows of the two alternatives into a

single investment, must the IRR of the combination be greater than 20% and less than 30%?

7. Is an IRR a dollar-weighted return or a time-weighted return? Why?
8. What is the primary cause of the shape of the J-curve of interim private equity fund returns?
9. In which scenario will a clawback clause lead to payments?
10. What is the difference between a hard hurdle rate and a soft hurdle rate?

NOTE

1. Ludovic Phalippou, *Private Equity Laid Bare* (CreateSpace Independent Publishing Platform, 2017).

CHAPTER 4

Statistical Foundations

T his chapter provides foundational material regarding statistical methods for the study of alternative investments in general and for the subsequent material in this book in particular. The use of statistics in performing hypothesis tests is addressed in detail in Chapter 8.

4.1 RETURN DISTRIBUTIONS

Risky assets experience unexpected value changes and therefore unexpected returns. If we assume that investors are rational, the more competitively traded an asset, the more these unexpected price changes may be random and unpredictable. Hence, asset prices and asset returns in competitively traded markets are typically modeled as random variables. Frequency and probability distributions therefore provide starting points for describing asset returns.

4.1.1 Ex Ante and Ex Post Return Distributions

Ex post returns are realized outcomes rather than anticipated outcomes. Future possible returns and their probabilities are referred to as expectational or **ex ante returns**. A crucial theme in understanding the analysis of alternative investments is to understand the differences and links between ex post and ex ante return data.

Often, predictions are formed partially or fully through analysis of ex post data. For example, the ex ante or future return distribution of a stock index such as the S&P 500 Index is often assumed to be well approximated by the ex post or historical return distribution. The direct use of past return behavior as a predictor of future potential return behavior requires two properties to be accurate. First, the return distribution must be stationary through time, meaning that the expected return and the dispersion of the underlying asset do not change. Second, the sample of past observations must be sufficiently large to be likely to form a reasonably accurate representation of the process. For example, equity returns were very high during the bull market decade of the 1990s, very low during the early years of the financial crisis (2007–08), and high in the decade subsequent to the crisis. Using any of these time periods in isolation would likely overstate or understate the realistic long-run equity market returns.

Taken together, the requirements for the past returns to be representative of the future returns raise a serious challenge. If the past observation period is long, the sample of historical returns will be large; however, it is likely that the oldest observations reflect different risks or other economic conditions than can be anticipated in the future. If the sample is limited to the most recent observations, the data may be more representative of future economic conditions, but the sample may be too small to draw accurate inferences from it.

For a traditional asset, such as the common stock of a large, publicly traded corporation, it may be somewhat plausible that the asset's past behavior is a reasonable indication of its future behavior. However, many alternative investments are especially problematic in this context. For example, historical data may not exist for venture capital investments in new technology or may be difficult to observe or to obtain in cases such as private equity, where most or all trades are not publicly observable. Especially in alternative investments such as hedge funds, return distributions are expected to change as the fund's investment strategies and use of leverage change through time. In these cases and many others, ex ante return distributions may need to be based on economic analysis and modeling rather than simply projected from ex post data.

Nevertheless, whether based on prior observations or on economic analysis, the return distribution is a central tool for understanding the characteristics of an investment. The normal distribution is the starting point for most statistical applications in investments.

4.1.2 The Normal Distribution

The **normal distribution** is the familiar bell-shaped distribution, also known as the Gaussian distribution. The normal distribution is symmetric, meaning that the left and right sides are mirror images of each other. Also, the normal distribution clusters or peaks near the center, with decreasing probabilities of extreme events.

Why is the normal distribution so central to statistical analysis in general and the analysis of investment returns in particular? One reason is empirical: The normal distribution tends to approximate many distributions observed in nature or generated as the result of human actions and interactions, including financial return distributions. Another reason is theoretical: The more a variable's change results from the summation of a large number of independent causes, the more that variable tends to behave like a normally distributed variable. Thus, the more competitively traded an asset's price is, the more we would expect that the price change over a small unit of time would be the result of hundreds or thousands of independent financial events and/or trading decisions. Therefore, the probability distribution of the resulting price change should resemble the normal distribution. The formal statistical explanation for the idea that a variable will tend toward a normal distribution as the number of independent influences becomes larger is known as the **central limit theorem**. Practically speaking, the normal distribution is relatively easy to use, which may explain some of its popularity.

4.1.3 Log Returns and the Lognormal Distribution

For simplicity, funds often report returns based on discrete compounding. However, log returns offer a distinct advantage, especially for modeling a return probability distribution. In a nutshell, the use of log returns allows for the modeling of different time intervals in a manner that is simple and internally consistent. Specifically, if daily log returns are normally distributed and independent through time, then the log returns of other time intervals, such as months and years, will also be normally distributed. The same cannot be said of simple returns. Let's take a closer look at why log returns have this property.

The normal distribution replicates when variables are added but not when they are multiplied. This means that if two variables, x and y, are normally distributed, then the sum of the two variables, $x + y$, will also be normally distributed. But because the normal distribution does not replicate multiplicatively, $x \times y$ would not be normally distributed. Aggregation of discretely compounded returns is multiplicative. Thus, if R_1, R_2, and R_3 represent the returns for months 1, 2, and 3 using discrete compounding, then the product $[(1 + R_1)(1 + R_2)(1 + R_3)] - 1$ represents the return for the calendar quarter that contains the three months. If the monthly returns are normally distributed, then the quarterly return is not normally distributed, and vice versa, since the normal distribution does not replicate multiplicatively. Therefore, modeling the distribution of discretely compounded returns as being normally distributed over a particular time interval (e.g., monthly) technically means that the model will not be valid for any other choice of time interval (e.g., daily, weekly, annually).

However, the use of log returns, discussed in Chapter 3, solves this problem. If $R_1^{m=\infty}$, $R_2^{m=\infty}$, and $R_3^{m=\infty}$ are monthly log returns, then the quarterly log return is simply the sum of the three monthly log returns. The normal distribution replicates additively; thus, if the log returns over one time interval can be modeled as being normally distributed, then the log returns over all time intervals will be lognormal as long as they are statistically independent through time.

Further, log returns have another highly desirable property. The highest possible simple (non-annualized) return is theoretically $+\infty$, while the lowest possible simple return for a cash investment is a loss of -100%, which occurs if the investment becomes worthless. However, the normal distribution spans from $-\infty$ to $+\infty$, meaning that simple returns, theoretically speaking, cannot truly be normally distributed; a simple return of -200% is not possible. Thus, the normal distribution may be a poor approximation of the actual probability distribution of simple returns. However, log returns, like the normal distribution itself, can span from $-\infty$ to $+\infty$. There are two equivalent approaches to model returns that address these problems: (1) use log returns and assume that they are normally distributed, or (2) add 1 to the simple returns and assume that it has a lognormal distribution. A variable has a **lognormal distribution** if the distribution of the logarithm of the variable is normally distributed. The two approaches are identical, since the lognormal distribution assumes that the logarithms of the specified variable (in this case, $1 + R$) are normally distributed.

In summary, it is possible for returns to be normally distributed over a variety of time intervals if those returns are expressed as log returns (and are independent through time). If the log returns are normally distributed, then the simple returns (in the form $1 + R$) are said to be lognormally distributed. However, if discretely compounded returns (R) are assumed to be normally distributed, they can only be normally distributed over one time interval, such as daily, since returns computed over other time intervals would not be normally distributed due to compounding.

4.2 MOMENTS OF THE DISTRIBUTION: MEAN, VARIANCE, SKEWNESS, AND KURTOSIS

Random variables, such as an asset's return or the timing of uncertain cash flows, can be viewed as forming a probability distribution. Probability distributions have an infinite number of possible shapes, only some of which represent well-known shapes, such as a normal distribution.

The moments of a return distribution are measures that describe the shape of a distribution. As an analogy, in mathematics, researchers often use various parameters to describe the shape of a function, such as its intercept, its slope, and its curvature. Statisticians often use either the raw moments or the central moments of a distribution to describe its shape. Generally, the first four moments are referred to as mean, variance, skewness, and kurtosis. The formulas of these four moments are somewhat similar, differing primarily by the power to which the observations are raised: mean uses the first power, variance squares the terms, skewness cubes the terms, and kurtosis raises the terms to the fourth power.

4.2.1 The Formulas of the First Four Raw Moments

Statistical moments can be raw moments or central moments. Further, the moments are sometimes standardized or scaled to provide more intuitive measures, as will be discussed later. We begin with raw moments, discussing the raw moments of an investment's return, R. Raw moments have the simplest formulas, wherein each moment is simply the expected value of the variable raised to a particular power:

$$n\text{th Raw Moment} = E(R^n) \tag{4.1}$$

The most common raw moment is the first raw moment and is known as the **mean,** or expected value, and is an indication of the central tendency of the variable. With $n = 1$, Equation 4.1 is the formula for expected value:

$$1\text{st Raw Moment} = E(R^1) = E(R) \tag{4.2}$$

The expected value of a variable is the probability-weighted average of its outcomes:

$$E(R) = \sum_i prob_i \times R_i \tag{4.3}$$

where $prob_i$ is the probability of R_i.

Equation 4.3 expresses the first raw moment in terms of probabilities and outcomes. Using historical data, for a sample distribution of n observations, the mean is typically equally weighted and is estimated by the following:

$$\text{Mean} = \overline{R} = \frac{1}{n} \sum_i R_i \tag{4.4}$$

Thus, Equation 4.4 is a formula for estimating Equation 4.2 using historical observations. The historical mean is often used as an estimate of the expected value when observations from the past are assumed to be representative of the future. Other raw moments can be generated by inserting a higher integer value for n in

Equation 4.1. But the raw moments for $n > 1$ are less useful for our purposes than the highly related central moments.

4.2.2 The Formulas of Central Moments

Central moments differ from raw moments because they focus on deviations of the variable from its mean (whereas raw moments are measured relative to zero). Deviations are defined as the value of a variable minus its mean, or expected value. If an observation exceeds its expected value, the deviation is positive by the distance by which it exceeds the expected value. If the observation is less than its expected value, the deviation is a negative number. Each central moment applies the following equation to the deviations:

$$n\text{th Central Moment} = E[(R - \mu)^n] \tag{4.5}$$

where μ = the expected value of R. The term inside the parentheses is the deviation of R from its mean, or expected value. The first central moment is equal to zero by definition, because the expected value of the deviation from the mean is zero. When analysts discuss statistical moments, it is usually understood that the first moment is a raw moment, meaning the mean, or expected value. But the second through fourth moments are usually automatically expressed as central moments because in most applications the moments are more useful when expressed in terms of deviations.

The **variance** is the second central moment and is the expected value of the deviations squared, providing an indication of the dispersion of a variable around its mean:

$$2\text{nd Central Moment} = \text{Variance} = E[(R - \mu)^2] \tag{4.6}$$

The variance is the probability weighted average of the deviations squared. By squaring the deviations, any negative signs are removed (i.e., any negative deviation squared is positive), so the variance $[V(R)]$ becomes a measure of dispersion. In the case of probability-weighted outcomes, this can be written as:

$$V(R) = \sigma^2 = \sum_i prob_i \times (R_i - \mu)^2 \tag{4.7}$$

The variance shown in Equation 4.7 is often estimated with a sample of historical data. For a sample distribution, the variance with equally weighted observations is estimated as:

$$\text{Variance} = \frac{1}{n-1} \sum_i (R_i - \overline{R})^2 \tag{4.8}$$

The mean in Equation 4.8, $\overline{R}$, is usually estimated using the same sample. The use of $n - 1$ in the equation (rather than n) enables a more accurate measure of the variance when the estimate of the expected value of the variable has been computed from the same sample. The square root of the variance is an extremely popular and useful measure of dispersion known as the **standard deviation**:

$$\text{Standard Deviation} = \sqrt{\sigma^2} = \sigma \tag{4.9}$$

In investment terminology, **volatility** is a popular term that is used synonymously with the standard deviation of returns. Other central moments can be generated by inserting a higher integer value for n in Equation 4.5. But the central moments for $n = 3$ (skewness) and $n = 4$ (kurtosis) are typically less intuitive and less well-known than their scaled versions. In other words, rather than using the third and fourth central moments, slightly modified formulas are used to generate scaled measures of skewness and kurtosis. These two scaled measures are detailed in the next two sections.

4.2.3 Skewness

The third central moment is the expected value of a variable's cubed deviations:

$$3\text{rd Central Moment} = E[(R - \mu)^3] \qquad (4.10)$$

A problem with the third central moment is that it is generally affected by the scale. Thus, a distribution's third central moment for a variable measured in daily returns differs dramatically if the daily returns are expressed as annualized returns. To provide this measure with a more intuitive scale, investment analysts typically use the standardized third moment (the relative skewness or simply the skewness). The **skewness** is equal to the third central moment divided by the standard deviation of the variable cubed and serves as a measure of asymmetry:

$$\text{Skewness} = E[(R - \mu)^3]/\sigma^3 \qquad (4.11)$$

Skewness is dimensionless, since changes in the scale of the returns affect the numerator and denominator proportionately, leaving the fraction unchanged. By cubing the deviations, the sign of each deviation is retained because a negative value cubed remains negative. Further, cubing the deviations provides a measure of the direction in which the largest deviations occur, since the cubing causes large deviations to be much more influential than the smaller deviations. The result is that the measure of skewness in Equation 4.11 provides a numerical measure of the extent to which a distribution flares out in one direction or the other. A positive value indicates that the right tail is larger (the mass of the distribution is concentrated on the left side), and a negative value indicates that the left tail is larger (the mass of the distribution is concentrated on the right side). A skewness of zero can result from a symmetrical distribution, such as the normal distribution, or from any other distribution in which the tails otherwise balance out within the equation. The top illustration of Exhibit 4.1 depicts negatively skewed, symmetric, and positively skewed distributions.

4.2.4 Excess Kurtosis

The fourth central moment is the expected value of a variable's deviations raised to the fourth power:

$$4\text{th Central Moment} = E[(R - \mu)^4] \qquad (4.12)$$

As with the third central moment, a problem with the fourth central moment is that it is difficult to interpret its magnitude. To provide this measure with a more intuitive scale, investment analysts do two things. First, they divide the moment by

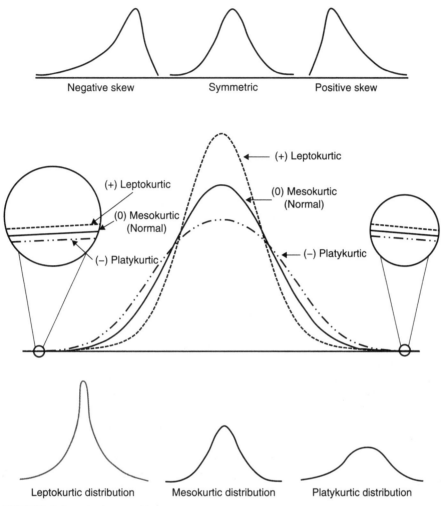

EXHIBIT 4.1 Skewness and Kurtosis

the standard deviation of the variable raised to the fourth power (to make it dimensionless):

$$\text{Kurtosis} = E[(R - \mu)^4]/\sigma^4 \qquad (4.13)$$

The resulting measure, known as **kurtosis,** is shown in Equation 4.13 and primarily serves as an indicator of the size of the extreme tails of a distribution. In the case of a normally distributed variable, the estimated kurtosis has a value that approaches 3.0 (as the sample size is increased). The second adjustment that analysts often perform to create a more intuitive measure of kurtosis is to subtract 3.0 from the result to derive a measure, known as excess kurtosis. **Excess kurtosis** provides a more intuitive measure of kurtosis relative to the normal distribution because it has a value of zero in the case of the normal distribution:

$$\text{Excess Kurtosis} = \{E[(R - \mu)^4]/\sigma^4\} - 3 \qquad (4.14)$$

Since 3.0 is the kurtosis of a normally distributed variable, after subtracting 3.0 from the kurtosis, a positive excess kurtosis signals a level of kurtosis that is higher than observed in a normally distributed variable, an excess kurtosis of 0.0 indicates a level of kurtosis similar to that of a normally distributed variable, and a negative excess kurtosis signals a level of kurtosis that is lower than that observed in a normally distributed variable.

Kurtosis is typically viewed as capturing the fatness of the tails of a distribution, with high values of kurtosis (or positive values of excess kurtosis) indicating fatter tails (i.e., higher probabilities of extreme outcomes) than are found in the case of a normally distributed variable.

In summary, the mean, variance, skewness, and kurtosis of a return distribution indicate the location and shape of a distribution, and are often a key part of measuring and communicating the risks and rewards of various investments. Familiarity with each can be a critical component of a high-level understanding of the analysis of alternative investments.

4.2.5 Platykurtosis, Mesokurtosis, and Leptokurtosis

The level of kurtosis is sufficiently important in analyzing alternative investment returns that the statistical descriptions of the degree of kurtosis and the related terms have become industry standards. If a return distribution has no excess kurtosis, meaning it has the same kurtosis as the normal distribution, it is said to be mesokurtic, mesokurtotic, or normal tailed, and to exhibit **mesokurtosis**. The tails of the distribution would have the same magnitude as the normal distribution.

The middle illustration in Exhibit 4.1 depicts that kurtosis can be viewed by the fatness of the tails of a distribution. If a return distribution has negative excess kurtosis, meaning less kurtosis than the normal distribution, it is said to be platykurtic, platykurtotic, or thin tailed, and to exhibit **platykurtosis**. If a return distribution has positive excess kurtosis, meaning it has more kurtosis than the normal distribution, it is said to be leptokurtic, leptokurtotic, or fat tailed, and to exhibit **leptokurtosis**.

The bottom illustration in Exhibit 4.1 depicts leptokurtic, mesokurtic, and platykurtic distributions. A leptokurtic distribution (positive excess kurtosis) with fat tails is illustrated on the left. A platykurtic distribution (negative excess kurtosis) with thin tails and a rounded center is illustrated on the right. In the middle is a normal mesokurtic distribution (no excess kurtosis). The key to recognizing excess kurtosis visually is comparing the thickness of the tails of both sides of the distribution relative to the tails of a normal distribution.

4.3 COVARIANCE, CORRELATION, BETA, AND AUTOCORRELATION

An important aspect of a return is the way that it correlates with other returns. This is because correlation affects diversification, and diversification drives the risk of a portfolio of assets relative to the risks of the portfolio's constituent assets. This section begins with an examination of covariance, then details the correlation coefficient. Much as standard deviation provides a more easily interpreted alternative to variance, the correlation coefficient provides a scaled and intuitive alternative to covariance. Finally, the section discusses the concepts of beta and autocorrelation.

4.3.1 Covariance

The **covariance** of the return of two assets is a measure of the degree or tendency of two variables to move in relationship with each other. If two assets tend to move in the same direction, they are said to covary positively, and they will have a positive covariance. If the two assets tend to move in opposite directions, they are said to covary negatively, and they will have a negative covariance. Finally, if the two assets move independently of each other, their covariance will be zero. Thus, covariance is a statistical measure of the extent to which two variables move together. The formula for covariance is similar to that for variance, except that instead of squaring the deviations of one variable, such as the returns of fund i, the formula cross multiplies the contemporaneous deviations of two different variables, such as the returns of funds i and j:

$$\text{Covariance} = E[(R_i - \mu_i)(R_j - \mu_j)] \tag{4.15}$$

where R_i is the return of fund i, μ_i is the expected value or mean of R_i, R_j is the return of fund j, and μ_j is the expected value or mean of R_j.

The covariance is the expected value of the product of the deviations of the returns of the two funds. Covariance can be estimated from a sample using Equation 4.16:

$$\text{Cov}(R_i, R_j) = \sigma_{ij} = \frac{1}{(T-1)} \sum_{t=1}^{T} [(R_{it} - \overline{R}_i)(R_{jt} - \overline{R}_j)] \tag{4.16}$$

where R_{it} is the return of fund i in time t, and $\overline{R}_i$ is the sample mean return of R_{it} and analogously for fund j. T is the number of time periods observed.

The estimation of the covariance for a sample of returns from a market index fund and a real estate fund is shown in Exhibit 4.2. Column 8 multiplies the fund's deviation from its mean return by the index's deviation from its mean return. Each of the products of the deviations is then summed and divided by $n - 1$, where n is the number of observations. The result is the estimated covariance between the returns over the sample period, shown near the bottom right-hand corner of Exhibit 4.2.

Because covariance is based on the products of individual deviations and not squared deviations, its value can be positive, negative, or zero. When the return deviations are in the same direction, meaning they have the same sign, the cross product is positive; when the return deviations are in opposite directions, meaning they have different signs, the cross product is negative. When the cross products are summed, the resulting sum generates an indication of the overall tendency of the returns to move either in tandem or in opposition. Note that the table method illustrated in Exhibit 4.2 simply provides a format for solving the formula, which can be easily solved by software. Covariance is used directly in numerous applications, such as in the classic portfolio theory work of Markowitz.

4.3.2 Correlation Coefficient

A statistic related to covariance is the correlation coefficient. The **correlation coefficient** (also called the Pearson correlation coefficient) measures the degree of association between two variables, but unlike the covariance, the correlation coefficient can be easily interpreted. The correlation coefficient takes the covariance and scales its value to be between $+1$ and -1 by dividing by the product of the standard deviations

EXHIBIT 4.2   Covariance, Correlations, and Beta

	(1) Month	Market Index			RE Fund			
		(2) Return	(3) Deviation	(4) Dev2	(5) Return	(6) Deviation	(7) Dev2	(8) Cross
	1	−0.060	−0.062	0.004	−0.008	−0.018	0.000	0.001
	2	−0.032	−0.034	0.001	−0.032	−0.042	0.002	0.001
	3	−0.004	−0.006	0.000	0.065	0.055	0.003	0.000
	·	·	·	·	·	·	·	·
	·	·	·	·	·	·	·	·
	·	·	·	·	·	·	·	·
	37	0.024	0.022	0.000	0.033	0.023	0.001	0.000
	38	0.034	0.032	0.001	0.047	0.037	0.001	0.001
	39	0.000	−0.001	0.000	−0.016	−0.026	0.001	0.000
	40	0.030	0.028	0.001	0.057	0.047	0.002	0.001
	Sum	0.075	0.000	0.146	0.402	0.000	0.468	0.215
	Mean	0.002	0.000		0.010	0.000	0.012	0.005
			Variance	0.37%		Variance	1.20%	
Autocorrelation of market	0.292		Std. dev.	6.11%		Std. dev.	10.95%	
Autocorrelation of fund	0.142					Cov.	0.006	
Durbin-Watson of market	1.393					Cor.	0.822	
Durbin-Watson of fund	1.697					Beta	1.474	

Source: Data from Bloomberg.

of the two variables. A correlation coefficient of −1 indicates that the two assets move in the exact opposite direction and in the same proportion, a result known as **perfect linear negative correlation**. A correlation coefficient of +1 indicates that the two assets move in the exact same direction and in the same proportion, a result known as **perfect linear positive correlation**. A correlation coefficient of zero indicates that there is no linear association between the returns of the two assets. Values between the two extremes of −1 and +1 indicate different degrees of association. Equation 4.17 provides the formula for the correlation coefficient based on the covariance and the standard deviations:

$$\rho_{ij} = \sigma_{ij}/(\sigma_i \sigma_j) \tag{4.17}$$

where ρ_{ij} (rho) is the notation for the correlation coefficient between the returns of asset i and asset j; σ_{ij} is the covariance between the returns of asset i and asset j; and σ_i and σ_j are the standard deviations of the returns of assets i and j, respectively.

Thus, ρ_{ij}, the correlation coefficient, scales covariance, σ_{ij}, through division by the product of the standard deviations, $\sigma_i \sigma_j$. The correlation coefficient can therefore be solved by computing covariance and standard deviation as in Exhibit 4.2 and inserting the values into Equation 4.17. The result is shown in Exhibit 4.2.

4.3.3 The Spearman Rank Correlation Coefficient

The Pearson correlation coefficient is not the only measure of correlation. There are some especially useful measures of correlation in alternative investments that are based on the ranked size of the variables rather than the absolute size of the variables. The returns within a sample for each asset are ranked from highest to lowest. The numerical ranks are then inserted into formulas that generate correlation coefficients that usually range between −1 and +1. The Spearman rank correlation coefficient is a popular example.

The **Spearman rank correlation** is a correlation designed to adjust for outliers by measuring the relationship between variable ranks rather than variable values. The Spearman rank correlation for returns is computed using the ranks of returns of two assets. For example, consider two assets with returns over a time period of three years, illustrated here:

Time Period	Return of Asset #1	Return of Asset #2
1	61%	12%
2	−5%	6%
3	0%	4%

The first step is to replace the actual returns with the rank of each asset's return. The ranks are computed by first ranking the returns of each asset separately, from highest (rank = 1) to lowest (rank = 3), while keeping the returns arrayed according to their time periods:

Time Period	Rank of Asset #1	Rank of Asset #2	Difference in Ranks (d_i)
1	1	1	0
2	3	2	1
3	2	3	−1

This table demonstrates the computation of d_i, the difference in the two ranks associated with time period i. The Spearman rank correlation, ρ_s, can be computed using those differences in ranks and the total number of time periods, n:

$$\rho_s = 1 - \frac{\sum d_i^2}{n(n^2 - 1)} \tag{4.18}$$

Using the data from the table, the numerator is 12, the denominator is $3 \times 8 = 24$, and ρ_s is 0.5. Rank correlation is sometimes preferred because of the way it handles the effects of outliers (extremely high or low data values). For example, the enormous return of asset 1 in the previous table is an outlier, which will have a disproportionate effect on a correlation statistic. Extremely high or very negative values of one or both of the variables in a particular sample can cause the computed Pearson correlation coefficient to be very near +1 or −1 based, arguably, on the undue influence of the extreme observation on the computation, since deviations are squared as part of the computation. Some alternative investments have returns that are more likely to contain extreme outliers. By using ranks, the effects of outliers are lessened, and in

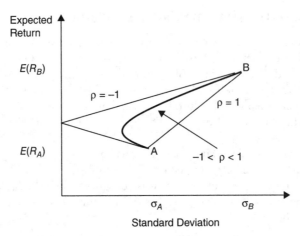

EXHIBIT 4.3 Diversification between Two Assets

some cases it can be argued that the resulting measure of the correlation using a sample is a better indicator of the true correlation that exists within the population. Note that the Spearman rank correlation coefficient would be the same for any return that would generate the same rankings. Thus, any return in time period 1 for the first asset greater than 0% would still be ranked 1 and would generate the same ρ_s.

4.3.4 The Correlation Coefficient and Diversification

The correlation coefficient is often used to demonstrate one of the most fundamental concepts of portfolio theory: the reduction in risk found by combining assets that are not perfectly positively correlated. Exhibit 4.3 illustrates the results of combining varying portions of assets A and B under three correlation conditions: perfect positive correlation, zero correlation, and perfect negative correlation.

The highest possible correlation and least diversification potential is when the assets' correlation coefficient is +1: perfect positive correlation. The straight line to the lower right between points A and B in Exhibit 4.3 plots the possible standard deviations and mean returns achievable by combining asset A and asset B under perfect positive correlation. The line is straight, meaning that the portfolio risk is a weighted average of the individual risks. This illustrates that there are no benefits to diversification when perfectly correlated assets are combined. The idea is that diversification occurs when the risks of unusual returns of assets tend to cancel each other out. This does not happen in the case of perfect positive correlation, because the assets always move in the same direction and by the same proportion.

The greatest risk reduction occurs when the assets' correlation coefficient is −1: perfect negative correlation. The two upper-left line segments connecting points A and B in Exhibit 4.3 plot the possible standard deviations and mean returns that would be achieved by combining asset A and asset B under perfect negative correlation. Notice that the line between A and B moves directly to the vertical axis, the point at which the standard deviation is zero. This illustrates ultimate diversification, in which two assets always move in opposite directions; therefore, combining them into a portfolio results in rapid risk reduction, or even total risk reduction. This zero-risk portfolio illustrates the concept of a perfect two-asset hedge and occurs when the weight of the investment in asset A is equal to the standard deviation of asset B divided by the sums of the standard deviations of A and B.

But the most realistic possibility is represented by the curve in the center of Exhibit 4.3. This is the more common scenario, in which the assets are neither perfectly positively nor perfectly negatively correlated; rather, they have some degree of dependent movement. The key point to this middle line in Exhibit 4.3 is that when imperfectly correlated assets are combined into a portfolio, a portion of the portfolio's risk is diversified away. The risk that can be removed through diversification is called diversifiable, nonsystematic, unique, or idiosyncratic risk.

In alternative investments, the concept of correlation is central to the discussion of portfolio implications. Further, graphs with standard deviation on the horizontal axis and expected return on the vertical axis are used as a primary method of illustrating diversification benefits. Assets that generate diversification benefits are shown to shift the attainable combinations of risk and return toward the benefit of the investor, meaning less risk for the same amount of return. The key point is that imperfect correlation leads to diversification that bends portfolio risk to the left, representing the improved investment opportunities afforded by diversification.

In the case of asset returns, true future correlations can only be estimated. Past estimated correlation coefficients not only are subject to estimation error but also are typically estimates of a moving target, since true correlations should be expected to change through time, as fundamental economic relationships change. Further, correlation coefficients tend to increase (offer less diversification across investments and asset classes) in times of market stress, just when an investor needs diversification the most.

4.3.5 Beta

The **beta** of an asset is defined as the covariance between the asset's returns and a return such as the market index, divided by the variance of the index's return, or, equivalently, as the correlation coefficient multiplied by the ratio of the asset volatility to market volatility:

$$\beta_i = \text{Cov}(R_m, R_i)/\text{Var}(R_m) = \sigma_{im}/\sigma_m^2 = \rho_{im}\sigma_i/\sigma_m \tag{4.19}$$

where β_i is the beta of the returns of asset i (R_i) with respect to a market index of returns, R_m. The numerator of the middle expression in Equation 4.19 measures the amount of risk that an individual stock brings into an already diversified portfolio. The denominator represents the total risk of the market portfolio. Beta therefore measures added systematic risk as a proportion of the risk of the index.

In the context of the capital asset pricing model (CAPM) and other single-factor market models, R_m is the return of the market portfolio, and the beta indicates the responsiveness of asset i to fluctuations in the value of the market portfolio. In the context of a single-factor benchmark, R_m would be the return of the benchmark portfolio, and the beta would indicate the responsiveness of asset i to fluctuations in the benchmark. In a multifactor asset pricing model, the beta indicates the responsiveness of asset i to fluctuations in the given risk factor, as is discussed in Chapter 5.

Exhibit 4.2 illustrates the computation of beta using a market index's return as a proxy for the market portfolio. Beta is similar to a correlation coefficient, but it is not bounded by +1 on the upside and −1 on the downside.

There are several important features of beta. First, it can be easily interpreted. The beta of an asset may be viewed as the percentage return response that an asset will have on average to a one-percentage-point movement in the related risk factor, such as the overall market. For example, if the market were to suddenly rise by 1% in response to particular news, a fund with a market beta of 0.95 would be expected on average to rise 0.95%, and a fund with a beta of 2.0 would be expected to rise 2%. If the market falls 2%, then a fund with a beta of 1.5 would have an expected decline of 3%. But actual returns deviate from these expected returns due to any idiosyncratic risk. The risk-free asset has a beta of zero, and its return would therefore not be expected to change with movements in the overall market. The beta of the market portfolio is 1.0.

The second feature of beta is that it is the slope coefficient in a linear regression of the returns of an asset (as the Y, or dependent variable) against the returns of the related index or market portfolio (as the X, or independent variable). Thus, the computation of beta in Exhibit 4.2 using Equation 4.19 may be viewed as having identified the slope coefficient of the previously discussed linear regression. Chapter 8 discusses linear regression.

Third, because beta is a linear measure, the beta of a portfolio is a weighted average of the betas of the constituent assets. This is true even though the total risk of a portfolio is not the weighted average of the total risk of the constituent assets. This is because beta reflects the correlation between an asset's return and the return of the market (or a specified risk factor) and because the correlation to the market does not diversify away as assets are combined into a portfolio.

Similar to the correlation coefficient between the returns of two assets, the beta between an asset and an index is estimated rather than observed. An estimate of beta formed with historical returns may differ substantially from an asset's true future beta for a couple of reasons. First, historical measures such as beta are estimated with error. Second, the beta of most assets should be expected to change through time as market values change and as fundamental economic relationships change. In fact, beta estimations based on historical data are often quite unreliable, although the most reasonable estimates of beta that are available may be based at least in part on historical betas.

4.3.6 Autocorrelation

The **autocorrelation** of a time series of returns from an investment refers to the possible correlation of the returns with one another through time. For example, first-order autocorrelation refers to the correlation between the return in time period t and the return in the previous time period $(t - 1)$. Positive first-order autocorrelation is when an above-average (below-average) return in time period $t - 1$ tends to be followed by an above-average (below-average) return in time period t. Conversely, negative first-order autocorrelation is when an above-average (below-average) return in time period $t - 1$ tends to be followed by a below-average (above-average) return in time period t. Zero autocorrelation indicates that the returns are linearly independent through time. Positive autocorrelation is seen in trending markets; negative autocorrelation is seen in markets with price reversal (i.e., mean reversion) tendencies.

We start here by assuming the simplest scenario: The returns on an investment are statistically independent through time, which means there is no autocorrelation.

Further, we assume that the return distribution is stationary (i.e., the probability distribution of the return at each point in time is identical). Under these strict assumptions, the distribution of log returns over longer periods of time will tend toward being a normal distribution, even if the very short-term log returns are not normally distributed.

How do we know that log returns will be roughly normally distributed over reasonably long periods of time if the returns have no autocorrelation and if very-short-term returns have a stationary distribution? One explanation is that the log return on any asset over a long time period such as a month is the sum of the log returns of the sub-periods. Even if the returns over extremely small units of time are not normally distributed, the central limit theorem indicates that the returns formed over longer periods of time by summing the independent returns of the sub-periods will tend toward being normally distributed.

Why might we think that returns would be uncorrelated through time? If a security trades in a highly transparent, competitive market with low transaction costs, the actions of arbitrageurs and other participants tend to remove pronounced patterns in security returns, such as autocorrelation. If this were not true, then arbitrageurs could make unlimited profits by recognizing and exploiting the patterns at the expense of other traders.

However, markets for securities have transaction costs and other barriers to arbitrage, such as restrictions on short selling. Especially in the case of alternative investments, arbitrage activity may not be sufficient to prevent nontrivial price patterns such as autocorrelation. The extent to which returns reflect nonzero autocorrelation is important because autocorrelation can affect the shape of return distributions. The following material discusses the relationships between the degree of autocorrelation and the shapes of long-period returns relative to short-period returns.

Autocorrelation of returns can be used as a general term to describe possible relationships or as a term to describe a specific correlation measure. Equation 4.20 describes autocorrelation in the context of a return series with constant mean:

$$\text{Autocorrelation} = E[(R_t - \mu)(R_{t-k} - \mu)]/(\sigma_t \sigma_{t-k}) \tag{4.20}$$

where R_t is the return of the asset at time t with mean μ and standard deviation σ_t, R_{t-k} is the return of the asset at time $t - k$ with mean μ and standard deviation σ_{t-k}, and k is the number of time periods between the two returns. Equation 4.20 is the same equation used to define the Pearson correlation coefficient in Equation 4.17 (with substitution of Equation 4.15 for covariance) except that Equation 4.20 specifies that the two returns are from the same asset and are separated by k periods of time. Thus, autocorrelations, like correlation coefficients, range between -1 and $+1$, with $+1$ representing perfect correlation.

There are unlimited combinations of autocorrelations that could theoretically be nonzero in a time series; thus, in practice, it is usually necessary to specify the time lags separating the correlations between variables. One of the simplest and most popular specifications of the autocorrelation of a time series is first-order autocorrelation. The first-order autocorrelation coefficient is the case of $k = 1$ from Equation 4.20, which is shown in Equation 4.21:

$$\text{First-Order Autocorrelation Coefficient} = E[(R_t - \mu)(R_{t-1} - \mu)]/(\sigma_t \sigma_{t-1}) \tag{4.21}$$

Thus, **first-order autocorrelation** refers to the correlation between the return in time period t and the return in the immediately previous time period, $t - 1$. Note that in the case of first-order autocorrelation, the returns in time period $t - 1$ would also be correlated with the returns in time period $t - 2$; thus, the returns in time period t would also generally be correlated with the returns in time period $t - 2$, as well as those of earlier time periods. Because first-order autocorrelation is generally less than 1, the idea is that the autocorrelation between returns diminishes as the time distance between them increases.

While autocorrelation would be zero in a perfectly efficient market, substantial autocorrelation in returns can occur when there is a lack of competition, when there are substantial transaction costs or other barriers to trade, or when there are returns that are calculated based on nonmarket values, such as appraisals. Autocorrelation of reported returns due to the use of appraised valuations or valuations based on the discretion of fund managers raises important issues, especially in the analysis of alternative investments.

Autocorrelation in returns has implications for the relationship between the standard deviations of a return series computed over different time lengths. Specifically, if autocorrelation is positive (i.e., returns are trending), then the standard deviation of returns over T periods will be larger than the single-period standard deviation multiplied by the square root of T. If autocorrelation is zero, then the standard deviation of returns over T periods will be equal to the single-period standard deviation multiplied by the square root of T. Finally, if autocorrelation is negative (i.e., returns are mean-reverting), then the standard deviation of returns over T periods will be less than the single-period standard deviation multiplied by the square root of T.

An important task in the analysis of the returns of an investment is the search for autocorrelation. An informal approach to the analysis of the potential autocorrelation of a return series is through visual inspection of a scatter plot of R_t against R_{t-1}. Positive autocorrelation causes more observations in the northeast and southwest quadrants of the scatter plot, where R_t and R_{t-1} share the same sign. Negative autocorrelation causes the southeast and northwest quadrants to have more observations, and zero autocorrelation causes balance among all four quadrants.

Another common approach when searching for autocorrelation is to estimate the first-order autocorrelation measure of Equation 4.21 directly, using sample data. Exhibit 4.2 shows the estimated first-order autocorrelation coefficients for the two return series.

4.3.7 Higher-Order Autocorrelation and Partial Autocorrelation

Analysis of alternative investments often involves consideration of whether a particular return series trends (i.e., has positive autocorrelation of returns) or mean-reverts (has negative autocorrelation of returns). Substantial evidence indicates that the returns of some assets trend over some time intervals (e.g., monthly returns) and mean-revert over other time intervals (e.g., annual returns). The potential for returns to have positive and negative autocorrelation over different time horizons indicates that analysis of higher-order autocorrelations may be useful.

Equation 4.20 provides the formula for all orders or lags of autocorrelation. For example, in the case of second-order autocorrelation the equation specifies:

$$\text{Second-Order Autocorrelation} = E[(R_t - \mu)(R_{t-2} - \mu)]/(\sigma_t \sigma_{t-2})$$

Note, however, that the second-order autocorrelation between the returns in period t and $t - 2$ can be viewed as emanating both from the shared correlation of the two returns with the returns from period $t - 1$ as well as potential correlation that is unique between periods t and $t - 2$. For example, suppose that a return series has a strong positive first-order autocorrelation coefficient of 0.7. Even if there is no further *causality* of returns beyond one period, the second-order autocorrelation coefficient will be 0.49, found as 0.7×0.7. In this example, an observed second-order auto-correlation coefficient statistically equal to 0.49 would be an indication that there is no further relation between returns t and $t - 2$. An observed second-order autocor-relation coefficient significantly greater than 0.49 would be an indication that there is additional positive relation between returns t and $t - 2$ beyond the correlation caused by the first-order correlation. Further, an observed second-order autocorre-lation coefficient significantly less than 0.49 would be an indication that there is a negative second-order relation between returns t and $t - 2$ (apart from the positive correlation caused by the first-order correlation).

A **partial autocorrelation coefficient** adjusts autocorrelation coefficients to iso-late the portion of the correlation in a time series attributable directly to a particular higher-order relation. Equation 4.22 depicts the formula for a second-order partial autocorrelation coefficient based on regular autocorrelation coefficients.

$$\text{Second-Order Partial Autocorrelation Coefficient} = (\rho_2 - \rho_1^2)/(1 - \rho_1^2) \quad (4.22)$$

where ρ_i is the ith-order autocorrelation coefficient as defined in Equation 4.20. Note that the numerator of Equation 4.22 "removes" the effect of first-order autocorrela-tion (ρ_1^2) from the second-order autocorrelation (ρ_2) to isolate the *marginal* effect of the period $t - 2$ return on the return in period t.

☞ **APPLICATION 4.3.7A**

A returns series indicates first-order autocorrelation of 0.6 and second-order autocorrelation of 0.2. What is the partial second-order autocorrelation coef-ficient?

Inserting 0.6 for ρ_1 and 0.2 for ρ_2 generates: $[0.2 - (0.6 \times 0.6)]/([1 - (0.6 \times 0.6)] = -0.25$. Note that even though the returns in periods k and $k - 2$ are positively correlated, that correlation is primarily driven by first-order correla-tion. The marginal second-order effect is captured in the partial autocorrela-tion coefficient and indicates a mean-reverting effect (once the first-order effects have been removed).

To estimate partial autocorrelation coefficients for more than two periods, an analyst can use multiple regression with R_t as the dependent variable and R_{t-1}, R_{t-2},

R_{t-3}, and so forth as independent variables. The regression coefficients are estimates of the partial autocorrelation coefficients. Multiple regression is discussed in Level II of the CAIA curriculum.

4.3.8 The Durbin-Watson Test for Autocorrelation

A formal approach in searching for the presence of first-order autocorrelation in a time series is through the Durbin-Watson test. To test the hypothesis that there is no autocorrelation in a series involves calculating the Durbin-Watson statistic:

$$DW = \frac{\sum_{t=2}^{T} (e_t - e_{t-1})^2}{\sum_{t=1}^{T} e_t^2} \tag{4.23}$$

where e_t is the value in time period t of the series being analyzed for autocorrelation. In alternative investments, the series being analyzed (e_t) may be returns or a portion of returns, such as the estimated active return. A DW value of 2 indicates no significant autocorrelation (i.e., fails to reject the hypothesis of zero autocorrelation). If DW is statistically greater than 2, then the null hypothesis may be rejected in favor of negative autocorrelation; and if DW is statistically less than 2, then the null hypothesis may be rejected in favor of positive autocorrelation. The magnitude of the difference from 2 required to reject zero autocorrelation is complex, but a rule of thumb is that zero autocorrelation is rejected when DW is greater than 3, which is negative autocorrelation, or less than 1, which is positive autocorrelation. The DW statistics for the market index and the real estate fund are reported in the bottom left-hand corner of Exhibit 4.2. Note that the reported DW statistics for both of the return series fail to reject zero autocorrelation, even though the estimated autocorrelation coefficients appear quite positive.

4.4 INTERPRETING STANDARD DEVIATION AND VARIANCE

Perhaps the most important single risk measure in investments is the standard deviation of returns, or volatility. Unfortunately, the complexity of its formula and its computation can lead to a belief that standard deviation is not easily interpreted. But the standard deviation of returns is almost as easy to interpret as the mean (expected value) of the returns. The purpose of the next two sections is to demonstrate the ease with which the standard deviation of returns can be intuitively understood.

4.4.1 Standard Deviation and Typical Deviations

The standard deviation of an investment's returns can be very roughly approximated as the typical amount by which an investment's actual return deviates from its average. Standard deviation, or volatility, is such a central concept in investments that we present an example here to encourage an intuitive grasp.

Let's start with applying the concept of standard deviation to basketball scores. Observers of basketball might estimate that an average number of points for one team to score in one game might be 100 and that a typical amount by which the outcomes tend to differ from this expectation might be 15 points. In other words, among the higher-than-average scores, a typical score would be 115 points, while among the lower-than-average scores, a typical score would be 85 points. In this case, 15 points would be a rough estimate of the standard deviation of the basketball score for one team.

The idea is that standard deviation (volatility) is a measure of dispersion that can be roughly viewed on an intuitive basis. In statistics, the average distance between a variable and its mean is known as the mean absolute deviation, but it is usually not very different from the standard deviation. The exact relationship between the standard deviation and the mean absolute deviation depends on the underlying distribution. In the case of the normal probability distribution, the standard deviation is approximately 1.25 times the mean absolute deviation, which probably somewhat understates the magnitude of the difference observed in distributions of most returns from modern financial markets with high kurtosis. However, in most cases of investment returns without extreme events, the concepts of standard deviation and mean absolute deviation are close enough that viewing them as being similar in magnitude facilitates a reasonably clear understanding.

Let's take a look at a portfolio that has an annual expected return of 5% and a standard deviation of 2%. We should be able to develop a quick and easy intuitive feel for the range of outcomes. In a year of average performance, this portfolio will earn 5%. However, among those years with below-average performance, a typically bad year would generate a 2% lower return, or about 3%. Sometimes the portfolio would do worse than a 3% return in a bad year and sometimes perhaps a little better. Of those years with above-average performance, a typically good year would generate a return of perhaps 7%.

If the standard deviation of the asset's return fell to 1%, then we would understand that the returns were clustered closer to 5%, with typically good years producing a return of about 6% and typically bad years producing a return of around 4%, each found by either adding or subtracting 1 standard deviation to or from the expected return. Of course, returns could be much higher or much lower, indicating highly unusual circumstances in which the outcomes are many standard deviations from the average.

Once we are familiar with the concept of standard deviation, we can use its mathematical properties to clarify the behavior of risk in a portfolio context and to sharpen our intuition. With a little practice, standard deviation becomes as easy to use as averages.

4.4.2 Standard Deviation of Normally Distributed Returns

If the return distribution were exactly normal, we could develop more precise indications of the range of values and their associated probabilities.

Exhibit 4.4 depicts the use of standard deviation to specify confidence intervals for normally distributed variables. The diagram at the top of Exhibit 4.4 illustrates the range of outcomes that could be expected within 1, 2, or 3 standard deviations from the mean of the distribution. The table at the bottom of Exhibit 4.4 indicates the probabilities that a normally distributed variable will lie inside a range of 1, 2, or 3 standard deviations (two tails) from the mean, or outside the range in a prespecified direction (single tail).

EXHIBIT 4.4 Confidence Intervals for the Normal Distribution Using Standard Deviation

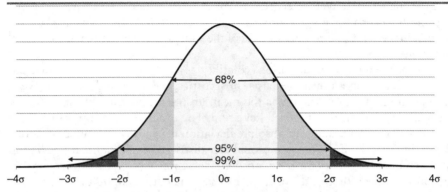

Number of σ's	Two-Tails Inside Probability	One-Tail Outside Probability
1	68.27%	15.87%
2	95.45%	2.28%
3	99.73%	0.13%

If returns were normally distributed, the standard deviation of the returns would help an investor know with precision what the probabilities of every outcome would be relative to its mean. Very roughly, two-thirds of the time the returns should lie within 1 standard deviation of the mean. The diagram illustrates this case of a −1-standard-deviation range using the lightest shading on each side of the mean, and illustrates larger ranges using darker shading. The diagram does not illustrate a particular value for the mean and standard deviation. The horizontal axis may be labeled to reflect the value of the mean and standard deviation. In the top panel of Exhibit 4.4, the value of the mean would lie on the horizontal axis at the point labeled 0σ. For all other points on the horizontal axis, the value is found by multiplying the standard deviation by the indicated number of standard deviations and adding the value to the mean. For example, with a mean return of 5% and a standard deviation of 2%, two-thirds of the outcomes (more exactly, 68.27%) would tend to lie between 3% and 7% (found as −2% and +2% from the mean of +5%). Also, roughly 95% of the time, the returns should lie within 2 standard deviations (between 1% and 9%). The one-tail probabilities would inform an investor that in this same example, there would be about a 16% probability that the return would be less than 3%, and a 2.28% probability that the return would be less than 1%. The normal distribution is symmetric, so there would be a 0.13% probability that the return would be more than 11%.

As discussed previously, actual return distributions are usually non-normally distributed. However, the large differences between the normal distribution and the actual distributions of returns typically observed in financial markets tend to occur farther out into the tails, such as 4 or more standard deviations. So for many actual return distributions, the probabilities just given would serve as reasonable approximations.

However, for huge return aberrations, such as a move of 10 standard deviations, the normal distribution provides an astoundingly underestimated indication of the actual probabilities of tail events. Extreme tail events, such as the U.S. equity market's decline during the fourth quarter of 2008, can be hundreds or even thousands of times more likely than indicated by probabilities from the normal distribution and historical standard deviations.

Standard deviation is analyzed so often in the context of the normal distribution that it is sometimes easy to forget that statements such as "Roughly 95% of the outcomes lie within 2 standard deviations of a mean" implicitly assume that the distribution is normally or near-normally distributed. Care should be taken to understand the assumed underlying probability distribution before associating outcomes with probabilities.

4.4.3 Properties of Variance

There are useful properties of variance in the analysis of alternative investments. Variance works well in many *formulas* regarding risk. This section demonstrates an important property of the variance of the returns of an asset through time. The variance of an investment's return over a time interval of T periods can be expressed as T times the variance measured over a single period under particular assumptions.

 FOUNDATION CHECK

The material in section 4.4.3 assumes familiarity with mean and variance as applied within a Markowitz framework.

We begin with the well-known formula for the variance of the return of a portfolio (p) of n assets as a weighted average of the variances and covariances of the returns of the assets in the portfolio:

$$\sigma_p^2 = \sum_{i=1}^{n} \sum_{j=1}^{n} w_i \, w_j \mathrm{Cov}(R_i, R_j) \tag{4.24}$$

where w_i and w_j are the weights of assets i and j in the portfolio.

Note that the covariance of any variable with itself is equal to its variance. Thus, Equation 4.24 contains n variances (one for each of the n assets) and $n^2 - n$ covariances (from the pairs of assets). The additivity of the formula assists in financial modeling, such as Markowitz's pioneering work on risk and return, in which variance measured risk. In the case of uncorrelated returns between securities, this formula is simplified because all of the covariances between nonidentical assets are zero:

$$V(R_p) = \sum_{i=1}^{n} w_i^2 \, \mathrm{Var}[R_i] \quad \text{when } \rho = 0 \text{ between all individual assets} \tag{4.25}$$

where R_p is the portfolio's return, and ρ is the correlation coefficient between all individual assets.

An important analogous concept involves the computation of the variance of a multiperiod return. The multiperiod continuously compounded rate of return of any asset is the sum of the continuously compounded returns corresponding to the sub-periods, as noted earlier in Chapter 3. For instance, the weekly rate of return expressed as log return is the sum of the five daily log returns:

$$R_w^{m=\infty} = R_1^{m=\infty} + R_2^{m=\infty} + \cdots + R_5^{m=\infty} \tag{4.26}$$

where $R_w^{m=\infty}$ represents the weekly log return.

If we assume that the returns are uncorrelated through time (i.e., there is no autocorrelation), all covariances vanish, and the variance of the weekly return is the sum of the variances of the daily returns:

$$V(R_w) = V(R_1) + V(R_2) + V(R_3) + V(R_4) + V(R_5) \text{ when } \rho_{t,t-k} = 0 \tag{4.27}$$

If we make the further assumption that the variances of the periodic returns of an asset are constant (i.e., homoskedastic), then the variance of the returns for a T-period time interval can be expressed as:

$$V(R_T) = T \times V(R_1) \text{ when } \rho_{t,t-k} = 0 \tag{4.28}$$

Since uncorrelated returns through time are consistent with market efficiency, this equation can be viewed as a starting point for understanding variance across different time horizons for asset returns that are reasonably independent through time. If returns are positively correlated in time (i.e., trending, or positively autocorrelated), then the variance will be larger than specified in Equation 4.28. If returns are negatively correlated in time (i.e., mean-reverting, or negatively autocorrelated), then the variance will be smaller than specified in Equation 4.28.

☞ **APPLICATION 4.4.3A**

The daily returns of Fund A have a variance of 0.0001. What is the variance of the weekly returns of Fund A assuming that the returns are uncorrelated through time?

Using Equation 4.28 and five days in a week, the variance is 0.0005.

4.4.4 Properties of Standard Deviation

The standard deviation has several especially useful properties in the study of the returns of alternative investments. One important property involves perfectly correlated cross-sectional returns. The standard deviation of a portfolio of perfectly correlated assets is a weighted average of the standard deviations of the assets in the portfolio:

$$\sigma_p = \sum_{i=1}^{n} w_i \times \sigma_i \qquad \text{when } \rho_{ij} = 1 \text{ for all } i, j \tag{4.29}$$

Another important property of the standard deviation involves a situation in which a return or any random variable can be expressed as a linear combination of another variable:

$$Y_t = mX_t + b$$

where Y_t is a random variable, such as the return of asset Y in time t; X_t is another random variable, such as the return of asset X at time t; m is a fixed slope coefficient; and b is a constant intercept. The standard deviation of Y is found as the product of the standard deviation of X and the slope coefficient:

$$\sigma_y = m \times \sigma_x \tag{4.30}$$

There are three especially useful applications of this property for investments. First, returns of a levered position in an asset can typically be well approximated as a linear function of the returns of an unleveraged position in the same asset. Therefore, the standard deviation of the levered position (σ_1) can be approximated as the product of the leverage (L) and the standard deviation of the unlevered asset σ_u:

$$\sigma_1 = L \times \sigma_u \tag{4.31}$$

 APPLICATION 4.4.4A

The daily returns of Fund A have a standard deviation of 1.4%. What is the standard deviation of a position that contains only Fund A and is leveraged with $3 of assets for each $1 of equity (net worth)?

Using Equation 4.31, the standard deviation of the levered returns is 4.2%.

For example, if a fund is levered 2:1 (i.e., the fund has $2 of assets for every $1 of equity investment), then its standard deviation of returns is generally twice the standard deviation of an unlevered fund with the same assets. The second useful application involves a portfolio that is a combination of proportion w in a risky asset (with return R_m) and proportion $1 - w$ in a risk-free asset (with return R_f). The portfolio's return (R_p) can be expressed as a linear function of the returns of the risky asset:

$$R_p = wR_m + (1 - w)R_f \tag{4.32}$$

Using the previous property of standard deviation and noting that the standard deviation of R_f is zero and that the correlation between risk-free and risky assets is zero, the standard deviation of the portfolio (σ_p) can be expressed as the product of the proportion invested in the risky asset, w, and the standard deviation of the risky asset, σ_m.

$$\sigma_p = w \times \sigma_m \tag{4.33}$$

APPLICATION 4.4.4B

The daily returns of Fund A have a standard deviation of 1.4%. What is the standard deviation of a position that contains 40% Fund A and 60% cash?

Using Equation 4.33, the standard deviation of the unlevered returns is 0.56%.

A third property of standard deviation involves the relationship between the standard deviations of single-period and multiple-period returns. Equation 4.28 in the previous section showed that the variance of a multiperiod log return is the number of periods multiplied by the single-period variance when the returns are homoskedastic and uncorrelated through time. Taking the square root of both sides of Equation 4.28 generates the relationship in terms of standard deviations:

$$\sigma_T = \sigma_1 \times \sqrt{T} \text{ when } \rho_{t,t-k} = 0 \qquad (4.34)$$

Equation 4.34 requires that the returns are independent through time and that the variances of the single-period returns are equal (i.e., homoskedastic). Note that the standard deviation of returns grows through the factor $\sqrt{T}$ as the time interval increases. Thus, a two-period return has $\sqrt{2}$ times the standard deviation of a one-period return, and a four-period return has two times the standard deviation of a one-period return. A popular annualization factor in alternative investments is to find the annual standard deviation by multiplying the standard deviation of monthly returns by $\sqrt{12}$.

Finally, it was previously noted that the standard deviation of a portfolio of perfectly correlated assets is the weighted average of the standard deviation of the constituent assets. Analogously, the standard deviation of a multiperiod return can be approximated as the sum of the standard deviations of the return of each sub-period if the returns are perfectly correlated. If we further assume that the standard deviation of each sub-period is equal (the standard deviation of the asset is constant through time), then:

$$\sigma_T = \sigma_1 \times T \text{ when } \rho_{t,t-k} = 1 \qquad (4.35)$$

Perfect positive correlation of returns through time does not make economic sense, so Equation 4.35 should be viewed as an upper bound. Let's compare the cases of independent and perfectly correlated returns through time. We see that the standard deviation of a multiperiod return varies from being proportional to $\sqrt{T}$ in the uncorrelated (independent) case to being proportional to T in the perfectly correlated case. If returns are mean-reverting, meaning negatively correlated through time, the standard deviation of the multiperiod return can be even less than indicated in Equation 4.34. Thus, comparing the standard deviations of an asset using different time intervals for computing returns (e.g., daily returns versus annual returns) provides insight into the statistical correlation of the returns through time (i.e., their autocorrelation). In other words, whether a return series is trending, independent, or mean-reverting drives the relationship between the asset's relative volatility over different time intervals. For example, if an asset's return volatility over four-week intervals is more than twice as large as its weekly return volatility, it may be that the weekly returns are positively autocorrelated.

☞ **APPLICATION 4.4.4C**

The daily returns of Fund A have a standard deviation of 1.2%. What is the standard deviation of the returns of Fund A over a four-day period if the returns are uncorrelated through time? What is the maximum standard deviation for other correlation assumptions?

With zero autocorrelation, the standard deviation of four-day returns is 2.4% (based on the square root of the number of time periods). As the correlation approaches +1, the upper bound would be 4.8%.

4.5 TESTING FOR NORMALITY

If a return distribution is normally distributed, then analysts can use well-developed statistical methods available for normally distributed variables and can be confident in the likelihood of extreme events. In practice, however, most return distributions are not normal. Some return distributions have substantial skews. Most return distributions have dramatically higher probabilities of extreme events than are experienced with the normal distribution (i.e., are leptokurtic).

4.5.1 Why Are Some Returns Markedly Non-Normal?

There are three main reasons for the non-normality often observed in alternative investment returns: autocorrelation, illiquidity, and nonlinearity. The first two can be related to each other.

1. AUTOCORRELATION: Price changes through time for many alternative investments will not be statistically independent in terms of both their expected direction and their level of dispersion. Autocorrelation is a major source of that statistical dependence. Short-term returns, such as daily returns, are sometimes positively autocorrelated if the assets are not rapidly and competitively traded. Many alternative investments, such as private equity and private real estate, cannot be rapidly traded at low cost. Further, when reported returns can be influenced by an investment manager, it is possible that the manager smooths the returns to enhance performance measures. Thus, autocorrelation of observed returns can exist and is often found.

   Positive autocorrelation causes longer-term returns to have disproportionately extreme values relative to short-term returns. The idea is that one extreme short-term return tends to be more likely to be followed by another extreme return in the same direction, to the extent that the return series has positive autocorrelation. The autocorrelated short-term returns can generate highly dispersed longer-term returns, such as the returns that appear to be generated in speculative bubbles on the upside and panics on the downside.

2. ILLIQUIDITY: Illiquidity of alternative investments refers to the idea that many alternative investments are thinly traded. For example, a typical real estate property or private equity deal might be traded only once every few years. Further, the trades might be based on the decisions of a very limited number of market participants.

   Observed market prices might therefore be heavily influenced by the liquidity needs of the market participants rather than driven toward an efficient price by the actions of numerous well-informed buyers and sellers. With a small number of potentially large factors affecting each trade, there is less reason to believe that the outcomes will be normally distributed and more reason to believe that extreme outcomes will be relatively common.

In illiquid markets, prices are often estimated by models and professional judgments rather than by competitive market prices. Evidence indicates that prices generated by models or professional judgments, such as those of appraisers, tend to be autocorrelated. The resulting returns are smoothed and tend to exhibit less volatility than would be indicated if true prices could be observed.

3. NONLINEARITY: A simple example of an asset with returns that are a nonlinear function of an underlying return factor is a short-term call option. As the underlying asset's price changes, the call option experiences a change in its sensitivity to future price changes in the underlying asset. Therefore, the dispersion in the call option's return distribution changes through time as the underlying asset's price changes, even if the volatility of the underlying asset remains constant. This is why a call option offers asymmetric price changes: A call option has virtually unlimited upside price change potential but is limited in downside price change potential to the option premium. The result is a highly nonsymmetric return distribution over long time intervals. A similar phenomenon occurs for highly active trading strategies (such as many hedge funds or managed futures accounts), which cause returns to experience different risk exposures through time, such as when a strategy varies its use of leverage.

Thus, many alternative investments tend to have markedly non-normal log returns over medium- and long-term time intervals. The shape of an investment's return distribution is central to an understanding of its risk and return. The following sections detail the analysis of return distributions through their statistical moments, which help describe and analyze return distributions even if they are not normally shaped.

Typically, the true underlying probability distribution of an asset's return cannot be observed directly but must be inferred from a sample. A classic issue that arises is whether a particular sample from a return distribution tends to indicate that the underlying distribution is normal or non-normal. The process is always one of either rejecting that the underlying distribution is normal or failing to reject that it is normal at some level of statistical confidence.

There are numerous types of tests for normality. Some methods are informal, such as plotting the frequency distribution of the sample and eyeballing the shape of the distribution or performing some informal statistical analysis. However, the human mind can be inaccurate when guessing about statistical relationships. Therefore, formal statistical testing is usually appropriate. The most popular formal tests use the moments of the sample distribution.

4.5.2 Moments-Based Tests for Normality with Data Samples

The statistical moments reviewed earlier in the chapter and statistics related to those moments, such as skewness and kurtosis, provide useful measures from which to test a sample for normality. The normal distribution has a skewness equal to zero and an excess kurtosis equal to zero. Even if a sample is drawn from observations of a normally distributed variable, the sample would virtually never have a sample skewness of exactly zero or an excess kurtosis exactly equal to zero. By chance, the observations included in the sample would tend to skew in one direction or the other, and the tails would tend to be fatter or skinnier than in the truly normal underlying distribution. Thus, tests are necessary to examine the level of departure of the sample statistics from the parameters of the normal distribution. Normality tests attempt to ascertain the probability that the observed skewness and kurtosis would occur if the sample had been drawn from an underlying distribution that was normal.

4.5.3 The Jarque-Bera Test for Normality

Numerous formal tests for normality have been developed. One of the most popular and straightforward tests for normality is the **Jarque-Bera test**. The Jarque-Bera test involves a statistic that is a function of the skewness and excess kurtosis of the sample:

$$JB = (n/6)[S^2 + (K^2/4)] \tag{4.36}$$

where JB is the Jarque-Bera test statistic, n is the number of observations, S is the skewness of the sample, and K is the excess kurtosis of the sample.

Both the sample skewness and the kurtosis are computed as detailed in the previous sections. The null hypothesis is that the underlying distribution is normal and that JB is equal to zero (since the skewness and excess kurtosis of the normal distribution are both zero).

While the Jarque-Bera test statistic is relatively easy to compute given the skewness and kurtosis, its interpretation is a little more complicated. Notice that S and K in the formula for the Jarque-Bera test statistic are both squared. Thus, the Jarque-Bera test will always be nonnegative. If the test did not square S and K, a negative skewness would offset a positive excess kurtosis, which would wrongly suggest normality. As a sample exhibits more of the tendencies of a normal distribution (less skewness and less excess kurtosis), the Jarque-Bera test statistic will tend to be closer to zero (holding n constant). Thus, the Jarque-Bera test for normality is whether the test statistic is large enough to reject the null hypothesis of normality. The Jarque-Bera test is more powerful when the number of observations is larger. If the underlying distribution is normal, the value of JB generated from a sample will exceed zero with the known magnitudes and probabilities given by the chi-squared distribution (with two degrees of freedom). Also, if the underlying distribution is normal, the size of the Jarque-Bera test statistic will tend to be small, since a sample drawn from a normal distribution will tend to have a low skewness and low excess kurtosis. The higher the JB statistic, the less likely it is that the distribution is normal. The probability that the Jarque-Bera test statistic will exceed particular values can be found from a chi-squared distribution table, shown here with the required two degrees of freedom. These critical values for the Jarque-Bera test are formed through simulations.

Confidence interval	0.90	0.95	0.975	0.99	0.999
Critical value	4.61	5.99	7.38	9.21	13.82

The analyst should perform the Jarque-Bera test in these four steps:

1. Select a confidence interval (e.g., 90%, 95%, 97.5%, 99%, or 99.9%).
2. Locate the corresponding critical value (e.g., 5.99 for 95% confidence).
3. Compute the *JB* statistic (using formula 4.36 and the sample skewness and excess kurtosis).
4. Compare the *JB* statistic to the critical value.

If the *JB* statistic exceeds the critical value, then the null hypothesis of normality is rejected using the stated level of confidence. If the *JB* statistic is less than the critical value, then the null hypothesis is not rejected, and the underlying distribution is assumed to be normal. The interpretation of this type of hypothesis test and the level of statistical confidence is actually quite complex and is discussed in detail in Chapter 8.

4.5.4 An Example of the Jarque-Bera Test

Assume that the sample skewness and excess kurtosis are computed as -0.577 and -0.042, respectively. The sample size, n, is 40. The Jarque-Bera test statistic is therefore given by:

$$JB = (n/6)[S^2 + (K^2/4)]$$
$$JB = 2.222$$

Using a statistical confidence of 95%, the critical value for the test is 5.99. Since the Jarque-Bera test statistic, 2.222, is less than 5.99, we cannot reject the null hypothesis of normality.

4.6 TIME-SERIES RETURN VOLATILITY MODELS

The previous sections often focused on the use of the past or historical standard deviation to express or measure risk. In most cases, however, analysts are concerned more with forecasting future risk than with estimating past risk. This section briefly reviews an approach to estimating future volatility based on past data.

Time-series models are often used in finance to describe the process by which price levels move through time. However, the analysis of how price variation moves through time is increasingly studied. Time-series models of how risk evolves through time are numerous and diverse. We will briefly summarize one of the most popular methods. **GARCH** (generalized autoregressive conditional heteroskedasticity) is an example of a time-series method that adjusts for varying volatility.

Let's examine generalized autoregressive conditional heteroskedasticity one word at a time. **Heteroskedasticity** is when the variance of a variable changes with respect to a variable, such as itself or time. **Homoskedasticity** is when the variance of a variable is constant. Clearly, equity markets and other markets go through periods of high volatility and low volatility, wherein each day's volatility is more likely to remain near recent levels than to immediately revert to historical norms. Thus, risky assets appear at least at times to exhibit heteroskedastic return variation. The GARCH method allows for heteroskedasticity and can be used when it is believed that risk is changing over time.

Autoregressive refers to when subsequent values to a variable are explained by past values of the same variable. In this case, *autoregressive* means that the next level of return variation is being explained at least in part by modeling the past variation, in addition to being determined by randomness. Casual observation of equity markets and other financial markets appears to support the idea that one day's variation, or volatility, can at least partially determine the next day's variation.

The term *conditional* in GARCH refers to a particular lack of predictability of future variation. Some securities have return variation that is somewhat predictable. For example, a default-free zero-coupon bond (e.g., a Treasury bill) can be expected to decline in return variation and price variation as it approaches maturity and as its price approaches face value. Conditioned on the time to maturity, the variance of a Treasury bill is at least somewhat predictable. Hence, the Treasury bill might only be unpredictable on an unconditional basis. Other financial values, however, do not exhibit a pattern like the default-free zero-coupon bond. For example, there is no apparent pattern to the volatility of the price of a barrel of oil or the value of an equity index.

When a financial asset exhibits a clear pattern of return variation, such as in the example of a Treasury bill near maturity, its variation is said to be unconditionally heteroskedastic. Most financial market prices are **conditionally heteroskedastic**, meaning that they have different levels of return variation even when specified conditions are similar (e.g., when they are viewed at similar price levels).

An example of conditional heteroskedasticity is as follows. Perhaps a major equity index reaches a similar price level, such as 800, several times in the course of a decade. There is no reason to believe, however, that the index will experience similar levels of return variation each time it nears that 800 level. Sometimes the index might be quite volatile at the 800 level, and other times the index might be quite stable at the same level, as a result of, for example, different macroeconomic environments. Thus, the asset's return variation is heteroskedastic even when such conditions as price levels are held constant. Hence, the index, like most financial assets, is conditionally heteroskedastic because its return variation is heteroskedastic even under similar conditions (i.e., even when conditioned on another variable).

Finally, *generalized* refers to the model's ability to describe wide varieties of behavior, also known as robustness. A less robust time-series model of volatility is **ARCH** (autoregressive conditional heteroskedasticity), a special case of GARCH that allows future variances to rely only on past disturbances, whereas GARCH allows future variances to depend on past variances as well. Developed subsequently to ARCH, GARCH is now generally the more popular approach in most financial asset applications.

Now we can summarize all of the terms in GARCH together. In the context of financial returns, GARCH is a robust method that can model return variation through time in a way that allows that variation to change based on the variable's past history and even when some conditions, such as price level, have not changed.

It has parameters that the researcher can set to allow closer fitting of the model to various types of patterns. The GARCH model is usually specified by two parameters like this: GARCH (p,q). The first parameter in the parentheses, p, defines the number of time periods for which past return variations are included in the modeling equation, and the second, q, defines the number of time periods for which autoregressive terms are included.

REVIEW QUESTIONS

1. Describe the difference between an ex ante return and an ex post return in the case of a financial asset.
2. Contrast the kurtosis and the excess kurtosis of the normal distribution.
3. How would a large increase in the kurtosis of a return distribution affect its shape?
4. Using statistical terminology, what does the volatility of a return mean?
5. The covariance between the returns of two financial assets is equal to the product of the standard deviations of the returns of the two assets. What is the primary statistical terminology for this relationship?
6. What is the formula for the beta of an asset using common statistical measures?
7. What is the value of the beta of the following three investments: a fund that tracks the overall market index, a riskless asset, and a bet at a casino table?
8. In the case of a financial asset with returns that have zero autocorrelation, what is the relationship between the variance of the asset's daily returns and the variance of the asset's monthly return?
9. In the case of a financial asset with returns that have autocorrelation approaching +1, what is the relationship between the standard deviation of the asset's monthly returns and the standard deviation of the asset's annual return?
10. What is the general statistical issue addressed when the GARCH method is used in a time-series analysis of returns?

CHAPTER 5

Foundations of Financial Economics

Financial economics serves as a vital foundation to asset pricing and the understanding of alternative investments. This chapter discusses informational market efficiency, asset pricing, forward contracts, and options.

5.1 INFORMATIONAL MARKET EFFICIENCY

The concept of informational market efficiency is especially important in the management of alternative investments. **Informational market efficiency** refers to the extent to which asset prices reflect available information. An informationally efficient market is a market in which assets are traded at prices that equal their values based on all available information. The concept of informational market efficiency is sometimes referred to as efficient market theory or the efficient market hypothesis.

In practice, all financial markets display at least some informational market efficiency, but no financial market is perfectly efficient. For example, many trades of large equities on the U.S. stock exchanges occur at one-cent intervals, implicitly indicating at least some degree of mispricing. It is more useful to describe markets as displaying varying degrees of informational market efficiency rather than attempting to divide markets into those that are and those that are not informationally efficient.

5.1.1 Further Definitions of Informational Market Efficiency

Definitions of informational market efficiency often extend beyond the terse definition that "prices reflect available information." For example, informationally efficient markets are sometimes described as markets in which the net present values (NPVs) of all investment decisions are zero.

Further, informationally efficient markets are often described as markets in which investors are unable to use information to consistently earn superior risk-adjusted returns. Note that investors bearing higher risk should tend to earn consistently higher returns, and that any investor bearing risk might occasionally earn high returns. However, in an informationally efficient market, investors cannot earn higher expected returns without bearing additional risk. Note that this is less a definition of an efficient market than it is an implication of an efficient market.

An informationally efficient market is often described as a market in which prices follow a "random walk." However, markets can be informationally efficient without following a random walk, and in theory, the opposite is also true: Prices in a totally irrational market could follow a random walk while being informationally inefficient.

It may be helpful to note that the term *efficient* is used in several distinct ways in investments. For example, an efficient portfolio typically denotes a portfolio that offers an unsurpassed combination of risk and return, and an economy that allocates its resources very well is said to be efficient. Accordingly, it is probably useful to specify *informational* market efficiency when the term is being used to denote the extent to which market prices reflect available information.

5.1.2 Forms or Levels of Informational Market Efficiency

Informational market efficiency is often discussed in the context of forms or levels that are related to information sets. First, **weak form informational market efficiency** (or weak level) refers to market prices reflecting available data on past prices and volumes (i.e., historical trading data). Weak form efficiency addresses the issue of whether technical analysis can be useful in earning consistent and superior risk-adjusted returns.

The concept of **semistrong form informational market efficiency** (or semistrong level) refers to market prices reflecting all publicly available information (including not only past prices and volumes but also any publicly available information such as financial statements and other underlying economic data). Semistrong form efficiency is designed to address the issue of whether technical analysis and, especially, fundamental analysis can be useful in earning consistent and superior risk-adjusted returns.

Finally, the concept of **strong form informational market efficiency** (or strong level) refers to market prices reflecting all publicly and privately available information. Strong form efficiency is designed to address the issue of whether any attempts to earn consistent and superior risk-adjusted returns can be successful, including insider trading.

Two clarifying details can be helpful. First, note that the three forms do not alter the general meaning of informational efficiency. The only thing that changes between the three levels or forms is the information set. Second, note that the information sets moving from weak form to semistrong form to strong form are cumulative. If weak form efficiency is violated, then all three forms will be violated, because the semistrong and strong forms include the information set used in the weak form. However, violation of strong form efficiency does not imply violation of the weak or semistrong forms.

The purpose of these three forms is to simplify and structure discussions of informationally efficient markets. Although the information sets are in fact cumulative, the three levels are often casually linked directly to the three major trading strategies: technical analysis to the weak form, fundamental analysis to the semistrong form, and insider trading to the strong form. The strong form is often criticized as being superfluous because it would seem to appear almost by definition that market prices cannot reflect information that is not publicly available. But an argument can be made that if insider trading generates consistent abnormal profits to insiders, then outsiders would perceive their informational disadvantage and would refuse any trading strategy other than an indexed buy-and-hold strategy. Put differently, strong form efficiency may not be a stable outcome, because if insiders consistently engage in NPV > 0 trading, it means that others irrationally persist in engaging consistently in NPV < 0 trading.

5.1.3   Informational Market Efficiency and "Efficient Inefficiency"

Informational market efficiency is the state in which available information regarding an asset is quickly reflected in the market price of that asset. For example, when does the market price of an equity, such as Tesla Inc., reflect the value of a new technology developed by the firm? Does the stock price rise when the idea for the technology is created, when the idea is made public, when the firm announces an investment to deploy the technology, when the technology is proved reliable, or when the firm begins receiving cash flows from sales based on the technology? In an information-ally efficient market, the answer is that the stock price reflects all potential cash flows (with their attendant probabilities), the moment the information regarding those cash flows is revealed to the marketplace. In such a market, no investor is able to consis-tently earn superior risk-adjusted returns based on available information, because the information is instantaneously reflected in market prices when it becomes publicly available.

A clear understanding of the implications of informational market efficiency is vital to being an effective overseer of assets. Informational market efficiency is a the-oretical idea rather than a precise description of actual markets. No asset market is perfectly efficient. Actual markets should be viewed as exhibiting different degrees of market efficiency. But perfect informational market efficiency is an important ideal. By way of analogy, consider a plumb line. A plumb line is a vertical line generally approximated using a suspended string with a weight attached at the bottom. A plumb line can be an important method of ensuring that a building's framework is well constructed. In practice, however, no building has perfect beams or walls. Simi-larly, the concept of perfect informational market efficiency creates a reference point against which market inefficiencies can be identified and the convergence of prices to the theoretically correct price can be forecast. In other words, perfect market effi-ciency is how financial analysts predict how prices *should* behave—allowing traders to identify mispriced assets and estimate their expected return and risk. Skill-based traders base their trades on perceived departures of actual asset prices from their informationally efficient prices.

How do empirics and economic reasoning inform asset allocators and their over-seers about the extent to which various asset markets are informationally efficient? Markets tend to be more informationally efficient to the extent that they (1) are being traded by large numbers of well-informed and financially sound traders com-peting for profits, (2) contain securities for which substantial amounts of reliable information are made broadly and quickly available, and (3) are subject to minimal transactions costs, taxes, and other impediments to trade. Large markets in modern economies with institutions that support free trade tend to exhibit high degrees of informational market efficiency.

The proposition that markets are perfectly efficient, however, is inconsistent with rational investing. If markets were perfectly efficient, no trader could earn a supe-rior profit by performing analyses using available information. Traders performing analysis would be wasting their valuable time processing information and would lose wealth relative to buy-and-hold investors because of higher trading levels and increased transaction costs. In the long run, it is only the existence of market inefficiencies that incentivizes analysts to use available information to drive markets toward efficiency.

Markets become more efficient through the efforts of speculators and other traders to identify mispriced assets and then to buy those perceived as being underpriced and to sell those perceived as being overpriced. The best traders are successful; they gain wealth, and they exert increasing influence on the pricing of assets.

The enigma as to how markets can become efficient when efficiency destroys the incentives to process information has led to the proposition that markets tend toward being *efficiently inefficient*.[1] The idea is that each market tends toward its own equilibrium degree of informational inefficiency, where that amount of inefficiency balances the marginal costs of additional skill-based trading with the marginal revenues from the skill-based trades.

Empirical studies of market efficiency reveal varying degrees of it in different markets and tend to indicate that opportunities to exploit particular inefficiencies decay through time as each successful trading strategy attracts additional capital. The empirical and theoretical evidence together suggest that skill-based trading strategies are more likely to be successful when (1) executed by the most skilled traders in any market and (2) executed in relatively new markets or with relatively new securities that have less competition among skill-based traders.

5.1.4 Six Factors Driving Informational Market Efficiency

The overall driver of informational market efficiency is greater competition among informed buyers and sellers. Thus, markets tend to attain higher degrees of informational market efficiency when there are more traders using all available information, and when those traders can transact with low costs. Informed traders will search to buy underpriced assets and sell (or short sell) overpriced assets, driving assets with similar risk toward offering equal expected returns (ignoring tax treatment differentials and other imperfections).

But what underlying factors cause the competition or analysis that drives prices toward informationally efficient levels? Let's look at six major factors. The first four factors serve to facilitate competition and to enhance liquidity; the last two factors facilitate better analysis.

1. The greater the value of the assets being traded, the greater the competition for potential profits and losses from mispricing, within limits. Higher profit potential motivates market participants to use more information and better analysis. Everything else equal, a $100 trade mispriced by 1% transfers only $1 of wealth between traders, whereas a $1,000,000 trade mispriced by only 0.1% transfers $1,000 of wealth. However, very large asset values, such as huge equity deals, may reduce competition if there are relatively few traders who have the resources to acquire the assets.

2. Greater trading frequency for the assets increases competition by providing greater incentives for investors, speculators, and arbitrageurs to analyze information and attempt to make favorable trades. Securities that are traded very infrequently typically have large bid-ask spreads due to the reduced profit potential for traders to benefit from mispricing.

3. Low levels of trading frictions facilitate higher competition by encouraging arbitrage and speculation with the lowering of total trading costs. Reduced trading frictions include lower transaction costs, such as brokerage fees, exchange fees, regulatory fees, and taxes.

4. Fewer regulatory constraints on trading also tend to lead to improved informational market efficiency by expanding competition and trading. Examples of regulatory constraints that may inhibit competition include restrictions on short selling and leverage.

5. Assets will also tend to trade at prices closer to their informationally efficient values when there is easier access to better information, as better information facilitates better financial analysis. In the United States, the Securities and Exchange Commission has as one of its primary goals requiring public companies to disclose meaningful information to the public.

6. Assets will also tend to trade at prices closer to their informationally efficient values when there is less uncertainty about their valuation. In other words, better valuation methods lead to better analysis. For example, the development of sound option pricing models in the 1970s led to improved informational market efficiency in options markets.

5.1.5 Factors Influencing Informational Efficiency in Alternative Asset Markets

As introduced in Chapter 1, alternative assets differ substantially from traditional assets. Many of these differences can cause the informational efficiency of alternative asset markets to differ from the informational efficiency of traditional markets.

Let's take a look at how these differences relate to the six factors that drive market efficiency, discussed in the previous section. Both traditional and alternative asset markets are quite diverse with regard to the first four factors. In other words, there are large, heavily traded markets, and small, thinly traded markets, in both traditional and alternative asset markets.

But it is primarily with regard to the fifth and sixth factors that many alternative markets possess features that lend themselves to less efficient pricing: substantial nonpublic information and substantial uncertainty with regard to valuation methods. The practices and tools for investing in traditional assets tend to be better developed and more widely accepted. Market participants tend to better understand the relationship between traditional asset values (such as bond prices) and information (such as expected inflation rates) than the relationship between alternative asset values (such as intellectual property values) and information (such as technological innovations).

The complex trading strategies inherent in some alternative investments rely on the discovery and exploitation of market inefficiencies in order to be successful. Hedge funds, discussed in detail in Chapters 14 through 19, tend to implement highly sophisticated trading strategies with frequent use of short positions, leverage, and high turnover. These strategies require the exceptional skills that are possessed only by top managers. The relatively low number of traders with the skills, models, data, and other resources needed to compete in the hedge fund arena increases the potential for the persistence of inefficient pricing. In contrast, long-only trading in traditional assets is accessible to numerous traders.

Private equity is another alternative investment that is accessible to a relatively limited number of traders and that requires highly specialized tools. Fewer investors are in the financial position to accommodate the specialized analytical tools, high minimum investments, and illiquidity of many private equity opportunities, meaning that the number of competitors may be limited. Thus, markets for traditional investments, such as publicly traded equity markets, may be more informationally efficient than markets for alternative assets, such as private equity.

An understanding of market informational efficiency, and especially the degree to which various markets may or may not be informationally efficient, is a vital tool in the practice of alternative investing.

5.2 THE TIME VALUE OF MONEY, PRICES, AND RATES

Cash is a financial asset that has an ultimate value that is based on its usefulness in obtaining real assets. Since the opportunities for converting cash into real assets change through time, cash flows to be received at different points in time are different commodities. This section, therefore, begins with a focus on the *prices* of prospective default-free cash flows.

5.2.1 Zero-Coupon Bond Prices and the Time Value of Money

Consider a set of default-free zero-coupon bonds with $1 face values (principal amounts) and with various maturities or longevities. In a perfect market with positive time value to money, a plot of the prices of these zero-coupon bonds against their longevities forms a monotonically declining function that asymptotically approaches zero as the longevities approach infinity. Exhibit 5.1 depicts this relationship, which is often termed the present value function.

The market price of $1 due in t years (i.e., a pure discount bond with a face value of $1) is expressed as $B(t)$. Viewing the time value of money through the lens of *prices*

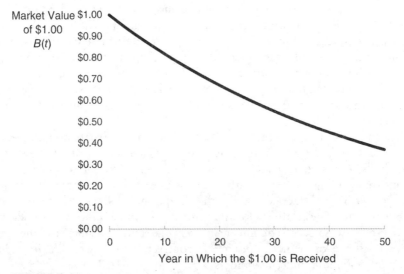

EXHIBIT 5.1   Value of a Zero-Coupon Bond

(as illustrated in Exhibit 5.1), offers some advantages. However, Exhibit 5.1 does not effectively communicate the *rates* at which the prices change through prospective time. Therefore, most applications in finance express the time value of money through the lens of *interest rates*. Interest rates are used to enable improved intuition, yet they introduce substantial complexities due to issues such as compounding intervals. Section 3.1 discusses compounding assumptions in the context of return computation. Section 5.2.2 discusses compounding in the context of discount rates and, more generally, interest rates.

5.2.2 Deriving Interest Rates from Zero-Coupon Bond Prices

Define $r_t^{m=1}$ as the interest rate corresponding to default-free cash flows due in t years, calculated under the assumption of annual compounding (i.e., $m = 1$). The rate can be calculated from the formula for a zero-coupon bond price based on annual compounding of interest:

$$B(t) = FV\left(1 + r_t^{m=1}\right)^{-t} \tag{5.1}$$

where FV is the face value or principal amount of the bond.

For expositional simplicity assuming $FV = \$1$, then $r_t^{m=1} = B(t)^{-1/t} - 1$. More generally, for any finite compounding assumption with r_t^m as the annual rate to be compounded m times per year:

$$B(t) = FV\left[1 + \left(r_t^m/m\right)\right]^{-tm} \tag{5.2}$$

$$r_t^m = \{[B(t)/FV]^{-1/(mt)} - 1\}m \tag{5.3}$$

Defining $r_t^{m=\infty}$ as the default-free interest rate corresponding to continuous compounding of the price, and continuing to assume the zero-coupon bond has a face value of $1, the price and rate can be found as:

$$B(t) = FVe^{-r_t^{m=\infty}t} \tag{5.4}$$

$$r_t^{m=\infty} = -(1/t)\ln[B(t)/FV] \tag{5.5}$$

Formulas 5.2 through 5.5 provide present values and interest rates for each compounding assumption. Continuous compounding is much easier to use once computational familiarity with the exponential function and the natural logarithmic function is achieved, although semiannual compounding is a convention in bond market quotations.

☞ APPLICATION 5.2.2A

Find the value of a $50 five-year zero-coupon bond for $m = 1, 2, 4, 12, 365$, and ∞, given an annual interest rate of 9%. Simply insert $50 in place of $1, 9% in place of r, 5 for t, and the given value for $m < \infty$ in Equation 5.2 (and analogously in Equation 5.4) to produce: $32.497, $32.196, $32.041, $31.935, and $31.883 (and $31.881 for continuous compounding).

5.2.3 Determination of the Short-Term Interest Rate

Although there is some evidence that markets price intraday lending, especially at times of crisis, the *short-term* interest rate generally refers to holding periods of one day, one week, or perhaps even one month. To the extent that a market is informationally efficient, the expected rate of return on various assets should be viewed on a real or after-inflation basis. The level of anticipated inflation is incorporated into any *nominal* rate of the time value of money. A **nominal interest rate** is the rate of return measured in terms of a given currency without a downward adjustment for the potential effects of positive inflation. **Inflation** is the rate of change in the value of a currency relative to a basket of real assets with a positive inflation rate indicating that the value of the currency is declining. The **anticipated inflation rate** (π) is generally defined as a measure of the expected rate of change in the value of a currency measured through changes in overall price levels. Expectations of inflation rates vary across market participants and are generally unobservable. Accordingly, indications of anticipated inflation are often based on surveys of consensus estimates, derived from past inflation, or inferred from other market information such as interest rates.

The **Fisher effect** (or **Fisher equation**) states that the nominal interest rate (r) is equal to the sum of the real interest rate (i) and the expected inflation rate (π), when interest rates are expressed as continuously compounded rates. The **real interest rate** is the annualized rate earned on default-free fixed-income investments, after adjusting the nominal rate downward for the effect of inflation. The real interest rate is usually expressed as an annualized short-term rate (e.g., daily or weekly) that is determined in the market by the supply and demand for short-term capital.

The traditional Fisher equation is sometimes modified for anticipated income taxes by assuming a uniform tax rate, T, on nominal interest income. The **modified Fisher equation** expresses the nominal interest rate as the combination of the after-tax real interest rate, r, and the anticipated rate of inflation (π), with an adjustment for the income tax rate, T, as shown in Equation 5.6:

$$r = (i + \pi)/(1 - T) \tag{5.6}$$

Equation 5.6 assumes that r, i and π are expressed as continuously compounded rates. If annualized rates are used a cross-term is introduced. Note that the Fisher equation is equal to the modified Fisher equation for the case of $T = 0$.

The CAIA Level II book, *Alternative Investments*, discusses the determination of the term structure of interest rates, interest rate risk, and inflation risk in detail. This chapter turns to the issue of estimating the term structure of interest rates.

5.2.4 Estimating the Term Structure of Interest Rates with Zero-Coupon Bonds

The **term structure of interest rates** is the relationship between spot interest rates and their associated longevities (i.e., times-to-maturity). Exhibit 5.2 depicts a common shape to the term structure of interest rates.

Given a large set of default-free zero-coupon bonds with a spectrum of maturities, the term structure can be estimated at each longevity corresponding to the maturities of the zero-coupon bonds. Fixed-income pricing focuses on yield to maturity. The **yield to maturity** of a fixed-income instrument is the rate that discounts all

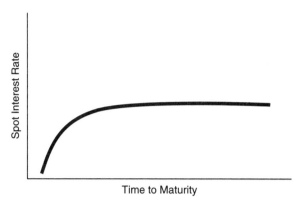

EXHIBIT 5.2 The Term Structure of Spot Interest Rates

of the promised cash flows of the instrument into a summed present value that equals the instrument's market price.

In the case of a zero-coupon bond with face value FV, T years to maturity, and a market price equal to P_T, the yield to maturity, y, can be determined with the following formula based on semiannual compounding:

$$y = 2 \left[\left(\frac{P_T}{FV} \right)^{\frac{-1}{2T}} - 1 \right] \tag{5.7}$$

Note that, in the case of a zero-coupon bond, the preceding formula for yield is equivalent to the formula for the spot interest rate in section 5.2.2. Therefore, the yields of zero-coupon default-free bonds can be used to represent the term structure of spot interest rates.

5.2.5 The Yield Curve and Its Approximation

Generally, fixed-income analysts wish to use coupon bonds to estimate most or all of the maturity ranges of the term structure of interest rates, because zero-coupon bonds are generally not available for longer maturities. A coupon bond with an annual coupon of C has the following formula for its price:

$$P_0 = \sum_{t=1}^{T} \frac{C}{(1+y)^t} + \frac{FV}{(1+y)^T} \tag{5.8}$$

The bond's yield to maturity (or simply its yield), y, is the rate that solves Equation 5.8. Substituting e^{yt} and e^{-yT} in place of the two denominators, respectively, generates an equation that can be solved for the yield expressed as a continuously compounded rate.

Note that a yield to maturity discounts each cash flow at the same rate regardless of its longevity and, therefore, is formed as a mixture of the spot rates associated with each cash flow. Yield to maturity does not have a market-based meaning except in the trivial case of a flat term structure of interest rates. In theory, each cash flow should be discounted with a rate associated with its longevity. However, yields are often used as a proxy for the term structure. In other words, yields-to-maturity are plotted against their corresponding terms-to-maturity and are described as yield curves that resemble the term structure of spot interest rates. Yields provide a somewhat close approximation to the spot rate corresponding to the bond's time-to-maturity, when coupon rates are small and when term structures are flat. However, for market environments with substantial coupons and sloped term structures, analysts often prefer to estimate spot rates. The next section discusses a method of deriving an estimate of the term structure of spot rates from coupon bonds.

Note however that in the case of zero-coupon bonds, the yield to maturity and the implied spot rate are identical because the zero-coupon bond has only one cash flow. Therefore, the zero-coupon bond's yield is not a mixture of rates from different times-to-maturity. Rather, it is a rate corresponding to a single time to maturity—the bond's time to maturity.

5.2.6 Bootstrapping the Term Structure of Interest Rates with Coupon Bonds

Bootstrapping the term structure is the process of recursively estimating spot rates using one or more zero-coupon bonds on the short end and coupon bonds on the medium- and long-term regions of the term structure. The idea is to start with a short-term spot rate (i.e., a six-month zero-coupon yield) and use that rate to discount the first coupon of a one-year bond (with semiannual coupon payments). Since the one-year bond has only two cash flows (assuming semiannual coupons), the value of the second cash flow (the principal plus coupon payment in 12 months) can be found by subtracting the discounted value of the six-month cash flow from the total value (price) of the one-year bond.

For example, consider: (1) a six-month zero-coupon bond with a face value of $100 and a price of $98, and (2) a 12-month 6% coupon bond with a face value of $100, semiannual coupons and a market price of $102. Note that the six-month zero-coupon bond is valued at 98% of its face value. The coupon bond's first coupon payment ($3) is due in six months and has a value of $2.94, found by multiplying the $3 coupon by 98% (the discount on six-month cash flows observed from the zero-coupon bond). The coupon bond also offers a $103 cash flow in 12 months, with a value that must equal the excess of the coupon bond's total price ($102) above the value of the coupon bond's first cash flow ($2.94), which equals $99.06. Note that the coupon bond's final cash flow is worth 96.175% of its undiscounted value ($103). The final step is to convert the discount factor (96.175% or 0.96175) into a one-year spot interest rate. The one-year spot rate can be expressed as 3.98% annually compounded, 3.94% compounded semiannually, or 3.90% compounded continuously.

The process could continue by analyzing an 18-month coupon bond, deriving the value of its final cash flow using the observed six-month and implied twelve-month spot rates, and converting the discounted value into an 18-month spot rate. Thus, an estimate of the entire term structure can be formed at six-month maturities if a bond can be found that matures on or very near each six-month interval.

☞ **APPLICATION 5.2.6A**

A six-month zero-coupon bond has a price of $97, while a 12-month 7.00% annual coupon bond (paid semiannually) has a price of $100.50. Both bonds have a face value of $100. Find the 12-month spot rate based on annual compounding, semiannual compounding, and continuous compounding. Solution: all six-month cash flows are worth 97% of their face value, so the coupon bond's first coupon is worth 0.97 × $3.50 = $3.395, leaving the 12-month cash flow to the coupon bond worth $100.50 − $3.395 = $97.105, which, based on a face value of $103.50 (including the semiannual coupon) means that 12-month cash flows are worth $97.105/$103.50 = 93.821% of face value. A 12-month discount factor of 0.93821 implies a 6.59% annually compounded yield, a 6.48% semiannually compounded yield, and a 6.38% continuously compounded yield.

5.3 THE THREE PRIMARY THEORIES OF THE TERM STRUCTURE OF INTEREST RATES

There are three primary theories (i.e., hypotheses) for the shape of the term structure of spot interest rates (default-free). The theories propose explanations of the relationship between interest rates corresponding to different longevities. These theories are vital tools that cut to the heart of fixed-income investment management. The following sections refer to each explanation of the term structure as a "theory," but each is also well known as a "hypothesis."

5.3.1 The Unbiased Expectations or Pure Expectations Theory

In a risk-neutral world, risk premiums are not required by market participants to bear interest rate risks. In that world, the unbiased expectations theory (i.e., the pure expectations theory) would hold. The **unbiased expectations theory** hypothesizes that all fixed-income securities offer the same expected return over the same time interval (i.e., there are no risk premiums), therefore serving as a useful tool in risk-neutral modeling in which all interest rates are formed purely on interest rate expectations. Put differently, under the unbiased expectations theory the expected value of every fixed-income security is expected to grow through time at the same rate over the same time interval and the shape of the term structure is driven purely by interest rate expectations (as opposed to being partly driven by risk aversion). Under the unbiased expectations theory the term structure should not be consistently upward sloping—which is inconsistent with historical observations.

5.3.2 The Liquidity Preference or Liquidity Premium Theory

Longer-term bonds tend to experience greater price volatility than shorter-term bonds, leading to the hypothesis that longer-term bonds are riskier and therefore require higher expected rates of return (i.e., higher risk premiums). Given risk aversion in a well-functioning market, the liquidity preference theory (i.e., the liquidity premium theory) would hold. The **liquidity preference theory** hypothesizes that longer-term fixed-income securities offer higher expected returns over the same time interval as shorter-term bonds, that risk premiums are positive and increasing in the bond's longevity, that all interest rates are formed based on both interest rate expectations and risk premiums, and that fixed-income management reflects a trade-off between risk and return. The liquidity preference theory hypothesizes that the expected return on zero-coupon fixed-income securities is an increasing function of the security's maturity, and that the shape of the term structure is formed as the sum of the term structure that would exist in a risk-neutral world (i.e., under the unbiased expectations theory) and the risk premiums associated with each maturity. The consistent upward slope to the term structure is consistent with the liquidity preference theory.

5.3.3 The Market Segmentation or Preferred Habitat Theory

Recall that the liquidity preference theory hypothesizes that fixed-income securities offer monotonically increasing expected returns (higher risk premiums) to securities with longer maturities. The market segmentation theory (i.e., preferred habitat theory) is based on an assumption that there may be localized imbalances in the supply and demand for bonds with different longevities. Specifically, some investors, such as pensions and insurance companies, may prefer or better tolerate the risks of longer-term bonds while others may prefer holding short-term bonds. Similarly, borrowers have their preferred longevities for obtaining funding.

The **market segmentation theory** hypothesizes that the preferred habitats of borrowers and lenders influence the expected returns of each maturity range, resulting in varying risk premiums and varying expected returns across maturity ranges that form humps and other non-monotonic shapes that are not eliminated by arbitrageurs (because the market is segmented). Economic theorists argue that the activities of speculators willing to form hedges that are long bonds within relatively underpriced maturity ranges and short bonds within relatively overpriced maturity ranges should minimize or eliminate expected return differentials based on habitat preferences.

5.3.4 Managerial Implications of the Three Term-Structure Theories

The three theories of the term structure prescribe different fixed-income strategies. The unbiased expectations hypothesis implies that borrowing and lending decisions should focus on issues of convenience such as cash-flow matching because all longevity-related choices offer equal expected returns to lenders and costs to borrowers. The liquidity premium theory asserts that lenders should seek longer longevities until the marginal aversion to risk offsets the higher expected returns, while borrowers should seek shorter maturities until risks associated with cash flow mismatches (funding risks) offset the lower expected costs. Finally, the market segmentation hypothesis introduces the complexities that different longevities offer expected returns to lenders and costs to borrowers that are driven by supply and demand factors that differ across maturity ranges and that may vary substantially through time.

5.4 FORWARD INTEREST RATES

The term structure of interest rates explicitly indicates spot rates—the time value of money from time zero to each prospective point. But it also *implicitly* indicates forward rates—the time value of money between any two points in time, such as between years 2 and 3.

5.4.1 Implied Forward Rates

Consider an investor holding a one-year zero-coupon bond with a face value of $100 and a market value of $90. If the investor holds that bond to maturity, the investor's return over the next year will be 11.11% (a $10 gain on a $90 position). The investor is contemplating selling the one-year bond immediately and rolling the proceeds into a two-year $100 face-value zero-coupon bond, with a market value of $80 per $100 of face value (offering a yield based on annual compounding of 11.8034%). If the investor rolled over the full sales price ($90) into the two-year bond, the principal amount or face value of the two-year zero-coupon bond that could be purchased would be $112.50, which is found as ($90/$80) × $100. The incremental cash flows of moving from a one-year bond to a two-year bond are shown in Exhibit 5.3.

The return on the incremental cash flows between years 1 and 2 would be:

$$(\$112.50 - \$100)/\$100 = 12.50\%$$

The incremental cash flows indicate that the investor would have $100 less in one year and $112.50 more in two years by exchanging the one-year bond for the two-year bond. The same incremental cash flows can be generated by any investor (in a perfect market) by simply short selling the one-year bond and using all the proceeds to buy the two-year bond.

In this example, 12.50% is the implied return of investing between periods 1 and 2 in the two-year bond, known as an implied forward rate. An **implied forward rate**, $F(t, T)$, is the annual return between time t and T (with $T > t$) inferred from the term structure of interest rates.

5.4.2 Implied Forward Rates with Annual and Continuous Compounding

The previous section simplified the computation of an implied forward rate by selecting a one-year interval between the starting and ending dates of the forward rate. This section generalizes the computation of the implied forward rates to other time intervals.

EXHIBIT 5.3 Incremental Cash Flows of Moving from a One-Year Bond to a Two-Year Bond

	Year 0	Year 1	Year 2
Current position	$0	$100	$0
Position with rollover	$0	$0	$112.50
Incremental cash flows	$0	−$100	+$112.50

Consider an investor weighing two choices:

1. Invest for T years at r_T.
   Or
2. Invest for a shorter period of time (t) at the rate r_t and then reinvest the proceeds into a forward rate, $F(t, T)$ for the remaining $T - t$ years.

In the absence of default risk, these two alternatives should generate identical returns in a perfect market since they each generate riskless proceeds in T years. Setting the future values of \$1 in T years from both alternatives equals:

$$(1 + r_T)^T = (1 + r_t)^t \times [1 + F(t, T)]^{T-t} \tag{5.9}$$

Solving for $F(t, T)$ generates:

$$F(t, T) = [(1 + r_T)^T / (1 + r_t)^t]^{1/(T-t)} - 1 \tag{5.10}$$

The formula is made simpler if the interest rates are expressed using continuous compounding:

$$e^{rT} = e^{rt} \times e^{F(t,T)(T-t)} \tag{5.11}$$

Factor the above equation by taking the natural log of each side to produce:

$$rT = rt + F(t, T)(T - t) \tag{5.12}$$

Then solve for $F(t, T)$ to produce the general formula (i.e., any T and t with $T > t$). The general implied forward rate (based on continuous compounding) is shown in Equation 5.13.

$$F(t, T) = (r_T T - r_t t)/(T - t) \tag{5.13}$$

Once again, continuous compounding makes the equation much simpler and intuitive. The intuition is straightforward: receiving r_T for T years exceeds r_T for t years by $F(t, T)$ per year (i.e., for each year from t to T). Inserting the previous example with $t = 1$ and $T = 2$:

$$F(1, 2) = [(2 \times 11.80434\%) - (1.11111\%)]/(2 - 1) = 12.50\% \text{ (rounded)}$$

For the case of $(T - t) = 1$ this equation simplifies to:

$$F(t, T) = r_T + (r_T - r_t) \times t \tag{5.14}$$

☞ APPLICATION 5.4.2A

The continuously compounded spot rates corresponding to years 3 and 5 are 6% and 7%, respectively. What is the implied continuously compounded annual interest rate from years 3 to 5? Using Equation 5.13: $F(t, T) = (r_T T - r_t t)/(T - t) = [(5 \times 7\%) - (3 \times 6\%)]/(5 - 3) = 17\%/2 = 8.5\%$. The investor in a five-year bond locks in an implied incremental (forward) 8.5% yield each year for two years by selecting the bond with the higher maturity.

EXHIBIT 5.4   The Term Structure of Single-Period Implied Forward Rates

5.4.3 The Term Structure of Implied Forward Rates

Note from Equation 5.13 that implied forward rates exist for any length time interval (i.e., from any t to any subsequent T). The two most common choices with which to plot a term structure of forward rates are one year ($T - t = 1$) and infinitesimal (when $T - t \to 0$). The formula for the implied forward rate for $T - t = 1$ is simply: $F(t, T) = (r_T T - r_t t)$.

A common structure in interest rate analysis is the term structure of implied forward rates. **The term structure of implied forward rates** is the relationship between implied forward rates and the starting point of each rate and is often superimposed on the term structure of spot rates. Exhibit 5.4 sketches the implied forward rates as lying above the estimated spot rates.

Given the relation for spot and forward rates derived in the previous section, $F(t, T) = (r_T T - r_t t)/(T - t)$, it is clear that the forward rate will lie above (below) the spot rate in the case of an upward (downward) sloping spot rate. The gap between the two tends to diminish from left to right. Also, the forward rate tends to "exaggerate" slope changes in the spot rate because the spot is an averaged rate while the forward rate is a marginal rate.

The concepts discussed in this section on implied forward rates serve as a foundation to the discussion of forward contracts in Chapter 6.

5.5 ARBITRAGE-FREE MODELS

Arbitrage is the attempt to earn riskless profits (in excess of the risk-free rate) by identifying and trading relatively mispriced assets. The implications of arbitrage activities form an important foundation for understanding finance in general and financial markets in particular. This section discusses arbitrage-free pricing models—a key technique in finance that has revolutionized both the field of finance and the world's financial markets.

5.5.1 Underlying Concept of Arbitrage-Free Models

An **arbitrage-free model** is a financial model with relationships derived by the assumption that arbitrage opportunities do not exist, or at least do not persist. The term *arbitrage* is sometimes used to describe attempts to earn profits that require the bearing of substantial risk due to uncertainty. For example, an equity portfolio manager might claim to be "arbitraging" the valuation differences between growth stocks and value stocks, but the manager is likely taking nontrivial risk. In its purest sense, often termed *pure arbitrage*, true arbitrage requires no risk bearing.

Pure arbitrage opportunities exist when identical assets can be traded at different prices, allowing the arbitrageur to buy at the lower price, sell at the higher price, and profit when arbitrage activities force the two identical assets to trade at identical prices. Arbitrage-free pricing models are based on the assumption that in the absence of transaction costs, taxes, or other trading restrictions, identical assets must trade at identical prices. In imperfect markets, arbitrageurs speculate that prices of identical assets will converge through time.

Arbitrage-free modeling provides a framework for understanding pricing relationships under idealized conditions. For example, in the absence of trading costs, if a euro is worth 1.10 Canadian dollars and a Canadian dollar is worth 1.10 U.S. dollars, then a euro will tend to be worth 1.21 U.S. dollars. We deduce this from the knowledge that any value other than 1.21 U.S. dollars would allow an arbitrage profit.

Arbitrage-free modeling is an important tool in modern financial analysis. For more than 50 years, finance has been applying arbitrage-free modeling to more and more assets and financial derivatives. Financial experts have done this by better identifying the relationships that exist among assets. This progress has not only changed the study of finance but has also dramatically changed the functioning of financial markets, as evidenced by the tremendous use of financial derivatives to manage risk.

A **key externality of arbitrage activities** is that they tend to drive similar assets toward similar prices which, in turn, improves global economic decisions. Better asset prices serve as signals of more accurate information to producers and consumers, which, in turn, enables supply and demand to be balanced at more efficient levels.

5.5.2 Applications of Arbitrage-Free Models

Arbitrage-free financial models vary in their complexity. In the next section, we discuss arbitrage-free pricing models that involve virtually instantaneous transactions, such that the arbitrage activity is concluded within seconds. In the section following that, we discuss arbitrage-free models that involve carrying positions for potentially extended periods of time. However, true to the purest definition of arbitrage, the models that are discussed are limited to those models containing little or no risk.

Arbitrage-free pricing models are used in the analysis of interest rates, foreign exchange rates, derivatives, and other areas, such as cash-and-carry trades. Arbitrage-free pricing models are relative pricing models. A **relative pricing model** prescribes the relationship between two prices. A trivial relative pricing model would specify that the price of a troy ounce of gold should sell for about 9.7% more than an avoirdupois ounce because a troy ounce of gold is about 9.7% larger. Note that this relative pricing model implies nothing about the overall price level of gold.

An **absolute pricing model** attempts to describe a value or a price level based on its underlying economic factors. For example, the price of a share of common stock typically involves substantial uncertainty with regard to its future growth. Attempts to model the stock's price (such as by using a dividend growth model) are absolute pricing models, since they estimate a price based on the stock's underlying fundamental factors. Absolute pricing models tend to be imprecise, since the model is based on bold assumptions and estimates about which investors have highly heterogeneous beliefs. However, relative pricing models are typically quite precise. It is the precision of relative pricing models that drives the usefulness of arbitrage-free pricing models. In effect, arbitrage-free pricing models tend to be used wherever relative pricing models are well developed and accurate.

5.5.3 Arbitrage-Free Pricing in Spot Markets

The **spot market** or **cash market** is any market in which transactions involve immediate payment and delivery: The buyer immediately pays the price, and the seller immediately delivers the product. Technically speaking, virtually all transactions involving financial securities have deferred delivery generated by the settlement period. But deferred delivery of spot (or cash) transactions is usually quite short and exists merely for convenience in facilitating the procedures necessary to settle the transaction.

Arbitrage-free pricing in spot markets involves identifying two sets of transactions with identical outcomes and requiring that their prices be equal. For example, consider an investor wishing to exchange euros for yen. In the spot foreign exchange market, the investor may find that one euro can be exchanged for 140 yen. However, there are numerous sets of transactions for converting euros to yen. For example, the investor may find that one euro can be converted to 1.40 U.S. dollars and that each U.S. dollar can then be converted into 100 yen. Of course, there are many other multiple-transaction paths that would lead to the same result: converting euros to yen. An arbitrage-free pricing model of the foreign exchange rates would describe the relationships that must exist between all of the exchange rates such that no investor or speculator could earn a profit through instantaneous trading among the currencies.

The skeleton of this arbitrage-free pricing model and other more sophisticated models is based on two steps: (1) identify two economically equivalent sets of assets or transactions, and (2) set their values equal to form a relationship based on the underlying determinants of their values. The next section extends this concept to the passage of time.

5.5.4 Carry Trades with and without Hedging

Carry trades are typically a set of long and short positions intended to generate perceived benefits through time, such as enhanced return, as the positions are "carried." Carry trades can either be hedged or be exposed to the risks of price changes.

For an unhedged example, consider an investor who observes that a one-year default-free bond in a particular foreign currency offers a 5% yield, whereas a default-free bond in the investor's domestic currency with the same maturity offers a yield of only 4%. The investor shorts the domestic bond (i.e., borrows in the domestic currency) at a cost of 4% and locks in a 5% yield in the foreign currency by purchasing the foreign bond with the borrowed cash. The carry trade offers an interest spread of 1% but is exposed to the risk that the foreign currency will weaken in value relative to the domestic currency. If the foreign currency weakens by more than 1% per year over the lifetime of the trade, the losses will exceed the 1% per year net income. In fact, to the extent that interest rate differentials reflect expectations of different inflation rates, the investor should *expect* the foreign currency to weaken by an amount that offsets the interest rate spread on a risk-adjusted basis.

The investor faces the risk that the proceeds of the foreign bond may be insufficient to settle the short position in the domestic bond at the end of the trade. The investor may decide to hedge the risk of this carry trade by locking in the exchange rate ahead of time between the foreign and domestic currencies. Specifically, the investor could use derivatives (such as a forward contract, discussed in Chapter 6) to lock in the rate to exchange the principal amount received in the foreign currency when the long position in the foreign bond matures for the amount due in the domestic currency. The key to the hedge is that it must allow the investor the opportunity to exchange the proceeds of the long position to cover the obligation of the short position at a prenegotiated value. However, since the investor is fully hedged against risk, the investor should only be able to receive the riskless return in an informationally efficient market.

5.6 BINOMIAL TREE MODELS

Binomial trees can be used to model a variety of risks, from equities to interest rates. Binomial models are often used as no-arbitrage models to value risky securities, especially financial derivatives. This section discusses an important arbitrage-free model for a call option using a binomial tree. A call option is a financial derivative that provides its owner with the right (but not the obligation) to purchase an asset at a prespecified price on (or perhaps before) the option's expiration date. Options are discussed in detail in Chapter 6.

5.6.1 The Mechanics of a Binomial Tree That Lead to a Normal Distribution

A **binomial tree** projects possible outcomes in a variable such as a security price or interest rate by modeling uncertainty as two movements: an upward movement and a downward movement. The movements are often modeled so that a pathway with an upward movement followed by a downward movement "recombines" with a pathway with a downward movement followed by an upward movement. Exhibit 5.5 illustrates how the current stock price in a binomial tree (S) can move up to S_u or down to S_d in the first step, moving from left to right. The second time step depicts the stock price as being one of three possible values under the very helpful (but not always necessary) recombining assumption that the stock price experiencing a downward move after an upward move (S_{ud}) is the same as one experiencing an upward move after a downward move (S_{du}). Trees recombine when upward movements are formed via a multiplicative shift factor, $S_u = S \times (1 + u)$, and downward movements are formed via division by the same factor, $S_d = S/(1 + u)$. A **recombining binomial tree** has $n + 1$ possible final outcomes for an n period tree, rather than 2^n outcomes, and is therefore much more manageable for models with 30 or more

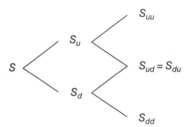

EXHIBIT 5.5   A Two-Step
Binomial Tree for a Stock Price (S)

time steps, since 2^{30} exceeds 1 billion, while a recombining 30-step tree would have 31 final outcomes.

Each step occurs over a unit of time specified by the modeler. An analyst may model a one-month period using 30 daily steps or a one-year period using 52 weekly steps. A key attribute of most binomial trees is that as the number of steps used increases (i.e., as the total time period is broken into smaller and smaller steps), the terminal distribution of the asset approaches a normal distribution. Therefore, the values obtained from the binomial model approach the values obtained using mathematical models (discussed in Chapter 6) that assume normally distributed returns.

5.6.2   A Simplified Binomial Tree Model for a Stock and a Call Option

As an illustration of the simplicity and power of these models, consider a very simplified scenario in which a stock price currently at $7 per share is expected to rise over the next year to $12 per share or fall to $0 per share, depending on the outcome of a very important event. Further, assume that there is a call option on that stock with a strike price (or exercise price) of $9 per share that expires in one year. At expiration, the call option will pay $3 if the stock rises to $12 (its excess above its strike price), or $0 if the stock falls to $0. Exhibit 5.6 illustrates single-period binomial trees for the stock and the call option.

Without knowing the probability of the stock rising or falling, it is still possible to know the value of a one-year call option (or a put option), using the principles of arbitrage-free modeling. The solution is found by noting that in this specialized case, the payoff of the call option is always 0.25 times the payoff of the stock (i.e., $0.25 \times \$12 = \$3$). Thus, the call option with a strike price of $9 must sell for one-quarter the price of the stock, or $1.75 (assuming no dividends). The idea is that four

EXHIBIT 5.6   Binomial Trees for Stock and Call Option with $9 Strike

call options are economically equivalent to owning one share of stock, so that call option must sell for one-quarter the price of the stock.

 APPLICATION 5.6.2A

A stock currently selling for $10 will either rise to $30 or fall to $0 in three months. How much would a three-month call sell for if its strike price were $20? The payoff of the call ($10 = $30 − $20) would be one-third the payoff of the stock ($10/$3 = 1/3). Therefore, the call must sell for $3.33 ($10 stock price × 1/3).

5.6.3 The Nature and Power of a Risk-Neutral Model

Note that the binomial model in Exhibit 5.6 was solved without specifying the probabilities of the up and down movements, without specifying the riskless interest rate, and without specifying the risk premium required for holding the stock. For example, perhaps the stock traded for $7 because the interest rate was zero, the stock had no systematic risk (and therefore required no risk premium), and the stock had a 7/12ths chance of rising and a 5/12ths chance of becoming worthless. Perhaps the chance of the stock rising was 2/3rds but investors demanded a 14.29% expected return for holding the stock and therefore it traded at $12. None of this matters, because the probabilities and interest rate were not required to find the solution.

A **risk-neutral model** is a framework for valuing financial derivatives in which risk preferences and probabilities of price changes do not alter the solution and are therefore irrelevant, and in which the analyst selects risk-neutrality as the model's underlying assumption with regard to risk preferences. Note that the probabilities and risk premiums can offset each other so there exist an infinite number of possible pairs of risk aversion and probabilities—two of which were given in the previous paragraph regarding Exhibit 5.6. Given that there exists an infinite number of possible probabilities and risk premiums, an analyst can therefore pick the most convenient scenario—which is the risk-neutral scenario. In the risk-neutral scenario all discount rates are the riskless rate and all probabilities found are the ones that allow the price of the risky asset to match its model value.

Risk neutral models are a very important tool in valuing financial derivatives and are discussed in numerous places throughout this book and in Level II.

5.6.4 The Advantage to Binomial Tree Models and Their Extensions

The primary advantage to binomial models is their *flexibility* to easily incorporate important features such as cash distributions, decisions by corporations to call (i.e., buy back) securities, and decisions by investors to exercise options prior to their expiration or to prepay loans.

In order to make the earlier binomial model extremely simple it was based on the highly unrealistic assumption that the stock price in one year would be either

$12 per share or zero. Obviously, actual binomial models relax that assumption. Binomial tree models can be based on interest rates (for valuing fixed-income securities), exchange rates (for currency derivatives), or two factors (e.g., interest rates and stock prices to value convertible bonds). Another extension is the use of trinomial models, in which each price is allowed to have three outcomes.

5.7 SINGLE-FACTOR DEFAULT–FREE BOND MODELS

A single-factor default-free bond model explains the systematic dispersion in bond returns using a single explanatory variable. This section discusses the most common single factor risk measure: bond duration.

5.7.1 Traditional Duration

The most popular single-factor approach to modeling default-free bond returns is traditional duration. Like any other single-factor measure of interest rate risk, duration is limited in its effectiveness to the type or types of interest rate risks for which it is designed. Throughout this section, the single interest rate risk being addressed is the risk of an instantaneous, parallel (or additive), and infinitesimal shift in the term structure of interest rates. Default risk is disregarded. These assumptions enable derivation of a bond's *duration* for a wide spectrum of securities. Duration-like risk measures exist for other types of shifts, but traditional duration is the most common such risk measure. Duration can be defined or interpreted in four primary ways, as detailed in this and subsequent sections.

The general definition of **duration** is the elasticity of a bond price with respect to a shift in its yield (or a uniform shift in the spot rates, corresponding to each prospective cash flow). Equation 5.15 expresses this general definition.

$$-(1/P_0) \times (dP_0/dy) = D \qquad (5.15)$$

where D is the duration, P_0 is the current bond price, and y is the bond yield. A key assumption of the preceding formula is the compounding assumption on which yields (or spot rates) are calculated. For simplicity, this section assumes that y (or each spot rate) is expressed as a continuously compounded rate.

Note that the elasticity described in Equation 5.15 is based on the bond's yield to maturity. Previous sections of this chapter noted the inconsistency of discounting each prospective cash flow of a bond using the same discount rate. In theory, each cash flow of a bond should be discounted with a spot rate based on its time to receipt. However, the use of spot rates raises two practical problems: (1) spot rates can be difficult to estimate, and (2) if spot rates are used to value each cash flow, the sum of the present values of each cash flow, in practice, will generally not be *exactly* equal to the bond's market price. So the use of yields in the computation of duration should be viewed as a practical approximation.

In the case of a fixed-coupon bond, the elasticity in Equation 5.15 can be expressed as the weighted average of the longevity of the bond's cash flows, as detailed in the next section.

5.7.2 Duration for a Fixed-Coupon Bond

The most common definition or characteristic of duration indicates how it is calculated in the case of *fixed-coupon* securities. The **duration of a fixed-coupon bond** is the weighted average of the longevities of the cash flows to a coupon bond where the weight of each of the bond's cash flows is the proportion of the bond's total value attributable to that cash flow. This standard formula for duration, D, is shown in Equation 5.16 for a fixed-coupon bond (with annual coupon payment and annual compounding for exposition simplicity):

$$D = \frac{\sum_{t=1}^{T} \frac{tC(t)}{(1+y)^t}}{P_0} \tag{5.16}$$

where t is time, $C(t)$ is the bond's promised cash flow for time t, y is the bond's yield to maturity, and P_0 is the bond's current value. Note that in the case of a fixed-coupon bond, the cash flows prior to T are coupons and the cash flow at period T is the principal payment.

But two important features involve challenges. First, when the interest rate compounding assumption is discrete (e.g., semiannual compounding), it introduces the need to adjust D in Equation 5.16 through division by $(1 + y/m)$, to create a risk measure entitled modified duration. Modified duration is a risk measure used with discrete compounding applications in which the traditional duration formula is adjusted through division by $(1 + y/m)$. Modified duration is discussed further in Chapter 22. With continuous compounding, the adjustment factor disappears (as m approaches infinity).

Second, the underlying assumption of the earlier duration formula is that the volatility of a default-free bond with respect to term-structure shifts is directly proportional to its longevity. This assumption is consistent with a parallel (or additive), instantaneous, and infinitesimal term-structure shift. In this case, each zero-coupon bond will shift in proportion to its maturity. Therefore, a fixed-coupon bond—which is equivalent to a portfolio of zero-coupon bonds—will experience a percentage price change directly proportional to its duration. The formula for duration in Equation 5.16 views a coupon bond as a portfolio of zero-coupon bonds and forming the risk of the portfolio as a value-weighted average of its components. The resulting duration is a measure of the bond's price sensitivity to a uniform shift—up or down—in interest rates, corresponding to all longevities.

Note that a bond that has a coupon rate that adjusts or floats to current interest rate levels can have a substantial average longevity but little or no interest rate risk. This exemplifies the importance of other definitions for duration that are detailed in subsequent sections.

5.7.3 Duration for a Bond Portfolio

Investors can use duration to manage the risk of a portfolio to a target level or to attempt to eliminate risk (hedge). **Interest rate immunization** is the process of protecting the value of a position against shifts in interest rates. A portfolio is said to be immunized with respect to specified shifts (or in some cases all interest rate shifts), if the value of the portfolio is independent of the shifts.

The traditional approach to interest rate risk management involves managing a portfolio's duration. The duration for a portfolio is simply a weighted average of the durations of the portfolio's constituent assets, much like the duration for a coupon bond is a weighted average of the durations of its prospective cash flows.

☞ APPLICATION 5.7.3A

Consider a simplified scenario in which all market interest rates are currently 5%, compounded semiannually. An investor has two bonds in a portfolio:

(1) A $1,000 face value one-year, 5% coupon bond (with semiannual coupon payments), and
(2) a $2,000 face value, five-year zero-coupon bond.

What is the duration of the investor's portfolio?
First, note that the duration of the five-year zero-coupon bond is 5.0. To calculate the duration of the one-year bond, view the bond as a portfolio of two cash flows: a $25 cash flow (coupon) due in six months with a present value (i.e., market value) of $24.39 (found as $25/1.025), and a $1,025 cash flow (principal plus interest) with a value of $975.61 (found as $1,025/1.025/1.025). The duration of the one-year bond is: [($24.39/$1,000) × 0.50] + [($975.61/$1,000) × 1.00] = 0.988.
The current value of the portfolio is found by summing the values of the $1,000 coupon bond ($1,000) and the zero-coupon bond [$1,562.40, found as $2,000 × (1.025)$^{-10}$], for a total value of $2,562.30. The duration of the portfolio is formed as a value-weighted average of the durations of its assets: [($1,000/$2,562.30) × 0.988] + [($1,562.40/$2,562.30) × 5.0] = 3.43 years.

5.7.4 Managing the Duration of a Long-Only Bond Portfolio to a Target

Traditional investing tends to focus on long-only positions in bonds. This section discusses the use of duration to manage interest rate risk in which the investor has a duration target. The target duration of the investor may emanate from several goals: (1) the investor has a horizon point in time at which she is concerned with the uncertainty of the portfolio's value, such as the end of a reporting period, (2) the investor has a set of projected cash needs and wants to be assured those needs can be funded by the portfolio, or (3) the investor views duration as a measure of short-term price risk and wishes to control the short-term price risk by controlling the duration—perhaps in tandem with efforts to predict interest rate shifts and use market timing in an attempt to add return.

For example, a pension fund likely prefers to have assets that hedge their liabilities in terms of interest rate risk. Accordingly, a pension fund with liabilities that average T years will be immunized by selecting assets with matching interest rate sensitivity (i.e., a duration of T years). As another example, an endowment attempting to fund a commitment in T years is concerned about the endowment's value in T years. The investor typically selects a target duration for the portfolio and manages the portfolio's duration to meet her goals through protection against infinitesimal, parallel, instantaneous shifts in interest rates.

☞ APPLICATION 5.7.4A

Consider a simplified scenario in which an investor has two bonds in a portfolio:

(1) $1,000 of market value in a 10-year zero-coupon bond, and
(2) $1,000 of market value in a five-year zero-coupon bond.

If the investor wishes to be immunized to a horizon point of 7.0 years, what transactions should be executed?

Note that the investor's current duration is 7.5, found as: $(0.50 \times 5) + (0.50 \times 10)$. To obtain the target duration of 7.0 years, she needs to select portfolio weights based on market values (w) for the five-year bond and $(1 - w)$ for the 10-year bond, such that the portfolio's duration is equal to the 7.0 year time horizon:

$$(w \times 5) + (1 - w) \times 10 = 7.0$$
$$5\,w = 10 - 7$$
$$w = 0.60$$

Thus, $200 of the 10-year bond should be sold to lower its weight to ($800/$2,000 = 40%) and used to purchase more of the five-year bond, to bring its weight to $1,200/$2,000 = 60%, so that the duration is 7.0, found as: $(0.6 \times 5.0) + (0.4 \times 10)$.

5.7.5 Duration for Securities with Stochastic Cash Flows

This section explores the challenges and solutions when the future cash flows of securities are stochastic. The section begins with floating-rate bonds and then discusses securities with embedded options. In a nutshell, the duration for securities with stochastic cash flows is calculated directly as an elasticity (based on Equation 5.15), not as the solution to the elasticity expressed in Equation 5.15 for the case of a fixed-coupon bond.

The responsiveness of the price of a floating-rate bond (i.e., with coupon rates that adjust with interest rate levels) to interest rate shifts approaches zero, as the speed with which the coupon adjusts to the short-term interest rate approaches zero. The idea that a floating-rate bond's duration is based on its coupon-reset period rather than its maturity is best understood by focusing on the sensitivity of the bond's price to interest rate changes. Simply put, fixed-coupon bonds are interest rate sensitive *because* their cash flows are fixed. Floating-rate bonds are only interest rate sensitive when their coupons adjust slowly or partially to interest rate changes.

Consider the cash flows from a hypothetical money market account that continuously pays its owners the short-term interest rate on its principal amount. The value of this fund is *immunized* against interest rate shifts. A money market asset paying a rate that instantaneously floats up and down with the short-term market interest rate is immunized with respect to any term-structure shift. A floating-rate or adjustable-rate bond offers the same future cash flow stream as this hypothetical money market account and is therefore fully immunized against any interest rate shifts, to the extent that the bond's rate adjusts instantaneously to market interest rate changes. However, a floating rate or adjustable rate bond that adjusts its coupon rate with a delay of *t* years will have the same interest rate sensitivity as a *t*-year zero-coupon bond:

Duration of Floating-Rate Bond = The Time to the Next Reset Period

The interest rate risks of floating-rate securities are discussed further in Chapter 22.

Many fixed-income securities contain options such as the prepayment option of a mortgage borrower and the callability of many corporate bonds. The durations for these securities require a valuation model for which the analysts may calculate an elasticity. Similarly, other securities potentially requiring advanced modeling include options on bond prices and interest rates.

5.7.6 Duration as the Longevity of a Zero-Coupon Bond of Equivalent Risk

A third interpretation of duration relates the risk of a given instrument to a zero-coupon bond. The duration of a zero-coupon bond is equal to its time to maturity, as is easily verified by examining the formula for duration in Equation 5.16 when the coupon rate is set to zero. There is only one cash flow (the principal at maturity) and so the weighted-average life of the zero-coupon bond is *T*—its time to maturity.

A coupon bond or other bond with a duration of, say, 5.0 years, responds identically to a parallel, infinitesimal, and instantaneous shift in the term structure as a 5.0-year zero-coupon bond. This can be verified from inspection of Equation 5.16 for both bonds. For a bond with a duration of, say, 5.4 years, its interest rate risk can be approximated as a portfolio with 60% in a five-year zero-coupon bond and 40% in a six-year zero-coupon bond. This interpretation of duration assists bond risk managers by allowing every security to be expressed using a reduced number of zero-coupon bonds.

An important feature of long-only bond portfolios that are immunized is that they tend to remain immunized as time passes, unless cash is received by the investor (i.e., coupon or principal payments). For example, consider the earlier example of matching a 7.0-year duration target with 60% of a portfolio invested in a five-year bond zero-coupon bond and 40% in a 10-year zero-coupon bond. As one year passes, for example, the 5- and 10-year bonds become 4- and 9-year bonds, leaving a weighted average of six years. It is likely that the investment horizon of the investor has also declined from seven years to six years. The portfolio's duration would tend to decline in line with the investor's target time horizon until the five-year zero-coupon bond matures. The point is that long-only portfolios tend to be somewhat reasonably hedged as time passes, but require rebalancing when cash flows are received.

5.7.7 Hedging or Immunizing a Long-Short Portfolio with Duration through Time

A portfolio with long and short positions (long-short) would be hedged and immunized if the long positions had a duration equal to the duration of the short positions. Further, a long-short portfolio can be immunized if the portfolio has a duration equal to the horizon point at which the investor anticipated using the proceeds from the portfolio. However, long-short portfolios raise a challenge with regard to the passage of time. This is a major reason why duration is said to be a perfect measure of risk when, among other things, there is an *instantaneous* term structure shift.

The following two applications illustrate these risk management techniques.

 APPLICATION 5.7.7A

An investor has a $1,000,000 portfolio with long positions that form a duration of 5.0 years. The investor wishes to consider two alternatives: adding $1,000,000 in short positions to hedge the portfolio or adding $500,000 in short positions to hedge the portfolio. What securities would provide immunization under the two scenarios? Solution: the $1,000,000 long position with a duration of 5.0 years can be hedged with $1,000,000 in short positions if the short positions have a duration of −5.0 years (i.e., short $1,000,000 of five-year zero-coupon bonds or other assets that would have a positive duration of 5.0 if held long). The negative position implicit in the short position will offset the positive duration exposure of the long position for an infinitesimal, parallel, and instantaneous shift in interest rates. In order to form a hedge with only $500,000 of short positions, the positions would have to have a duration of −10.0 years, such as having $500,000 of market value short sold in 10-year zero-coupon bonds. The proceeds of the short sales should be held in cash to avoid introducing further interest rate risk.

 APPLICATION 5.7.7B

An investor has a $1,000,000 portfolio with long positions that form a duration of 5.0 years. The investor's goal for the portfolio is to have a duration of 4.0 years because the portfolio is to be liquidated at that time to fund a project. The investor wishes to add short positions to hedge the portfolio to a duration of 4.0 years. There are many solutions to this problem. For example, the investor could short $200,000 of five-year zero-coupon bonds and hold the proceeds from the short sale in cash. Any combination of dollar amount V and duration D that solves the following equation would lower the duration to 4.0 years:

$$(\$1,000,000 \times 5.0) - (V \times D) = \$4,000,000$$
$$V \times D = (\$1,000,000 \times 5.0) - \$4,000,000 = \$1,000,000$$

The previous section noted that long-only bond portfolios matched to a horizon point duration tend to experience a decline in their duration that roughly matches the rate at which the time-to-the-horizon point is declining (until a cash flow occurs). The same cannot be said of a long-short portfolio. Take, for example, the portfolio in Application 5.7.7.A in which a five-year duration $1,000,000 portfolio is hedged with a $500,000 short position in a 10-year duration portfolio. Note that after one year the long side of the portfolio would tend (in the absence of intervening cash flows) to decline to having a duration of 9.0, while the short side would tend toward a duration of 4.0. The 2-1 hedge would no longer provide immunization.

Chapter 17 on relative value funds and Chapter 22 on private credit explore duration-based hedging further.

5.7.8 Extensions to Traditional Duration

As indicated previously, single (scalar) duration measures can be derived for any particular shift in the term structure. For example, the term structure often shifts in a non-parallel (i.e., non-additive) manner, so alternative duration measures for slope shifts and curvature shifts in the term structure have been engineered. However, this section discusses the challenge of controlling the risk of *finite* interest rate shifts. Duration was shown earlier to be an elasticity based on a first-order partial derivative. As a first-order derivative to a nonlinear function, traditional duration hedging is subject to errors that are nonlinearly related to the size of the interest rate shift.

The risk of finite-sized shifts in the term structure are typically managed by considering higher moments. Thus, whereas traditional duration is a first-order elasticity, financial engineers use *convexity* to address second-order shifts. Convexity is discussed in detail in Level II of the CAIA program. In a nutshell, risk managers can use convexity (in addition to duration) to provide better hedging or management of the risks of large interest rate shifts. Convexity functions as a second-order derivative.

5.8 SINGLE-FACTOR EQUITY PRICING MODELS

An **asset pricing model** is a framework for specifying the return or value of an asset based on its risk, as well as future cash flows. Although asset pricing models include the term *pricing* in their name, they are focused on the returns on assets rather than their prices. Also, the term is usually used to describe the returns of equities rather than assets such as bonds.

This section reviews single-factor asset pricing and discusses the distinction between ex ante asset pricing and ex post asset pricing. Asset pricing models are not simply mathematical exercises; they are ways of expressing the most fundamental issues related to investing: the nature of the risks and returns of investment opportunities.

5.8.1 Single-Factor Asset Pricing

The central theme of asset pricing involves return, systematic risk, and diversification. The **capital asset pricing model (CAPM)** provides one of the easiest and most widely understood examples of single-factor asset pricing by demonstrating that the risk of the overall market index is the only risk that offers a risk premium. The CAPM is a general equilibrium model, meaning that it prices all assets rather than simply describing one or more relative pricing relationships.

 FOUNDATION CHECK

This section assumes basic familiarity with the capital asset pricing model, including its underlying assumptions, the intuition of the model, the division of systematic and diversifiable risk, the interpretation of beta, and the estimation of beta.

Equation 5.17 provides the most common representation of the CAPM:

$$E(R_i) = R_f + \beta_i[E(R_m) - R_f] \tag{5.17}$$

where $E(R_i)$ is the expected return on asset i, β_i is the market beta of asset i, $E(R_m)$ is the expected return on the market portfolio, and R_f is the riskless rate of return.

The CAPM is frequently and correctly criticized for failing to explain and predict financial returns accurately. Nevertheless, this section discusses the CAPM as a foundation for developing more complex models and the concepts crucial to the analysis of alternative investments.

Equation 5.17 indicates that the expected return of any asset (the left side of the equation) has two parts: a risk-free rate to compensate the investor for the time value of money (R_f) and a risk premium to compensate the investor for bearing the risk. The asset's risk premium, $\beta_i[E(R_m) - R_f]$, is the product of the asset's risk, or beta, and the market risk premium, meaning the amount investors demand for bearing each unit of risk. The market return is the return of the market portfolio. The **market portfolio** is a hypothetical portfolio containing all tradable assets in the world (except riskless financial assets). Each asset in the market portfolio is held in a quantity based on its market weight. The **market weight** of an asset is the proportion of the total value of that asset to the total value of all assets in the market portfolio. Thus, if the combined market value of all shares of XYZ Corporation is $250 billion, and if the combined market value of all investable assets in the world is $250 trillion, then the market weight of XYZ's equity would be 0.10%.

The CAPM is an example of a single-factor asset pricing model. A **single-factor asset pricing model** explains returns and systematic risk using a single risk factor. Whereas the CAPM describes the entire economy, other single-factor models may simply describe relative prices and returns among a subset of the economy. For instance, consider an analyst modeling the returns of a group of REITs (real estate investment trusts) that have somewhat similar underlying assets. Equation 5.18 represents a REIT-based single-factor asset pricing model that differs in important ways from the CAPM:

$$E(R_i) = a_i + \beta_i[E(R_{index})] \tag{5.18}$$

where $E(R_i)$ is the expected return on $REIT_i$, a_i is a constant, β_i is the beta of $REIT_i$, and $E(R_{index})$ is the expected return on an index of REITs.

Note that the model in Equation 5.18 does not specify that all assets must be included in the index, or that the constant is the riskless rate. The beta in Equation 5.18 describes the behavior of a REIT with respect to an index of REITs, which would clearly differ from the beta from the CAPM, which describes the behavior of an asset with respect to the market portfolio.

Thus, the CAPM is a specialized case of a single-factor asset pricing model. The CAPM is the very important case that describes an economy in which all investors diversify perfectly among all assets and achieve an equilibrium in which all investors allocate their assets between two portfolios: the market portfolio and the riskless portfolio.

Within the context of single-factor asset pricing models such as the CAPM, the next two sections discuss the distinction between ex ante asset pricing and ex post asset pricing.

5.8.2 Ex Ante Asset Pricing

Equation 5.17 is primarily a cross-sectional representation of the CAPM that focuses on the expected returns of asset *i* rather than the realized returns of asset *i* subscripted for time (*t*). Equation 5.17 is the expectational (i.e., ex ante) form of the CAPM. **Ex ante models**, such as ex ante asset pricing models, explain expected relationships, such as expected returns. Ex ante means "from before." Ex ante models provide an understanding of how return expectations or requirements are formed.

The expected return expresses the central tendency of asset *i*'s return. The actual return of asset *i* in a particular time period may differ from the expected return either because the market earned more or less than expected or because asset *i* experienced an unexpected and idiosyncratic change in price.

☞ APPLICATION 5.8.2A

Using the CAPM equation, when the risk-free rate is 2%, the expected return of the market is 10%, and the beta of asset *i* is 1.25, what is the expected return of asset *i*? By placing each of these variables on the right side of Equation 5.17 and solving the left side, the expected return of asset *i* is 12%.

The ex ante form of the CAPM makes two powerful prescriptions that are especially relevant to an analysis of alternative investments. The first is the assertion that any and all rewards for bearing risk should only be available from bearing market risk, which can be fully measured by an asset's beta relative to the market portfolio. The second assertion is that investors should not be able to earn any additional expected return from bearing any other type of risk. The first assertion is driven by the single-factor nature of the CAPM, and the second assertion is common to equilibrium asset pricing models. In an equilibrium asset pricing model, participants do not seek to change their positions to exploit perceived pricing errors, because there are no discernible pricing errors based on available information, meaning there are no arbitrage opportunities.

The implications of the ex ante form of the CAPM are vast. If the CAPM were true, then every investor would hold all risky assets in proportion to their size. Risk-averse investors would hold a greater portion of their portfolio in risk-free assets, and risk-tolerant investors would hold a greater portion of their wealth in the risky market portfolio. Although individual investors might allocate different total amounts to the market portfolio, every investor would be exposed to exactly the same risk factor: the risk that the market portfolio will change in price. In the idealized world of the CAPM, no investor tries to beat the market by overweighting or underweighting any risky assets or by trying to time the market (i.e., trying to buy and sell assets immediately before favorable price changes).

The importance of alternative investments as a distinct category of investing must therefore emanate from the insufficiency of the CAPM to describe financial markets. This is because if the CAPM were true, all investors would hold the same portfolio of risky assets, and no further analysis or management would be required. To motivate a nontrivial approach to alternative investment management, we must relax some of the assumptions on which the CAPM is based. In other words, for there to be a need to analyze alternative investments, the CAPM must be an insufficient description of asset pricing. Alternative investment analysis must focus on assets for which prices are not well described by the CAPM and must implicitly or explicitly use models that differ from the CAPM.

The CAPM is derived from the assumption that many of the real-world features that are linked to alternative investments do not exist. The CAPM is typically derived assuming that no single trader can affect security prices, that all investors can focus exclusively on the market value of their wealth at the end of the same single period, that all assets are publicly traded, that all investors can short sell limitlessly, that all investors can borrow limitlessly at the risk-free rate, that there are no taxes or transaction costs, that all investors care only about the mean and variance of an asset's return distribution, and, in most cases, that all investors have equal expectations about security returns.

A foundation for alternative investment analysis must begin with ideas of how assets are priced when the CAPM's assumptions do not hold. In other words, what risks other than the CAPM beta might be compensated? If different risks are rewarded, are they rewarded with equally attractive risk premiums? If some securities are not publicly traded, how do their risks and returns compare and contrast with the risks and returns of publicly traded securities? If superior knowledge or skill can enhance expected returns, how would assets be priced? Understanding these important questions is critically linked to understanding asset pricing, the distinctions between ex ante and ex post pricing models, and the analysis of alternative investments.

5.8.3 Ex Post Asset Pricing

The previous description of the CAPM focused on the expected return of an asset. Expected returns were shown to depend on a common or systematic factor. **Systematic return** is the portion of an asset's return driven by a common association. **Systematic risk** is the dispersion in economic outcomes caused by variation in systematic return. **Idiosyncratic return** is the portion of an asset's return that is unique to an investment and not driven by a common association. **Idiosyncratic risk** is the dispersion in economic outcomes caused by investment-specific effects. This section focuses on realized returns and the modeling of risk.

Actual returns deviate from expected returns due to unexpected effects. The unexpected portions of returns result from systematic and idiosyncratic risks. Systematic effects occur when a systematic risk factor is higher or lower than expected. Idiosyncratic effects are all effects that are not systematic. The ex ante form of the CAPM does not include an added expected return from idiosyncratic effects, since the expected value (i.e., expected return) of all idiosyncratic effects must be zero. This is because idiosyncratic risk is diversifiable. If idiosyncratic risk bearing offered a risk premium, then investors could receive a higher expected return (rather than simply a lower total risk) from simply holding a diversified portfolio—which would represent an unsustainable arbitrage opportunity.

This section discusses an ex post (meaning "from afterward" or realized) form of the CAPM. An **ex post model** describes realized returns and provides an understanding of risk and how it relates to the deviations of realized returns from expected returns.

The realized return of an asset differs from its expected return due to systematic and idiosyncratic effects, which are illustrated as the right side of the following equation:

$$R_{it} - R_f = \beta_i(R_{mt} - R_f) + \varepsilon_{it} \tag{5.19}$$

The left side of the equation is the realized excess return of asset i in time period t. The **excess return** of an asset refers to the excess or deficiency of the asset's return relative to the periodic risk-free rate. The terms between the equal sign and the plus sign reflect the effect of the market's realized return in time period t, or the effect of systematic risk on the realized return of asset i in time period t. To the extent that the realized return of the market differs from its expected return, an asset with a nonzero beta realizes a return that differs from its expected return proportional to its beta. Finally, ε_{it}, the term to the far right, is the portion of the excess return that is due to the effect of idiosyncratic risk. Idiosyncratic returns include any effect on the return of asset i in time period t other than that which is correlated with the return of the market, such as the impact of firm-specific news. Taking the expected value of each side of the ex post CAPM equation and rearranging the terms returns the equation to the ex ante form of the CAPM (Equation 5.17).

☞ APPLICATION 5.8.3A

Returning to the previous example in which the risk-free rate is 2% and the beta of asset i is 1.25, if the actual return of the market is 22%, the ex post CAPM model would generate a return due to non-idiosyncratic effects of 27% for the asset: $2\% + [1.25(22\% - 2\%)]$. If the asset's actual return is 30%, then the extra 3% would be attributable to idiosyncratic return, ε_{it}.

Two essential attributes of the ex post CAPM are that (1) the return from idiosyncratic risk, ε_{it}, has an expected value of zero (otherwise, it would appear in the ex ante form of the CAPM), and (2) the return from idiosyncratic risk is not linearly correlated with the return of the market, because any such effects are captured through the beta of the asset. In this case, the asset pricing model is being used with its true idiosyncratic return component, ε_{it}, not an estimate, such as the residuals from a regression equation. Linear regression residuals are, by definition, uncorrelated with the regression's independent variables.

Equation 5.19, the ex post CAPM equation, can be viewed as both a cross-sectional and a time-series model, since one or more variables on each side are subscripted both by time (t) and by subject (i). Thus, the model might be used to describe the time-series properties for a single stock or might be used across many firms during a single time period in a cross-sectional study.

Equation 5.20 provides insight into risk. It is formed by taking the variance of both sides of Equation 5.19, assuming that R_f and β_i are constant and that the correlation between R_{mt} and ε_{it} is zero:

$$\sigma_i^2 = \beta_i^2 \sigma_m^2 + \sigma_\varepsilon^2 \tag{5.20}$$

where σ_i^2 is the variance of the returns of asset i, σ_m^2 is the variance of the returns of the market index, and σ_ε^2 is the variance of the idiosyncratic returns of asset i. The left side of Equation 5.20 is the total risk of asset i. The term $\beta_i^2 \sigma_m^2$ is the portion of the total risk that is attributable to the asset's systematic risk, and σ_ε^2 is the portion attributable to the idiosyncratic risk. The idiosyncratic risk vanishes when enough assets are added to a portfolio.

Although the ex post returns in Equation 5.20 (R_{it}, R_f, and R_{mt}) can be observed, the beta of the investment, β_i, is never observed, and therefore ε_{it} can only be estimated. When empirical tests of Equations 5.19 and 5.20 are performed, the measured idiosyncratic return in Equation 5.19 and the variance of the idiosyncratic risk in Equation 5.20 contain estimation errors to the extent that the estimated beta differs from the true beta of the investment.

This chapter discusses several asset pricing issues in the context of the CAPM because the CAPM provides a relatively simple representation of the concept of systematic and idiosyncratic risk and return. But the CAPM is generally faulted for its inability to describe the real world accurately, especially its inability to describe the behavior of alternative investments. Alternative investment analysis often focuses on the potential for multiple sources of systematic risk and on the potential to invest such that the expected idiosyncratic return, $E(\varepsilon_{it})$, is positive.

REVIEW QUESTIONS

1. Jane studies past prices and the volume of trading in major public equities and establishes equity market-neutral positions based on her forecasts of prices. Jane consistently outperforms market indices of comparable risk. Does the performance indicate that the equity market is informationally inefficient at the semistrong level?
2. List two major factors that drive informational market efficiency through facilitating better investment analysis.

3. What does the modified Fisher equation express regarding minimal interest rate determinants?
4. What does it mean to bootstrap a yield curve?
5. In which theory of the term structure of interest rates do all bonds have the same expected return?
6. What differentiates a relative pricing model from an absolute pricing model?
7. What makes a binomial tree a recombining tree?
8. What is the term used to describe a framework for specifying the return or price of an asset, based on its risk as well as future cash flows and payoffs?
9. What is the market portfolio and what is a market weight?
10. What is an ex post excess return?

NOTE

1. See, for example, Lasse Heje Pedersen, *Efficiently Inefficient* (Princeton, NJ: Princeton University Press, 2015).

CHAPTER **6**

Derivatives and Risk-Neutral Valuation

This chapter discusses basic financial derivatives. The chapter begins with forward and futures contracts that represent agreements for deferred delivery; it concludes with options—contracts that allow their owner the right to execute a transaction at one or more points in the future.

6.1 FOUNDATIONS OF FORWARD CONTRACTS

Forward contracts are important financial derivatives that facilitate risk management by transferring risk between the two parties to the contract.

6.1.1 Forward Contracts, Delivery, and Settlement

A **forward contract** is simply an agreement calling for deferred delivery of an asset or a payoff at a prespecified time, at a fixed price or rate on a prespecified date (i.e., the settlement or delivery date) or for an economically equivalent cash settlement. In the case of settlement by delivery, the entity holding the short side of the contract promises to deliver a specified asset to the entity holding the long side of the contract in exchange for the prespecified price (the forward contract price). Alternatively, the two parties may agree to cash settle the contract by exchanging the difference between the forward price and the market price at the settlement date in the case of a forward contract on a price. In the case of a forward contract on a rate, the settlement takes place according to the size and other details specified by the contract.

The long side of a forward contract on an asset is the participant who is obligated to *buy* the specified asset at the specified and fixed price (the forward price) on the delivery or settlement date. The short side of the forward contract is obligated to deliver the asset in exchange for receiving the forward price set in the contract at the contract's inception. Forward contracts are usually formed with no immediate cash exchange between the two parties (although parties may negotiate posting of collateral). In these cases, the forward contract price (i.e., the forward price) is set to a value that sets the value of the contract to zero. Throughout this chapter it is assumed that the forward contract is initiated with a zero market value so there is no immediate payment between the two parties.

A simple example of a forward contract is an agreement for a major bank to deliver a three-month U.S. Treasury bill (T-bill) with a face value (principal value) of $100,000 in exchange for F dollars from a bond investor, with delivery to take place in six months. F in this example denotes the forward price.

6.1.2 The No-Arbitrage Approach to Determining Forward Prices

Forward contracts on prices of financial assets are perhaps the simplest derivatives to model.

Arbitrage-free modeling, discussed in Chapter 5, demonstrates that the current spot market interest rates of six-month and nine-month U.S. Treasury bills can be used to determine the implied forward rate between their maturity dates. Similarly, spot market prices of the two bonds can be used to find the implied price for a forward contract based on prices. The forward price is set when the contract is formed to be equal to the implied forward price from spot prices because it is the only price for that forward contract that is arbitrage-free, with zero cash being exchanged to initiate the contract (i.e., for which arbitrageurs will not be able to earn a riskless profit in excess of the riskless rate).

The key to arbitrage-free modeling is to identify two identical assets or strategies that must offer the same returns. If two identical strategies can be identified with identical payoffs and returns they must have identical market prices; otherwise, there would be an arbitrage opportunity. The arbitrageur could profit from buying the relatively underpriced asset and shorting the relatively overpriced asset.

In an efficient market, the return of investing in a default-free bond that offers a total return of $R_{0,T}$ over the time interval from 0 to T (with maturity at T) must be the same as a strategy that offers: (1) a default-free total bond return of $R_{0,t}$ over the time interval (with maturity at t) from 0 to t (with $T > t$), and (2) uses a long position in a forward contract locking in the return $R_{t,T}$ over the time interval from t to T (assuming that the forward contract is initiated at time 0 with a value of zero):

$$(1 + R_{0,T}) = (1 + R_{0,t}) \times (1 + R_{t,T}) \tag{6.1}$$

Equation 6.1 indicates that a relatively long-term zero-coupon bond will offer the same total return as a strategy of investing in a shorter zero-coupon bond and using a forward contract to lock in the return from the maturity of the shorter bond to the maturity of the longer bond. Since both strategies offer riskless returns from time 0 to T, their prices must be such in a perfectly competitive market that the total returns will be equal (i.e., there will be no arbitrage opportunities).

6.1.3 Determining the Forward Contract Price of a Zero-Coupon Default-Free Bond

Let's return to the forward contract to deliver a three-month U.S. Treasury bill (T-bill) with a face value (principal value) of $100,000 in exchange for F dollars from a bond investor, with delivery to take place in six months. Let's find a no-arbitrage forward price (F) to deliver the three-month T-bill in six months given the cash market prices of two bonds that correspond to the starting and ending dates of a forward contract. Assume that a six-month T-bill has a market price of $98,000, and a nine-month T-bill has a market price of $96,900 (both with zero coupons and $100,000 face values). Assume that there are no transaction costs, taxes, or other imperfections, and that there is no risk that either side to a forward contract will default on its responsibilities.

Let's examine two strategies that have a nine-month life (i.e., $T = 9$ months). The first strategy is to simply invest in the nine-month T-bill. The second strategy is to invest in the six-month T-bill and roll the proceeds at maturity into a three-month T-bill using the forward price guaranteed through the forward contract. Both strategies have riskless returns at the nine-month horizon and must have identical returns to prevent arbitrage opportunities. Equation 6.1 can be used to solve for the return on the forward contract, $R_{t,T}$, from which the implied forward price will be $100,000/(1 + R_{t,T})$.

The wealth ratio (i.e., one plus the non-annualized return) of buying and holding the nine-month T-bill to maturity is $100,000/$96,900. The wealth ratio of the second strategy is the product of (1) the wealth ratio of buying and holding the six-month T-bill to maturity, and (2) the wealth ratio of reinvesting in the three-month T-bill using the forward contract. Setting the wealth ratios of the two strategies equal generates:

$$\$100,000/\$96,900 = (\$100,000/\$98,000)(\$100,000/F_{t,T})$$

where $98,000 is the current market value of the six-month T-bill and $F_{t,T}$ is the forward price at which the three-month T-bill is exchanged according to the forward contract. Note that the right side of the equation does not imply that the investor purchases $98,000 of the six-month T-bill. In fact, to make the dollar investments equal, the investor would purchase $96,900 of the six-month T-bill. But the scale of each investment does not change the values of the wealth ratios; thus, for simplicity, it is ignored. Solving for $F_{t,T}$ generates $F_{t,T} = \$98,878$.

☞ APPLICATION 6.1.3A

Nine-month riskless securities trade for $97,000, and 12-month riskless securities sell for P (both with $100,000 face values and zero coupons). A forward contract on a three-month, riskless, zero-coupon bond, with a $100,000 face value and a delivery of nine months, specifies a forward price of $99,000. What is the arbitrage-free price of the 12-month zero-coupon security (i.e., P)?

The 12-month bond offers a ratio of terminal wealth to investment of ($100,000/P). The nine-month bond reinvested for three months using the forward contract offers a 12-month wealth ratio of ($100,000/$97,000) ($100,000/$99,000).

Setting the two wealth ratios equal and solving for P generates $P = \$96,030$. The 12-month bond must sell for $96,030 to prevent arbitrage.

This section has demonstrated that the forward price of a default-free zero-coupon bond is a function of the spot prices of two default-free zero-coupon bonds corresponding to the inception and termination of the forward contract.

6.1.4 Forward Prices, Expected Spot Prices, and Risk Neutrality

This section introduces the analysis of expected spot prices. Note the prices per $100 of principal amount that were assumed or derived in the previous application:

Spot price of 9-month zero-coupon bond:	$97.00
Spot price of 12-month zero-coupon bond:	$96.03
Forward price of 3-month bond in 9 months:	$99.00

There are no explicit assumptions or predictions regarding the expected future prices of the bonds in the previous section (prior to their maturities). A key question is the relationship, if any, between the forward price of $99 and the *expected spot price* of the three-month bond in nine months. Note that the solution ($99) to the forward price of the three-month bond did not require knowledge of the current three-month bond price or how much added return investors require for bearing interest rate risk or any other risk!

While no assumptions were made regarding investor attitudes toward risk, it is highly instructive to consider a scenario that specifies that investors are neutral toward risk. In a risk-neutral world (in which investors do not require risk premiums for bearing risks), the forward price will be driven toward equaling the expected spot price because any other relationship would allow trading that offered abnormal expected return (note that due to the assumption of risk neutrality there would be no concern regarding risk). Specifically, trading by arbitrageurs in a world of risk neutrality will force all forward prices to equal their corresponding expected spot prices (i.e., the expected price of the contract's underlying bond at time of settlement). Thus, in a risk-neutral world, the expected price of the underlying bond is equal to the forward price ($99) of a forward contract on that bond. This relationship is *consistent* with the unbiased expectations theory detailed in section 5.3 but is inconsistent with a world dominated by risk aversion, as explained in the next section.

6.1.5 Forward Prices, Expected Bond Prices, and Term-Structure Theories

Note that the long side of a forward contract on the price of a bond is taking the risk that the value of the bond (e.g., a three-month bond received at the end of the contract) will be *less* than the forward price at which the long side must buy the bond at the delivery date. The short side of the contract takes the opposite risk. A forward contract therefore is a *transfer of risk* between the two parties with regard to the market price of the bond at settlement. In this case, the long side is taking the *classic* interest rate risk in which there will be gains when interest rates decline and losses when interest rates rise. This classic fixed-income exposure to rising interest rates has been generally regarded as requiring and offering a risk premium as expressed in the liquidity premium hypothesis discussed in section 5.3. Conversely, the short side to this forward contract is laying off interest rate risk and should expect in an efficient market that there is an expected cost to this protection.

In an unbiased expectations world, forward bond prices (whether implied by spot rates or observed in the forward prices of forward contracts) are unbiased estimates of subsequent spot or cash market prices. In a liquidity premium world, investors are compensated for bearing the risks of rising interest rates by being offered higher expected returns. So forward bond prices (yields) will understate (overstate) expected spot prices (yields) in order to provide an expected risk premium to the long side for bearing the risk of rising rates (and to exact an expected cost to the short side of the contract for laying off the risk of rising rates). The market segmentation or preferred habitat theory does not predict a monotonic spread between forward prices and expected spot prices since the theory assumes that forward prices and rates cannot be perfectly arbitraged because there are impediments or limits to the ability of arbitrageurs to form hedges across different sections of the term structure.

6.2 FORWARD CONTRACTS ON RATES

Forward contracts on interest rates and currency exchange rates facilitate risk management of funding costs and currency conversions by operating firms and others. They are also foundational to many alternative investment strategies that use the contracts to engineer desired risk exposures.

6.2.1 Forward Rate Agreements

Chapter 5 demonstrated how an investor with a long position in one zero-coupon bond and a short position in another zero-coupon bond could be viewed as having locked in a borrowing rate or a lending rate during the time interval between the maturities of the bonds (ignoring default risk). This section discusses financial derivatives that accomplish the same objective of locking in borrowing and lending *rates* (and currency conversion rates). Two common short-term rates that serve as the reference rates in forward rate agreements are LIBOR for U.S. dollars and Euribor for Euros. A **reference rate** is a market rate specified in contracts such as a forward contract that fluctuates with market conditions and drives the magnitude and direction of cash settlements.

A **forward rate agreement** (FRA) is a cash-settled contract in which one party agrees to offer a specified or fixed *rate* (the FRA rate), such as an interest rate on a specified principal amount and over a specified time in the future (or a currency exchange rate at a specified time in the future) while the other party agrees to provide that rate. In the case of a forward rate agreement on an interest rate, the payer in the contract effectively agrees to pay the interest rate over a specified time interval based on a specified notional amount while the receiver in the contract effectively agrees to receive that rate. The term *notional principal* is used to indicate that the principal amount is not actually exchanged, but rather serves to scale the size of the rate-related payments. The contract is settled with a payment based on the amount by which the FRA rate differs from the actual market rate at the time of settlement (the reference rate) multiplied by the notional amount.

The buyer of the FRA uses the FRA for protection against interest rate increases by locking in a fixed future rate (the FRA rate) to borrow (e.g., meet funding needs) rather than pay whatever subsequent borrowing rates occur (e.g., LIBOR). The FRA buyer receives cash at settlement when the reference rate exceeds the FRA rate and makes payment to the FRA seller when the reference rate is less than the FRA rate.

For example, consider a three-month FRA (to be settled in several years) with an FRA rate of 5% and a notional value of $1,000,000. At the time of settlement the actual market interest rate (LIBOR) rises to 6%. The FRA would require the FRA seller to pay the buyer $2,500 because LIBOR, the reference rate, is above the FRA, found as follows: [$1,000,000 × (3 mos./12 mos.) × (6%–5%)]. Had the reference rate fallen to 4%, the buyer would pay the seller $2,500. In practice, the cash settlement amount is usually based on a discounted value (i.e., the $2,500 would be discounted for the length of the loan—three months in this example) and would be payable at the start of the period when the market rate is observed. The example illustrates the important ability of an FRA to allow financial entities to control their borrowing costs and lending revenues.

6.2.2 Forward Rate Agreements and Implied Forward Interest Rates

Chapter 5 detailed the concept of implying forward default-free interest rates from observing default-free spot rates. In a perfect market, the FRA rate will be equal to:

$$F_{T-t} = [(T \times r_T) - (t \times r_t)]/(T - t) \tag{6.2}$$

In practice, continuous compounding is not used, nothing is truly default-free, and markets are not perfect. Nevertheless, Equation 6.2 works well as an approximation and it conveys the primary point of risk-neutral pricing of forward contracts: Initial forward contract prices and rates are not driven toward equaling expected future spot prices and rates. Rather, they are implied from spot rates. Equation 6.2 is quite intuitive. The forward rate is shown to be the difference between the longer-term interest rate and the shorter-term interest rate, with each rate being averaged over its longevity. For example, if the five-year rate is 5% and the four-year rate is 4%, the forward rate on a one-year security settling in four years must be 9% (i.e., 25% – 16%).

☞ APPLICATION 6.2.2A

A three-year riskless security trades at a yield of 3.4%, whereas a forward contract on a two-year riskless security that settles in three years trades at a forward rate of 2.4%. Assuming that the rates are continuously compounded, what is the no-arbitrage yield of a five-year riskless security?

Inserting 3.4% as the shorter-term rate in Equation 6.2 and 2.4% as the left side of Equation 6.2, the longer-term rate, R_T, can be solved as 3.0%, noting that $T = 5$ and $t = 3$. Note that earning 3.0% for five years (15%) is equal to the sum of earning 3.4% for three years (10.2%) and 2.4% for two years (4.8%). The rates may be summed due to the assumption of continuous compounding.

6.2.3 Forward Rates and Their Extensions

The point being made in this chapter is that given the prices (section 6.1) or rates (this section) from the spot market for the underlying cash instruments (i.e., the prices of shorter-term and longer-term securities), there is only one arbitrage-free price or rate of the forward contract that spans the maturity dates. Arbitrage-free price and rate relationships will hold in a perfectly efficient market, but no market is perfectly efficient. When actual market prices deviate from arbitrage-free prices, investors may use skill-based strategies that attempt to earn superior profits by anticipating that relative prices will tend to revert toward their arbitrage-free levels. Relative value hedge fund strategies (discussed in Chapter 17) are examples of such strategies.

Another type of financial derivative is a swap. A **swap** is a string of forward contracts grouped together that vary by time to settlement. Thus, a commodity swap is a portfolio of commodity forwards. Typically, the settlement times are equally spaced. For example, an oil refinery might regularly need to purchase crude oil. Rather than bear the risk of fluctuating oil prices, the refinery may decide to lock in the purchase price of the oil by entering various forward contracts to purchase the oil at prespecified prices (i.e., to swap cash for oil). Instead of entering into a series of separate forward contracts, the refinery may enter into a single swap that calls for quarterly or monthly exchanges through time at prices set at the initiation of the swap. Swaps are discussed in greater detail in Chapter 24.

Some alternative investment strategies use swaps to manage risk exposures. The risk of a swap is formed from the risk exposures of the forward contracts that comprise it. Thus, like forward contracts, interest rate swaps allow for the transfer of interest rate risk. Analogously, commodity swaps and currency swaps allow for the transfer of commodity risks and currency risks.

6.3 FORWARD CONTRACTS ON EQUITIES

This section discusses the forward prices set when forward contracts are initiated and when the deliverable or reference asset is a risky asset such as a stock price or an index value. To the extent that the asset underlying the forward contract has systematic risk, the underlying asset will have an expected return that exceeds the riskless interest rate. Financial derivatives on individual equities and equity indices are widely used in alternative investments.

6.3.1 Determining the Forward Contract Price of a Stock with No Dividends

This section describes the model for determining the no-arbitrage forward price of risky assets, such as common stocks and stock indices, that pay no dividends. Consider a long position in a growth stock currently valued at P_0 that will not pay dividends for a long time. Any investor who buys the stock at time 0 at P_0 receives no dividends but can sell the stock at any time T at its market price, P_T. As an alternative strategy an investor can establish a long position in a forward contract on that stock at time 0 for settlement at time T. What would be the equilibrium forward price on this stock, F_T, for a forward contract initiated at time 0 for settlement at time T? The answer to this question reveals the essence of forward pricing and lays a foundation on which to build more robust models.

Long positions in forward contracts are commonly and correctly described as financed positions. **Financed positions** enable economic ownership of an asset without the posting of the purchase price. A long position in a forward contract provides the same economic exposure as a cash position but is obtained without bearing the opportunity cost of funding a cash position. Thus, the key difference between owning the previously mentioned stock versus having a long position in a forward contract on that stock is that the forward position does not require an initial cash outlay (although it may require posting collateral).

A long position in a forward contract held to settlement has only one cash flow, which occurs at time T and is based on the difference between the stock's value at time T and the forward price for the contract on the stock that settles at time T: $P_T - F_T$. The short side to the forward contract has the same cash flow with the opposite sign: $F_T - P_T$. Throughout this chapter, it is assumed that forward contracts are established such that the immediate market value of the contract is zero (i.e., there is no cash payment required from either side to initiate the contract).

Consider an arbitrageur who buys the stock at time 0 and simultaneously establishes a short position in a forward contract to sell the stock at time T for F_T. The cash flows to the arbitrageur are $-P_0$ at time 0 to buy the stock, $+P_T$ from selling the stock at time T, and $F_T - P_T$ at time T from the settlement of the forward contract. Equivalently, the arbitrageur can be viewed as delivering the stock $(-P_T)$ to the long side and receiving the forward price $(+F_T)$ instead of settling the contract with cash $(F_T - P_T)$. Since the arbitrageur's short position in the forward contract hedges the risk of the long cash position in the stock, the transaction is riskless and competition will drive the expected return to zero. The net present value (NPV) of the arbitrage is zero and the proceeds at time T are discounted (note that P_T cancels out):

$$NPV = 0 = -P_0 + F_T e^{-rT} \tag{6.3}$$

Note that the subscript to the riskless interest rate has been dropped for expositional simplicity. In all cases where the subscript is dropped, the rate refers to the riskless spot rate with a longevity equal to the time to the respective cash flow or contract settlement. Factoring generates the formula for F_T—the formula for the forward value in Equation 6.5 of a financial asset with no dividends or other distributions:

$$F_T = P_0 e^{rT} \tag{6.4}$$

6.3.2 The Forward Contract Price and Accrued Funding Costs

An important way to conceptualize Equation 6.4 is that $P_0 e^{rT}$ is the amount of debt that an arbitrageur (with a short position in a forward contract on the stock) would accrue from borrowing P_0 dollars at time 0 (to buy the stock), continuously accruing interest on the loan at the rate r and then delivering the stock to the short side of the forward contract at F_T. This riskless transaction must have no return in a perfectly competitive market.

☞ APPLICATION 6.3.2A

A stock sells for $100 and is certain not to make any cash distributions in the next year. A forward contract on that stock trades with a settlement in one year. Assuming that the interest rate corresponding to one year is 5% compounded continuously, what is the no-arbitrage price of this forward contract?

A one-year forward contract on the stock must trade at $105.13 using Equation 6.4. At settlement, a long position in the forward contract obligates the holder to pay $105.13 in exchange for delivery of the stock. If the holder of the forward contract places the stock's initial value ($100) in an account (or as collateral) offering at 5% continuously compounded return, the $100 investment will enable the purchase of the stock at the end of the year without further cash.

Application 6.3.2A starkly illustrates the simplicity of forward pricing by showing that in the case of risky assets with no intervening cash flows (e.g., no dividends), the forward price of the asset is very simply the current market price grossed up for the time value of money rather than being a forecast of the stock's future market value.

6.3.3 The Forward Price, the Riskless Interest Rate, and Risk Neutrality

Note that the forward price, F_T, in Equation 6.4 depends on the riskless rate rather than a rate with a risk premium associated with the risk of the equity that underlies the forward contract. The forward price is established at time 0 and in the case of Equation 6.4 is the *risk-neutral future value* of P_0 because it is compounded forward at a riskless rate as if market participants were risk-neutral rather than risk-averse. This use of riskless rates to compound forward risky values at the riskless rate (and to discount risky cash flows at the riskless rate) is central to risk-neutral modeling. The astonishing simplicity of valuation when cash flows can be compounded forward and discounted backward at easily observable riskless interest rates is why financial derivative valuation models are so powerful and derivatives can be such effective risk management tools. Risk-neutral modeling and the resulting valuation models for financial derivatives (e.g., binomial tree models) are key breakthroughs.

Let's examine the intuition of Equation 6.4. It is only by setting the forward contract price equal to $P_0 e^{rT}$ at the initiation of the contract that the long position in a forward contract (who bears the risk of fluctuations in the stock) has an expected profit equal to the risk premium of the stock. Because an asset with systematic risk is expected to grow at a rate higher than the riskless rate, the long side of the forward contract in Equation 6.4 can expect to earn a profit because the forward price uses a lower rate (the riskless rate) to discount future cash flows. Conversely, the short side—who can use the forward contract to lay off the risk of holding the stock—should expect to incur a loss on average from the forward contract because the forward contract transfers the risk of the stock from the entity holding the short position to the entity holding the long position. It therefore makes sense that the forward contract should contain a forward price that offers an expected profit to the long side and an expected loss to the short side.

Another way to view the result is that the only difference, in theory, between the forward contract and cash possession of the stock is that the forward contract is "financed"—it does not require an investment of P_0 at inception. These "savings" relative to buying the stock now must raise the forward contract price by the riskless rate so that the two can coexist in equilibrium—but not by so much (the risky rate) that there would be no expected profit for bearing the risks of being long a forward contract on a risky asset.

6.3.4 The Forward Price of a Financial Asset Is an Equality Given the Riskless Interest Rate

A final important point is that Equation 6.4 is an equality, not just an inequality. The relationship between the forward price and the spot price was justified by the potential for arbitrage if the relationship did not hold. The discussion of that arbitrage in section 6.3.1 described the ability of an arbitrageur to establish a short position in the forward contract and a long position in the underlying asset. This arbitrage makes sure that the forward price is not too high. But the opposite arbitrage approach (establishing a long position in the forward contract and a short position in the underlying asset) will make sure that the forward price is not too low; thus the ability to buy or short sell the underlying asset forces Equation 6.4 to be an equality.

Exhibit 6.1 plots hypothetical forward prices on a non-dividend-paying financial asset against the forward contract's time to delivery (or settlement). The relationship depicted is consistent with Equation 6.4 and a flat term structure of riskless interest rates. Forward contracts with greater longevity tend to have higher forward prices because the contracts offer the long-side investors exposure to the underlying financial asset at a purchase price that is deferred until delivery. Exhibit 6.1 may be viewed as the cumulative savings on funding costs (i.e., the opportunity cost of the capital) by using a forward contract to obtain its underlying asset on a deferred-payment basis rather purchasing the asset in the cash market.

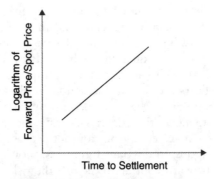

EXHIBIT 6.1   The Term Structure of
Forward Contracts on an Equity Index

6.3.5 Determining the Forward Contract Price of a Stock with Dividends

Let's return to the example of a forward contract on a stock (or stock index) in Application 6.3.2A (section 6.3.2). Recall the forward contract was found to have a \$105.13 forward price, which was simply found by compounding the stock's current \$100 value forward for one year at the riskless interest rate of 5%. The result emanated from the perspective of an arbitrageur with a long position in the stock and a short position in the forward contract that generated the following NPV:

$$NPV = 0 = -P_0 + F_T e^{-rT} \tag{6.5}$$

Let's relax the assumption of no dividends in that example by including a non-zero dividend. Specifically, let's assume that the stock will pay a \$3 dividend with certainty immediately prior to the expiration of the forward contract. The arbitrageur now collects \$3 extra at time T. So the new NPV is:

$$NPV = 0 = -P_0 + F_T e^{-rT} - \$3 e^{-rT},$$

so

$$F_T = P_0 e^{rT} - \$3$$

Here is the key result: The anticipated dividend of the stock lowers the forward price. A more realistic assumption is to recognize smaller, more frequent dividends. However, the assumption that dividends are paid continuously offers a simple and convenient formula for the forward price of a forward contract on a dividend-paying risky asset such as a stock:

$$F_T = P_0 e^{(r-q)T} \tag{6.6}$$

where q is the dividend yield on the forward contract's underlying asset expressed as a continuously paid annual dividend rate. For example, consider the stock with no dividend in Application 6.3.2A (with a riskless rate of 5%). Let's change the dividend assumption to having the stock distribute a continuous dividend at an annual rate of 3% (i.e., the stock's annual dividend yield). The forward price would be \$102.02 using Equation 6.6.

$$F_T = \$100 e^{(.05-.03) \times 1} = \$102.02$$

☞ APPLICATION 6.3.5A

A stock sells for \$50 and it pays a continuous dividend yield of 1% per year. Assuming a 5% continuously compounded riskless rate, what is the no-arbitrage price of this forward contract with a time to settlement or delivery of 0.25 years?

The formula for the forward contract on a dividend-paying risky asset is:

$$F_T = P_0 e^{(r-q)T}$$
$$F_T = \$50 e^{(.05-.01) \times 0.25}$$
$$F_T = \$50.5025$$

To the holder of a long position in a forward contract on a dividend-paying stock, the dividend is a *cost* that drains value out of the stock before the forward contract holder is able to take possession of the stock. Inspection of Equation 6.6 reveals two key results:

1. Higher funding costs to cash positions (i.e., higher riskless rates) make forward contracts more valuable because higher forward contracts are "financed positions." Therefore, the riskless rate enters Equation 6.6 with a positive sign.
2. Higher dividend payouts reduce the value of a forward contract by eroding the value of its underlying asset prior to settlement or delivery. Therefore the dividend yield enters Equation 6.6 with a negative sign.

These two results are why the funding rate (the riskless rate) and the dividend have opposite signs in Equation 6.6 and will guide the derivation of a formula for a forward price on physical assets in section 6.4.

6.3.6 Four Cases of the Forward Curves of Financial Asset Prices

The forward prices for financial assets are described in Equation 6.6. This section expounds on Equation 6.6 and analyzes the model in four cases with regard to its two parameters: the riskless rate, r (the funding cost), and q, the continuous rate of dividends (or other distributions, such as coupons). The forward curve (i.e., the term structure of forward prices) is derived for each case.

CASE 1: NO DIVIDENDS AND NO INTEREST: In this simplest case, all forward prices with different delivery dates are equal, and are all equal to the spot price, P. This can be verified using Equation 6.6 with $r = q = 0$. The logic of this case is that in the absence of dividends and financing costs, there are no differences between transactions with immediate delivery (spot market) or deferred delivery (forward market). Thus, forward prices must equal spot prices. Thus, any slope or curvature of the forward curve must be driven entirely by dividend rates and financing costs.

Exhibit 6.2 illustrates the case of a flat term structure of forward prices, using the horizontal line in the middle of the three structures. The length of time, if any, by which the transaction is deferred (i.e., the time to delivery of the contract) does not change the price at which delivery will take place, since cash pays no interest and the asset pays no dividends. Buyers and sellers are indifferent between immediate exchange and deferred exchange at the same price. Exhibit 6.2 also illustrates an

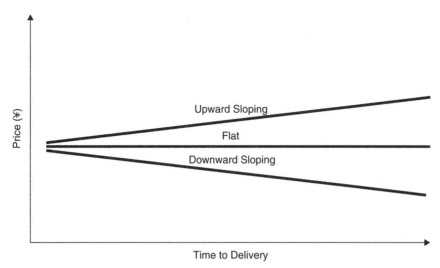

EXHIBIT 6.2   Forward Term Structures

upward-sloping and a downward-sloping relationship. In the case of forward contracts on financial securities, the slopes must be related to the cost-of-carry factors of interest rates and dividends (both of which were assumed to be equal to zero in the previous discussion).

CASE 2: INTEREST RATES EQUAL THE DIVIDEND RATE: When $r - q = 0$, Equation 6.6 is the same as when both rates are zero. Hence, all the forward prices are equal to the spot price, and the term structure of forward prices is flat. The intuition is that when the benefit of using the spot market (being able to receive dividends) equals the cost of using the spot market (the borrowing cost or opportunity cost of purchasing the asset for cash), the spot and forward prices must be equal.

☞ **APPLICATION 6.3.6A**

If the spot price of an equity index that pays a dividend yield equal to the riskless rate is $500, what is the one-year forward price on the equity index?

The forward contract of every time to delivery has a forward price of exactly $500. Market participants would be indifferent between buying and selling the index in the spot market with instant delivery or in the forward market with delayed delivery because the interest payments and dividends offset each other.

CASE 3: INTEREST RATES EXCEED THE DIVIDEND RATE: When $r > q$, then $e^{(r-q)T} > 1$, and forward prices will be higher for higher values of T. Hence, forward prices are increasing in T, and the term structure of forward prices will be upward sloping. Thus, if the spot price of an equity index that pays dividends is $500 and if the riskless interest rate exceeds the dividend rate, then every forward contract of every time to delivery will have a forward price equal to $\$500e^{(r-q)T}$, where $(r - q)$ is positive and $e^{(r-q)T}$ is increasing in T.

 APPLICATION 6.3.6B

Assuming a continuously compounded annual interest rate of 5%, if the spot price of an equity index with 2% continuously paid dividends is $500, what would be the forward price on the equity index with settlement in three months? The price of every forward contract on that index for every time to settlement would be $500e^{(0.05-0.02)T}$. The three-month forward price would be $500e^{(0.03 \times 0.25)}$, or $503.76. Six-month and 12-month forward prices would be $507.56 and $515.23, respectively (found by inserting 0.50 and 1.00 for T, and 0.03 for $r - q$).

Market participants would be indifferent between (1) using cash to buy the index in the spot market and (2) using forward markets, saving interest (r), forgoing dividends (q), and paying a higher price in the forward market than the spot price. The higher forward price than spot price offsets the net gains that forward market participants receive in the form of interest savings that exceed lost dividends.

CASE 4: THE DIVIDEND RATE EXCEEDS THE INTEREST RATE: When $r < q$, then $e^{(r-q)T} < 1$, and forward prices will be lower for higher values of T. With $(r - q) < 0$, $e^{(r-d)T}$ is less than one and decreasing in T. The case of $(r - q) < 0$ is illustrated in Exhibit 6.2 with a downward-sloping forward curve.

 APPLICATION 6.3.6C

Assuming a continuously compounded annual interest rate of 2%, if the spot price of an equity index with 3% continuously paid dividends is $500, what would be the forward price of a contract with settlement in three months? The price of every forward contract of every time to delivery would be $500e^{(-0.01)T}$, with $(r - q) = -1\%$. The three-month forward price would be $500e^{-0.01 \times 0.25}$, or $498.75. Six-month and 12-month forward prices would be $497.51 and $495.02, respectively (found by inserting 0.50 and 1.00 for T).

An intuitive explanation of why prospective dividends and coupon payments reduce forward prices is that the cash distributions lower the value of a financial asset (i.e., financial asset prices generally fall on days when dividend payments are made). These anticipated declines in spot prices are reflected in the reduction of the prices of forward contracts that call for delivery after the cash distributions.

There is another way to view why forward prices are less than spot prices when q is high and r is low: The value of the deliverable security may be viewed as the sum of the present value of its dividend stream up to time T and the present value of its market price at time T. Conceptually, the underlier of a forward contract is only the second term (the present value of the security's future market price). In effect, the inclusion of q in Equation 6.4 may be viewed as lowering the value of the financial asset to remove the present value of the dividend stream.

In summary, for forward contracts on financial securities, the slope and curvature of the term structure of forward prices (the forward curve) are driven entirely by the relationship between the underlying security's dividend yield and the riskless interest rate (both of which may vary in T). The forward curve will be flat when $r = q$, upward sloping when $r > q$, and downward sloping when $q > r$. An understanding of these relations serves as an important foundation for understanding many of the issues involved with investing in commodities through futures contracts.

6.4 FORWARD CONTRACTS ON ASSETS WITH BENEFITS AND COSTS OF CARRY

This section discusses the economic benefits and costs of carrying or holding a cash position versus holding a forward position and the implication of those benefits and costs for the pricing of forward contracts. The section moves the focus from financial assets toward physical assets such as commodities.

6.4.1 The Benefits and Costs of Carry

In the context of forward contracts, a **cost of carry** (or **carrying cost**) is any direct financial difference between maintaining a position in the cash market and maintaining a position in the forward market. For example, being physically long wheat requires storage (and generates storage costs), whereas being long a forward contract on wheat does not require physical storage.

Cost-of-carry models use projections of carrying costs and benefits to value derivatives such as forward contracts. The modeling approach is to identify two strategies that have identical payoffs (cash market vs. forward market) and attribute differences in current prices to differences in the costs of carrying each strategy. A cost-of-carry model assumes that in an informationally efficient market, when two positions converge to an equivalent value at some point in the future, any differences in their current values will be determined exactly by the differences in their carrying costs (and benefits).

Exhibit 6.3 lists the categories of carrying costs and benefits for real (physical) assets and for financial assets.

There are two key entries in Exhibit 6.3 that warrant special consideration: convenience and storage. Convenience, expressed in a rate as **convenience yield** (y), is the economic benefit that the holder of a physical inventory (e.g., a commodity) receives from directly holding the inventory rather than having a long position in a forward contract on the physical assets.

Gold provides a vivid example of convenience yield. For a firm that uses gold in its production process, such as a jewelry manufacturer, an inventory of gold helps

EXHIBIT 6.3   Benefits and Costs of Direct Ownership

	Real Assets	Financial Assets
Benefits	Convenience (y)	Dividends + Coupons (d)
Costs	Interest (r) + Storage (c)	Interest (r) + Custody (zero)

protect it from supply disruptions. A forward contract on gold might offer protection from changes in the market price of gold, but ultimately the jewelry manufacturer needs physical inventory to ensure that production will not be disrupted. For another holder of gold, the convenience yield of the gold inventory may be the value to the holder of having an emergency asset that might offer exchange value during even the most terrible times for the economy. In both cases, physical ownership of the asset may be viewed as more valuable than synthetic ownership (i.e., ownership through a forward contract to take delivery), since the physical ownership provides a more immediate and certain ability to use the asset for an intended purpose.

Convenience yield serves the holder of a nonfinancial commodity in the same direction that the dividend yield serves the owner of a financial asset; therefore, dividends and convenience yield both enter pricing models with the same sign (a negative sign to denote that a benefit is the same as a negative cost). However, a key distinction is that different market participants have different convenience yields for a given physical asset that vary based on their individual circumstances, whereas each holder of a particular financial asset receives the same dividends (or interest). For example, natural gas can have substantially different convenience yields—which in turn can vary based on seasons and weather (due to its use as a heating fuel). This is in contrast to the benefits of financial assets shown in Exhibit 6.3 (dividends and other distributions), which tend to have clear and somewhat unanimously perceived economic values.

Storage costs of physical assets (e.g., commodities) involve such expenditures as warehouse fees, insurance, transportation, and spoilage. Storage costs are of the sign opposite to that of dividends, since they are costs of holding the underlying asset rather than benefits. Accordingly, the storage costs expressed as a continuous rate, c, can be an important determinant in the pricing relationship. Storage costs enter using the same sign as r, the opportunity cost of capital, since both reflect costs of ownership of a physical commodity. In fact, the financing cost, r, of holding the physical commodity can be included as part of c. However, storage costs for physical assets such as natural gas can vary substantially between market participants. This is in contrast to the opportunity cost of capital (r) of both financial assets and physical assets, which tend to have clear and somewhat unanimously perceived economic values.

Note that Exhibit 6.3 depicts carrying costs of holding physical assets. The storage costs are positive carrying costs that, everything else equal, make holding a physical inventory unattractive. Forward contracts on the same commodity do not have storage costs. Therefore the storage costs of physical assets, c, make forward contracts more attractive than physical inventories, everything else equal. Of course everything else is usually not equal. Physical inventories typically offer convenience yield, y, which is an attractive feature that forward contracts do not offer. This explains why $c - y$ must appear in a model of the relative values of forward prices and spot prices on commodities.

6.4.2 The Forward Price of a Commodity

Equation 6.6 provides the formula for a forward price on a financial asset based on the spot price of the underlying asset that uses two variables: the riskless interest rate and the underlying asset's dividend yield. The right side of Exhibit 6.3 lists these two variables as costs (the riskless rate reflects the cost of carry of a cash position) and benefits (the dividend yield is a benefit of a cash position), respectively. Replacing the costs and benefits of carrying a cash position of a financial asset with the costs and benefits of carrying physical inventory (the left side of Exhibit 6.3) generates the formula for a forward contract on a commodity in Equation 6.7.

$$F_T \leq P_0 e^{(r+c-y)T} \tag{6.7}$$

where r is the spot interest rate corresponding to a time to maturity of T years, c is the commodity's storage cost, and y is the commodity's convenience yields, all expressed as continuously compounded annual rates.

Note that the relationship is expressed as an inequality in Equation 6.7 in contrast to the equality relationship for a financial asset in Equation 6.6. This is due to potential problems with short-selling a physical asset.

☞ APPLICATION 6.4.2A

Consider a six-month forward contract on a commodity that trades at a spot price of $50. The commodity has marketwide convenience yields of 3%, storage costs of 2%, and financing costs (interest rates) of 7%. What is the price of the six-month forward contract on the commodity? The forward price is $51.52, found by placing $0.5(7\% + 2\% - 3\%)$ in as the exponent of Equation 6.7, $50 as P_0, and solving for F_T.

Dividing through Equation 6.7 by P_0, assuming that it is an equality, and taking the logarithm of each side and factoring, generates:

$$\text{Implied growth rate of forward over spot} = r + c - y$$

In words, the price ratio of the forward price to the spot price (expressed as a continuously compounded rate) is the sum of the two benefits to having the forward position (avoiding the carrying costs of a physical inventory including financing costs and storage costs) minus the cost to an investor of using a forward contract rather than a physical inventory (losing the convenience yield).

6.4.3 Four Factors Differentiating Forward Pricing on Financial and Physical Assets

Previous sections detailed the arbitrage-free price of a forward contract on a financial security based on comparing the carrying costs of a spot market transaction with those of a forward market transaction. This section contrasts the determinants of forward prices for financial securities with the determinants of forward prices for commodities.

A central concept in understanding forward contracts is that in the simple case of forward contracts on financial securities, the forward prices of the contracts are driven entirely by spot prices including the level and shape of the term structure of interest rates (and prospective dividend yields). Formulas for the forward prices therefore contain current market values, such as spot prices, and current rates, such as risk-free interest rates and dividend yields. Arbitrageurs able to hedge either long or short positions in the forward contracts force the relationship to hold.

Forward prices on financial assets do not reveal information on future price changes beyond the information already contained in spot prices. For example, it is a mistake to interpret the shape of forward interest rate curves as containing information beyond what is in the term structure of spot rates because there is a one-to-one relationship between the two structures. Similarly, expected spot prices do not drive the spread between forward prices and spot prices for financial assets.

However, forward prices on physical assets are different. Many alternative investment strategies involve forward contracts (or futures contracts, detailed later in this chapter) on assets other than financial securities, in particular, commodities. Commodity forward prices and the term structure of forward prices on commodities often do not adhere to a strict cost-of-carry relationship for several reasons. The forward structure's shape for commodities and other real assets can be driven by at least four additional factors: (1) forecasts of supply and demand changes, (2) storage cost differentials, (3) convenience yield differentials, and (4) difficulties with short selling.

6.4.4 Challenges Involving Measuring Storage Costs and Convenience Yields

If c and y are observable marketwide values and if physical assets can be limitlessly short sold, forward contracts would be strictly priced according to Equation 6.7 in perfect and competitive markets. However, storage costs and convenience yields of physical assets have a very important difference relative to the dividend yield on financial assets: Storage costs and convenience yield can be expected to vary with location and market participants, as well as with supply and demand.

For example, storage costs for natural gas are seasonal on account of increased winter demand. Storage costs for agricultural and other products can be seasonal as well, relating to harvest times. Since anticipated supply and demand factors can cause storage costs to vary through time, the pricing relationships between forward contracts of different delivery dates (i.e., the term structure of forward prices) can reflect anticipated supply and demand. Further, storage costs vary between participants.

From the perspective of an individual entity, Equation 6.7 can be viewed as associating the entity's storage costs and convenience yields with the relative values of the spot and forward prices of the commodity. From the marketwide perspective, Equation 6.7 can be viewed as relating the relationship between the forward and spot prices of a commodity to the spread between the storage costs and convenience yield $(c - y)$ of the *marginal market participant*. The **marginal market participant** to a derivative contract is any entity with individual costs and benefits that make the entity indifferent between physical positions and synthetic positions.

As in the case of storage costs, convenience yield can be expected to vary through time and across market participants and locations. One entity might perceive tremendous advantage from having a large supply of a commodity in inventory (i.e., being able to meet unexpected demand or unforeseen supply disruptions), and another entity might perceive little advantage.

The convenience yield of a particular commodity to a consumer or a producer would typically be much higher when there is a general shortage of the commodity (i.e., low inventories). Thus, a manufacturer of silver-plated products would derive

Natural Gas Futures Prices

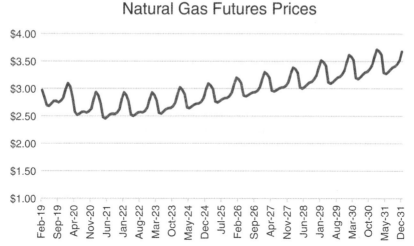

EXHIBIT 6.4   Term Structure of Natural Gas Futures Closing Prices
Source: Data from Bloomberg.

more convenience yield from holding an inventory of silver at a time when silver is scarce and the danger of being unable to obtain adequate silver supplies is higher.

The potential for storage costs and convenience yield to vary through time and have predictable changes through time adds to the reasons that the term structure of forward prices will not be monotonically upward sloping or downward sloping as depicted in Exhibit 6.2. In the case of a commodity such as natural gas, Exhibit 6.4 demonstrates a pronounced wave pattern of the term structure of forward prices to reflect the anticipated effects of seasonal demand on storage costs and convenience yield.

Further, the idea that the slope and shape of the term structure of forward prices depends not only on observed values (e.g., the riskless rates and dividend yields) but also on predictions of supply and demand means that superior supply and demand forecasting may offer superior returns to market participants better able to predict supply and demand. In other words, market participants can speculate on the shapes and slopes of the term structure of forward prices and may consistently generate superior returns if their abilities to forecast supply and demand (and, to a lesser extent, storage costs and convenience yields) are superior.

6.4.5   Short Selling of Physical Assets

Section 2.8 discussed short-selling of financial assets, wherein there is a well-organized market for the lending and borrowing of stocks and bonds. Previous sections in this chapter have relied on the actions of hypothetical arbitrageurs to force specific relations between forward prices and spot prices based on carrying costs and benefits. Specifically, Equation 6.6 is premised on the ability of arbitrageurs to establish long positions in a forward contract to hedge a short position in its underlying asset and establish short positions in a forward contract to hedge a long position in its underlying asset because the asset is a financial asset.

But developed markets for lending *physical* assets such as commodities do not exist to the extent that such markets exist for lending financial assets. Without commodity lending, the arbitrageurs cannot short-sell commodities to form a hedge against a long position in a forward contract. This inability to hedge a long position in a forward contract inhibits the ability of arbitrageurs to take on long positions in a forward contract, thereby preventing arbitrage from driving underpriced forward prices to their theoretical values. As a result, Equation 6.7 expresses the forward price as being less than or equal to its theoretical value in the case of a forward contract on a physical asset when that physical asset (the underlying asset) cannot be shorted.

6.4.6 Forward Contracts with Nonzero Market Value

The material on forward contracts in the previous sections has focused on the forward price (or rate) that is set at the initiation of the forward contract under the assumption that the contract is initiated with a market value of zero (i.e., no cash is exchanged between the parties to initiate the contract). It is possible that the long and short sides of the contract agreed to a forward price that caused the contract to have a nonzero initial value, especially if one of the sides of the contract made an immediate payment to the other side to initiate the contract. Further, it is expected that forward contracts will take on various positive or negative values to each side of the contract after the contract is initiated as the market price (or rate) of the contract's underlying asset (or rate) moves up or down.

Equation 6.8 expresses the value to the long side of a forward contract under the assumption that the underlying asset can be readily short-sold.

$$\text{Value of long position in forward contract at time } t = P_t e^{(r+c-y)(T-t)} - F_0 \quad (6.8)$$

where P_t is the price of the contract's underlying (deliverable) asset at time t, F_0 is the forward price of the contract (set at the contract's initiation to generate a zero value to the contract), and other variables are as previously defined (included at their time t values). The value to the short side has the opposite sign in a perfect market. Note that at $t = T$, the value of the forward contract is $P_T - F_0$, which is the cash settlement to (from) the long side from (to) the short side when $P_T - F_0$ is positive (negative).

👉 APPLICATION 6.4.6A

Consider a forward contract with three-month delivery on a commodity that currently trades at a spot price of $110. The commodity has a current market-wide convenience yield of 2%, storage costs of 4%, and financing costs (interest rates) of 6%. If the forward price in the contract is $101.00, what is the value of the contract to the long side assuming that the underlying commodity can be readily short sold? The value of the contract to the long side is found using Equation 6.8, the forward price of $101.00, and using $0.25(6\% + 4\% - 2\%)$ as the exponent of Equation 6.8. Noting that the time remaining $(T - t)$ is 0.25 and using $110 as P_0 solves for the contract's value, $11.22, to the long side of the contract (and a value of –$11.22 to the short side).

6.5 FORWARD CONTRACTS VERSUS FUTURES CONTRACTS

Forward contracts were discussed in moderate detail in sections 6.1–6.4. This section discusses futures contracts on underlying financial assets and physical assets (i.e., commodities).

Both forward contracts and futures contracts are binding agreements for the purchase or sale of an asset but with deferred exchanges of the asset and the cash.

6.5.1 Trading Differences between Forward Contracts and Futures Contracts

In introductory material, the terms *forward contract* and *futures contract* are often used interchangeably due to their similarities: The hallmark of both contracts is the deferred delivery, and both contracts are priced with similar principles. One major distinction between the two is that forward contracts are typically over-the-counter (OTC) contracts, whereas futures contracts are exchange traded. Since futures contracts are traded on an organized exchange, they share the same advantages as other listed securities: a central marketplace and transparent pricing. Compared to most forward contracts, futures contracts also enjoy clearinghouse security, uniform contract size and terms, and daily liquidity.

Forward contracts are ad hoc contracts negotiated between two parties, with flexibility regarding the details to help meet the needs and preferences of each party. As exchange-traded contracts, futures contracts are standardized. Each futures contract trades with a relatively high degree of uniformity with regard to the quantity and quality of the underlying asset and the location and time of delivery.

The standardization of futures contracts permits active trading and liquidity. At any point in time, the long futures position holder can close a position by establishing an identical short position (so that the long position and short position net to zero). Similarly, the short futures position can close a position by entering an offsetting long position. The outstanding quantity of unclosed contracts is known as **open interest**. If the buyer (i.e., long) of the futures contract does not wish to take delivery of the underlying asset, the buyer closes out the long futures position at the prevailing market price of the contract by taking on a short position. Similarly, if the holder of a short position does not wish to deliver the underlying asset, the holder can establish an offsetting long position prior to delivery. Only a very small percentage of futures contracts (usually less than 1%) result in delivery of the underlying asset. The point is that the primary purpose of futures (and forward) contracts is to exchange risks, rather than to serve as vehicles for arranging physical transfers of goods. The idea is that by using futures markets to manage risk, a party can take or make delivery of physical goods using the cash market with the lowest transportation or other costs.

Forward contracts are over-the-counter contracts between two parties that contain the terms and conditions agreed on by the two parties. These terms and conditions include how much, if any, collateral is required; the size of the contract; and the delivery details (including time, quality, and location). Since the contracts are not standardized, there are usually no market prices that can be observed to directly value the position. If the holder of a long or short position in a forward contract wishes to terminate or hedge the exposure, there is no ready secondary market of identical contracts available. The entity wishing to terminate the exposure to a forward may attempt to negotiate an exit with the counterparty to the forward or establish a new forward contract with another party, which will serve to offset the risk. Whereas long and short positions in the same futures contract will close a position, the same is not true for forward contracts. Because forward contracts are specific to a given counterparty, a transaction can only be closed with the same counterparty. Although a long and short forward position with two different counterparties will neutralize market exposure, counterparty risk remains. Nevertheless, the flexibility of forward contracts makes them very popular. The most prominent forward market is the currency forward market, which is substantially more liquid than the currency futures market.

Many of the distinctions between forward and futures contracts may disappear over time. Due to the Dodd-Frank Act in the United States and new regulations throughout the world, market structures are changing. If OTC markets are required to offer greater transparency and participate in a central clearing system, forwards will become more like exchange-traded futures contracts.

6.5.2 The Mechanics of Marking-to-Market

A critical distinction between most futures and forward contracts is that futures contracts are marked-to-market. The term **marked-to-market** means that the side of a futures contract that benefits from a price change receives cash from the other side of the contract (and vice versa) throughout the contract's life. The cash exchanges resulting from positions being marked-to-market are intended to cause each side of the derivative to have a zero market value at the end of each day. The reason that each contract has a zero value at the end of the day is that the price at which the commodity is promised to be delivered is adjusted to the current futures price as a result of the marking-to-market process.

The following example provides a closer examination of the process of marking-to-market. Consider a trader who establishes a long position in a gold futures contract at €1,000 per ounce on Monday morning. The trader has promised to buy gold for €1,000 per ounce unless the trader closes the position by establishing a short position that offsets the original long position prior to the required delivery date. Suppose that the gold futures contract rises in price to close on Monday afternoon at €1,005 per ounce. In effect, the futures exchange collects €5 per ounce from the trader who established the short position and delivers €5 per ounce into the account of the trader who established the long position. Now the futures contract calls for delivery of the gold at €1,005 per ounce. Suppose that on Tuesday the futures contract falls to €998 per ounce. The exchange then takes €7 per ounce out of the account of the trader with the long position and delivers €7 per ounce to the trader with the short position (assuming that they both continue to hold their respective positions). The contract would then be changed to call for delivery of the gold at €998 per ounce.

The process continues each day until delivery day. Suppose that at the delivery date the price of gold has risen to €1,500. The holder of the long position must now pay €1,500 per ounce for the gold. But recall that the trader entered a contract to buy gold at €1,000, not €1,500. The final economic result is accomplished because, throughout the life of the contract, there was a net transfer of €500 per ounce from the short side of the contract to the long side of the contract through the marking-to-market process as the closing futures price of gold rose from €1,000 per ounce to €1,500 per ounce. The long position effectively combines the €500 of marked-to-market profit with the original promise to pay €1,000 and delivers €1,500 in exchange for the gold. The short position effectively nets the €500 loss accrued from marking-to-market from the €1,500 received at delivery to receive the promised net value of €1,000 per ounce.

The net result is the same: Both sides of the trade perform as originally promised unless one or both close their positions prior to delivery.

☞ APPLICATION 6.5.2A

Futures contracts on crude oil are often denominated in 1,000-barrel sizes. In other words, each contract calls for the holder of a short position at the delivery date of the futures contract to deliver to the long side 1,000 barrels of the specified grade of oil using stated delivery methods. Assume that a trader establishes a long position of five contracts in crude oil futures at the then-current futures market price of $100 per barrel. Both the trader on the long side of the contract and the trader on the short side of the contract post collateral (margin) of, say, $10 per barrel. At the end of the day, the market price of the futures contract falls to $99. How much money will each side of the contract have, assuming that the required collateral was the only cash and that there were no other positions?

The five contracts call for delivery of 5,000 barrels (5 contracts × 1,000 barrels). The long side of the contract loses $5,000 as a result of the decline in price of $1 per barrel. Each side posted collateral of $50,000 (5,000 barrels × $10 per barrel). The long side experiences a decline in collateral position (cash) to $45,000, and the short side experiences an increase in collateral position (cash) to $55,000.

An exchange-traded futures contract can be viewed as a forward contract that is settled in cash at the end of each day (i.e., marked-to-market) and then restruck at the prevailing price for new futures contracts. Thus, the long position in the first example began with a contract to buy gold at €1,000 per ounce and ended with a contract to buy gold at €1,500 per ounce. During the price move from €1,000 to €1,500, the holder of the long position in the contract received €500 from the holder of the short position. If the holder of the long position takes delivery of the gold at €1,500, the net cost will be the originally agreed-upon price of €1,000 (when the €500 of receipts from marking-to-market profits are included). Correspondingly, the short position holder delivers gold at €1,500 but nets only €1,000 after considering the mark-to-market losses of €500. In advanced pricing models, the impact of interest rates on the marking-to-market process is included in the original pricing of the futures contract. In this discussion, these minor interest effects were ignored.

6.5.3 Marking-to-Market and Counterparty Risk

Each side of a derivative contract refers to the other side of the contract as its counterparty to the contract. Forward contracts and, to a lesser extent, futures contracts expose each party to the risk that the counterparty holding the other side of the contract will default on its obligations. This risk of failure of the counterparty to perform contractual duties is known as counterparty risk and is discussed in greater detail in subsequent chapters.

The importance of the marking-to-market process is to avoid the counterparty risk known as the crisis at maturity. A **crisis at maturity** is when the party owing a payment is forced at the last moment to reveal that it cannot afford to make the payment or when the party obligated to deliver the asset at the original price is forced to reveal that it cannot deliver the asset. The key point is that the potential for a crisis at maturity creates uncertainty throughout the life of the contract when information is asymmetric. Rather, through the marking-to-market process, the party accruing an increasingly expensive obligation to the other party is forced each day to deliver the necessary funds or to reveal any financial problem.

Consider the previous example of a contract to deliver gold at €1,000. When the market price of gold soared from €1,000 to €1,500, the holder of an unhedged short position would be required to deliver the gold at a loss of €500. In the absence of a marking-to-market process, the holder of the long position would be incurring larger and larger counterparty risk as the price of gold soared. With marking-to-market, the short position would settle a portion of the loss each day that the price of gold rose, thus avoiding the crisis at maturity.

If a party does not have the financial resources to meet the requirements of daily marking-to-market, the party's position is closed into the market, and a new counterparty to the position takes over. Hence, daily marking of a position to market typically limits counterparty risk to one day's price movement.

During the marking-to-market process, financial settlement of the contract effectively takes place daily throughout the contract's life rather than simply at the delivery date. In essence, a long-term futures contract is a string of daily contracts that is restruck every day. Marking-to-market of exchange-traded futures contracts minimizes counterparty risk. In addition to the protection provided by the marking to-market process, the exchange's clearing mechanism combines capital from all exchange members to guarantee the trades of any individual members who may default on their obligations. However, the failure of a large futures commission merchant (FCM), such as Lehman Brothers Europe, could create counterparty risk, depending on the jurisdiction and the legal segregation of the assets.

As an OTC-traded product, forward contracts are not usually marked-to-market and are therefore subject to greater counterparty risk. Some market participants prefer the forward market because of the lack of a marking-to-market process. Although forwards have greater counterparty risk than futures do, corporate users may prefer to participate in the forward market to avoid the volatility that futures positions can create in a firm's cash flow and financial statements.

6.5.4 Marking-to-Market and the Time Value of Money Effect on Risk

A critical difference between futures and forward contracts is that the marking-to market feature of futures contracts accelerates the receipt of profits and losses relative to forward contracts. This acceleration has two distinct effects: one on risk and the other on pricing.

Let's first examine the effect of marking-to-market on risk. Acceleration of cash flows due to marking-to-market is tantamount to higher price volatility and higher risk.

For example, consider the difference between being long a futures contract and being long a forward contract on oil. For simplicity, let's assume that although the contract is a one-year contract, due to an important announcement in the first week of the contract the price of oil will either rise by $10 or fall by $10 per barrel. A $10 rise in the oil price in the first week generates a $10 profit for the long side of either the futures contract or the forward contract. But the long side of the futures contract receives that $10 profit in the form of cash during the first week through the marking-to-market process, whereas the long side of the forward contract receives the profits as cash at settlement in one year. If the price were to fall, the long side of the futures contract would pay $10 in one week, whereas a forward contract payment for the loss would be deferred until delivery in one year.

The marking-to-market process effectively requires participants to pay as they go. Paying now rather than later increases the present value, and therefore futures contracts have higher price risk than otherwise identical forward contracts.

6.5.5 Marking-to-Market and the Time Value of Money Effect on Prices

The second effect of the marking-to-market process can be to alter the market price of a futures contract relative to an otherwise identical forward contract. At inception, there should be no difference between the price of a futures contract and an otherwise identical forward contract *if interest rate changes are uncorrelated with the spot price underlying the contracts*.

To understand this complex issue, consider otherwise identical futures and forward contracts with underlying assets that contain no systematic risk and therefore offer no expected profit to the long position and no expected loss to the short position. Because of the marking-to-market process, the futures contract will generate daily cash flows between the long side and the short side as the futures price changes through time. The expected value of these cash flows is zero, since the underlying asset contains no systematic risk.

However, the expected *discounted* value of these cash flows will be positive to the long side of the contract if the interest rate is positively correlated with the spot price underlying the futures contract. If the interest rate and spot price are positively correlated, then the long position in the futures contract will receive cash flows from the marking-to-market process, which will be invested at a high interest rate (because high spot prices and high interest rates will tend to occur together). Conversely, the long side will deliver payments due to the marking-to-market process when the spot price falls, at which time the interest rate will tend to be low (due to the assumed positive correlation between spot prices and interest rates).

The net result is that with positive correlation between spot prices and interest rates, the long side of a futures contract tends to receive marking-to-market cash flows when interest rates move higher and tends to deliver marking-to-market cash flows when interest rates move lower. This asymmetric relationship, which tends to benefit the long side, forces the price of the futures contract above the price of an otherwise equivalent forward contract.

Conversely, with a negative correlation between spot prices and interest rates, the long side of a futures contract tends to deliver marking-to-market cash flows when interest rates move higher and tends to receive marking-to-market cash flows when interest rates move lower. This asymmetric relationship, combined with the opportunity cost of money, forces the price of the futures contract below the price of an otherwise equivalent forward contract when the spot price is negatively correlated with interest rates.

In summary, the price of a contract that is marked-to-market will be greater than, equal to, or less than the price of an otherwise identical contract that is not marked-to-market depending on whether interest rates are positively correlated, uncorrelated, or negatively correlated with the spot price of the contract's underlier.

6.5.6 Futures Trading and Initial Margin

Market participants in futures contracts are required to make a collateral deposit of a size determined by the futures exchange. The collateral deposit made at the initiation of a long or short futures position is called the **initial margin**. This margin requirement is a small percentage of the full purchase price of the underlying commodity, usually less than 10%. Margin requirements are set by the exchanges, are subject to change, and are expressed as currency per contract. For example, at a particular point in time, the initial margin requirement for each futures contract on silver might be $11,000. This means that the entity initiating a long or short position in silver futures must have $11,000 of available collateral per silver futures contract being traded to enter the order and establish the position. Thus, a jewelry-manufacturing firm wishing to take a long position in 10 silver contracts would have to have $110,000 of available collateral to place the trade order.

> ☞ **APPLICATION 6.5.6A**
>
> To lock in sales prices for its anticipated production, HiHo Silver Mining Company wishes to take short positions in five silver futures contracts, settling in each quarter for the next four quarters (20 contracts total). If the initial margin requirement is $11,000 per contract, what is the firm's total initial margin requirement?
>
> The firm must have $220,000 of available collateral to establish the positions.

The initial margin reduces counterparty risk by ensuring the payment of daily losses on futures market positions (except in the case of very extreme price movements). Any collateral deposits for forward contracts are determined through negotiations between the parties.

6.5.7 Marking-to-Market and Maintenance Margin

When commodity prices change substantially, the promise of the long position to pay for delivery or the promise of the short position to make delivery could be placed in peril. To protect the integrity of the contracts, futures exchanges require that positions be marked-to-market, as discussed previously. After initiation of the position (which is done subject to initial margin requirements), market participants with open futures positions are subject to maintenance margin requirements. A **maintenance margin requirement** is a minimum collateral requirement imposed on an ongoing basis until a position is closed. Like the initial margin, the maintenance margin is expressed as units of currency per contract and is usually set at 75% to 80% of the initial margin. If the collateral of a market participant falls below the maintenance margin requirement, typically due to the marking-to-market of losses, a margin call is issued. A **margin call** is a demand for the posting of additional collateral to meet the *initial* margin requirement. If the investor cannot meet the margin call, the futures commission merchant has the right to liquidate the investor's positions in the account. (The positions may be closed at market prices without the investor's direction.) This daily process ensures that promises to make and take delivery have reduced counterparty risk.

Returning to the example of the jewelry manufacturer with a long position in 20 silver contracts, assume that the position was established at a futures price of $25 per ounce and that each contract called for delivery of 5,000 ounces. Thus, the manufacturer has promised to buy 100,000 ounces (20 contracts) at $25 per ounce, for a total purchase price of $2,500,000. Now suppose that the market price of the futures contract drops from $25 to $24. As holder of a long position, the jewelry manufacturer has lost $1 per ounce, and its position has dropped in value by $100,000 (based on all 100,000 ounces underlying the 20 contracts). The futures exchange marks the position to market by transferring $100,000 out of the account of the jewelry manufacturer and placing it into the accounts of entities with short positions in silver futures contracts. The silver manufacturer now has $100,000 less cash in its account, but now its promise is to buy the silver at $24 an ounce rather than $25 per ounce.

Suppose that the jewelry manufacturer originally had only enough collateral to meet the initial margin requirement of $220,000. After the $100,000 loss due to the marking-to-market process, the account contains only $120,000. If the required maintenance margin is not met, the jewelry manufacturer will receive a margin call and will be required to post an additional $100,000 in collateral to return the account to meeting the initial margin requirement and to prevent a forced closure of its positions. The process continues on a daily basis to provide assurances that each trader's obligations will be met. The exchange or the broker can alter margin requirements during a contract's lifetime, often in response to changes in past or anticipated volatility.

☞ APPLICATION 6.5.7A

Returning to the previous example of an oil trader with a long position of five contracts established at an initial futures price of $100 per barrel, the five contracts call for delivery of 5,000 barrels (5 contracts × 1,000 barrels). The trader posts exactly the required initial margin of $50,000 ($10,000 per contract). Suppose that the maintenance margin requirement is $25,000 ($5,000 per contract) and that the price of oil drops $6 per barrel. What is the trader's margin balance after the price decline? Also, describe any margin call that might be made and what it would require.

The long side of the contract loses $6,000 per contract ($30,000 total) as a result of the decline in price of $6 per barrel. The initial collateral of $50,000 falls to a remaining margin balance of $20,000 ($4,000 per contract). The trader receives a margin call, since the remaining margin is less than the maintenance margin requirement. The amount of the margin call is $30,000 to bring the margin back to the initial margin requirement.

Futures contracts have other characteristics that differ from forward contracts, including transparent pricing and, usually, higher liquidity. Although these differences are often important, to focus on the basic principles of commodities futures, the remainder of this chapter generally ignores the distinction between forward and futures contracts, usually using the terms interchangeably.

6.6 MANAGING LONG-TERM FUTURES EXPOSURES

Long positions in equities and real assets can typically be held indefinitely using a simple buy-and-hold strategy. However, futures and forward positions expire at settlement. To maintain a long-term exposure using futures or forward contracts, it is necessary to *roll* the positions over at or prior to their settlement dates. In other words, to maintain an exposure in the forward market, it is necessary to close a position in one contract as it approaches or reaches settlement and open a new position in a contract with the same underlying commodity but with a longer time to settlement. **Rolling contracts** refers to the process of closing positions in short-term futures contracts and simultaneously replacing the exposure by establishing similar positions with longer terms. The rolling of contracts is an important part of maintaining long-term commodity exposures or hedges through futures and forward markets; this section provides foundational concepts on the issues involved.

6.6.1 Futures Contracts with Different Settlement Dates

Futures contracts have regular settlement dates, as determined by the exchanges that created the contracts. A typical interval for settlement dates is quarterly, but especially among the shorter-term contracts, the interval can be monthly or even weekly. On an exchange, the futures contract with the shortest time to settlement is often referred to as the **front month contract**. The front month contract is sometimes referred to as the front contract, the nearby contract, or the spot contract. Contracts with longer times to settlement are often called **distant contracts**, deferred contracts, or back contracts. Deferred contracts are sometimes ranked as first deferred, second deferred, and so forth, denoting their order, with first deferred representing the deferred contract with the shortest time to settlement (after the front month) and so on.

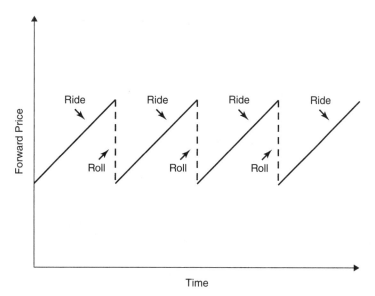

EXHIBIT 6.5 Riding and Rolling of Forward and Futures Contracts

Exhibit 6.5 illustrates the concept of regularly extending the settlement dates of the positions by closing nearby positions and opening deferred positions simultaneously to maintain a continuous exposure to the underlying commodity. Exhibit 6.5 simplifies the diagram by assuming that all of the opening trades occur at one price and that all of the closing trades occur at another price. In practice, the opening and closing prices would vary.

To be consistent with concepts of finance other than commodities, the terminology for the process in Exhibit 6.5 would be that an investor holds, or rides, a given position as its time to settlement nears. At the point that the old position is closed and is replaced by a new position in the same commodity with a longer time to settlement, the investor is said to have rolled the position over. Thus, a long-term exposure can be constructed and maintained with a series of rides and rolls.

However, in commodities, the expression *roll* can also be used to describe the holding of a forward position through time.

6.6.2 Rollover Decisions Alter Long-Run Returns

The timing of each rollover transaction is at the discretion of the investor. Some investors may wait until the contract settles or is about to settle before closing the old position and initiating a new position with a longer settlement date. Others may extend their settlement dates while their positions still have considerable time to settlement. Further, some investors may move into contracts with only a slightly longer time to settlement, whereas others may move into contracts with a much longer time to settlement.

The critical point is that, unlike financial assets such as equities, the long-term returns on futures contracts vary based on the particular decisions made by the holder of the position regarding the procedures used to extend the position into a longer position. The result is that the long-term returns of futures and forward contracts can be calculated only by making important assumptions about how and when the contracts are rolled over. Traders with different preferences for rolling contracts experience different long-term returns.

6.7 OPTION EXPOSURES

This section is the first of three sections on options. An understanding of options is central to a thorough understanding of many alternative investments, not only because many strategies use options and securities with embedded options but also because many trading strategies are best understood through option analysis. For example, the classic strategy of rebalancing to maintain a fixed-leverage ratio can be shown to have optionlike payoffs.

An option is a contract that allows its owner the right (but not the obligation) to execute a specified transaction in the future. The essence of an option is driven by the likelihood that additional information may arrive over the lifetime of the option. Any arrangement that allows a participant the opportunity to make or alter a decision on the basis of the arrival of new information may be viewed as an option. In this context, almost all economic activity contains abundant options, and therefore option analysis is an important tool in almost all decision-making involved in the management of alternative investments.

This section builds on foundational knowledge of options by reviewing risk exposures, primarily through the use of risk exposure diagrams.

 FOUNDATION CHECK

This section assumes knowledge of the terminology and mechanics of options, including call options, put options, European options, American options, strike or exercise prices, moneyness, option writing, intrinsic value, time value, and the expiration/exercise process.

6.7.1 Option Risk Exposure Diagrams

Risk exposure diagrams express the outcomes of establishing a position in one or more options (or other securities) and holding that position until maturity of the option(s), at which time the options are exercised if in-the-money. The vertical axis above the origin indicates profits, and below the origin indicates losses. The profits and losses ignore the time value of money and transaction costs. The horizontal axis expresses the price of the underlying asset.

6.7.2 Long and Short Positions in an Underlying Asset

The two diagrams in the top panel of Exhibit 6.6 begin this discussion of risk exposures by illustrating long and short positions in the underlying asset rather than positions in options. A long position in an underlying asset, such as a share of stock, is illustrated on the left, and a short position is illustrated on the right. In the top panel,

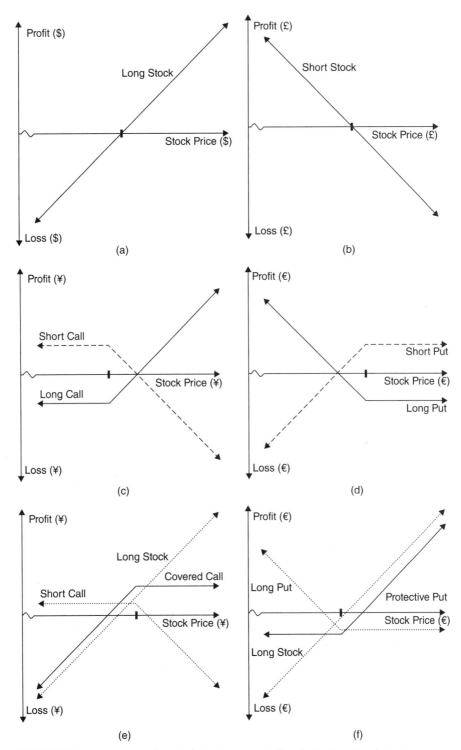

EXHIBIT 6.6 Diagrams of Underlying Assets and Simple Option Combinations

the diagrams express the trivial case of the risk exposure of an asset to itself. Long positions have unlimited profit potential to the upside of the underlying asset and limited loss potential to the downside of the underlying asset. Short positions, which are an important part of many alternative investment strategies, have the opposite exposures: limited profit potential to the downside and unlimited loss potential to the upside. The intersection of each of these exposures with the horizontal axis can indicate the current price or opening price of the position. The long and short positions in the top panel of Exhibit 6.6 may be viewed as cash positions, such as a share of stock or a physical commodity, or forward contracts on an asset, such as a commodity. As with all such diagrams, the risk exposure of the long position is the mirror image of the risk exposure of the short position.

6.7.3 Call and Put Exposures

The diagrams in the middle panel of Exhibit 6.6 illustrate the risk exposure of long and short positions in call options and put options. Both the short position and the long position are illustrated in the same diagram, with the short position denoted with a dashed line. Strike prices of the options are indicated with a mark on the horizontal axis. Whereas call options generate unlimited exposures to the upside of the underlying asset, put options do not have unlimited exposures in either direction, since the underlying asset's price cannot go below zero. Note that all kinks in option diagrams occur directly above or directly below the option's strike price. A short option position that is unhedged is often referred to as a **naked option**.

6.7.4 Covered Call and Protective Put Exposures

The bottom panel of diagrams in Exhibit 6.6 illustrates the risk exposures of two popular combinations of an option and an underlying asset: a covered call and a protective put. A **covered call** combines being long an asset with being short a call option on the same asset. Note from the diagrams that a covered call has the same net risk exposure as a naked put.

A **protective put** combines being long an asset with a long position in a put option on the same asset. Note from the diagrams that a protective put has the same net risk exposure as a call option. The underlying components of the combinations are indicated with dotted lines, and the net exposure of the combination is indicated with a solid line.

 FOUNDATION CHECK

The material in this section and the diagrams in the exhibits assume familiarity with the netting of individual risk exposure diagrams to form diagrams of the net exposures of portfolios of options and/or underlying assets.

Both diagrams illustrate the put-call parity relationship among a call, a put, an underlying asset, and a zero-coupon default-free bond. Note that the diagram on the left illustrates that the risk exposure of an asset minus a call is equal to a short position in a put. The diagram on the right illustrates that the risk exposure of an asset plus a put is equal to a call. The zero-coupon default-free bond in the put-call parity relationship has no risk exposure but merely serves to balance the netted sizes of the positions. Put-call parity is discussed in section 6.7.7.

6.7.5 Exposures of Two-Position Spreads

The top panel of Exhibit 6.7 illustrates major option spreads, containing two positions each. An **option spread** (1) contains either call options or put options (not both), and (2) contains both long and short positions in options with the same underlying asset. Option spreads contain options that differ with regard to strike price, expiration date, or both. Option spreads based on differences only in expiration date are termed calendar spreads, or horizontal spreads. The illustrated option spreads differ only by strike price and are often referred to as vertical spreads. Diagonal spreads differ by both expiration date and strike price.

Consider a combination of one long position and one short position in either two calls or two puts that differ only by strike price. An option combination in which the long option position is at the lower of two strike prices is a **bull spread**, which offers bullish exposure to the underlying asset that begins at the lower strike price and ends at the higher strike price. The left side of the top panel of Exhibit 6.7 illustrates a bull spread. An option combination in which the long option position is at the higher of two strike prices is a **bear spread**, which offers bearish exposure to the underlying asset that begins at the higher strike price and ends at the lower strike price. The right side of the top panel of Exhibit 6.7 illustrates a bear spread. Note that bull spreads have long positions in the option with the lower strike price (and bear spreads have long positions in the option with the higher strike price) whether the spreads are formed with calls or with puts.

Spread positions termed **ratio spreads** can be formed in which the number of options in each position differ. For example, a ratio spread might contain two long call positions at one strike price and one short call position at another strike price, both with the same underlying asset. Ratio spreads tilt the option exposures to provide greater sensitivity (i.e., leverage) in one direction (e.g., bullish) than in the other. Spread ratios serve as an illustration of using greater degrees of leverage through establishing relatively large directional bets. The creation of positions that, over some ranges, are highly sensitive to changes in the value of the underlying asset is shown in Chapter 24 to be an important component of some structured products.

6.7.6 Exposures of Two-Position Combinations

An **option combination** contains both calls and puts on the same underlying asset. The middle panel of Exhibit 6.7 illustrates two major option combinations containing two positions each: option straddles and option strangles. An **option straddle** is a position in a call and put with the same sign (i.e., long or short), the same underlying asset, the same expiration date, and the same strike price. An **option strangle** is a position in a call and put with the same sign, the same underlying asset, the same

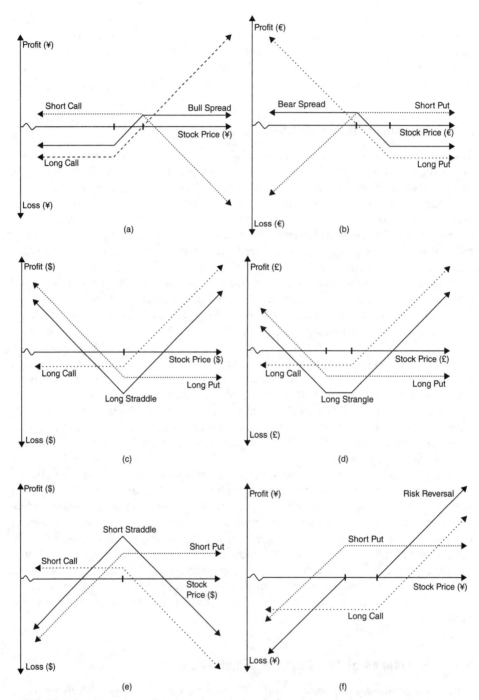

EXHIBIT 6.7   Diagrams of Options Spreads and Combinations

expiration date, but *different strike prices*. When the call and put options are both long, the resulting position is a long straddle (or strangle); and when the call and put options are both short, the resulting position is a short straddle (or strangle). An option straddle is illustrated on the left side of the middle panel of Exhibit 6.7, and an option strangle is illustrated on the right side of the panel. The bottom left side of Exhibit 6.7 illustrates a short straddle.

The straddles and strangles discussed previously involved calls and puts with the same sign (i.e., long or short). Consider an option combination with a single call option and a single put option with the same underlying asset, the same time to expiration, but *opposite signs*. If the strike prices of the call and put are the same, the combination is a synthetic position in the underlying asset. If the call option is the long position and the put is short, the result is a synthetic long position in the underlying asset. If the call option is the short position and the put is long, the result is a synthetic short position in the underlying asset. By varying the strike prices of the options relative to the market price of the underlying asset, the synthetic positions can be designed to require no financing, to require some financing, or even to generate financing.

Consider a position similar to the previously discussed synthetic long position (long a call and short a put) but with different strike prices. A long out-of-the-money call combined with a short out-of-the-money put on the same asset and with the same expiration date is termed a **risk reversal**. The right side of the bottom panel of Exhibit 6.7 depicts the risk exposure of a risk reversal. Note that the position resembles a synthetic long position except for the level range between the strike prices. Reversing the signs of the option positions (i.e., a short position in a risk reversal) generates a synthetic short position outside of the range between the strike prices.

There are specialized names for option combinations that have differently sized positions in puts and calls (e.g., straps and strips), which tilt the exposures to be more sensitive in one direction than the other. There are also positions of three or more options that are sometimes described with specialized terms, such as butterflies and condors. These more arcane terms are less frequently used in alternative investments.

6.7.7 Put-Call Parity and Option Collars

In practice, the risk of an asset is often *collared* by buying a put option at strike price K_1 and writing a call option at strike price K_2 with $K_1 < K_2$ to limit the range over which the investor is exposed to the risk of the underlying asset to movement of the underlying asset within the range between K_1 and K_2.

An **option collar** uses positions in options to limit the upside and downside exposure of a position to a price or rate, with the most common example being when the risk of a price or rate is limited by establishing a long position in a put option with a strike price K_1 and a short position in a call option with a strike price or rate of K_2, in which $K_1 < K_2$. The resulting position is collared and has the same net exposure of a bull call spread in Exhibit 6.7a. A short position in a price or rate can be collared by a long position in a call option with a strike price K_1 and a short position in a put option with a strike price or rate of K_2, in which $K_1 < K_2$. The resulting position is collared and has the same net exposure of a bear call spread in Exhibit 6.7b.

One of the most important relationships within option analysis is put-call parity. **Put-call parity** is an arbitrage-free relation among the values of an asset, a riskless bond, a call option, and a put option. This relation was discussed briefly in the context of Exhibit 6.7. The options are European options on the same non-dividend-paying underlying asset, with identical strike prices and expiration dates. The riskless bond is a zero-coupon default-free bond, with a face value equal to the strike price of the options and a maturity date equal to the expiration date of the options. Equation 6.9 illustrates one arrangement of put-call parity:

$$\text{Call} + \text{Bond} - \text{Put} = \text{Underlying Asset} \qquad (6.9)$$

There are many ways to rearrange Equation 6.9. As shown, the relation has the following intuition: A long position in both the call option and the bond, combined with a short position in the put option, will have the same value at the expiration date as a long position in the asset that underlies the options. The long call provides the upside exposure, and the short put provides the downside loss exposure. The riskless bond balances the amount of cash that must be invested when the positions are initiated (and will be received when the positions are terminated at the option expiration date). Since the left and right sides of the relation both have the same exposures and require the same investment, their values at all points in time must be the same in well-functioning capital markets.

Note also in Equation 6.9 that rearranging the equation to put both of the options on the right side generates the result that an asset combined with a long put position and short call position (with the same strike price) is equivalent to a zero-coupon bond. The long put and short call with the same strike price hedge all the risk from the underlying stock price at the option's expiration.

6.8 OPTION PRICING MODELS

Modern option pricing models are precise tools with applications that permeate investment analysis, especially alternative investment analysis. This section provides a somewhat nontraditional view of continuous time option-pricing models, starting with the generalized case of an exchange option rather than with the classic Black-Scholes call option pricing model.[1] Throughout the analysis, it is assumed that the underlying asset does not pay any cash distributions.

 FOUNDATION CHECK

This section assumes basic familiarity with applying the Black-Scholes option pricing model, including application of the cumulative normal distribution.

6.8.1 An Option on a Portfolio

Most option pricing models can be shown as special cases of the simple model introduced in Equation 6.10. Consider a portfolio that has both one or more long positions and one or more short positions, with a current net market value that may be positive or negative. An investor has an option either to take ownership of both sides of the portfolio or to walk away from the transaction and let the option expire at some fixed expiration date. The value for the option on this portfolio is given by this simple equation:[2]

$$P_o = P_l N(d) - P_s N(d - v) \tag{6.10}$$

where P_o = the value of the option, P_l = the value of the long positions, P_s = the value of the short positions, $N(\cdot)$ = the cumulative normal distribution, $d = [\ln(P_l/P_s)/v] + (v/2)$, and v = the return volatility of the portfolio integrated over the time to expiration.

Note that the relevant measure of volatility, v, is based on the volatility of the combined long and short positions. The volatility of the portfolio is therefore based on the volatility of the long positions, the volatility of the short positions, and the correlation between the two positions.

The distinction between calls and puts is simplified by viewing this generalized case. A call option is when the short position is a fixed cash flow (i.e., a zero-coupon bond), and a put option is when the long position is a fixed cash flow. If both positions are fixed cash flows, denominated in different currencies, then Equation 6.10 becomes an FX (foreign exchange) or currency option.

6.8.2 The Black-Scholes Call and Put Option Formulae

As indicated previously, a call option is the special case of Equation 6.10 in which the long position is an asset, such as a share of common stock, say S, and the short position is a zero-coupon bond with a face value of K that matures when the option expires. Substituting into Equation 6.10 produces the famous Black-Scholes (1973) call-option formula (continuing to assume no dividends) for the price of a call.[3] The **Black-Scholes call option formula** expresses the price of a call option as a function of five variables: the price of the underlying asset, the strike price, the return volatility of the underlying asset, the time to the option's expiration, and the riskless rate, as shown in Equation 6.11:

$$c = SN(d_1) - e^{-rT}KN(d_2) \tag{6.11}$$
$$d_1 = [\ln(S/e^{-rT}K)/v] + (v/2)$$
$$d_2 = d_1 - v$$
$$v = \sigma_s\sqrt{T}$$

where c is the call option price, r is the riskless rate, T is the time to the option's expiration, and σ_s is the constant volatility of the returns of S. The Black-Scholes model assumes that the riskless rate and the volatility of the stock, σ_s, are constants.

The constant volatility assumption and the absence of correlation between the stock price and the strike price simplify v to being $\sigma_s \sqrt{T}$. If the short position is an asset, such as a share of common stock, and the long position is a zero-coupon bond with a face value of K that matures when the option expires, then Equation 6.9, with some rearrangement, is the familiar Black-Scholes put option formula.

6.8.3 The Black Forward Option Pricing Model

Black (1976) derived an option pricing model for a call option on a forward contract:[4]

$$c = e^{-rT}[FN(d_1) - KN(d_2)] \tag{6.12}$$
$$d_1 = [\ln(F/K)/v] + (v/2)$$
$$d_2 = d_1 - v$$

where F is the forward price. Note that the model is easily derived from the Black-Scholes formula by substituting for S from the cost-of-carry model in section 6.4: $S = e^{-(r-d)T}F(T)$, and setting the dividend yield to zero. It should be noted that e^{-rT} vanishes from d_1 in the case of an option on a forward. The intuition of the model is that since neither the forward contract nor the strike price requires an initial investment, both variables need to be discounted, so r drops out of the model.

6.8.4 The Currency Option Pricing Model

A currency option pricing model was derived by Biger and Hull (1983).[5] The distinguishing feature of the currency or currency exchange model is that there are two riskless interest rates corresponding to the two currencies being exchanged:

$$\text{Option Price} = e^{-r^*T}S^*N(d_1) - e^{-rT}SN(d_2) \tag{6.13}$$

Equation 6.13 is an option to exchange S^* units of one currency with an associated riskless interest rate of r^* for S units of another currency with an associated riskless interest rate of r. Both interest rates also appear in the formula for d_1 in the case of a currency exchange option.

6.9 OPTION SENSITIVITIES

The sensitivities of option prices to the variables that determine their prices are important inputs to many hedging strategies and risk management techniques. These sensitivities can be derived for all of the option pricing models discussed in section 6.7. This section discusses these sensitivities primarily in the context of the Black-Scholes option pricing model of call and put options on an underlying asset, such as a share of stock.

6.9.1 The Five Most Popular Sensitivities

Call and put options usually have four underlying variables that normally change: the underlying asset (S), the return volatility of the underlying asset, the time to expiration, and the riskless interest rate. For the purposes of this analysis, it is assumed that the strike price cannot change and that there are no dividends. The partial derivatives of a call option's price, c, with respect to each of these four variables are assigned names as follows:

$$\text{Delta} = \partial c / \partial S$$
$$\text{Vega} = \partial c / \partial \sigma_s$$
$$\text{Theta} = \partial c / \partial T$$
$$\text{Rho} = \partial c / \partial r$$

Delta, the first partial derivative of the option price with respect to the price of its underlying asset, is so important that the second derivative is also commonly used:

$$\text{Gamma} = \partial^2 c / \partial S^2$$

Delta, gamma, vega, and theta are discussed in more detail in the sections on hedge fund strategies, including convertible bond hedging, in Chapter 17. **Rho** is the sensitivity of an option price with respect to changes in the riskless interest rate. Option sensitivities are also discussed in other parts of this book, including Chapter 17.

6.9.2 Unlimited Sensitivities

An infinite number of potential option sensitivities can be formed by inserting additional variables into an option pricing model or by using higher-order derivatives. Second-order partial derivatives are common, and some third-order derivatives, although usually uncommon, have been named. Other first-order partial derivatives can be formed by assuming that the price of the underlying asset to an option is itself a function of other variables. For example, consider an option on an asset that in turn is a function of several variables, such as a credit spread. By inserting the underlying security price formula in place of the price of the underlying asset, S, a first-order partial derivative can be formed for each variable contained in the formula for S. For example, **omicron** is the partial derivative of an option or a position containing an option to a change in the credit spread and is useful for analyzing option positions on credit-risky assets.

Most option sensitivities indicate value changes, such as a delta of 0.4, indicating that the price of a call option will rise 0.4 units for each 1 unit change in the underlying asset (for infinitesimal changes). Ignoring nonlinearity, a call option with a delta of 0.7 would therefore rise in price by 7 cents if the underlying asset rose 10 cents.

Another measure of option price sensitivity can be formed by computing the elasticity rather than the partial derivative. An **elasticity** is the percentage change in a value with respect to a percentage change in another value. Generally, the elasticity of x with respect to y can be formed by multiplying the derivative of x with respect to y by the ratio of y to x. For example, a call option price elasticity of 2.0 with respect to the underlying asset would indicate that the call option price would change by 2% when the underlying asset changed by 1%.

Lambda and omega are often used to indicate the elasticity of an option price with respect to the price of the option's underlying asset. Elasticities can be formed by multiplying the partial derivative by the ratio of the price of the asset in the denominator of the partial derivative to the price of the asset in the numerator. Thus, **lambda** or **omega** for a call option is the elasticity of an option price with respect to the price of the underlying asset and is equal to delta multiplied times the quantity (S/c). Another type of sensitivity is cross-derivatives. For example, an analyst may be concerned about how delta changes when volatility changes ($\partial^2 c/\partial S \partial S\sigma_s$).

6.9.3 Using Option Sensitivities for Risk Management

Option sensitivities have multiple uses. A convertible bond trader may focus on a particular risk, such as the risk that the stock price underlying the convertible bond will change. The trader uses the sensitivities to establish hedge ratios. Option sensitivities may also be integrated into a comprehensive approach to managing all potential risk exposures. For example, many portfolios or strategies can be well represented as responding to a specific set of factors or underlying prices.

The risk manager can analyze the risk of the portfolio by taking the total derivative of the portfolio with respect to each potential source of risk. Unlike a partial derivative, a total derivative does not assume that all other variables remain constant. A total derivative measures the direction of the change and is accurate for infinitesimal changes. In many cases, the total derivative depends only on first-order derivatives, discussed in the previous section.

Another approach involves attempting to incorporate the effect of finite changes in the value of a position. In those applications, the analyst may use the concept of a total differential, which would generally include the higher-order effects, such as gamma in the case of an option and convexity in the case of a bond.

REVIEW QUESTIONS

1. What two spot interest rates imply the value of a six-month forward contract from a six-month Treasury bill?
2. What is the relationship between a forward interest rate and its expected value at settlement under the unbiased expectations hypothesis and the liquidity premium hypothesis?
3. What are the carrying costs (and benefits) of physical inventory such as a commodity?
4. Which is likely to be more liquid, a forward contract or a futures contract?
5. What does it mean when a future is marked-to-market?
6. What is maintenance margin?
7. What two assets form a long straddle?
8. What is the equation for put-call parity?
9. What are the five variables that determine the price of an option on a non-dividend stock according to the Black-Scholes option pricing model?
10. What are the names of the first and second derivatives of an option price with respect to the price of the option's underlying asset?

NOTES

1. William Margrabe, "The Value of an Option to Exchange One Asset for Another," *Journal of Finance* 33, no. 1 (1978): 177–86.
2. Compared to most option pricing models!
3. Fischer Black and Myron Scholes, "The Pricing of Options and Corporate Liabilities," *Journal of Political Economy* 81, no. 3 (1973): 637–54.
4. Fischer Black, "The Pricing of Commodity Contracts," *Journal of Financial Economics* 3, no. 1/2 (January/March 1976): 167–79.
5. Nahum Biger and John Hull, "The Valuation of Currency Options," *Financial Management* 12 (1983): 24–28.

CHAPTER 7

Measures of Risk and Performance

Foundational concepts in alternative assets include risk measurement and performance analysis.

7.1 MEASURES OF RISK

Standard deviation of returns, also known as volatility, is the most common measure of total financial risk. If the return distribution is a well-known distribution such as the normal distribution, then the standard deviation reveals much or even all of the information about the width of the distribution. If the distribution is not well-known, then standard deviation is usually a first pass at describing the dispersion. However, standard deviation can be an ineffective measure of risk when a distribution is nonsymmetrical. Standard deviation incorporates dispersion from both the right-hand side (typically profit) and the left-hand side (typically loss) of the distribution. The two sides are identical in a symmetrical distribution, but in a nonsymmetrical distribution the sides differ; and in the case of risk, the analyst is primarily concerned with the left, or downside, half of the distribution.

The following section includes risk measures that focus on the left or loss side of the return distribution, as well as other popular measures. This section is not intended as a comprehensive listing; it does not discuss the computation of systematic risk measures (betas) or other less frequently used measures.

7.1.1 Semivariance

Some risk measures focus entirely on the downside of the return distribution, meaning that they are computed without use of the above-mean outcomes other than to compute the mean of the distribution. One of the most popular downside risk measures is the semivariance.

Variance, as a symmetrical calculation, is an expected value of the squared deviations, including both negative and positive deviations. The **semivariance** uses a formula otherwise identical to the variance formula except that it considers only the negative deviations inside the summation. Semivariance is therefore expressed as:

$$\text{Semivariance} = \frac{1}{T} \sum_t [R_t - E(R)]^2 \text{ For all } R_t < E(R) \tag{7.1}$$

where T is the total number of observations. Semivariance's summation includes only the observations with values below the mean. Semivariance provides a sense of how much variability exists among losses or, more precisely, among lower-than-expected outcomes.

The equation for the semivariance of a sample is given as:

$$\text{Semivariance} = \frac{1}{T-1} \sum_t (R_t - \bar{R})^2 \text{ For all } R_t < \bar{R} \qquad (7.2)$$

where $\bar{R}$ is the sample mean.

7.1.2 Semistandard Deviation

Semistandard deviation, sometimes called semideviation, is the square root of semivariance. Most statisticians define T in the computation of the semivariance and semistandard deviation as the total number of observations for a series. Some practitioners define T as the number of observations that have a negative deviation. Defining T as including all observations has desirable statistical properties and is the standard in statistics. Defining T as including only the number of negative deviations tends to scale semistandard deviation and standard deviation comparably, allowing easier comparisons of semistandard deviations with standard deviations. Both specifications of T should provide identical rankings when comparing samples with equal numbers of total observations and with equal numbers of negative observations.

The semivariance and semistandard deviation for a return series are rather easily computed. The idea is to include only those observations that have a deviation (return minus its mean) that is negative. All of the negative deviations are squared and summed. In this case, the semistandard deviation is often termed a downside deviation.

7.1.3 Semivolatility

Semivolatility has been proposed as an improved measure of risk compared to semistandard deviation. **Semivolatility** is similar to semistandard deviation except that it is unambiguously based on only the number of observations below the mean or threshold (T^*) and it subtracts 0.5, rather than 1.0, from that number.

$$\text{Semivolatility} = \sqrt{\frac{1}{T^* - 0.5} \sum (R_t - \bar{R})^2} \text{ For all } R_t < \bar{R} \qquad (7.3)$$

where T^* is the number of observations less than the mean (or threshold).

By using the new term (*semivolatility*) and defining it as using T^* rather than T in the denominator, semivolatility avoids the ambiguity of the computation of semistandard deviation discussed in section 7.1.2 from the conflicting definitions of semistandard deviation. Further, by subtracting 0.5 from T^* rather than 1, the originators of the measure claim that semivolatility becomes ". . . an unbiased measure of dispersion that is defined in the case of a sample with only one negative deviation."[1]

7.1.4 Shortfall Risk, Target Semivariance, and Target Semistandard Deviation

In addition to measuring return risk relative to a mean return or an expected return, some analysts measure risk relative to a target rate of return (such as 5%), chosen by the investor based on the investor's goals and financial situation. Generally, the target return is a constant. **Shortfall risk** is simply the probability that the return will be less than the investor's target rate of return.

The concept of a target return can also be used in measures of downside dispersion. **Target semivariance** is similar to semivariance except that target semivariance substitutes the investor's target rate of return in place of the mean return. Thus, target semivariance is the dispersion of all outcomes below some target level of return rather than below the sample mean return. **Target semistandard deviation** (TSSD) is simply the square root of the target semivariance.

When the target is the mean, target semivariance equals semivariance. A very high target return eliminates only the highest outcomes, whereas a very low target eliminates most of the outcomes. The target should typically be set equal to the investor's target rate of return, such as the minimum return consistent with achieving the investor's goals.

7.1.5 Tracking Error

Tracking error indicates the dispersion of the returns of an investment relative to a benchmark return, where a benchmark return is the contemporaneous realized return on an index or peer group of comparable risk. Although tracking error is sometimes used loosely simply to refer to the deviations between an asset's return and the benchmark return, the term *tracking error* is usually defined as the standard deviation of those deviations, as shown in Equation 7.4:

$$\text{Tracking Error} = \sqrt{\frac{1}{T-1}\sum_{t=1}^{T}(R_t - R_{Bench,t} - \bar{R}^*)^2} \qquad (7.4)$$

where $R_{Bench,t}$ is the benchmark return in time period t, and $\bar{R}^*$ is the mean of $(R_t - R_{Bench,t})$, which is often assumed to be zero.

Note that the benchmark return in Equation 7.4 is subscripted by t, denoting that it differs from period to period. As a standard deviation, tracking error has the advantage of being able to be roughly viewed as a typical deviation, as discussed in Chapter 4. Since tracking error is formed based on deviations from a benchmark rather than deviations from its own mean, it is an especially useful measure of the dispersion of an asset's return relative to its benchmark. Therefore, whereas standard deviation of returns might be used for an asset with a goal of absolute return performance, tracking error might be used more often for an asset with a goal of relative return performance.

7.1.6 Drawdown

Drawdown is defined as the maximum loss in the value of an asset over a specified time interval and is usually expressed in percentage-return form rather than currency. For example, an asset reaching a high of $100 and then falling to a subsequent low of $60 would be said to have suffered a drawdown of 40%. **Maximum drawdown** is defined as the largest decline over *any* time interval within the entire observation period. Smaller losses during smaller intervals of the observation period are often referred to as drawdowns or individual drawdowns. For example, an asset might be said to have experienced a maximum drawdown of 33% since 1995 (for example, between 2000 and 2002), with individual drawdowns of 23% in 2000 and 14% in 2007.

The measured size of a drawdown can vary based on the frequency of the valuation interval, meaning the granularity of the return and price data. For example, if only quarter-end valuations and quarterly returns are used, the true highest values and lowest values of an asset would not be included unless the high and low happened to coincide with dates at the end of a quarter. Thus, a March 31 quarter-ending value of $60 to an asset may be the lowest quarter-ending figure, but the asset may have traded well below $60 sometime during that quarter. A drawdown figure based on only end-of-quarter values would almost always miss the true highs and lows. More frequent observations have a greater likelihood of capturing the true highs and lows. Thus, using monthly, daily, or even tick-by-tick data generally produces higher measures of drawdown.

7.1.7 Value at Risk

Value at risk (VaR) is the loss figure associated with a particular percentile of a cumulative loss function. In other words, VaR is the maximum loss over a specified time period within a specified probability. The specification of a VaR requires two parameters:

1. The length of time involved in measuring the potential loss
2. The probability used to specify the confidence that the given loss figure will not be exceeded

Thus, we might estimate the VaR for a 10-day period with 99% confidence as being $100,000. In this case, the VaR is a prediction that over a 10-day period, there is a 99% chance that performance will be better than the scenario in which there is a $100,000 loss. Conversely, there is a 1% chance that there will be a loss in excess of $100,000, but VaR does not estimate the expected loss or maximum possible loss in extreme scenarios. Additional VaR values could be obtained for other time horizons and with other probabilities, such as a VaR for a one-day period with 90% confidence.

The time horizon selected is often linked to how long the decision maker thinks it might be necessary to take an action, such as liquidating a position. The probability is linked to whether the manager wants to analyze extremely bad scenarios or more likely scenarios. Longer time horizons generally produce larger VaRs because there is more time for the financial situation to deteriorate further. Higher confidence probabilities produce larger VaRs because they force the loss estimate to be based on more unusual circumstances. There is nothing to prevent management from analyzing a number of VaRs based on multiple time periods and/or confidence levels.

Exhibit 7.1 illustrates the concept of a $100,000 VaR for a portfolio based on a confidence level of 99%. The investor can be 99% confident that the portfolio will not lose more than $100,000 over the specified time interval. Thus, there is a 1%

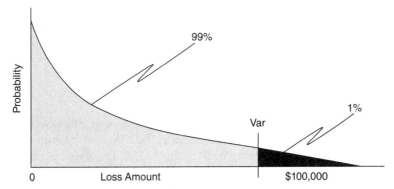

EXHIBIT 7.1   Example of the Distribution of a $100,000 VaR for a Portfolio Based on a Confidence Level of 99%

probability that the investor will suffer a loss of $100,000 or more over that time interval.

The VaR summarizes potential loss in a condensed and easy-to-understand way to facilitate understanding and comparison. However, as a single measure of potential loss, the information that it can contain is limited unless the user knows the shape of the distribution of the potential losses.

Variations of VaR exist, such as conditional value-at-risk. **Conditional value-at-risk** (CVaR), also known as expected tail loss, is the expected loss of the investor given that the VaR has been equaled or exceeded. Thus, if the VaR is $1 million, then the CVaR would be the expected value of all losses equal to or greater than $1 million. The CVaR provides the investor with information about the potential magnitude of losses beyond the VaR.

7.1.8   Strengths and Weaknesses of VaR

The VaR provides a first glance at risk. It can be computed for a single risk exposure (such as a single security), for a portfolio, for an entire division, or for the entire firm. The VaR is a simplified risk measure that can be relatively uniformly computed and interpreted across divisions within a fund or across funds. Numerous entities request or require the reporting of VaR, and they test through time whether a fund's reported VaR is consistent with the actual risk that is experienced. The VaR is especially useful in situations in which a worst-case analysis makes no sense, such as in derivatives, where some positions have unlimited downside risk.

As a single risk measure, VaR provides rather limited information. Further, in some circumstances, VaR can be extremely deceptive. For example, consider a situation in which there is a 1 in 60 chance that a fund will lose $1 million, and under all other situations, the fund will make $30,000 (such as a fund writing an out-of-the-money binary option with a probability of being exercised of 1/60). The VaR using 90%, 95%, or 98% confidence is $0. But the VaR using 99% confidence is $1 million. A manager seeing only the 99% confidence number will perceive a very different risk exposure than a manager seeing VaR from a lower probability.

The VaR is an important risk measure and can be estimated in a variety of ways based on a variety of circumstances. The estimation of VaR is sufficiently important to warrant an entire section.

7.2 ESTIMATING VALUE AT RISK (VaR)

Consider JAC Fund, which has accumulated a position of 50,000 shares of an exchange-traded fund (ETF) that tracks the S&P 500. This hypothetical ETF trades at $20 per share for a total holding of $1 million. JAC Fund wishes to know how much money could be lost if the ETF fell in value. The theoretical answer is that the fund could lose the entire $1 million, under the highly unlikely scenario that the ETF becomes completely worthless.

JAC Fund's management realizes that to make this number meaningful, they must specify a length of time and a probability of certainty. Thus, they might ask how much is the most money that could be expected to be lost 99% of the time over a 10-business-day interval. A reasonable answer to that question is $100,000. In other words, 99 times out of 100, the position in the ETF will do better than losing $100,000 over 10 business days. But on average, during one two-week period out of every 100 such periods, JAC Fund should expect to lose $100,000 or more. It could compute other VaR estimates using time horizons other than 10 days (1, 2, 5, and 30 days are also common) or probabilities other than 99% (90%, 95%, and 98% are also common).

It is easy to assume that VaR analysis is based on the normal probability distribution, because most VaR applications use the statistics of that distribution. However, VaR computation does not require the use of a normal probability distribution or any other formal probability distribution. It merely requires some method or model of predicting the magnitudes and probabilities of various loss levels.

For example, debt securities do not offer a payout at maturity that is normally distributed. Rather, there is usually a high probability that the debt will be paid off in full and various probabilities that only partial payments will be received. If the potential losses of a position or a portfolio of positions cannot be modeled accurately using the normal distribution or another common distribution, the VaR can be estimated in other ways. If the potential losses form a normal distribution, then a parametric approach can be used.

The following section details the parametric estimation of VaR when the losses are normally distributed. Later sections discuss other methods of estimating VaR.

7.2.1 Estimating VaR with Normally Distributed Returns

If the potential losses being analyzed follow a normal distribution, a parametric approach can be used (i.e., VaR can be based on the parameters of the normal distribution). A VaR computation assuming normality and using the statistics of the normal distribution is known as **parametric VaR**. Computing parametric VaR begins with estimating a standard deviation and inserting the standard deviation into the following formula based on daily price changes:

$$\text{Parametric VaR} = N \times \sigma \sqrt{\text{Days}} \times \text{Value} \qquad (7.5)$$

The formula can use time periods other than days by adjusting N and σ. For simplicity, the formula assumes that the expected return of the investment is zero. The four components to this formula are:

1. N is the number of standard deviations, which depends on the confidence level that is specified. The value 2.33 should be used if the user wants to be 99% confident, 1.65 should be used if the user wants to be 95% confident, and so forth, with values that can be found using tables or spreadsheets of confidence intervals based on the normal distribution.

2. σ is the estimated daily standard deviation expressed as a proportion of price or value (return standard deviation). The standard deviation is a measure of the volatility of the value. For example, the ETF discussed earlier might be viewed in a particular market as having a daily standard deviation of perhaps 1.35%. Given a stock price of $20, we can think of the ETF's daily standard deviation measured in absolute terms as being about $0.27. If the standard deviation is expressed as a dollar value of the entire position, then the formula would omit the last term. The standard deviation can be estimated using historical data, observed through option volatilities, or forecasted in some other way, such as with fundamental analysis.

3. $\sqrt{\text{Days}}$ is the square root of the number of days used for the VaR analysis, such as 1, 2, 5, or 10 days. The reason we use the square root is that risk as measured by VaR often grows proportionally with the square root of time, assuming no autocorrelation. Thus, a two-day VaR is only 41.4% bigger than a one-day VaR.

4. Value is the market value of the position for which the VaR is being computed. For example, it might be the value of a portfolio.

☞ APPLICATION 7.2.1A

Let's return to the example of JAC Fund's $1 million holding of the ETF with an expected return of zero. Estimating roughly that the daily standard deviation of the ETF is 1.35%, for a 99% confidence interval, the 10-day VaR is found through substituting the known values into the equation:

$$2.33 \times \sigma \times \sqrt{\text{Days}} \times \text{Value}$$
$$2.33 \times 1.35\% \times \sqrt{10} \times \$1,000,000$$

The first three values multiplied together produce the percentage change in the value that is being defined as a highly abnormal circumstance. In this case, the answer would be very roughly 10%, indicating that there is a 1% chance that the ETF could fall 10% or more in 10 business days. This percentage is then multiplied by the position's value (the fourth term) to produce the dollar amount of the VaR. In the example, the 10% loss on the $1 million stock holdings would produce a VaR of approximately $100,000.

In many cases, such as in this case of a single position, these four inputs are simply multiplied together to find the VaR. In other cases, a further adjustment might be necessary, such as subtracting the collateral that is being held against the potential loss to find the amount that is at risk, or adjusting for the expected profit on the position over the time interval.

7.2.2 Estimating VaR with Normally Distributed Underlying Factors

The approach just described is the simplest case of the analytic approach to computing VaR. Note that the standard deviation used in the equation was the standard deviation of the value or returns of the position being studied. In more complex examples of the analytic approach, the values being studied (e.g., security prices) are modeled as functions of one or more underlying economic variables or factors, such as when an option price is modeled as a function of five or more variables. In these instances, the VaR equation is expressed using the volatilities and correlations of the underlying factors, as well as the sensitivity of the security prices to those factors.

In the case of highly nonlinear price functions, such as options, the sensitivities include terms to capture the nonlinearity of large movements (e.g., by using convexity). Thus, the parametric VaR equation that is rather simple for a single position with value changes that are normally distributed can become quite complex for positions with highly nonlinear relationships to underlying factors and/or positions that depend on several factors.

7.2.3 Two Primary Approaches to Estimating the Volatility for VaR

In most parametric VaR applications, the biggest challenge is estimating the volatility of the asset containing the risk. A common approach is to estimate the standard deviation as being equal to the asset's historical standard deviation of returns. Much work has been done and is being devoted to developing improved forecasts of volatility using past data. These efforts focus on the extent to which more recent returns should be given a higher weight than returns from many time periods ago. Models such as ARCH and GARCH emphasize more recent observations in estimating volatility based on past data and were discussed in Chapter 4.

Another method of forecasting volatility is based on market prices of options. Estimates of volatility are based on the implied volatilities from option prices. These estimates, when available and practical, are typically more accurate than estimates based on past data, since they reflect expectations of the future. For example, in our case of estimating the VaR on a position linked to an ETF tracking the S&P 500, the analyst may use implied volatilities from options on products that track the S&P 500 or may examine the CBOE Volatility Index (VIX) futures contract that reflects S&P 500 volatility.

7.2.4 Two Approaches to Estimating VaR for Leptokurtic Positions

The VaR computations are sensitive to misestimation of the probabilities of highly unusual events. If a position's risk is well described by the normal distribution, then the probabilities of extreme events are easily determined using an estimate of volatility. But leptokurtic positions have fatter tails than the normal distribution, so VaR is sensitive to the degree to which the position's actual tails exceed the tails of a normal distribution.

One solution is to use a probability distribution that allows for fatter tails. For example, the *t*-distribution not only allows for fatter tails than the normal distribution but also has a parameter that can be adjusted to alter the fatness of the tails. Also, the lognormal distribution is often viewed as providing a more accurate VaR for skewed distributions. Some applications involve rather complicated statistical probability distributions, such as mixed distributions, to incorporate higher probabilities of large price changes. In these cases, the parametric VaR (Equation 7.5) must be modified to reflect the new probability distribution.

A second and potentially simpler approach to adjusting for fat tails is simply to increase the number of standard deviations in the formula for a given confidence level. The increase should be based on analysis (typically historical analysis) of the extent of the kurtosis. An analyst computing VaR for a 99% confidence level might adjust the number of standard deviations in the VaR computation from the 2.33 value that is derived using a normal distribution to a value reflecting fatter tails, such as 2.70. The higher value would likely be based on empirical analysis of the size of the tails in historical data for the given position or similar positions. It is usually necessary to adjust the number of standard deviations only in the cases of very high confidence levels, since most financial return distributions are reasonably close to being normally distributed within 2 standard deviations of the mean. The adjustment may need to be large for very high confidence levels that focus on highly unusual outcomes. Extreme value theory is often used to provide estimates of extremely unlikely outcomes.

7.2.5 Estimating VaR Directly from Historical Data

Rather than using a parameter such as the standard deviation to compute a parametric VaR, a very simple way to estimate VaR can be to view a large collection of previous price changes and compute the size of the price change for which the specified percentage of outcomes was lower.

For example, consider a data set with a long-term history of deviations of an ETF's return from its mean return. We wish to estimate a five-day 99% VaR. We might collect the daily percentage price changes of the ETF for the past 5,000 days and use them to form 1,000 periods of five days each. We then rank the five-day deviations from the highest to the lowest. Suppose we find that exactly 10 of these 1,000 periods had price drops of more than 6.8%, and all the rest of the periods (99%) had better performance. The 99% five-day VaR for our ETF position could then be estimated at 6.8% of the portfolio's current value, under the assumption that past price changes are representative of future price changes.

The value of this approach is its conceptual simplicity, its computational simplicity, and the fact that it works even if the underlying probability distribution is unknown. The approach requires the process to be stable, meaning that the risk of the assets hasn't changed and that the number of past observations is sufficiently large to make an accurate estimate. The requirement of unchanging asset risk throughout the many previous observation periods usually disqualifies this approach for derivatives and some alternative investments with dynamically changing risk exposure, such as hedge funds. The requirement of sufficient past observations is a challenge for illiquid alternative investments, such as private real estate and private equity.

7.2.6 Estimating VaR with Monte Carlo Analysis

Monte Carlo analysis is a type of simulation in which many potential paths of the future are projected using an assumed model, the results of which are analyzed as an approximation to the future probability distributions. It is used in difficult problems when it is not practical to find expected values and standard deviations using mathematical solutions.

An example outside of investments illustrates the method. An analyst might be trying to figure out the best strategy for playing blackjack at a casino, such as whether a gambler should "stay" at 16 or 17 when the dealer has a face card showing. Solving this problem with math and statistics can get so complex that it may be easier to simulate the potential strategies. To perform a Monte Carlo analysis, a computer program is designed to simulate how much money the gambler would win or lose if the gambler played thousands and thousands of hands with a given strategy. The computer simulates play for thousands of games, one at a time, using the known probabilities of drawing various cards. The strategy that performs best in the simulations is then viewed as the strategy that will work best in the future.

In finance, it can be very complex to use a model to solve directly for the probability of a given loss in a complex portfolio that experiences a variety of market events, such as interest rate shifts. To address the problem with Monte Carlo simulation, the risk manager defines how the market parameters, such as interest rates, might behave over the future and then programs a computer to project thousands and thousands of possible scenarios of interest rate changes and other market outcomes. Each scenario is then used to estimate results in terms of the financial outcomes on the portfolio being analyzed. These results are then used to form a frequency distribution of value changes and estimate a VaR. A Monte Carlo simulation might project one million outcomes to a portfolio. In that case, a 99% VaR would be the loss that occurred in the 10,000th worst outcome.

7.2.7 Three Scenarios for Aggregating VaR

Once VaR has been computed for each asset or asset type, how are the VaRs aggregated into a VaR for the entire portfolio? For example, consider a hedge fund with equally weighted allocations to its only two positions. The fund's analyst reports a VaR of $100,000 for position #1 and a VaR of $100,000 for position #2. The critical question is the VaR of the combined positions. Let's consider three scenarios based on correlations between the returns of the two positions:

1. Perfect positive correlation: If the two positions are identical or have perfectly positive correlated and identical risk exposures, then the VaR of the combination is simply the sum of the individual VaRs, $200,000.
2. Zero correlation: If the two positions have statistically independent risk exposures, then under some assumptions, such as normally distributed outcomes, the VaR of the combination might be the square root of the sum of the individual VaRs, or $141,421, which can be derived from the equation for the variance of

uncorrelated normally distributed returns and the formula for parametric VaR based on the normal distribution.

3. Perfect negative correlation: If the two positions completely hedge each other's risk exposures, then the VaR of the combination would be $0.

Thus, VaRs should be added together to form a more global VaR only when the risks underlying the individual VaRs are perfectly correlated and have identical risk exposures. In other words, the addition of VaRs assumes that every asset or position will experience a highly abnormal circumstance on the same day. If the risks of the assets or positions are imperfectly correlated with each other, the VaRs should be combined using a model that incorporates the effects of diversification using statistics and the correlation between the risks.

7.3 BENCHMARKING AND PERFORMANCE ATTRIBUTION

Benchmarking and performance attribution are especially important and challenging in alternative investment management. These two important topics are covered in greater detail in Level II.

7.3.1 Benchmarking Overview

The starting point for analyzing the risk and return of an investment is often to compare the investment with a benchmark. **Benchmarking**, often referred to as performance benchmarking, is the process of selecting an investment index, an investment portfolio, or any other source of return as a standard (or benchmark) for comparison during performance analysis. Benchmarking is typically performed by investors and analysts external to an investment pool for the purpose of monitoring performance. Fund managers may be reluctant to adopt or declare a benchmark because they may believe that the performance of their investment strategy cannot be properly linked to a benchmark or may prefer the investment flexibility of not having their performance tied to a specific benchmark.

7.3.2 Types of Benchmarks

The return on a benchmark is usually calculated as an average of the returns from a number of assets. There are two general types of benchmark returns that might be used in the analysis of fund performance: peer and index.

Peer benchmarks are based on the returns of a comparison or peer group. The **peer group** is typically a group of funds with similar objectives, strategies, or portfolio holdings. The group may include virtually all possible comparison funds, known as a universe group, or a sampling. Instead of using a peer group of highly similar funds, a comparison group may be formed that contains many or all of the underlying securities that a fund might have in its portfolio. Unlike indices, comparison groups and peer groups tend to be customized for the specific needs of an investor analyzing one or more holdings. Thus, a particular financial institution, such as a pension fund or a pension consulting firm, might create comparison groups to benchmark managers against similar funds. Often the mean or median return of the group is subtracted from the return of the fund being analyzed to estimate abnormal returns. Also, the return of a fund being analyzed might be displayed in a graph or table alongside all the returns from a comparison group, rather than simply summarized using the mean or median return. The returns of a fund relative to its peer group are often expressed as a ranking or percentile in relation to the group.

Indices such as the MSCI World Index, a highly diversified equity index including stocks from 23 developed countries, and the Russell 2000 Index are commonly used as benchmarks. Indices typically reflect weighted averages of the returns of a set of securities or funds. Indices tend to be used for a more general audience and are often available for use by a variety of investors to gauge the performance of an investment, a market, or a sector.

7.3.3 Performance Attribution

Performance attribution, also known as **return attribution**, is the process of identifying the components of an asset's return or performance. Performance attribution seeks to separate the total return of an investment into quantities that can be linked to various determinants such as market factors (e.g., the return of one or more indices) and managerial factors (e.g., market timing and superior asset selection).

Benchmarking is a simpler, popular, and practical form of attributing return. In benchmarking, the return of an asset is simply divided into two components: the benchmark return and the active return. The active return is the deviation of an asset's return from its benchmark. The benchmark's return is subtracted from the asset's return for the same time period to form the active return. In effect, the benchmark return is attributed to the systematic performance of the asset, and the active return is attributed to the idiosyncratic performance of the asset.

7.4 RATIO-BASED PERFORMANCE MEASURES

There are two major types of performance measures. The first uses ratios of return to risk. With this method, return can be expressed in numerous ways in the numerator, and risk can be expressed in numerous ways in the denominator. This section discusses the most useful and common return-to-risk ratios. A second method for measuring performance involves estimating the risk-adjusted return of an asset that can be compared with a standard. This and other approaches are discussed in this section.

The numerator of ratio-based performance measures is based on the expected return or the average historical return of the given asset. The numerator usually takes one of three forms: (1) the asset's average return, (2) the asset's average return minus a benchmark or target rate of return, and (3) the asset's average return minus the riskless rate.

The denominator of the ratio can be virtually any risk measure, although the most popular performance measures use the most widely used risk measures, such as volatility (standard deviation) or beta. The risk measure may be an observed estimate of risk or the investor's belief regarding expected risk. This section discusses the most common ratio-based performance measures in alternative investment analysis.

7.4.1 The Sharpe Ratio

The most popular measure of risk-adjusted performance for traditional investments and traditional investment strategies is the Sharpe ratio. The **Sharpe ratio** has excess return as its numerator and volatility as its denominator:

$$SR = [E(R_p) - R_f]/\sigma_p \qquad (7.6)$$

where SR is the Sharpe ratio for portfolio p, $E(R_p)$ is the expected return for portfolio p, R_f is the riskless rate, and σ_p is the standard deviation of the returns of portfolio p. The numerator is the portfolio's expected or average excess return, where expected or average excess return is defined as expected or average total return minus the riskless rate.

The following examples further illustrate use of the Sharpe ratio.

☞ **APPLICATION 7.4.1A**

Consider a portfolio that earns 10% per year and has an annual standard deviation of 20% when the risk-free rate is 3%. The Sharpe ratio is (10% − 3%)/20%, or 0.35. When using annual returns and an annual standard deviation of returns, the Sharpe ratio may be interpreted as the annual risk premium that the investment earned per percentage point in annual standard deviation. In this case, the investment's return exceeded the riskless rate by 35 basis points for each percentage point in standard deviation. In an analysis of past data, the mean return of the portfolio is used as an estimate of its expected return, and the historical standard deviation of the sample is used as an estimate of the asset's true risk. Throughout the remainder of this analysis of performance measures, the analysis may be viewed as interchangeable between using historical estimates and using expectations.

The Sharpe ratio facilitates comparison of investment alternatives and the selection of the opportunity that generates the highest excess return per unit of total risk. However, the denominator of the Sharpe ratio (the standard deviation) does not reflect the marginal contribution of risk that occurs when an asset is added to a portfolio with which it is not perfectly correlated. In other words, the actual additional risk that the inclusion of an asset causes to a portfolio is less than the standard deviation whenever that asset helps diversify the portfolio. Accordingly, it can be argued that the Sharpe ratio should be used only on a stand-alone basis and not in a portfolio context.

It should be obvious that both the numerator and the denominator of the Sharpe ratio should be measured in the same unit of time, such as quarterly or annual values. The resulting Sharpe ratio, however, is sensitive to the length of the time period used to compute the numerator and the denominator. Note that the numerator is proportional to the unit of time, ignoring compounding. Thus, the excess return expressed as an annual rate will be two times larger than a semiannual rate and four times larger than a quarterly rate, ignoring compounding. However, the denominator is linearly related to the square root of time, assuming that returns are statistically independent through time:

$$\sigma_T = \sigma_1 \sqrt{T} \tag{7.7}$$

where σ_T is the standard deviation over T periods; σ_1 is the standard deviation over one time period, such as one year; and T is the number of time periods.

This formula assumes that the returns through time are statistically independent. Thus, a one-year standard deviation is only $\sqrt{2}$ times a semiannual standard deviation, and a one-year standard deviation is only twice ($\sqrt{4}$) the quarterly standard deviation. Thus, switching from quarterly returns to annualized returns roughly increases the numerator fourfold but increases the denominator only twofold, resulting in a twofold higher ratio.

☞ APPLICATION 7.4.1B

Ignoring compounding for simplicity, and assuming statistically independent returns through time, the Sharpe ratios based on semiannual returns and quarterly returns are, using the same annual values as illustrated earlier, as follows:

Annual: $(10\% - 3\%)/20\% = 0.350$

Semiannual: $[(10\% - 3\%)/2]/(20\% \sqrt{0.5}) = 0.247$

Quarterly: $[(10\% - 3\%)/4]/(20\% \sqrt{0.25}) = 0.175$

Note that the Sharpe ratio declines from 0.350 to 0.175, which is a 50% decrease, as the time interval for measurement is reduced by 75%, from annual to quarterly.

If returns were perfectly correlated through time, the Sharpe ratio would not be sensitive to the time unit of measurement; it would be dimensionless. However, in a perfect financial market, returns are expected to be statistically independent through time, and in practice, returns are usually found to be somewhat statistically independent through time. The point is that Sharpe ratio comparisons must be performed using the same return intervals.

Sharpe ratios should be computed and compared consistently with the same units of time, such as with annualized data. Sharpe ratios can then be easily intuitively interpreted and compared across investments. However, Sharpe ratios ignore diversification effects and are primarily useful in comparing returns only on a stand-alone basis. This means that Sharpe ratios should typically be used when examining total portfolios rather than evaluating components that will be used to diversify a portfolio. Of course, if the investments being compared are well-diversified portfolios, then the Sharpe ratio is appropriate, since systematic risk and total risk are equal in well-diversified portfolios. It should be noted that in the field of investments, the term **well-diversified portfolio** is traditionally interpreted as any portfolio containing only trivial amounts of diversifiable risk.

Finally, a Sharpe ratio is only as useful as volatility is useful in measuring risk. In the case of normally distributed returns, the volatility fully describes the dispersion in outcomes. But in the many alternative investments with levels of skew and kurtosis that deviate from the normal distribution, volatility provides only a partial measure of dispersion. Thus, the Sharpe ratio is a less valuable measure of risk-adjusted performance for asset returns with non-normal distributions.

7.4.2 Four Important Properties of the Sharpe Ratio

As detailed in the previous section, the Sharpe ratio has the following four important properties:

1. It is intuitive. Using annual or annualized data, the Sharpe ratio reflects the added annual excess return per percentage point of annualized standard deviation.
2. It is a measure of performance that is based on stand-alone risk, not systematic risk. Therefore, it does not reflect the marginal risk of including an asset in a portfolio when there is diversifiable risk.
3. It is sensitive to dimension. The Sharpe ratio changes substantially if the unit of time changes, such as when quarterly rates are used rather than annualized rates.
4. It is less useful in comparing investments with returns that vary by skew and kurtosis.

The Sharpe ratio should be used with caution when measuring the performance of particular alternative investments, such as hedge funds. Research has shown that the Sharpe ratio may be manipulated (to the benefit of a hedge fund manager) using optionlike strategies that prevent extreme returns.

7.4.3 The Treynor Ratio

Another popular measure of risk-adjusted performance for traditional investments and traditional investment strategies is the Treynor ratio, which differs from the Sharpe ratio by the use of systematic risk rather than total risk. The **Treynor ratio** has excess return as its numerator and beta as the measure of risk as its denominator:

$$TR = [E(R_p) - R_f]/\beta_p \qquad (7.8)$$

where TR is the Treynor ratio for portfolio p; $E(R_p)$ is the expected return, or mean return, for portfolio p; R_f is the riskless rate; and β_p is the beta of the returns of portfolio p.

☞ **APPLICATION 7.4.3A**

Consider a portfolio that earns 10% per year and has a beta with respect to the market portfolio of 1.5 when the risk-free rate is 3%. The Treynor ratio is (10% − 3%)/1.5, or 0.0467 (4.67%). The Treynor ratio may be interpreted as the risk premium that the investment earns per unit of beta. In this example, the investment's expected return is 4.67% higher than the riskless rate for each unit of beta.

The Treynor ratio offers the intuition of estimating the excess return of an investment relative to its systematic risk. The Treynor ratio can be directly compared to the equity risk premium discussed in Chapter 8.

Unlike the Sharpe ratio, the Treynor ratio should not be used on a stand-alone basis. Beta is a measure of only one type of risk: systematic risk. Therefore, selecting a stand-alone investment on the basis of the Treynor ratio might tend to maximize excess return per unit of systematic risk but not maximize excess return per unit of total risk unless each investment were well diversified. Beta does, however, serve as an appropriate measure of the marginal risk of adding an investment to a well-diversified portfolio. In this way, the Treynor ratio is designed to compare well-diversified investments and to compare investments that are to be added to a well-diversified portfolio. But the Treynor ratio should not be used to compare poorly diversified investments on a stand-alone basis. The Treynor ratio is less frequently applied in alternative investments, as beta is not an appropriate risk measure for many alternative investment strategies.

The Treynor ratio depends on the unit of time used to express returns. Generally, the beta of an asset (the denominator of the ratio) would be expected to be quite similar, regardless of the unit of time used to express returns. However, ignoring compounding, the quarterly returns would be expected to be one-quarter the magnitude of annual returns, and monthly returns would be expected to be one-twelfth the magnitude of annual returns. Thus, the numerator is proportional to the time unit, and the denominator is roughly independent of the time unit, meaning that the ratio is proportional to the unit of time.

7.4.4 Four Important Properties of the Treynor Ratio

As detailed in the previous section, the Treynor ratio has the following four important properties:

1. It is highly intuitive. Using annual or annualized data, the Treynor ratio reflects the added annual excess return per unit of beta.
2. It is a measure of performance that is based on systematic risk, not stand-alone risk. Therefore, it does not reflect the marginal total risk of including an asset in a portfolio that is poorly diversified.
3. It is directly proportional to its dimension. The Treynor ratio varies directly with the unit of time used, such that ratios based on annualized rates tend to be four times larger than ratios based on quarterly rates.
4. It is less useful in comparing investments with returns that vary by skew and kurtosis, because beta does not capture higher moments.

7.4.5 The Sortino Ratio

A measure of risk-adjusted performance that tends to be used more in alternative investments than in traditional investments is the Sortino ratio. The **Sortino ratio** subtracts a benchmark return, rather than the riskless rate, from the asset's return in its numerator and uses downside standard deviation as the measure of risk in its denominator:

$$\text{Sortino Ratio} \, [E(R_p) - R_{Target}]/TSSD \tag{7.9}$$

where $E(R_p)$ is the expected return, or mean return in practice, for portfolio p; R_{Target} is the user's target rate of return; and *TSSD* is the target semistandard deviation (or downside deviation), discussed earlier in the chapter.

As a semistandard deviation, the *TSSD* focuses on the downside deviations. As a target semistandard deviation, *TSSD* defines a downside deviation as the negative deviations relative to the target return, rather than a mean return or zero. Thus, the Sortino ratio uses the concept of a target rate of return in expressing both the return in the numerator and the risk in the denominator.

☞ APPLICATION 7.4.5A

Consider a portfolio that earns 10% per year when the investor's target rate of return is 8% per year. The semistandard deviation based on returns relative to the target is 16% annualized. The Sortino ratio would be (10% – 8%)/16%, or 0.125.

Even if the target return is set equal to the riskless rate, the Sortino ratio is not equal to the Sharpe ratio. Although they would share the same numerator, the denominator would be the same only when distributions were perfectly symmetrical. The point is that the emphasis of the Sortino ratio is the use of downside risk rather than the use of a target rate of return. To the extent that a return distribution is nonsymmetrical and the investor is focused on downside risk, the Sortino ratio can be useful as a performance indicator.

7.4.6 The Information Ratio

The information ratio provides a sophisticated view of risk-adjusted performance. The **information ratio** has a numerator formed by the difference between the average return of a portfolio (or other asset) and its benchmark, and a denominator equal to its tracking error:

$$\text{Information ratio} = [E(R_p) - R_{Benchmark}]/TE_p \qquad (7.10)$$

where $E(R_p)$ is the expected or mean return for portfolio p, $R_{Benchmark}$ is the expected or mean return of the benchmark, and TE_p is the tracking error of the portfolio p relative to its benchmark return.

Tracking error, which was discussed earlier in this chapter, may be approximately viewed as the typical amount by which a portfolio's return deviates from its benchmark. Technically speaking, tracking error is the standard deviation of the differences through time of the portfolio's return and the benchmark return.

The numerator is the average amount by which the portfolio exceeds its benchmark return (if positive). Thus, the information ratio is the amount of added return, if positive, that a portfolio generates relative to its benchmark for each percentage by which the portfolio's return typically deviates from its benchmark.

☞ **APPLICATION 7.4.6A**
_____

If a portfolio consistently outperformed its benchmark by 4% per year, but its performance relative to that benchmark typically deviated from that 4% mean with an annualized standard deviation of 10%, then its information ratio would be 4%/10%, or 0.40.

Like the Sharpe ratio, the information ratio is sensitive to whether it is computed using annualized returns or periodic (e.g., quarterly) returns. The information ratio is higher when the portfolio's average return is higher, and lower when the portfolio deviates from its benchmark by larger amounts. Accordingly, the use of the information ratio is an attempt to drive the portfolio toward investments that track the benchmark well but consistently outperform the benchmark.

7.4.7 Return on VaR

Value at risk (VaR) was detailed earlier in this chapter as a measure of potential risk for a specified time horizon and level of confidence. **Return on VaR (RoVaR)** is simply the expected or average return of an asset divided by a specified VaR (expressing VaR as a positive number):

$$RoVaR = E(R_p)/VaR \tag{7.11}$$

In cases in which VaR is a good summary measure of the risks being faced, RoVaR may be a useful metric. In such cases, the risks of the investment alternatives typically share similarly shaped return distributions that are well understood by the analysts using the ratio.

7.5 RISK-ADJUSTED RETURN MEASURES

The previous section focused on ratio-based performance measures. This section discusses three performance measures that are not return-to-risk ratios. Other performance measures exist, and some firms use performance measures unique to their particular firm. In practice, a variety of performance measures should be viewed in a performance review, each of which is selected to view performance from a relevant perspective.

7.5.1 Jensen's Alpha

Jensen's alpha is based on the single-factor market model discussed in Chapter 5. In terms of expected returns, **Jensen's alpha** may be expressed as the difference between its expected return and the expected return of efficiently priced assets of similar risk. The return of efficiently priced assets of similar risk is usually specified using the single-factor market model, as shown in the following equation:

$$\alpha_p = E(R_p) - R_f - \beta_p[E(R_m) - R_f] \tag{7.12}$$

The right-hand side expresses the alpha as the expected return of the portfolio in excess of the riskless rate and the required risk premium. Any return above the riskless rate and the required risk premium is alpha, which represents superior performance.

☞ APPLICATION 7.5.1A

A portfolio is expected to earn 7% annualized return when the riskless rate is 4% and the expected return of the market is 8%. If the beta of the portfolio is 0.5, the alpha of the portfolio is 1%, found by substituting into Equation 7.12 and solving:

$$\alpha_p = 7\% - 4\% - [0.5(8\% - 4\%)] = 1\%$$

Jensen's alpha is a direct measure of the absolute amount by which an asset is estimated to outperform, if positive, the return on efficiently priced assets of equal systematic risk in a single-factor market model. It is tempting to describe the return in the context of the CAPM, but strictly speaking, no asset offers a nonzero alpha in a CAPM world, since all assets are priced efficiently. In practice, expected returns on the asset and the market, as well as the true beta of the asset, are unobservable. Thus, Jensen's alpha is typically estimated using historical data as the intercept (a) of the following regression equation adapted from Chapter 8.

$$R_t - R_f = a + b(R_{mt} - R_f) + e_t \tag{7.13}$$

where R_t is the return of the portfolio or asset in period t, R_{mt} is the return of the market portfolio in time t, a is the estimated intercept of the regression, b is the estimated slope coefficient of the regression, and e_t is the residual of the regression in time t. The error term e_t estimates the idiosyncratic return of the portfolio in time t, b is an estimate of the portfolio's beta, and a is an estimate of the portfolio's average abnormal or idiosyncratic return. Since the intercept, α, is estimated, it should be interpreted subject to levels of confidence.

7.5.2 M² (M-Squared) Approach

The **M² approach**, or M-squared approach, expresses the excess return of an investment after its risk has been normalized to equal the risk of the market portfolio. The first step is to leverage or deleverage the investment so that its risk matches the risk of the market portfolio. The superior (or inferior) return that the investment offers relative to the market when it has been leveraged or deleveraged to have the same volatility as the market portfolio is M². A fund is leveraged to a higher level of risk when money is borrowed at the riskless rate and invested in the fund, and a fund is deleveraged when money is allocated to the riskless asset rather than invested in the fund.

EXHIBIT 7.2 Sample Computations of M^2

(1) Fund	(2) Excess Return	(3) Fund Volatility	(4) Sharpe Ratio	(5) Portfolio Weight	(6) Portfolio Volatility	(7) Portfolio Excess Return	(8) Fund M^2
A	3%	5%	.60	200%	10%	6%	$6\% + R_f$
B	5%	10%	.50	100%	10%	5%	$5\% + R_f$
C	6%	15%	.40	67%	10%	4%	$4\% + R_f$

Consider three funds with excess returns and volatilities as expressed in the second and third columns of Exhibit 7.2. Note that the three funds differ in volatility (column 3), so their returns cannot be directly compared.

The Sharpe ratio in column 4 reveals that Fund A provides the best excess return per unit of standard deviation. The M^2 approach shows Fund A's superior potential with a different metric in light of the opportunity provided by the market portfolio. Assuming that the volatility of the market portfolio is estimated to be 10%, the first step of the M^2 approach is to leverage or deleverage each of the funds into a total portfolio that has the same volatility as the market portfolio, which is 10%. Columns 5, 6, and 7 indicate leveraging (Fund A) and deleveraging (Fund C) to create risk levels equal to that of the market. To invest in Fund A, which has a volatility of 5%, with a total volatility of 10%, a manager would use 2:1 leverage, effectively allocating a weight of +200% to Fund A and –100% to the riskless asset, as indicated in column 5. To invest in Fund B with a total volatility of 10%, the manager can simply allocate 100% of a portfolio to Fund B. Finally, to invest in Fund C with a total volatility of 10%, the manager allocates 67% of the portfolio to Fund C and the remaining 33% to the riskless asset. Using leverage and deleverage, all three alternatives can be used to generate portfolios with the same expected volatility as the market, or 10%, as indicated in column 6. The excess returns of the portfolios, found by multiplying the alphas of the funds in column 2 by the weight of the fund in the portfolio column 5, are shown in column 7.

The most attractive alternative, using Fund A with leverage, is the alternative with the highest excess return, since all three portfolios have the same volatility. The expected return of each portfolio is M^2, which is shown in column 8 by adding the riskless rate to the excess return in column 7; M^2 provides an estimate of the expected return that an investor can earn using a specified investment opportunity and taking a level of total risk equal to that of the market portfolio. Equation 7.14 provides the formula for M^2:

$$M^2 = R_f + \{(\sigma_m/\sigma_p)[E(R_p) - R_f]\} \tag{7.14}$$

where R_f is the riskless rate, σ_m is the volatility of the market portfolio, σ_p is the volatility of the portfolio or asset for which M^2 is being calculated, and $E(R_p)$ is the mean or expected return of the portfolio.

APPLICATION 7.5.2A

Consider a portfolio with $M^2 = 4\%$. The portfolio is expected to earn 10%, whereas the riskless rate is only 2%. What is the ratio of the volatility of the market to the volatility of the portfolio? Inserting the given rates generates $4\% = 2\% + [(\text{ratio of volatilities}) \times 8\%]$. The ratio of the volatility of the market to the volatility of the portfolio must be 25%.

 APPLICATION 7.5.2B

Consider the following information:

	Expected Return	Volatility
Market	12%	14%
Portfolio	14%	28%
Riskless Asset	2%	0%

M^2 is found by inserting four of the values into Equation 7.14:

$$M^2 = 2\% + \{(0.14/0.28)[0.14 - 0.02]\}$$
$$M^2 = 2\% + 6\% = 8\%$$

It should be noted that there is an alternative formula for M^2, sometimes called M^2-alpha, which is slightly different from Equation 7.14. This alternative formula can be found both in Modigliani and Modigliani's original paper as well as in subsequent analyses by other authors.[2] However, this text focuses on the M^2 formula in Equation 7.14, which is more reflective of the totality of the original work.

The formula for M^2 is an expected return or, in the case of an estimation using sample data, the mean return. Specifically, it is an estimated expected return on a strategy that uses borrowing or lending to bring the total volatility of the position equal to the volatility of the market portfolio. The first term on the right-hand side of the formula for M^2 is the riskless rate, the compensation for the time value of money. The term in brackets is a risk premium specific to the portfolio or fund being analyzed. The ratio inside the first set of parentheses is the leverage factor that brings the volatility of the portfolio to the same level as the volatility of the market. That leverage factor is multiplied by the excess return of the underlying fund to form the excess return of the leveraged position.

7.5.3 Average Tracking Error

An important concept in all investing is tracking error, discussed earlier in this chapter. Most applications of the concept of tracking error refer to it as the standard deviation of these differences. Thus, tracking error is most commonly viewed as a standard deviation. However, some sources use the term *tracking error* to refer generally to the differences through time between an investment's return and the return of its benchmark. When tracking error is used in the latter sense, the term **average tracking error** simply refers to the excess of an investment's return relative to its benchmark. In other words, it is the numerator of the information ratio.

REVIEW QUESTIONS

1. What are the two main differences between the formula for variance and the formula for semivariance?
2. What are the main differences between the formula for semistandard deviation, semivolatility, and the target semistandard deviation?
3. Define tracking error and average tracking error.
4. What is the difference between value at risk and conditional value at risk?
5. Name the two primary approaches for estimating the volatility used in computing value at risk.
6. What are the steps involved in directly estimating VaR from historical data rather than through a parametric technique?
7. When is Monte Carlo analysis most appropriate as an estimation technique?
8. What is the difference between the formulas for the Sharpe and Treynor ratios?
9. Define return on VaR.
10. Describe the intuition of Jensen's alpha.

NOTES

1. Donald R. Chambers and Qin Lu, "Semivolatility of Returns as a Measure of Downside Risk" *The Journal of Alternative Investments*, 19 (3) (Winter 2017): 68–74.
2. Franco Modigliani and Leah Modigliani, "Risk-Adjusted Performance," *Journal of Portfolio Management* 23, no. 2 (Winter 1997): 45–54.

CHAPTER 8

Alpha, Beta, and Hypothesis Testing

C hapter 6 discussed a number of measures of the price risk of options using Greek letters, such as delta, theta, and gamma. Greek letters and other similar-sounding words, such as vega, are not limited to option analysis. This chapter begins with a detailed discussion of alpha and beta. Alpha and beta are central concepts within alternative investment analysis. Consider the following hypothetical example of a discussion of investment performance:

During an investment committee meeting, the chief investment officer (CIO) comments on the performance of a convertible arbitrage fund named MAK Fund: "MAK generated an alpha of 8% last year and 10% two years ago. I think we can expect an alpha of 4% next year." A portfolio manager debates the point: "MAK Fund takes positions in convertible bonds with high credit risk. I think that MAK's alpha during the last two years was really beta." The CIO replies: "But MAK is delta hedged. And even though the fund is long gamma, is there really any beta in being long gamma?"

8.1 OVERVIEW OF BETA AND ALPHA

The preceding example illustrates how Greek letters are often used in investments to represent key concepts. This chapter focuses on alpha and beta, two critical concepts in the area of alternative investments. In a nutshell, alpha represents, or measures, superior return performance; and beta represents, or measures, systematic risk. A primary purpose of this chapter is to explore their meanings and nuances. The second purpose of this chapter is to discuss hypothesis testing, since alpha and beta are generally estimated rather than observed.

8.1.1 Beta

In the CAPM (capital asset pricing model), the concept of beta is precisely identified: Each asset has one beta, and the beta is specified as the covariance of the asset's return with the return of the market portfolio, divided by the variance of the returns of the market portfolio. This is also the definition for a regression coefficient in a simple linear regression of an asset's returns on the returns of the market portfolio. Intuitively, beta is the proportion by which an asset's excess return moves in response to the market portfolio's excess return (the return of the asset minus the return of the riskless asset). If an asset has a beta of 0.95, its excess return can be expected, on average, to increase and decrease by a factor of 0.95 relative to the excess return of the market portfolio.

But beta has a more general interpretation outside the CAPM, both within traditional investment analysis and especially within alternative investment analysis. Beta refers to a measure of risk, or the bearing of risk, wherein the underlying risk is systematic (shared by at least some other investments and usually unable to be diversified or fully hedged without cost) and is potentially rewarded with expected return. Outside the CAPM model, assets can have more than one beta, and a beta does not have to be a measure of the response of an asset to fluctuations in the entire market portfolio.

Chapter 5 detailed the idea of beta in asset pricing models. For example, when a particular investment, such as private equity, locks the investor into the position for a considerable length of time, is this illiquidity a risk that is rewarded with extra expected return? If so, then a benchmark should reflect that risk and reward, and a beta measuring that illiquidity and a term reflecting its expected reward should be included as an additional factor in an ex ante asset pricing model.

In alternative investments, the term *beta* can be used to refer to any systematic risk for which an investor might be rewarded. The term can apply to a specific systematic risk, from a single-factor or a multifactor model, or to the combined effects of multiple systematic risks from multiple factors. Beta is commonly used in phrases such as "This strategy has no beta," "Half of the manager's return was (from) beta," and "That product is a pure beta bet."

Bearing beta risk is generally viewed as a source of higher expected return. The attempt to earn consistently higher returns without taking additional systematic risk leads to the topic of the next section: alpha.

8.1.2 Alpha

Alpha refers to any excess or deficient investment return after the return has been adjusted for the time value of money (the risk-free rate) and for the effects of bearing systematic risk (beta). For an investment strategy, alpha refers to the extent to which the skill, information, and knowledge of an investment manager generate superior risk-adjusted returns (or inferior risk-adjusted returns in the case of negative alpha).

The measurement of alpha, and even the existence of alpha, is an important issue in investments in general and in alternative investments in particular. One person may believe that a high return was generated by skill (alpha), whereas another person may argue that the same return was a reward for taking high risks (beta) or a result of being lucky (idiosyncratic risk). Therefore, the concept of alpha and the estimation of alpha are inextricably linked to the view of how financial assets and financial markets function. Asset pricing models, discussed in detail in Chapters 5 and 7, are expressions of asset and market behavior. The demarcation between return from alpha, beta, and idiosyncratic risk depends on one's view of the return-generating process (or asset pricing model) as implicitly or explicitly expressed. If the return-generating process is misspecified and relevant beta risks are excluded from the analysis, then manager skill may be overstated, because the perceived alpha may include compensation for beta risks omitted from a benchmark or asset pricing model.

The concept of alpha originated with Jensen's work in the context of the CAPM. Jensen's analysis was a seminal empirical application of the single-factor market model. Jensen measured the net returns from mutual funds after accounting for the funds' returns based on the single-factor market model. He subtracted the single factor market model's estimated return from the actual returns, and what was left over (either positive or negative) was labeled alpha. However, the term *alpha* is not limited to the context of the CAPM. Regressions based on single-factor or multifactor market models are commonly performed with the value of the intercept referred to as alpha to reflect the common notation of the intercept of a linear regression.

8.2 EX ANTE VERSUS EX POST ALPHA

Although in a very general sense there is consensus in the alternative investment community regarding the general meaning of alpha as superior risk-adjusted performance, the term is often used interchangeably for two very distinct concepts. Sometimes alpha is used to describe any high risk-adjusted returns, and sometimes it is used to describe superior returns generated through skill alone. This section distinguishes these two views of alpha using the terms *ex ante alpha* and *ex post alpha*. Considerable confusion regarding alpha originates from the failure to distinguish between these different uses of the term *alpha*.

8.2.1 Ex Ante Alpha

Ex ante alpha is a term that is not commonly used in industry or academics; rather, it is used in this book to denote an issue of critical importance in understanding alpha. **Ex ante alpha** is the expected superior return if positive (or inferior return if negative) offered by an investment on a forward-looking basis after adjusting for the riskless rate and for the effects of systematic risks (beta) on expected returns. Ex ante alpha is generated by a deliberate over- or underallocation to mispriced assets based on investment management skill. Simply put, ex ante alpha indicates the extent to which an investment offers a consistent superior risk-adjusted investment return.

In the context of the single-factor market model, ex ante alpha may be viewed as the first term on the right-hand side of the following equation:

$$E(R_{it} - R_f) = \alpha_i + \beta_i[E(R_{mt}) - R_f] \tag{8.1}$$

where α_i is the ex ante alpha of asset i.

In a perfectly efficient market, α_i (alpha) in this equation would be zero for all assets. The use of a single-factor market model in Equation 8.1 and throughout most of this chapter is for simplicity. A multifactor model would simply insert a set of beta terms and factor returns in Equation 8.1 in addition to or in place of the market beta and market factor.

Equation 8.1 is described as representing a single-factor market model rather than the CAPM because the CAPM implies that no competitively priced asset would offer a positive or negative ex ante alpha, since every asset would trade at a price such that its expected return would be commensurate with its risk. In practice, market participants often seek expected returns that exceed the expected return based on systematic risk, a goal that is illustrated in Equation 8.1 using the term α_i.

☞ **APPLICATION 8.2.1A**

Consider the Sludge Fund, a fictitious fund run by unskilled managers that generally approximates the S&P 500 Index but does so with an annual expense ratio of 100 basis points (1%) more than other investment opportunities that mimic the S&P 500. Using Equation 8.1 and assuming that the S&P 500 is a proxy for the market portfolio, the ex ante alpha of Sludge Fund would be approximately −100 basis points per year. This can be deduced from assuming that $\beta_i = 1$ and that $[E(R_{it}) - E(R_{mt})] = -1\%$ due to the expense ratio. Sludge Fund could be expected to offer an ex ante alpha, meaning a consistently inferior risk-adjusted annual return, of −1% per year. This example illustrates that ex ante alpha can be negative to indicate inferior expected performance, although alpha is usually discussed in the pursuit of the superior performance associated with a positive alpha.

In practice, ex ante alpha is typically a concept rather than an observable variable. This can be seen from Equation 8.1 in a number of ways. First, β_i is a sensitivity that must be estimated with approximation. If the true value of β_i is not clear, then the true value of α_i cannot be known. Second, all of the expected returns in Equation 8.1, except the risk-free rate, are unobservable and must be estimated. Thus, ex ante alpha can only be estimated or predicted. A positive ex ante alpha is an expression of the belief that a particular investment will offer an expected return higher than investments of comparable risk in the next time period. As an illustration, consider the manager of an equity market-neutral hedge fund who desires to maximize ex ante alpha while maintaining a beta close to zero. The manager's strategy creates a hedge against systematic risk factors while attempting to exploit abnormal performance of individual stocks within the same sector or industry. Once the ex ante alpha of each stock is estimated, the portfolio is built using an optimization process seeking to maximize the positive alpha of long positions and the negative alpha of short positions, while requiring the systematic risk exposures of the long portfolio to match the short portfolio. The intended result is a zero-beta, or market-neutral, portfolio with a high ex ante alpha.

8.2.2 Ex Post Alpha

The ex ante alpha discussed in the previous section is a common interpretation of the term *alpha*. This section provides details about another potential interpretation of the term: the ex post alpha. As in the case of ex ante alpha, ex post alpha is a term used primarily for the purposes of this book.

Ex post alpha is the return, observed or estimated in retrospect, of an investment above or below the risk-free rate and after adjusting for the effects of beta (systematic risks). Whereas ex ante alpha may be viewed as expected idiosyncratic return, ex post alpha is *realized* idiosyncratic return. Simply put, ex post alpha is the extent to which an asset outperformed or underperformed its benchmark in a specified time period. Ex post alpha can be the result of luck or skill. Unlike ex ante alpha, ex post alpha can usually be estimated with a reasonable degree of confidence.

Considerable and valid disagreement exists with describing the concept of ex post alpha as being a type of alpha. The reason is that alpha is sometimes associated purely with skill, whereas ex post alpha can be generated by luck. Nevertheless, the use of the term to describe past superior performance is so common that it is labeled as such throughout this book. In the context of the single-factor market model, ex post alpha may be viewed as the last term on the right-hand side of the following equation (ε_{it}):

$$R_{it} - R_f = \beta_i(R_{mt} - R_f) + \varepsilon_{it} \tag{8.2}$$

Note that Equation 8.2 refers to theoretical values rather than actual values estimated using a linear equation or other statistical technique. Some analysts would correctly refer to ε_{it} as the idiosyncratic return or the abnormal return and might object to having the return labeled as any type of alpha, because there might be no reason to think of the return as being generated by anything other than randomness or luck. Nevertheless, many other analysts use the term *alpha* synonymously with idiosyncratic return or abnormal return; therefore, the term *ex post alpha* is used here to distinguish the concept from the other interpretation of alpha (ex ante alpha).

☞ APPLICATION 8.2.2A

Consider the Trim Fund, a fund that tries to mimic the S&P 500 Index and has managers who are unskilled. Unlike the Sludge Fund from the previous section, Trim Fund has virtually no expenses. Although Trim Fund generally mimics the S&P 500, it does so with substantial error due to the random incompetence of its managers. However, the fund is able to maintain a steady systematic risk exposure of $\beta_i = 1$. Last year, Trim Fund outperformed the S&P 500 by 125 basis points. Using Equation 8.2, assuming that $\beta_i = 1$ and that $(R_{it} - R_{mt}) = +1.25\%$, it can be calculated that $\varepsilon_{it} = +1.25\%$. Thus, Trim Fund realized a return performance for the year that was 1.25% higher than its benchmark, or its required rate of return. In the terms of this chapter, Trim Fund generated an ex post alpha of 125 basis points, even though the fund's ex ante alpha was zero.

In this example, Trim Fund must have been lucky, because the fund outperformed its benchmark by 125 basis points despite the managers being unskilled. Alpha-based analysis typically involves two steps: (1) ascertaining abnormal return performance (ex post alpha) by controlling for systematic risk, and (2) judging the extent to which any superior performance was attributable to skill (i.e., was generated by ex ante alpha). The more problematic issue can often be in the second step of the analysis, differentiating between the potential sources of the ex post alpha: luck or skill.

A key difference between ex ante and ex post alpha is that ex ante alpha reflects skill, whereas ex post alpha can be a combination of both luck and skill. For example, a manager might have enough skill to select a portfolio that is 1% underpriced but that happens to experience some completely unexpected good news that results in the portfolio outperforming other assets of similar risk by 11%. The manager had an ex ante alpha of 1% (purely skill) and an ex post alpha of 11% (1% from skill plus 10% from luck).

When discussing alpha, many analysts do not explicitly differentiate between the ex ante and ex post views. If an analyst identifies an alpha of 5% because a fund's risk-adjusted returns were 5% higher the previous year than the risk-adjusted returns of other funds, then in this book's terminology, the alpha is an ex post alpha. However, if the analyst expects that a fund will have a 5% higher expected return than other funds of similar risk, then in this book's terminology, the analyst believes that the fund has an ex ante alpha of 5% and that the fund's superior return is probably attributable to the better skill of the manager in selecting superior investment opportunities.

8.3 SINGLE-FACTOR MODELS AND REGRESSION

Chapter 5 discussed single-factor equity pricing models. The best-known single-factor market model is the capital asset pricing model (CAPM), which states that the expected return and realized return of an asset are linearly related to its market beta. This section begins by detailing the application of simple linear regression to the ex post version of the single-factor market model.

8.3.1 Simple Linear Regression and the Single-Factor Market Model

A **regression** is a statistical analysis of the relationship that explains the values of a dependent variable as a function of the values of one or more independent variables based on a specified model. The **dependent variable** is the variable supplied by the researcher that is the focus of the analysis and is determined at least in part by other (independent or explanatory) variables. **Independent variables** are those explanatory variables that are inputs to the regression and are viewed as causing the observed values of the dependent variable.

In a linear regression, the model that describes the relationship between the dependent variable and the independent variable or variables is linear. A **simple linear regression** is a linear regression in which the model has only one independent variable. For example, the ex post version of the single-factor market model describes realized excess returns of a security or fund as a linear function of an intercept, the market beta, the market portfolio's realized excess return, and an error term that reflects idiosyncratic risk. An excess return is a total return minus the periodic riskless rate. The single-factor market-model-based regression equation for asset i, based on a time series of total return data, is as follows:

$$R_{it} - R_f = \alpha_i + b_{im}(R_{mt} - R_f) + e_{it} \tag{8.3}$$

Where R_{it} is the return of asset i in time period t, R_f is the periodic riskless rate, α_i is the estimated intercept, b_{im} is the estimated slope coefficient, R_{mt} is the return of the market portfolio in time period t, and e_{it} is the residual or estimated error term for asset i at time t.

Equation 8.3 seeks to predict or explain the values of the dependent variable, excess returns $E(R_{it}) - R_f$, through movements in the independent variable, the excess return of the market portfolio $(R_{mt} - R_f)$, b_{im} is the estimated slope coefficient of the regression and is an estimate of the beta for asset i. The **slope coefficient** is a measure of the change in a dependent variable with respect to a change in an independent variable. In this example, the slope coefficient estimates the linear sensitivity of the return of asset i to the excess return of the market. The estimate of the intercept of the regression is α_i. The **intercept** is the value of the dependent variable when all independent variables are zero. In the case of Equation 8.3, the intercept can be interpreted as an estimate of the average ex post alpha of asset i. Finally, the **residuals** of the regression, e_{it}, reflect the regression's estimate of the idiosyncratic portion of asset i's realized returns above or below its mean idiosyncratic return (i.e., the regression's estimates of the error term).

8.3.2 Ordinary Least Squares Regression

There are unlimited estimated values that can be inserted for the intercept (α_i) and slope coefficient (b_{im}) in Equation 8.3. Ordinary least squares regression, the most common regression procedure, selects the intercept and slope that minimize the sum of the squared values of the residuals (the values of e_{it}). In simple linear regression, the process may be envisioned as drawing a regression line through a scatter plot of the dependent variable and independent variable. The vertical distance between the regression line and each observation is the residual. The least squares fitting criterion minimizes the sum of those distances squared. The use of ordinary least squares has several advantages: It is quick and easy, and the slope coefficient that results has an intuitive interpretation. Least squares regression has been shown to generate unbiased and most likely estimates of the slope coefficient and intercept if the error terms in the model are (1) normally distributed, (2) uncorrelated, and (3) homoskedastic (i.e., having the same finite variance). Violations of these assumptions are discussed in the next three sections. Other criteria for fitting a model to data also exist.

8.3.3 Outliers

Violations of the assumption that the error term in the model is normally distributed often occur when the data are subject to very large outliers, as is often the case in investment returns.

PROBLEM 1 : OUTLIERS. Fat tails (leptokurtic distributions) are synonymous with frequent outliers. Alternative investment returns are especially prone to being leptokurtic. Large outliers dominate a regression, potentially causing the estimates of the slope and intercept to be driven too much by the outliers, rather than by the remaining, more representative data. Ordinary least squares regression seeks to minimize the sum of squared residuals, and the squaring of residuals can cause outliers to have disproportionately higher influence than observations closer to the mean.

RESPONSE 1: A critical but often overlooked task in linear regression is visual observation of the residuals of the regression. At least two plots are advisable for important regressions. Residuals should be plotted on the vertical axis against the independent or explanatory variable on the horizontal axis, and time-series residuals should be plotted on the vertical axis against time on the horizontal axis. The analyst should note extreme outliers to determine if the residuals reflect data errors or economic fact. If the extreme residuals are not the result of errors, the analyst should determine if the underlying economic behavior causing the observation warrants the large level of influence that the outlier has on the estimated parameters. If the outlier is caused by an event that can be reasonably expected to not recur, perhaps the outlier should be removed. An example is a fund experiencing a catastrophic event from short option positions that has amended its investment strategy to disallow short option positions. It is important not to remove outliers corresponding to gains or losses that are likely to be repeated.

For example, if an analyst regressed the monthly returns of a U.S. financial stock on U.S. stock market returns over a period including 2007 and 2008, the analyst would probably obtain a very high estimate of the stock's beta due especially to the months in which financial stocks experienced tremendously negative returns and in which the overall market experienced negative returns as well. The analyst would detect these outliers with a plot and then need to decide whether the observed correlations were a representative sample on which to forecast future systematic risk (beta) or the outliers generated an estimate of beta that is unduly indicative of behavior under stressed conditions and therefore unrepresentative of anticipated market conditions.

8.3.4 Autocorrelation

The simplest statistical regression procedures assume that the model's error terms are uncorrelated—including through time. Autocorrelation of the error terms is a violation of that assumption.

PROBLEM 2 : AUTOCORRELATION. Violations of the assumption that the error term is uncorrelated through time most often occur when returns are autocorrelated. Many alternative investment return series are especially prone to autocorrelation due to smoothed pricing or illiquidity.

RESPONSE 2: The Durbin-Watson statistic, detailed in Chapter 4, is used to test for autocorrelation of residuals. If the Durbin-Watson statistic indicates autocorrelation, there are several well-established statistical procedures for performing adjusted regressions that provide better results. First-order autocorrelation is a common phenomenon in alternative investments and is reasonably easy to address. For example, if an analyst regresses the percentage changes in a real estate project's value based on monthly appraisals against the overall market return, the residuals of the regression might exhibit autocorrelation based on a Durbin-Watson test. The autocorrelation may indicate that the appraisal valuations were reflecting value changes on a delayed basis. Such a regression should be corrected for autocorrelation in order to provide a more accurate measure of the correlation between true real estate values and the overall market.

8.3.5 Heteroskedasticity

The simplest statistical regression procedures assume that the variance of the model's error terms is homoskedastic.

PROBLEM 3 : HETEROSKEDASTICITY: Heteroskedasticity is the opposite of homoskedasticity. In a regression, heteroskedasticity refers to a situation in which the variance of the error term varies. For example, the variance of the error term may be correlated with an independent variable, may vary through time, or may be related to some other variable or dimension. With homoscedasticity, the variance of the error term is constant.

RESPONSE 3: The same plots used for outlier examination should be used to detect heteroskedasticity (i.e., residuals should be plotted against the independent variable and against time). In this visual analysis, the analyst should look for a pattern in the dispersion of the residuals, such as a <, >, <>, or >< pattern. For example, a < pattern would show generally increasing dispersion of the residuals moving from left to right in the diagram. Heteroskedasticity can be formally detected using various tests. The problem with regression results from data exhibiting heteroskedasticity is that the estimated regression parameters are unduly influenced by the data related to the greatest variance in the error term. The most popular correction is weighted least squares, in which a weighting scheme is developed and applied to the data to reduce the importance of the data subject to higher error-term volatility.

For example, an analyst regressed the returns of a corporate bond against a constant maturity Treasury index. A plot of the residuals through time tends to indicate a > pattern, with earlier observations (to the left) having more dispersion than more recent observations (to the right). The heteroskedasticity is attributable to the declining price volatility of the corporate bond as its maturity nears and its duration declines. The earliest observations with the highest dispersion dominate the regression, generating inefficient estimates. A weighted least squares approach should be used to adjust the influence of the observations toward being more equal over time.

In summary, the accuracy of a regression's results may be adversely affected by three primary issues: outliers, autocorrelation, and heteroskedasticity. The statistical approach should be adjusted as necessary to correct for any of these challenges before using the estimated parameters.

8.3.6 Interpreting a Regression's Goodness of Fit

The first major interpretation of a regression's results is evaluating the overall explanatory power of the regression. The explanatory power of the regression is evaluated as its goodness of fit. The **goodness of fit** of a regression is the extent to which the model appears to explain the variation in the dependent variable. The *r*-squared value of the regression, which is also called the coefficient of determination, is often used to assess goodness of fit, especially when comparing models. In a simple linear regression, the *r*-squared is simply the squared value of the estimated correlation coefficient between the dependent variable and the independent variable. Correlation, discussed in Chapter 4, ranges from −1 to +1, with negative values showing an inverse relationship between two variables, and positive values denoting a direct relationship between two variables. Because the *r*-squared is equal to a correlation coefficient squared, the range of possible values for *r* squared is between zero and 1 and is often expressed as a percentage. When building or explaining financial relationships, larger values of *r*-squared are preferred, everything else being equal, as the independent variable is explaining a greater portion of the variance in the dependent variable.

R-squared is also interpreted in an absolute sense. For example, a long-only mutual fund may have an r-squared of perhaps 0.90 (i.e., 90%) in a regression of its returns on the returns of a market index. An r-squared such as 0.90 would often be described as meaning that the independent variable (in this case, the returns of the market index) explained 90% of the variation in the dependent variable (in this case, the returns to the mutual fund). This can be interpreted as indicating that 90% of the fund's returns were explained by the systematic risk (i.e., exposure to the market risk represented by the index). The remaining value, $1 - r^2$, is the idiosyncratic risk, or the risk that is not explained by the market index. In this case, the idiosyncratic risk is 10% of the fund's total risk. The fund's idiosyncratic risk might be due to incomplete diversification, such as holding only 25 stocks and being compared to a very well-diversified benchmark index.

8.3.7 Performing a *t*-Test on Regression Parameters

The second major interpretation of a regression's results is testing the significance of the parameter estimates. In an application of Equation 8.3, the intercept of the regression is usually interpreted as an estimate of the ex ante alpha, or skill of the fund manager (if a fund's return is being analyzed), or the superior risk-adjusted return of a security (if a security's return is being analyzed). The slope coefficient of the regression is usually interpreted as the beta of the asset, a measure of the asset's systematic risk.

The parameter estimates of the regression are typically examined for statistical significance using a *t*-test. A *t*-test is a statistical test that rejects or fails to reject a hypothesis by comparing a *t*-statistic to a critical value.

For each alpha and beta estimate, the *t*-statistic is formed. The *t*-statistic of a parameter is formed by taking the estimated absolute value of the parameter and dividing by its standard error. The resulting *t*-statistic is compared to a critical value. If the *t*-statistic exceeds the critical value, the parameter estimate is deemed to be significantly different from zero. The critical value of the *t*-statistic is found from published lists of critical values based on two parameters: (1) the degrees of freedom and (2) the desired significance level of the test.

☞ APPLICATION 8.3.7A

Consider a regression with an alpha estimate of 0.5% (with a standard error of 0.3%) and a beta estimate of 1.1 (with a standard error of 0.3). Are the regression parameters statistically significant? The *t*-statistic of the alpha is 1.67, whereas the *t*-statistic of the beta is 3.67, each found by dividing the parameter estimates by the corresponding standard error. At a 5% confidence level, the *t*-statistic needs to exceed 1.96 to be deemed statistically significant (assuming a very large number of degrees of freedom). In this case, the alpha is not deemed to be significantly different from zero because the *t*-statistic is less than 1.96 (the critical value); however, the beta does differ significantly from zero, as its *t*-statistic exceeds 1.96.

8.4 INFERRING EX ANTE ALPHA FROM EX POST ALPHA

One of the most central functions of alternative investment analysis is the process of attempting to identify ex ante alpha. Ex ante alpha estimation would be simplified if the expected returns of all assets could be observed or accurately estimated. In practice, expectations of returns on risky assets vary from market participant to market participant. In fact, the existence of ex ante alpha comes from different investors having different expectations of risk-adjusted return.

A key method of identifying ex ante alpha for a particular investment fund is a thorough and rigorous analysis of the manager and the manager's processes and methods. Analysis of historical data should typically also play a role, though not too large a role, in identification of ex ante alpha. In this section, these empirical methods are discussed. Empirical methods estimate ex ante alpha through attempting to differentiate between the roles of luck and skill in generating past risk-adjusted returns. The objective of these empirical analyses is to understand how much, if any, of an investment's past returns are attributable to skill and might be predicted to recur.

8.4.1 Two Steps to Empirical Analysis of Ex Ante Alpha

Two critical steps are used to identify ex ante alpha from historical performance. First, an asset pricing model or benchmark must be used to divide the historical returns into the portions attributable to systematic risks (and the risk-free rate) and those attributable to idiosyncratic effects. Second, the remaining returns, meaning the idiosyncratic returns (i.e., ex post alpha), should be statistically analyzed to estimate the extent, if any, to which the superior returns may be attributable to skill rather than luck.

The first step, identifying ex post alpha, requires the specification of an ex post asset pricing model or benchmark and can be challenging. Ex post alpha estimation is the process of adjusting realized returns for risk and the time value of money. Ex post alpha is not perfectly and unanimously measured, because it relies on accurate specification of systematic risks and estimation of the effects of those systematic risks on ex post returns.

Given estimates of ex post alpha (idiosyncratic returns), the second step is the statistical analysis of the superior or inferior returns to differentiate between random luck and persistent skill. The second part of this chapter (starting with section 8.8) discusses hypothesis testing and statistical inference. The idea is that, given a set of assumptions with regard to the statistical behavior of idiosyncratic returns, historical returns can be used to infer central tendencies. If historical risk-adjusted returns are very consistently positive or negative, the analyst can become increasingly confident that the underlying investment offered a positive or negative alpha.

8.4.2 Lessons about Alpha Estimation from a Fair Casino Game

To frame the discussion of the role of idiosyncratic risk and model misspecification in alpha estimation, we discuss a hypothetical scenario in which skill is clearly not a factor, such as in the casino game roulette. This simplified scenario enables a clearer illustration of the challenges raised by model misspecification. **Model misspecification** is any error in the identification of the variables in a model or any error in identification of the relationships between the variables. Model misspecification inserts errors in the interpretation and estimation of relations.

For example, assume that there is a perfectly balanced roulette wheel in a casino with perfectly honest employees and guests. For simplicity, the payouts of all bets are assumed to be fair gambles rather than gambles offering the house an advantage. In other words, every possible gamble has an expected payout equal to the amount wagered, meaning an expected profit or loss of zero. Gamblers use a variety of strategies, and they wager different amounts of money.

Based on these assumptions, a model can be derived that states that the expected gain or loss to each gambler should be $0 and 0%. By assumption, any realized gambling returns that differ from zero will be based purely on luck. When the actual profits and losses to the gamblers at the end of a day are observed, some gamblers ended up winning large amounts of money, some gamblers lost a lot of money, and many gamblers won or lost smaller amounts.

Based on the assumption that the roulette wheel is perfectly balanced, all of the observed profits and losses are idiosyncratic (i.e., all ex post alphas were generated by luck, since all ex ante alphas were zero).

Let's assume that there is a researcher who believes that some gamblers have skill in predicting the outcomes of the roulette wheel. That researcher would hypothesize that some or all of the observed profits were due to that skill and should thus be viewed as ex ante alpha. The researcher decides to perform statistical tests to identify the skilled gamblers.

Even in this simplified example, it would be easy for the researcher to make incorrect inferences. For example, assume that thousands of gamblers were observed. The researcher might focus on the gambler who won the most money, conclude that the odds were extraordinarily low that a gambler could win so much money in one night, and therefore falsely conclude that the chosen gambler was skilled. Another researcher might expand the search to multiple nights and multiple casinos and find a gambler with even higher winnings. But in this example, no level of winnings can prove that skill was involved, because skill was eliminated by assumption.

Unfortunately, some financial analysts use the analogous approach to analyze investment opportunities. They examine the past returns from a large set of investment pools and conclude that the top-performing funds must have achieved that success through skill. This example highlights the challenges faced in investment analysis. Does ex ante alpha exist in a particular market? Do we have models that can accurately separate ex post alpha from systematic risk bearing? Finally, will our statistical tests enable us to differentiate between idiosyncratic outcomes (luck) and ex ante alpha (skill)?

8.5 RETURN ATTRIBUTION, ALPHA, AND BETA

Return attribution (performance attribution) was introduced in Chapter 7. This section focuses on return attribution and distinguishing between the effects of systematic risk (beta), the effects of skill (ex ante alpha), and the effects of idiosyncratic risk (luck).

8.5.1 A Numerical Example of Alpha

For simplicity, consider an example that uses a single-factor market model and for which expected returns are known. Assume that Fund A trades unlisted securities that are not efficiently priced, has a beta of 0.75, and has an expected return of 9%. Additionally, assume that the expected return of the market is 10% and that the risk-free rate is 2%. During the next year, the market earns 18% and Fund A earns 17%.

Given these assumptions, we can answer the following questions:

- What was the fund's ex ante alpha?
- What was the fund's ex post alpha?
- What was the amount of ex post alpha that was luck?
- What was the amount of the ex post alpha that was skill?

First, the ex ante alpha is found as the intercept of the ex ante version of the single-factor market model, in this case a CAPM-style model. Inserting the market's expected return, the fund's beta, and the risk-free rate into Equation 8.1 generates the required return, $E(R_A{}^*)$, for Fund A in an efficient market:

$$E(R_A{}^*) - 2\% = [0.75(10\% - 2\%)]$$
$$E(R_A{}^*) = 8\%$$

The return of 8% is the expected return that investors would require on an asset with a beta of 0.75, which is also the expected return that Fund A would offer in an efficient market. The ex ante alpha of Fund A is any difference between the expected return of Fund A and its required return:

Ex Ante Alpha = Expected Return − Required Return → 9% − 8% → 1%

Thus, Fund A offers 1% more return than would be required based on its systematic risk (i.e., an ex ante alpha of 1%). Next, the ex post alpha is found from the ex post version of the single-factor market model. Inserting the two realized returns, the beta and the risk-free rate, into Equation 8.2 generates the following:

$17\% - 2\% = [0.75(18\% - 2\%)] + \varepsilon \rightarrow$ Ex Post Alpha $(\varepsilon) = 15\% - 12\% = +3\%$

The analysis indicates that even though Fund A underperformed the market portfolio prior to risk adjustment, it performed 3% better than assets of similar risk. Thus, in the terminology introduced earlier in the chapter, the ex post alpha (idiosyncratic return) was 3%.

Finally, since the analysis assumes that the fund offers an expected superior return, or ex ante alpha, of 1%, then 1% (i.e., one-third) ex post alpha of 3% could be said to be attributable to skill and 2% (i.e., two thirds of 3%) attributable to good luck (positive idiosyncratic return).

In practice, true beta and expected returns are difficult to estimate. The beta is necessary to estimate either ex ante alpha or ex post alpha. The expected returns are necessary only to estimate ex ante alpha and to distinguish between luck and skill. It is common for a return attribution analysis to estimate ex post alpha but not consider ex ante alpha, and not estimate the distinction between luck and skill.

☞ APPLICATION 8.5.1A

Consider the following data on Target Fund: $\beta = 1.5$ and its expected return is 14%. Assume that the expected return of the market is 11% and that the risk-free rate is 3%. During the next year, the market earns 8% and Target Fund earns 7%. What was: (1) the Fund's ex ante alpha, (2) the Fund's ex post alpha, (3) the Fund's return that was skill, and (4) the Fund's return that was luck?

(1) Inserting the market's expected return, the Fund's beta, and the risk-free rate into the ex ante CAPM generates the expected return of an efficiently priced asset with a beta of 1.5:

$$E(R) = 3\% + [1.5(11\% - 3\%)] \Rightarrow E(R) = 15\%$$

Because the Fund's expected return is only 14%, it represents an ex ante alpha of –1%.

(2) Given the market return was 5% more than the risk-free return of 3%, an asset with a beta of 1.5 should have earned 7.5% ($5\% \times 1.5$) more than the riskless rate (i.e., 10.5%). Because it earned 7%, it had an ex post alpha (ε) of –3.5%.

(3) The answer to (1) means that the Fund is expected to underperform by 1%. Therefore, –1% of the actual subsequent return was skill.

(4) The Fund underperformed by –3.5%. Since the expected loss on the fund is –1% based on skill (perhaps due to fees), the return attributed to bad luck (negative idiosyncratic return) was –2.5%.

8.5.2 Three Types of Model Misspecification

The previous example assumed that the investment's systematic risks were fully and accurately captured in a single market beta and that the single-factor market model was accurate. Errors in estimating alpha can result from model misspecification, including misspecification of a benchmark. Three primary types of model misspecification can confound empirical return attribution analyses:

1. **Omitted (or misidentified) systematic return factors** is the failure to include relevant factors in an analysis of returns such as momentum or size.
2. **Misestimated betas** is estimation error due to randomness or econometric errors such as failure to correct for heteroskedasticity.
3. **Nonlinear risk-return relation error** is the failure to model nonlinearity such as quadratic or cubic effects.

In each case of misspecification, the component of the return attributable to systematic risk is not precisely identified. Because systematic risks have a positive expected return, omitting a significant risk factor or underestimating a beta tends to overstate the manager's skill by attributing beta return to alpha.

The bias caused by omitted systematic return factors in estimating alpha can be illustrated as follows. Assume that a fund's return is driven by four betas, or systematic factors. If an analyst ignores two of the factors (e.g., factor 3 and factor 4), then the estimate of the idiosyncratic return will, on average, contain the expectation of the two missing effects, both of which would have positive expected values.

In the second case of model misspecification, misestimated betas, when the systematic risk, or beta, of a return series is over- or underestimated, the return attributable to the factors is also over- or underestimated. Underestimation of a beta is a similar but less extreme case of omitting a beta.

The final major problem with misspecification is when the functional relationship between a systematic risk factor and an asset's return is misspecified. For example, most asset pricing models assume a linear relationship between risk factors and an asset's returns. If the true relationship is nonlinear, such as in the case of options, then the linear specification of the relationship generally introduces error into the identification of the systematic risk component of the asset's return.

8.5.3 Beta Nonstationarity

Beta nonstationarity is one reason why return can be attributed to systematic risk with error. **Beta nonstationarity** is a general term that refers to the tendency of the systematic risk of a security, strategy, or fund to shift through time. For example, a return series containing leverage is generally expected to have a changing systematic risk through time if the leverage changes through time. An example is the stock of a corporation with a fixed dollar amount of debt. As the assets of the firm rise, the leverage of the equity falls (or if the assets fall, leverage of the equity rises), causing the beta of the equity to shift.

A type of beta nonstationarity that is sometimes observed in hedge funds is beta creep. **Beta creep** is when hedge fund strategies pick up more systematic market risk over time. When assets pour into hedge funds, it might be expected that the managers of the funds will allow more beta exposure in their portfolios in an attempt to maintain expected returns in an increasingly competitive and crowded financial market. This causes the creeping effect: Over time, as the alphas of available investment opportunities decline, the amount of systematic risk in portfolios will creep upward.

The betas of funds may also be nonstationary because of market conditions, such as market turmoil, rather than changes in the fund's underlying assets. In periods of economic stress, the systematic risks of funds have been observed to increase. **Beta expansion** is the perceived tendency of the systematic risk exposures of a fund or asset to increase due to changes in general economic conditions. Beta expansion is typically observed in down market cycles and is attributed to increased correlation between the hedge fund's returns and market returns.

Another example of beta nonstationarity is market timing, the intentional shifting of an investment's systematic risk exposure by its manager. Consider the case of a skilled market timer. The fund manager takes on a positive beta exposure when his or her analysis indicates that the market is likely to rise and takes on a negative beta, or a short position, when he or she perceives that the market is likely to decline. This beta nonstationarity (or beta shifting) makes return attribution more problematic, since the level of beta between reporting periods would typically be very difficult to estimate accurately.

This market-timing example raises an interesting issue in the attribution of returns to alpha or beta. Assume for the sake of argument that a market-timing fund manager possesses superior skill in timing markets. The manager is successful at designing and implementing the strategy to generate superior returns but is unable to enhance returns through picking individual stocks. Would the fund's superior return better be described as alpha or beta?

At first glance, the answer may appear to be ex ante alpha, since the market timing manager's return is superior. But in each sub-period, the manager earns a rate of return commensurate with the fund's systematic risk exposure; that is, whether the fund's risk exposure is positive or negative, its returns are commensurate with risk. Thus, in each sub-period, the portfolio earns the predicted return and exhibits an ex post alpha of zero. However, when viewed over the full time period, the fund earns a high ex post alpha, since the portfolio outperformed the market through superior market timing.

This example illustrates an important lesson: Evaluation of investment performance over a full market cycle can alleviate difficulties with shifting betas and misspecified models. A **full market cycle** is a period of time containing a large representation of market conditions, especially up (bull) markets and down (bear) markets. Although use of a full market cycle does not eliminate return attribution difficulties, it can mitigate the impact of modeling misspecifications and estimation errors.

8.5.4 Can Alpha and Beta Be Commingled?

The difficulty of identifying the return attributable to systematic risk is not limited to beta nonstationarity. Sometimes the line between alpha and beta can be blurred, even on a conceptual basis. Consider a specialized type of private equity transaction involving target firms in financial distress. An investment strategy directed at these opportunities requires sophisticated investors with keen negotiating skills and large amounts of available cash, since transactions must be made quickly. Very skilled investors can identify attractive opportunities, but the strategy requires exposures to systematic risks that cannot be hedged. One could argue that any superior return is ex ante alpha, since it takes superior skill to participate successfully in this market. However, one could also argue that the superior return is at least partially beta, since high returns are achieved only through bearing the systematic risk of the sector. Should highly attractive returns that require skill as well as the bearing of systematic risk be attributed to alpha or beta? Perhaps there is no clear answer, such as in trying to attribute the dancing superiority of a pair of competitive dancers to each performer. In some cases, performance may be better viewed as indistinguishably related to both.

8.6 EX ANTE ALPHA ESTIMATION AND RETURN PERSISTENCE

Numerous investment advertisements warn that "past performance is not indicative of future results." That admonition would be true with regard to alpha if markets were perfectly efficient. But there is no doubt that inefficiencies exist and that abnormally good and bad performance has been predictable based on past data in many instances. However, there are also many instances in which investors have incorrectly used past performance to indicate future results.

Abnormal return persistence is the tendency of idiosyncratic performance in one time period to be correlated with idiosyncratic performance in a subsequent time period. This section focuses on return persistence in interpreting idiosyncratic return and identifying ex ante alpha.

8.6.1   Separating Luck and Skill with Return Persistence

Assume that a reasonably accurate performance attribution has distinguished returns due to systematic risks from those due to idiosyncratic risks. The next step is to attribute the idiosyncratic returns to their sources: luck, skill, or both. Proper attribution of the idiosyncratic returns (the ex post alpha) to luck or skill is typically a statistical challenge.

Attempting to identify ex ante alpha through an abnormal return persistence procedure can be summarized in the following three steps:

1. Estimate the average idiosyncratic returns (ex post alpha) for each asset in time period 1.
2. Estimate the average idiosyncratic returns (ex post alpha) for each asset in time period 2.
3. Statistically test whether the ex post alphas in time period 2 are correlated with the ex post alphas in time period 1.

8.6.2   Interpreting Estimated Return Persistence

A statistically significant positive correlation between average idiosyncratic returns in consecutive periods implies positive return persistence. To the extent that the return model has been correctly specified, consistent and statistically significant positive correlation would lead to increased confidence that managerial skill has driven some or all of the investment results.

Note that this approach differs markedly from the more common approach of using a single time period to identify top returns and assuming that the top returns were driven by skill. However, just because an investment experiences positive return persistence in two consecutive periods does not prove that the returns are based on skill. The most that a researcher can do is use careful statistical testing to develop increased confidence that persistence has been successfully identified.

The later part of this chapter discusses hypothesis testing with statistics and the care that should be used in constructing tests and interpreting their results.

8.7   RETURN DRIVERS

The term **return driver** represents the investments, the investment products, the investment strategies, or the underlying factors that generate the risk and return of a portfolio. A conceptually simplified way to manage a total portfolio is to divide its assets into two groups: beta drivers and alpha drivers. Briefly, in the context of a portfolio, an investment that moves in tandem with the overall market or a particular risk factor is a **beta driver**. An investment that seeks high returns independent of the market is an **alpha driver**.

For example, consider an investor who owns a portfolio consisting of one mutual fund indexed to the FTSE 100 and one market-neutral fund with offsetting long and short exposures that attempts to earn superior rates without bearing systematic risk. The allocation to the FTSE 100 Index fund is a beta driver, since the holding will generate systematic risk but will not offer ex ante alpha. That allocation is designed simply to harvest the average higher returns of bearing beta (systematic) risk. The allocation to the market-neutral fund is an alpha driver, since it is an attempt to earn superior rates of return through superior security selection rather than through systematic risk bearing.

Viewed from a portfolio management context, various investments and investment strategies can be viewed as alpha drivers, beta drivers, or mixtures of both. Alternative investing tends to focus more on alpha drivers, whereas traditional investing tends to focus more on beta drivers.

8.7.1 Beta Drivers

Beta drivers capture market risk premiums, and good or pure beta drivers do so in an efficient (i.e., precise and cost-effective) manner. Beta drivers capture risk premiums by bearing systematic risk.

Bearing beta risk as defined by the CAPM has been extremely lucrative over the long run. The long-term tendency of beta drivers to earn higher returns from equity investments than are earned on risk-free investments is attributed to the equity risk premium. The **equity risk premium** (ERP) is the expected return of the equity market in excess of the risk-free rate. This risk premium may be estimated from historical returns or implied by stock valuation models, such as through the relationship between stock prices and forecasts of earnings.

Especially in the United States, stocks have outperformed riskless assets tremendously, and these high historical returns form the equity risk premium puzzle. The **equity risk premium puzzle** is the enigma that equities have historically performed much better than can be explained purely by risk aversion, yet many investors continue to invest heavily in low-risk assets. Based on the data of the past 100 years or so, it seems that most investors are foolish not to place more of their money in equities rather than riskless assets. There is no consensus, however, on whether the superior equity returns of the past century that generated the high equity premium will persist in magnitude through the twenty-first century.

8.7.2 Passive Beta Drivers as Pure Plays on Beta

Passive investing, such as employing a buy-and-hold strategy to match a benchmark index, is a pure play on beta: simple, low cost, and with a linear risk exposure. A **linear risk exposure** means that when the returns to such a strategy are graphed against the returns of the market index or another appropriate standard, the outcomes tend to lie on a straight line. Options and investment strategies with shifting betas have nonlinear risk exposures.

A **passive beta driver** strategy generates returns that follow the up-and-down movement of the market on a one-to-one basis. In this sense, pure beta drivers are linear in their performance compared to a financial index.

Some managers can deliver beta drivers for annual fees of as little as a few basis points per year, whereas others may charge more than a half percent per year and deliver performance before fees that is virtually identical to that of a pure beta driver. **Asset gatherers** are managers striving to deliver beta as cheaply and efficiently as possible, and include the large-scale index trackers that produce passive products tied to well-recognized financial market benchmarks. These managers build value through scale and processing efficiency.

8.7.3 Alpha Drivers

Alpha drivers seek excess return or added value through generating returns that exceed the returns on investments of comparable risk. Many alternative assets fall squarely into the category of alpha drivers. They tend to seek sources of return less correlated with traditional asset classes, which reduces risk in the entire portfolio in the process. Alpha drivers are the focus of much alternative investing. Alternative investments are often touted as being able to generate greater combinations of return and risk by providing return streams that have relatively low correlation with traditional stock and bond markets but comparable average returns.

8.7.4 Product Innovators and Process Drivers

Historically, most investment pools were mixes of beta drivers and alpha drivers. In other words, the funds derived considerable return variation from bearing substantial systematic risk but implemented active investment strategies intended to generate alpha. In recent decades, the distinction between alpha drivers and beta drivers has increased. Thus, much of the asset management industry has moved into the tails of the alpha driver–beta driver spectrum. At one end of the spectrum are **product innovators**, which are alpha drivers that seek new investment strategies offering superior rates of risk-adjusted return. At the other end are passive indexation strategies, previously described as asset gatherers, which offer beta exposure as efficiently as possible without any pretense of alpha seeking.

Another development among beta drivers is the growth of process drivers. **Process drivers** are beta drivers that focus on providing beta that is fine-tuned or differentiated. As an example, these index trackers have introduced a large number and wide variety of exchange-traded funds (ETFs) that track specific sectors of the market rather than broadly diversifying across most or all sectors. For example, many new ETFs provide beta for a particular market-capitalization range, industry, asset class, or geographic market. These process drivers carve up systematic risk exposure into narrower risk factors as they identify investors desiring targeted risk exposures.

The increased difficulty for a fund manager to capture alpha or to compete with the extremely low-cost asset gatherers has put pressure on beta drivers with high fees. It has been argued that some managers following a pure beta driver strategy do not disclose the true nature of their strategy accurately, perhaps because it would be difficult to justify their high fees when their performance before fees is virtually indistinguishable from that of other beta drivers with fees near zero.

8.8 USING STATISTICAL METHODS TO LOCATE ALPHA

Suppose that a manager running a fund called the Trick Fund claims the ability to consistently outperform the S&P 500 Index using a secret strategy. It turns out that for each $100 of value in the fund, the manager initially holds $100 in a portfolio that mimics the S&P 500, and then on the first of each month, the fund manager writes a $0.50 call option on the S&P 500 that is far out-of-the-money and expires in a few days. If the fund manager has bad luck and the S&P 500 rises dramatically during the first week, so that the call option rises to, say, $2.50, and is about to be exercised, the fund manager purchases the call at a loss (covering the option position). The fund manager purchases the call option back using money obtained from writing large quantities of new out-of-the-money call options for the second week at combined prices of $2.50. If the second group of options rises in value to, say, $12.50, the fund manager repeats the process by selling even more call options for the third week to generate proceeds of $12.50, which are used to cover the second option positions. The strategy continues into the fourth week, such that if the third set of short options rises to, say, $62.50, a fourth set of out-of-the-money options is sold for $62.50. By the end of the fourth week, either the fourth set of options is worthless or the fund is ruined.

If at any point during the month one of the sets of options expires worthless, the fund manager ceases writing options for the rest of the month, and the fund is $0.50 (i.e., 50 basis points) ahead of its benchmark for the month. There is very little likelihood (perhaps once every 200 months) that all four sets of options would finish in-the-money and therefore that the option strategy would lose a large amount of money. In perhaps 199 of every 200 months, the fund outperforms the S&P 500 by 50 basis points (ignoring any transaction costs or fees). Since there is no open option position at the end of any month, the fund manager's strategy has been kept a secret; the manager shows the fund's positions and risks only at the end of each month.

If we assume that the options market is efficient, this manager is not generating ex ante alpha; the manager is simply taking a gamble on a very large chance of making a small amount of money and a very small chance of losing a very large amount of money (relative to the benchmark). But the returns that this manager generates would typically be very hard to distinguish from those of a manager who truly generated a small but consistent return advantage. Could statistical analysis of the fund's returns help us figure out what the Trick Fund was doing and help us differentiate truly superior performance from luck?

8.8.1 Four Steps of Hypothesis Testing

Hypotheses are propositions that serve as a foundation on which to analyze an issue. Two hypotheses regarding the Trick Fund example could be that the fund has a system that generates ex ante alpha or that it does not have such a system. Hypothesis testing is the process of developing and interpreting evidence to support and refute the various hypotheses. Hypothesis tests typically follow the same four steps, in which the analyst does the following:

1. States a null hypothesis and an alternative hypothesis to be tested
2. Designs a statistical test
3. Uses sample data to perform the statistical test
4. Rejects or fails to reject the null hypothesis based on results of the analysis

STATING THE HYPOTHESES: Hypothesis testing requires the analyst to state a null hypothesis and an alternative hypothesis. The **null hypothesis** is usually a statement that the analyst is attempting to reject, typically that a particular variable has no effect or that a parameter's true value is equal to zero. For example, common null hypotheses are that a fund's alpha is zero or that a fund's exposure to a particular risk factor, or beta, is zero.

The **alternative hypothesis** is the behavior that the analyst assumes would be true if the null hypothesis were rejected. The alternative and null hypotheses are often stated in such a way that they are mutually exclusive. That is, if one is true, the other must be false, and vice versa. For example, if the null hypothesis is that an alpha, beta, or other variable is zero, the alternative hypothesis is that the variable is not equal to zero.

DESIGNING A TEST OF THE HYPOTHESES: The test's plan describes how to use sample data to reject or to not reject the null hypothesis. This stage involves specifying the variables for a model, the relationships between the variables, and the statistical properties of the variables. Typically, the test involves a test statistic, which is a function of observed values of the random variables and typically has a known distribution under the null hypothesis. The **test statistic** is the variable that is analyzed to make an inference with regard to rejecting or failing to reject a null hypothesis. Given a test statistic and its sampling distribution, an analyst can assess the probability that the observed values of the random variables of interest could come from the assumed distribution and can determine if the null hypothesis should be rejected.

The plan should specify a significance level for the test before the test is run. Generally, the term **significance level** is used in hypothesis testing to denote a small number, such as 1%, 5%, or 10%, that reflects the probability (that a researcher will tolerate) of the null hypothesis being rejected when in fact it is true. The selection of a smaller probability for the significance level is intended to reduce the probability that an unusual statistical result will be mistakenly used to reject a true null hypothesis. For example, a hypothesis tested with a significance level of 1% has a 1% likelihood of rejecting a true null hypothesis.

Statistical analyses of parameter estimates often utilize confidence intervals. A **confidence interval** is a range of values within which a parameter estimate is expected to lie with a given probability. The confidence interval is typically based on a large probability, such as 90%, 95%, or 99%. A 90% confidence interval defines the range within which a parameter estimate is anticipated to lie in 90% of the tests given that the null hypothesis is true. An outcome outside the confidence interval provides the researcher with an indication that the true parameter lies outside the confidence interval. For example, suppose that a 95% confidence interval for the estimated beta of an asset ranges from 0.8 to 1.2. If the null hypothesis is true, a statistical estimate of that beta has a 95% chance of falling within that range and a 5% chance of falling outside that range.

RUNNING THE TEST TO ANALYZE SAMPLE DATA: Using sample data, the analyst performs computations called for in the plan. These computations allow calculation of the test statistic that is often standardized in the following form:

Test statistic = (Estimated value − Hypothesized value)/(Standard error of statistic)

(8.4)

This standardization creates a test statistic that has zero mean and unit standard deviation under the null hypothesis. The assumptions of the model are used to derive a probability distribution for the test statistic. Using that distribution, a p-value is estimated based on the data. The **p-value** is a result generated by the statistical test that indicates the probability of obtaining a test statistic by chance that is equal to or more extreme than the one that was actually observed (under the condition that the null hypothesis is true). The p-value that the test generated is then compared to the level of significance that the researcher chose.

REJECTING OR FAILING TO REJECT THE NULL HYPOTHESIS: The analyst rejects the null hypothesis when the p-value is less than the level of significance. A p-value of 2% obtained in a statistical test indicates that there is only a 2% chance that the estimated value would occur by chance (under the assumption that the null hypothesis is true). So a p-value of 2% in a test with a significance level of 5% would reject the null hypothesis in favor of the alternative hypothesis. However, that same p-value of 2% would fail to reject the null hypothesis if the significance level of the test had been set at 1%.

8.8.2 The Error of Accepting a Hypothesis

In the previous example, the p-value of 2% was referred to as "fail[ing] to reject the null hypothesis" when the significance level was set at 1%. Why wouldn't the analyst simply conclude that the null hypothesis was *accepted*? If a test indicates that a variable has not been found to be statistically different from the predictions of the null hypothesis, it does not mean that the null hypothesis is true or even that it is true with some known probability. For example, the test may assume that returns are normally distributed and that the means are equal. If the test indicates inequality, it could mean simply that the returns were not normally distributed.

The results of statistical tests are misunderstood or misused in many investment applications. The famous twentieth-century philosopher Karl Popper helped formulate the modern scientific view that knowledge progresses by proving that propositions are false and that no important proposition can be proven to be true. Popper's philosophy should be used in conducting empirical analyses of alternative investments.

Tests should be designed to disprove things that are thought possibly to be true, not to try to confirm those things that are hoped to be true. Unfortunately, the strong desire of investors to confirm their beliefs and to locate an investment that offers positive alpha can lead them to search for confirmation of their hopes and beliefs. Popper's philosophy encourages research that focuses on refuting one's beliefs and is viewed by some as the recipe for greater success in alternative investing.

8.8.3 Four Common Problems Using Inferential Statistics

Results of hypothesis testing are very often interpreted incorrectly. A discussion of four common problems with interpreting p-values follows.

First, outcomes with lower p-values are sometimes interpreted as having stronger relationships than those with higher p-values; for example, an outcome of $p < 0.01$

is interpreted as indicating a stronger relationship than an outcome of $p < 0.05$. But at best, a p-value indicates whether a relationship exists; it is not a reliable indicator of the size and strength of the relationship.

A second major problem is failure to distinguish between statistical significance and economic significance. **Economic significance** describes the extent to which a variable in an economic model has a meaningful impact on another variable in a practical sense. One can be very statistically confident that one variable is related to another, but the size of the estimated parameter and the degree of dispersion in the explanatory variable may indicate that the parameter has only a minor economic effect in the model. Conversely, one might be less statistically confident that another variable has a true relationship, but given the absolute size of the estimated parameter and the dispersion in the related explanatory variable, we might determine that the relationship, if true, would have a very substantial impact on the model.

Third, the p-value is only as meaningful as the validity of the assumption regarding the distribution of test statistic. Researchers should carefully examine the data for indications that the distributional assumptions are violated.

Finally, a major problem is when the p-value from a test is interpreted as the unconditional probability that a statistically significant result it true. For example, assume that an analyst has a null hypothesis that hedge fund managers cannot earn superior returns using skill and an alternative hypothesis that hedge fund managers can earn superior returns using skill. Assume that the analyst has correctly applied a statistical procedure and finds that the mean performance of the hedge fund managers is higher than the benchmark's mean performance with a p-value of 1%.

The incorrect statement that is often made regarding such a result is that the research indicates that there is a 99% probability that fund managers are able to outperform the benchmark using skill, or that there is a 99% probability that fund managers will earn higher expected returns than the benchmark. In fact, researchers have no reasonable basis for making this assertion. The relatively uncharted waters of alternative investments make these erroneous assertions even more problematic.

Since the body of knowledge is less well-established, false beliefs based on erroneous statistical interpretations are less easily identified and corrected with alternative investment analytics. To explain this important concept carefully, the next section details two types of errors.

8.8.4 Type I and Type II Errors

Two types of errors can be made in traditional statistical tests: type I errors and type II errors. A **type I error**, also known as a false positive, is when an analyst makes the mistake of falsely rejecting a true null hypothesis. The term α is usually used to denote the probability of a type I error and should not be confused with investment alpha. The symbol α is the level of statistical significance of the test, and $1 - \alpha$ is defined as the specificity of the test.

A **type II error**, also known as a false negative, is failing to reject the null hypothesis when it is false. The symbol β is usually used to denote the probability of a type II error and should not be confused with the use of that symbol to denote systematic risk. The statistical power of a test is equal to $1 - \beta$. An analyst may lower the

EXHIBIT 8.1   Errors in Hypothesis Testing

	Null Hypothesis True	Null Hypothesis False
Reject null hypothesis	Type I error	Correct
Fail to reject null hypothesis	Correct	Type II error

chances of both types of errors by increasing the sample size. Exhibit 8.1 shows a matrix that is often used to denote the four possible outcomes.

When a statistical test is performed with a significance level of 5%, it can best be viewed as differentiating between the upper left and lower left shaded boxes of the matrix. Given that the null hypothesis is true, there is a 5% probability that the null hypothesis will be mistakenly rejected (upper left shaded box) and a 95% probability that the correct decision will be made and the null hypothesis will not be rejected (lower left shaded box).

But the key is that the probability that the truth lies on the left-hand side of the matrix is not known. Accordingly, the unconditional probability of the error rate is not known. It cannot be claimed unconditionally that there is only a 5% chance of error in the test, because it is not certain that the null hypothesis is true. It can only be known that *if* the null hypothesis is true, one has only a 5% chance of error, if that is the significance level. The next section provides an example of this important point.

8.8.5 An Example of Erroneous Conclusions with Statistical Testing

Assume that all traders have equal skill but that one of every 10,000 traders cheats by using inside information. Thus, the probability of picking a trader at random who uses inside information is one in 10,000, or 0.01%. The null hypothesis is that a trader is honest and does not use inside information. A test has been developed that, when applied to an honest trader's transaction record, gives a correct answer that the person does not trade illegally 99% of the time and a false accusation 1% of the time.

This test has a type I error rate of 1%, meaning the probability of falsely rejecting the null hypothesis by alleging that an honest trader is cheating is 1%. To simplify the problem, assume that when the test is given to a dishonest trader, the test always correctly identifies the trader as a cheater. In other words, there is no possibility of a type II error. What is the probability that a trader whose transaction record indicates cheating, according to the test, has actually cheated? The answer is not 99%; it is only 1%.

To understand this astounding result, note the assumption that only 0.01% of traders (10 traders out of 100,000 traders) actually cheat. However, from a population of 100,000 honest traders who are tested, the test would falsely indicate that 1,000 of the traders have cheated, since the test has a 1% type I error rate. Since, on average, 10 traders in a sample of 100,000 traders have actually cheated, whereas

1,000 have been falsely accused, approximately 99% of the indications of cheating will be false.

In summary, many analysts interpret a significance level or confidence interval as indicating the probability that a test has reached a correct conclusion. For example, an analyst using a 5% significance level or 95% confidence interval might interpret the finding of a nonzero mean or a nonzero coefficient as being 95% indicative that the mean is not zero or the coefficient is not zero. But this would be an erroneous interpretation of the test results.

Using a 5% level of significance as an example, this is what is known: If the null hypothesis is true, then there is only a 5% chance that the null hypothesis will be incorrectly rejected.

8.9 SAMPLING AND TESTING PROBLEMS

This section discusses potential problems when the sample being analyzed is not representative of the population or is not correctly interpreted.

8.9.1 Unrepresentative Data Sets

The validity of a statistical analysis depends on the extent to which the sample or data set on which the analysis is performed is representative of the entire population for which the analyst is concerned. When a sample, subsample, or data set is a biased representation of the population, then statistical tests may be unreliable.

A bias is when a sample is obtained or selected in a manner that systematically favors inclusion of observations with particular characteristics that affect the statistical analysis.

For example, as privately placed investment pools, the total population or universe of hedge funds is unknown. Suppose that a researcher forms a sample of 100 funds for an in-depth analysis. If the 100 funds were selected at random, then the sample would be an unbiased representation of the population. However, if the 100 funds were selected on the basis of size or years in existence, then the sample would not be representative of the general hedge fund population. Statistical inferences about the entire population should not be made based on this biased sample with regard to such issues as return performance, since return performance is probably related to size and longevity. If the sample tends to contain established and large funds, the sample is likely to contain an upward bias in long-term returns, since these large, established funds probably became large and established by generating higher long-term returns. This is an example of selection bias. **Selection bias** is a distortion in relevant sample characteristics from the characteristics of the population, caused by the sampling method of selection or inclusion. If the selection bias originates from the decision of fund managers to report or not to report their returns, then the bias is referred to as a **self-selection bias.**

A number of other related biases have been recognized in alternative investment analysis, especially with regard to the construction of databases of hedge fund returns. For example, **survivorship bias** is a common problem in investment databases in which the sample is limited to those observations that continue to exist through the end of the period of study. Funds that liquidated, failed, or closed, perhaps due to poor returns, would be omitted.

8.9.2 Data Mining versus Data Dredging

Data mining typically refers to the vigorous use of data to uncover valid relationships.[1] The idea is that by using a variety of well-designed statistical tests and exploring a number of data sources, analysts may uncover previously missed relationships. **Data dredging**, or data snooping, refers to the overuse and misuse of statistical tests to identify historical patterns. The difference is that data dredging involves performing too many tests, especially regarding historical relationships for which there are not *a priori* reasons for believing that the relationships reflect true causality. The problem with data dredging is not so much the number of tests performed as the failure to take the number of tests performed into account when analyzing the results.

The primary point is this: Any empirical results should be analyzed not only in the context of other research and economic reasoning but also through an understanding of how many tests have been performed. Not only can this information be difficult to obtain or estimate, but it may also be intentionally masked by researchers attempting to bolster a particular view.

8.9.3 Backtesting and Backfilling

Backtesting is the use of historical data to test a strategy that was developed subsequent to the observation of the data. Backtesting can be a valid method of obtaining information on the historical risk and return of a strategy, which can be used as an indication of the strategy's potential going forward. However, backtesting combined with data dredging and numerous strategies can generate false indications of future returns. The reason is that the strategy identified as most successful in the past is likely to have had its performance driven by luck. One must be especially careful of allocating funds to investment managers who choose to report backtested results of their new model rather than the actual returns of the disappointing old model that traded client money in real time.

Backtesting is especially dangerous when the model involves overfitting. **Overfitting** is using too many parameters to fit a model very closely to data over some past time frame. Models that have been overfit tend to have a smaller chance of fitting future data than a model using fewer and more generalized parameters.

In alternative investments, **backfilling** typically refers to the insertion of an actual trading record of an investment into a database when that trading record predates the entry of the investment into the database. An example of backfilling would be the inclusion of a hedge fund into a database in 2015, along with the results of the fund since its inception in 2010.

Backfilling of actual results can be an appropriate technique, especially when done with full disclosure and when there is a reasonable basis to believe that the results will not create a substantial bias or deception. Thus, data sets of investment fund returns sometimes include past actual results of funds in the data set when the sample of funds being included is not being assembled on the basis of past investment results. The danger with backfilling is backfill bias. **Backfill bias**, or instant history bias, is when the funds, returns, and strategies being added to a data set are not representative of the universe of fund managers, fund returns, and fund strategies.

Instead, the additions would typically generate an upward return bias because it would be likely that the data set would disproportionately add the returns of successful funds that are more likely to survive and that may be more likely to want to publicize their results.

Backfilling can also refer to the use of hypothetical data from backtesting. In investments in general, backfilling sometimes refers to the insertion of hypothetical trading results into a summary of an investment opportunity. A reason that backfilling rarely refers to the inclusion of hypothetical trading results in the case of alternative investments is that alternative investments often focus on active trading strategies, in which hypothetical trading results would be highly discretionary and would be unsuited to hypothetical backfilling.

For example, an investment firm may have two funds with highly similar strategies, except that one fund uses two-to-one leverage and the other fund is unleveraged. Suppose that the unleveraged fund has been trading for 10 years and the leveraged fund has been trading for five years, and that, over the past five years, the leveraged fund has shown a very consistent relationship to the unleveraged fund. If clearly disclosed as being hypothetical, it may be reasonable to indicate the 10-year return that could have been expected if the leveraged fund had been in existence for 10 years, based on the observed relationship.

Backfilling can be deceptive even with innocent intentions. Often investors change or evolve their strategies as time passes, conditions change, and performance declines. Traders are especially likely to adapt their strategies in response to poor performance. An investor who backtests a revised trading strategy and backfills the hypothetical performance into the track record of the current and revised strategy is clearly providing a biased indication of forward-looking performance. The indication would be especially biased if the revision in the strategy were in response to data from the same time interval on which the backfilling was performed.

8.9.4 Cherry-Picking and Chumming

Cherry-picking is the concept of extracting or publicizing only those results that support a particular viewpoint. Consider an investment manager who oversees 10 funds.

If the manager is not particularly skillful but takes large risks, half of the funds might be expected to outperform their benchmark in a given year, and half might be expected to underperform. After three or four years, there would probably be one fund with exceptionally high returns, and perhaps most of the remaining funds might be liquidated. Cherry-picking is the advertising and promotion of the results of the successful fund without adequately disclosing the number and magnitude of failed or poorly performing funds. If an investment firm has a large number of funds and is regularly opening new funds and closing old funds, it should be no surprise if many of the remaining funds are historical performance leaders.

Chumming is a fishing term used to describe scattering pieces of cheap fish into the water as bait to attract larger fish to catch. In investments, we apply this term to the practice of unscrupulous investment managers broadcasting a variety of predictions in the hope that some of them will turn out to be correct and thus be viewed as an indication of skill. For example, consider an unscrupulous Internet-based newsletter writer who sends 10 million emails, 5 million of which forecast that a particular stock will rise and 5 million of which forecast that it will fall. After observing whether the stock rises or falls, the writer sends follow-up emails to the 5 million recipients of the email with the predictions that were correct in retrospect. This second email notes the success of the previous prediction and makes another bold prediction. One version of that second email predicts that a second stock will rise and is sent to 2.5 million addresses, and an opposite prediction is sent to the remaining 2.5 million addresses. The process continues perhaps six or seven times until the writer has a list of 100,000 or so addresses that received six or seven correct predictions in a row. The people who received the string of correct predictions are encouraged to pay money for additional newsletter forecasts.

Would the recipient of six or seven correct predictions be persuaded that the results were generated by skill? Perhaps if the recipients understood that 9.9 million recipients received one or more bad predictions, it would be clear that the good predictions were based on luck. That is the key problem also observed in data dredging: Attractive results are usually not interpreted in the context of the total number of experiments being conducted.

8.10 STATISTICAL ISSUES IN ANALYZING ALPHA AND BETA

Two of the most central tasks in alternative investments are estimating alpha and beta in the sense that alpha and beta represent return and risk. This section applies the concepts of hypothesis testing and other statistical issues from previous sections of this chapter to the estimation of alpha and beta. Alternative investment is a field that emphasizes emerging asset groups, and therefore its empirical analysis must be on the cutting edge of investment research. But with that pioneering task comes the need to use exceptionally solid methods, as the body of knowledge is less established.

8.10.1 Non-Normality and the Cross-Sectional Search for Alpha

Cross-sectional searches for alpha are especially prone to error when performance is analyzed with methods that assume normally distributed returns.

Suppose that an analyst is studying the return performance of 40 hedge fund managers. Assuming that all 40 funds have highly similar systematic risk exposures, the analyst uses a one-way statistical test assuming normality to determine which, if any, funds had a mean return that was 1.96 standard deviations or more above the average returns of the sample (a 97.5% confidence interval). If a fund's return exceeded the test's threshold, the analyst judged the fund as having generated superior returns.

A well-trained analyst would note that one out of 40 funds would typically exceed the 1.96 standard deviation threshold simply by randomness. But suppose that the analyst observes that eight of the 40 fund managers achieved statistically superior returns by this criterion. Should the analyst conclude that such a high number of funds with superior performance must be attributable to the superior skill of most or all of those eight managers?

The logic of this analysis is appealing. If the null hypothesis is true (that returns are normally distributed and that all managers possess equal skill), it would be expected on average that only one fund manager in 40 would achieve statistically significant superior returns using a 97.5% confidence interval. It would seem that eight managers in 40 having statistically significant superior performance would be indicative of a cluster of skill.

A potential explanation of the finding is simply that the returns are not normally distributed.[2] Cross-sectional return differentials exist, but dispersion alone does not mean that skill is involved. In fact, the existence of any thickness or length to the tails of a frequency distribution of fund returns provides little or no evidence that the dispersion is caused by skill rather than luck.

8.10.2 Outliers and the Search for Alpha

Another area of concern is whether empirical findings are being driven by one or more outliers. An **outlier** is an observation that is markedly further from the mean than almost all other observations. Outliers tend to have large impacts on results, and an exceptionally unusual outlier may severely distort the measurement of the economic tendencies of the data in traditional tests, especially in the case of small samples. Many statistical methodologies use squared values. When an outlier value is squared, its impact on the analysis can be huge. However, outliers also represent behavior that can be reasonably expected to recur, and therefore their inclusion in a sample may be useful in generating results that predict behavior well. Outliers often result from non-normally distributed variables, and they are often detected through visual inspection of plots or listings of observations ranked by the size of the regression residuals.

Visually examining plots of variables used in a statistical test can provide insight regarding their distribution, as well as the extent to which outliers may be driving the results. If past results are attributable to an outlier, an analysis based on those results may provide a poor indication of the future unless it is clear that the outlier is as likely to occur in the future as it was likely to occur in the past.

8.10.3 Biased Testing and the Search for Alpha

Two issues of biased testing are: (1) Was the fund being analyzed selected at random, or was the fund identified prior to the sample period being analyzed? (2) Were the test procedures (such as the number of tests and the confidence levels) fully specified prior to the analysis of any results?

The first issue speaks to the tendency to observe a fund that has performed well and then to test if the performance is statistically superior. Did the person performing the test identify this fund based on noticing that it had performed well, or did a salesperson or financial publication bring this fund to the analyst's attention? If so, this test would be tantamount to standing outside a casino, observing a person who has won a great deal of money, and then testing to see if that person's winnings were statistically high.

The second issue speaks to the specification of the test and the importance of avoiding data dredging. Each statistical test typically involves numerous decisions, such as (1) the specification of the return model and benchmark or peer group, (2) the specification of the sample period, and (3) the specification of the significance level. It is vital that these decisions are made prior to the conduct of the test to avoid varying the specifications in search of a more favorable result.

8.10.4 Spurious Correlation, Causality, and Beta Estimation

Beta estimation is a crucial task in measuring systematic risk for use in risk adjustment of returns. As a measure of correlation rather than a measure of central tendency, beta is inherently more difficult to analyze and more subject to complexities. Further, estimates of betas and correlations based on historical data can be highly unreliable. This section overviews the major challenges of estimating beta.

Virtually all of the challenges discussed in the previous sections regarding alpha estimation apply to the estimation of beta: non-normality of the underlying data, outliers, and biased testing. The primary additional challenges with estimation of beta discussed in this section are (1) differentiating between spurious correlation and true correlation, and (2) differentiating between true correlation and causality.

The difference between spurious correlation and true correlation is that **spurious correlation** is idiosyncratic in nature, coincidental, and limited to a specific set of observations. Estimates of security betas, even using a single-factor market model, are remarkably unstable over different time periods. Thus, the beta of an individual stock, a sophisticated hedge fund strategy, or an alternative investment such as a commodity tends to vary enormously based on the time period being analyzed. The estimated beta of individual stocks is regarded as so erratic that published estimates of beta are automatically adjusted for their historical tendencies toward 1.0 when used to predict future betas. Thus, if XYZ Corporation's beta over the past 60 months is estimated to be 2.0, a forecast of its future beta is often adjusted toward 1.0 (to a value of perhaps a little over 1.5) to provide a more realistic prediction of future correlation. This does not mean that there is no true correlation between XYZ and the market; it means that the correlation is changing or is difficult to measure, so estimates of beta are erratic over different time periods. The estimated correlation is being driven both by true correlation and by spurious correlation.

The difference between true correlation and causality is that **causality** reflects when one variable's correlation with another variable is determined by or due to the value or change in value of the other variable. Clearly, when the overall economy performs very well, it causes the net asset value of a long-only equity fund to rise.

The net asset value of one long-only equity fund might be highly correlated with another long-only equity fund, but there is no reason to believe that one fund's net asset value *causes* the other fund's net asset value to rise; they are rising together due to common underlying factors.

When economic reasoning indicates a causal relationship between two variables, an analyst or a researcher can be more confident that an observed correlation is true rather than spurious.

8.10.5 Fallacies of Alpha and Beta Estimation

Alpha estimation is central to detecting potentially enhanced returns, while beta estimation is central to measuring the nondiversifiable risks of investments. This section discusses three common misunderstandings about alpha estimation and two common misunderstandings regarding beta estimation. To the extent that analysts are ignoring these issues, their conclusions are likely to be unsupported.

THREE FALLACIES OF ALPHA ESTIMATION: Suppose that an analyst is studying a group of funds to identify possible investment opportunities that offer consistent superior risk-adjusted returns (ex ante alpha).

Fallacy 1. If all funds being analyzed can reasonably be assumed to have highly similar systematic risk exposures, then if the analyst identifies numerous funds with statistically better performance (e.g., 12 managers out of 100 in a test with a 5% level of significance), the analyst should infer that some of the superior performance is attributable to managerial skill.

This conclusion is inaccurate. The results can be explained, and probably are explained, by the distribution of the unexplained returns being non-normal. The managers could all be skilled, all be unskilled, or be any combination in between. In fact, even if every fund manager studied had superior skill and there was absolutely no luck involved, if the skill differentials were normally distributed, only 5% of the managers on average would have statistically higher-than-average returns within the sample. The lesson is this: Returns should be analyzed using a risk-adjusted standard, such as a benchmark or an asset pricing model of efficiently priced assets, rather than compared to each other, and the results should be visually examined.

Fallacy 2. If the analyst examines an investment and estimates ex post alpha as the intercept of a time-series regression of the investment's returns using a multifactor asset pricing model, then a statistically positive alpha indicates that the investment earned a higher-than-average risk-adjusted return.

This conclusion is inaccurate. The test is a joint hypothesis of the appropriateness of the particular model of returns and of whether a particular fund has ex ante alpha. The observed result can be explained by model misspecification. It is very possible that the omission of a type of a systematic risk factor will cause the estimate of idiosyncratic performance, or alpha, to contain returns from bearing systematic risk. Thus, some of the funds being analyzed may have simply speculated on a risk that this model ignores, and happened to benefit from that risk with higher returns. The lesson is this: A hypothesis test is usually based on critical assumptions, so a test using a particular asset pricing model is only as reliable as the model itself.

Fallacy 3. Assuming that the asset pricing model is well specified, meaning it correctly captures and models all important systematic risks, if a statistically significant positive alpha is estimated using a significance level of 1%, we can conclude that there is a 99% chance that the investment had a positive ex ante alpha, which denotes managerial skill.

This conclusion is inaccurate. As detailed in this chapter, the level of significance used in a hypothesis test is not the probability that the null hypothesis is false if a statistically significant result is found. The proper conclusion is that with a well-specified model, a fund that has zero ex ante alpha has only a 1% chance of being incorrectly estimated as having a nonzero ex ante alpha.

Two Fallacies of Beta Estimation: Beta estimation fallacies include the third fallacy of alpha estimation: that a statistically significant result with a significance level of 10% indicates that the null hypothesis has a 90% chance of being false. This section lists two additional common fallacies.

Fallacy 1. If an analyst performs a test of the relationship between a particular return series and a potential return factor, a consistent result that the coefficient is statistically equal to zero means that the investment's return was not related to that return factor, according to the observed data.

This conclusion is inaccurate. Traditional correlation measures indicate a linear response between the variables but may not capture some nonlinear relationships, such as U-shaped or V-shaped relationships. For example, the correlation between the returns of an at-the-money option straddle and the returns of the underlying assets may be zero, since the V-shaped relationship generates positive returns for large increases or decreases in the underlying asset. The lesson is that alternative assets tend to contain nonlinear risk exposures and that complex statistical techniques suited to studying nonlinear relationships may need to be employed.

Fallacy 2. A statistically significant nonzero beta in a well-specified model indicates that the return factor causes at least part of the investment's return. This conclusion is inaccurate. Correlation can be different from causation. The price levels of most goods measured over the past century tend to be highly correlated because of inflation in the currency used to measure the prices. Thus, the long-term price level of gold might be highly correlated with the price level of a haircut, but neither of the prices causes the other price. The lesson is that economic intuition should play a role alongside empirical techniques to avoid misinterpretation of spurious correlation and to lessen the possibility of data dredging.

To conclude this chapter, recall the Trick Fund example, which introduced section 8.8. Can it be determined whether the Trick Fund offers ex ante alpha on the basis of empirical analysis alone? The answer is probably not. The reported returns for Bernard L. Madoff Investment Securities LLC generated an incredibly definitive empirical proof of ex ante alpha. However, the reported investment performance turned out to have been fictitious and fraudulent. Generally, high-quality alternative investment analysis requires economic reasoning as well as statistical and quantitative analysis.

REVIEW QUESTIONS

1. Provide two common interpretations of the investment term *alpha*.
2. Provide two common interpretations of the investment term *beta*.
3. Does ex ante alpha lead to ex post alpha?
4. What are the two steps to an analysis of ex ante alpha using historical data?
5. List the three major types of model misspecification in the context of estimating systematic risk.
6. What is the goal of an empirical investigation of abnormal return persistence?
7. What is the term for investment products designed to deliver systematic risk exposure with an emphasis on doing so in a highly cost-effective manner?
8. Does an analyst select a p-value or a significance level in preparation for a test?

9. What is the relationship between selection bias and self-selection bias in hedge fund data sets?
10. What are two methods of detecting outliers in a statistical analysis?

NOTES

1. The term *data mining* used to be commonly used to indicate overuse of data synonymous with data dredging.
2. For example, assume that each of the 40 managers has the same level of skill. Each manager follows a strategy of making very short-term investment bets until one of two events happens: Either the fund rises 4% or it falls 1%. All managers stop investing once they have hit either the 4% profit level or the 1% loss level. Assuming zero average returns for simplicity, there is an 80% probability that a manager will lose 1% and a 20% probability that a manager will earn 4%. These are the only probabilities that sum to 1 and generate a zero expected return. Thus, on average, we could expect that eight of the managers would perform very well (+4%) and 32 of the managers would lose a little (−1%). The standard deviation of the returns would be approximately 2%, using the formula for standard deviation and the true probabilities of the outcomes. To exceed a 97.5% confidence interval, a manager would need to outperform the mean by 1.96 standard deviations or more, found with a cumulative normal distribution table. Each of the managers who earn 4% will outperform the mean by 2 standard deviations and therefore will have generated statistically significant superior returns.

Two

Real Assets

Chapters 9 to 13 cover a broad range of assets that may generally be described as real assets. The five chapters are roughly ordered by the assets' focus on operations and management, from those involving the least focus to those involving the greatest focus. Chapter 9 discusses natural resources and land, Chapter 10 covers commodities, and Chapter 11 covers enterprises engaged in operationally intensive management of real assets, including infrastructure and intellectual property. A discussion of real estate closes out Part 2, with Chapter 12 focusing on fixed-income claims on real estate and Chapter 13 emphasizing equity claims on real estate.

Natural Resources and Land

R eal assets are economic resources that create or add to the consumption opportunities available to people. All consumption ultimately originates from real assets.

Financial assets are the counterpart to real assets. Financial assets serve as conduits of value rather than as direct creators of consumption opportunities.

This chapter discusses institutional-quality investments in two types of real assets: natural resources and land. **Natural resources** are real assets that have received no or almost no human alteration. Commodities are often categorized as natural resources, but since they are typically processed or otherwise altered, they are discussed in later chapters. Undeveloped land and timberland are almost always classified as natural resources. This chapter concludes with a discussion of the challenges raised in examining past return data when valuations are based on appraisals rather than market prices.

9.1 NATURAL RESOURCES OTHER THAN LAND

Examples of natural resources include oil, natural gas, coal, ore, land, water, wind, and other inputs to production that largely remain in a natural state and location. Most natural resources are related to facilitating energy consumption because energy is such a major input to the world economy. For example, energy consumption tends to represent approximately 8% to 10% of gross domestic product in the United States. Other substantial sectors of natural resources include land and metal ores and other minerals.

9.1.1 Economic Roles and Vehicles of Natural Resources

A large portion of natural resources is under the earth's surface. In most jurisdictions, private land ownership is limited to surface rights, with the ownership of underground mineral and energy rights retained by governments. However, in the United States, private land ownership has typically included mineral rights. Although much U.S. land is publicly owned, some states allow split estates. A **split estate** is when surface rights and mineral rights are separately owned.

Public or private owners of natural resources often lease their natural resource rights to developers for eventual extraction. Thus, effective economic ownership of a natural resource is often accomplished through the purchase or leasing of rights rather than through transfer of recorded property ownership.

Pure plays on a private investment in natural resources are rare. A **pure play** on an investment is an investment vehicle that offers direct exposure to the risks and returns of a specific type of investment without the inclusion of other exposures. Since most underground natural resources are not privately owned and most U.S. privately owned natural resources are commingled with surface rights, there are few institutional-quality investments with returns determined almost solely by the values of the underlying natural resources.

An example of a somewhat pure play on natural resources is Natural Resource Partners L.P., which might also be viewed as a liquid alternative. Natural Resource Partners L.P. is an MLP (master limited partnership) that trades on the NYSE under the ticker symbol NRP. (MLP structures were introduced in Chapter 2). NRP is principally engaged in owning and managing mineral reserve properties including coal, aggregates, and oil and gas reserves across the United States. Its performance over the financial crisis tended to follow the overall market, while its performance since then has been linked to the prospects for profits from its coal properties. This highlights the challenge of using public markets to access pure plays on natural resources. As is discussed later in this chapter, the lack of such publicly-traded investment opportunities limits the evidence available from observing market prices on natural resource investments.

In summary, institutional ownership of natural resources can be achieved through land ownership that includes underground rights, ownership of mineral rights, or leasing of mineral rights. There are some opportunities for pure plays on natural resources through private partnerships or listed partnerships (MLPs); however, most global natural resources are either owned by governments or leased to operating firms.

9.1.2 Natural Resources as Exchange Options

Viewing natural resources as options to develop commodities and other real assets offers important insight regarding the analysis of natural resources. A potential developer of a natural resource anticipates expending money to develop the natural resource into a commodity or another improved real asset just as a call option holder anticipates expending cash to acquire an asset. However, an essential element of natural resources as options is that the amount of money necessary to develop the resources is uncertain. Therefore, a key aspect of natural resources as options is that they are better analyzed as an exchange option rather than as a call option with a fixed strike price. An **exchange option** is an option to exchange one risky asset for another rather than to buy or sell one asset at a fixed exercise or strike price.

The process of developing a resource involves using the mineral rights along with fuel, materials, labor, management, and equipment to bring a commodity to market. It is for this reason that a natural resource should be viewed as an exchange option in which the developer exchanges one set of resources with stochastic prices (the production inputs) to obtain the output (with a price that is also stochastic).

For example, a firm that owns mineral rights to gold ore can be viewed as owning an option to exchange the mineral rights, fuel, mining equipment, labor, management, and materials necessary to extract the gold for a long position in the underlying gold, as depicted more generally in Exhibit 9.1.

The market prices of both the receivables and the deliverables change. As discussed in Chapter 6, like all options, the value of an exchange option depends on

EXHIBIT 9.1 Receivables and Deliverables in Exchange Option

Receivables	Deliverables
Processed minerals (e.g., gold)	Mineral rights (e.g., mining rights), fuel, equipment, labor, management, materials

volatility. In the case of an exchange option, the volatility depends on (1) the volatility of the price of the asset(s) being delivered, (2) the volatility of the price of the asset(s) being received, and (3) the covariance or correlation coefficient between the prices.

The volatility underlying the exchange option adheres to the familiar formula of Markowitz, which defines the volatility of a two-asset portfolio as depending on both the individual volatilities of the assets and their correlation. If the cost of development is highly correlated with the value of the commodity, the volatility of the value of the exchange will be lower and the value of the option will be lower (everything else being equal). The option can be especially valuable when development costs and commodity prices are not highly positively correlated.

The prices of developing a resource can change due to technological advances and other factors, such as environmental and regulatory concerns. Recent technological breakthroughs in drilling for oil and gas (e.g., hydraulic fracturing, or fracking) have enabled development of resources previously deemed economically infeasible. The transformation of previously worthless shale oil formations into highly valuable producing wells is an illustration of the importance of volatility in development costs that are uncorrelated with commodity prices.

9.1.3 Moneyness as a Crucial Factor in Natural Resource Development

Exhibit 9.2 illustrates a value diagram for natural resource development as an option that is similar to the value diagram of a call option. However, there is an important distinction between the diagram in Exhibit 9.2 and the diagram of a traditional call option (shown in Chapter 6). The horizontal axis of Exhibit 9.2 is the *ratio* of the current price of the developed natural resource to the current cost of development. The key idea is that both the price of the developed natural resource and the cost of developing the resource are stochastic, so the moneyness depends on the spread between the benefits and the costs of development.

Moneyness in Exhibit 9.2 reflects the direct benefit-to-cost ratio of developing the natural resource immediately. Exhibit 9.2 has three ranges of moneyness: in-the-money (to the right of 1.0 on the horizontal axis), at-the-money (1.0 on the horizontal axis), and out-of-the-money (to the left of 1.0 on the horizontal axis). Being in-the-money means that if the mineral rights are mined at the current price of the commodity (e.g., gold), then the revenues from the sale of the commodity will exceed the current costs of developing the commodity (i.e., mineral rights, fuel, labor, management, materials, and equipment).

The option to develop rights to a natural resource may have no expiration date or may be leased on a temporary basis. We examine here the case of a perpetual option. A **perpetual option** is an American option with no expiration date. All perpetual options are American options, since a European perpetual option could never be exercised and therefore would have no value.

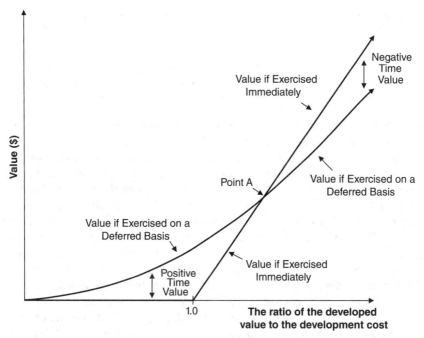

EXHIBIT 9.2 Natural Resource Development as a Call Option

In traditional option theory, most options should be held until expiration. There are limited cases in which an option should be exercised early, such as deep-in-the-money put options and call options prior to ex-dividend dates. Since the option to develop a natural resource is generally a perpetual option, the critical issue is how the owner makes the decision of when to exercise the option.

A natural resource should generally not be developed until the option is substantially into the money. But how far into the money should the option be to justify it being exercised?

Consider the following scenario: A tract of land has moderate quantities of ore containing gold. Suppose that at a market price of $1,500, the gold can be mined at a cost of $1,400 per ounce, for a profit of $100 per ounce. Does it make sense to mine the gold now because of the positive time value of money? The answer is that it depends on three things: the volatility in the price of gold, the volatility in the cost of mining the gold, and the correlation between the two.

9.1.4 Moneyness Differences and Natural Resource Development

Exhibit 9.2 illustrates a key insight into natural resource development when the moneyness depicted on the horizontal axis is viewed as representing different properties. Different properties containing natural resources have different benefit-to-cost ratios from development. Returning to the gold example, consider two properties: (1) a property in a jurisdiction supportive of development, with easily accessible material that is rich in gold ore, and (2) a property subject to strict environmental regulations, and poorly accessible material with low concentrations of gold ore. Obviously the first property reflects a development option that is deep in-the-money, whereas the second property reflects a development option that is deep out-of-the-money.

Common sense indicates that the first property should be developed before the second property. In economics, this is known as the low-hanging-fruit principle. The **low-hanging-fruit principle** states that the first action that should be taken is the one that reaps the highest benefits over costs. Thus, the *order* in which natural resource properties are developed should tend to be driven by the low-hanging-fruit principle.

9.1.5 Why Some In-the-Money Options Should Not Be Exercised Immediately

Option theory guides the distinction between the properties that are sufficiently in-the-money to justify immediate development and the properties for which development should be postponed awaiting subsequent price changes.

The value of delaying a decision to exercise an in-the-money development option, as in all in-the-money options, is based on the time value of money and an analysis of the benefit of awaiting further information. The convex nature of the payoff diagram in Exhibit 9.2 illustrates the asymmetric payoff to options. A long position in an option has increased value at an increasing rate in one direction (in the case of Exhibit 9.2, moving to the right) and decreased value at a decreasing rate in the other direction. The essence of this convexity to holders of long positions in options is to consider the advantage generated by the volatilities of market prices when deciding on the optimal time to exercise an option.

To illustrate, consider a perpetual option with a current intrinsic value of $100. An **intrinsic option value** is the greater of $0 and the value of an option if exercised immediately. Assume that the option's owner believes that future changes in the moneyness of the option are random and, for simplicity, are symmetric. If the moneyness of the option grows substantially higher by increments of, say, $200, then the option's intrinsic value will rise to $300. But if the moneyness falls by the same amount ($200), the option's intrinsic value will not fall to –$100; it can only fall to $0.

These numbers illustrate why the owner of the option should be reluctant to exercise the option. If the owner exercised the option now, it would be worth $100. But the owner might very well prefer a 50% chance of receiving $300 and a 50% chance of having an out-of-the-money option that might become valuable someday.

In this simplified analysis, the option should not be exercised until the time value of the option is zero. The **time value of an option** is the excess of an option's price above its intrinsic value. The sum of an option's intrinsic value and its time value is equal to the option's total value (or price), as depicted in Equation 9.1:

Option Price or Value = Intrinsic Option Value + Time Value of Option   (9.1)

Returning to Exhibit 9.2, the point at and above which a development option should be exercised is depicted by point A, where the time value of the option is zero. Above that point, the developer gains more wealth from immediately reaping the profit of development than from delaying the decision to exercise the option and potentially benefit from the option's convexity and stochastic market prices. The financial economics are similar to the decision to exercise an American put option early.

From a macroeconomic perspective, the price of the associated commodity rises or falls to either increase or decrease development rates so that the supply of the commodity matches the demand for the commodity.

9.1.6 Implications of Moneyness for Risk of Natural Resources

Exhibit 9.2 and the related discussions provide insight into the risks of natural resources. For natural resources that represent in-the-money development options, the short-term financial risks are primarily driven by the price of the underlying commodity. The steep slope of the option curve in Exhibit 9.2 for options that are far in-the-money indicates that changes in the price of the commodity are the dominant source of short-term volatility in the value of the option to develop the natural resource. Higher moneyness shortens the time horizon of the exercise of the option and reduces the chance that the option's price will be substantially altered directly by changes in the costs of developing the natural resource.

Conversely, natural resources that represent out-of-the-money development options have substantial sensitivity to uncertainty other than the price of the underlying commodity. The more distant time horizon for possible development increases the sensitivity of the natural resource's price to changes in development costs, interest rates, and other factors.

9.2 LAND

Raw, undeveloped, or unimproved land is land that is not currently generating substantial scarce resources, such as food, shelter, or recreation. The value of any such land must be attributable to the possibility or option that the land can be developed, improved, or otherwise transformed into being productive. The vast majority of land, by area, falls into the category of undeveloped and unimproved. In most jurisdictions, rights to minerals and other natural resources under the land are titled separately.

9.2.1 Land in Anticipation of Development

A term for investment in and acquisition of undeveloped land or vacant lots is *land banking*. **Land banking** is the practice of buying vacant lots for the purpose of development or disposition at a future date. This practice is common in the home-building industry and allows home builders to secure land tracts for eventual use in the fulfillment of housing development pipelines.

Land banking most commonly refers to the acquisition of unimproved or raw land that sits in the anticipated path of residential growth, but the term also references improved vacant lots held by a third-party entity for home builders who have option agreements to use these lots as needed. This has allowed for the more efficient use of capital by home builders. The key investment strategy is to purchase at a relatively low cost land that is vacant, rural, or underutilized and hold it in anticipation of substantial value increases as the location emerges in the path of future development.

The value of land or lots is distinguished not only by location but also by the level of improvement or development. Generally, three types of lots can be purchased for investment:

Paper lots are sites that are vacant and approved for development by the local zoning authority but for which construction on streets, utilities, and other infrastructure has not yet commenced.

Blue top lots are at an interim stage of lot completion in which the owner has completed the rough grading of the property and the lots, including the undercutting of the street section, interim drainage, and erosion control facilities, and has paid all applicable fees required. At this stage, a home builder can obtain a building permit upon payment of the ordinary building permit fee.

Finished lots are fully completed and ready for home construction and occupancy. All entitlements, including infrastructure to the lot, finished grading, streets, common area improvements, and landscaping, have been completed. All development fees, exclusive of the building permit and inspection, have been paid.

In times past, home builders banked land and developed lots for their own accounts. As they have become increasingly sophisticated public companies, they have largely changed this practice, relying on joint ventures or third-party investors to bank land for them. Because of this, there has been an increased disintermediation of investment in raw land development. Institutional investors now provide a substantial share of the paper lots and finished lot inventories to home builders on an as-needed basis.

The attraction of land investment is based on the ability to purchase land at an attractive price relative to its potential value in development. However, this is a long-term investment strategy. The key risks depend on the type of residential land purchased and where it is located. Finished lots near a major metropolitan area are safer investments than is raw, undeveloped land. Lots far from urban areas trade at steep discounts to potential value because their development is longer-term and less likely, which implies higher risk and possibly more expenses from, for example, building paved roads and providing electricity and sewerage in a pioneering effort. Unfinished lots also face steep discounts because of the expenses required to develop lots into finished products. These concepts are best understood when land is viewed as a call option.

9.2.2 Land as an Option

Investment in undeveloped land is an option on development much like investment in land with mineral rights.[1] The strike price of the option is the cost of developing or improving the land (e.g., constructing an apartment building). The time to expiration of the option is typically unlimited. The receivable asset of the option is the combination of the land and its improvement or development (e.g., a finished apartment building with the land beneath it). The payoff of the option is the spread between the value of the completed project and the cost of constructing the project.

The cost of construction (i.e., the strike price of the option) tends to be correlated with the price of improved real estate. This is because the actions of developers tend to arbitrage the relative prices whenever the price of improved real estate substantially increases relative to the cost of development. The value of land as an option on development is therefore positively related to the excess of the value of completed real estate projects over the costs of construction. The volatility of the underlying asset is the volatility of the spread between the costs of construction and the value of the improved property. As with any option, the value of land is positively related to the anticipated volatility in the underlying asset. But since construction costs and completed real estate values are positively correlated, the value of the option is reduced relative to the value that would be obtained if the exercise price (construction costs) were fixed.

Land that has multiple potential uses is more valuable than land with a single potential use, all other things being equal. As long as the possible values to the various potential uses are imperfectly correlated, multipurpose land will have higher expected payouts and higher values. The reason is that each potential purpose for the land provides possible payouts that, if imperfectly correlated with the payouts of other purposes, generate higher volatility.

While land is generally a perpetual option, it should be exercised (i.e., developed) when the net benefits of development exceed the net value of retaining the option. Therefore, the decision to develop property can be modeled using option theory and depends on the moneyness of the option. The option value also depends on the volatility of the spread; the dividend yield (income) of the completed project; the risk-free rate; and any costs of holding the undeveloped land, such as property taxes, insurance, and maintenance.

9.2.3 Example of Land as a Binomial Option

Chapter 5 discussed binomial tree models and provided a single-period example of pricing an option when the price of the underlying asset for the downward branch had a price of zero. In this section, the binomial approach is expanded to allow nonzero prices for the underlying asset in both branches of the tree.

For simplicity, this example is single period and assumes that the risk-free interest rate is zero. These assumptions allow the use of a simplified version of a powerful option-modeling technique called binomial option pricing. **Binomial option pricing** is a technique for pricing options that assumes that the price of the underlying asset can experience only a specified upward movement or downward movement during each period.

Consider a parcel of land that can be improved at a construction cost that depends on the overall health of the economy. If the economy improves (the up state), the land can be improved at a construction cost of $100,000 and will create an improved property worth $160,000. If the economy falters (the down state), the construction cost drops to $80,000 and the improved property would be worth $70,000. Comparable improved properties now sell for $100,000.

The first step in valuing the land is to use the current price of comparable improved properties ($100,000) and the two possible values of improved properties at the end of the period ($160,000 and $70,000) to determine the risk-neutral probability that the economy will improve. A **risk-neutral probability** is a probability that values assets correctly if, everything else being equal, all market participants were risk neutral. A risk-neutral probability may be viewed as being equal to a statistical probability that has been adjusted for risk so that it can be used to price risky assets in a risk-neutral framework. More details are provided regarding risk-neutral probabilities in Part 5. By assuming that the riskless interest rate is zero, we enjoy the simplicity in this example of not needing to discount future cash flows. So the current value of a comparable property must equal its end-of-period expected value based on risk-neutral probabilities, as shown in Equation 9.2:

$$\text{Current Value} = \text{Expected Value} = (\text{UpValue} \times \text{UpProb}) + [\text{DownValue}$$
$$\times (1 - \text{UpProb})] \tag{9.2}$$

where UpValue equals value in the up state, DownValue equals value in the down state, UpProb equals the risk-neutral probability of the up state, and (1 − UpProb) equals the risk-neutral probability of the down state (a faltering economy).

Inserting the comparable property's current value and possible property values into Equation 9.2 generates a solution for the probabilities:

$$\$100,000 = (\$160,000 \times \text{UpProb}) + [\$70,000 \times (1 - \text{UpProb})]$$

Solving this equation generates UpProb = 1/3, which means that the risk-neutral probability that the economy will falter is 2/3.

The second step is to insert the probabilities calculated in the first step into Equation 9.2 to compute the value of the option (the land). The key is to compute the value of the two development outcomes. In the up state, the developer earns $60,000 ($160,000 − $100,000). In the down state, the developer loses $10,000 ($70,000 − $80,000) by developing, so let's assume for simplicity that the developer donates the land to a nature conservancy rather than suffering a cash loss. The value of the option (the land) is the weighted average of the outcomes, since the riskless interest rate is zero.

$$\text{Option Price} = (\$60,000 \times 1/3) + (\$0 \times 2/3) = \$20,000$$

Thus, the value of the land is $20,000. Simply put, there is a one-third chance that the economy will do well, netting the developer $60,000, and a two-thirds probability that the land will be abandoned to charity. The power of binomial option pricing models emanates from setting or calibrating the probabilities of each path based on market-observed values of efficiently priced assets and then using those probabilities to price an option.

While extremely simplified, this binomial option pricing framework can demonstrate important principles, as illustrated in the following examples.

☞ APPLICATION 9.2.3A

Using the same values except that the construction costs are fixed at $86,667 (the original expected value), find the value of the land.

The math is the same except the up-state payoff to the option is $73,333 ($160,000 − $86,667) and the value of the option is $24,444 ($73,333 × 1/3). Thus, having fixed construction costs increases the volatility of the spread, which in turn increases the value of the option. The implication is that land values benefit from decreased correlation between construction costs and improved real estate values.

The option model approach may be used for a variety of purposes, such as computing volatility given an option price and computing probabilities given an option price. The application of binomial option pricing, even in this simplified example, demonstrates the ability of option theory to provide insight into risk. In addition to including a nonzero riskless interest rate, an analyst may wish to consider multiple time periods in applying the option approach.

9.2.4 Risk and Return of Investing in Land

Investment in land is a departure from the traditional forms of real estate investment by institutional investors, who tend to purchase commercial real estate that is then leased, providing both capital appreciation and an annual cash flow. As a result, land development tends to be riskier and more speculative than other real estate investing, owing primarily to its lack of revenue, its long holding period, and its uncertain prospects. However, raw land does not deteriorate in value the way developed real estate does. Whereas developed properties require constant upkeep to maintain their value, the downside risk of owning undeveloped land can be low.

Land may be viewed as a call option. As with the expected return of a call option on an equity, the expected return of land depends on its systematic risk. The expected return of land is a probability-weighted average of the expected return of the land if it remains undeveloped and the expected return of the land if it is developed:

$$E(R_l) = [P_d \times E(R_d)] + [(1 - P_d) \times E(R_{nd})] \qquad (9.3)$$

where $E(R_l)$ equals expected return on land, P_d equals probability of development, $E(R_d)$ equals expected return conditioned on land being developed, and $E(R_{nd})$ equals expected return conditioned on land not being developed.

☞ APPLICATION 9.2.4A

Land that remains undeveloped is estimated to generate an expected return of 5%, and land that is developed is estimated to generate an expected single-period return of 25%. If the probability that a parcel of land will be developed is 10% over the next period, what is its expected return?

Inserting the values into Equation 9.3 generates $[(0.10 \times 0.25) + (0.90 \times 0.05)] = 7\%$.

Undeveloped land is sometimes criticized as an investment with poor returns, based on the observation that values of undeveloped land do not increase substantially through time. However, historical returns of undeveloped land may suffer from a negative survivorship bias. A **negative survivorship bias** is a downward bias caused by excluding the positive returns of the properties or other assets that successfully left the database. In this case, a return index on properties that remained undeveloped excludes the high returns obtained on the properties that were developed.

Returning to the option view of land, land that does not get developed tends to be land that in retrospect was a bad investment (unexercised options). Land that gets developed tends to have been a successful investment (exercised options). Consequently, price indices of undeveloped land tend to understate the expected returns of all undeveloped land because they ignore the success stories, meaning the land that became developed during the period in which the returns are being observed.

☞ APPLICATION 9.2.4B

Land that remains undeveloped is estimated to generate an expected return of 5%, and land that is developed is estimated to generate an expected single-period return of 25%. If 20% of land in a database is developed in a particular year, by how much will an index based on land that remains undeveloped understate the average return on all land?

Inserting the realized values into Equation 9.3 in place of the expected values generates that the mean return of a portfolio with 20% development is $[(0.20 \times 0.25) + (0.80 \times 0.05)] = 9\%$. The historical index of returns based on land that remained undeveloped was 5%. The negative survivorship bias was 4%.

In most investment analyses, survivorship bias is positive. In the cases discussed in subsequent chapters, the problem is that the index ignores the negative returns of investments that fail. In the case of undeveloped land, the properties that remain in the category tend to be the failures. By excluding the favorable outcomes, historical indices of undeveloped property may substantially understate mean returns and falsely portray undeveloped land as a poor investment.

9.3   TIMBER AND TIMBERLAND

Timber is investment in existing forestland for long-term harvesting of wood. Institutional investors have long recognized the benefits of investing in timberland assets.

9.3.1   The Structure of Timber and Timberland Ownership and Management

Forests may be owned by the public sector or by firms or individuals in the private sector. Public ownership refers to the situation in which a government body exercises ownership jurisdiction over lands. Private ownership describes the situation in which individuals, firms, businesses, corporations, and even nongovernmental organizations possess ownership rights to forests. Overall, approximately 86% of the world's 4 billion hectares of forests are under public ownership. Africa, Asia, and Europe have the highest percentage of public forestland by continent at 90% or higher. The United States is unique among countries with large forest resource endowments because of the dominant role of private forests. In the United States, forests currently occupy about a third of the total land mass. Approximately 50% of the forests are privately owned.

Timber ownership has changed in recent decades. At one time the forest products industry was integrated, with firms owning all of the components of the process: trees, pulp mills, and sawmills. More recently there has been reduced integration. **Reduced integration in the forest products industry** refers to the increased separation of ownership of trees, pulp mills, and sawmills and is a key reason for changes in timberland ownership. The reduced integration occurred over the past 30 years, with timberland increasingly viewed not so much as part of an entire system but as an input into a different system. A rise in leveraged buyouts in the 1970s and 1980s helped break up the integrated companies. These buyouts followed the buyout strategy of purchasing companies that have multiple operating divisions and then breaking them up into their component parts and selling them off to the highest bidders. Corporate raiders in the 1980s recognized that timberlands owned by forest product companies were undervalued assets. Some forest product companies, such as International Paper and Boise Cascade, responded with preemptive action by selling off their timberland and establishing long-term wood supply agreements with the new owners.

A second reason for the change in ownership was the rise of timberland investment management organizations. **Timberland investment management organizations (TIMOs)** provide management services to timberland owned by institutional investors, such as pension plans, endowments, foundations, and insurance companies, and have been a key reason for changes in timberland ownership. The growth of TIMOs facilitated the migration of timber ownership from longtime corporate manufacturers of timber-related products. Most institutional investors rely on TIMOs to advise them about their investments in forestland. Instead of actually owning the timberland, TIMOs arrange for investors to buy the timberland and then manage the timberland on behalf of those investors. TIMOs usually collect a management fee and a share of the profits at harvest.

A key concept in timber management is rotation. **Rotation** is the length of time from the start of the timber (typically the planting) until the harvest of the timber. Natural stands of pine frequently require a rotation of 45 to 60 years. Hardwoods may need 60 to 80 years to produce high-quality saw-timber products. Even though intensive management of planted pine can shorten the rotation to approximately 25 to 35 years, the investment is still very long-term and subject to risk—such as fire, drought, and other natural disasters—as well as obsolescence due to innovation or government restrictions on ownership rights, such as harvesting.

But timber does offer harvesting flexibility, which is a timing option. A harvest schedule can be accelerated or postponed by several years in most cases, giving the owner the opportunity to time a harvest to coincide with personal income needs or to wait for a more favorable price situation. There can be a substantial value to delaying the harvest of timber for an additional year. Depending on age, weather, and location, Forest Research Group estimates that northern hardwood experiences a biological growth rate of 1% to 3.33% per year.[2] Delaying harvest during a year of low timber prices earns an additional year of growth while waiting for timber to rise to a more profitable sales price. Also, timber can be used for a variety of purposes (firewood, pulpwood, chip-n-saw, home building), offering the option to put the timber into a variety of products. To the extent that the prices of the associated products are imperfectly correlated, the multipurpose option can add considerable value.

EXHIBIT 9.3 Returns Based on Market Price

June 2008–Jan. 2019	Mean	Vol
WOOD	6.02%	23.77%
CUT	6.57%	25.00%
MOO	2.46%	21.89%
NRP	−7.62%	55.56%
Russell 3000	8.41%	15.57%

9.3.2 Four Publicly Traded Ways to Obtain Exposure to U.S. Timber Returns

Most timberland is directly owned and privately traded by institutional investors. There are four key publicly traded ways to invest in timber in the United States. First, investors can directly own shares in publicly traded timber-related firms. Second, there are two major ETFs (exchange-traded funds in the United States, with ticker symbols WOOD and CUT) that have been developed to track timber firm values. The two ETFs have a combined market value of very roughly $1 billion, track different indexes, and have returns that can differ substantially. The most popular way for retail investors to gain exposure to timber is through real estate investment trusts (REITs), which are discussed in Chapters 12 and 13. There are four primary REITs that specifically invest in timberland and have combined values of over $30 billion. Finally, there is a futures contract (Random Length Lumber contracts) that trades on the CME and offers exposure to timber prices, which are part of—but not perfectly correlated—with timberland prices. See Exhibit 9.3.

9.3.3 Three Key Benefits and Three Key Disadvantages of Timber Investment

The three key potential benefits of timber investment are: (1) it has the potential for returns that have a low correlation with traditional stocks and bonds (i.e., diversification potential), (2) timber offers flexibility in the timing of its harvesting (i.e., timing options that may lessen the risk exposure to short-term economic fluctuations), and (3) timber may serve as an effective inflation hedge.

The three key disadvantages to timber include: (1) timber values are tied to cyclical industries such as housing that can experience prolonged slumps, such as the housing slump that began in 2007, (2) timber's long growth cycle makes its value subject to risks of changes in technology and other factors affecting demand that may occur during the long rotation periods, and (3) the potential for losses due to natural disasters or adverse changes in legal standards.

9.4 FARMLAND

Farmland represents ownership of a real asset (land), yet unlike many real assets, farmland also generates current cash flow, as crop income is a potentially steady and renewable stream of cash. Farmland differs from traditional real estate in that the annual cash flow is more closely linked to commodity prices (i.e., crop prices)

EXHIBIT 9.4 Farmland

Purchase price	$300,000
Financing	$150,000
Equity investment	$150,000
Annual revenues	$30,000
Less real estate taxes	$6,000
Less insurance	$2,000
Operating income	$22,000
Less interest	$12,000
Net income	$10,000
ROE = $10,000/$150,000 = 6.67%	

rather than rent; therefore, the market price of farmland may be closely linked to commodity prices.

9.4.1 Farmland Valuation

The value of farmland, like all assets, is the sum of the discounted future cash flows. As a potentially perpetual asset, farmland value can be modeled with the perpetuity formula.

Exhibit 9.4 provides an example of the potential return to farmland before income taxes. Assume that farmland costs $10,000 per acre and that the investor purchases 30 acres, for a total investment of $300,000. The landowner finances half the farmland with debt at 8%, for a total interest expense of $12,000 per year. The landowner receives as rent $1,000 per acre, for an annual income of $30,000. There are property taxes of $200 per acre, for a total property tax expense of $6,000. Insurance and other costs are $2,000.

Exhibit 9.4 shows that the return on equity (ROE) (net income/equity) is 6.67%. The return on assets (operating income/assets) is $22,000/$300,000, or 7.33%. In real estate, the **cap rate** (capitalization rate) or yield is a common term for the return on assets (7.33% in this example). The concept is often used to value real estate so that the value of a property might be viewed as equal to the property's expected annual net operating income divided by an estimate of an appropriate cap rate:

$$\text{Value of Real Estate} = \text{Annual Operating Income}/\text{Cap Rate} \qquad (9.4)$$

The annual operating income is the income before financing costs. When Equation 9.4 is used to value real estate, the cap rate (or yield) is a ratio based on observation of comparable real estate and professional judgment.

 APPLICATION 9.4.1A

If the annual revenue in Exhibit 9.4 is expected to rise to $40,000 and the market cap rate rises to 8%, then with all other values remaining constant, the farmland's price would rise to $400,000 [($40,000 – $6,000 – $2,000)/0.08].

With a price of $360,000 and an annual operating income of $40,000, what would the cap rate be?
From Equation 9.4:

$$\$360,000 = \$40,000/\text{Cap Rate}$$

$$\text{Cap Rate} = \$40,000/\$360,000 = 11.11\%$$

9.4.2 The Structure of Farmland Ownership and Management

Row crops are crops that need to be replanted each year, such as soybeans and grains, including corn and wheat. **Row cropland** is annual cropland that produces row crops, such as corn, cotton, carrots, or potatoes from annual seeds. Row cropland comprises approximately 55% of the NCREIF Farmland Index, a major U.S. index of farmland values.

Permanent crops are crops that do not need to be replanted annually, such as tree-based crops (e.g., apples, oranges, nuts). **Permanent cropland** refers to land with long-term vines or trees that produce crops, such as grapes, cocoa, nuts, or fruit. To provide an indication of relative sizes, permanent cropland comprises approximately 45% of the NCREIF Farmland Index.

An investor in farmland does not necessarily actively manage the crops. Typically, the owner of the farmland leases the land to a local farmer, a cooperative, or even an agricultural corporation. Since lease payments are made on a calendar basis, the cash rents provide a steady stream of payments that are not tied to a particular growing season. Investment in farmland and other real assets operated by another party introduces agency risk. **Agency risk** is the economic dispersion resulting from the consequences of having another party (the agent) making decisions contrary to the preferences of the owner (the principal). Agency relationships are discussed in greater detail in subsequent chapters. In the case of farmland, the agency risk is the possibility, and perhaps the likelihood, that a farmer will fail to maximize the net economic benefits to the owner.

Farmland can be contrasted to the prior discussion of timberland. Timberland has great flexibility in terms of its harvest schedule, which can be timed to take advantage of better pricing. Conversely, farm crops must be harvested annually and generally within a window of just a few weeks. Some crops—such as wheat, soybeans, and corn—can be stored for one to two years, but beyond that, the crop begins to deteriorate (rot). Timber has a long growth cycle between seeding and harvesting. Farmland allows the farmer to harvest from seed to crop within one year. Farmland's shorter growth cycle provides annual cash flows and allows for a more valuable multipurpose option than timberland, since farmland's crop selection is a shorter-term decision, and there are numerous potential crops.

Another risk faced in farmland ownership as well as other forms of land ownership is political risk. **Political risk** is economic uncertainty caused by changes in government policy that may affect returns, perhaps dramatically. Political risk can arise both from government's failure to take beneficial actions and its initiation of harmful actions. For example, political risk of farmland ownership includes the risk that the government will terminate support payments, such as corn ethanol subsidies, and the risk that the government will abrogate ownership rights or expropriate land, as reportedly occurred in recent years in Venezuela.

9.4.3 Demand for and Supply of Agricultural Products

The future *demand* for agricultural products could be driven by: (1) worldwide population growth rates, (2) substantially changed incomes in emerging markets leading to changing diets, including increasing consumption of animal protein and (3) the use of agricultural products in biofuels and other non-food-based end uses.

To the extent that the global population becomes wealthier and disposable incomes rise, dietary habits tend to shift toward agriculturally more intensive food products, such as increased consumption of meat and other animal proteins, as well as higher-value horticultural crops, such as fruit, vegetables, seeds, and nuts. This demand shift, in turn, leads toward increased demand for animal feed grains (corn, soybeans, etc.), as well as the land and infrastructure necessary for the production of horticultural crops. On a calorie basis, the production of feed grains needed for livestock production requires much more land than the production of the same calories were they consumed by humans directly in plant form.

Biofuels typically use agricultural products with food value, especially corn and sugar, to generate usable fuels or fuel additives. Biofuel production has engendered some controversy regarding its impact on food prices, particularly during periods of high commodity prices. Efforts to produce biofuels from nonfood agricultural products, like corn stalks and various high-biomass grasses, have met limited success to date. The growth in biofuels usage has created additional pressure on productivity. In the United States, a significant portion of acreage is devoted to producing corn destined for ethanol plants.

The future *supply* of agricultural products could be driven by: (1) changing agricultural yields, (2) changing quantities and qualities of agricultural infrastructure (including irrigation, transportation networks, and processing), and (3) the quantity of land under cultivation and/or changing use of aquaculture.

Growth in yields, particularly in the developed world, has occurred largely as a result of four advances: (1) improved technology (including advancement of seed stock through plant breeding and, in certain cases, transgenic modification); (2) improved agronomy; (3) increasing use of inputs, such as fertilizer; and (4) increasing use of capital assets, like machinery and agricultural infrastructure. **Agronomy** is the science of soil management, cultivation, crop production, and crop utilization. Agricultural infrastructure, like other forms of infrastructure, derives economic return largely from the value of efficiency gains. The key economic function of agricultural infrastructure is to increase productivity of the agricultural value chain.

9.4.4 Three Key Benefits and Three Key Disadvantages
of Farmland Investment

The key benefits of farmland investment are: (1) farmland as an inflation hedge, since farmland is a real asset linked to food and energy production and prices; (2) farmland as a diversifying source of return being subject to distinct physical and economic dynamics and not, in the short run, directly linked to financial markets; and

(3) the supply of farmland may be more constrained than the demand for agricultural products.

Disadvantages of farmland investment include: (1) like most other forms of real estate investing, farmland is illiquid, with potential exposures to natural disasters; (2) the transaction costs of searching for, buying, and selling farmland tend to be high, with sales that are arranged through brokers that can charge fees of 3% to 5% for negotiating the sale of the land and with potentially high search costs; and (3) farmland ownership can involve high levels of agency costs.

9.4.5 Methods of Accessing Exposure to U.S. Farmland Returns

There are three primary approaches for institutional investors to access agricultural asset returns: (1) direct ownership of farmland to earn lease income, (2) direct ownership of listed equities in agricultural firms or through pooled funds, and (3) long positions in agricultural futures contracts or similar financial derivative instruments. Note that the third use provides exposure to agricultural prices, not directly land prices, and may not be highly correlated with farmland values.

Regarding publicly traded pools related to agriculture and farmland, there are several stock indices that track the agribusiness industry. These industries vary in their exposure to publicly traded companies in four areas of the agribusiness industry: (1) agricultural products, (2) seed and fertilizer, (3) farm machinery, and (4) packaged foods.

The VanEck Vectors Agribusiness ETF (ticker MOO, a creatively descriptive ticker name) began trading in August 2007, and holds a portfolio of globally diversified stocks in the agribusiness industry. Publicly available REITs with farmland include Gladstone Land (LAND) and Farmland Partners (FPI). Returns are previously shown in Exhibit 9.3.

9.4.6 Three Factors of Multiple-Use Option Values

The agricultural value of farmland is driven by the profitability of its agricultural use, which in turn is related to commodity prices and farming expenses. A prolonged surplus of a commodity, like corn, generates substantially lower commodity prices. Lower commodity prices, such as lower corn prices, can lead to depressed farmland prices, especially for land areas where corn production has traditionally served as the land's best use.

This highlights the value and importance of assets with multiple purposes, such as farmland. The value of the multiple purposes of farmland is driven by three factors related to the multiple uses (other than the moneyness of the current best use): (1) the current closeness of the profitability of each alternative to each other, (2) the volatility of the profitability of each alternative, and (3) the lack of correlation between the alternatives as to profitability.

For example, suppose that a farmer has two main crops that are suitable for the farmer's land and equipment: corn and soybeans. The option to plant *either* crop has *high value* if: (1) each crop becomes the best choice at least periodically, (2) both corn and soybeans have profitability that varies substantially through time, and (3) if corn and soybean profitability is only mildly or negatively correlated. In all three cases, the option to switch from one crop to the other has higher value.

Consider a region where planting one particular crop is consistently the best use of farmland. For example, in the United States, there is a major corn-producing region. In this region, other uses of the land often substantially lower profitability. In such cases, the options for alternative use may be viewed as being far out-of-the-money. Therefore, the multipurpose aspect of the option has little value, and the land behaves more like a single-use option that is in-the-money. However, having several viable crops with volatile and uncorrelated prices is a valuable option.

The possible multipurpose option of farmland often extends well beyond multiple agricultural uses. Land that is currently most profitably deployed as farmland can become more valuable for other uses, such as development (residential, industrial) and mineral rights. Multiple-use options can be especially valuable when they include both agricultural and nonagricultural uses, because the correlation between the profitability of diverse uses tends to be lower than the correlation between the profitability of similar uses. Low correlation of uses generates higher option value, because when underlying assets diverge in profitability or value, the call option holder can benefit from the rise in the value of one use with limited harm from the fall in the value of the alternative use.

9.5 VALUATION AND VOLATILITY OF REAL ASSETS

Private real assets and other assets that are not publicly traded do not have observable market values and instead are often valued by appraisals. This section discusses the effects that smoothing from the appraisal process can exert on return and price volatility.

9.5.1 Smoothing of Reported Values Can Reduce the Perceived Riskiness of an Asset

Smoothing is reduction in the reported dispersion in a price or return series. Smoothed returns can mask true risk. An example from money markets illustrates this important concept. Consider a one-year U.S.-government-guaranteed certificate of deposit (CD) and a one-year U.S. Treasury bill (T-bill). The two investments offer the same risk-free cash flow in one year. Assuming that the one-year CD is nonnegotiable and has a substantial withdrawal penalty, the CD is riskier than the one-year T-bill because the T-bill offers the investor better liquidity.

However, the methods of reporting the values of the two securities may vary. Most investors receive financial statements of their positions in T-bills indicating that the market prices of the T-bills fluctuate as interest rates fluctuate. In many financial statements, on the other hand, CDs are given a very stable value that accrues slowly at the CD's coupon rate and ignores the impact of interest rate changes on present values. This accounting simplification causes a smoothed reported price series relative to the economic reality.

The smoothing of the CD prices causes the CD returns to be smoothed. When interest rates change, the true value of a fixed-rate CD changes regardless of whether the valuation method used for accounting purposes recognizes the volatility. The owner of a CD observing the smoothed prices might wrongly conclude that the CD is less risky than the T-bill because its reported value is more stable. Of course, the reality is that the T-bill is less risky because it offers better liquidity.

9.5.2 Smoothing of True Values to Reduce Reported Risk Measures

The previous section discussed when reported prices are smoothed relative to their true values. This section discusses smoothing the true values of a portfolio, such as when market transactions are executed by an investment manager with the goal of reducing high returns and buttressing low returns. For example, consider an investment manager with a large portfolio of actively managed equities. The manager regularly buys out-of-the-money put options on a market index while simultaneously writing out-of-the-money calls on that same index during each reporting period. The manager obtains enough cash from writing the calls to fund the purchase of the put options each period. The puts eliminate large losses, and the calls eliminate large profits. The net result is a series of returns in which both the extreme upside and downside returns are smoothed. The result is lower actual and reported volatility.

For simplicity, consider an investment that experiences the following six months of returns (not necessarily in this order): $-3\%, -2\%, -1\%, +1\%, +2\%,$ and $+3\%$. Since this series has a sample mean of 0%, the sample variance of the series is simply $(1/5) \times [(-0.03^2) + (-0.02^2) + (-0.01^2) + (0.01^2) + (0.02^2) + (0.03^2)]$. The sample volatility (or standard deviation) of the monthly return series is 2.37% (rounded). Now consider the measured volatility if the returns of the best and worst months are changed to $+2\%$ and -2% from $+3\%$ and -3% using the option strategy discussed in the previous section. The sample variance of this new series is $(1/5) \times [(-0.02^2) + (-0.02^2) + (-0.01^2) + (0.01^2) + (0.02^2) + (0.02^2)]$, and the sample volatility is 1.90% (rounded). The reduction in volatility can be a legitimate risk-management technique or can be used to "game" reported risk.

If the highest and lowest returns are smoothed, the observed volatility can be substantially reduced. In the above example, the observed volatility of the smoothed series is approximately 80% of the size of the unsmoothed series. Smoothing also affects the measured correlation between returns on different assets, as is discussed in detail in Level II of CAIA, wherein portfolio issues are emphasized.

☞ APPLICATION 9.5.2A

A fund manager follows a strategy that is expected to generate equally likely outcomes of $+7\%, +3\%, +2\%,$ or -4% per period. The manager enters into financial derivatives at zero initial cost that cap the fund's returns at 3% while providing a downside protective floor of a 0% return. What is the reduction in the fund's true volatility from using the financial derivatives? A true mean and volatility can be calculated because the probabilities provided are known rather than estimated based on a sample. The true mean is 2%. The true variance without the derivative strategy is simply the average of the squared deviations $(1/4)[(.05^2) + (.01^2) + 0 + (-.06^2)] = 0.00155$ for a volatility of $.03937$. The true variance with the derivative strategy is $(1/4)[(.01^2) + (.01^2) + 0 + (-.02^2)] = 0.00015$, for a volatility of $.01225$. The derivative-protected strategy has a volatility that is roughly 31% of the original strategy.

9.5.3 Managed Returns and Volatility

Managed returns are returns based on values that are reported with an element of managerial discretion. There are four primary ways that values and returns can be managed: favorable marks, selective appraisals, model manipulation, and market manipulation.

A **favorable mark** is a biased indication of the value of a position that is intentionally provided by a subjective source. For example, a trader may ask a brokerage firm to provide an indication of the value of a thinly traded asset for reporting purposes when the trader has reason to believe that the brokerage firm has an incentive to bias the valuation process in a particular direction to assist its client. Favorable marks may be used to obtain high real estate appraisals that enable larger mortgages.

Selective appraisals refers to the opportunity for investment managers to choose how many, and which, illiquid assets should have their values appraised during a given quarter or some other reporting period. Appraisals are relatively expensive, so the normal practice is to appraise a subset of assets infrequently (e.g., annually or even once every three years) and to quote asset values between appraisals using inexpensive internal updates. This practice enables investment managers to alter the timing of appraisals and the selection of properties to be appraised to manage reported returns.

Model manipulation is the process of altering model assumptions and inputs to generate desired values and returns. Model manipulation can occur in complex unlisted derivative transactions and other unlisted assets that are valued using models. The reported values can be manipulated by altering the parameter values that are inserted into the model. For example, use of higher estimates of asset volatilities can generate higher option prices.

Market manipulation refers to engaging in trading activity designed to cause the markets to produce favorable prices for thinly traded listed securities. As an example of this extreme practice, a buy order may be placed very near the close of trading to generate a higher closing price (or, conversely, a sell order may be placed to generate a lower closing price) in order to report more favorable returns for the current period or to smooth price variations, since valuations are frequently based on closing prices. To the extent that investment managers and fund managers are rewarded for exhibiting stable returns, there is an incentive to reduce observed volatility by managing returns. Smoothing can also be generated inadvertently. In the case of real assets, the appraisal process can introduce smoothing, as discussed in the next section.

9.5.4 Appraisals and Return Smoothing Due to Behavioral Biases

The valuation of many real assets is based on appraisals—that is, by an expert's opinion of value. Appraisals are performed with a variety of methods, including comparative sales, analysis of net assets, and discounted cash flows (or income). Real asset appraisals, such as those of land, timberland, farmland, and other real estate, can be especially subjective because of the heterogeneity of the assets and the resulting ambiguities in comparative analyses. A key issue in appraised valuation is the tendency of appraisals to generate a smoothed series of prices that stray from market-based indicators of values and changes in values.

Much has been written about human nature and the potential tendency of appraisers to be overly conservative and reluctant to modify their beliefs regarding valuation levels. Behavioral finance theory cites an *anchoring* effect in which participants place an inordinate importance on previously accepted beliefs. Appraisers in 2007 had reported virtually continuous quarterly price increases in commercial real estate for 12 years. It is possible that these appraisers were reluctant to conclude that the trend suddenly had reversed until well into the financial crisis when substantial evidence had emerged of a directional change. Note also that transaction prices may be deceptive if real estate sellers are reluctant to sign contracts for sales at a price substantially lower than the previous appraisal.

9.5.5 Four Causes of Return Smoothing Due to Reliance on Infrequent Transactions or Stale Data

The raw data behind an index based on appraisals are subjective estimates that often rely heavily on analyses of transactions data. This section discusses five potential causes of return and price smoothing.

First, in highly illiquid markets such as those for natural resources, timberland and farmland, there can be a substantial gap in time between the date at which a deal is struck and the date at which the transaction is consummated. Appraisers often are forced to rely on data observed from the dates on which transactions are consummated because the transactions and prices are not typically revealed publicly until after the deal is completed. The delay between the agreement on a price and its revelation to the public can cause a substantial delay in the recognition of price changes in appraisals.

Second, the transactions that occur in illiquid markets may be biased indications of widespread valuation changes. For example, it is possible that transaction data in the early stages of an economic slowdown might focus on sales of high-quality properties at relatively high prices, whereas the data in the early stages of a recovery might be drawn more from sales of lower quality properties at or near the previously observed lowest prices.

Third, managerial discretion can often be used to time or select appraisals to smooth performance. In some cases, the property manager's decision of when to update particular appraisals are not random but rather are selected carefully to manage apparent returns—delaying bad news and sometimes saving some of the good news for a future time. In addition, returns can be managed through model manipulation defined as inflated or deflated model inputs to generate particular values. One example of this practice is the use of an unrealistically low discount rate that has the effect of elevating the property's value. A favorable mark (i.e., a biased indication of value that is provided by a third party) can be used to inflate the reported value of a portfolio of real assets.

Fourth, appraisals may rely on data regarding revenues (e.g., rental income) and expenses (e.g., maintenance contracts) that themselves exhibit time delays in reflecting the effects of changes in market conditions. For example, actual rental revenue does not change to reflect changes in market conditions until leases are renewed. Note that variable delays in recognition of changes in market conditions tend to dampen the volatility of appraisal-based prices.

In addition to its effect on volatility, smoothing can also reduce, perhaps substantially, the estimates of correlation such as the correlation between a price series of real assets based on appraisals and a price series of financial securities based directly on market prices. However, in a later section of this chapter smoothing will be shown to have a minimal impact on estimated long-term average rates of return.

9.6 PRICING AND HISTORIC DATA ANALYSIS

Stale prices are indications of value derived from data that no longer represent current market conditions. This section provides a simplified example of the effects of stale data on estimations of risk and return.

9.6.1 A Model of Stale Prices

Consider asset i, a real asset with true return of $r_{i,t}$ in period t. Assume that the true prices of asset i are observed on a delayed basis and are used by an appraiser. Thus, the appraiser's estimates of the value of asset i are based on transaction prices revealed on a delayed basis. To simplify the analysis, assume that the return reported by the appraiser for asset i in period t, $r_{i,t}^*$, is a blend of the contemporaneous true return $(r_{i,t})$ and prior period's true return $(r_{i,t-1})$ of asset i, with α proportion of the return based on the contemporaneous true return and $(1 - \alpha)$ based on the previous period's return:

$$r_{i,t}^* = \alpha r_{i,t} + (1 - \alpha) r_{i,t-1} \tag{9.5}$$

For example, if the true return of asset i in period 1 was 10%, the true return in period 2 was –5%, and the value of α is 0.6, the appraiser reports a return of 1% for period 2. This return is found as: $(.6 \times -5\%) + (.4 \times 10\%)$.

The next two sections use this model to evaluate the effect of stale pricing on estimated means, volatilities, and correlations.

9.6.2 The Effect of Stale Pricing on Historic Mean Returns

Consider a sample of $T+1$ true returns for asset i from period 0 to period T, as well as a sample of T stale (e.g., appraisal-based) returns for asset i from period 0 to period T, which are calculated as discussed in the previous section. The estimated mean return using the stale return data for the T periods from period 1 to T, u^*, and the estimated mean return using the true return data for the T periods from period 1 to T, u:

$$u^* = (1/T) \sum_{t=1}^{T} r_{i,t}^*$$

$$u = (1/T) \sum_{t=1}^{T} r_{i,t}$$

Equation 9.5 can be used to create a relation containing the mean of the stale return series, u^*, based on the mean of the true return series, u.

$$u^* = u + (1/T)[(1 - \alpha) r_{i,0} - \alpha r_{i,T}] \tag{9.6}$$

Note that the term in brackets on the rightmost side of Equation 9.6 is the error of approximating u based on the use of a stale price from period 0 when $r_{i,t}^*$ was used in place of $r_{i,t}$, as well as a correction for using only α as the weight on $r_{i,T}$ rather than the full weight for period T. In other words, the only differences between calculating a mean with the stale returns and the true returns occurs as follows: The mean based on stale data overweights the return in period 0 and underweights the return in period T.

For example, consider a true series from time 0 to 6: 4%, –2%, 8%, 0%, 2%, 6%. The true mean based on the last five returns is 2.8%. Using Equation 9.5, the series based on stale prices and $\alpha = 0.5$ is: 1%, 3%, 4%, 1%, 4% (each calculated as an average of the current and previous period's true value) and has a mean of 2.6%. Equation 9.6 isolates the source of the difference, which is due to the stale data's improper use of the period 0 true return (4%) and the underweight of the period T true return of 6%. Substituting the numbers from this example into Equation 9.6 verifies the relation:

$$2.6\% = 2.8\% + (1/5)\,(.5 \times 4\% - .5 \times 6\%)$$

Note that the above equation can be used to explain the *difference* between the mean returns of the true and stale return series without knowing the true returns from periods 1 to $T - 1$.

☞ APPLICATION 9.6.2A

An analyst observes a stale return series over a period of 50 weeks and finds a mean weekly return of 0.24%. The analyst notes that the returns of the week prior to the most recent 50 returns (week 0) was 2.50% and the return of the most recent period (week 50) was 5.00%. What is the mean return of the true returns for weeks 1 to 50 based on the analyst's assumption that $\alpha = 0.60$? Substituting into Equation 9.6:

$$0.24\% = u + (1/50)\,[(1 - 0.6)\,2.50\% - 0.6 \times 5.00\%]$$
$$u = 0.24\% - (1/50)\,(1.00\% - 3.00\%) = 0.24\% - (-2.00\%/50) = 0.28\%$$

The large period 0 and T returns caused a relatively minor error (0.04%) from using a stale mean to estimate a true mean.

Here is the key point. The error in estimating the true mean of a return series by using stale returns based on stale prices occurs from overweighting the return prior to period 1 (i.e., it is included in the computation in the mean when it should not be included) and underweighting the return in the final period (T) (by including only a partial weight). But, as the number of observations in the sample increases, the magnitude of the difference between the averages decreases. Therefore, for large samples there would typically be only a small difference between the mean based on stale returns and the mean based on true returns, so the use of stale valuation tends to have little effect on estimations of long-run returns. This is important information to understand when stale (or smoothed) return series are used.

9.6.3   The Effect of Stale Pricing on Volatility

The key issue regarding volatility and stale (or smoothed) data is to infer the true but unobservable underlying return volatility from the volatility of the available return data (the return series with stale pricing).

Consider a smoothed return series that is formed as an equally weighted average of the true returns of the current time period and one or more previous time periods:

$$(r_{i,t}^*) = (1/N)\,[r_{i,t} + r_{i,t-1} + \cdots + r_{i,t-(N-1)}] \tag{9.7}$$

Note that the stale return averages the returns of the true series using the N returns from the true return of the same period and the $N-1$ previous true returns (i.e., the stale returns are a simple moving average of the true returns).

The volatility of the left side of Equation 9.7 must equal the volatility of the right side since the two sides are always equal:

$$\sigma(r_{i,t}^*) = \sigma\{(1/N)[r_{i,t} + r_{i,t-1} + \cdots + r_{i,t-(N-1)}]\}$$

If the true return series on the right side of the above equation is homoskedastic (constant volatility) and has no autocorrelation, the equation can be factored as shown in Equation 9.8:

$$\sigma(r_{i,t}^*) = \sigma(r_{i,t})/\sqrt{N} \tag{9.8}$$

Simply put, the observed volatility of the stale return series will equal the volatility of the true return series divided by the square root of N. For $N=2$, the return volatility of the true series will be higher than the volatility of the observed (stale) series by a factor of $\sqrt{2}$. For $N=4$, the stale price series will exhibit only half the volatility of the true return series.

The key point is that the observed volatility of a return series based partially on current data and partially on old data (i.e., stale valuations) will understate the true return volatility by a factor that can be economically significant.

☞   APPLICATION 9.6.3A

An analyst observes a stale return series for an index based on appraised values and finds an annualized volatility of 16% over the same time period in which an index based on market values of otherwise identical assets exhibited an annualized volatility of 27.7%. Based on the assumption that the returns from the series using appraisals is based on an equally weighted average of N data points (including the contemporaneous data point), how many data points are being averaged in order to estimate an appraised value? Substituting into Equation 9.8:

$$16.0\% = 27.7\%/\sqrt{N}$$
$$N \approx 3$$

Another challenge with using historical data based on appraisals is in the attempt to measure true return correlations. Correlations are a vital part of portfolio management because they are an important determinant of diversification. CAIA Level II provides details on adjusting for smoothed prices in measuring correlation and forming portfolios.

9.7 CONTAGION, PRICE INDICES, AND BIASES

The previous sections implicitly viewed returns based on market prices as true indications of risk while viewing smoothed returns based on appraisals as flawed indications that underestimate the true risks. However, in some cases, there is considerable debate regarding the reliability of market prices versus appraisals. This section discusses whether the listing of real assets reveals risk or increases risk.

For U.S. real estate, there are reliable data on both appraised prices from unlisted properties and market prices of similar real estate held inside funds that trade in liquid markets. Often the returns computed from appraised values diverge substantially from the returns computed from market prices, even though the underlying real assets are similar. Specifically, the volatility of returns based on market prices is often substantially higher than the volatility of returns based on appraised values. A critical issue is whether the price volatility of listed real assets reflects true changes in the value of the real assets or whether the price changes reflect trading conditions in the equity markets. For example, if the equity market experiences a huge sell-off and the listed prices of real assets similarly decline, do the large losses correctly reflect actual diminished value of real assets or do they overstate the true losses?

Consider Exhibit 9.5. The prices underlying the column based on market data can be observed daily and reflect up-to-the-minute indications from traders with regard to the value of publicly traded real estate held in REITs. According to the market data, the financial crisis began driving down real estate prices in February 2007. The total decline over the next 25 months was 73%. The appraisal-based data is derived from U.S. commercial real estate appraisals, which are reported quarterly. The appraisal-based data did not reflect the start of a major decline in real estate prices until after the end of the third quarter of 2008—more than 1.5 years later—and indicated that the decline in real estate values lasted only six quarters. Further, as can be seen in Exhibit 9.5, the full decline based on quarterly appraisals

EXHIBIT 9.5 Market Prices and Appraisals Spanning the Financial Crisis

	Market Data	Appraisal Data
Date of pre-crisis high	2/2007	6/30/2008
Date of subsequent low	3/2009	12/31/2009
Duration of decline	25 months	6 quarters
Size of decline	−73%	−24%

Sources: Market Data based on NAREIT daily closing prices from Bloomberg. Appraisal data from NCREIF Property Index (NPI) quarterly returns.

was only 24%. It should be noted, however, that the market data is based on REITs that tend to be substantially leveraged. The difference in leverage could explain the large difference between the reported magnitudes of the declines during the financial crisis. However, it is the *timing* of the declines that raises a clear distinction between the information being signaled.

Did actual U.S. real estate values plunge from February 2007 to March 2009 or from June 2008 to December 2009? Did agreements regarding sales of commercial real estate begin to reflect lower prices in the United States as early as 2007? Did unleveraged commercial real estate in the United States decline only 24% from the quarterly high to the quarterly low during the financial crisis? Traditional expert-based appraisals and prices from listed equity markets provided entirely different indications. There is no consensus, but, clearly, indices based on traditional appraisals indicated the declines on a delayed basis. However, the market prices of REITs traded in the U.S. equity markets appear in retrospect to be driven at least in part by contagion.

Contagion is the general term used in finance to indicate any tendency of major market movements—especially declines in prices or increases in volatility—to be transmitted from one financial market or sector to other financial markets or sectors. When comparing the high volatility of listed real estate prices relative to appraised real estate prices, it may be argued that the high volatility of listed real estate prices is driven by contagion effects from other listed securities, such as the equities of operating firms that are listed on the same exchange. Within this interpretation, the high volatility of listed real estate prices were driven by potentially temporary contagion effects rather than indicating true volatility in the value of the underlying properties.

The primary question is: Do listed real asset prices overstate underlying asset volatility because they are unduly influenced by liquidity swings or mood swings in financial markets, or do appraised real asset values understate underlying asset volatility because they fail to reflect value changes on a full and timely basis due to smoothing?

One clue to the resolution of this question can be found in the definition of fair market value, as appraisers seek to measure it. A typical definition is "the amount of cash that a property would bring if exposed for sale in the open market under conditions in which neither buyer nor seller could take advantage of the exigencies of the other."[3] For example, a liquidity crisis that motivated an owner to accept a relatively low price to convert a real asset into cash would be explicitly ignored in the process of appraising the value of that asset. In contrast, asset values and returns that are measured using actual transaction prices incorporate events such as liquidity crises, as the market events of October 2008 through March 2009 showed. Such events indisputably affect the values at which assets can be sold.

This issue of whether market prices or appraised values better reflect risk is central to the analysis of real assets and important to consider in the analysis of their risks and returns. In section 9.8, both appraised values and market values of real assets are used to estimate historical mean returns and volatility. Clearly, the results need to be viewed in light of the likelihood that the reported volatility of farmland and timberland based on appraisals substantially underestimated the true volatility because of the use of smoothed valuations rather than market prices.

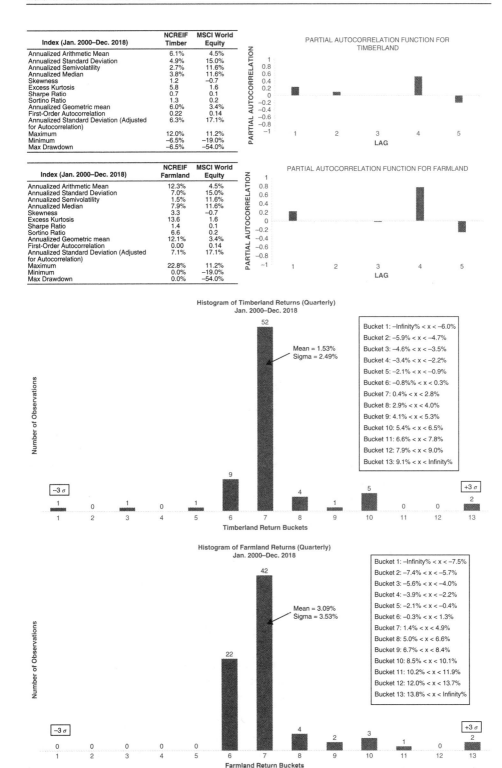

EXHIBIT 9.6 Statistical Summary of Returns

9.8 KEY OBSERVATIONS REGARDING HISTORICAL RETURNS OF TIMBERLAND

Timber returns are quarterly returns observed from the first quarter of 2000 to the last quarter of 2018. Exhibit 9.6 provides univariate return statistics in the top panel, partial autocorrelations of returns (discussed in section 4.3.7) in the middle panel, and a histogram of returns in the bottom panel.

Key observations on timber returns that are consistent with economic reasoning (and are consistent with and driven by the use of appraisals for valuations) are an essential component of knowledge and include the following:

1. Timber returns had low historic volatility relative to world equities.
2. Timber returns generated an attractive Sharpe ratio of 0.7.
3. Timber returns had a modestly positive skew.
4. Timber returns had a markedly positive excess kurtosis.
5. Timber returns enjoyed a very mild maximum drawdown (i.e., only –6.5%).
6. Timber returns had a markedly high fourth-order partial autocorrelation, indicating a large one-year lag in recognizing changes in value.
7. Timber returns were very tightly clustered around their mean.

9.9 KEY OBSERVATIONS REGARDING HISTORICAL RETURNS OF FARMLAND

Farmland returns are quarterly returns observed from the first quarter of 2000 to the last quarter of 2018. Exhibit 9.6 provides univariate return statistics in the top panel, partial autocorrelations of returns (discussed in section 4.3.7) in the middle panel and a histogram of returns in the bottom panel.

Key observations on farmland returns that are consistent with economic reasoning (and are consistent with and driven by the use of appraisals for valuations) are an essential component of knowledge and include the following:

1. Farmland returns had low historic volatility relative to world equities.
2. Farmland returns generated a very attractive Sharpe ratio of 1.4.
3. Farmland returns had a markedly positive skew.
4. Farmland returns had a markedly positive excess kurtosis.
5. Farmland returns reported an incredibly small drawdown (i.e., a 0% drawdown).
6. Farmland returns had a markedly high fourth-order partial autocorrelation, indicating a large one-year lag in recognizing changes in value.
7. Farmland returns were very tightly clustered around their mean.

In conclusion, note that both timberland and farmland have highly smoothed returns, as noted by the strong autocorrelation results. Analysts need to adjust for this artificially low level of volatility before using these risk estimates in asset allocation models.

REVIEW QUESTIONS

1. What is the difference between row cropland and permanent cropland?
2. What is the name of an option with no expiration date? Would that option typically be a European option or an American option?
3. What is the name of a lot of land that is vacant and approved for development but for which infrastructure construction has not commenced?
4. When and why are risk-neutral probabilities used?
5. What is the role of a timberland investment management organization (TIMO)?
6. How do agency risks and political risks relate to institutional ownership of farmland?
7. Other than moneyness of the best available use, what are three factors regarding the uses that would cause a multiple-use option to have a low value?
8. What is the effect of smoothed or stale asset values on the estimation of long-term average returns?
9. What is the effect of smoothed or stale asset values on the estimation of historic return volatility?
10. What is contagion in a financial market?

NOTES

1. For previous discussions of underdeveloped land as options, see Sheridan Titman, "Urban Land Prices under Uncertainty," *American Economic Review* 75, no. 3 (June 1985): 505–14; and Joseph T. L. Ooi, C. F. Sirmans, and Geoffrey K. Turnbull, "The Option Value of Vacant Land," March 2006, http://ssrn.com/abstract=952556 or http://dx.doi.org/10.2139/ssrn.952556.
2. Jack Lutz, "Biological Growth Rates and Rates of Return," *Forest Research Notes* 2, no. 3 (2005).
3. California State Board of Equalization, *Assessors' Handbook* (emphasis added).

CHAPTER 10

Commodities

Commodities are introduced in Chapter 1. The use of forward contracts and futures contracts to gain exposure to commodities is introduced in Chapter 6. This chapter dives more deeply into commodities and the methods institutions use to gain exposure to commodity returns. Throughout this chapter, the terms *futures* and *forward contracts* will be used interchangeably unless an important difference (e.g., marking-to-market) is being analyzed.

10.1 INVESTING IN COMMODITIES WITHOUT FUTURES

One of the most popular methods of obtaining investment exposure to commodity returns is through positions in futures and forward contracts on commodities. This section discusses four other popular methods of obtaining exposure to commodity returns: direct physical commodity ownership, equity-related commodity investments, exchange-traded funds (or notes), and commodity-linked notes.

10.1.1 Three Disadvantages of Direct Investment in Physical Commodities

Institutional-quality investment opportunities in commodities focus on those commodities that are used in large quantities. Institutional investors generally obtain exposure to commodities through derivative contracts such as futures contracts rather than through physical inventories for several reasons: (1) to avoid storage costs and other disadvantages of moving, maintaining, and managing inventories; (2) to avoid wasting the convenience yield implicit in physical inventories; and (3) to avoid the opportunity cost of capital or financing costs of purchasing physical inventories. These three factors are detailed next.

Physical ownership of commodities can be problematic. Storage and transportation costs associated with direct investments in commodities make this an unattractive alternative for most institutional investors. Most institutional investors do not have expertise in managing the storage and transportation issues of physical commodities, and are unwilling to bear these costs of ownership associated with possession of physical commodities.

Convenience yield is the marginal economic benefit that an investor obtains for having physical ownership of a commodity rather than synthetic ownership through futures contracts or other financial securities. Some operating firms prefer physical ownership of a commodity because the firms place a high value in possessing physical inventory (and are perhaps able to maintain an inventory of the commodity at low storage costs). An example is a manufacturer with excess storage capacity and with concerns that commodity supply disruptions (e.g., transportation failures) could disrupt vital operations.

While users of commodities typically derive convenience yield from inventories, speculators or investors who hold inventories of commodities that they do not use are wasting the convenience yield of the commodity. To the extent that convenience yield is efficiently priced, firms that perceive no convenience yield from a particular commodity should prefer investing in commodities in a form other than physical ownership.

Lastly, physical ownership of commodity inventories requires outlay of the purchase costs (which creates opportunity costs to the capital) or borrowing the funds (which entails direct financing costs).

Some firms are purely in the business of storing commodities. Natural gas is an example of a commodity held by storage operators that do not consume that commodity in their business. The seasonal nature of natural gas demand causes periods of physical inventory buildup and drawdown throughout the year. Natural gas storage operators possess the option to receive natural gas during low-demand periods (summer) and deliver the gas during high-demand periods (winter). These firms generally do not invest in commodities to seek exposure to general commodity price levels, but rather are seeking implicit or explicit reimbursement of storage costs (and profits) from providing storage services.

The essential point is that physical ownership of commodities offers the benefit of convenience yield but also the costs of storage and transportation. Physical storage of commodities is typically a poor method of obtaining commodity exposure for institutional investors without a competitive advantage to storing the commodity and without a high convenience yield for the commodity (relative to other market participants).

10.1.2 Hotelling's Theory and Attractive Direct Commodity Returns

Theories vary with respect to the expected returns from direct investment in physical commodity inventories. This section and the next discuss two views—or hypotheses—regarding the long-run expected returns of holding direct long positions in commodities. The two hypotheses propose distinct views on direct commodity investments: (1) the expected long-run returns of direct commodity investment are attractive, or (2) they are unattractive.

In 1931, Hotelling discussed the long-run investment prospects of investing directly in a commodity that is available in a fixed quantity such as copper. **Hotelling's theory** states that prices of exhaustible commodities, such as various forms of energy and metals, should increase by the prevailing nominal interest rate—perhaps with a risk premium. Therefore, ignoring storage costs, expected spot prices of commodity i at a horizon point of T years, $E(P_{i,T})$, should be equal to the future value of the current spot price compounded at the nominal riskless rate plus a risk premium as indicated in Equation 10.1.

$$E(P_{i,T}) = P_{i,T}e^{rT} \tag{10.1}$$

where r = the risk-adjusted continuously compounded return required for holding commodity i for T years. In theory it is conceivable that r for a particular commodity could be less than the default-free nominal interest rate if there were inflation risk-reducing or systematic risk-reducing attributes of the particular commodity that were perceived by the marginal investor to be so attractive as to justify investment with a negative risk premium. Generally, however, Equation 10.1 expresses Hotelling's theory and indicates that spot commodity prices are expected grow at a rate equal to an appropriately risk-adjusted nominal rate.

Hotelling reasoned this relation by noting the perspective of the owners of natural resources containing the commodities (e.g., oil). Consider the decision faced by the owner of an oil field who can leave the oil in the ground indefinitely or extract and sell it right away. In other words, the owner can keep the oil as a physical asset or turn it into a financial asset and begin to earn interest. In a competitive market, the expected long-run equilibrium price of oil in the market must cause owners of oil to be indifferent between the two alternatives. This will happen if the price of oil (net of extraction costs) is expected to increase at the prevailing rate of interest plus a premium to compensate the owner for the risks associated with keeping the oil in the ground. The logic draws from the profit-maximizing behavior of commodity owners and may be extended to include many other resources.

Although Hotelling's argument does not apply to agricultural commodities whose supplies are not exhaustible, it does suggest that the expected long-run return to various forms of direct investment in energy, industrial metals, and precious metals should be equal to the long-term real interest rate and perhaps a risk premium.

10.1.3 Simon and Unattractive Direct Commodity Returns

Some commentators (e.g., Stanford University biology professor Paul Ehrlich) have argued that exhaustible commodities reach peak extraction rates and that future declines in extraction rates will lead in some cases to massive shortages, price increases, and economic crises. Others (e.g., University of Maryland business professor Julian L. Simon) argued that innovation and technological advances would cause long-term spot commodity prices to tend to *decline* in real terms.

Simon and Ehrlich entered into a famous 10-year wager in 1980 that allowed Ehrlich to select five commodity metals he believed would rise in price over the ensuing 10 years. Ehrlich, with the aid of the experts he consulted, picked copper, chromium, nickel, tin, and tungsten. Ehrlich lost the bet: The inflation-adjusted prices of all five commodities trended downward during the 10-year wager period.

As discussed in Chapter 9, the decision to extract and sell a natural resource is based on option theory and a benefit-cost analysis. The most easily extracted reserves will tend to be developed first (the low-hanging fruit theory). Technologies typically emerge to make the cost of extraction decline in real terms. Salt, viewed as a precious commodity centuries ago, now sells for less than $100 per ton. The net result is that long-run expected spot prices of commodities (in real or inflation-adjusted terms) can be consistently less than predicted by Hotelling's theory, as indicated in Equation 10.2.

$$E(P_{i,T}) \leq P_{i,T} e^{rT} \tag{10.2}$$

Equation 10.2 views Hotelling's theory as ignoring technological changes. Equation 10.2 uses an inequality to set only an upper bound on expected spot prices. If the current price, $P_{i,T}$, is such that the left side of Equation 10.2 exceeds the right side, arbitrageurs could purchase commodities (continuing to ignore storage costs) and hold them, with the expectation of selling them at time T at a price that offers a superior expected return. However, restrictions and frictions on short-selling do not allow arbitrage in the other direction. Therefore, models that allow technological innovation predict that commodities can have expected spot prices that are lower than those predicted by Hotelling's theory, making direct investment in physical inventories unattractive in the absence of benefits derived from convenience yield.

10.1.4 The Idiosyncratic Risks and Two Betas of Commodity-Related Equities

Another way to gain exposure to commodities is to own the securities of firms that derive a substantial part of their revenues from the sale of physical commodities, such as natural resource companies. A major problem with this approach is that most firms have revenues related to a variety of commodities or have operations that extend outside of activities directly related to the ownership and extraction of commodities. As a result, the share price of most firms will often be poorly correlated with the price of a single commodity.

There are several reasons why even a firm focused on a single commodity might not be a good proxy for a direct investment in the firm's underlying commodity. First, a high correlation between the stock price and the commodity price assumes that the firm has not hedged its exposure to the commodity through short positions in forward or futures contracts. Also, the firm must own the underlying commodities (or rights) rather than purchasing the commodities or leasing the rights at market prices.

Next, consider how the price of a common stock can be viewed as the product of the earnings per share (EPS) and a price-to-earnings (P/E) ratio. Although the EPS of a commodity-producing firm may be somewhat highly correlated to the price of the underlying commodity, the P/E ratio may not be. If the stock market declines quickly, P/E ratios tend to fall throughout the various sectors. When commodity prices and inflation are increasing, the decline in overall market P/E ratios could arguably lead to a decline in the P/E ratio and prices of commodity-producing firms.

Commodity equities therefore may be viewed as having two *betas*: one to the underlying commodity market and a second to the equity market. Only the first is attractive for investors with a goal of direct exposure to a commodity. If the goal of commodity investment is to diversify the portfolio away from equity market exposure, commodity-related equity investments may retain more equity market risk than is desirable to meet this diversification goal.

Also, commodity-related equities may generate returns uncorrelated with the price of the commodity that the firm produces (e.g., oil) due to idiosyncratic risk. Investments in commodity-producing firms can have substantial idiosyncratic risks (i.e., stock-specific risks) caused by the operating risks associated with an operating company including major accidents, labor problems, and managerial effectiveness.

Also, the firm may have other operations with substantial exposures to other risks.

Note that most diversified investors in the stock market already have a substantial exposure to commodity-related equities. For example, in the United States, the Russell 1000 Index (consisting of roughly the largest 1,000 U.S. stocks) has a weight of nearly 10% in firms that produce energy, metals, and materials.

10.1.5 Commodity-Linked Exchange-Traded Funds and Notes

One of the easiest ways to invest in a basket of commodities or, in some cases, individual commodities, is through an exchange-traded fund (ETF). There are several structures through which commodity ETFs can obtain exposure to commodity prices: futures markets, equity markets, and physical ownership. Many ETFs have underlying commodity exposures diversified across energy, metals, and agricultural commodities. Other ETFs focus on a specific commodity sector, such as energy, or can invest in a single commodity, such as gold. The largest gold ETF has held more than $30 billion in client assets. Those ETFs based purely on physical commodities typically invest in a single commodity, such as gold or silver. Investors in these ETFs hold a share of a physical stock of bullion held in a secure warehouse.

Most ETFs offer direct, unleveraged exposures. However, some offer leveraged returns and others offer bear exposures (exposures negatively correlated with commodity prices by holding short positions in futures contracts). Most ETFs tend to be cost-effective for retail investors but may not be adequately cost-effective for institutional-sized portfolios.

Exchange-traded notes (ETNs) are similar to ETFs. Whereas investors in ETFs have a direct claim on an underlying pooled portfolio, investors in ETNs purchase a debt security with cash flows that are directly linked to the value of a portfolio. This debt security is typically issued by an investment bank or a commercial bank that agrees to pay interest and principal on the debt at a rate tied to the change in price of a referenced portfolio (or index). Investors need to be aware of a key difference between ETNs and ETFs: ETNs incur the credit risk of the issuing bank (i.e., counterparty risk), whereas ETF investments do not. The risk of ETNs was highlighted during the 2008 bankruptcy of Lehman Brothers, when related ETNs were delisted as exchange-traded products, and investors holding these notes became general creditors of the firm. Both ETNs and ETFs investing directly in physical commodities have become extremely popular in recent years, especially in the metals markets.

Exposure to commodities obtained through ETFs investing in commodity futures can be complicated by a lack of correlation between futures returns and spot returns due to reasons detailed in later sections. Other issues arising from the use of futures and forwards to obtain commodity exposure are also detailed in later sections.

Finally, some commodity ETFs obtain commodity price exposure by investing in the equity securities of commodity-producing firms. These ETFs may be diversified across commodity sectors or focused on the producers in a single sector, such as energy, metals, or agriculture. Similar to investments in commodity-producing equities, these ETFs are correlated to both the equity market and the commodity market.

In a falling equity market, equity-based commodity ETFs can decline in value, even if prices of commodities are rising in the spot or futures markets.

10.1.6 Three Advantages and One Disadvantage of Commodity-Linked Notes

A **commodity-linked note** (CLN) is an intermediate-term debt instrument whose value at maturity is a function of the value of an underlying commodity or basket of commodities. CLNs are often structured products created through financial engineering so that the commodity risk exposures are generated through positions in commodity derivatives. CLNs are often issued by large banks to meet the risk and return preferences of investors; however, they can also be issued by firms that produce the commodities as a source of financing. Whether issued as innovative sources of financing for a commodity-producing firm or financially engineered as structured products, CLN returns and prices can be closely linked to commodity prices.

One major advantage to CLNs is that a commodity-producing issuer of a CLN can benefit by better matching the risks of its assets and liabilities. For example, a gold-mining firm has assets and revenues highly positively correlated with the price of gold. A CLN offers the firm the opportunity to be financed with debt securities that hedge risk by having the expenses of the CLN's coupon or principal payments directly related to the same commodity price that drives its revenues.

CLNs have two major advantages to investors. First, an investor does not have to execute the rolling of commodity futures contracts to maintain exposure. If the CLN uses futures contracts to obtain its commodity exposure, the mechanics of rolling the positions becomes the problem of the issuer of the note (who must roll futures contracts to hedge the commodity exposure embedded in the note). Second, the note is, in fact, a debt instrument. Although some institutional investors may have investment restrictions on direct positions in futures contracts (due to their implicit leverage and potentially large losses), they may be able to obtain commodity exposure through CLNs because they are debt instruments. They are recorded as a liability on the balance sheet of the issuer and as a bond investment on the balance sheet of the investor, and they can have a stated coupon rate and maturity just like any other debt instrument.

A major potential disadvantage of CLNs is that they contain the idiosyncratic default risk of the issuing firm.

10.1.7 Commodity-Linked Notes Example

Suppose that a pension fund is not allowed to trade commodity futures directly (due to restrictions on leverage) but wishes to invest in the commodity markets as a hedge against inflation. To diversify its portfolio, the fund purchases at par value from an investment bank a $1 million structured note tied to the value of an index on commodities, such as the S&P GSCI (discussed later). Assume that the note has a maturity of one year and is principal guaranteed. The principal guarantee means that the pension fund will receive at least the face value of the note at maturity unless the issuer defaults. However, if the S&P GSCI exceeds a prespecified level at the maturity of the note, the pension fund will receive this appreciation. Thus, principal repayment can be higher than the original principal amount, depending on the settlement price of the S&P GSCI at the note's maturity. The pension fund therefore has a call option embedded in the note. If the S&P GSCI exceeds a predetermined level (the strike price) at the maturity date, the pension fund will participate in the price appreciation. However, if the S&P GSCI declines, the pension fund has a promise of receiving the original principal amount.

The embedded call option on the S&P GSCI is not free. Thus, an investor such as a pension fund pays for this option by receiving a reduced coupon payment (or no coupon) on the note. When issued, the closer the call option is to being in-the-money (or the further that it is in-the-money), the lower the coupon payment of the CLN. Let's assume that a plain-vanilla note (i.e., a note with no unusual features) with a face value of $1 million from the issuer might carry a coupon rate of 6%. Under normal circumstances, a CLN with the embedded call option might carry a coupon of only 2%. In this case, the pension fund is sacrificing 4% of coupon income as the price of the call option on the S&P GSCI.

Assume that at the time the note is issued, the S&P GSCI is at $1,000. Further assume that the strike price on the call option embedded in the note is set 10% out-of-the-money, at $1,100. If at maturity of the note the value of the S&P GSCI is above $1,100, in addition to receiving the original principal the investor receives its 2% coupon plus the appreciation of the S&P GSCI above $1,100 (assuming no default occurs). If the S&P GSCI is at or below $1,100, the investor is owed only the original principal and the coupon. Therefore, the final payout of the $1 million CLN with a one-year maturity can be expressed as follows:

$$\{[1 + \max(0, (GSCI_T - GSCI_X)/GSCI_X)] \times \$1,000,000\} + \$20,000$$

where $GSCI_T$ is the value of the S&P GSCI at maturity of the note, and $GSCI_X$ is the strike price for the call option embedded in the note. The $20,000 is found as the 2% coupon multiplied by the $1 million face value of the note, assuming annual coupon payments.

If the option expires out-of-the-money (the S&P GSCI is less than or equal to the strike price of $1,100 at maturity), then the investor receives the return of its principal plus a 2% coupon ($1,020,000). If the option expires in-the-money, then the investor is owed the strike price, the 2% coupon, plus the percentage gain of the index above the strike price applied to the principal.

For example, if the S&P GSCI is at $1,155 at maturity, the CLN returns a principal payment of $1,050,000 in addition to the coupon payment of $20,000. The $1,050,000 principal payment is found as follows:

$$\$1,000,000 \times [1 + (\$1,155 - \$1,100)/\$1,100]$$

The investor (the pension fund) shares in the upside of the commodity price but is protected on the downside. The trade-off for the upside potential is a lower coupon payment relative to a note without the embedded call option. The issuer of the note presumably purchases a one-year call option on the S&P GSCI as a hedge and, in effect, pays for that call option using savings from issuing a note with an otherwise below-market coupon.

> ☞ **APPLICATION 10.1.7A**
>
> A plain-vanilla note from a particular issuer carries a coupon rate of 7%. The firm issues a CLN with a coupon of 4%. The CLN contains an implicit call option on the S&P GSCI (currently at 1,500) with a strike price set 10% out-of-the-money, at 1,650. How much would the CLN distribute as a principal payment on a $1,000,000 note under the following four scenarios: The S&P GSCI value at the notes maturity is: 1,500, 1,600, 1,700, or 1,800?
>
> The principal payment is simply $1,000,000 for the two scenarios in which the implicit call option finishes out of the money (S&P GSCI is 1,500 or 1,600). For S&P GSCI = 1,700, the payout is $1,000,000 × [1 + (1,700 − 1,650)/1,650] = $1,030,303. For S&P GSCI = 1,800, the payout is $1,000,000 × [1 + (1,800 − 1,650)/1,650] = $1,090,909.

The previous examples have the CLN's principal protected from downside commodity exposure and therefore had the payout of a call option. However, not all CLNs are principal protected. Some notes have principal payments that share fully in the change in value of commodity price changes—up or down. Thus, in this case the value of the principal owed at maturity can be either higher or lower than the note's face value. This may be viewed as a CLN linked to a futures contract instead of an option contract. Further, coupons may be linked to the commodity price or commodity index as well as to the principal.

10.2   THE TERM STRUCTURE OF FORWARD PRICES ON COMMODITIES

Chapter 6 focuses on the term structure of forward contracts with *financial securities* as their underlying asset. The slope and shape of the forward curve for these financial contracts is shown in Chapter 6 through an arbitrage-free model (the cost-of-carry model) to depend on only two factors: market (riskless) interest rates and the distribution rate (e.g., divided yield) of the underlying asset. This section discusses the term structure of forward prices on *commodities*. The slope and shape of the forward curve for certain commodities were shown in Chapter 6 to depend on three factors: market interest rates, storage costs, and convenience yield. This chapter includes the effects of anticipated changes in supply and demand, in particular the supply effects of harvests.

10.2.1   Costs of Carry for Commodities

Chapter 6 discusses the costs of carrying physical inventories as important inputs to the pricing of forward contracts on commodities. The forward price of a commodity, F_T, is found based on carrying costs and the spot price of the commodity, P_0, as depicted in Equation 6.8 and reproduced below:

$$F_T \leq P_0 e^{(r+c-y)T} \tag{10.3}$$

EXHIBIT 10.1   Cost of Carry

Cost of Carry	Per Month	Three Months
Spot price per bushel		$ 4.25
Financing rate	0.20%	$ 0.026
Spoilage rate	0.165%	$ 0.021
Convenience yield	0.20%	−$ 0.026
Storage cost per bushel	$0.010	$ 0.030
Total cost of carry		$ 0.051
Break-even futures price		$ 4.301

where r is the spot (riskless) interest rate corresponding to a time-to-maturity of T years, c is the commodity's storage cost, and y is the commodity's convenience yields, all expressed as continuously compounded annual rates. Cost-of-carry models assume that in an informationally efficient market, when two positions converge to an equivalent value at some point in the future, any differences in their current prices will be determined exactly by the differences in their carrying costs.

In addition to the costs of carry introduced in Chapter 6, in some cases other carrying costs are included. For example, in the case of perishable commodities, spoilage costs may be modeled separately as a cost of carry or may be included as a storage cost. **Spoilage cost** is the loss of value that may naturally occur through time during storage due to physical deterioration. **Inventory shrinkage** is loss of inventory through time due to theft, decline in moisture content, and so forth.

Exhibit 10.1 displays an example of the cost of carry. In this case, the spot price per bushel of corn is $4.25. For simplification, the costs of carry are assumed to be payable at the end of the carry period (three months). Given the components of the cost of carry presented in the exhibit, one would be indifferent when choosing between purchasing the corn in the spot market for $4.25 and carrying the commodity for three months, and purchasing the corn in the futures market for $4.301 and taking delivery in three months.

As noted in the previous equation, the cost-of-carry model indicates a maximum forward price. When arbitrageurs cannot borrow a commodity without incurring expenses (other than the time value of money), it is possible that forward prices will be less than those implied by the cost-of-carry model. Two clear examples would be the forward price of a grain deliverable after the next harvest or the forward price of natural gas after the winter heating season. When there is a convenience yield, c, forward prices tend to be less than those implied by the cost-of-carry model. Therefore, the futures price of $4.301 is a maximum price above which arbitrage would be possible and below which arbitrage may or may not be possible based on convenience yield and the ability to short-sell the commodity.

☞ APPLICATION 10.2.1A

The spot price of a commodity is $10.00 while its six-month futures price is $10.12. Given that the annual financing rate is 3%, the annual spoilage rate is 2%, and the storage cost per month is $0.02, what is the implied annual convenience yield?

Use the table in Exhibit 10.1 to find the cost of carry, assuming that the futures price of $10.12 must equal the spot price of $10.00 plus the cost of carry. The six-month financing cost is $10.00 × 0.03 × 6/12, or $0.15; the six-month spoilage cost is $10.00 × 0.02 × 6/12, or $0.10; and the storage cost ($0.02 × 6) is $0.12. The convenience yield (CY) must satisfy the following equation:

$$\text{Futures Price} = \$10.12 = \$10.00 + \$0.15 + \$0.10 + \$0.12$$
$$- (CY \times \$10.00 \times 6/12)$$

Convenience Yield = 5% per year

Note that the computations are illustrated with simple interest rather than compounded interest for simplicity and because of the relatively short period of time. Of course, any one of the variables in the relationship could be solved, given the values of all the other variables.

10.2.2 Harvests, Supply Elasticity, and Shifts in Demand

A key issue in understanding the term structure of forward prices is the rate at which and the extent to which changes in the supply and demand of a commodity can be predicted. Those predictions (such as a bumper crop of grain after several years of drought) can substantially influence the shape of the forward price curve of the commodity.

With regard to supply, on one end of the spectrum is a perfectly elastic supply. **Perfectly elastic supply** describes a market in which any quantity demanded can be instantaneously and limitlessly supplied without changes in the market price, and is associated with little or no convenience yield. Currencies provide an example of an item with a supply that can be changed rapidly (in this case, by a central bank).

On the other end of the spectrum are commodities with inelastic supply. **Inelastic supply** is when supplies of the item change slowly in response to market prices or when large changes in market prices are necessary to effect supply changes, and is associated with high convenience yield. An example of sluggishly responding supply is an agricultural commodity that is harvested annually. At any particular point in time, not only is additional supply not available until the next harvest, but the size of the next harvest may have already been determined by such decisions as the acreage planted. When the supply of a commodity cannot respond quickly to meet changing demand, it is likely that its convenience yield will be higher, since users of the commodity may have greater fear of shortages.

Demand for commodities can shift, based on factors such as levels of economic activity and consumer preferences. Demand for some goods, such as grain, may shift slowly or moderately as needs for livestock feed shift. The demand for other goods, such as natural gas, may change more rapidly due to factors such as weather. When demand can change quickly, the convenience yield is likely to be higher, since users of the commodity may have greater fear of shortages. **Inelastic demand** is a market condition in which the demand for a good does not increase or decrease substantially due to changes in price and therefore is a potential cause of higher price volatility and higher convenience yield.

Forecasts of supply and demand shifts can affect not only the current price level of a commodity but also the slope and shape of the term structure of forward prices. These potential complexities add to both the threats and the opportunities for commodities traders and managers of managed futures programs. The challenges can be addressed with both fundamental and technical analysis, with those performing and implementing superior analysis earning better returns than those performing and implementing poor analysis.

10.2.3 Backwardation and Contango

The slope of the term structure of futures and forward contracts on financial assets is discussed Chapter 6. The term structure (i.e., futures or forward curve) is formed as the relation between delivery dates and price (or rates in the case of contracts on rates). In the case of futures contracts, the possible delivery (settlement) dates are determined by the exchange on which the futures are traded and are typically spaced in weeks, months, or quarters. Forward contract settlement dates are usually negotiated between the parties and can therefore occur on virtually any trading day.

Exhibit 10.2 illustrates the possible slopes of the term structure of forward prices on commodities along with the terms for those slopes in the study of commodities.

When the term structure of forward prices is upward sloping (i.e., when more distant forward contracts have higher prices than contracts that are nearby), the market is said to be in **contango**. Contango also refers to a forward price exceeding the current spot price (viewing a spot price as a forward price with zero time to delivery may provide clarity). When the slope of the term structure of forward prices is negative, the market is in **backwardation,** or is backwardated. The concept of backwardation is the complement to contango.

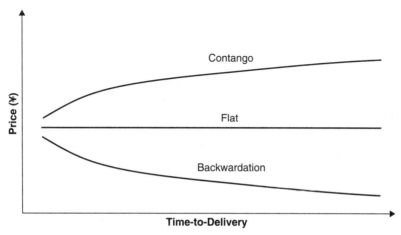

EXHIBIT 10.2 Term Structure of Forward Prices: Contango, Flat, and Backwardation

Recall from Chapter 6 that the term structure of forward prices on financial securities is upward sloping (i.e., in contango) when the riskless rate exceeds the underlying asset's dividend yield. In rare cases, the slope may be downward (i.e., in backwardation) if the dividend yield on the deliverable (underlier) exceeds the risk-free rate.

10.2.4 How Backwardation and Contango Reflect Cost of Carry in a Perfect Market

Chapter 6 demonstrated that in the case of forward contracts on financial assets, the slope of the term structure of forward prices was driven entirely by the two costs of carry: interest rates and dividends (the benefits of dividends are included as a negative cost). A critical assumption was that of perfect financial markets in which there are no transactions costs, or restrictions on transactions—especially short-selling.

In a perfect and informationally efficient market for financial assets, contango and backwardation occur to prevent arbitrage opportunities that would otherwise exist if the term structure of forward contracts on financial assets were flat when the riskless rate differed from the dividend yield.

A close look at the determination of financial forward prices illustrates two important points: (1) backwardation, contango, and, in fact, the entire slope and shape of the term structure are determined by differences in cost of carry, and (2) in an efficient market, all forward contracts offer equal risk-adjusted expected returns, regardless of the slope and shape of the term structure of forward prices.

10.2.5 Backwardation and Contango in an Imperfect Market

Three major issues inhibit the arbitrage activity that ensures the relation between carrying costs and the shape of forward curves discussed in the previous section.

First, unlike the cost of carry to a financial security (the cost of financing), the storage costs of commodities can vary substantially through time and among market participants. The supply of physical storage facilities is inelastic, meaning that changes in demand for storage can dramatically affect marginal storage costs. Exhibit 6.4 indicated the effects of predictable demand patterns on forward natural gas prices in the presence of storage constraints.

Second, unlike the benefit of carry to a financial security (dividends and other distributions), the convenience yield to commodities can vary substantially through time and among market participants. The marginal benefits of holding inventories can change dramatically based on current and anticipated inventory levels. Exhibit 10.3 indicates the effects of predictable supply patterns (i.e., harvests) on forward corn prices in the presence of demand inelasticity, where the July futures tend to be higher than in other expiration months.

Finally, difficulties in borrowing commodities—especially those that are in short supply—inhibit the ability of arbitrageurs to short-sell such that forward prices are driven to levels based on the cost-of-carry model including convenience yield.

As a result, the slope of the forward curves for commodities (backwardation vs. contango), as well as the shape, is driven by complex factors. Understanding the complex dynamics of commodity forward prices is a challenge with substantial potential

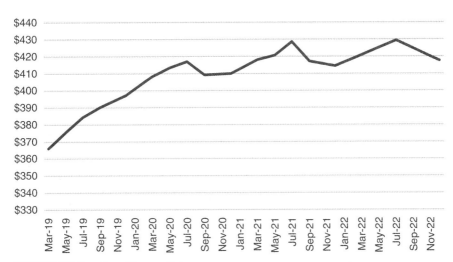

EXHIBIT 10.3 Corn Futures Prices

benefits to those market participants with superior knowledge or skill. Commodities that have tremendous variations in demand (e.g., natural gas across winter vs. summer in the northern hemisphere) and variations in supply (grains across growing seasons) lead to price changes that in turn lead to challenges and opportunities for investors and speculators.

10.2.6 The Basis of Forward and Futures Contracts

The **basis** of futures or forward contracts is commonly defined as the spot price minus the futures or forward price, although in some literature the basis is defined as the forward price minus the spot price. **Basis risk** is the dispersion in economic returns associated with changes in the relation between spot prices and futures prices. The basis of a forward contract with delivery in T years, F_T, on a referenced asset with price, S, is depicted in Equation 10.4:

$$\text{Basis} = S - F_T \tag{10.4}$$

Again, in some sources the basis is defined as the forward price minus the spot price. The basis is equal to the present value of the carrying costs (perhaps multiplied by -1, depending on the definition used). Note that at delivery (i.e., time T) $S = F_T$ (i.e., the prices converge at delivery, since a forward contract with zero time to delivery is a spot transaction). Analysts study the behavior of the basis through time, recognizing convergence. Convergence, previously defined as the spot price approaching the forward price as delivery approaches, can also be viewed as the basis approaching zero as the time of delivery approaches.

An arbitrageur or trader hedging spot positions against forward positions analyzes the basis, compares it to carrying costs, and attempts to identify mispricing. To the extent that markets are informationally efficient, a position that is short the forward contract and long the spot price is hedged and should offer an expected return equal to the cost of carry (before transaction costs). The opposite position (long the futures and short the spot) is, in effect, borrowing money by selling or short selling an asset. That trade is also riskless and generates a borrowing cost equal to the carrying costs.

10.2.7 Calendar Spreads on Forward Contracts

Traders hedging forward contracts against each other focus on the calendar spread between the prices of the contracts, as depicted in Equation 10.5:

$$\text{Calendar Spread} = F_{T+t} - F_T \tag{10.5}$$

where t is the length of time separating the settlement dates of the contracts. A **calendar spread** can be viewed as the difference between futures prices (or forward prices) on the same underlying asset but with different settlement dates. A calendar spread can also be viewed as a position: the simultaneous long and short positions in forward contracts with the same underlying commodity but with different times to delivery. Thus, the trader may *calculate* the calendar spread as a numerical concept, and may *put on* a calendar spread by taking hedged positions in the contracts. Other types of spreads may be formed based on distinctions between contracts other than settlement dates.

Calendar spread trading focuses on the search for relatively mispriced futures or forward contracts on the same commodity but with different settlement dates. Calendar spread trading is therefore a speculation on changes in the shape and slope of the term structure of forward prices.

10.2.8 The Return on a Calendar Spread

The return on a calendar spread (ignoring dividends, which are common in financial futures) must depend on the same variables that determine forward prices, which in Equation 10.2 are the spot price (S), the riskless financing rate (r), the storage costs (c), and the convenience yield (y).

☞ **APPLICATION 10.2.8A**

Consider a calendar spread that is long the two-year forward contract and short the one-year forward contract on a physical commodity with a spot price of $100. Assume that the number of contracts in the long position equals the number of contracts in the short position. The trader puts on a spread in anticipation that storage costs, c, will rise. Assume that the forward prices adhere to Equation 6.8 and that $r = 2\%$, $c = 3\%$, and $y = 5\%$. Note that these values were chosen for the simplicity that $r + c - y = 0\%$ so that the forward prices equal the spot prices. (a) What would the profit or loss be to the trader if spot prices rose $1? (b) What would the profit or loss be to the trader if the storage costs rose one percentage point (from 3% to 4%)? (a) Changes in the spot price will not affect calendar spreads as long as none of the carrying costs change from $r + c -$

$y = 0$. All forward prices will continue to match the spot price, and the basis of all contracts will remain zero. The trader is hedged against changes in the spot price by holding an equal number of long and short contracts. (b) In the second scenario, when storage costs rise from 3% to 4%, $r + c - y$ will no longer equal 0, and forward prices will rise relative to spot prices. In this example, the longer delivery date of the long position (two years) will cause the forward price of the two-year forward to rise in price in relation to the one-year forward, netting the trader a profit from correctly speculating that the storage costs would rise. Specifically, the two-year forward rises from $100 to $102.020, and the one-year forward rises from $100 to $101.005, netting the trader a profit of $1.015 from being long the two-year forward and short the one-year forward. Note that the values are based on continuous compounding.

Note that in the previous example, the trader had equally sized long and short positions. In this unique situation of a level-term structure of forward contracts, a trader can have the same notional value in each position by having the same number of contracts. If the term structure of forward prices has a slope, then the notional value of each contract differs, and a trader with offsetting positions with equal numbers of contracts will not be hedged in terms of notional values.

In summary, calendar spreads that contain long and short positions of equal notional value are hedged against changes in the spot price. Changes in the spot price (everything else being equal) may be viewed as causing a parallel or additive shift in the entire term structure of forward prices. Changes in the costs of carry cause a slope change in the term structure of forward prices. Returns on calendar spreads are primarily driven by two equivalent concepts: changes in the slope of the term structure of forward prices, and changes in carrying costs.

10.2.9 The Risks of a Calendar Spread

Individual positions in forward contracts are quite sensitive to the price of the underlying asset. But as illustrated in section 10.2.8, a calendar spread based on notional values may have little or no sensitivity to the price of the underlying asset.

Note from Equation 6.8 that the sensitivity of the price of a forward contract with respect to the carrying costs is proportional to the time to settlement of the contract (T). This leads to two properties regarding the risks of calendar spreads:

1. The value of a calendar spread is sensitive to carrying costs. The degree of sensitivity that a calendar spread has to carry costs is driven by the amount of time that separates the times to settlement of the contracts that form the spread. Thus, spreads with underlying contracts that differ more in longevity tend to be riskier.
2. Spreads that are long the longer-term contract benefit when costs of carry rise, and suffer when costs of carry decline. The intuition is that the benefit of a forward contract is avoiding the costs of carrying a cash position in an asset. When carrying costs rise, longer-term forward contracts enjoy a larger increase in total benefits than is enjoyed by shorter-term contracts.

The concept that longer-term forward contracts are positively related to carrying costs and more sensitive than shorter-term contracts can be confirmed by noting that the partial derivative of $F(T)$ in Equation 6.8 with respect to carrying costs (r and c) is $T F(T)$.

10.3 ROLLING OF FORWARD AND FUTURES CONTRACTS

Chapter 6 discussed the process of rolling futures and forwards positions from one contract to a more distant contract for the purpose of maintaining a long-term exposure to a commodity. Contracts may be rolled over from any point in time to any available contract. This section discusses the implications of these timing and longevity decisions. The **excess return of a futures contract** is the return generated exclusively from changes in futures prices and is not to be confused with the definition of excess return of a cash security, which is its return minus the riskless rate. Thus, if the futures price of a particular contract on gold rises from $1,000 per ounce to $1,050 per ounce, the contract experiences an *excess return* of 5%.

10.3.1 Why Returns on a Futures Contract Can Differ from the Spot Return

The previous section defined the basis as the difference between the spot price and the futures or forward price. Consider a fully collateralized position in a futures contract. A **fully collateralized position** is a position in which the cash necessary to settle the contract has been posted in the form of short-term, riskless bonds. The total returns from fully collateralized futures or forward returns differ from returns on spot positions on the same asset primarily due to basis risk. The basis risk that causes realized returns on a fully collateralized commodity futures contract or forward contract to differ from the total return on the underlying spot position may be divided into three primary sources: (1) when the costs of carry to a marginal investor for the spot position are not the same as the costs implied by the basis, (2) when the convenience yield from the spot position differs from its storage costs, and (3) when the basis changes. The first issue would tend to indicate informational market inefficiency in the pricing of the futures contract. The second issue is that, in equilibrium, if a spot position offers a convenience yield that does not exactly offset its storage costs, $c - y$ is positive and the spot price must be lower than when the convenience yield is high. While the inventory holder may not earn the convenience yield, there is an indirect benefit of having sufficient inventories preventing a stock-out that slows their business operations. The third issue is simply a consequence of uncertainty.

10.3.2 Components of Futures Returns

There are two especially useful formulas depicting the components of the total return of a collateralized futures position: a two-component formula and a three-component formula.

The return on a fully collateralized position, R_{fcoll}, can be expressed as the sum of two components:

$$R_{fcoll} = \text{Collateral Yield} + \text{Excess Return} \tag{10.6}$$

Equation 10.6 expresses the total return from an unleveraged, fully collateralized commodity futures position as the sum of the interest earned from the riskless bonds used to collateralize the futures contract (the collateral yield) and the percentage price change in the futures contract (the excess return).

The price of a futures or forward contract may be viewed as equaling the spot price minus the basis. Thus, the excess return in Equation 10.6 (the change in the futures price) may be broken into the change in the spot price and the change in the basis. By substituting the change in the spot price and the change in the basis into Equation 10.6 in place of the excess return, the total return from this unleveraged, fully collateralized commodity futures position can be expressed as coming from three primary sources.

The three primary sources are depicted in Equation 10.7 as: (1) changes in the spot price of the underlying commodity, (2) the interest earned from the riskless bonds used to collateralize the futures contract, and (3) changes in the contract's basis (i.e., roll yield):

$$R_{fcoll} = \text{Spot Return} + \text{Collateral Yield} + \text{Roll Yield} \tag{10.7}$$

Each of the three components can be an important part of the return of a commodity futures position. Let's look at each of these three components closely.

The first component in Equation 10.7, **spot return**, is the return on the price of the underlying asset in the spot market. The returns of unhedged futures positions are primarily driven by the spot return. Exposure to spot price changes is the primary reason that most market participants enter futures contracts, and is also why market participants wishing to gain exposure to commodity prices establish positions in futures contracts on commodities. It should be noted that there is not a single centralized spot market or a single network of spot markets that provides a single universally recognized spot price for most physical assets.

The second component, **collateral yield**, is the interest earned from the riskless bonds or other money market assets used to collateralize the futures contract. Positions in futures contracts are often partially collateralized in that they only post collateral that is equal to the margin required by the futures exchanges. Partial collateralization generates leveraged returns, since the value changes of the entire futures position is borne by a smaller collateral amount. Fully collateralized positions are unleveraged, since the cash invested equals the economic exposure of the futures contract. Depending on interest rate levels, the collateral yield can be a substantial part of the total return to a fully collateralized commodity futures position.

The third component of a futures position is changes in its basis, also known as roll yield or roll return. **Roll yield** or **roll return** is properly defined as the portion of the return of a futures position from the change in the contract's basis through time. The basis of a futures contract changes for two reasons. First, as time passes, the time to settlement of the futures contract shortens, and the contract's price (and basis) rolls up or down the term structure of forward prices toward the spot price. Second, as components of the cost of carry vary (interest rates, dividend yields for financial futures contracts, storage costs, or convenience yields), the basis will also vary, since the basis depends directly on the four components of cost of carry. This very important concept is detailed in the next several sections.

☞ **APPLICATION 10.3.2.A**

Consider a one-year, fully collateralized commodity futures position on a commodity that experiences a 3% decline in its spot price. Over that same year, the basis in the commodity fell from the spot price exceeding the futures price by 2% to a basis of 0%. The riskless interest rate was 4% and the storage cost of the commodity was 2.4% per year. Compute the spot return, collateral yield, excess return, roll yield (i.e., roll return), and the return on a fully collateralized position.

The spot return is the change in the spot price, which is given as –3%. The collateral yield on a fully collateralized position would be equal to the riskless rate, which is given as 4%. The excess return of the futures contract is the percentage price change in the futures contract. Since the spot price fell 3% and the futures price rose relative to the spot price from being 2% lower to being equal, the excess return on the futures contract was –1%. The roll yield or roll return is the 2% gain in the futures contract relative to the spot price from the basis going from the futures price being 2% less than the spot price to being equal. The return on a fully collateralized position may be calculated using either Equation 10.6 (Collateral Yield + Excess Return = 4% – 1% = 3%) or Equation 10.7 (Spot Return + Collateral Yield + Roll Yield = –3% + 4% + 2% = 3%). The 2.4% storage costs are subsumed within the roll yield and are superfluous to the exercise.

10.3.3 Two Interpretations of Rolling Contracts

One of the sources of futures returns just discussed is the roll yield, or roll return, which is the subject of alternative understandings. Conflicting interpretations of roll return emanate from ambiguity in the concept of rolling a futures position.

Rolling a contract has two common interpretations. Sometimes it is used to describe the transactions involved in switching, or rolling from, a short-term futures contract to a futures contract with a longer term to settlement in the process of maintaining a continuous exposure to the underlying asset. Other times the rolling of a contract describes how its price "rolls up" (or down) the term structure of forward prices as its time to settlement nears.

The two interpretations of rolling a contract lead to two interpretations of roll return or roll yield.

When rolling a contract is viewed as holding a futures position while its time to settlement nears and its price potentially rolls up or down the forward curve, then roll return is viewed as the change in the contract's basis through time. This view of roll return tends to be associated with a financial economics view of risk and return.

When rolling a contract is viewed as a transaction, roll return is viewed as the profit or loss recognized at the time that a position in a futures contract is rolled from one contract to another. This view of roll return is used to adjust excess futures returns in the process of reporting returns of continuous commodity exposures. This view of roll return tends to be associated with an accounting view of returns.

It should be noted that the transactions of closing a position in a short-term contract and opening a position in a longer-term contract do not directly and immediately cause a gain or loss. Rolling between contracts can be viewed as *recognizing* a gain or loss that was previously accrued. But recognition of accrued gains (and rolling of contracts) does not create wealth or return.

10.3.4 Roll Yield and the Slope of the Forward Curve

Section 10.2 discussed the concepts of contango (an upward-sloping term structure of forward prices) and backwardation (a downward-sloping term structure of forward prices). An important topic in commodity futures is the relation between the slope of the term structure of forward prices (i.e., the forward curve) and the sources of return from holding a futures contract.

It is often claimed that holding a long position in a futures contract when a market is in backwardation tends to be a successful strategy because it earns roll return (or roll yield). The idea is that as time passes and the time to settlement of a futures contract diminishes, the future's price rises as the futures contract "rolls up" the downward-sloping curve of a backwardated market. In other words, it is often argued that market participants can earn consistently superior risk-adjusted returns from the positive roll yield generated from long positions in futures contracts when markets are backwardated.

The argument that roll return generates superior returns in backwardated markets for long futures positions implies that roll return generates superior returns in contango markets for short futures positions. Also, roll return could be similarly argued to lead to inferior returns for long positions in markets that are in contango and inferior returns for short positions in markets that are backwardated. Can alpha be consistently generated by alternating between long and short positions based on the slope of the forward curve?

Previous sections have demonstrated that the slope of the term structure of forward prices depends on the costs of carry. In an informationally efficient market, a nonzero slope of the term structure of forward prices exists to *prevent* superior risk-adjusted returns. In other words, the term structure takes on a positive or negative slope (contango or backwardated) based on carrying costs, so that the risk-adjusted returns of spot positions and fully collateralized futures positions will be equal. Commercial holders of inventories can benefit from convenience yield, which would drive the futures price to be less than or equal to the spot price adjusted for interest rates and storage costs.

In an informationally efficient market, roll return is simply the change in the basis that allows identical exposures in cash and futures markets to offer identical total returns. However, no market is perfectly efficient, especially those involving real assets, such as commodities.

10.3.5 Roll Yield, Carrying Costs, the Basis, and Alpha

There are three ways of expressing the relation between spot and forward prices through time: (1) the basis, (2) carrying costs, including convenience yield, and (3) roll yield. All three of these terms express the same concept.

In an informationally efficient market (and when the carrying costs are expressed as present values rather than as rates or percentages), the absolute value of the carrying costs will equal the absolute value of the basis. The carrying costs and the basis will have different signs, according to the most common definition of the basis being the spot price minus the forward price.

The roll yield is the same as the basis (and the carrying costs) when viewing the return on a futures contract through its settlement. Note that the roll yield is defined as the change in the basis. Since the basis of a futures contact or forward contract is zero at settlement, the roll yield of a futures contract to settlement must equal the contract's starting basis.

Let's examine the relations first in the context of futures on financial assets and then in the context of futures on real assets (e.g., commodities).

In the case of futures contracts on financial assets, the costs of carry for the underlying financial asset are the financing costs expressed as an interest rate (r) and the rate of dividends, coupons, or other distributions (d) that are received and are entered as a negative cost ($-d$). While r is observable, d is assumed to only be predictable. We assume that all market participants are unanimous with regard to these values and can engage in transactions to receive or pay the same values of r and d. Therefore, the actions of arbitrageurs in these markets should force financial futures toward a high degree of informational efficiency in which roll yield equals the cost of carry, which, in turn, determines (and equals) the basis.

In the case of real assets, the carrying costs of holding the real asset include the storage cost, c, and the convenience yield, y. Storage costs and convenience yields on real assets are heterogeneous between market participants. A **heterogeneous** value differs across one or more dimensions. In this case, individual market participants may have different costs and benefits (c and y) from holding a real asset. Further, these costs and benefits may be unobservable to others.

A clear benefit of futures markets on real assets is the market's ability to facilitate the efficient bearing of storage costs and reaping of convenience yields. For example, an efficient storage operator of natural gas can store natural gas while hedging its price risk in the futures market. A manufacturer that depends on silver as a raw material can enjoy the convenience of large inventories (e.g., protection from supply disruptions) while hedging the price risk of silver in the futures market.

A major source of potentially superior risk-adjusted returns using futures contracts on real assets emanates from the heterogeneous costs of carry across market participants. The key for a market participant to generate alpha through analysis of carrying costs and the basis is to execute trades when the prices of futures contracts imply costs of carry that deviate from the participant's costs of carry. For example, a trader can generate alpha if the trader's storage costs are less than the storage costs implicit in the basis of the futures contract.

10.3.6 The Strategy of Rolling Contracts Affects Return Expectations

This section and the next discuss the rolling of futures or forward positions: the closing of a position prior to or at settlement, and the opening of an otherwise identical contract with a later settlement date in order to maintain continuous exposure. What is an appropriate measure of the return for a long-term continuous exposure to a commodity? The issue is how to establish an appropriate return standard or expectation for a long-term continuous futures contracts exposure to a commodity. There are two issues: rollover decisions and collateral investment decisions.

Within futures markets, individual investors roll their futures positions over at different times relative to settlement and may differ in the selection of which settlement date to use for the new positions. The rollover decision has two components: when to exit a position and which longevity to select for the new futures or forward position. Accordingly, it is not possible to identify a pattern of rollovers that is common to all investors and to identify the return of a particular pattern of rollovers as being representative of the returns achieved by all investors. Returns are determined by the particular rollover strategy implemented.

Finally, the return of a fully collateralized strategy depends on the interest rate that is earned on the collateral. Collateral investment positions are often in default-free fixed-income securities. These positions can differ by their duration and therefore their returns can differ.

10.3.7 The Impact of Rolling Contracts on Alpha

What is the relation between risk-adjusted *expected* returns and the selection of a particular rolling strategy (e.g., entry and exit longevities)? Can a particular rollover strategy consistently generate attractive risk-adjusted returns (alpha)? These issues are greatly simplified by viewing the difference between two rollover strategies as being equal to a simple calendar spread strategy.

To illustrate, consider two investors with continuous long positions in the same commodity futures. Suppose that Investor A rolls over contracts one month prior to settlement and establishes a new position in the first deferred contract. Investor B rolls over contracts at settlement and establishes a new position in the new nearby contract. As long as the nearby contract has one month or more to settlement, Investors A and B have the same position. However, when the nearby contract has one month or less to settlement, Investor A rolls into the first deferred contract while Investor B remains in the nearby contract. The difference between the returns of the two strategies occurs only during the month prior to settlement and is equal to the returns of a calendar spread.

For purposes of discussion, let's title the strategy followed by Investor B as a classic rollover strategy: Each contract is held to settlement and then is rolled over into the shortest available contract. All other rollover strategies generate a return that is equal to the return of that classic rollover strategy plus, at some or all times, the return of a short calendar spread. If markets are inefficient, it may be possible to earn a consistently superior or inferior risk-adjusted return through the adoption of a particular rollover strategy (which is to say that superior return is possible if calendar spreads are inefficiently priced). In other words, any advantage between two rollover strategies is identical to the advantage of an equivalent strategy using calendar spreads (in a perfect market). Speculating on rollover strategies is tantamount to speculating on calendar spreads.

It should be noted that, in practice, markets are imperfect and have transaction costs. When transaction costs are included, some rollover strategies may be more cost-effective than others.

10.3.8 Three Propositions Regarding Roll Return

The more common definition of roll return (or roll yield) is that it is the return accrued in a futures position through time, attributable to changes in the basis of the futures contract. This section distinguishes this definition of roll return from the accounting usage of the term regarding the closing of one futures position and the opening of another. The following three propositions highlight key issues.

PROPOSITION 1: Roll return is *not* generated when one position is closed and a new position is opened. For example, roll return is not generated by closing the nearby contract at $95 and opening the first deferred contract at $92, for a $3 profit. The lack of logic to that view of rollover is analogous to selling a short-term Treasury bill for $99, buying a longer-term Treasury bill for $98, and claiming that the transaction generated a profit of $1.

Roll return occurs throughout the time that a particular futures or forward contract is held. Roll return can be viewed as the difference between the price at which a particular contract is opened and the price at which that *same* contract is closed in excess of the return on a spot position in the contract's underlying commodity. The price difference is based on the same contract at two different points in time.

PROPOSITION 2: Roll return is not necessarily positive when markets are backwardated for holding periods shorter than being held to settlement. It is true that roll return is positive in backwardated markets if none of the components of the costs of carry change. However, if the costs of carry change, then even in backwardated markets there is no guarantee that roll return will be positive prior to settlement. In other words, it is reasonably likely for the term structure of forward rates to shift such that roll return will be negative in a backwardated market.

PROPOSITION 3: A position that generated a positive roll return does not indicate that the position's total returns were superior (i.e., that there was alpha). Roll return is a part of the total returns that make futures contracts and cash positions equally attractive. Roll return is usually negative, to punish the forward position (relative to the cash position) for not requiring a cash investment relative to a spot position. But roll return can clearly be positive, when, for example, there is a high dividend or coupon rate on the underlying asset. In the case of a forward contract or futures contract on a financial asset held to settlement, roll return equals carrying costs times -1: $(d - r)$. Thus, if the dividend yield of a financial asset exceeds the riskless rate, then roll return is positive if the position is held to settlement.

10.4 NORMAL BACKWARDATION AND NORMAL CONTANGO

Backwardation and contango are typically discussed as the relationship between *current* spot prices and the prices of futures contracts of various settlement dates. This section discusses *expected* spot price and futures prices.

10.4.1 Normal Backwardation

A somewhat subtle distinction exists between backwardation and *normal* backwardation. In **normal backwardation**, the forward price is believed to be below the expected spot price. We say "believed to be" because we cannot observe the expected spot price; we can only estimate it, and those estimations may differ between market participants. Since in normal backwardation the expected spot price exceeds the forward price, there is a positive expected return from holding the futures contract. Thus, a long position in a forward contract involves an expected profit in the case of normal backwardation (with no investment other than the posting of collateral that can earn interest).

Normal backwardation does not mean that markets are informationally inefficient, even though a forward contract in a market with normal backwardation would offer an expected profit with no investment; this is because any expected profit could be due to compensation for bearing risk. The concept of normal backwardation is silent on whether the expected profit of a long position is alpha or is a risk premium for bearing systematic risk. The entity on the long side of the forward contract should expect to earn a profit (a risk premium) for bearing the risk of being long the commodity whenever the underlying systematic risk (i.e., beta) is positive.

10.4.2 Normal Contango

Normal contango is an infrequently used term that refers to the relationship between forward prices and expected spot prices in which the forward price is believed to be *above* the expected spot price. In normal contango, the entity on the *short* side of the forward contract should expect to earn a profit from bearing the risk of being short the commodity. Conversely, the entity on the long side of the forward contract should expect to bear a loss. In an informationally efficient market, normal contango would only exist for commodity forwards with negative betas (i.e., with returns that tend to hedge systematic risk). Since it would be relatively rare to expect a commodity to have negative beta, normal contango should be viewed as a rare occurrence. In an informationally inefficient market, normal contango would exist because a particular forward contract is overpriced and offers negative ex ante alpha to the long side and positive ex ante alpha to the short side.

10.4.3 Interpreting Normal Backwardation and Normal Contango

Unlike backwardation and contango, normal backwardation and normal contango cannot be directly observed, because expected spot prices cannot be observed. It should be noted that the literature on commodities differs with regard to the distinction between backwardation and normal backwardation. The literature also differs about the distinction between contango and normal contango, and many sources do not even use the term *normal contango*. The definitions used in this chapter may not match the definitions that are found elsewhere, but they reflect the most consistent and useful definitions of the terms. The concepts involved are central to an organized understanding of the risks and returns of commodities and forward contracts on commodities, so it is necessary to use these terms with precision, even at the risk of having definitions that conflict with other sources.

Novices to forward markets sometimes assume that forward or futures prices are equal to expected spot prices. But in an efficient market, forward and futures prices must differ from expected spot prices whenever the position involves *systematic* risk. The excess of the expected spot price over the forward price is the expected reward for bearing the risk of being long the forward contract when the underlying asset has positive systematic risk. The expected loss to the short side of the contract is the cost of using the forward contract to hedge systematic risk. The only time that forward or futures prices should equal expected spot prices in an informationally efficient market is when the underlying asset contains no systematic risk.

In highly liquid futures markets such as the market for futures contracts on the S&P 500, futures contracts are viewed as being cost-effective methods of obtaining exposure that is otherwise identical to a cash position in the S&P 500. Unlike commodity futures, the components of the cost of carry on S&P 500 futures contracts are somewhat easily observed (interest rates) or forecasted (dividend yields). Unlike some commodities, there are no harvests or inventory shortages for S&P 500 exposure. Accordingly, issues such as the slope of the futures curve for S&P 500 futures are largely ignored, since participants understand that the slope simply reflects the spread between interest rates and dividend yields. Also, decisions as to which S&P 500 futures contracts to use (e.g., the nearby or deferred contracts) are based more on convenience and less on speculation with regard to changes in the basis.

In summary, in perfect capital markets, the price (or rates) of forward contracts on *financial* assets have term structures with slopes and curves that are driven entirely by the observable costs of carry (interest rates and distributions). In this case the relation between forward prices and *expected* spot prices is driven by risk premiums based on the systematic risks of the assets underlying the forwards. This understanding helps put the concepts of normal backwardation and normal contango in context: The relationship between expected spot prices and futures prices is not directly observable, it is determined by risk premiums, and it is distinct from the relation between current spot prices and current futures prices (which is determined by the costs of carry).

10.4.4 Keynes and Normal Backwardation

John Maynard Keynes argued that commodity futures prices should typically be lower than the expected future spot prices (i.e., futures and forward markets should be in normal backwardation). Keynes's reasoning was based on the assumption that *producers* of a commodity have a strong incentive to lock in a sales price today for future production by selling futures contracts (artificially pushing down futures prices), but that *users* of the commodity have a strong incentive to purchase at spot prices (artificially raising spot pricing). If there is a natural oversupply of futures contracts, then speculators will enter the market to purchase the excess supply, but only at a discount to the expected future spot price. This exerts downward pressure on long-term futures prices relative to expected spot prices, leading to markets with normal backwardation.

In the fixed-income world, this argument is similar to the liquidity preference hypothesis. The liquidity preference hypothesis holds that producers of bonds (borrowers) prefer issuing long maturities, whereas consumers of bonds (lenders) prefer purchasing short maturities, distorting relative prices or rates from reflecting unbiased expectations. Producers offer attractive longer-term yields, which would mean relatively low long-term bond prices, to entice borrowers to extend their maturity or to induce speculators to borrow at short maturities and lend at long maturities. Thus, speculators are compensated for providing a service (time intermediation) to the market. They provide demand by establishing long positions in long-term futures contracts to counter the excess supply generated by net short producers. This supports futures prices at a level above where they might lie in the absence of speculators. The positive risk premium entices speculators to enter the market despite the risk.

10.4.5 Commodity Forward Curves, Storage Costs, and Inventory Variation

Models of a commodity forward curve predict that the curve will be upward sloping when the current inventory levels are much greater than the threshold levels of demand (low convenience yield), and that it will be downward sloping when inventories are exceptionally tight (high convenience yield). Storage models are unique to real assets. They do not have a corresponding model in fixed income because, except for financing, there is no cost of carry for bonds.

Another factor incorporated into storage models is the risk of **stock-out**, which occurs when storage effectively drops to zero, resulting in consumption being entirely dependent on production and transportation networks, and typically occurs in markets with peak seasonal demand, such as natural gas or heating oil, or with annual crop cycles, such as grains. To avoid stock-out, users of a commodity have an incentive to hedge more actively at points on the forward calendar that are most susceptible to stock-out. These would be the months just before harvest for annual crops, and the later part of the heating season for natural gas and heating oil.

The theory of storage is illustrated in the **Working curve**, which positively relates the slope of the forward curve to current levels of inventory such that low inventory levels tend to be associated with a negative and nonlinear forward curve slope. The nonlinearity is due to embedded real options related to inventory levels. When inventory is low, users of the commodity may face costs related to searching, delays, rush charges, and transportation. In the extreme, they may face significant costs from stock-outs as inventory is depleted.

10.4.6 Commodity Forward Prices and the Market Segmentation Hypothesis

Section 10.4.4 discusses the possibility that commodity forward curves are determined by a liquidity preference or liquidity premium and the desire of producers to hedge their anticipated commodity sales with short positions in long-term forwards or futures. In some markets, the users of a commodity rarely use the forward market to hedge future commodity needs. These particular markets typically exist for products that are directly consumed by the public, such as gasoline.

In some cases, the forward curve may be better explained by the reasoning used in fixed-income markets in discussions of the preferred market segmentation (i.e.,

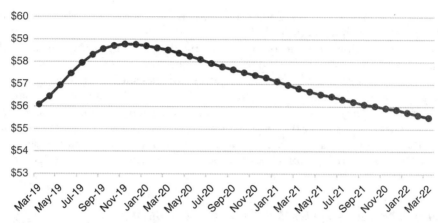

EXHIBIT 10.4   Crude Oil Futures Curve

preferred habitat) hypothesis, in which the relation between expected spot rates and forward rates varies nonmonotonically throughout the range of delivery dates due to supply and demand pressures in localized regions of the curve.

Under the market segmentation hypothesis, the net supply or demand for specific futures contracts by natural hedgers could be positive or negative depending on market conditions and preferences of producers and users to hedge their risks. As a result, speculators may need to take short or long positions to absorb the excess demand or the excess supply of futures contracts created by hedgers. To the extent that market participants demand substantial risk premiums to stray from using their preferred time to settlement to another longevity, the risk premium in the futures markets could vary across times to settlement. In other words, if participants have a preferred habitat (i.e., time to settlement) and the market is segmented (participants are reluctant to hedge contracts of varying times to settlement), there could be nonmonotonic slopes to forward curves, such as a humped curve.

The crude oil futures market has often exhibited a **humped curve**, which in the typical case of commodity futures means that the market is in contango in the short term, but gives way to backwardation for longer-maturity contracts. Exhibit 10.4 depicts a humped curve.

10.4.7   Option-Based Models of the Forward Curve for Commodities

Option-based models of the term structure focus on two types of real options embedded in commodity markets. Real options embedded in commodity markets are implied options involving real assets.

The first type of real option is the option to extract a natural resource. A copper mine can be shut down if the price of copper falls below the marginal cost of production. Although there may be times when the spot price of copper falls below its marginal cost of production due to a temporary glut, producers will not sell forward production below cost for long; that is, they will shut down the mine. The option to extract (or defer extraction of) the resource dampens the volatility of commodity prices for future delivery.

The second real option embedded in the commodity forward curve is related to inventories. Commodity markets generally have a volatility asymmetry. A **volatility asymmetry** is a difference in values between two analogous volatilities, such as is the case with commodities, in which volatility tends to be higher when prices are rising than when they are falling. This is because shortages tend to cause more serious problems than surpluses. The volatility asymmetry favors owning physical inventory (or short-dated futures contracts) over longer-dated futures contracts. All other things being equal, this factor will tend to flatten commodity futures curves or lead to backwardation.

10.5 COMMODITY EXPOSURE AND DIVERSIFICATION

A key justification for allocations to commodities is diversification—however, the exact meaning of *diversification* and the role of commodities as diversifiers varies. We begin with a discussion of commodities and their diversification with traditional assets.

10.5.1 Four Explanations of Commodities as Diversifiers

Commodities are often viewed as an asset class that helps diversify a portfolio of traditional assets (stocks and bonds) through a lack of return correlation between commodities and traditional assets. Here we discuss four reasons why commodity returns may have low correlation with stock prices and bond prices.

First, unlike financial securities, commodities have prices that are not directly determined by the discounted value of future cash flows. Accordingly, commodity prices are not as directly related to changes in forecasted cash flows and changes in market discount rates. Instead, commodity prices are evaluated primarily on forecasts of the commodity's supply and demand. Since commodity prices are driven by different economic fundamentals than are stocks and bonds, they should be expected to have little correlation, or even negative correlation, with the prices of financial assets.

Second, nominal commodity prices should be positively correlated with inflation largely because commodity prices form part of the definition and computation of inflation. Inflation is the decline in the value of money relative to the value of a general bundle of goods and services. A **nominal price** refers to the stated price of an asset measured using the contemporaneous values of a currency. Thus, the 2020 nominal price of a bushel of corn in U.S. dollars is simply the market price observed in 2020. A **real price** refers to the price of an asset that is adjusted for inflation through being expressed in the value of currency from a different time period. The 2020 real price of a bushel of corn based on 2010 dollars deflates the 2020 nominal price for the inflation that occurred in the dollar between 2010 and 2020. Since prices of physical commodities such as oil are an important component of the computation of inflation, we should generally expect that the nominal prices of commodities and other real assets would move in tandem with inflation. Thus, real commodity prices would tend to be unaffected by inflation. On the other hand, both the real and the nominal prices of stocks and especially bonds tend to be negatively correlated with inflation because inflation raises the discount rates applied to their valuations. To the extent that changing rates of inflation drive the prices of real assets differently than they drive the real prices of financial assets, there should be low correlation or perhaps even negative correlation between commodity prices and the prices of most stocks and bonds.

A third reason why commodity price changes may be negatively correlated with the returns of stocks and bonds is that they may react very differently at different parts of the business cycle. The value of stocks and bonds is derived from expectations regarding long-term earnings or coupon payments. Commodities are often priced more on the state of current economic conditions and factors regarding short-term supply and demand. For example, in the midst of a severe and prolonged drought, the price of corn and other agricultural products may be extremely high, despite the long-term expectation that the drought will undoubtedly end and the prices will revert toward more normal levels.

A fourth argument for low or negative correlation between commodity prices and financial assets is based on commodities being a major cost of some corporate producers. In the short run, a major increase in commodity prices (e.g., oil) may cause a substantial decline in corporate profits, and a decline in commodity prices may result in an increase in profits. Thus, as commodity prices soar, corporate stocks and bonds may falter (except those of commodity-producing firms). The result is a negative correlation between commodity prices and the prices of financial assets.

All four of these arguments indicate why there tends to be a low or negative correlation of commodity prices and returns to the prices and returns of financial assets.

10.5.2 Commodities as Diversifiers in a Perfect Market Equilibrium

A market is in equilibrium when current market prices equate supply and demand such that further transactions cannot benefit market participants. In an ideal equilibrium, all market participants are well diversified, and the differences between market risk and idiosyncratic risk can be precisely delineated. With a perfect capital market in equilibrium, the role of commodities in diversifying a portfolio is clear, as summarized here.

Diversification is the process of eliminating exposure to idiosyncratic risks while constructing a portfolio that matches the risk characteristics of a perfectly diversified portfolio. In the CAPM (capital asset pricing model), the perfectly diversified portfolio is the market portfolio that contains exposure to all assets and contains exposure to each of those assets in proportion to their total market value (i.e., size). The percentage of the total market portfolio attributable to each asset in that portfolio is known as the market weight. In other words, the market weight of an asset is equal to the percentage of the total global value of that asset relative to the total global value of all assets. For example, if crude oil represents 5% of the total wealth of the world, then a perfectly diversified portfolio of risky assets should have a 5% weight in oil. In a perfect market in equilibrium, any investor with a portfolio of risky assets that has an asset exposure greater than or less than its market weight is speculating on idiosyncratic risk. In a perfect market equilibrium, bearing idiosyncratic risk does not offer higher expected returns.

Commodities are a substantial part of total wealth; therefore, commodities should be a substantial part of all portfolios, according to classic equilibrium models such as the CAPM. So, based on the CAPM, the only issue in determining appropriate exposure to each commodity is determining the market weight of that commodity. However, ascertaining the total global market value of a commodity is difficult in practice. Returning to the example of oil, even this simplified view of portfolio allocations introduces a number of difficult questions: How much oil is expected to be discovered? How much oil that is already discovered can be extracted? What price should be attached to oil reserves that are years from being extracted? Further, ascertaining the exposure of financial assets to each commodity is difficult. How much of an oil company's stock price is attributable to oil? How have an oil company's hedging activities modified the company's exposure to oil prices?

10.5.3 Commodities as Diversifiers in the Presence of Market Imperfections

In practice, markets are in a continuous state of disequilibrium and might remain substantially out of equilibrium for extended periods of time, which may offer the opportunity for an asset class to offer benefits as a diversifier without also offering commensurately lower returns. Often commodity shortages and oversupplies cannot be quickly corrected by price mechanisms. In disequilibrium, participants tend to hold substantially different exposures to various asset classes—especially commodities—than exposures based on market weights.

Some nations have vast holdings of oil and other resources that cannot be quickly developed and divested, and therefore the nation remains poorly diversified (i.e., highly concentrated), with a very high percentage of wealth exposed to oil prices or other commodity prices. If one market participant holds an asset in a higher proportion than its market weight, then some other market participants must hold that asset in a lower proportion than its market weight. In imperfect markets and in disequilibrium, it is no longer clear that all market participants can or should hold oil or any other commodity in their portfolios with a weight equal to the market weight of that commodity. In that case, investors seek to hold commodities in the proportion that provides the highest return-to-risk ratio based on their existing portfolios and such circumstances as the structure of their liabilities.

10.5.4 Commodities as Diversifiers against Unexpected Inflation

One of the most often cited virtues of commodity investment is its ability to diversify a portfolio against the risk of unexpected inflation. When rates of inflation are steady, asset prices tend to adjust such that the expected nominal returns of each asset reflect anticipated inflation. Therefore, steady and anticipated inflation is not generally a serious investment risk or a determinant of real returns. However, unexpected inflation can be a serious risk to investors. For example, a fixed-income security tends to underperform in an environment of unexpectedly high inflation because the value of the promised future cash flows is being diminished at an unexpectedly high rate.

Real assets in general and commodities in particular offer protection against inflation risk. **Inflation risk** is the dispersion in economic outcomes caused by uncertainty regarding the value of a currency and it emanates from the divergence between realized and anticipated rates of inflation (i.e., unanticipated inflation).

There are two intuitive explanations for the protection from inflation risk provided by commodities. First, as mentioned in a previous section, commodity prices are an important component (i.e., determinant) of the price indices that measure inflation. Therefore, general price indices (and realized inflation rates) tend to be positively correlated with commodities. Second, the value of a commodity is its perceived ability to provide consumption. Because of their homogeneity and their ability to be transported, commodity prices tend to be determined by global factors rather than local factors. Therefore, in each country local commodity prices should adjust quickly to changes in the value of the local currency. For example, when a country's currency experiences hyperinflation, the nominal price of oil in that currency rises, but the real price of oil in the currency of other nations is unaffected. The real returns of commodity investments in each country should be unaffected by the inflation rate of the investor's home currency.

10.6 EXPECTED RETURNS ON COMMODITIES

This section compares the expected returns of commodity exposures through both physical inventories and derivatives.

10.6.1 Empirical Evidence on Long-Run Commodity Price Changes

Substantial debate exists as to the long-term performance of *spot* commodity prices. Consider the two major forms of analysis: empirical and theoretical. The preponderance of the empirical very-long-term evidence on the direction of commodity prices is that spot prices do not rise at or above the riskless nominal rate. Although it is true that nominal prices of many commodities have increased in the past 50 or so years, the very-long-term real returns on many commodities have been negative. For example, from the middle of the nineteenth century until recently, the real prices of aluminum, copper, iron, nickel, silver, and zinc have declined. Virtually every commodity is now less expensive in real terms than they were many centuries ago.

10.6.2 Theoretical Evidence on Expected Commodity Returns

Consider three points that argue against investment in physical inventories by financial institutions: lack of systematic risk premia, increasing technologies, and wasted convenience yield.

A starting point in the theoretical analysis of expected returns on investments is to consider a general equilibrium model of expected returns, such as the capital asset pricing model. To the extent that commodities have little or no systematic risk (and serve as effective diversifiers relative to equities and bonds), the required and expected returns on commodities would be modest in equilibrium—perhaps near the riskless rate. However, physical commodity returns have generally failed to keep up with riskless rate, as noted in the previous section.

Theory provides an explanation for the long-term history of commodity price declines (due to increasing technologies) and supports the likelihood that the very-long-term downward trends of real commodity prices will continue. Technology is likely to continue to improve efficiency in the extraction (i.e., lower the cost of extraction) and efficiency in the use of commodities (reducing demand). Technology is also likely to improve the rate of reclamation of many commodities and to develop alternatives to utilizing commodities that experience increasing real prices.

Finally, physical commodities often offer convenience yield. However, financial institutions generally seek only financial returns because they do not benefit from the convenience yield of physical inventories of commodities. Therefore, holding of physical inventories of commodities by financial institutions is generally a waste of any convenience yield.

10.6.3 Irrelevancy of Commodity Price Expectations to Returns on Futures Contracts

The previous sections have discussed physical (i.e., direct) ownership of commodity inventory and have provided both empirical and theoretical evidence of the unattractiveness of long-term physical ownership of commodities. This section discusses exposure through forward and futures contracts and demonstrates that derivative contracts can offer competitive returns on commodities even when *expected* spot prices are dramatically lower than *current* spot prices.

Consider the market for popular memory chips used in electronics. For decades, the long-term direction in the price of memory chips on a basis of cost per bit has been steeply downward in real terms as technology has advanced. It would make little economic sense to speculate on memory chip prices by accumulating a large physical inventory in the hope of long-term price increases. However, the market for memory chips includes contracts that call for future delivery of the chips. The prices for future delivery of particular memory chips are consistently lower than the spot prices (for immediate delivery)—as should be expected for a "commodity-like" item such as memory chips, for which technology is improving so rapidly. The price of contracts on memory chips with future delivery adjusts with both sides of the contract taking into account the likely decline in spot prices over the life of the contract.

The dynamics are similar to the case of a very-high-coupon bond selling at an enormous premium to its face value. Investors know that the bond is expected to decline in price but are still able to enter into appropriately priced forward contracts on that bond by simply adjusting the forward price to reflect the high distribution rate of the bond. Chapter 6 detailed the relation between the spot and forward prices of financial assets and discussed the effect of high distributions rates on forward prices relative to spot prices. The relation between forward prices and spot *commodity* prices similarly adjusts for anticipations of declining spot prices such as in the long run when improved technologies emerge that are expected to drive down real prices (e.g., memory chips) or in the short-run when a huge harvest is anticipated that will drive down grain prices.

The point is this: Commodity price exposure obtained through financial derivatives occurs at prices that adjust for anticipated spot price changes, leaving holders of long positions in commodity futures the ability to earn competitive returns even when long-term commodity prices are anticipated to decline. Financial institutions therefore have theoretical justifications to invest in commodities through derivative contracts based on the pursuit of broader diversification.

In order for the demand for commodities as an investment to equal the supply of available commodity investment opportunities, some market participants need to be incentivized to overrepresent commodities in their investment portfolios relative to market weights when others underrepresent commodities. The mechanism by which this would occur is through price adjustments, until commodities offered both enhanced returns and diversification benefits sufficient to induce more sophisticated and innovative investors to make large allocations to commodities. Simply put, to the extent that commodity investing is ignored or rejected by some investors, prices would adjust so that other investors would find superior investment opportunities through making higher allocations to commodities. The result would be that commodity beta exposure would offer higher expected returns per unit of risk than would other beta exposures. This is consistent with the view that hedging by commodity producers will drive down futures prices to a point where financial investors find commodity futures to be attractive investments.

The bottom line is this: Commodities do not enhance expected returns when they are efficiently priced and when their systematic risk exposures (betas) are low. If markets are perfect and in equilibrium, market participants should hold exposures to commodities and other asset classes, expecting lower returns in exchange for enjoying lower risk. Financial institutions can utilize forward contracts and futures contracts to attain those exposures.

10.7 COMMODITY FUTURES INDICES

In this section, we review several investable commodity futures indices, analyze their construction, and discuss their use as benchmarks. An **investable index** has returns that an investor can match in practice by maintaining the same positions that constitute the index.

10.7.1 Construction and Uses of Commodity Futures Indices

Financial securities are generally traded in centralized spot markets, so most indices related to traditional investments focus on prices (or returns) from cash markets. Returns on physical commodities are generally better measured using prices of futures contracts rather than spot or cash prices. Spot prices of physical commodities are not generally traded in a single centralized market, and therefore the spot prices vary between locations (a difference that cannot be arbitraged to near zero due to transportation costs). Also, while shares of a particular security are homogeneous and trade at the same price, some commodities have different qualities or grades that trade at different prices. For these reasons, commodity price indices are commonly constructed using futures prices on commodities rather than cash commodity prices.

The construction and the application of commodity futures indices raise several complexities relative to indices of traditional assets. As discussed in Chapter 3, returns on derivative positions such as futures can be based on fully collateralized positions or on leveraged positions. Commodity futures indices are generally constructed as being unleveraged. The face value of the futures contracts is fully supported (collateralized) either by cash or by riskless bonds (e.g., Treasury bills). The commodity indices discussed here are long-only (i.e., hypothetical long positions are established in derivatives to provide economic exposure to commodities equal to the amount of cash dollars being invested in the index).

An investment manager can use commodity futures indices in several ways. First, a commodity futures index can be used as a benchmark for investment performance analysis and return attribution. Second, an investable commodity futures index can be used to implement an active tactical bet by the investment manager that the underlying commodities will generate superior expected or average returns. Finally, an investable commodity futures index can be used in a passive strategy as a strategic long-term exposure, often for the purpose of reducing risk through portfolio diversification.

10.7.2 Commodity Futures Indices

The construction or selection of a long-only commodity index involves numerous decisions, including:

1. The roll strategy (when is a position liquidated relative to its settlement date and what time-to-settlement is selected for the new exposure)
2. Which commodities are represented
3. How the commodities are weighted

There are literally hundreds of regularly published commodity indices in the world. The following three sections discuss three index approaches that are widely used in academia and industry: production-weighted indices, market-liquidity-weighted indices, and tier-weighted indices.

10.7.3 Production-Weighted Long-Only Commodity Indexes

A **production-weighted index** weights each underlying commodity exposure using estimates of the quantity of each commodity produced. A production-weighted index is designed to reflect the relative importance of each of the constituent commodities to the world economy in terms of production levels. The **Standard & Poor's GSCI** is a very popular production-weighted long-only index of physical commodity futures. The S&P GSCI (formerly the Goldman Sachs Commodity Index) is composed of the first nearby futures contract in each commodity. Perhaps the most distinctive feature of the S&P GSCI is that a futures contract trades on the index itself (on the Chicago Mercantile Exchange [CME]). In other words, investors can purchase a futures contract tied to the spot value of the S&P GSCI. The weights in the S&P GSCI are based on five years of data and are heavily dominated by energy commodities (at times well over 70%) due to their dominant role in global production. The S&P GSCI is constructed with 24 physical commodities across five main groups of real assets: energy, precious metals, industrial metals, livestock, and agriculture.

10.7.4 Market-Liquidity-Weighted Long-Only Commodity Indexes

Another approach to commodity weighting in a commodity index is based on market liquidity as a measure of global economic significance. As an example, the **Bloomberg Commodity Index** (BCOM), formerly the Dow Jones-UBS Commodity Index (and before that the Dow Jones-AIG Commodity Index), is a market-liquidity-weighted long-only index composed of futures contracts on 23 physical commodities in six sectors: energy, grains, precious metals, industrial metals, livestock, and softs. These commodities are diversified and include petroleum products, natural gas, precious metals, industrial metals, grains, livestock, soybean oil, coffee, cotton, and sugar. The weights of each commodity in the index rely primarily on liquidity data, such as *trading activity*. This index considers the relative amount of trading activity associated with a particular commodity to determine its weight in the index.

The Bloomberg Commodity Index bands the weights within upper (15%) and lower (2%) limits to smooth the relative roles played by each commodity in the return of the index. While the bands appear arbitrary, they serve the role of preventing the index from being dominated by any one sector (e.g., energy), as no commodity sector can comprise more than 33% of the index weight.

10.7.5 Tier-Weighted Long-Only Commodity Indices

Another approach to commodity index weighting is a tier-based approach. A tier-based commodity-weighting approach groups commodities of similar characteristics into tiers and then assigns weights to each tier. For example, the **Thomson Reuters/CoreCommodity CRB Index** is the oldest major commodity index and is currently made up of 19 commodities traded on various exchanges. Originally the CRB Index (Commodity Research Bureau Index), the Thomson Reuters CoreCommodity CRB Index uses four tiers or groups to weight the commodities. The system is designed to reflect the importance of each commodity to global economic development. For example, Tier I currently has 33% of the index weight and includes only petroleum products. The second tier represents agricultural commodities and is weighted 42%. Tiers III and IV represent precious metals and base/industrial metals with weights of 20% and 5%, respectively. Weights are described as being determined to make the index a representative indicator of global commodity markets.

10.8 COMMODITY RISK ATTRIBUTES

Many non-commodity-based investment strategies are exposed to large and often simultaneous event risk, such as losses from international tensions or financial turmoil (e.g., the global financial crisis of 2007–2008). Simply put, when a major global or economic crisis arises, long positions in most risky assets decline in value.

10.8.1 Four Favorable Characteristics of Commodities with Respect to Event Risks

There are four characteristics of commodity investments that suggest that many major events actually enhance returns to investors with long positions in commodities.

First, most major global events cause increases in commodity prices due to anticipated decreases in commodity supplies or increases in demand. Events that may lead to unexpectedly reduced supply of one or more commodities include disrupted trade and disrupted production. Events such as trade wars, military wars, major weather events, and political instability can inhibit production and/or trade and drive up commodity prices. Trade disputes, wars, and political unrest tend to drive energy prices higher. Droughts, floods, and crop freezes tend to reduce the supply of agricultural products. Major labor unrest or global political instability can drive up the prices of and demand for both precious and industrial metals.

Second, commodity price increases due to events tend to be larger and more sudden than the price decreases resulting from events that lower commodity prices. These shocks to the commodity markets should provide long positions in commodities with positively skewed returns.

Third, many commodity shocks are likely to be uncorrelated with each other. For example, OPEC agreements to cut oil production should be uncorrelated with droughts in the agricultural regions around the world or with labor strikes affecting mining. The implication is that the commodity price changes due to major events should be relatively uncorrelated with each other and therefore somewhat diversifiable.

Fourth, shocks to the commodities markets are generally uncorrelated with shocks to the financial markets—or perhaps even negatively correlated. The reason is that most sudden large events have negative short-term implications to global production and trade. These shocks tend to reduce the supply of commodities, causing commodity prices to rise while simultaneously depressing equities and corporate bonds. For example, a shock such as a trade dispute or weather event may cause a sudden decrease in the supply of raw materials, which should have a positive impact on commodity prices but a negative impact on financial asset prices through its anticipated reduction in corporate profits.

10.8.2 Commodities as a Defensive Investment

Fluctuations in aggregate global wealth are an unfortunate consequence of economic activity. When major declines in aggregate wealth occur (i.e., when major economic recessions or depressions occur), most major classes of investments tend to decline in response. A number of studies have examined the correlation of global equity markets during periods of market stress or decline. The conclusion is that equity markets around the world tend to be more highly correlated during periods of economic stress than during normal times. This means that in very bad times, when the benefits of diversification are most needed, equity markets throughout the world tend to decline at the same time, and global equity diversification fails to protect the investor. The major reason that traditional assets often do not provide downside risk protection is that almost all traditional assets react in similar fashion to major macroeconomic events. For example, a spike in oil prices is felt across almost all traditional asset classes.

Most traditional investments do not offer both protection from global turmoil and attractive returns. This is a major reason that investors are drawn to alternative investing. The greatest concern for most investors is downside risk. The ability to protect the value of an investment portfolio in hostile or turbulent markets is the key to the value of any macroeconomic diversification. Commodities may be especially useful at reducing downside risk.

10.8.3 Commodity Prices and Institutional Investing Demand

One potential risk to long-only commodity investing is the impact of changes in institutional demand for long-only commodity positions. Historically, there was slow acceptance of commodity futures as a long-only investment by institutions such that institutional investment capital committed to commodity futures was considerably smaller than that invested with hedge funds. In the years prior to the global financial crisis of 2007–2008, large institutional investors sought greater diversification in their investment portfolios and established major long positions in commodities. This massive increase in the popularity of long-only commodity investing has been cited as a cause of large increases in the prices of commodities. Commodity prices collapsed during the financial crisis along with economic activity and prices in financial markets. While some attributed declining commodity prices to decisions by institutional investors to reduce long-only commodity exposures, there is evidence that there are many other factors at play. Notably, the prices of commodities without futures contracts or institutional investment also saw prices drop sharply during the global financial crisis (GFC).

Black (2009)[1] seeks to downplay the role that institutional investors have played in commodity price volatility. Although it is plausible that their trading activity can influence commodity prices, other factors are likely more influential, especially in the energy markets, which are the largest sector in most commodity indices. Supply and demand for energy commodities, especially from biofuels, has a strong effect on prices. As many commodities worldwide are priced in U.S. dollars, a strong U.S. dollar likely contributes to weakness in commodity prices. Analysts also need to follow demand for commodities from China and other emerging markets, which can consume the majority of the world's commodity supplies despite having less than 20% of the value of global equity markets.

Irwin and Sanders (2010)[2] suggest that commodity index investing, with some caveats, may have decreased price volatility during the GFC. To the extent that commodity index investing provides more capital for taking the other side of hedging by commodity inventory holders, this means that more inventories can be held than otherwise would be the case. More inventories can help to reduce the chance of price spikes, which reduces price volatility.

Simply put: Short-term to medium-term long-only commodity returns may have volatility emanating from many sources, including commodity supply and demand, interest rates, inflation, trading activity, and currency markets.

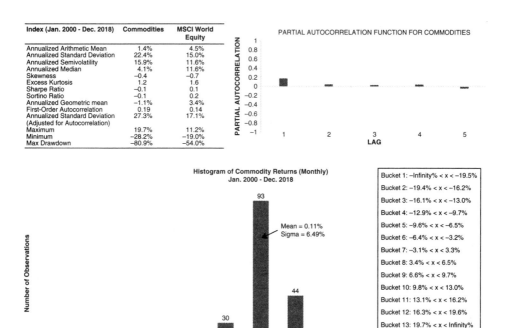

Index (Jan. 2000 - Dec. 2018)	Commodities	MSCI World Equity
Annualized Arithmetic Mean	1.4%	4.5%
Annualized Standard Deviation	22.4%	15.0%
Annualized Semivolatility	15.9%	11.6%
Annualized Median	4.1%	11.6%
Skewness	−0.4	−0.7
Excess Kurtosis	1.2	1.6
Sharpe Ratio	−0.1	0.1
Sortino Ratio	−0.1	0.2
Annualized Geometric mean	−1.1%	3.4%
First-Order Autocorrelation	0.19	0.14
Annualized Standard Deviation (Adjusted for Autocorrelation)	27.3%	17.1%
Maximum	19.7%	11.2%
Minimum	−28.2%	−19.0%
Max Drawdown	−80.9%	−54.0%

PARTIAL AUTOCORRELATION FUNCTION FOR COMMODITIES

Histogram of Commodity Returns (Monthly)
Jan. 2000 - Dec. 2018

Mean = 0.11%
Sigma = 6.49%

Bucket 1: −Infinity% < x < −19.5%
Bucket 2: −19.4% < x < −16.2%
Bucket 3: −16.1% < x < −13.0%
Bucket 4: −12.9% < x < −9.7%
Bucket 5: −9.6% < x < −6.5%
Bucket 6: −6.4% < x < −3.2%
Bucket 7: −3.1% < x < 3.3%
Bucket 8: 3.4% < x < 6.5%
Bucket 9: 6.6% < x < 9.7%
Bucket 10: 9.8% < x < 13.0%
Bucket 11: 13.1% < x < 16.2%
Bucket 12: 16.3% < x < 19.6%
Bucket 13: 19.7% < x < Infinity%

EXHIBIT 10.5 Statistical Summary of Returns

10.9 OBSERVATIONS BASED ON HISTORICAL RETURNS

Commodity returns are monthly returns observed from January of 2000 to December of 2018, for a total of 228 observations. Exhibit 10.5 provides univariate return statistics in the top panel, partial autocorrelations of commodities in the middle panel, and a histogram of returns in the bottom panel.

Key observations on commodity returns that are consistent with economic reasoning are an essential component of knowledge and include the following:

1. Commodity returns had historic volatility moderately exceeding that of global equities.
2. Commodity returns generated a negative Sharpe ratio.
3. Commodity returns had moderate positive first-order autocorrelation.
4. Commodity returns had a maximum calendar month loss of almost 30% (1.5 times that of global equities).
5. Commodities experienced a massive maximum drawdown (i.e., about –80%).

REVIEW QUESTIONS

1. Explain the implications of Hotelling's Theory on long-term commodity prices.
2. What are the three costs of carry that determine the price of a forward contract on a physical asset?
3. What is the name of the condition in which the expected spot price of a commodity in one year exceeds the one-year forward price of the commodity?
4. What is the primary reason that causes a commodity futures market to be in contango or backwardation?
5. What is the name of the following quantity: the spot price of a commodity minus a forward price on the commodity?
6. What is the primary reason that the forward price of an asset could be substantially smaller than the price generated by the cost-of-carry model?
7. In the context of analyzing the returns of futures contracts, what is excess return?
8. What is the definition of roll return that is earned through holding futures contracts?
9. List three important propositions regarding the accrual of roll return through holding futures contracts through time.
10. List four reasons why commodities should help diversify a portfolio of traditional assets.

NOTES

1. K. Black, "The Role of Institutional Investors in Rising Commodity Prices," *Journal of Investing* 18, no. 3 (2009): 21–26.
2. S. H. Irwin and D. R. Sanders "The Impact of Index and Swap Funds on Commodity Futures Markets: Preliminary Results," *OECD Food, Agriculture and Fisheries Working Papers*, No. 27 (2010), OECD Publishing. doi:10.1787/5kmd40wl1t5f-en.

CHAPTER 11

Other Real Assets

This chapter focuses on other real assets, including commodity producers, publicly traded partnerships of natural resources, infrastructure, and intellectual property.

11.1 COMMODITY PRODUCERS

Chapter 9 discussed natural resources as real assets that have experienced little or no alteration by humans. Investments in natural resources attract investor interest based on their perceived ability to serve as diversifiers against general economic fluctuations and the risk of unexpected inflation. However, direct and liquid institutional investment opportunities in natural resources are somewhat limited by the large extent to which global natural resources are owned by the public. Investments in firms with operations involved in *developing* natural resources are much more accessible. This section discusses investment opportunities of firms that transform natural resources into commodities and other goods and services available for consumption.

Each investment opportunity related to a natural resource may be viewed as lying on a spectrum, ranging from the purest plays on the value of a natural resource to those that are driven more by their operational focus than by the value of the natural resource related to their operations. For example, the rights to the mineral reserves of land containing copper ore are highly driven by the price of copper. The market price of an operating firm that mines and smelts the copper ore is presumably driven by a mixture of the effects of copper prices and other factors. Finally, ownership of the firms that provide products and services to the copper mine operators represents another potential avenue of diversifying into exposures to natural resources.

11.1.1 Natural Resource Prices as a Driver of Operating Firm Performance

A key issue is the extent to which investments in firms that process natural resources provide reasonably similar risk and return characteristics to direct investments in the underlying natural resources. For example, are the returns of firms that explore, mine, or refine gold driven by the prices of refined gold?

In many industries, there would seem to be unclear links between the performance of an operating company and the price of the good that underlies the company's production. Thus, the price changes of the equities of manufacturers, technology firms, communications firms, and health-care firms tend to be only moderately correlated with the price changes of their products. For example, when airline ticket prices soar due to rising fuel costs, the stocks of airlines usually decline. In this example, the higher prices for tickets are driven by higher costs to the airline companies, not higher profits. In other cases, operating firms may hedge the exposure of their revenues to commodities, such as in the case of large oil companies that use derivatives to hedge their revenue from oil sales to smooth their profits.

In theory, the correlations between the returns of firms and price changes for their associated goods are driven by three primary factors: the price elasticity of the demand for the good, the price elasticity of the supply of the good, and the extent to which an operating firm is exposed to or has hedged changes in its profits.

There are sound economic reasons to believe that the market prices of firms that provide goods and services related to the extraction and processing of natural resources should be substantially correlated with the prices of the natural resources themselves or the commodities that emanate from the processing. The reasoning is that a dramatic rise in the price of a commodity, such as a metal or an agricultural product, indicates that demand vastly exceeded supply at the previous price. The relatively high demand for a commodity should generally coincide with increased demand for the services of firms that process those commodities. Thus, for example, when a commodity price such as oil soars, the firms that explore for oil, drill for oil, extract oil, and transport oil should generally expect that their services will have much higher demand than during a period following a large decrease in price. Accordingly, absent hedging strategies, large price increases in a commodity should tend to drive anticipation of higher profits in the firms that provide goods and services in the production of that commodity. For example, soaring oil prices have clearly been a boon to the oil and gas development industry.

11.1.2 Evidence on Commodity Prices and the Equity Prices of Operating Firms

Empirical evidence can also provide insight into the relationship between commodity prices and the equity prices of operating firms. Let's examine an extreme 10-year price move in a major commodity. The price of gold in U.S. dollars soared roughly sixfold, from about $300 per ounce in 2002 to a peak of $1,800 per ounce in 2012. Did investors in the shares of gold mining firms realize similar profits? No. Roughly, the price of gold mining shares (as represented by the Dow Jones U.S. Gold Mining Index) experienced only a threefold increase. It would appear likely that much of the gain from rising gold prices went to the owners of gold bullion and gold reserves rather than to the firms that explore, develop, extract, and process the resource. But gold mining stocks outperformed the overall market, which rose about 50% from 2002 to 2012.

Now let's turn to a shorter-term example of gold price changes. In the turbulent economic times of the global financial crisis (October 2008), overall equity prices varied widely. The price of gold in U.S. dollars fluctuated roughly between $700 and $900 per ounce from early September 2008 to the end of November 2008. At the end of October, gold was down only about 10% from its value in early September. Over the entire three-month period, the price of gold was slightly up. Gold therefore provided protection to investors from the panic that devastated equity markets.

On the other hand, U.S. gold mining firms did not fare so well over the same period. The average price of these firms was quite volatile and generally moved downward. As represented by the VanEck Vectors Gold Miners ETF (which tracks the NYSE Arca Gold Miners Index), shares of gold mining firms dropped on average by almost half from early September to their low in October and recovered only partially by the end of November to a net decline of about one-third. Thus, in the short run, it appeared that the publicly traded firms related to gold production were driven more by the volatility of the equity markets than by the volatility of gold prices.

Gold provides evidence that firms related to a commodity have short- and long-term performance that differs substantially from the price performance of the related commodity. The empirical evidence cited in this section substantiates the intuition that the share prices of firms related to a commodity depend only partially on the value of the commodity. If the firms are publicly traded, their performance tends to be substantially correlated with the overall performance of public equity markets.

11.1.3 Commodity Prices and Operating-Firm Equity Return Correlations

Let's turn to another commodity for a more formal analysis of correlations based on returns. From an economic perspective, energy is the largest sector of natural resources, and oil is the largest underlying resource within the energy sector. Oil prices vary between quality and location. Based on the private ownership of natural resources in the United States and data availability, we examined data on U.S. oil and equity prices. This analysis uses monthly calendar returns related to U.S. oil and ETF prices from August 2006 through December 2018.

Exhibit 11.1 lists the correlation coefficients between the returns of four investments: (1) the price of West Texas Intermediate light, sweet crude oil, as represented by United States Oil ETF (ticker USO); (2) the value of the SPDR S&P Oil & Gas Equipment & Services ETF (ticker XES); (3) the value of the SPDR S&P Oil & Gas Exploration & Production ETF (ticker XOP); and (4) the value of the SPDR S&P 500 (ticker SPY).

Are the returns of oil-industry-related equities related more to oil prices or to stock prices? In Exhibit 11.1, the first column depicts correlations of two oil industry ETFs (XES and XOP) with oil prices (USO). The second column depicts correlations of the same ETFs with general U.S. equity prices (SPY, which proxies the S&P 500).

The results indicate relatively high and positive return correlations that are rather uniform. The ETFs of firms related to oil production (XES and XOP) had reasonably high correlations with oil prices but also had reasonably high correlations with U.S. equity prices. XES focuses on publicly traded oil equipment and services firms, such as Schlumberger and Halliburton. XOP focuses on publicly traded oil exploration and production firms, such as Goodrich Petroleum Corporation.

The correlation between the monthly returns of USO and SPY over the same period was 0.45 (not shown). Thus, the relatively high return correlations between

EXHIBIT 11.1 Return Correlations of Oil Operating Firms to Oil (USO) and Equities (SPY)

	USO	SPY
XES	0.71	0.65
XOP	0.69	0.62

the ETFs of the oil firms and the U.S. equity market indicate that much of the return variation in oil-related industries is driven by overall equity valuations and general economic conditions rather than as a pure play on the price of oil.

The empirical analysis summarized in Exhibit 11.1 reinforces the intuition that investments in firms are not pure plays on the returns of the real assets related to the firm's industry. Rather than the returns of these firms being driven entirely by the contemporaneous prices of related commodities, they are presumably also driven by the market's anticipation of dynamic supply and demand factors more related to the long-term profitability of the goods and services directly offered by those firms, which in turn tend to be correlated with overall equity markets. To the extent that the returns of firms within the ETFs in Exhibit 11.1 are driven substantially by operational issues, the investments will serve more as traditional equity investments rather than as diversifiers or any other type of alternative investment vehicle.

11.2 LIQUID ALTERNATIVE REAL ASSETS

One of the largest and most rapidly growing alternative investment areas in the United States has been the use of master limited partnerships (MLPs) to provide liquid investment access to operationally intensive real assets.

11.2.1 Structure of MLPs and the MLP Sector

MLPs are simply limited partnerships in which the limited partnership ownership units are listed (publicly traded). Limited partners of MLPs are unit holders. MLPs receive tax treatment predicated on adhering to regulations, including that at least 90% of the entities' revenues come from specified businesses, such as energy.

Although MLPs have existed in the United States since 1981, they have thrived more recently. There are now more than 100 MLPs in the United States with an aggregate market value of over roughly $500 billion.

MLPs are typically traded on major exchanges, such as the NYSE, in the same manner as are corporate operating firms. MLPs are not shares in the equity of taxable corporations; they are limited partnership units representing direct ownership of a firm. Many publicly traded securities are described as investments in natural resources, but a closer look indicates that the investment is subjected to substantial development, extraction, and processing operational risks.

Most MLPs are involved in the energy sector, although some MLPs invest in real estate, timber, or other assets as permitted by regulations. The oil and gas sector is divided into upstream, midstream, and downstream operations. **Upstream operations** focus on exploration and production; midstream operations focus on storing and transporting the oil and gas; and **downstream operations** focus on refining, distributing, and marketing the oil and gas. **Midstream operations** and midstream MLPs—the largest of the three segments—process, store, and transport energy and tend to have little or no commodity price risk. For example, a gas pipeline is paid a transportation fee for the quantity of oil or gas transported without regard for the value of the product being transported. Similar to infrastructure investments, midstream MLPs have been called a toll road for energy.

EXHIBIT 11.2 Summary of Three Forms of Ownership

	Subject to U.S. Corporate Income Tax?	Distributions Subject to U.S. Individual Income Tax?
C corporation	Yes	Yes
Investment company	No[*]	Yes
Limited partnership	No[†]	No[‡]

[*]Investment companies distributing almost all income to shareholders are not taxed at the corporate level. Examples include mutual funds.

[†]The revenues and expenses of limited partnerships pass through the partnership directly into the tax forms of the partners.

[‡]Investors in limited partnerships are subject to taxes on net income, whether or not that income was distributed.

11.2.2 Tax Characteristics of MLPs

MLPs have an ownership structure distinct from most traditional investments. Exhibit 11.2 highlights three major types of major U.S. business entities: taxable corporations (C corporations), tax-exempt corporations (investment companies), and limited partnerships.

Exhibit 11.2 highlights the critical issue of how income is taxed. Investors in the equity of traditional operating corporations in the United States experience double taxation. **Double taxation** is the application of income taxes twice: taxation of profits at the corporate income tax level and taxation of distributions at the individual income tax level. Most investment companies in the United States, including mutual funds and REITs, can avoid paying corporate income taxes if they distribute almost all of their profits to the corporation's shareholders—a practice generally followed. The distributions are taxed at the individual income tax level.

Limited partnerships in general and MLPs in particular are not directly subject to income taxes at the partnership level. The revenues, expenses, and profits of the partnerships flow directly through the partnerships and into the tax forms of the partners. The limited partners are subject to tax on profits that flow from the partnership, whether or not the profits are distributed to them. Thus, Exhibit 11.2 indicates that partnership *distributions*, per se, are not taxed at the individual level.

Energy development enterprises in the United States tend to have opportunities to enjoy substantial tax benefits, including credits and accelerated expensing. MLP structures allow tax benefits to pass through the firm level directly to the tax forms of the limited partners. These benefits manifest themselves in the ability of limited investors to enjoy large tax-free distributions, because it is income that is taxed, not distributions. Many of the large distributions from MLPs are sheltered in the short run as *return of capital* due to generous rules regarding the expensing of costs. Return of capital distributions are tax-free when received. Distributions that represent return of capital serve to lower the tax basis of the MLP investment to the investor. Upon the sale of the MLP, the lowered tax basis tends to cause more of the sales proceeds to be taxable. The recaptured gains attributable to the distributions tend to be taxed at full rates rather than preferred capital gain rates. Thus, the tax-free distributions of MLPs are likely to serve as tax deferrals.

The potential tax benefits of MLPs to U.S. investors need to be weighed against three potential drawbacks. First, MLPs report income on K-1 forms rather than 1099s, which may add substantial complexities and delays to federal tax filing. Second, MLP income is usually subject to income taxation in the states in which the MLPs operate, which means that limited partners with moderate to large holdings may be required to file numerous state income tax returns. Finally, MLPs can cause **unrelated business income tax (UBIT)** liability for some pension plans and not-for-profit corporations in the United States, as the income generated through businesses unrelated to the tax-exempt purpose of the organization can be taxable. That is, although the income generated from educational activities is tax-exempt for a university, some investment activities may be taxable if determined to be outside of the charitable scope of the organization.

11.2.3 MLP Valuations and Distribution Rates

There has been controversy regarding the prospective risks and returns of the MLP sector in general and MLPs with high distribution rates in particular. As noted earlier, MLP investors are taxed on income, not distributions, from MLPs. The MLP structures themselves are not required to pay income taxes. Whereas mutual funds and REITs generally set distributions to be approximately equal to their income, MLPs are free to make distributions as high as their cash flows allow. As previously noted, these distributions are tax-free and are attractive to investors focused on cash income.

Some MLPs are alleged to make distributions at rates that are not sustainable based on the MLP's current and prospective income. It is further alleged that the market prices of these MLPs are inflated by high demand from brokers and investors who are drawn to the high tax-free distributions and who overestimate the sustainability of the distribution rates.

Proponents of the high valuations of MLPs with high distribution rates argue that the high rates are reasonable and sustainable due to the highly profitable transactions and operations underlying the MLPs. New acquisitions are often financed by issuing new partnership units at high market valuations, which enables attractive future cash flow projections. Exceptional prospects for success can be captured as the present value of exceptional growth opportunities.

Analysts who say that MLPs are overpriced often argue that the high cash flows are being driven by proceeds from the secondary offerings of the MLP units and that eventually the distributions will have to be cut when new financings and acquisitions end. Can the proceeds from secondary offerings buy and develop new capacity that will lead to growing cash flows that can support higher levels of cash distributions? While required by law to be factually correct, prospectuses often indicate intricate and complicated arrangements between affiliated entities that make analysis exceedingly complex relative to many traditional investments.

Perhaps one thing is certain: MLP investing, like many other forms of alternative investing, is skill based. Even a broad indexation strategy in which an MLP ETF, an MLP exchange-traded note, or a representative basket of individual MLPs is purchased requires the skillful evaluation of whether the entire MLP sector is fairly valued.

11.3 INFRASTRUCTURE

In finance, infrastructure refers to the underlying and fundamental assets and systems that facilitate functions that are necessary to the well-being of an economy. Not all infrastructure assets are conducive to being privately financed. Infrastructure assets are a means for ensuring the delivery of goods and services that promote prosperity and growth and contribute to quality of life, including the social well-being, health, and safety of citizens and the quality of their environments. For example, it may be argued that agricultural ventures are part of infrastructure in view of their being essential to the economy and population of a country. However, in most economies, agricultural assets are privately financed.

11.3.1 Seven Elements That Help Identify Investable Infrastructure

Defining investable infrastructure is challenging. Some market participants define investable infrastructure based on having risks and returns that are distinct from those of traditional investments and that require specialized tools of analysis. Other market participants focus on the extent to which the investments are financial claims on infrastructure assets. For our purposes, **investable infrastructure** is typically differentiated from other assets with seven primary characteristics: (1) public use, (2) monopolistic power, (3) government related, (4) essential, (5) cash generating, (6) conducive to privatization of control, and (7) capital intensive with long-term horizons.

1. Public use refers to the idea that the associated economic activity is accessed by a large segment of the population or is viewed as serving the general welfare of a society.
2. Monopolistic power refers to the extent to which services are offered by a single provider or are offered such that the provider can set prices relatively free from competition.
3. Government related refers to the extent to which the underlying assets are typically created by, owned by, managed by, or heavily regulated by government.
4. Infrastructure assets tend to provide essential goods or services, such as electricity distribution. Hence, the demand for the goods or services is usually price inelastic, and cash inflows tend to be stable and inflation-protected.
5. Investable infrastructure tends to be focused on assets that directly generate cash, such as toll roads, rather than similar assets that are supported by general tax revenues, such as highways other than toll roads.
6. Investable infrastructure may possess attributes that make the underlying assets and systems relatively conducive to privatization of managerial control.
7. Investable infrastructure is usually capital intensive, with underlying assets that are long-term in nature.

To the extent that these elements are satisfied, an asset is more likely to be considered an investable infrastructure asset. However, no single element is necessary or sufficient. For example, a municipal bond backed by revenues from a toll road would generally not be considered investable infrastructure even though it may satisfy almost all of the aspects found in investable infrastructure discussed here. In

EXHIBIT 11.3   Infrastructure Investment Universe

Economic Infrastructure	Social Infrastructure
Transport	Education facilities
Toll roads, bridges, tunnels	Schools
Airports	Universities
Seaports	Health-care facilities
Rail networks	Hospitals
Utilities	Aged care
Distribution of gas, electricity, and other energy sources	Child care
Treatment and distribution of water	Correctional facilities
Renewable energy	Courts
Communications infrastructure	Jails, prisons
Specialty sectors	
Car parks	
Storage facilities	
Forests	

Source: Asieh Mansour and Hope Nadji, "Opportunities in Private Infrastructure Investments in the U.S.," RREEF Research, September 2006.

the case of a municipal bond, there is no privatization of the toll road or change in managerial control if the toll road remains under the full authority of a governmental organization. The equity of a firm that manufactures a common and essential vaccine may satisfy all of the listed aspects of investable infrastructure except that such equity is not traditionally governmentally owned. Fortunately, the major types of investable infrastructure are reasonably well defined, as shown in Exhibit 11.3.

Investable infrastructure can originate as a new, yet-to-be-constructed project, referred to as a **greenfield project**, that was designed to be investable. Investable infrastructure can also be an existing project, or **brownfield project**, that has a history of operations and may have converted from a government asset into something privately investable. New projects may be funded by private capital rather than through government control and financing in order to promote efficiency and enable construction without straining government resources. Existing projects are converted to investable infrastructure primarily to raise capital for government and to earn cash flow for private investors.

The **critical property of infrastructure** (i.e., the most important distinction between investable infrastructure and traditional investments) is in the nature of the revenues, with investable infrastructure generating a cash flow stream in a monopolistic environment rather than in a competitive environment. An investment in infrastructure generally relies on the purchase or long-term lease of a facility that generates stable cash flows, ideally growing with the rate of inflation.

11.3.2 Economic versus Social Infrastructure

As shown in Exhibit 11.3, infrastructure investments can be divided into the two broad categories of economic and social infrastructure. **Economic infrastructure** assets are assets with economic value that is driven by the revenue they generate, typically with end users paying for the services provided by these assets. Examples of these are toll roads and bridges, railways, airports, and maritime terminals. **Social infrastructure** assets are assets that have end users who are unable to pay for the services or that are used in such a way that it is difficult to determine how many services were used by each person; examples include schools, public roads, prisons, administrative offices, and other government buildings.

Notice how these infrastructure categories fit the previous discussion, as transportation or utility assets often have the characteristics of a natural or regulated monopoly, in which users have a low price elasticity of demand. When necessary services are provided, users do not typically reduce their usage substantially as a result of price increases; this means that the service providers have pricing power, which allows price increases to result in revenue increases.

Infrastructure assets can be categorized according to who the payer is, with a distinction that is similar to the difference between economic and social infrastructure. Often the end user pays to use the assets. Examples of these are toll roads, utilities, and communications networks. Government and taxpayers pay for the use of assets. In this case, the asset is mostly or partially free for the end users. Examples of these are many schools and some hospitals, administrative buildings, and parks.

11.3.3 Public-Private Partnerships in Infrastructure Investing

Governments have long recognized that investments in infrastructure produce positive externalities, contribute to economic growth, expand market access, and reduce inefficiencies. From a public policy perspective, improvements in regulation, governance, transparency, ethics, property rights, and external checks are necessary and go a long way in encouraging private-sector participation in infrastructure projects. Given the extremely high up-front capital costs in establishing projects, infrastructure assets exhibit natural monopoly characteristics; often a single firm can produce essential social service outputs at greater efficiencies and at lower social costs than can multiple competitive firms. Recognizing this, governments restrict competition and create statutory monopolies.

Many existing infrastructure assets were built with public funds and then sold into the private sector. When a governmental entity sells a public asset to a private operator, this is termed **privatization**. While some argue that the private sector operates assets more efficiently, others argue that privatization is unfair to public-sector workers or otherwise contrary to the public interest. Although many privatizations take the form of the outright sale of an asset, in other cases, the governmental entity retains a stake in the asset. A **public-private partnership** (PPP) is a collaboration between public bodies, governments, and the private sector that occurs when a private-sector party is retained to design, build, operate, or maintain a public building (e.g., a hospital), for a lease payment with a finite time. Popular are leases or concessions wherein the government leases an asset to a private operator for 20 to 99 years, with the full equity interest in the facility reverting to public ownership at the end of the concession term. The partnerships extend across a variety of sectors, which can include transportation, water supply, and waste management, as well as the building and managing of hospitals, schools, public housing, and prisons. PPPs can take a wide variety of forms, with varying involvement of the private sector and varying degrees of risk transfer from government to the private sector.

PPPs and regulated assets (as in economic regulation, with the regulator setting prices) are normally mutually exclusive. A PPP is a finite concession with a price mechanism agreed to contractually up front. Privatized assets are owned by the private sector under a license, and prices are periodically set (or at least reviewed) by a regulator to ensure that they are appropriate and fair to the owner and to customers.

In order to enter into a greenfield PPP contract to design, build, operate, and own an infrastructure asset under a long-term government concession, private-sector investors form a special purpose vehicle (SPV) to act as concessionaire. Based on the concession contract and projected revenues from usage fees, the SPV receives equity capital from investors and enters into a contract with a design and construction company to build the asset. It may also enter into a separate contract with an operating company for the operation and maintenance of the infrastructure asset. The SPV also raises debt that can range from 60% to 90% of total project costs. Upon completion and commissioning of the infrastructure asset, the revenue generated through usage fees after payment of the concessionaire at the agreed-upon tariff rate is used to partly pay down debt, with the surplus passed on to equity contributors.

PPPs have faced opposition from advocacy groups and, sometimes, from the public. Criticism often takes the form of allegations of reduced accountability and the profit motive of the private sector, which may be at odds with the public interest. This criticism tends to be more intense in projects in which fees charged to the public are highly visible, such as in the case of toll roads. There have also been instances (although rare) of privatization reversals in response to allegations of underinvestment and poor asset upkeep. Many issues are driven by public perception. For example, municipalities may be reticent to declare future toll increases and may have minimal incentives to publish aggressive projections, for these can be politically unpalatable. Private concessionaires, in contrast, are less reluctant to establish explicit future increases.

Ideally, regulatory public policy with respect to PPPs would be consistent with technological innovation, capital needs, market developments, public opinion, and changing needs to create a balance between the multiple and often opposing constituencies. Issues that inevitably feature in policy discussions relate to economic transfers and distributional effects: for example, who benefits and at what cost to others, rents, accountability, regional development, jobs, prices, and tariffs. To preclude excess rent-seeking monopolistic behavior, infrastructure services may be procured under PPP with an agreed-upon pricing mechanism or may be heavily regulated. In some cases, regulation has not kept pace with the swift pace of innovation in this arena.

The degree of private investment within infrastructure depends on the commercial viability of the sector or subsector, as well as the governmental policy within a given country. Private-sector participation in economic infrastructure relies on a government that is content with essential assets being operated by the private sector, which charges citizens for its services (often within a regulated pricing structure). It also relies on customers' propensity to pay. For example, toll roads have been historically unpopular with many electorates; consequently, new roads are often procured as "shadow toll" PPPs, meaning that motorists do not pay the tolls. In developing countries, users may be unable to pay, resulting in the need for government support. Private investment in social infrastructure depends both on the government's ability to pay the private sector for the service and on the government's political support for the PPP.

11.3.4 Risks and Government Regulation of Infrastructure Investing

Investors in infrastructure need to be keenly aware of governmental issues related to their investments, which can be either positive or negative. The scope and quality of a nation's infrastructure can influence its economic growth, with weaker infrastructure often blamed for reducing the economic growth potential of a nation. One positive aspect of governmental issues on the infrastructure sector is the vast need for new or improved infrastructure assets combined with the constrained fiscal budgets of governments. In developed economies, infrastructure is aging and needs to be repaired, replaced, or improved. In developing economies, especially those with rapid population and income growth, there is a substantial demand for the creation of new infrastructure. In most countries, the scale of infrastructure needs far outstrips the ability of the government to fund the investment. Governments can use the proceeds from infrastructure leases or sales to fund other infrastructure projects or divert them to other fiscal needs. However, some governmental entities use those proceeds for spending or debt reduction, neither of which directly and immediately enhances the quality or availability of the infrastructure in an economy.

The revenues of infrastructure are closely linked to the prices of the services provided—which in turn is driven by the degree of pricing regulation. **Regulated pricing** occurs in most countries and the pricing for goods and services deemed essential is largely determined by price changes that must be approved by public entities and are most common in the energy sector. There is a growing trend toward unregulated pricing of certain infrastructure investments in mature countries.

There can be regulatory risk in a transaction. **Regulatory risk** is the economic dispersion to an investor from uncertainty regarding governmental regulatory actions and includes uncertain regulation regarding the initiation of a project or its operation. In some circumstances, a sale to investors may need to be approved by voters or a governing body, and therefore the consummation of a purchase is uncertain until all approvals have been obtained. Even after the completion of a purchase, investors in many infrastructure assets continue to find operations being regulated. Governmental entities, especially in the transport or utility sectors, are often involved in monitoring service quality and regulating prices or profit margins. Although regulating prices or margins may reduce profit potential, the right to run a monopoly business often leads to relatively stable cash flows. When assets are leased, the governmental entity may retain the right to revoke the lease if the service and maintenance of the assets do not meet the stated standards.

One example of regulatory risk can be seen in the case of Gassco, a joint venture between the Norwegian government and a number of large institutional investors that operated pipelines that delivered Norwegian natural gas to continental Europe. After 10 years of stable tariffs that allowed investors the ability to earn predictable returns, litigation was filed after the government proposed a sharp decline in the pipeline tariff that made gas more affordable for customers, but substantially reduced the return to the investors in the pipeline project. Similarly, a number of foreign investors sued the government of Spain in 2013, charging that regulatory changes regarding renewable energy projects violated the Energy Charter treaty. After foreign investors allocated more than EUR 13 billion to investments in renewable energy projects in Spain, Spain reduced the subsidies to these projects and added a tax on power generation. Both regulatory changes reduced the return previously anticipated by the investors.

Political infrastructure risk includes regulatory risk and nonregulatory risks, such as the risk of expropriation. In developing countries, political infrastructure risk is a key consideration given the essential nature of the assets to the local economy, the long life of the assets, and the fact that they cannot be moved, making them vulnerable to expropriation. To mitigate this risk, many investors target only developed countries or developing countries with robust legal frameworks.

Some projects also carry the risk that revenues will be insufficient to cover the interest expense on the debt issued to buy or rebuild the asset. In September 2014, the concession running the Indiana Toll Road was forced to sell the asset as a result of the bankruptcy process after increasing interest rates and traffic counts that were lower than anticipated. Managers were cautioned regarding financial projections, as the high price of this project required significant debt financing. If the price of the concession had been significantly lower, and based on more reasonable projections, the debt load would have been more manageable and the concession might not have needed to have been sold as part of the bankruptcy process.[1]

11.3.5 Stages of Infrastructure

This section describes an important determinant of infrastructure risk-return characteristics: stage of maturity. Investment in assets under construction is riskier than investment in completed assets; investment in newly completed assets with no operating history (including usage) is riskier than investment in mature assets with established operations and usage history. Depending on its phase, an infrastructure investment may be referred to as being in a greenfield or brownfield stage.

The **greenfield phase** covers the initial stages of infrastructure, from (1) building and development (including the design), to (2) the construction of the project itself, and (3) the project's ramp-up period (i.e., its start-up). By their nature, infrastructure assets tend to involve major construction work, in which risk can be quite high. The greenfield phase of a project contains many risks. The phase can be long and complex, requiring the coordination of many participants. At the greenfield stage, the risks can range from technical to political. Environmental issues are particularly important at this stage, as investors and lenders are becoming increasingly sensitive to these issues.

The **brownfield phase** involves operations and takes place when assets are already constructed. Assets in the operating phase have a history of operations that provides good visibility into revenue, usage rates, and operating costs. Exhibit 11.4 depicts the levels of risk of these phases.

11.3.6 Infrastructure Investment Vehicles

Infrastructure investments can be accessed indirectly through a number of vehicles: listed stocks, listed funds, open-end funds, and closed-end unlisted funds. Open-end funds permit further investment or withdrawal of funds by investors, whereas closed-end funds have a fixed size.

Estimates of total global listed infrastructure assets vary around $3 trillion. In 2019, the S&P Global Infrastructure Index (S&P GII) comprised over $1.4 trillion of publicly traded stocks, with approximate weights of 40% utilities, 40%

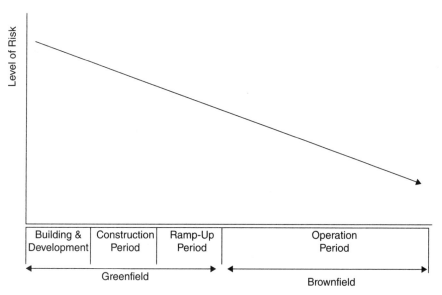

EXHIBIT 11.4   Risk Profile of Infrastructure Investment Development Stages
Source: World Economic Forum (2014).

industrials, and 20% energy firms by asset size. Infrastructure stocks are generally regarded as having higher dividend yields and lower volatility than stocks from other sectors. The higher dividend yields can reflect, for example, the relatively inelastic demand for infrastructure services or the generally reduced growth potential for infrastructure assets compared to overall equities. The lower volatility can be attributed to the monopolistic and regulated nature of infrastructure assets, as well as the price-inelastic demand for the goods and services generated by many infrastructure assets.

Investing in listed infrastructure stocks or funds of infrastructure stocks over unlisted funds has the advantages of greater liquidity and a clearer valuation process. However, these funds have exhibited higher volatility and a greater correlation to equity markets than non-market-based valuations on unlisted infrastructure funds. **Closed-end infrastructure funds** are typically structured like private equity funds, have a life of typically 10 to 15 years, and draw down investor capital commitments over a stated investment period of four to five years. Management fees typically range from 1% to 2% annually, in addition to carried interest of 10% to 20% over a preferred return of 8% paid at the exit of the fund or liquidation of specific investments. The appraised prices of these unlisted funds have experienced lower volatility and lower correlation to equity markets than the market prices of listed funds. However, this may be due to the appraisal-based nature of the valuation and the illiquid nature of the fund. Also, while listed funds may use 30% to 40% leverage, unlisted funds can reach 60% to 90% leverage when financing markets allow that level of borrowing. Due to the short track record and the private nature of unlisted funds, reliable benchmark index data have not yet been disseminated or studied.

Unlisted open-end funds, also called **evergreen funds**, allow investors to subscribe to or redeem from these funds on a regular basis. This provision of liquidity works only when investor redemption demands match the underlying liquidity of the fund's assets. To fund net investor redemptions, an open-end fund must have the ability to liquidate assets, attract new investors, borrow on a line of credit, or draw down cash balances. Should the demand of investors to redeem exceed these resources, gates may form. **Gates** are fund restrictions on investor withdrawals. Infrastructure funds may erect gates, especially during difficult markets, requiring that investor shares be redeemed over time rather than on an as-requested basis.

Some institutional investors have chosen to invest directly in infrastructure assets, in addition to or as a substitute for investing in unlisted infrastructure funds. This method of access has become increasingly popular over the past decade, especially among the larger institutions that have built in-house teams with the experience to source, analyze, structure, negotiate, and manage infrastructure assets. Direct infrastructure ownership by institutional investors was pioneered by large Canadian and Australian pension plans.

Infrastructure investments are global in nature, with approximately equal weights in the publicly listed companies of North America, Europe, and the rest of the world. Investors in a global fund accept currency risk, as the assets, debt, and cash flows of each project are typically denominated in the currency of the country where each asset is located. Investors in these funds have a risk that the value of the currency where the asset is located might depreciate relative to the value of the currency of the home country of the investor.

Exhibit 11.5 provides a summary of the characteristics of investing in infrastructure using three types of approaches: unlisted direct investment, unlisted funds, and listed securities.

11.3.7 Twelve Determinants of Infrastructure

The fundamental drivers of infrastructure performance (and risk) consist of the following 12 common attributes. Each of these 12 characteristics tends to generally

EXHIBIT 11.5 Types of Infrastructure Investments

	Unlisted Direct Investment	Unlisted Fund	Listed Securities
Investment size	Very high	Moderate	Low
Ease of access	Difficult; takes considerable time	Moderate difficulty; takes moderate time	Easy and immediate
Length of investment	Long term	Long term	Flexible
Capacity	Limited	Moderate	High
Liquidity	Low	Low to medium	High
Leverage	Low but varies	High	Moderate
Fees/expenses	No fees; very high expenses	High fees; low expenses	Low fees and expenses
Diversification	Concentrated risk; low correlation to other assets	Medium to high; low correlation to other assets	High; high correlation to other assets
Control	Maximum control over assets	High level of control	Limited control

provide for reduced risk, making many infrastructure assets a relatively defensive investment.

1. **Inelastic demand**

   Most infrastructure assets and businesses provide essential services that support the functioning of society and the economy, such as power, water, and basic transportation. The indispensable nature of most infrastructure investments results in their demand being relatively inelastic to price changes and economic downturns; their long-term growth is generally proportional to overall economic growth.

2. **Monopolistic market positions**

   More often than not, infrastructure assets and businesses are natural monopolies, with high barriers to entry. For example, suppose an airport is the only airport for a particular city. It may be uneconomical to build a competing airport, it may be difficult to get planning approval, and the government may explicitly promise the existing operator not to permit the development of a competing airport in the catchment area.

3. **Regulated entities**

   Given the monopolistic nature of such infrastructure assets, governments (or government-sponsored agencies) often regulate their activities and pricing to preclude undue monopolistic practices and extra-market returns at the expense of the consumer. As regulated entities, they are often required to sell their services at approved tariffs, which are intended to generate sufficient revenues to fund operating costs plus a certain return on capital. Gas, electric, and water utilities as well as transmission assets are examples of these regulated businesses. Their effective management necessitates specialized understanding of the applicable regulatory framework as well as technical and industry expertise to generate attractive risk-adjusted returns.

   Under the right management, regulated assets may be particularly attractive investments because price regulation mitigates downside risk if costs increase. This is because prices will be allowed to increase to maintain the target return rate. Moreover, returns can still be improved by outperforming the regulator's assumptions for operating costs, capital costs, and cost of capital. On the other hand, because regulated prices tend to be more stable, they may tend to be lower than unregulated prices. In addition, while improved services resulting from capital spending can lead to higher prices in unregulated investments, such increases are less likely to occur in regulated industries. Finally, depending on the provisions of the long-term contract, regulated prices may not be allowed to rise fast enough to reflect the increased cost of operations when these costs increase faster than the overall rate of inflation.

4. **Capital-intensive setup, low operating costs**

   While infrastructure assets are capital intensive to set up (e.g., airports, bridges, and tunnels), once established, they generally have relatively low operating costs. This provides for strong operating margins. This attribute, combined with long projected service lives, can support high levels of leverage.

5. **Low volatility of operating cash flows**

   In most instances, infrastructure investment revenue streams are relatively stable and predictable, often resulting from either a captive customer base or long-term contracts, regulated pricing schedules, and limited competition or licensing. Utilities are one example. Stable cash flows can also support value-enhancing financial leverage at a more attractive cost of debt capital than similar financings undertaken by more risky assets, such as private equity buyouts.

6. **Resilience to economic downturns**

Due to their essential role in the economy, infrastructure businesses, once operational, are less likely to suffer from a significant permanent decline in demand, traffic, or patronage than are businesses in other industries. They are expected to better weather downturns, with the possible exception of cases in which inappropriate capital structures have been used to finance their development (e.g., too much leverage) or when demand forecasts have been grossly inaccurate. Infrastructure investments have varying levels of sensitivity to economic conditions and business cycles.

To the degree that returns from certain infrastructure investments are not sensitive to business cycles, they will help reduce the volatility of an investor's overall performance during various stages of a business cycle. Exhibit 11.6 illustrates the general economic sensitivity of various infrastructure investments. Typically, if the cash flow of an investment is contractually fixed, the value of the investment will tend to be less sensitive to changes in economic conditions.

7. **Technology risk**

Many infrastructure assets are less exposed to technology obsolescence risk. However, for greenfield infrastructure that is reliant on technology (e.g., power generation), it is important to ensure that the technology used is proven or that the risk of technology failure is otherwise mitigated.

8. **Long-term horizons**

Infrastructure assets have long and useful economic lives (often over 50 years), producing stable revenues with relatively stable cash flows. This long-term predictability may be helpful to investors seeking to match long-term yielding assets against long-term liabilities (e.g., pension plan and insurance company liabilities).

EXHIBIT 11.6   Infrastructure versus Other Asset Classes

Type	Financing	Operating Costs	Return	Others
Infrastructure	Long-term with leverage	Medium	Medium	Long duration and inflation protection
Real estate	Long-term with leverage	Medium	Medium	Long duration and inflation protection
Private equity	Medium-term with some leverage	Low	High	Exposure to equity risks; high leverage and interest rate risk for buyouts
Public equity	Highly liquid	Very low	High	Volatile and limited protection against inflation
Public debt	Flexible maturity and varied liquidity	Very low	Low to medium	No protection against inflation and exposure to interest rates

9. **Inflation-indexed cash flows**

   Infrastructure assets may have contractual or regulatory revenue structures that are adjusted for changes in measures of inflation, such as the Consumer Price Index, thus making for an effective inflation hedge. Their long-term inflation-linked cash flow characteristics are attractive duration hedges for long-term liabilities. Foreign infrastructure investment projects expose investors to currency fluctuations. If cash flows are contractually fixed, this will make future cash flows more predictable and may reduce the cost of financing these projects. However, the real value of the cash flows will suffer if there is an unexpected increase in inflation. To the degree that the local currency may depreciate in response to higher inflation, foreign investors will see the value of the cash flows converted into their own currency decline as well.

10. **Stable yield**

    A consequence of the low operating costs and stable revenues is the ability of mature infrastructure businesses to support relatively high dividend yields, typically in the mid-to-high single digits per annum, in conjunction with moderate capital appreciation. This contrasts with private equity or venture capital investments, which are focused on capital growth for the great majority of the investment return.

11. **Low correlation with other asset classes**

    Infrastructure businesses typically display low correlation with traditional asset classes. One reason for this apparent low correlation is that valuation may be appraisal-based, which leads to smoothed returns. When returns are smoothed, their volatilities are artificially reduced and their correlations with traditional asset classes are moved toward zero. The other reason is that infrastructure businesses are regulated and have inelastic demand, leading to stable cash flows. Therefore, while infrastructure investments are expected to provide significant diversification benefits when added to a portfolio consisting of traditional asset classes, empirical estimates of these benefits could be overstated.

12. **Potentially low total and idiosyncratic risks**

    Many infrastructure investments have relatively low idiosyncratic risks. Total historical average returns from mature infrastructure investments have tended to depend on various factors, including the sector and jurisdiction in which the business operates. For example, with exceptions, a mature regulated gas utility has tended to have low idiosyncratic risks and to provide a lower return to investors (due to the lower risk as a result of the regulated nature of the business and the reliability of future cash flows). Returns from investments in sectors such as airports and ports (in part due to the variability of revenue as a result of exogenous factors) tend to have higher volatility.

11.3.8 Opportunities and Allocations in Infrastructure Investments

Infrastructure has traditionally been under the purview of governmental bodies. Its importance from a public interest perspective cannot be overstated. For several reasons, there has been globally widespread historical underinvestment, resulting in degradation of existing assets with a simultaneous failure to add sufficient new capacity. As this issue is unlikely to reverse course any time soon, forward-thinking countries and government entities have sought to encourage the convergence of public and private sector activity. Their aim is to help the creation of economically viable new infrastructure assets and upgrade, properly maintain, manage, and operate existing ones. Formal contracting structures through active PPPs supported by recent government initiatives have made progress in encouraging private capital investment in infrastructure. However, there remains a lot to be done.

The market opportunities in developed countries remain substantial. These opportunities are in civil aviation, bridges, roads, mass transit, railways, greenfield and brownfield projects, dams, water, waste management, and energy. The success of many new fund launches exclusively dedicated to infrastructure investing is suggestive of the vital role that private finance will continue to play in infrastructure development. This overall positive sentiment notwithstanding, many institutional investors have yet to ramp up their investment capabilities in this area. Some of them have not made dedicated allocations to infrastructure, perhaps reflecting the relative infancy of this asset class. Consequently, possibilities for early-mover advantages may remain in developed countries and are arguably even higher elsewhere. Government policy, changing legislation and regulatory norms, and private capital flows will strongly influence the evolution of infrastructure investments.

There is a debate about where infrastructure fits in an investor's asset allocation, as infrastructure has commonalities with fixed-income (institutional bonds), institutional real estate, and private equity investments. Exhibit 11.7 summarizes the four investments across seven characteristics. Some investors consider infrastructure as a fixed-income investment due to its high current yield, steady cash flows, and long duration. Infrastructure is similar to real estate and physical assets in terms of generating cash flows. Social infrastructure may have more in common with real estate investments than energy or utility infrastructure. Investors considering infrastructure as a private equity investment focus on the control aspect of infrastructure operating companies and the ability to add value through financial engineering or operating improvements. A CFA Institute paper estimates that 34% of investors consider infrastructure as part of their private equity allocation, 16% place it in the real estate or real assets allocation, and 50% consider it a unique asset class.[2]

From an alternative investment perspective, infrastructure assets exhibit different risk-return profiles from other private investments; they can be a source of alpha as well as a valuable diversification tool in portfolio construction. They provide exposure through both illiquid long-term private vehicles and liquid publicly traded funds. This versatility makes them attractive for various investor segments.

11.4 INTELLECTUAL PROPERTY OVERVIEW

A substantial portion of gross domestic product (GDP) is now generated by and composed of intangible assets, namely intellectual property (IP). For an asset to be owned, it must be excludable. An **excludable good** is a good others can be prevented from enjoying. Exclusivity distinguishes private goods and private property (e.g., houses) from public goods (e.g., air). Many intangible assets are nonexcludable goods, especially in the long run. For example, everyone benefits from ancient inventions such as the wheel without having to pay its inventor. But some intangible assets are naturally

EXHIBIT 11.7 Characteristics Associated with Infrastructure and Other Asset Categories

	Infrastructure	Institutional Bonds	Institutional Real Estate	Private Equity
Nature of asset	Typically an operating company dependent on control of large, physical assets	Financial security	Physical property	Operating company
Asset availability	Asset scarcity; many in unique, monopoly situations	Deep volumes in most markets	Moderate to deep volumes in most markets	Moderate volumes in most markets
Acquisition dynamic	Competitive tenders; regulatory, environmental, social, and political issues; often held for the long run	Efficient, on-market purchase	Competitive tenders; environmental and social issues common	Competitive tenders, management buyout, negotiated trade sale, typically medium-term exit strategy
Liquidity	Moderate	Very high	Moderate in most sectors	Moderate
Income	Once assets mature, very stable; inflation/GDP growth relative; typically higher than bonds and core real estate	Fixed coupon; sensitive to interest rates	Mixture of fixed and variable interest rates and sector dependent	Typically dominated by capital returns
Growth	Dependent on asset stage; modest (late stage) to high (early stage/development assets)	Low	Dependent on asset characteristics; moderate to high	Dependent on asset characteristics; typically high
Volatility	Moderate (early stage) to low (late stage)	Moderate (market factors)	Low/moderate	High (early stage) to moderate (late stage) depending on industry sector
Typical return expectation per annum post fees	Mature portfolio: 7%–10%; development portfolio: > 10%	Approximately 5%–7%	Core: ~7%–9%; value added: ~12%–18%; opportunistic: > 18%	Diversified portfolio: > 15%

Source: Data from "Understanding Infrastructure," RREEF, 2005.

excludable (e.g., reputation) or are protected by law (e.g., patents, trademarks, and copyrights).

Intangible assets are excludable, do not have a physical form, are real assets (not financial assets), and can include ideas, technologies, reputations, artistic creations, and so forth. **Intellectual property (IP)** is an intangible asset that is a creation of the human mind and that is excludable, such as copyrighted artwork. Like tangible assets, IP assets are important components in the production of goods, and have many of the same characteristics as tangible assets. This section provides an overview of IP and then discusses three categories as examples: (1) film production and distribution, (2) visual works of art, and (3) patents and research and development (R&D).

11.4.1 Characteristics of IP

Intangible assets, including IP, are necessary inputs to economic productivity, along with labor, capital, and raw materials. Intangible assets such as technology are the primary source of productivity that determines the relative level of the wealth of societies, both through time and across societies. Much of the value of the stocks and bonds of a modern corporation, such as a pharmaceutical firm or a computer technology firm, is composed of IP.

Historically, most intellectual property was bundled with tangible corporate assets and was available for investment through traditional means, such as an equity investment in a software (or other intellectual property–oriented) company. However, in recent years, there has been an increased interest in unbundling and isolating intangible assets, IP in particular, for stand-alone investment purposes. Examples of such assets include patent portfolios, film copyrights, art, music or other media, research and development (R&D), and brands. **Unbundled intellectual property** is IP that may be owned or traded on a standalone basis.

Unbundled IP may be acquired or financed at various stages in its development and exploitation. Ex ante, newly created IP may have widely varying value and use. The value of property such as exploratory research, new film production, new music production, or pending patents will typically be widely uncertain prior to production or implementation. Similar to venture capital investments, many of these types of IP may fail to recapture initial investment or costs, whereas a proportionately small number of cases will capture a large asymmetric return on investment. For example, most movies lose money; yet films, on average, are still profitable. De Vany and Walls (2004) report that, for a sample of more than 2,000 films, 6.3% of the films generated 80% of the total profits. **Mature intellectual property** is IP that has developed and established a reliable usefulness and will have a more certain valuation and a more clear ability to generate licensing, royalty, or other income associated with its use.

The duration of IP varies by type. Most forms of IP, such as patents and copyrights, are wasting assets—that is, assets with relatively large immediate benefits but with value that is expected to diminish through time. Intellectual property generally diminishes in value through time, as its productive advantages are displaced by new creativity or its excludability wanes (e.g., patents expire). However, some IP offers substantial capital accumulation through time. Clearly, many instances of artwork and brand names have exhibited substantial long-term growth in value.

11.4.2   Intellectual Properties and Six Characteristics of Real Assets

Financial economists use the term *real assets* as the counterpart to financial assets, and in this context IP is clearly a real asset despite its intangible nature. A number of investment managers have advanced the idea that certain intellectual property assets have properties that characterize them as real assets in the context of organizing alternative investment portfolio allocations. Recent changes to U.S. gross domestic product (GDP) accounting, which allow certain intellectual property assets to be treated as fixed investments, are consistent with this idea.

Six characteristics recognized as belonging to real assets have been analyzed as generally being common among typical intellectual property assets (Martin 2014). The six general characteristics of real assets that follow are each used to ascertain the extent to which IP fits the investment classification of being a real alternative asset.

1. **Low operating risk**

   Investing in proven and established intellectual property (such as established pharmaceutical technology), owning existing media assets rather than funding the creation of new assets (such as movie slates), and using established patents or technological IP that is already in use are lower-risk ways to invest in patents. As with traditional tangible assets, these assets may derive their value from their use in established economic processes and have value that is largely transferable from one owner to another, with less emphasis on strategic complementarities and hence niche value. The preservation of value under transfer of ownership or control is particularly emphasized in IP assets that are subject to license and sale (such as technology patents or pharmaceutical IP). Ownership rights in IP are long-lasting and used repeatedly in the production process.

2. **Positive correlation with inflation**

   Positive correlation between rates of inflation and investment returns provides investors with protection from inflation risk. However, Martin (2010) notes that there is no definitive evidence on the correlation of intellectual property assets and inflation. Nevertheless, this lack of certainty also pertains to certain other assets that have been classified as real, such as real estate. Casual observation and economic reasoning indicates that it is likely that intellectual property assets have low correlation with inflation and, like other real assets, represent a diversifier of inflation risk, unlike other traditional assets in institutional portfolios (e.g., equities and nominal bonds).

3. **Preserving value in periods of macroeconomic instability**

   In general, excluding some industries such as technology and biotech, intellectual property products have low beta to the overall market. For example, five-year rolling betas to the Fama-French market factor indicates that the pharmaceutical sector has a beta in the lower half of all sectors, and that it is generally in the lowest quartile of sector betas. Elevated intermediate cash flows serve to reduce risk generally while also reducing the asset's sensitivity to exit risk in a temporarily unfavorable market environment.

4. **Benefits from the scarcity of inputs in sectors like energy, manufacturing, and agriculture**

   Most real assets are viewed as benefiting from scarcity of key inputs. However, IP assets have been established as *not* possessing this characteristic and, therefore, in this sense do not conform to this traditional characteristic of real assets (in the context of institutional asset classifications).

5. **Are essential parts of economic infrastructure**

Intellectual property, and in particular "intellectual property products" as defined by the Bureau of Economic Analysis in its definition of GDP, is of growing importance. As indicated by the accounts behind the calculation of GDP, long-lived intellectual property products are considered a significant part of the U.S. GDP and therefore are likely an essential part of an economy's infrastructure.

6. **Offers long-term risk and return properties suitable for supporting funding with long-term liabilities**

The focus on intellectual property products with low operating risk, ready transferability or license, and long lives provides a basis for the generation of relatively stable cash flows which in turn supports the proposition that IP assets may be suitable for funding long-term liabilities.

In summary, IP tends to exhibit five of the six characteristics commonly ascribed to the category of real assets in institutional portfolios.

11.4.3 A Simplified Model of Intellectual Property

Based on the generalized behavior of IP, a very simplified model of IP values may be constructed as the present value of expected future cash flows. Assume that the value of IP at its creation is the sum of the discounted expected cash flows generated by the property. Further assume that the property has two possible outcomes: the probability (p) of generating large positive cash flows and the probability ($1 - p$) of generating no positive cash flows. Denote the first-year cash flows of the project, if positive, as CF_1. Finally, assume that the cash flows in years 2 and beyond are equal to CF_1 adjusted annually by the rate g: $CF_t = CF_1 (1 + g)^{t-1}$. If the model is being used to value a wasting asset, then the rate g is a negative number that indicates the rate at which the cash flows are decaying through time as a result of obsolescence or other causes of diminished value. Using the perpetual growth model commonly used to value common stock (where g is typically positive), the value of the IP at time zero, $V_{ip,0}$, discounted at the rate r can be expressed as depicted in Equation 11.1:

$$V_{ip,0} = p \times CF_1/(r - g) \qquad (11.1)$$

Equation 11.1 is identical to the perpetual growth model used for common stocks except for the use of $p \times CF_1$ to denote the expected cash flow in the first year and the idea that g is likely to be negative. Note that the present value of the future cash flows, $V_{ip,0}$, is positively related to p and g. Given estimates of p, CF_1, r, and g, a value may be estimated for $V_{ip,0}$.

☞ **APPLICATION 11.4.3A**

Loosely following some of the values indicated earlier in this section for films, assume that the probability of substantial success for an investment in IP (p) is 6%, the rate at which expected cash flows diminish each year after their initial potential (g) is 5%, and the required rate of return (r) is 12%. How much would this investment in IP be worth per dollar of projected possible first-year cash flow (CF_1)?

This example normalizes the analysis to a value of $1 for CF_1. Using Equation 11.1 produces $(0.06 \times \$1)/[0.12 - (-0.05)]$, which equals approximately $0.35. Roughly estimated, the value of the IP might be only 35 cents for each dollar of initial annual cash inflow that would be generated, assuming that the initial cash flow is a potential cash flow and therefore represents a very successful outcome.

The previous computation reflects the idea that investment in new IP may have risk similar to that of an out-of-the-money call option. To illustrate another perspective, Equation 11.1 can be rearranged to solve for the total annual rate of return, r, as shown in Equation 11.2:

$$r = p \times (CF_1/V_{ip,0}) + g \tag{11.2}$$

The total rate of return is the expected cash flow in the first year expressed as a percentage of the value of the IP minus the rate of decay. The intuition of Equation 11.2 is that an investment in undeveloped IP is a chance (p) at a potential stream of income (CF_1) that is likely to diminish $(g < 0)$ through time as the productivity of the IP wanes.

☞ APPLICATION 11.4.3B

Assume that Equation 11.2 is an appropriate valuation model and that $CF_1/V_{ip,0}$ is 3.0, p is 0.06, and g is –0.05. What is the investment's annual rate of return?

Inserting the values generates the result that r is 13%.

Financial analysis of IP requires specialized skills, including legal knowledge that should be accessed to reap potential benefits through return and diversification. The reason that legal knowledge is especially important in the case of IP is the tendency of property rights to be complex and dynamic for intangible assets.

11.5 CASH FLOWS OF INTELLECTUAL PROPERTY

Film production and distribution comprise a subset of IP that often has relatively substantial accounting data availability and thus provides a good example of the methods for estimating and modeling expected future cash flows and accounting profitability.

11.5.1 Film Production and Distribution Revenues

Film production and distribution fall into the IP category of artwork. Total global box office revenues were estimated to be over $38 billion in 2016. Film revenues

EXHIBIT 11.8   Schedule of Film Exhibition Venues

Exhibition Form	Window	Time after Release
Theatrical	6 months	0
Home Video	10 years +	4 months
Pay-per-View	2 months	8 months
Pay TV	18 months	12 months
Network	30 months	30 months
Pay TV Second Window	12 months	60 months
Basic Cable	60 months	72 months
Television Syndication	60 months	132 months

Source: Data from Wood Creek Capital Management (2011).

are generated almost exclusively by exhibition, which has a generally stable set and sequence of stages, though not all films will be licensed for exhibition in all forms (Exhibit 11.8). The revenues from home media and broadcast are larger than global box office revenue, but include programming made both as films and directly for television.

Exhibition forms include theatrical, cable-based and web-based home video, television networks, and DVDs. The expected size of the revenues, the starting time of the revenue streams, and the projected length of the revenue streams are aggregated to project the total revenues through time. While total revenues from film have demonstrated relative stability, the mix of revenue sources has been changing relatively quickly, due in part to technology but also to other financial imperatives, such as the availability (or lack) of capital for new film production. Examples of changing revenue sources include the rise and subsequent relative decline in revenues associated with DVD and similar exhibition technologies, as well as the increasing importance of online and non-U.S. revenues to overall revenue.

Translating revenue numbers into profits is typically impossible without direct knowledge of and participation in the production of particular film assets. However, there are regularities that arise in contracting that can be exploited to conduct an analysis and forecast cash flows. For example, empirical evidence indicates that sequels tend to generate more revenue at lower risk, and different film genres have different risk-return properties. To maximize the potential returns and portfolio benefits from investments in IP, investors should develop or retain analysts with expertise in the underlying assets of the IP.

11.5.2   Film Production and Distribution Expenses

Film production itself has several stages. First, the costs of producing the film are collectively called negative costs. **Negative costs** refer not to the sign of the values but to the fact that these are costs required to produce what was, in the predigital era, the film's negative image. These costs include story rights acquisition; preproduction (script development, set design, casting, crew selection, costume design, location scouting); principal photography and production (compensation of actors, producers, directors, writers, sound stage, wardrobe, set construction); and postproduction (film editing, scoring, titles and credits, dubbing, special effects). These costs are coupled with the substantial cost of prints and advertising, which is the cost of the film prints to be used in theaters, whether digital or physical, and a film's advertising and marketing costs.

11.5.3 Film Financing

Financing is achieved through equity or debt financing, or a combination of both. Equity financing structures include slate equity financing, corporate equity, coproduction, and miscellaneous third-party equity financing:

- SLATE EQUITY FINANCING: In slate equity financing, an outside investor (e.g., hedge fund or investment bank) funds a set of films to be produced by a studio. These slates typically reflect a set of parameters regarding diversification, risk, the number of films to be released, minimum and maximum budgets for film production and P&A (prints and advertising), and genre diversification requirements. Slate deals emerged to spread financial risk across a series of films, thus limiting the impact of one film's losses on an overall financial investment. Slate financings may have further provisions to ensure against moral hazards; such provisions would, for example, deter a studio from assigning films with lower expected returns or greater risk to slate financings.
- CORPORATE EQUITY: This is equity fund-raising (private placement or public offering) to fund the activities of a production company.
- COPRODUCTION: In coproduction, two or more studios partner on a film, sharing the equity costs and, correspondingly, the risks and returns.
- MISCELLANEOUS THIRD-PARTY EQUITY: Some combination of high-net-worth individuals, institutional investors, and other third-party investors fund costs not covered by other types of financing; this is particularly common for smaller independent films.

Debt financing structures include senior secured debt, gap financing, and super gap financing/junior debt.

- SENIOR SECURED DEBT: A bank or another financial institution lends funds to a movie studio or producer to finance the production and/or P&A of a film. This loan can come in various structures and forms, backed by specific collateral, such as the following:
  - *Negative pickup deal.* A negative pickup deal occurs when a film distributor agrees to purchase a film from a producer for a fixed sum upon delivery of the completed film.
  - *Foreign presales.* A foreign presale occurs before the film is made, when the producer sells distribution rights for specific foreign territories for a fixed price; all, or nearly all, of this payment is due upon delivery of the completed film.
  - *Tax credits/grants.* The producer receives tax credits (which are salable) or grants (paid in cash) for filming in a specific state or country.
- GAP FINANCING: Gap financing covers the difference between the production budget and the senior secured debt, which can be collateralized by sales of unsold territories to distributors.
- SUPER GAP FINANCING/JUNIOR DEBT: Super gap financing is a second level of gap financing, often syndicated, representing the final gap that the senior lender or gap financier does not want to risk.

Further, financing may be supported directly or indirectly with royalty participations. These may, in the case of talent, be in lieu of salary or other noncontingent compensation; or, in the case of financial investors, they may be used to lower the cost of up-front financing. These participations are usually assignable (i.e., transferable to third parties) after a film has been produced.

11.5.4 Film Profitability

Films offer profit potential with a right skew. The ratio of estimated worldwide revenues to investment can be 1,000% or more. According to "The Numbers,"[2] there have been 17 movies with profits of over $500 million, with Avatar earning well over $1 billion. Only eight movies generated losses in excess of $100 million, with *Mars Needs Moms* having the largest estimated loss of $143.5 million.

11.6   VISUAL WORKS OF ART AND HISTORICAL PERFORMANCE DATA

Within IP, art tends to provide superior long-term pricing data for analysis of historical returns. **Visual works of art** include paintings and have a rich history of prices and returns, but they do not represent a major component of *institutional* portfolios. Further, returns from previous centuries are probably not reflective of returns related to modern market conditions. It should be noted that art is a major component of some high-net-worth investor portfolios.

There is a wide range of studies regarding the returns to art, typically differentiated by style or geography, as reflected in Exhibit 11.9. The median real return to holding art over extended periods of time is 2.2% (methods used to estimate returns do not vary substantially in outcomes). However, most studies of the returns to art investment consider only hammer prices, which are final auction prices that do not include commissions to the auction house. Commissions that may be charged to both the buyer and the seller amount to as much as 15%. If we assume that the typical round-turn transaction cost for a sale is 25%, then it would be expected to take 10 years of price appreciation to cover the transaction costs associated with a piece of art.

Spaenjers (2010) considers data on more than 1 million art transactions across 13 countries from the 1960s onward, accounting for both geographical and currency effects. The results are consistent with the preceding: Annualized real returns to a diversified basket of art have been in the neighborhood of 2% and do not vary significantly across geographies or markets. In addition, the volatility of art indices has a median of 17% per year. This combination of risk and return compares unfavorably to historical experience in equity markets. In other words, the Sharpe ratio is relatively unattractive.

Forsyth (2012) suggests that high-net-worth investors invest in art as a hedge against inflation or confiscation of wealth by governments. For those with a net worth above $100 million, he suggests, an important goal is to maintain rather than grow wealth. Artworks can protect against monetary debasement, confiscation, and social unrest. Forsyth quotes Richard Morais: "Any private banker will tell you that, as soon as a centimillionaire...makes their fortune, the first thing they do is figure out

EXHIBIT 11.9 Estimated Returns to Art from Various Studies

Author	Sample	Period	Method	Nominal Return	Real Return
Anderson (1974)	Paintings in general	1780–1960	Hedonic	3.3%	2.6%
	Paintings in general	1780–1970	Repeat sales	3.7%	3.0%
Stein (1977)	Paintings in general	1946–1968	Assumes random sampling	10.5%	
Baumol (1986)	Paintings in general	1652–1961	Repeat sales		0.6%
Frey and Pommenihne (1989)	Paintings in general	1635–1949	Repeat sales		1.4%
		1950–1987	Repeat sales		1.7%
Buelens and Ginsburgh (1993)	Paintings in general	1700–1961	Hedonic		0.9%
Pesando (1993)	Modern prints	1977–1991	Repeat sales		1.5%
Goetzmann (1993)	Paintings in general	1716–1986	Repeat sales	3.2%	2.0%
Barre et al. (1996)	Great impressionist	1962–1991	Hedonic	12.0%	5.0%[a]
	Other impressionist	1962–1991	Hedonic	8.0%	1.0%[a]
Chanel et al. (1996)	Paintings in general	1855–1969	Hedonic		4.9%
	Paintings in general	1855–1969	Repeat sales		5.0%
Goetzmann (1996)	Paintings in general	1907–1977	Repeat sales		5.0%
Pesando and Shum (1996)	Picasso prints	1977–1993	Repeat sales	12.0%	1.4%
Czujack (1997)	Picasso printings	1966–1994	Hedonic		8.3%
Mei and Moses (2001)	American, impressionist, and old master	1875–2000	Repeat sales		4.9%
Graeser (1993)	Antique furniture	1967–1986	Neither[b]	7.0%	2.2%
Ross and Zondervan (1989)	Stradivarius violins	1803–1986	Hedonic		2.2%

[a] As many of the surveys report only nominal returns, the authors calculated the real return rates as follows. For the Anderson and Baumol studies, an inflation rate of 0.7% a year was used. This number is based on Baumol's estimate of inflation during the 300-year period of his study using the Phelps-Brown and Hopkins price index. Goetzmann's estimate of inflation during the period of his study (also based on Phelps-Brown and Hopkins) is 1.2%. French price inflation between 1962 and 1992 according to OECD statistics was 7%.
[b] Assumes random sampling within a portfolio of fixed furniture types.
Source: Ashenfelter and Graddy (2003).

how they can ferret away large chunks of that wealth to countries that guarantee political and personal freedoms, have sound legal systems, a favorable tax environment, good security and good schools for their kids." A substantial portion of this newfound wealth may be invested in real estate in cities such as New York or London, and in art, which can be easily shipped to the residences in these safe, global cities.

Another explanation of low financial returns to art is that the investment in art provides a total return that is a combination of the financial return to art (price appreciation) and the aesthetic benefit to being the owner of the art. The **aesthetic benefit** is the nonfinancial benefit to owning art and includes the joy of viewing and otherwise controlling the art. To the extent that competition drives the total return to similar risk-adjusted levels, there is a trade-off between the financial return and the aesthetic benefit. In artwork overall, and perhaps in some artwork in particular, prices are driven higher (and expected financial returns are driven lower) in anticipation of the nonfinancial benefits from ownership.

The historical evidence of modest real returns and nontrivial risk indicates disappointing risk-adjusted financial returns. Economic reasoning indicates that one explanation is that art offers part of its return in the form of aesthetic benefits. Although art can be attractive as a wealth-preservation technique for high-net-worth investors, there is little basis for viewing it as an attractive asset class for traditional financial institutional portfolios.

11.7 R&D AND PATENTS AS UNBUNDLED INTELLECTUAL PROPERTY

Research and development (R&D) and patents provide important insights into intellectual property (IP) in the context of unbundled IP and in the establishment and preservation of property rights for intangible assets. Unlike tangible assets, for which property rights are typically indicated by possession and usually clearly established, IP often raises challenges regarding its potential nonexcludability. Although this section focuses on R&D and patents, much of the discussion is applicable to other unbundled IP, such as royalties on music, books, and other copyrights.

11.7.1 Accessing R&D through Patents

Investors have historically accessed the returns to R&D through private or public equity investments in operating entities. However, to the extent that patents or other protected IP represent the crystallization of prior R&D, ownership of patents may represent a mechanism for accessing the benefits of R&D without bearing the operational risk associated with broader investments in companies that own such IP. Investments in patents can take multiple forms, such as direct acquisition or indirect acquisition through firms or funds that specialize in the acquisition and monetization of IP.

Five key strategies for acquisition of and exit from (monetizing) patent-related IP are:

1. Acquisition and licensing
2. Enforcement and litigation
3. Sale license-back
4. Lending strategies
5. Sales and pooling

11.7.2 Patent Acquisition and Licensing Strategies

Acquisition and licensing strategies are generally built around agreements regarding royalty streams. Examples of key terms between the licensor/grantor and the licensee include:

■ MINIMUM ROYALTY PROVISION: If the royalties do not hit the contracted amount within a specified commercialization period, the licensor may either terminate the license or make the license nonexclusive.

- FIELD-OF-USE PROVISION: A licensor may grant an exclusive license for a geographical region or a particular market.
- RESERVATION OF RIGHTS PROVISION: The grantor may make use of the patent, most often for noncommercial research uses.
- IMPROVEMENT PROVISIONS: These are provisions dealing with improvements to the patent whereby a more efficient method is created (but the new method would arguably infringe on the claims of the patent); improvements are a difficult part of the license negotiations, because either the licensor or the licensee may be the originator of the improvement.
- AUDIT/REPORTING/PAYMENT DUE DATE OBLIGATIONS: Licensors may want to monitor the licensee's royalty payments.
- EXCLUSIVITY RESPONSIBILITIES: Generally, the licensor has (sometimes limited) duties to enforce exclusivity, whereas the licensee has to report infringement cases to the licensor. This varies a great deal from license to license.

In general, license rates are typically specified as a function of revenues associated with products built on the licensed technology.

11.7.3 Patent Enforcement and Litigation Strategies

Ownership of patents may require patent enforcement and litigation to protect the value of the IP, meaning that the owner of the IP monitors the use of the patent and takes legal action against those who make uncompensated or unauthorized use of the patent. In fact, an IP investment strategy can be to acquire patents or other protected intellectual property that the potential purchaser believes is being infringed on in the marketplace. This strategy has received increasing scrutiny and public debate, as "non-practicing" holders of patents seek to monetize their intellectual property portfolios.

Typically, an investor who believes that his patent is the subject of infringement will approach users of the technology and seek to negotiate a license agreement with them. This is usually far more cost-effective than litigation. However, should agreement and licensing not be achieved, the owner of the patent may seek litigation against the infringers.

While subject to risks and requiring substantial expertise, in addition to the time and costs of the litigation, actual patent litigation tends to proceed in a relatively orderly fashion, with most patent cases being resolved through settlement. For example, Janicke (2007) finds that most patent litigation (~80%) is resolved through settlement rather than trial. Evidence indicates that settlement rates have been relatively stable through time.

The difficulty with settlements, however, is that their terms are not generally reported, so it is difficult to evaluate from public data the extent to which settlement-based outcomes generate sufficient risk-adjusted returns. However, although these outcomes are difficult to evaluate, it is known that cases resolved through trial generate median awards of $10 million—a figure generally confirmed by Mazzeo, Hillel, and Zyontz (2013).

In evaluating the returns to litigation, a key factor is the amount of time it takes to resolve a case, in part because length of time is positively correlated with costs; it takes longer to redeploy capital in new cases as old cases drag on; and, of course, there is the time value of money. The timing of resolutions can be summarized with the following stylized facts:

- Defaults have the shortest time to resolution. Summary judgments range from 5 months to 35 months in duration.
- Trials generally take between 35 and 50 months to resolve.
- Late dispositions take the most time to resolve: upwards of 50 months.

11.7.4 Patent Sale License-Back Strategies

In a strategy that parallels the sale leaseback transactions of the corporate and real estate worlds, the patent sale license-back (SLB) strategy is in use when the patent holder sells one or more patents to a buyer, who then licenses those patents back to the original holder. In doing so, a patent seller is benefiting from the ability to monetize a portion of the intangible assets. The patent buyer then places the patent in a pool of similar technologies for out-licensing to other parties. Often, the patent buyer will participate in the licensing revenue from new licensees. By allowing the patent to be pooled with other patents, the patent owner can benefit from revenue participation generated from the potential synergies of the pooled patents.

There is also a potentially substantial tax benefit if a company lends a patent to an IP holding company in a jurisdiction with a lower tax regime than that of the previous patent holder. However, it is important to note that SLBs can incur structural problems. A borrower who has transferred title of a patent may have difficulty bringing infringement actions.

11.7.5 Patent Lending Strategies

Lending strategies backed by patents are typically separated into two classes of transactions, depending on the quality of the underlying IP:

1. SECURITIZATION: Lending backed by IP collateral allows separation of the IP owner's credit risk from the risk of holding the IP through the bankruptcy process.
2. MEZZANINE IP LENDING: Lending secured by IP collateral usually includes warrants or other upside. Fischer and Ringler (2014) discuss the use of patents as collateral in debt financings and find that actual collateralizations are driven primarily by the direct economic value of the patent rather than by strategic considerations, such as the ability to potentially exclude other parties from using technology in the case of liquidations.

11.7.6 Patent Sales and Pooling

Patent owners seeking to divest patents must find buyers. Traditionally, patent buyers have entered the market for one of three reasons:

1. To purchase patents for operational use
2. To purchase patents to use as "trading cards"
3. To purchase a patent for strategic use; in this scenario, the purchaser may use the patent for defensive protection in negotiating with patent dealers.

A fourth (and emerging) class of patent buyers is made up of IP asset managers looking to buy patents for monetary exploitation. Patent pooling, in which multiple owners of related patents agree to jointly license a number of patents to external users, is more complex than in-house licensing because of the need to divide royalty income based on revenue-sharing formulas. This can be a practical solution in industries with set standards and large quantities of patented technologies.

Two fairly recent patent pools that were highly effective at setting industry standards were the Moving Picture Experts Group (MPEG) patent pools and the DVD patent pools. Even though multiple pools had to be formed (for different MPEG formats and different DVD formats), it meant that licensees dealt with only one of a couple of pools rather than a myriad of individual companies. This simplification led to the success of both technologies.

11.7.7 Risks to Investment in Patents

While there are many strategies involving patent assets, there are also many risks:

- ILLIQUIDITY: IP assets are highly illiquid assets, which often cannot be easily monetized.
- TECHNOLOGY/OPERATIONAL RISK: For investors buying cash flow streams generated by IP or purchasing debt collateralized by IP, technological risk and operational risk (which may limit the investors' ability to capitalize on the IP) are major concerns; cash flows depend on successful operation of the asset, particularly when the asset is prone to heavy competitive pressure (e.g., brands or technology in a fast-moving space).
- OBSOLESCENCE: If new technology displaces current IP, the asset may be rendered worthless.
- MACROECONOMIC/SECTOR RISK: If macroeconomic or sector-specific factors drive down an industry, this can have significant effects on the value of a patent or a company's ability to produce cash flows from the patent.
- REGULATORY RISK: IP represents government-issued rights; at any point, the government could change the structure of IP authority or impose regulation on licensing/sales activities.
- LEGAL RISK: IP transactions require a thorough understanding of IP law; failure to account for all legal implications of a transaction could result in a loss of IP value.
- EXPIRATION RISK: A patent's life is 20 years (with some exceptions for extensions, primarily in the pharmaceutical space).

11.8 INTELLECTUAL PROPERTY CONCLUSIONS

This chapter has reviewed three primary forms of IP. In the case of film production and distribution, revenue and profitability forecasts are difficult. Generally, film production can be viewed as offering return distributions skewed to the right, similar to venture capital returns. Art provides a long and somewhat plentiful history of transaction data from which estimation of historical risk and return is possible. Art has offered relatively low returns with moderate levels of risk and is subject to high transaction costs. R&D and patents are emerging as stand-alone investments, potentially of offering high returns but requiring expertise in evaluation of the underlying assets.

The case for intellectual property as the bedrock of future long-term economic growth is persuasive. The case for substantial allocation of institutional portfolios to IP is less clear. However, stand-alone, institutional-quality IP appears to be likely to be an important investable sector, and may eventually offer superior returns to first-movers.

REVIEW QUESTIONS

1. Name three factors that theory suggests should drive the extent to which natural resource price changes drive the performance of firms that process those natural resources.
2. To what extent have gold prices driven the short-term equity values of gold mining firms based on data from the United States during the financial crisis in late 2008?
3. Why are most listed MLPs in the United States involved in producing, processing, and distributing energy products?
4. Do infrastructure assets need to have all seven of the elements that identify investable infrastructure? Why or why not?
5. What is the difference between economic and social infrastructure? Provide an example of each.
6. What is the primary defining difference between greenfield projects and brownfield projects?
7. What is the term used to describe when a governmental entity sells a public asset to a private operator?
8. Is investable intellectual property a public good or a private good?
9. What are the four inputs to the simplified model of intellectual property values?
10. What is the empirical evidence on the very long-term annual financial returns of works of art?

NOTES

1. "Infrastructure Investing: A Key Source of Growth in the Global Economy," CFA Institute, Financial Analysts Seminar, July 2010.
2. https://www.the-numbers.com/movie/Mars-Needs-Moms#tab=summary

REFERENCES

De Vany, A., and W. Walls. 2004. "Motion Picture Profit, the Stable Paretian Hypothesis, and the Curse of the Superstar." *Journal of Economic Dynamics and Control* 28:1035–57.
Fischer, T., and P. Ringler. 2014. "What Patents Are Used as Collateral? An Empirical Analysis of Patent Reassignment Data." *Journal of Business Venturing* 29 (5): 633–50.
Forsyth, R. 2012. "Art for Art's Sake? Or to Protect Wealth?" *Barron's*, May 1.
Janicke, P. 2007. "Patent Litigation Remedies: Some Statistical Observations." PowerPoint presentation.

Martin, G. 2010. "The Long-Horizon Benefits of Traditional and New Real Assets in the Institutional Portfolio." *Journal of Alternative Investments* 13 (1): 6–29.

———. 2014. "Real Assets: An Institutional Perspective." Presentation to CISDM, Amherst, MA.

Mazzeo, M., J. Hillel, and S. Zyontz. 2013. "Explaining the 'Unpredictable': An Empirical Analysis of US Patent Infringement Awards." *International Review of Law and Economics* 35: 58–72.

Spaenjers, C. 2010. "Returns and Fundamentals in International Art Markets." November. www.hec.unil.ch/documents/seminars/ibf/430.pdf.

Wood Creek Capital Management. 2011. "Film Industry Overview."

CHAPTER 12

Real Estate Assets and Debt

This is the first of two chapters on real estate. This chapter provides an overview of real estate assets, followed by a detailed discussion of fixed-income investments backed by real estate. It also discusses liquid alternatives that provide exposure to real estate.

Real estate has been a very large and important portion of wealth for thousands of years. Even as recently as a century ago, real estate dominated institutional portfolios and was classified as property. During recent decades, the preeminence of real estate has yielded to the growing importance of intangible assets, yet real estate remains a valuable part of any well-diversified portfolio. The transition of private real estate from dominating traditional institutional-quality investments to being an alternative investment raises important issues in terms of how to evaluate real estate on a forward-looking basis.

12.1 CATEGORIES OF REAL ESTATE

This section describes the main characteristics of various real estate assets, beginning with five especially common categories that can be used to differentiate real estate:

1. Equity versus debt
2. Domestic versus international
3. Residential versus commercial
4. Private versus public
5. Market size of geographic location

Each of these categories is briefly discussed in the following five sections.

12.1.1 Equity versus Debt

The traditional method of distinguishing between equity claims and debt claims is to use the legal distinction between a residual claim and a fixed claim. A **mortgage** is a debt instrument collateralized by real estate, with a value that is more closely associated with the value of the real estate than the profitability of the borrower. Mortgages with substantial credit risk can behave more like real estate equity, and equity ownership of properties with very-long-term leases can behave like debt. Real estate equity investments will be discussed in Chapter 13.

12.1.2 Domestic versus International

One of the primary motivations of real estate investing is diversification. International investing (i.e., cross-border investing) in general and international real estate investing in particular are regarded as offering substantially improved diversification. However, the heterogeneity of most real estate and the unique nature of many real estate investments make international real estate investing more problematic than international investing in traditional assets. **Seven challenges to international real estate investing** include: (1) a lack of knowledge and experience regarding foreign real estate markets, (2) a lack of relationships with foreign real estate managers, (3) the time and expense of travel for due diligence, (4) liquidity concerns, (5) political risk (particularly in emerging markets), (6) risk management of foreign currency exposures, and (7) taxation differences. For these reasons, a large share of international real estate investing is done through shares of listed property companies in foreign countries. The continuing emergence of derivative products related to real estate investments in particular nations or regions is an important potential opportunity for exploiting the benefits of international diversification without the challenges of direct international investment.

These challenges are addressed in detail in Chapter 40 of the Level II CAIA curriculum, which is entitled "Complexity and the Case of Cross-Border Real Estate Investing." That chapter includes extensive discussion of the potential risks and solutions to currency differentials. Briefly, all of these challenges introduce complexities to cross-border real estate investment that require substantial time, expertise, and resources.

The extent of appropriate international investing depends on the locale of the asset allocator. An asset allocator in a very large economy may be able to achieve moderate levels of diversification without foreign real estate investing. However, an asset allocator in a nation with a small or emerging economy may experience high levels of idiosyncratic risk in the absence of foreign investments.

12.1.3 Residential versus Commercial

One of the most important drivers of the characteristics of a real estate investment is the nature of the real estate assets underlying the investment. A broad distinction, especially in mortgages, is residential real estate versus commercial real estate. **Residential real estate** or housing real estate includes many property types, such as single-family homes, townhouses, condominiums, and manufactured housing. The housing or residential real estate sector is traditionally defined as including owner-occupied housing rather than large apartment complexes.

Within residential real estate, institutional investors are primarily concerned with investing in mortgages backed by housing and residential real estate. Institutional ownership in these instruments is usually established through pools of mortgages.

Commercial real estate properties include the following property sectors: office buildings, industrial centers, data centers, retail (malls and shopping centers, also referred to as "strips"), apartments, health-care facilities (medical office buildings and assisted-living centers), self-storage facilities, and hotels. Small properties may be directly and solely owned by a single investor. Alternatively, collections of numerous smaller properties and large commercial properties may be managed by a real estate company or through private equity real estate funds, which, in turn, are owned by several institutional investors as limited partners.

The volume of transactions fluctuates significantly depending on the stage of the business cycle, but it is generally high enough to support large investments by institutional investors. For the most part, residential and commercial real estate require very distinct methods of financial analysis. For example, the credit risk of mortgages on residential real estate is typically analyzed with a focus on the creditworthiness of the borrower. Mortgages on commercial real estate tend to focus on the analysis of the net cash flows from the property.

12.1.4 Private versus Public

Exposure to the real estate market, especially the equity side, can be achieved via private and public ownership. **Private real estate equity** investment involves the direct or indirect acquisition and management of actual physical properties that are not traded on an exchange. **Public real estate investment** entails the buying of shares of real estate investment companies and investing in other indirect exchange-traded forms of real estate (including futures and options on real estate indices and exchange-traded funds linked to real estate). **Private real estate** is also known as physical, direct, or non-exchange-traded real estate, and may take the form of equity through direct ownership of the property or debt via mortgage claims on the property.

The **private real estate market** comprises several segments: housing or residential real estate properties, commercial real estate properties, farmland, and timberland. Farmland and timberland, which were discussed in Chapter 9, are often discussed as real assets rather than as real estate. The relative advantages of investing in the private side of real estate equity are that investors or investment managers have the ability to choose specific properties, exert direct control of their investments, and enjoy the potential for tax-timing benefits.

12.1.5 Real Estate Categorization by Market Size

Institutional investors often categorize private commercial real estate equity investments by the size of the real estate market in which the property is located. Real estate assets are said to trade in a **primary real estate market** if the geographic location of the real estate is in a major metropolitan area of the world, with numerous large real estate properties or a healthy growth rate in real estate projects with easily recognizable names. Using the United States for illustration, examples range from cities such as Orlando, Florida, to very large metropolitan areas within huge cities, such as Manhattan in New York City. Large institutional investors focus on investments in these primary markets. Secondary real estate markets include moderately sized communities as well as suburban areas of primary markets. Tertiary real estate markets tend to have less recognizable names, smaller populations, and smaller real estate projects.

12.2 ADVANTAGES, DISADVANTAGES, AND STYLES OF REAL ESTATE INVESTMENTS

This section introduces potential determinants of allocations to institutional-quality real estate assets.

12.2.1 Five Potential Advantages of Real Estate

There are five common attributes of real estate that can encourage its inclusion in an investment portfolio:

1. Potential to offer absolute returns
2. Potential to hedge against unexpected inflation
3. Potential to provide diversification with stocks and bonds
4. Potential to provide cash inflows
5. Potential to provide income tax advantages

These potential advantages, the first three of which are related to portfolio risk, do not necessarily come without costs. In particular, to the extent that markets are competitive and efficient, market prices of real estate will tend to adjust, such that any risk-reducing advantages will be offset by lower expected returns. However, some of the disadvantages of private real estate ownership may lead to higher expected returns in the form of premiums for bearing risks, such as liquidity.

This list of potential advantages to real estate investment is not comprehensive. For example, another motivation could be to own all or part of a trophy property that offers name recognition, prestige, and enhanced reputation to the owner, such as a large, high-quality office property in a prominent location.

12.2.2 Three Potential Disadvantages of Real Estate

There are also aspects of real estate that can discourage its inclusion in an investment portfolio (unless the investor receives appropriate compensation in the form of higher expected returns). Included are these three potential disadvantages:

1. Heterogeneity
2. Lumpiness
3. Illiquidity

Real estate is a highly heterogeneous asset. This heterogeneity may be particularly burdensome in the initial and ongoing due diligence processes. As indicated in a previous section, real estate differs, as evidenced by the numerous categories of real estate. However, real estate can also be highly heterogeneous *within* its subcategories due to instances where there may be tremendous differences in their economic nature.

For example, consider two office buildings that are similar in size, construction, and location. The first office building has a 20-year noncancellable lease with a large well-capitalized and well-hedged corporation. The lease essentially locks in the rental revenues for the entire property for the next two decades. In this case, the annual income of the property will be similar to that of a corporate bond, and the value of the property to the investor will tend to fluctuate in response to the same factors affecting the value of a corporate bond issued by the tenant (i.e., riskless interest rate changes and changes in the credit spread on the debt of the tenant).

The second office building in the example is vacant. Both buildings are located in a geographic area with an economy strongly linked to oil prices. The value of this empty real estate asset will be especially sensitive to the supply of and demand for office space in the local real estate market. Thus, the value of this property will be driven by the forces that affect the region's economy—in this case, oil prices. The vacant property's value may behave more like equity prices in general and like oil stock prices in particular.

This example shows that assets within a specific type of real estate (e.g., private commercial real estate) may behave like debt or equity securities depending on the characteristics of the individual properties. A particular property may experience dramatic changes in its investment characteristics due to a specific event, such as the signing or termination of a very-long-term, noncancellable lease.

The second potential disadvantage to private real estate is lumpiness. **Lumpiness** describes when assets cannot be easily and inexpensively bought and sold in sizes or quantities that meet the preferences of the buyers and sellers. Listed equities of large companies are not lumpy, because purchases and sales can easily be made in the desired size by altering the number of shares in the transaction. Direct real estate ownership may be difficult to trade in sizes or quantities desired by a market participant. The indivisible nature of private real estate assets leads to problems with respect to high unit costs (i.e., large investment sizes) and relatively high transaction costs.

The final major disadvantage relates to the liquidity of private real estate. As a non-exchange-traded asset with a high unit cost, private real estate can be highly illiquid, especially when compared to stocks and bonds. An important implication of illiquidity is its effect on reported returns as well as its added risk challenges.

12.2.3 Real Estate Styles Overview

The premier approach to organizing private commercial real estate is through styles of real estate investing. **Styles of real estate investing** refers to the categorization of real estate property characteristics into core, value added, and opportunistic. In 2003, the National Council of Real Estate Investment Fiduciaries (NCREIF) defined these three styles as a way to classify real estate equity investment or real estate managers. Real estate investment styles assist an asset allocator in organizing and evaluating real estate opportunities, facilitate benchmarking and performance attribution, and help investment managers monitor style drift.

The three NCREIF styles divide real estate opportunities from least risky (core) to most risky (opportunistic), with value added in the middle. In terms of risk, core properties are most bond-like, and opportunistic properties are most equity-like. Core properties tend to offer reliable cash flows each year from rents and lease payments, whereas opportunistic properties offer potential capital appreciation and typically have little or no reliable income. Each of the three styles is more fully described in the following three sections.

12.2.4 Core Real Estate Style

Core real estate includes assets that achieve a relatively high percentage of their returns from income, are expected to have low volatility, are the most liquid, most developed, least leveraged, and most recognizable properties in a real estate portfolio, and include five specific categories: office, retail, industrial, multifamily, and hotels.

Although these properties have the greatest liquidity, they are not traded quickly relative to traditional investments. Core properties tend to be held for a long time to take full advantage of the lease and rental cash flows that they provide. The majority of their returns comes from cash flows rather than from value appreciation, and very little leverage is applied. Core properties are somewhat bond-like in the reliability of their income.

12.2.5 Value-Added Real Estate Style

Value-added real estate includes assets that exhibit one or more of the following characteristics: (1) achieving a substantial portion of their anticipated returns from appreciation in value, (2) exhibiting moderate volatility, and (3) not having the financial reliability of core properties. Value-added properties begin to stray from the more common and lower-risk real estate investments included in the core real estate style. The value-added real estate style includes hotels, resorts, assisted-care living facilities, low-income housing, outlet malls, hospitals, and the like. These properties tend to require a subspecialty within the real estate market to be managed well and can involve repositioning, renovation, and redevelopment of existing properties.

Relative to core properties, value-added properties are anticipated to produce less current income and to rely more on property appreciation to generate total return. However, property appreciation is subject to substantial uncertainty, and value-added properties as a whole have experienced prolonged periods of poor realized appreciation. Value-added properties can also include new properties that would otherwise be core properties except that they are not fully leased. A value-added property can also be an existing property that needs a new strategy, such as a major renovation, new tenants, or a new marketing campaign. These properties tend to use more leverage and generate a total return from both capital appreciation and income.

Pennsylvania's Public School Employees' Retirement System (PSERS) identifies value-added real estate as follows:

> *Value-added real estate investing typically focuses on both income and growth appreciation potential, where opportunities created by dislocation and inefficiencies between and within segments of the real estate capital markets are capitalized upon to enhance returns. Investments can include high-yield equity and debt investments and undervalued or impaired properties in need of repositioning, redevelopment, or leasing. Modest leverage is generally applied in value-added portfolios to facilitate the execution of a variety of value creation strategies. (PSERS 2007)*

12.2.6 Opportunistic Real Estate Style

Opportunistic real estate properties are expected to derive most or all of their returns from property appreciation and may exhibit substantial volatility in value and returns. The higher volatility of opportunistic properties relative to the other two styles may be due to a variety of characteristics, such as exposure to development risk, substantial leasing risk, or high leverage.

Opportunistic real estate moves away from a core/income approach to a capital appreciation approach. The majority of the returns from opportunistic properties comes from value appreciation over a three- to five-year period, at which time the investor exits or refinances the property. The capital appreciation of opportunistic real estate can come from development of raw property, redevelopment of property that is in disrepair, or acquisition of property that experiences substantial improvement in prospects through major changes, such as urban renewal.

12.2.7 Differentiating Real Estate Styles with Eight Attributes

The three NCREIF styles can be differentiated using eight major real estate attributes, or characteristics. These attributes were developed by NCREIF to distinguish the three types of real estate asset styles:

1. Property type (purpose of structure, e.g., general office versus specialty retail)
2. Life-cycle phase (e.g., new/developing versus mature/operating)
3. Occupancy (e.g., fully leased versus vacant)
4. Rollover concentration (tendency of assets to trade frequently)
5. Near-term rollover (likelihood that rollover is imminent)
6. Leverage
7. Market recognition (extent that properties are known to institutions)
8. Investment structure/control (extent of control and type of governance)

The styles and their attributes can be used to organize individual properties. Exhibit 12.1 provides descriptions of the three NCREIF styles using the eight attributes of individual real estate properties. Real estate style analysis can be applied to real estate managers (i.e., portfolios) in addition to individual properties. Exhibit 12.2 provides summary descriptions of the characteristics of real estate portfolios classified into the three NCREIF styles.

12.2.8 Three Purposes of Real Estate Style Analysis

Real estate styles are essentially locators. In other words, they are categories designed to help identify the space in which each property resides or a real estate manager operates. There are three main reasons for introducing styles into real estate portfolio analysis:

1. Performance measurement: Investors continually look for tools that can provide them with a better understanding of an investment's or a sector's objectives and success in accomplishing those objectives. This includes identifying peer groups, return objectives, range of risks, return or performance attribution, and peer performance. Simply put, styles may be useful in identifying appropriate benchmarks.
2. Monitoring style drift: Tracking style drift is another benefit of assessing the style of a portfolio. It is a fact of investing that portfolio managers occasionally drift from their stated risk, return, or other objectives. Classifying different styles of real estate investments allows an investor to assess the association between a portfolio and its underlying investment products as the portfolio changes over time. Identifying the concentration of a portfolio in terms of the styles for each

EXHIBIT 12.1 The Underlying Eight Attributes of the Three Real Estate Styles

	Core Attributes	Value-Added Attributes	Opportunistic Attributes
Property type	Major property types only: office, apartments, retail, and industrial	Major property types plus specialty retail, hospitality, senior/assisted-care housing, storage, low-income housing	Nontraditional property types, including speculative development for sale or rent and undeveloped land
Life-cycle phase	Fully operating	Operating and leasing	Development and newly constructed
Occupancy	High occupancy	Moderate to well-leased and/or substantially preleased development	Low economic occupancy
Rollover concentration	Tend to be held for a long period of time, forming the central component of the real estate portfolio, which is geared toward generating income rather than sales appreciation	Moderate rollover concentration—a higher percentage of the assets are held for a short- to intermediate-term sale and rollover into new assets	High rollover concentration risk—most of the assets are held for appreciation and resale
Near-term rollover	Low total near-term rollover	Moderate total near-term rollover	High total near-term rollover
Leverage	Low leverage	Moderate leverage	High leverage
Market recognition	Well-recognized institutional properties and locations	Institutional and emerging real estate markets	Secondary and tertiary markets and international real estate
Investment structure/control	Investment structures often have substantial direct control	Investment structures often have moderate control, but with security or a preferred liquidation position	Investment structures often have minimal control, usually in a limited partnership vehicle and with unsecured positions

EXHIBIT 12.2 Real Estate Portfolio Style Definitions

Core Portfolio	Value-Added Portfolio	Opportunistic Portfolio
A portfolio that includes a preponderance of core attributes. As a whole, the portfolio will have low lease exposure and low leverage. According to the NCREIF Open-End Diversified Core Equity (ODCE) index for Q3 2018, the long-run average leverage of core funds was 21.8%. A low percentage of noncore assets is acceptable. Such portfolios should achieve relatively high-income returns and exhibit relatively low volatility. The portfolio attributes should reflect the risk and return profile of the NCREIF Property Index (NPI).	A Portfolio that generally includes a mix of core real estate with other real estate investments that have a less reliable income stream. The portfolio as a whole is likely to have moderate lease exposure and moderate leverage. According to the NCREIF Fund index-CEVA for Q3 2017, the maximum leverage of value-added funds was 40%. Such portfolios would achieve a substantial portion of the return from the appreciation of real estate property values and should exhibit moderate volatility. A risk-and-return profile moderately greater than the MPI is expected.	A portfolio predominantly of noncore investments that is expected to derive most of its return from the appreciation of real estate property values and that may exhibit substantial volatility in the total return. The increased volatility and appreciation risk may be due to a variety of factors, such as exposure to development risk, substantial leasing risk, high degree of leverage, or a combination of moderate risk factors. A risk-and-return profile substantially greater than the NPI is expected.

property facilitates a better understanding of the portfolio's risk level at any given point in time.

3. Style diversification: The ability to compare the risk-return profile of a manager relative to the manager's style may allow for a better diversification of the portfolio, since an investor may be able to construct a portfolio that has a more robust risk-return profile if there is a better understanding of each real estate manager's style location. Simply put, style may be useful in understanding risk, diversifying risk, and managing or controlling risk.

It should be noted that the preceding real estate styles are primarily applied to private commercial real estate equity, although the concepts can also be applied to publicly traded real estate.

12.3 REAL ESTATE STYLE BOXES

The first part of this chapter detailed the use of NCREIF real estate styles to differentiate real estate properties and portfolios by their risks and returns. These categories can be used to create and use real estate style boxes.

Real estate style boxes use two categorizations of real estate to generate a box or matrix that can be used to characterize properties or portfolios. Exhibit 12.3

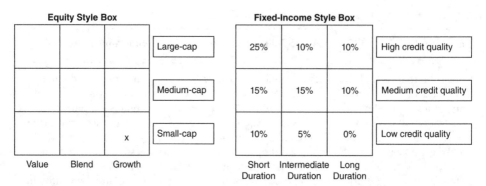

EXHIBIT 12.3   Equity and Fixed-Income Style Boxes

illustrates style boxes for traditional investments. In the case of the equity style box on the left, the box has equity style on the horizontal axis (e.g., value versus growth) and capitalization size on the vertical axis. In traditional bond analysis, duration is usually on the horizontal axis, with credit quality on the vertical axis.

Style boxes are applied to individual assets, managers, or portfolios. For a style box of an individual stock or bond, the box contains an X in the square most descriptive of the asset. Similarly, managers can be identified with an X in a style box to denote their primary focus. The equity style box in Exhibit 12.3 illustrates the use of an X in a single square to denote the primary characteristic of a hypothetical small-cap growth fund. Portfolios and funds are often identified with percentages in each square denoting how much of the fund's or portfolio's holdings are invested in assets of each location. The fixed-income box on the right of Exhibit 12.3 illustrates the use of percentages in each of the nine squares.

Exhibit 12.4 illustrates real estate style boxes. There is no uniform standard for style boxes in the real estate industry. Clearly, for private commercial equity, the styles of NCREIF are prime candidates for the horizontal axis. Primary, secondary, and tertiary real estate markets are potentially useful for the vertical axis. The left side of Exhibit 12.4 illustrates a potential style box and hypothetical allocations. In this illustration, a real estate style box serves as a method of better understanding the top-down allocations of a real estate portfolio. A real estate style box can also be

Real Estate Allocation Style Box				**Gross Expected Returns Style Box**			
50%	15%	5%	Primary	$E(R) = 7\%$	$E(R) = 7.5\%$	$E(R) = 10\%$	Primary
10%	5%	5%	Secondary	$E(R) = 7.5\%$	$E(R) = 8\%$	$E(R) = 11\%$	Secondary
5%	5%	0%	Tertiary	$E(R) = 8\%$	$E(R) = 9.5\%$	$E(R) = 12\%$	Tertiary
Core	Value-Added	Opportunistic		Core	Value-Added	Opportunistic	

EXHIBIT 12.4   Real Estate Style Boxes

used to denote the location of a single manager or a single property by placing an X in the relevant square.

12.4 RESIDENTIAL MORTGAGES

This section examines residential mortgages from the perspective of the investor. The primary issues regarding residential mortgage investments are the timing and safety of the payments.

A mortgage loan can be simply defined as a loan secured by property. The property serves as collateral against the amount borrowed. If the borrower defaults on the loan, then the lender can take possession of the property. The borrower can usually partially or fully prepay the mortgage before the contractual due date. These partial prepayments may be made by borrowers to save on future interest payments. However, lenders may add prepayment penalties to mortgages to discourage borrowers from refinancing prior to maturity.

A major distinction between mortgages is whether the interest rate used to determine mortgage payments is fixed or variable. A **fixed-rate mortgage** has interest charges and interest payments based on a single rate established at the initiation of the mortgage. A **variable-rate mortgage** has interest charges and interest payments based on a rate that is allowed to vary over the life of the mortgage based on terms established at the initiation of the mortgage.

Another major distinction between mortgages is residential versus commercial. Residential and commercial mortgages and their markets differ in a number of ways, such as in the structure of the actual loans and with regard to the characteristics of the securitized markets. **Residential mortgage loans** are typically taken out by individual households on properties that generate no explicit rental income, since the houses are usually owner occupied. Therefore, the credit risk of residential mortgages depends on the borrower's income and financial position, in addition to the characteristics of the property. In contrast, commercial mortgage loans are largely taken out by corporations or other legal entities. The risk of mortgages on commercial properties often focuses on the rental income generated by the property, which can be used to make the mortgage payments. Another feature of residential mortgage loans is their tendency to be more homogeneous in terms of their price behavior than commercial loans.

12.4.1 Fixed-Rate Mortgages

A fixed-rate, constant payment, fully amortized loan has equal monthly payments throughout the life of the loan. These loans give the residential mortgage market some of its unique characteristics, as discussed later in the chapter. The fixed-rate and constant payment nature of these loans make the value of the loans subject to interest rate risk and inflation risk. The monthly payments of a fixed-rate loan can be calculated using the formula for the present value of a constant annuity, with the payment amount factored into the left-hand side of Equation 12.1:

$$MP = MB \times \{i/[1 - (1 + i)^{-n}]\} \tag{12.1}$$

where *MP* is the constant monthly payment, *MB* is the mortgage balance or total amount borrowed, *i* is the monthly interest rate (defined as the stated annual rate divided by 12), and *n* is the number of months in the term of the loan.

☞ APPLICATION 12.4.1A

Assume that a borrower takes out a $100,000, 25-year mortgage (300 months), at a 6% annual nominal interest rate (a monthly interest rate of 6%/12, or 0.5%). What is the mortgage's monthly payment?

The monthly payments (principal plus interest) can be calculated using Equation 12.1 directly, as follows:

$$MP = \$100,000 \times \{0.005/[1 - (1.005)^{-300}]\} = \$644.30$$

Using a financial calculator, the monthly mortgage payment is calculated by inputting the following values: *n* (number of periods) = 12 × 25 = 300 months, *i* (interest rate per period) = 6%/12 = 0.5%, *PV* (present value) = +/− $100,000, *FV* (future value) = $0, and solving for (compute) *PMT* (payment).

The *PV* is entered as either a positive or a negative number, depending on the calculator that is used. Note that some financial calculators require that the interest rate of 0.5% be entered as .005 and some as .5. Also, some financial calculators require prior clearing, input of negative numbers, or output of negative numbers and may or may not require input of other values, such as the *FV*. Spreadsheets contain functions analogous to the financial calculator functions that are demonstrated throughout this chapter. In Excel, the payment can be calculated using = pmt (annual rate/12, number of months, loan amount).

Note that payment amounts in practice are rounded to the nearest cent.

An important feature of the fixed-rate mortgage is that the proportion of the monthly payments that is applied against the principal and the proportion that consists of interest charges change over the lifetime of the loan, as the outstanding principal balance declines. In the early years of the mortgage, the largest portions of the payments represent interest payments rather than principal repayments. The interest component is equal to the monthly interest rate multiplied by the outstanding loan amount from the beginning of the current month or the end of the previous month.

The principal repayment component of the monthly mortgage payment is the residual between the total payment and the interest portion. Reduction in principal due to payments is known as **amortization**. Exhibit 12.5 illustrates the amortization schedule for the example just presented: a $100,000 mortgage with a fixed-rate (0.5% a month) constant payment ($644.30 per month) that is fully amortized. An asset is **fully amortized** when its principal is reduced to zero.

As can be seen in Exhibit 12.5, the first interest payment is equal to $100,000 × 0.5% = $500.00. Given that the fixed monthly mortgage payment is $644.30, the principal repayment in the first month will be $644.30 − $500.00 = $144.30, and the end-of-month mortgage balance will decline from $100,000 to $99,855.70.

EXHIBIT 12.5 Amortization Schedule for a Fixed-Rate (6% per year), Constant Payment ($644.30 per month), Fully Amortized 25-Year Mortgage of $100,000, Assuming No Unscheduled Principal Payments

Month	Beginning-of-Month Mortgage Balance	Mortgage Payment	Interest Payment	Principal Payment	End-of-Month Mortgage Balance
1	$100,000.00	$644.30	$500.00	$144.30	$99,855.70
2	$99,855.70	$644.30	$499.28	$145.02	$99,710.68
3	$99,710.68	$644.30	$498.55	$145.75	$99,564.93
⋮	⋮	⋮	⋮	⋮	⋮
59	$90,318.56	$644.30	$451.59	$192.71	$90,125.86
60	$90,125.86	$644.30	$450.63	$193.67	$89,932.18
61	$89,932.18	$644.30	$449.66	$194.64	$89,737.55
⋮	⋮	⋮	⋮	⋮	⋮
299	$1,279.96	$644.30	$6.40	$637.90	$642.06
300	$642.06	$644.30	$3.21	$641.09	$1 (rounded)

☞ APPLICATION 12.4.1B

What would be the outstanding mortgage balance at the start of month 61 in terms of remaining principal of a $100,000, 25-year mortgage (300 months), at a 6% annual nominal interest rate?

As shown in Exhibit 12.5, the outstanding mortgage balance at the start of month 61 in terms of remaining principal is $89,932.18, five years after the loan has been taken out. This amount does not correspond exactly to a present value computation of the balance using the exact payment amount of $644.30 (using a financial calculator: $n = 12 \times 20 = 240$, $i = 6.0\%/12 = 0.5\%$, $PMT = \$644.30$, $FV = \$0$, solve for PV). The reason is that mortgage payments are values that in practice are rounded to the nearest cent, and mortgage amortization computations (such as Exhibit 12.5) are based on this rounded payment amount ($644.30) rather than a more exact payment amount ($644.3014).

For simplicity, this discrepancy caused by rounding error is disregarded in the computations that follow. Notice that, over time, the proportion of interest payment to principal payment declines, and increasingly a larger portion of the total payment is allocated to paying down the principal.

Fixed-rate residential mortgages are valued similarly to bonds. As the market level of interest rates increases, the present value of the future payments declines. If the appropriate market interest rate remains at 6% per year, the market value of the mortgage would be equal to the outstanding principal balance. However, at a new and higher market interest rate, the value of the mortgage would drop below the principal balance.

Exhibit 12.5 illustrates the amortization of a fixed-rate mortgage in the absence of unscheduled principal repayments. If the borrower makes **unscheduled principal payments,** which are payments above and beyond the scheduled mortgage payments, the mortgage's balance will decline more quickly than illustrated in Exhibit 12.5, and the mortgage will terminate early. In traditional mortgages, payments that exceed the required payment reduce the principal payment but do not lower required subsequent payments until the mortgage is paid off.

☞ **APPLICATION 12.4.1C**

Suppose that the market interest rate for the mortgage in Exhibit 12.5 rises to 7.5%. What is the market value of the mortgage, assuming it is the start of month 61? The market value is equal to $79,978.33 (using a financial calculator: $n = 12 \times 20 = 240, i = 7.5\%/12 = 0.625\%, PMT = \$644.30, FV = \$0$, solve for PV). At a new and lower market interest rate of 4.5%, the market value of the mortgage is equal to $101,841.56 (found as before except that $i = 4.5\%/12 = 0.375\%$). These values illustrate that the market value of fixed-rate mortgages, as fixed-income securities, varies inversely with market interest rates.

Unscheduled principal payments cause a wealth transfer between the borrower and the lender, depending on the relationship between the mortgage's interest rate and current market interest rates. When market rates are lower than the mortgage rate, unscheduled principal payments generally benefit the borrower and harm the lender. The lender receives additional cash flows that, if reinvested at prevailing interest rates, will earn less return than the mortgage offers. Borrowers can make unscheduled prepayments to reduce the total interest costs of their mortgage by an amount greater than the amount that they could earn from interest income in the market. Thus, borrowers have an incentive to make prepayments on mortgages when interest rates decline below the mortgage's rate.

When market rates are higher than the mortgage rate, unscheduled principal payments generally benefit the lender and harm the borrower. The lender receives additional cash flows that can be reinvested at prevailing interest rates that will earn more return than the mortgage offers. Borrowers are harmed by prepaying a low-rate mortgage when they could earn more by investing in the market at the new and higher rates. Borrowers may make such payments due to idiosyncratic reasons, such as selling the property, refinancing due to liquidity problems, or other personal reasons.

The ability of the borrower to make or not make unscheduled principal payments is an option to the borrower: the borrower's **prepayment option**. The option is a call option in which the mortgage borrower, much like a corporation with a callable bond, can repurchase its debt at a fixed strike price. Therefore, a mortgage borrower benefits from increased interest rate volatility. The lender, on the other hand, has written the call option and suffers from increased interest rate volatility. The key point is that fixed-rate mortgage investing has interest rate risk that includes the interest rate risk of the borrower's prepayment option. While the prepayment option may be viewed as a call option on the value of the debt, the option may also be viewed as a put option on interest rates. Just like a call option on a price, a put option on a rate rises in value when rates fall and prices rise. Both option views illustrate that during times of declining interest rates and rising fixed-income prices, it may be to the borrower's advantage to refinance the loan, replacing the current high-interest-rate, high-priced debt with a new loan at a lower interest rate.

It must be remembered, however, that options are not free goods. The lender demands compensation for writing the prepayment call option to the borrower.

Although the option may not be explicitly priced as part of the loan, it is implicitly priced in the form of a higher interest rate on the mortgage loan or in up-front points, or fees, charged to the borrower.

12.4.2 Interest-Only Mortgages

Some fixed-rate mortgages are interest-only mortgages, which means that the monthly payments consist entirely of interest payments for some initial period. The two most widely used interest-only loans are both 30-year mortgages. The first begins with a 10-year interest-only period, followed by a 20-year fully amortizing period; this type of loan is known as 10/20. The second begins with a 15-year interest-only period, followed by a 15-year fully amortizing period; this type of loan is known as 15/15. A 25-year mortgage with a 10-year interest-only period would be referred to as a 10/15 interest-only mortgage. In each case, the interest-only payments are equal to the product of the principal balance and the monthly rate. When the mortgage commences amortization, the payments are computed like fixed-payment mortgages except that they are based on the remaining and shorter period of the mortgage's life.

☞ APPLICATION 12.4.2A

Consider a $100,000, 25-year mortgage that is structured as a 10/15 interest only mortgage, with an annual rate of 6%. What would the payments be for the first 10 and the last 15 years?

For the first 10 years, the monthly payments, which are interest only, would be $500 ($100,000 × 6.0%/12). Between years 11 and 25, the monthly fixed payment necessary to fully amortize the mortgage for the remaining 15 years would be $843.86 (using a financial calculator: $n = 12 \times 15 = 180$, $i = 6\%/12 = 0.5\%$, $PV = +/- \$100,000$, $FV = \$0$, solve for PMT).

Interest-only mortgages have the potential advantage that the monthly payments during the interest-only period are lower than those in the case of a fully amortized loan ($500 versus $644.30). However, during the amortization period the monthly payments are higher ($843.86 versus $644.30), as the borrower has fewer years to amortize the loan (15 years versus 25 or 30 years).

12.4.3 Variable-Rate Mortgages

Particularly during the period from 2004 to 2006, mortgage markets shifted toward increased use of variable-rate or adjustable-rate mortgages (ARMs) and away from fixed-rate mortgages. Although the initial payments in the case of ARMs are calculated in the same manner as conventional fixed-rate loans, the payments are not necessarily constant during the life of the loan, as the interest rate is periodically adjusted by the lender, generally to reflect changes in underlying short-term market interest rates, as prescribed in the mortgage agreement.

Consider a hypothetical variable-rate mortgage in which the interest rate changes each month and is set equal to the one-month interest rate prevailing at the time.

In this extreme and hypothetical example, the mortgage lender would receive the same interest as if the lender had placed funds in a series of short-term (one-month) interest-bearing accounts. Therefore, investors in this hypothetical variable-rate mortgage would have the same interest rate risk that investors face in the short-term money market. In effect, and ignoring default and reset limits, a variable-rate mortgage that fully resets every X months behaves to the lender or mortgage investor like a series of investments in short-term fixed-income accounts, each with a maturity of X months.

The market value of a variable-rate mortgage (absent default) behaves like a money market account to the extent that the mortgage's rate adjusts quickly and without limits. Therefore, an obvious advantage of a variable-rate type of mortgage to a lender is that it protects the lender from the valuation fluctuations due to interest rate changes experienced with fixed-rate mortgages. An obvious disadvantage of variable-rate loans is the risk to the borrower that interest rates will increase. A variable-rate loan provides the advantage to the borrower of substantially lower initial interest rates.

Exhibit 12.6 demonstrates the payment changes for a variable-rate mortgage.

Suppose that a $100,000, 25-year mortgage is taken out. The initial interest rate that will apply for the first full year is 7%, compounded monthly. This implies that the monthly mortgage payment during the first year is $706.78 ($n = 12 \times 25 = 300$, $i = 7\%/12$, $PV = +/- \$100,000$, $FV = \$0$, solve for PMT) and that at the end of the first year, the mortgage balance will be $98,470.30 ($n = 12 \times 24 = 288$, $i = 7\%/12$, $PMT = \$706.78$, $FV = \$0$, solve for PV). The variable-rate mortgage begins the same as a fixed-rate mortgage in terms of computational methods, although it usually has a lower initial rate. The payments change when the variable rate changes, as illustrated in Exhibit 12.6.

The monthly payments of the variable-rate mortgage in Exhibit 12.6 are based on an adjustable rate that can vary from the 7% initial rate beginning in month 13 (end of year 1). This variable rate, which applies for the whole next year, is based on an index rate. An **index rate** is a variable interest rate used in the determination of the mortgage's stated interest rate. Index rates fluctuate freely in the money markets and can be based, for example, on the yield of one-year Treasury securities. Variable rates typically include a margin rate. A **margin rate** is the spread by which the stated

EXHIBIT 12.6   Amortization Schedule for a Variable-Rate, Variable Payment, Fully Amortized 25-Year Mortgage of $100,000, Assuming No Unscheduled Principal Payments

Year	Index Rate	+	Margin Rate	=	Interest Rate	Beginning of Year	Monthly	End of Year
1					7.0%	$100,000.00	$706.78	$98,470.30
2	8.5%		1.5%		10.0%	$98,470.30	$903.36	$97,430.75
3	10.0%		1.5%		11.5%	$97,430.75	$1,006.05	$96,515.25
4	8.0%		1.5%		9.5%	$96,515.25	$872.94	$95,150.13

mortgage rate is set above the index rate. (This should not be confused with the same term used to describe a rate associated with margin debt in a brokerage account.)

This example uses a margin rate of 1.5%. This margin rate is determined as part of the original terms of the mortgage and is added to compensate for the expected or assessed degree of risk, including interest rate risk and the riskiness of the borrower.

The total interest rate is the sum of the index rate and the margin rate.

☞ APPLICATION 12.4.3A

What would the monthly payment be for the mortgage in Exhibit 12.6 in the second year, when the mortgage's rate climbs to 10.0%? Note that it is necessary to decrease the mortgage's original principal to reflect amortization and decrease the months remaining by 12, to 288.

From Exhibit 12.6, the monthly mortgage payment that the borrower would have to make during the second year, for which a higher index rate of 8.5% applies, is equal to \$903.36 ($n = 12 \times 24 = 288$, $i = 10\%/12$, $PV = +/- \$98,470.30$, $FV = \$0$, solve for PMT). Notice that the increase in interest rates between the first year and the second year has caused a substantial increase (27.81%) in the monthly payment that the borrower is obligated to make.

The process of determining payments continues into the third year, with the interest rate and longevity of the mortgage being adjusted at each reset in order to determine the new payment. The mortgage balance at the end of the second year is equal to \$97,430.75, which is determined from the amortization, assuming no unscheduled principal payments (using a financial calculator: $n = 12 \times 23 = 276$, $i = 10\%/12$, $PMT = \$903.36$, $FV = \$0$, solve for PV). The mortgage balance at the end of the second year, \$97,430.75, is then used, along with the third-year mortgage rate, 11.5%, to compute the payments for the third year. This process of computing the remaining mortgage balance and using that balance to compute the new monthly payments, considering the new interest rate that applies each year, continues over the life of the variable-rate portion of the mortgage.

It is also common for interest rates on ARMs to be capped. An **interest rate cap** is a limit on interest rate adjustments used in mortgages and derivatives with variable interest rates. In the previous example, suppose that the increase in interest rates was capped to 2% during any one year and to a total increase of 4% during the life of the mortgage. The effect of these interest rate caps on the mortgage balance and on the monthly payments would be to prevent the mortgage's rate from rising above the annual or lifetime caps. Thus, with the given 2% cap, the mortgage rate for the second year would be capped at 9% and would be used in place of 10% for the second-year calculations. Further, the mortgage rate for the third year would be capped at 11% and would be used in place of 11.5% for the third-year calculations due to the limitation of lifetime interest rate increases to 4% over the mortgage's lifetime ($7\% + 4\% = 11\%$) as well as the 2% per year limitation. Obviously, the borrower must pay for these caps in the form of a higher initial mortgage rate or index rate to compensate the lender for the potential negative effects that the cap rates may have on the lender's future income from the mortgage if future uncapped interest rates were to rise above the mortgage's cap.

12.4.4 Other Types of Mortgages

Fixed-rate and variable-rate mortgage loans have other variations as well. For example, it is common, particularly with variable-rate mortgages, for the initial interest rate to be low when compared to short-term market rates and for that low rate to be fixed for an initial period. After this period, the mortgage rate is calculated based on the lender's standard variable interest rate. Another type of loan with relatively low initial payments is a graduated payment loan. This loan is made at an initially fixed interest rate that is relatively low but scheduled to increase slowly over the first few years. Both of these variations are designed to help borrowers qualify for the loan and be able to make the initial payments on the loan. Historically, defaults on mortgage loans tend to be concentrated in the first few years of a loan. Therefore, by offering a reduced rate for the initial years, the lender is not only using the lower rate as a tool for attracting business but also attempting to mitigate the default risk in the early years of the mortgage. Note that in an environment of steadily increasing housing prices, if a mortgage defaults several years after being initiated, the losses to the lender should be minimal, since the collateral would most likely exceed the loan amount.

Another variation in variable-rate mortgages provides payment flexibility. An **option adjustable-rate mortgage (option ARM)** is an adjustable-rate mortgage that provides borrowers with the flexibility to make one of several possible payments on their mortgage every month. The payment alternatives from which borrowers may select each month typically include an interest-only payment, one or more payments based on given amortization periods, or a prespecified minimum payment amount. Thus, borrowers are granted flexibility to make lower payments than would be required in a traditional mortgage. Option ARMs typically offer low introductory rates and may allow borrowers to defer some interest payments until later years.

One feature of option ARMs that can exacerbate default risk is that they may not be fully amortizing. In fact, when an option ARM allows payments that are below the interest charged on the loan, the loan has negative amortization. **Negative amortization** occurs when the interest owed is greater than the payments being made such that the deficit is added to the principal balance on the loan, causing the principal balance to increase through time. This negative amortization can generate higher probabilities of default from borrowers taking on too much debt or failing to prepare for future payments.

A further mortgage variation is a loan that includes some form of balloon payment. A **balloon payment** is a large scheduled future payment. Rather than amortizing a mortgage to $0 over its lifetime (e.g., 25 years), the mortgage is amortized to the balloon payment. In other words, at the end of the loan, there is an outstanding principal amount due that is equal to the balloon payment. The balloon payment allows for a lower monthly payment, given the same mortgage rate, since the mortgage is not fully amortized to $0. Balloon payments due in a relatively short time period (compared to traditional mortgage maturities of 15 to 30 years) may lower the interest rate risk to the lender and permit a lower mortgage rate.

☞ APPLICATION 12.4.4A

To illustrate balloon payments, assume that the borrower and the lender in the original example decide that the $100,000 loan made at the fixed rate of 6% per year compounded monthly for 25 years will amortize to a $70,000 balance on the 25-year maturity date rather than being fully amortized to $0. This amount of $70,000 is known as a balloon payment and will be due at the end of 25 years. In this case, the monthly payment would be equal to $543.29 (using a financial calculator: $n = 12 \times 25 = 300$, $i = 6\%/12 = 0.5\%$, $PV = +/- \$100,000$, $FV = \$70,000$, solve for PMT). Notice that the $543.29 monthly payment is less than the $644.30 payment that was computed for the case of the fully amortizing loan, even though the interest rates in both mortgages are equal to 6%.

An extreme example of a balloon payment mortgage is when the loan payments are only interest, which means that no regular principal repayments are required. Therefore, at the end of the loan, all the capital is due. In the previous example, the mortgage's initial value of $100,000 would be inserted as the balloon payment, or *FV*. The remaining payment would simply be the interest on $100,000 at 6% per year, or $500 per month. This interest-only form reduces monthly payments.

In an ideal scenario, the capital appreciation of the actual property's value will be substantial, and the borrower will gain substantial equity in the property even though the principal amount of the mortgage remains constant.

12.4.5 Residential Mortgages and Default Risk

Default risk is dispersion in economic outcomes due to the actual or potential failure of a borrower to make scheduled payments. For most residential mortgages, the full repayment of the mortgage is backed by a public or private guarantee, such that mortgage investors are focused on interest rate risk rather than default risk—that is, mortgages may be insured by a governmental entity or a commercial insurance company that specializes in backing mortgage loans. These firms that insure the performance of the borrower on mortgage loans will reimburse the lender if the borrower does not pay principal and interest as scheduled and the proceeds from the property sale do not fully repay the balance on the mortgage loan.

Insured mortgage loans are generally extended based on an analysis of the underlying property and the creditworthiness of the borrower. However, especially in the years prior to the 2007 global credit crisis, increasing percentages of newly issued mortgages were uninsured and had borrowers with relatively high credit risk. Uninsured mortgages with borrowers of relatively high credit risk are generally known as **subprime mortgages. Prime mortgages** are offered to borrowers with lower levels of credit risk and higher levels of creditworthiness.

Analysis of the creditworthiness of the borrower and the protection provided to the lender by the underlying real estate asset is fundamental analysis that generally relies substantially on ratio analysis. Ratios regarding the creditworthiness of the borrower often focus on the ratio of some measure of the borrower's housing expenses to some measure of the borrower's income. For example, a debt-to-income ratio is computed as the total housing expenses (including principal, interest, taxes, and insurance) divided by the monthly income of the borrower, and it might be required to be below a specified percentage for the borrower to qualify for mortgage insurance.

The front-end ratio, including only housing costs, may be limited to 28% of gross income; the back-end ratio, including both housing costs and other debts, such as credit cards and automobile loans, may be limited to 36% of gross income. The exact definitions of these types of ratios vary and are part of a larger fundamental analysis that includes indicators of creditworthiness, such as credit scores and credit history.

Fundamental analysis of the real estate property underlying the mortgage typically includes an appraisal and analysis of factors regarding the property, such as availability of services and structural integrity. Ratio analysis is also important in the analysis of the property. Specifically, the **loan-to-value ratio** (**LTV ratio**) is the ratio of the amount of the loan to the value (either market or appraised) of the property. Residential mortgages with LTV ratios of 80% are often viewed as being very well collateralized. LTV ratios of up to 95% are commonly allowed for insured residential mortgages.

12.5 COMMERCIAL MORTGAGES

Commercial mortgage loans are loans backed by commercial real estate (multifamily apartments, hotels, offices, retail and industrial properties) rather than owner-occupied residential properties. In contrast to the relative standardization of residential mortgage loans, there is far greater variety when it comes to mortgages in the commercial sector, a fact that has hindered trading of commercial mortgages in secondary markets.

12.5.1 Commercial Mortgage Characteristics

Mortgage loans on commercial real estate differ in a number of respects from those in the residential market. Almost all commercial loans involve some form of balloon payment on maturity, since the loan term is almost always shorter than the time required to fully amortize the loan at the required payment. Furthermore, due to the large size of commercial real estate projects, few individuals participate in this market as borrowers or lenders. Most of the borrowers are commercial or financial firms that possess greater financial sophistication than the average homeowner.

An important distinction when examining commercial mortgages is the nature of the loan and, in particular, whether it is for completed projects or for development purposes. Most development loans are shorter-term and phased, wherein the developer draws down funds only as required during the construction phase. This is in contrast to loans for existing properties, which tend to have a longer horizon, usually in the region of 5 to 10 years, and for which the full amount of the loan is drawn immediately.

12.5.2 Commercial Mortgage Default Risk

Whereas residential mortgage investors are primarily concerned about interest rate risk and prepayment rates, commercial mortgage investors typically face substantial default risk related to the credit risk of the borrower as well as the price risk of the underlying collateral (i.e., property). Default risk is related to covenants and recourse.

In general, the covenants in a commercial mortgage are more detailed than those in a corresponding residential loan document. **Covenants** are promises made by the borrower to the lender, such as requirements that the borrower maintain the property in good repair and continue to meet specified financial conditions. Failure to meet the covenants can trigger default and make the full loan amount due immediately. The view that covenants benefit lenders at the expense of borrowers is naïve. Although covenants lower the credit risk to the lender, they are presumably offered by the borrower in exchange for better terms on the loan (e.g., a lower interest rate). The severity and details of covenants required by lenders vary across firms. To some extent, borrowers choose to offer particular covenants by selecting lenders that demand those covenants, because they prefer the lower rates of loans attached to those covenants.

Commercial loans tend to contain far more detail concerning such issues as the seniority of the loan. As with all debts, particularly at the corporate level, lenders need to know their position with respect to seniority in the event of default or financial difficulty. For instance, it may be the case that if the loan is senior or is the original debt (also called the first lien or first mortgage) on the property, the lender has to provide permission before subsequent debts (such as second liens or second mortgages) can be incurred. Another key element in any commercial debt deal is the recourse that the lender has to the borrowing entity. **Recourse** is the set of rights or means that an entity such as a lender has in order to protect its investment. Recourse may include how the loan is secured, such as the potential ability of the lender to take possession of the property in the event of a default and the potential ability of the lender to pursue recovery from the borrower's other assets. Another type of covenant included in many commercial mortgages but not included in residential mortgages is restriction on the distribution of the rental income from the property, with perhaps a specified proportion being redirected to a reserve account rather than paid straight to the owner. A lender may also insist on a minimum deposit or balance to be maintained in an account with the lender.

In addition to explicit covenants with regard to the debt, commercial mortgages may come attached with a proviso (i.e., condition or limitation) relating to the management and operation of the property. Lenders may insist that minimum levels of cash flow, net operating income, and earnings before interest and taxes need to be achieved or that rental levels may not fall below a previously specified level. Such provisions are designed to ensure that the property is able to generate sufficient income on an ongoing basis for the borrower to service the loan. Lenders may even insist on having some form of either control or consultation with regard to leasing policies, such as examination of new lease terms or credit checks on potential tenants.

Finally, in order to mitigate the risk to which they are exposed, lenders commonly use a **cross-collateral provision**, wherein the collateral for one loan is used as collateral for another loan. For example, say a corporation has borrowed twice, securing each loan with a property; with a cross-collateral provision, both properties would be used as collateral for both loans. If the corporation fully pays off one of the loans and wishes to sell the related property, the lender may prevent the sale because the property is still serving as collateral to the other loan.

12.5.3 Financial Ratios for Commercial Mortgages and Default Risk

Whereas a large number of residential mortgages are insured against default risk, commercial mortgages are generally exposed to default risk. Therefore, commercial mortgage investing usually involves fundamental analysis of default risk. Further, while fundamental analysis of residential mortgage default risk focuses on the credit risk of the borrower, fundamental analysis of commercial mortgage default risk focuses primarily on the role of rental income from the property in covering the mortgage payments.

As with residential loans, the LTV ratio, both at the origination of the loan and on an ongoing basis, is a key measure used by lenders. The LTV ratio at which a lender will issue a loan varies depending on the lender, the property sector, and the geographic market in which the property is located, as well as the stage of the real estate cycle and other circumstances, such as the borrower's creditworthiness. Financial institutions tend to lend at lower LTV ratios in the commercial sector than in the residential sector. It would be rare for senior debt in commercial properties to be lent at an LTV ratio in excess of 75%. Commercial borrowers, then, typically need a larger down payment or equity contribution than do borrowers purchasing residential real estate.

Given that commercial real estate generates rental income, lenders also examine a variety of income-based measures, in addition to the LTV ratio, when assessing the credit risk of a loan. For instance, lenders typically examine the **interest coverage ratio**, which can be defined as the property's net operating income divided by the loan's interest payments. The interest coverage ratio allows lenders to analyze the level of protection they have in terms of a borrower's ability to service a debt from the property's operating income. Senior secured debt lenders usually require that borrowers meet a minimum coverage ratio of 1.2 to 1.3. This means that the projected net income must be at least 20% to 30% greater than the projected interest payments. A related measure is the **debt service coverage ratio (DSCR)**, which is the ratio of the property's net operating income to all loan payments, including the amortization of the loan. A final typically used key ratio with an even broader definition of expenses is the fixed charges ratio. The **fixed charges ratio** is the ratio of the property's net operating income to all fixed charges that the borrower pays annually. The risk of default needs to be constantly monitored by mortgage investors. Research by Esaki notes that default rates of commercial mortgages are highly cyclical and tend to be explained by both market conditions and lender policies.[1] Loans taken out, for example, during the real estate booms of the late 1980s and mid-2000s—periods that witnessed not only a booming real estate market but also liberal lending policies (including LTV ratios greater than 100%, along with fewer or weaker covenants)—eventually recorded high default rates. In contrast, loans issued during the 1990s experienced much lower default rates, due in part to more conservative lending policies during that period. A major difference between residential and commercial lending is that it is far more likely that defaulting commercial loans will be restructured rather than moved directly to foreclosure, due in part to the size of the individual loans. Esaki, for instance, finds that 40% of defaulting commercial loans were restructured.[2]

12.6 MORTGAGE-BACKED SECURITIES MARKET

This section discusses the mortgage-backed securities market. **Mortgage-backed securities (MBS)** are a type of asset-backed security that is secured by a mortgage or pool of mortgages. In recent decades, MBS have facilitated cost-efficient real estate financing but have also been blamed for facilitating destabilizing speculation. Although most attention has been focused on the **residential mortgage-backed securities (RMBS)** market, which is backed by residential mortgage loans, there was substantial growth in the commercial mortgage-backed securities market in the years leading up to the real estate and financial crisis that began in 2007.

There are two basic types of MBS differing by the extent, if any, to which they partition risk within different classes of securities. A **pass-through MBS** is perhaps the simplest MBS and consists of the issuance of a homogeneous class of securities with pro rata rights to the cash flows of the underlying pool of mortgage loans. **Collateralized mortgage obligations (CMOs)** extend this MBS mechanism to create different security classes, called tranches, which have different priorities to receiving cash flows and therefore different risks. CMOs are discussed in Part 5 on structured products.

12.6.1 Residential Mortgage Prepayment Options

Residential mortgage markets have been dominated in size by insured mortgages for which there is little or no risk of default to the lender. Most mortgages have scheduled principal repayments that amortize the mortgage's principal value from the initial mortgage amount to zero over the mortgage's scheduled lifetime. Most mortgages also allow the borrower the option to make additional and unscheduled principal payments without penalty. Future unscheduled prepayments are the key unknown variable in determining the values of insured mortgages and mortgage pools.

Residential mortgages are callable bonds. The lender is short a call option on the value of the loan, which may also be viewed as being short a put option on mortgage rates. Borrowers may exercise this option by refinancing if interest rates decline. Exercise of this prepayment option when interest rates fall acts to the detriment of lenders, which presumably must reinvest the prepaid principal at the lower rates.

Unscheduled mortgage principal payments include full mortgage prepayments (e.g., when a loan is refinanced or when it is repaid because a homeowner is moving) and partial repayments, when borrowers decide to make one or more mortgage payments that exceed the minimum required payment (e.g., when the mortgage rate is higher than the interest rate that the borrower can earn on excess cash).

The main problem with unscheduled principal repayments is that the mortgage investor cannot predict the size of the prepayments or the rate at which the unscheduled principal repayments will be received and can be reinvested. Unscheduled repayments on a mortgage issued at an interest rate of 6% cease earning 6% to the mortgage investor and presumably begin earning current interest rates, which may be higher or lower than 6%.

The option to make or not make unscheduled principal repayments rests with the borrower. Mortgage borrowers have an incentive to make unscheduled mortgage payments when interest rates are low, for several reasons. First, borrowers are more likely to refinance when rates are low. Second, borrowers are more likely to move and fully prepay mortgages when rates are low. Finally, borrowers are more likely to use excess cash to prepay mortgages when the interest rate on their mortgages substantially exceeds the rate at which the excess cash can be invested. The same incentives reverse when interest rates are high, making borrowers less likely to prepay mortgages. Simply put, borrowers have a prepayment option, and they tend to exercise that option in their favor based on interest rates. However, there are also idiosyncratic factors related to the borrower, such as the ability to make prepayments and the decision to sell a house, that affect prepayment decisions. These factors are not fully driven by interest rates, and they may cause or prevent otherwise optimal exercise of the prepayment option based purely on interest rates. Thus, mortgage prepayments are difficult to predict even under specific interest rate scenarios.

Mortgage lenders write the prepayment options at the initiation of the mortgage, and therefore the lenders, and any subsequent mortgage investors, are short those options until the mortgage is fully repaid. Mortgage investors suffer losses when the borrower's prepayment option moves into-the-money relative to an investor in a similar fixed-income security without the prepayment option. The borrower harvests gains by exercising the prepayment option. Specifically, rational exercise of the prepayment option by borrowers tends to generate higher unscheduled prepayments to lenders when interest rates are low and reinvestment opportunities are least desirable.

Unscheduled principal payments to lenders when interest rates are high and reinvestment opportunities are most desirable would be made only due to the borrowers' idiosyncratic factors. Although they would typically work to the advantage of the mortgage investor, such unscheduled principal payments would be relatively less likely.

Each long-term mortgage has hundreds of scheduled future payments and hundreds of future potential prepayment options. The cash flows, or payments, of individual mortgages are aggregated and form the available cash flows of the mortgage pools underlying the RMBS. These cash flows include the unscheduled principal payments that are passed from the mortgage pool to the RMBS investors. Thus, the main risks of RMBS with insured underlying mortgages involve the prepayment behavior of the underlying pool and its relationship with reinvestment opportunities. These unscheduled payments create uncertainty on the part of investors regarding both the timing of the principal repayments they will receive and the longevity of the interest payments they will receive.

12.6.2 Measuring Unscheduled Prepayment Rates

Mortgage returns that are not driven by default risk are primarily driven by the interest rate risk inherent in prepayment risk. Mortgage investors therefore focus on the unscheduled principal payments and the forecasted speed of prepayments.

In essence, the market value of each mortgage or pool of mortgages is a function of its anticipated rate of prepayment. Attempts to earn superior rates of return are generally exercises in predicting prepayment rates and investing in those mortgages or pools of mortgages that will experience more desirable rates of prepayment than are reflected in the current price. With stable interest rates, high rates of prepayment are usually beneficial to the mortgage investor because they reduce the expected longevity of the cash flow stream. However, when mortgages have interest rates higher than prevailing market interest rates, slower prepayment rates may be desirable to the mortgage investor.

More sophisticated insured mortgage analysis focuses on models that combine interest rate behavior with unscheduled principal payment rates. The secondary mortgage market has developed models for deriving interest rate scenarios, correlating those interest rate scenarios with prepayment scenarios, and using the framework to price MBS. This section describes the major metric by which unscheduled principal payments are expressed.

The annualized percentage of a mortgage's remaining principal value that is prepaid in a particular month is known as the **conditional prepayment rate (CPR)**. The exact computation of the CPR involves principal balances and specifies such details as the use of monthly compounding. But the CPR for a particular month is clearly intuitive: It roughly reflects the annual reduction in the mortgage principal that would be anticipated if the same percentage of principal were repaid each month for 12 consecutive months. For example, if 1% of a mortgage's remaining principal payment is prepaid in a particular month, the CPR for that month would be 11.4% (which is less than 12% due to compounding with a declining balance).

The Public Securities Association (PSA) established the **PSA benchmark**, a benchmark of prepayment speed that is based on the CPR and that has become the standard approach used by market participants. The PSA prepayment benchmark is shown in Exhibit 12.7.

As indicated in Exhibit 12.7, the benchmark assumes that for a 30-year mortgage, a CPR of 0.2% will apply for the first month of the security. The monthly benchmark CPR then increases by 0.2% per month for the next 30 months until it reaches a level of 6%. The benchmark CPR is then assumed constant at this rate of 6% for the rest of the life of the mortgage. The reason behind the initially increasing CPR rate is that only a few borrowers will be expected to prepay in the early years of their loans (e.g., due to moving or refinancing), as their circumstances and market interest rates have had little time to change since they made the decision to take out the loan. However, as time passes, prepayments are assumed to pick up until they level off at a CPR of 6%.

EXHIBIT 12.7   PSA Benchmark Pattern

Month	CPR
1	0.2%
2	0.4%
3	0.6%
⋮	⋮
29	5.8%
30	6.0%
31	6.0%
32	6.0%
⋮	⋮

The key to the benchmark is that it is used as a standard against which each mortgage or mortgage pool is indexed. If a mortgage experiences the same CPR for a particular month, as is listed in Exhibit 12.7, then it is described as prepaying at 100% PSA. For example, if Mortgage A has a steady CPR of 1% for every month, in month 2 it would be referred to as 250% PSA because the actual CPR (1%) is 2.5 times the PSA standard rate (0.4%) for the second month of a mortgage's life. In month 30 or beyond in the mortgage's life, a CPR of 1% would be referred to as 16.7% PSA because the actual CPR (1%) is one-sixth the PSA standard rate for those months (6%).

☞ APPLICATION 12.6.2A

Mortgage B experiences a CPR of 2% in its 20th month. How would this prepayment rate be expressed using the PSA benchmark? Mortgage B has a PSA prepayment speed of 50% in month 20. Mortgage B's prepayment rate of 2% is 50% of the 4% benchmark. The 4% benchmark is 0.2% × 20 months, since the month number is less than 30.

☞ APPLICATION 12.6.2B

Mortgage C experiences a PSA rate of 200% in each month and is now five years old. What is its CPR? The PSA standard is 6% at 30 months and beyond, and 200% of 6% is 12%. Since the mortgage is already at or beyond month 60, the CPR for the mortgage is now 12%.

12.6.3 Pricing RMBS with PSA Rates

The cash flows of insured residential mortgage pools can be projected, assuming a given PSA speed. Those cash flows can then be discounted to form an estimated present value or price to the pool. However, the selection of an appropriate discount rate is complicated by the interest-rate-related options of mortgages. Expected cash flows cannot simply be discounted at expected interest rates, since larger cash flows (i.e., higher unscheduled principal repayments) tend to occur when interest rates are lowest. Thus, RMBS pricing models should be based on option pricing technology.

However, mortgage prepayment options are not exercised based purely on interest rates. Some mortgage borrowers prepay mortgages during high-interest rate environments due to personal circumstances (e.g., moving due to a change in employment), and some mortgage borrowers fail to prepay mortgages even when interest rates are low and refinancing appears beneficial. Factors affecting prepayment decisions other than interest rates or other systematic factors are known as **idiosyncratic prepayment factors**. Idiosyncratic prepayment factors prevent the specification of a precise relationship between unscheduled prepayments and interest rate levels, and option pricing models that include this behavior should be used.

Mortgage prepayment rates can also vary due to systematic prepayment factors other than interest rates. For example, a rise in economic activity or higher housing prices can generate widespread prepayments as borrowers change residences to move into larger houses or accept new jobs. Changes in prepayment rates from systematic factors can also be due to interest-rate-related factors other than current interest rate levels, including the path that mortgage rates have followed to arrive at the current level. For instance, when mortgage rates drop further after having declined substantially in the recent past, refinancing may not occur at a rapid rate, since those who ascertain a benefit from refinancing at lower interest rates will probably have done so when the mortgage rate first dropped. Reduced refinancing speeds due to high levels of previous refinancing activity is known as **refinancing burnout**.

The prepayment rates experienced by mortgage pools will vary based on such factors as the characteristics of the underlying mortgage pool. These factors include the maturities of the mortgages, the rates of the fixed-rate mortgages, and the terms of any variable-rate mortgages. Another factor is the geographic location of the pool. There are regional prepayment tendencies, regional economic performance levels, and regional impacts on prepayment speeds even within the same country. Geography also comes into play in relation to factors such as the risk of destruction of properties. For example, if a large number of properties in the pool are located closer to major storm risks or earthquake risks, there can be substantial effects on the potential speeds of prepayments of insured and uninsured mortgages. Analysts build fundamental models of prepayment speeds based on these characteristics and include analysis of past prepayment rates to predict future prepayment rates.

Ownership of mortgage pools is often divided or structured into investment products that have widely varying exposures to prepayment risks. These structured products are discussed in detail in Part 5.

12.6.4 Commercial Mortgage-Backed Securities

Commercial mortgage-backed securities (CMBS) are mortgage-backed securities with underlying collateral pools of commercial property loans. CMBS provide liquidity to commercial lenders and to real estate investors. Commercial lenders can sell commercial loans that they have issued into the CMBS pools. Real estate investors may purchase CMBS and enjoy higher liquidity and diversification than they would through direct ownership of commercial loans.

The emergence of the CMBS market in the United States in the early 1990s can be explained, at least partially, by a large market correction in the U.S. real estate market at that time, which caused a severe lack of liquidity in the sector. The correction damaged many traditional commercial lenders and decreased the level of activity of many others. At that point, CMBS facilitated investment by mortgage investors other than traditional commercial lenders. The use of CMBS rose over the years, along with real estate prices, leading to the financial crisis that began in 2007.

The global financial crisis of 2007–2009 can be partially attributed to real estate markets, especially residential loans to subprime borrowers. In the years leading up until 2007, home ownership substantially increased in the United States, with much of the increase coming from borrowers with lower income or creditworthiness purchasing homes. With lower levels of due diligence, down payments, and creditworthiness, lenders made it easier to purchase homes than in the past. The increase in demand for homes, combined with weakened lending standards, led to increases in home prices, and, by extension, increases in prices in commercial properties. When it became clear that these marginal borrowers could not service their loans, their properties went into foreclosure, moving the strong increase in demand into an increased supply of properties that drove prices quickly lower. With low to no down payments providing equity in the property, borrowers were forced out or abandoned the properties, leaving banks and mortgage lenders to suffer nearly all of the losses from declining property values. When bank and lender capital was found to be insufficient to cover the losses, numerous banks failed both in the United States and in Europe, leading to bailouts from government and taxpayer funds.

Compared to an insured RMBS, a CMBS provides a lower degree of prepayment risk because commercial mortgages are most often set for a shorter term. Fixed-rate commercial mortgages typically charge a prepayment penalty, which makes commercial borrowers substantially less likely to refinance than residential borrowers. However, CMBS are more subject to credit risk. Because they are not standardized, there are lots of details associated with CMBS that make default risks difficult to ascertain and thus make these instruments difficult to value. Many of these differences relate to the more heterogeneous nature of CMBS issues relative to RMBS issues and to their underlying real estate properties. In particular, default risks are complex and heterogeneous due to the unique risks of commercial real estate assets. Factors that may affect CMBS default probabilities include property type, location, borrower quality, tenant quality, lease terms, property management, property seasoning, and year of origination. Further, given the large size and indivisible nature of properties, CMBS issues tend to contain fewer loans. This means that investors in the CMBS market have concentrated risk to a relatively small number of potential defaults.

LTV ratios and debt yields (cash flow divided by the amount of the loan) play a big role in the analysis of CMBS issues, as they do for the underlying commercial mortgages. Most U.S. CMBS issues have had historical average LTV ratios in the 65% to 80% region, and CMBS issues with average LTV ratios greater than 75% would be viewed as risky. However, what is perhaps more important to consider is the percentage of the individual loans in a CMBS with LTV ratios above 75%. In many cases, rating agencies allow a maximum of 15% of loans with LTV ratios in excess of 75%. The risk of CMBS is also driven by the level of diversification in the pools' mortgages. For example, rating agencies often discourage issues (refuse to assign high ratings) when an individual loan is more than 5% of a specific CMBS issue.

12.7 LIQUID ALTERNATIVES: REAL ESTATE INVESTMENT TRUSTS

This section introduces the concept of REITs (real estate investment trusts). The final section of the chapter reports historical risks and returns of mortgage REITs. Although REITs are not popular in all countries, they are central to illustrating and understanding central points with regard to real estate, liquidity, and liquid alternatives.

Legislation facilitating REITs dates back to 1960 in the United States. Perhaps due to their long-term popularity, REITs are not usually included in lists of liquid alternatives. But REITs fit the definition of a liquid alternative very well; they are publicly traded vehicles that allow retail access to an asset class (real estate) that is often considered to be an alternative asset class.

A **real estate investment trust (REIT)** is an entity structured much like a traditional operating corporation, except that the assets of the entity are almost entirely real estate. Because most major REITs are listed on major stock exchanges, they are a simple and liquid way to bring real estate exposure into an investor's portfolio. They operate in much the same fashion as mutual funds, especially closed-end mutual funds. They pool investment capital from many small investors and invest the larger collective pool in real estate properties that would not be available to the small investor.

Equity REITs invest predominantly in equity ownership within the private real estate market. **Mortgage REITs** invest predominantly in real estate–based debt. REITs that invest substantially in both markets have been termed hybrid REITs—a category that has shrunk into very limited use. There are three key advantages of REITs as vehicles to real estate investment. First, REITs provide management services in the selection and operation of properties. Second, REITs provide liquid access to an illiquid asset class. Investors can add to or trim their exposure to real estate quickly and easily through purchase and sale of shares in REITs. Finally, REITs avoid double taxation of income that comes with paying taxes at both corporate and individual levels. REITs avoid corporate income taxation to the extent that they distribute their income and capital gains to their shareholders. Distributions from REITs tend to be subject to income taxation at the individual level.

These potential advantages to REITs may be offset—especially to large, sophisticated real estate investors—by disadvantages, including management fees and lack of influence over management. Also, some analysts argue that exchange-traded real estate investments (i.e., REITs) have greater price risk than private real estate investments because the market prices of REITs take on the volatility of financial markets. Others argue that market prices of REITs reflect the true price risk of real estate, which is masked by other valuation methods, such as appraisals.

An investor can use REITs to form asset allocations to real estate as an asset class. The diverse nature of REITs allows investors to refine their asset allocation within real estate by tilting their real property exposure to particular parts of the real estate market. For example, an investor can choose different categories of REITs, such as mortgage-based versus equity-based REITs, and various subcategories of real estate, such as office buildings, health-care facilities, shopping centers, and apartment complexes.

REITs offer professional asset management of real estate properties to passive investors. These real estate professionals know how to acquire, finance, develop, renovate, and negotiate lease agreements with respect to real estate properties to get the most return for their shareholders. REITs are also overseen by independent boards of directors, which are charged with seeing to the best interests of the shareholders. This provides a level of corporate governance protection similar to that employed for other public companies. REITs strive to provide a consistent dividend yield for their shareholders.

To enjoy the freedom from corporate income taxation in the United States, REITs are subject to the following two main restrictions: 75% of the income they receive must be derived from real estate activities, and they must pay out 90% or more of their taxable income in the form of dividends. Other restrictions relate to the ownership structure of the REIT, such as restrictions on the percentage of the shares that can be held directly or indirectly by a small group of investors. As long as a REIT is in compliance with the relevant restrictions, it may deduct dividends from its income in determining its corporate tax liability, which means it pays corporate income taxes only on the retained income. The returns of mortgage REITs are used in the next section to indicate the general risks and returns to mortgage investments.

12.8 KEY OBSERVATIONS REGARDING HISTORICAL RETURNS OF MORTGAGE REITs

Mortgage REITs returns are monthly returns observed from January of 2000 to December of 2018, for a total of 228 observations. Exhibit 12.8 provides univariate return statistics in the top panel, partial autocorrelations of returns in the middle panel, and a histogram of returns in the bottom panel.

Key observations on Mortgage REITs returns that are consistent with economic reasoning are an essential component of knowledge and include the following.

1. Mortgage REITs returns had historic volatility moderately exceeding that of global equities.
2. Mortgage REITs returns generated a moderate Sharpe ratio.
3. Mortgage REITs returns had a moderate negative skew.
4. Mortgage REITs returns had a markedly positive excess kurtosis.
5. Mortgage REITs experienced a massive maximum drawdown (i.e., almost −70%).

In conclusion, mortgage REITs are more similar to stocks than bonds, with volatility and returns significantly exceeding those found in the investment-grade bond market.

Index (Jan. 2000–Dec. 2018)	Mortgage REITs	MSCI World Equity
Annualized Arithmetic Mean	10.3%	4.5%
Annualized Standard Deviation	18.8%	15.0%
Annualized Semivolatility	16.7%	11.6%
Annualized Median	18.6%	11.6%
Skewness	−1.3	−0.7
Excess Kurtosis	4.4	1.6
Sharpe Ratio	0.4	0.1
Sortino Ratio	0.5	0.2
Annualized Geometric Mean	8.5%	3.4%
First-Order Autocorrelation	0.12	0.14
Annualized Standard Deviation (Adjusted for Autocorrelation 1)	21.2%	17.1%
Maximum	14.2%	11.2%
Minimum	−24.1%	−19.0%
Max Drawdown	−69.1%	−54.0%

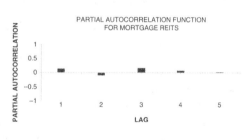

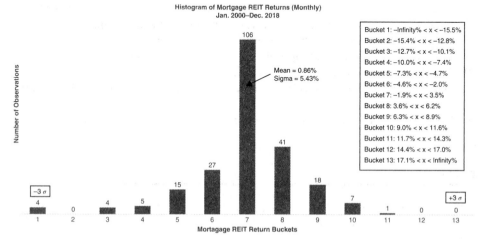

EXHIBIT 12.8 Statistical Summary of Returns

REVIEW QUESTIONS

1. List three potential disadvantages of real estate as an investment.
2. Name the three styles of real estate investing.
3. Provide an example of a common real estate investment for each of the three styles of real estate investing.
4. Define mortgage.
5. How do unscheduled principal payments affect the lender of a fixed-rate mortgage at different levels of market interest rates?
6. How does increased interest rate volatility affect the borrower of a fixed-rate mortgage in which the borrower can make unscheduled principal payments?
7. How does the interest rate risk of a variable-rate mortgage compare to that of a fixed-rate mortgage from the perspective of the lender?
8. What is the "option" in an option adjustable-rate mortgage?
9. Are investors in commercial mortgages typically more or less concerned than investors in residential mortgages about (a) rental income, (b) default risk, and (c) prepayment risk?
10. Describe the three major advantages of REIT ownership relative to direct real estate ownership.

NOTES

1. H. Esaki, "Commercial Mortgage Defaults: 1972–2000," *Real Estate Finance* (Winter 2002): 43–52.
2. Ibid.

CHAPTER 13

Real Estate Equity

T his chapter discusses equity participations in real estate investments. Real estate equity investments are residual claims. In other words, the value of an equity investment in real estate is equal to the value of the underlying real estate property minus the value of mortgage claims, if any, against that real estate. The previous chapter provided detailed information about mortgages. This chapter provides details about the valuation and analysis of the equity claims on real estate and begins with a discussion of real estate development.

13.1 REAL ESTATE DEVELOPMENT

Real estate development projects can include one or more stages of creating or improving a real estate project, including the acquisition of raw land, the construction of improvements, and the renovation of existing facilities. The development phase may terminate with the sale of improved parcels to interested buyers or through the leasing of improved properties. Typically, real estate development entails (1) acquiring land or a site; (2) estimating the marketing potential and profitability of the development project; (3) developing a building program and design; (4) procuring the necessary public approvals and permits; (5) raising the necessary financing; (6) building the structure; and (7) leasing, managing, and perhaps eventually selling the property.

13.1.1 Real Estate Development as Real Options

This section focuses on issues related to the initial stages of development. Development is one of the most entrepreneurial as well as one of the riskiest sectors in the real estate investment space. The primary risks involved in real estate development center around the possibility that a project will fail to progress successfully into realization of the perceived potential. Two key factors differentiate development projects from standing real estate investments. First, real estate development is a process in which a new asset is being created. Second, during the lifetime of the development, there is a high degree of uncertainty regarding the estimates of the revenues and costs of the investment.

Most real estate development projects may be viewed as a string of real options. A **real option** is an option on a real asset rather than a financial security. The real option may be a call option to purchase a real asset, a put option to sell a real asset, or an exchange option involving exchange of nonfinancial assets.

Each expenditure in the development process may be viewed as the purchase of a call option. Consider a stylized three-stage real estate project that involves (1) an initial feasibility analysis, (2) the purchase of a suitable tract of land, and (3) the construction of a building, all of which lead to the ownership of a completed project. The potential to move forward with the third stage (after the second stage has been completed) may be viewed as a call option in which the developer has the option to pay money and contribute vacant land in exchange for an improved property. The potential to move forward with the second stage (after the first stage has been completed) may be viewed as a call option in which the developer has the option to pay money to receive vacant land, which is itself an option on further development. The first stage, payment for a feasibility analysis, may be viewed as the purchase of a call option on a call option (the second stage), which is in turn a call option on the final stage.

A view of the stages of real estate development as a string of call options provides intuition into understanding the risks of real estate development. But the option view can also reveal important insights into the value of a project. The following sections illustrate the application of option theory to a simplified real estate development project.

13.1.2 An Example of a Real Estate Project with Real Options

Consider a decision of whether to build a large hotel next to a stadium that is trying to obtain a franchise for a major sports team. The project being considered is to be the official hotel of the stadium. The sports league will announce its decision regarding whether to award the franchise in exactly one year. If the sports franchise is granted, the need for the hotel will begin two years later (a total of three years from the present time). To be the official hotel, the hotel must be finished when the games begin. It will take three years to build the hotel. Therefore, any decision to build the hotel must be made now. Assume the following costs to getting the hotel opened:

First Year	Purchase of rights, land, plans, and permits	$10,000,000
Second Year	Construction of building shell	$20,000,000
Third Year	Construction of building interior and furnishings	$20,000,000
Total		$50,000,000

Assume for simplicity that if the sports franchise is successful, the hotel will be a terrific investment worth $80 million when it opens. However, if the sports franchise is denied, then the hotel will struggle to attract guests and be worth only $20 million. Should the project be begun?

To begin the analysis, assume that there is a 50% chance that the franchise will be granted, whereby the hotel will be worth $80 million, and a 50% chance that the hotel will be worth only $20 million. Using these probabilities, the expected value of the hotel is $50 million.

To make the analysis as simple as possible, assume that interest rates are 0%. Thus, the expected value of the hotel and the total cost of the completed project are both $50 million, and it would appear that the project would have a zero expected value (i.e., net present value). Ignoring options theory, it appears as though the only way this project would be viable would be if the probability of the franchise being granted were more than 50%.

But this analysis ignores an important real option that exists throughout such construction projects: the right to abandon the project or change plans if events unfold that make the continuation of the existing project undesirable. Ignoring interest rate and other risks, when the option to abandon is included, the sports hotel project should be undertaken even if there is only a 25% chance of the franchise being granted.

Here's how the abandonment option may be viewed. First, the developer pays $10 million for all first-year expenses to acquire the rights, land, plans, and permits. If after that first year the franchise is granted, then the developer has the right to continue the project by building the hotel for another $40 million. The investors would then make a $30 million profit, since the hotel costs $50 million and is worth $80 million. On the other hand, if after one year the franchise is denied, the investors would abandon the hotel for a total loss of $10 million. In most real situations, some of the investment might be recouped, such as would be the case in this example if the land still had value.

Thus, if there is a 25% chance that the franchise would be granted, there would be a 75% chance of losing $10 million and a 25% chance of making $30 million, and the project would represent a fair investment. Any higher probability of the franchise being granted would create a positive expected value.

13.1.3 Decision Trees

In the sports hotel example, there were two decision points. The first was whether to begin the project, and the second was whether to abandon the project after the first year. In practice, a real estate development project can have numerous decision points at which a project can be terminated or modified. Projects can also be delayed, expanded, reduced, or otherwise altered, such as by devising a change in purpose.

To analyze more complex problems, it is often useful to construct a decision tree. A **decision tree** (as depicted in Exhibit 13.1) shows the various pathways that a decision maker can select, as well as the points at which uncertainty is resolved. A decision tree enables analysis and solutions regarding the choices that should be made

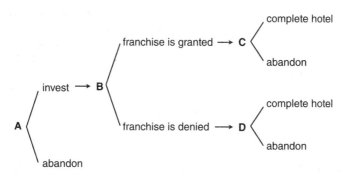

EXHIBIT 13.1   Decision Tree for the Sports Hotel

based on various decision-making points and on new information as that information becomes available.

The decision tree models two types of events: the arrival of new information and decisions. Alternative outcomes of decisions are illustrated vertically. Each potential decision is modeled as two or more branches that emanate from a decision node. The starting node in Exhibit 13.1 is labeled A and represents a decision node. A **decision node** is a point in a decision tree at which the holder of the option must make a decision. In the case of node A, the decision is that the investor must decide whether to start the project. Node B represents an information node. An **information node** denotes a point in a decision tree at which new information arrives. In the case of node B, the information is the decision by the league as to whether a sports franchise will be granted.

13.1.4 Backward Induction and Decision Trees

Backward induction is used to solve a problem involving options and using a decision tree. **Backward induction** is the process of solving a decision tree by working from the final nodes toward the first node, based on valuation analysis at each node. Backward induction guides the decision maker to resolve the final decisions first, since those decisions involve a single period and have no real options remaining unresolved. Then, working backward through time one period at a time, the decision maker can resolve decisions until the only remaining decision is the first one. Backward induction is also used in pricing financial derivatives.

Exhibit 13.2 illustrates backward induction. In Exhibit 13.2A, the ends of each path have been valued using the assumed information and based on all possible paths of outcomes and decisions; all uncertainty has been resolved. The analysis now moves to nodes C and D, which are decision nodes representing points in time at which the investor can decide which path to take. The decisions of the investor at nodes C and D can be solved under the continuing and simplifying assumption that the appropriate discount rate is 0%. For example, at node C, the investor would prefer to complete the hotel (receive $30 million), and at node D, the investor would prefer to abandon the hotel (lose only $10 million). These decisions are reflected in Exhibit 13.2B. The process is repeated to value the project at node B, yielding a value of $10 million

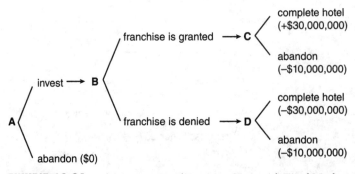

EXHIBIT 13.2A The Sports Hotel Decision Tree with Final Nodes Value

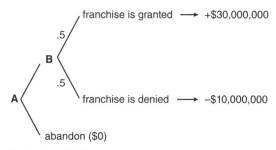

EXHIBIT 13.2B Sports Hotel Decision Tree with Final Decision Included

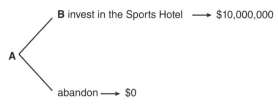

EXHIBIT 13.2C Sports Hotel Decision Tree with Final Decision and New Information Included

(multiplying $30 million by 0.5 and multiplying –$10 million by 0.5, and summing). The results are reflected in Exhibit 13.2C.

Exhibit 13.2 illustrates that the investor's decision is simple. Proceeding with the first-year plans for the hotel produces an expected profit of $10 million. The project appeared to have no value, meaning expected benefits equaled expected costs, when options were ignored. However, when options are priced, the project has tremendous value. The essential driver of value emanating from an option analysis is the ability to revise plans when new information arrives. Real estate investment involves risk, and real estate development typically involves great risk. However, the risk that a developer might not be able to sell or lease when a real estate development is completed (e.g., because of adverse general market conditions) can be mitigated by preselling or preleasing all or part of the real estate development before its completion. Analysis using real options can help structure the problem such that the value of being able to defer decisions until after new information has arrived and uncertainty has been resolved can be assessed and appreciated.

13.2 COMMERCIAL REAL ESTATE VALUATION

Valuation is central to finance and essential to real estate analysis. The distinction between the terms valuation and appraisal, if any, vary by source and by context (e.g., residential vs. commercial). In the context of commercial real estate analysis, **real estate valuation** is often used as a general term describing processes of estimating the worth of a property from various perspectives (especially the perspective of a financial analyst) with regard to the price at which informed investors would be willing to both buy and sell a property.

In the context of commercial real estate analysis, a **real estate appraisal** is generally viewed as a formal opinion of a value provided by an appraiser and often used in financial reports and in decision-making including lending. For institutional investors, appraisals are often performed once a year on real estate properties and are used in reporting.

In the case of private commercial real estate equity, valuation challenges arise because the respective assets are heterogenous and are not exchange-traded like stocks or bonds of public companies. Each real estate asset valuation is unique, dealing with its unique individual characteristics such as location. Real estate assets are also notorious for their illiquidity, as an individual property may not be traded for a considerable number of years. Nevertheless, in spite of the difficulties, and perhaps because of those difficulties, commercial real estate valuation is necessary.

13.2.1 Three Reasons for the Emphasis on Commercial Real Estate Equity

Most of the focus in the remainder of this chapter is on the valuation of equity exposures to private commercial (i.e., income producing) real estate rather than on public real estate, residential real estate, or commercial mortgages. There are three major reasons for institutional focus on equity participations in commercial real estate:

1. Most commercial real estate throughout the world is privately held rather than publicly traded (whether owned directly or held through limited partnerships).
2. Most of the equity of residential real estate is held by the occupier of the property rather than by an institutional investor.
3. The valuation of equity claims to private commercial real estate drives the pricing of the credit risk in the valuation of commercial mortgages. In other words, real estate debt may be viewed through the structural model (detailed in Level II of the CAIA program) as being well explained through an understanding of the risks of the equity in the same property (since assets equal debt plus equity).

13.2.2 The Comparable Sales Approach as a Major Valuation Approach

This section summarizes the first of five approaches used for valuing private commercial real estate equity: the comparable sale prices approach. The other four approaches are the profit approach, the cost approach, the income approach, and multifactor transaction-based approaches.

For non-income-producing properties, such as an owner-occupied single-family residence, a discounted cash flow approach is not viable. In these cases, when there are sufficient transactional data available, valuations are often based on the comparable sale prices approach.

The **comparable sale prices approach** values real estate based on transaction values of similar real estate, with adjustments made for differences in characteristics by a valuation professional such as an appraiser. The comparable sales approach is one of the two primary valuation methods in real estate (the other being the income approach). In the comparable sales approach, the real estate asset is evaluated against the reported prices of comparable (substitute) properties that have recently transacted. Value adjustments may be made for characteristics such as square footage, date of sale, location, and amenities.

In this approach, the real estate appraiser looks at sales of similar properties in the same geographic region (if not city) as the property being appraised. These actual sale prices give the appraiser an estimate of the cost (i.e., price) per square foot of similar real estate properties. The appraiser then adjusts this cost per square foot for the unique characteristics of the property being appraised: better parking or access, better location, newer lobby, longer-term tenants, and so on.

The comparable sales approach has the advantage of being based on actual sales transactions. However, the approach tends to contain substantial subjectivity in the valuation of most characteristics other than the focal point (e.g., price per square foot). Multifactor transaction-based approaches, detailed later, objectively quantify multiple factors.

The accuracy of the comparable sale approach (and other transaction-based approaches) is lower when there is a lack of frequency of property sales. Every property is unique, so it is hard to adjust a square-foot calculation value from one property to form the value of another accurately. When the comparable sale prices approach is not viable because the number of recent and relevant real estate transactions is very limited, alternative approaches may be used based on either or both of two components: (1) the replacement construction costs of the structure and (2) indications of the market value of the site for its most profitable use. These two approaches are briefly discussed in the next section. More sophisticated approaches based on transaction prices are also discussed briefly later in this chapter and are detailed in Level II of the CAIA curriculum.

13.2.3 The Profit and Cost Approaches

The **profit approach** to real estate valuation is typically used only for properties with a value driven by the actual business use of the premises; it is effectively a valuation of the business rather than a valuation of the property itself. Thus the profit approach should only be used when the value of the property is based primarily on the value of the business that occupies the space. The profit approach is a special case of the income approach, detailed later.

The **cost approach** assumes that a buyer will not pay more for a property than it would cost to build an equivalent one. In this approach, a property's value is initially based on its cost and can be further refined by adding the values of any improvements to the land value of the property and applying economic depreciation as appropriate. This approach is often suggested when valuing newer structures and in markets with substantial new construction.

13.2.4 Cap Rates and the Perpetuity Valuation Approach

A somewhat crude but widespread metric in real estate valuation is the capitalization (cap) rate. The cap rate of a real estate investment is the net operating income (NOI) of the investment divided by some measure of the real estate's total value, such as purchase price or appraised value:

$$\text{Cap Rate} = \text{NOI/Value} \tag{13.1}$$

where NOI is usually viewed on an annualized basis and represents the expected, normalized cash flow available to the owner of the real estate, ignoring financing costs (e.g., cash flows from rent, net of operating expenses). The variable "Value" used in Equation 13.1 is an estimate of the market value of the real estate on an unlevered basis.

☞ APPLICATION 13.2.4A

Assume that a real estate project has a current market value of $125 million and expected annual cash flows from rent, net of operating expenses, of $10 million. What is its cap rate?

The answer is found using Equation 13.1: Cap Rate = ($10 million/ $125 million) = 8%.

The exact specifications of the NOI for the numerator of the cap rate (recent, current, forecasted) and the value (beginning of period versus end of period, transaction price versus appraised price) for the denominator of the cap rate vary between users and purposes. Note that NOI does not reflect financing costs, and therefore the NOI-based approach for estimating value depicted in Equation 13.1 is intended for analysis of unleveraged property values.

Cap rates are often viewed as direct estimates or forecasts of expected returns or required returns. Thus, according to this view, a property with a cap rate of 9% is expected to generate a return of 9% to the investor on an unleveraged basis. The view of a cap rate as an estimated expected return is at best a crude approximation in that it typically ignores anticipated capital gains or losses as well as anticipated growth or decline in income. Nevertheless, cap rates are a good starting point for an analysis of expected returns.

Cap rates can be viewed as required rates of return and used as risk-adjusted discount rates to perform risk-adjusted present values in the valuation of properties using discounted cash flow approaches. To illustrate the risk adjustment, an investor may search for a core property that offers a cap rate of at least 7% while demanding a cap rate of at least 9% on a value-added property because it is perceived as having higher risk.

Observed cap rates are often used to establish values for particular properties. Note that Equation 13.2 can be formed by rearranging Equation 13.1 to express property value as depending on NOI and cap rate:

$$\text{Value} = \text{NOI/Cap Rate} \tag{13.2}$$

A prospective buyer or analyst divides the estimated NOI of a property by an observed cap rate on properties of similar risk or characteristics to obtain an estimate of the property's unleveraged value.

 APPLICATION 13.2.4B

An investor is considering the purchase of a core real estate property that offers $350,000 per year in net operating income. The investor's analysis of cap rates on similar properties finds an average cap rate of 7%. What is the value of the property based on Equation 13.2 and the investor's estimates of the net operating income and appropriate cap rate?

The answer is found using Equation 13.2:

$$\text{Value} = \text{NOI/Cap Rate} = (\$350,000/0.07) = \$5,000,000.$$

Other metrics that are commonly used to assess real estate investment opportunities mirror the approaches discussed in private equity, including the internal rate of return (IRR) approach and the multiple of the cash in (the cash projected to be received from an investment on a project) to the cash out (the investment in the project). Numerous ratios of operating performance, interest coverage, and leverage are also used, most of which are analogous to financial ratios used throughout corporate finance. Cap rates represent a tool that is widely used in real estate but less so in other areas of finance.

NCREIF and other organizations estimate cap rates for various commercial property types in the United States. The overall weighted average of cap rates for core commercial property in the United States has varied between 5% and 10% since the mid-1980s. The higher end of the range was reached in the mid-1990s and again in 2002 in the United States, whereas the lower end of the range preceded the financial crisis that began in 2007 and was observed again in 2018.

13.2.5 The Income Approach as a Major Valuation Approach

The **income approach** values real estate by projecting expected income or cash flows, discounting for time and risk, and summing them to form the property's total value and is similar to the discounted cash flow method (DCF method) used for valuing stocks and bonds. The income approach is one of the two primary valuation methods in real estate. Sections 13.3 and 13.4 discuss this important approach in detail.

In the income approach, several years of net operating income are projected for a specific property (or portfolio of properties) and then discounted using an estimate of an appropriate discount rate. This approach is particularly useful when valuing income-producing real estate assets, such as commercial real estate. The income approach (or discounted cash flow method) has become the most accepted practice by real estate appraisers for commercial properties. The approach has the advantage of valuing the unique characteristics of the property being appraised. However, it requires the estimation of an appropriate discount rate and is subject to forecasting errors of cash flows due to errors in forecasting occupancy rates, lease growth rates, expenses, the holding period for the property, the terminal value of the property, inflation estimates, and the like.

13.2.6 Transaction-Based Methods (Repeat-Sales and Hedonic)

Transaction-based real estate valuation methods are based on relatively large data sets of actual transaction prices of properties within a specified time period and include the repeat-sales and hedonic methods. They may be viewed as more systematic, comprehensive and quantitatively sophisticated forms of the comparable sales approach. Quantitative techniques such as multiple regression are used on relatively large data sets (compared to most comparable sales applications) to build a property's valuation based on multiple attributes.

Transaction-based methods can form a reliable basis for real estate valuation when:

1. They are performed with adequate data and with rigorous econometric methods.
2. Differences among the properties are modeled well.
3. Statistical noise in the data is minimal.

The two main methods used to estimate transaction-based price indices are the repeat-sales method (RSM) and the hedonic pricing method (HPM). Both methods are detailed in Level II of the CAIA curriculum.

13.2.7 Two Advantages of Appraisal-Based Models over Transaction-Based Models

All valuation methods discussed earlier except the two purely transaction-based methods (the repeat-sales and hedonic methods) are viewed as appraisal-based methods, even though the comparable sales approach includes transactions prices as input data.

There are two primary advantages of appraisal-based models:

1. In general, they do not suffer from a small sample size problem.
2. All properties can be appraised frequently and by multiple experts, although this is a costly process.

13.2.8 Four Disadvantages of Appraisal-Based Models over Transaction-Based Models

There are four primary disadvantages of appraisal-based models:

1. Appraisals are inherently subjective and backward-looking, thus introducing potential errors in the resulting valuation.
2. In the case of real estate price indices based on appraisals, not all properties are reappraised as frequently as the index is reported. For example, an appraisal-based real estate price index published every quarter is likely to be based on appraisals that are fully performed only annually. This may cause a **stale appraisal effect** (i.e., errors from the use of dated appraisals), which contributes to the lagged recognition of price changes observed in appraisal-based indices.

3. Appraisal-based indices are smoothed compared with actual changes in real estate market values, meaning that substantial value changes tend to be reflected on a delayed basis. Thus, measures of volatility of the value of commercial real estate assets based on appraisal-based models are underestimated. Fortunately, unsmoothing techniques (detailed in Level II of the CAIA curriculum) help mitigate this problem.

4. Appraisal-based methods tend to rely on data from comparable properties. Therefore, the quality of the appraisal will depend critically on the relevance and quality of available data. As a result, appraisals may not be accurate in situations in which multiple comparable properties cannot be identified (e.g., the current property is rather unique) or when there is a significant time lag between the time the data have become available and the time the appraisal takes place.

13.2.9 The NCREIF Property Index as an Appraisal-Based Index

The National Council of Real Estate Investment Fiduciaries (NCREIF) is a large U.S. not-for-profit institutional real estate investment industry association that collects data from its members, which include, for the most part, institutional real estate investment managers. NCREIF maintains a massive data set of real estate income and pricing data and uses those data to publish a major real estate index and subindices of commercial properties as well as several other indices, such as a farmland index and a timberland index. The **NCREIF Property Index** (**NPI**) is a large, popular, value-weighted index published quarterly and is based on unleveraged commercial-property appraisals (or leveraged data adjusted to an unleveraged basis). NCREIF sub-indices are available on sub-categories, including property types and geographical differentiation by region, division, state, and zip code.

The NPI is based on financial information from member institutional investors. Members are required to report information on their real estate holdings on a quarterly basis. The NPI started in the fourth quarter of 1977. Recently the NPI consisted of over 7,500 properties (including the five major categories of apartment, industrial, hotel, office, and retail properties) with a gross fair market value of roughly $600 billion. Most valuations are appraisal-based. The reason for the use of appraisals is the illiquid nature of real estate: Properties simply do not turn over frequently enough to compute short-term returns using prices from transactions performed in an arm's-length manner.

The change in value of each property in the NPI is calculated every quarter on an "as if" basis: as if the property were purchased at the beginning of the quarter at its appraised value, held for income during that quarter, and sold at the end of the quarter at its end-of-quarter appraised value. If the property was actually acquired or sold during the quarter, the transaction price is used in place of either the beginning or the ending value.

The total return on the index is calculated as the sum of an income return and a capital value return. The income portion of the total return of each property is a fraction, with net operating income (NOI) in the numerator and an estimate of the property value in the denominator. The estimate of the property value is based on the beginning-of-period appraised value, with adjustments for any capital improvements, any partial sales, and reinvestment of NOI.

The numerator of the capital value return is the change in the estimated value of the property from the beginning of the quarter to the end of the quarter, adjusted for capital improvements and partial sales such that increases in the value due to further investments are not included as profits, and declines in value due to partial sales are not deducted as losses. The denominator of the capital value return is the same as the denominator for the income portion.

The NPI is calculated on an unleveraged basis, as if the property being included in the index were purchased with 100% equity and no debt. As a result, the returns are less volatile, and there are no interest charges deducted. The **calculation of the returns to the NPI** is performed on a before-tax basis (and therefore do not include income tax expense) and is performed for each individual property and then value-weighted in the index calculation. The turnover of most real estate properties is infrequent (every six or seven years, on average), so the NPI is based primarily on appraised values rather than market transactions.

Although the NPI is a quarterly index, NCREIF properties are not formally appraised every quarter. Most properties are formally valued at least once per year, but many are appraised only every two or even three years. Appraisals cost money; therefore, there is a trade-off between the benefits of having frequent property valuations and the costs of those valuations as a drain on portfolio performance. In fact, many institutional real estate investors value their portfolio properties only when they believe there is a substantial change in value based on new leases, changing economic conditions, or the sale of a similar property close to the portfolio property.

Even when properties have been recently appraised, it is possible that the appraisal process will be driven by old information, such as previous transactions on comparable properties, or by delays in the willingness of appraisers to adopt new valuation standards brought on by changes in market conditions, such as capitalization (cap) rates. Thus, even recent appraisals can cause smoothing due to delays in fully reflecting changes in true value. Note that the NPI is published quarterly but that quarter-end values are published with a time lag. Thus, even ignoring appraisal-based smoothing, a major decline in asset prices that occurs in October would not be reflected in quarterly index figures until the December 31 appraisal, and the December 31 value would not be published until almost a month later. The Investment Property Databank (IPD) Index is another example of an appraisal-based index. It tracks retail, office, and industrial properties in the United Kingdom and includes data on actual property transactions from property companies and institutional investors. The IPD Index is available monthly and annually.

In contrast, real estate market indices, such as real estate indices based on REIT market prices, are continuously updated and may be able to reflect the market's quickly changing perception of real estate values. Transaction-based indices may offer more timely recognition of appraisal-based indices. NCREIF has begun producing the Transaction Based Index (TBI). The TBI is a hedonic index (discussed in a previous section) that uses transaction data from the NCREIF database. The relative merits of market-based indications of real estate values (i.e., REITs), transaction-based indications of real estate values, and appraisal-based indications of real estate values is a very important topic in the estimation of the risks of real estate investments and therefore the appropriate risk premium. This topic is explored in detail in Level II of the CAIA program.

13.3 DETAILS OF THE INCOME APPROACH TO REAL ESTATE VALUATION

This section details the estimation of cash flows and the estimation of the discount rate for the income approach along with a discussion of taxes and financing costs.

13.3.1 Cash Flows for the Income Approach

The value of a commercial property depends on the benefits it can offer to its investors. The benefits are the future incomes or, preferably, cash flows that are expected over the life of the property being held as a standing investment. The income approach to real estate valuation consists of forecasting a property's future expected revenues (e.g., rents) and expenses and then discounting the income, which is revenues minus expenses, at an appropriate rate to find an estimate of the property's value. The income approach is also known as the **discounted cash flow (DCF) method** when cash flows are discounted rather than accounting estimates of income.

Since most properties are unlimited in longevity, cash flows are often projected to some horizon point in time, at which a liquidation value is forecasted. Alternatively, a property may be valued using a perpetuity formula. For long-term horizons, annual values and annual discounting are common.

The investment value (*IV*) or intrinsic value of the property is based on the discounted expected cash flows, $E[CF_t]$, for each time period, t, as illustrated in Equation 13.3:

$$IV = \frac{E[CF_1]}{(1+r)} + \frac{E[CF_2]}{(1+r)^2} + \cdots + \frac{E[CF_{T-1}]}{(1+r)^{T-1}} + \frac{E[CF_T]}{(1+r)^T} + \frac{NSP}{(1+r)^T}$$

$$= \sum_{t=1}^{T} \frac{E[CF_t]}{(1+r)^t} + \frac{NSP}{(1+r)^T} \tag{13.3}$$

The final term in the equation is the present value of the net sale proceeds. The **net sale proceeds** (NSP) is the expected selling price minus any expected selling expenses arising from the sale of the property at time *T*. In the case of real estate, interim or operating cash flows are usually estimated using the concept of net operating income. **Net operating income (NOI)** is a measure of periodic earnings that is calculated as the property's rental income minus all expenses associated with maintaining and operating the property. Equating the expected cash flow at time *t*, $E[CF_t]$, with the net operating income, $E[NOI_t]$, generates the following equation:

$$IV = \frac{E[NOI_1]}{(1+r)} + \frac{E[NOI_2]}{(1+r)^2} + \cdots + \frac{E[NOI_{T-1}]}{(1+r)^{T-1}} + \frac{E[NOI_T]}{(1+r)^T} + \frac{NSP}{(1+r)^T}$$

$$= \sum_{t=1}^{T} \frac{E[NOI_t]}{(1+r)^t} + \frac{NSP}{(1+r)^T} \tag{13.4}$$

We illustrate the income approach with the following example. Suppose that an investor is considering the purchase of an office building. The **potential gross income** is the gross income that could potentially be received if all offices in the building were occupied. For this example, the potential gross income of the first year of operations has been estimated at $300,000. However, it is unlikely that the building will be fully occupied all year round. In the case of commercial properties, there typically needs to be some consideration for possible vacancies and therefore the loss of rental income. The **vacancy loss rate** is the observed or anticipated rate at which potential gross income is reduced for space that is not generating rental income. The **effective gross income** is the potential gross income reduced for the vacancy loss rate. Assuming a 10% vacancy loss rate and no other income, the effective gross income from the building in the first year will be $300,000 − ($300,000 × 0.1) = $270,000.

To be able to estimate the NOI, the operating expenses arising from the property need to be estimated and then subtracted from the gross income. **Operating expenses** are non-capital outlays that support rental of the property and can be classified as fixed or variable. **Fixed expenses**, examples of which are property taxes and property insurance, do not change directly with the level of occupancy of the property. **Variable expenses**, examples of which are maintenance, repairs, utilities, garbage removal, and supplies, change as the level of occupancy of the property varies. This simplified example does not consider depreciation, which is discussed later. Continuing with the example, assume that fixed and variable expenses were estimated at $42,000 and $75,000, respectively, for a total operating expense of $117,000 for the first year, or 43.3% of the first-year effective gross income. Therefore, the NOI arising from this property in the first year is estimated to be:

$$\text{NOI} = (\text{Potential Gross Income} - \text{Vacancy Loss}) - \text{Fixed Expenses}$$
$$- \text{Variable Expenses} \qquad\qquad (13.5)$$

or

$$\text{NOI} = \text{Effective Gross Income} - \text{Operating Expenses}$$
$$= \$270,000 - \$117,000 = \$153,000$$

Now, assuming that the investor expects to maintain the property for seven years, that rents are estimated to increase by 4% per year, that the vacancy loss rate will remain constant at 10%, and that annual operating expenses will continue to represent the same fraction of effective gross income (117/270), the projected annual NOI for each year in the seven-year period is as shown in Exhibit 13.3.

Finally, assume that the net sale proceeds in year 7 have been estimated at $1,840,000.

13.3.2 Discount Rate for the Income Approach

To be able to calculate the investment value of the office building in the previous section, a discount rate needs to be estimated to compute the present value of the expected cash flows. There are several approaches that can be used to estimate an appropriate discount rate. In the case of real estate investments, the discount rate is often estimated using a risk premium approach. The **risk premium approach** to

EXHIBIT 13.3 Estimates of Annual Net Operating Income

	Year 1	Year 2	Year 3	Year 4	Year 5	Year 6	Year 7
Potential gross income	$300,000	$312,000	$324,480	$337,459	$350,958	$364,996	$379,596
Vacancy loss	−$30,000	−$31,200	−$32,448	−$33,746	−$35,096	−$36,500	−$37,960
Effective gross income	$270,000	$280,800	$292,032	$303,713	$315,862	$328,496	$341,636
Operating expenses	−$117,000	−$121,680	−$126,547	−$131,609	−$136,873	−$142,348	−$148,042
Net operating income	$153,000	$159,120	$165,485	$172,104	$178,989	$186,148	$193,594

estimation of a discount rate for an investment uses the sum of a riskless interest rate and one or more expected rewards—expressed as rates—for bearing the risks of the investment. The following formulas use a risk premium approach with two risk premiums: one for liquidity and one for risk.

$$r = [1 + R_f][1 + E(R_{LP})][1 + E(R_{RP})] - 1 \tag{13.6}$$

$$r \approx R_f + E(R_{LP}) + E(R_{RP}) \tag{13.7}$$

where r is the required return on the respective real estate investment, R_f is the risk-free rate of return (the return or yield on a Treasury security of similar maturity to the real estate investment), $E(R_{LP})$ is a liquidity premium that is inherent to direct real estate investments, and $E(R_{RP})$ is the required risk premium or extra return demanded for bearing the remaining risks of investing in the specific real estate project.

☞ APPLICATION 13.3.2A

Assume that U.S. Treasury notes with a seven-year maturity are currently yielding 5.8%, that the liquidity premium is 1% per year, and that the required or anticipated risk premium for the systematic risk of the real estate project is 2.2% per year. With these numbers, the required rate of return for this real estate project is 9%. The required return using Equation 13.6 is found as $(1.058 \times 1.01 \times 1.022) - 1$, or 9.21%. Using Equation 13.7, the three rates sum to 9% (i.e., $5.8\% + 1.0\% + 2.2\% = 9\%$).

Equation 13.6 expresses r using a multiplicative relationship that generates a generally more accurate measure of r using traditional interest rate conventions and annual compounding. Equation 13.7 expresses r as an approximation. The three summed components on the right-hand side of Equation 13.7 ignore the cross products of R_f and the risk premiums. For many situations, the approximation is adequate.

Using a discount rate of 9%, the investment value of the office building is as follows:

$$IV = \frac{\$153,000}{(1.09)} + \frac{\$159,120}{(1.09)^2} + \frac{\$165,485}{(1.09)^3} + \frac{\$172,104}{(1.09)^4} + \frac{\$178,988}{(1.09)^5}$$
$$+ \frac{\$186,148}{(1.09)^6} + \frac{\$193,594}{(1.09)^7} + \frac{\$1,840,000}{(1.09)^7}$$
$$IV = \$1,863,772$$

In practice, the cash flow estimates typically involve a far more detailed projection of cash flows than were illustrated in the example. Full pro forma appraisals usually incorporate the following key elements: rental income on a lease-by-lease basis, other sources of income, a deduction for factors such as allowances for unanticipated vacancies and downtime between leases in a given space, detailed operating expenses, capital items, tenant improvements, and leasing commissions.

For large properties, rental income calculations can become complicated if the property has multiple leases. In such a case, total rental income is estimated by calculating and summing the annual rental income received for each lease in the property. Future demand-and-supply dynamics in the relevant real estate market and the impact of market conditions on the cash flows of the property are vital concerns. As the largest factor in the cash flows will be the net rental income, rent estimates must be as unbiased as possible. A simplistic approach is to assume that rents will increase through all of the years at an estimated and fixed rate of growth that reflects anticipated inflation and any other relevant factors.

The operating expenses incurred by the property include a wide variety of items. Some of them, such as general property management expenses, are recurring and contracted and can therefore be regarded as fixed expenses. Other expenses are considered variable because they depend on the level of property vacancy. It is important to take into consideration the terms of the leases, as some leases may be gross and some may be net. In a **net lease**, the tenant is responsible for almost all of the operating expenses.

The other major expense items on the pro forma cash flow are primarily related to capital improvements and leasing costs. These are irregular payments that are dependent on such factors as the terms of the lease and the condition of the property. In addition, it is common to include a capital reserve for the anticipated level of unexpected costs.

The issue of tenant improvements depends on the exact nature of the property. However, office and retail space is generally offered in such a condition as to allow tenants to tailor it to their own needs. It is common for a landlord to at least partially contribute to these fitting-out costs. The extent to which this is a major cost largely depends not only on the magnitude of the costs but also on the frequency of tenant turnover in the property. The final major item is leasing commissions, which are the costs payable to the brokerage firm for marketing the space.

There are other important issues in applying the DCF approach. First, there is a difference between income and cash flow, especially with real estate when depreciation is involved. **Depreciation** is a noncash expense that is deducted from revenues in computing accounting income to indicate the decline of an asset's value. To convert income to cash flow, it is necessary to add depreciation back into income. Importantly, depreciation is tax deductible, and its role in decreasing taxable income and increasing after-tax cash flows is essential to the analysis. The importance of depreciation for taxable investors is detailed later in this chapter.

13.3.3   Taxes and Financing Costs in the Income Approach

The example in Exhibit 13.3 ignored income taxes and implicitly used a required rate of return that would be appropriate for pre-tax cash flows. In the case of institutional investors without income taxes, there is no need to incorporate taxes. For investors subject to income taxes, there are two ways to view income taxation. The **pre-tax discounting approach** is commonly used in finance, where pre-tax cash flows are used in the numerator of the present value analysis (as the cash flows to be received), and the pre-tax discount rate is used in the denominator. An alternative is to use an after-tax approach. In an **after-tax discounting approach**, the estimated after-tax cash flows (e.g., after-tax bond payments) are discounted using a rate that has been reduced to reflect the net rate received by an investor with a specified marginal tax rate.

☞   APPLICATION 13.3.3A

Investment A offers $80 per year in taxable income and an additional final non-taxable cash flow in five years of $1,000. An investor in a 40% tax bracket requires a pre-tax return of 8% and an after-tax return of 4.8% on investments. What is the value of Investment A on both a pre-tax basis and an after-tax basis? On a pre-tax basis, Investment A is worth $1,000, found on a financial calculator as $PMT = \$80, FV = \$1,000, N = 5, I = 8\%$, solve for PV. On an after-tax basis, the $80 annual income is worth $48 [$80 × (100% − 40%)]. On an after-tax basis, Investment A is also worth $1,000, found on a financial calculator as $PMT = \$48, FV = \$1,000, N = 5, I = 4.8\%$, solve for PV.

Note that in this simplified example, the investor's required after-tax rate of return was simply the pre-tax required rate of return reduced for the tax rate being applied to the cash flows. Further, every cash flow except the final return of the investment was taxed at the same rate, which caused the two approaches to generate identical results. In more realistic scenarios, the taxability of different cash flows and the tax rate of the investor are likely to vary through time.

The pre-tax analysis in the simplified example contains a theoretically inconsistent feature. The $80 coupon payments and $1,000 principal payment to a taxable investor are all discounted at the same high rate (8%) in order to adjust for the effect of taxes. In theory, it is inappropriate to adjust for taxes by attaching a higher discount rate to both the coupon payments and the principal payment because only the coupon payments are taxed. Care should be exercised in interpreting the pre-tax yield in the case of a taxable investor. Nevertheless, both approaches are used in fixed-income analysis.

Finally, the example using Exhibit 13.3 ignored financing flows, such as interest payments and principal payments on a mortgage. The approach valued ownership of the entire real estate property as if there were no mortgage on the property. If there is a mortgage on the property, then the resulting value ($1,863,772) should be equal to the sum of the values of the property's mortgage and equity. The value of the equity in the property could then be estimated as $1,863,772 minus the value of the mortgage. An alternative approach, often termed the **equity residual approach**, focuses on the perspective of the equity investor by subtracting the interest expense and other cash outflows due to mortgage holders (in the numerator) and by discounting the remaining cash flows using an interest rate reflective of the required rate of return on the equity of a leveraged real estate investment (in the denominator). The resulting value would estimate the value of the equity in the real estate project.

In summary, the income or DCF approach involves projecting all cash flows, including a terminal value (net sale proceeds), and discounting the cash flows using a rate commensurate with the investment's longevity and risk. The accuracy of the approach depends on the accuracy of the cash flow projections and the accuracy of the estimation of the discount rate (required rate of return).

13.4 ILLUSTRATION OF THE INCOME METHOD OF REAL ESTATE VALUATION

Valuation of the income approach may be viewed as having three stages: estimating the cash flows, estimating a discount rate, and calculating the value using the DCF method.

To illustrate the mechanics of the income approach (discounted cash flow model) using an example, suppose a German-based real estate company needs to estimate the value of an office building that it just purchased in Munich. First, project the net operating income for the next four years (see Exhibit 13.4).

The *potential* gross income and operating expenses of the first year of operations have been estimated at €10 million and €3.8 million, respectively. For simplicity, assume that these amounts are received at the end of the year. A 10% vacancy loss rate is being assumed for this investment for the first two years, decreasing to 8% for the subsequent two years. Assume that the real estate company expects to maintain the office building for four years, and that rents and operating expenses are estimated to increase by 5% per year.

EXHIBIT 13.4 Projection of Net Operating Income over Next Four Years

	Year 1	Year 2	Year 3	Year 4
Potential gross income	€10,000,000	€10,500,000	€11,025,000	€11,576,250
Vacancy loss	€ 1,000,000	€ 1,050,000	€ 882,000	€ 926,100
Effective gross income	€ 9,000,000	€ 9,450,000	€10,143,000	€10,650,150
Operating expenses	€ 3,800,000	€ 3,990,000	€ 4,189,500	€ 4,398,975
Net operating income	€ 5,200,000	€ 5,460,000	€ 5,953,500	€ 6,251,175

The office building is projected to be sold in four years, providing estimated net sales proceeds of €75 million at that time. Using discounted cash flow analysis, appraise the value of this office building. The real estate company is using a required rate of return of 6% for comparable investments. Ignore taxes for simplicity. First, project the net operating income for the next four years (see Exhibit 13.4). The present value of the four years of NOI and the net sales proceeds to be received in four years, discounted at 6%, is €79,122,255. This is the appraised value of the office building using the income approach.

13.5 ALTERNATIVE REAL ESTATE INVESTMENT VEHICLES

Several alternative real estate investment vehicles are available, some of which have been recently introduced. (New alternative real estate investment vehicles are anticipated to be launched in the coming years.) These alternative investments include both private and exchange-traded products. This section begins by discussing the main characteristics of the following private real estate alternative investments: commingled real estate funds, syndications, joint ventures, and limited partnerships. The remainder of the section focuses on public real estate investments, including open-end real estate mutual funds, closed-end real estate mutual funds, and equity real estate investment trusts (REITs).

13.5.1 Private Equity Real Estate Funds

Private equity real estate funds are privately organized funds that are similar to other alternative investment funds, such as private equity funds and hedge funds, yet have real estate as their underlying asset. Three specific types of private equity real estate funds (commingled real estate funds, syndications, and joint ventures) are discussed in the sections that follow. These funds collect capital from investors with the objective of investing in the equity or the debt side of the private real estate space. The funds follow active management real estate investment strategies, often including property development or redevelopment. Private equity real estate funds usually have a life span of 10 years: a two- to three-year investment period and a subsequent holding period during which the properties are expected to be sold.

The primary advantage to an investor is the access to private real estate, especially useful for smaller institutions that are limited in the size of the real estate portfolios they are able to construct directly. However, even for larger institutions, there are advantages to investments in private equity real estate funds (and also to commingled real estate funds, explained in the next section), as these investment vehicles can provide access to larger properties in which an institution may be reluctant to invest alone because of the unique asset risk it would need to bear and because a single asset could account for a portfolio allocation that might be too high. The use of private equity real estate funds can also provide access to local or specialized management or to specific sectors and markets in which the institution does not feel it has sufficient market knowledge or expertise.

However, investments through private equity funds do not allow investors direct control over the real estate portfolio and its management. In addition to the loss of control, private equity fund investors often lack a sufficiently liquid exit route.

Another major issue with private equity funds is the difficulty of reporting the values of the underlying properties. Hence, the reported performance may not be accurate, and there may be considerable time or uncertainty in realizing reported performance. The finite life of this vehicle tends to make the funds a "hold to liquidation" instrument.

13.5.2 Commingled Real Estate Funds

Commingled real estate funds (CREFs) are a type of private equity real estate fund that is a pool of investment capital raised from private placements that are commingled to purchase commercial properties. The investors are primarily large financial institutions that receive a negotiable, although non-exchange-traded, ownership certificate that represents a proportionate share of the real estate assets owned by the fund. Generally, CREFs are closed-end in structure (i.e., without additional shares issued or old shares redeemed), with unit values reported through annual or quarterly appraisals of the underlying properties. Other than the negotiability of the ownership certificates, the advantages and disadvantages of CREFs are similar to those of other private equity real estate funds.

13.5.3 Syndications

Syndications are private equity real estate funds formed by a group of investors who retain a real estate expert with the intention of undertaking a particular real estate project. A syndicate can be created to develop, acquire, operate, manage, or market real estate investments. Legally, real estate syndications may operate as REITs, as corporations, or as limited or general partnerships. Most real estate syndications are structured as limited partnerships, with the syndicator performing as general partner and the investors performing as limited partners. This structure facilitates the passing through of depreciation deductions, which are normally high, directly to individual investors, and potentially circumvents double taxation.

Syndications are usually initiated by developers who require extra equity capital to raise money to begin a project. Syndications can be a form of financing that offers smaller investors the opportunity to invest in real estate projects that would otherwise be outside their financial and management competencies. Syndicators profit from both the fees they collect for their services and the interest they may preserve in the syndicated property.

13.5.4 Joint Ventures

Real estate joint ventures are private equity real estate funds that consist of the combination of two or more parties, typically represented by a small number of individual or institutional investors, embarking on a business enterprise such as the development of real estate properties. An example of a joint venture would be the case of an institutional investor with an interest in investing in real estate, but with no expertise in this area, that agrees to form a joint venture with a developer. A joint venture can be structured as a limited partnership, an important form of real estate investment that is explained in the next section.

13.5.5 Limited Partnerships

Private equity real estate funds, including the three types described in the previous sections, are increasingly organized as limited partnerships. Not only have real estate funds increasingly adopted limited partnership structures, but existing limited partnerships—such as private equity and hedge funds—have increasingly entered the real estate market. As with other limited partnership structures, a private real estate equity fund's sponsors act as the general partner and raise capital from institutional investors, such as pension funds, endowments, and high-net-worth individuals, who serve as limited partners. Generally, the initial capital raised is in the form of commitments that are drawn down only when suitable investments have been identified.

Limited partnership funds in real estate have largely adopted a more aggressive investment, reflected by gearing. **Gearing** is the use of leverage. The degree of gearing can be expressed using a variety of ratios. In real estate funds, a popular gearing ratio is the percentage of a fund's capital that is financed by debt divided by the percentage of all long-term financing (e.g., debt plus equity). This ratio is often called the LTV (loan-to-value) ratio or the debt-to-assets ratio. Many traditional real estate funds have limited, if any, gearing, whereas a large proportion of the new private equity real estate limited partnerships have LTVs as high as 75%. Gearing ratios are also commonly expressed as the ratio of debt to equity.

☞ APPLICATION 13.5.5A

Private real estate fund A has $100 million of assets and $50 million of debt. Private real estate fund B has $20 million of equity and $30 million of debt. What are the LTV and debt-to-equity ratios of each of these geared funds? Fund A is 50% debt, and has an LTV of 50% and a debt-to-equity ratio of 1.0. Fund B is 60% debt, and has an LTV of 60% and a debt-to-equity ratio of 1.5.

Limited partnerships have also tended to adopt the fee structures commonly in place in private equity funds. In addition to an annual management fee, commonly in the region of 1% to 2% of assets under management, the newer funds have introduced performance-related fees, commonly in the region of 20% of returns. Generally, the incentive-based performance fees are subject to some form of hurdle rate or preferred return. The fund sponsors (or general partners) usually contribute some capital to the fund (e.g., 8% to 10%), thus potentially benefiting not only from the explicit incentive and management fees but also from their share of the limited partnership's return through their investments.

13.5.6 Open-End Real Estate Mutual Funds

Open-end real estate mutual funds are public investments that offer a non-exchange-traded means of obtaining access to the private real estate market. These funds are operated by an investment company that collects money from shareholders and invests in real estate assets following a set of objectives laid out in the fund's prospectus. Open-end funds initially raise money by selling shares of the funds to the public and generally continue to sell shares to the public when requested. Open-end real estate mutual funds allow investors to gain access to real estate investments with relatively small quantities of capital. These funds often allow investors to exit the fund freely by redeeming their shares (potentially subject to fees and limitations) at the fund's net asset value, which is computed on a daily basis.

However, these funds may limit investors' ability to redeem units and exit the fund when, for example, a significant percentage of shareholders wish to redeem their investments and the fund is encountering liquidity problems. These liquidity problems can be exacerbated when the real estate market is either booming or declining. Given that upward and downward phases in real estate prices may last a considerable length of time, some analysts may view real estate valuations used in some net asset value computations as trailing true market prices in a bull market (and trailing declines in a bear market).

The use of prices that lag changes in true market prices is known as **stale pricing**. Stale pricing of the net asset value of a fund provides an incentive for existing shareholders to exit (sell) during declining markets and new investors to enter (buy) during rising markets. These actions of investors exploiting stale pricing may be viewed as transferring wealth from long-term shareholders in the fund to the investors exploiting the stale prices. The reason that the purchase transactions in a rising market transfer wealth from existing shareholders to new shareholders is that the stale prices are artificially low and permit new shareholders to receive part of the profit when the fund's net asset value catches up to its true value. Conversely, sales transactions during declining markets transfer wealth from remaining shareholders to exiting shareholders because the stale prices are artificially high and permit the exiting shareholders to receive proceeds that do not fully recognize the true losses, leaving the true losses to be disproportionately borne by the remaining shareholders when the fund's net asset value falls to its true value.

During declining markets, an open-end fund may face redemption problems and be forced to sell some of its real estate assets at deep discounts to obtain liquidity. To protect long-term investors and fund assets, many open-end real estate mutual funds increasingly opt to reserve the right to defer redemption by investors to allow sufficient time to liquidate assets in case they need to do so.

In summary, investors in open-end mutual funds are typically offered daily opportunities to redeem their outstanding shares directly from the fund or to purchase additional and newly issued shares in the fund. This attempt to have high liquidity of open-end real estate fund shares contrasts with the illiquidity of the underlying real estate assets held in the fund's portfolio. This liquidity mismatch raises issues about the extent to which investors will receive liquidity when they need it most and whether realized returns of some investors will be affected by the exit and entrance of other investors who are timing or arbitraging stale prices.

13.5.7 Options and Futures on Real Estate Indices

Derivative products allow investors to transfer risk exposure related to either the equity side or the debt side of real estate investments without having to actually buy or sell the underlying properties. This is accomplished by linking the payoff of the derivative to the performance of a real estate return index, thus allowing investors to obtain exposures without engaging in real estate property transactions or real estate financing.

Challenges to real estate derivative pricing and trading include difficulties that arise with the highly heterogeneous and illiquid assets comprising the indices that underlie the derivative contracts. The indices underlying the derivatives may not correlate highly to the risk exposures faced by market participants, and therefore use of the derivatives for hedging may introduce basis risk, discussed in Chapter 10. Nevertheless, real estate derivatives may offer the potential for increased transparency and liquidity in the real estate market.

13.5.8 Exchange-Traded Funds Based on Real Estate Indices

Exchange-traded funds (ETFs) represent a tradable investment vehicle that tracks a particular index or portfolio by holding its constituent assets or a subsample of them. They trade on exchanges at approximately the same price as the net asset value of the underlying assets due to provisions that allow for the creation and redemption of shares at the ETF's net asset value. The actions of speculators attempting to earn arbitrage profits by creating and selling ETF shares when they appear overpriced in the market or buying and redeeming ETF shares when they appear underpriced in the market tend to keep ETF market prices within a narrow band of the underlying value of the ETF. These funds have the advantage of being a relatively low-trading cost investment vehicle (in the case of those ETFs that have reached a particular size or popularity among investors); they can be tax efficient; and they offer stock-like features, such as liquidity, dividends, the possibility to go short or to use with margin, and, in some cases, the availability of calls and puts. Exchange-traded funds based on real estate indices track a real estate index such as the Dow Jones U.S. Real Estate Index, which raises issues of basis risk to hedgers. Other ETFs, such as the FTSE NAREIT Residential, track a REIT index. Since REITs are publicly traded, the use of ETFs on REITs may offer cost-effective diversification but may not offer substantially distinct hedging or speculation opportunities.

13.5.9 Closed-End Real Estate Mutual Funds

A closed-end fund is an exchange-traded mutual fund that has a fixed number of shares outstanding. Closed-end funds issue a fixed number of shares to the general public in an initial public offering, and in contrast to the case of open-end mutual funds, shares in closed-end funds cannot be obtained from or redeemed by the investment company. Instead, shares in closed-end funds are traded on stock exchanges.

A **closed-end real estate mutual fund** is an investment pool that has real estate as its underlying asset and a relatively fixed number of outstanding shares. Unlike open-end funds, closed-end funds do not need to maintain liquidity to redeem shares, and they do not need to establish a net asset value at which entering and exiting investors can transact with the investment company. Most important, unlike with open-end funds, the closed-end funds themselves and their existing shareholders are not disrupted by shareholders entering and exiting the fund, especially in an attempt to arbitrage stale prices. This is because shareholders buy and sell shares on secondary markets rather than affecting fund liquidity by redeeming shares or subscribing to new shares.

Since closed-end funds are not required to meet shareholder redemption requests, the fund structure is generally more suitable for the use of leverage than that of open-end funds. The closed-end structure is frequently used to hold assets that investors often prefer to hold with leverage, such as municipal bonds. Similarly, the closed-end fund structure has advantages for investment in relatively illiquid assets, and is often used for such assets as real estate and emerging market stocks.

Like other closed-end funds, closed-end real estate mutual funds often trade at premiums or substantial discounts to their net asset values, especially when net asset values are not based on REITs, since REITs have market values. Closed-end real estate mutual funds usually liquidate their real estate portfolios and return capital to shareholders after an investment term (typically 15 years), the length of which is stated at the fund's inception.

13.5.10 Equity Real Estate Investment Trusts

This introduction to public equity real estate investment products concludes with a discussion of equity REITs. As introduced and briefly described in Chapter 12, REITs are a popular form of financial intermediation in the United States. This discussion focuses on equity REITs, which are REITs with a majority of their underlying real estate holdings representing equity claims on real estate rather than mortgage claims.

An equity REIT acquires, renovates, develops, and manages real estate properties. It produces revenue for its investors primarily from the rental and lease payments it receives as the landlord of the properties it owns. An equity REIT also benefits from the appreciation in value of the properties it owns as well as any increase in rents. In fact, one of the benefits of equity REITs is that their rental and lease receipts tend to increase along with inflation, making REITs a potential hedge against inflation.

One of the biggest advantages is that REITs are publicly traded. Most REITs fall into the capitalization range of $500 million to $5 billion, a range typically associated with small-cap stocks and the smaller half of mid-cap stocks. The market returns on equity REITs have been observed to have a strong correlation with equity market returns, especially the returns of small-cap stocks (and to a slightly lesser extent those of mid-cap stocks).

The strong correlation of equity REIT returns with the returns of similarly sized operating firms raises a very important issue. Are the returns of equity REITs highly correlated with the returns of small stocks because the underlying real estate assets are highly correlated with the underlying assets of small stocks? Or is this correlation due to the similar sizes (total capitalization values) of REITs and small-cap stocks and the fact that they are listed on the same exchanges? The explanation that REIT returns are highly correlated with the returns of similarly sized operating firms due to the similarity of the risks of their underlying assets seems dubious.

Commercial real estate valuations tend to depend on projected rental income, whereas operating firm valuations tend to depend on sales of products and services that are generally unrelated to real estate. However, the idea that the shared size and shared financial markets explain the correlation runs counter to traditional efficient capital market theory. Financial theory implies that market prices reflect underlying economic fundamentals rather than trading location and size or total capitalization. To the extent that REIT prices are substantially influenced by the nature of their trading would mean that observed returns are more indicative of stock market fluctuations and less indicative of changes in underlying real estate valuations. However, due to problems with other approaches, REIT returns form the basis for the empirical analyses presented at the end of this chapter.

There is no consensus on whether the high correlation of REIT returns with equity market returns is unique to public REITs or is simply masked in private REITs and appraisal-based returns. Further, there is no consensus on the implications of the observed strong correlation of public REIT returns and overall equity market returns on the risk premiums offered by public REITs.

13.6 EQUITY REIT RETURNS

Equity REITs can be either publicly traded or organized as a private fund. Investors are concerned about how the risk and return varies across these two structures.

13.6.1 Private versus Public REITs

As introduced and briefly described in Chapter 12, REITs are a popular form of financial intermediation in the United States. This discussion focuses on *public* equity REITs, which are REITs with a majority of their underlying real estate holdings representing equity claims on real estate rather than mortgage claims. Private REITs are also an important form of real estate investment that are offered to investors through private structures that are exempt from SEC registration in the United States. However, throughout this chapter and the discussion in Chapter 12 on REITs, the focus is on publicly traded REITs. Publicly traded REITs incur higher costs in order to be registered as a public security and to trade on an exchange. However, many investors prefer the liquidity of public REITs and the potential safety from the regulatory oversight as well as the price revelation available from public trading.

13.6.2 Do Public REITs Offer an Illiquidity Premium?

As in the case of products such as closed-end funds, REITs hold illiquid private investments, which generate returns that are passed through public REIT structures to form ownership units (shares) that are liquid. A fascinating and unresolved issue is whether owners of publicly traded REITs receive an expected return that includes a risk premium for illiquidity. On the one hand, the underlying properties are illiquid and it is possible that they are acquired at prices that are discounted for their illiquidity given that the real estate trades in a market dominated by private investors. On the other hand, competition by investors to receive a positive illiquidity premium while holding a liquid REIT would appear to drive property values up to the point that they no longer offer a risk premium for illiquidity. Dividend yields on private REIT structures tend to be moderately higher than those on public REITs, suggesting that public REITs offer little or no risk premium for holding illiquid real estate.

13.6.3 Real Estate Indices Based on Financial Market Prices

Unlike private commercial real estate, the reported returns of REITs are based on observations of frequent market prices. The ability to observe frequent market prices offers a huge potential advantage to measuring risk and return. Publicly traded real estate, especially REITs in the United States, provides regular market prices with which to observe, measure, and report real estate returns. The **FTSE NAREIT US Real Estate Index Series** is a family of REIT-based performance indices that covers the different sectors of the U.S. commercial real estate space. As with most investment categories of listed securities, there are numerous indices published.

13.7 KEY OBSERVATIONS REGARDING HISTORICAL RISKS AND RETURNS OF EQUITY REITs

Equity REIT returns are monthly returns observed from January of 2000 to December of 2018 for a total of 228 observations. Exhibit 13.5 provides univariate return statistics in the top panel, partial autocorrelations of returns in the middle panel, and a histogram of returns in the bottom panel.

Key observations on Equity REITs returns that are consistent with economic reasoning are an essential component of knowledge and include the following:

1. Equity REITs returns had historic volatility substantially exceeding that of global equities.
2. Equity REITs returns generated a moderate Sharpe ratio.
3. Equity REITs returns had a moderate negative skew.
4. Equity REITs returns had a markedly positive excess kurtosis.
5. Equity REITs experienced a massive maximum drawdown (i.e., almost −70%).

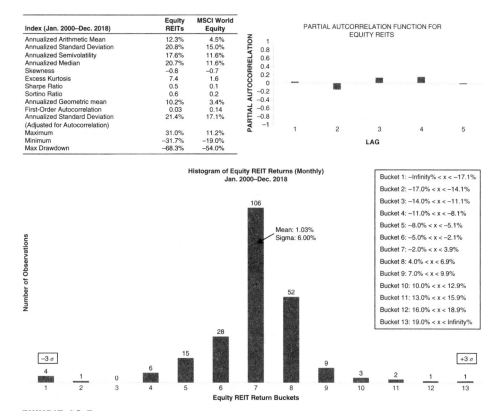

Index (Jan. 2000–Dec. 2018)	Equity REITs	MSCI World Equity
Annualized Arithmetic Mean	12.3%	4.5%
Annualized Standard Deviation	20.8%	15.0%
Annualized Semivolatility	17.6%	11.6%
Annualized Median	20.7%	11.6%
Skewness	−0.8	−0.7
Excess Kurtosis	7.4	1.6
Sharpe Ratio	0.5	0.1
Sortino Ratio	0.6	0.2
Annualized Geometric mean	10.2%	3.4%
First-Order Autocorrelation	0.03	0.14
Annualized Standard Deviation (Adjusted for Autocorrelation)	21.4%	17.1%
Maximum	31.0%	11.2%
Minimum	−31.7%	−19.0%
Max Drawdown	−68.3%	−54.0%

PARTIAL AUTCORRELATION FUNCTION FOR EQUITY REITS

Histogram of Equity REIT Returns (Monthly) Jan. 2000–Dec. 2018

Mean: 1.03%
Sigma: 6.00%

Bucket 1: −Infinity% < x < −17.1%
Bucket 2: −17.0% < x < −14.1%
Bucket 3: −14.0% < x < −11.1%
Bucket 4: −11.0% < x < −8.1%
Bucket 5: −8.0% < x < −5.1%
Bucket 6: −5.0% < x < −2.1%
Bucket 7: −2.0% < x < 3.9%
Bucket 8: 4.0% < x < 6.9%
Bucket 9: 7.0% < x < 9.9%
Bucket 10: 10.0% < x < 12.9%
Bucket 11: 13.0% < x < 15.9%
Bucket 12: 16.0% < x < 18.9%
Bucket 13: 19.0% < x < Infinity%

EXHIBIT 13.5   Statistical Summary of Returns

REVIEW QUESTIONS

1. What is the complementary option type to financial options?
2. What is the name of the point in a decision tree at which new information arrives?
3. List the two *major* approaches to valuing private commercial real estate equity.
4. Define *net operating income*.
5. How does the numerator of a pre-tax discounting approach differ from the numerator of an after-tax discounting approach?
6. How does the equity residual approach to real estate valuation differ from a DCF approach applied to the assets of a real estate project?
7. What are the characteristics that distinguish syndications from other real estate investment vehicles?
8. A real estate project is estimated to offer a 10% after-tax rate of return when the depreciation allowed for tax purposes is equal to the true economic depreciation. In what direction would the expected rate of return change if the depreciation allowed for tax purposes were accelerated relative to the true economic depreciation, and why?
9. Summarize two major unresolved issues risk-related issues of equity REIT returns.
10. Contrast the NAREIT and NCREIF real estate indices as measures of private commercial real estate performance.

Three

Hedge Funds

Part 3 on hedge funds begins with an introductory chapter, overviewing the industry and discussing how an institutional investor can establish a program of investing in hedge funds. Chapters 15 to 19 discuss five categories of hedge funds: macro and managed futures funds, event-driven hedge funds, relative value hedge funds, equity hedge funds, and funds of funds. Each of these categories groups hedge funds with similar investment strategies—for example, hedge funds that focus their investment ideas around certain events are grouped together in the event-driven hedge fund category. Each category is then further refined into strategies. For instance, there are four strategy groups within the event-driven hedge fund category: activist funds, merger arbitrage funds, distressed securities funds, and event-driven multistrategy funds.

CHAPTER 14

Structure of the Hedge Fund Industry

The term *hedge fund* originated with the first hedge fund, A.W. Jones & Co., which was established in 1949 and invested in both long and short equity positions. The intent was to limit market risk while focusing on stock selection. This hedge fund operated in relative obscurity until an article published in *Fortune* magazine in April 1966 spotlighted Alfred Winslow Jones.[1] The interest in Jones's product was large, and within two years, a survey conducted by the SEC established that the number of hedge funds had grown from 1 to 140. Many hedge funds were liquidated during the bear market of the early 1970s, and the hedge fund industry did not regain popularity until the end of the 1980s. The appeal of hedge funds increased tremendously in the 1990s, and by 2018, there were around 10,000 hedge funds with more than $3.2 trillion in total assets. For comparison, the amount of total assets for mutual funds, exchange-traded funds (ETFs), and institutional funds was $40 trillion in 2017.

14.1 DISTINGUISHING HEDGE FUNDS

The term *hedge fund* has evolved and expanded to include funds that do not necessarily hold hedged positions. In this book, hedge funds are distinguished from their traditional counterpart, mutual funds, with the definition in the next section.

14.1.1 Three Primary Elements of Hedge Funds

A hedge fund is an investment pool or investment vehicle that (1) is privately organized in most jurisdictions; (2) usually offers performance-based fees to its managers; and (3) can usually apply leverage, invest in private securities, invest in real assets, actively trade derivative instruments, establish short positions, invest in structured products, and generally hold relatively concentrated positions.

First, hedge funds are privately organized and generally unlisted. They are designed in this way to pool the resources of sophisticated investors and provide opportunities that are not available through traditional, regulated pools or that are more easily or cost effectively executed using private vehicles. Hedge funds are typically less regulated than public investment vehicles because of their privately organized nature. (In some jurisdictions, the fund management company of a hedge fund has to be registered in the same manner as the fund management company of a mutual fund.)

Hedge funds are designed to be private by using one or more safe harbor provisions. In investments, a **safe harbor** denotes an area that is explicitly protected by one set of regulations from another set of regulations. In the United States, for example, hedge funds are specifically exempt from the disclosure requirements of the U.S. Investment Company Act of 1940 through one of two exemptions, or safe harbors, available to funds that are not advertised or offered to the general public.

Second, hedge funds typically offer incentive-based fees to attract and motivate top managers. These fees are designed to align the interests of the managers with the investors, as is detailed in a subsequent section of this chapter. The potentially high and performance-based compensation to managers is central to the idea that hedge fund management implements highly sophisticated investment strategies that offer investment opportunities distinct from those available in the public investment space. How managers are compensated can change the nature of an investment, including its risks and returns.

Third, hedge funds typically allow one or more aspects of greater investment flexibility than do traditional investment vehicles. This investment flexibility is detailed in the next section.

14.1.2 Six Investment Flexibilities of Hedge Funds

The six major investment flexibilities used by hedge funds are:

1. Hedge fund strategies often invest in nonpublic, unlisted securities—that is, securities that have been issued to investors without the support of a prospectus and a public offering and that are not publicly traded.
2. Hedge funds often use leverage, at times very large amounts. Mutual funds in the United States are limited in the amount of leverage they can employ, able to borrow up to 33% of their net asset base. Hedge funds do not have this restriction. Consequently, it is not unusual to see some hedge fund strategies employing leverage up to 10 times their net asset base.
3. Hedge funds often use derivative strategies much more predominantly than do traditional investment vehicles such as mutual funds. In some strategies, such as convertible arbitrage or managed futures, the ability to sell or buy options or futures is a key component of executing the fund's strategy. The use of derivative strategies may result in nonlinear cash flows that may require more sophisticated risk management techniques. Derivative strategies can also increase fund leverage.
4. Hedge funds take short positions in securities to increase return or reduce risk. The ability to take very large short positions in public securities is one of the key distinctions between hedge fund managers and traditional money managers. Hedge fund managers explicitly incorporate their ability to short sell securities into their investment strategies. For example, equity long/short hedge funds tend to buy and short sell securities within the same industry to maximize their return but also to control their risk. This is very different from the actions of most traditional money managers, who are tied to a long-only securities benchmark. Shorting can also have the effect of increasing fund leverage.
5. Hedge funds sometimes trade in more esoteric or riskier underlying investments, such as those that are structured.

EXHIBIT 14.1 Comparing Mutual Funds and Hedge Funds

	Mutual Funds	**Hedge Funds**
Manager registration	Required	Required
Offering method (documentation)	Prescribed, detailed	Flexible, voluntary
Disclosure requirements	Prescribed, detailed	Flexible, voluntary
Investment strategies available	Restricted	Unrestricted
Concentration limits	Restricted	Unrestricted
Use of leverage	Restricted	Unrestricted
Use of derivatives	Restricted	Unrestricted
Allowable investors	Unrestricted (anyone)	Restricted (accredited only)

6. Hedge funds tend to be more actively managed than traditional investment vehicles, with more complex strategies and with more dynamic risk exposures than traditional funds, which are often constrained to generating performance that is linked to a benchmark.

Some funds are considered hedge funds even though they possess only one or two of the characteristics discussed in this section. Hedge funds are not defined by sharp lines of division from other investments; in fact, as alternative investments evolve, it is becoming increasingly difficult to distinguish hedge funds from other alternative investment vehicles, such as private equity funds.

The side-by-side comparison of mutual funds and hedge funds in Exhibit 14.1 summarizes distinctions between mutual funds and hedge funds commonly observed in various jurisdictions throughout the world.

The greater restrictions on mutual funds facilitate the distribution of shares more broadly to the public, whereas the lesser restrictions on hedge funds are consistent with limited distribution to the accredited investors or qualified purchasers whom regulators deem able to properly evaluate the risks inherent in the offering.

There are many reasons for the huge interest in hedge funds. First, hedge fund returns can offer low correlation with traditional investments and therefore serve as diversifiers. Strong bear markets over the past 25 years have fueled the interest of those investors who saw their traditional stock portfolios decline in value. Second, many investors recognize the advantage that hedge funds have with regard to investment flexibility, such as being able to go both long and short to maximize the value of their information about stocks, bonds, and other securities. Third, many investors sought the potential double-digit returns of the hedge fund industry, especially when other investment opportunities, such as bonds, offered low or even negative returns after taxes and anticipated inflation.

While hedge funds enjoyed enormous growth prior to 2007, the industry saw a decline in both the assets and the number of funds after 2007. The financial crises that began in 2007 caused the hedge fund industry to post negative returns and experience the first asset net outflows since 1994. Between the end of 2007 and the end of 2009, Hedge Fund Research, Inc. (HFR), a major firm specializing in the indexation and analysis of hedge funds, estimates that hedge fund industry assets declined by 25%, as fund losses totaled $176 billion and investors withdrew an additional $285 billion.

Exhibit 14.2 shows the change in the number of hedge funds over time. Notice that the hedge fund industry added new funds each year from 1996 to 2007. After

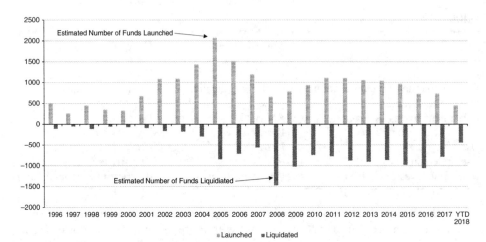

EXHIBIT 14.2 Estimated Number of Funds Launched/Liquidated
Source: Data from HFR Industry Reports, HFR, Inc. © 2018,
www.hedgefundresearch.com.

significant net attrition in 2008 and 2009, the number of hedge funds continued to grow through 2014, as more funds were launched than liquidated. More recently, we've witnessed net attrition from 2015 through 2017, as performance has been challenging and asset flows have experienced more volatility.

14.1.3 Industry Concentration

The year 2008 was an especially difficult year for hedge fund investing, with several prominent hedge fund frauds and massive fund liquidations. These events served to accelerate the trend of consolidation within the hedge fund industry. **Consolidation** is an increase in the proportion of a market represented by a relatively small number of participants (i.e., the industry concentration). While there were more than 9,700 hedge funds and funds of funds at the third quarter of 2018, institutional investors are showing a clear preference for the largest funds. An explanation is that hedge fund investors are seeking to invest with stable firms with demonstrated risk management processes and strong operational risk controls. Simply put, large funds are perceived as being less risky.

Another reason for hedge fund industry consolidation is the expense to hedge funds of facilitating due diligence by investors. Due diligence processes, discussed in Level II of the CAIA program, are performed by prospective investors prior to consummating their investment in a hedge fund. These due diligence processes place a substantial burden on the managers of hedge funds targeted for investment. The largest hedge funds can best afford the investments in staff and systems required to pass the strict investigations made by today's post-crisis institutional investors.

Exhibit 14.3 shows the consolidation in the hedge fund industry, as the largest funds continue to grow as a percentage of industry assets. Approximately 27.8% of hedge fund management firms manage more than $500 million. Combined, these funds manage over 94% of all industry assets. These large funds may be successful at raising assets because they have made large investments in compliance and risk

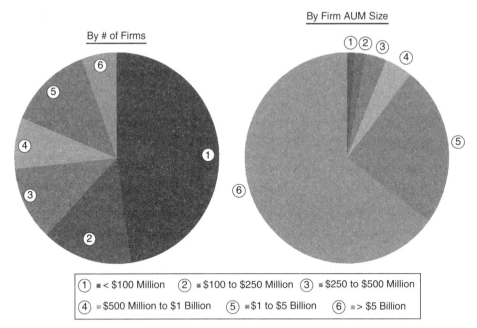

EXHIBIT 14.3   Distribution of Industry Assets by Firm AUM Tier
Source: Data from HFR Industry Reports, HFR, Inc. © 2018,
www.hedgefundresearch.com.

management infrastructures necessary to pass the enhanced due diligence processes of large institutional investors. This leaves more than 7,000 hedge funds competing for less than 6% of industry assets under management (AUM).

14.2   HEDGE FUND FEES

What attracts talented managers to the hedge fund industry? Hedge funds allow managers the flexibility to implement sophisticated strategies and to reap financial gains from high returns through fees and through their own investment in the fund. A typical hedge fund fee arrangement has two components: a management fee and an incentive (or performance) fee. The management fee is a constant percentage applied to the net asset value (NAV) of the fund. The NAV is the value of the fund's assets minus its liabilities. An incentive fee is a form of profit sharing wherein managers receive a stated percentage of profits. The incentive fee is applied to the profits of the firm after the management fee has been deducted. Incentive fees are received only if the hedge fund manager earns a profit for investors, and may be subject to other conditions and limitations. The management and incentive fees are typically expressed as a pair of numbers—such as 2 and 20, which would represent annual management fees of 2% and incentive fees of 20% of profit.

Fund managers usually have their own capital invested in the fund. The primary reason for fund managers to devote a substantial portion of their capital to their own fund is to align their financial interests with the financial interests of the limited partners and to communicate their faith in the fund and their alignment of interests to prospective investors. Fund managers therefore can benefit from high fund returns both through the incentive fees and through their investment in the fund.

The attraction of high potential returns and the associated fees generated as a result of high returns, along with the satisfaction of the freedom to use more flexible investment tools and trading strategies, fueled the exodus of talent from traditional investment vehicles to the hedge fund industry, and this pool of talent continues to drive the growth of assets to this brand of investing. In some cases, especially since the financial crisis of 2007 to 2009, investors can negotiate with the manager to reduce the total amount of fees paid. A hedge fund fee arrangement often includes other terms, such as hurdle rates, clawback provisions, and details regarding exact computations and payment dates.

14.2.1 Computation of Hedge Fund Fees

Although management fees vary, 1.5% annual management fees are common in the hedge fund industry and can substantially exceed the management fees of most traditional investment pools, such as mutual funds. Further, a 17.5% incentive fee is common in hedge funds in addition to the management fee. Incentive fees are generally not found in traditional investment vehicles. Typical hedge fund fees range from 1% to 3% for management fees and up to 30% for incentive fees. The management fee may be collected on a quarterly, semiannual, or annual basis, and the incentive fee is usually collected annually. Incentive fees can be very large when returns are high. The total annual fee as a percentage of fund assets is expressed in Equation 14.1:

$$\text{Annual Fee} = \text{Management Fee} + \{\text{Max}[0, \text{Incentive Fee} \\ \times (\text{Gross Return above HWM} - \text{Management Fee} - \text{Hurdle Rate})]\} \quad (14.1)$$

In Equation 14.1, management fee, incentive fee, and hurdle rate are expressed as percentages. HWM denotes the high-water mark of the fund, which is discussed in detail in the next section. The total annual fee in currency can be found by multiplying the percentage fees by the fund's NAV.

☞ APPLICATION 14.2.1A

TTMAR Hedge Fund has a 1.5 and 30 fee arrangement, with no hurdle rate and an NAV of $200 million at the start of the year. At the end of the year, before fees, the NAV is $253 million. Assuming that management fees are computed on start-of-year NAVs and are distributed annually, find the annual management fee, the incentive fee, and the ending NAV after fees, assuming no redemptions or subscriptions.

The annual management fee is simply 1.5% of $200 million, or $3 million. After the management fee of $3 million, the fund earned a profit of $50 million ($253 − $3 − $200). The incentive fee on the profit is $15 million ($50 × 30% = $15). Therefore, the ending NAV after distribution of fees to the fund manager is $235 million ($253 − $3 − $15).

It can be more challenging to back out the fees from observations of NAVs that are reported on an after-fee basis.

☞ APPLICATION 14.2.1B

VVMAR Hedge Fund has a 1.5 and 30 fee arrangement, with no hurdle rate and an NAV of $200 million at the start of the year. At the end of the year, after fees, the NAV is $270 million. Assuming that management fees are computed on start-of-year NAVs and are distributed annually, find the annual management fee, the incentive fee, and the ending NAV before fees, assuming no redemptions or subscriptions.

The incentive fee represents 30% of the total profits for the general partner and 70% of the net profits to the limited partners. Since the profit to the limited partners is $70 million, the incentive fee to the manager must be $30 million (i.e., $70 million × 30%/70%). Thus, the NAV after management fees but before incentive fees must be $300 million. The management fees are 1.5% of the starting NAV: 1.5% × $200 million = $3 million, inferring an ending NAV of $303 million before fees. To recap: $303 million is reduced to $300 million by the 1.5% management fee on the starting value of $200 million. The fund therefore earned a profit of $100 million after management fees ($300 million − $200 million). The incentive fee to the manager was 30% of $100 million, or $30 million. The profit after fees to the limited partners was $70 million, leaving an NAV of $270 million after all fees.

Note that in the previous application, the fund's NAV before fees grew by $103 million, whereas the NAV after fees grew by only $70 million. The key figure of $100 million growth (after the management fee) is found by dividing $70 million by (100% − 30%), where 30% is the incentive fee.

14.2.2 Hedge Fund Fees through Time

The concept of a high-water mark is crucial to understanding incentive fees through time. The **high-water mark** (HWM) is the highest NAV of the fund on which an incentive fee has been paid. Thus, the HWM is the highest NAV recorded on incentive fee computation dates but not necessarily the highest overall NAV. If incentive fees are calculated at the end of each calendar year, the HWM would be the maximum of the NAVs corresponding to the last day of each year. In practice, it would be unlikely that the overall highest NAV would happen to occur on the incentive fee computation date.

The idea of paying fees relative to an HWM ensures that fees subsequent to the date on which a fund reached its HWM will not be paid on recouped losses. To illustrate, if a fund's annual year-ending NAV fluctuated between $100 million and $110 million, the HWM would be $110 million. The managers could receive an incentive fee on the profits that were generated to reach the $110 million value the first time. However, when the fund's value declined back to $100 million and then returned to $110 million, the manager would not receive additional incentive fees on the recouped losses. Of course, if managers had returned earlier incentive fees due to a clawback arrangement (discussed in Chapter 3), then the incentive fees would apply to recouped losses.

Consider the following example, which is detailed in the spreadsheet shown in Exhibit 14.4. A hedge fund charges an annual management fee of 2%, and an incentive fee is paid in the amount of 20% of profits net of the management fee. Fees are paid annually subject to an HWM provision. Each time the annual NAV makes a new high at the end of a period, incentive fees are paid, and a new HWM is set. No incentive fee is paid during a drawdown, which is when losses in NAV have pushed the fund value below its HWM. The idea of an HWM is that incentive fees should be paid only once on each dollar of cumulative net profit to the fund.

The manager of the fund shown in the top panel in Exhibit 14.4 is not subject to a hurdle rate. A hurdle rate is a specified minimum return that must be earned by the investor before the incentive fee is applied to profits. Everything else being equal, hurdle rates tend to lower the total fees paid by the investor. In year 1 and year 2, the fund's investors pay an annual incentive fee of 20% of the 3% return net of management fees (incentive fee in this period is 0.6% of assets) in addition to the 2% management fee. Notice that the managers do not receive an incentive fee in either year 4 or year 5. It is clear why no incentive fee applies in year 4, as the fund posted a negative return, and there are no gains to share between the manager and the investor. The reason that no incentive fee is paid in year 5 is the HWM provision, as the 15.6% gain in year 5 is offset by the 10% loss in year 4, as well as the 2% management fee paid in each year. Because the gains in year 5 are simply offsetting prior losses, no incentive fee is paid in year 5.

The arithmetic average of the gross returns is 7.27%, while the manager in the first example earned average annual fees of 3.00% over the six-year period. Of course, the investor may not be pleased with this level of fees, as the manager's fee income was nearly as great as the investor's average net return of 4.27% over the same period. The idea of offering 2 and 20 fee arrangements is to attract managerial talent and effort to design and implement investment strategies that generate high enough returns to provide generous fees to managers and returns net of fees to investors.

One way to reduce the total fees paid is to have a hurdle rate provision included in the investor's subscription agreement. The bottom panel of Exhibit 14.4 illustrates a hard hurdle rate, as discussed in Chapter 3. With a 2% annual management fee and a 3% annual hurdle rate, the manager earns an incentive fee only when the NAV of the fund before fees exceeds that of the HWM by at least 5% annually. Notice that the insertion of the 3% hurdle rate leaves the investor $2.9 million richer over the six-year period, as the manager's average annual fee has fallen to 2.6%. The hurdle rate provision saved the investor 0.6% (that is, the incentive fee of 20% multiplied by the hurdle rate of 3%) in each year the incentive fee was paid. In the example of the lower panel of Exhibit 14.4, with a positive hurdle rate, the investor paid incentive fees only in years 3 and 6, whereas the investor without the hurdle rate provision also paid incentive fees in years 1 and 2.

14.2.3 Incentive Fees and Manager Behavior

Whereas management fees are widely accepted throughout the money management industry, it is the incentive fee that draws the most scrutiny and publicity to the hedge fund community. Unlike hedge fund managers, most traditional investment managers do not receive fees based on performance. In some cases, managers are prohibited by

EXHIBIT 14.4 Fee Calculations with and without Hurdle Rate

Year	Gross Return	Hurdle Rate	Management Fee (%)	Incentive Fee (% of Profits)	Incentive Fee (% of Assets)	Total Fee	Net Return	Beginning NAV	Ending NAV	Ending HWM
Year 1	5.00%	0.00%	2.00	20.00	0.60	2.60%	2.40%	$100.0	$102.4	$102.4
Year 2	5.00%	0.00%	2.00	20.00	0.60	2.60%	2.40%	$102.4	$104.9	$104.9
Year 3	20.00%	0.00%	2.00	20.00	3.60	5.60%	14.40%	$104.9	$120.0	$120.0
Year 4	−10.00%	0.00%	2.00	20.00	0.00	2.00%	−12.00%	$120.0	$105.6	$120.0
Year 5	15.60%	0.00%	2.00	20.00	0.00	2.00%	13.60%	$105.6	$119.9	$120.0
Year 6	8.00%	0.00%	2.00	20.00	1.20	3.20%	4.80%	$119.9	$125.7	$125.7

Year	Gross Return	Hurdle Rate	Management Fee (%)	Incentive Fee (% of Profits)	Incentive Fee (% of Assets)	Total Fee	Net Return	Beginning NAV	Ending NAV	Ending HWM
Year 1	5.00%	3.00%	2.00	20.00	0.00	2.00%	3.00%	$100.0	$103.0	$103.0
Year 2	5.00%	3.00%	2.00	20.00	0.00	2.00%	3.00%	$103.0	$106.1	$106.1
Year 3	20.00%	3.00%	2.00	20.00	3.00	5.00%	15.00%	$106.1	$122.0	$122.0
Year 4	−10.00%	3.00%	2.00	20.00	0.00	2.00%	−12.00%	$122.0	$107.4	$122.0
Year 5	15.60%	3.00%	2.00	20.00	0.00	2.00%	13.60%	$107.4	$122.0	$122.0
Year 6	8.00%	3.00%	2.00	20.00	0.60	2.60%	5.40%	$122.0	$128.6	$128.6

law from earning fees directly related to investment performance. Incentive fees, like management fees, are designed to compensate managers for their time, effort, and expertise. Further, incentive fees are designed to align manager and investor interests by encouraging fund managers to generate superior returns. The alignment of manager and investor interests can reduce agency costs. However, incentive fees can encourage managers to be aggressive in risk taking, and hence regulators often discourage them, especially for investments open to the public and to smaller, possibly unsophisticated investors. For example, **asymmetric incentive fees**, in which managers earn a portion of investment gains without compensating investors for investment losses, are generally prohibited for stock and bond funds offered as '40 Act mutual funds in the United States.

Perfect alignment of manager and investor interest is not possible, because contracting is not costless and because the parties differ with regard to risk tolerance, diversification, and other factors. **Optimal contracting** between investors and hedge fund managers attempts to align the interests of both parties to the extent that the interests can be aligned cost-effectively, with marginal benefits that exceed marginal costs.

Managerial coinvesting is an agreement between fund managers and fund investors that the managers will invest their own money in the fund. The idea is that by having their own money in the fund, managers will work hard to generate high returns and control risk. However, the downside to managerial coinvesting can be excessive conservatism by the hedge fund manager. **Excessive conservatism** is inappropriately high risk aversion by the manager, since the manager's total income and total wealth may be highly sensitive to fund performance. Note that investors tend to be better diversified than managers, meaning they are less exposed to the idiosyncratic risks of the fund in relation to their total wealth.

The idea of incentive fees is to provide managers with a share of upside profits without promoting excessive conservatism through high exposure to losses, as is possible in the case of substantive coinvesting. But incentive fees can generate higher agency costs through perverse incentives. A **perverse incentive** is an incentive that motivates the receiver of the incentive to work in opposition to the interests of the provider of the incentive. Specifically, the behavior of fund managers may become especially contrary to the interests of the investors depending on the relative values of the fund's NAV and HWM. Kouwenberg and Ziemba suggest that this perverse incentive is substantially reduced when the fund manager invests in the fund along with investors, especially when the investment exceeds 30% of the manager's personal net worth, as the upside from additional incentive fees earned on risky investments is offset by the potential losses of the manager's personal investment in the fund.[2]

14.2.4 The Present Value of a Hedge Fund Fee Annuity

The purpose of this section is to demonstrate the potential value of an annuity of fees available to hedge fund managers to illustrate the manager's incentive to maintain profitability. The **annuity view of hedge fund fees** represents the prospective stream of cash flows from fees available to a hedge fund manager. The example assumes a standard 2% management fee and a 20% incentive fee that is distributed to the fund manager each year. The example allows for a hurdle rate (or preferred return), even though hedge funds are less likely to have these provisions than are private equity funds. For simplicity, it is assumed that the fund earns a constant rate of return and uses that same rate as a discount rate in present value computations. No additional capital is invested in the fund, no partners withdraw their funds, and no distributions are made to the limited partners until the fund liquidates.

For example, consider Fund A with an initial NAV of $100 million. Fund A earns 17% each year, and there is no preferred return. Thus, at the end of year 1, Fund A has gross earnings of $17 million, from which it distributes $2 million as a management fee (2% of the starting-year NAV of $100 million) and $3 million in incentive fees (20% of the net profit of $15 million). Fund A begins year 2 with an NAV of $112 million ($117 – $2 – $3), on which it again earns 17% before fees. In the second year, Fund A earns $19.04 million (17% of $112 million), pays a management fee of $2.24 million (2% of the starting-year NAV of $112 million) and an incentive fee of $3.36 million (20% of the net profit of $16.8 million), and ends year 2 with an NAV of $125.44 million.

Now suppose that Fund A liquidates its $125.44 million in assets and distributes the proceeds to its limited partners at the end of year 2. The value of this distribution to the limited partners, discounted at 17%, is $91.636 million, as shown in the following equation:

$$PV = \$125.44 \, \text{million}/(1.17)^2 = \$91.636 \, \text{million}$$

Since Fund A began with $100 million, the remaining $8.364 million represents the present value (PV) of the fees distributed to the managers in years 1 and 2:

$$PV = (\$5.00 \, \text{million}/1.17) + [\$5.60 \, \text{million}/(1.17)^2] = \$8.364 \, \text{million}$$

Thus, 8.36% of Fund A's present value was distributed to managers in the form of management and performance fees. Note that Fund A's investors received a 12% annual return, which is the IRR (internal rate of return) from investing $100 million and receiving proceeds of $125.44 million after two years. This 12% return is a result of earning 17% before fees each year, while paying 2% in management fees and 3% (20% × 15%) in incentive fees each year. It is reasonable to believe that investors will be happy with earning 12% from providing capital and taking risk, and that managers will be happy with dedicating their talent and time in generating superior fund profits in return for receiving management and incentive fees.

The same approach is used to examine the effects of changing rates of return, hurdle rates, and fund longevity on the percentage of a fund's value that is received by fund managers. Exhibit 14.5 summarizes the results under a variety of scenarios.

The second-to-last row of Exhibit 14.5 contains the values for a fund that earns 17% per year before fees and has no hurdle rate. For two-year investments, the present value of fees equals approximately 8.4% of the NAV, as previously demonstrated in the example of Fund A. Note that if the time horizon is extended to 10 years, the percentage rises to 35.4%. It may initially appear surprising that the number is so large when fees are being discounted at 17%. However, the key factor that drives the magnitude of the percentages associated with longer-term horizons is that fees are distributed annually from the fund to the managers while the profits of the investors are reinvested. Thus, long-term time horizons enable managers to collect

EXHIBIT 14.5   Percentage of NAV Earned by the Hedge Fund before Fees and Distributed to Managers in the Form of 2%/20% Fees

Returns	Hurdle Rate	1	2	5	Longevity (years) 10	25	100	500
7%	0%	2.8%	5.5%	13.3%	24.8%	50.9%	94.2%	100.0%
7%	5%	1.9%	3.7%	9.0%	17.2%	37.6%	84.8%	100.0%
12%	0%	3.6%	7.0%	16.6%	30.5%	59.7%	97.4%	100.0%
12%	5%	2.7%	5.3%	12.7%	23.8%	49.3%	93.4%	100.0%
17%	0%	4.3%	8.4%	19.6%	35.4%	66.4%	98.7%	100.0%
17%	5%	3.4%	6.7%	16.0%	29.4%	58.1%	96.9%	100.0%

fees on retained earnings in addition to fees on the initial investments. When the fees on reinvested earnings are included and are expressed as a percentage of the initial investment, the percentage becomes large.

It should be noted that Exhibit 14.5 does not indicate that investors suffer poor returns. As indicated earlier, investors earned 12% per year after fees when the assets generated 17% before fees. To the extent that the returns generated on the fund's assets substantially exceed the returns available on other investments, the investors can enjoy superior rates of return under a 2 and 20 fee arrangement. As long as the gross returns are high, the investors will do well.

Exhibit 14.5 indicates two primary implications of a traditional hedge fund compensation scheme, such as a 2 and 20 arrangement. First, there is an enormous incentive for fund managers to generate high returns. The significant benefits of doing so attract the best managers to the hedge fund space. Note that in Exhibit 14.5, the value of the potential fees that managers can collect does not include the fees that they can ultimately receive on additional investments attracted by the high returns. With growth opportunities from new investors included, managers can reap even higher financial benefits from superior performance. Exhibit 14.5 also does not reflect the managers' profit on their own investment in the fund.

Second, Exhibit 14.5 illustrates the importance to fund managers of being able to remain in operation. It is the ability to earn fees on reinvested money and on newly attracted capital that offers managers the highest long-run benefits. Thus, managers have a very strong incentive to avoid poor returns, retain existing investors, and attract new investors.

The numerical analysis of this section assumed a constant rate of asset returns, essentially ignoring uncertainty. In practice, returns are likely to experience volatility and vary between high returns and low returns. If a fund experiences negative returns within a reporting period, the fund's manager may view the fund as likely to close, in which case the manager may have a strong incentive to take excessive risks in an attempt to recoup losses and stay in business. Even if the manager does not fear that the fund will close, if the fund's NAV falls substantially below its HWM, the manager may foresee no realistic chance of earning incentive fees in the near term unless the fund's risk is increased. Thus, an incentive fee structure may encourage enormous risk taking by managers.

Further, one of the benefits to fund managers of incentive fees is the ability to earn fees on high returns while not being liable for losses, other than possibly returning incentive fees due to clawback provisions. This asymmetric arrangement is another factor that may encourage enormous risk taking by managers. Thus, uncertainty in fund returns can have enormous implications on the behavior of managers with regard to risk taking. The next section explores the implications of uncertainty using option theory.

14.2.5 Hedge Fund Fees and Option Theory

The previous section illustrated the importance to a manager of maintaining high performance through an annuity view of hedge fund fees. The analysis assumed that the fund generated a constant profit. Of course, hedge fund returns contain volatility. This section illustrates the effect of return volatility on the value of managerial incentive fees using option theory. The **option view of incentive fees** uses option theory to demonstrate the ability of managers to increase the present value of their fees by increasing the volatility of the fund's assets.

This section focuses on a one-period model of incentive fees and assumes that the fund's hurdle rate is zero. In a more realistic framework, the manager not only has to be concerned with the value of the current period's incentive fees but also has to examine the effects of decisions on the future value of incentive and asset management fees.

Hedge fund incentive fees can be considered a call option on a portion of the profits that the hedge fund manager earns for investors. If the fund earns a profit, the manager collects an incentive fee. The hedge fund manager who does not generate a profit collects no incentive fee. The call option is on the fund's NAV, with a strike price equal to the HWM and an expiration date equal to the end of the period to which the incentive fee applies. This payoff is described using Equation 14.2:

$$\text{Payout on Incentive Fee Option} = \text{Max}[i(\text{ENAV} - \text{BNAV}), 0] \qquad (14.2)$$

where i is the incentive fee rate (e.g., 20%), ENAV is the ending NAV of the hedge fund, and BNAV is the strike price of the call option, which is equal to the NAV of the hedge fund at the start of the period or the fund's HWM if it is larger.

The maturity, or expiration, of the incentive fee option is one year. The manager pays for the option by providing time, effort, and talent. If the option is out-of-the-money at maturity (the end of the year), the hedge fund manager receives no incentive fee. Alternatively, if the option is in-the-money at the end of the year, the hedge fund manager can be considered as exercising the option and collecting the incentive fee. At the beginning of every year, the hedge fund manager receives a new call option. The new call option is at-the-money whenever an incentive fee has just been paid and there is no hurdle rate. The new call option is out-of-the-money to the extent that either the fund's NAV is below its HWM or the fund's hurdle rate exceeds zero.

The **incentive fee option value** is the risk-adjusted present value of the incentive fees to a manager that have been adjusted for its optionality. The incentive fee option value is often expressed using the Black-Scholes option pricing model, which generates the price of an option using five inputs. These five inputs, with their corresponding values in parentheses, are the current value of the underlying assets (the fund's

NAV), the strike price (the higher of the beginning-of-period NAV or the HWM), the time until maturity of the option (in this discussion, one year), the risk-free rate (a one-year risk-free bond yield), and the volatility of the underlying asset's returns (the standard deviation of the returns of the fund's NAV). Note that in the case of a hurdle rate, the strike price is the future value of the NAV using the hurdle rate.

The Black-Scholes option pricing model can be easily solved on a spreadsheet given these five values. However, a much easier approximation for at-the-money option prices can be used for discussion purposes. The **at-the-money incentive fee approximation** expresses the value of a managerial incentive fee as the product of 40%, the fund's NAV, the incentive fee percentage, and the volatility of the assets (σ_1) over the option's life. This approximation, which assumes that the incentive fee option is at-the-money and interest rates are very low, is shown in Equation 14.3 and provides a reasonably accurate approximation of the value of a manager's incentive fee over one incentive fee computation period:

$$\text{Incentive Fee Call Option Value} \approx i \times 40\% \times \text{NAV} \times \sigma_1 \qquad (14.3)$$

Consider a $100 million hedge fund with a 20% incentive fee for its managers. At the beginning of a one-year period, when the incentive fee option has been reset to being at-the-money, the approximated value of the incentive fee call option is as shown in Equation 14.3:

$$\text{Incentive Fee Call Option Value} \approx 8\% \times \$100 \, \text{million} \times \sigma_1$$

Inserting annual volatilities of 5%, 10%, and 20% would generate values of the one-year incentive fee of $0.4 million, $0.8 million, and $1.6 million, respectively. Equation 14.3 demonstrates the tremendous influence of the volatility of the fund's assets on the value of the incentive fee held by managers. Simply put, the fund manager can manipulate the value of the single-period incentive fee call option into any value desired by simply changing the volatility of the fund's assets through the fund's investment strategy. Note that the relationship is not intended to be applied when the incentive fee call option is in-the-money or out-of-the-money.

☞ APPLICATION 14.2.5A

Consider a $1 billion hedge fund with a 20% incentive fee at the start of a new incentive fee computation period. If the hedge fund computes incentive fees annually and begins the year very near its high-water mark, what would be the value of the incentive fee over the next year for annual asset volatilities of 10%, 20%, and 30% using the at-the-money incentive fee approximation formula?

Inserting $i = 20\%$, NAV = $1 billion, and the three given volatilities generates approximations of $8 million, $16 million, and $24 million.

Option analysis reveals several important implications of how the incentive fee can affect hedge fund manager behavior. First, hedge fund managers can increase the value of their incentive fee call options by increasing the volatility of a hedge fund's NAV. The holder of a call option will always prefer more volatility in the value of the underlying asset, because the greater the volatility, the greater the upside profits, whereas downside losses are limited.

Unlike managers, investors have more symmetric payoffs, since they must bear all of the losses when a fund's NAV falls below its HWM. This establishes a key conflict of interest between investors in the hedge fund and the hedge fund manager. Investors in the hedge fund own the underlying partnership units and receive payoffs offered by the entire distribution of return outcomes associated with the hedge fund NAV.

The costs associated with perverse incentives, meaning a potential increase in strategic risk taking, must be compared to the potential benefits that the performance fee provides, such as the alignment of other interests. In the absence of an incentive fee, managers may become pure asset gatherers, driven by the annuity view of fees. A **pure asset gatherer** is a manager focused primarily on increasing the AUM of the fund. A pure asset gatherer is likely to take very little risk in a portfolio and, like mutual fund managers, become a closet indexer. A **closet indexer** is a manager who attempts to generate returns that mimic an index while claiming to be an active manager.

A second important implication of the option view of hedge fund fees is how hedge fund managers react when their incentive fee call option is far-out-of-the-money. This happens when the hedge fund NAV has declined substantially below the HWM or when the fund has an unrealistically high hurdle rate, causing the strike price for the incentive fee option to be substantially higher than the NAV of the hedge fund. When an option is out-of-the-money, the hedge fund manager has two choices for increasing the value of the option. The first is to increase the volatility of the underlying asset, as demonstrated with option theory. The second is to pursue repricing of the option. When the incentive fee call option is far-out-of-the-money, it is unlikely that the hedge fund manager's current investors will allow the manager to lower the HWM. Therefore, hedge fund managers with incentive fees that are far-out-of-the-money have an incentive to close the existing fund and start a new hedge fund.

14.2.6 Hedge Fund Fees and Managerial Behavior

There is no doubt that hedge fund incentive fees motivate managers to try to generate higher expected returns. The primary issue that arises is the extent to which managerial decisions with regard to risk taking conflict with the preferences of the fund's investors. The annuity view of hedge fund fees indicates the enormous fees available to managers for being able to sustain long-term growth in assets. The option view of hedge fund fees indicates the enormous gains in single-period expected incentive fees that managers can generate by increasing the volatility of a fund's assets. The literature demonstrates some interesting facts regarding hedge fund fees and how they may influence the behavior of hedge fund managers.

1. Managers May Take Fewer Risks after a Period of High Returns and Take More Risks after a Period of Negative Returns

Hodder and Jackwerth's "Incentive Contracts and Hedge Fund Management" has a number of interesting theoretical results regarding incentive fees.[3] They model the financial preferences for hedge fund managers being compensated with incentive fees and find that consistent with a single-period option view, fund managers have an incentive to take large risks, and that this preference for risk taking depends "dramatically" on fund value. When the incentive option is far-into-the-money, the wealth effects to managers from risk taking are nearly symmetrical, and therefore excessive risk taking is not encouraged. Rather, managers have an incentive to lower risk to preserve their fees, known as the lock-in effect. The **lock-in effect** in this context refers to the pressure exerted on managers to avoid further risks once high profitability and a high incentive fee have been achieved.

Hodder and Jackwerth further note that as fund values decline and the incentive option becomes far-out-of-the-money, the payoff to managers is skewed to the right, and risk taking is strongly encouraged. In a multiple-period framework, Hodder and Jackwerth find that risk-taking behavior is rapidly moderated, or brought into reasonable bounds, when the fund experiences acceptable levels of positive subsequent return performance. They also find that if the fund asset value continues to decline, there is a point at which it is optimal for the fund manager to close the fund to pursue other opportunities. However, as a fund's value approaches the point that will trigger a decision to close, the manager acquires an especially strong incentive to take even higher risks. These managerial behaviors are not optimal from the perspective of the fund's investors. Common sense says that fund investors would prefer that risk-taking behavior be governed by analysis of market opportunities rather than by the effect of risk on the manager's compensation.

2. Managers May Modify the Time Series of Returns to Enhance Risk-Adjusted Performance or to Improve the Number of Profitable Months

A possible role of incentive fee structures in influencing managerial decisions involves dynamic behavior during the period in which the incentive fee is being applied. Agarwal, Daniel, and Naik examine the hypothesis that hedge funds have incentives to manage or massage reported returns upward as the accounting period for computing incentive fees is ending.[4] The terms *managing returns* and *massaging returns* refer to efforts by managers to alter reported investment returns toward preferred targets through accounting decisions or investment changes. Consistent with this hypothesis, Agarwal and colleagues find that December returns for hedge funds were higher than other months by 1.5% and that, after controlling for risk, residual returns continued to be 0.4% higher. The authors conclude that hedge funds may be managing, or massaging, their reported returns. However, they cannot explain why returns were unusually low between June and October of each year.

Kazemi and Li show that hedge fund managers may manage the volatility of their return processes to balance several risks and incentives.[5] A fund manager has an incentive to increase the fund's volatility, especially if the option is about to expire out-of-the-money, meaning that the fund's NAV is below its HWM near the end of the period. However, higher volatility increases the probability that the fund may experience negative performance. This can negatively affect the manager's welfare in four ways: (1) a manager who has personal capital invested in the fund will have to share in the losses; (2) negative performance means that the fund's NAV will be further below the HWM, making it less likely that the manager can collect incentive fees in the future; (3) negative performance could lead investors to redeem their capital, reducing the asset management fees of the fund for current and future periods; and (4) negative performance, along with higher volatility, could damage the fund manager's reputation, reducing future income. Kazemi and Li empirically test the impact of all these incentives on the behavior of hedge fund managers. They show that a manager tends to increase the fund's return volatility if (1) the incentive option is at-the-money, (2) the fund's NAV has spent a significant amount of time under the HWM, and (3) the fund's assets are liquid enough to allow the manager to adjust the fund's volatility. Further, they show that small and young funds do not tend to adjust their volatility: At a time when fund managers are trying to establish their reputations, they are reluctant to risk losing their assets by adjusting the volatility of their funds.

Thus, both theoretical and empirical analyses indicate that managers respond to incentive fees in ways that include behavior other than attempts to serve fund investors. The implications of incentive fees are numerous and substantial. Hedge fund managers usually understand options and the implications of their management decisions on their wealth. However, managerial behavior should not be overgeneralized based on potentially perverse incentives. Most managers may be driven toward serving investors based on ethical considerations or in order to preserve their professional reputations and their ability to continue to work in their chosen field. Further, to the extent that incentive fees generate perverse incentives, hedge fund investors have an incentive to demand compensation arrangements that ameliorate the difficulties of excessive risk taking, such as requiring substantial co-investment by managers. The primary conclusions should be the importance of understanding the potential conflicts of interest caused by incentive fees and the need to perform careful due diligence and monitor managerial behavior.

14.3 HEDGE FUND CLASSIFICATION

A critical dimension in understanding hedge funds is the spectrum of trading strategies that underlie their performance. Hedge funds as a group are identified, at least in part, by their use of sophisticated trading strategies, and hedge funds are primarily differentiated from one another by their trading strategies. The diverse strategies that comprise the universe of hedge funds are often organized into a classification of hedge fund strategies. A **classification of hedge fund strategies** is an organized grouping and labeling of hedge fund strategies. Hedge funds are classified differently by different commentators, authors, and database managers. This book uses the classification of hedge fund strategies shown in the following list. The organization of the last five chapters of Part 3 (Chapters 15 to 19) follow this organization closely, with categories I through V corresponding to Chapters 15 to 19.

CAIA Classification of Hedge Fund Strategies

  I. Macro and Managed Futures Funs
    (A) Macro
    (B) Managed Futures
 II. Event-Driven Hedge Funds
    (A) Activists
    (B) Merger Arbitrage

The hedge fund industry is composed of single-manager funds (Chapters 15 to 18) as well as funds of funds (Chapter 19). The distinction between single-manager hedge funds and funds of funds is important. A **fund of funds** in this context is a hedge fund with underlying investments that are predominantly investments in other hedge funds. A **single-manager hedge fund**, or single hedge fund, has underlying investments that are not allocations to other hedge funds.

A single hedge fund may be a multistrategy fund. A **multistrategy fund** deploys its underlying investments with a variety of strategies and sub-managers, much as a corporation would use its divisions. In a multistrategy fund, there is a single layer of fees, and the sub-managers are part of the same organization. The underlying components of a fund of funds are themselves hedge funds, with independently organized managers and a second layer of hedge fund fees to compensate the manager for activities relating to portfolio construction, monitoring, and oversight.

An analogy can be made between hedge funds and stocks in understanding the distinction between single-manager funds, multistrategy funds, and funds of funds. As single stocks are to mutual funds, single-manager hedge funds are to funds of funds. For example, investing in a single stock is like investing in a single-manager hedge fund in that in both cases there is a substantial amount of idiosyncratic risk. The company's industry or the hedge fund manager's style may go out of favor, or the CEO of the company or the fund manager may make some consequential mistakes. There is substantial dispersion in returns across single stocks or single hedge funds, so concentrating wealth in a single investment can lead to riches or ruin. Continuing with the analogy, investing in a multistrategy fund rather than a single-manager hedge fund is akin to investing in a conglomerate stock rather than a stock focused on a single line of business.

Funds of funds can also be compared to mutual funds. Just as mutual funds invest in a large number of stocks across industries to diversify risk, funds of funds invest in multiple hedge fund managers and strategies to control risk. If a fund of funds includes a fund or strategy that experiences dramatic losses, investors' percentage losses are likely to be reduced by other managers or strategies in the fund of funds that maintained or grew their value. Whereas portfolio concentration in a few stocks or hedge funds can lead to success or failure, mutual funds and funds of funds offer returns in a much narrower range due to the diversification inherent in multiple investments.

Fund mortality, the liquidation or cessation of operations of funds, illustrates the risk of individual hedge funds and is an important issue in hedge fund analysis. The data underlying Exhibit 14.2 shows that more than 13,000 hedge funds have liquidated since 1996, including 11,000 funds that have liquidated since 2006. These numbers reflect only a subset of total hedge fund liquidations, as HFR can only track fund liquidations among the funds that chose to report to its database. Of the hedge funds alive in 2010, HFR estimates that approximately half have survived more than five years, 29% are less than three years old, and 21% are between three and five years old. In a study of commodity trading advisers, Gregoriou and associates estimate that the average hedge fund life was 4.4 years. The study also notes that funds with larger AUM and lower volatility tended to exist longer.[6] Later, we will discuss survivor bias, which can be an important issue in the performance analysis of hedge funds.

14.4 HEDGE FUND RETURNS AND ASSET ALLOCATION

This section overviews the process of designing and implementing a hedge fund program. A **hedge fund program** refers to the processes and procedures for the construction, monitoring, and maintenance of a portfolio of hedge funds. We begin by providing an overview of available funds and strategies.

A starting point of hedge fund analysis is to organize and analyze funds by their type of strategy. Before hedge funds are included in a portfolio, the risks of various hedge fund strategies should be understood. Specifically, the historical distribution of returns of each hedge fund strategy should be analyzed to determine its shape and properties. Empirical evidence presented in later chapters shows that many hedge fund return distributions have exhibited properties that are distinctly non-normal. The issue is how to apply this information in constructing a hedge fund program.

One observation is as follows: Do not construct a hedge fund program based on only one type of hedge fund strategy, as each hedge fund style exhibits different return distributions. Therefore, benefits can be obtained by diversifying across hedge fund strategies. This is classic portfolio theory: Do not put all of your eggs into one hedge fund basket.

An alternative to aggregating the returns of individual hedge funds into hypothetical portfolios is to observe the return of actual portfolios of hedge funds, known as funds of funds (FoFs). A fund of funds (or fund of hedge funds) is a hedge fund that has other hedge funds as its underlying investments. The three advantages of observing the returns of funds of funds are that (1) FoFs directly reflect the actual investment experience of diversified investors in hedge funds,[7] (2) the databases on FOFs have fewer biases than those on individual hedge funds, and (3) the net performance of FoFs is net of the costs of due diligence and portfolio construction from investing in hedge funds. These costs, which are borne directly by investors who invest directly in individual hedge funds, are not reflected in the returns of individual hedge funds.

14.4.1 Grouping Strategies by Systematic Risk

For the purposes of risk management and asset allocation, the various hedge fund strategies are often grouped according to their risk exposures. Within this view there are generally four groupings of hedge fund strategies: (1) **equity strategies**, which exhibit substantial market risk; (2) **event-driven strategies**, which seek to earn returns by taking on event risk, such as failed mergers, that other investors are not willing or prepared to take, and **relative value strategies**, which seek to earn returns by taking risks regarding the convergence of values between securities; (3) **absolute return strategies**, which seek to minimize market risk and total risk; and (4) **diversified strategies**, which seek to diversify across a number of different investment themes. This grouping of hedge fund strategies is designed to facilitate risk management and asset allocation rather than to serve as a detailed classification system, such as the CAIA classification system discussed in section 14.3. The next four sections detail each group.

14.4.2 Equity Strategies

Hedge funds that are substantially exposed to stock market risk include equity hedge and short bias funds. These hedge fund strategies invest primarily in equities and always retain some net stock market exposure. For example, many long/short equity funds may have 100% gross long exposures, 60% gross short exposures, and 40% net market exposure. While the fund is exposed to only 40% of the beta risk of the underlying market, investors are taking 160% exposure to the manager's stock selection skill. Note that funds with such low net exposure are likely to outperform stocks in a rapidly declining market while underperforming stocks in a strong bull market.

Short bias funds average a strong negative beta to global equity markets, essentially holding all stocks in a short sale position. These funds, with a negative correlation to global stocks, are a great risk reducer, serving to substantially reduce losses in a time of equity bear markets. However, these funds offer the lowest returns of any hedge fund strategy, underperforming global stocks over a full market cycle. While this may seem to be a disappointing return, short sellers may be highly skilled at stock selection, as evidenced by a large estimated alpha. In other words, the historical average returns of short sellers are estimated to be higher than the returns of the market portfolio when adjusted for their negative systematic risk.

14.4.3 Event-Driven and Relative Value Strategies

Returns of hedge funds in the event-driven and relative value categories have historically experienced the lowest standard deviation as well as the largest values of negative skewness and excess kurtosis. These strategies have consistently earned small profits but are prone to posting large losses over short periods of time. The return pattern is similar to what is earned by an insurance company that collects small premiums on a regular basis but once in a while experiences a large negative return. Event-driven and relative value strategies typically hold hedged positions.

Merger Arbitrage In merger arbitrage, managers seek to hold equal and offsetting amounts of stock market risk in their long and short positions involved in a merger. Similarly, positions with substantially offsetting risks are used in fixed-income and convertible bond arbitrage strategies that seek to minimize some risks, such as equity market and interest rate risk, but are exposed to other risks, such as credit risks.

Consider merger arbitrage, wherein the majority of the time investors experienced monthly returns in the 0%–2% range. These results are very favorable, as evidenced by their standard deviation being less than one-third of the MSCI World Index compared to equity markets, in which the returns are much more dispersed. The consistency with which merger arbitrage funds delivered moderately positive performance indicates less risk relative to overall equity market performance.

However, merger arbitrage is exposed to extreme losses due to significant event risk, as the returns exhibit large values of negative skewness and excess kurtosis. Merger arbitrage is similar to selling a put option or selling insurance, which in effect allows managers to underwrite the risk of loss associated with a failed merger or acquisition.

14.4.4 Event Risk and Volatility

Many financial transactions that contain event risk, such as merger arbitrage positions, can be viewed or described as writing options, although the underlying positions do not literally contain traditional options. Actual sales of option securities, as well as the effective sale of options through event-related arbitrage strategies, are known as short volatility exposures.

Short Volatility   **Short volatility exposure** is any risk exposure that causes losses when underlying asset return volatilities increase. Event risk and short volatility trading strategies tend to have short volatility exposures because they are negatively exposed to event risk, and events cause market volatility.

During stable or normal market conditions, a short volatility exposure makes a profit through the collection of premiums as long as realized volatility is less than the market's anticipated volatility. But in rare cases, short volatility strategies incur a substantial loss when the unexpected happens and event-driven hedge funds experience losses associated with the failure of the expected event. Losses occur when volatility increases beyond expectations or when anticipated events do not materialize.

Insurance Contract   Another way to consider the risk of event-driven strategies is that it is similar to the risk incurred in the sale of an insurance contract. Insurers sell insurance policies and collect premiums. In return for collecting the insurance premium, they take on the risk of unfortunate economic events. If nothing happens, the insurance company gets to keep the insurance/option premium. However, if there is an event, the insurance policyholder can put the policy back to the insurance company in return for a payout. The insurance company must then pay the face value, or the strike price, of the insurance contract and bear a loss.

Off-Balance-Sheet Risk   Event risk is effectively an **off-balance-sheet risk**—that is, a risk exposure that is not explicitly reflected in the statement of financial positions. The balance sheet of a typical merger arbitrage hedge fund manager would have offsetting long and short equity positions reflecting the purchase of the target company's stock and the sale of the acquiring company's stock. Looking at these offsetting long and short equity positions, an investor might conclude that the hedge fund manager has a hedged portfolio with long positions in stock balanced against short positions in stock. Yet the balance sheet positions alone do not explicitly indicate the true risk of merger arbitrage: The fund has effectively issued financial market insurance against the possibility that the deal will break down. This short volatility strategy will not show up from just a casual observation of the hedge fund manager's investment statement.

Relative Value   Although merger arbitrage was used as an example to highlight the downside risk exposure, the risks are similar for relative value or event-driven strategies. Each of these strategies has a similar short put option exposure with outlier event risk. Relative value trading strategies bet that the prices of two similar securities will converge in valuation over the investment holding period. These strategies often earn a return premium for holding the less liquid or lower-credit-quality security while going short the more liquid or creditworthy security. Through time, the strategy is a speculation that the two securities will converge in valuation and the hedge fund manager will earn a spread, or premium, that once existed between the two securities. **Convergent strategies** profit when relative value spreads move tighter, meaning that two securities move toward relative values that are perceived to be more appropriate.

14.4.5 Event Risk and Insurance Contracts

Convergent strategies may be viewed as selling financial market insurance against market events. If unusual market events do not occur, the hedge fund manager earns an insurance premium for betting correctly that the spread between the two securities will decline through time. However, if there is an unusual or unexpected event in the financial markets, the two securities are likely to diverge in valuation, and the hedge fund manager loses on the trade. Relative value strategies are essentially short volatility strategies, much like event-driven hedge fund strategies.

Long-Term Capital Management and the Russian Default   Consider the demise of Long-Term Capital Management (LTCM), a prestigious relative value hedge fund manager established in the mid-1990s. Its strategy was simple: Securities with similar economic profiles should tend to converge in price subsequent to perceived dislocations. Year in and year out, LTCM was able to collect option-like premiums in the financial markets for insuring that the valuations of similar securities would converge.

However, a disastrous economic event eventually occurred: the default by the Russian government on its bonds in the summer of 1998. A rapid flight to quality ensued in the financial markets as investors sought the safety of the most liquid and creditworthy instruments. Instead of valuations converging as LTCM had bet they would, valuations of many similar securities diverged. The hedge fund's short put option profile worked against it, and it lost massive amounts of capital.[8] The huge leverage LTCM employed exacerbated its short put option exposure, and it was forced to liquidate its positions, realize its massive losses, and close. This collapse further disrupted financial markets, vividly illustrating the dangers of short volatility exposure.

Credit   Event-driven and relative value hedge fund strategies may also be viewed as bearing similarities to investing in credit-risky securities, such as high-yield bonds. Credit risk distributions are generally exposed to significant downside risk. This risk is embodied in the form of credit events, such as downgrades, defaults, and bankruptcies. Consequently, credit-risky investments are also similar to insurance contracts or the sale of put options.

An investment in high-yield bonds is essentially the sale of an insurance contract (or put option) that says that the insurance seller (or option writer) is liable for losses due to credit events that may occur. Under normal market conditions, the investor collects the high coupons (insurance or option premiums) associated with the high-yield bond. But if large or numerous credit events occur, such as defaults, downgrades of credit ratings, or bankruptcy filings, the high-yield investor is liable for the losses.

Credit-risky investments experience negative skew and leptokurtosis because they are exposed to event risk: the risk of downgrades, defaults, and bankruptcies. These events cause more of the probability mass to be concentrated in the extreme left-hand tail of the return distribution, leading to the negative skew. The combination of leptokurtosis and negative skew reflects the considerable downside risk. This downside risk is sometimes referred to as fat tail risk because it reflects the fact that credit-risky investments have a relatively large probability mass in the downside tail of their return distributions.

In summary, many types of hedge funds act like insurance companies or option writers: If there is a disastrous financial event, they bear the loss.[9] This exposure is exacerbated to the extent that arbitrage funds apply leverage.

14.4.6   Absolute Return Strategies

Many hedge funds are often described as absolute return products. Absolute return products are investments in which the returns are designed to be consistently positive rather than being linked to or assessed against broad market performance. Hedge fund managers generally claim that their investment returns are derived from their skill at security selection, with the market risk of the portfolio hedged by short positions in broad indices or overvalued stocks from the same industry. Therefore, the returns should be evaluated on an absolute basis, meaning whether or not they were positive, rather than on a relative basis, meaning whether or not they exceeded a broad market index.

Many hedge fund managers build concentrated portfolios of relatively few investment positions and do not attempt to ensure that their returns match the returns of a particular stock or bond index. Some hedge funds appear to have been able to minimize their exposure to credit risk and equity market risk. These hedge funds tend to have a small skew or none at all and to exhibit low values of leptokurtosis or even generate platykurtosis, in which the tails of the distribution are thinner than in a normal distribution.

Hedge funds can offer a quite different return profile than mutual funds, which are often described as relative return products. A **relative return product** is an investment with returns that are substantially driven by broad market returns and that should therefore be evaluated on the basis of how the investment's return compares with broad market returns. Given that most mutual funds are constrained to hold long positions and follow a narrow mandate, they are destined to lose money when their market segment declines. Many hedge fund managers are judged by their level of consistently positive returns, whereas mutual fund managers are judged by their return relative to their benchmark index.

A single-strategy hedge fund may struggle to earn positive absolute returns in any and all market conditions, especially if its strategy is event driven or directional. Carefully selected diversification across hedge fund strategies should allow investors to earn more consistent absolute returns. Two strategies that seem to come close to meeting this goal of absolute returns are equity market-neutral and market-defensive funds of funds. These strategies stand out for their low standard deviations, low drawdowns, low correlations to equity markets, and skewness and kurtosis statistics that are close to indicating normality.

14.4.7 Diversified Fund Strategies

Global macro, systematic diversified funds (i.e., managed futures funds), multistrategy funds, and funds of hedge funds can be an attractive addition to an investor's portfolio from the perspective of diversification. These funds can offer high returns, reasonable risks, and low drawdowns. In addition, global macro and systematic diversified funds have exhibited a return pattern that is remarkably symmetrical, very close to the normal distribution—an elusive pattern sought by asset managers. For risk-averse investors, these would be the ideal investment from a risk perspective, provided that attractive performance persists.

When conducting risk management, one of the questions that should be asked is: What is the worst that can happen to this strategy? The returns generated by various funds and fund strategies in 2008 may provide examples of near-worst-case outcomes. An analysis of hedge fund return patterns shows that managed futures funds profited in 2008, whereas macro funds generally maintained their value. Undoubtedly, the credit and liquidity crisis that swept through global financial markets had an impact on other hedge fund returns, potentially skewing those returns toward the negative side and expanding the tails of the distributions.

14.5 EVALUATING A HEDGE FUND INVESTMENT PROGRAM

This section discusses the evaluation of a hedge fund investment program.

14.5.1 Hedge Fund Investment Program Parameters

Setting specific parameters will determine how the hedge fund program is constructed and operated and should include risk and return targets, as well as the type of hedge fund strategies that may be selected. Absolute return parameters should operate at two levels: that of the individual hedge fund manager and that of the overall hedge fund program. For example, the investor should set target return ranges for each hedge fund manager and a specific target return level for the entire absolute return program. Parameters for the individual managers may be different from those for the program.

The program parameters for the hedge fund managers may be based on such factors as volatility, expected return, types of instruments traded, leverage, and historical drawdown. Other factors may be included, such as length of track record, periodic liquidity, minimum investment, and assets under management. Liquidity is particularly important, because an investor needs to know the time frame for cashing out of an absolute return program if hedge fund returns appear unattractive or cash is needed.

Before considering how to incorporate hedge funds as part of a strategic investment program, the following question must be asked: Should hedge funds be included? Both the return potential of hedge funds and their role in diversifying or otherwise altering the aggregate risk of a portfolio that includes stocks and bonds should be considered.

Hedge funds can expand the investment opportunity set for investors, as many hedge fund strategies have offered risk-adjusted returns above those of stocks and bonds as well as provided risk management tools.

14.5.2 Three Research Findings Regarding Hedge Fund Performance

Recent research on hedge funds indicates consistent positive performance and low correlation with traditional asset classes. Although these conclusions may present opportunity, there are several caveats to keep in mind with respect to the documented results for hedge funds.

First, research provides clear evidence that shocks to one segment of the hedge fund industry can be felt across many different hedge fund strategies.[10] Second, future results generally differ from past results. In the case of hedge fund returns, there are reasons to believe that past results may consistently overestimate future results. Most of the research to date on hedge funds has still not factored in the tremendous growth of this industry over the past 10 years. Thus, the impact on returns of this explosive growth has yet to be fully documented.

Third, some form of bias—either survivorship bias or selection bias—exists in the empirical studies. All of the cited studies make use of hedge fund databases that have biases embedded in the data. These biases, if not corrected, can unintentionally inflate the estimated returns to hedge funds. It has been estimated that these biases can add from 70 to 450 basis points to the estimated total annual returns of hedge funds.

Most of the prior studies of hedge funds have generally examined hedge funds within a mean-variance efficient frontier framework. Generally, Sharpe ratios are used to compare hedge fund performance to that of stock and bond indices. However, hedge funds may pursue investment strategies that have nonlinear payoffs or are exposed to significant event risk, both of which may not be apparent from a Sharpe ratio analysis because this type of analysis assumes that returns are symmetric and normally distributed, meaning that the mean and the variance fully explain returns. Bernardo and Ledoit demonstrate that Sharpe ratios are misleading when the distribution of returns is not normal, and Spurgin shows that fund managers can enhance their Sharpe ratios by selling off the potential return distribution's upper end—for example, by entering a swap to pay the year's highest monthly return and be compensated for the year's lowest monthly return.[11]

14.5.3 Opportunistic Hedge Fund Investing

Several hedge fund investment strategies can be referred to as **opportunistic**, which is when a major goal is to seek attractive returns through locating superior underlying investments. Opportunistic investing is driven by the identification of and potentially aggressive exposure to investments that appear to offer superior returns (ex ante alpha), typically on a temporary basis. Opportunistic investing can be contrasted to traditional portfolio management, which is dominated by longer-term positions and acceptance of risks and returns commensurate with broad market conditions. The opportunistic nature of hedge funds can provide an investor with new investment opportunities that cannot otherwise be obtained through traditional long-only investments.

The Approach   There are several ways hedge funds can be opportunistic. First, many hedge fund managers can add value to an existing investment portfolio through specialization in a sector or in a market strategy. These managers seek to contribute above-market returns through application of superior skill or knowledge of a narrow market or strategy. In fact, this style of hedge fund investing describes most of the sector hedge funds in existence.

Consider a portfolio manager whose particular expertise is the biotechnology industry. He has followed this industry for years and has developed a superior information set to identify winners and losers. In a traditional investing approach, the manager purchases those biotech stocks he believes will increase in value and avoids those biotech stocks he believes will decline in value. Often, the selections are made with an effort to be moderately diversified within the sector, and positions are adjusted slowly. However, this strategy may be criticized for not using the manager's superior information set to its fullest advantage. The ability to go both long and short biotech stocks in a hedge fund is the only way to maximize the value of the manager's information set. Furthermore rapid trading, more concentrated positions, and use of leverage can maximize the benefits of the manager's superior information. Therefore, a biotech hedge fund provides a new opportunity: the ability to extract value on both the long side and the short side of the biotech market, and to do so aggressively in terms of concentration, turnover, and leverage. This is consistent with the fundamental law of active management, which is described in detail in the CAIA Level II curriculum. The long-only constraint is the most expensive constraint in terms of lost alpha generation that can be applied to active portfolio management.

Benchmarks   Sector hedge funds tend to have well-defined benchmarks. For the previous example of the biotech long/short hedge fund, an appropriate benchmark would be the AMEX Biotech Index, which contains 17 biotechnology companies. The point is that opportunistic hedge funds are generally not absolute return vehicles; their performance should typically be measured relative to a benchmark.

Traditional long-only managers are benchmarked to passive indices. The nature of benchmarking is such that it forces managers to focus on their benchmark and their fund's tracking error associated with that benchmark. This focus on benchmarking leads traditional active managers to make portfolio allocation decisions at least partly based on keeping the tracking error low, ensuring that the fund's returns are correlated with the benchmark. Even if a manager has the skills to outperform the benchmark in the long run, the manager might not take full advantage of these skills because it could substantially increase the tracking error of the portfolio relative to the benchmark. If the correlation between the benchmark and the portfolio is low, the manager runs the risk that the portfolio could underperform the benchmark over a short period of time, leading to loss of assets. The necessity to consider the impact of every trade on the portfolio's tracking error relative to its assigned benchmark reduces the flexibility of the investment manager.

In addition, long-only active managers are constrained in their ability to short securities. Generally, they may underweight a security only up to its weight in the benchmark index. If the security is only a small part of the index, the manager's efforts to underweight the stock are further constrained. The long-only constraint is a well-known limitation on the ability of traditional active management to earn excess returns.[12]

Summary   Opportunistic hedge fund investing is used to expand the set of available investments rather than to hedge traditional investments. Constructing an opportunistic portfolio of hedge funds depends on the constraints under which such a program operates. For example, if an investor's hedge fund program is not limited in scope or style, then diversification across a broad range of hedge fund styles will be appropriate. If, however, the hedge fund program is limited in scope to, for instance, expanding the equity investment opportunity set, then the choices will be less diversified across strategies.

14.6   THREE RESEARCH STUDIES ON WHETHER HEDGE FUNDS ADVERSELY AFFECT THE FINANCIAL MARKETS

Throughout history, speculators, speculation, and asset volatility are frequently observed together. Some commentators allege that hedge fund activity causes financial crises. But it is not clear whether speculation causes market volatility or market volatility attracts speculation. Theoretical work is mixed, but it should be noted that speculators profit only when they buy low and sell high—so successful speculation should generally stabilize prices, since buying low and selling high pushes price levels toward their mean. Empirical evidence throughout history is also mixed, but clearly there is little long-term evidence to suggest that markets that allow speculative activity are made substantially more volatile in the long run by allowing such activity.

More recently, hedge funds have often been accused of causing market volatility and exacerbating times of crisis in financial markets. The idea of headline risk deters some investors from allocating assets to hedge funds. **Headline risk** is dispersion in economic value from events so important, unexpected, or controversial that they are the center of major news stories. Some investors may be especially sensitive to negative publicity from investing with a manager who makes unfavorable headlines. For example, a charitable endowment fund may suffer reduced donations if its endowment is associated with a famous catastrophic loss or a financial scandal.

Hedge fund activity that can provoke controversy includes currency speculations, such as those attributed to George Soros. In 1992, Soros apparently bet against the British pound sterling and the Italian lira in correctly anticipating that the currencies would devalue, and generated a combined total profit of close to $3 billion. In 1997, Soros was once again blamed for a currency crisis by Malaysian prime minister Mahathir bin Mohammad. The prime minister attributed the crash in the

Malaysian ringgit to speculation in the currency markets by hedge fund managers, including Soros.

Brown, Goetzmann, and Park tested specifically whether hedge funds caused the crash of the Malaysian ringgit.[13] They regressed the monthly percentage change in the exchange rate on the currency exposure held by hedge funds. Reviewing the currency exposures of 11 large global macro hedge funds, they concluded that there is no evidence that the Malaysian ringgit was affected by hedge fund manager currency exposures. Additionally, they tested the hypothesis that global hedge funds precipitated the slide of a basket of Asian currencies, known as the Asian contagion, in 1997, and found no evidence that hedge funds contributed to the decline of Asian currencies in the fall of that year.

Fung and Hsieh measured the market impact of hedge fund positions on several financial market events, from the October 1987 stock market crash to the Asian contagion of 1997.[14] They found that there were certain instances in which hedge funds did have an impact on the market, most notably with the devaluation of the pound sterling in 1992. However, in no case was there evidence that hedge funds were able to manipulate the financial markets away from their natural paths driven by economic fundamentals. For instance, the sterling came under pressure in 1992 due to large capital outflows from the United Kingdom. The conclusion is that, for instance, George Soros bet correctly against the sterling and exacerbated its decline, but he did not trigger the devaluation.

Khandani and Lo analyzed the extraordinary stock market return patterns observed in August 2007, when losses to quantitative hedge funds in the second week of the month were presumably started by a short-term price impact that was the result of a rapid unwinding of large quantitative equity market-neutral hedge funds.[15] These authors argue that the return patterns of that week were a sign of a liquidity trade that can be explained as the consequence of a major hedge fund strategy liquidation. Khandani and Lo also contend that, unlike banks, hedge funds can withdraw liquidity at any time and that a synchronized liquidity withdrawal among a large group of funds could have devastating effects on the basic functioning of the financial system. In spite of the potential harm brought about by hedge funds, Khandani and Lo argue that the hedge fund industry has facilitated economic growth and generated social benefits by providing liquidity, engaging in price discovery, discerning new sources of returns, and facilitating the transfer of risk. Additionally, hedge funds engaging in short-selling activity may actually be reducing market volatility, as they seek to sell assets as prices rise and buy assets as prices fall.

14.7 HEDGE FUND INDICES

Most traditional investment funds can be reasonably benchmarked to an index of traditional investments. But Brown, Goetzmann, and Ibbotson contend that a hedge fund investment is almost a pure bet on the skill of a specific manager.[16] Hedge fund managers tend to seek out arbitrage or mispricing opportunities in the financial markets, using a variety of cash and derivative instruments. They typically take small amounts of market exposure to exploit mispricing opportunities but employ large amounts of leverage to extract higher potential value. The key point is that hedge fund managers pursue investment strategies that usually cannot be clearly associated with a conventional financial market benchmark. The investment styles of hedge funds are alpha driven rather than beta driven. Capturing the risk and returns of skill-based investing in a benchmark index can be problematic. Still, hedge fund indices are constructed and published for two key reasons. First, they can serve as a proxy for a hedge fund asset class, which is important for asset allocation studies. Second, they can serve as performance benchmarks to judge the success or failure of hedge fund managers.

Hedge fund indices start with the collection of a hedge fund database. Unlike returns on traditional listed assets, the returns on hedge funds are not centrally reported. Hedge fund managers may choose to report their returns to one or more database collectors. The databases, in turn, may be used by hedge fund index providers to construct indices and to calculate and publish returns.

There are more than 15 hedge fund index providers, each with its own unique way of constructing databases and benchmarks. Each index is computed with a different number of constituent hedge funds, and there is relatively little overlap. Most of the indices use equally weighted returns across hedge funds, whereas the others use assets under management to weight the returns on individual hedge funds. Also, some index providers collect the underlying data themselves, whereas others allow the hedge fund managers to enter the data. Some hedge fund indices include managed futures, whereas some do not. In sum, there are many different construction techniques of hedge fund indices. We discuss the challenges of implementing these methodologies in the following sections.

14.7.1 Management and Incentive Fees

According to Fung and Hsieh, more than 70% of live hedge funds (in Trading Advisor Selection System [TASS], HFR, and Center for International Securities and Derivatives Markets [CASAM/CISDM] databases) charge a management fee between 1% and 2%.[17] The same authors also find that the majority of live hedge funds in the aforementioned three databases charge a 20% incentive fee. Fees have fallen since this study was published, with most incentive fees now between 15% and 20% with management fees of 1.5% as common as 2%.

All hedge fund indices calculate hedge fund performance net of fees. However, two issues related to fees can result in different performance than portrayed by a hedge fund index.

First, incentive fees are normally calculated on an annual basis. However, all of these indices provide month-by-month performance. Therefore, on a monthly basis, incentive fees must be forecasted and subtracted from performance. Since the forecasted fees may be different from the actual fees collected at year-end, the estimated monthly returns may contain estimation errors.

Second, hedge funds are a form of private investing. Indeed, virtually all hedge funds are structured as private limited partnerships. As a consequence, often the terms of specific investments in hedge funds may not be negotiated in a consistent manner among different investors or across different time periods. The lack of consistency means that the net-of-fee returns earned by one investor may not be what another investor can negotiate. In fact, the more successful the hedge fund manager, the greater the likelihood that the manager will increase the fee structure to take advantage of that success. We call this fee bias. **Fee bias** is when index returns overstate what a new investor can obtain in the hedge fund marketplace because the fees used to estimate index returns are lower than the typical fees that a new investor would pay.

14.7.2 Inclusion of Managed Futures

Managed futures funds, or commodity trading advisers (CTAs), are sometimes considered a subset of the hedge fund universe and are therefore included in index construction. These are investment managers who invest in the commodity futures markets using either fundamental economic analysis or technical analysis such as trend-following models. They may invest in financial futures, energy futures, agriculture futures, metals futures, livestock futures, or currency futures. Because their trading style (mostly trend-following models) and the markets in which they invest are different from those of other hedge fund managers, CTAs and managed futures accounts are sometimes segregated from the hedge fund universe. Thus, returns may vary across hedge fund indices due to the decision to include or exclude managed futures funds.

14.7.3 Asset Weighted versus Equally Weighted

A hedge fund index return is constructed as an average of the returns on the underlying funds. Some databases report returns on an equally weighted basis, in which the returns to each fund have the same influence on the index return. Other databases report asset-weighted returns, in which the largest funds have the most significant impact on returns. HFR data indicate that the largest 19% of hedge fund managers now control nearly 90% of hedge fund industry assets, and the smallest half of hedge fund managers, those with AUM below $100 million, control only 1.2% of industry assets.

Equal weighting has the advantage of not favoring large funds or hedge fund strategies that attract a lot of capital, like global macro or relative value. The downside to an equally weighted index is that the small funds together have an extremely large weight in the reported index returns, yet a relatively small role in determining the returns experienced by actual investors in hedge funds. An asset-weighted index is dominated by large funds and is therefore influenced by the flows of capital. Some of the largest funds choose not to report their data to public databases, so it may be difficult to interpret an asset-weighted index return that does not include some of the larger hedge funds. Most hedge fund index providers argue that a hedge fund index should be equally weighted to fully reflect all strategies.

There are further worthwhile arguments for and against an asset-weighted hedge fund index. First, smaller hedge funds can transact with a smaller market impact, which enables them to do so at more favorable prices. An asset-weighted index more accurately reflects the market impact experienced by the majority of the money invested in hedge funds. Second, many other asset classes are benchmarked against capitalization-weighted (cap-weighted) indices. The S&P 500 and the Russell 1000, for example, are cap-weighted equity indices. Large institutional investors use these cap-weighted indices in their asset allocation decision models. Therefore, to compare on an apples-to-apples basis, hedge fund indices should also be asset weighted when used for asset allocation decisions. However, this argument might be moot. Empirically, equally weighted and asset-weighted hedge fund indices have similar correlations to equity and fixed-income indices.

14.7.4 The Size of the Hedge Fund Universe

One of the problems with constructing a hedge fund index is that the size of the total universe of hedge funds is not known with certainty. This uncertainty regarding the true size of the hedge fund industry stems from its loosely regulated nature. Especially in the past, hedge funds enjoyed relative secrecy compared to their mutual fund counterparts. For example, in the United States, mutual funds are regulated investment companies that are required, along with investment advisers, to register with the SEC, since mutual funds are considered public investment companies that issue public securities on a continual basis. Further, they are required by law to report and publish their performance numbers to the SEC and to the public. Recent regulatory changes around the world are resulting in more hedge fund managers having a more public profile, as registration with local authorities is now more frequently mandated than in the past.

Although the hedge fund industry has become more transparent, Liang demonstrates a good example of the lack of knowledge about the exact size of the hedge fund universe.[18] He studied the composition of indices constructed by two well-known providers: TASS and Hedge Fund Research, Inc. At the time of his study, there were 1,627 hedge funds in the TASS index and 1,162 hedge funds in the HFR Index. He found that only 465 hedge funds were common to both hedge fund indices. Further, of these 465 common hedge funds, only 154 had data covering the same time period.

Another problem with measuring the size of the hedge fund universe is that the attrition rate for hedge funds is quite high. Brown, Goetzmann, and Ibbotson and Park, Brown, and Goetzmann find that the average life of a hedge fund manager is 2.5 to 3 years, meaning that there will be considerable differences with respect to hedge fund index composition.[19] In conclusion, there are large differences in the compositions of various hedge fund indices with relatively little overlap. As a result, many investors purchase access to several databases and combine the funds listed to get a more complete view of the universe. Hedge fund mortality may increase over time. Getmansky, Lee, and Lo show that the attrition rate from the Lipper TASS database was 6% to 10% each year from 1996 to 2006, but increased to between 15% and 22% each year from 2007 to 2012.[20]

14.7.5 Representativeness and Data Biases

Representativeness is a key aspect of hedge fund databases and indices. The **representativeness** of a sample is the extent to which the characteristics of that sample are similar to the characteristics of the universe. If the sample consistently favors inclusion of observations based on a particular characteristic, then the sample is biased in favor of that characteristic. There are several important data biases associated with hedge fund databases.

Survivorship bias arises when an index is constructed that disproportionately includes past returns of those investments that remain in operation, meaning they have survived, while excluding the return histories of those investments that have not survived. This means that the past performance of the index contains an upward bias in comparison to the true performance of all funds that were available in the past. The reason for the bias is that surviving funds are likely to have outperformed those funds that have left the industry. In other words, an investor in a diversified portfolio of funds several years ago would have earned a return lower than what is reported by an index that is constructed today using the past performance of surviving funds. The survivorship bias can be measured as the average return of surviving funds in excess of the average return of all funds, both surviving and defunct. Survivorship bias has been estimated as 2.6% to 5% per year. This bias is also common with mutual funds and other traditional investments.

A common misperception is that available published hedge fund indices have substantial survivorship bias. Survivorship is a problem that often affects databases but not usually return indices. The reason is that most published hedge fund indices use all available managers who report to a database to create the index at each period in time. Subsequently, some of these managers may stop reporting to the database for a variety of reasons. These managers' performance is not reflected in the future returns of the index. However, the historical performance of these managers continues to be reflected in the past returns and values of the index. In this sense, published hedge fund indices are similar to public equity indices. For example, the historical performance of defunct companies, such as Lehman Brothers and Enron, continues to be part of the historical performance of the Russell 1000 Index.

Survivorship bias occurs when the historical returns of a defunct fund are dropped from a database, are dropped from historical index return computations, or are not proportionately reflected in the construction of indices. Specifically, if one were to start a new index today based on the managers who report as of today, then the historical performance of this index prior to today would suffer from survivorship bias because it would not include the performance of all those managers who stopped reporting to the database during previous periods.

The lack of a regulatory environment for hedge funds creates the opportunity for other data biases that are unique to the hedge fund industry. In addition to survivorship bias, there are three other biases that may affect average performance figures estimated from databases.

First, there is selection bias, which occurs when an index disproportionately reflects the characteristics of managers who choose to report their returns. Essentially, it is voluntary for hedge fund managers to report their returns to a database provider. This managerial self-selection in reporting may cause a database to disproportionately represent those funds that have characteristics that make reporting more desirable. In particular, managers with lower returns and higher risks may disproportionately choose to conceal their track records relative to managers with higher returns and lower risks (those demonstrating excellent performance). However, it is also possible that fund managers with the most attractive performance may disproportionately fail to report their returns if their funds have reached capacity and are no longer seeking new investors (participation bias, discussed later). It is very difficult to quantify the magnitude of this important bias, as it affects past values of the indices as well as their future values.[21]

Closely related to selection bias is instant history bias, also referred to as backfill bias. **Instant history bias** or **backfill bias** occurs when an index contains histories of returns that predate the entry date of the corresponding funds into a database and thereby cause the index to disproportionately reflect the characteristics of funds that are added to a database. These biases therefore arise only when a hedge fund manager begins to report return performance to a database provider, and the provider includes or backfills the hedge fund manager's historical performance into the database.

Because it is more likely that a hedge fund manager will begin reporting performance history after a period of good performance, this bias pushes the historical performance of managers upward. For example, consider a manager who has compiled an excellent three-year track record. Based on this success, the manager chooses to begin reporting fund performance to the database. Backfill (instant history) bias pertains to the inclusion of fund returns that were generated prior to the fund's decision to report performance to the database. If successful funds are more likely than unsuccessful funds to begin reporting to a database, and if the database includes return histories, then the database will disproportionately reflect successful funds.

When a fund is added to a database, all future returns should be flagged by the database as live returns, and returns from the inception of the fund until the first reporting date should be excluded or flagged as backfilled returns. Again, similar to survivorship bias, this bias does not affect the historical performance of most published indices. The reason is that most index providers do not revise the history of an index once a new manager is added to the index. That is, only current and future performance of the manager affects the index on a forward-looking basis once the index has been established.

Estimates for backfill bias are highly dependent on the database that is being used. In general, the estimated average value of backfilled performance can be as low as 1% to as much as 5% per year higher than the performance of the manager after being listed in a database.

Last, there is **liquidation bias**, which occurs when an index disproportionately reflects the characteristics of funds that are not near liquidation. Frequently, hedge fund managers go out of business, especially to shut down an unsuccessful hedge fund. When the return histories of these funds are excluded from a database or an index, it causes survivorship bias. Liquidation bias is different in that it involves the partial reporting of the returns of defunct funds. When a hedge fund ceases operations, the fund manager typically stops reporting its performance in advance of the cessation of operations. Delayed reporting exacerbates the problem. If a fund's performance recovers, the manager is more likely to report returns. But if its performance does not recover, several months of poor performance are probably lost because the hedge fund manager is more concerned with winding down operations than with reporting final performance numbers to an index provider. To the degree that liquidating managers do not report large negative returns to databases, these figures do not get reflected in published databases. Therefore, this bias increases the reported performance of published indices. The flip side to liquidation bias is participation bias. **Participation bias** may occur for a successful hedge fund manager who closes a fund to new investors and stops reporting results because the fund no longer needs to attract new capital.

A related concept is that of the hazard rate, which is defined in this context as the proportion of hedge funds that drop out of a database at a given fund age. For example, Fung and Hsieh found that the highest dropout rate occurs when a hedge fund is 14 months old. This is a type of selection bias. The impact of this bias is that if an index is constructed that requires at least 24 months of performance history, a large number of funds may be excluded, introducing a bias relative to the overall universe of funds.

It is possible that in some applications, these biases can add up to 10% of annual enhancement to the average performance of the managers who report to a database. However, indices may or may not reflect these biases, because index computations may not be based on all of the data in the database. It is important to take note of these biases, because all indices suffer from one or more of them. Exhibit 14.6 summarizes the literature that estimates the size of these biases and their impact on hedge fund returns.

14.7.6 Strategy Definition and Style Drift

Hedge fund databases and indices subdivide their funds based on strategies. Index providers determine their own hedge fund strategy classification system, and this varies from index to index. An index must have enough strategies to represent the broad market for hedge fund returns accurately and enough funds in each strategy to be representative. **Strategy definitions**, the method of grouping similar funds, raise two problems: (1) definitions of strategies can be very difficult for index providers to establish and specify, and (2) some funds can be difficult to classify in the process of applying the definition.

Consider a hedge fund manager who typically establishes a long position in the stock of a target company subject to a merger bid and a short position in the stock of the acquiring company. The strategy of this hedge fund manager may be classified alternatively as merger arbitrage by one index provider (e.g., HFR), relative value by another index provider (e.g., CASAM/CISDM), or event driven by yet another index provider (e.g., CSFB/Tremont). In summary, there is no consistent definition of hedge fund styles among index providers. Indeed, the dynamic trading nature of hedge funds makes them difficult to classify, which is part of their appeal to investors.

Further complicating the strategy definition is that most hedge fund managers are classified according to the disclosure language in their offering documents. However, consider the following language from a hedge fund private placement memorandum: "Consistent with the General Partner's opportunistic approach, there are no fixed limitations as to specific asset classes invested in by the Partnership. The Partnership is not limited with respect to the types of investment strategies it may employ or the markets or instruments in which it may invest."

How should this manager be classified? Relative value? Global macro? Market neutral? Unfortunately, with hedge funds, this type of strategy description is commonplace. The lack of specificity may lead to guesswork on the part of index providers with respect to the manager's strategy. Alternatively, some index providers may leave this manager out because of lack of clarity, but this adds another bias to the index by purposely excluding these types of hedge fund managers. In sum, there is no established format for classifying hedge funds. Each index provider develops its own scheme without concern for consistency with other hedge fund index providers, and this makes comparisons between hedge fund indices difficult.

Even if an index provider can successfully classify a hedge fund manager's current investment strategy, there is the additional problem of style drift. **Style drift** is a consistent movement through time in the primary style or strategy being implemented by a fund, especially a movement away from a previously identified style or

EXHIBIT 14.6 Biases Associated with Hedge Fund Data

Bias	Park, Brown, and Goetzmann, 1999	Brown, Goetzmann, and Ibbotson, 1999	Fung and Hsieh, 2000	Ackermann, McEnally, and Ravenscraft, 1999	Barry, 2003	Ibbotson and Chen, 2011
Survivorship	2.60%	3.00%	3.00%	0.01%	3.70%	3.16%
Selection	1.90%	Not estimated	Not estimated	No impact	Not estimated	Not estimated
Instant history	Not estimated	Not estimated	1.40%	No impact	0.40%	1.97%
Liquidation	Not estimated	Not estimated	Not estimated	0.70%	Not estimated	Not estimated
Total	4.50%	3.00%	4.40%	0.71%	4.10%	5.13%

Sources: James Park, Stephen Brown, and William Goetzmann, "Performance Benchmarks and Survivorship Bias for Hedge Funds and Commodity Trading Advisors," *Hedge Fund News*, August 1999; Stephen Brown, William Goetzmann, and Roger Ibbotson, "Offshore Hedge Funds: Survival and Performance, 1989–1995," *Journal of Business* 72, no. 1 (1999): 91–117; William Fung and David Hsieh, "Performance Characteristics of Hedge Funds and Commodity Funds: Natural versus Spurious Biases," *Journal of Financial and Quantitative Analysis* 25 (2000): 291–307; Carl Ackermann, Richard McEnally, and David Ravenscraft, "The Performance of Hedge Funds: Risk, Return, and Incentives," *Journal of Finance* (June 1999): 833–74; Ross Barry, "Hedge Funds: A Walk through the Graveyard," *Journal of Investment Consulting* (2003); and Roger Ibbotson and Roger Chen, "The ABCs of Hedge Funds: Alphas, Betas, and Costs," *Financial Analysts Journal* 67, no. 1 (January/February 2011): 15–25.

strategy. Because of the mostly unregulated nature of hedge fund managers, there is no requirement for a hedge fund manager to notify an index provider when an investment style has changed.

Consider the potential for style drift among merger arbitrage managers. During the recession of 2001 and the financial crisis of 2008, the market for mergers and acquisitions declined substantially except for investment banks, brokerage firms, and traditional banks. There were simply too few deals to fuel all that merger arbitrage managers need for investment opportunities. Consequently, many of these managers changed their investment style to invest in the rising tide of distressed debt deals, which are countercyclical from mergers and acquisitions. In addition, many merger arbitrage managers expanded their investment portfolios to consider other corporate transactions, such as spin-offs and recapitalizations. However, once a hedge fund manager has been classified as merger arbitrage by a particular database manager, it will typically remain in that category despite substantial changes in its investment focus.

Finally, a growing recent trend in the industry has been for hedge funds to evolve from single-strategy specialists into multistrategy hedge funds. In addition, Fung and Hsieh comment on the growing trend of so-called synthetic hedge funds. **Synthetic hedge funds** attempt to mimic hedge fund returns using listed securities and mathematical models. These funds are designed to replicate the returns of successful hedge fund strategies but at a lower cost to investors as a result of lower fees.[22] Both of these trends further complicate the classification of hedge funds into strategy types.

14.7.7 Index Investability

A key issue is whether a hedge fund index can be or should be investable. The **investability** of an index is the extent to which market participants can invest to actually achieve the returns of the index. This issue is usually more of a problem for hedge fund indices than it is for their traditional investment counterparts. Indices of listed securities are generally investable through holding the same portfolio described in the index.

There are numerous reasons that a market participant cannot simply hold a portfolio equivalent to the portfolio implied by a hedge fund index. First, hedge fund investments often have capacity limitations. **Capacity** is the limit on the quantity of capital that can be deployed without substantially diminished performance. Hedge funds generally have or develop capacity issues, since as a particular strategy performs well, there may be increasing competition to exploit the available opportunities. Limited capacity often leads hedge fund managers to refuse further investments of capital into the fund (i.e., to close the fund to new investment and new investors) when the managers have achieved a level of assets under management that makes it more difficult to generate strong returns with further capital. Market participants are inhibited from achieving the returns of an index that contains funds that are closed. Thus, to the extent that an index contains closed funds, there is less investability of the index.

A related issue is whether hedge fund indices should be investable. The argument is that an investable index excludes hedge fund managers that are closed to new investors and therefore excludes a large section of the hedge fund universe. Most index providers argue that the most representative index acts as a barometer for current hedge fund performance and that both open and closed funds should be included. The trade-off, therefore, is between having a very broad representation of current hedge fund performance and having a smaller pool of hedge fund managers that represent the performance that may be accessed through new investment. Billio, Getmansky, and Pelizzon compare the characteristics of investable and noninvestable databases and determine that investability affects the distributions of hedge fund returns.[23] Investable indices have generally underperformed noninvestable indices.

14.8 CONCLUSION

Research indicates that hedge fund investments can expand the investment opportunity set for investors. The returns to hedge funds have generally been positive, have had lower volatility than equity markets, and have had less-than-perfect correlation with traditional asset classes. Consequently, hedge funds have provided, and will probably continue to provide, a good opportunity to diversify a portfolio and an excellent risk management tool.

REVIEW QUESTIONS

1. List the three primary elements that differentiate a hedge fund from other investment pools.
2. Describe consolidation in the hedge fund industry in recent years.
3. Define the high-water mark in the context of hedge fund fee computation.
4. How can managerial coinvesting contribute to optimal contracting?
5. What is an example of a perverse incentive caused by incentive fees?
6. How does the annuity view of hedge fund fees differ from the option view of hedge fund fees?
7. What is the primary difference between a fund of funds and a multistrategy fund?
8. Define short volatility exposure.
9. When do convergent strategies generate profit?
10. What is fee bias?

NOTES

1. Carol Loomis, "The Jones Nobody Keeps Up With," *Fortune*, April (1966): 237–47.
2. Roy Kouwenberg and William T. Ziemba, "Incentives and Risk Taking in Hedge Funds," *Journal of Banking and Finance* 31, no. 11 (2007): 3291–310.
3. James E. Hodder and Jens Carsten Jackwerth, "Incentive Contracts and Hedge Fund Management," *Journal of Financial and Quantitative Analysis*, 42, no. 4 (2007), 811–26.
4. Vikas Agarwal, Noveen Daniel, and Narayan Naik, "Role of Managerial Incentives and Discretion in Hedge Fund Performance," *Journal of Finance* 64 (October 2009): 2221–56.
5. Hossein Kazemi and Ying Li, "Managerial Incentives and Shift of Risk-Taking in Hedge Funds" (working paper, Isenberg School of Management, University of Massachusetts, Amherst, 2008).
6. Greg N. Gregoriou, Georges Hubner, Nicolas Papageorgiou, and Fabrice Rouah, "Survival of Commodity Trading Advisors: 1990–2003," *Journal of Futures Markets* 25, no. 8 (2005): 795–815.

7. William Fung and David Hsieh, "Performance Characteristics of Hedge Funds and Commodity Funds: Natural versus Spurious Biases," *Journal of Financial and Quantitative Analysis* 25 (2000): 291–307.

8. Philippe Jorion, "Risk Management Lessons from Long-Term Capital Management" (working paper, University of California at Irvine, January 2000).

9. See William Fung and David Hsieh, "A Primer on Hedge Funds," *Journal of Empirical Finance* 6, no. 3 (1999): 309–31.

10. See Goldman, Sachs & Co. and Financial Risk Management Ltd., "The Hedge Fund 'Industry' and Absolute Return Funds," *Journal of Alternative Investments* 1, no. 4 (Spring 1999): 11–27; Goldman, Sachs & Co. and Financial Risk Management Ltd., "Hedge Funds Revisited," Pension and Endowment Forum (January 2000); Mark Anson, "Financial Market Dislocations and Hedge Fund Returns," *Journal of Alternative Assets* 5, no. 3 (Winter 2002): 78–88.

11. Antonio Bernardo and Oliver Ledoit, "Gain, Loss, and Asset Pricing," *Journal of Political Economy* 108, no. 1 (2001): 144–72; Richard Spurgin, "How to Game Your Sharpe Ratio," *Journal of Alternative Investments* 4, no. 3 (Winter 2001): 38–46.

12. See Richard Grinold and Ronald Kahn, *Active Portfolio Management* (New York: McGraw-Hill, 2000).

13. Stephen Brown, William Goetzmann, and James Park, "Hedge Funds and the Asian Currency Crisis," *Journal of Portfolio Management* 26, no. 4 (Summer 2000): 95–101.

14. William Fung and David Hsieh, "Measuring the Market Impact of Hedge Funds," *Journal of Empirical Finance* 7, no. 1 (2000): 1–36.

15. Amir Khandani and Andrew Lo, "What Happened to the Quants in August 2007?" *Journal of Investment Management* 5 (2007): 29–78.

16. Stephen Brown, William Goetzmann, and Roger Ibbotson, "Offshore Hedge Funds: Survival and Performance, 1989–1995," *Journal of Business* 72, no. 1 (1999): 91–117.

17. William Fung and David Hsieh, "Hedge Funds: An Industry in Its Adolescence," Federal Reserve Bank of Atlanta *Economic Review* 91, no. 4 (May 2006): 1–33.

18. Bing Liang, "Hedge Funds: The Living and the Dead," *Journal of Financial and Quantitative Analysis* 35, no. 3 (2000): 309–26.

19. Brown, Goetzmann, and Ibbotson, "Offshore Hedge Funds"; James Park, Stephen Brown, and William Goetzmann, "Performance Benchmarks and Survivorship Bias for Hedge Funds and Commodity Trading Advisors," *Hedge Fund News*, August 1999.

20. Mila Getmansky, Peter A. Lee, and Andrew W. Lo, "Hedge Funds: A Dynamic Industry in Transition" (working paper, MIT Laboratory for Financial Engineering, 2014).

21. As we mentioned in the previous chapter, a contrary argument can be made for selection bias: that good hedge fund managers choose not to report their data to hedge fund index providers because they have no need to attract additional assets.

22. Fung and Hsieh, "Hedge Funds."

23. Minica Billio, Mila Getmansky, and Loriana Pelizzon, "Dynamic Risk Exposure in Hedge Funds" (Yale Working Paper 07-14, September 2007).

CHAPTER 15

Macro and Managed Futures Funds

This first of five chapters on hedge fund strategies begins at, literally, the macro level. This chapter explores macro funds (i.e., global macro funds) and managed futures funds. Macro and managed futures strategies can differ substantially from other hedge fund strategies. Many investment strategies, especially in the arbitrage sector, focus on inefficiencies within markets at the security level. Macro and managed futures funds focus on the big picture, placing trades predominantly in futures, forward, and swap markets that attempt to benefit from anticipating price level movements in major sectors or to take advantage of potential inefficiencies at sector and country levels. At the end of 2018, Hedge Fund Research (HFR) estimated that macro and managed futures funds managed $581 billion, which is 18.7% of the hedge fund universe.

15.1 MACRO AND MANAGED FUTURES STRATEGIES

Macro (i.e., global macro) and managed futures funds share many common features. They tend to have substantially greater liquidity and capacity and, when focused on exchange-traded futures markets, lower counterparty risks than hedge funds that follow other strategies. **Capacity** refers to the quantity of capital that a fund can deploy without substantial reduction in risk-adjusted performance. **Counterparty risk** is the uncertainty associated with the economic outcomes of one party to a contract due to potential failure of the other side of the contract to fulfill its obligations, presumably due to insolvency or illiquidity. This section focuses on the major distinctions within the category of macro and managed futures funds.

15.1.1 Discretionary versus Systematic Trading

Discretionary fund trading occurs when the decisions of the investment process are made according to the judgment of human traders. The trader may rely on computers for calculations and other data analysis, but in discretionary trading, the trader must do more than simply mechanically implement the instructions of a computer program. Despite the fact that computer programs are obviously written with human judgment, in discretionary trading there must be an ongoing and substantial component of human judgment.

Systematic fund trading, often referred to as **black-box model trading** because the details are hidden in complex software, occurs when the ongoing trading decisions of the investment process are automatically generated by computer programs. Although these computer programs are designed with human judgment, the ongoing application of the program does not involve substantial human judgment. Traders make decisions about when to use the program and may even adjust various parameters, including those that control the size and risk of positions. The key is that individual trades are not regularly subjected to human judgment before being implemented.

The concept of discretionary versus systematic trading applies to all investment processes, not just macro and managed futures funds. However, the distinction is especially relevant in discussing macro and managed futures funds. Global macro funds tend to use discretionary trading, and managed futures funds tend to use systematic trading. However, there are many exceptions, and some funds use discretionary trading for some of their trading activity and systematic trading for their other trading activity.

15.1.2 Fundamental and Technical Analysis

Trading strategies are based on analysis of information. A major distinction is whether the investment strategy analyzes information with fundamental analysis, technical analysis, or both. Briefly, **technical analysis** relies on data from trading activity, including past prices and volume data. **Fundamental analysis** uses underlying financial and economic information to ascertain intrinsic values based on economic modeling. Trading decisions can be based purely on technical or fundamental analysis or on a combination of the two. For example, some investment processes rely on fundamental analysis to determine potential long and short positions and on technical analysis to determine the timing of entering and exiting those positions.

Technical analysis focuses on price movements due to trading activity or other information revealed by trading activity to predict future price movements. Typically, technical analysis quantitatively analyzes the price and volume history of one or more securities with the goal of identifying and exploiting price patterns or tendencies.

One motivation for using technical analysis is based on the idea that prices already incorporate some economic information, but price patterns may be identified that could be exploited for profit opportunities. The underlying assumption is that prices may not instantaneously and completely reflect all available information (i.e., prices may be slow to react to new information). For instance, if there is asynchronous global economic growth, one might forecast exploitable price movements as some local markets (e.g., in country-specific equity indices) react on a delayed basis to information already reflected in larger and more efficient markets. A common strategy in macro and managed futures funds is to attempt to exploit currency exchange rate movements, such as trends resulting from announced government intervention in foreign exchange markets. The key to this technical trading is the assumption that although prices are predominantly based on underlying economic information, analysis of trading activity can reveal consistent patterns of how prices respond to new information.

A second motivation to pursuing strategies based on technical analysis is a belief that market prices are substantially determined by trading activity that is unrelated to a rational analysis of underlying economic information. These technical strategies attempt to identify price patterns generated by trading activity and to identify those patterns on a timely basis. An example would be a prediction that an index is not likely to pass through a particular level as it approaches that level (e.g., an index nearing a round number such as 1,000), but if that level is breached, then the price is likely to continue moving in the same direction.

Fundamental analysis attempts to determine the value of a security or some other important variable through an understanding of the underlying economic factors. Fundamental analysis can be performed at a macro level using economy-wide information, such as economic growth rates, inflation rates, unemployment rates, and data on commodity supply and demand. It can also be performed at the micro level using firm-specific data, such as revenues, expenses, earnings, and dividends, or security-specific information. Fundamental analysis often focuses on predicting price changes to securities based on current and anticipated changes in underlying economic factors. Underlying economic factors can include (1) market or economy-wide factors, such as changes to monetary or fiscal policies; (2) industry-wide factors, such as changes in relevant commodity prices or consumer preferences; and (3) firm-specific factors, such as product innovations, product failures, labor strikes, or accidents. Fundamental analysis and technical analysis are used throughout alternative investment strategies, but the distinction in macro and managed futures funds is especially interesting. As in the case of distinguishing between discretionary and systematic trading, some funds focus on strategies using fundamental analysis, some focus on strategies using technical analysis, and some have a mix. However, systematic trading strategies tend to be built around technical analysis.

15.1.3 Organization of the Chapter

There are sufficient similarities between macro funds and managed futures funds to combine the two in this chapter. Global macro funds are more likely to be discretionary and emphasize fundamental analysis, whereas managed futures tend to be more systematic and emphasize technical analysis. So although exceptions are frequent, the remainder of this chapter begins with a section on global macro funds to discuss the use of discretionary trading and strategies based on fundamental analysis. Then, the section on managed futures funds discusses futures contracts, systematic trading, and technical analysis.

15.2 GLOBAL MACRO

Most macro funds employ discretionary trading and are often concentrated in specific markets or themes. As their name implies, global macro hedge funds take a macroeconomic approach on a global basis in their investment strategy. These are top-down managers who invest opportunistically across national borders, financial markets, currencies, and commodities. They take large positions that are either long or short, depending on the hedge fund manager's forecast of changes in equity prices, interest rates, currencies, monetary policies, and macroeconomic variables such as inflation, unemployment, and trade balances.

Global macro funds have the broadest investment universe: They are not limited by market segment, industry sector, geographic region, financial market, or currency, and therefore tend to offer high diversification. Macro funds tend to have low correlation to stock and bond investments, as well as to other types of hedge funds. Given their broad mandate, the returns earned by macro managers may also have relatively low correlation to other macro funds.

The ability to invest widely across currencies, commodities, financial markets, geographic borders, and time zones is a double-edged sword. On the one hand, this mandate allows global macro funds the widest universe in which to implement their strategies. On the other hand, it lacks a predetermined focus. As more institutional investors have moved into the hedge fund marketplace, they are demanding fund managers who offer greater investment focus rather than investing with managers who have free rein.

Global macro funds tend to have large amounts of investor capital. In addition, they may apply leverage to increase the size of their macro bets. As a result, global macro hedge funds tend to receive the greatest attention and publicity in the financial markets. Although macro managers have broad latitude in their trades, examples of trading strategies that are common or classic across managers are discussed here, to illustrate the essence of global macro fund investing.

15.2.1 Global Macro Strategies: The Case of Exchange Rates

Profit opportunities may exist when national governments impose fixed or managed exchange rates. Macro managers often seek to invest in markets that they perceive to be out of equilibrium or that exhibit a risk-reward trade-off skewed in the manager's favor. High levels of competition tend to drive market prices to approximate their informationally efficient values. However, actions by powerful national governments can, at least temporarily, cause market prices to diverge substantially from their expected long-run values in the absence of government actions. Perhaps the best example of these types of trades can be found in countries where the government has mandated fixed or managed currency rates between its currency and the currency of one or more other nations. Managers of macro funds monitor these currencies and estimate the likelihood of a currency revaluation or devaluation to a price other than the official rate.

Fund manager George Soros speculated famously in currency markets in the 1990s through the Quantum Fund. Soros made substantial gains in 1992 by successfully wagering that the British pound would devalue. In the days before the euro, the British pound (GBP) was a member of the European Exchange Rate Mechanism (ERM), which sought to keep currencies within a specified range of values relative to other European currencies. When the pound reached below the target rate, the British government would intervene to raise the value of the GBP relative to the DM. For the GBP, this scheme fell apart in September 1992. Hedge funds and other market participants were short selling the GBP, betting that the British government would stop purchasing the GBP in order to defend the ERM rate and system. Finally, the GBP moved to a floating rate and exited the ERM. The GBP suffered an overnight loss of 4% and fell 25% versus the U.S. dollar by the end of 1992. Those who were short GBP against DM were able to book a large and swift profit as the market forced the GBP to trade at a rate more reflective of the fundamentals. At the time, Germany had stronger monetary and fiscal policy fundamentals.

Soros was accused of contributing to the Asian contagion in the fall of 1997, when Thailand devalued its currency, the baht, triggering a domino effect in currency movements throughout Southeast Asia. In this case, Thailand, Malaysia, and Indonesia had currency rates that were pegged relative to a basket of currencies, with a heavy weighting to the U.S. dollar. Each country had high interest rates, large external debt, and large current account deficits, in which the value of imports exceeded the value of exports. Soros and other market participants increasingly short sold these currencies at the government-supported fixed exchange rates, and the respective governments seemed to be the only buyers. Eventually, each government exhausted its official reserves and was forced to stop the defense of its currency. Once the governments stopped buying their currency at the official rate, each currency moved to a freely floating value. Within a short time, the Thai baht and other Asian currencies declined by 40% to 70%.

15.2.2 Global Macro Strategies: The Case of Bonds

Markets for sovereign bonds may also present global macro funds with potential trade and profit opportunities. In addition to attempting to control currency rates, national governments exert enormous influence on the interest rates of their bonds, which are known as sovereign bonds. Global macro hedge fund managers often speculate on sovereign bond prices. Between 1994 and 1998, a bullish bet was to take large positions on new entrants into the euro currency. The sovereign bonds of Portugal, Italy, Greece, and Spain—the countries that joined the euro currency in 2001—were extraordinarily profitable investments as the countries prepared to enter the economic union. As with all countries seeking to enter the union, these nations were required to meet the terms of the Maastricht Treaty, which required annual government budget deficits below 3% of GDP, total national debt below 60% of GDP, an inflation rate no higher than 1.5% above the strongest member countries, and long-term interest rates within 2% of the current members of the union.

As indications of the profits earned by funds establishing long positions in the debt and equity of countries entering the economic union, note that Greek sovereign bonds denominated in drachmas yielded 25% in 1994 and declined to 11% by 1998, whereas the Greek stock market increased by 130% between 1998 and 1999. More recently, some funds have profited from shorting sovereign debt.

15.2.3 Global Macro Strategies: The Case of Economic Policy

Macro managers are expert at understanding the impact of central bank intervention in the markets. A recent example is the election of Shinzo Abe as the prime minister of Japan. His 2012 campaign focused on economic reform, seeking to restore inflation and economic growth after two decades of malaise. Abe's plan, now deemed "Abenomics," had three arrows: aggressive monetary easing, large public investments, and structural reforms. In just over one year, the monetary supply doubled, which led to a quick increase in the Nikkei index of over 50% and a decline in the yen against many world currencies of approximately 20%. Macro managers with long stock and short yen positions made quick and substantial profits by buying into the short-term stimulus measures implemented by Abe shortly after his election. As the value of the yen declines, exports become more competitive and profitable. The goal is for these increased profits of large exporting firms to result in increased investment, productivity, employment, and wages. Ideally, these higher incomes would lead to increased domestic spending and consumption.

Fighting against Abenomics are demographics, a consumption tax increase, and the delay of a decline in corporate tax rates from 35% to a desired 29%. Demographics are difficult, as the population of 127 million is expected to decline to less than 87 million by 2060, according to the National Institute of Population and Social Security Research. As the number of retirees increases and the number of births declines, old age benefits deplete government budgets faster than young entrants can increase the productive workforce and the resulting income tax payments. When sales taxes were increased from 3% to 5% in 1997, a multiyear recession ensued. The consumption tax increased to 8% in 2014. These tax increases offset the optimism that higher stock prices and easing monetary policy are meant to provide. While exports have increased, domestic job growth and consumer demand remain weak, even in the face of import price inflation.

15.2.4 Global Macro Strategies: Thematic Investing

Thematic investing is a trading strategy that is not based on a particular instrument or market; rather, it is based on secular and long-term changes in some fundamental economic variables or relationships—for example, trends in population, the need for alternative sources of energy, or changes in a particular region of the world economy. The last type is exemplified by the rise of China. Investors who believe that Chinese GDP growth will remain strong have a wide variety of trading ideas, many of them outside the Chinese markets. One such view might be the decline of the developed markets of the United States and Europe as they continue to deal with large trade and budget deficits. China's rise may have benefits for other Asian countries, including Japan, India, and South Korea. The strength of the Chinese economy may cause even the Chinese to outsource, which could lead to economic growth and additional wage income in less developed Asian countries, such as Vietnam.

The power of China is, perhaps, most clearly seen in the commodity markets. China's rise accounted for a substantial portion of the world's increased demand for a number of commodities. As China continued to urbanize and industrialize, building new roads, cities, workplaces, and consumer goods stoked the demand for commodities. As China's growth has slowed, commodity prices moved lower for a number of years. Savvy global macro managers who are able to better predict these major global economic themes may use bets in commodity markets and other markets to attempt to generate superior returns.

15.2.5 Global Macro Strategies: Macro and Micro

These examples of common global macro investing illustrate the role of macroeconomics in the implementation of the strategy. Many of the hedge fund strategies discussed in the remaining chapters of Part 3 are implemented through an understanding of individual firms, individual securities, and market microstructure. **Market microstructure** is the study of how transactions take place, including the costs involved and the behavior of bid and ask prices. But each of the examples of global macro investing just discussed is more concerned with the economic workings of economy-wide or even global markets, institutions, and forces. The illustrations involved exchange rates, interest rates, inflation rates, country economic growth rates, regional growth rates, and so forth.

Success in global macro investing requires superior skills in forecasting changes at the macroeconomic level. The necessary macroeconomic analysis can be performed qualitatively or quantitatively. Quantitative macroeconomic models can be empirical models of how markets have behaved (i.e., positive models) or theoretical models of how they ought to behave (i.e., normative models). The models vary in size and sophistication. However, the importance of experience, intuition, and data gathering should not be underestimated.

15.2.6 Three Primary Risks of Macro Investing

Macro funds often have higher risk exposures than most other strategies to market risk, event risk, and leverage risk.

Market risk refers to exposure to directional moves in general market price levels. Macro funds typically do not focus on equity markets, as equities can be highly influenced by microeconomic factors, such as company-specific events. However, macro funds can take substantial and concentrated risks in currency, commodity, and sovereign debt markets, especially when it is believed that changes in governmental policies will lead to large moves in the underlying markets.

Event risk refers to sudden and unexpected changes in market conditions resulting from a specific event (e.g., Lehman Brothers bankruptcy). Macro funds attempt to benefit from particular events. They seek profits from large market dislocations, especially those involving governmental financial policies. However, because macro funds seek out situations of event risk at the macroeconomic level, these funds can have substantial changes in value over short periods of time.

Leverage refers to the use of financing to acquire and maintain market positions larger than the assets under management (AUM) of the fund. Leverage is typically established through borrowing or derivatives positions and poses risks. Funds with leverage may be forced to deploy additional capital if they experience losses, and if they are unable to do so, they may be forced to liquidate positions at the least opportune time. Magnifying the risk of their concentrated positions in markets with substantial event risks, many macro funds use futures, swap, and forward markets to increase the leverage of the fund. While gains can be substantial, leverage can also lead to dramatic losses. Leverage in these derivatives markets, though, is less problematic than leverage in single securities sourced through prime brokers, as derivatives markets are less likely to require large changes in margin without notice.

15.3 MANAGED FUTURES

The term **managed futures** refers to the active trading of futures and forward contracts on physical commodities, financial assets, and exchange rates. Managed futures is a subclass of alternative investment strategies. For these strategies, professional money managers (also known as commodity trading advisers [CTAs]) manage client assets by actively taking positions primarily in futures markets, forward markets, options and other liquid derivatives, and structured products. Using highly liquid marked-to-market contracts, they typically provide their clients access to a wide range of asset classes, including fixed income, currencies, equity indices, soft commodities, energy, and metals. They apply leverage either directly via margin or indirectly via the use of derivative products, such as futures and options. Another key feature of this strategy group is the ability to go long or short with relative ease. The flexibility and liquid nature of managed futures strategies coupled with the wide array of markets they trade provide risk and return patterns not easily accessible through traditional asset classes (such as long-only stock and bond portfolios) or other alternative investments (such as hedge funds, real estate, private equity, or long-only commodities).

15.3.1 Background on Futures Contracts

The "futures" in "managed futures" denotes the industry's primary focus on using futures contracts or similar instruments. These products are desirable for these strategies because of the transparency and reduced counterparty and credit risk associated with exchange-traded instruments. For example, futures contracts are transparent because they are standardized and highly specified and are traded on markets that pool the collateral of all participants. For these contracts, the clearinghouse takes the other side of the trade, and pooling funds reduces the counterparty and credit risks of bilateral transactions. The pooling of positions and the futures exchange structure allow for substantial reduction in the margin capital required for establishing positions in futures contracts. For example, according to the CME Group, the eurodollar contract, which is one of the most liquid, can have margins as low as $175, or 0.017% of a $1 million notional contract. By comparison, the required margin for a long position in an exchange-traded stock is 50%.

Futures contracts emerged in the agricultural markets of the 1800s as cost-effective vehicles for the transfer and management of the risk related to uncertain crop prices. The history of managed futures products goes back to the middle of the 1900s. The first public futures fund began trading in 1948 and was active until the 1960s. That fund was established before financial futures contracts were invented, and it consequently traded primarily in agricultural commodity futures contracts. The success of that fund spawned other managed futures vehicles, and a new industry was born. Financial futures contracts emerged in the 1970s and eventually offered opportunities for market participants to transfer and manage a variety of financial risks, including equity market risk, interest rate risk, exchange rate risk, and credit risk. With the advent and rapid growth of financial futures contracts, more and more managed futures trading funds and strategies were born.

Previous chapters provide detailed foundational material on the pricing of futures contracts and forward contracts. For the purposes of this chapter, it suffices to know that futures and forward contracts are similar and can be cost-effective means of establishing positions with risk exposures that very closely approximate those that can be established in the cash market. For example, a market participant may wish to speculate that a particular price, such as the price of corn, gold, a stock index, or a Japanese government bond, is likely to rise. The speculator could buy those assets in the cash market, store them, and then sell them to close the trade. However, cash positions can have numerous disadvantages, such as storage costs, financing costs, higher transaction costs, inconvenience, and restrictions on short selling. Market participants with short-term trading horizons often prefer futures and forward contracts. Futures and forward contracts usually offer lower transaction costs, higher liquidity, more observable pricing, and more flexibility to short sell.

15.3.2   The Structure of the Managed Futures Industry

Investors can access the managed futures industry either by investing in a futures trading fund (via a managed account or a commingled fund) or through a commodity pool—a commingled investment vehicle that resembles a fund of funds and is managed by a **commodity pool operator (CPO)**, who invests in a number of underlying CTAs. Investments from a number of investors are pooled together and then invested in futures contracts, either directly by the CPO or through one or more commodity trading advisers. CPOs may be either public or private. In the United States, the requirements for investing in public futures funds generally differ from state to state; globally, the requirements vary from country to country.

Globally, the futures trading industry has a relatively short history of regulation. In the United States, the **Commodity Futures Trading Commission (CFTC)** was initiated in 1974 as a federal regulatory agency for all futures and derivatives trading. This regulatory body was later supplemented with U.S. futures exchanges and the **National Futures Association (NFA)**, an independent, industry-supported, self-regulatory body created in 1982. In Europe and Asia, managed futures funds are regulated under the same framework as hedge funds. For example, in Europe, managed futures managers are classified as alternative investment fund managers (AIFMs). AIFMs are regulated under the Alternative Investment Fund Managers Directive (AIFMD). In order to solicit business, a manager of such a fund must register as an AIFM and follow certain regulatory and reporting rules in order to qualify for a European passport to solicit business in the EU. Historically, foreign exchange has been one area of the managed futures industry that has remained largely unregulated. The vast majority of currency trading is conducted in the over-the-counter (OTC), interbank (spot), and forward markets, which are subject to only limited regulation. After the 2008 financial crisis, there has been increased regulatory tightening on all OTC markets.

Title VII of the Dodd-Frank Act in the United States and the European Market Infrastructure Regulation (EMIR) in Europe push for increased transparency and standardization of OTC products. This regulatory push has created an incentive to move many traditionally OTC contracts from bilateral contracts to the multilateral cleared contract structure of futures markets. Many in the industry term this movement from traditional OTC contracts to multilateral cleared contracts the **futurization** of OTC contracts. For the managed futures industry, this means that there is an incentive for growth in futures and a potential increase in the number of tradable futures contracts going forward. Managed futures programs and assets under management have grown substantially over the past several decades. Futures markets have grown in tandem.

15.3.3   The Purpose of the Managed Futures Industry

The purpose of the managed futures industry is to enable investors to receive the risk and return of active management within the futures market while enhancing returns and diversification.

The managed futures industry provides a skill-based style of investing. Investment managers attempt to use their special knowledge and insight to establish and manage long and short positions in futures and forward contracts for the purpose of generating consistent, positive returns. These futures managers tend to argue that their superior skill is the key ingredient in generating profitable returns from the futures markets.

Managed futures strategies tend to be based on systematic trading more than discretionary trading. Further, futures managers tend to use more technical analysis, as opposed to trading based on fundamental analysis. This section on managed futures takes a detailed look at systematic trading and technical analysis. The section begins, however, with an overview of futures contracts and futures markets.

15.3.4 Regulation and Organization of the Managed Futures Industry

Until the early 1970s, the managed futures industry was largely unregulated. Anyone could advise an investor regarding commodity futures investing or form a fund for the purpose of investing in the futures markets. Recognizing the growth of this industry, the industry's potential impacts on an economy, and the lack of regulation associated with the industry, regulatory authorities have been established for managed futures funds, futures contracts, and, to a lesser extent, forward contracts. For example, in the United States in 1974, Congress enacted the Commodity Exchange Act (CEA) and created the Commodity Futures Trading Commission (CFTC). Under the CEA, Congress first defined the terms *commodity pool operator* (CPO) and *commodity trading adviser* (CTA). In addition, Congress established standards for financial reporting, offering memorandum disclosure, and bookkeeping. Congress required CTAs and CPOs to register with the CFTC. Last, Congress required CTAs and CPOs to undergo periodic educational training in cooperation with the National Futures Association (NFA), the designated self-regulatory organization for the managed futures industry.

Commodity trading advisers may invest in both exchange-traded futures contracts and forward contracts. The economic structure of forward contracts is highly similar to that of futures contracts, with the most major difference being that futures contracts are exchange-traded while forward contracts are usually traded over the counter. Forward contracts are private agreements. Therefore, they can have terms that vary considerably from the standard terms of exchange-listed futures contracts. Forward contracts accomplish virtually the same economic goal as a futures contract but with the flexibility of custom-tailored terms. However, futures contracts provide substantial protection against counterparty risk as a result of being backed by the exchange's clearinghouse, whereas forward contracts are exposed to full counterparty risk. In the remainder of this chapter, both types of contracts are referred to as futures contracts.

15.3.5 Three Ways to Access Managed Futures

There are three ways to access the skill-based investing of the managed futures industry:

1. Public commodity pools
2. Private commodity pools
3. Individually managed accounts

Commodity pools are investment funds that combine the money of several investors for the purpose of investing in the futures markets. **Public commodity pools** are open to the general public for investing in much the same way that a mutual fund sells its shares to the public. In the United States, public commodity pools must file a registration statement with the SEC (Securities and Exchange Commission) before distributing shares in the pool to investors. An advantage of public commodity pools is the low minimum investment and the high liquidity that they provide for investors, allowing them to withdraw their investments with relatively short notice (compared to other hedge fund strategies).

Private commodity pools are funds that invest in the futures markets and are sold privately to high-net-worth investors and institutional investors. They are similar in structure to hedge funds and are increasingly considered a subset of the hedge fund marketplace. Commodity pools are managed by a general partner. In the United States, the general partner for the pool must typically register with the CFTC and the NFA as a CPO. However, there are exceptions to the general rule. Private commodity pools are organized privately to avoid lengthy or burdensome initial regulatory requirements, such as registration with the SEC in the United States, and to avoid ongoing reporting requirements, such as those of the CFTC in the United States. Otherwise, their investment objective is the same as that of a public commodity pool. Advantages of private commodity pools are usually lower fees and greater flexibility to implement investment strategies.

The CPOs for either public or private pools typically hire one or more CTAs to manage the money deposited with the pool. **Commodity trading advisers (CTAs)** are professional money managers who specialize in the futures markets. Some CPOs act as a fund of funds, diversifying investments across a number of CTA products. Like CPOs, CTAs in the United States must register with the CFTC and the NFA before managing money for a commodity pool. In some cases, a managed futures investment manager is registered as both a CPO and a CTA. In this case, the general partner for a commodity pool may also act as its investment adviser.

In addition, wealthy investors and institutional investors may use a managed account. A **managed account** (or separately managed account) is created when money is placed directly with a CTA in an individual account rather than being pooled with other investors. When large enough to be cost-effective, managed accounts offer numerous advantages over pooled arrangements. These separate accounts have the advantage of representing narrowly defined and specific investment objectives tailored to the investor's preferences. With a managed account, the investor retains custody of the assets with the investor's regular broker and only needs to allow the CPO or CTA to exert trading authority in the account. Other advantages to the investor include transparency and control, which allow the investor to see all of the trading activity, as well as the ability to increase or decrease the leverage applied. Like hedge funds, CTAs and CPOs charge management fees and incentive fees. The standard hedge fund fees of 2 and 20 (2% management fee and 20% incentive fee) are equally applicable to the managed futures industry, although management fees can range from 0% to 3% and incentive fees can range from 10% to 35%.

15.4 SYSTEMATIC TRADING

Systematic trading is usually quantitative in nature and often referred to as computer-based, model-based, or black-box trading. Systematic trading in this context refers to the automation of the investment process, not to systematic risk. Systematic trading models apply a fixed set of trading rules in determining when to enter and exit positions. Deviation from the system's rules is generally not permitted.

15.4.1 Derivation of Systematic Trading Rules

Systematic trading rules are generally derived from backtests. In the context of systematic trading rules, a backtest is an identification of a price or return pattern that appears to persist, as located and verified through a quantitative analysis of historical prices. Trading systems are generally based on the expectation that historical price patterns will recur in the future. However, many trading systems that appear to perform well using backtested data end up performing poorly when they are implemented in real time. Statistics show that when many analysts search through many data sets with many hypothetical trading systems, very many trading systems appear ex post to be profitable but in fact are generated purely by randomness or by market regimes that no longer exist. Being able to avoid data dredging and false identification of attractive trading rules is the key to successful backtesting.

Backtests should also have reasonable estimates for transaction costs and slippage. **Slippage** is the unfavorable difference between assumed entry and exit prices and the entry and exit prices experienced in practice. Thus, an analyst observing a long history of daily closing prices should assume that an actual trading strategy is likely to generate less favorable price executions due to the tendency of buy orders to push prices up, or be executed at an offer price, and of sell orders to push prices down, or be executed at a bid price. Care should also be taken to ensure that reported prices on which backtests are performed are executable prices rather than stale prices or published indications of prices, and that they are free from large errors. Systematic traders rarely employ only a single trading system with a single security.

Managers who have success with one trading system in one market typically search for other markets in which that trading system, or a modified version of it, can be successfully applied. Over time, managers may modify their trading systems, develop new ones, and abandon others.

15.4.2 Three Questions in Evaluating a Systematic Trading System

There are three useful questions to ask when evaluating an individual trading strategy:

1. What is the trading system, and how was it developed? Here, one is looking to understand the broad underlying trading approach (e.g., trend following versus countertrend) and specific characteristics of the strategy itself. It is also important to understand the research methods used to identify and develop the trading strategy to avoid strategies based on spurious results from data dredging. Poor

research methods can lead to overfitting of historical data, such that a historical price series may appear to have a recurring pattern yet be in fact random.

2. Why and when does the trading system work, and why and when might it not work? It is important to understand the underlying hypothesis of a specific trading strategy. If the trading system is making money for its investors, from where or from whom is that money coming? Such understanding is important in and of itself but is also critical in identifying market conditions that are likely to be supportive of the strategy (e.g., trend accompanied by low volatility). Although it may be difficult to forecast market conditions, understanding what impact various market conditions are likely to have on the strategy's performance is important in interpreting the potential success or failure of a strategy over time.

3. How is the trading system implemented? Many operational factors contribute to a successful systematic trading strategy, including selection of data sources, determination of periodicity of data, establishment of protocols to clean the data, processing of the data into a trading signal, placement of trades, record keeping, and broker reconciliation.

The key to systematic trading systems is to differentiate spurious results from results that will persist. Similarly, analysts seek to ascertain whether trading systems that were successful in the past but have stopped working recently will perform poorly on a temporary basis or on a permanent basis. In other words, at what point should a trading system be abandoned or modified if the system worked very well in the past but has generated poor results recently?

15.4.3 Validation and Potential Degradation of Systematic Trading Rules

Systematic managed futures strategies rely on quantitative research methods that backtest trading rules using historical price data. **Validation** of a trading rule refers to the use of new data or new methodologies to test a trading rule developed on another set of data or with another methodology. For example, a trading rule developed analyzing data during five calendar years should be tested first in subperiods of those five years to see if the results are robust across data sets and sub-intervals. **Robustness** refers to the reliability with which a model or system developed for a particular application or with a particular data set can be successfully extended into other applications or data sets. Most important, validation of the trading rule should be performed with out-of-sample data. **Out-of-sample data** are observations that were not directly used to develop a trading rule or even indirectly used as a basis for knowledge in the research. For example, the trading rule should be validated on the most recent data, which, of course, should not have been used explicitly or implicitly in the model's development. **In-sample data** are those observations directly used in the backtesting process. Out-of-sample data consist of more recent data than were used in the backtest. Out-of-sample data should be used to test the profitability of a trading strategy beyond the period covered by the backtest. The goal is to avoid data dredging and to ensure that a trading rule generates persistent performance.

Further, it is vital to know how many trading rules were tested, how many were subjected to validation, and how many were rejected in the validation process. If 20 trading rules (e.g., one model with 20 different parameter values) are subjected to validation, one of them on average will survive a validation process with a confidence interval of 95%, even if none of the rules truly offers value-added properties. More to the point, if several analysts test hundreds of strategies (e.g., hundreds of parameter values) on numerous data sets (e.g., securities), then numerous trading strategies will survive the validation process unless the validation process is carefully designed to incorporate into its statistical approach the total number of tests performed.

Trading rules typically evolve over time as analysts try to optimize profitability. Analysts perform ongoing research to estimate and refine trading parameters, add new trading parameters, and drop old trading parameters. Markets also typically evolve over time. A once-profitable price pattern that becomes identified and exploited by numerous CTAs eventually ceases to exist or substantially changes. Therefore, a trading model or trading strategy that has been successful over the past 10 years often experiences degradation and is not profitable over the next 10 years. In this context, **degradation** is the tendency and process through time by which a trading rule or trading system declines in effectiveness. The key is to differentiate between (1) trading rules that are being changed to better identify true price patterns, and (2) trading rules that are data dredging for a pattern that no longer exists. Both an effective trading system and a fully degraded trading system experience episodes of high returns and episodes of poor returns due to randomness. Identifying which systems remain effective and which have degraded requires careful statistical analysis as well as informed qualitative analysis.

15.4.4 Systematic Trading Strategies Overview

Systematic trading strategies are generally categorized into three groups: trend-following, non-trend-following, and relative value.

Trend-following strategies are designed to identify and take advantage of momentum in price direction (i.e., trends in prices). **Momentum** is the extent to which a movement in a security price tends to be followed by subsequent movements of the same security price in the same direction. Trend-following strategies use recent price moves over some specific time period (e.g., ranging from a few minutes to several hundred days) to identify a price trend. The goal is to establish long positions in assets experiencing an upward trend, establish short positions in assets experiencing a downward trend, and avoid positions in assets not experiencing a trend.

Mean-reverting refers to the situation in which returns show negative autocorrelation—the opposite tendency of momentum or trending. An asset that consistently tends to return toward its previous price level after a move in one direction is typically said to be mean-reverting or to exhibit mean reversion. Mean reversion is the extent to which an asset's price moves toward the average of its recent price levels. Trending markets exhibit returns with positive autocorrelation. A price series with changes in its prices that are independent from current and past prices is a **random walk**. Therefore, momentum and mean reversion are properties that are not consistently displayed by prices that follow a random walk.

15.4.5 Simple Moving Averages in Systematic Trading Strategies

One of the most popular classes of trend-following strategies uses moving averages to signal trades. A **moving average** is a series of averages that is recalculated

EXHIBIT 15.1 Simple Moving Average Summary

Description:	In a simple moving average, the daily prices are equally weighted. As each new price observation is added to the series, the oldest observation falls away, creating a window of averaged prices that is often charted.
Signals:	Enter long if current price $P_t > SMA_t(n)$ Enter short if current price $P_t < SMA_t(n)$

through time based on a window of observations. The most basic approach uses a **simple moving average**, a simple arithmetic average of previous prices. More sophisticated averaging techniques place a greater weight on more recent prices. The formula for calculating a simple moving average, $SMA_t(n)$, is shown in Equation 15.1, where t is the current time period and n is the number of time periods used in the computation:

$$SMA_t(n) = \frac{1}{n}p_{t-1} + \frac{1}{n}p_{t-2} + \cdots + \frac{1}{n}p_{t-n} \qquad (15.1)$$

The window of observations is composed of a fixed number of lagged prices. For example, a current 10-day moving average price (day 0) is formed using the 10 prices corresponding to the 10 days immediately preceding the current price (days –1 to –10). Yesterday's (day –1) 10-day moving average would be composed of the prices corresponding to the 10 days prior to that day (days –2 to –11). Exhibit 15.1 summarizes the process along with the classic trading signals based on a simple trend following rule.

☞ APPLICATION 15.4.5

A stock price experiences the following 10 consecutive daily prices corresponding to days –10 to –1: 100, 102, 99, 97, 95, 100, 109, 103, 103, and 106. What are the simple (arithmetic) moving average prices on day 0 using 3-day and 10-day moving averages, as well as the 3-day moving average for days –2 and –1? Using the data, the three-day moving average on day 0 is [(103 + 103 + 106)/3], or 104. For days –2 and –1, the three-day moving averages are 104 and 105, respectively. The 10-day moving average for day 0 is 101.4. Because the price on day –1 moved above the recent three-day moving averages, a classic interpretation of a simple moving average trading system would be that a long position should have been established.

Like the underlying market itself, the moving average price changes every day, but the moving average changes value in a lagged and muted fashion relative to the current price. The shorter the time period used to calculate the moving average, the more quickly the average will respond to changes in the level of more current prices, the more volatile the average will be, and, generally, the more times the current price will cross over the moving average price (i.e., the more trading signals will be generated).

Numerous variations of moving average computations exist:

- The number of periods (and the length of the time period) used in the moving average, n, can vary (e.g., 10-day versus 30-day versus 60-minute).
- The entry and exit levels can be a percentage of the moving average (e.g., enter when the current price exceeds the moving average by 1%).
- An unequally weighted moving average can be calculated, using an averaging process that weights recent prices more heavily than older prices.

There are trading signals other than the comparison of the current price to a single moving average. For example, trading signals to establish long positions may be identified as follows:

- When the current price exceeds two or more moving averages (e.g., both the 10-day and the 30-day moving averages)
- When a shorter-term moving average crosses up and over a longer-term moving average
- When moving averages align upward (i.e., are all in the same direction, with the shorter moving averages exceeding the longer moving averages)

The three computational variations taken together with the various signal identification rules generate an astounding number of possible strategies. The abundance of potential strategies leads to the potential problem of data dredging, in which so many potential strategies can be tested that strategies will be identified that satisfy empirical tests with high levels of statistical confidence even when true patterns do not exist. There are two major approaches to weighting more recent prices more heavily than older prices: weighted moving averages and exponential moving averages.

15.4.6 Weighted and Exponential Moving Averages in Systematic Trading Strategies

Although simple moving averages are the most commonly used measures, weighted and exponential moving averages are also used and have the potential advantage of assigning larger weights to the most recent prices.

☞ **APPLICATION 15.4.6A**

A stock price experiences the following 10 consecutive daily prices corresponding to days −10 to −1: 100, 102, 99, 97, 95, 100, 109, 103, 103, and 106. What are the five-day weighted moving average prices on days −1 and 0?

The sum of the digits 1 through 5 is 15. The five-day weighted moving average on day 0 is as follows:

$$[(106 \times 5) + (103 \times 4) + (103 \times 3) + (109 \times 2) + (100 \times 1)]/15, \text{ or } 104.6$$

The five-day weighted moving average on day −1 is as follows:

$$[(103 \times 5) + (103 \times 4) + (109 \times 3) + (100 \times 2) + (95 \times 1)]/15, \text{ or } 103.27$$

A **weighted moving average** is usually formed as an unequal average, with weights arithmetically declining from most recent to most distant prices. To illustrate, the length of the averaging interval (i.e., the number of observations used in the computation of each average) is denoted as n. The oldest price is multiplied by 1, the second oldest price is multiplied by 2, and so forth, until the most recent price is multiplied by n. Each product is then divided by the sum of the digits. The n-period weighted moving average, $WMA_t(n)$, is shown in Equation 15.2:

$$\text{Define } N = 1 + 2 + 3 + \cdots + n$$
$$WMA_t(n) = \frac{n}{N}P_{t-1} + \frac{n-1}{N}P_{t-2} + \cdots + \frac{1}{N}P_{t-n} \tag{15.2}$$

In the case of $n=4$, the sum of the labels, N, is 10 (the sum of 1 through 4). The most recent previous price (P_{t-1}) is weighted 40% (4/10), the second most recent price is weighted 30% (3/10), and so forth, until the oldest price is weighted only 10% (1/10). Note that the weights decline arithmetically: 40%, 30%, 20%, and 10%.

The **exponential moving average** is a geometrically declining moving average based on a weighted parameter, λ, with $0 < \lambda < 1$. The most recent observation is weighted through multiplication by the weighted parameter, λ. All other previous observations are weighted by $\lambda (1 - \lambda)^n$, in which n is the length of the time lag. For example, with $\lambda = 0.4$, the most recent observation is multiplied by 0.4. The second and third most recent observations are weighted by $\lambda (1 - \lambda)^1$ and $\lambda (1 - \lambda)^2$ (0.24 and 0.144), respectively. The formula for the exponential moving average at time t, $EMA_t(\lambda)$, is given next in an expanded form (Equation 15.3a) and a reduced form (Equation 15.3b):

$$EMA_t(\lambda) = \lambda P_{t-1} + \lambda(1 - \lambda)P_{t-2} + \lambda(1 - \lambda)^2 P_{t-3} + \lambda(1 - \lambda)^3 P_{t-4} + \dots \tag{15.3a}$$
$$EMA_t(\lambda) = (\lambda \times P_{t-1}) + [(1 - \lambda) \times EMA_{t-1}(\lambda)] \tag{15.3b}$$

Equation 15.3a illustrates the intuition of the exponential moving average. The most recent price receives the weighted parameter, λ. The terms after the first term are multiplied both by λ and by $(1 - \lambda)^n$. Since $(1 - \lambda)$ is less than 1, the weight assigned to each previous price declines as the price becomes more distant. The problem with Equation 15.3a is that to compute $EMA_t(\lambda)$ using that equation requires input of the entire history of the price series.

☞ **APPLICATION 15.4.6B**

A stock price experiences the following five consecutive daily prices corresponding to days −5 to −1: 100, 109, 103, 103, and 106. What are the exponential moving average prices on days –1 and 0 using λ = 0.25? Assume that the exponential moving average up to and including the price on day –3 was 100. The exponential moving average on day –1 is found as 0.25 × 103 (the day –2 price) plus 0.75 × 100 (the previous exponential moving average), which equals 100.75. The exponential moving average on day 0 is found as 0.25 × 106 (the day –1 price) plus 0.75 × 100.75 (the previous exponential moving average), or 102.0625.

Equation 15.3b denotes how the exponential moving average is calculated in practice. In this view, today's exponential moving average is a weighted average of the current price and yesterday's exponential moving average. Inspection of either equation reveals that the formula requires an infinitely long history of previous prices. Therefore, in practice, computation is performed by seeding some initial value to EMA_t–1. Once an initial approximation is set for a previous value of the exponential moving average, all subsequent exponential moving averages are simply computed as the sum of λ times the most recent price (1 – λ) times the most recent exponential moving average.

15.4.7 An Illustration of a System Using Two Moving Averages

Exhibit 15.2 illustrates a strategy employing two moving averages to generate trading signals. In the example, the strategy uses a 10-day and a 45-day moving average as the shorter-term and the longer-term indicators, respectively. The first signal in the example (denoted with a vertical line) is a sell signal (i.e., a signal to establish a

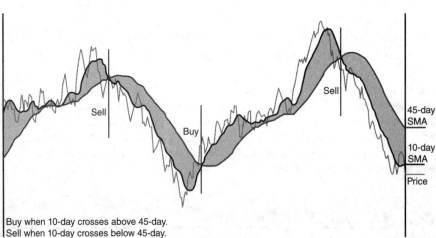

EXHIBIT 15.2   Example with Two Moving Averages

short position), because the 10-day moving average line (the shorter average) crossed below the 45-day moving average line (the longer average). Some days later, a signal to establish a long position emerged when the 10-day moving average line crossed above the 45-day moving average line.

Exhibit 15.2 appears to illustrate a highly successful trading period with two sell signals at prices much higher than the buy signal. Trend-following strategies perform well when there is an extended move in the price from one level to another, and tend to be more powerful when that move is accompanied by low daily price volatility. This low volatility makes it less likely that the trend-following manager will be whipsawed. **Whipsawing** is when a trader alternates between establishing long positions immediately before price declines and establishing short positions immediately before price increases and, in so doing, experiences a sequence of losses. In trend-following strategies, whipsawing results from a sideways market. A **sideways market** exhibits volatility without a persistent direction. Exhibit 15.2 contains several regions in which whipsawing may take place. Midway between the starting point and the first indicated trade signal are two instances where the two moving averages appear to touch and then return to their previous relationship. When trading signals are clustered, whipsawing generally takes place, and traders lose from the accompanying back-and-forth price pattern as well as the trading costs (bid-ask spreads and commissions).

Visual exhibits with discrete prices tend to mask the potential for whipsawing and its trading costs. Also, when a market price consistently reverts toward previous values (i.e., is mean-reverting), trend-following strategies tend to generate negative alphas. The primary challenge of implementing a moving average strategy is forecasting when markets are likely to trend, meaning the strategy should be applied, and forecasting when markets are likely to be random or to mean-revert, meaning the strategy should not be applied. Thus, implementation of moving average strategies focuses on developing methods of determining when to apply the strategy in addition to specifying which particular moving average strategy to apply. There has been considerable academic debate over the viability of trend-following strategies.

15.4.8 Breakout Strategies

Breakout strategies focus on identifying the commencement of a new trend by observing the range of recent market prices (e.g., looking back at the range of prices over a specific time period). If the current price is below all prices in the range, the strategy identifies this as a breakout and possibly the beginning of a downward trend, and a short position is initiated. Breakout strategies lead to long trade entry points when prices break above these ranges. If a price is within the range, then the system might continue to hold the previous position or no position at all. The concept can apply to both prices and volatilities, and these are often used in tandem. Exhibit 15.3 describes a simple channel breakout strategy.

The simplest way to think of this is in terms of a look-back. For example, a 20-day look-back means that the trading system observes today's price in relation to all prices over the past 20 days. Exhibit 15.3 provides a summary.

EXHIBIT 15.3 Channel Breakout Strategy Summary

Description:	Channels are created by plotting the range of new price highs and lows. When one side grows disproportionately to the other, a trend is revealed.
Signals:	Buy when channel breaks upward.
	Sell when channel breaks downward.
Equation:	UpperBound = HighestHigh(n)
	LowerBound = LowestLow(n)
	Most commonly, $n = 20$ days

☞ **APPLICATION 15.4.8**

A stock price experiences the following 10 consecutive daily high prices corresponding to days –10 to –1: 100, 102, 99, 98, 99, 104, 102, 103, 104, and 100. What is the day 0 price level that signals a breakout and possibly a long position, using these 10 days of data as representative of a trading range?

A price of 105 exceeds the maximum of the past 10 days of the data and signals that a long position should be established. If the price series represented the low prices for each day, a current price of 97 would signal a breakout on the downside and would typically be interpreted as a sell signal.

15.4.9 Analysis of Trend-Following Strategies

Trend following is generally believed to be the dominant strategy applied in managed futures, in terms of both numbers of managers and the amount of industry assets. Empirical analysis by Fung and Hsieh confirms that trend following is the dominant style employed by CTAs.[1]

Lhabitant explains two drawbacks of trend-following systems based on moving average rules.[2] First, they are slow to recognize the beginning or end of trends. That is, an entry signal occurs after the trend has already been in effect for a while and profits have been missed, and the exit signal occurs after the trend has reversed and losses have occurred. The second drawback is that moving average rules are designed to exploit trends or momentum that should not persist in competitive markets. Perfect competition causes randomness rather than trending in price. But even at modest levels of competition, trends may cease to exist at approximately the same time that they become easily identified. In this case, moving average rules tend to generate useless and costly signals; that is, the trader may end up incurring substantial transaction costs and being whipsawed.

Some observers have described trend-following strategies as long volatility strategies. The idea is that trend-following strategies profit when market prices make large unidirectional changes and that large unidirectional changes generate higher reported volatility, as indicated by some measures of volatility. However, large unidirectional changes can also be consistent with low volatility. For example, a prolonged period of consistently positive daily or weekly returns compounds into large monthly returns and a large unidirectional change. But the standard deviation of the daily or weekly returns will be low if most of the returns are near the mean return. Thus, depending on how volatility is viewed or measured, trend-following systems may or may not be accurately described as being long volatility.

Malek and Dobrovolsky provide an extended discussion of the volatility exposure of managed futures programs.[3] Rather than describing CTAs as managers who take long volatility positions, Malek and Dobrovolsky assert that a better view is that CTAs take long gamma positions. Gamma is more completely discussed in Chapter 17. In this context, gamma refers to the risk exposure from increasing long positions in rising markets and decreasing short positions in falling markets.

Managed futures programs can benefit when markets trade in wide ranges, making prolonged moves between levels that vary substantially. Trend-following programs struggle to profit when markets trade in narrow ranges and exhibit negative autocorrelation. Predicting those markets that will consistently experience trends, and identifying when those markets are going to trend—and when they will not trend—is the goal of many CTAs and the source of alpha.

15.4.10 Non-Trend-Following Strategies

Non-trend-following strategies are designed to exploit nonrandomness in market movements, such as a pattern of relative moves in prices of related commodities (e.g., oil and gasoline). Non-trend-following strategies generally fall into the major categories of countertrend or pattern recognition. **Countertrend strategies** use various statistical measures, such as price oscillation or a relative strength index, to identify range-trading opportunities rather than price-trending opportunities. The **relative strength index (RSI)**, sometimes called the relative strength indicator, is a signal that examines average up and down price changes and is designed to identify trading signals such as the price level at which a trend reverses (Exhibit 15.4). The formula for RSI is shown in Equation 15.4.

$$RSI = 100 - \frac{100}{1 + \frac{U}{D}} \tag{15.4}$$

where U = average of all price changes for each period with positive price changes for the last n periods, D = average of all price changes (expressed as absolute values)

EXHIBIT 15.4   Relative Strength Index (RSI)

Description:	The RSI is an oscillator based on an index of 0 (a market low) to 100 (a market high), with 50 being neutral. The RSI attempts to determine the relative market strength of the current price. To do this, the RSI compares the average price change for each period having a positive price change with the average price change for each period having a negative price change.
Signals:	Establish long position when RSI < 30 (oversold market). Establish short position when RSI > 70 (overbought market).

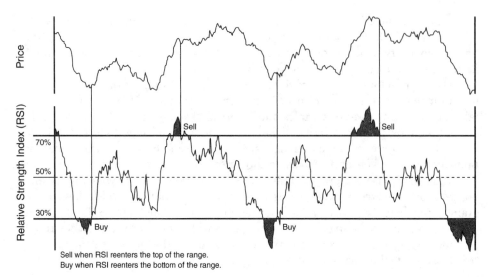

EXHIBIT 15.5   Relative Strength Index (RSI); Sometimes Termed Relative Strength Indicator

for each period with negative price changes for the last *n* periods, and *n* = number of periods (most commonly, *n* = 14 days).

An example of applying the RSI is summarized in Exhibit 15.5. The RSI is a simple form of a pattern recognition system. A **pattern recognition system** looks to capture non-trend-based predictable abnormal market behavior in prices or volatilities. The RSI can be implemented with any periodicity or unit of time. The periodicity, *N*, is defined as days, and the number of periods is often set at 14 days. But the periodicity can be expressed in hours, in minutes, or even in terms of individual price ticks; the user sets the number of periods.

The RSI trading signals are based on numerical levels. When an RSI is less than 30, the market is typically considered oversold (i.e., underpriced), and a long position is established. When its value is more than 70, the market is considered overbought, and a short position is taken. Exhibit 15.5 illustrates the use of an RSI graphically using hypothetical data. As can be seen in the diagram, the price of a futures contract declined sharply early in the series, eventually reaching a level for which the corresponding RSI was less than 30, indicated by the dark-shaded area below the 30% RSI horizontal line. At or below this level, the countertrend strategy would buy (i.e., go long) the futures contract and hold the position (subject to other risk management rules in the strategy) until the RSI moved back into its midrange, where it might be liquidated. As prices continued to move higher, so did the RSI, eventually reaching levels associated with an overbought market. The strategy would then signal the trader to establish a short futures position, once again hoping to liquidate the position when the RSI returned to its midrange.

Relative strength index applications vary in terms of the timing of transactions. For example, a buy or entering trade might be made when the RSI reaches 30 from above, when it returns to 30 from below, or even using more sophisticated analysis to select a point while the RSI is below 30. Exhibit 15.5 illustrates basing buy decisions on when the RSI reaches 30 from below and sell decisions when the RSI reaches 70 from above.

Exhibit 15.5 portrays a very successful example of using the RSI. Prolonged downtrends and uptrends can generate losses. Non-trend-following strategies trade frequently, usually much more often than do most trend-following systems, although short-term trend-following strategies are likely to have high turnover as well. In the managed futures industry, most countertrend strategies operate within a relatively short time frame, using periods ranging from minutes to a few days. This higher frequency price sampling, at least relative to trend followers, more often than not results in substantially higher daily trading volumes. For instance, many trend followers trade between 1,000 and 2,000 contracts annually per $1 million AUM, whereas nontrend managers frequently trade 5,000 or more contracts per $1 million AUM.

15.4.11 Relative Value Strategies and Technical Analysis

Relative value strategies attempt to capture inefficient short-term price divergences between two empirically or theoretically correlated prices or rates. Technical strategies commonly applied to prices and rates can also be applied to spreads or ratios between prices and rates in relative value strategies. For example, RSIs can be applied to the price spread between related assets, such as the spread between the futures price of corn and the futures price of wheat.

In managed futures, relative value strategies focus on short time frames (e.g., measured in seconds to days) or long time frames (e.g., measured in months). Relative value strategies analyze the correlation structure between two or more futures contracts and attempt to exploit deviations in prices as individual futures contracts respond differently to new information or to liquidity imbalances.

Exhibit 15.6 illustrates a relative value futures trade. It depicts the price evolution of two contracts, A and B, which are assumed to be highly correlated (e.g., oil and gasoline). Assume that earlier in the series, prior to the time period graphed in

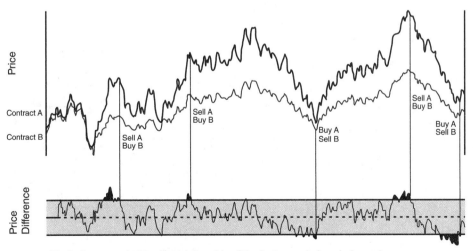

Trade the spread when the relationship of the instruments is unbalanced.

EXHIBIT 15.6 Relative Value Strategy

Exhibit 15.6, the prices of both contracts behaved very similarly. However, as illustrated in Exhibit 15.6, after reaching an initial low, the price of contract A rose much faster than the price of contract B. Relative value strategies look to exploit the price gap that developed between these two contracts by selling (i.e., going short) contract A and buying (i.e., going long) contract B when the spread becomes large relative to past spreads. The trade is unwound as the two price series converge.

The relative value strategy does not directly rely on the separate behavior of either price series. In other words, it is not essential that price A or price B experience trending or mean reversion. Rather, the focus is on the behavior of the relationship between the two prices.

The strategies outlined here are just a few of those used in managed futures trading. In practice, these trading strategies are often quite complex, containing a variety of rules and filters, entries, exits, position sizing, and risk management.

15.5 FOUR CORE DIMENSIONS OF MANAGED FUTURES INVESTMENT STRATEGIES

Managed futures strategies can be divided across four core dimensions: data sources, implementation style, strategy focus, and time horizon. Exhibit 15.7 presents a diagram of managed futures strategies.

15.5.1 Data Sources as a Core Managed Futures Dimension

Managed futures strategies are often denoted as either fundamental or technical. Fundamental strategies rely on such data as economic forecasts, supply and demand estimates, and crop rotation schedules, whereas technical strategies typically analyze

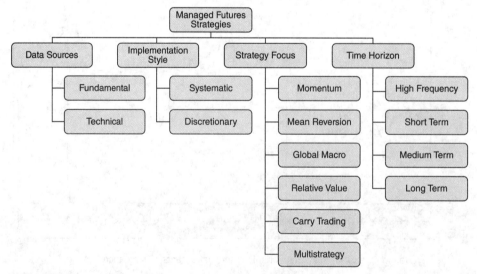

EXHIBIT 15.7 Dimensions of Managed Futures Strategies

historical information such as price and volume. Strategies are also categorized into implementation styles of either systematic or discretionary. Systematic (or quantitative) strategies follow a series of rules to determine entry and exit conditions, position scaling, and position sizes. These strategies rely mostly on the outputs of quantitative models rather than the manager's direct intervention. In terms of turnover, systematic strategies may vary greatly in terms of trade horizon, where trades are held from seconds to months. Over time, systematic strategies have grown in complexity, designed by quant teams that develop the models and automate trading execution. Systematic trading programs also require extensive data capabilities, trading support, and technical support. Systematic implementation is often used in the futures space, given the complexities of futures trading. Trading systems allow a CTA to allocate across many futures markets, maintain collateral, and control and monitor a large number of positions.

15.5.2 Implementation Style as a Core Managed Futures Dimension

Systematic programs are typically more broadly diversified than discretionary traders, both in the number of markets analyzed and in the types of strategies employed. Discretionary managed futures strategies are implemented at the discretion of a CTA manager. These strategies seek to participate opportunistically in market-driven price actions, with the final trading decision being made at the discretion of the fund manager. Since many discretionary managers also use quant models to determine positions, the line between purely discretionary and systematic can sometimes be blurred.[4]

15.5.3 Strategy Focus as a Core Managed Futures Dimension

Given the range of possible asset classes in futures markets, the range of strategies is relatively broad. Common strategies in the space, discussed in previous sectors, include momentum, mean reversion, and relative value. Other strategies include carry trading, multistrategy, and global macro.

Global macro managed futures strategies use fundamental information to determine long and short allocations across the global range of futures markets. Global macro futures strategies will take positions in foreign exchange, commodities, domestic and international equity, and fixed-income markets based on fundamental analysis. A global macro strategy can develop economic models that attempt to explain how the global economy will react to various changes in economic regimes. For example, if the U.S. dollar appreciates, this improves the purchasing power of the U.S. dollar while decreasing the attractiveness of U.S. exports. A global macro manager can construct an economic model that attempts to predict both U.S. dollar exchange rates and the economic impact on commodities, global stock markets, and short- and long-term rates. Another macro strategy may use fundamental inputs and data to gauge the change in the demand for oil. If a global macro manager's model predicts an increase in demand, the manager will go long oil; if demand is predicted to decrease, the manager will short oil. Global macro managers and trend-following strategies use different inputs to determine where global trends will occur. Because of this, the performance of discretionary versus systematic managed futures can vary. Another key difference between the two is that a fundamentally based strategy is more likely to enter a global trend earlier than a trend-following strategy will. This is because trend-following strategies need to measure momentum in prices to begin a position. Although global macro strategies often get in earlier, the market may not agree with the fundamentals for long periods of time, causing difficulty for global macro strategies.

Mean-reversion and countertrend strategies focus on prices reverting to the mean in the short term. Mean-reversion strategies are typically implemented in days to weeks, whereas trend following is often implemented in months. A strategy is considered contrarian if it trades against the prevalent trend. Mean-reversion strategies often take contrarian positions. A contrarian strategy would have the opposite sign of a trend-following strategy. Carry strategies are designed to take advantage of differences in the carry of various commodities. In general, the carry of an asset is the return obtained from holding it (if positive) or the cost of holding it (if negative). For instance, commodities are usually negative carry assets, as they incur storage costs and may suffer from depreciation; however, appropriately hedged commodities can be positive carry assets if the futures market is willing to pay a sufficient premium for future delivery. Carry trades involve long positions in fixed-income investments of high interest rate countries and short positions in fixed-income investments of low interest rate countries. **Multistrategy CTAs** combine a variety of strategy focuses to provide a diversified set of potential return sources and risk-reward profiles.

15.5.4 Time Horizon as a Core Managed Futures Dimension

The final aspect that differentiates managed futures strategies is time horizon. Time horizons can range from high frequency to long term. Trading speed is often measured by the average holding period for each trade. High-frequency trading is reserved for a special group of strategies that do not attempt to benefit from trends in prices and traditionally have not been classified as managed futures strategies. Short-term CTA trading strategies are often classified as intraday to one month, with an average holding period of around 10 days or less. Medium term can be one month to six months. Long term can be greater than six months. Mean reversion and countertrend tend to be shorter term, whereas trend following is often medium to long term. It is very common for systematic funds to combine a large range of approaches, from short term to long term.

A core issue in dynamic futures trading strategies is transaction costs, trading capacity, and slippage. Transaction costs are incurred on a per trade basis. As a result, transaction costs are very important for short-term strategies that may require frequent transactions. Medium- to long-term strategies focus on longer-term effects. As a result, they do not adjust their positions as quickly or as often as do shorter-term programs. Trading capacity is important for strategies that take large positions relative to open interest. If a strategy requires large short-term changes in positions, the strategy may move the market against the strategy. Since CTAs manage accounts on behalf of clients, they often trade multiple accounts simultaneously. This could lead to slippage. Slippage occurs when actual performance deviates or "slips away" from the expected trading results using the computer's signal.

15.6 SYSTEMATIC FUTURES PORTFOLIO CONSTRUCTION

Position taking is a particular feature of futures trading, which differs from investment in traditional assets. In futures markets, one takes positions as opposed to holding underlying assets. The way futures markets approach risk has important implications for the way CTAs do business and for the way someone may choose to invest in these markets: (1) futures markets require gains and losses to be settled in cash daily, (2) futures contracts have no net liquidating value, and (3) futures markets require participants to post collateral to cover potential daily losses. For systematic futures trading portfolios, the key is in building a system for determining positions in futures markets. This section is dedicated to taking a closer look at the basic building blocks in a systematic futures trading system.

15.6.1 The Four Core Decisions of a Futures Trading System

The typical futures trading system is composed of the following four core decisions:

1. Entry: When to enter a position
2. Position sizing: How large a position to take on
3. Exit: When to get out of a position
4. Market allocation: How much risk or capital to allocate to different sectors and markets

Given these four core decisions, a systematic futures trading system is a dynamic system that processes price data inputs, generates trading signals, and outputs automated executable trading decisions. A trading system can simultaneously take into account large amounts of data, process the data, create trading signals, and calculate and allocate risks, as well as determine position sizes, stops, and limits across futures positions. Inside these systems, there are several components that are integrated into portfolio construction: (1) data processing, (2) position sizing, (3) market allocation, and (4) trading execution. Each of these is described in the following sections.

15.6.2 Data Processing in Futures Portfolio Construction

Data inputs for futures trading systems can include both fundamental and technical data. When dealing with futures prices, the aspect of rolling forward futures contracts must be taken into consideration. More specifically, positions will need to be rolled from expiring contracts to newer ones. The rolling aspect of futures contracts creates gaps in price series, requiring adjustments around futures expiration dates. Continuous price series are created by removing these gaps.

15.6.3 Position Sizing in Futures Portfolio Construction

Futures trading systems systematically allocate capital to positions across many different asset classes. Position sizing must take into account the volatility of a particular market. One approach to this is **volatility targeting**, where the size of the position is determined by the trader's conviction in the signal, the volatility of the particular futures market, and a volatility target that is determined by the trader. In particular,

$$\text{Number of Futures Contracts} = \text{Sizing Function} \times \frac{\text{Risk Loading} \times \text{Equity}}{\text{Notional Value}} \times \frac{\text{RVol}_T}{\text{RVol}_R}$$

$$(15.5)$$

where the sizing function reflects the direction of the bet (i.e., long or short) as well as the confidence that the trader has in the signal (i.e., signal strength). For example, a value of 1 indicates that a long position should be taken and that the signal is strong, whereas a value of 0.5 indicates a long position when the signal is not as strong. The risk loading is a parameter selected by traders to reflect the amount of exposure they want to have to the particular market. The value of risk loading is determined by the trader, based on the market environment and the amount of risk the trader wishes to take. Notice that risk loading is multiplied by the amount of equity in the portfolio. The risk loading times the equity or capital is sometimes termed the **capital at risk**. For example, if $1 million is the available equity or capital, and the risk loading is 0.02, then $20,000 is the capital at risk. The denominator is the notional value of the futures contract. The last term on the right-hand side of Equation 15.5 is related to volatility targeting. Here, RVol_T is the realized volatility target, and RVol_R is an estimate of future volatility. This estimate could either be obtained from implied volatility of option prices or be based on realized volatility, calculated using a prespecified window (e.g., 30 daily observations).

☞ **APPLICATION 15.6.3A**

Consider a CTA with $30 million capital. The CTA has determined that 10% of this capital should be allocated to trading in the Brent Crude Oil market. The sizing function is estimated to be 0.8, which means the trader's signal is strong and indicates a long position in this market. The size of each futures contract is 1,000 barrels, and assuming a current price of $50 per barrel, the notional value of each contract will be $50,000. Finally, assume that the annualized volatility target is 20% and that the annualized realized volatility using near-term futures prices of the past 30 days has been 30%.

Given these figures, the number of futures contracts based on Equation 15.5 will be as follows:

$$\text{Number of Futures Contracts} = 0.8 \times \frac{10\% \times 30,000,000}{50,000} \times \frac{20\%}{30\%} = 32$$

If oil markets become calmer, and the estimate of price volatility declines to 25%, the trader will need to rebalance his position to have 38 contracts in the portfolio.

An alternative approach would be to determine the position size based on a range of factors other than a volatility target. This approach can be expressed as follows:

$$\text{Number of Contracts} = \text{Sizing Function} \times \frac{\text{Risk Loading} \times \text{Capital}}{\text{PVol}_R \times \text{Contract Size}} \quad (15.6)$$

In this expression, the sizing function is similar to what was discussed in Equation 15.5, and it reflects the direction of the bet (i.e., long or short) as well as the confidence that the trader has in the signal (i.e., signal strength). In this case, the risk loading is a parameter selected by the trader to reflect the amount of exposure she wants to have to the particular market and will incorporate a volatility target as well as other information she wants to take into account when determining allocation to this market. Similar to the previous case, the risk loading is multiplied by the amount of equity or capital to determine the allocation to this market. In the denominator of Equation 15.6, PVol_R is daily price volatility of the futures contract, which is multiplied by the size of the futures contract.

☞ APPLICATION 15.6.3B

Continuing with the previous example in which the CTA's capital is assumed to be $30 milllion, suppose the sizing function is 0.8 and the risk loading is 0.2%. The daily price volatility of oil is estimated to be $1.1, and each contract is for 1,000 barrels.

Given these figures, the trader will take a long position in futures contracts based on Equation 15.6:

$$\text{Number of Contracts} = 0.8 \times \frac{0.2\% \times 30,000,000}{1.1 \times 1,000} \approx 44$$

In Equation 15.6, the sizing function is multiplied by the total adjusted dollar risk allocated, which is equal to the allocated dollar risk (risk loading times capital) divided by the volatility of price changes measured over the last K trading periods times the point value of the contract. The **point value** is the gain or loss in the contract from a one-point change (e.g., $1) in the futures prices. The allocated dollar risk is the amount of capital that is put into active risk, which is the notional amount times the scalar for how much risk will be taken (risk loading). This amount of risk must then be divided by the futures contract dollar risk. The **futures contract dollar risk** is a measure of the riskiness of the underlying asset of the futures contract during the most recent K trading periods and is the denominator in Equation 15.6. It depends on the contract size or point value and volatility of each particular futures contract. It is important to remember that the notional value of one contract is equal to the point value (multiplier) times the contract price. For example, given the size of the Brent Crude Oil futures contract (1,000 barrels) and the price per barrel ($50), the notional value of each contract is $50,000.

15.6.4 Market Allocation in Futures Portfolio Construction

Market allocation is the process with which both risk and capital are allocated across various futures positions. The process of allocation comes from both capital allocation schemes and risk allocation. Using the equations for the nominal positions in the previous section, there are two avenues by which market allocation can be adjusted based on risk. Risks can be adjusted by the risk loading and the volatility adjustment for risk per contract.

In the simplest case, the risk loading can be set to be equal for all markets. The risk loading is set up in this way to allow for a simple increase or decrease in the overall exposure of the futures trading system. Capital allocation can also vary from market to market. In the simplest case, capital allocation can equal dollar risk weighted. This means that the capital for an individual market is equal to the total capital divided by the number of traded markets.

Consider a $100 million portfolio that is trading 100 futures markets. If each strategy trades equal dollar risk, each market will be allocated $100 million/100, or $1 million. The size of the position for each market will depend on the allocated risk and the amount of realized volatility in each market. This means that the notional exposure in each market can vary substantially depending on each market's volatility. Although the risk allocation will be equal, the notional exposures may differ.

There is a wide range of methodologies for implementing capital allocation. Several of these methods fit easily into the simple structure proposed in this section. Others may require either more complicated or new structures to implement them. The main ways to allocate risk are through equal dollar risk allocation; equal risk contribution, which is similar to risk parity, a topic discussed earlier in this book; and market capacity weighting, in which an allocation is adjusted to reduce the market impact of the futures trading system. In summary:

- **Equal dollar risk allocation** is a strategy that allocates the same amount of dollar risk to each market. This approach does not consider the correlation between markets and is similar to the $1/N$ approach.
- **Equal risk contribution** is a strategy that allocates risk based on the risk contribution of each market, taking correlation into account. This approach is similar to risk parity.
- **Market capacity weighting** is an approach in which capital is allocated as a function of individual market capacity. In futures markets, a market capacity weighting will depend on the market size, as measured by both daily volume and price volatility.

A managed futures fund with larger assets under management cannot allocate capital to markets with lower open interest and volumes. These constraints may cause a larger managed futures fund to tend to allocate risk similarly to market capacity weighting.

15.6.5 Trading Execution in Futures Portfolio Construction

The final component of a futures trading system is trading execution. Implementation approaches for turning trading signals into actual positions can vary from one system to another. **Alpha decay** is the speed with which performance degrades as execution is delayed. In the long-term perspective, alpha decay is much less important for trend following than it is for many shorter-term futures strategies. As a result, the more important consideration related to execution for trend-following systems is cost rather than execution speed. Slower futures trading systems create orders that can be executed in a rather passive manner. Some managers may also choose to sample the price throughout the liquid periods of the day to generate signals, and split daily orders into several intraday orders. For the case of trend following, execution is generally done via simple market orders. Stop-loss orders and more complicated limit orders are less commonly used.

15.7 EIGHT CORE BENEFITS OF MANAGED FUTURES FOR INVESTORS

Managed futures provide a number of benefits in terms of risk-return trade-offs to investors, eight of which are introduced here:

1. DIVERSIFICATION. Managed futures constitute an alternative asset class that has achieved strong performance in both up and down equity, commodity, and currency markets, and has exhibited low correlation to traditional asset classes, such as stocks, bonds, cash, and real estate. Managed futures, when used in conjunction with traditional asset classes, may reduce risk while potentially increasing portfolio returns.
2. PERFORMANCE. Historically, managed futures have provided risk-return profiles comparable to those of many traditional asset classes and superior to those offered by long-only investments in commodities. For example, the historical Sharpe ratio of a diversified portfolio of managed futures could be four times higher than that of a long-only portfolio of commodities.
3. ACCESS TO MULTIPLE MARKETS. There are more than 150 liquid futures products across the globe, including stock indices, currencies, interest rates, fixed income, energies, metals, and agricultural products. CTAs are able to take advantage of potential opportunities in various asset classes in many geographical locations. The fundamental law of active management states that the information ratio of an investment increases as the breadth of the investment strategy increases (holding other variables constant). This means that CTAs have the potential to provide performance with a superior risk-return profile.
4. TRANSPARENCY. Futures prices are determined competitively and are marked to market daily. The fact that futures prices tend to be determined in single-price discovery markets in which everyone can see the limit order book and in which the settlement prices are, in most cases, tradable makes them more accurate and more reliable than prices determined in nearly any other market. The prices used to mark portfolios to market are not stale. There are no dark pools of liquidity, like those found in equity markets. There are no interpolation methods similar to those of some bond markets, in which only a handful of bonds actually trade on any given day. Moreover, there are no models needed to determine the value of structured securities. As a result, the returns experienced are real and have not been smoothed.

5. LIQUIDITY. Liquidity has already been mentioned, but only in the context of liquidating positions and extracting cash. In fact, transaction costs in futures are lower than in their underlying cash markets. As a result, the benefits of the kind of active management and trading that CTAs implement are available with less drag from market impact than one would incur with the same type of trading in underlying markets.

6. SIZE. As an investment alternative, managed futures have been available since the 1970s and experienced significant growth over the past several decades. As of 2018 the size of the market was estimated at about $320 billion. This means the market has reached a level at which it can accommodate allocations from institutional investors.

7. NO WITHHOLDING TAXES. In a number of the world's stock and bond markets, foreign investors are taxed more heavily than are domestic investors. With futures, all of the tax benefits that accrue to domestic investors can be passed through to those who use futures in the form of simple cash/futures arbitrage.

8. VERY LOW FOREIGN EXCHANGE RISK. Futures on foreign assets or commodities have little exposure to foreign exchange risk. A futures contract has no net liquidating value. As a result, a long position in a European equity index futures contract has no exposure to the change in the price of the euro, whereas an investment in European equities exposes the investor not only to changes in the price of European stocks but to changes in the price of the euro as well. In the case of futures, the investor's currency risk is limited to the comparatively small amounts of margin that must be posted at exchanges around the world and to any realized profit or loss that has not yet been converted back into the investor's home currency.

To understand this benefit, note that a position in a futures contract is similar to a long position in the same asset in the cash market, where the position is financed through borrowing. This means a futures position in a foreign-currency-denominated asset is similar to a cash position in the same asset with investment financed through borrowing in the same foreign currency. As a result, currency fluctuations will have equal effects on assets and liabilities of the investors, with zero net effect. For instance, from a Japanese investor's viewpoint, a position in Euro Stoxx futures makes or loses money only when the index rises or falls. A change in the yen price of the euro would, by itself, produce neither a gain nor a loss, because the investor has no cash position in euros.

In contrast, the yen return to a fully funded, currency-unhedged investment in Euro Stoxx would be, to a first approximation, the sum of the return on Euro Stoxx, as viewed by a euro-based investor, and the yen return on the euro. Conventional money managers are well aware of the problems raised by currency risk because currency volatility is potentially very large. During periods of increased uncertainty in global markets, currency volatility may contribute as much to the risk of a fully funded position as does the volatility of the underlying asset, the Euro Stoxx.

For CTAs, the only foreign currency risk associated with using futures to trade comes from the value of cash or collateral balances that are the result of either posting margin collateral or accumulating gains or losses in currencies in which the contracts are denominated. Because these balances tend to be small relative to the notional values of the positions taken, foreign currency risk is, for all practical purposes, separate from the risks associated with the underlying assets or commodities. This decoupling allows CTAs to take much more nuanced views on currency exposure than would be possible for most conventional money managers, for whom hedging currency exposure can be costly.

15.8 EVIDENCE ON MANAGED FUTURES RETURNS

There are a number of key questions with respect to managed futures: Can managed futures products produce consistent alpha? Can managed futures provide downside risk protection? What are the sources of returns, and what are the potential risks?

15.8.1 Evidence on Managed Futures Alpha

There are two types of relevant empirical research on the issue of consistent alpha. The first type examines the actual returns of managed futures funds. The second type estimates returns to funds based on simulations of well-known trading strategies using historical prices.

The first empirical approach is addressed by Kazemi and Li, who use the direct examination of actual managers to show that systematic CTAs have demonstrated statistically significant, positive market-timing ability.[5] Returns to trend-following systematic CTAs are achieved through long positions in rising markets and short positions in falling markets. Kazemi and Li conclude that CTAs have demonstrated skill in differentiating between upward- and downward-trending markets.

The simulation-based approach is studied by Miffre and Rallis, who simulate well-known momentum strategies, such as trend following.[6] By examining historical returns of 31 U.S.-based commodity futures contracts for evidence of shorter- and longer-term price momentum or reversal characteristics for the period January 31, 1979, through September 30, 2004, they find that 13 of the momentum strategies they studied were profitable for the period of their analysis.

In general, the empirical research supports the inclusion of managed futures in a diversified portfolio context. However, the potential benefits of managed futures may be neutralized if the investments take place through CPOs managing a pool of CTAs. The second layer of fees charged by these CPOs effectively eliminates most of the benefits associated with this asset class.

15.8.2 The Evidence on Downside Risk Protection

The greatest concern for investors is typically downside risk. The ability to protect the value of an investment portfolio in hostile or turbulent markets is the key to the value of diversification. An asset class distinct from traditional financial asset classes has the potential to diversify and protect an investment portfolio from hostile markets. In 2008, the downside risk of the market crisis was severe. While some investors bemoaned that there was nowhere to hide from the market losses and risks, the last three lines of Exhibit 15.8 indicate that macro and managed futures funds emerged relatively unscathed from the turbulence of the financial crisis that began in 2007.

EXHIBIT 15.8   Returns of Various Asset Classes and Hedge Fund Strategies, 2007 to 2009

	Asset Returns			
	2007	2008	2009	2007–2009
GSCl Commodities	32.7%	−46.5%	13.5%	−19.4%
MSCI World Index	9.0%	−40.7%	30.0%	−16.0%
S&P 500	5.5%	−37.0%	26.5%	−15.9%
Convertible Arb	5.2%	−31.6%	47.3%	6.0%
Emerging Markets Hedge	20.2%	−30.4%	30.0%	8.8%
Fixed Income Arb	3.8%	−28.8%	27.4%	−5.9%
60% MSCI World, 40% Barclays Global	9.4%	−24.9%	20.7%	−0.8%
Equity Long/Short	13.7%	−19.7%	19.5%	9.0%
Hedge Fund Index	12.6%	−19.1%	18.6%	8.0%
Event-Driven Multistrategy	16.8%	−16.2%	19.9%	17.3%
Macro	17.4%	−4.6%	11.5%	24.9%
Barclays Global Aggregate	9.5%	4.8%	6.9%	22.7%
Managed Futures	6.0%	18.3%	−6.5%	17.2%

Source: Data from Bloomberg.

15.8.3   Mechanical Managed Futures Indices

The Mount Lucas Management Index provides a useful comparison for evaluating trend-following futures strategies. The **Mount Lucas Management (MLM) Index** is a passive, transparent, and investable index designed to capture the returns to active futures investing. It provides a useful benchmark for evaluating trend following futures strategies. The MLM Index mechanically applies a simple price trend-following rule for buying and selling commodity, financial, and currency futures. Each of the three sub-baskets is weighted by its relative historical volatility, whereas markets within each sub-basket are equally weighted. The MLM Index can take long or short positions in any of its 22 constituent markets; there are no neutral positions. Because the MLM Index is investable, its performance is representative of what investors may actually obtain if they use the index's simple strategy in their portfolios. One of the biggest advantages of the MLM Index is the observed symmetry of its past returns. The distribution of returns has shown a somewhat bell-shaped curve, albeit with larger tails than those of a normal distribution. Also, there has been lower volatility in the MLM Index compared to all of the managed futures indices.

15.8.4   Why Might Managed Futures Provide Superior Returns?

Whether managed futures funds can be a source of alpha can be addressed intuitively, not just empirically. Having an intuitive or theoretical explanation of the sources of superior returns can provide valuable information in differentiating between empirical results that help predict future performance and empirical results that do not indicate future performance because they are spurious or apply only to past specific market regimes. This section introduces a conceptual framework that could explain why managed futures funds may provide alpha to investors.

Managed futures funds tend to trade futures contracts in which the underlying assets are broad asset classes, such as equities, commodities, currencies, and fixed-income instruments. Further, managed futures funds trade in futures contracts that are highly liquid, with rather narrow bid-ask spreads. Finally, note that futures contracts represent zero-sum games: Any dollar received on one side of a futures contract is paid to managed futures funds by the other side of the futures contract. Therefore, capital gains earned must result from capital losses by other futures market participants. Thus, it appears that the typical arguments put forth to describe the economic sources of alpha for other investment strategies do not apply in this case. For instance, there is no illiquidity premium to be earned by managed futures funds. So, what is the potential source of alpha for typical managed futures funds? If a theoretical argument for the presence of ex ante alpha cannot be provided, then any empirically estimated ex post alpha must be looked at with an especially skeptical eye.

The starting point of this conceptual framework is the observation that most futures contracts are used as hedging instruments by some market participants and as speculating instruments by other market participants. A large group of futures market participants are natural hedgers. A **natural hedger** is a market participant who seeks to hedge a risk that springs from its fundamental business activities. Natural hedgers participate in futures markets to hedge their risks rather than to earn profits through speculation.

If there are more natural hedgers on one side of a market (e.g., long) than on the other side of the market, then speculators (e.g., managed futures funds) step in and fill the gap between supply and demand in futures contracts. In this case, managed futures funds, much like insurance agents, earn positive excess return for providing a valuable service to natural hedgers. In other words, managed futures funds earn a return by accepting risks that natural hedgers want to avoid. Managed futures funds are able and willing to accept this risk because, unlike natural hedgers, they tend to hold diversified portfolios of futures contracts.

The motive of managed futures funds is to make a profit. When demand by natural hedgers for short positions in a particular futures contract is strong, prices fall to the point that managed futures funds perceive a profit opportunity by taking an offsetting long position. When demand by natural hedgers for long positions in a particular futures contract is strong, prices rise to the point that managed futures funds perceive a profit opportunity by taking an offsetting short position. An example of a natural hedger seeking a long position in a futures contract is a manufacturer requiring a metal or other material for a production process.

The presence of natural hedgers with different time horizons, risk profiles, and break-even points could also explain the presence of trends in futures. As more producers come to market to hedge their positions, managed futures funds are willing to take larger long positions only if they expect ongoing increases in futures prices. In this context, managed futures funds may be viewed as providing protection from price risk for a group of natural hedgers who are willing to pay the cost for the protection that the futures contract provides.

Often there is approximately equal demand from potential natural hedgers on each side of a futures contract. If there are enough natural hedgers on each side of the market, the managed futures fund's potential source of alpha tends to disappear. However, even when long-term demand for long and short positions by natural hedgers is equal, there are occasional mismatches, provided the natural hedgers do not come to the market at the same time. These temporary mismatches between demand and supply of futures contracts provide a role for managed futures funds to play. They also explain why managed futures funds are not always long or short in a particular market. If there are more corn producers who are trying to hedge their income, then managed futures funds need to be long; and when more corn users come to the market to hedge their cost, managed futures funds need to take short positions.

One implication of this conceptual framework is that managed futures funds are likely to earn positive alphas in those markets in which there is a great need for hedging when natural hedgers come to market at different points in time. For example, futures markets for industrial metals, agricultural products, and currencies are more likely to be sources of alpha than are futures markets for equities and precious metals. There are fewer natural hedgers in the equity and precious metal markets and therefore less need for managed futures funds to provide a service to other market participants.

Additional arguments for a consistent source of alpha to managed futures funds are available. For example, central banks may be willing to manipulate exchange rates in the short run away from levels consistent with long-term market forces for the purpose of pursuing their domestic policy agenda. The massive level of governmental resources involved in these interventions raises the possibility that exchange rates are periodically, substantially, and temporarily dislocated, thereby generating profitable speculative opportunities to managed futures funds. In other words, ongoing intervention by central banks could cause persistent trends in exchange rates or sovereign debt yields until the intervention ceases, at which point the trend may reverse. Managed futures funds may profit from these patterns at the expense of the central banks.

15.8.5 Six Potentially Important Risks of Managed Futures Funds

The risks of managed futures funds can be summarized as follows.

Many investors find it difficult to invest in black-box systems, in which trading algorithms are not disclosed, as it gives rise to transparency risk. **Transparency** is the ability to understand the detail within an investment strategy or portfolio. **Transparency risk** is dispersion in economic outcomes caused by the lack of detailed information regarding an investment portfolio or strategy. Trusting investment capital to an automated system may also bring fears of computer bugs, viruses, or connectivity issues, not unlike those that may cause flash crashes or rare instances of enormous market price changes for no apparent reason other than massive intentional or unintentional trades.

A second major risk is model risk. **Model risk** is economic dispersion caused by the failure of models to perform as intended. Systematic trend-following managers rely on algorithmic models to generate trade signals. Model risk arises if a model is not adequately tested before deployment and could therefore break down under particular market conditions. For example, the model may not have been tested for the situation in which the price of a futures contract rises substantially during one day and therefore hits a prespecified limit set by the exchange.

Capacity risk arises when a managed futures trader concentrates trades in a market that lacks sufficient depth (i.e., liquidity). The performance of a trader who has developed expertise in trading a thinly traded futures contract will suffer if investors decide to substantially increase their allocations to this fund.

A fourth risk, **liquidity risk**, is somewhat related to capacity risk in that it refers to how a large fund that is trading in a thinly traded market will affect the price should it decide to increase or decrease its allocation. However, liquidity risk can also arise in markets with high volume. If too many funds seek to trade the same markets at the same price, competition for trades can lead to increased slippage and trading costs. If trading volume among other market participants declines, managed futures funds become a larger part of the market and find it difficult to execute in less liquid markets.

Given their association with speculation, futures exchanges are especially prone to change margin terms or to face actions by governmental entities that tax or restrict futures trading. This exposes managed futures to a fifth risk, **regulatory risk**, which is the risk of unanticipated changes in taxation or regulations.

Trend-following managed futures funds need trending markets to profit. Volatile, trendless markets can leave managed futures funds with substantial losses. This gives rise to the final risk, **lack of trends risk**, which comes into play when the trader continues allocating capital to trendless markets, leading to substantial losses. Therefore, the attrition rate among managed futures funds is relatively high.

15.8.6 Managed Accounts and Platforms

Once investors decide to make an allocation to managed futures, they must tackle the problem of just how to structure the investment. The choice of vehicle employed to make an allocation is dependent on the size of the allocation as well as on the level of expertise and experience the investor possesses.

To tackle the problem of structuring the investments, investors will need to follow a decision-making process that proceeds along the following lines. First, the investor must determine how many managed futures funds he wants in the portfolio. Many family offices, and even some larger institutional investors, will decide to invest in a single managed futures fund. This decision has the virtue of simplicity and is possible to implement by choosing one of the large, diversified trend-following managed futures funds, whose performance correlates highly with a trend-following benchmark. If the investor decides to use this approach, the focus should be on examining differences between investing in a fund sponsored on behalf of the managed futures funds versus a managed account.

Generally, the single managed futures funds route exposes the investor to a greater amount of risk. In this scenario, the results depend on the performance of a single manager, concentrate risk to a single organization, and may be exposed to a limited number of trading models. To avoid these constraints, the investor may decide to form a diversified portfolio of managed futures funds.

Second, if the investors are large enough, they must decide how to create a diversified portfolio of managed futures funds. Initially, the most cost-effective approach to achieving diversification is to allocate to a multi-managed futures fund. Then, as the size of the allocation to managed futures funds increases, more options become available to the investor. Eventually, the investor must decide whether to assemble an in-house team to manage the portfolio and whether to use a managed account platform. There are cost issues associated with each choice.

Related to the size of allocation to managed futures funds, two issues arise as the investor decides on the best approach to creating a diversified portfolio of CTAs. The first issue is related to the level of allocation at which it becomes cost effective to move from working with a multi-managed futures fund's investment program to assembling an in-house team to create and manage a diversified portfolio of managed futures funds. While no exact figure exists for this cost threshold, it is primarily affected by four factors:

1. The extra layer of fees that the investor will have to pay the multi-managed futures fund
2. The cost of assembling a team of analysts who can construct and manage a managed futures fund portfolio
3. The minimum size of the investment that managed futures funds are willing to accept
4. The number of managed futures funds that should be included in the portfolio to achieve diversification

For example, in order to achieve a reasonable degree of diversification, a portfolio may consist of about six managed futures funds. If the minimum investment size for large institutional-quality funds is assumed to be $5 million, an investment of at least $30 million is required to make it cost-effective to create a portfolio of managed futures funds. The management fee associated with a $30 million portfolio is around $300,000 or more. This amount may not be enough to create a team that can select and manage a portfolio of managed futures funds. As the size of the investment increases, the extra level of fees paid increases as well, and it will eventually become economical to create an in-house team to manage a portfolio of managed futures funds and forgo allocations to multi-managed futures funds.

The second issue is related to the next level of allocation, when it becomes viable for the investor to use a managed account platform. Managed accounts offer a number of very important advantages over managed futures funds, including transparency, security of collateral, and ease of opening and closing positions. However, they require the investor to have experienced people and reliable systems in place, which can be costly.

Some funds are structured with different share classes, which may differ in fee structure and withdrawal rights. For example, someone who wants daily liquidity might be willing to pay a higher management fee than someone willing to accept annual liquidity. A new investment may be held in a temporary share class until it reaches the same high-water mark as the rest of the fund. Some classes may be invested in additional assets that are not part of the main fund.

15.8.7 Multimanager Funds

Multi-managed futures funds are known variously as managed futures funds of funds or commodity pools. From the investor's standpoint, both accomplish the same thing: They provide a single vehicle for investing in a diversified portfolio of managed futures funds. The differences are chiefly regulatory, relating to the way the funds are structured and where they are offered. Commodity pool operators (CPOs), for example, create vehicles that are distributed in the United States. They are common investment vehicles for retail investors, high-net-worth individuals, and even some small institutions. Some funds launch offshore funds and tend to attract larger institutional investors. The expression *fund of funds* derives from a time when the primary investment vehicle at the individual managed futures funds level was a fund. As the industry has evolved, multimanager funds have migrated to the use of managed accounts.

The primary benefits of a multi-managed futures fund structure are accessing the expertise that the fund manager has in choosing the managers, structuring the portfolio, performing both investment and operational due diligence, reporting performance, monitoring risk, and accounting. In addition, the fund manager performs less obvious tasks, such as collecting data, meeting managers, running background checks, analyzing performance and strategies, negotiating contracts and fees, monitoring performance, and rebalancing the portfolio as necessary. From an investor's perspective, the investment offering and services of such a structure consolidate much of the work into choosing and reviewing a single organization. Because individual multi-managed futures funds have different investment objectives, investors need to find a fund that is consistent with their needs for risk and return as well as for reporting and transparency.

With a multimanager futures fund, the manager assembles a portfolio of managed futures funds and then accepts investments in the entire portfolio. The multi-managed futures fund manager charges a fee for portfolio construction and oversight services. Each of the managers in the fund also charges a fee. Although investors negotiate contracts and fees with the multi-managed futures fund manager directly, and the investment is consolidated into a single organization, investors still have due diligence and monitoring obligations.

The fees charged by multi-managed futures fund managers raise important questions about how to structure the investment. If the level of allocation is relatively small, the investor would likely invest in managed futures funds. However, if investors intend to allocate a large amount to managed futures funds, they might be better advised to save the fees that would be paid to a multi-managed futures fund manager and simply hire the staff and consultants needed to select managed futures funds, perform the due diligence, construct the portfolios, and so on. Managed accounts, which are the vehicle of choice for most multi-managed futures fund managers, are a much bigger undertaking than are managed futures funds. To warrant the work involved in setting up brokerage accounts, negotiating agreements, monitoring the accounts, reconciling trades, complying with anti-money-laundering regulations, managing cash flows, and so forth, a reasonable break-even point is an investment in managed futures funds of around $500 million.

15.8.8 Structuring Managed Futures Products with Managed Accounts

A managed account is a brokerage account held by a brokerage firm that is also registered as a futures commission merchant, in which investment discretion has been assigned to the managed futures fund manager. The investor is responsible for opening and maintaining the account, reconciling brokerage statements, and maintaining cash controls, as well as negotiating contracts with managers, including investment management agreements and powers of attorney. The limited power of attorney gives the manager authority to trade on the investor's behalf, but the money has to remain in the investor's account. The investor controls the terms of the power of attorney, including the right to revoke trading privileges.

The key advantage to a managed account is complete control. By pulling trading privileges, the investor has the ability to manage the cash and liquidate the account at any time. Managed accounts, then, avoid the lockup and gating provisions frequently found in hedge fund investments. In theory, this gives the investor better than daily liquidity, as the account can be liquidated whenever the market is open. That alone is enough to make some investors demand managed accounts, especially investors with in-house staff to handle the paperwork.

Managed accounts have other advantages. The money is within the investor's control, not the fund manager's, at all times. The accounts offer complete transparency. The investor can see the positions, trades, and details at any time. Managed accounts, then, virtually eliminate the risk of fraud, as the transparency and security of these accounts prevent the manager from misstating leverage, manipulating returns, or stealing the investor's assets. The investor can choose the parameters for leverage based on the targeted volatility of returns. The choice of leverage makes it easier for the investor to manage the underlying cash. In fact, this type of managed futures fund account structure is often looked at as an overlay on the cash position in an investor's portfolio, rather than a separate asset class.

Of course, these advantages come at a cost. The first is the reduced pool of managers to choose from. Many large managers do not accept managed accounts, whereas those that do require a large minimum investment and other administrative stipulations. In addition, the previously mentioned transparency and control come with the responsibility for establishing and maintaining brokerage accounts that require legal, administrative, risk, and investment oversight in accordance with each organization's investment standards. Further, unless procured by the investor, there is no administrator or auditor.

Managed accounts can be set up in a variety of ways to meet different portfolio policy requirements. The limited partnership structure of hedge funds limits investor liability to the amount invested. For example, an investor who allocates $10 million to a failed hedge fund cannot lose more than $10 million, even if the hedge fund is highly leveraged and sustains losses greater than the amount of contributed client assets. Managed accounts, however, do not automatically have a limited liability structure. Especially in futures markets, where the required margin is much smaller than the notional value of contracts, investor losses in high margin-to-equity investments can be larger than the amount of contributed capital. Therefore, managed accounts must be carefully designed with a legal structure that ensures that limited liability is obtained. Structures offering limited liability vary by legal jurisdiction but may include limited liability companies, limited partnerships, special purpose vehicles (SPVs), or bankruptcy-remote entities. Each structure is designed to limit investor losses to the amount of cash invested, even if trading activity incurs greater losses.

In many managed account situations, the investor begins by setting up an SPV or another holding entity to fence off any trading liabilities from the rest of the money that the investor controls. It is not a necessary step, however, as there are other ways to manage the potential liability. In most cases, the investor uses the SPV to open an account at a brokerage firm where the managed futures funds manager has trading authority. The investor gives the manager the authority to trade in the account.

15.8.9 Structuring Managed Futures Products with Platforms

An alternative way to structure a managed futures funds investment is through a platform. This is a relatively new product, offered by a handful of financial services firms. It operates almost like a multi-managed futures fund, except that investors can select their own leverage and create their own portfolios from the mix of funds offered through the platform.

Platform companies argue that a key advantage of their structure is having objective, independent boards of directors and vendors that are selected by the platform company, not a manager. The platform structure may also reduce custody concerns. Usually, these platforms pass on some of the advantages of managed accounts, such as transparency, liquidity, and customized leverage.

Investors can have a series of fund investments in the platform's participating money managers, receiving consolidated performance information as well as consolidated subscription and redemption paperwork from the platform. It is relatively easy to move money from one manager to another. Because of the transparency and liquidity, these are a hybrid of managed accounts and managed futures funds.

Exhibit 15.9 consolidates much of the previous discussion into a summary table, providing an overview of the primary characteristics of the four types of investment structures: managed futures funds, multi-managed futures funds, managed accounts, and platforms. While there are definitely exceptions to the assignment of characteristics in this table, it should serve as a good starting point when considering an investment structure.

15.9 BENEFITS OF MANAGED FUTURES FUNDS

A more direct way to examine the attractiveness of a managed futures investment is to analyze the performance of managed futures traders.

15.9.1 Research Regarding the Benefits of Managed Futures Funds

In 1983, John Lintner presented one of the first academic papers on the topic of managed futures funds and their benefits. His analysis was designed to examine the risk-return characteristics of managed futures accounts or funds.[7] In this study, Lintner concluded that "the combined portfolios of stocks (or stocks and bonds) after including judicious investments . . . in managed futures accounts (or funds) show substantially less risk at every possible level of expected return than portfolios of stocks (or stocks and bonds) alone."

Lintner's work provided an initial academic basis for investing in managed futures. Other early studies that followed his research both challenged and supported his results. A series of studies by Elton, Gruber, and Rentzler in 1987, 1989, and 1990, known as the EGR studies, examined public commodity pools and, unlike Lintner, found little evidence of the benefits of managed futures.[8] However, other analyses of managed futures supported their inclusion in investment portfolios. Some of these

EXHIBIT 15.9 Structural Characteristics of Managed Futures Funds, Multi-Managed Futures Funds, Managed Accounts, and Platforms

	Liability	Liquidity	Funding and Leverage	Oversight and Control of Assets	Maintenance	Position and Trade Transparency	Availability	Due Diligence Burden
CTA Fund	Limited	Monthly	Manager determined	Directors selected by manager	Low	Usually not	Most managers offer flagship fund.	Medium
Multi-CTA Fund	Limited	Weekly/ Monthly	Manager determined	Directors selected by manager	Low	Usually not	Most managers offer flagship fund.	Low
Managed Account	Unlimited	Daily	Customer determined	Investor	High	Yes	Not all managers accept managed accounts.	High
Platform	Limited	Weekly/ Monthly	Hybrid	Directors selected by platform	Medium	Varies; manager determined	Not all managers have an established relationship with a platform.	Low

later analyses attempted to address data issues in the EGR studies. The EGR studies looked at public commodity pools, known to have been a very expensive way to invest in managed futures. Later analyses directly examined the returns of managed futures traders and found evidence that, on average, managed futures provide attractive risk-adjusted returns, especially if the performance is measured in the context of a diversified portfolio of stocks and bonds.

Unlike previous studies that examined the benefits of CTAs either as a standalone investment or in the context of portfolios consisting of traditional asset classes, Kat (2002) examined the possible role of managed futures in portfolios of stocks, bonds, and hedge funds.[9] He found that allocating to managed futures allows investors to achieve a very substantial degree of overall risk reduction at limited costs in terms of lower returns or skewness. Apart from their lower expected returns, managed futures appear to be more effective diversifiers than hedge funds. The paper concluded that adding managed futures to a portfolio of stocks and bonds will reduce that portfolio's standard deviation more and quicker than hedge funds will, and without the undesirable side effects in terms of lower skewness and higher kurtosis. Finally, Kat observed that overall portfolio standard deviation can be further reduced by combining both hedge funds and managed futures with stocks and bonds. Again, it is worth repeating that these results are, to some degree, time dependent and can change dramatically over short periods of time.

Some studies have shown that systematic trend-following strategies tend to outperform discretionary strategies on a risk-adjusted basis.[10] These studies show that on the basis of absolute monthly returns, systematic funds outperform discretionary funds whenever the relevant markets are falling. When markets are rising, however, discretionary funds tend to deliver higher absolute returns than do systematic funds. Across a variety of metrics, systematic funds perform better than discretionary funds. In particular, on an ex post basis, systematic funds produce less extreme drawdowns, higher Sharpe ratios, and higher Jensen's alpha (measured against traditional asset classes). Furthermore, systematic funds exhibit lower skewness and kurtosis than do discretionary funds. Results suggest that much of systematic funds' outperformance comes from a better ability to manage extreme events, performing better than discretionary funds in crisis conditions. Managed futures managers and trend followers, in particular, are supposed to be able to time their chosen markets (e.g., currencies or commodities). A study by Kazemi and Li (2009) investigated the return and volatility market-timing ability of managed futures funds and examined whether there is a difference in market-timing abilities between systematic and discretionary traders.[11] For this purpose, a set of risk factors was developed based on returns from the most heavily traded futures contracts. The study made two conclusions:

1. Managed futures funds exhibit both return and volatility market-timing ability in markets that they have declared to be their focus, most notably for currencies, interest rates, and commodities. However, managed futures funds display negative return timing in equity markets.
2. Systematic traders are generally better market timers than are discretionary traders. Systematic traders show timing ability for currency futures and physical product (corn, crude oil, natural gas, gold) futures.

15.9.2 Sources of Return for Managed Futures Funds

The sources of return to managed futures are essentially different from those related to traditional stocks, bonds, or even hedge funds. For instance, futures, swaps, and forward contracts can provide direct exposure to underlying financial and commodity markets but often with greater liquidity and less market impact. Futures and options allow traders to take short positions without the need to borrow the securities from other investors. This allows traders to actively allocate assets between long and short positions within the futures/options market-trading complex. In addition, options traders may also directly trade market/security characteristics, such as price volatility, that underlie the contract. The unique return opportunities of managed futures may also stem from the global nature of futures contracts available for trading and the broader range of trading strategies.

It is important to note that many managed futures strategies trade primarily in futures markets, which in aggregate are zero-sum games. This means that for each amount that is gained by a group of traders, there is an equal amount that is lost by another group of traders. (In traditional equity and fixed-income markets, investor gains are not offset by losses by other investors.) The implication is that if, as an asset class, managed futures funds provide positive returns on a consistent basis, then other investors must be earning negative returns on a consistent basis. This may appear to be implausible. Futures markets are not subject to this implication of a zero-sum game if one considers that many participants have positions in cash markets and that losses in futures markets may be offset by gains in cash markets. In other words, some spot market participants may be willing to lose money in futures markets because the loss is offset by gains in other parts of their operations. These gains could be in the form of higher income or lower risk. The classic case of a corn farmer who hedges and is willing to experience a small loss on the futures contract in exchange for avoiding exposure to fluctuations in future corn prices highlights this scenario. Without a hedge, this farmer could lose her entire business if the price of corn unexpectedly declines. Thus, she would be willing to suffer a small loss in the futures market to avoid the risk of ruin.

Since in broader terms futures are not a net zero-sum game, managed futures strategies can earn a positive rate of return if they provide a service or benefit to those market participants who are willing to accept small losses in futures markets while experiencing higher profits, lower losses, or lower risks in other markets. Managed futures managers may fulfill the following functions: (1) they allow other participants to hedge a position and therefore reduce their risks, (2) they provide liquidity so that other participants satisfy their need for liquidity, and (3) they take offsetting positions for rebalancing and other demands from other market participants. These activities allow managed futures funds to earn a premium, which is highly time varying. This means that the premium is not earned by always taking the same long or short position in a given market; rather, the premium is earned by taking both long and short positions during different periods. Hedging and liquidity provision is an important aspect of the benefits provided to other market participants. Whereas futures contracts are used by some participants to hedge their risks, spot markets serve a different purpose. Therefore, the same level of premiums may not be earned by a managed futures fund if the trading strategy involves the spot market.

EXHIBIT 15.10 The Total Futures Price and Spot Price Only Performance for a Representative Pure Trend-Following System, 1980–2013

		Sharpe Ratio	Monthly Return (%)	Monthly Risk (%)
All	Futures	0.74	1.01	4.65
	Spot	0.46	0.63	4.64
Fixed Income	Futures	0.51	1.45	9.64
	Spot	0.21	0.60	9.63
Short-Term Interest Rates	Futures	1.12	2.95	8.90
	Spot	0.98	2.57	8.88
Equity	Futures	0.08	0.20	8.08
	Spot	0.09	0.21	8.08
Commodity	Futures	0.73	1.00	4.60
	Spot	0.35	0.47	4.59
Currency	Futures	0.93	0.93	8.10
	Spot	0.28	0.66	8.10

Source: Greyserman and Kaminski, *Trend Following with Managed Futures: The Search for Crisis Alpha* (Wiley, 2014).

One simple way to examine this effect is to compare the performance of a simple trend-following strategy on both spot and futures prices. Both spot and futures prices are available at the same time, but they represent different things. Spot prices represent the price to purchase or sell something at the current time. Futures prices represent the price to purchase or sell something in the future. Futures contracts allow for risk transfer and hedging. Exhibit 15.10 lists the Sharpe ratio, monthly return, and monthly risk for the performance of a representative trend-following strategy on both the spot price series and the futures price series across all asset classes from 1980 to 2013. The Sharpe ratio for trend following on spot prices is 0.46, whereas the Sharpe ratio on futures prices is 0.74. This demonstrates how futures prices may tend to offer more hedging benefits to other market participants, leading to profit opportunities for CTAs. Another interesting aspect of Exhibit 15.10 is the variation in performance across asset classes. The outperformance of the futures prices is most pronounced in fixed-income and commodity markets. This is consistent with the hedging of long-term fixed-income and commodity risk. The performance of equity futures prices is roughly the same as direct investments in equities. This suggests that there may be fewer hedging or liquidity provision opportunities in equities for managed futures.

Index (Jan. 2000–Dec. 2018)	HFRI Macro: Systematic Diversified	MSCI World Equity
Annualized Arithmetic Mean	5.0%	4.5%
Annualized Standard Deviation	7.6%	15.0%
Annualized Semivolatility	4.2%	11.6%
Annualized Median	4.6%	11.6%
Skewness	0.2	-0.7
Excess Kurtosis	0.1	1.6
Sharpe Ratio	0.3	0.1
Sortino Ratio	0.6	0.2
Annualized Geometric Mean	4.7%	3.4%
First-Order Autocorrelation	-0.04	0.14
Annualized Standard Deviation (Adjusted for Autocorrelation)	7.4%	17.1%
Maximum	6.5%	11.2%
Minimum	-6.4%	-19.0%
Max Drawdown	-13.6%	-54.0%

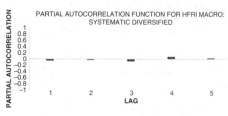

Index (Jan. 2000–Dec. 2018)	HFRI Macro (Total)	MSCI World Equity
Annualized Arithmetic Mean	4.3%	4.5%
Annualized Standard Deviation	5.1%	15.0%
Annualized Semivolatility	2.9%	11.6%
Annualized Median	3.1%	11.6%
Skewness	0.3	-0.7
Excess Kurtosis	0.6	1.6
Sharpe Ratio	0.4	0.1
Sortino Ratio	0.6	0.2
Annualized Geometric Mean	4.2%	3.4%
First-Order Autocorrelation	0.01	0.14
Annualized Standard Deviation (Adjusted for Autocorrelation)	5.1%	17.1%
Maximum	5.7%	11.2%
Minimum	-3.7%	-19.0%
Max Drawdown	-8.0%	-54.0%

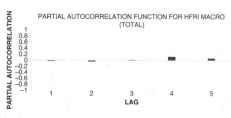

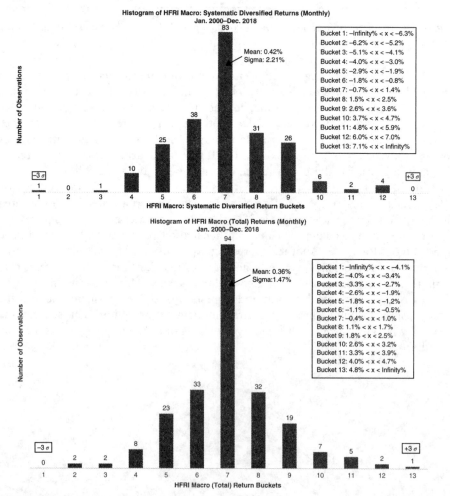

EXHIBIT 15.11   Statistical Summary of Returns

15.10 KEY OBSERVATIONS REGARDING HISTORICAL RETURNS OF MACRO AND SYSTEMATIC DIVERSIFIED FUNDS

Monthly returns to macro and systematic diversified funds are observed from January of 2000 to December of 2018. Exhibit 15.11 provides univariate return statistics in the top panel, partial autocorrelations of returns in the middle panel, and histograms of returns in the bottom panel.

Key observations on the returns to systematic diversified funds that are consistent with economic reasoning are an essential component of knowledge and include the following:

1. The historic return distribution of systematic diversified funds resembled that of a normal distribution, with no indication of a pronounced skew or fat tails (excess kurtosis).
2. Volatility of returns was moderately low relative to world equities.
3. Returns exhibited little or no autocorrelation.
4. Maximum drawdown was much better than observed for global equities.

Key observations on the returns to macro funds that are consistent with economic reasoning are an essential component of knowledge and include the following:

1. The historic return distribution of Macro (Total) resembled that of a normal distribution, with no indication of a pronounced skew or fat tails (excess kurtosis).
2. Volatility of returns was low relative to world equities.
3. Returns exhibited little or no autocorrelation.
4. Maximum drawdown was much better than observed for global equities.

REVIEW QUESTIONS

1. Distinguish discretionary fund trading from systematic fund trading.
2. Describe the strategy of a global macro fund.
3. What does market risk mean in the context of macro investing?
4. Describe the strategy of a managed futures fund.
5. What is a commodity trading adviser (CTA)?
6. List three questions to ask when evaluating a systematic trading system.
7. In a market trending upward, explain how the value of a simple moving average compares to the value of an exponential moving average.
8. Does whipsawing tend to occur in a trending market or a sideways market?
9. What is a breakout strategy?
10. List the six major potential risks of managed futures funds.

NOTES

1. William Fung and David Hsieh, "Empirical Characteristics of Dynamic Trading Strategies: The Case of Hedge Funds," *Review of Financial Studies* 10, no. 2 (April 1997): 275–302.

2. François-Serge Lhabitant, *Hedge Funds: Origine, Strategies, Performance* (Paris: Dunod, 2008).
3. Marc H. Malek and Sergei Dobrovolsky, "Volatility Exposure of CTA Programs and Other Hedge Fund Strategies," *Journal of Alternative Investments* 11, no. 4 (2009): 68–89.
4. Peter Park, Oguz Tanrikulu, and Guodong Wang, "Systematic Global Macro: Performance, Risk and Correlation Characteristics" (January 2009). Working paper. Available at https://www.researchgate.net/profile/Oguz_Tanrikulu2/publications.
5. Hossein Kazemi and Ying Li, "Market Timing of CTAs: An Examination of Systematic CTAs vs. Discretionary CTAs," *Journal of Futures Markets* 29, no. 11 (2009): 1067–99.
6. Joelle Miffre and Georgios Rallis, "Momentum Strategies in Commodity Futures Markets," *Journal of Banking and Finance* 31, no. 6 (2007): 1863–86.
7. Lintner, J. 1996. "The Potential Role of Managed Commodity-Financial Futures Accounts (and/or Funds) in Portfolios of Stocks and Bonds." In *The Handbook of Managed Futures: Performance, Evaluation and Analysis*, edited by Carl Peters and Ben Warwick, 99–137. New York: McGraw-Hill Professional. Originally presented to the Analysts Federation in 1983.
8. Edwin J. Elton, Martin J. Gruber, and Joel C. Rentzler, "Professionally Managed, Publicly Traded Commodity Funds," *Journal of Business* 60, no. 2 (1987): 175–99; "New Public Offerings, Information, and Investor Rationality: The Case of Publicly Offered Commodity Funds," *Journal of Business* 62 (1989): 1–15; "The Performance of Publicly Offered Commodity Funds," *Financial Analysts Journal* 46 (1987): 23–30.
9. Harry M. Kat, "Managed Futures and Hedge Funds: A Match Made in Heaven" (November 1, 2002). Research paper, Cass Business School, London.
10. Irene Aldridge, "Systematic Funds Outperform Discretionary Funds" (December 2, 2009). Working paper, BigDataFinance.org.
11. Kazemi, Li, "Market Timing of CTAs."

CHAPTER 16

Event-Driven Hedge Funds

The **event-driven** category of hedge funds includes activist hedge funds, merger arbitrage funds, and distressed securities funds, as well as special situation funds and multistrategy funds that combine a variety of event-driven strategies. Event-driven hedge funds search for mispriced securities during both the anticipation of and the realization of events. Events include mergers and acquisitions, spinoffs, tracking stocks, accounting write-offs, reorganizations, bankruptcies, share buybacks and secondary offerings, special dividends, and any other corporate events that are generally associated with substantial market price reactions in the securities related to the transactions.

The most common transaction for an event-driven strategy fund is to enter positions in one or more corporate securities during a period of event risk. For example, an event-driven strategy fund may purchase the equity of a target firm and short sell the equity in the acquiring firm in a proposed merger and hold those positions until the merger is completed or the deal falls through. Event-driven funds profit when events unfold as predicted and suffer losses when events unfold with the opposite consequences. In the case of a traditional merger arbitrage transaction, the fund benefits if the specified event (such as a merger) takes place and suffers a loss if the event fails.

Within the event-driven class of hedge funds, four styles will be discussed: activist funds, merger arbitrage funds, distressed securities funds, and multistrategy event-driven funds. Hedge Fund Research (HFR) estimates that event-driven hedge funds totaled nearly $820 billion at the end of 2018. This includes nearly $120 billion in activist funds, $24 billion in merger arbitrage funds, and over $200 billion in distressed securities funds. Multistrategy and special situation funds add another $460 billion in assets under management.

16.1 THE SOURCES OF MOST EVENT STRATEGY RETURNS

By their very nature, special events are nonrecurring and usually contain unique or unusual circumstances. Therefore, market prices may not fully adjust to the information associated with these transactions in a timely manner. This provides an opportunity for event-driven managers to act quickly and capture a return premium—perhaps a risk premium—associated with these transactions. Event-driven hedge funds are generally exposed to substantial event risk. **Corporate event risk** is dispersion in economic outcomes due to uncertainty regarding corporate events. A central issue in the analysis of event-driven strategies is the extent, if any, to which returns are driven by beta (systematic risks) or alpha (superior risk-adjusted returns).

16.1.1 Insurance-Selling View of Event Strategy Returns

Consider the case of a proposed merger that, if completed, will result in a $100 per share payment to the shareholders of the target firm in exchange for their shares. In this scenario, the shares of the target firm jumped from $70 per share to $90 per share when the proposed merger was announced. Although the news of the proposed merger is public knowledge, it will be several months before it will be known whether the necessary approvals can be obtained. Thus, there is a period of event risk during which share prices will be expected to react to news on whether the proposed merger will be consummated. It is common for existing shareholders of a target firm to sell shares soon after the share prices jump as a result of the proposed merger announcement. It is also common for event-driven hedge funds to purchase shares during the period between the proposed merger announcement and the resolution of uncertainty regarding the event.

After the merger announcement, existing shareholders of the target firm need to decide whether to continue to hold their shares, in hopes that the merger will be approved and share prices will rise from $90 to $100 per share, or to sell their shares at $90, avoiding the risk that the merger will fail and that the share price will fall back to $70 or perhaps lower. Some shareholders wish to avoid the event risk and choose to sell their shares to hedge funds at a discount to this $100 offer, such as the $90 price described in the example. Presumably, they reinvest their sales proceeds in firms that are not subject to substantial event risk and, in so doing, reduce the total event risk of their portfolio. These shareholders are often viewed as having purchased insurance against the failure of the firms to complete the anticipated merger.

Event-driven hedge funds may be viewed as seeking to earn risk premiums for selling insurance against failed deals. **Selling insurance** in this context refers to the economic process of earning relatively small returns for providing protection against risks, not the literal process of offering traditional insurance policies. Further, a merger arbitrage hedge fund's portfolio typically consists of several potential mergers, and therefore its exposure to each deal might be relatively small, similar to an insurance company with relatively small exposure to each contract or set of contracts. Finally, a merger arbitrage manager is typically able to use derivative securities to manage its exposure to large deals, a relatively complicated alternative that other investors may not be able to employ because of legal restrictions on the use of derivative securities.

Other types of event-driven funds may have other return drivers. Distressed funds might earn returns for providing liquidity, purchasing securities from investors who need to sell when there are few bidders. Activist fund managers benefit from event risk, often in the case when the actions of the activist help to make that event possible.

16.1.2 Binary Option View of Event Strategy Returns

Continuing with this example, the hedge fund purchases the shares at $90 and holds the shares until either the merger succeeds, in which case the fund receives $100 per share, or the merger fails, in which case the fund receives perhaps $70 per share. In this simplistic example, a long position in the merger target may be viewed as a long position in a riskless bond with a $70 face value and a long position in a binary call option that pays $30 if the deal is consummated and $0 if the deal fails. A **long binary call option** makes one payout when the referenced price exceeds the strike price at expiration and a lower payout or no payout in all other cases. A long binary call option would be priced at $20 in this example if it were assumed for simplicity that riskless interest rates were 0%. A **long binary put option** makes one payout when the referenced price is lower than the strike price at expiration and a lower payout or no payout in all other cases. A long binary put option pays higher cash when the referenced price falls and would be priced at $10 in this example, assuming a 0% riskless rate. Thus, using put options rather than call options, the hedge fund's long position in the merger target may be viewed as a long position in a riskless bond with a $100 face value and a short position in a binary put option that pays $30 if the deal fails. Note that whether the fund's position is described with long calls or short puts, the initial cost of $90 and the final payout of either $100 or $70 are the same.

☞ APPLICATION 16.1.2A

ABC Corp. has offered to purchase DEF Corp. for $25 per share. Immediately before the merger proposal announcement, DEF was trading at $18 per share. Immediately after the announcement, DEF is trading at $23 per share. Assuming that the share price of DEF would fall to $16 if the deal fails and that the riskless interest rate is 0%, describe a long position in DEF taken by an event-driven hedge fund both as a combination of positions in a risk-free bond and a binary call option and as a combination of positions including a binary put option.

The hedge fund's position may be viewed as a long position in a riskless bond with a face value of $16 and a long position in a binary call option with a potential payout of $9 in case the merger is successful and shares of DEF rise to $25 per share. The hedge fund may also be viewed as a long position in a riskless bond with a face value of $25 and a short position in a binary put option with a potential payout of $9 in case the merger is not successful and shares of DEF decline to $16 per share.

The binary put option view of the hedge fund's position illustrates that the hedge fund has, among other things, written a put option on the event such that the hedge fund will bear a loss if the merger does not occur. In this view, event-driven hedge funds are writing put options and will tend to have payouts consistent with writing out-of-the-money options, meaning modest upside potential with large downside potential. In many cases, this asymmetric payout is an accurate description of the event risks that a hedge fund takes. It should be noted that in the previous merger examples, the downside risk of owning the target firm's stock was that the target firm's stock price could fall to a prespecified price. However, in practice, the downside risk could be substantial, and a long position in the target firm's stock could include losses due to a general market decline in addition to a failed deal.

16.1.3 Binary Call Option View of Events

Not all positions of hedge funds in event-driven strategies offer the potential for large losses and small profits. Thus, not all positions can be well approximated as being short an out-of-the-money put option. For example, event-driven hedge funds may play either side of an event such as a merger: the side that benefits if the event is consummated or the side that loses. The fund tries to use superior information or analysis to ascertain whether market prices overestimate, underestimate, or properly reflect the outcomes of various events. This may be possible because these are unique and rare events, and long-only investors may not typically have the skills and the data to make accurate predictions about the eventual outcome. The hedge fund seeks to earn higher returns from formulating better predictions of the event outcomes than are reflected in market prices.

The binary call option view of the hedge fund's position illustrates that the hedge fund has, among other things, purchased a call option on the event such that the hedge fund will gain if the merger is consummated and lose if the event deal does not occur. This view of the transaction as a long position in a call option illustrates the expected risk premium that the hedge fund's position should earn. A long position in a call option on equity is a very bullish bet. In competitive markets, long positions in equities tend to have positive beta risk and should generally earn expected risk premiums. Long positions in call options in equities tend to have higher betas than their underlying stocks and in theory should offer even higher expected risk premiums. Thus, using this long binary call option view, it may be argued that typical event-driven strategies contain substantial systematic risk and that higher returns for this strategy may reflect bearing systematic risk, or beta, rather than alpha.

By their nature, events are primarily firm specific and cause idiosyncratic risks. However, some events, such as mergers, have probabilities of consummation that are positively correlated with the performance of the overall market. In bull markets and good economic times, mergers and other deals are more likely to be proposed and consummated. Thus, some of the event risk may be systematic. Event-driven fund managers may take both long and short positions in equity or debt securities. However, they will find it difficult to fully hedge against both the event risk and the overall movement in the market and thus achieve complete market neutrality. The result is a tendency to bear systematic risks in addition to the obvious idiosyncratic risks of the events. Therefore, event-driven funds typically profit during normal and healthy market conditions, when deals are consummated on a timely basis. However, substantial losses can result during times of market crisis and failed deals, when market participants back away from deals and, typically, sell off securities that exhibit illiquidity and high risk.

This call option binary view of event-driven investing is most applicable to events with binary outcomes, such as mergers and spin-offs. Distressed investing and activist investing are complex areas of investments which may have longer investment time horizons and different paths of potential outcomes.

The following sections examine each of the major subcategories of the event strategy more closely, starting with activist investing.

16.2 ACTIVIST INVESTING

Corporate governance describes the processes and people that control the decisions of a corporation. Activist investing is involvement in corporate governance as an alpha-driven investment strategy. The **activist investment strategy** involves efforts by shareholders to use their rights, such as voting power or the threat of such power, to influence corporate governance to their financial benefit as shareholders. An activist investment strategy often involves (1) identification of corporations whose management is not maximizing shareholder wealth; (2) establishment of investment positions that can benefit from particular changes in corporate governance, such as replacement of existing management; and (3) execution of the corporate governance changes that are perceived to benefit the investment positions that have been established.

16.2.1 Background on Corporate Governance

The equity investors in a firm literally establish the corporation and legally own the corporation. But in major corporations, it is impractical for several thousand or million individual shareholders to manage the company on a day-to-day basis. Corporations are therefore set up with a corporate governance process, wherein shareholders elect a board of directors. The board of directors selects and contracts with the executive management team and delegates the management of the company to the executive managers, who are compensated for running the day-to-day business. The top executive managers usually serve as directors of the corporation but with insufficient seats to form a majority.

The firm's executive management team typically provides information to the board regarding the firm's operations and initiates proposals. Although the procedures and levels of consensus vary widely, it is common for the board's decisions to be agreeable with the management team. In other words, the management team and the board of directors tend to work cooperatively. To the extent that the management team is in substantial and irresolvable conflict with the majority of the directors, the management team will be replaced.

The board periodically conducts voting by shareholders for election of new board members and with regard to major proposals. Typically, proposals clearly identify those actions recommended by the board of directors. Shareholders approve the vast majority of board recommendations.

Although shareholders vote for the board of directors and the board selects managers charged with serving the interests of the shareholders, there are typically substantial conflicts between the interests of shareholders and managers. The divergence between the preferences of shareholders and managers is the foundation for most shareholder activism. **Shareholder activism** refers to efforts by one or more shareholders to influence the decisions of a firm in a direction contrary to the initial recommendations of the firm's senior management. These efforts can include casting votes, introducing shareholder resolutions, and taking legal action. The divergence between the preferences of shareholders and those of managers is a critical issue in understanding shareholder activism and is discussed in detail in a subsequent section.

The terms used to discuss activist investing overlap with terminology used elsewhere in investments and are not used entirely uniformly in discussing shareholder activism. This book defines an activist investment strategy as any investment strategy with the objective of generating superior rates of return through shareholder activism.

One of the most important events of shareholder activism is a shareholder vote. Shareholder votes occur at regular annual meetings and at special shareholder meetings. Shareholders attend meetings to cast their votes, cast direct votes prior to meetings using ballots provided to them by the firm, or complete proxies that allow others to vote on their behalf—either with regard to a specific issue or in general. The outcome of these votes typically depends on the results of a proxy battle. A **proxy battle** is a fight between the firm's current management and one or more shareholder activists to obtain proxies (i.e., favorable votes) from shareholders. These proxies permit them to vote the shares of the other shareholders in support of their activism. The board of directors can also solicit proxies from shareholders for their support. The proxies help determine the winner of the shareholder vote.

Shareholders can be inundated with multiple copies of the proxy from each side, since each shareholder's ultimate vote is governed by the latest dated or most recently submitted proxy, if any, that the shareholder completed. Proxy battles can be very expensive. Shareholder activists pay for their direct costs of these proxy battles in the hope of financial gains from success. The firm's current board of directors generally uses the corporation's financial resources to wage the battle, which, of course, ultimately belong to the shareholders. Thus, shareholder activists not only pay for their side of the battle but also pay their pro rata share of the other side.

16.2.2 Five Dimensions of Shareholder Activists

The players in the arena of shareholder activism differ on several dimensions:

1. FINANCIAL VERSUS SOCIAL ACTIVISTS: Efforts by shareholder activists can have social objectives or financial objectives. Social objectives include attempts to steer a firm toward behavior deemed by some as more beneficial to society as a whole, such as reduced pollution, better treatment of employees, better treatment of animals, or refusal to manufacture goods such as weapons, alcohol, and tobacco. Financial objectives may vary in some regards, but the underlying motivation is increased shareholder wealth through increased share prices. For the purposes of this chapter, shareholder activist investment strategies refer entirely to shareholder activism driven by financial objectives.

2. ACTIVISTS VERSUS PACIFISTS: Activists oppose current management and seek major changes in a firm's leadership or decision-making. Pacifists oppose the proposed activism. Instead, pacifists support current management, the status quo, and any proposed changes outlined by the current management. Activists attempt to intervene in the corporate governance process, whereas pacifists oppose making any changes. Pacifists, however, are not necessarily dormant; they may be aggressive in their opposition to the activists.

3. INITIATORS VERSUS FOLLOWERS: Some shareholders initiate activism, whereas others actively follow the activists. Activists can be followed through stories in the media or through required regulatory filings, such as 13D forms. Initiators of activism search for suitable targets, develop activist plans, establish positions, and implement the plans. Importantly, initiators pay for the direct expenses of activism. Active followers support the plans of the initiators and establish positions in the firms being targeted by activists.

4. FRIENDLY VERSUS HOSTILE ACTIVISTS: Activism is executed with different degrees of confrontation with management. Hostile activists tend to threaten managers with adverse consequences, whereas friendly activists tend to work with managers to develop mutually beneficial outcomes. Whereas some activists prefer to engage corporate management behind closed doors, others conduct very public campaigns, with their demands distributed through the media. When conversations are public, other large shareholders—both hedge funds and pension funds—may get involved in the conversation or voting process.

5. ACTIVE ACTIVISTS VERSUS PASSIVE ACTIVISTS: This dimension refers to the motive for investing. Active activists establish positions for the purpose of activism. Passive activists participate in activism when they happen to hold positions in firms that become targets of activism. It is also possible but less likely for passive activists to be initiators rather than followers. A passive activist can be an initiator by first establishing a position for purposes other than activism but then deciding to initiate activism, perhaps due to frustration with current management.

16.2.3 Shareholder Activists' Strategies

The key players in successful financial activism are active initiators, active followers, and passive followers. The role of active initiators is obvious, since they serve as the catalysts for the actions and typically bear the potentially large direct costs involved. But active initiators rarely have sufficient voting power to implement change unless others join in. Activists need to be careful about hunting in packs, as securities laws may be violated if activists work together without the proper regulatory disclosures. In order to avoid the appearance of working in groups, Orol encourages activists to choose separate law firms and to avoid emailing one another.[1]

Passive activists, those who have positions in firms where an activist is leading the efforts, may be viewed as free riders. A **free rider** is a person or entity that allows others to pay initial costs and then benefits from those expenditures. An example of a free rider is a citizen who stands by while a subgroup pays for an improvement, such as the beautification of a park, and then enjoys the enhancement. Shareholder activism can have large direct costs, including legal costs and the costs of proxy contests. Active followers search public records and other sources of information to identify firms that are most likely to be profitable targets of shareholder activism. For example, active followers can directly or indirectly learn of potential activism targets from observing that known shareholder activists are acquiring positions in particular firms. Regulators often require information on large holdings by market participants. Active followers have a symbiotic relationship with active initiators. Although they act as free riders to the active initiators who pay the direct costs of activism, active followers typically help the initiators by voting in support of the activism, which serves to increase the influence of the initiators without their having a larger investment in the target firm.

Most investors are passive in the context of this analysis; that is, these investors, like those in mutual funds, established positions in the equity of public companies for reasons other than anticipation of activism. Passive followers, or the lack thereof, often make or break shareholder activism. Passive followers are a subgroup of the passive investors who happen to be holding stock in a firm that becomes the target of activist initiators. These existing shareholders who retain their shares must ultimately decide whether they will support the activist proposals as passive followers or vote against the proposals as pacifists. They can become the object of intense battles between activist initiators and agents of the firm's management, receiving mailings, overnight correspondence, phone calls, and even personal contacts from both sides soliciting their support.

The key players in unsuccessful financial activism are pacifists. These shareholders do not establish equity positions in the target firm for the purposes of supporting or opposing activism. They are brought into the fray from holding previously established positions in firms that became the targets of activism. They opt to support current management due to confidence in the management or a belief that the activists would be harmful. In addition, some shareholder pacifism results from concerns that support for the activists might damage their business relationships with current management and other entities that oppose the activism. Shareholder votes are not secret ballots; thus, corporate management generally has direct knowledge of which shareholders vote to support their position and which shareholders oppose them.

16.2.4 Why Managers Are Not Viewed as Maximizing Shareholder Wealth

As their name implies, activist investors believe that value can be unlocked within a public company through active engagement with the executive management of the corporation or its board of directors. A common question is why the executive management of the company does not undertake the necessary changes to unlock the intrinsic value of the company without pressure from activists. The fundamental reason is the existence of conflicts of interest between managers and shareholders. Simply put, managerial goals can differ from shareholder goals.

Agency theory studies the relationship between principals and agents. A **principal-agent relationship** is any relationship in which one person or group, the principal(s), hires another person or group, the agent(s), to perform decision-making tasks. The principals enter this relationship with the objective of having their utility maximized, while the agents seek to maximize their own utility. Preferences and goals generally differ among all people and all groups of people. Therefore, conflicts of interest typically exist within all organizations and among all groups within those organizations.

Shareholders are the principals and the executive management team members are their agents. It is generally reasonable to assume that as principals, the shareholders wish to have the managers pursue shareholder wealth maximization (share price plus dividends), whereas the managers wish to pursue their goals, including salary maximization, bonus maximization, prestige, career opportunities, job security, job satisfaction, and perhaps improved leisure time and other aspects of their lives. To the extent that shareholder wealth maximization is inconsistent with the goals and preferences of managers, there will be conflicts of interest.

Agency theory focuses on optimal contracting in the presence of conflicts of interest—specifically on the process of designing managerial compensation schemes that maximize shareholder wealth. An **agent compensation scheme** is all agreements and procedures specifying payments to an agent for services, or any other treatment of an agent with regard to employment. A perfect compensation scheme would be costless to implement and would maximize shareholder wealth by resolving all conflicts of interest between shareholders and managers at minimal cost.

In practice, however, perfect compensation schemes do not exist, resulting in agency costs. In a nutshell, **agency costs** are any costs, explicit (e.g., monitoring and auditing costs) or implicit (e.g., excessive corporate perks), resulting from inherent conflicts of interest between shareholders as principals and managers as agents. These agency costs have two sources: (1) the costs of aligning the interests of shareholders and managers when those interests can be cost-effectively aligned, and (2) the costs to the shareholders of unresolved conflicts of interest between shareholders and managers. Regarding the latter source, not all conflicts of interest can be cost-effectively resolved; therefore, in an optimal compensation scheme, agents will generally not always act in the best interests of the principals. Simply put, in some cases, it is cheaper for shareholders to accept managerial actions that conflict with their best interests than to try to bring managers' interests into perfect alignment with their own interests.

16.2.5 Consequences of Shareholder and Manager Misalignment

The misalignment between shareholders' and managers' interests stemming from unresolved conflicts of interest often results in potentially major and inefficient consequences, including the following:

- Managers receiving excessive compensation from running the corporation for their own personal entitlement at disproportionately large costs to shareholders
- Managers being overly risk averse in their decision-making for fear of being associated with large failures and possibly losing job security
- Managers making decisions (with disproportionately large costs to shareholders) based on the comfort they obtain from protecting their jobs and existing pay packages
- Managers imposing risk preferences in corporate decision-making based on their disproportionate participation in the upside of the company's fortunes and their limited downside exposure
- Managerial preferences to avoid hard work or reject optimal change, such as updating the business plan or model of the company, which disproportionately harm shareholder wealth
- Managerial preferences to avoid sharp conflicts, such as challenging unions, demoting employees, firing employees, or closing divisions

In each case, there is nothing suboptimal about a manager receiving generous compensation or avoiding a personally undesirable outcome as long as there is not a net unnecessary cost to shareholders. To illustrate, it may be economically efficient for a firm to offer free parking to a manager in exchange for reduced taxable salary if there is a net benefit to that combination that increases shareholder wealth. Further, it may serve the best interests of shareholders to offer first-class airfare, or even corporate jet travel, to managers if such actions ultimately create value and a net benefit to shareholders, perhaps through employee satisfaction and resulting improved performance. The examples were designed to emphasize conflicts of interest that tend to be inefficient when managers receive benefits or engage in behavior that has high costs without offsetting benefits to shareholders. Shareholders are not averse to paying generous financial and other benefits to managers who are thereby incentivized to offer services that provide net benefits to shareholders. Rather, shareholders are concerned with compensation to managers or behavior by managers with costs deemed excessive or disproportionate relative to the benefits these managers generate.

In large public corporations, the practical ability of shareholders to understand, monitor, and correct conflicts of interest with managers may be very limited. As a result, conflicts of interest may emerge and grow that are inefficient and, in aggregate, may become highly costly to shareholders. As a result of these conflicts based on managerial preferences dominating shareholder interests, a public company's stock price may trade substantially below its intrinsic value. Therein lies the source of untapped value that shareholder activist strategies pursue.

16.2.6 Corporate Governance Battles

Rather than waiting for untapped value, or alpha, to be exploited through external events, activists attempt to accelerate the realization of the alpha by seeking to expedite change to the operations of a corporation. The intense engagement required to be an active initiator means that activists must typically hold very concentrated portfolios of 5 to 15 equity positions in publicly traded corporations. These positions are long, are large, and usually represent 1% to 10% of the outstanding stock of the company. There is a considerable amount of systematic and idiosyncratic risk embedded in the resulting portfolios. Although the fee structures and liquidity risks clearly categorize activist fund managers as hedge fund managers, some investors may view investments in activist funds to be sufficiently similar to traditional long-only equity investments that they include the activist fund holdings in the computation of their allocation to equity.

Activist hedge fund positions in target firms can be kept secret as long as the activist owns less than 5% of the target firm. In the United States, **Form 13D** is required to be filed with the Securities and Exchange Commission (SEC) within 10 days, publicizing an activist's stake in a firm once the activist owns more than 5% of the firm and has a strategic plan for the firm. Many activists will acquire a 4.9% stake in the firm, just below the threshold for filing a Form 13D, to keep their holdings secret and to allow time for conversations with the firm to progress. A **toehold** is a stake in a potential merger target that is accumulated by a potential acquirer prior to the news of the merger attempt becoming widely known.

In addition to Form 13D, several other forms may be required to provide investors with additional information regarding potential mergers. In the United

States, **Form 13 G** is required of passive shareholders who buy a 5% stake in a firm, but this filing may be delayed until 45 days after year-end. **Form 13F** is a required quarterly filing of all long positions by all U.S. asset managers with over $100 million in assets under management, including hedge funds and mutual funds, among other investors. These forms must list all long positions; however, disclosure of short positions is not required.

Many investors regularly track these filings, some taking positions in the holdings of famous or profitable activists and other hedge fund managers. Brav, Jiang, Partnoy, and Thomas show that companies listed as holdings of activists on Form 13D have a one-month excess return of 7% during the month of the 13D disclosure while earning returns similar to the market in the following year.[2] This return is not consistent across activist objectives, as activist goals of mergers earn 10% returns and exploring strategic alternatives earns 5.9% returns, whereas corporate governance issues have no statistically significant excess returns.

Well-respected activists may have a strong following or wolf pack of other hedge funds (active followers). A **wolf pack** is a group of investors who may take similar positions to benefit from an activists' engagement with corporate management. This wolf pack investment team can magnify the activists' influence, as the combined positions of similarly minded investors serve to make the target firm's management more responsive to the activists' agenda.

Activists typically publicize a single issue that is believed to add substantial value to the shares of the target firm. Activist agendas have targeted a wide variety of corporate governance issues, including executive compensation, composition of the board of directors, potential mergers or divestitures, and capital structure issues such as cash positions that are too large and debt loads or dividends that are too low.

Activist investors usually demand a meeting with the target company's board of directors or senior management to discuss and publicize the desired change in corporate governance. In addition, activist investors may attempt to work with management to implement their preferred business plan. This manner of investing is friendly and is also called corporate engagement, as activist investors pursue a direct dialogue with management and the board of directors. Alternatively, or subsequently, activist investors may resort to hostile actions, such as attempts to remove senior management who are perceived as unresponsive or ineffective.

Although activists have been accused of thinking only about short-term stock price movements, the management of the target firm may be more inclined to agree to the activists' agenda when it is perceived to be likely to lead to longer-term creation of value for the corporation. Activists can have quite lengthy holding periods, frequently owning a stock for one to three years before the value has been unlocked.

The success of investors such as CalPERS and Hermes has encouraged other investors to engage corporation management to reap the rewards of better corporate governance. Using a large hand-collected data set from 2001 to 2006, Brav, Jiang, Partnoy, and Thomas find that hedge fund activists succeed in at least part of their agenda at two-thirds of the target firms.[3] Target firms in the United States experience increases in operating performance, payout, and CEO turnover after activism from hedge funds.

It can be more difficult for activist investors to earn a large number of board seats when the terms of the board members are staggered. **Staggered board seats** exist when instead of having all members of a board elected at a single point in time, portions of the board are elected at regular intervals. For example, if one-third of the board seats are elected each year, it would take at least two years to elect a majority of the board. Corporations are more vulnerable when the entire board is up for election in a single year, as activists can more quickly take control of the board.

16.2.7 Activist Agenda 1: CEOs, Compensation, and Boards of Directors

Good corporate governance efficiently resolves those conflicts of interest that are worth resolving. **Interlocking boards** occur when board members from multiple firms—especially managers—simultaneously serve on each other's boards and may lead to a reduced responsiveness to the interests of shareholders. Interlocking boards and exorbitant CEO compensation are typical conflicts of interest that merit resolution and are near the top of the activist agenda. Conflicts of interest and resulting agency costs can become particularly inefficient when a CEO effectively controls the board of directors in one of two forms. First, the CEO might also be the chairman of the board of directors. In such a position, the CEO-chairman controls both the company's operations and the board of directors, with limited checks and balances. Second, the board of directors can become too comfortable or friendly with the CEO. This can lead to excessive pay packages for the CEO.

An unfortunate example of the latter situation is UnitedHealth Group of Minnesota. For years, UnitedHealth Group's board of directors lavished compensation on William McGuire, the company's CEO and founder. However, more egregiously, the board granted McGuire stock options that were backdated to a point in time when the stock price of the company was lower. The result was that McGuire received a stock option payout in 2006 of $1.6 billion, the largest payout for a U.S. corporate CEO at that time. Outrage by activist investors led to a class action lawsuit filed by CalPERS in 2006, which was joined by several other state pension funds. The class action lawsuit was filed against UnitedHealth, 20 executives, and the board of directors, and was quickly followed by an SEC enforcement against McGuire. The result was a settlement reached by the company to return to share owners approximately $900 million from backdated stock option grants. Of this amount, $300 million came from current executives of UnitedHealth, who agreed to forfeit amounts previously paid. McGuire personally agreed to return more than $600 million of his backdated stock option gains. In addition, the SEC fined McGuire $7 million and barred him from being a director of a public company for 10 years. McGuire also lost his job at UnitedHealth.

Although it can be appropriate for CEOs to earn large salaries and bonuses, activists believe that total compensation should be incentive based and appropriate relative to the value generated by the management team. For very large corporations, the direct cost of generous compensation schemes is often minor when viewed as a percentage of the firm's equity or income. The concerns with high compensation in very large firms are often more a matter of other issues and can include information signaling and agency costs. Information signaling is the intentional or unintentional conveying of information through actions.

What sort of information signals can large compensation packages to top managers send to the firm's other employees, lenders, and customers? Does a huge managerial compensation package encourage the firm's stakeholders to negotiate more aggressively with the firm or to be less cooperative?

Large non-incentive-based compensation schemes can exacerbate agency conflicts and costs. Managers who are generously paid without serving shareholder interests may focus their energies on serving the stakeholders and the corporate cultures that sustain their pay. The costs to shareholders of ineffective management, from their perspective, may greatly exceed the direct costs of compensation.

16.2.8 Activist Agenda 2: Capital Structure and Dividend Policy Issues

Another popular agenda among activists is to request a change in the capital structure or dividend policy of the firm. As a profitable firm accumulates cash, managers have an incentive to reinvest the cash inside the firm so that the firm grows in size and profitability, and presumably the compensation and prestige of the manager will similarly grow. Investors want the firm to exploit those opportunities for which the firm has a comparative advantage through managerial expertise or other capabilities. However, due to unresolved conflicts of interest, managers may have an incentive to invest in opportunities even if they do not exploit the firm's advantages and do not maximize shareholder wealth. Perhaps some investments diversify the firm's assets and thereby provide job security. Improperly incentivized managers may intentionally or inadvertently advocate reinvestment of earnings into projects that are not in the best interests of the shareholders.

Shareholders may believe that it is better to use the cash to pay dividends or execute stock buybacks or share repurchases rather than to reinvest the cash in new businesses through retained earnings. Both dividends and stock buybacks return cash to shareholders. In theory, both can generate equivalent outcomes, since they both reduce the firm's cash and the total market value of the firm's equity. In practice, tax laws often favor share repurchases because personal income taxes on capital gains are usually lower than taxes on dividends. Activists frequently call for increases in dividends or stock buybacks, believing that the cash can be better deployed in the hands of the shareholders. There is an additional benefit of share buybacks in that earnings growth can accelerate. Given that Earnings per Share = Net Income/Shares Outstanding, a decrease in shares outstanding increases earnings per share even when net income is unchanged.

Consider the case of Microsoft, which came under attack after amassing cash of more than $56 billion while not paying shareholder dividends. Shareholders were benefiting from the software business, a business that is extremely profitable but usually not capital intensive. Shareholders feared that Microsoft's management would use the cash to expand into unrelated capital-intensive businesses, such as video game consoles and cable television boxes. Microsoft initiated its dividend in 2003, shortly after U.S. tax laws changed to reduce the tax on dividend income. In 2005, Microsoft paid a one-time dividend of $32 billion, announced a stock buyback of $30 billion, and doubled the amount of the quarterly dividend. Would retention of the cash have allowed Microsoft to exploit valuable new opportunities, or did the distribution of the cash allow shareholders to deploy the capital more effectively? To the extent that large unresolved conflicts of interest and resulting agency costs exist between shareholders and managers, shareholders have an incentive to serve as activists and intervene to assure the efficient deployment of excess cash.

Activists may also criticize firms for not having enough debt on the balance sheet. In some cases, it is argued that the after-tax cost of debt capital can be below that of the risk-adjusted cost of equity capital, due, for instance, to the tax deductibility of interest expense from corporate taxable income. However, higher leverage increases the risk of the firm's equity and generally increases the probability of the firm experiencing financial distress or bankruptcy. The reason is that, unlike equity financing, debt financing obligates the firm to make mandatory principal and interest payments, which may push the firm into bankruptcy.

Interestingly, once debt has been issued, a firm that is struggling may find that risk taking that causes higher probabilities of financial distress can increase shareholder wealth. Equity in a corporation can behave like a call option on the firm's assets. Option theory demonstrates that increased volatility in an option's underlying assets increases the value of a call option. Therefore, shareholders may benefit from high levels of risk taking. Simply put, shareholders can receive full upside benefits from gains while enjoying limited downside exposure to losses because of their ability to declare bankruptcy and leave further losses to be borne by debt holders. Of course, this risk taking can be limited by other constraints, since a firm with increasing levels of distress may find it difficult to continue attracting the efforts and resources of employees and suppliers.

Managers are very likely to have different preferences than shareholders with regard to risk taking, meaning there is a conflict of interest. Managers would typically be expected to prefer lower probabilities of corporate financial distress so that their compensation packages and careers are protected. The result can be that managers underutilize debt, leaving wealth-increasing opportunities unexploited. Corporate leverage can also provide benefits to shareholders by disciplining a firm's management to deploy the capital wisely and oversee the firm more closely. The managers of a highly leveraged firm may become more disciplined in their investments and other decisions in order to protect their salaries and careers, since they are aware of the need to meet required debt payments. Conversely, managers of firms with limited leverage and with excess cash obtained through retained earnings may be less disciplined, may have greater conflicts of interest with shareholders, and may subject the firm to greater losses due to agency costs. Accordingly, companies that are underleveraged can be targets of shareholder activism or targets for acquisition as the market attempts to correct the inefficiency.

16.2.9 Activist Agenda 3: Mergers or Divestitures

Some mergers and related corporate activity are not driven by shareholder activism but are often related to asset-driven motivations, such as operational efficiencies, conglomeration, integration, and reduction in competition. Merger activity driven by shareholder activism is better understood through viewing such corporate reorganizations as battles for control of assets and analyzing those battles with respect to the interests of managers and shareholders.

Activists are constantly searching to understand business models and the valuations of corporations and their subsidiaries. When an activist finds a portion of a large corporation that is not maximizing shareholder wealth, the activist encourages the corporation to sell or spin off the shares of the business. This situation is especially likely in a conglomerate, in which one firm manages a wide variety of businesses, or in a large firm that has faster-growing, smaller divisions.

A **spin-off** occurs when a publicly traded firm splits into two publicly traded firms, with shareholders in the original firm becoming shareholders in both firms. For example, a shareholder who owns 300 shares of Company A before a spin-off may own 300 shares of Company A and 100 shares of Company B after the spin-off if each three shares of Company A spun out one share of Company B. A **split-off** occurs when investors have a choice to own Company A or B, as they are required to exchange their shares in the parent firm if they would like to own shares in the newly created firm.

Consider the case of McDonald's (MCD), which owned a fast-growing business named Chipotle Mexican Grill. McDonald's was encouraged by activists to split the two firms in the belief that the value of the two businesses as independent firms would be higher than the value of the two combined. McDonald's split off Chipotle Mexican Grill (eventually trading as CMG) by performing an initial public offering (IPO) of a small portion of CMG shares and distributing the remaining shares to those MCD shareholders who chose to exchange their shares. The split-off appeared highly successful for investors in both firms, as MCD shares doubled and CMG shares increased by more than 300% in the first five years after the split-off, while the U.S. stock market was relatively unchanged.

The Chipotle investment was profitable for McDonald's, which purchased 90% of the young burrito chain for $360 million in a series of transactions beginning in 1998. In 2006, the IPO and split-off of CMG earned McDonald's $1.5 billion in proceeds. By 2014, it was clear why the split-off occurred, as McDonald's is a large, slow-growing firm with a market capitalization of $92.5 billion and a forward price-to-earnings ratio of 17. Chipotle had grown quickly to a market capitalization of $21 billion and a forward price-to-earnings ratio of 50. While the share price of McDonald's increased by 300% from 2006 to 2014, Chipotle dramatically outperformed by increasing by 1,200% over the same period. It is not clear if the value of the CMG business would have increased at such a high rate if it had continued to be housed within the larger MCD holding company.

Another popular activist agenda is to separate hard assets from intellectual property. One example is the trend to separate retail firms from their real estate holdings. In the United States, Pershing Square proposed to separate Target Stores into two companies, one to hold the retail operations and another to restructure the real estate holdings into a REIT (real estate investment trust).

Several explanations can be set forth as to why such corporate reorganizations could increase shareholder wealth. For example, an agency theory–based explanation would be that agency costs are reduced. In both cases, by separating the assets, each resulting management team could manage with better focus. Other explanations are based on capital market inefficiencies or imperfections. For example, some may argue that separation of the ownership of the two units allows different clienteles of shareholders to invest in the business they prefer rather than being allowed to invest only in the combined businesses. Similarly, some may argue that earnings are priced inefficiently in financial markets, such that higher price-to-earnings ratios are applied to the separated earnings streams than to the combined earnings stream.

Index (Jan. 2005–Dec. 2018)	HFRX Event-Driven: Activist	MSCI World Equity
Annualized Arithmetic Mean	6.7%	6.6%
Annualized Standard Deviation	12.9%	14.7%
Annualized Semivolatility	10.2%	12.1%
Annualized Median	9.0%	11.6%
Skewness	−0.8	−0.9
Excess Kurtosis	2.8	2.7
Sharpe Ratio	1.0	0.3
Sortino Ratio	1.3	0.3
Annualized Geometric Mean	5.9%	5.5%
First-Order Autocorrelation	0.43	0.15
Annualized Standard Deviation (Adjusted for Autocorrelation)	9.5%	17.2%
Maximum	9.7%	11.2%
Minimum	−16.3%	−19.0%
Max Drawdown	−37.4%	−54.0%

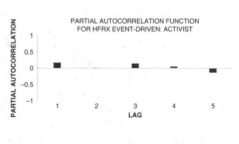

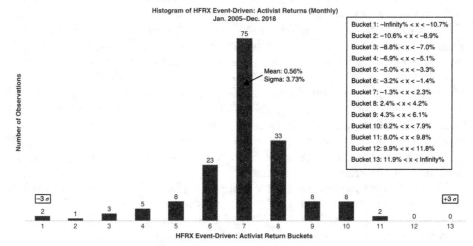

EXHIBIT 16.1 Statistical Summary of Returns

16.2.10 Key Observations Regarding Historical Returns of Activist Funds

Monthly returns to activist funds are observed from January of 2000 to December of 2018 for a total of 228 observations. Exhibit 16.1 provides univariate return statistics in the top panel, partial autocorrelations of returns in the middle panel, and a histogram of returns in the bottom panel.

Key observations on the returns to activist funds that are consistent with economic reasoning are an essential component of knowledge and include the following:

1. The volatility, skew, maximum drawdown, and Sharpe ratio are comparable to world equity indices.
2. Activist returns exhibited a markedly high level of excess kurtosis.
3. Activist returns exhibited substantial positive first- and third-order autocorrelation.

16.3 MERGER ARBITRAGE

Merger arbitrage attempts to benefit from merger activity with minimal risk and is perhaps the best-known event-driven strategy. The acquiring firm in a merger purchases shares in the target firm through cash; through exchange of shares; or through a combination of cash, equity shares, and other securities.

Cash-for-stock mergers occur wherein the acquirer pays cash for the shares of the firm being acquired. In a cash offer, speculators often focus solely on the shares of the target firm and the relationship between the target share price and the bid price.

Stock-for-stock mergers acquire stock in the target firm using the stock of the acquirer and typically generate large initial increases in the share price of the target firm. For example, a firm may offer to issue 2.5 shares of its common equity in exchange for each existing share in the target firm. Speculators in stock-for-stock mergers typically take offsetting hedged positions in the shares of the two firms based on the ratio of shares in the merger offer. Between the time of the merger announcement and its ultimate resolution, long positions in the equity of the target firm are generally exposed to relatively modest increases if a merger is completed and larger decreases if no merger occurs. Thus, long positions in the target firm are substantially exposed to event risk over this period, and price relationships between the firms' share prices should be based on a combination of the return demanded in the market to bear the event risk and the perceived probabilities of various merger outcomes.

Traditional merger arbitrage generally uses leverage to buy the stock of the firm that is to be acquired and to sell short the stock of the firm that is the acquirer. Thus, the traditional strategy cannot be used for small firms or other firms for which there is insufficient liquidity to take short positions. The simultaneous long and short positions provide a hedge, with the numbers of shares on each side driven by the ratio of shares in the exchange offer. This traditional merger arbitrage strategy seeks to capture the price spread between the ratio-adjusted spreads of the current market prices of the merger partners and the spreads upon the successful completion of the merger.

Being long the target and short the bidder exposes the arbitrageur to risk that the merger will fail. Therefore, the arbitrageur should expect to receive a premium for bearing the risk. Superior returns, beyond premiums for bearing risk, can be earned when arbitrageurs identify those mergers in which the share price of the target firm does not reflect the probability that the merger will fail. In the traditional strategy of undervalued target firms, profit opportunities may be driven by the strong desire of the target firm's shareholders to sell their shares to harvest profits and avoid event risk. Arbitrageurs step in to provide liquidity, possibly requiring high expected returns, which exiting shareholders may be willing to sacrifice. If arbitrageurs believe that the target firm is overvalued relative to the probability that the merger will succeed, the arbitrageur can short the target and buy the acquirer.

16.3.1 Stock-for-Stock Merger Arbitrage

The simplest form of merger arbitrage is a stock swap deal. Consider an acquiring firm that offers two shares of its stock, currently trading at $10, for each share of the target firm. The target firm's shares rise from $14 to $18 after the deal is announced. The traditional arbitrage for this deal would be to buy one share of the target firm for $18 and sell short two shares of the acquiring firm for proceeds of $20. The hedge ratio is determined by the merger offer. Note that if the merger is consummated, shares of the target held long can be exchanged for the exact number of shares necessary to cover the short position.

The fund receives $2 in net proceeds from the hedge and hopes to earn this $2 as a profit when the merger deal closes. Note that as long as the merger is consummated as proposed, the arbitrageur's final profit is completely protected from fluctuations in either of the share prices. Regardless of share prices, as long as the merger occurs as proposed, the arbitrageur can deliver each share in the target in exchange for two shares in the acquirer and deliver those two shares in satisfaction of the short position. Note that for simplicity, this example ignores the fact that the arbitrageur's ultimate profit or loss also depends on transaction costs, any intervening dividends, and financing proceeds or costs related to the positions. However, if the merger fails, the target share price would probably fall. The arbitrageur would lose $4 per share on the long position in the target if the target shares fell back to their previous value of $14 and would also be subject to changes in the value of the acquiring firm.

☞ **APPLICATION 16.3.1A**

Prior to a merger announcement, MegaStock, trading at $102, plans to offer one share of MegaStock for 3.5 shares of MiniStock, trading at $20. After the announcement, MegaStock trades at $100, MiniStock jumps to $25, and an arbitrageur takes a traditional and hedged merger arbitrage position. Ignoring transaction costs, interest, and dividends, how much money would the arbitrageur earn per share of MegaStock if the merger consummates, and how much money would be lost if the deal fails and the prices revert to their preannouncement levels?

The short position in one share of MegaStock generates proceeds of $100. Buying 3.5 shares of MiniStock costs $87.50. If the deal goes through, the arbitrageur pockets the $12.50 net proceeds as profit and delivers the exchanged

> shares to cover the short. If the deal fails, the arbitrageur sells the 3.5 shares at $20 for $70 in proceeds, buys back MegaStock at $102, and expends $32, which is a $19.50 loss after netting the proceeds of $12.50.

If the arbitrageur believes that current market prices imply that a merger consummation is unlikely, the arbitrageur may take the opposite position by purchasing the acquirer and shorting the target. In this side of the transaction, the arbitrageur would be negatively subjected to event risk and would not expect to earn any return as a premium for bearing event risk. Rather, the arbitrageur would be purely speculating on her ability to predict the probabilities of the outcomes of the event better than is reflected in the relative market prices. Other deal types are hedged differently. As illustrated near the start of this chapter, to participate in an all-cash deal, typically the arbitrageur simply buys the target stock. If the acquirer offers cash and stock for the target firm, the arbitrageur may hedge only the part of the deal consideration that is offered in stock.

Traditional merger arbitrage is a form of insurance underwriting. In the case of a stock-for-stock deal, if the merger goes through, the merger arbitrage hedge fund manager collects an insurance premium equal to the initial stock price spread between the target and the acquirer. If the merger fails, the merger arbitrage hedge fund manager has to pay out on the insurance policy and loses money on the failed merger.

Merger arbitrage is more deal driven than market driven. Merger arbitrage derives its return from the number of deals and the values and relative values of the companies involved in the events. Consequently, merger arbitrage returns should be driven more by the economics of the individual deals than by the levels of the general stock market. However, during periods of market downturns, merger activity dries up, and many announced mergers fall through. As a result, the merger arbitrage strategy shows some correlation with the overall stock market and tends to perform poorly during market declines.

16.3.2 Third-Party Bidders and Bidding Wars

There is also a possibility that another company will enter into a bidding contest. A **bidding contest** or bidding war is when two or more firms compete to acquire the same target. A bidding contest dramatically changes the initial dynamics of the arbitrage. A traditional merger arbitrage position typically benefits from the onset of a bidding war due to its long position in the target and short position in the original bidder. The onset of a bidding war can create lucrative returns to traditional merger arbitrage transactions, but these deals can be among the riskiest situations.

Consider the bidding war that started in 2010 for control of the Dollar Thrifty Automotive Group (DTG). The market for rental cars at U.S. airports was concentrated, and whichever firm was able to control the target, DTG, would become the leader in the U.S. rental car market. In April 2010, Hertz (HTZ) made a $1.2 billion bid ($41-per-share bid in cash and stock) for the shares of DTG. DTG shares had traded below $1 in 2009 and had still traded below $25 in February 2010, but they had rallied to over $38 at the time of the bid. After shares of HTZ rallied on the day of the announcement, the combined value of the stock and cash offered in the deal rose to $42.15 per share. Yet the price of DTG shares closed at $43.07, a premium of 2.2% to the value of HTZ's bid. Apparently, the market had been anticipating that the first offer from Hertz would not be high enough to win the approval of DTG shareholders and some higher offer might be made.

At this point, arbitrageurs with traditional positions had a difficult choice, as they would lose money going forward on their long positions in DTG if the deal closed at the stated terms and existing prices. Although some of the arbitrageurs passed this deal by, others continued to hold their traditional positions in expectation of a sweetened bid at a later date. These arbitrageurs were richly rewarded in the coming months, as the anticipated bidding war materialized. The bids kept rising after Budget entered the fray with a $46.50 cash and stock deal announced at the end of July. Hertz raised its bid to $50 in September, and then Avis went to $53 per share just 10 days after the final Hertz bid. After several rounds of bidding, and even an abandonment of its bid for some period of time, Hertz completed the deal for $87.50 per share in cash in December 2012.

Because the U.S. rental car market is highly concentrated, the Federal Trade Commission performed an antitrust review designed to limit the decline in competition that can result from mergers and acquisitions. An **antitrust review** is a government analysis of whether a corporate merger or some other action is in violation of regulations through its potential to reduce competition. In order to complete the acquisition, Hertz was required to divest a portion of the business, selling Advantage Rent A Car and 26 locations of Dollar or Thrifty. These locations were specifically selected to limit the market share of Hertz, Thrifty, and Dollar locations at specific U.S. airports. Post-merger, the U.S. car rental business was highly concentrated, with the top three firms—Hertz/Dollar/Thrifty, Enterprise, and Avis/Budget—having an 82% market share. In some cases, antitrust authorities may deny some merger proposals if they find that market concentration is too great to have a competitive market, even after some divestitures.

Not all bidding contests turn out this well for arbitrageurs. Some deals with multiple bidders are never completed with any suitor, leaving the target stock to continue life as a stand-alone firm, often returning to the pre-deal price. Usually when merger arbitrage funds make money, they do so slowly, as the price of the target moves ever closer to that of the deal price over the 6- to 18-month life of the deal. Conversely, when a deal falls apart, the price of the target moves rapidly to lower prices, often losing as much as 30% in one day. Therefore, merger arbitrage funds tend to make money slowly and lose money quickly. This positive exposure to event risk can be seen in the negative skewness and excess kurtosis of the returns to merger arbitrage funds. The returns of these funds can be generated by risk premiums for bearing event risk or by superior returns from identifying mispriced stocks.

16.3.3 Overview of Risks of Merger Arbitrage

Merger arbitrage is subject to several sources of event risk. The primary risks affecting whether a deal will fail are regulatory risk and financing risk, which are detailed in the next two sections. There are also risks from defensive actions taken by the management of the target company, bidding war risks, and the simple risk that one or both companies will simply walk away from the deal. Merger arbitrageurs specialize in assessing these risks and maintaining a diversified portfolio across several industries to spread out the risks.

Merger arbitrageurs conduct substantial research on the companies involved in the merger. They review current and prior financial statements, SEC EDGAR filings, proxy statements, management structures, cost savings from redundant operations, strategic reasons for the merger, regulatory issues, press releases, and the competitive position of the combined company within the industry in which it competes. Merger arbitrageurs calculate the rate of return that is implicit in the current spread and compare it to the event risk associated with the deal. If the spread is sufficient to compensate for the expected event risk, they execute the traditional arbitrage. Less often, they may speculate that the deal will fail. Some merger arbitrage managers invest only in announced deals. However, other hedge fund managers will put on positions, especially in possible target firms, on the basis of rumor or speculation.

16.3.4 Regulatory Risk

Regulatory risk is the economic dispersion caused by uncertain outcomes of decisions made by regulators. Various U.S. and foreign regulatory agencies may not allow a proposed merger to take place for a variety of reasons, primarily that it could substantially reduce competition in the given market. There are three possible outcomes to an antitrust ruling: yes, no, and conditional. Governing bodies typically allow most proposed mergers, especially in fragmented industries in which market share is so widely spread that antitrust issues are not a concern. Conditional approval of mergers may require divestiture of some assets before the merger is completed, bringing more balance to the market share across firms. A key skill of merger arbitrage managers is the ability to determine the likely outcome of antitrust concerns before the governing bodies rule. In deals for which antitrust issues are a concern, the spread between the price of the target and the price of the acquiring firm may start out wide and then narrow substantially when and if the deal is cleared by regulators, as moving beyond this potential roadblock makes the deal more likely to close and the timing of such a deal more certain.

Regulators can also disallow deals for nationalistic or tax-related reasons. Cross-border mergers of commodity-producing firms or national-defense-related firms tend to be especially politically sensitive. In 2005, the China National Offshore Oil Corporation withdrew its bid for the U.S.-based oil company Unocal after the U.S. House of Representatives criticized the $18.5 billion merger on concerns of national security. The U.S. firm Chevron later acquired Unocal. In August 2010, the Australian firm BHP Billiton made a $130-per-share bid for the Canadian firm Potash Corporation of Saskatchewan. BHP Billiton, the world's largest mining firm, sought control of Potash, which controls between 25% and 50% of the world's potash supplies, a key ingredient in fertilizer. On the day of the bid, the stock price of Potash rose from $112 to over $143, showing the market's clear expectation that BHP would need to offer more than $130 per share to complete the merger. But in November 2010, the Canadian national government, at the urging of the Saskatchewan provincial government, rejected the proposed merger deal. Canadian law requires that foreign takeovers of Canadian firms offer continued benefits to the nation, a promise that BHP was either unable or unwilling to make.

16.3.5 Financing Risk

Financing risk is the economic dispersion caused by failure or potential failure of an entity, such as an acquiring firm, to secure the funding necessary to consummate a plan. Whenever a merger is announced, arbitrageurs need to analyze the probability that a deal will be completed on the proposed terms. For stock swap deals, investors focus on the regulatory issues and the fit between the two firms. Whenever there is a cash component to the merger offer, there also needs to be an evaluation of the financing risk, which is the ability of the acquiring firm to acquire the cash necessary to fund the purchase of the target firm. Financing risk should be seen as minimal when a large firm with a strong balance sheet acquires a smaller firm. But a firm with $4 billion in market capitalization and $1 billion in cash may find it challenging to fund a $3 billion cash merger if its balance sheet already shows $3 billion in debt. In this case, the arbitrage spread may be wide, showing that the market is not confident in the ability of the acquiring firm to fund the purchase of the target firm. The merger spread is likely to tighten substantially when the financing is arranged, perhaps through a bank loan, a bond issue, or asset sales.

A commonly cited example of financing risk is the proposed 1989 management and employee buyout of United Airlines. After the potential acquirers failed to secure financing for the $6.7 billion transaction, the deal collapsed and the U.S. stock market declined nearly 7% in one day on fears that the time of easily financing mergers through the issuance of junk bonds was coming to an end. On that day, merger arbitrage managers experienced both deal risk and systematic risk, as the falling market and the difficulty of financing future deals simultaneously hit returns.

More recently, John Paulson of Paulson & Co. invested in a number of merger arbitrage transactions in his event-driven fund. Leveraged buyouts are particularly sensitive to financing risk and were a key source of merger activity between 2005 and 2007. Near the start of the 2008 financial crisis, Paulson correctly predicted that difficulties in obtaining financing for leveraged buyouts would be a driver of failed deals. Paulson sought to hedge this financing risk. He concluded that the subprime mortgage market was particularly vulnerable to financing risk and selected that market to hedge the financial risk of the fund's merger arbitrage activity. Paulson bought credit default swap (CDS) protection (credit default swaps are discussed in Part 5). His conviction of the financing risk in the subprime mortgage market also led him to start two credit funds that generated legendary levels of profitability (300% and nearly 600%, respectively). Although questions were raised as to the conformity of the fund's strategy to its original goals, the hedging strategy illustrates financing risk as extending beyond being merely a deal-by-deal phenomenon.

A final risk to the merger arbitrage strategy is that deals need to be approved by the shareholders of each publicly traded company involved in a transaction. After shareholders of both the acquiring firm and the target firm have approved the deal, the spread between the deal price and the price of the target firm tends to decline, reflecting another risk that has been overcome and, potentially, moving the date at which the merger will close forward.

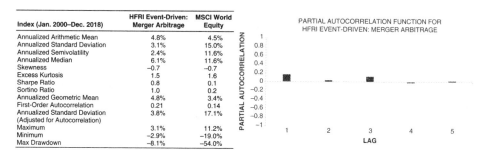

Index (Jan. 2000–Dec. 2018)	HFRI Event-Driven: Merger Arbitrage	MSCI World Equity
Annualized Arithmetic Mean	4.8%	4.5%
Annualized Standard Deviation	3.1%	15.0%
Annualized Semivolatility	2.4%	11.6%
Annualized Median	6.1%	11.6%
Skewness	−0.7	−0.7
Excess Kurtosis	1.5	1.6
Sharpe Ratio	0.8	0.1
Sortino Ratio	1.0	0.2
Annualized Geometric Mean	4.8%	3.4%
First-Order Autocorrelation	0.21	0.14
Annualized Standard Deviation (Adjusted for Autocorrelation)	3.8%	17.1%
Maximum	3.1%	11.2%
Minimum	−2.9%	−19.0%
Max Drawdown	−8.1%	−54.0%

PARTIAL AUTOCORRELATION FUNCTION FOR
HFRI EVENT-DRIVEN: MERGER ARBITRAGE

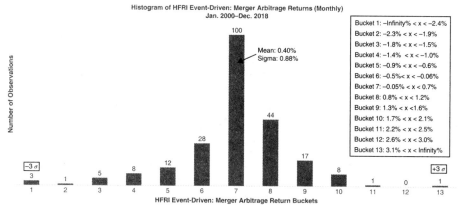

Histogram of HFRI Event-Driven: Merger Arbitrage Returns (Monthly)
Jan. 2000–Dec. 2018

Mean: 0.40%
Sigma: 0.88%

Bucket 1: −Infinity% < x < −2.4%
Bucket 2: −2.3% < x < −1.9%
Bucket 3: −1.8% < x < −1.5%
Bucket 4: −1.4% < x < −1.0%
Bucket 5: −0.9% < x < −0.6%
Bucket 6: −0.5% < x < −0.06%
Bucket 7: −0.05% < x < 0.7%
Bucket 8: 0.8% < x < 1.2%
Bucket 9: 1.3% < x <1.6%
Bucket 10: 1.7% < x < 2.1%
Bucket 11: 2.2% < x < 2.5%
Bucket 12: 2.6% < x < 3.0%
Bucket 13: 3.1% < x < Infinity%

HFRI Event-Driven: Merger Arbitrage Return Buckets

EXHIBIT 16.2 Statistical Summary of Returns

16.3.6 Key Observations Regarding Historical Returns of Merger Arbitrage Funds

Monthly returns to activist funds are observed from January of 2000 to December of 2018 for a total of 228 observations. Exhibit 16.2 provides univariate return statistics in the top panel, partial autocorrelations of returns in the middle panel, and a histogram of returns in the bottom panel.

Key observations on the returns to merger arbitrage funds that are consistent with economic reasoning are an essential component of knowledge and include the following:

1. Merger arbitrage returns exhibited much lower volatility than world equities.
2. Merger arbitrage returns exhibited similar skew and kurtosis to world equities.
3. Merger arbitrage returns had a very favorable maximum drawdown.
4. Merger arbitrage returns exhibited moderate positive autocorrelation.

16.4 DISTRESSED SECURITIES FUNDS

Distressed debt hedge funds invest in the securities of a corporation that is in bankruptcy or is likely to fall into bankruptcy. Companies can become distressed for any number of reasons, such as too much leverage on their balance sheet, poor operating performance, accounting irregularities, or even competitive pressure. Some of these strategies can overlap with private equity strategies. Distressed debt is discussed in detail in Chapter 22, since distressed debt is an important area of investment within private equity. The key difference is that private equity investors take a long-term view on the value and reorganization potential of the corporation, whereas hedge funds typically take a shorter-term trading view on distressed investments.

When evaluating investments across multiple layers of the capital structure, investors need to estimate the long-term value of each layer of the capital structure, which can be highly influenced by the priority of claims in a bankruptcy proceeding. The bankruptcy process is more fully covered in Chapter 22 on private equity; however, the following section covers material on the bankruptcy process that is essential to understanding distressed hedge fund strategies.

16.4.1 The Bankruptcy Process

When the face value of the liabilities of a firm exceeds the market value of its assets, the bankruptcy process allocates the assets across various security holders and stakeholders of the firm. The **bankruptcy process** is the series of actions taken from the filing for bankruptcy through its resolution. Those who are paid after the most senior claims such as wages are paid are the holders of senior, secured, and collateralized debt. Once these senior claims have been satisfied, junior, subordinated, and convertible bondholders are next in line. In many cases, these junior debt holders do not receive a full recovery during the bankruptcy proceedings but may receive equity in the firm if it is reorganized. Last in line come preferred stock and equity holders in the firm, who often receive little or no value during the bankruptcy reorganization process.

In the United States, firms declaring bankruptcy may either liquidate or reorganize operations, but European firms typically face liquidation when they are deemed unable to meet their debt obligations. In a **liquidation process** (chapter 7 in U.S. bankruptcy laws), all of the assets of the firm are sold and the cash proceeds are distributed to creditors. A firm is liquidated when it is viewed as not viable as an ongoing entity. Firms with liquidity problems but with reasonable chances of being viable are reorganized. In a **reorganization process** (chapter 11 in U.S. bankruptcy laws), the firm's activities are preserved. The goal of a reorganization process is to stabilize the operations and finances of the company in a way that allows the firm to continue operations after the bankruptcy process has been completed. To strengthen the firm, contracts such as labor union contracts, pension programs, and real estate leases can be substantially revised during the process. Debt holders may agree to lengthen maturities, reduce coupon rates, or accept equity in the reorganized firm as a way of reducing the emerging company's cash outflows and debt burdens. During the reorganization process, the equity in the pre-bankrupt firm is typically canceled and becomes worthless as shares in the newly reorganized firm are either offered to subordinated debt holders or sold to new investors.

Distressed securities investments can be inefficiently priced and require active management. Positions in investment-grade equities require almost no ongoing involvement other than periodic voting. However, management of positions in distressed securities may require frequent participation in the bankruptcy process to negotiate and litigate better outcomes. Most distressed securities investments are one-off transactions. A **one-off transaction** has one or more unique characteristics that cause the transaction to require specialized skill, knowledge, or effort. Investors in traditional equity positions may rely to some extent on the availability of public information and the high level of competition in financial markets to drive market prices toward reflecting available information, meaning that the prices are informationally efficient. As securities involving unique situations, rapidly changing situations, information asymmetries, and limited numbers of institutional owners, distressed securities are less likely to trade at informationally efficient prices. Information asymmetries occur when individual economic actors possess different knowledge.

Thus, investing in distressed securities requires specialized, skillful, and ongoing analysis and involvement. Therein lies the potential of the strategy both to generate alpha and to contribute risk to the investor. However, seeking alpha through distressed investing does not necessarily mean involvement in an asset type that is a zero-sum game, wherein each investor with a positive alpha must be balanced by an investor with a negative alpha. Most institutions either do not want to directly invest in distressed securities or are unable to invest in distressed securities. Many institutions, such as insurance companies and pension funds, are prevented through regulation from purchasing or even holding substantial quantities of non-investment-grade securities. Other institutions may divest speculative holdings prior to bankruptcy for the following reasons: (1) to avoid the increased monitoring needs; (2) to avoid ending up with inappropriate securities (e.g., bond funds that might receive equity in the reorganization process); or (3) to avoid revelation of embarrassing investment holdings in future portfolio disclosures, meaning to window-dress the public view of the portfolio. It is argued that the dumping of securities by institutions as they spiral downward in quality causes low price levels that permit generous alphas to those providing liquidity to the market by purchasing the unwanted securities. Overall positive average alphas to distressed securities investing may therefore be generated by institutional factors and offered to distressed investors as a reward for the provision of liquidity.

16.4.2 Short Sales of Equity as Writing Naked Call Options

There are many variations on how a hedge fund plays a distressed situation. The declaration of bankruptcy by a firm can vary from being made by viable firms seeking temporary protection from cash flow problems to highly distressed firms with virtually no chance of survival. When a firm known to be in financial trouble seeks bankruptcy protection and reorganization (chapter 11 in the United States), the stock price often rises in recognition of the firm's decision to use the technique to solve its financial problems. However, surprise bankruptcy filings and chapter 7 (liquidation) bankruptcy filings usually cause share price declines. Most of the following discussion focuses on firms for which bankruptcy is perceived to be likely to end in liquidation.

Prior to a bankruptcy, if an analyst views a situation as likely to deteriorate financially, the simplest trade is to sell short the stock of the distressed firm. This requires the hedge fund manager to borrow stock from its prime broker and sell the stock with the expectation that it will be able to purchase the stock back at a lower price in the future after the fundamentals of the firm have deteriorated. This is an unhedged speculation and nothing more than an attempt to sell high and buy low.

Short selling of a distressed company exposes the hedge fund manager to substantial risk if the company's fortunes suddenly improve. Perhaps the riskiest trade in the equity market is to be short the stock of a firm that is rumored to be descending into bankruptcy but recovers vigorously. Consider the stock of American Airlines, which traded below $2 in March 2003, shortly after both United Airlines and US Airways declared bankruptcy. Similarly, shares of Ford traded below $2 in November 2008 as General Motors approached bankruptcy. Unfortunately for short sellers, the shares of each firm traded above $11 one year later, when it became clear that neither American Airlines nor Ford would declare bankruptcy anytime soon.

As is detailed in Part 5 on structured products, shares in highly leveraged firms resemble call options. Short selling distressed equities is therefore analogous to writing naked call options on the firm's assets and generates a negatively skewed return distribution. An investor has a naked option position when the investor is short an option position for which the investor does not also have a hedged position, such as owning the underlying asset when short a call and being short the underlying asset when short a put. The negative skew is seen in the previous examples in the potential gain of $2 and potential loss of $9 or more in the shares of American Airlines and Ford. Conversely, an analyst who views share prices as reflecting overestimated probabilities of further deterioration in the firm's financial condition may establish long positions in the firm's equity and typically receive a positively skewed return distribution.

After most bankruptcy filings, the stocks are delisted. In some cases, there is almost no probability that the firm will distribute any cash to equity holders, and therefore the stocks are virtually worthless. Nevertheless, it is sometimes the case that the shares trade at values that reflect unrealistic probabilities of survival. Some investors are comfortable selling short shares in companies after bankruptcy is declared, even at prices of $0.50 per share or less. However, a caveat must be provided regarding the potential danger. Shares of USG Corporation (USG) and General Growth Properties (GGP) rallied sharply while in bankruptcy. USG shares, which traded below $3 in 2002, rallied to over $110 per share early in 2006 before exiting bankruptcy. Similarly, GGP shares, which traded below $0.20 in late 2008, increased in value to over $15 by the end of 2010, as it became clear that the value of the firm's real estate holdings exceeded the outstanding value of the debt.

16.4.3 Searching for Distressed Undervalued Securities and Estimating Recovery Value

The prices of debt in distressed firms can trade substantially below face value before and during the bankruptcy process. Senior debt typically has higher prices than subordinated debt of the same firm due to the higher priority of claims on the assets of the firm. At the time of the bankruptcy filing, many debt holders sell their bonds due to restrictions on the credit quality of holdings that may be imposed by insurance or pension plan regulators or simply because of investors' unwillingness to stomach the risk or tolerate the time-intensive nature of holding and evaluating distressed securities. In cases of poor market liquidity, debt securities of these firms may be undervalued and therefore offer return from alpha in addition to a systematic risk premium for their market risks.

The job of a distressed investor sounds simple: Estimate the recovery value. The **recovery value** of the firm and its securities is the value of each security in the firm and is based on the time it will take the firm to emerge from the bankruptcy process and the condition in which it will emerge. Unfortunately, analyzing probabilities and outcomes and making both of these estimations can be difficult and firm-specific processes. The estimated liquidation or reorganized value of assets is analyzed with the priority of claims to arrive at the estimated recovery rates for each bond issue. The recovery rate of a bond is the portion of face value that is ultimately received by an investor in a bond issue at the end of the bankruptcy proceedings. Securities with higher seniority in bankruptcy generally experience higher recovery rates and are therefore worth more than junior securities. Thus, a firm may have senior debt issues trading at 60% of par value and subordinated debt issues trading at 30% of par value, even though they share the same underlying assets.

The recovery value of distressed securities at liquidation can be especially sensitive to market conditions in the industry. Consider the bankruptcy of an electric utility such as Enron. When the firm is liquidated, hard assets, such as power plants, need to be sold in a relatively short time frame. When the entire industry is in distress and overleveraged, it may be necessary to sell these assets at depressed prices. Some distressed investors—especially when the firm will need to sell substantial industry-specific assets—hedge the recovery rate risk by selling short shares in firms that have similar assets.

The time that firms spend in bankruptcy can vary widely, even when the firms are of relatively similar size and from the same industry. For example, US Airways spent just seven months in bankruptcy court, from August 2002 to March 2003, but United Airlines spent over three years, from December 2002 to February 2006, finally reemerging as a reorganized firm.

16.4.4 Estimating Returns from Undervalued Securities

The annualized returns of deals involving distressed investing are highly influenced by the time the company spends under the supervision of the bankruptcy court. For example, consider an investor who buys a senior debt issue at 60% of face value and a subordinated debt issue at 30% of face value that yield eventual recovery values of 80% and 50%, respectively. These recovery values would generate non-annualized returns of 33.3% on the senior debt and 66.7% on the subordinated debt, assuming no coupon income. These returns are computed as the difference in the percentage of face value invested relative to the percentage of face value recovered, expressed as a percentage of the invested quantity. In the example of a six-month bankruptcy process, these returns represent annualized returns of 67% ($33.33\% \times 2$) on the senior debt and 133% ($66.7\% \times 2$) on the subordinated debt, ignoring compounding. But for a deal that takes 3.33 years to work out, the same deal generates annualized returns of 10% on the senior debt and 20% on the subordinated debt, ignoring compounding.

☞ APPLICATION 16.4.4A

A bond is purchased at 40% of face value. After bankruptcy, 30% of the bond's face value is ultimately recovered. Express the rate of return as a non-annualized rate, as an annualized rate based on a four-month holding period, and as an annualized rate based on a four-year holding period, ignoring compounding and assuming no coupon income. The non-annualized rate is –25%, found as a 10% loss on a 40% investment. The annualized rate based on a four-month holding period is –75%, found as –25% × (12 months/4 months); and an annualized rate based on a four-year holding period is –6.25%, found as –25%/4.

Investors may also profit from determining if and when the company will declare bankruptcy. An understanding of the financial condition of the firm based on financial statements and other information is key, as the investor needs to estimate how cash flows, including interest expense and debt maturities, can affect the timing of the bankruptcy. An investor who predicts that a bankruptcy filing will not occur for two years, perhaps a longer view than the market's, can profit if correct by buying debt issues with less than two years until maturity while selling short debt issues with more than two years until maturity. If the first debt issue is repaid at its full face value before the company files for bankruptcy and before the maturity of the later debt issue, the distressed investor has probably earned alpha.

16.4.5 Distressed Activists

Many distressed investors do not take an activist approach; rather, they simply buy distressed securities and wait for the events related to reorganization to unfold. Activist investors in distressed securities seek to influence both the recovery value and the timing of the exit from the bankruptcy process. The activist approach is an intense process that requires a substantial amount of legal work as the manager negotiates with the court and other investors.

The activist investor may simply choose to expedite the bankruptcy process by cooperating with other parties, which may lower ultimate recovery rates but increase annualized returns. Alternatively, the activist may attempt to improve its position relative to other parties in the priority of claims with a less cooperative approach that may generate higher recovery values as well as delays in distributions.

16.4.6 Capital Structure Arbitrage

Unhedged positions in distressed firms, such as simple long positions or short positions in equity or other securities, involve relatively high risk. Unhedged positions in distressed securities are plays on absolute value and are subject to substantial idiosyncratic and systematic risks. Most hedge fund managers typically use a hedging strategy known as capital structure arbitrage. **Capital structure arbitrage** involves offsetting positions within a company's capital structure with the goal of being long relatively underpriced securities, being short overpriced securities, and being hedged against risk. These hedged positions have reduced exposure to the general risks of the economy or the firm and are plays on relative values within the firm's capital structure.

For a traditional capital structure arbitrage trade, investors typically buy the more senior claim and sell short the more junior claim. Consider a company that has four levels of outstanding capital: senior secured debt, junior subordinated debt, preferred stock, and common stock. Two standard distressed security investment strategies are (1) to buy the senior secured debt and short the junior subordinated debt, or (2) to buy the preferred stock and short the common stock.

In a bankruptcy, the senior secured debt stands in line in front of the junior subordinated debt for any bankruptcy-determined payouts. The same is true for the preferred stock compared to the common stock. In both of the common capital structure arbitrage strategies just detailed, there is a long position in the more senior security and a short position in the more junior security for each pair. Therefore, in both cases, the strategy is long the security with the higher standing in the bankruptcy process.

Consider the case of buying the senior secured debt and shorting the junior subordinated debt. Assume that equal dollar positions of $10,000 (of opposite sign) are established in both bonds at discounts to face value, with the senior debt trading at a smaller discount than the junior debt. The gains and losses on this hedged position depend on the relative movements of the constituent positions. There are four cases that provide insight into the risks of this traditional hedge:

1. At the bearish extreme for the firm's assets, no recovery is ever received on either bond, and the hedge breaks even by gaining $10,000 on the short position and losing $10,000 on the long position.
2. On the bullish extreme for the underlying assets, full recovery is made on both bonds, and the loss on the short exceeds the gain on the long, causing the hedge to lose money.
3. If the senior debt is fully recovered and the junior debt has no recovery, the hedged position gains on both legs of the trade and generates a large profit.
4. If recovery rates of the bonds are equal, the junior bond gains more and the hedge generates a net loss.

Thus, capital structure arbitrage is not a simple bullish or bearish bet on the eventual value of the firm's assets that can be distributed to security holders. The key to traditional capital structure arbitrage profitability is when the more senior security improves more, or deteriorates less, than the junior security. Note that the analysis assumed equal sizes for the long and short positions. Other hedge ratios are common, and they can generate substantially different profits and losses for various outcomes.

Senior claims in distressed debt securities tend to offer higher loss potential and lower profit potential than do junior claims. For example, the equity can resemble a call option or a lottery ticket, with a small investment required and a small chance of a large payout. If less sophisticated investors prefer the return distributions of the junior claims, it is possible that more sophisticated investors can consistently profit from the traditional capital structure arbitrage strategies to the extent that the market overprices the more junior claims and underprices the more senior claims.

Derivative securities can expand the opportunities available for capital structure arbitrage and make strategies more versatile and riskier. In some cases, especially pre-bankruptcy, it is argued that financial market segmentation occurs such that the stock market and the bond market may be valuing securities based on very different appraisals of the firm's prospects. **Financial market segmentation** occurs when two or more markets use different valuations for similar assets due to the lack of participants who trade in both markets or who perform arbitrage between the markets. The idea is that each market attracts its own clientele, and the different clienteles generate different values.

For example, the bonds of General Motors (GM) were rated as CCC at a time when GM stock was trading at over $20 per share. Assuming that these observations indicated sharply divergent valuation standards in the debt and equity markets, investors could have chosen to perform capital structure arbitrage with the legs of the trade in different markets. A hedge fund manager could have bought put options on GM stock to hedge a long position in GM bonds. Derivatives expand the set of markets pricing a deal by adding derivative markets. Thus, a capital structure arbitrage opportunity may be designed to exploit perceived mispricing due to financial market segmentation. The CDS market is also a key component of capital structure arbitrage strategies, providing cost-effective vehicles for hedging credit risk in long or short positions in corporate debt. CDS protection is bought and sold in the over-the-counter market, further increasing opportunities to exploit financial market segmentation.

16.4.7 Buying the Firm Using Distressed Securities

A distressed securities hedge fund can become involved in the bankruptcy process as a strategy for establishing a controlling position in firms that the fund perceives as substantially undervalued. This is where an overlap with the strategies of private equity firms can occur. To the extent that a distressed securities hedge fund is willing to learn the arcane workings of the bankruptcy process and participate in its steps, including sitting on creditor committees, substantial value can be realized if the distressed company can be successfully restructured and is able to regain its profitability. This strategy, with its intention of gaining a controlling interest, differs from that of hedge fund managers who purchase the securities of a distressed company shortly before it announces its reorganization plan to the bankruptcy court. The latter case is based on the expectation of a positive resolution with the company's creditors, whereas the former case includes a desire to obtain control.

Index (Jan. 2000–Dec. 2018)	HFRI Event-Driven: Distressed / Restructuring Index	MSCI World Equity
Annualized Arithmetic Mean	6.9%	4.5%
Annualized Standard Deviation	6.0%	15.0%
Annualized Semivolatility	5.0%	11.6%
Annualized Median	9.5%	11.6%
Skewness	−1.0	−0.7
Excess Kurtosis	3.2	1.6
Sharpe Ratio	0.7	0.1
Sortino Ratio	0.9	0.2
Annualized Geometric Mean	6.8%	3.4%
First-Order Autocorrelation	0.53	0.14
Annualized Standard Deviation (Adjusted for Autocorrelation)	10.8%	17.1%
Maximum	5.5%	11.2%
Minimum	−7.9%	−19.0%
Max Drawdown	−27.4%	−54.0%

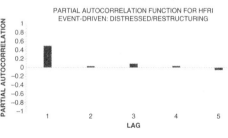

PARTIAL AUTOCORRELATION FUNCTION FOR HFRI EVENT-DRIVEN: DISTRESSED/RESTRUCTURING

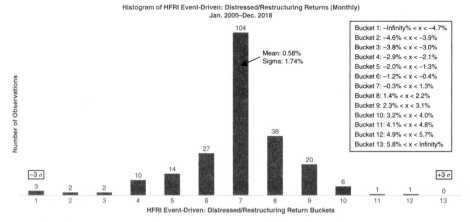

Histogram of HFRI Event-Driven: Distressed/Restructuring Returns (Monthly)
Jan. 2000–Dec. 2018

Mean: 0.58%
Sigma: 1.74%

Bucket 1: −Infinity% < x < −4.7%
Bucket 2: −4.6% < x < −3.9%
Bucket 3: −3.8% < x < −3.0%
Bucket 4: −2.9% < x < −2.1%
Bucket 5: −2.0% < x < −1.3%
Bucket 6: −1.2% < x < −0.4%
Bucket 7: −0.3% < x < 1.3%
Bucket 8: 1.4% < x < 2.2%
Bucket 9: 2.3% < x < 3.1%
Bucket 10: 3.2% < x < 4.0%
Bucket 11: 4.1% < x < 4.8%
Bucket 12: 4.9% < x < 5.7%
Bucket 13: 5.8% < x < Infinity%

EXHIBIT 16.3 Statistical Summary of Returns

16.4.8 Key Observations Regarding Historical Returns of Distressed Funds

Monthly returns to distressed funds are observed from January of 2000 to December of 2018 for a total of 228 observations. Exhibit 16.3 provides univariate return statistics in the top panel, partial autocorrelations of returns in the middle panel, and a histogram of returns in the bottom panel.

Key observations on the returns to distressed funds that are consistent with economic reasoning are an essential component of knowledge and include the following:

1. Event-driven distressed returns exhibited substantially lower volatility than world equities.
2. Event-driven distressed returns exhibited somewhat fat tails and, like world equities, a negative skew.
3. Event-driven distressed returns exhibited a moderate maximum drawdown, much less than world equities.
4. Event-driven distressed returns exhibited substantial positive first-order autocorrelation.

16.5 EVENT-DRIVEN MULTISTRATEGY FUNDS

Event-driven multistrategy funds diversify across a wide variety of event-driven strategies, participating in opportunities in both corporate debt and equity securities. Merger activity and debt defaults occur in waves or cycles. Merger activity is usually higher when equity returns are strong, and default rates on debt tend to rise during times of weak equity market performance. Because these two strategies are countercyclical to each other, many managers mix a number of event-driven strategies into a single fund. This combination can increase the capacity of the fund to manage higher levels of assets, as well as smooth out the opportunity set over time and various market conditions. **Special situation funds** invest across a number of event styles and are typically focused on equity securities, especially those with a spin-off or recent emergence from bankruptcy.

Index (Jan. 2000–Dec. 2018)	Credit Suisse Event-Driven: Multistrategy	MSCI World Equity
Annualized Arithmetic Mean	5.8%	4.5%
Annualized Standard Deviation	6.2%	15.0%
Annualized Semivolatility	5.3%	11.6%
Annualized Median	8.7%	11.6%
Skewness	−1.0	−0.7
Excess Kurtosis	2.1	1.6
Sharpe Ratio	0.5	0.1
Sortino Ratio	0.6	0.2
Annualized Geometric Mean	5.6%	3.4%
First-Order Autocorrelation	0.29	0.14
Annualized Standard Deviation (Adjusted for Autocorrelation)	8.2%	17.1%
Maximum	4.8%	11.2%
Minimum	−6.2%	−19.0%
Max Drawdown	−17.5%	−54.0%

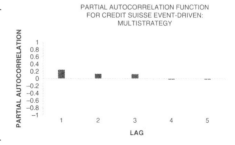

PARTIAL AUTOCORRELATION FUNCTION FOR CREDIT SUISSE EVENT-DRIVEN: MULTISTRATEGY

Index (Jan. 2000–Dec. 2018)	HFRI Event-Driven (Total)	MSCI World Equity
Annualized Arithmetic Mean	6.3%	4.5%
Annualized Standard Deviation	6.1%	15.0%
Annualized Semivolatility	5.0%	11.6%
Annualized Median	8.9%	11.6%
Skewness	−1.0	−0.7
Excess Kurtosis	2.9	1.6
Sharpe Ratio	0.6	0.1
Sortino Ratio	0.8	0.2
Annualized Geometric Mean	6.1%	3.4%
First-Order Autocorrelation	0.39	0.14
Annualized Standard Deviation (Adjusted for Autocorrelation)	9.2%	17.1%
Maximum	4.7%	11.2%
Minimum	−8.2%	−19.0%
Max Drawdown	−24.8%	−54.0%

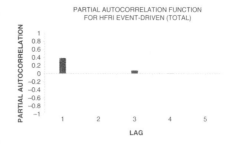

PARTIAL AUTOCORRELATION FUNCTION FOR HFRI EVENT-DRIVEN (TOTAL)

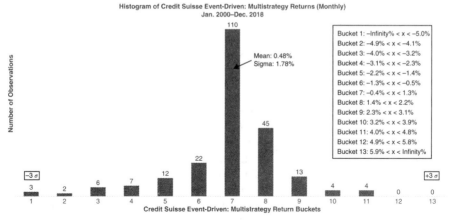

Histogram of Credit Suisse Event-Driven: Multistrategy Returns (Monthly) Jan. 2000–Dec. 2018

Mean: 0.48%
Sigma: 1.78%

Bucket 1: −Infinity% < x < −5.0%
Bucket 2: −4.9% < x < −4.1%
Bucket 3: −4.0% < x < −3.2%
Bucket 4: −3.1% < x < −2.3%
Bucket 5: −2.2% < x < −1.4%
Bucket 6: −1.3% < x < −0.5%
Bucket 7: −0.4% < x < 1.3%
Bucket 8: 1.4% < x < 2.2%
Bucket 9: 2.3% < x < 3.1%
Bucket 10: 3.2% < x < 3.9%
Bucket 11: 4.0% < x < 4.8%
Bucket 12: 4.9% < x < 5.8%
Bucket 13: 5.9% < x < Infinity%

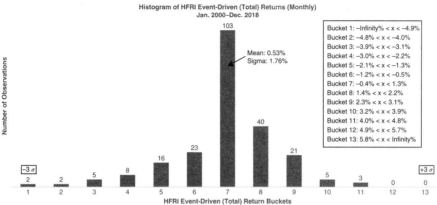

Histogram of HFRI Event-Driven (Total) Returns (Monthly) Jan. 2000–Dec. 2018

Mean: 0.53%
Sigma: 1.76%

Bucket 1: −Infinity% < x < −4.9%
Bucket 2: −4.8% < x < −4.0%
Bucket 3: −3.9% < x < −3.1%
Bucket 4: −3.0% < x < −2.2%
Bucket 5: −2.1% < x < −1.3%
Bucket 6: −1.2% < x < −0.5%
Bucket 7: −0.4% < x < 1.3%
Bucket 8: 1.4% < x < 2.2%
Bucket 9: 2.3% < x < 3.1%
Bucket 10: 3.2% < x < 3.9%
Bucket 11: 4.0% < x < 4.8%
Bucket 12: 4.9% < x < 5.7%
Bucket 13: 5.8% < x < Infinity%

EXHIBIT 16.4 Statistical Summary of Returns

16.5.1 Key Observations Regarding Historical Returns of Event-Driven Multistrategy Funds

Monthly returns to event-driven multistrategy funds are observed from January of 2000 to December of 2018 for a total of 228 observations. Exhibit 16.4 provides univariate return statistics in the top panel, partial autocorrelations of returns in the middle panel, and histograms of returns in the bottom panel.

Key observations on the returns to event-driven multistrategy funds that are consistent with economic reasoning are an essential component of knowledge and include the following:

1. Event-driven multistrategy returns exhibited substantially lower volatility than world equities.
2. Event-driven multistrategy returns exhibited somewhat fat tails and, like world equities, a negative skew.
3. Event-driven multistrategy returns exhibited a moderate maximum drawdown, much less than world equities.
4. Event-driven multistrategy returns exhibited some positive first-, second-, and third-order autocorrelation.

REVIEW QUESTIONS

1. List the three primary categories of single-strategy event-driven hedge funds.
2. Why are event-driven hedge funds often characterized as selling insurance?
3. Why would activist hedge fund managers need to understand corporate governance?
4. List the five dimensions of shareholder activists.
5. What is the economic term for a person or an entity that allows others to pay initial costs and then benefits from those expenditures?
6. Is Form 13F a U.S.-required form targeted toward activist hedge funds?
7. What is the difference between a spin-off and a split-off?
8. What are the positions used in a traditional merger arbitrage strategy?
9. What is financing risk in the context of an event-driven investment strategy?
10. How is short selling of equity in a distressed firm similar to an option position?

NOTES

1. Ronald D. Orol, *Extreme Value Hedging: How Activist Hedge Fund Managers Are Taking on the World* (Hoboken, NJ: John Wiley & Sons, 2008).
2. Alon Brav, Wie Jiang, Frank Partnoy, and Randall Thomas, "Hedge Fund Activism, Corporate Governance and Firm Performance," *Journal of Finance* 63, no. 4 (August 2008): 1730.
3. Ibid., 1729.

CHAPTER 17

Relative Value Hedge Funds

Relative value strategies attempt to capture alpha through predicting changes in relationships between prices or between rates. For example, rather than trying to predict the price of oil, a relative value strategy might predict that there will be a narrowing of the margin between the price of oil and the price of gasoline.

17.1 OVERVIEW OF RELATIVE VALUE STRATEGIES

Relative value fund managers take long and short positions that are relatively equal in size, volatility, and other risk exposures. Ideally, the combined positions have little net market risk but can profit from short positions in relatively overvalued securities and long positions in relatively undervalued securities. Relative value funds tend to profit during normal market conditions when valuations converge to their equilibrium values. **Convergence** is the return of prices or rates to relative values that are deemed normal. Since returns to these convergence strategies are normally very small, managers have to employ substantial leverage to generate acceptable returns for these strategies. Therefore, relative value funds can experience substantial losses during times of market crisis, as leveraged funds may be forced to liquidate positions and wind down leverage at times when relative values appear dramatically abnormal.

Within the relative value class of hedge funds, four styles will be discussed: convertible bond arbitrage, volatility arbitrage, fixed-income arbitrage, and relative value multistrategy funds. Hedge Fund Research (HFR) estimates that relative value hedge funds hold more than a quarter of hedge fund industry assets, totaling over $830 billion at the end of 2018. This includes nearly $50 billion in convertible arbitrage funds, $18 billion in volatility arbitrage, and $316 billion in fixed-income arbitrage. Within fixed-income arbitrage, nearly $150 billion is invested in corporate bond strategies, $26 billion in sovereign bonds, and over $90 billion in asset-backed securities. Many relative value hedge funds mix these styles, as evidenced by the $487 billion in relative value multistrategy fund assets under management.

The **classic relative value strategy trade** is based on the premise that a particular relationship or spread between two prices or rates has reached an abnormal level and will, therefore, tend to return to its normal level. This classic trade involves taking a long position in the security that is perceived to be relatively underpriced and a short position in the security that is perceived to be relatively overpriced. The normal level to which the price or rate relationship is anticipated to return is usually a level deemed by the fund manager to represent a long-term tendency as observed empirically or derived theoretically.

Relative value strategies tend to perform well during periods of decreasing volatility and increasing market calm when positions with diverse values converge and credit spreads narrow. However, relative value strategies can experience large losses in crisis markets when there is a flight-to-quality response to risk, with increased volatility and widening credit spreads, resulting in returns that have large exposures to kurtosis and negative skewness.

17.2 CONVERTIBLE BOND ARBITRAGE

The **classic convertible bond arbitrage trade** is to purchase a convertible bond that is believed to be undervalued and to hedge its risk using a short position in the underlying equity. The hedge is usually adjusted as the underlying stock rises or falls in value. If the underlying equity experiences volatility that is higher than the volatility implied by the original market price of the bond, then the strategy generates favorable returns. The convertible bond arbitrage strategy includes variations to the classic trade, such as using alternative hedging strategies, as well as to the reverse trade, involving a short position in a convertible bond perceived to be overvalued. Before discussing the actual trading strategy and describing its potential sources of return, we need to note the important characteristics of convertible bonds and explain the factors that affect the prices of these instruments.

17.2.1 Defining and Pricing Convertible Bonds

Convertible bonds are hybrid corporate securities, mixing fixed-income and equity characteristics into one security. In their simplest form, convertible bonds can be thought of as a combination of an unsecured corporate bond and a call option on the issuer's stock. In a bankruptcy proceeding, convertible bonds are senior to equity securities and subordinated to senior and collateralized debt issues. The yield to maturity on convertible bonds is lower than the yield on otherwise equivalent straight debt because the convertible bond's conversion feature provides an option with substantial value to the holder. Because the holder of the convertible bond owns straight debt plus an equity call option, the owner is willing to pay a higher price (and accept a lower yield) than would be acceptable for an otherwise similar straight bond. Following are formulas for the value of a convertible bond, the conversion ratio, the option strike price, the conversion value, and the conversion premium of a convertible bond:

$$\text{Convertible Bond Price} = \text{Value of Straight Corporate Debt} \qquad (17.1a)$$
$$+ \text{Value of the Implicit Equity Call Option}$$
$$\text{Conversion Ratio} = \text{Number of Shares per Convertible Bond} \qquad (17.1b)$$
$$\text{Option Strike Price} = \text{Convertible Bond Face Value/Conversion Ratio} \qquad (17.1c)$$
$$\text{Conversion Value} = \text{Current Stock Price} \times \text{Conversion Ratio} \qquad (17.1d)$$
$$\text{Conversion Premium} = (\text{Convertible Bond Price} - \text{Conversion Value})/ \qquad (17.1e)$$
$$\text{Conversion Value}$$

☞ **APPLICATION 17.2.1A**

Consider a firm with a borrowing cost of 8% on unsecured, subordinated straight debt and a current stock price of $40. The firm may be able to issue three-year convertible bonds at an annual coupon rate of 4% by offering a conversion ratio such as 20. What is the bond's strike price, and what does the conversion option allow the bond investors to do?

The conversion ratio of 20 is equivalent to a $50 strike price using Equation 17.1c, assuming that the bond's face value is $1,000. On or before maturity, bond investors can opt to convert each $1,000 face value bond into 20 shares of the firm's equity rather than receive the remaining principal and coupon payments.

Thus, the firm in Application 17.2.1a can borrow $10 million today in a bond issue and potentially never have to repay the loan in cash, as investors may opt to be repaid with 200,000 shares of stock at some date at or before the three-year maturity of the convertible bond. Valuing the convertible bond is typically accomplished by unbundling the structure into its component parts of straight debt and the equity call option, valuing each component, and summing their values.

☞ **APPLICATION 17.2.1B**

Returning to the previous example of an 8% unsecured bond rate, a $40 stock price, and a conversion ratio of 20, and assuming that a three-year European-style call option—given a current stock price of $40, a strike price of $50, and other parameters, such as volatility and dividends—is valued at $5.14 per share according to the Black-Scholes option pricing model, what are the values of the convertible bond, the conversion value, and the conversion premium?

Starting with the straight debt issue, the three-year bond in the example can be valued with a 4% coupon and an 8% discount rate, found from observing corporate bonds of similar credit risk, at $896.92, using a financial calculator with annual coupons and compounding for simplicity. Using representative calculator inputs $n = 3$, $I = 8$, $PMT = 40$, and $FV = 1,000$ and computing PV yields 896.92. Adding the straight bond value of $896.92 to the value of 20 options, $102.80 (i.e., 5.14×20), yields a convertible bond valuation of $999.72, a value that is very close to the bond's face value of $1,000. The current stock price multiplied by the conversion ratio gives a conversion value of $800 (i.e., 40×20). Therefore, this convertible bond is selling at a conversion premium of 24.97% [i.e., ($999.72 − $800)/$800].

In practice, convertible bonds are not valued by the Black-Scholes option pricing model that is used to value short-term equity options, as assumptions (including that of constant volatility) do not apply to long-dated convertible bond issues.

17.2.2 Busted, Hybrid, and Equity-Like Convertibles

The characteristics of convertible bonds vary widely with the moneyness. **Moneyness** is the extent to which an option is in-the-money, at-the-money, or out-of-the-money. In the case of a convertible bond, moneyness indicates the relationship between the strike price implied by the conversion option and the price of the underlying stock. Bonds with very high conversion premiums (see Equation 17.1) are often called **busted convertibles,** as the embedded stock options are far out-of-the-money. These bonds behave like straight debt because when the stock option is far out-of-the-money, the convertible bond's value is primarily derived from its coupon and principal payments.

Bonds with very low conversion premiums have stock options that are deep in-the-money, where the convertible bond price and the conversion value are very close. The further in-the-money that the option is, the more the convertible bond behaves like the underlying stock. An **equity-like convertible** is a convertible bond that is far in-the-money and therefore has a price that tracks its underlying equity very closely. Interest rates and credit spreads matter less on equity-sensitive convertibles.

Convertible bonds with moderately sized conversion ratios have stock options closer to being at-the-money and are called **hybrid convertibles.** Hybrids are usually the most attractive bonds for use in convertible arbitrage strategies. These hybrid convertibles are attractive for convertible arbitrage due to their asymmetric payoff profile. Exhibit 17.1 illustrates the effect of moneyness on convertible bond prices and their sensitivity to the underlying equity prices. Note the convexity in the convertible bond price for hybrid convertibles. This convexity is the essential characteristic that drives the traditional convertible arbitrage strategy. The following section on delta, gamma, and theta provides a further foundation for understanding the dynamics of convertible arbitrage.

17.2.3 Delta, Gamma, and Theta

The concepts of delta and gamma are keys to understanding the convertible arbitrage strategy. **Delta** is the change in the value of an option (or a security with an implicit option) with respect to a change in the value of the underlying asset (i.e., it measures

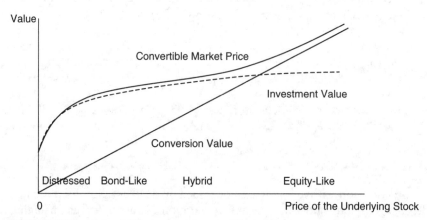

EXHIBIT 17.1 Price Behavior of a Convertible Security

the sensitivity of the option price to small changes in the price of its underlying asset). For example, if a $1 rise in the value of a stock price causes a call option to rise $0.60, then the delta of the call option is roughly 0.6.[1] Call options that are very far out-of-the-money have deltas near 0.0, whereas options very far in-the-money have deltas near 1.0. The delta of a put option is negative. Delta is the first derivative of an option's price with respect to the price of the underlying asset and is a key concept in setting the hedge ratio of a convertible arbitrage position. In a graph of an option price against the price of the underlying asset, delta is the slope of the relationship at each point along the curve.

Gamma is the second derivative of an option's price with respect to the price of the underlying asset—or, equivalently, the first derivative of delta with respect to the price of the underlying asset. That is, it measures how delta changes as the price of the underlying asset changes. Graphically, gamma is the degree of curvature in the option price versus the underlying asset price relationship. Gamma measures the rate of change in the value of delta as the price of the underlying asset changes. Gamma is near zero when an option is extremely far out-of-the-money and the delta is very small. Gamma is also near zero when an option is extremely far in-the-money and the delta is near one. Gamma tends to be largest when the option is near-the-money. As illustrated in the next section, the gamma of a position can be used to describe how hedged positions earn money during periods of high volatility in the underlying asset.

Finally, **theta** is the first derivative of an option's price with respect to the time to expiration of the option. Theta is negative for a long position in an option, since as time passes and all other values remain the same, the option declines in value. In a nutshell, theta reflects the loss in an option's time value as time passes, which can be referred to as time decay. Theta is a key concept in understanding how hedged positions lose value if there are no changes in the underlying asset or its volatility. That is, theta is a cost to the buyer of the option and a benefit to the seller of the option, as the time value decays as the option approaches expiration. The goal of many active long-option trading strategies, including convertible bond arbitrage, is to earn sufficient profits from gamma trading to overcome the predictable losses from theta.

In summary, delta is used to establish the hedge ratio in a traditional convertible arbitrage position. The positive gamma or long gamma nature of the convertible bond ensures that the hedged position will make money if the underlying asset quickly rises or falls in value. This profit is generated by the unlimited upside and limited downside nature of a long position in an option (i.e., its curvature). Finally, the theta of the long option position indicates that as time passes, the hedged position loses value in the absence of underlying asset changes. Thus, a traditional convertible arbitrage strategy's return varies directly with the level of volatility experienced in the underlying asset. The goal in convertible arbitrage is to purchase undervalued options and short sell overvalued options while hedging other risks.

17.2.4 Stylized Illustration of Convertible Arbitrage

Consider a $1,000 face value convertible bond that can be converted into one share of stock, for mathematical simplicity. The stock currently sells for about $1,000, so the implicit option is at-the-money. Exhibit 17.2 shows the five prices that the convertible bond can currently have for five possible stock prices. Notice that the convertible bond's price moves nonlinearly with respect to large changes in the underlying asset

EXHIBIT 17.2 Example of a Delta-Neutral Position in Stocks and Convertible Bonds

Stock Price	$960	$980	$1,000	$1,020	$1,040
Convertible bond price	$1,085	$1,090	$1,100	$1,110	$1,125
Long 1 bond and short 0.5 shares	$605	$600	$600	$600	$605

price, just like a call option does, with smaller losses to the downside and larger gains to the upside. This behavior is due to convexity and is a key to the profit potential.

Assume that the current price of the stock is $1,000 and the price of the convertible bond is $1,100. If the stock rises or falls $20, the convertible bond moves in the same direction but with half the magnitude (i.e., $10).[2] The delta of the convertible bond is therefore 0.50, and the hedged position would be a long position of one convertible bond and a short position of 0.5 shares of stock. The hedged position is said to be delta-neutral. A **delta-neutral** position is a position in which the value-weighted sum of all deltas of all positions equals zero. In this example, the sensitivity of the 0.5 short-sold shares to the equity price equals the sensitivity of one convertible bond to the equity price, offsetting each other and leaving the combined positions insensitive to small changes (i.e., a change of $20) in the stock price.

The last line of Exhibit 17.2 illustrates that the hedged position breaks even for very small changes in the stock price; the combined positions retain a constant value of $600. But the combined positions are profitable for either a $40 up or a $40 down movement in the underlying asset. This illustrates that even though the positions are delta-neutral, the hedge benefits from large movements in either direction. The profit is generated by the positive gamma of the convertible bond, wherein losses of the bond slow down when the stock declines, and profits accelerate when the stock rises. If a large price change in the underlying asset takes place, the hedged position makes a profit, and the positions are adjusted to being delta-neutral based on a new hedge ratio at the new price levels. If the underlying stock price does not move, the convertible bond will slowly decline to its par value at maturity, and the hedged position will fall to $500, illustrating the negative theta.

In a convertible arbitrage strategy, when the underlying stock price has changed and the positions (i.e., the hedge ratio) have been adjusted to bring the exposure back to being delta-neutral, it does not matter whether the stock price moves back to its original value or continues moving in the same direction. The reason it does not matter is that once the stock price has changed and the arbitrageur has reset the hedge to reflect the new hedge ratio by expanding or contracting the short position in the stock, the positions are returned to being delta-neutral. Once the positions are returned to delta neutrality, the positions return to the profit and loss exposures illustrated in Exhibit 17.2, and the arbitrageur returns to being able to profit whether the next move in the stock is up or down.

Note, however, that for the arbitrageur to make more money on gamma than is being lost on theta, which is known as time decay, the stock must keep experiencing substantial price changes. These price changes dictate the relationship between realized volatility and implied volatility. **Realized volatility** is the actual observed volatility (i.e., the standard deviation of returns) experienced by an asset—in this case, the underlying stock. The **implied volatility** of an option or an option-like position—in this case, the implied volatility of a convertible bond—is the standard deviation of returns that is viewed as being consistent with an observed market price for the option. A traditional convertible arbitrage strategy is a play on whether the realized volatility is equal to, less than, or greater than the implied volatility of the convertible bond price when the position was established. The keys to convertible arbitrage success are to buy convertible bonds with underpriced conversion options (i.e., implied volatility that is too low), short sell convertible bonds with overpriced conversion options (i.e., implied volatility that is too high), and maintain hedges by taking offsetting positions in the underlying equity to control for risk. By far the most common strategy is to take a long position in the convertible bond and hedge the market risk of the position by taking a short position in the underlying equity. Fund managers who follow this strategy believe that the implied volatilities of convertibles are too low when compared to the expected realized volatility of the stock.

17.2.5 Convertible Arbitrage and Short Selling

The most common convertible arbitrage strategy involves short selling large quantities of the common stock underlying the convertible bond's embedded option. As detailed in Chapter 2, the steps in selling assets short include the following:

1. Borrowing the assets from an entity that currently owns them. There is an active market between entities that borrow assets and entities that lend assets, known as securities lending. Securities lending is generally facilitated by an intermediary, usually an investment bank or a brokerage firm.
2. Selling the borrowed assets into the market.
3. Eventually closing the position by purchasing the assets from the market and delivering them to the entity from which they were borrowed.

17.2.6 Convertible Bond Arbitrage Background

Convertible bond arbitrage offers the potential to earn alpha when the options implicit in the bonds are mispriced. Why might convertible bond prices be attractive? As a small and complex asset class, convertible bonds may offer liquidity or complexity premiums to skilled hedge fund managers who are able to evaluate them and identify the potential mispricing that results from their complexity. A **complexity premium** is a higher expected return offered by a security to an investor to compensate for analyzing and managing a position that requires added time and expertise. Convertible bonds, already made complex by the conversion options, become especially complex when the bonds stray from the plain-vanilla package of corporate debt plus a conversion option to having the additional complexities of callable or putable convertibles, dual currencies, and/or forced conversions.

Convertible bond arbitrage funds develop computerized systems to scan the universe of convertible bonds and compare convertible bond prices to the price of the straight debt and equity call option package. Each hedge fund creates customized assumptions for the straight bond yield and the volatility of the underlying equities. The analysis of the underlying straight bond focuses on the firm's credit risk, whereas the analysis of the equity volatility focuses on historical return volatilities and current option prices. When the convertible bond is undervalued relative to the sum of its parts, the hedge fund purchases the convertible bond and shorts the underlying equity. Less often, the convertible bond is viewed as overvalued and sold short with a long position in the underlying equity. Also, the convertible bond position is sometimes hedged with positions in equity options in addition to or in place of positions in equities. Further, to hedge the interest rate risk and credit risk of the convertible bonds, the manager sometimes establishes positions in interest rate derivatives or credit derivatives.

17.2.7 Four Sources of Returns to Convertible Bond Arbitrage

Fund managers who are able to develop accurate predictions of equity volatility relative to the volatility implied by convertible bond prices can earn superior returns by buying undervalued convertible bonds and shorting the underlying equity. In the past two decades, convertible bond arbitrage trading tended to focus on long positions in convertible bonds and to generate superior returns, especially in the mid- to late 1990s, indicating that convertible bonds themselves offered consistently superior returns.

Note, however, that if investors in convertible bonds consistently earned superior returns, the bonds might offer higher than necessary yields, which make convertible bonds an expensive source of corporate financing (i.e., the return earned by the bond investor is the cost of capital to the firm). In perfect capital markets, the risk-adjusted costs of all sources of financing would be forced toward equality, since investors would avoid buying securities with returns too low and corporations would avoid issuing securities with returns too high. There are two elements necessary to support the argument that convertible bonds should consistently offer superior risk-adjusted returns. First, demand to buy convertible bonds must be restricted such that it prevents convertible bond prices from increasing to the point of offering normal risk-adjusted returns. Second, suppliers of convertible bonds (corporations) must be of sufficient size to suppress convertible bond prices to the point of allowing superior returns.

The argument that there is limited demand from convertible bond investors appears plausible. The complexity of convertible bond analysis and hedging, combined with restrictions on the ability of traditional investment managers such as mutual fund managers to short equity, may limit the number of investors willing and able to perform convertible bond arbitrage. But why would corporations issue convertible bonds if they were consistently underpriced? More broadly, are there solid reasons to believe that convertible bonds will continue to be issued at prices that offer consistently high risk-adjusted returns to investors and therefore higher costs to issuers? There are four especially persuasive reasons to believe that issuers may, at least periodically, continue to offer convertible bonds at attractive prices:

1. Agents (corporate managers) may underestimate the true costs of issuing convertible bonds. Convertible bonds offer yields that substantially underestimate expected returns when those yields are based on coupons and principal amounts. Issuers may find the lower yields to be attractive, as the coupon interest rate on convertible bonds is lower than the interest rate paid on the straight bonds issued by the firm. The issuers may not fully appreciate the potential harm to share prices from dilution when the implicit options are exercised. **Dilution** takes

place when additional equity is issued at below-market values, and the per-share value of the holdings of existing shareholders is diminished.

2. Agents of small firms may have no choice but to issue convertible bonds at attractive prices. Convertible bonds are rarely registered in a public offering. In the United States, most convertible bonds are sold as 144A exempt securities, meaning they are exempt from the registration requirements of the SEC (Securities and Exchange Commission). As a result, most convertible bonds cannot be sold to retail investors, and trade only among institutional investors. The lack of a public market for these convertible bonds makes them less liquid than stocks or regular bonds. Consequently, their prices may be lower and their returns higher as a premium for bearing liquidity risk.

3. There is a potentially substantial conflict of interest between straight bond investors and shareholders with regard to preferred corporate asset volatility. Straight bondholders prefer low asset volatility to decrease the probability of bankruptcy. Equity holders have a risk exposure that can be viewed as a call option on the firm's assets, and, therefore, they may prefer high asset volatility. Shareholders have an incentive to increase the volatility of the firm's assets after the issuance of debt, in order to transfer wealth from bondholders to themselves. Since bondholders are aware of this potential risk, they demand a higher yield for compensation, and suboptimal corporate investment decisions may result. The incentive to take on excessive risk is reduced if convertible bonds are issued, as any increase in volatility benefits the convertible bondholders as well as the equity holders. In short, convertible bonds reduce agency costs and lead to a lower cost of capital for the firm. Asymmetric information between corporate managers and investors regarding asset volatility can exacerbate the problems with issuing straight debt. Since convertible bonds are hybrid investments, their prices are less sensitive to the credit risk of the issuing firm. This insensitivity makes it easier for the firm and potential bondholders to agree on the value of the bond when convertible debt is used and there is substantial uncertainty about the riskiness of corporate assets.

4. Indirect equity issuance costs are a factor. Corporations use convertible bonds as an indirect way to issue equity because their cost of directly issuing new equity may be high. For instance, when managers opt to issue new stock at current price levels, potential buyers of the new shares may conclude that managers and current shareholders view the current price as being above its fair value, making them willing to bring in new investors. The inadvertent information signal caused by issuing equity could depress share prices as market participants react to the concern that the firm is in worse financial condition than originally believed and as reflected in the share price. Since most convertibles are converted into equity only if the stock price increases, the signal conveyed to the market is not viewed as negatively as when equity is issued.

17.2.8 Components of Convertible Arbitrage Returns

The **components of convertible arbitrage returns** include interest, dividends, rebates, and capital gains and losses. Exhibit 17.3 depicts these components for the case of a traditional convertible bond strategy of being long the convertible bond and short the underlying stock. The first component of the return of a traditional convertible

EXHIBIT 17.3   Components of the Return of a Traditional Convertible
Arbitrage Strategy

Convertible Bond Arbitrage Income
(Bond Interest − Stock Dividends + Short Stock Rebate − Financing Expenses)
+
Convertible Bond and Stock Net Capital Gains and Losses
(Capital Gains on Stock and Bond − Capital Losses on Stock and Bond)

---

arbitrage strategy is the income component. Assuming a long position in the convertible bond and a short position in the stock, the investor earns the coupon interest paid on the bond, pays any dividends due on the short stock position, and earns a rebate on the cash proceeds from the short sale of the stock. If there are any costs to financing the position, such as the cost to borrow the stock or the interest paid on leveraged positions, those costs are deducted from the arbitrage income.

The second source of the return to the convertible bond arbitrageur is the gain on stock trading (and, to a lesser extent, the possible gain or loss on the eventual sale of the convertible bond), as illustrated in Exhibits 17.2 and 17.3. In the traditional convertible arbitrage trade of being long the convertible bond, the larger and more frequent the stock price moves, the greater the profits from gamma trading. Profits from gamma trading, though, are offset through theta, or time decay. The goal of gamma trading is to earn more in profits from gamma than the option value loses in time decay. This goal is met when the realized volatility of the stock exceeds the implied volatility priced into the option on the day the convertible bond is purchased.

This simplified discussion of convertible arbitrage has held constant other sources of risk and return, such as interest rates, credit spreads, and implied volatility. Although some convertible bond managers are content to maintain a simple hedge of the convertible bond against the underlying stock, other managers may seek to hedge other risks or add further value through derivative strategies related to interest rates, credit spreads, volatility, or stock price anticipation. For example, more sophisticated hedging strategies use interest rate and credit derivatives to hedge interest rate and credit spread risks such that the arbitrage is more of a pure play on realized volatility relative to implied volatility.

Some convertible arbitrage hedge funds attempt to identify and hedge the underpriced embedded options of a convertible bond by buying the convertible bond and selling short an exchange-traded call option on the underlying stock. This technique can be effective when there is a large spread in implied volatility between exchange-traded and embedded call options. However, there is rarely a clean match between listed and embedded options in terms of exercise periods, and many convertible bond issuers do not have options listed on their stock. Interest rate hedges are less common in convertible arbitrage funds. Given that much of the convertible bond universe is below investment grade, credit spread changes can be significantly more important than changes in risk-free or investment-grade interest rates. Credit derivatives, detailed in Chapter 24, can be useful vehicles with which to hedge credit risk.

Rather than hedging various risk exposures, managers may speculate on them. Profits from a convertible arbitrage position can be substantially enhanced when managers have the ability to consistently predict the future path of interest rates, credit spreads, stock prices, or volatility. For example, to add value through credit spread anticipation, the manager may perform fundamental credit analysis on each issuer, seeking to purchase bonds with improving credit quality and tightening credit spreads, while avoiding bonds whose credit quality is deteriorating, which can lead to widening credit spreads. For stock price anticipation, the manager deviates from delta neutrality in an attempt to profit from stock price moves in a particular direction. The manager applies heavy delta hedges (a net short position) to stocks expected to underperform, and light delta hedges (a net long position) to stocks for which higher prices are anticipated. Fund managers are also likely to diversify their portfolios across issuer, sector, maturity, and so forth to reduce both idiosyncratic risk and exposures to industries and sectors.

17.2.9 Details Regarding Convertible Bond Arbitrage

Let's take a close look at how a traditional convertible arbitrage strategy tries to enhance returns. Specifically, this section details how a position that is delta hedged can earn gains from gamma (convexity) that more than offset the losses from theta (time decay).

Delta hedging is shown in this example to reduce risk; however, delta hedging does not eliminate the potential for net capital gains. Due to the nonlinear nature of their payoff, most at-the-money convertible bonds exhibit a desirable property known as positive convexity, or high gamma. That is, they appreciate in value from an immediate upward stock price change more than they depreciate from the same sized downward change in the underlying stock price. This section shows that a delta-hedged position will actually benefit from *any* movement in the underlying stock due to this convexity. The traditional arbitrage strategy speculates that there will be enough movements in the stock price (i.e., volatility) to generate gains from gamma that more than offset the losses from theta (the time decay of the position).

Consider an example of convertible bond XYZ with a conversion ratio of 8. A convertible bond arbitrageur believes that the implicit option in the bond is undervalued and that therefore the entire bond is underpriced based on the arbitrageur's estimate of the future volatility of the underlying asset (stock). How can the arbitrageur exploit such a mispricing? Buying the cheap convertible bond is clearly part of the solution, but it is not sufficient. Simply waiting for market prices to adjust is not an arbitrage because the long convertible position comes with a variety of risks that could easily wipe out the expected gains. To arbitrage, it is necessary to both buy the cheap convertible bond and hedge its risks, a dynamic process that is very similar to what arbitrageurs of listed options do on a regular basis.

The primary risk of holding a long convertible position comes from the potential variations in the underlying stock price. This equity risk can be easily eliminated by selling short an appropriate quantity of the underlying stock. This quantity corresponds to the convertible's delta multiplied by the number of shares into which the bond may be converted. Let's assume that the delta of the XYZ convertible bond is 0.625. To hedge the equity risk, an arbitrageur would need to sell short delta times the conversion ratio ($0.625 \times 8 = 5.0$) shares of stock per \$1,000 face value of the convertible bond bought. If the stock price gains \$1, the convertible bond will gain approximately delta (times 8) dollars and the short stock position will lose delta (times 8) dollars, so that the overall variation will be near zero. Conversely, if the stock price drops by \$1, the convertible bond will lose approximately the same

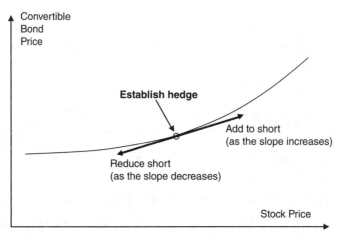

EXHIBIT 17.4 Delta Hedging a Convertible Bond

number of dollars that the short stock position will gain. As illustrated in Exhibit 17.4, for a small change in the price of the stock, the arbitrageur's position will be hedged.

But this approximation ignores a key aspect to the hedge: Although delta hedging reduces the risk from changes in the underlying stock price, it does not eliminate return. Return of the strategy can be enhanced because, ignoring theta, the hedged position generates a small gain whether the underlying stock moves up or down, due to the position's gamma. This important concept is detailed later.

First let's focus on the need to rebalance the original delta-hedged position. In our example, when the stock price changes, the delta of the convertible bond will no longer be 0.625, and, therefore, the net delta of the position will no longer be equal to zero. The **net delta** of a position is the delta of long positions minus the delta of short positions.

As the stock price increases, the option component moves further in-the-money and the convertible bond becomes more equity sensitive (see Exhibit 17.4). The delta of the convertible bond increases, so the arbitrageur must adjust the hedge by shorting more shares. Conversely, as the stock price declines, the option moves out-of-the-money, the delta of the convertible bond declines, and the arbitrageur must reduce the hedge by buying back some shares.

For example, if the delta rises to 0.70 due to a stock price increase, the short position must be expanded from 5.0 shares to 5.6 shares (8×0.70). If the delta falls to 0.50 due to a stock price decrease, the short position must be contracted to 4.0 shares (8×0.50). The hedge needs to be rebalanced repeatedly as the stock price moves, in a strategy known as dynamic delta hedging. **Dynamic delta hedging** is the process of frequently adjusting positions in order to maintain a target exposure to delta, often delta neutrality.

A key question for most arbitrageurs is how often they should rebalance their hedges. Arbitrageurs usually rehedge based on a time or price formula. In the former case, rehedging takes place at prespecified time intervals, such as every day or every hour. In the latter case, rehedging takes place whenever the stock price changes by a certain amount (e.g., every $1 move or every 1% move in the stock price) or when the size of the necessary adjustment reaches a certain threshold.

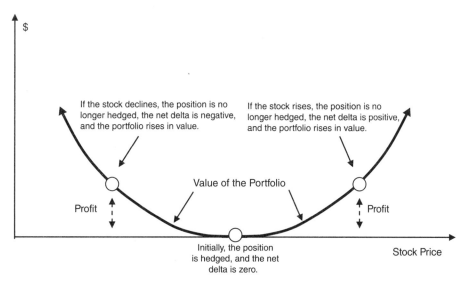

EXHIBIT 17.5 Profit on a Delta-Hedged Position (Long Convertible, Short Stock)

Let's look more closely at the convexity, or gamma, that drives the traditional convertible bond arbitrage strategy. Gamma refers to the asymmetric valuation profile generated by movements in the underlying stock price. In other words, gamma is illustrated by the curvature in Exhibit 17.5.

Exhibit 17.5 illustrates why the gamma of the convertible bond generates a gain to the hedged position when the underlying stock moves up or down. But Exhibit 17.5 does not illustrate the downside risk. The worst outcome for the traditional convertible bond arbitrageur is when the stock price remains unchanged. When the stock price does not change, the hedged position loses value due to the theta (time decay) of the long position in the implicit option. When the underlying stock price experiences less volatility than is implied by the bond price, the losses from the theta of the option more than offset the gains from the gamma, and the strategy underperforms.

Saying that a convertible bond is cheap is equivalent to saying that the corresponding implied volatility is too low. If realized volatility is higher than implied volatility, then the profits illustrated in Exhibit 17.5 should dominate the theta, resulting in net profits for the strategy. Conversely, if the realized volatility is below the implied volatility, the loss due to theta will outweigh the profit made from the realized volatility, and the position will underperform a risk-free investment, perhaps even incurring a loss.

17.2.10 Return Drivers of Convertible Bond Arbitrage

The mispricing of convertible bonds can be relatively large or small. Minor differences in the volatility used to price the embedded stock option in a convertible bond can generate substantial price differences. For example, if a three-year convertible bond is mispriced by two volatility points (e.g., 25% volatility is used to price the bond rather than 27%), the convertible bond may be underpriced by 1%, a mispricing that may take three years to fully correct. In cases of small degrees of mispricing, convertible bond arbitrage hedge funds may apply leverage to increase the expected returns. Before the 2008 financial crisis, it was not uncommon to see convertible bond hedge funds trade at leverage of over eight times investor capital. Since 2008, it has become more difficult to leverage positions, with the result that some convertible bond funds may now forgo leverage, while others may be able to reach a maximum leverage of only four times investor capital.

It is easy to see why hedge fund managers are tempted to use leverage, as they earn incentive fees on each additional dollar of returns they earn. But leverage is a two-edged sword to investors, as it magnifies both gains and losses. However, incentive fee–based hedge fund managers disproportionately participate in the gains but not the losses; thus, as detailed in Chapter 14, the managers may increase the value of their incentive fee option by taking larger risks.

The market crisis of 2008 created unprecedented risks and opportunities for convertible bond arbitrage. The Credit Suisse Convertible Bond Arbitrage Index declined by more than 25% during the last four months of 2008. This decline may have been caused by illiquidity and large amounts of forced selling of convertible bonds, as prime brokers forcibly reduced the availability of leverage, and the large portfolio of the now-defunct Lehman Brothers was quickly sold into the market. Once this selling subsided, the opportunities in the convertible bond market were unprecedented, as mispricing reached record levels. The yield on U.S. investment-grade convertible bonds reached 14.9% in March 2009, wider than the straight bond yield of 11.0% of the same issuers. A convertible bond arbitrage fund could apparently buy the convertible bond and sell short the straight bond of the same issuer, receiving a free option and an extra yield of 3.9%. Exhibit 17.6 summarizes the risks of convertible bond arbitrage.

EXHIBIT 17.6 Summary of Convertible Bond Arbitrage Risks

Risk	Position	Effect
Interest rates	Long convertible bond, long duration, long convexity	Convertible bonds have an exposure to risk-free interest rates. As rates rise, bond prices fall. Some funds hedge these risks through the use of sovereign bond futures or interest rate swaps.
Equity and volatility	Short stock, delta-neutral, long gamma, long vega, long theta	When the convertible bond arbitrage manager takes a short equity position of the appropriate size, the equity risk of the convertible bond is hedged. The embedded long positions in vega and gamma can increase profits when volatility rises. However, the passage of time works against the investor, as the option's time value, measured by theta, decays over time.
Correlation	Long bond-equity correlation	The strategy is long correlation: When interest rates rise, losses may be offset by gains on the short equity positions. When interest rates fall, losses on the short equity position offset the fixed-income gains. When correlation declines, stock and bond prices move in opposite directions, causing losses on both components of the convertible bond.

(Continued)

EXHIBIT 17.6 (*Continued*)

Risk	Position	Effect
Credit	Long convertible, short equity	Convertible bonds have an exposure to credit risk. As credit spreads widen, bond prices fall. All bonds have a senior claim relative to equities during bankruptcy proceedings.
Legal	Long convertible	Adverse regulatory rulings can negatively affect convertible bond arbitrageurs. Reductions in leverage ratios, short-selling restrictions, and accounting changes that make convertible issuance more restrictive can cause unexpected losses for arbitrageurs.
Liquidity and crisis	Short equity, long convertible	Convertible bond investors sell economic disaster insurance as credit spreads widen during times of economic crisis. Convertible bond arbitrageurs are exposed to liquidity risks, such as equity short squeezes, widening bid-ask spreads of convertible bonds, and increases in both the short stock borrowing rate and the prime broker borrowing rate.

Adapted from Alexander Ineichen, *Absolute Returns* (Hoboken, NJ: John Wiley & Sons, 2003).

17.2.11 Key Observations Regarding Historical Returns of Convertible Arbitrage Funds

Monthly returns to convertible arbitrage hedge funds are observed from January of 2000 to December of 2018, for a total of 228 observations. Exhibit 17.7 provides univariate return statistics in the top panel, partial autocorrelations of returns in the middle panel, and a histogram of returns in the bottom panel.

Key observations on convertible arbitrage returns that are consistent with economic reasoning are an essential component of knowledge and include the following:

1. The historical return distribution of convertible arbitrage exhibited moderately greater left skew and extraordinarily high excess kurtosis relative to global equities.
2. Volatility of returns was moderately lower than that of world equities.
3. Returns exhibited strong positive first-order autocorrelation.
4. Maximum drawdown was moderately milder than observed for global equities.

Index (Jan. 2000–Dec. 2018)	HFRI Relative Value: Fixed Income-Convertible Arbitrage Index	MSCI World Equity
Annualized Arithmetic Mean	5.7%	4.5%
Annualized Standard Deviation	7.0%	15.0%
Annualized Semivolatility	7.2%	11.6%
Annualized Median	7.7%	11.6%
Skewness	−2.8	−0.7
Excess Kurtosis	26.0	1.6
Sharpe Ratio	0.5	0.1
Sortino Ratio	0.4	0.2
Annualized Geometric Mean	5.5%	3.4%
First-Order Autocorrelation	0.57	0.14
Annualized Standard Deviation (Adjusted for Autocorrelation)	13.5%	17.1%
Maximum	9.7%	11.2%
Minimum	−16.0%	−19.0%
Max Drawdown	−35.3%	−54.0%

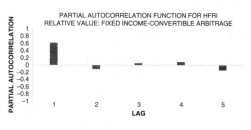

Index (Jan. 2000–Dec. 2018)	HFRI Relative Value (Total)	MSCI World Equity
Annualized Arithmetic Mean	6.1%	4.5%
Annualized Standard Deviation	4.0%	15.0%
Annualized Semivolatility	4.1%	11.6%
Annualized Median	7.5%	11.6%
Skewness	−2.6	−0.7
Excess Kurtosis	16.5	1.6
Sharpe Ratio	0.9	0.1
Sortino Ratio	0.9	0.2
Annualized Geometric Mean	6.0%	3.4%
First-Order Autocorrelation	0.53	0.14
Annualized Standard Deviation (Adjusted for Autocorrelation)	7.2%	17.1%
Maximum	3.9%	11.2%
Minimum	−8.0%	−19.0%
Max Drawdown	−18.0%	−54.0%

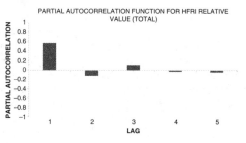

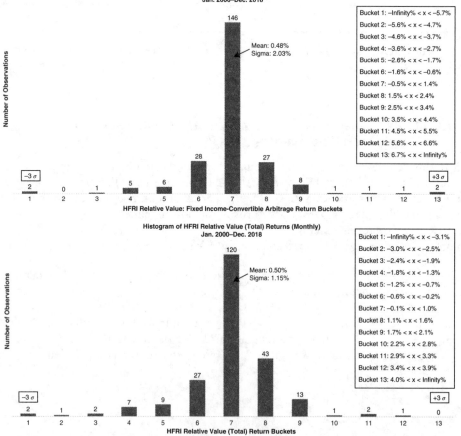

EXHIBIT 17.7   Statistical Summary of Returns

17.3 VOLATILITY ARBITRAGE

Trading on the basis of prices is as old as money itself. The concept of explicitly trading on the basis of asset price volatility is relatively new. **Volatility arbitrage** is any strategy that attempts to earn a superior and riskless profit based on prices that explicitly depend on volatility.

17.3.1 Volatility and Vega Overview

Any security that contains a nontrivial option feature may be viewed as having a direct relationship between its price and the volatility of the underlying asset, holding all other values constant. Often multiple security prices depend on the same underlying asset volatility (or related asset volatilities). Examples include options on the same asset that differ with regard to strike price, expiration date, type of option (e.g., European, American, Bermuda, range, and knockout), and being calls or puts. This permits traders to speculate on the relative performance of the multiple securities with option characteristics and with the same underlying asset.

A key concept in volatility arbitrage and options in general is vega. **Vega** is a measure of the risk of a position or an asset due to changes in the volatility of a price or rate that helps determine the value of that position or asset. For example, in the case of an option, vega is the first derivative of the option price with respect to the implied volatility of the returns of the asset underlying the option. **Vega risk** is the economic dispersion caused by changes in the volatility of a price, return, or rate.

A key distinction in volatility involves differences between implied volatility, anticipated volatility, and realized volatility. In all three cases, volatility is defined as the standard deviation of returns. Implied volatility, as discussed earlier, is the level of volatility in an option's underlying asset inferred by the current price of the option based on a particular option pricing model. Implied volatility is a mathematical computation performed by searching for the level of asset volatility that, when inserted into a specified option pricing model, generates a model price that equals the current market price of the option. **Anticipated volatility** is the future level of volatility expected by a market participant. Realized volatility, as discussed previously, is a statistically based estimate of the actual historical volatility experienced in the marketplace. Market participants often develop anticipations of volatility based on observations of realized volatility. They then compare the anticipated volatility with the implied volatility of options, taking long option positions when their anticipations of volatility exceed the implied volatility and short option positions when their anticipations of volatility are lower than the implied volatility.

It is especially important in discussing volatility arbitrage funds to be careful regarding the use and meaning of the term *volatility*. Outside investments, volatility is interpreted as simply indicating dispersion. Within investments, volatility is typically used specifically as and synonymously with standard deviation. However, in the area of volatility derivatives and variance derivatives, the terminology is evolving, and it is not always clear that volatility refers solely to standard deviation or that variance derivatives reference only variance.

Sinclair presents some stylized observations regarding volatility, many of which are key assumptions behind some volatility arbitrage portfolio strategies and risk management techniques:

1. Volatility is not constant, but it mean-reverts, clusters, and has long memory. As such, many traders will model volatility using a regime-switching model.
2. Volatility tends to stay low for some extended period of time until a market shock occurs and volatility transitions to a higher level for some period of time.
3. The volatility of volatility can be high, but in the long run, volatility tends to revert toward some long-term average level.
4. In equity markets, volatility tends to increase as price levels decline.
5. Volatility tends to rise more quickly in response to stock prices falling than it falls in response to stock prices rising.[3]

The final two observations may partially explain volatility skew levels, in which equity put option prices often trade at higher implied volatility levels than equity call option prices of similar deltas.

17.3.2 Instruments Used by Volatility Arbitrage Funds

Managers of volatility arbitrage funds have substantial latitude in the choice of assets to trade in their funds. Broadly speaking, these funds may have positions in any instrument with volatility exposure. These assets include exchange-traded options, warrants, convertible bonds, other bonds with embedded options, over-the-counter (OTC) options, and OTC variance swaps. In recent years, a robust exchange-traded market has arisen in volatility futures and options, trading specifically on the Chicago Board Options Exchange (Cboe) Volatility Index (VIX), which measures the implied volatility of options on the S&P 500 Index. A given volatility arbitrage fund may focus on these assets within one market, such as equities, while others may mix instruments across currency, debt, equity, credit, and commodity markets. In addition to holding assets with option characteristics, volatility arbitrage funds also hold assets without option characteristics in order to hedge or reduce their net exposure to moves in the underlying markets. The simplest examples of positions taken by volatility arbitrage funds involve exchange-traded options and warrants, whose performance is tied to price moves in single-equity securities or futures contracts in the equity, commodity, currency, or debt markets. In order to focus trading on volatility, traders follow a strict delta-hedging process to hedge away moves in the underlying market.

Bonds with embedded options can also be attractive to managers of volatility arbitrage funds. Convertible bonds have an embedded long call option on the issuer's stock, whereas mortgage-backed securities (MBS) are short a put option on interest rates (which is a short call option on bond prices), meaning borrowers are allowed to prepay their mortgages without penalty. Complex or illiquid securities may offer higher expected returns and more frequent opportunities from mispricing. For example, valuation of MBS requires assumptions regarding future interest rate paths and volatility, as well as the potential prepayment rates of the borrowers under various interest rate scenarios.

Variance swaps are forward contracts in which one party agrees to make a cash payment to the other party based on the realized variance of a price or rate in exchange for receiving a predetermined cash flow. Variance swaps are OTC products and are commonly traded by volatility arbitrage funds. These contracts offer cash flows based on the annualized variance in the returns on a referenced asset. In a variance swap, one party (the variance buyer) pays a predetermined variance (referred to as a swap strike price or strike variance) and receives realized variance. The counterparty (the variance seller) has the opposite cash flow exposure, receiving a fixed variance and paying realized variance. The amount of the net cash flow is the difference between the realized variance and the strike variance multiplied by the variance notional value of the contract. The **variance notional value** of the contract simply scales the size of the cash flows in a variance swap. The annualized variance is simply the squared value of the annualized standard deviation. At maturity, a variance swap pays off according to the following formula:

$$\text{Variance Swap Payoff} = \text{Variance Notional Value} \times (\text{Realized Variance} - \text{Strike Variance}) \quad (17.2a)$$

For example, consider a 30-day variance swap on the returns of the S&P 500 Index with a variance notional value of $100,000. The strike variance of the swap is 4.00 (corresponding to a 4% annualized variance). After the 30-day reference period is observed, the realized annualized variance in the index is, for example, 4.50. The payoff of the variance swap would be as follows:

$$\text{Variance Swap Payoff} = \$100,000 \times (4.50 - 4.00) = \$50,000$$

 APPLICATION 17.3.2A

Consider a 30-day variance swap with a notional value of $250,000. The strike variance is 9.00. The realized variance of the index is 7.00. What would be the payment or payoff of the swap?

The variance swap payoff:

$$\$250,000 \times (7.00 - 9.00) = \$-500,000$$

The swap buyer received the realized variance and pays the strike variance, so in this example the swap buyer pays $500,000 to the variance swap payer.

A **volatility swap** mirrors a variance swap except that the payoff of the contract is linearly based on the standard deviation of a return series rather than the variance. In a volatility swap, the payoff is determined by multiplying the spread between the realized volatility and the strike volatility by the vega notional value. Similar to the variance notional value, the **vega notional value** of a contract serves to scale the contract and determine the size of the payoff in a volatility swap. The vega notional value provides a simple payoff formula for volatility swaps:

$$\text{Volatility Swap Payoff} = \text{Vega Notional Value} \times (\text{Realized Volatility} - \text{Strike Volatility}) \quad (17.2b)$$

For example, a volatility swap with a vega notional value of $50,000 would pay off $100,000 if the realized volatility was 22.00 when the strike volatility was 20.00.

 APPLICATION 17.3.2B

Consider a 30-day volatility swap with a notional value of $500,000. The strike volatility is 17.50. The realized volatility of the reference asset is 18.25. What would be the payment of the swap?

The volatility swap payoff:

$$\$500,000 \times (18.25 - 17.50) = \$375,000$$

The swap buyer receives the realized volatility and pays the strike volatility, so in this example the swap payer pays $375,000 to the swap buyer.

The payoff to a variance swap in Equation 17.2a is often expressed using an expression that includes the vega notional value in place of the variance notional value. The variance notional value is equal to the vega notional value divided by 2 times the square root of the strike variance. In other words, the vega notional value is equal to the variance notional value multiplied by 2 times the square root of the strike variance. Inserting the formula for variance notional based on vega notional value into Equation 17.2a offers the following more common but less simple and less intuitive payoff formula:

$$\text{Variance Swap Payoff} = \frac{\text{Vega Notional Value} \times (\text{Realized Variance} - \text{Strike Variance})}{2 \times \sqrt{\text{Strike Variance}}}$$

(17.8)

APPLICATION 17.3.2C

The payoff of a variance swap is $120,000. The strike variance is 9.00 and the realized variance is 10.00. What are the vega notional value and the variance notional value?

From the formula for variance swap payoff (Equation 17.8):

$$\text{Variance Swap Payoff}$$
$$= \frac{\text{Vega Notional Value} \times (\text{Realized Variance} - \text{Strike Variance})}{2 \times \sqrt{\text{Strike Variance}}}$$
$$\$120,000 = \frac{\text{Vega Notional Value} \times (10.00 - 9.00)}{2 \times \sqrt{9.00}}$$
$$\rightarrow \text{Vega Notional Value} = \$720,000$$

From the definition of variance notional value:

$$\text{Variance Notional Value} = \frac{\text{Vega Notional Value}}{2\sqrt{\text{Strike Variance}}}$$

$$\text{Variance Notional Value} = \frac{\$720,000}{2\sqrt{9.00}} \rightarrow \$120,000$$

It should be noted that the exact computation methods are specified in the documentation but are not perfectly standardized.

The attraction to variance swaps is that they offer a pure play on asset return variance without exposure to the direction of moves in the underlying instrument. To speculate on the spread between implied and realized volatility in the exchange-traded options market without variance swaps, traders need to buy one set of options, sell another set of options, and frequently rebalance the hedges to keep exposures to the underlying markets close to delta-neutral. Options can be complex, exposing traders not only to volatility exposure (vega risk) but also to moves in the underlying assets (delta and gamma risk). Variance swaps give pure volatility exposure without the directional risk of moves in the underlying assets, which eliminates the obligation to continually rehedge the delta risk of the portfolio. As OTC products, variance swaps create counterparty risk, which must be monitored at all times.

17.3.3 Risks of Exchange-Traded versus OTC Derivatives

Standardized, exchange-traded derivatives and other instruments can be less risky than some OTC instruments. Exchange trading is physically or electronically centrally located. Each instrument traded on the exchange is listed by the exchange, a process that specifies and unifies the characteristics of each instrument. OTC instruments are typically traded by investment banks and fixed-income brokerage houses and vary from being uniform (e.g., shares of common stock) to being unique (e.g., currency swaps with specific delivery dates). Generally, there are three major risks that positions in OTC-traded instruments have relative to positions in exchange-traded instruments:

1. Exchange-traded instruments tend to offer less counterparty risk. Options involve an ongoing obligation by the party with the short position (the option writer) to pay cash or deliver assets to the other party (the option owner). Swaps offer an ongoing obligation by each party to pay cash to the other party. Counterparty risk is the potential dispersion in economic outcomes caused by the potential or actual failure of the other side of a contract to fulfill its obligations. In this case, the investor and the swap dealer have counterparty risk that the other might fail to fulfill the contract. By contrast, exchange-traded derivatives have clearinghouses that back the obligations of the members associated with each listed security.

   Clearinghouses have capital and the incentives and powers to demand collateral and creditworthiness of market participants, greatly mitigating the concerns with regard to the integrity of each contract. Moreover, clearinghouses diversify risk away from a single dealer and spread the risk across multiple members (or broker-dealers), making it less exposed to a single counterparty.

2. Exchange-traded instruments tend to offer higher price transparency and less pricing risk. **Price transparency** is information on the prices and quantities at which participants are offering to buy (bid) and sell (offer) an instrument. **Pricing risk** is the economic uncertainty caused by actual or potential mispricing of positions. For example, complex and unique derivative OTC instruments might have no information on prices other than estimations derived through complex models or price indications offered by dealers. Conversely, exchange-traded instruments have easily observable prices at which trades have taken place, and bids and offers of prices at which participants are currently willing to transact.

3. Exchange-traded instruments tend to offer higher liquidity. Owing to price transparency, standardization of the terms of a security, reduced counterparty risk, and centralized trading, exchange-traded instruments tend to offer substantially higher liquidity than do OTC instruments. Liquidity provides market participants with the ability to manage their risks more effectively by being able to transact without substantially affecting market prices.

These three major risks were vividly illustrated during the global financial crisis of 2007 to 2009. For example, counterparty risk was experienced in 2008. Traders with counterparty risk exposure to particular subsidiaries of Lehman Brothers were not paid the gains on their derivative positions when Lehman Brothers defaulted. Further losses to counterparties were avoided when the U.S. government was called on to guarantee the payment of OTC derivative contracts that had been sold by American International Group, Inc.

The price transparency of exchange-traded products facilitates the use of mark-to-market pricing. **Marking-to-market** refers to the use of current market prices to value instruments, positions, portfolios, and even the balance sheets of firms. The use of OTC derivatives often partially or fully relies on pricing based on a mark-to-model methodology. **Marking-to-model** refers to valuation based on prices generated by pricing models. The pricing models generally involve two components. An instrument that is not frequently traded, and therefore does not offer price transparency, is modeled as being related to one or more market prices, rates, or factors. The current values of the determinants of the model price are then input into the model to approximate the value of the instrument. Thus, marking-to-model requires the specification of a model and its inputs. A problem with marking-to-model is that different investors holding similar securities may report widely different valuations to their investors based on the assumptions underlying their proprietary pricing model or the inputs used. In comparison, exchange-traded products are marked-to-market, wherein all investors value their holdings at a single, exchange-disseminated price.

17.3.4 Volatility Arbitrage Strategies

An essential concept to understanding volatility arbitrage strategies is vega. As previously defined, vega is the sensitivity of an option or a security with an embedded option to changes in the volatility of the price or the returns of the asset underlying the option. A long position in an option has a positive vega, a short position in an option has a negative vega, and a position without option characteristics has a vega of zero. Note that vega indicates the sensitivity of an asset to changes in volatility assuming all other values are held constant. In practice, when volatility changes, there are usually changes in price levels.

Volatility arbitrage funds trade a variety of assets, typically taking long positions in instruments in which volatility is underpriced (or underestimated), and short positions in instruments in which volatility is overpriced (or overestimated). Other market risks are often hedged out, leaving the fund with less directional risk to the underlying markets. Instead, the positions are exposed to volatility risk and correlation risk. **Volatility risk** is dispersion in economic outcomes attributable to changes in realized or anticipated levels of volatility in a market price or rate. **Correlation risk** is dispersion in economic outcomes attributable to changes in realized or anticipated levels of correlation between market prices or rates.

As markets move, the fund manager needs to continue to implement rebalancing trades to remain delta-neutral. These rebalancing trades are profitable for long volatility positions that have positive gamma and unprofitable for short volatility positions that have negative gamma. However, positions long in vega are usually exposed to theta risk (negative theta), such that as time passes in a period with low asset volatility, the positions decline in value.

There are two main types of volatility arbitrage funds: those that are market (volatility) neutral and those that are intentionally exposed—typically long—to volatility. An example of a long volatility strategy is a variance buyer in a variance swap. The position either generates a payoff or requires a payoff based entirely on realized volatility. Long volatility funds can provide valuable tail risk protection during times of rising volatility, when markets are likely to decline. Market-neutral volatility funds seek to earn a profit without exposure to changes in volatility levels. An example of a market-neutral volatility strategy would be offsetting positions in two options with different implied volatilities in the same or similar underlying assets. The profit or loss is primarily driven by changes in the relationship between the two implied volatilities rather than the level of volatilities.

17.3.5 Market-Neutral Volatility Funds

The most common strategy pursued by market-neutral volatility funds has been to make the assumption that there is an arbitrage opportunity between the higher implied volatility and the lower realized volatility for some options. In other words, the assumption is that some options are overpriced, and the trading strategy involves writing those options. The fund hedges the overall exposure of short positions in the options perceived as being overpriced by taking one or more offsetting positions in securities deemed to be more appropriately priced. As an example, a fund may sell equity index options and hedge the risk with a dynamically adjusted replicating portfolio of equity index futures that approximates the returns of the realized variance of the underlying equity market.

One example of why implied volatility of some options might consistently overestimate realized volatilities involves out-of-the-money index puts. Due to the demand for index put options to serve as protection from downside risk, implied volatility of out-of-the-money index put options is frequently believed to trade higher relative to realized volatility. The spread between implied and realized volatility compensates volatility sellers for providing insurance against rising volatility and falling markets. This spread is likely to continue as long as sellers of index volatility continue to demand a risk premium for providing insurance coverage to other market participants and as long as insurance buyers continue to be willing to pay for the protection.

17.3.6 Challenges of Estimating Dispersion

Care is necessary in interpreting measures of dispersion in the context of volatility derivatives. First, there are numerous conventions for calculating dispersion, so implied versus realized computations should be compared only when both series are calculated with consistent methodologies. Second, the payoff of variance swaps is linearly related to the square of volatility (i.e., variance is the square of standard deviation) and is therefore highly nonlinear relative to volatility, or standard deviation. Estimates of implied standard deviation based on observation of derivative prices with payouts linearly related to variance, such as those shown in Equation 17.8, are biased as predictors of volatility.

Suppose that the realized volatility of an asset has exactly six equally likely outcomes: 1%, 2%, 3%, 4%, 5%, or 6%. The expected value of the volatility is 3.5%. Now consider the same dispersion expressed in term of variance: 0.0001, 0.0004, 0.0009, 0.0016, 0.0025, and 0.0036. The expected value of the variance is approximately 0.152. The volatility corresponding to this variance is approximately 39%. The square root of the expected variance differs substantially from the expected volatility (standard deviation). Special care should be taken in comparing volatility computations and variance computations.

☞ APPLICATION 17.3.6A

Suppose that the realized volatility of an asset has exactly five equally likely outcomes: 1%, 3%, 4%, 5%, or 7%. Calculate: (1) The expected value of the realized volatility, (2) the five equally likely realized variances corresponding to the five given outcomes (volatilities), (3) the expected value of the five variances, and (4) the value of volatility that corresponds to the value found in Step 3 (i.e., the volatility that corresponds with the expected variance).

(1) The expectation of the five outcomes provided (i.e., realized volatilities) is 4%, found as the sum of the five outcomes divided by 5. (2) The five variances (expressed as a decimal) corresponding to the five volatilities are: 0.0001, 0.0009, 0.0016, 0.0025, and 0.0049. (3) The expected value of the five equally likely values found in Step 2 is the sum divided by five: $(0.0100/5) = 0.0020$. (4) The value of volatility that corresponds to a variance of 0.0020 is found as its square root: 4.47%. Note that the expected variance—expressed as a volatility—differs substantially from the expected volatility (standard deviation). This issue needs to be considered in comparing derivatives with payoffs based on expected volatility with those based on expected variance.

17.3.7 Tail Risk Strategies

Tail risk is the potential for very large loss exposures due to very unusual events, especially those associated with widespread market price declines. Entities with undesirably high exposures to tail risk may seek protection from tail risk that is often termed portfolio insurance. **Portfolio insurance** is any financial method, arrangement, or program for limiting losses from large adverse price movements. Portfolio insurance can be provided through dynamic trading strategies that hedge losses, such as taking short positions in corresponding futures contracts that are adjusted in size based on market levels. Portfolio insurance can also be provided by establishing positions in investments that thrive during periods associated with tail risk. A straightforward solution is to purchase long positions in put options that are very far out-of-the-money. The problem with buying puts that are far out-of-the-money is that they are often viewed as being priced very high. In other words, market participants often view those options as having implied volatility that substantially exceeds expectations of realized volatility. Purchasing out-of-the-money put options at high implied volatilities can be a substantial drag on portfolio performance when, as usually happens, there are no crises and the options expire worthlessly. The explanation for the high implied volatilities is that there is tremendous demand from institutional investors to hold the options for protection against tail risk and a limited number of market participants with the financial resources and desire to provide such protection by writing the puts.

Tail risk strategies may be viewed as attempts to fill the market need for portfolio protection without the potentially large costs of purchasing put options that regularly expire worthlessly and that therefore generate losses during normal market conditions. Some volatility arbitrage funds attempt to design tail risk strategies that earn substantial profits during times of stress, panics, crises, and widespread losses, and generate only small losses or perhaps even small gains during most other market conditions.

For example, a fund may develop a strategy of taking long positions in options with implied volatilities that are deemed low and writing options with implied volatilities that are deemed high. The fund may believe that these particular option positions will permit large profits in the event of a major market decline while having very limited losses in normal markets. It should be noted that option-like payoffs can be attempted using non-option securities through dynamic rebalancing strategies. For example, a strategy that buys additional assets when asset prices rise and liquidates positions when asset prices decline exhibits high upside potential and low downside risk, similar to that of a long call option position. However, such strategies are likely to fail during periods of extreme market stress or over times when markets are closed, since prices and volatility can jump before the necessary dynamic adjustments can be implemented.

The payoff profile of tail risk funds is designed to be negatively correlated to price levels in major markets, especially equity and credit markets. As equity markets decline and credit spreads widen, volatility and correlation tend to increase. Tail risk funds that can profit during these times of crisis can serve as a hedge to the risk exposures of traditional equity and credit market investors. These tail risk funds are used by investors who mix the tail risk strategies into portfolios with substantial long exposure to equity and credit investments to provide a combined portfolio with the goal of profitability during normal market conditions and little or no downside risk during periods of market stress.

Funds that offer the attractive payoff profile of providing tail risk protection may be relatively delta-neutral for small changes in market conditions but lose their delta neutrality for large changes so that they can generate gains during large market drops. In other words, the strategies are long gamma. The strategies are also long vega, since they benefit from rising levels of volatility.

Correlation among assets is a crucial issue in tail risk strategies. During normal market conditions, it is observed that, for example, stocks have modest correlation with each other, simultaneously rising or falling by different amounts. However, during periods of market stress, it is often said that correlations go to one. The term **correlations go to one** means that during periods of enormous stress, stocks and bonds with credit risk decline simultaneously and with somewhat similar magnitudes. However, some analysts prefer to describe this phenomenon by breaking movements in risky assets into market risks and idiosyncratic risks. During normal market conditions, price changes due to idiosyncratic factors are not dominated by changes due to market factors, so correlations between risky assets are modest. The reason is that idiosyncratic movements are uncorrelated by definition. However, during periods of stress, the market factors dominate the idiosyncratic factors, causing risky assets to have highly correlated returns. The reason is that the market-related movements of the individual assets are perfectly correlated by definition. The point of this analysis is that the underlying correlations, parameters, and processes do not change during periods of market stress. Rather, during these periods of stress, market factors experience larger volatility and therefore exert larger effects than do idiosyncratic factors. However, not all assets have returns that increase in correlation with each other during a market crisis. There are defensive assets that have historically been able to maintain their value or even post profits in a market crisis, actually moving toward negative one in terms of correlation with risky assets. These defensive assets may include long put options, long call options on volatility, sovereign debt, and even some hedge fund strategies, such as global macro or managed futures.

Tail risk funds tend to be less focused on pure arbitrage and therefore take positions across markets, attempting to sell overpriced volatility and buy underpriced volatility in whatever markets can be found. If tail risk strategies are able to post large gains during times of market crisis, owners of these funds gain access to valuable cash when other investors may have constrained liquidity in their portfolios. This improved cash position can provide substantial benefits to investors. Investors may be able to avoid losses due to liquidity concerns, such as by being able to fund capital calls to real estate and private equity funds without selling equity and credit investments after sharp market declines. The cash generated from the tail risk portfolio can also be used to opportunistically purchase assets at fire-sale prices from distressed investors who need to raise cash. Although the benefits of a tail risk fund are clear, the challenge to the fund manager is to provide protection during crisis markets without paying too much in option premiums during normal market conditions, which can persist for a very long time. In essence, the strategy attempts to mimic the payouts to out-of-the-money put protection at a lower cost through the implementation of sophisticated trading strategies.

17.3.8 The Dispersion Trade

The **classic dispersion trade** is a market-neutral short correlation trade, popular among volatility arbitrage practitioners, that typically takes long positions in options listed on the equities of single companies and short positions in a related index option. For example, a fund may buy options on 50 different large-capitalization, U.S.-listed firms and take a short position in options listed on the S&P 500 Index. Typically, the goal is to create a basket of options on individual assets that mimics the composition of the index closely, perhaps by matching the industry weights of the portfolio.

The key to the dispersion trade is the relationship between a portfolio of options and a single option on a portfolio. That relationship is driven by volatility, which in turn is driven by correlations across assets. Portfolio variance is lower when the constituent stocks have lower volatility and lower correlation with each other. Conversely, as the correlations between stocks rise, portfolio variance increases, as there are fewer stocks experiencing offsetting price moves. Thus, the relative returns of options on indices and options on individual assets are driven by changes in the anticipated correlation among the assets. In practice, individual assets are not highly correlated with each other, so the realized volatility of individual assets tends to be substantially higher than the realized volatility of a related index. Therefore, the implied volatilities of options on individual assets tend to be higher than the implied volatility of an option on a related index. Equation 17.9 expresses the variance of the return of a portfolio as depending on the variance of the constituent assets and their correlations:

$$V(R_p) = \sum_{i=1}^{n} \sum_{j=1}^{n} w_i w_j \sigma_i \sigma_j \rho_{ij} \qquad (17.9)$$

where $V(R_p)$ is the variance of the portfolio, R_p is the return on the portfolio, n is the number of assets in the portfolio, w_i is the weight of asset i in the portfolio, σ_i is the standard deviation of returns for asset i, and ρ_{ij} is the correlation coefficient between returns on assets i and j. When $i = j$, $\rho_{ij} = 1$.

In summary, correlation drives the magnitude of the differences between the volatilities of individual assets and portfolios. Lower values of correlation generate lower portfolio risk through diversification, whereas higher correlation inhibits diversification. Dispersion trades are speculations on correlation. The classic dispersion trade is that realized correlations between assets will be lower than the correlation implied by the pricing of index options relative to options on individual assets. Therefore, the classic dispersion trade is referred to as a **short correlation** trade because the trade generates profits from low levels of realized correlation and losses from high levels of realized correlation.

17.3.9 Profit and Loss on Dispersion Trades

Profits from the classic dispersion trade (long individual asset options and short index options) are the greatest during times of declining correlation, and losses occur when correlations rise significantly. The logic and terminology of dispersion trades parallel those of most option trading. Fund managers focus on the difference between implied correlations and realized correlations rather than implied volatility and realized volatility. The ideal condition for a classic dispersion trade is when implied correlation between stocks is high and the fund manager can consistently predict when realized correlation is going to be lower. Conversely, traders may implement a reverse dispersion trade—buying the index options and writing the single stock options—when implied correlation is lower than the trader's expectation for realized correlation.

As an example, consider a basket of four stocks (stocks A, B, C, and D), each of which is one-quarter of the weight of an index. Begin by assuming that the classic dispersion trade is implemented by purchasing equal quantities of four call options that are near-the-money on the four individual stocks and writing call options on the index. The short position in the index calls is assumed to have an aggregated magnitude in terms of underlying asset value equal to the sum of the underlying asset values of the four individual options. Assume that the options have three months to expiration, that the implied correlation among the four individual stocks in the index is equal to 0.30, and that the implied annualized volatilities of the individual options are all 0.40.

The profits from the classic dispersion trade are high when the realized correlation is lower than the implied correlation (i.e., when realized volatilities on individual stocks are relatively high, and realized volatilities on the index are relatively low). For example, if stocks A and B rise in value by 50% during the lifetime of the options, and stocks C and D fall by 50% over the same time period, the profitability of the single stock call options on A and B is extremely high due to the large upward movement in the underlying stocks. The call options on stocks C and D are worthless. The positive gamma ensures that the profits on the options on A and B will exceed the losses on C and D, so that the aggregated long positions in the individual options perform very well. Note that although the stocks experienced large moves, the stock market index was unchanged, as the positive returns on A and B were offset by the negative returns on C and D. The correlations among the assets in the index were a mix of positive and negative values. Since the stock market index was unchanged, the index options that had been written expire worthless, making for an extremely profitable dispersion trade. In a nutshell, the realized correlation was lower than the implied correlation.

Note that the dispersion trade in this example would also be very profitable using put options instead of call options. In that case, the put options on C and D would pay off well, while the losses on the put options on A and B would be limited. Further, the short position in the index put would generate a profit by expiring worthlessly. The reason that either calls or puts would generate profits is that the market remained unchanged.

Having analyzed the profitability of the classic dispersion trade, it is easy to compute the profitability of the reverse trade (buying the index option and writing the individual options). The reverse trade would have lost money using calls or puts, since the classic trade and reverse trade are mirror images of each other. Delta neutrality can be pursued either by mixing calls and puts (i.e., using straddles and strangles) or by hedging with the underlying assets of the options.

Now consider what would happen in a classic dispersion trade using call options if all four stocks moved up 50% together or down 50% together. In other words, what would happen if the realized correlation was 1.00? If all four stocks rose 50%,

EXHIBIT 17.8 Summary of Volatility Arbitrage Risks

Risk	Effect
Underlying markets: equity, credit, commodity, currency, and interest rates	Market-neutral volatility arbitrage funds seek to minimize risks to underlying markets through delta-hedging trades. Tail risk funds may retain substantial exposure to changes in underlying markets.
Correlation	Market-neutral and dispersion trades are short correlation trades that seek to benefit from market convergence. Tail risk funds are long correlation trades, seeking to benefit during times of market crisis.
Volatility	Market-neutral funds try to minimize volatility exposure, seeking to take offsetting long and short volatility positions. Tail risk funds typically benefit during times of rising volatility.
Counterparty	Exchange-traded positions have minimal counterparty risks, whereas OTC trades can incur substantial counterparty risks, which need to be monitored and controlled.
Liquidity	Some positions, especially those in credit instruments and structured products, incur substantial liquidity risks. Trades placed on exchange-traded markets have much lower liquidity risks.

all four call options on the individual stocks, as well as the index option, would pay approximately 50% of the value of the underlying assets; and given the weighting assumptions, the aggregated payoff would be zero, due to the loss on the short position in the index option. If all four stocks fell by 50%, all four call options as well as the index option would expire worthlessly, and the aggregated payoff would again be zero. However, the classic trade would generate losses in either scenario, since the positions required an initial outlay of capital. The reason that establishing the positions required an initial outlay was that the options on the individual stocks cost more than the income the writing of the index option generated; this is because the implied volatilities of the individual options exceeded the implied volatility of the index, which is always the case when the implied correlation is less than one.

17.3.10 Summary of Five Volatility Arbitrage Risks

Exhibit 17.8 summarizes the risks of various volatility arbitrage strategies. Note that five major determinants of performance are the returns in the underlying market, correlation, volatility, counterparty solvency, and market liquidity. Knowledge of the risks related to volatility arbitrage performance is essential.

Index (Jan. 2005–Dec. 2018)	HFRX Relative Value: Volatility Index	MSCI World Equity
Annualized Arithmetic Mean	3.3%	6.6%
Annualized Standard Deviation	5.3%	14.7%
Annualized Semivolatility	6.2%	12.1%
Annualized Median	2.5%	4.7%
Skewness	−2.4	−0.9
Excess Kurtosis	8.7	2.7
Sharpe Ratio	0.1	0.3
Sortino Ratio	0.1	0.3
Annualized Geometric Mean	3.1%	5.5%
First-Order Autocorrelation	0.09	0.15
Annualized Standard Deviation (Adjusted for Autocorrelation)	8.2%	17.2%
Maximum	2.8%	11.2%
Minimum	−7.7%	−19.0%
Max Drawdown	−15.4%	−54.0%

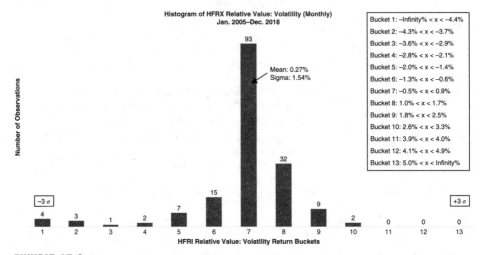

EXHIBIT 17.9   Statistical Summary of Returns

17.3.11 Key Observations Regarding Historical Returns of Relative Value Volatility Funds

Monthly returns to relative value volatility funds are observed from January of 2000 to December of 2018, for a total of 228 observations. Exhibit 17.9 provides univariate return statistics in the top panel, partial autocorrelations of returns in the middle panel, and a histogram of returns in the bottom panel. Due to a shorter track record, the following statistics mix data from the HFRX and HFRI Relative Value: Volatility indices.

Key observations on relative value volatility returns that are consistent with economic reasoning are an essential component of knowledge and include the following.

1. The historical return distribution of HFRI Relative Value: Volatility exhibited modestly greater left skew and quite high excess kurtosis relative to global equities.
2. Volatility of returns was very substantially lower than that of world equities.
3. Returns exhibited modest positive first-order autocorrelation.
4. Maximum drawdown was very much better than that observed for global equities.

17.4 FIXED-INCOME ARBITRAGE

Fixed-income arbitrage involves simultaneous long and short positions in fixed-income securities with the expectation that over the investment holding period, the security prices will converge toward a similar valuation standard.

17.4.1 The Core of Fixed-Income Arbitrage Strategies

At the core of any arbitrage strategy is a model of how prices should behave. This model may be based on theory, empirical observations, or both. The arbitrage is often performed on a pair of securities with a long position in one security offset by a short position in the other security. However, the arbitrage can involve any number of longs and shorts.

An example of a three-security trade is as follows: Assume that based on theoretical reasons or past observations, a fund manager predicts that the yield on 9-month debt will trade at a particular relationship to the yields on 6-month and 12-month debt. Assume that the fund manager predicts that the 9-month yield will trade within five basis points of the mean between the other two yields in a particular market. The fund manager might take a long position in the 9-month debt whenever its yield trades above this relationship, while taking offsetting short positions in the 6-month and 12-month bonds. The fund manager is speculating that the yield on the 9-month debt will decline relative to the average yields of the other two bonds as its yield returns toward the long-term relationship that the fund manager predicts. Note that the manager is not speculating necessarily that the 9-month yield is absolutely high or that the 6- and 12-month yields are absolutely low. Rather, the manager is speculating on the relative values and, in particular, that the relative values will converge as predicted by the manager's model.

Fixed-income arbitrage managers search continuously for pricing inefficiencies across all fixed-income markets. These arbitrage strategies are similar to the traditional goal of buying low and selling high. However, in arbitrage, the trade is based on relative value rather than absolute value, and the goal is to hedge the aggregated position against all risks other than the specific behavior on which the manager is speculating. The arbitrageur hedges the positions against market factors such as credit risks and general interest rate risks, then waits for the relatively under-valued security (or securities) to increase in value, the relatively overvalued security (or securities) to decline in value, or both to occur.

In most cases, trades are designed to be duration-neutral. **Duration** is a measure of the sensitivity of a fixed-income security to a change in the general level of interest rates, as discussed in Chapter 5. A duration-neutral position means that the returns to the position are relatively insensitive to changes in the general level of market interest rates. However, fixed-income positions can also be exposed to other risks, such as changes in credit spreads, changes in yield curve shapes, changes in volatility, and changes in liquidity. Generally, the perceived relative mispricing between fixed-income securities is small. Thus, the potential profit of the fixed-income arbitrageur is typically small relative to the sizes of the long and short positions. By controlling for other risks, the hedge fund manager attempts to generate returns driven solely by the behavior of the pricing discrepancy. If the pricing discrepancy converges over time, the strategy should generate a profit. If the pricing discrepancy diverges further, the positions generate losses.

Given the relatively small potential profits as a proportion of position sizes, hedge fund managers typically add more profit potential through leveraging their portfolios with direct borrowings from their prime brokers or with swaps and other derivative securities. This leverage can lead to substantial positive returns when prices return to their predicted levels, which typically happens in normal markets but can create disastrous losses in turbulent environments. Key issues in such arbitrage strategies are managing liquidity and adjusting the size of the positions as perceived price discrepancies diverge further and further in turbulent markets. If positions are reduced, the fund may have reduced its profit potential when the prospects for future profits are at their highest. However, if positions are maintained or increased as losses mount, the firm runs the risk of being forced to liquidate when price discrepancies and losses are at their highest levels.

17.4.2 Types of Fixed-Income Arbitrage Strategies

There are numerous ways to categorize fixed-income arbitrage strategies. Within a particular bond market, positions may be established by anticipating various changes in relationships. These strategies include speculations that the yield curve will become less steeply sloped (yield flattener), that the yield curve will become more steeply sloped (yield steepener), or that portions of the curve will become more curved or less curved (yield butterflies). These are examples of **intracurve arbitrage positions** because they are based on hedged positions within the same yield curve.

A **yield curve** is the relationship between the yields of various securities, usually depicted on the vertical axis, and the term to maturity, usually depicted on the horizontal axis. The terms *yield curve* and *term structure of interest rates* are often used interchangeably. Sometimes the **term structure of interest rates** is distinguished from the yield curve because the yield curve plots yields to maturity of coupon bonds, whereas the term structure of interest rates plots actual or hypothetical yields of zero-coupon bonds.

There are also **intercurve arbitrage positions**, which means arbitrage (hedged positions) using securities related to different yield curves. Examples include swap spread trading (arbitraging differences in swap rates) and carry trades. **Carry trades** attempt to earn profits from carrying or maintaining long positions in higher-yielding assets and short positions in lower-yielding assets without suffering from adverse price movements. For further examples, see Duarte, Longstaff, and Yu's "Risk and Return in Fixed-Income Arbitrage: Nickels in Front of a Steamroller?"[4] They discuss swap-spread arbitrage, yield-curve arbitrage, mortgage arbitrage, volatility arbitrage, and capital-structure arbitrage.

Fixed-income arbitrage funds are often differentiated by the markets in which they speculate. These markets fall into a number of categories, including sovereign debt and asset-backed or mortgage-backed securities.

17.4.3 Fixed-Income Arbitrage Strategies: Sovereign Debt

Sovereign debt is debt issued by national governments. Sovereign debt possesses distinct credit risks from corporate debt because governments can choose to default on their obligations even when they are technically able to meet them. Further, most national governments can use monetary policy to alter the value of their currency and thereby change the real value of their outstanding obligations. In other words, most national governments can literally print money to pay their debts but can choose to default anyway. Sovereign debt ranges in creditworthiness from the low-credit-risk obligations of the largest and most secure nations to the obligations of the least creditworthy nations. Fixed-income arbitrage and hedging using the obligations of the U.S. government are illustrated here. Fixed-income arbitrage does not need to use exotic securities. For example, it can be nothing more than buying and selling U.S. Treasury securities. In the U.S. bond market, the most liquid securities are on-the-run U.S. Treasury bonds. On-the-run Treasury bonds are the most currently issued bonds for each common maturity issued by the U.S. Treasury Department (e.g., 3-month, 6-month, and 12-month Treasury bills; 10-year notes; and so forth). There are other U.S. Treasury bonds outstanding (known as off-the-run) that have similar maturities and coupons to the on-the-run Treasury bonds. However, off-the-run bonds were issued much earlier than on-the-run bonds and are now less liquid, as dealers are less actively trading them and many of them have been bought and held by long-term investors. As a result, price discrepancies occur among off-the-run issues, as well as between on-the-run and off-the-run issues. The difference in prices may be very small, just a few 32nds of 1%, but can increase in times of high uncertainty, when there are high and erratic levels of trading as investors shift money into and out of the most liquid U.S. Treasury bonds in response to the market crisis.

Another form of fixed-income arbitrage involves trading among maturity ranges of fixed-income securities, especially those that are relatively close to maturity. This is a form of yield-curve arbitrage. These types of trades are driven by temporary imbalances in the supply of and demand for the securities that apparently cause temporary distortions in the yield curve. Kinks in the yield curve can happen at any maturity and usually reflect a change in liquidity demand around the focal point. These kinks provide an opportunity to speculate on changes in the shape of the yield curve by purchasing and selling Treasury securities that are similar in maturity. Investors who hold bonds can view their returns as being driven not just by shifts in the yield curve but also by the change in a bond's yield if the yield curve remains constant and the maturity of the bond shortens. The process of holding a bond as its yield moves up or down the yield curve due to the passage of time is known as **riding the yield curve**. Consider a yield curve with an upward slope between the two-year and five-year maturities. The holder of the five-year Treasury bond can profit by rolling down or riding down the yield curve toward the two-year rate if the yield curve does not shift. **Rolling down** the yield curve is the process of experiencing decreasing yields to maturity as an asset's maturity declines through time in an upward-sloping yield curve environment. In other words, if the yield curve remains static, the five-year Treasury note ages into a lower-yielding part of the yield curve.

Continuing the example of a yield curve that slopes upward, the investor might buy a five-year note at a yield of 5.2% and hold it for three years. If the yield curve has not changed over this holding period, the resulting two-year note position will now fall to a yield of perhaps 5.1%. As the bond's yield falls from 5.2% to 5.1% with the passage of time, the owner of this bond has a profit from rolling down the curve. Moving down the yield curve generally means positive price appreciation as a bond's yield declines. Conversely, Treasury bonds with maturities in a downward-sloping range of the yield curve roll up the yield curve to higher yields if the yield curve remains static. This means that the bond prices would underperform if the yield curve remains static and the bond ages into a higher-yielding maturity range. The slope of the yield curve usually differs across various maturity ranges. Based on differences in the slopes along the yield curve, an arbitrage trade might be to purchase bonds in an upward-sloping maturity range and short bonds in a downward-sloping maturity range. As the short bond positions roll up the yield curve, their values should decline as yields rise, while the long bond positions should increase in value as they roll down the yield curve. This arbitrage trade will work as long as the yield curve is static. In an efficient market, the yield curve could be expected to shift in a manner to make expected risk-adjusted returns equal.

Attempts to arbitrage yield curves have risks. First, shifts in the yield curve up or down can affect the profitability of the trade if it is not duration-neutral. A **duration-neutral** position is a portfolio in which the aggregated durations of the short positions equal the aggregated durations of the long positions weighted by value. A duration-neutral position is protected from value changes due to shifts in the yield curve that are small, immediate, and parallel. A **parallel shift** in the yield curve happens when yields of all maturities shift up or down by equal (additive) amounts. However, a hedge that is duration-neutral does not necessarily provide perfect interest rate immunization. **Interest rate immunization** is the process of eliminating all interest rate risk exposures. Duration-neutral positions may still be exposed to the risks of large or nonparallel interest rate shifts. To provide immunization against more general interest rate behavior, the hedge fund manager needs to regularly adjust the positions to maintain duration neutrality and possibly needs to introduce other positions to provide protection from other sources of risk, such as large and nonparallel yield curve shifts.

For fixed-income securities without option characteristics, duration is calculated as the value-weighted average time to maturity of the security's principal and coupon cash flows. A zero-coupon bond pays only the principal value at maturity with no coupon payments, so its duration equals its maturity. Thus, the duration of a five-year zero-coupon bond is five. The derivative of that bond's log price with respect to its continuously compounded yield to maturity is minus five. So for each small change in its continuously compounded yield, the price moves in the opposite direction with a magnitude of five. If the bond's continuously compounded yield instantaneously falls by 0.1% (e.g., from 4.0% to 3.9%), the bond's price would rise by approximately 0.5%. Rather than expressing the relationship with continuous compounding, the sensitivity of a bond price with respect to discretely compounded yields can be expressed as the modified duration. **Modified duration** is equal to traditional duration divided by the quantity $[1 + (y/m)]$, where y is the stated annual yield, m is the number of compounding periods per year, and y/m is the periodic yield. With continuous compounding, m is infinity, and traditional duration equals modified duration. Although duration can be used as a linear approximation of a bond price's change to small yield changes, bond prices have nonlinear relationships to their yields, making the approximation inaccurate for large yield changes. The nonlinear relationship between a bond's price and its yield is measured by its convexity. Consider a two-year note with a 2% yield to maturity and a five-year note with a 3% yield to maturity, both paying semiannual coupon interest. The two-year note has a duration of 1.97 years, and the five-year note has a duration of 4.68 years. Because the five-year note is expected to be 2.376 times (i.e., 4.68/1.97) more volatile than the two-year note for a given change in yield, a trade that equally weights the long five-year note positions and the short two-year note positions will be exposed to the risk of increases in the market level of interest rates. To make this trade market-neutral to a parallel shift in the yield curve (such as yields rising by 0.1% at both maturities), a duration-neutral weighting must be used. The trader would sell short $2.376 million of the two-year note for each $1 million held long in the five-year note. The total profit or loss of the position would depend on interest rate behavior. For example, the potential benefits of rolling up the yield curve with the short position and down the yield curve with the long position could add considerably to the final profits.

☞ APPLICATION 17.4.3A

What would be the short position in a four-year zero-coupon bond that would form a duration-neutral hedge with a $2 million long position in a bond with a duration of 2.5?

The duration of the four-year zero-coupon bond is 4.0 (i.e., equal to its maturity). The size of the short position must be $2,000,000 × (2.5/4.0), or $1,250,000.

There is a strong parallel between duration hedging in fixed-income securities and delta hedging in options. Both are linear approximations to nonlinear relationships; therefore, they hold only as approximations, with increasing inaccuracy when there are large shifts. The nonlinearity is addressed in both cases by second-order risk measures: convexity for bonds and gamma for options.

17.4.4 Asset-Backed and Mortgage-Backed Securities Strategies

Still another subset of fixed-income arbitrage trades is **asset-backed securities** (ABS), which are securitized products created from pools of underlying loans or other assets. ABS can diversify the idiosyncratic risk of the underlying assets through the use of pooling, while the securitization or structuring of such a pool can create a security that meets the risk and return preferences of investors. Moreover, ABS transform assets that are not easily traded into securities that can be much more easily traded. These loans are originally issued for a variety of purposes, including credit cards, university tuition, automobiles, and mortgages on residential and commercial properties. Banks and other financial institutions originate loans to individual borrowers and then sell the loans into the financial markets through the pooling and securitization process.

After loan originators sell these loans into the securitized pools, capital is returned to the banks or other institutions that issued the loans, restoring their capacity to make new loans. Cash flows from ABS are difficult to predict due to the borrowers' option to prepay the loans and the probabilities of various default rates. Therefore, the valuation of ABS is complex, requiring advanced modeling and sophisticated analysis. The complexity of these securities and their valuations makes them a fertile area for fixed-income arbitrage.

17.4.5 Prepayment Risk and Option-Adjusted Spreads

Most consumer loans, including auto loans and mortgage loans, allow borrowers to make principal payments in excess of that required by the loan's amortization schedule. Although the loans have a stated maturity, unscheduled principal payments or prepayments cause the loans to be repaid ahead of schedule, leaving ABS and MBS with an uncertain duration. When securities have option characteristics that alter the interest rate risk, risk is usually measured as effective duration. **Effective duration** is a measure of the interest rate sensitivity of a position that includes the effects of embedded option characteristics. Thus, the effective duration of a 30-year mortgage, or any callable bond, is substantially lower than its traditional duration (i.e., the weighted average of the times to maturity of the mortgage's scheduled cash flows).

Chapter 12 provided details on the measurement of prepayment rates for mortgages. Modeling prepayment risk is a complex and important part of ABS and MBS investments. Investors who model ABS prices by assuming a prepayment speed that is too fast typically overvalue a security by underestimating its longevity. Those underestimating prepayment speeds project receiving payments too slowly, overestimate longevity, and typically undervalue the security.

Prepayment risk is typically to the detriment of ABS and MBS investors, since prepayment is a short option position to the investor. When interest rates rise, borrowers prepay more slowly, which leads to rising duration during times of falling bond prices. Conversely, when interest rates decline, consumers rush to refinance their mortgages and other debts, reducing the longevity of the payment streams received by ABS investors. The higher prepayment rates in falling interest rate environments increase the cash received by the investors in an interest rate environment with low reinvestment rates. In short, the option for borrowers to prepay their debt when interest rates fall is valuable to borrowers. Optimal exercise of those options benefits the borrowers and harms the investors in ABS. Investors in ABS are well aware of the embedded option and are therefore careful to price securities properly by taking into account the value of the embedded short positions in options.

Mortgage-backed securities arbitrage attempts to generate low-risk profits through the relative mispricing among MBS or between MBS and other fixed-income securities. For example, MBS arbitrage can be performed between fixed-income markets, such as buying MBS and selling U.S. Treasuries. This investment strategy is designed to capture inefficiencies between U.S. Treasuries and MBS while hedging underlying interest rate risk with short positions in U.S. Treasuries. To reflect the uncertainties associated with MBS, these securities trade at a spread over U.S. Treasuries. This spread reflects any credit risk of the MBS along with the value of the short call option (the prepayment option) embedded into the MBS.

MBS arbitrage can be quite sophisticated. Hedge fund managers use proprietary models to price the value of the prepayment options and to value the MBS. The short call option implicit in a prepayable fixed-income security causes the price of the security to be lower and the yield of the security to be higher than in an otherwise comparable security without the prepayment option. A key concept in pricing fixed-income securities with embedded prepayment options is the **option-adjusted spread** (OAS), which is a measure of the excess of the return of a fixed-income security containing an option over the yield of an otherwise comparable fixed-income security without an option after the return of the fixed-income security containing the option has been adjusted to remove the effects of the option. For example, a prepayable mortgage may have a yield of 7%. A Treasury security of comparable maturity and with no call features may have a yield of only 5.5%. Analysis indicates that 90 basis points, or 0.9% of the mortgage's yield, is attributable to the prepayment option. The OAS would be the remaining difference in yield, 0.6%, or 60 basis points. The difference in yield may be attributable to credit risk, liquidity differences, mispricing, or taxability differences.

$$\text{Prepayable Mortgage Yield} = \text{Treasury Yield} + \text{OAS}$$
$$+ \text{Spread Due to Prepayment Option} \quad (17.10)$$

☞ APPLICATION 17.4.5A

A prepayable mortgage has an option-adjusted spread of 50 basis points. Analysis indicates that 70 basis points of the prepayable mortgage yield is attributable to the prepayment option. If the prepayable mortgage has a yield of 6.00%, what is the yield on a comparable treasury security?

Inserting into Equation 17.10 and solving identifies that the corresponding Treasury yield is 4.80%.

More formally, the OAS is calculated as the spread over the Treasury spot curve that equates the present value of a bond's cash flows to its market price, incorporating the fact that the bond's cash flows may change under different interest rate environments. The calculations are based on a specific model, and thus OAS is model dependent. Hedge fund managers can use mortgage pricing models that rely on the concept of OAS to evaluate the market prices of ABS. In effect, the hedge fund manager estimates the option-adjusted price of various ABS using OAS and searches for relatively mispriced securities.

A hedge fund manager may attempt to arbitrage perceived pricing differentials within the ABS and MBS markets. The options embedded in ABS in general and MBS in particular are enormously complex. Some borrowers may make prepayments to exploit interest rate changes (i.e., refinancing when rates fall). However, other pre-payments are made for idiosyncratic factors, such as when the homeowner moves or needs to refinance to withdraw equity from the house. Default represents a pre-payment when the mortgage is covered by mortgage insurance. Prepayments due to default can be a benefit or a disadvantage to lenders, depending on the interest rate of the mortgage and current interest rate levels. The substantial cash flow timing uncertainty and highly complex option characteristics of ABS provide potential for security mispricing and arbitrage.

17.4.6 Five Risks of Asset-Backed and Mortgage-Backed Securities Arbitrage

Many risks are associated with MBS arbitrage. Mortgage-backed securities have complex risks that are driven not just by changes in interest rate levels but also by changes in the shape of the yield curve, the prepayment rates of borrowers, and the default rates of borrowers. Hedging these risks may require the purchase or sale of MBS derivative products or other derivative products—including exchange-traded products—and OTC products, such as interest rate forwards, swaps, and OTC options.

The use of OTC derivatives for hedging adds counterparty risk. If a hedging strategy is accomplished using exchange-traded futures and options, counterparty risk is negligible, as the exchange's clearinghouse stands behind every trade. However, if the hedge fund manager hedges with an OTC instrument such as a swap, it is a private transaction for which the hedge fund manager accepts the risk that the counterparty may not complete the transaction by paying cash flows according to the terms of the swap. Although this risk can be minimized through collateral and standardized contractual agreements, it is not foolproof, as the sudden collapse of Lehman Brothers in 2008 demonstrated.

As noted earlier, during a flight to quality, some investors tend to seek out the most liquid markets, such as the on-the-run U.S. Treasury market, and bid the prices of these securities up to induce their holders to sell them at a time of crisis. Conversely, some investors liquidate riskier positions and offer them at low prices in order to induce other investors to buy them at a time of crisis. The decline in Treasury yields and the increase in yields of risky assets cause credit spreads to temporarily increase beyond what is historically, or perhaps even economically, justified. In this case, sophisticated investors with sufficient liquidity may speculate that the MBS market is priced very cheaply compared to U.S. Treasuries. The arbitrage strategy would be to buy MBS and sell U.S. Treasury securities when the interest rate exposure of both instruments is sufficiently similar to eliminate most (if not all) of the risk with regard to Treasury yield levels. The expectation is that the credit spread between MBS and U.S. Treasuries will decline and that MBS will increase in value relative to U.S. Treasuries.

What should be noted about fixed-income arbitrage strategies is that they are generally designed to have profitability that is independent of the direction of the general financial markets. Arbitrageurs seek out pricing inefficiencies based on rela-tive valuations between securities instead of making bets on the absolute pricing of the overall market.

EXHIBIT 17.10   Summary of the Five Risks of Fixed-Income Arbitrage Funds

Risk	Effect
Interest rates/duration	ABS and MBS are securitized products for which investors have short call options on the underlying pool of bonds. Duration lengthens in times of rising rates, and duration declines in times of falling rates. This duration extension and contraction is exactly the opposite exposure desired by investors.
Credit spreads	ABS and MBS are pools of loans made to consumers borrowing to purchase homes, automobiles, or consumer products. As such, ABS and MBS investors assume the credit risks of these underlying loans. The credit risks of some MBS are guaranteed by agencies of the U.S. government, whereas investors retain all of the credit risk of student loans, automobile loans, and credit card pools.
Prepayment risk	Consumers who borrow to purchase a home have the option to refinance their loan at any time. MBS investors need to accurately model the size and timing of refinancing activity. Prepayment risk is heightened during times of falling interest rates and robust refinancing activity.
Volatility/convexity	MBS and ABS securitized products contain embedded short call options, causing bond prices at or above par to experience negative convexity. As interest rate volatility rises, the risk of prepayments and the degree of negative convexity can increase.
Liquidity and crises	MBS and ABS can substantially underperform sovereign debt during times of a market crisis and a flight-to-quality investor response. Due to the complexity of these issues, as well as the embedded options and credit risks, liquidity of ABS and MBS can decline substantially, whereas OAS can increase dramatically during crisis markets.

Exhibit 17.10 summarizes the five major risks of fixed-income arbitrage funds and provides key summaries of the responses of fixed-income arbitrage funds to five major risks with a focus on MBS and ABS products.

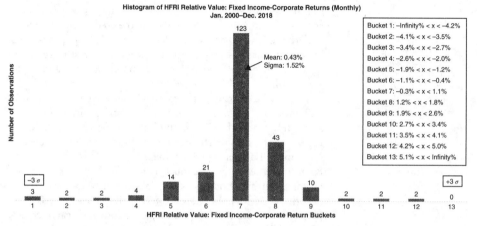

Index (Jan. 2000–Dec. 2018)	HFRI Relative Value: Fixed Income-Corporate Index	MSCI World Equity
Annualized Arithmetic Mean	5.1%	4.5%
Annualized Standard Deviation	5.3%	15.0%
Annualized Semivolatility	5.2%	11.6%
Annualized Median	8.0%	11.6%
Skewness	−2.1	−0.7
Excess Kurtosis	13.0	1.6
Sharpe Ratio	0.5	0.1
Sortino Ratio	0.5	0.2
Annualized Geometric Mean	5.0%	3.4%
First-Order Autocorrelation	0.51	0.14
Annualized Standard Deviation (Adjusted for Autocorrelation)	9.2%	17.1%
Maximum	4.5%	11.2%
Minimum	−10.6%	−19.0%
Max Drawdown	−28.2%	−54.0%

Histogram of HFRI Relative Value: Fixed Income-Corporate Returns (Monthly)
Jan. 2000–Dec. 2018

Mean: 0.43%
Sigma: 1.52%

Bucket 1: −Infinity% < x < −4.2%
Bucket 2: −4.1% < x < −3.5%
Bucket 3: −3.4% < x < −2.7%
Bucket 4: −2.6% < x < −2.0%
Bucket 5: −1.9% < x < −1.2%
Bucket 6: −1.1% < x < −0.4%
Bucket 7: −0.3% < x < 1.1%
Bucket 8: 1.2% < x < 1.8%
Bucket 9: 1.9% < x < 2.6%
Bucket 10: 2.7% < x < 3.4%
Bucket 11: 3.5% < x < 4.1%
Bucket 12: 4.2% < x < 5.0%
Bucket 13: 5.1% < x < Infinity%

EXHIBIT 17.11 Statistical Summary of Returns

17.4.7 Key Observations Regarding Historical Returns of Fixed-Income Arbitrage Strategies

Monthly returns to fixed-income arbitrage funds are observed from January of 2000 to December of 2018, for a total of 228 observations. Exhibit 17.11 provides univariate return statistics in the top panel, partial autocorrelations of returns in the middle panel, and a histogram of returns in the bottom panel.

Key observations on fixed-income arbitrage strategy returns that are consistent with economic reasoning are an essential component of knowledge and include the following:

1. The historical return distribution of HFRI Fixed Income: Corporate exhibited moderately greater left skew and very high excess kurtosis relative to global equities.
2. Volatility of returns was substantially lower than that of world equities.
3. Returns exhibited strong positive first-order autocorrelation.
4. Maximum drawdown was moderately milder than observed for global equities.

17.5 RELATIVE VALUE MULTISTRATEGY FUNDS

Relative value multistrategy (RVMS) funds simply combine one or more relative value strategies within a single fund. Rather than focusing on a single relative value strategy, such as convertible arbitrage, volatility arbitrage, or fixed-income arbitrage, managers diversify positions across these strategy types. The category of multistrategy relative value funds is extremely large.

17.5.1 Rationale of Relative Value Multistrategy Funds

What is the rationale for building a RVMS fund rather than a single-strategy relative value fund? First, we know that some of the largest funds in the hedge fund universe are RVMS funds. Funds focusing on a smaller market may have capacity issues, finding that their assets have grown too large to effectively invest exclusively in one strategy, such as convertible arbitrage. Second, opportunities may be cyclical. If a manager believes that asset-backed securities currently offer a lower-risk or higher return investment than corporate debt arbitrage, allocations to the more attractive investment sector can be opportunistically increased. Finally, there is an opportunity for diversification. By investing across sectors, a multistrategy fund may be able to offer cost-effective access to diversification.

17.5.2 Key Observations Regarding Historical Returns of Relative Multistrategy Funds

Monthly returns to relative value multistrategy funds are observed from January of 2000 to December of 2018, for a total of 228 observations. Exhibit 17.12 provides univariate return statistics in the top panel, partial autocorrelations of returns in the middle panel, and a histogram of returns in the bottom panel.

Key observations on relative value multistrategy returns that are consistent with economic reasoning are an essential component of knowledge and include the following.

1. The historic return distribution of HFRI Multi-Strategy exhibited moderately greater left skew and very high excess kurtosis relative to global equities.
2. Volatility of returns was very substantially lower than that of world equities.
3. Returns exhibited strong positive first-order autocorrelation.
4. Maximum drawdown was moderately milder than observed for global equities.

In conclusion, we note similar observations regarding the returns across all relative value strategies. These strategies tend to invest in fixed-income securities, some of which are less liquid, which is noted by the strong autocorrelation of returns. These strategies also tend to have extreme levels of negative skewness and excess kurtosis, as the large losses during liquidity crisis events are out of character with the smooth positive returns experienced in normal markets.

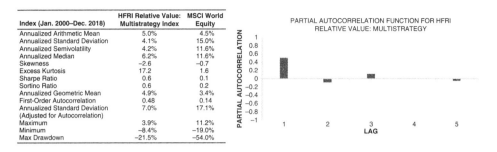

Index (Jan. 2000–Dec. 2018)	HFRI Relative Value: Multistrategy Index	MSCI World Equity
Annualized Arithmetic Mean	5.0%	4.5%
Annualized Standard Deviation	4.1%	15.0%
Annualized Semivolatility	4.2%	11.6%
Annualized Median	6.2%	11.6%
Skewness	−2.6	−0.7
Excess Kurtosis	17.2	1.6
Sharpe Ratio	0.6	0.1
Sortino Ratio	0.6	0.2
Annualized Geometric Mean	4.9%	3.4%
First-Order Autocorrelation	0.48	0.14
Annualized Standard Deviation (Adjusted for Autocorrelation)	7.0%	17.1%
Maximum	3.9%	11.2%
Minimum	−8.4%	−19.0%
Max Drawdown	−21.5%	−54.0%

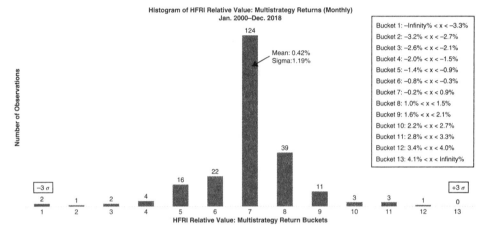

EXHIBIT 17.12 Statistical Summary of Returns

REVIEW QUESTIONS

1. Describe the positions used in a classic convertible bond arbitrage trade.
2. What are the three terms used to describe convertible bonds differentiated by whether their implicit option is in-the-money, at-the-money, or out-of-the-money?
3. What is the difference between delta and theta in measuring the price sensitivity of an option?
4. What is the term that describes additional equity being issued at below-market values, causing the per-share value of the holdings of existing shareholders to be diminished?
5. List the components of the returns of a traditional convertible arbitrage strategy.
6. What is the key difference between a volatility swap and a variance swap?
7. What is the primary term for financial arrangements that protect an investor's portfolio from tail risk?
8. What are the differences between duration, modified duration, and effective duration?
9. What is the difference between a yield curve and a term structure of interest rates?
10. For what type of interest rate shift is a duration-neutral position best protected?

NOTES

1. This relation holds only when there are very small changes in the value of the stock.
2. Technically speaking, Exhibit 17.2 should not depict a linear relationship in the convertible bond for stock prices from $980 to $1,020, since the relationship is convex. The linearity was allowed to make computation of the delta more straightforward.
3. Euan Sinclair, *Volatility Trading* (Hoboken, NJ: John Wiley & Sons, 2013).
4. Jefferson Duarte, Francis A. Longstaff, and Fan Yu, "Risk and Return in Fixed-Income Arbitrage: Nickels in Front of a Steamroller?" *Review of Financial Studies* 20, no. 3 (2006): 769–811.

CHAPTER 18

Equity Hedge Funds

Equity hedge funds follow the most popular hedge fund strategy, whether measured in terms of assets under management (AUM) or in terms of the number of funds. As of the end of 2018, Hedge Fund Research estimated that equity hedge funds of all styles constituted 28% of hedge fund industry AUM and 40% of the number of hedge funds. Although this sector is the largest by AUM, equity hedge funds have a smaller average asset size than funds in the event-driven, macro, or relative value categories.

18.1 COMMONALITIES OF EQUITY HEDGE FUNDS

At their heart, equity hedge funds of all styles share a common strategy focused on taking long positions in undervalued stocks and short positions in overvalued stocks. A major difference among equity hedge fund strategies is the typical net market exposure maintained by managers. Positive systematic risk levels are typically maintained by equity long/short hedge funds. **Equity long/short funds** tend to have net positive systematic risk exposure from taking a net long position, with the long positions being larger than the short positions. **Equity market-neutral funds** attempt to balance short and long positions, ideally matching the beta exposure of the long and short positions and leaving the fund relatively insensitive to changes in the underlying stock market index. Finally, **short-bias funds** have larger short positions than long positions, leaving a persistent net short position relative to the market index that allows these funds to profit during times of declining equity prices.

The success of funds within each of these strategies is primarily related to the extent to which a manager is successful in establishing long positions in stocks that outperform the market and short positions in stocks that underperform the market. It is not necessary for the long positions to increase in value and the short sales to decline in price for the equity manager to profit.

Consider a market-neutral manager with an 8% return target attributable to a 3% alpha on long positions, a 5% alpha on short positions, and equal long and short positions that are equivalent to the fund's net asset value. When the market is rising, it is unrealistic to expect the short positions to earn absolute profits. If the market index rises by 20%, the goal would be for the long positions to rise by 23% and for the short positions to lose only 15%. The key is for the returns of the stocks underlying the long positions to exceed the returns on the stocks underlying the short positions by 8%.

This chapter focuses on equity long/short funds, equity market-neutral funds, and short-bias funds, which control $690 billion, $70 billion, and $3.7 billion, respectively. Hedge Fund Research also covers a number of other styles within the equity category, most notably sector managers who focus exclusively on a particular sector, such as energy or technology stocks.

18.2   SOURCES OF RETURN

What are the potential sources of ex-ante alpha to equity hedge funds? In markets with relatively low transaction costs, such as major equity markets, any return in excess of the equity market portfolio received by one market participant must be offset by deficient returns to another market participant. This section provides three explanations of why some equity hedge funds might be able to generate consistently superior returns.

18.2.1   Providing Liquidity

Some equity hedge funds provide liquidity to the market by buying securities at relatively small discounts from large anxious sellers and selling securities at small premiums to large anxious buyers. **Liquidity,** in this context, is the extent to which transactions can be executed with minimal disruption to prices. The term *anxious* refers to market participants placing orders, especially large orders, with more concern about getting the full order executed on a timely basis and less concern about getting the most favorable possible price based on short-term movements.

For example, consider a major financial institution that decides to substantially alter its portfolio composition by liquidating one holding to establish another holding. Suppose that the current price of the stock the institution wishes to buy is $50.00 bid and $50.01 offered. A short-term equilibrium for the stock currently holds, wherein there are no traders currently preferring to buy at $50.01 and no traders preferring to sell at $50.00. For the institution to substantially increase its holding in the shares, other market participants need to be induced to decrease their holdings. If the institution is anxious to increase its holding, it will begin purchasing the shares currently available at the offer price of $50.01 and continue buying shares at higher and higher prices to find more and more willing sellers. Depending on the size and urgency of the institution's trades, the buying pressure may drive the price of the stock up perhaps 5 cents, 10 cents, or even more to find a sufficient number of willing sellers. A hedge fund or other market participant may intervene to offer the shares at the increased price in hopes that the price will decline once the buying pressure of the institution dissipates. If the hedge fund does not hold any position in the stock, it may short the stock to satisfy this temporarily increased demand for the stock.

The institution modifying its portfolio may be described as taking liquidity, since the institution's trading activities reduce the current supply of available sellers. More generally, **taking liquidity** refers to the execution of market orders by a market participant to meet portfolio preferences that cause a decrease in the supply of limit orders immediately near the current best bid and offer prices. The institution is trading to attain its preferred long-term positions.

Market participants who list their bid orders to purchase and offer orders to sell, or who stand by willing to enter the market to take positions offsetting the price pressure, may be described as providing liquidity. **Providing liquidity** refers to the placement of limit orders or other actions that increase the number of shares available to be bought or sold near the current best bid and offer prices. These providers of liquidity are trading with the primary purpose of making short-term trading profits, not to adjust their positions toward long-term preferences.

A **market maker** is a market participant that offers liquidity, typically both on the buy side by placing bid orders and on the sell side by placing offer orders. A market maker meets imbalances in supply and demand for shares caused by idiosyncratic trade orders. Typically, the market maker's purpose for providing liquidity is to earn the spread between the bid and offer prices by buying at the bid price and selling at the offer price.

Most hedge funds do not explicitly make markets by bidding to buy and offering to sell the same security at the same time. But many hedge fund managers provide liquidity by searching markets to detect price movements that appear to be driven by orders that are large relative to existing liquidity. For example, when one or more large sellers of a stock cause a drop in a stock price, it entices these hedge fund managers to intervene by buying the stock at the depressed price. In so doing, the hedge fund manager is providing liquidity. The goal of the fund manager in buying at a depressed price is to subsequently liquidate the position when the price recovers from the selling pressure. Conversely, large urgent buy orders can cause price increases that lead hedge funds and other providers of liquidity to short sell shares at the increased price levels.

In the case of an imbalance between buy and sell orders, providers of liquidity should be concerned that they might be taking positions in a firm whose share price is rising or falling due to factors other than liquidity, such as news regarding an unexpected change in anticipated earnings. A quick price movement in a stock may reflect idiosyncratic and temporary trade imbalances, or it may be the first leg of a large unidirectional move due to important fundamental information regarding the stock that is not widely known. If a hedge fund or other provider of liquidity notices a quick price movement and provides liquidity, the provider is taking the risk that the price movement will trend rather than revert toward its previous level. A provider of liquidity succeeds or fails based on the ability to distinguish between liquidity-driven price movements that will reverse and fundamentally driven price movements that will continue to trend.

It should be noted that the institution taking liquidity is very happy that there are hedge funds or other arbitrageurs providing liquidity. Every time an arbitrageur that is providing liquidity executes a trade, the taker of liquidity on the other side of that trade is receiving a price that is better than the price offered by any other market participant. Thus, provision of liquidity can be a long-term source of higher returns to market participants who are skilled at detecting illiquidity and executing appropriate trades. The situation is similar to antique dealers, ticket scalpers, and other traders in used goods who provide liquidity to their markets by being available to buy goods from anxious sellers and sell goods to anxious buyers. Providers of liquidity make money only when they execute trades, and they can execute trades only when they provide the highest available bid price or the lowest available offer price.

Provision of liquidity as a source of long-term superior returns is further discussed later in this chapter in the section on pairs trading.

18.2.2 Providing Informational Efficiency

Another explanation of consistently superior returns with an equity hedge fund is that the profitability results from exploiting the inefficiencies caused by poorly informed traders or traders making decisions based on behavioral biases rather than evidence. Although many academics believe in efficient markets, most hedge fund managers believe that markets are not always efficient and that they can take advantage of temporary inefficiencies in prices. Markets are said to be **informationally efficient** when security prices reflect available information. Stated another way, when markets are efficient, there is no reliable, consistent way to outperform the market at a risk level that is similar to the market.

Abnormal profit opportunities tend to come from market inefficiencies, and market inefficiencies tend to come from reduced competition. Theoretically, the competition for finding overvalued securities is less than that experienced in the search for undervalued securities, as fewer market participants can or do engage in short selling. The reduced competition for short selling is evidenced in the volume of short interest. **Short interest** is the percentage of outstanding shares that are currently held short. Choie and Hwang demonstrate that stocks with high short interest tend to underperform the market, with the implication that short sellers are skilled at selecting overpriced securities.[1] Thus, a potential source of return to equity hedge funds is short selling overpriced securities. By doing so, hedge fund managers provide increased confidence to all market participants that there is a mechanism tending to keep security prices from remaining grossly overpriced for long periods of time.

Asynchronous trading is an example of market inefficiency in which news affecting more than one stock may be assimilated into the price of the stocks at different speeds. A hedge fund manager may observe the release of information or may observe that a particular stock has experienced an abnormally large price change, presumably due to news that affected that stock. The hedge fund manager then establishes a position in another firm that the manager has fundamentally or empirically identified as being expected to experience similar price movements but on a delayed basis.

Another potential source of abnormal profits for hedge funds is **overreacting/underreacting**, in which short-term price changes are too large or too small, respectively, relative to the value changes that should occur in a market with perfect informational efficiency. For example, analysis of past market prices may indicate tendencies of the stocks of some firms to consistently overreact in the short term to some types of bad news regarding the firm and to eventually correct for the overreaction. If patterns of overreacting and underreacting exist, hedge fund managers can generate consistently superior returns by identifying the patterns and establishing positions that would benefit from repetition of the pattern.

Consistently superior returns from market inefficiencies are a transfer of wealth to the market participant recognizing the inefficiency from the market participant on the other side of each trade. Efforts by market participants to exploit market inefficiencies by purchasing underpriced assets and selling overpriced assets drive prices toward their efficient levels. In a society in which resources are allocated by prices, informationally efficient pricing provides substantially improved resource allocation.

Trading profits are the market-based incentive for participants to perform the analysis that ensures that prices are more efficient, resulting in better-allocated resources. In a market-based economy, the best producers of any goods (based on market values) tend to earn superior profits. Secondary security markets provide liquidity and reveal prices that convey valuable information. Therefore, the most talented and best-informed market participants should be able to earn superior rates of return in excess of their costs of analysis. Otherwise, no market participants would have an incentive to analyze information. The added return may be viewed as a complexity premium. A complexity premium is a higher expected return offered through the consistently lower prices of securities that are difficult to value with precision and therefore must be priced to offer an incentive to market participants to perform the requisite analysis.

18.2.3 Identifying Factors That Can Create Profit Opportunities

Some equity hedge fund managers analyze the factors that drive the equity returns of each company in search of those that offer the ability to predict the equities that offer ex ante alpha. These quantitative hedge fund managers use factor models to find those financial variables that explain stock price changes and that might be used in predicting price changes. These are bottom-up models that concentrate on firm-specific financial information as opposed to macroeconomic or industrial data.

As discussed in Level II of the CAIA curriculum, Fama and French show that exposure to value stocks, measured as firms having relatively high ratios of book value to stock price, and small-capitalization stocks explained returns and added average returns, even for portfolios with similar beta exposure, as defined using the capital asset pricing model (CAPM).[2] Simply put, small-capitalization stocks and stocks viewed as value stocks have demonstrated consistently higher returns than large-capitalization stocks and growth stocks. Debate exists as to why these return differentials have existed in the past and whether they will be exhibited in the future. Since Fama and French's seminal work, numerous factor models have been proposed to explain past returns and, potentially, to predict future returns.

The key issues are twofold: (1) Are expected returns for equities predictable based on past return factors? (2) Would any return factor offering a high expected return be attributable to alpha or beta? As discussed in Chapter 5, if the CAPM holds, then expected returns are determined entirely by one beta: the beta of each asset with the market portfolio. But the CAPM clearly does not hold exactly. It is possible that equity returns are driven by more than one beta and that some betas offer higher rewards for risk than do other betas. Identifying those systematic risk factors (i.e., betas) that offer disproportionate returns is a potential source of consistently superior returns. For example, suppose that equity markets continue to offer higher returns to small-cap value stocks, as identified using historical returns by Fama and French. Would a portfolio manager earning superior future returns with a portfolio of small cap value stocks be better described as having earned those returns from alpha or beta?

The provision of liquidity and attempts to find inefficiently priced assets or lucrative return factors all involve some level of speculation. In this context, **speculation** is defined as bearing abnormal risk in anticipation of abnormally high expected returns.

Abnormal risk and abnormal expected returns are defined here as including any risk and return other than those consistent with and commensurate with a market equilibrium, as described by the CAPM. Speculators have been defended as providing a valuable role in a market-based economy by moving market prices toward more informationally efficient levels. Extensive empirical analysis in various markets has investigated whether increased speculative activity stabilizes or destabilizes market prices. Generally, the results either are inconclusive or tend to find that speculators contribute to reduced price volatility. Note that speculators make profits by buying at low prices and selling at high prices, two actions that tend to stabilize prices.

18.3 MARKET ANOMALIES

Investment strategies that can be identified based on available information and that offer higher expected returns after adjustment for risk are known as **market anomalies**, which are violations of informational market efficiency. In the equity markets, these anomalies focus on such attributes as value, market capitalization, accounting accruals, price momentum or reversal, earnings surprise, net stock issuance, and insider trading. Good overviews of all anomalies, including the segregation of performance across the micro-cap, small-cap, and large-cap stock sectors, are presented by Fama and French, and by Stambaugh, Yu, and Yuan.[3] Interestingly, Stambaugh et al. argue that the timing of anomaly profits can be influenced by sentiment. Although anomaly profits accruing to holders of long stock positions are relatively constant over time, short sellers have earned their greatest profits after periods of above-average sentiment.

Several major anomalies that equity hedge fund managers have used to generate ex ante alpha are reviewed in the following sections. First, however, is a discussion of key issues in the identification and verification of anomalies.

18.3.1 Market Efficiency Tests as Joint Hypotheses

Practitioners and academics have debated the existence of a variety of market anomalies using empirical tests based primarily on asset pricing models, especially the CAPM. An empirical test of market efficiency is a **test of joint hypotheses** because the test assumes the validity of a model of the risk-return relationship to test whether a given trading strategy earns consistent risk-adjusted profits.

Thus, any finding of consistent superior risk-adjusted returns may be caused by model misspecification for adjusting returns for risk differentials rather than by market inefficiency. A return model is misspecified when the model omits explanatory variables or incorrectly describes the relationships between variables. Empirical indications of market inefficiency should be viewed as reliable only to the extent that the risk-adjustment procedures are viewed as well specified.

Extensive empirical analysis through the 1970s and 1980s provided indications of numerous anomalies based on single-factor models, such as the CAPM. But the multifactor models discussed in Level II of the CAIA curriculum indicate that returns can be substantially better explained by a multiple-factor model than by a single-factor market model. Empirical studies based on the CAPM may have falsely indicated that a strategy offers superior returns because the model for risk adjustment was misspecified, resulting in a failure in the research to adjust fully for risk. For example, if a strategy of investing in young firms is shown to have earned abnormal returns, it might be due to the fact that young firms tend to be relatively small. Thus, the strategy might be earning extra returns because of exposure to the size factor rather than because the firms are young. Consequently, to be seen as a valid market anomaly, a perceived anomaly needs to earn excess returns using a well-regarded model of returns.

18.3.2 Predicting Persistence of Market Anomalies

There are several critical issues regarding the application of investment strategies based on evidence of the past performance of anomaly-based strategies. Is the statistical result due to spurious correlations or to true underlying correlations? Even if the statistical results are reliable, is there a basis for believing that the anomaly will continue? How long should a manager continue implementing a strategy based on a perceived anomaly when the strategy begins suffering losses?

Anomalies based entirely on empirical observation should be viewed with more skepticism than anomalies that also appear to be consistent with reasoning. Accordingly, the search for reasoned explanations of empirical findings should be used in tandem with the empirical search for return patterns. In other words, both the decision of when to implement a strategy based on a perceived anomaly and the decision of when to abandon the strategy should be based on the extent to which the explanations for the anomaly can be reasoned. When the success of a strategy has a reasonable explanation, the empirical results are more trustworthy, and the decision of when to abandon a strategy can be based at least in part on whether the explanation for the anomaly remains valid. A reasonable explanation for the anomaly should include (1) from whom the excess returns are being earned, and (2) why the entity on the other side of the trade is willing to transact at prices that the fund manager perceives as beneficial to the fund and harmful to the other trader.

The rest of this section discusses major anomalies, with a focus on their potential behavioral explanations.

18.3.3 Accounting Accruals and Market Anomalies

Sloan discusses the role of accounting accruals in equity valuation.[4] An **accounting accrual** is the recognition of a value based on anticipation of a transaction. Sloan contrasts the cash flow of a firm with its net income. Net income includes the effects of accounting accruals. For example, sales of products on credit enter into the calculation of net income but have very little or no impact on free cash flow. According to this anomaly, investors seem to focus too much on net income, even though free cash flow appears to be the main driver of long-term returns. Since managers can manipulate accruals to generate positive net income and to meet the market's expectations of quarterly earnings, it is argued that investors should ignore higher net incomes that are mostly caused by large accruals (i.e., noncash items). The reason is that when current net income is largely due to accounting accruals rather than cash flows, the inflated short-term profits evolve into reduced subsequent profits when the cash flows associated with those accruals are received, since profits have already been recognized. Subsequent profits may also not be received and therefore must have their associated profits written off. For instance, a firm that is trying to meet particular earnings targets may be tempted to sell too many products on credit, which will create higher net income and larger accounts receivable. If some of these receivables cannot be collected later, then future net income will be adversely affected by the current urge to increase sales. In behavioral finance terms, investors are overreacting to the temporary accounting profitability of the accruals while underreacting to the more reliable indications provided by cash flows.

Accruals are reflected by changes in noncash items. Equation 18.1 provides an accounting definition of total accruals (ignoring accrued taxes):

$$\text{Total Accruals} = \Delta CA - \Delta CL - \Delta Cash + \Delta STDEBT - D\&A \qquad (18.1)$$

where ΔCA is the change in current assets, ΔCL is the change in current liabilities, $\Delta Cash$ is the change in cash, $\Delta STDEBT$ is the change in short-term debt, D&A is depreciation and amortization expenses.

According to the anomaly, an increase in noncash current assets ($\Delta CA - \Delta Cash$), such as accounts receivable and inventory, can indicate lower future earnings if customers do not eventually pay for the goods and services provided, if the inventory becomes obsolete, or if the inventory is sold at a discounted price. Similarly, current liabilities and short-term debt ($-\Delta CL + \Delta STDEBT$) may include deferred accounts payable or tax liabilities that increase earnings but defer current-period expenses until a future date. Finally, a decline in depreciation and amortization expenses (D&A) increases current-year income but actually reduces free cash flow, as the higher reported net income incurs a larger tax expense.

Bradshaw, Richardson, and Sloan conduct an empirical analysis that indicates that firms with especially large accruals, in which net income is significantly higher than operating cash flow, tend to have negative future earnings surprises that lead to stock price underperformance.[5] The implication is that equity hedge fund managers can buy stocks with negative accruals (higher ratio of free cash flow to net income) and sell short stocks with positive accruals (lower ratio of free cash flow to net income). To the extent that this is a true anomaly and that the anomaly continues, the strategy would generate superior risk-adjusted returns.

18.3.4 Price Momentum and Market Anomalies

Although many anomalies focus on the fundamental analysis of items on corporate financial statements, there is also evidence that technical factors, such as price and volume, may be used to predict superior returns. **Price momentum** is trending in prices such that an upward price movement indicates a higher expected price and a downward price movement indicates a lower expected price. A strategy based on price momentum is a trend-following strategy in which stock prices are believed to have positive serial correlation (i.e., positive autocorrelation).

Chan, Jegadeesh, and Lakonishok demonstrate the price momentum effect by measuring the performance of stocks ranked by their return over the prior six months.[6] For the subsequent six to 12 months, they provide evidence that superior risk-adjusted profits can be earned by buying stocks that performed well over the previous six months (winners) and selling stocks that performed poorly over the previous six months (losers). Thus, price momentum appears to prevail using six-month intervals. However, a reversal effect is seen at very short- and long-term horizons, as stocks with the strongest price performance at one-month or five-year time frames underperform over a similar time horizon, whereas losers over the same time period outperform. Thus, both consistent price momentum and price reversals have been observed, each based on different time intervals.

Many reasons have been put forth to explain the presence of momentum. One potential explanation is that well-informed investors cannot take large positions in stocks because their superior information is likely to be leaked to the market. Thus, these investors have to build positions in equities gradually. For instance, if a hedge fund manager through hard work and detailed analysis discovers that a particular firm is undervalued, rather than buying a large number of shares immediately, the optimal strategy would be to build a position in the stock a little at a time so that the price impact of its purchase is minimized. The stock of the firm is still likely to increase gradually through time, especially if it is a small firm, as the hedge fund builds its position. Eventually, the rest of the market learns about the firm and the stock price increases further, leading to the presence of momentum. This line of reasoning is consistent with available empirical evidence showing that momentum is strongest in small-cap stocks.

18.3.5 Earnings Momentum and Market Anomalies

Earnings are primary drivers of idiosyncratic stock returns. Unlike patterns in share prices, patterns in corporate earnings may exist in an efficient market, since speculators cannot trade directly on earnings. In an efficient market, share prices respond quickly to changes in a firm's prospects, whereas earnings may tend to respond on a delayed basis. For example, firms that experience rapid growth in earnings in one year due to a successful new product are likely to continue to experience earnings growth in the subsequent year. In other words, accounting numbers are often conservative in the speed with which they recognize increases in underlying value. There is no doubt that earnings show patterns; the key question is whether patterns in earnings can be used to find patterns in share prices.

Brown summarizes the research on earnings momentum and earnings surprise.[7] **Earnings momentum** is the tendency of earnings changes to be positively correlated. **Earnings surprise** is the concept and measure of the unexpectedness of an earnings announcement.

Earnings surprise may be estimated using mechanical rules applied to historical earnings or may be calculated by comparing actual earnings to the forecasts of analysts. Equity analysts working for large banks and brokerage firms routinely publish estimates of quarterly earnings per share (EPS) for thousands of corporations worldwide. When a corporation announces a new EPS, the market compares the actual result to the average, or consensus, of the estimates produced by analysts. A positive earnings surprise results when actual profits exceed estimates, and a negative earnings surprise occurs when earnings fall below estimates. **Standardized unexpected earnings** (SUE) is a measure of earnings surprise. Although exact definitions of the SUE vary, a representative example of the SUE for a firm based on analysts' expectations in the most recent quarter is defined as follows:

$$\text{SUE} = \frac{\text{EPS} - \text{Analyst Consensus EPS Estimate}}{\text{Standard Deviation of Earnings Surprises}} \qquad (18.2)$$

The denominator of Equation 18.2 is a measure of the dispersion in previous earnings or in the amount by which analysts' estimates missed actual earnings. For example, one popular computation of the denominator in Equation 18.2 is the standard deviation of (EPS – Analyst Consensus EPS Estimate) over the previous eight quarters.

On average, stock prices have been shown to continue to drift in the same direction of the SUE even after the announcement of quarterly profit figures, meaning that stocks with positive earnings surprises outperform the market, and stocks with negative earnings surprises underperform the market. In an efficient market, prices should immediately and fully react to the earnings announcement and return to a random walk immediately thereafter. However, a **post-earnings-announcement drift** anomaly has been documented, in which investors can profit from positive surprises by buying immediately after the earnings announcement or selling short immediately after a negative earnings surprise.

If markets are perfectly efficient, there should be no post-earnings-announcement drift in risk-adjusted share prices. The post-earnings-announcement drift anomaly indicates a tendency of market participants to underestimate serial correlation in quarterly earnings, as earnings surprises tend to repeat in the same direction. In other words, traders underestimate earnings momentum. Once companies report a positive earnings surprise, earnings in future quarters tend to exceed analyst estimates.

Trading strategies can be developed to predict earnings surprises rather than merely react to them. Brown, Han, Keon, and Quinn build a model to predict earnings surprises.[8] The most relevant factors for predicting an earnings surprise in the next quarter are the prior quarter's SUE and the market capitalization of the stock. Small-capitalization stocks and stocks for which analysts have been increasing their earnings estimates are factors found to correspond to higher earnings surprises.

18.3.6 Net Stock Issuance and Market Anomalies

Corporations can expand and contract the number of their shares outstanding, and research has indicated that there may be anomalies associated with these activities. When a company chooses to reduce its shares outstanding, a **share buyback program** is initiated, and the company purchases its own shares from investors in the open market or through a tender offer. These shares are retired from the share count, thereby increasing the proportional ownership of all other shareholders. Reduced shares outstanding can immediately increase earnings per share, reduce dividends payable, and even generate earnings-per-share growth. Share repurchase activity directly increases the demand for shares and reduces the supply of shares, both of which may exert upward pressure on the stock price in the absence of other effects, such as signals that the firm lacks superior investment opportunities.

Whereas share repurchases reduce the number of shares outstanding, issuance of new stock increases the number of shares outstanding. **Issuance of new stock** is a firm's creation of new shares of common stock in that firm and may occur as a result of a stock-for-stock merger transaction, through a secondary offering, or the issuance of employee and executive stock options. Issuance of new stock causes positive net stock issuance. **Net stock issuance** is issuance of new stock minus share repurchases. Companies that issue large amounts of new shares, such as more than 20% of the shares currently outstanding, frequently see their stock price substantially underperform the market. Singal documents the subsequent five-year underperformance of acquiring firms that pay for their acquisition in shares, noting that the decision to issue shares in a merger transaction indicates management's view that the price of its own firm's stock is overvalued.[9] Conversely, acquirers who pay for their acquisition in cash outperform the market over a five-year period, as management's decision not to issue new shares signals management's confidence that its firm's shares are undervalued.

There is evidence that positive or negative net stock issuance has been one of the most profitable anomalies. Continued informational market inefficiency with respect to net stock issuance offers equity hedge fund managers another fundamental-analysis based strategy for identifying sources of alpha.

18.3.7 Insider Trading and Market Anomalies

Singal also documents an insider-trading anomaly.[10] **Illegal insider trading** varies by jurisdiction but may involve using material nonpublic information, such as an impending merger, for trading without required disclosure. In many countries, senior executives of a corporation are required to report their trading in company shares to regulatory authorities, who disseminate that information to market participants. These company insiders may also be subject to trading windows, which restrict trades to only those times when they are assumed to not have material information regarding sensitive topics, such as profitability or an upcoming merger. Such windows may occur immediately after an earnings announcement, because known accounting results have recently been disclosed and it is too early in the quarter to have strong knowledge of future results. Trading by insiders can be **legal insider trading** when it is performed in accordance with legal requirements.

Legal insider trading by senior executives can signal potentially valuable information. Evidence indicates that even during the restricted trading windows, corporate insiders tend to execute especially prescient trades, as should be expected given that their knowledge of the firm's operations is better than that of nearly all other market participants.

The key to implementing information from announced legal insider trading is differentiating insider trading driven by personal financial circumstances from trading driven by perceived mispricing of shares. Many of these executives acquire shares as compensation in the form of options, grants, or bonuses. Selling shares is frequently driven by idiosyncratic factors, such as the insider's desire for liquidity, for diversification, or to meet large personal expenses. Insider selling, then, especially by a single executive in small amounts, is not likely to indicate that the insider believes that the stock is overvalued. However, if multiple insiders at a single firm sell large portions of their holdings in a short time period, that signal is likely to be more negative.

The rationale for insider buying is much clearer than that for insider selling, as the predominant motive for buying is to earn a profit from investing in undervalued shares. Generally, insiders would have little motivation to increase their holdings in the firm if they viewed the shares as fairly valued or overvalued. Insider buying can also be used to forecast the direction of the stock market as a whole, as insider buying across firms tends to be more prevalent near a bottom in the stock market.

18.4 IMPLEMENTING ANOMALY STRATEGIES

Equity hedge fund managers do not typically select a single anomaly that governs all trading decisions. This section discusses a factor model approach to integrating multiple anomalies into a single trading signal and other practical issues in the implementation of anomaly-based strategies.

18.4.1 Integrating Anomalies Using Factor Models

To integrate a set of anomalies into a single trading signal, a manager assigns scores to each stock based on each anomaly. The scores are based on that manager's perception of the relationship between returns and the variables that the manager believes are linked to the anomaly. Many quantitative equity managers adopt a nonparametric or ranking approach to convert the underlying information regarding an anomaly into a single trading signal. These managers rank stocks into percentiles, deciles, or quintiles according to variables linked to several perceived anomalies. For example, some factors, such as momentum, have returns that are monotonically related to the momentum rank, meaning that stocks ranked in the top quintile outperform those ranked in the second quintile, second-quintile stocks outperform those in the third quintile, and so on. The corresponding factor would signal monotonically increasing strength, so that stocks with higher momentum would receive a higher factor score for momentum. Other factors, such as net stock issuance, may have substantial excess returns only in the extreme quintiles, so the net stock issuance factor would have only nonzero values for extreme levels of net stock issuance. Firms with somewhat normal stock issuance would have a zero factor score for net stock issuance, since there is little explanatory power for returns found in the middle three quintiles.

Most quantitative equity managers employ multiple-factor scoring models. **Multiple-factor scoring models** combine the factor scores of a number of independent anomaly signals into a single trading signal. The idea is that when trading signals for anomalies such as earnings surprise and price momentum are not perfectly correlated, combining both factors into a multiple-factor model should show improved trading signals and improved profitability. Thus, a factor model is constructed that integrates various anomaly-based signals.

Further, trading signals associated with anomalous events can be combined with trading signals associated with ongoing valuation factors, such as price-to-earnings and momentum, to improve the risk-adjusted returns of quantitatively selected portfolios. Modeling can be performed to take into consideration that each factor may have a different effective time period, with some factors—such as value factors—exerting longer-term effects, and other factors—such as earnings momentum and earnings surprise—exerting shorter-lived effects.

There are two reasons that equity managers may prefer multifactor approaches over strategies based on single anomalies. First, a trading signal based on several anomalies simultaneously should offer improved expected returns if each underlying anomaly offers increased expected returns and if the signals generated by the anomalies are not perfectly positively correlated. Second, portfolios selected on multiple factors are more diversified against the risk that an underlying anomaly will generate perverse results, as long as the performance of the anomaly trading strategies are not perfectly positively correlated. In other words, the risk that a trading strategy based on one particular anomaly, such as stock issuance, generates negative returns may be offset by the possibility that the effects of trading based on another anomaly will be positive.

18.4.2 Integrating Anomalies Using Pairs Trading

Pairs trading is a strategy of constructing a portfolio with matching stocks in terms of systematic risks but with a long position in the stock perceived to be relatively underpriced and a short position in the stock perceived to be relatively overpriced. The approach is designed to hedge systematic risks (beta) and exploit patterns in relative idiosyncratic returns (ex-post alpha).

The first step in constructing the portfolio is to identify pairs of stocks—based on fundamental analysis (e.g., being in the same industry and having the same size) or technical analysis (having very high return correlations)—that are believed to have similar systematic risks. This is done both so that offsetting positions in the stocks will hedge away the systematic risk and so that patterns in their relative pricing can focus on idiosyncratic performance.

The second step is to track the price spread or recent return spread between the two stocks. When the spread is abnormally wide, the recently outperforming stock is sold short, and the recently underperforming stock is purchased, with the assumption that the spread will be mean-reverting. The key to successful pairs trading is the ability to detect patterns in spreads and correctly identify when a spread has become abnormally large and is likely to converge.

As Gatev, Goetzmann, and Rouwenhorst write: "The concept of pairs trading is disarmingly simple. Find two stocks whose prices have moved together historically. When the spread between them widens, short the winner and buy the loser. If history repeats itself, prices will converge and the arbitrageur will profit."[11]

For example, a pairs trader may identify shares of Coca-Cola (Coke) and Pepsi as having especially highly correlated total returns or may identify through fundamental analysis that the two firms should be driven by similar systematic factors. The pairs trader programs a computer system to analyze the historical performance spread between Coke and Pepsi (along with the spreads of thousands of other pairs of stocks). The pairs trader develops and uses a quantitative model of the spread, based on its historical size and volatility, to identify an abnormal level of spread.

Furthering the example, if Coke experiences a large price drop whereas Pepsi's stock remains stable, the fund's automated system will recognize the performance spread, and the firm's trading system will take a long position in Coke and a short position in Pepsi. Over the next hours or days, the manager bets that the market overreacted when shares of Coke fell too much or underreacted to the tendency of Pepsi to decline when Coke declines. Perhaps the abnormal performance spread was caused by the trading impact of a major sale of Coke shares by a financial institution; in this case, when the order is completed, the spread might be expected to revert to its previous range. Or perhaps the drop in Coke was the result of bad news. Either way, the fund manager is anticipating that the abnormal spread is likely to revert. Note that the strategy is concerned only about the relative performance of the two stocks, not the absolute performance of either.

Successful pairs traders have automated systems constantly searching for abnormal price movements in thousands of pairs, probably trading dozens of pairs each day in reaction to short-term performance divergences.

18.4.3 Short Selling and Reducing Risk versus Increasing Alpha

Consider a skilled manager not only able to select positions with ex ante alpha but also able to evaluate from among those favorable opportunities those positions that have very high ex ante alpha and those that have moderately high ex ante alpha. In other words, the manager is able to rank investment opportunities from most attractive to marginally attractive with some consistency and accuracy. However, the manager would probably not decide to hold a highly concentrated portfolio in only the most attractive opportunities, as the portfolio would lack sufficient diversification. Therefore, in adding securities to the portfolio for the purpose of diversification, the manager is compelled to establish positions in opportunities with smaller and smaller ex ante alpha. The net result is that there is a trade-off to the manager between maximizing alpha through concentration in the best opportunities and minimizing risk through diversification into less favorable opportunities. This concept is illustrated in Exhibit 18.1 in the context of the expected return of the portfolio, $E(Rp)$, and the portfolio's tracking error.

Exhibit 18.1 illustrates two managers with different levels of breadth. The higher curve represents a portfolio manager with greater breadth, perhaps due to an ability to short sell. The rate of change in the trade-off between performance and risk is indicated by the degree of concavity in Exhibit 18.1. The improvement in the risk-return opportunities (e.g., the information ratio) of an investment manager with the ability to short sell relative to the long-only manager follows from the greater breadth that the manager has from the flexibility to short sell. An increase in tracking error leads to an increase in the portfolio's expected rate of return for both managers. For example, with a long-only constraint, the increases in portfolio size lead to smaller

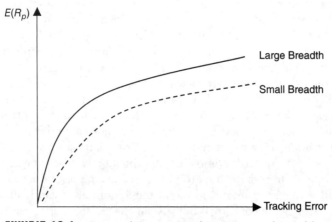

EXHIBIT 18.1 Expected Return, Tracking Error, and Breadth

and smaller increases in expected return due to the limited breadth. By not having a long-only constraint, an equity long/short fund manager is allowed to short sell, which leads to a better expected return for each level of active risk taking.

18.4.4 The Limits to Arbitrage

If the anomalies are as well-known as indicated in this chapter, and if the trading of anomalies moves security pricing toward more efficient pricing, then why aren't these profits arbitraged away? The answer lies in the limits to arbitrage, which is nicely summarized by Singal.[12] The **limits to arbitrage** refer to the potential inability or unwillingness of speculators, such as equity hedge fund managers, to hold their positions without time constraints or to increase their positions without size constraints. Taking higher portfolio risks through higher leverage increases expected return but there is a limit to the risk that an arbitrager can tolerate and/or is allowed to take. This provides a limit on the level of arbitrage activity by a single manager.

As discussed in this chapter, many equity hedge fund managers attempt to arbitrage mispriced equities by taking simultaneous and aggressive long and short positions. These portfolios underperform when the subsequent return spreads between the long positions and the short positions are the reverse of the forecasted tendencies. However, even though the basis for a strategy may include well-established historical tendencies, or the hedge fund manager may have discovered truly overvalued or undervalued stocks, the periods of loss can be long and severe. For example, one of the longest observed anomalies was the tendency of value stocks to outperform growth stocks in the United States for many decades prior to 1998. But from January 1998 to early 2000, large U.S. growth stocks outperformed large U.S. value stocks by well over 50%. Value stocks as a group lost money over periods of time in which the most aggressive large-cap growth stocks were experiencing triple-digit gains.

Managers with aggressive bets that value stocks would outperform growth stocks ran the risk of ruin. In other words, a manager who placed a substantial bet that value stocks would revert to their long-term tendency to outperform growth stocks either abandoned the bet or was ruined. Managers who want to be successful in the long run must limit the risk of a fund; by doing so, they provide one of the reasons for the limit to arbitrage. The success of growth stocks in the late 1990s was short-lived. Within approximately one year (by early 2001), the superior performance of growth stocks from 1998 to early 2000 had been fully eroded. And in the 10 years following 2001, value stocks continued their tendency toward higher returns.

Finally, market structures may prevent successful arbitrage in some cases. Especially in micro-cap stocks, institutional investors may be too large to participate, as a $1 billion fund may find that the impact of its trading on a stock with a $50 million market capitalization may be too large. For stocks with small market capitalization, the liquidity is typically low. Low liquidity means that the bid-ask spread is wide, the volume is thin, and the market impact of a large order can be prohibitive. **Market impact** is the degree of the short-term effect of trades on the sizes and levels of bid prices and offer prices. Studies of market anomalies must be careful to properly account for the total transaction costs, including the effect of market impact, before concluding that an anomaly is truly profitable.

Another limit to arbitrage is restrictions on short selling in some stocks or even in entire markets. Some countries do not allow short selling. Even in developed markets, short-term bans on short sales may be enacted. Stocks floating recent IPOs or spin-offs may not have shares available to be shorted. Finally, the shares of some companies may be temporarily unavailable for borrowing when the demand to sell the shares short exceeds the supply of borrowable shares. Whenever it is not feasible to sell short shares of a specific firm, the firm may be obviously overvalued but can remain at that valuation for a very long time, as investors do not have a mechanism to profit from the stock's return to a fair value.

18.5 THE THREE EQUITY STRATEGIES

This section discusses the three major types of equity hedge funds: short-bias funds, equity long/short funds, and equity market-neutral funds. Each of these discussions is framed in the context of the CAPM. The CAPM is used for simplicity as a well-known model with only one factor. The concepts could also be demonstrated with multiple factor models of risk and return but would involve more complexity in mathematical examples.

18.5.1 Mechanics of Short Selling

The main factor separating most equity hedge fund managers from traditional equity managers is the use of short selling. The basics of short selling were discussed in Chapter 17 in the context of convertible bond arbitrage.

The mechanics of short selling are quite distinct, and short selling requires special skills and risk management techniques. Given the importance of short selling in equity hedge fund strategies, let's explore how the mechanics and risks of short positions differ from those of long positions. Theoretically, a short position can lead to unlimited losses. When an investor purchases a $100 stock, the worst loss that can occur is $100 if the stock falls to zero. But when an investor short sells a stock at $100, there is virtually no limit to how high the stock can go and how large the loss can become. Conversely, long positions can lead to unlimited profits because there is no limit to how high a stock price can go. Short positions can generate only limited profits because the stock price cannot fall below zero. Thus, short selling offers an unattractive profile of limited profit potential and unlimited loss potential, the opposite of long positions.

Short selling also raises potential liquidity problems, because the lender of the security demands collateral to protect its loan. A long/short equity manager can typically post long positions as collateral on the short positions. However, suppose a long/short manager has two investments, A and B, and suppose she holds a long position of $100 in A and a short position of $100 in B. She posts the long position as collateral for the security loan. Now suppose that both positions go against her by 10% in one day. Thus, stock A goes down from $100 to $90, and stock B goes up from $100 to $110. The manager now needs to have $110 in collateral to cover the short position that has risen to $110. But the collateral that was posted—stock A—has fallen to $90. A highly leveraged fund manager may eventually be forced to liquidate the long positions that have fallen in value and buy back the stocks that have risen and that underlie the short positions—both of which may generate poor price executions in a period of illiquidity.

Another potentially huge complexity from short selling is that the lender of the security may demand that the shares be returned. Most securities are lent on a short-term basis, with the lender retaining the right to demand that the shares be returned at any moment. Usually when this happens, the broker simply arranges for another securities lender to loan shares so that the short seller maintains a seamless exposure.

But especially in times of overall market turbulence, or in times of turbulence for a particular stock, the shares become difficult to borrow. In those cases, the short seller may be forced to cover the position. This means that the short seller must purchase the shares in the market so that they can be returned to the securities lender. The short seller is therefore forced to close his position during a period of turbulence rather than at a time of his choosing. Note that an investor with a long position in a stock does not face this risk. The short seller's potential problem of being forced to liquidate a position is especially acute during a short squeeze, discussed in Chapter 2.

Calculating the total return from short selling is a little more complex than calculating the total return of long positions. For long positions, the return on a stock is the percentage capital gain or loss expressed as a proportion of price, plus any dividends received also expressed as a percentage of price. When the short seller provides cash as collateral for borrowing shares (including the posting of the proceeds from the short sale), the seller typically receives interest in the form of a rebate on the collateral from the securities lender.

The returns on a short position involve three major components: (1) capital gain or loss, (2) dividends, and (3) the short stock rebate on the collateral.

☞ APPLICATION 18.5.1A

Suppose that a short seller establishes a short position in one share of XYZ Corporation at $50 per share and that XYZ pays a dividend of $0.30 per share each calendar quarter. The current rebate on XYZ shares is 1% per year. What would be the dollar return to the short seller if XYZ rose to $51 at the end of one year?

First, the short position loses $1 (a capital loss) when the stock rises from $50 to $51. When the stock pays four quarterly dividends of $0.30, it is up to the short seller to make a cash payment to the securities lender in lieu of dividends, so the short seller loses another $1.20. Finally, an institutional short seller typically receives a short stock rebate; in this case, the rebate would be $0.50 (1% × $50). The total loss is $1.70 ($1.00 + $1.20 − $0.50).

18.5.2 The Basics of Short-Bias Funds

Managers of short-bias hedge funds may be distinguished from equity long/short managers in that they generally maintain a net short exposure to the stock market.

However, short-selling hedge funds tend to adjust their short exposures in an effort to time markets. That is, they trim their short positions when they anticipate that the stock market is more likely to rise, and they go fully short when they anticipate that the stock market is more likely to decline.

Short-bias fund managers face a difficult challenge: Equity markets typically rise over time due to the equity risk premium, so short-bias funds should be expected to rise very little or perhaps even decline in an efficient market. To earn consistent profits as a short-bias manager, the manager must identify stocks that generally decline in value, even though the overall stock market generally rises.

In theory, short-bias funds should be evaluated on performance relative to their negative systematic risk. Thus, negative performance should be tolerated or even praised if the fund's beta is substantially negative, if equity markets have risen, and if the negative performance is minimal. The reason that low or even negative returns from short-bias funds should be tolerated is that short-selling strategies provide good downside protection for bear markets. Short-bias funds can be included in a portfolio with a positive beta for the hedging and protection against downside risk, but short-bias funds should not be the focal point for generating excess returns.

For example, consider a world in which the CAPM holds, the expected return of the market portfolio is 12%, and the riskless rate is 2%. Assume that a long-only fund with a beta of 1.0 offers an expected return of 14%, and a short-bias fund with a beta of −1.0 offers an expected return of −4%. Using the CAPM, the ex ante alpha of the long-only fund is 2%, and the ex-ante alpha of the short-bias fund is 4%. Should an asset allocator consider the short-bias fund to be a valuable addition to a portfolio? The answer is yes. Consider a portfolio invested 50% in the long-only fund and 50% in the short-bias fund. This portfolio of two funds would have a net beta exposure of zero. However, the expected return of the combination would be 5% (found as 50% × 14% for the long-only fund, and 50% × −4% for the short-bias fund). With zero systematic risk, the ex ante alpha of the combination is its expected return in excess of the riskless rate: 3%. The computation of the ex ante alpha is confirmed by summing 50% of the ex ante alpha of the long-only fund (50% × 2%) and 50% of the ex ante alpha of the short-bias fund (50% × 4%).

This example shows that, in theory, a negative expected return to a short-bias fund may be acceptable if the fund offers a sufficiently negative beta to hedge the positive beta of other funds. The focus in evaluating a short-bias fund should be its returns relative to the systematic risk, not the fund's absolute returns.

Finally, there are reputational and regulatory risks to short selling that do not exist for funds that establish only long positions. During the 2008 financial crisis some countries restricted short selling altogether, while others restricted short sales in particular stocks, such as the shares of firms in the financial sector. Hedge funds that require the short sales of stock, such as short-bias funds, convertible bond funds, and merger arbitrage funds, may not be able to properly implement their strategies during times of short sale restrictions. Specifically, without short selling being allowed, some hedge funds may have a greater than desired net long exposure to the underlying market. Regulations may also have or institute an **uptick rule** that permits short sellers to enter a short sale only at a price that is equal to or higher than the previous transaction price of the stock. The goal of regulators is to prevent short sales from directly causing a downward spiral in the price of a stock by completing executions at lower and lower prices. Short sellers may also be politically unpopular, as they may be perceived to revel in a company's failure, or even to be the cause of a sharp decline in a company's stock price.

18.5.3 Key Observations Regarding Returns of Short-Bias Funds

Short bias fund returns are observed from January of 2005 to December of 2018 for a total of 168 observations. Exhibit 18.2 provides univariate return statistics in the top panel, partial autocorrelations of returns in the middle panel, and a histogram of returns in the bottom panel.

Key observations on long-short equity returns that are consistent with economic reasoning (and are consistent with and driven by the use of appraisals for valuations) are an essential component of knowledge and include the following:

1. Short bias historical equity returns averaged annual returns of roughly −4%, which is to be expected given the average returns of world equities of roughly +6.5%.
2. Short bias historical equity returns indicated somewhat less volatility than world equities.
3. Returns had the reverse skew as world equities and similar excess kurtosis.
4. Maximum drawdown was slightly higher than that of world equities.
5. Returns had very slight but consistently positive first through fourth order partial autocorrelations.

In summary, these short-biased returns exhibited mean returns and risk levels expected from being the opposite exposure of an index of long world equities.

Index (Jan. 2005–Dec. 2018)	HFRX Equity Hedge: Short Bias	MSCI World Equity
Annualized Arithmetic Mean	−4.2%	6.6%
Annualized Standard Deviation	11.2%	14.7%
Annualized Semivolatility	6.5%	12.1%
Annualized Median	−8.0%	11.6%
Skewness	0.5	−0.9
Excess Kurtosis	1.9	2.7
Sharpe Ratio	−0.6	0.3
Sortino Ratio	−1.0	0.3
Annualized Geometric Mean	−4.8%	5.5%
First-Order Autocorrelation	0.11	0.15
Annualized Standard Deviation (Adjusted for Autocorrelation)	10.4%	17.2%
Maximum	12.2%	11.2%
Minimum	−11.8%	−19.0%
Max Drawdown	−68.6%	−54.0%

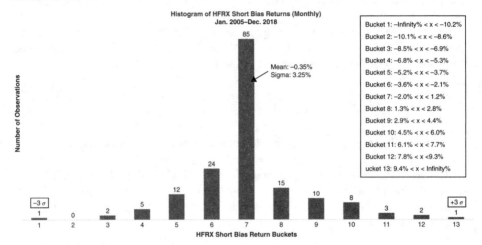

EXHIBIT 18.2 Statistical Summary of Returns

18.5.4 The Basics of Equity Long/Short Funds

Equity long/short managers build their portfolios by combining a core group of long stock positions with short sales of stock, or bearish positions in stock index options and futures. Their net market exposure of long positions minus short positions tends to have a positive bias. That is, equity long/short managers tend to be long market exposure by typically having a larger long position than short position.

As a simplified example, consider a hedge fund manager who at the beginning of 2008 held 150% of the portfolio value in a long position in the SPDR XME, an exchange-traded fund (ETF) that passively replicates exposure to the metals and mining sector of the S&P 500. Simultaneously, the hedge fund manager established a short position of 50% of the portfolio value in the SPDR XLF, an ETF that passively replicates exposure to the financial sector of the S&P 500. Assume that the relevant market index is the S&P 500, that the estimated beta of the XME is 0.99, and that the estimated beta of the XLF is 0.98. Therefore, the weighted average beta of this equity long/short portfolio is $(1.5 \times 0.99) - (0.5 \times 0.98) = 0.995$.

This long/short equity portfolio has approximately the same systematic risk as the S&P 500. In the period from January 2008 through August 2008, the return on the S&P 500 was −13.64%, and the risk-free rate was about 2.25%. Given the realized return on the market portfolio and the beta of the hedge fund, the realized return on this portfolio, ignoring idiosyncratic risk and using the CAPM, should be as follows:

$$\text{Return} = 2.25\% + 0.995(-13.6\% - 2.25\%) = -13.52\%$$

However, from January to August 2008, the return on the XLF was −33%, and the return on the XME was +23%. This portfolio, with a beta of approximately one, would have earned the following return, ignoring fees and transaction costs:

$$(1.5 \times 23\%) + (-0.5 \times -33\%) = 51\%$$

This is a much higher return than that predicted by the CAPM. The ability to go both long and short in the market is a powerful tool for magnifying idiosyncratic risk without necessarily magnifying systematic risk. Higher idiosyncratic risks offer skilled managers greater breadth and an opportunity to generate higher ex ante alpha. The long/short nature of the portfolio can be misleading with respect to the risk exposure. This manager appears to have risk similar to that of the S&P 500, and an investor might conclude that returns similar to those of the S&P 500 will be realized. However, what the hedge fund manager has done is make two idiosyncratic bets: that financial stocks will underperform and that metals and mining stocks will outperform. Even though the fund has market exposure similar to that of the index, the extreme industry exposures can create substantial risk.

Many hedge fund managers build concentrated positions in an attempt to take advantage of forecasted deviations of expected returns from the predictions of the CAPM. The important question is whether hedge fund managers, with their flexible mandates and strong incentives, are able to identify and to take advantage of mispricings.

Equity long/short hedge funds essentially come in two varieties: quantitative or fundamental. Quantitative managers use precise, objective models to identify trading opportunities. These models are often focused on technical analysis but may use fundamental measures in addition to or instead of technical indicators.

Fundamental equity long/short hedge funds conduct fundamental analysis on a company's business prospects, including its competition and the current economic environment. These managers may visit with management, talk with Wall Street analysts, contact customers and competitors, and essentially conduct bottom-up analysis. A difference between these hedge funds and long-only managers is that hedge fund managers can short the stocks that they predict will be poor performers. In addition, they may leverage their positions.

Fundamental equity long/short hedge funds may invest broadly or in one economic sector. Equity long/short managers who focus on one sector are called sector hedge funds. For example, sector hedge funds are equity long/short managers who specialize in a specific sector, such as biotechnology, health care, or natural resources. These are typically fundamental stock pickers who have considerable knowledge and experience in analyzing companies in a specialized sector of the economy. They go both long and short, using their fundamental information advantage to find both excellent and poorly performing companies in that sector. Typically, they have a long beta exposure—sometimes a very long beta exposure—with only a few short positions offsetting many long positions.

18.5.5 Key Observations Regarding Historical Returns for Equity Long/Short Funds

Equity long-short fund returns are observed from January of 2000 to December of 2018 for a total of 228 observations. Exhibit 18.3 provides univariate return statistics in the top panel, partial autocorrelations of returns in the middle panel, and a histogram of returns in the bottom panel.

Key observations on long-short equity returns that are consistent with economic reasoning (and are consistent with and driven by the use of appraisals for valuations) are an essential component of knowledge and include the following:

1. Long-short historical equity returns indicated roughly half the volatility of world equities.
2. Long-short returns were symmetrical but with substantially higher excess kurtosis than world equities.
3. Maximum drawdown was less than half that of world equities.
4. Returns had slightly positive first-order partial autocorrelations.

In summary, these hedged returns exhibited generally lower risk than a long-only index of world equities, except in the case of excess kurtosis.

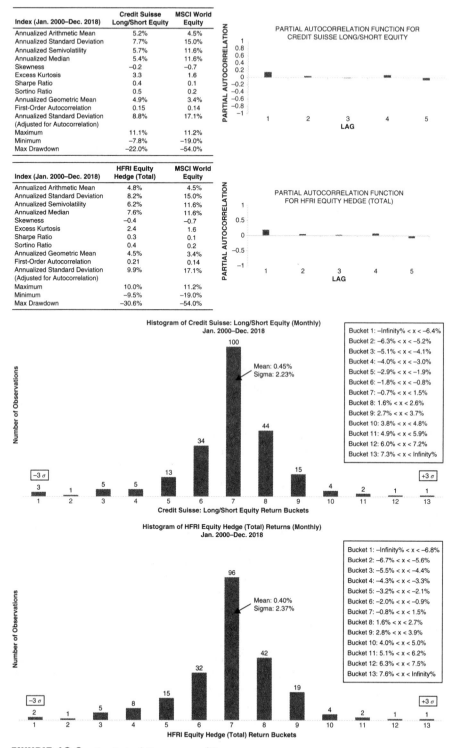

EXHIBIT 18.3 Statistical Summary of Returns

18.5.6 The Basics of Equity Market-Neutral Funds

Like equity long/short funds, equity market-neutral hedge funds establish both long and short positions in the equity market. The difference is that equity market-neutral funds maintain integrated portfolios that are designed to neutralize equity market risk, bringing beta risk to zero. This generally means a target of being neutral not just to the overall stock market but also across sectors. The idea of equity market-neutral funds is to neutralize market and industry risk and concentrate purely on stock selection in both the long and short positions. Although equity market-neutral fund managers seek alpha through security selection, unlike equity long/short managers they strive for market neutrality rather than engaging in market timing.

Patton discusses a number of definitions of market neutrality.[13] More than 70% of funds in the merger arbitrage, convertible arbitrage, relative value arbitrage, and equity market-neutral categories are found to be statistically indistinguishable from being market neutral. This is in contrast to the hedge fund strategies commonly known to be directional, in which perhaps half to two-thirds of the funds are shown to have statistically significant directional market exposure. The standard definition of market neutrality is mean neutrality. **Mean neutrality** is when a fund is shown to have zero beta exposure or correlation to the underlying market index. In other words, when the market experiences a move in one direction, mean-neutral funds are no more likely to move in the same direction as in the opposite direction. In addition, investors may consider whether their hedge fund exhibits variance neutrality. **Variance neutrality** is when fund returns are uncorrelated to changes in market risk, including extreme risks in crisis market scenarios. The concept of variance neutrality can be extended into other measures of risk, such as value-at-risk neutrality or tail neutrality. Patton found evidence that perhaps one-fourth of funds failed to be independent from market risk.

Some equity market-neutral managers use leverage. But being market beta neutral is not a zero-risk strategy. Consider the years 1998 and 1999, in which some quantitative equity investors were long value stocks and short growth stocks. Even with a zero market beta, substantial losses were experienced when managers were not sector or industry neutral. For example, profits from long positions in retail stocks were not able to overcome losses from the short positions in Internet stocks.

Generally, equity market-neutral managers follow a three-step procedure in their strategy. The first step is to build an initial screen of investable stocks. These are stocks that are traded on the exchanges the manager follows, that have sufficient liquidity to enable the fund to enter and exit positions quickly, and that may be borrowed from the hedge fund manager's prime broker for short positions. Additionally, the hedge fund manager may limit her universe by using other criteria, such as a capitalization segment (e.g., mid-caps). Next, the manager analyzes investable stocks to identify those stocks that are attractive candidates for long positions, in that they are perceived to be underpriced, and those that are attractive candidates for short positions, in that they are perceived to be overpriced. Finally, the portfolio is constructed. The hedge fund manager uses a computer program to identify portfolio weights so as to be neutral to the overall market as well as potentially neutral across sectors.

Most equity market-neutral managers use optimizers to neutralize market and sector exposure. However, more sophisticated optimizers attempt to keep the portfolio neutral to several risk factors, including size, price-to-earnings ratio, book-to-market ratio, leverage, liquidity, and currency sensitivity. The idea is to have no intended or unintended risk exposures that might compromise the portfolio's neutrality.

Because equity market-neutral portfolios are designed to produce returns independent of the market, these strategies are especially sensitive to the manager's or the model's stock-picking skill. Crowded trades, in which hedge funds control a significant portion of the stock's outstanding shares, are a special risk, especially among leveraged managers trading factor models. To the extent that multiple quantitative managers are using similar factor models, many managers have similar positions. If these managers need to liquidate positions rapidly, such as occurred in August 2007, losses may occur as long positions are sold and short positions are covered without regard for market impact.

18.5.7 Key Observations Regarding Historical Returns of Equity Market-Neutral Funds

Equity market-neutral returns are observed from January of 2000 to December of 2018 for a total of 228 observations. Exhibit 18.4 provides univariate return statistics in the top panel, partial autocorrelations of returns in the middle panel, and a histogram of returns in the bottom panel.

Key observations on long-short equity returns that are consistent with economic reasoning (and are consistent with and driven by the use of appraisals for valuations) are an essential component of knowledge and include the following:

1. Equity market-neutral historical equity returns indicated a mere fifth of the volatility of world equities.
2. Equity market-neutral returns were roughly symmetrical but exhibited moderately higher excess kurtosis than world equities.
3. Maximum drawdown was approximately 20% the size of that of world equities.
4. Returns had small but consistently positive first-through fourth-order partial autocorrelations.

In summary, these hedged returns exhibited generally lower risk than a long-only index of world equities, except in the case of excess kurtosis.

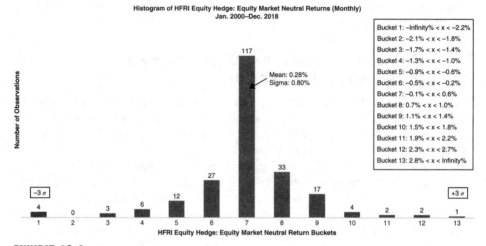

Index (Jan. 2000–Dec. 2018)	HFRI Equity Hedge: Equity Market Neutral	MSCI World Equity
Annualized Arithmetic Mean	3.4%	4.5%
Annualized Standard Deviation	2.8%	15.0%
Annualized Semivolatiltiy	2.2%	11.6%
Annualized Median	4.0%	11.6%
Skewness	−0.5	−0.7
Excess Kurtosis	3.1	1.6
Sharpe Ratio	0.3	0.1
Sortino Ratio	0.4	0.2
Annualized Geometric Mean	3.4%	3.4%
First-Order Autocorrelation	0.08	0.14
Annualized Standard Deviation (Adjusted for Autocorrelation)	3.0%	17.1%
Maximum	3.1%	11.2%
Minimum	−2.9%	−19.0%
Max Drawdown	−9.2%	−54.0%

PARTIAL AUTOCORRELATION FUNCTION FOR HFRI EQUITY HEDGE: EQUITY MARKET NEUTRAL

Histogram of HFRI Equity Hedge: Equity Market Neutral Returns (Monthly)
Jan. 2000–Dec. 2018

Bucket 1: −Infinity% < x < −2.2%
Bucket 2: −2.1% < x < −1.8%
Bucket 3: −1.7% < x < −1.4%
Bucket 4: −1.3% < x < −1.0%
Bucket 5: −0.9% < x < −0.6%
Bucket 6: −0.5% < x < −0.2%
Bucket 7: −0.1% < x < 0.6%
Bucket 8: 0.7% < x < 1.0%
Bucket 9: 1.1% < x < 1.4%
Bucket 10: 1.5% < x < 1.8%
Bucket 11: 1.9% < x < 2.2%
Bucket 12: 2.3% < x < 2.7%
Bucket 13: 2.8% < x < Infinity%

Mean: 0.28%
Sigma: 0.80%

EXHIBIT 18.4 Statistical Summary of Returns

EXHIBIT 18.5 Summary of Equity Hedge Fund Risks

Risk	Effect
Equity markets	Long/short equity funds typically maintain net long exposure to equity markets, whereas short-bias equity funds maintain net short exposure. As such, long/short equity funds can post losses in bear markets, and short-bias funds can post losses in bull markets.
Quantitative versus fundamental	Quantitative, or black box, models assume that stock prices behave according to a specified factor model. If stock prices do not react as expected, equity hedge fund strategies may produce a negative alpha. Similarly, fundamental strategies rely on the judgment of a person or a team, which may or may not add value in a given market environment.
Concentrated positions and liquidity	As position sizes become larger and the market capitalization of the stocks declines, managers may find that their trades have significant market impact. As a risk management tool, a limit on position sizes relative to average daily volume in a specific stock should be implemented.
Regulatory	Restrictions on short selling, from the uptick rule to periodic bans on short positions, can have a substantial impact on equity hedge fund strategies.

18.6 EQUITY HEDGE FUND RISKS

Exhibit 18.5 summarizes the risks of major types of equity hedge funds. Investors in these funds must understand the risks of equity markets, the difference between quantitative and fundamental strategies, the importance of liquidity and concentrated positions, and the impact of changing regulatory environments.

REVIEW QUESTIONS

1. Name the three major types of equity hedge funds, and describe their typical systematic risk exposures.
2. Describe the role of a market maker in the context of taking or providing liquidity in a market with anxious traders.
3. Why is an empirical test of informational market efficiency a test of joint hypotheses?
4. Define *standardized unexpected earnings*, and describe how the measure is used.
5. What have empirical studies generally concluded about the relationship between the net stock issuance of a firm and the subsequent returns of the firm's shareholders?
6. What is the name of the measure that describes managerial skill as the correlation between managerial return predictions and realized returns?
7. Explain how limits to arbitrage prevent markets from being perfectly efficient.
8. What is the name of the modeling approach that combines the factor scores of a number of independent anomaly signals into a single trading signal?

9. Consider a skilled manager implementing a pairs trading strategy. What is the concern that tends to limit the size of the positions that the manager might take in attempting to increase expected alpha?
10. What distinguishes mean neutrality from variance neutrality in equity market-neutral strategies?

NOTES

1. Kenneth S. Choie and S. J. Hwang, "Profitability of Short-Selling and Exploitability of Short Information," *Journal of Portfolio Management* 20, no. 2 (1994): 33–38.
2. Eugene Fama and Kenneth French, "The Cross Section of Expected Stock Returns," *Journal of Finance* 47, no. 2 (1992): 427–65.
3. Eugene Fama and Kenneth French, "Dissecting Anomalies," *Journal of Finance* 63 (August 2008): 1653–78; and Robert F. Stambaugh, Jianfeng Yu, and Yu Yuan, "The Short of It: Investor Sentiment and Anomalies," *Journal of Financial Economics* 104, no. 2 (May 2012): 288–302.
4. Richard G. Sloan, "Do Stock Prices Fully Reflect Information in Accruals and Cash Flows about Future Earnings?" *Accounting Review* 71, no. 3 (1996): 289–315.
5. Mark T. Bradshaw, Scott A. Richardson, and Richard G. Sloan, "Do Analysts and Auditors Use Information in Accruals?" *Journal of Accounting Research* 39, no. 1 (1996): 45–74.
6. Louis K. C. Chan, Narasimhan Jegadeesh, and Josef Lakonishok, "The Profitability of Momentum Strategies," *Financial Analysts Journal* 55, no. 6 (1999): 80–90.
7. Lawrence D. Brown, "Earnings Surprise Research: Synthesis and Perspectives," *Financial Analysts Journal* 53, no. 2 (1997): 13–19.
8. Lawrence D. Brown, Jerry C. Y. Han, Edward F. Keon Jr., and William Quinn, "Predicting Analysts' Earnings Surprise," *Journal of Investing* 5, no. 1 (Spring 1996): 17–23.
9. Vijay Singal, *Beyond the Random Walk: A Guide to Stock Market Anomalies and Low Risk Investment* (New York: Oxford University Press, 2003).
10. Ibid.
11. Evan Gatev, William Goetzmann, and K. Rouwenhorst, "Pairs Trading: Performance of a Relative-Value Arbitrage Rule," *Review of Financial Studies* 19, no. 3 (2006): 797–827.
12. See Singal, *Beyond the Random Walk*.
13. Andrew J. Patton, "Are 'Market-Neutral' Hedge Funds Really Market Neutral?" *Review of Financial Studies* 22, no. 7 (2009): 2295–330.

CHAPTER 19

Funds of Hedge Funds

T he preceding five chapters have described the universe of hedge funds and its constituent categories of macro and managed futures, event-driven, relative value, and equity strategies. Few investors allocate their entire hedge fund investment to a single hedge fund manager or even a single hedge fund strategy. Investors realize that each manager and each strategy has its own specific risks and cyclicality of returns and that diversification across managers and strategies can reduce the risks of hedge fund investing.

The hedge fund industry includes funds of funds (FoFs) as well as single-manager funds. Funds of funds are hedge funds with an underlying portfolio of other hedge funds. The primary advantages of a fund of funds are diversification, professional manager selection, and portfolio management processes. The primary disadvantage of a fund of funds is a second layer of fees imposed by the fund of funds manager.

Investors may also want to consider multistrategy funds, which manage multiple strategies within a single entity. Multistrategy funds offer strategy diversification without the additional layer of fees, but there are also trade-offs involved when selecting these funds.

19.1 OVERVIEW OF FUNDS OF HEDGE FUNDS

A fund of hedge funds is a diversified fund run by a single hedge fund manager, in which assets are allocated among other hedge funds. This structure creates two layers of fees: the fees of the fund of funds structure, and the fees of the underlying hedge fund investments. A key goal of investing in a fund of funds is to improve portfolio diversification, as a fund of funds quickly diversifies both the risks of concentrated hedge fund styles and the idiosyncratic risks of investing with single hedge fund managers.

19.1.1 Benefits and Costs of Diversification

The benefits of holding a diversified portfolio of assets result from correlations among asset returns being less than 1, meaning that returns are not perfectly positively correlated. Exhibit 19.1 shows that there have been varying correlations across hedge fund strategies, ranging from 0.248 between macro and relative value to 0.907 between event-driven and equity hedge. Because each hedge fund strategy has its own risks and varying correlations to other hedge fund strategies, diversifying across hedge

EXHIBIT 19.1 Correlation of Returns across Investment Strategies, January 2000 to December 2018

(Jan. 2000–Dec. 2018)	MSCI World Index	JPM Aggregate Global Bond Index	HFRI Fund Weighted Composite Index	HFRI Fund of Funds Composite Index	HFRI Macro (Total) Index	HFRI Event-Driven (Total) Index	HFRI Relative Value (Total) Index	HFRI Equity Hedge (Total) Index
MSCI World Index	1.000							
JPM Aggregate Global Bond Index	0.221	1.000						
HFRI Fund Weighted Composite Index	0.841	0.188	1.000					
HFRI Fund of Funds Composite Index	0.715	0.157	0.941	1.000				
HFRI Macro (Total) Index	0.279	0.370	0.549	0.582	1.000			
HFRI Event-Driven (Total) Index	0.796	0.118	0.926	0.877	0.380	1.000		
HFRI Relative Value (Total) Index	0.666	0.163	0.789	0.807	0.248	0.831	1.000	
HFRI Equity Hedge (Total) Index	0.854	0.156	0.982	0.914	0.454	0.907	0.767	1.000

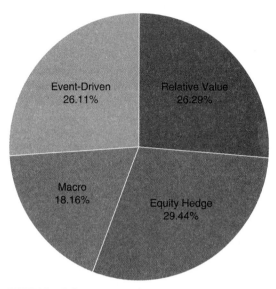

EXHIBIT 19.2   Estimated Strategy Composition by
Assets Under Management, 4Q 2018
Source: HFR Industry Reports, HFR, Inc. © 2018,
http://www.hedgefundresearch.com.

fund strategies reduces the risk of a hedge fund portfolio. As shown in Exhibit 19.1, with a correlation of 0.841 to the MSCI World Index and 0.188 to the JPMorgan Global Aggregate Bond Index, the HFRI Fund Weighted Composite Index also brings diversification and risk reduction to a portfolio of traditional stock and bond investments.

Exhibit 19.2 shows how investors have chosen to allocate their total investment in hedge funds to various strategy types. The largest allocation to single-strategy managers has been to equity hedge, and relative value managers and event-driven funds have earned larger allocations than have macro managers. At the end of 2018, Hedge Fund Research (HFR) estimated that the industry was composed of 8,331 single hedge funds and 1,324 funds of funds. Whereas the number of single-manager hedge funds continues to grow, there has been consolidation in the funds of funds sector, as there were 2,462 funds of funds at the end of 2007.

19.1.2   Four Functions of Fund of Funds Management

Delegated management using a fund of funds (FoF) approach provides investors with professional management to perform the following four important functions:

1. STRATEGY AND MANAGER SELECTION: The FoF manager is responsible for selecting the strategies and the managers who will implement those strategies. FoF managers may have access to closed managers as well as insights regarding strategies that are likely to perform better going forward. Many of the largest institutional investors and their investment consultants have teams dedicated to finding, vetting, and investing directly in hedge funds.

2. PORTFOLIO CONSTRUCTION: Once the strategies and managers have been selected, the FoF manager has to decide on how much to allocate to each strategy and manager. The allocation will depend on the risk and return characteristics of the individual managers and the expected correlations between funds, as well as other fund features, such as the lockup period, the liquidity of the positions, the size of the fund, and the length of each manager's track record.

3. RISK MANAGEMENT AND MONITORING: The FoF manager will monitor each hedge fund to ensure that its ongoing performance profile is consistent with the fund's overall objectives. Some FoFs employ sophisticated risk-management processes to monitor the underlying hedge funds' positions. Other FoFs may employ multifactor sensitivity analysis to gauge the risk exposure to various market factors and to analyze the funds' potential tail risk.

4. DUE DILIGENCE: For hedge fund investing, due diligence is the process of monitoring and reviewing the management and operations of a hedge fund manager. This is perhaps one of the more important functions and value-added features of an FoF manager to consider when deciding between a direct and a delegated hedge fund investment program. Unfortunately, some of the large FoFs have been marred by blowups and fraud scandals, which have caused some institutional investors to become wary about the value of an FoF's due diligence process. There is, however, some academic evidence justifying the payment of an additional layer of fees in return for operational due diligence. **Operational due diligence** is the process of evaluating the policies, procedures, and internal controls of an asset management organization. Brown, Fraser, and Liang[1] estimate that net of fees, the largest FoFs tend to outperform the smallest FoFs. Larger FoFs may outperform because their scale allows them to invest greater resources in due diligence and risk management processes.

19.1.3 Eleven Benefits to Investing in Funds of Funds

In addition to accessing professional management for the four functions just discussed, there are a number of other benefits to investing in funds of funds. These potential benefits include the following 11 advantages:

1. DIVERSIFICATION: Prudent investing dictates that portfolios be well diversified. Some investors lack the necessary asset size and expertise to invest directly in hedge funds to reach an appropriate level of diversification and risk reduction. By contrast, through a single FoF investment, investors can access a well-diversified portfolio in terms of managers or strategies. However, the diversification level of an FoF portfolio is not necessarily a straightforward function of the number of underlying funds or strategies analogous to stock investing. This is because hedge funds are not single securities; rather, they are previously diversified portfolios of securities.

2. ACCESSIBILITY: The median minimum investment for a single hedge fund is $500,000, which makes diversification into numerous funds unaffordable for most individual investors. By comparison, minimum investment levels for FoFs are relatively low. This allows more individual investors and small institutions

to gain diversified access to hedge funds even though their capital base is comparatively small.

3. ECONOMIES OF SCALE: Investors essentially share costs, such as those associated with the manager selection, reporting, analysis, and due diligence processes, with their FoF co-investors, thereby reducing their individual costs.

4. INFORMATION ADVANTAGE: As professional asset allocators, FoF managers have the ability to access, collect, and interpret data gleaned from various channels, such as data providers, prime brokers, and industry contacts. This gives them an informational advantage over nonprofessional investors.

5. LIQUIDITY: Investments in hedge funds are relatively illiquid, due to lock-ups, potential redemption gates, notice periods, and limited redemption dates. By comparison, the liquidity terms offered by FoFs are typically more flexible. Most FoFs offer quarterly or monthly liquidity in normal market conditions. Some FoFs even offer daily liquidity, either through a listing on an exchange or via an over-the-counter secondary market that matches demand and supply.

6. ACCESS TO CERTAIN MANAGERS: Access to the best talent and ideas in the hedge fund community is a scarce resource. The most desirable hedge funds may be closed to new investments. Many investors do not have the necessary networks and protocol for obtaining investment capacity in these funds when it becomes available. Investing in an existing FoF that is already allocated to these desirable hedge funds is the fastest way to immediately participate in their performance.

7. NEGOTIATED FEES: Thanks to the power of their collective assets, some FoFs have successfully negotiated access to certain managers at reduced fees. This is normally beyond the capabilities of most individual investors.

8. REGULATION: In order to facilitate their distribution to a wider audience, some FoFs choose to register in regulatory jurisdictions that offer better investor protection than their underlying investments, even though the cost and administrative and operational burdens may be higher. The improved investor protections can often be reassuring for first-time investors and can ensure that they will receive sufficient transparency, oversight, and quarterly reports.

9. CURRENCY HEDGING: Although the currency of choice in the hedge fund world is the U.S. dollar, some FoFs offer share classes denominated in various currencies with the currency risk hedged. Whereas institutional investors often wish to manage their own currency risks, many small or private investors prefer to be shielded from currency fluctuations and thus delegate the hedging aspects to professional managers.

10. LEVERAGE: Some FoFs provide leverage to their investors. They borrow money in addition to the capital provided by their investors and invest it in a portfolio of hedge funds. This allows them to produce higher returns than would be produced with an unlevered FoF, as long as the leverage and interest costs incurred are surpassed by the unlevered returns of the underlying hedge fund portfolio.

11. EDUCATIONAL ROLE: Many first-time hedge fund investors look at FoFs not simply as an investment vehicle but as a way of learning about hedge fund strategies and hedge fund managers. Larger investors may switch to direct investments in hedge funds after gaining a few years of experience.

19.1.4 Six Disadvantages to Investing in Funds of Funds

Conversely, there are disadvantages to investing in funds of funds. These include the following six potential disadvantages:

1. DOUBLE LAYER OF FEES: FoF managers effectively pass on to their investors all fees charged by the underlying hedge funds in their portfolios, while also charging an extra set of fees for their own work, as well as for an additional layer of service providers. Many FoFs charge a 1% management fee and a 10% performance fee on top of an underlying hedge fund management fee of sometimes 2% and an incentive fee of 20% for the hedge funds. Due to economies of scale, institutional investors making large allocations have recently been paying much lower fees than the 1% and 10%. Fees have been falling in recent years, due to both disappointing hedge fund performance and the increased buying power of large investors. As of 2018, the median hedge fund charges a management fee of 1.5% and an incentive fee of 17.5%, with just 30% charging 2% and 20%. As far as funds of funds go, the median is now a 0.8% management fee and an incentive fee of 9%. Funds of funds are increasingly available, with incentive fees between 0% and 5%.

2. PERFORMANCE FEES NOT NETTED: In an FoF, the investor must pay performance fees for each of the underlying hedge funds that are profitable, regardless of the performance of the overall portfolio. Thus, if half the managers are down 10% and the other half are up 10% on a gross basis, the investor will have to pay a performance fee to the positive performers despite no positive returns at the aggregate level. The fees are the same for portfolios of funds using direct investing. However, the fees are generally lower using a multistrategy fund, discussed later, because performance fees are charged on a netted or aggregate basis.

3. TAXATION: Because of their offshore registration, many hedge funds and FoFs may be tax inefficient for certain investors in certain countries. As an illustration, in Germany, most FoFs invest in hedge funds that fail to meet the extensive notification and disclosure duties requested by the German authorities. As a result, their gains are subjected to heavy taxation penalties, which ultimately affect the investor.

4. LACK OF TRANSPARENCY: Some FoF managers do not disclose the content of their portfolio or their asset allocation. They contend that it represents the valuable skills that they bring to the table, and they are reluctant to reveal their full strategy. In such cases, it becomes relatively difficult for their investors to understand what is really happening in terms of risk and returns beyond the information that can be ascertained from the stream of net asset values (NAVs).

5. EXPOSURE TO OTHER INVESTORS' CASH FLOWS: FoFs commingle the assets of a number of investors. As a result, investors are affected jointly by inflows and outflows, since co-investors in the same fund may trigger cash increases or decreases or undesirable leveraging to finance redemptions. Furthermore, to satisfy investors' requests for redemption, the FoF manager will typically sell the most liquid funds first, leading to a potential change in the FoF's style. Custom portfolios for a single investor (managed accounts) are not exposed to this type of problem.

6. LACK OF CONTROL: In an FoF, investors give up control over how the assets are managed. Moreover, they lose the direct relationship with the hedge funds in which the FoF invests. Direct investment in hedge funds allows investors to create allocations that fit their overall portfolios, but investors in FoFs can't control this style allocation. For example, the pension fund of a bank may not wish to have exposure to distressed credit instruments because of the business risk of the pension fund's sponsor.

19.1.5 Three Major Ways for FoF Managers to Add Value

One of the most important debates with respect to FoFs concerns whether they deserve their second layer of fees. For example, do funds of funds add value relative to a direct investing approach that randomly selects a portfolio of, say, 20 to 40 hedge funds? In practice, there are essentially three major ways for FoF managers to add value from portfolio selection and asset allocation:

1. THROUGH STRATEGIC ALLOCATIONS TO VARIOUS HEDGE FUND STYLES: Running an FoF is not just simply a matter of assembling a large collection of good managers. Having such a collection can still result in a concentration of risks, with somewhat illusory diversification if there is a high level of correlation in the trades or underlying exposures of these managers. The first choice that an FoF manager must make when organizing a portfolio is the long-term strategic asset allocation. The strategic allocation sets the long-term weights across strategies, such as static weights of 20% on macro strategies and 30% on equity strategies.

   This normally implies analyzing the long-term risk and return profiles of the different strategies, as well as examining the correlation of their observed and expected returns. The goal is then to determine an initial portfolio allocation consistent with the fund's long-term objectives and constraints. This task determines the long-run beta of the fund with respect to various sources of risks. Superior strategic asset allocations would be an important way for a fund of funds manager to add value.

2. THROUGH TACTICAL ALLOCATIONS ACROSS HEDGE FUND STYLES: Tactical asset allocation refers to active strategies that seek to enhance short-term portfolio performance by opportunistically shifting the asset allocation in response to the changing environment. Many FoFs argue that they implement a top-down, tactical allocation process. In theory, this involves making three key style-weighting decisions periodically: (1) what to do (i.e., overweighting or underweighting a particular investment style); (2) when to do it (i.e., implementing the changes based on levels of certain indicators or factors); and (3) how much to do (i.e., deciding whether the overweight should be, for example, 1% or 3%).

   In practice, however, an FoF's tactical allocations are limited due to the underlying hedge funds' liquidity constraints unless the fund of funds invests in the most liquid areas of alternative investments or uses managed accounts. However, new investment flows received by the FoF can be used to reallocate to the most attractive tactical opportunities. Thus, tactical allocation may be a way for fund of funds managers to add value by determining how much the FoF adjusts its asset allocations in response to changes in the market environment.

3. THROUGH SELECTION OF INDIVIDUAL MANAGERS: FoF managers can add value within a strategy through the decision of how much money to invest with each manager. Although this manager selection activity seems very similar to a traditional stock selection activity, the reality is that FoF managers need to consider the liquidity of the funds. Managers have to make a trade-off between their ability to add value through dynamic manager allocations in highly liquid funds and the potential contribution of less liquid funds (those with lockups, etc.). Managerial selection can be a major source of added value for an FoF manager.

19.1.6 How Many Hedge Funds Provide Reasonable Diversification?

The first issue to consider when constructing a portfolio of hedge funds is how many funds are needed to achieve appropriate diversification. That is, how many funds are required to reduce manager- and style-specific risks while maintaining manager weights large enough for superior manager selection to have a positive impact on the portfolio? We discuss two methods of estimating the relationship between number of funds and level of diversification: empirical and theoretical.

Using the empirical approach, Fothergill and Coke suggest that a broadly diversified portfolio of between 15 and 20 hedge funds can reduce portfolio volatility to the level of fixed-income investments.[2] Amo, Harasty, and Hillion measure the impact of each additional hedge fund investment on the standard deviation of terminal wealth.[3] At a one-year time horizon, a portfolio of eight hedge funds has half of the standard deviation of a single hedge fund, and investing in as few as five funds cuts the risk by more than half at a time horizon of 5 or 10 years. The marginal risk reduction benefit of adding more than 15 to 20 hedge funds is minimal. Gregoriou states that portfolios of more than 40 hedge funds dilute manager skill and approach the risk and return of a hedge fund index.[4]

The problem with the empirical approach to estimating the benefits to diversification is differentiating between systematic and diversifiable risks and the assumption that future returns will offer the same levels of diversification indicated by analysis of past returns. A theoretical approach is to model the returns of a portfolio as depending on the weights, variances, and covariances of the returns of the constituent assets. Equation 4.25 from Chapter 4, replicated here, reflects Markowitz's pioneering expression for the variance of a portfolio when the assets are uncorrelated:

$$V(R_p) = \sum_{i=1}^{n} w_i^2 \text{Var}[R_i]$$

when $\rho = 0$ between all n individual assets.

To derive a simple rule, this equation is used while assuming that all assets in the portfolio are equally weighted, all assets have no systematic risk, and all assets have equal variances, σ^2. In this case, the variance of the portfolio is σ^2/n. Given these assumptions, the standard deviation of the rate of return on the portfolio is directly related to the number of funds, as indicated in Equation 19.1:

$$\sigma_p = \sigma_f/\sqrt{n} \tag{19.1}$$

where σ_p is the standard deviation of the portfolio's return, σ_f is the standard deviation of every constituent fund, and n is the number of assets in the portfolio.

Equation 19.1 provides a simple approximation of risk reduction based on the number of funds. If there are four funds, Equation 19.1 approximates that the standard deviation of the portfolio will be half the standard deviation of a single fund. Portfolios with 16 and 100 funds will have 75% and 90% less standard deviation than a single fund. Equation 19.1 assumes zero correlation between fund returns, which overstates the benefits to diversification. However, these results may provide reasonable indications of the potential reduction in the idiosyncratic risks.

19.1.7 Identifying Funds for an Institutional Portfolio or Fund of Funds

The second issue to consider is that of manager selection and due diligence, described in the Level II curriculum of CAIA. Out of thousands of single-manager hedge funds, how does the portfolio manager attempt to select the best mix of perhaps 20 managers? Many hedge fund investors have one or more simple rules that immediately reduce the number of hedge funds under consideration. For example, how does the portfolio manager attempt to select the best mix of perhaps 20 managers? Many hedge fund investors have one or more simple rules that immediately reduce the number of hedge funds under consideration. For example, a size rule requiring minimum assets under management (AUM) of $200 million immediately reduces the number of funds under consideration to less than 1,400.

The manager funnel, as shown in Exhibit 19.3, shows the steps taken to select a small number of managers from the vast sea of candidates. Quantitative screens, such as a minimum length of track record, minimum returns, or maximum risk when compared to funds in the same style, can also quickly reduce the number of hedge

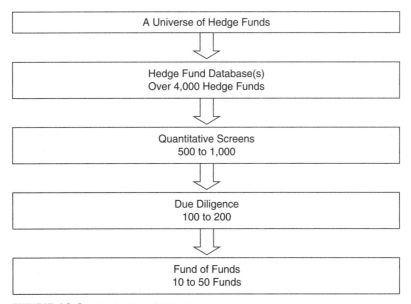

EXHIBIT 19.3 Hedge Fund Selection

funds under investment consideration. Other criteria may include manager capacity and the ability of the fund of funds manager to build a long-term relationship with the hedge fund manager. The next step, due diligence, is the most expensive and most challenging, beginning with locating and meeting each hedge fund manager. Although locating managers can be accomplished through database searches, many fund of funds managers have an edge through proprietary knowledge of managers who do not report their returns to databases. Large investors are also frequently contacted by managers who wish to present their funds for investment consideration.

Suppose that after the quantitative screens and the first manager interview, the portfolio manager has selected an initial 100 to 200 funds for further consideration. Perhaps there are 10 to 20 funds in each investment style. Once the portfolio manager is initially satisfied with this group of candidates, the in-depth due diligence process begins. After reviewing a completed due diligence questionnaire, the investor visits the hedge fund manager's office. The on-site visit gives the investor an opportunity to interview a broad number of staff members from the hedge fund to determine the manager's level of skill and ability to manage market risks and minimize operational risks. The prospective investor should also conduct reference checks, contact service providers, and verify systems and trading programs.

19.2 INVESTING IN MULTISTRATEGY FUNDS

A growing number of hedge fund managers are adopting a multistrategy approach to investing, in which a single hedge fund diversifies its trading and its positions across the macro and managed futures, event-driven, relative value, and equity hedge fund strategies. In many cases, the multistrategy fund designates one portfolio manager to allocate funds across strategies to various sub-managers, moving assets across teams trading each of the underlying strategies.

19.2.1 Incentive Fees as a Potential Advantage of Multistrategy Funds

The key advantage of a multistrategy fund over a fund of funds is the lack of an explicit second level of fees. Many multistrategy funds charge fees similar to those of a single-strategy hedge fund manager, such as 1.5 and 17.5. Although funds of funds pay each of their underlying managers similar fees, the fund of funds manager also earns an additional fee, perhaps 0.5 and 7.5. The second layer of fees can cause a fund of funds to have total fees of 2 and 25.

Reddy, Brady, and Patel discuss the importance of fee netting when evaluating multistrategy funds versus funds of funds.[5] Most multistrategy funds charge the incentive fee on the aggregated returns of the combined portfolio of underlying strategies. **Fee netting**, in the case of a multistrategy fund, is when the investor pays incentive fees based only on net profits of the combined strategies, rather than on all profitable strategies. This is a distinct advantage over a fund of funds. With a fund of funds arrangement, each underlying fund can charge 1.5 and 17.5, irrespective of the performance of other funds; there is no netting of profits and losses across funds in determining incentive fees charged by the underlying funds in an FoF.

For example, consider an otherwise identical multistrategy fund and a fund of funds, each having a 0% aggregated return after management fees but before considering incentive fees. The multistrategy fund manager clearly earns no incentive fee, as there are no aggregated profits to share between the manager and the investors. Suppose, however, that half of the funds underlying the fund of funds posted 10% returns before incentive fees, while the other half posted 10% losses before incentive fees. The fund of funds, like any other limited partner in the funds posting a profit, has to pay 20% incentive fees to those funds that have earned a profit. Thus, the fund of funds pays incentive fees in the amount of 1% of AUM to the half of the underlying managers earning 10% returns (assuming no hurdle rates). However, ignoring possible clawbacks, the fund of funds does not receive an offset on incentive fees from the funds posting 10% losses. Thus, even though the fund of funds does not pay incentive fees to the funds posting losses, the incentive fees on the funds showing profits place the fund of funds at a disadvantage to the multistrategy manager.

Incentive fees were discussed in Chapter 14 as call options on the NAVs of the fund. Limited partners in funds with incentive fees can be viewed as having written call options to the managers. An investor in a fund of funds can be viewed as having written a portfolio of call options, one on each fund. An investor in a multistrategy fund may be viewed as having written a call option on the portfolio of the aggregated strategies. Because the volatility of a portfolio is generally much lower than the volatilities of the constituent assets, the call options written by the multistrategy fund's investors are less expensive (i.e., the incentive fees owed through the multistrategy fund are generally lower than the incentive fees owed through a fund of funds). Lomtev, Woods, and Zdorovtsov estimate that the mean savings from fee netting gives multistrategy managers a 0.23% annual return advantage relative to funds of funds.[6]

19.2.2 Flexibility and Transparency

Multistrategy funds also have a greater ability to make tactical strategy allocation and risk management decisions than do funds of funds. When a fund of funds manager invests with 20 underlying managers, each investment is subject to possible liquidity terms and limited transparency. The fund of funds manager may agree to an initial lockup period of one year, with quarterly redemption periods thereafter. Whereas some managers may provide monthly portfolio snapshots, other managers jealously guard the details of their holdings. Thus, the fund of funds manager may not be able to obtain financial information or act on information in a timely manner.

Using a multistrategy fund approach, the portfolio manager has real-time access to all positions, making it easy to identify the exact positions, performance, and risks at all times. The multistrategy manager has the ability to direct trading teams to reduce or expand positions. For example, if the portfolio manager tactically believes that macro funds will underperform other funds over the coming quarter, capital can be quickly reallocated across traders from macro funds to other funds within the multistrategy fund without the complications of lockups and redemption periods experienced by fund of funds managers. Also, the transparency allows the portfolio manager to determine and implement portfolio-level hedges to manage the total risk of the multistrategy fund, since the manager has timely and complete information on the composition of the portfolio.

A recent development in the hedge fund world is the emergence of hedge fund companies that build their own internal funds of funds. These hedge fund companies offer several different hedge fund strategies to their investors, housing such funds as equity hedge, event-driven, relative value, merger arbitrage, and global macro all under one roof. These companies then create another hedge fund that optimally rebalances across the underlying hedge funds, effectively creating an internal fund of funds from their existing hedge fund offerings. Although this approach can be used to address transparency issues and liquidity constraints, it focuses the fund of funds investment opportunities on the products of a single company.

Reddy, Brady, and Patel discuss the potential returns to tactical reallocation across hedge fund strategies as adding less value than tactical reallocation between traditional stock and bond investments.[5] Whereas the best- and worst-performing hedge fund reallocation strategies had returns differing by 3.8% per year, the value of switching between stock and bond investments was 8.6% per year. Although it is difficult to measure the style timing skill of multistrategy managers, several papers, including Beckers, Curds, and Weinberger, and Gregoriou, have concluded that funds of funds have not convincingly demonstrated positive market timing skill.[7]

19.2.3 Managerial Selection and Operational Risks

Whereas multistrategy managers have potential advantages in fees, risk management, and tactical allocation, funds of funds may have a greater ability to add value through manager selection. At a multistrategy fund, the portfolio manager hires a number of trading teams, each of which executes a specific strategy and agrees to have its capital allocation regularly increased or decreased at the discretion of the portfolio manager. The number of traders employed in a multistrategy approach may range from one trader in each of four strategies to possibly five traders in each of 10 strategies. Thus, the multistrategy manager has hired anywhere from four to 50 traders, among whom the manager can manage risks and make capital allocation decisions. In contrast, the fund of funds manager may have the ability to allocate to any of the more than 8,000 single-strategy fund managers, clearly a wider selection than the multistrategy fund has to choose from once the multistrategy team has been formed.

Although asset allocation is much more important than manager selection in traditional investments, the opposite is probably true in the hedge fund universe. Reddy, Brady, and Patel estimate a 7% annual difference in returns between top quartile and bottom-quartile hedge fund managers within hedge fund styles, with only a 3.8% spread across strategies.[8]

Some investors may be concerned with the operational risks of investing in a multistrategy fund. Whereas funds of funds diversify operational risk across 10 to 20 independent managers and organizations, a multistrategy fund has a single operational infrastructure. Market risk may also be a concern, as a catastrophic loss in even one of the multistrategy fund's underlying strategies may sink the entire fund. Conversely, the failure of one of a fund of funds' 20 managers may subject investors to only a 5% loss and not affect the fund's other investments.

Empirical evidence indicates that multistrategy funds have historically outperformed funds of funds on a risk-adjusted basis, predominantly due to the extra layer of fees charged by fund of funds managers. Agarwal and Kale estimate that multi-strategy funds outperform funds of funds by a net-of-fees alpha of 3.0% to 3.6% per year after accounting for exposure to market risks.[9] Agarwal and Kale attribute the superior performance of multistrategy managers to a self-selection effect. The self-selection effect in this case is when only the most successful and confident single-strategy hedge fund managers choose to become multistrategy managers by hiring a team of experts and expanding into the world of multistrategy funds. However, it can be argued that the best and brightest among the available hedge fund managers do not remain satisfied in the role of multistrategy fund manager, preferring to manage their own single-strategy fund in order to link their compensation to their own money management skill rather than to the performance of the managers they oversee.

19.3 INVESTING IN FUNDS OF HEDGE FUNDS

The primary purposes of funds of funds are to reduce the idiosyncratic risk of an investment with any one hedge fund manager and to tap into the potential skill of the fund of funds manager in selecting and monitoring hedge fund investments. Also, some funds of funds have continued access to investing with managers whose funds are closed to new investors. Fund **access** is an investor's ability to place new or increased money in a particular fund. The access to otherwise closed funds is a potential advantage of a fund of funds for an investor relative to the investor forming his own portfolio. Additionally, some funds of funds arrange to have a liquidity facility that can bridge the fund's mismatches between subscriptions and redemptions. A **liquidity facility** is a standby agreement with a major bank to provide temporary cash for specified needs with prespecified conditions.

19.3.1 Funds of Hedge Funds as Diversified Pools

There is safety in numbers. An analogy is that as mutual funds are to single stocks, funds of funds are to single managers. Funds of funds offer diversification and professional management, just like mutual funds. Just as mutual funds invest in a large number of stocks across industries to diversify risk, funds of funds invest in multiple hedge fund managers and strategies to control risk. Investing in a single stock has some commonalities to investing in a single hedge fund manager in that there is a substantial amount of idiosyncratic risk. The company's industry or the hedge fund manager's style may be out of favor, or the CEO of the company or the fund manager may make some substantial mistakes. If a fund of funds invested in a single manager or strategy that experienced dramatic losses, the investor's losses would be reduced by the other investments that maintained or grew their value. Whereas concentrated investments in single stocks or hedge funds can lead to riches or ruin, diversified investments in mutual funds and funds of funds earn returns in a much narrower range, due to the reduction in idiosyncratic risk inherent in portfolios that contain multiple investments.

A fund of funds may seek to reduce operational risk and improve transparency for the fund of funds manager by placing the fund's money in managed accounts or separate accounts. Rather than investing as a limited partner and allowing the individual hedge fund managers as general partners to take custody of the assets of the fund of funds, the manager of the fund of funds can invest using a managed account or separate account that allows the hedge fund managers to trade the assets while the fund of funds controls the custody of the assets. This arrangement nearly eliminates the ability of the hedge fund managers to steal the funds or misrepresent performance. Because the assets are controlled by the fund of funds, the manager has perfect transparency, allowing the fund of funds manager to see all performance and positions in real time, which improves the manager's ability to manage risk and oversee investors. The liquidity of the fund of funds portfolio also increases, as the underlying hedge funds typically can't enforce lockup and gating provisions in a managed account framework.

Empirical evidence indicates that the returns to funds of funds have underperformed the returns of a broad hedge fund index. However, it may be inappropriate to directly make this comparison. Fung and Hsieh use hedge fund databases to document findings that funds of funds suffer less from survivor bias and selection bias than do individual hedge funds.[10] Hedge fund survivor bias was found to be 3% annually, whereas the survivor bias of funds of funds was 1.4% annually. Instant history bias was also less for funds of funds, 0.7%, than for hedge funds, 1.4%. In fact, Fung and Hsieh suggest that analyzing the returns to funds of funds may give a more realistic view of the performance of the hedge fund universe. There are several reasons that funds of funds would give a less biased view of hedge fund performance, including the following:

- Survivor bias arises when returns from dead funds are removed from, or never included in, a database. Funds of funds that invested in funds that eventually liquidated, however, retain the returns of those funds in their track records.
- Similarly, instant history bias is reduced, as funds of funds count the returns to their investments in single hedge funds from the date of investment.
- Funds of funds use actual investment weights, which may better reflect the weights used by typical investors.

Because of the second layer of fees, the after-fee returns of funds of funds are, on average, lower than hedge fund returns. However, it would be a mistake to conclude that funds of funds do not add value. In addition to reducing the due diligence cost of building a diversified portfolio of single-manager hedge funds, funds of funds may have skill in evaluating the hedge fund managers. In one study, Ang, Rhodes-Kropf, and Zhao argue that funds of funds should not be evaluated relative to hedge fund returns from reported databases.[11] Instead, the correct fund of funds benchmark is the return an investor would achieve from direct hedge fund investments individually, without recourse to funds of funds. Once fund of funds performance is compared to the correct benchmark, Ang and colleagues conclude that on average, funds of funds add value on an after-fee basis.

Ammann and Moerth find that larger funds of funds have statistically significant levels of higher returns and alpha than do smaller funds.[12] In addition, the larger funds also have significantly lower standard deviations, which lead to higher Sharpe ratios. The authors surmise that the larger funds of funds have greater operational resources, which can be used to invest in stronger risk management, portfolio construction, and manager due diligence capabilities. The larger funds may also cater to a more institutionally focused clientele. If the large institutional investors demand lower fees from their fund of funds managers, this fee difference may explain a portion of the return advantage experienced by the larger funds of funds. Brown, Fraser, and Liang argue that the difference in returns between smaller and larger funds of funds represents economies of scale from the fixed cost of performing operational due diligence.[13]

19.3.2 Funds of Hedge Funds Have Varying Investment Objectives

Funds of funds, like any other investor, can choose to build a portfolio with a wide range of investment objectives. HFR maintains indices that measure the performance of funds of funds, including composite, conservative, diversified, market-defensive, and strategic indices. The composite and diversified indices look most like the hedge fund universe, investing across the macro, equity, event-driven, and relative value strategies, and can be most closely compared to the HFRI Fund Weighted Composite Index of single-strategy hedge funds. Funds of funds included in the conservative index focus on strategies with lower standard deviations, such as equity market-neutral, relative value, and event-driven. Investors in funds included in the strategic index seek to maximize total returns, which is quite different from the risk-reduction goal espoused by many funds of funds. To earn these higher returns, strategic funds tend to make larger allocations to directional strategies, such as equity hedge or emerging markets funds.

Managers of funds of funds included in the market-defensive index seek returns that are uncorrelated to stock and bond markets and have lower downside risk. Defensive funds are likely to have minimal investments in event-driven and relative value strategies, as these managers prefer to overweight investments in macro, systematic diversified, and short selling funds.

Although the vast majority of funds of funds are diversified across a number of strategies, some funds of funds eschew this diversification to focus on a single sector. The most popular of these focused funds invest only in equity strategies, only in managed futures, only in smaller and emerging managers, or only in funds within a specific geographic region. These single strategy or sector-focused funds of funds may be attractive to investors who seek the specific return profile of one strategy, such as managed futures, but believe that it is important to invest in a number of managers to reduce the fund-specific risk.

19.3.3 Funds of Funds as Venture Capitalists

In some cases, it can be difficult to tell the difference between private equity funds and hedge funds. Within the specific strategies of distressed investments or equity activists, the line between private equity funds and hedge funds becomes increasingly blurred, especially when hedge funds invest in private securities or private equity funds invest in public securities.

Some funds of funds also blur the line between hedge fund and private equity investments. **Seeding funds,** or seeders, are funds of funds that invest in newly created individual hedge funds, often taking an equity stake in the management companies of the newly minted hedge funds. One reason that a seeding fund may create new funds is to obtain transparency and capacity in its underlying hedge fund managers, which can be difficult to obtain with existing hedge funds. Perhaps the best way for a fund of funds to guarantee transparency and capacity over the long run with specific hedge fund managers is for the fund of funds to own a stake in the hedge fund management company.

Further, although hedge fund managers are experts at trading strategies, not all hedge fund managers have the time, connections, or skill to raise funds, and some may not have the resources or knowledge to build the infrastructure of a new hedge fund. Funds of funds are experts at raising capital from investors and structuring new investment vehicles. These complementary needs and skills can form the basis for a seeding relationship, or an incubating relationship, between a fund of funds and a start-up hedge fund manager. In a seeding relationship, the fund of funds may provide the fledgling hedge fund manager with $20 million or so in capital, in addition to the legal and accounting documents, infrastructure, and relationships needed to start the hedge fund. The fund of funds manager may also serve as a third-party marketer, soliciting investors for the new hedge fund. In return, the hedge fund manager guarantees capacity to the fund of funds, even when the hedge fund has closed its doors to other investors. The fund of funds also has an equity stake in the hedge fund manager, which may earn the fund of funds 20% of the hedge fund's total fees and/or the value of the firm upon the sale of the hedge fund management company to an external investor.

The seeding activity of a fund of funds may eventually reach 10 managers across a number of strategies. At $20 million per manager, the fund of funds has $200 million of investor capital placed with the underlying managers, quite similar to a traditional fund of funds without the seeding activity. The seeding fund of funds earns the return to the underlying hedge fund portfolio, perhaps at preferential fees. In addition to the return on the hedge fund portfolio, the fund of funds also receives an equity kicker. To the extent that any of the underlying managers becomes extremely successful, perhaps raising $500 million in investor capital, the value of the fee and equity sharing agreement with the fund of funds can become quite valuable, possibly exceeding the return on the investment in the underlying hedge fund strategy.

19.4 INVESTING IN PORTFOLIOS OF SINGLE HEDGE FUNDS

Although funds of funds provide instant diversification, they do so at the cost of an extra layer of fees. Whereas investors with a small amount to invest in hedge funds may find these fees to be cost-effective, larger investors need to compare the value of paying fees to funds of funds relative to building a portfolio of hedge funds using in-house resources.

There are a number of costs involved with the hedge fund due diligence process. It is expensive to subscribe to hedge fund databases, to hire and retain internal staff skilled in manager selection and portfolio construction, and to fund the expenses of visiting and evaluating each hedge fund manager. In addition, since the minimum investment in hedge funds tends to be rather large, only investors with very large portfolios can hold a diversified portfolio of hedge funds.

Keith Black discusses a buy-versus-build heuristic that institutional investors should consider.[14] Assume that a fund of funds approach has a second layer of hedge fund fees, including a management fee of 1% and an incentive fee of 10%. Black estimates that a full internal program has a minimum annual cost of $1 million for building and maintaining an internal fund evaluation program. Investors may find it cost-effective to build their own hedge fund portfolio once assets allocated to hedge funds exceed $50 million. This result is found by dividing $1 million by 2%, which is the total fee, assuming a typical incentive fee of 1% of AUM. However, for investors with less than $50 million to invest in hedge funds, paying 2% fees to a fund of funds manager can be seen as a lower-cost alternative to spending $1 million annually inhouse.

Exhibit 19.4 describes the minimum initial investment sizes required by individual hedge funds. The information presented in the exhibit can be used to help set an investment minimum for building an internal hedge fund portfolio. The median hedge fund has a minimum investment size of $500,000. If investors need approximately 20 hedge funds to be well diversified, then investors would need a minimum hedge fund portfolio of $10 million to consider investing directly in single-manager hedge funds. Yet even if an investor has $10 million to commit to hedge funds, the expenses of building the fund may be prohibitive (e.g., $1 million of expenses, as discussed, would represent 10% of the $10 million investment). Accordingly, small investors are attracted to funds of funds.

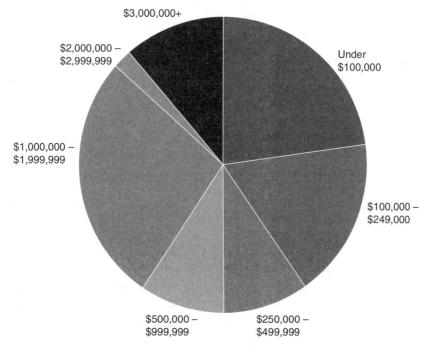

EXHIBIT 19.4   Minimum Investments Required by Hedge Funds, 4Q 2018
Source: HFR Industry Reports © HFR, Inc. 2018.
http://www.hedgefundresearch.com.

19.5   MULTIALTERNATIVES AND OTHER HEDGE FUND LIQUID ALTERNATIVES

Liquid exposure to hedge fund strategies is a large and relatively new category of the liquid alternatives introduced in Chapter 2.

19.5.1   Emergence of Liquid Alternatives

As the quality and the number of liquid strategies increase, the business model of funds of funds could be negatively affected. When individual investors can easily access transparent, liquid hedge funds with a low minimum investment, the advantages of a fund of funds to diversify investments and offer a low minimum subscription become much less compelling. Not only do liquid alternatives provide access to hedge fund strategies at lower fees and small minimum investments, but search costs are also reduced, as exchange-traded strategies have regulatory-mandated disclosures that allow both large and small investors to quickly access information regarding all exchange-traded hedge fund strategies.

Historically, most hedge funds have been offered mainly as illiquid and less-than-transparent private placements, sold to high-net-worth and institutional investors. Liquid alternative investments are innovative products that democratize alternative investments by allowing all investors to easily access these strategies in an exchange-traded and transparent format.

A hedge fund is an investment pool or investment vehicle that is privately organized in most jurisdictions and usually offers performance-based fees to its managers. Hedge funds can usually apply leverage, invest in private securities, invest in real assets, actively trade derivative instruments, establish short positions, invest in structured products, and hold relatively concentrated positions.

Investment managers in private placement vehicles have the ultimate flexibility, in that they can take as much or as little risk as investors or counterparties allow. In private placement formats, long lockup periods can encourage holding illiquid or complex assets, which may earn higher long-term returns. If there is a liquidity premium, in which less liquid assets tend to earn higher returns, then some fund managers may choose to hold most or all of their assets in less liquid holdings.

Whereas hedge funds are relatively unregulated, exchange-traded or liquid alternative investments must comply with local regulations, such as the Investment Company Act of 1940 (commonly referred to as "the '40 Act") in the United States, National Instrument 81-102 in Canada, and Undertakings for Collective Investment in Transferable Securities (UCITS) in Europe. These regulations specifically legislate minimum levels of liquidity and transparency, and maximum levels of leverage, derivatives, shorting, and investment concentration.

On average, private placement funds will have higher returns and higher risks due to the extra freedom allowed in the portfolio management process. Exchange-traded liquid alternatives will generally have lower returns and lower risks than private placements trading similar strategies, as the regulatory restrictions reduce investment manager flexibility. The investors attracted to liquid alternative products are those who may value the lower fees, greater transparency and liquidity, as well as the reduced risk of these products over the potentially higher returns from private placement products. There is also evidence of retail investors, or those not legally allowed to access private placement products due to low net worth levels, increasingly investing in liquid alternative products to diversify their portfolios in ways that were previously not possible.

19.5.2 UCITS Framework for Liquid Alternatives

UCITS funds were introduced in Chapter 2. UCITS-compliant funds were generally managed as long-only stock and bond funds for the first 15 years of the regulatory regime. When UCITS III was enacted in 2001, the regulations allowed the use of options, futures, and other strategies for the first time, which opened the door for managers to offer hedge-fund-like strategies in a UCITS-compliant vehicle. UCITS IV, enacted in 2011, allows fund mergers and master-feeder structures, which gives even greater flexibility to hedge fund managers. UCITS V, enacted in 2016, tightened requirements for custody of assets, requiring the use of a single depository to be responsible for explicit safekeeping requirements.

Although private placements offer the investment manager a great deal of flexibility when implementing an investment strategy, UCITS regulations have strict requirements for transparency, risk, and liquidity of compliant funds. UCITS regulations require reporting of holdings at least every two weeks to enable investors to view the composition of their funds on a regular basis.

In some aspects, UCITS regulations are less flexible than those of the U.S. Investment Company Act of 1940. For example, investments in property, private equity, and commodities are generally not permitted in UCITS funds. Leverage and concentration risks are also tightly controlled in UCITS funds, with leverage and risk typically limited to 200% of the NAV or risk of the underlying index. UCITS-compliant funds are required to be highly diversified, meaning that there are limits on the size of specific holdings within each fund. For example, UCITS regulations limit the holdings of a single European Union sovereign debt issuer to 35% of fund assets, the holdings of a single investment fund to 20%, the holdings of illiquid investments to 10%, and the amount of assets deposited within a single institution to 20%. Finally, there is a 10% limit on holdings of a single corporate issuer, or 20% when derivatives are included.

The liquid alts regulations in Canada under National Instrument 81-102 are largely similar to those of UCITS, which allows liquid alternative funds to charge asymmetric incentive fees similar to those found in private hedge funds. Canadian funds are limited to borrowing at 50% of NAV, leverage with an aggregate gross exposure of three times NAV, a concentration of 20% in a single issuer, and a hard cap on illiquid holdings of 15%.

19.5.3 Funds Registered under the '40 Act

Unlike the less liquid regime of private placements, funds compliant with the '40 Act regulations must offer regular liquidity, with redemptions being paid within seven days. Fund holdings must also be disclosed on a regular basis. Perhaps the most interesting aspect of the '40 Act regulations is that performance fees for funds that trade securities must be symmetric. That is, the sharing of investment profits by investment managers must be matched by the sharing of investment losses. In the private placement world, hedge fund or private equity managers frequently earn asymmetric incentive fees. Hedge fund managers typically have incentive fee structures that allow managers to receive 20% of all fund profits without the requirement of compensating investors for 20% of their losses. This asymmetric fee structure, which is very attractive to managers of private placement products, is not compliant with the regulations of the '40 Act. Although most managers of '40 Act funds do not charge performance fees, there are a few managers who charge symmetric performance fees. These performance-based fees are unlikely to ever be as popular with liquid alternative managers as the asymmetric performance fees that can be earned in the private placement world.

The '40 Act also places limits on each fund's leverage. There is a 300% asset coverage rule, which requires a fund to have assets totaling at least three times the total borrowings of the fund, thus limiting borrowing to 33% of assets. A fund with 150% long positions and 50% short positions would comply with the regulations, whereas a fund with 200% long positions and 100% short positions would not. The concentration limits of the '40 Act are less complex than those of UCITS. Under the '40 Act, diversification regulations apply to 75% of the fund's portfolio, while the remaining 25% of the fund has no concentration limits. In the diversified portion of a fund, investment concentrations cannot exceed 5% of assets invested in one issuer, 25% in one industry, or more than 10% of the shares outstanding of a single company. Finally, there are limits on liquidity risk, specifying that no more than 15% of the fund can be invested in illiquid assets.

19.5.4 Availability of Liquid Alternative Strategies

Let's review our four key hedge fund strategies in the context of the regulatory framework for liquid alternative investments.

Macro and managed futures funds are broadly available as liquid alternative products, given that the underlying holdings of futures and forward contracts can be extremely liquid. Funds using a '40 Act fund structure can access managed futures returns by holding funds as collateral and entering into swap agreements that transport the returns of managed futures into the liquid alternative structure. Liquid alternative funds, though, may be managed with less concentration and leverage than typical macro funds. Investors need to perform due diligence carefully on funds in this sector, as leverage and asymmetric incentive fees may be buried in the swap products that are often used inside the liquid alternative vehicles.

Event-driven hedge funds are a broad variety of strategies that focus on corporate events. Strategies such as merger arbitrage or activism are likely to be compliant with liquid alternative regulations but aren't yet broadly available in a liquid alternative format. Other strategies, such as distressed investing, are likely to be too illiquid to be offered in an exchange-traded format. Similarly, traditional private equity strategies are typically not available as liquid alternatives, as the time to exit may be years away, far longer than the daily or weekly liquidity expected by investors in liquid alternative funds.

Relative value hedge funds focus mainly on convertible bond arbitrage and fixed-income arbitrage strategies. These funds generally hold long positions in underpriced bonds and short positions in bonds or stocks meant to hedge the long positions. Because the divergences between the long positions and fair value are often small in these strategies, relative value funds are often managed at levels of leverage far in excess of those allowed under the UCITS or '40 Act regulations. As such, relative value funds are not generally available in a liquid alternative format.

Compared to other hedge fund styles, equity hedge fund strategies have attracted the largest AUM in the liquid alternative sector. Long/short equity funds are the most popular strategy, with equity market-neutral funds following closely behind. Perhaps the availability of equity funds in a liquid alternative format is so prevalent due to the similarity of the strategy in the private and public formats. That is, a large number of equity hedge funds are likely to be compliant with the regulatory requirements for alternative investments, even when managed in a private placement structure.

The liquid alternative space is broader than hedge funds, including funds with exposure to commodities, currencies, and nontraditional bonds. **Nontraditional** or **unconstrained bond funds** do not simply take long positions in investment-grade sovereign and credit securities, but may also invest in high-yield or emerging markets debt, often including leverage and short positions. These funds may increase exposure to credit risk while reducing the risk to changes in the level of investment-grade interest rates.

19.5.5 Engineering Illiquid and Leveraged Strategies into Multialternatives

Multialternative funds are liquid alternative funds that offer a strategy similar to that of funds of funds, in that they diversify across fund managers and strategies. Long/short equity and multialternative funds comprise more than half of assets under management within the category of liquid alternatives focused on hedge-fund-like strategies.

Both investors and hedge fund managers may find multialternative funds attractive. Investors can buy a single multialternative fund as a diversified offering, similar to that of a fund of funds. Hedge fund managers may wish to serve as a sub-adviser to a multialternative fund, especially when their stand-alone strategy does not comply with the liquid alternative regulations.

For example, some hedge fund strategies, such as highly levered fixed-income arbitrage or event-driven, are difficult to manage within the leverage constraints of the '40 Act. However, these fund managers are finding success within the multialternative or multimanager structure, as the provisions of the '40 Act apply to the full fund, not to the individual strategies. That is, highly levered fixed-income strategies can be mixed with strategies that tend to use less leverage, such as equity long/short strategies. By combining strategies with varying levels of target leverage within a multialternative fund, the total fund may comply with the leverage provisions of the '40 Act without materially changing the strategy or positions preferred by more highly levered managers.

Managers may also prefer to be a sub-adviser to a multialternative fund rather than offering their own liquid alternative funds, as that role more clearly delineates between the manager's private placement and liquid alternative investments. Managers who offer both a private placement fund and a liquid alternative fund following similar strategies must be careful to demonstrate that the private placement fund adds value relative to the greater liquidity and lower fees offered in the exchange-traded market.

19.5.6 Performance of Liquid Alternative Vehicles

Next, let's look closely at the empirical evidence: the studies of actual historical returns of alternative investments. We will look at return performance using various approaches: matched-sample tests, comparison of U.S. indices to one another, and comparison of U.S. indices to European Union indices.

We begin with matched-sample tests. Perhaps the best way to determine the true risk and return difference between liquid alternative funds and private placements is to find a subset of funds in which each manager offers both a hedge fund and a mutual fund running similar strategies. Of course, this matched-sample performance analysis technique is not perfect, as only a small number of funds will be included in each study.

A study by Cliffwater LLC does just that, comparing two investment vehicles offering the same strategy.[15] Its finding is that, on average, liquid alternative funds have lower risks than limited partnership (LP) funds that employ the same strategy. This makes sense to us, as the regulatory restrictions constrain the investment flexibility of managers in the mutual fund vehicle. The good news for mutual fund investors is that net of fees, returns for liquid alternative funds trail returns of the LP fund offered by the same manager by less than 1% per year. Some strategies, such as equity long/short, credit, market-neutral, and macro and managed futures funds, had return differences between 0.42% and 0.94% per year. Other strategies, namely event-driven and multistrategy funds, had return differences as large as 2.18%. As previously stated, the higher leverage employed in these strategies exacerbates the difference between the more highly levered LP vehicle and the much less levered mutual fund.

A study by David McCarthy looks at a sample of LP and registered funds and finds that equity long/short funds have had similar returns and market exposures across the two fund types.[16] This is good news for retail investors, as it means that retail investors in hedged equity mutual funds are getting a qualitatively similar experience to investors in equity hedge funds.

Finally, a study by Barclays segregates '40 Act fund offerings by whether the manager has had experience managing hedge funds or long-only mutual funds.[17] This study finds that all '40 Act funds with net long positions have earned a return of 0.9% per year, the HFRI Fund Weighted Composite Index have earned a return of 2.3% per year, and mutual funds run by hedge fund managers have earned 1.6% per year. This study also shows that during the crisis year of 2008, liquid alternative funds experienced lower drawdowns than the average long-only mutual fund.

19.6 KEY OBSERVATIONS REGARDING HISTORICAL RETURNS OF FUNDS OF FUNDS

Monthly returns to funds of funds are observed from January of 2000 to December of 2018 for a total of 228 observations. Exhibit 19.5 provides univariate return statistics for six styles of funds of hedge funds.

Market-defensive funds of funds tend to have underlying and unhedged short positions. According to HFR, market-defensive funds of funds invest in funds that "generally engage in short-biased strategies such as short selling and managed futures."[18] Ideally, this category of funds of funds should have low to negative correlations with respect to major market indices.

Conservative funds of funds have underlying hedged positions. According to HFR, conservative funds of funds tend to seek consistent returns primarily through "investing in funds that generally engage in more 'conservative' strategies such as Equity Market Neutral, Fixed Income Arbitrage, and Convertible Arbitrage."[19]

Strategic funds of funds tend to have underlying directional bets. According to HFR, strategic funds of funds seek superior returns primarily through "investing in funds that generally engage in more opportunistic strategies such as Emerging Markets, Sector Specific, and Equity Hedge."[20]

Diversified funds of funds represent a broad mix of funds. According to HFR, diversified funds of funds invest "in a variety of strategies among multiple managers."[21]

The composite index of funds of funds invests across the various styles of funds of funds investments.

Key observations on funds of funds returns that are consistent with economic reasoning are an essential component of knowledge and include the following:

1. All of the fund of funds sub-indices and the composite index exhibited historic return volatility less than one-third that of world equities except the strategic index, which was a little less than one-half.
2. Only the conservative index exhibited returns that were quite negatively skewed and had very large positive excess kurtosis.
3. All of the fund of funds sub-indices and the composite index exhibited high first-order return autocorrelation except the defensive index.
4. All of the fund of funds sub-indices and the composite index exhibited less than half the maximum drawdown of the world equities. The defensive index had a maximum drawdown of only 10.9%, less than one-fifth that of world equities.

In conclusion, we note that returns to funds of hedge funds exhibit volatility and drawdowns substantially lower than those of equity markets. For most styles of funds of hedge funds, autocorrelation is present, showing that many of the underlying assets and strategies may have lower levels of liquidity.

EXHIBIT 19.5 Statistical Summary of Returns

Index (Jan. 2000 – Dec. 2018)	HFRI Fund of Funds: Market Defensive Index	HFRI Fund of Funds: Conservative Index	HFRI Fund of Funds: Strategic Index	HFRI Fund of Funds: Diversified Index	HFRI Fund of Funds: Composite Index	MSCI World Equity
Annualized Arithmetic Mean	4.2%	3.0%	3.2%	3.2%	3.2%	4.5%
Annualized Standard Deviation	4.9%	3.6%	6.8%	4.8%	4.9%	15.0%
Annualized Semivolatility	2.8%	3.6%	5.4%	4.0%	4.1%	11.6%
Annualized Median	3.9%	4.9%	6.7%	5.4%	5.3%	11.6%
Skewness	0.2	−2.2	−0.6	−1.0	−1.0	−0.7
Excess Kurtosis	0.3	10.2	3.1	4.1	3.9	1.6
Sharpe Ratio	0.3	0.1	0.1	0.1	0.1	0.1
Sortino Ratio	4.1	0.1	0.1	0.2	0.2	0.2
Annualized Geometric Mean	4.1%	3.0%	3.0%	3.1%	3.1%	3.4%
First-Order Autocorrelation	0.01	0.45	0.25	0.30	0.31	0.14
Annualized Standard Deviation (adjusted for autocorrelation)	4.9%	5.8%	8.5%	6.5%	6.6%	17.1%
Maximum	4.9%	2.4%	8.7%	5.4%	5.2%	11.2%
Minimum	−3.2%	−5.9%	−7.7%	−6.5%	−6.5%	−19.0%
Max Drawdown	−10.9%	−20.4%	−26.8%	−21.8%	−22.2%	−54.0%

REVIEW QUESTIONS

1. List the four functions of fund of funds management.
2. Name four benefits to investing in funds of funds that may lead to higher net returns to limited partners without causing higher risk.
3. Name five benefits to investing in funds of funds that may lead to lower investment risk to limited partners without sacrificing expected return.
4. Describe the double layer of fees in funds of funds.
5. In theory, how would the volatility of an equally weighted portfolio of 16 uncorrelated and equally risky funds compare to the volatility of a single such fund?
6. Why might the incentive fees of a multistrategy fund differ substantially from the incentive fees of an otherwise similar fund of funds even if the stated fees are equal?
7. Why might the operational risks of a multistrategy fund differ substantially from the operational risks of a fund of funds?
8. What is a seeding fund?
9. What investment pools in the United States and Europe provide liquid access of investors to alternative investment strategies?
10. List the four major categories of funds of funds.

NOTES

1. Stephen J. Brown, Thomas L. Fraser, and Bing Liang, "Hedge Fund Due Diligence: A Source of Alpha in a Hedge Fund Portfolio Strategy," January 21, 2008. Available at SSRN: http://ssrn.com/abstract=1016904 or doi:10.2139/ssrn.1016904.
2. Martin Fothergill and Carolyn Coke, "Funds of Hedge Funds: An Introduction to Multi-Manager Funds," *Journal of Alternative Investments* 4, no. 2 (Fall 2001): 7–16.
3. Anne-Valere Amo, Helene Harasty, and Pierre Hillion, "Diversification Benefits of Funds of Hedge Funds: Identifying the Optimal Number of Hedge Funds," *Journal of Alternative Investments* 10, no. 2 (Fall 2007): 10–21.
4. Greg Gregoriou, "Are Managers of Funds of Hedge Funds Good Market Timers?" *Journal of Wealth Management* 7, no. 3 (Winter 2004): 61–76.
5. Girish Reddy, Peter Brady, and Kartik Patel, "Are Funds of Funds Simply Multi-Strategy Managers with Extra Fees?" *Journal of Alternative Investments* 10, no. 3 (Winter 2007): 49–61.
6. Igor Lomtev, Chris Woods, and Vladimir Zdorovtsov, "Fund of Hedge Fund vs. Multi-Strategy Providers: Implications for Cost-Effectiveness and Portfolio Risk," *Journal of Investment Strategy* 2, no. 1 (2007): 73–82.
7. See, for example, Stan E. Beckers, Ross Curds, and Simon Weinberger, "Funds of Hedge Funds Take the Wrong Risks," *Journal of Portfolio Management* 33, no. 3 (Spring 2007): 108–21; and Gregoriou, "Are Managers of Funds of Hedge Funds Good Market Timers?"
8. Reddy, Brady, and Patel, "Are Funds of Funds Simply Multi-Strategy Managers with Extra Fees?"
9. Vikas Agarwal and Jayant R. Kale, "On the Relative Performance of Multi-Strategy and Funds of Hedge Funds," *Journal of Investment Management* 5, no. 3 (2007): 41–63.
10. William Fung and David A. Hsieh, "Performance Characteristics of Hedge Funds: Natural versus Spurious Biases," *Journal of Financial and Quantitative Analysis* 35, no. 3 (2000): 291–307.

11. Andrew Ang, Matthew Rhodes-Kropf, and Rui Zhao, "Do Funds-of-Funds Deserve Their Fees-on-Fees?" NBER Working Paper, 2007.
12. Manuel Ammann and Patrick Moerth, "Impact of Fund Size on Hedge Fund Performance," *Journal of Asset Management* 6, no. 3 (2007): 219–38.
13. Brown, Fraser, and Liang, "Hedge Fund Due Diligence."
14. Keith H. Black, *Managing a Hedge Fund* (New York: McGraw-Hill, 2004).
15. Cliffwater LLC, "Performance of Private versus Liquid Alternatives: How Big a Difference?," 2013.
16. David McCarthy, "Hedge Funds versus Hedged Mutual Funds: An Examination of Equity Long/Short Funds," *Journal of Alternative Investments* 16, no. 3 (2014): 6–24.
17. Barclays, "Going Mainstream: Developments and Opportunities for Hedge Fund Managers in the '40 Act Space," April 2014.
18. www.hedgefundresearch.com/index.php?fuse=indices-str.
19. Ibid.
20. Ibid.
21. Ibid.

Private Securities

C hapter 20 is the first of the three chapters on private securities. It provides general background information on the assets underlying private equity investments with a focus on venture capital, growth equity, and buyouts. Chapter 21 discusses private equity funds and Chapter 22 discusses private credit.

CHAPTER 20

Private Equity Assets

P rivate equity is defined broadly in the CAIA curriculum, to such an extent that some private equity securities that are not equity and some that are publicly traded are included in the category. There are no universal categories of private equity. The CAIA curriculum divides private equity into three major categories: (1) venture capital (VC), the financing of start-up companies, (2) growth equity, noncontrolling interests in successfully emerging enterprises, and (3) buyouts, where established companies are purchased for full control.

20.1 INTRODUCTION TO PRIVATE EQUITY TERMS AND BACKGROUND

At the most general level, private securities can be divided into private equity and private credit, although the term private equity is sometimes used as an umbrella term that includes some private credit.

20.1.1 Private Equity Securities

Private equity is as old as commerce itself. Virtually every major enterprise began as a small, unlisted firm. Private equity is a long-term investment process that requires patience, due diligence, and hands-on monitoring. Private equity provides the capital investment and working capital that are used to help private companies grow and succeed. The payouts to most private equity investments resemble the payouts to long positions in out-of-the-money calls: The risks are great, but the potential rewards are even greater. This call option view of private equity from the perspective of the investor reflects the frequent total losses and occasional huge gains of private equity investments, especially venture capital.

Consider the three types of assets underlying private equity: VC, growth equity, and buyouts. Venture capital and buyouts focus on opposite ends of the life cycle of a company. Whereas VC represents nascent, start-up companies, buyouts represent established and mature companies. Growth equity tends to lie in the middle between VC and buyouts with underlying firms that are too large and established to be considered VC but too small to be publicly traded firms subject to buyouts.

Several private securities are often termed private equity that are legally or traditionally considered to be fixed-income securities, including mezzanine financing and distressed debt, when the risk characteristics of the securities resemble the risk exposure of equity positions. These securities are introduced briefly in the next three subsections and are covered in detail in Chapter 22.

20.1.2 Introduction to Mezzanine Debt

Mezzanine debt blurs the line between equity and debt because it contains both equity-like and debt-like features. It is referred to as *mezzanine* because it is inserted into a company's capital structure between the floor of equity and the ceiling of senior secured debt. Mezzanine debt is often viewed as a form of private equity because of its high risk and because it often comes with potential equity participation, although it appears as debt on an issuer's balance sheet. More often than not, mezzanine debt represents a hybrid, meaning a combination of debt and equity.

Typically, mezzanine financing is constructed as an intermediate-term bond, with some form of equity kicker thrown in as an additional enticement to the investor. An **equity kicker** is an option for some type of equity participation in the firm (e.g., options to buy shares of common stock) that is packaged with a debt financing transaction. The equity kicker portion provides the investor with an interest in the upside of the company, whereas the debt component provides a steady payment stream. The gap that mezzanine finance fills can be quite large and include several tranches of junior debt or preferred equity.

20.1.3 Introduction to Distressed Debt

Distressed debt investing is the practice of purchasing the debt of troubled companies, requiring special expertise and subjecting the investor to substantial risk. These troubled companies may have already defaulted on their debt, may be on the brink of default, or may be seeking bankruptcy protection. Like the other forms of private equity, this form of investing requires a longer-term horizon and the ability to accept the lack of liquidity for a security for which often no trading market exists.

Similar to the mezzanine debt just discussed, the returns to distressed debt tend to depend little on the overall performance of the stock market. This is because the value of the debt of a distressed or bankrupt company is more likely to rise and fall with the fortunes of the individual company, which in turn are driven mostly by idiosyncratic factors. In particular, the company's negotiations with its creditors have a much greater impact on the value of the company's debt than does the performance of the general economy.

A key to understanding distressed debt investing is to recognize that the term *distressed* has two meanings. First, it means that the issuer of the debt is troubled; the face value of its liabilities may exceed the value of its assets, or it may be unable to meet its debt service and interest payments as they come due. Therefore, distressed debt investing almost always means that some workout, turnaround, or bankruptcy solution must be implemented for the bonds to appreciate in value. Second, distressed refers to the price of the bonds. Distressed debt often trades for a small percentage of face value. This affords a savvy investor the opportunity to earn extraordinary returns by identifying a company with a viable business plan but a short-term cash flow problem.

Distressed debt investors are often referred to as vulture investors or just vultures because they are alleged to feast on the remains of underperforming companies. They buy the debt of troubled companies, including subordinated debt, junk bonds, bank loans, and obligations to suppliers. Their investment plan is to buy the distressed debt at a fraction of its face value and then seek improvement of their position through major changes in the assets, capital structure, or management of the company.

Both hedge funds and private equity funds invest in distressed debt. The goal of hedge funds in the distressed debt space is mainly to earn short-term trading profits from their event-driven strategy, typically waiting for a catalyst from the resolution of issues in the bankruptcy court. Private equity investors in distressed debt typically have a longer time horizon. In fact, many private equity investors may take control of a company's equity through their distressed debt position, or even hold publicly traded equity that may be distributed through the bankruptcy process.

20.1.4 Introduction to Leveraged Loans

Another asset class of fixed-income securities that private equity firms have moved into is leveraged loans. Leveraged loans are the more senior debt security in the capital structure of a firm relative to subordinated debt such as mezzanine financing. They are issued by firms with substantial debt (hence the name leveraged loans) or poor credit. Leveraged loans typically have high interest rates and low credit ratings (i.e., below investment grade). The loans are often created in order to provide the borrower with capital to finance an acquisition, as part of a refinancing, or to provide working capital.

Mezzanine debt, distressed debts, and leveraged loans are detailed in Chapter 22 on private credit.

20.2 OVERVIEW OF THREE FORMS OF PRE-IPO PRIVATE EQUITY INVESTING

A key investment strategy is to invest in firms that grow into publicly traded corporations.

Most large publicly traded firms began as small, nascent enterprises. For example, Apple was founded as Apple Computer Company in April 1976 by Steve Wozniak, Steve Jobs, and Ronald Wayne. Ronald Wayne soon sold his 10% share in the company for $500. In August 2018 Apple's market capitalization reached $1 trillion. This section discusses three major forms of investing in private companies with a goal of exiting the investment through an IPO (initial public offering).

20.2.1 Venture Capital to Initial Public Offering

Virtually every attempt to start a new business is venture capital, from the smallest retail store to the largest energy exploration. In terms of numbers, most of these ventures are financed fully by their founders, with little or no capital from others. However, this book is about investing in institutional-quality alternative investments, which form the vast majority of the total financial value of venture capital.

Venture capital (VC), the best known of the private equity categories, is early financing for young firms with high potential growth that do not have a sufficient track record to attract investment capital from traditional sources, like public markets or lending institutions. Entrepreneurs develop business plans and then seek investment capital to implement those plans, since start-up companies are unlikely to produce positive cash flow or earnings for several years. The equity stakes that venture capitalists initially acquire begin as a substantial but minority position in the company. Control by VC investors is not absolute.

A VC project is primarily distinguished by its small size, lack of revenues, and high risk. The typical investment into a VC project is $5 million or more, with a company value of $10 million to $100 million. The eventual goal of VC investors is to work with the original owners (typically the founders) to build products, revenues, and income to the point of the firm going public via an IPO and, eventually, for the VC investor to exit the investment through sales of the investor's now-listed equity stake. The pathway to an IPO typically includes additional funding and assistance by the VC investors in management of the firm.

Return targets for VC are large multiples such as 10- or 20-fold increases in value. VC is a large asset class that is often listed separately from other forms of private equity by investment managers.

20.2.2 Growth Equity to Initial Public Offering

Growth equity focuses on companies that have established a reliable base of revenues, an established business model, and have opportunities to expand that require more cash than can be funded by existing revenues. Growth equity is provided as additional working capital and/or to facilitate growth by increasing production capacity and developing markets or products. Typical investments in this stage can be $25 million or more, to firms of $100 million or more in size (middle market size), and annual revenues of $25 million to $50 million or more.

Growth equity typically does not involve substantial control by the new investors (as opposed to buyouts). Growth equity is usually the last financing round before an IPO or other exit (e.g., a buyout). Return expectations for equity growth are more modest (e.g., less than 10-fold) than the large multiples targeted in VC.

20.2.3 Buyout to Initial Public Offering

The largest forms of buyout, detailed in later sections, involve buying out a public company and taking the company private. However, buyouts of private companies commonly take full control of a company, typically with the eventual goal of taking the firm public. A private company that is a buyout target is typically founder-owned. The key distinction is control. Buyouts typically involve total control by the new investor.

20.2.4 Contrasting Venture Capital, Growth Equity, and Buyouts

Exhibit 20.1 summarizes eight major distinctions between VC, growth equity, and buyouts based on assets, revenues, control, time horizon, and so forth. Note how growth equity lies between VC and buyouts with respect to most of the distinctions.

EXHIBIT 20.1   Major Distinctions between VC, Growth Equity, and Buyouts

	Venture Capital	Growth Equity	Buyouts
Asset Size	$10 million+	$100 million+	$100 million+
Annual Revenue Size	$0 to $10 million	$25 million+	$25 million+
Control by Investor	A Team Approach	No Control Change	Buyer in Control
Use of Capital	Establish Product	Revenue Expansion	Earnings Growth
Time Horizon	5–10 Years	3–7 Years	3–5 Years
Potential Upside	5- to 20-fold	3- to 8-fold	2- to 5-fold
Target IRR	30%–60%	25%–40%	20%–35%
Investment Risk	Very High	Moderately High	Moderate

20.3   VENTURE CAPITAL

Venture capital is the most well-known category of private equity. Venture capital focuses on equity or equity-like claims of enterprises that are early stage in terms of growth. They are attempting to grow into large firms but have not yet established substantial and reliable revenues.

The foundation of VC is the underlying start-up businesses and the entrepreneurs who create and build them. Venture capitalists provide financing for these businesses using their own capital and the capital of their investors. Venture capitalists are not passive investors. Once they invest in a company, they take an active role either in an advisory capacity or as a director on the board of the company. They monitor the progress of the company, implement incentive plans for the entrepreneurs and management, and establish financial goals for the company. Besides providing management insight, venture capitalists usually have the right to hire and fire key managers, including the original entrepreneur. They also provide access to consultants, accountants, lawyers, investment bankers, and, most important, other businesses that might purchase the start-up company's product.

Venture capitalists are involved in numerous stages of a firm's growth. Different financing needs are required for each of these stages, and different product technology is found at each stage. In terms of company characteristics, start-up companies generally have a new or innovative technology that can be exploited with the right amount of capital. The management of the company is typically idea driven rather than operations driven. A proven revenue model may not yet be established, and the capital consumption is probably high.

The cash flows from VC are related to the operations of these nascent firms and are typically expected to be negative for several years. The **cash burn rate** of a business describes the speed with which cash is being depleted through time and can be used to project when the organization will deplete its cash and require outside funding. The time until the cash runs out is estimated by dividing the current cash balance by the organization's cash burn rate. For example, a company that has $30 million of cash and a burn rate of $2 million per month either needs new cash injections in 15 months or needs to reduce its burn rate.

Banks, other lending institutions, and the public stock market are generally unwilling to provide capital to support business plans of firms without collateral or without reasonably high probabilities of positive cash flows in the short run. As the source of equity financing to start-up companies, VC is risky, illiquid, and backed by unproven ideas. The VC investment strategy is to strive for very high rates of return to compensate for the considerable risks.

20.3.1 Securities and Goals Used in Venture Capital

Venture capital securities are the privately held stock, preferred stock, or equity-linked securities that venture capitalists obtain when investing in business ventures that are striving to become larger and to go public. Investors in venture capital securities must be prepared to invest for the long haul; investment horizons may be as extended as 5 to 10 years. During this time, venture capitalists often take active roles in providing managerial guidance and, to varying degrees, exercising managerial control. The ultimate goal of the venture capitalist is for the venture to be successful, usually to the point that the firm can exit the investment at a profit. **VC exits** typically focus on going public (i.e., conducting an initial public offering of the company's securities), but can also include sales to acquiring firms or even a leveraged recapitalization, where the proceeds from the debt are paid to the venture capitalist. Successful start-up companies funded by venture capital include Cisco Systems, Google, Microsoft, and Genentech.

Attractive VC investment opportunities can be difficult to assess and are usually concentrated in a few high-technology sectors, often resulting in a relatively high number of small investments. Returns stem from taking large risks to develop new businesses and concentrating efforts and capital through several incremental funding rounds. The goal is to build companies that can be sold or taken public with a high multiple of invested capital. These few big wins need to compensate for many failures. VC-funded companies can be seen as works in progress, with intermediate stages of completion. These stages of completion are often distinguished by milestones, such as rounds of financing (rounds A, B, and C) or, in the case of biotech companies, phases of clinical trials (phases I, II, and III). In this respect, they are development projects that cannot be prematurely exited without risking the loss of most, if not all, of one's invested capital. Thus, VC transactions should be viewed as long-term investments.

Venture capitalists usually invest in the convertible preferred stock of the start-up company. **Investment structures** used by venture capitalists include convertible preferred equity, convertible notes, or debentures that provide for the conversion of the principal amount of the note or bond into either common or preferred shares at the option of the venture capitalist, or other positions such as warrants.

Convertible preferred stock is used by VC investors to provide higher priority than common stock along with an implicit call option to share in upside potential similar to the upside potential of equity. In other words, venture capitalists have the option to convert their shares to common stock when exiting via an initial public offering (IPO) and are the favored manner of investment because they are senior to common stock in terms of dividends, voting rights, and liquidation preferences. Convertible notes and debentures may also allow conversion upon the occurrence of an event, such as a merger, an acquisition, or an IPO. There may be several rounds (or series) of preferred stock financing before a successful start-up company goes public.

Venture capitalists sometimes receive warrants to purchase the common equity of the start-up company, as well as stock rights in the event of an IPO.

VC funding by venture capitalists does not typically involve straight debt (i.e., nonconvertible). Venture capitalists gain control of a company over time through a series of equity investments. Venture capitalists typically provide not only financing for building businesses but also industry know-how, relevant contacts, and management expertise. Returns stem from building companies and from managing growth. The investments can be relatively small and are overwhelmingly equity or quasi-equity financed, with little or no leverage. Successful exit strategies usually require VC managers to secure follow-on financing.

20.3.2 The Option-Like Payout of Venture Capital

The venture capitalist has a simple binary choice with respect to every potential investment in a start-up business: Invest or don't invest. Investing in a start-up company is similar to the purchase of a call option. The price of the option is the capital that the venture capitalist invests in the start-up company. If the company fails, the venture capitalist forfeits the option premium—the capital invested. However, if the start-up company is successful, the venture capitalist shares in all of the upside, much like a call option.

Most start-ups fail. Clearly, this investment class is not for the fainthearted. Given that venture capitalists are dealing with nascent companies that may or may not burst onto the scene (some just burst), a wide range of returns should be expected. When a company does well, it can result in dramatic upside gains, like a 20-bagger, for its VC investors. The term **20-bagger** indicates a company that appreciates in value 20-fold compared to the cost of the VC investment. This return pattern is similar to a call option and tends to post a return pattern with a large positive skew and a large positive value of kurtosis.

20.3.3 History of Venture Capital

Institutional investing in VC remained limited until 1979, due in part to the so-called prudent person standard, or prudent man rule, in the United States. The **prudent person standard** is a requirement that specifies that the levels of care that should be exercised in particular decision-making roles, such as investment decisions made by a fiduciary, be equal to or greater than the care that a prudent person would exercise for his or her own portfolio. Prudent person rules were established to ensure competent investment decision-making with regard to the large and growing pension assets of U.S. corporations.

The prudent person standard or rule as interpreted prior to 1979 effectively prohibited U.S. pension funds from investing in venture capital funds because of their illiquidity and risk. In 1979, a clarification of the prudent person rule in the United States indicated that venture capital and other high-risk investments should not be considered on a stand-alone basis but on a portfolio basis. Thus, an investment with considerable total risk may be prudent if the marginal contribution of that investment to the risk of the portfolio is reduced through diversification. In addition, the rule clarified that the prudent person test should be based on an investment review process, not on the ultimate outcome of investment results. Therefore, as long as a pension fund investment fiduciary follows sufficient due diligence in considering the portfolio effects of investing in venture capital, the prudent person test is met.

The **change in the prudent person standard** was to base analysis on a portfolio basis (rather than a standalone basis) and to test for prudence based on analysis (rather than outcome), allowing U.S. pension funds for the first time to wholly endorse and engage in venture capital investing. In doing so, it opened venture capital to a vast source of capital: retirement assets.

20.3.4 Angel and Other Very Early Stages of Venture Capital

Although some VC firms classify themselves by geography or industry, by far the most distinguishing characteristic of VC investing is the stage of financing. However, the names and descriptions of these stages are not universal. Further, some investors do not differentiate between VC and growth equity, especially in the description of stages. This section does not include those stages that are viewed as growth equity.

Angel investing refers to the earliest stage of venture capital, in which investors fund the first cash needs of an entrepreneurial idea. Angel investors often come from F & F—that is, friends and family. But sometimes venture capitalists include a third F, for fools. At this earliest stage of the venture, typically a lone entrepreneur has just an idea, possibly sketched out at the kitchen table. There is no formal business plan, no management team, no product, no market analysis, just an idea.

In addition to family and friends, angel investors can be wealthy individuals who dabble in start-up companies. Many angel investors are successful businesspeople themselves who may prefer to focus their investments in the industry in which they have built their careers, so that they can offer industry-specific skills or analysis to the entrepreneur. This level of financing is typically done without a private placement memorandum or subscription agreement. It may be as informal as an agreement written on a cocktail napkin. Yet without the angel investor, many ideas would wither on the vine before reaching more traditional venture capitalists.

At the angel stage of financing, the task of the entrepreneur is to begin the development of a prototype product or service. The entrepreneur drafts or revises a business plan, assesses market potential, and possibly even assembles some key management team members. No marketing is done at this stage. This stage often includes or leads to alpha testing of the product or service. **Alpha testing** is the process of analyzing a product or service to determine its ability to perform its tasks, potentially under laboratory-like conditions, to generate feedback for developers.

The amount of financing at this stage is typically very small: $50,000 to $500,000. Any more than that would strain family, friends, and other angels. The money is used primarily to flesh out the concept to the point at which an intelligent business plan can be constructed.

The **seed capital stage** is typically the first stage where institutional investors commit their capital into a venture and is typically prior to having established the viability of the product. At this stage, a business plan is completed and presented to outside investors. Some members of the management team have been assembled at this point, and the entrepreneur and a small team have performed a market analysis and addressed other parts of the business plan. Financing is provided to complete the product development and possibly begin initial marketing of the prototype to potential customers.

This seed-capital phase of financing usually raises $1 million to $5 million. At this stage of financing, a prototype is developed and product testing begins. This is often referred to as **beta testing**, in which a prototype is sent to potential customers free of charge to get their input into the product's viability, design, and user-friendliness.

Very little, if any, revenue has been generated at this stage, and the company is definitely not profitable. Venture capitalists invest in this stage based on their due diligence of the management team, their own market analysis of the demand for the product or service, the viability of getting the product to market while there is still time and no other competitor, the additional management team members who need to be added, and the likely timing for additional rounds of capital from the same investors and/or new investors. Unfortunately, the entrepreneur might have to rely on angel investors through this stage as well.

20.3.5 First-Stage, Start-Up, and Early-Stage Venture Capital

The **first-stage, start-up stage, or early-stage of venture capital** begins when the start-up company has a viable product that has been beta tested and involves testing of the second-generation prototype with potential end users and funding after seed capital but before commercial viability has been established. Typically, a price or fee is being charged for the company's product or service. Revenues are being generated, and the product or service is now demonstrating its commercial viability. These early VC financing stages usually require investment totaling $2 million or more.

Start-up, first-stage, and early-stage financing is typically used to build out commercial-scale manufacturing services. The product is no longer being produced out of the entrepreneur's garage or some vacant space above a store. The company is now a going concern with an initial, if not complete, management team. At this stage, at least one venture capitalist is sitting on the board of directors of the company. In addition, the business and marketing plans are refined, manufacturing has begun, and initial sales have been established.

The goal of the start-up venture is to achieve market penetration with its product. Some of this will have been accomplished with the beta testing of the product. However, additional marketing must now be done. In addition, distribution channels should be identified by now, and the product should be established in these channels. Reaching a break-even point is the financial goal.

20.3.6 Second and Later Stages of Venture Capital

Second- or late-stage/expansion venture capital begins as the start-up company may have generated its first profitable quarter or be near the point of breaking even, and the company and its products are demonstrating commercial viability. Additional terms for the latter stages of VC (before reaching the classification of equity growth) can include third stage and formative stage. The number and names of further stages depend in part on whether a distinction is being made between venture capital and growth equity. Cash flow management is critical at this stage, as the company is not yet at the level where its operating cash flows alone can sustain its own growth.

At this late-stage/expansion VC stage, the start-up venture incurs the growing pains of all successful companies. The future is bright, but working capital is short.

Sales and receivables are growing, but the receivables have not yet been translated into a solid and stable cash flow. The start-up may need additional working capital because it has been focusing on product development and product sales but now finds itself with a huge backload of accounts receivable that it must collect from customers. Inevitably, start-up companies are very good at getting the product out the door but very poor at collecting receivables and turning sales into cold, hard cash. Also at this stage, market penetration has been established, and the company has met some initial sales goals. A break-even point has been achieved, and the company is now starting to generate profits, even though its cash is still lagging.

This is when expansion capital can help. Late-stage venture financing helps the successful start-up get through its initial cash crunch. Eventually, the receivables will be collected, and sufficient internal cash will be generated to make the start-up company a self-sustaining force. Until then, one more round of financing may be needed.

Mezzanine venture capital, or pre-IPO financing, is the last funding stage before a start-up company goes public (via an IPO) or is sold to a strategic buyer (via a buyout). At this point, a second-generation product may already be in production, if not distribution.

The financing at this stage is considered bridge or mezzanine financing to keep the company from running out of cash until the IPO or strategic sale. At this stage, the company is a proven winner with an established track record.

Mezzanine financing is halfway between equity and secured debt. Mezzanine financing may be in the form of convertible debt. In addition, the company may have sufficient revenue and earning power to qualify for a traditional loan. Mezzanine financing may also be used to buy out earlier investors and pay for other costs incurred before going public.

20.3.7 The J-Curve for Private Equity Projects

Chapter 3 discusses the concept of the J-curve in private equity, based on accounting conventions, including prompt recognition of early losses and deferral of unrecognized gains. The initial years of a start-up tend to generate a reported accounting-based loss. Money is spent in development, such as turning an idea into a prototype product and beta testing the product with potential customers. Little or no revenue is generated during this time, causing the initial dip in reported performance. Note, however, that the money being spent in development is being spent with the assumption that it is an investment that is creating value for the firm. In an economic sense, the firm may not be losing money, but rather exchanging cash for assets such as information, even if traditional accounting methods do not recognize the information as an asset on the balance sheet. Management believes that the firm is being made more valuable by the development work. It may only be in an accounting sense that the firm is sure to lose money at this stage.

Additional rounds of financing may be needed to get the company to generate cash and profit. Once critical mass is achieved—when products are sold, when sales are turned into profits, and when accounts receivable are turned into cash—the company turns a profit using traditional accounting. As the company realizes its profit potential, it enters into the higher range of profits on the right-hand side of the

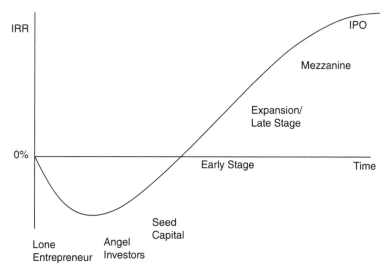

EXHIBIT 20.2   The Life Cycle of a Start-Up Company and the J-Curve

J-curve. The ultimate goal is at the rightmost part of the J-curve, when the start-up company achieves a public offering and the venture capitalists can exit the deal successfully.

The internal rates of return (IRRs) in Exhibit 20.2, except for the rightmost IRR, are generally computed as interim IRRs. Each interim IRR is therefore based on the nonmarket value (net asset value) that was estimated at that point in time. Exhibit 20.2 includes labels for the typical stages at various points on the curve. The concept of a J-curve for private equity *funds* is discussed in Chapter 21.

20.3.8   The Valuation of Venture Capital Companies Based on Operating Income

Valuation of venture capital is challenging because estimates of future cash flows are highly uncertain. While, in theory, the value of an investment is the sum of the discounted cash flows, in the case of VC the cash flow projections over long periods of time may be too unreliable to form the basis of a valuation. Numerous methods are used. This section uses a simple multiple of operating income to illustrate the types of rule-of-thumb methods that can be used to estimate the values of highly speculative ventures.

Valuation is also complicated by the lack of appropriate comparisons, which explains why venture capitalists carry out more extensive sector/product due diligence and more limited financial due diligence, compared to other private equity managers such as growth equity or buyout managers. A popular expression of VC worth is enterprise value. **Enterprise value** is the total value of the company, which adds the equity value of the firm to its outstanding debt and subtracts the cash on the firm's balance sheet. This definition leaves the question of the method of asset valuation unanswered.

In venture capital, assets are commonly valued based on EBITDA and EBITDA multiples (although other valuation metrics are often used in addition to or in place of EBITDA multiples) when reliable estimates of long-term cash flows are not possible. EBITDA is a firm's earnings or operating income before interest, taxes, depreciation, and amortization and is therefore used as a measure of before-tax cash flow rather than being a net-of-debt measure. **EBITDA multiples** are general levels of the perceived ratio between the enterprise value of a firm's assets and its estimated or projected earnings before income taxes, depreciation, and amortization. Thus, the enterprise value can be expanded into the product of the EBITDA and the EBITDA multiple.

A popular method of modeling the tremendous uncertainty of future value is to discount the projected enterprise value (projected to the estimated point of exit) with a very high required rate of return. VC investors target high IRRs. The reason is simple: There is substantial risk in funding a nascent company with brand-new technology relative to investments in more established companies with regular and predictable cash flows. These required rates of return are typically entitled IRRs consistent with the focus of IRR as a metric for private investments. Equation 20.1 calculates the value of the venture as a discounted analysis of the enterprise value.

$$\text{Value of Venture} = (\text{EBITDA} \times \text{EBITDA multiple})/(1 + \text{IRR})^T \qquad (20.1)$$

where IRR is the investor's required rate of return and T is the number of years estimated before exit.

Consider a VC investor contemplating a \$4 million investment in a venture targeted to take six years to reach the point of being bought out or going public. The investor requires a 60% IRR, given the highly uncertain nature of the venture and the risk that the venture will not succeed. The investor projects an EBITDA of \$20 million (if successful) and an EBITDA multiple of 7.5. Inserting these values into Equation 20.1 generates:

$$\text{Value of Venture} = (\$20 \text{ million} \times 7.5)/(1.60^6) = \$8.94 \text{ million}$$

Taking into consideration the percentage of the firm that the investor will own, the costs of providing oversight and managerial assistance, and any other existing claims to the firm such as indebtedness, the VC investor must decide whether the \$8.94 million discounted enterprise value warrants the \$4 million investment.

☞ APPLICATION 20.3.8A

A potential VC investment has a projected EBITDA of \$25 million (if successful) and an EBITDA multiple of 8, if the project can be exited in 7 years. Ignoring the percentage of the firm that the investor will not own, the costs of providing oversight and managerial assistance, and any other existing claims to the firm such as indebtedness, what is the estimated value of the venture if its required IRR is 65%?

$$\text{Value of Venture} = (\$25 \text{ million} \times 8.0)/(1.65^7) = \$6.01 \text{ million}$$

Note from inspection of Equation 20.1 that the model focuses on three especially crucial determinants: (1) the potential operating income of the venture (the EBITDA), (2) the time that it is expected to get to the potential operating income (T), and (3) the level of required rate of return necessary, taking into account the tremendous uncertainties and risks of the venture.

20.3.9 Venture Capital Business Plans

How does a venture capitalist select investments? The most important document to a venture capitalist deciding whether to invest in a start-up company is the business plan of the entrepreneur. The **venture capital business plan** should clearly state the business strategy, identify the niche that the new company will fill, and describe the resources needed to fill that niche, including the expenses, personnel, and assets. It must be comprehensive, coherent, and internally consistent. The business plan of the entrepreneur has two key objectives: (1) to provide the information necessary to attract financing from a venture capitalist, and (2) to serve as an internal game plan for the development of the start-up company.

Business plans should typically have an executive summary and sections that analyze or detail the plans for the market, the product or service, intellectual property rights, the management team, operations, the prior operating history, financial statement projections, the amount of and schedule for financing, and exit opportunities.

The **exit plan** describes how venture capitalists can liquidate their investment in the start-up company to realize a gain for themselves and their investors. Facilitating exit strategies is a way venture capitalists can add value beyond providing start-up financing. Venture capitalists often have many contacts within established operating companies. An established company may be willing to acquire the start-up company for its technology as part of a strategic expansion of its product line (i.e., an exit based on a buyout). Additionally, venture capitalists maintain close ties with investment bankers. These bankers are necessary if the start-up company decides to seek exit via an IPO. In addition, a venture capitalist may ask other venture capitalists to invest in the start-up company. This helps to spread the risk and also provides additional sources of contacts with operating companies and investment bankers.

20.4 VENTURE CAPITAL AS A COMPOUND OPTION

Previous sections in this chapter describe the call-option-like payoff and nature of venture capital. Further valuable insight can be derived from viewing VC as a compound option. A **compound option** is an option on an option. In other words, a compound option allows its owner the right but not the obligation to pay additional money at some point in the future to obtain an option.

For example, consider a project requiring $100,000 of angel capital and expected to last one year to explore a business idea potentially capable of receiving $2 million of seed capital. If successfully deployed, the seed capital may lead to early-stage financing of $5 million, which in turn could lead to later stages with even higher capital requirements, ultimately leading to the possibility of an IPO.

Money invested in each of these stages of a venture can be viewed as the purchase of a call option on investing in the next stage of the venture, which in turn is a call option. In the very first investment of $100,000, the $100,000 is the price or premium of the first option on the project, which has an expiration date of one year and a strike price of $2 million. If that option is exercised, the venture capitalist acquires another option costing $2 million, with a strike price of $5 million.

The compound option view of VC is synonymous with the analysis of real estate development as a string of real options in Chapter 13. In both cases, the key to the process is that the option's owner delays committing further capital until *new information* has arrived. Entrepreneurs may be charged with reaching milestones. A **milestone** is a set of goals that must be met to complete a phase and usually denotes when the entrepreneur will be eligible for the next round of financing. That is, the venture capitalist may explicitly state the specified operating goals of the firm that must be met before more funds are invested in the venture. Milestones may include patents on a product, revenue from a product, improvements in EBITDA, and so on. It is the ability to defer investment decisions until uncertainty has diminished that gives these options their primary value, not the time value of money.

When viewing each VC investment as a compound call option, the option's expiration date is the point in time at which either additional capital has to be invested or the project is abandoned or sold. Options are exercised when the option holder perceives that the value of the next option being acquired exceeds the strike price of the current option. If all options are successfully exercised, even the option to exit via an IPO, the resulting equity in the leveraged public company itself can be viewed and analyzed as a call option. In a VC project, each call option is purchased far out-of-the-money and typically has modest chances of being exercised.

The compound option view of VC facilitates an understanding of the high value to a venture capitalist of being able to make relatively small investments in projects that generate high profits if successful and can be abandoned if unsuccessful. The compound option view also clarifies the **two keys to successful VC investing**: (1) identifying underpriced options by locating potentially valuable projects for which substantial information regarding likely profitability can be obtained prior to commitment of substantial capital, and (2) abandoning worthless out-of-the-money options when they are expiring by ignoring sunk costs and judiciously assessing likely outcomes of success based on the objective analysis of new information.

20.5 GROWTH EQUITY

There is no clear demarcation between financing for the later stages of venture capital and growth equity. The later stages of venture capital are often described as the expansion stage (second or third stage), borrowing stage, late stage, mezzanine stage, and so forth. These stages occur after the VC firm has established the technology and market for its new product or services. The stages can overlap with growth equity.

Growth equity (also called growth capital or expansion capital) covers investment in firms after the VC stage and prior to a buyout, such as becoming publicly traded (exited by IPO). Firms seeking financing in the form of growth equity have been successful in establishing a strong base of revenues, as opposed to VC companies that are striving to be recognized as a leading provider of a good or service. Growth equity financing is the final financing prior to exit via an IPO.

A primary demarcation between a project being in the later part of VC or in the growth equity stage involves control: If the financing includes a "team approach" to managing the nascent enterprise, it is likely late-stage/expansion venture capital. To the extent that the financing comes with limited ongoing managerial involvement by the investor, then it is more like growth equity than VC. Growth equity is used to tap into distribution channels, establish call centers, expand manufacturing facilities, and attract the additional management and operational talent necessary to ramp up operations and transform the company into a longer-term success.

20.5.1 Describing Growth Equity Investments

As discussed in section 20.2.4, Exhibit 20.1 summarizes and compares key characteristics of growth equity alongside venture capital and buyouts. The exhibit provides approximate ranges for quantitative characteristics such as asset size, annual revenue, potential upside ratios, and target IRRs. This section focuses on qualitative characteristics.

SECURITIES: **Growth equity securities** are newly originated securities that have a minority position in terms of control but a relatively high position in terms of liquidation priority, such as convertible preferred equities or debt.

SOURCE OF GROWTH: Large increases in the value of a VC company come from increased probability of the successful launch of a product or service. Increases in the value of growth equity primarily come from growth in the firm's revenues and profitability. That growth is enabled or accelerated by financing from growth equity that enables enhanced production and injects working capital to meet the expanded capital requirements of increased production costs and increased accounts receivable.

CASHFLOW: VC companies have little or no net cash flow. Growth equity companies have little or no interest payments (little or no debt), moderate cash inflow from revenues, but little or no free cash flow.

20.5.2 Protective Provisions as a Key Deal Characteristic

Matt Stewart (2012) describes the importance of protective provisions in growth equity investing.[1] **Protective provisions in growth equity** provide operational control such as investor consent rights on key transactions, with key growth transactions including changes in capital structure, major assets, tax or accounting policies, key employees, and significant operational activities. Also, growth equity investors should require notification and consent on substantial deviations from the budget or changes in the business plan. These provisions help facilitate the monitoring and, if necessary, the control of the enterprise by its growth equity investors, which lies between total control and no control.

20.5.3 Redemption Rights as a Key Deal Characteristic

Stewart describes the importance of redemption rights and details their characteristics.[2] **Redemption rights** grant powers to investors to redeem their position in the company by specifying the triggers and actions that demark the remedies available to the investors.

> FOUR PRINCIPAL CONSIDERATIONS IN REDEMPTION RIGHTS: **Four principal considerations in redemption rights are** (1) redemption triggers, (2) redemption value, (3) sources of funds, and (4) remedies for defaulted redemption.
>
> REDEMPTION TRIGGERS: The **three common redemption triggers** are time, performance, and violations of covenants. (1) Time: the time-based trigger for redemption trigger is typically 60–66 months after the original issuance date; (2) performance: performance-based triggers are milestones typically benchmarked to revenue or profitability, and may be tested multiple times during the life of the investment; and (3) covenant-based: covenant-based triggers are similar to default triggers in credit and are typically based on failure to satisfy financial and other covenants.
>
> REDEMPTION VALUE: If redemption is triggered, the investor has a right to the prenegotiated redemption value. A **growth equity redemption value** is typically set as the maximum of one of the following or the maximum of two or more of the following: (1) the original issuance price plus a preferred return, (2) a multiple of the original issuance price, and (3) the fair market value of the equity interest.
>
> SOURCES OF FUNDS: Growth equity investors often obtain contractual requirements of the efforts that the issuer must use to meet requested redemptions. **Growth equity redemption sources** can be required to include: (1) all "legally available funds," (2) undertaking a "forced sale" or other capital raising transaction, (3) issuing a promissory note for the redemption value, and/or (4) using all other available means in order to effect a required redemption.
>
> DEFAULT REMEDIES: Growth equity contracts may include default remedies. **Growth equity default remedies** include springing board remedies and forced sales. A **springing board remedy** occurs when the investor designates a majority of the defaulting issuer's board of directors. A **forced sale remedy** occurs when an investor compels a liquidating transaction, such as sale of the entire company or other transactions, to generate cash to meet the redemption obligation.

20.5.4 The Valuation of Growth Equity Based on Revenue

The valuation of growth equity is similar to the valuation of venture capital in the sense that most of the value emanates from the uncertain potential for large growth and a favorable exit. As in the case of venture capital, sophisticated techniques for valuation, such as discounted annual cash flow analysis, may not be viable given a high level of uncertainty. This valuation example focuses on a company within a service industry. A popular method of modeling the value of a service company such as an asset manager or consulting firm is based on a multiple of revenues. The **times revenue method** values an enterprise as the product of its projected annual revenue and a multiple derived from analysis of the value of similar firms.

An enterprise-value-to-revenue (EV/R) multiple value may be estimated based on observation of publicly traded firms or previous deals. The EV/R multiple is often adjusted to reflect deal-specific attributes such as anticipated levels of operating costs, compared to industry norms, and anticipated levels of cash or other assets.

Equation 20.2 discounts the estimate of the enterprise value on exit.

$$\text{Value of Venture} = (\text{Annual Revenue} \times \text{Revenue Multiple})/(1 + \text{IRR})^T \quad (20.2)$$

where annual revenue is the estimated sales revenues in T years and revenue multiple is the EV/R anticipated at time T (the exit time).

Consider a growth equity investor requiring a 40% IRR on a growth equity investment in a firm that has substantial uncertainty with regard to its likely growth. The investor projects potential annual revenues of $50 million in five years (if successful), at which point an IPO is anticipated. Analysis of similar firms that are publicly traded indicates a typical ratio of enterprise value to annual revenues (EV/R) of 2.0. Inserting these values into Equation 20.2 generates:

$$\text{Value of Venture} = (\$50 \text{ million} \times 2.0)/(1.40^5) = \$18.59 \text{ million}$$

Taking into consideration the percentage of the firm that the investor will own, the growth equity investor must decide whether the $18.59 million discounted enterprise value for the entire firm warrants any proposed investment in growth equity for a share of the firm.

☞ APPLICATION 20.5.4A

A potential growth equity investment has projected annual revenues of $80 million in six years, at which point an IPO is anticipated. Similar publicly traded firms have enterprise-value-to-revenue multiples of 2.25. The firm seeks growth equity financing and offers a 25% stake in the company. Based on Equation 20.2, and ignoring any cash or debt in the existing firm, determine the estimated value of the growth equity if the required IRR is 45%.

$$\text{Value of Venture} = (\$80 \text{ million} \times 2.25)/(1.45^6) = \$19.37 \text{ million}$$
$$\text{Value of Growth Equity Stake} = 25\% \times \$19.37 \text{ million} = \$4.84 \text{ million}$$

Note from inspection of Equation 20.2 that the model focuses on three especially crucial determinants: (1) the potential revenue of the mature firm, (2) the time that it is expected to get to maturity and exit (T), and (3) the level of required rate of return necessary, taking into account the substantial uncertainties of reaching the revenue potential.

20.6 BUYOUTS AND LEVERAGED BUYOUTS

Buyout is a generic term that denotes a change of ownership. A **buyout** occurs when capital, often as a mix of debt and equity, is used to acquire an entire existing company (private or publicly traded) from its current shareholders and to operate the company as an independent organization—as opposed to an *acquisition,* in which the acquired company is folded into the buyer's existing company. Distinctions between buyouts tend to focus on the purpose of the buyout and the management team that will operate the target firm. The largest type of buyout is a leveraged buyout, which is discussed in detail in section 20.8.

20.6.1 Overview of Buyout Types

A **buyout of a private company** is a form of private equity that is often executed in lieu of an IPO exit, from the perspective of the shareholders who are selling the company. Buyouts focus on enterprises that are candidates to be transformed into being more profitable and to grow in potential value prior to an IPO. Buyouts of private companies are detailed in section 20.7.

20.6.2 Overview of Leveraged Buyouts

A **leveraged buyout (LBO)** is distinguished from a traditional investment by three primary aspects: (1) an LBO buys out control of the assets or the firm, (2) an LBO uses substantial leverage, and (3) the resulting leveraged firm is not immediately publicly traded. The target firm of an LBO is typically a publicly traded firm, but the term may also be used to describe buyouts of private firms. Thus, most LBOs transform the target company from being publicly traded to being highly leveraged private equity. LBOs are distinguished from mergers and acquisitions that typically fold the structure and operations of the target firm into the acquiring firm.

When a public company is bought entirely and delisted from the stock exchange, the transaction is referred to as public-to-private (P2P). Target companies for a buyout are established enterprises with tangible assets and are normally beyond the cash-burning stage, which allows the use of debt to finance part of the transaction. Thus these buyouts are referred to as leveraged buyouts.

Control of the new company is concentrated in the hands of the buyout firm and the target company's management, and there are usually no public shares left outstanding. The goal of the buyout is to increase the value of a corporation by unlocking hidden value, maximizing the borrowing capacity of a company's balance sheet, taking advantage of the tax benefits of using debt financing, and/or exploiting existing but underfunded opportunities. Private companies often state that it is easier to make long-term investments without the oversight of investors in public companies, who may focus on short-term results and quarterly earnings.

LBOs are detailed in section 20.8.

20.6.3 Types of Private Equity Buyouts and Resulting Management

A **management buy-in (MBI)** is a type of LBO in which the buyout is led by an outside management team. Control of the new company is taken over by the new (outside) management team, and the old (incumbent) management team leaves. The compensation package, if any, offered to or negotiated by the incumbent managers can be a critical issue, which is discussed in a subsequent section.

A buyout that is termed an LBO often involves bringing in a new management team to replace the firm's existing management. An LBO led by the firm's existing managers that retains most top members of the management team is usually referred to as a management buyout. A **management buyout (MBO)** occurs when the current management acquires the company.

A **buy-in management buyout** is a hybrid between an MBI and an MBO in which the new management team is a combination of new managers and incumbent managers.

A secondary buyout is an increasingly important sector of buyouts. In most large buyouts, a public company is being taken private. In a **secondary buyout (SBO)**, one private equity firm typically sells a private company to another private equity firm. In effect, a secondary buyout is typically an ownership change among private equity firms. Secondary buyouts provide a secondary-market-like opportunity for private equity firms to exit a buyout. Phalippou notes that the performance of secondary buyouts in a PE fund depends on when the deal is closed relative to the fund's investment period. A buyout fund that purchases a portfolio company through an SBO in the first half of the fund's investment period sees that portfolio company perform inline with other investments in the fund. SBOs purchased late in the fund's investment period, when the GP might be racing to close on deals simply to increase invested capital and subsequent management fees, tend to underperform SBOs purchased earlier in the life of the fund as well as underperforming investments directly in portfolio companies.[3]

20.6.4 Private Equity Strategies Based on Their Purpose

Other private equity strategies that do not fit neatly into the above categories include:

Rescue capital (or turnaround capital) refers to a strategy in which capital is provided to help established companies recover profitability after experiencing trading, financial, operational, or other difficulties.

Replacement capital (also called secondary purchase capital) refers to a strategy in which capital is provided to acquire existing shares in a company from another PE investment organization.

20.7 BUYOUTS OF PRIVATE COMPANIES

This section details buyouts of private companies by an entity that has a private ownership structure. Buyouts are distinguished from mergers by the extent to which the firm that is bought out is intended to function as a stand-alone business rather than to be folded into the organization of the purchaser. In a buyout of a private company, all of the equity is typically acquired and control is absolute. The terms for purchasing control of a company are not universal or clearly delineated. Since this chapter is on private equity, the focus is on buyout transactions that generate privately owned claims with equity or equity-like exposures. The most broad and generic term for these transactions is buyouts.

20.7.1 Buyout Objectives

Investors in buyouts target lower internal rates of return (IRRs) than in venture capital, although both are quite high. The reason the VC-required IRRs are higher is simple: There is more risk funding a nascent company with brand-new technology than an established company with regular and predictable cash flows.

A buyout of a private company is an alternative exit from an IPO, from the perspective of an early investor such as a venture capitalist. Typically the target company has an established product. The management of the company going forward is driven not by idea generation but often by improving efficiency. Revenues are established, recurring, and fairly predictable. With a buyout, capital is necessary not for product or service development (as in VC) but to optimize the company's efficiencies with the likely ultimate goal of an IPO exit.

Ultimately buyouts must have a value-creating purpose. The next two sections discuss two important potential objectives.

20.7.2 Buyouts and Capital Structure Optimization

Large capital requirements and lower risk levels relative to VC result in most buyout managers making a smaller number of investments compared to venture capitalists. Buyout transactions typically use both equity and debt financing to acquire companies. Assets of the acquired company are used as collateral for the debt, and the company's cash flow is used to pay off the debt. Buyout managers conduct intensive financial due diligence and occasionally rely on sophisticated financial engineering. Financial engineering, in this context, refers to the process of creating an optimal capital structure for a company.

In private equity, the capital structure is often made up of different types of financial instruments, such as multiple layers of debt, mezzanine, and equity, each carrying a different risk-reward profile. Buyouts typically use debt financing, either through bank loans or with newly issued debt to purchase the outstanding equity of the target company. Typically, these loans and bonds are secured by the underlying assets of the company being bought.

Mezzanine financing relates to capital provided through the issuance of subordinated debt, with warrants or conversion rights to finance the expansion or transition capital for established companies (usually privately held or below investment grade, or both). While mezzanine financing gives a more predictable cash-flow profile, it is unlikely to provide capital returns comparable to other PE financing forms.

20.7.3 Buyouts and Operational Efficiency Optimization

A multitude of approaches to improving operational efficiency can be combined in a transaction, such as divestment of unrelated businesses, vertical or horizontal integration through acquisition, and company turnaround. Buyout managers need to give extensive advice on strategic and business planning, and they tend to focus on consistent rather than outsized returns. Because they target established enterprises, buyout firms experience fewer outright failures but have upside potential that is more limited.

The ability to analyze a company's operations and increase efficiencies, as opposed to the implementation of capital structure changes, is the primary driver of a successful transaction.

20.8 LEVERAGED BUYOUTS (LBOs)

A buyout is described as an LBO when, after the buyout, the debt-to-equity ratio is much greater than before the acquisition. In fact, the debt-to-equity ratio can be as high as 9:1, meaning the capital structure of the company after the buyout is 90% debt and 10% equity. An LBO typically includes an effort to make fundamental changes in the management and/or operations of the target.

20.8.1 History of Leveraged Buyouts

Although buyouts began after World War II, it was not until the 1970s that their investment value became apparent. In 1976, a new investment firm, Kohlberg Kravis Roberts & Co. (KKR), was created on Wall Street with just $3 million of its own funds to invest. The founders of KKR had previously worked at Bear Stearns Companies, where they helped pioneer buyout transactions as early as 1968. No firm has had a greater impact on the buyout market than KKR, which has conducted landmark transactions, such as the buyout of RJR Nabisco.

The 1980s witnessed the rise of a key element of the growth in buyouts: financing of the buyouts using bonds with low credit ratings, known as junk bonds. Junk bonds are debt instruments with high credit risk, also referred to as high-yield, non-investment-grade, or speculative-grade debt. Bonds with low credit ratings previously existed, primarily as a result of a decline from an initial investment-grade rating. Michael Milken of Drexel Burnham Lambert helped pioneer the use of high-yield debt as a financing tool by issuing junk bonds to finance buyouts.

Fueled by junk bond financing, buyout deals reached an initial peak in 1989, when KKR bought the giant food conglomerate RJR Nabisco Inc. for $31 billion in a deal that was documented in the book and movie *Barbarians at the Gate*.[4] This buyout would stand as the largest buyout for many years, until KKR surpassed the RJR Nabisco deal in 2006 with its bid for TXU Corporation, a major Texas-based utility company. The subsequent large debt load of Energy Future Holdings, the holding company successor to TXU, led to its bankruptcy in 2014. The bankruptcy is also attributed to the company's heavy reliance on coal-fired generation facilities, which struggled to compete with natural gas power production due to the depressed prices of natural gas and the increased supply of natural gas from improved production techniques (e.g., fracking).

In the 1990s, buyout activity declined for two reasons. First, the recession of 1990–91, that affected most major world economies, briefly pushed credit spreads to high levels and thus dampened the attractiveness of junk bond financing for buyouts. Second, in 1998, the Russian government defaulted on its sovereign bonds, which once again sent credit spreads spiraling upward. Whereas debt represented as much as 95% of the financing of some buyout deals during the 1980s, by the end of the 1990s, buyouts financed with more than 75% debt were viewed as unattractive.

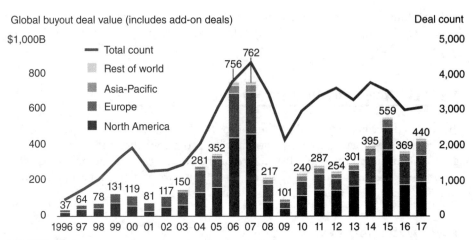

EXHIBIT 20.3   Global Buyout Deal Values and Counts
Source: Bain *Global Private Equity Report 2018*, https://go.bain.com/rs/545-OFW-044/
images/BAIN_REPORT_2018_Private_Equity_Report.pdf.

Bain publishes an annual *Global Private Equity Report* that in 2018 reported global buyout deal values and numbers as reproduced in Exhibit 20.3. As evidenced in Exhibit 20.3, the new millennium started quietly for the buyout market, but availability of credit increased in the United States and elsewhere, leading to an unparalleled boom in buyouts from 2003 into early 2007. This buyout boom culminated in the largest buyout ever: the $45 billion buyout of TXU Corporation. But by late 2007, the liquidity bubble had burst, leading to the credit problems of 2008 and the swift decline of buyout activity. Thus, buyout activity is driven not just by economic growth but also by interest rates and credit spreads. Note that in the 10 years subsequent to the global financial crisis, deal sizes and counts have resumed growth but have yet to reach the pre-crisis levels of 2006 and 2007.

20.8.2   Three Key Economic and Agency Issues of Buyouts

Three economic and agency issues related to buyouts are key:

Are Buyout Markets Segmented and Informationally Inefficient?   Buyout activity was previously thought to take place in a segmented market. **Segmentation**, in this context, denotes the grouping of market participants into clienteles that focus their activities within specific areas of the market, rather than varying their range of activities more broadly throughout all available opportunities. When a market is segmented, the valuations in that market can vary based on the preferences of the clienteles that dominate the particular segments. For example, it is often argued that the fixed-income market is segmented, based on the maturity ranges in which different investors (clienteles) prefer to invest. Thus, short-term yields might be argued to be driven by money market investors, whereas longer-term yields are driven by pension and insurance firms in a segmented market.

Buyout activity was also previously thought to take place in an inefficient market. Inefficiency refers to informational inefficiency, the idea that transactions take place with relatively large divergences between the actual prices of the transactions and the true underlying values of those transactions, based on all available information. Segmentation can lead to informational market inefficiency.

An **evolution of the buyout market** has occurred that has been driven by substantial buyout activity and has resulted in a less segmented market that has grown into a more efficient, auction-driven asset market, in which greater competition has reduced abnormal profit opportunities.

Are Management Buyouts a Violation of Fiduciary Duties? Buyouts can have large economic consequences to both the managers and shareholders of the target firm. There is an inherent conflict of interest between the shareholders as principals and the managers as agents with regard to most buyouts. That conflict of interest can become especially important in the high-stakes environment of buyouts. The primary conflicts involved in management buyouts are quite distinct from the conflicts involved in management buy-ins.

In an MBO, the existing management team takes over ownership of the firm from the firm's existing shareholders.

Managers clearly owe a fiduciary duty to the shareholders of the firm in which they are employed. Managers tend to have superior information regarding the firm and its potential value. Presumably, in a management buyout, the incumbent managers perceive that there are substantial gains that can be unlocked through their actions. A critical issue is whether managers choosing to pursue a path of unlocking those gains through a management buyout are violating their fiduciary responsibilities to the firm's shareholders. In other words, if a management team leads a buyout that unlocks tremendous value for themselves rather than implementing those changes for the firm's existing owners, has the management team as agents enriched themselves at the expense of the principals? Or do the existing shareholders receive a generous sales price based on the anticipated benefits that the new management team will be able to unlock after the buyout—benefits that could not be unlocked under the current ownership structure and incentives? In the latter case, the managers might be best fulfilling their fiduciary responsibility by initiating an MBO.

Are Managers Perversely Incentivized with Regard to Management Buyins? In an MBI, an external management team replaces the existing management team. The outcome of an MBI for incumbent managers can vary tremendously depending on the extent to which the managers are compensated upon their departure.

A generous compensation scheme, known as a **golden parachute**, is often given to top managers whose careers are being negatively affected by a corporate reorganization. Two primary conflicts of interest emanate from these potentially lucrative compensation schemes. First, incumbent managers have a strong incentive to resist any buyout attempt (no matter how lucrative to shareholders) that displaces them as managers if the buyout does not provide them with generous compensation. Second, incumbent managers have a strong incentive to encourage buyouts that offer them generous compensation. Thus, incumbent managers are incentivized to interfere with buyouts or promote buyouts based on the financial implications to themselves rather than based purely on their duties to serve the interests of the shareholders.

20.8.3   Five General Categories of LBOs That Can Create Value

Most LBOs can be identified with one of five major categories based on the motivation or circumstances of the deal.

1. EFFICIENCY BUYOUTS: **Efficiency buyouts** are LBOs that improve operating efficiency. A company may be bought out because it is shackled with a noncompetitive operating structure. For large public companies with widespread equity ownership, management may have little incentive to create shareholder value because it has a small stake in the company's profit. Under these circumstances, management is likely to be compensated based on revenue growth, which may result in excessive expansion and operating inefficiencies. These examples often occur in mature industries with stable cash flows.

   Efficiency buyouts often lead to a reduction in firm assets and revenue with the goal of eventually increasing firm profits. Such a buyout introduces more concentrated ownership and a better incentive scheme to mitigate agency problems. Management is given a stake in the company with an incentive scheme tied not to increasing revenues but to increasing operating margins and equity value. In addition, a high leverage ratio is used to ensure that management has little discretion to invest in inefficient projects. Last, the LBO firm replaces the diverse shareholder base and provides the active oversight that was lacking with the prior widespread equity owners.

2. ENTREPRENEURSHIP STIMULATORS: **Entrepreneurship stimulators** are LBOs that create value by helping to free management to concentrate on innovations. One frequently used strategy focuses on an unwanted or neglected operating division. Often an operating division of a conglomerate is chained to its parent company, which may impede its ability to implement an effective business plan. An LBO can free the operating division to control its own destiny.

3. THE OVERSTUFFED CORPORATION: One of the main targets of many LBO firms is conglomerates. **Conglomerates** have many different divisions or subsidiaries, often operating in completely different industries. Wall Street analysts are often reluctant to follow or cover conglomerates because they do not fit neatly into any one industrial category. As a result, these companies can be misunderstood by the investing public and perhaps undervalued. Sometimes conglomerates drain profits from profitable divisions within the firm and use them to prop up failing divisions rather than reinvesting them in successful divisions or distributing them to shareholders as dividends. An LBO can be used to dismantle inefficient conglomerates, shut down or sell inefficient operations, and allow profitable divisions to reinvest and meet their growth potential.

4. BUY-AND-BUILD STRATEGY: A **buy-and-build strategy** is an LBO value-creation strategy involving the synergistic combination of several operating companies or divisions through additional buyouts. The LBO firm begins with one buyout and then acquires more companies and divisions that are strategically aligned with the initial LBO portfolio company. The strategy seeks to benefit from synergies realized through the combination of several different companies into one. In some respects, this strategy is the reverse of that for conglomerates. Rather than strip a conglomerate down to its most profitable divisions, this strategy

pursues an assembling approach. This type of strategy is also known as a lever-aged buildup or roll up.

5. TURNAROUND STRATEGY: Traditional buyout firms often look for successful, mature companies with low debt-to-equity ratios and stable management. The economic recession that began in 2007 highlighted another form of LBO: the turnaround LBO. A **turnaround strategy** is an approach used by LBO funds that look for underperforming companies with excessive leverage or poor man-agement. The targets for turnaround LBO specialists come from two primary sources: (1) ailing companies on the brink of bankruptcy, and (2) underperform-ing companies in another LBO fund's portfolio. In some cases, the private equity firm does not buy out the complete company but makes a large equity contribu-tion at a price discounted to the public market price of the stock and takes seats on the target company's board of directors.

20.8.4   The Appeal and Four Benefits of a Leveraged Buyout to Targets

Leveraged buyouts can have a number of appealing characteristics to corporate man-agement and investors of the target firm. From the perspective of the shareholders of the target firm, LBO offers are usually accepted because the bid price for their shares is typically at a large premium compared to the market price. More to the point, LBO firms often target companies that have a depressed stock price. Conse-quently, shareholders often welcome an LBO bid. From the perspective of the target firm's corporate management, the benefits to those who are retained can include the following:

1. The use of leverage where interest payments are tax deductible
2. Less scrutiny from public equity investors and regulators
3. Freedom from a distracted (and potentially distracting) corporate parent
4. The potential of company management to become substantial equity holders and thereby benefit directly from building the business

The benefit of an LBO to the acquiring LBO investor is the potential for attrac-tive risk-adjusted returns. The following section provides a simplified example of the profit potential from a successful LBO.

20.8.5   Valuation of an LBO

The potential payoffs of an LBO are like a call option: large upside potential relative to downside risk. Consider a publicly traded firm that is viewed by a private equity firm as a potential target, since it is failing to use its potential to generate earnings. The company has equity with a market value of $500 million and debt with a face value of $100 million. The company is currently generating earnings before interest, taxes, depreciation, and amortization (EBITDA) of $80 million, which represents the free cash flow from operations that is available for the owners and debtors of the company. This equates to a 13.3% before-tax return on assets for the company's shareholders and debt holders.

An LBO fund uses $700 million to purchase the equity of the company and pay off the outstanding debt. The debt is paid off at a face value of $100 million, while the remaining $600 million is offered to the equity holders to entice them to tender their shares to the LBO fund (i.e., a 20% premium is offered over the current market value). The $700 million LBO is financed by the LBO fund with $600 million in debt at a 10% coupon rate and $100 million in equity. Thus, the company must pay $60 million in annual debt service to meet its interest payment obligations. (The debt load in this example is not realistic, but used for illustration only, as buyouts in 2017 had average equity contributions of five times equity and six times debt for a debt-to-enterprise value ratio of 54.5%.)

After the LBO, the management of the company improves operations, stream-lines expenses, and implements better asset utilization. One explanation for the improved managerial performance might be that the LBO fund brought in new man-agement. Another possibility is that some or all of the existing top management ini-tiated the LBO and became highly incentivized to improve profitability. As a result, assume that the cash flow from operations of the company improves from $80 mil-lion to $120 million per year. By forgoing dividends and using the free cash flow to pay down the remaining debt, the LBO fund can own the target company free and clear of the debt used to finance the acquisition in about seven years. This means that after seven years and ignoring potential growth in cash flows, the LBO firm as the sole equity owner can claim the annual cash flow of $120 million completely for itself.

After the seven-year point, assume a forward-looking long-term growth rate of 2% per year and a discount rate of 12%. The value of the unlevered firm in seven years can be projected using the constant dividend growth model, as follows:

$$\$120 \text{ million}/(0.12 - 0.02) = \$1.2 \text{ billion}$$

Under these assumptions, the LBO fund can own the $1.2 billion company free and clear in seven years, starting with an equity investment of only $100 million. The total return on the investment for the LBO transaction would be as follows:

$$(\$1.2 \text{ billion}/\$100 \text{ million})^{1/7} - 1 = 42.6\%$$

The total return of 42.6% represents the annual compounded return on the equity portion of the LBO fund's investment. Notice the impact that leverage has on this transaction. The company is financed with a 6:1 debt-to-equity ratio. This is a very high leverage ratio for any company. The cash flows generated by the company were used to pay down the debt to a point where the company is completely owned by the equity holders. The equity holders receive a very high return because the debt used to finance the transaction is locked in at a 10% coupon rate. This means that most operating efficiencies and capital gains generated from the business accrue to the benefit of the equity holders—a keen incentive for equity holders to improve the operations of the company.

Notice that the total return to the leveraged equity investment is 42.6%, far greater than the 8% unlevered return found as:

$$(\$1.2 \text{ billion}/\$700 \text{ million})^{1/7} - 1 = 8\%$$

The larger the leverage multiple, the larger the difference between the levered and unlevered return to equity.

 APPLICATION 20.8.5A

Returning to the previous example, suppose that all other facts remain the same except that the discount rate used at the end of seven years is 15%. The projected value of the company becomes $120 million/(0.15 − 0.02) = $923 million and the seven-year rate of return becomes ($923 million/$100 million)$^{1/7}$ − 1 = 37.4%.

 APPLICATION 20.8.5B

Returning to the original example, suppose that all other facts remain the same except that the growth rate used at the end of the seven years is 5%. The projected value of the company becomes $120 million/ (0.12 − 0.05) = $1.714 billion, and the seven-year rate of return becomes ($1.714 billion/$100 million)$^{1/7}$ − 1 = 50.1%.

 APPLICATION 20.8.5C

Returning to the original example, suppose that all other facts remain the same except that the investment requires eight years to exit. The projected value of the company becomes $120 million/(0.12 − 0.02) = $1.2 billion, and the eight-year rate of return becomes ($1.2 billion/$100 million)$^{1/8}$ − 1 = 36.4%.

Note that the numerator of the constant dividend growth model is the cash flow that is anticipated one year beyond the valuation date. Thus, if the valuation is being performed in year 7, the cash flow that should be used as the numerator in the dividend growth model is the cash flow anticipated in year 8. Often this is expressed as the year 7 cash flow multiplied by $(1 + g)$, where g is the projected annual growth rate. This aspect is introduced in the following application.

 APPLICATION 20.8.5D

Returning to the original example, suppose that all other facts remain the same except that the $120 million cash flow estimate given is a year 7 cash flow that is anticipated to grow by year 8. The $120 million seven-year cash flow is therefore estimated to grow to an eight-year cash flow as $120 million $\times$ (1.02) = $122.4 million. The projected value of the company becomes $122.4 million/(0.12 – 0.02) = $1.224 billion, and the seven-year rate of return becomes ($1.224 billion/$100 million)$^{1/7}$ – 1 = 43.0%.

These applications illustrated a simplified LBO as being financed with a combination of debt and equity, with debt being the large majority of the financing. Generally in LBO deals there are three tranches of financing: senior debt, mezzanine debt, and equity. Senior debt typically entails financing from banks, credit/finance companies, insurance companies, or public debt offerings. Mezzanine debt is purchased by mezzanine debt funds (another form of private equity to be discussed in Chapter 22), insurance companies, and other institutional investors. Last is the equity tranche, held by the LBO firm that has taken the company private, and it often includes some form of equity kicker for the mezzanine debt tranche.

20.8.6 Five LBO Exit Strategies

A key assumption in each of the previous examples is that the LBO transaction can be exited at the estimated values. Leveraged buyout funds can exit investments through any one or any combination of five methods:

1. SALE TO A STRATEGIC BUYER: This is the most common exit strategy. Management can sell the company to a competitor or another company that wishes to expand into the industry.
2. INITIAL PUBLIC OFFERING (IPO): If the underlying company would make an attractive stand-alone and publicly traded company, an investment bank could be retained to take the firm public.
3. ANOTHER LBO: The firm could be refinanced by the current owners using another LBO deal, in which debt is reintroduced into the company to compensate management for its equity stake. In fact, the existing management team may even remain the operators of the company with an existing stake in the second LBO transaction, providing them with the opportunity for a second round of leveraged equity appreciation. In this transaction (and the next transaction example), proceeds of the debt are used to purchase shares of the company from the sponsor of the initial LBO.
4. STRAIGHT REFINANCING: This is similar to the preceding example, in which a company takes on debt to pay out a large cash distribution to its equity owners.
5. BUYOUT-TO-BUYOUT DEAL: Buyout-to-buyout deals are increasingly common in the private equity industry. A **buyout-to-buyout deal** takes place when a private equity firm sells one of its portfolio companies to another buyout firm. The second buyout firm believes that it can create a second leg of growth after the original buyout firm sells the company. It is estimated that almost one-third of private equity deals are now buyout-to-buyout deals, also known as secondary buyouts. Initially, secondary buyouts were rare. Private equity firms were reluctant to sell a portfolio company to another private equity firm in a buyout-to-buyout deal because of the stigma of failure associated with not being able to take a company

public or sell it to a strategic partner. Increasingly, private equity firms are selling to one another as an exit strategy.

20.8.7 Four Spillovers of Corporate Governance to the Public Market

The principles of corporate governance that LBO firms apply to their private companies have four important benefits for the public market.

First, the strong governance principles that an LBO implements in its private firms should remain when those firms are taken public again. Second, LBO transactions serve as a warning to the management team of other public companies: If a company has a poor incentive scheme and minimal shareholder monitoring, it may be ripe for an LBO acquisition. Third, the incentive and monitoring schemes implemented by LBO firms for their portfolio companies provide guidance to managers and shareholders of other firms searching for more efficient governance methods. Last, as indicated earlier, conglomerates can be popular targets for LBO firms, and this can help stop unnecessary and inefficient diversification of large corporations.

20.9 MERCHANT BANKING

Merchant banking is so closely related to buyouts that it is sometimes difficult to distinguish between the two. **Merchant banking** is the practice whereby financial institutions purchase *nonfinancial* companies as opposed to merging with or acquiring other financial institutions. Most major banks have merchant banking units. These units buy and sell nonfinancial companies for the profits that they can generate, much as in the case of buyouts. In some cases, the merchant banking units establish limited partnerships, similar to buyout funds. At that point, there is very little distinction between a merchant banking fund and the buyout funds discussed earlier, other than that the general partner is a financial institution.

Merchant banking started as a way for investment banks and money center banks to establish an equity participation in the enterprises they helped fund. If a bank lent money to a buyout group to purchase a company, its merchant banking unit also invested some capital as equity capital and received an equity participation in the deal. Soon, the merchant banking units of investment banks established their own buyout funds and created their own deals.

Whereas merchant banking is designed to earn profits for the bank, it also allows the bank to expand its relationship with the buyout company into other money-generating businesses, such as underwriting, loan origination, merger advice, and balance sheet recapitalization. All of this ancillary business translates into fee generation for the investment bank.

20.10 DYNAMICS OF PRIVATE EQUITY OPPORTUNITIES

This section concludes the chapter with a discussion of dynamics that have implications for private equity investing, especially VC and growth equity.

20.10.1 Implications of Winner-Take-All Markets

The process of bringing a venture from a nascent company to a huge enterprise increasingly resembles a winner-take-all market. A **winner-take-all market** refers to a market with a tendency to generate massive rewards for a few market participants that apparently provide products or services that are only marginally better than their competitors. Perhaps the most successful venture was a little quicker to market or possessed a charismatic founder. The implication of winner-take-all markets for venture capitalists is that being the second- or third-best entrant in a market may result not only in forgone profits but also in losses and bankruptcy.

VC performance is increasingly driven by participation in successful ventures known as unicorns. A **unicorn** is a VC-backed firm that soars to $1 billion or more in private market capitalization over a relatively short period of time. While in previous centuries, growth of firms to huge sizes required decades of successful operations, in recent years the unicorns have been able to explode to enormous market capitalizations with little or no history of profitable operations.

The implications to VC investors of winner-take-all markets and the preeminence of unicorns in generating attractive returns include the importance of diversification and superior management. Private equity investors may increasingly: (1) seek smaller investments in more enterprises, and (2) seek investments only with the most talented private equity managers.

20.10.2 Implications of Longer Time Horizons to Exits

VC investments are taking increased time to exit via an IPO relative to the time taken in previous decades. Mäkiaho (2016) finds "strong evidence that the private equity holding periods have significantly lengthened from the pre-crisis average of 4.7 years to 5.8 years after the financial crisis, despite the exit route.[5] Additionally, only 42% of the post-crisis exits were made in less than five years, compared to 61% for the pre-crisis period."

With the average time for a start-up firm to exit via an IPO increasing, VC investors and private equity funds (discussed in detail in Chapter 21) must be prepared for longer-term investment horizons. The lengthening time horizons for venture capital add to the illiquidity of private equity and the importance of growth equity.

20.10.3 Three Potential Reasons for the Declining Number of Public Firms in the United States

VC investing and growth equity bridge the gap between nascent private firms and established public firms. The economic environment has undergone major changes in the last few decades. For example, the number of listed firms in the United States has declined markedly from well over 7,000 in the mid-1990s to less than 4,000 in 2018.

The reasons for the decline in the *number* of publicly listed equities (but not the total value of those equities) are not entirely clear. An article by Schumpeter in the *Economist* (2017) notes: (1) concerns over increasing regulations, (2) pressure from shareholders of public companies regarding short-term stock price performance, and (3) the decline in IPOs "from 300 a year on average in the two decades to 2000 to about 100 a year since."[6]

The decline in IPOs provides fewer entrants to public listings. Further, many publicly traded firms are delisting due to: consolidation of public companies (e.g., through mergers), companies going from public to private (e.g., Equity Office Properties Trust), and bankruptcies. Public listing comes with listing fees, pressures such as disgruntled shareholders regarding recent market performance or headline news, and inefficiencies in governance such as nuisance shareholder proposals. Events such as the $20 million fine levied by the SEC against Tesla in 2018 (for tweets by its founder, Elon Musk), and the subsequent resignation of Musk as chairman, have increased concern over the efficacy of being listed in markets that are increasingly driven by rapid technological change and young entrepreneurs.

20.10.4 Competition between Private and Public Ownership Structures

A key issue in equity markets is the relative strengths of the private equity governance structure and the public equity governance structure. While both structures are sure to persist, the key question is, which structure is better for a particular enterprise at a particular point in time?

Clearly, nascent firms lack the size to be public and can benefit greatly from the managerial expertise and connections that venture capitalists bring to the organization. As discussed in Chapter 21, private equity fund managers can bring enormous skill, experience, and contacts to ventures. But under what conditions does it make sense for very large and/or established firms to go private or remain private for the reason that the private equity governance structure better serves the investors?

The key takeaway is to view the choice between being public or private as depending upon relative strengths (e.g., the efficiency and effectiveness) of the private equity and public equity governance structures. Chapter 21 delves deeply into the role of private equity funds in generating advantages emanating from governance structures.

REVIEW QUESTIONS

1. What are the three major forms of private debt introduced in the chapter?
2. List major contrasts between venture capital, growth, equity, and buyouts with respect to asset size, investor control, time horizon, and investment risk.
3. Identify three major methods of executing an exit from VC.
4. What differentiates the angel investing stage of VC from the seed stage of venture capital financing?
5. What is a compound option and how do compound options relate to VC?
6. What is a springing board remedy?
7. What is the primary difference between a management buy-in LBO and a management buyout LBO?
8. Describe the evolution of the buyout market.

9. What are the two primary conflicts of interest that emanate from the potentially lucrative compensation schemes offered to exiting management teams in a management buy-in?
10. List the five general categories of LBOs that can create value.

NOTES

1. Matt Stewart, "Growth Equity: The Intersection of Venture Capital and Control Buyouts," PE Hub Network, November 9, 2012, http://www.pehub.com/2012/11/growth-equity-the-intersection-venture-capital-control-buyouts/.
2. Ibid.
3. Ludovic Phalippou. *Private Equity Laid Bare*. (CreateSpace Independent Publishing Platform, 2017).
4. Bryan Burrough and John Helyar, *Barbarians at the Gate: The Fall of RJR Nabisco* (New York: Harper & Row, 1990).
5. Juho Mäkiaho, "Prolonged Private Equity Holding Periods: European Evidence" (Master's thesis, Department of Finance, Aalto University, 2016), https://pdfs.semanticscholar.org/6d0f/f368844b7caf3fca9b25d33d258adbbeaca2.pdf.
6. Schumpeter, "Why the Decline in the Number of Listed American Firms Matters," *The Economist*, April 22, 2017.

CHAPTER **21**

Private Equity Funds

T his chapter focuses on the investment pools through which investors gain access to private equity (PE) exposures. The organized PE market is dominated by PE funds. **PE funds** are unregistered investment vehicles in which investors, or limited partners (LPs), pool money to invest in privately held companies under the management of general partners (GPs). Fund management companies, referred to as PE firms, set up these funds and typically serve as the GPs.

21.1 OVERVIEW OF PRIVATE EQUITY FUNDS

PE funds were discussed at the end of Chapter 20 as utilizing a potentially superior governance structure for venture capital (VC), growth equity, and buyouts. This chapter begins with an in-depth discussion of VC funds. Later, leveraged buyout (LBO) funds are detailed.

Start-up ventures have been created and financed throughout history, but the first modern VC firm was American Research and Development, formed in 1946 as a publicly traded closed-end fund. The first VC limited partnership fund was formed in 1958, and the limited partnership form of organization eventually became the standard tool for investing in VC. A **VC fund** is a PE fund that pools the capital of large sophisticated investors to fund new start-up companies.

21.1.1 The Organizational Structure of Private Equity Funds

Each PE fund is managed by a general partner. The general partner is typically the PE firm that raised the capital for the fund. The general partner sources investment opportunities for the fund, reviews business plans, performs due diligence, and, once an investment is made, in the case of a VC fund, typically takes a seat on the board of directors of the start-up company and works with the management of the company to develop and implement the business plan.

PE funds usually have a contractually limited life of seven to 10 years, often with a provision for an extension of two to three years. The VC funds deploy capital by purchasing PE securities in underlying business enterprises, which are referred to as the portfolio companies. VC funds and other PE funds are typically structured as limited partnerships, as discussed in Chapter 2 and illustrated in Exhibit 2.1 for the case of hedge funds. The case of PE is illustrated in Exhibit 21.1.

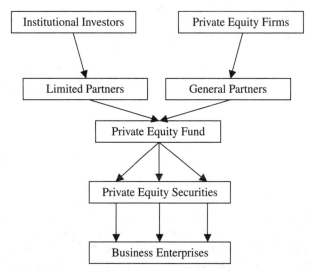

EXHIBIT 21.1   Private Equity Investment Process

A potentially confusing aspect of PE arises from differentiating between the multiple layers of PE investments. Exhibit 21.1 illustrates the three main levels at which PE is discussed. Discussions of PE often refer to the three levels in Exhibit 21.1 with interchangeable terms, due in part to the multiple relationships that can exist. Each level is sometimes referred to as PE, and therefore it is sometimes unclear whether the term is being used to describe a manager, an investment fund, or an underlying investment.

At the base of the diagram is the underlying PE investment, which consists of the private business enterprises from which all cash flows to investors must ultimately be derived. Examples include new ventures for VC funds, firms seeking growth equity for growth equity funds, and so forth. The key point is that these are the private enterprises that produce goods or services and that underlie PE investing. The securities of these enterprises (e.g., common stock in these enterprises) are often referred to as PE investments.

The middle level of Exhibit 21.1 represents PE funds, which are investment pools created to hold portfolios of PE securities (i.e., the equity securities at the bottom of the exhibit). The funds serve as intermediaries between the underlying business enterprises (called the portfolio companies when they are owned by a fund) and the investors in the PE funds. Institutional investors typically invest in PE as LPs in these funds rather than through direct ownership of PE securities. These PE funds are also often referred to as PE investments.

21.1.2 Private Equity Firms

Large PE firms serve as fund managers. The managers serve as GPs and attract institutions as LPs. The fund manager's objective is to realize, or exit, all investments before or at the liquidation of the fund. If successful, the fund managers will launch multiple PE funds through time.

The top right side of Exhibit 21.1 depicts PE firms that invest in PE and serve as managers to PE funds. PE firms, such as Kohlberg Kravis Roberts & Co. (KKR), often serve as the GPs of PE funds, usually invest their own capital, and sometimes fully own the underlying business enterprises. However, PE firms usually obtain additional capital through forming limited partnerships, which attract LPs (e.g., institutions) to invest in a series of ventures. Thus, Exhibit 21.1 depicts both PE firms and institutions investing in PE funds. As indicated in the exhibit, the institutional investors are the LPs.

Typically, a major PE firm serves as the general partner for a series of limited partnerships that span a few decades and may be numbered sequentially or with years (e.g., KKR European Fund III or KKR Fund 1996). Large PE firms may also manage multiple funds concurrently, based on geographic sectors or industry sectors.

Further, the limited partnership funds, indicated as PE funds, in the middle of Exhibit 21.1 are also referred to as PE investments, since the partnership units are usually not publicly traded. Of course, the underlying business enterprises at the bottom of Exhibit 21.1 are PE investments. Ownership of these underlying business enterprises is through PE securities, as illustrated with the second to last row of Exhibit 21.1.

Exhibit 21.2 provides detail on the entities used to structure the responsibilities and compensation of the relation between the PE firm and the PE fund. The PE firm (which can be an LLC) typically creates an LLC to serve as the general partner (GP) of the partnership. The general partner typically makes a minimal investment in the partnership (e.g., 1%) but receives a large share (e.g., 20%) of the distributions (forming the incentive fee). The PE firm typically creates another LLC to serve as the investment adviser to the partnership. The investment adviser receives the management fee (e.g., 2% annually). As discussed in Chapter 2, the personnel from the PE firm in the LLCs may be overlapping or even identical. The structures are used to

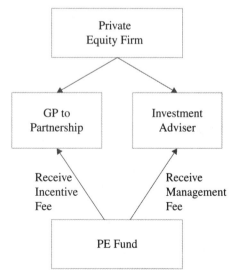

EXHIBIT 21.2 Dual Roles and Entities of a Private Equity Firm

preserve limited liability, delineate compensation, and provide clarity with regard to responsibilities.

Tax, legal, and regulatory requirements drive the structuring of the entities in Exhibits 21.1 and 21.2, as well as goals that include reducing taxation and limiting liability (investors' liabilities are limited to the capital committed to the fund).

The term *PE firm* is used in this chapter to describe firms such as KKR at the top level, and the term *PE funds* is used to describe limited partnerships such as KKR European Fund III at the middle level.

21.1.3 Private Equity Portfolio Companies

Finally, PE securities, portfolio companies, or underlying business enterprises are used to describe the underlying investments in the unlisted businesses seeking growth, shown at the bottom level of Exhibit 21.1.

In summary, a PE firm creates a PE fund that purchases PE securities. Further, each type of PE investment, such as VC, is sometimes used in place of the more generic term PE. Thus, in the VC area of PE, the concepts illustrated in Exhibit 21.1 might be referred to as a VC firm creating a VC fund that purchases VC securities.

The structures in Exhibits 21.1 and 21.2 can be used for growth equity funds and buyout funds as well as VC funds. VC funds can be further distinguished by the stage of VC that the fund focuses on, such as first- or early-stage VC, second- or late-stage/expansion VC, and mezzanine financing. Different expertise is required for managing investments at each stage of financing.

A PE limited partnership fund typically invests in 10 to 30 portfolio companies. This translates to approximately two to six companies per year that are sourced, reviewed, and purchased in the first three to five years of the fund's life. In a buyout, the PE fund takes seats on the board of directors. The general partner of the PE firm supplies these new directors, usually picking one to four of its partners to sit on the company's board. As directors, the PE firm interacts with the management of the private company on a weekly, if not daily, basis. A buyout fund assists the company in developing a new business plan. This plan might entail expansion or contraction, adding new employees or deleting part of the workforce, and introducing new products or cutting off unproductive and distracting product development. In a majority of cases, the PE firm gets the company to streamline its workforce, reduce its expenses, and increase its balance sheet capacity for more leverage.

21.1.4 Private Equity Investment by Institutional Investors

Many institutions outsource their PE fund investment program either through a dedicated account or by pooling assets with other investors. PE funds of funds are probably the most common type of institutional investment program. PE funds of funds, which are mainly organized by specialist asset managers, are vehicles that pool capital from a group of investors to invest in a diversified portfolio of PE funds. Some funds of funds specialize in certain PE sectors or geographies, whereas others follow a more generalist approach.

PE funds of funds primarily invest in newly formed limited partnerships. Because of the **blind pool** nature of such investments, in which investors don't know the underlying portfolio companies before committing capital, the initial assessment and ongoing monitoring of the fund management team's skills are key.

PE funds of funds also co-invest alongside primary investors. This activity requires direct investment experience and skills. PE funds of funds can also use secondary investments in existing funds or portfolios of direct investments. This is generally a niche activity for most funds of funds. This activity requires both co-investment skills for the assessment of the companies already in the portfolio and primary investment skills for the blind-pool part of the transaction. Co-investment is discussed in detail in Level II of the CAIA curriculum.

While investment in a particular PE fund can have a blind-pool nature, a fund of funds can have established relationships with fund managers via existing investments. Therefore, its future portfolio is somewhat predictable and is not necessarily a blind pool investment. A newly created portfolio is likely to be largely composed of follow-on funds raised by these known managers. In fact, funds of funds are marketed on either a partially blind or a fully informed basis. For a partially blind pool, some of the intended partnership groups are identified, while for a fully informed pool, virtually all of the intended partnerships have been identified.

Institutions such as pension funds, endowments, PE funds of funds, public institutions, banks, insurance companies, and high-net-worth individuals or family offices invest in PE funds as LPs by committing specified amounts of money to the fund. These commitments are drawn as needed to fund investments. The amount committed but not yet called is an **undrawn commitment or dry powder**.

For institutional investors, direct investment can be problematic because many institutions cannot offer adequate performance-related pay to attract and retain top employees and analysts. For typical conservative and seniority-based institutions like banks, pension funds, and insurance companies, a theoretically unlimited carried interest does not always fit well with the institution's traditional compensation scheme.

While institutional investors do not lack staff with the intellectual caliber to evaluate investment proposals and to structure transactions, generating profitable exits in PE programs requires very hard work over protracted periods of time. Moreover, the lack of incentive to take risk and to find value (or the conflict of interest therein) may affect investment decisions.

There is a substantial learning curve, and without performance-related pay, employees may jump ship as soon as they are competent in the area and understand their opportunities better. Finally, for larger institutions, intermediation through funds of funds allows them to focus on their core businesses.

21.2 PRIVATE EQUITY FUNDS AS INTERMEDIARIES

PE funds serve as financial intermediaries by facilitating investment in PE. There are several motivations to using PE funds as intermediaries.

21.2.1 Private Equity Fund Intermediation and Risk

Basically, PE funds step into the funding process when traditional lenders are not willing or able to provide funding. For example, banks may be unwilling to lend to an entrepreneur or be involved in LBOs because of the substantial risks that are involved. In the case of lending to an entrepreneur, the product or the intellectual property is not well understood, and of course the firm has no track record that the bank could use to evaluate its riskiness. Also, some of these lenders (e.g., banks) are not willing or allowed to take equity positions in these firms. This means they cannot fully participate in the significant upsides that PE investments could provide. These significant upside returns can justify the risks PE investors are willing to take by investing in new and untested companies or by taking significant credit and leverage risk and investing in poorly performing firms. PE investors take advantage of the inefficiencies in financial markets while satisfying the needs of these borrowers.

PE funds are generally organized as limited partnerships designed to provide limited liability to the investors. Limited liability is the protection of investors from losses that exceed their investment. LPs are not responsible for liabilities beyond the total loss of their investment, even if the partnership has further losses and unmet liabilities due to the use of leverage or from lawsuits. To have limited liability, a partner must be a limited partner and must not take an active role in the partnership's management. The general partner does not have limited liability and takes an active role in the management of the partnership.

21.2.2 Private Equity Fund Intermediation and Efficient Incentives

Another reason for the existence of PE firms is the presence of certain economic inefficiencies in the traditional corporate structure. In some cases, management may not be given proper incentives to maximize the value to the shareholders of a corporation. PE seeks to address this problem by tightly aligning the interests of managers and shareholders to achieve increased efficiency and higher return to shareholders.

21.2.3 Private Equity Funds Serve the Following Five Primary Functions

PE funds may be viewed as providing five primary functions:

1. Pooling investors' capital for investing in private companies
2. Screening, evaluating, and selecting potential companies with expected high-return opportunities
3. Financing companies to develop new products and technologies, foster their growth and development, make acquisitions, or allow for a buyout or a buyin by experienced managers
4. Controlling, coaching, and monitoring portfolio companies
5. Sourcing exit opportunities for portfolio companies

21.2.4 Forms of Private Equity Fund Intermediation

There are different routes for investing in PE (see Exhibit 21.3). Few institutional investors have the experience, the incentive structures, and the access that would allow them to invest directly in nonpublic companies, so most investors seek intermediation through funds. For institutions, the most relevant approaches to investing

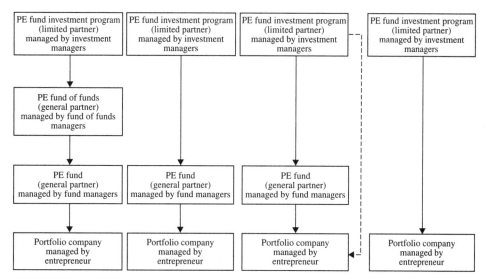

EXHIBIT 21.3 PE Funds Investment Program

in PE are through fund-of-funds specialists as intermediaries or through similarly structured dedicated in-house PE investment programs that invest directly in funds. Other routes are via publicly quoted PE vehicles or through a dedicated account managed by a PE specialist.

Reading Exhibit 21.3 from left to right, the various programs are defined as follows:

In a fund of funds structure, an institutional PE investor buys LP units of a PE fund of funds, which in turn purchases LP units of a PE fund, which, in turn, invests in portfolio companies.

In the second column, an institutional PE investor buys LP units directly in a PE fund that invests in portfolio companies.

In the third column, a PE fund adds a co-investment to the process in the second column. The co-investment leg is where the PE fund has an additional investment in a certain portfolio company, typically at preferential management and performance fee terms. **Co-investment** involves investors being invited by GPs to make direct investments in portfolio companies, as is discussed in detail in the second level of the CAIA program.

Finally, the fourth column depicts direct investment by the institutional PE investor who eschews PE fund structures altogether and makes investments straight into a portfolio company (without intermediation), similar to a co-investment but without the input of a PE fund manager.

21.2.5 The Life Cycle of a Venture Capital Fund

A VC fund is a long-term investment. Typically, investors' capital is locked up for a minimum of 10 years, the standard term of a VC limited partnership. There is a PE fundraising cycle that begins anew each time GPs need to raise capital for another fund. Typically, limited partnership agreements do not allow follow-on funds by the same manager before the end of the initial fund's investment period or until a large part of the initial fund has been invested.

During this long investment period, a VC fund normally goes through five stages of development.

THE FUNDRAISING STAGE: The first stage of a VC fund is the fundraising stage, in which the VC firm raises capital from outside investors. Capital is committed, not collected. This is an important distinction. Investors sign a legal agreement (typically a subscription) that legally binds them to make cash investments in the VC fund up to a specified amount. This is the committed, but not yet drawn, capital. The VC firm or general partner also posts committed capital. Fundraising normally takes six months to a year. However, the more successful VC funds can raise the funds in just a few months.

Commitments (capital pledges by investors in PE funds) are drawn down as needed, or just in time, to make investments or to pay costs, expenses, or management fees. Because PE funds do not typically retain large pools of uninvested capital, their GPs make capital calls (or drawdowns) once they have identified a company in which to invest. Therefore, the main part of the drawdown gets invested immediately.

SOURCING INVESTMENTS: The second stage is **sourcing investments**, the process of locating possible investments (i.e., generating deal flow), reading business plans, performing intense due diligence on start-up companies, and determining the attractiveness of each start-up company. This period begins the moment the fund is closed to investors and normally takes up the first three to five years of the venture fund's existence to complete. As the general partner, the manager has full operating authority to manage the fund, subject to restrictions placed in the covenants of the fund's documents. During the first two stages, no profits are generated by the VC fund. In fact, quite the reverse happens: The VC fund generates losses because the manager continues to draw annual management fees based on the total committed capital. These fees generate a loss until the manager begins to extract value from the investments of the venture fund at a later stage.

INVESTING STAGE: Stage three is investment of capital. During this stage, the VC fund manager determines how much capital to commit to each start-up company, at what level of financing, and in what form of investment (convertible preferred shares, convertible debentures, etc.). At this stage, the fund manager also makes capital calls to the investors in the fund to draw the committed capital of the LPs. Note that no cash inflow is generated yet; the venture fund is still in a deficit.

Generally, the year in which the fund first draws down capital from investors for the purpose of investing in a company is called the **vintage year**; some data providers use the year that the fund commences operations as the vintage year.

A substantial portion, though not typically all, of the committed capital is drawn down during the investment period, typically the first three to five years, during which new opportunities are identified. After that, during the divestment period, only the existing portfolio companies with the highest potential are further supported, with some follow-on funding provided to extract the maximum value through exits. The manager's efforts during this time are concentrated on realizing or selling investments.

It might surprise many investors to learn that they should expect the accounting value of their investment in a VC fund to drop over the first three to five years. This is because the organizational expenses of the VC partnership are deducted immediately. In addition, management fees are charged on committed capital by the VC fund's general partner. Further, those investments that fail quickly are posted as losses, while investments that are showing excellent potential are not posted as profits (if they have not already been sold). All of this means that investors must be braced for a loss on their investments for the first three to five years of a VC fund's life. Truly, VC is for the long-term investor.

OPERATIONS AND MANAGEMENT: Stage four, which includes operation and management of the portfolio of companies, begins after all the funds have been invested, and lasts almost to the end of the term of the VC fund. During this time, the manager works with the portfolio companies in which the VC fund has invested. The manager may improve each portfolio company's management team, establish distribution channels for the new product, refine the prototype product to generate the greatest sales, and generally position the start-up company for an eventual public offering or sale to a strategic buyer. During this period, the VC fund manager begins to generate profits for the fund. These profits initially offset the previously collected management fees and other expenses until a positive cumulative profit is established for the venture fund.

WINDUP AND LIQUIDATION: The last stage of the VC fund is its windup and liquidation. At this point, all committed capital has been invested, and the fund is now in the harvesting stage. Each of the fund's portfolio companies faces three possible outcomes: being sold to a strategic or a financial buyer, being brought to the public markets in an initial public offering (IPO), or being liquidated through a bankruptcy liquidation process. Profits are distributed to the LPs, and the general partner/fund manager now collects the incentive/profit-sharing fees.

When realizations (sales of portfolio companies) are made, or when interest payments, dividends, or recapitalizations are received, they are distributed to investors as soon as is feasible. Under this scenario, the fund liquidates as the underlying investments are realized. However, these returns come mostly in the second half of the fund's lifetime. However, some funds have a **reinvestment provision**, normally subject to a cap amount, wherein the proceeds of realizations within the investment period or a similar time frame may be reinvested in new opportunities and not distributed to investors.

Distributions to investors can also take the form of securities of a portfolio company, known as **in-kind distributions**, provided that these securities are publicly tradable or distributed when the fund gets liquidated. Legal documentation may also allow for some reinvestment of realizations.

21.2.6 The Fund J-Curve

The life stages of a VC fund follow the life stages of the portfolio companies that are contained within the fund. The life cycles of portfolio companies often follow similar stages and lead to what is known as the J-curve effect, as shown in Exhibit 21.4. The J-curve is the classic illustration of the early losses and later likely profitability of VC. The central return measurement for PE is the IRR method detailed in Chapter 3. Although Exhibit 21.4 plots interim IRRs and the lifetime IRR of a typical portfolio company, the shape of the curve (i.e., the J-curve) approximates the IRRs of VC funds through time, since a VC fund is composed of a set of portfolio companies.

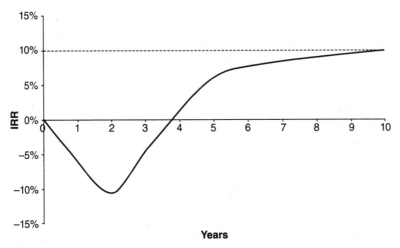

EXHIBIT 21.4   Fund Standard J-Curve

Exhibit 21.4 shows that during the early life of a portfolio company, the company generates losses and negative IRRs, but profits may eventually be harvested in the case of a successful company. Similarly, VC fund profitability often follows a J-curve. It should be noted that the J-curve focuses on computing IRRs with an accounting view of profits and losses. In a financial economics sense, many of the early accounting losses are due to writing off fees that, in many cases, may be better viewed as necessary and valuable investments in the fund's future. An analogy is the investment of a young person in a college education. A student accumulating debt to finance an education may experience declining net worth during those college years if the increase in the value of human capital is ignored. Instead of viewing the expenses of the education as a period of financial loss, the student should see herself as building human capital and the time period as being quite profitable.

Other J-curves can also be observed in PE funds: the cash flow J-curve and the net asset value (NAV) J-curve. The NAV of a fund is calculated by adding the value of all the investments held in the fund and dividing by the number of outstanding shares of the fund. The **NAV J-curve** is a representation of the evolution of the NAV of a fund versus the net paid in (NPI), which first decreases during the early years of the fund's existence and then improves in its later years.

The **cash flow J-curve** is a representation of the evolution of the net accumulated cash flows from the investors to the fund, which are negative during the early years of existence before making a U-turn and becoming positive in the later years of the fund's life. This is explained by the fact that in standard PE fund structures, commitments are drawn down as needed, or just in time, and when realizations are made after having successfully developed these newly founded companies, they are distributed as soon as is practical.

21.2.7 Undrawn Capital Commitments

Undrawn capital commitments are a liability of the associated investors. While they are often viewed as irrelevant to the investment's value (since the calls of capital commitments are used to fund investments that belong to the partnership), undrawn commitments caused serious problems for some LPs during the global financial crises and coined the terms *commitment risk* or *funding risk*. **Commitment risk** describes the situation in which an LP may become a defaulting investor if the proceeds of exiting funds are not sufficient to pay the capital calls of newly committed funds. Commitment risk is discussed in the next section.

21.2.8 Four Substantial Risks of Private Equity

PE has specific characteristics that are not shared by other asset classes. The most substantial risks in this asset class are market risk, liquidity risk, commitment or funding risk, and realization risk (EVCA 2013):[1]

1. MARKET RISK: Market risk is economic uncertainty with regard to the value of an asset, in this case an illiquid asset. Listed assets are valued using market prices. Illiquid assets are often valued using an analysis of the present value of the estimated future cash flows from that asset. Market prices and professional valuations often signal different levels of market risk.
2. LIQUIDITY RISK: LPs can sell their stakes in PE partnerships to fund their outstanding commitments. However, the secondary market for PE investments is relatively small and inefficient. Secondary market prices may be influenced by factors beyond the fair value of the partnership, which often means that prices are discounted. Liquidity risk plays a far less important role for public equities.
3. COMMITMENT OR FUNDING RISK: The unpredictable timing of cash flows over the life of a fund poses funding risk for the limited partner. Fund managers call most or all of the committed capital over the investment period of the fund. LPs then have to meet their commitments within a fixed short-notice period. Because commitments are contractually binding, a limited partner who cannot meet his obligations is forced to default on payments and lose a substantial portion of or even his entire share in the partnership.
4. REALIZATION RISK: PE investors face the long-term risk of not recovering the value of their invested capital at realization. This long-term capital risk can be affected by a number of factors, namely (1) the ability of managers to create value and extract cash from exiting the companies, and (2) the level of equity markets and IPO activity at the time of exit.

21.3 THE LP AND GP RELATIONSHIP LIFE CYCLE

Most PE funds have a finite life of very roughly 10 years. A key aspect of PE fund investing is that successful management teams that serve as GPs of PE funds oversee multiple funds through time. Further, satisfied institutional investors in those funds seek to invest in the new funds being offered by successful GPs. This section discusses this practice in detail.

21.3.1 The Relationship between LPs and GPs in Private Equity

The LP–GP relationship is a classic principal-agent relationship, which, because information in PE markets is incomplete and highly asymmetric, has evolved to address the problems of moral hazard and conflict of interest. There is a symbiotic relationship between LPs and GPs. An LP's investment strategy is built around a number of relationships with GPs, who focus on specific segments (such as stages or sectors) of the market. This specialized focus can often limit the scalability of a particular fund, especially in the case of VC, in which LPs may find it difficult to identify and access additional fund managers of comparable quality.

GPs, for their part, want financially strong, dependable, knowledgeable, and long-term LPs. LPs should have industry expertise and familiarity with the nuts and bolts (particularly valuations and benchmarking) of the PE business. Adverse selection exists in the PE market: Poor-quality GPs, be they lacking experience or falling into decline, will court inexperienced LPs. Because of poor results, both will eventually exit the market.

To maintain continuous investment in new portfolio companies, GPs need to raise new funds as soon as the capital from their latest active fund is fully invested (or reserved for follow-on investments), that is, about every three to five years. Thus, relationships between LPs and GPs follow a life cycle and are forged through various rounds of investment, eventually resulting in a virtuous circle of growing experience and fund size.

Anecdotal evidence suggests that experienced market players profit from these relationships over protracted periods of time. Initially, criteria are very stringent, and fund managers usually cannot get rich through their first funds. However, a favorable track record is an asset in itself. For more reputable funds, fundraising is less costly. To minimize their expenses, fund managers generally turn first to those who invested in their previous partnership, provided that the fund's performance was satisfactory. While it is easy to see how fund managers benefit from a loyal and reliable investor community, these long-term relationships can also be advantageous for LPs. In the opaque PE market, the search for and due diligence of funds is a costly exercise, and LPs often prefer familiar fund managers to unproven investment proposals.

Such long-term relationships may provide access to a quality deal flow of co-investment opportunities in portfolio companies within an established framework. It is especially desirable for an investor to hold on to good fund managers, as the best teams will have an established investor base (i.e., a set of established and loyal clients), which may eliminate the need to seek out new funding sources to the detriment of adding value to the portfolio companies when making new investments or exits. There is likely to be better planning, as LPs make clear their intentions to participate in follow-on funds. As LPs form a network, even if they do not have the means to continue, they often refer other investors to a good team. Predictable closings put money to work more efficiently.

21.3.2 The Three Phases in the Relationship between LPs and GPs

The life cycle of the GP–LP relationship (see Exhibit 21.5) focuses on the long-term pattern of GPs as they create multiple funds through time. The GP–LP life cycle can be divided into three phases: (1) entry and establish (the phase involving the initial funds); (2) build and harvest (or grow and compete), the phase in which the funds thrive and grow; and (3) the three potential outcomes: decline (lost competitiveness), exit (gave up or made it), or transition to new managers (spinouts).

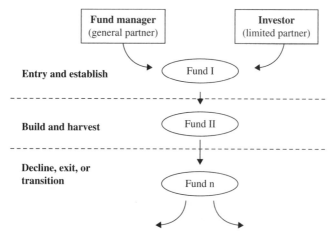

EXHIBIT 21.5 Fund Manager–Investor Relationship Life Cycle

The main differences between these phases are summarized in Exhibit 21.6.

During the entry and establish phase, substantial entry barriers into the PE market exist for both GPs and LPs. Lacking a verifiable track record, new teams find it difficult to raise their first fund. Furthermore, analysis of historical benchmark data supports the hypothesis that new teams suffer from higher mortality than do established or institutional-quality fund managers. First-time funds note the importance of differentiation or innovation as applied to fundraising and thus often pursue specialized investment strategies.

EXHIBIT 21.6 GP–LP Relationship Life Cycle Model

Fund's characteristics	Entry and establish	Build and harvest	Decline or exit
Investment strategy	Differentiation	"Star" brand	Unexciting
Fundraising	Difficult fundraising	Loyal limited partner base	Limited partners leave and are replaced by other types of investors (secondary plays, new entrants in market)
Performance	Unknown: either "top" or "out"	Likely "top" performer	Not "top" but consistent performer
Size	Fund is too small	Fund size is right	Fund size too large/too many funds
Economies of scale	Fund too small to get rich	Best alignment of interests	Senior managers "made it"
Management team	Management team forming	Management team performing	Succession issues, spinouts

New LPs also face entry barriers, suffering the initial informational disadvantages that make it extremely difficult to identify or gain access to the best managers, particularly when those funds are oversubscribed. For LPs, it takes the disciplined execution of a long-term investment strategy to build up a portfolio of funds that gives attractive and sustainable returns.

Since investors are mainly interested in the cash returned, the fund manager–investor relationship tends to be relatively stable throughout the build and harvest phase. Lerner and Schoar present evidence on the high degree of continuity in the investors of successive funds, and the ability of sophisticated investors to anticipate funds that will have poor subsequent performance.[2]

It is an oversimplification to assume that investors invest only in top performers and that below-average funds are unable to continue. As in most relationships, there is a certain degree of tolerance for mistakes and failures, at least over a limited period of time. It is clear that there are limits to disappointing results, but all things being equal, investors will tend to go with fund managers they already know or who have been referred to them through their network, even if the fund's performance has been subpar at times.

Eventually, the relationship ends in the decline, exit, or transition (spinout) phase. Not surprisingly, the terms *marriage* and *divorce* are often used in the context of relationships between fund managers and their investors. A gradual decline may occur either as a result of past successes, which potentially decrease the financial motivation of senior fund managers, or due to an improperly planned succession, which leads to the departure of middle management. In addition, the LPs may eventually end the relationship if they lose confidence or trust in the team (for example, if the team becomes arrogant or fails to deliver). Some LPs do not invest in follow-on funds and may be replaced by less deep-pocketed or experienced investors, or by secondary investors who choose to invest as a one-off financial play.

21.4 PRIVATE EQUITY FUND FEES AND TERMS

Chapter 3 introduced the fees and terms found in limited partnerships for private structures in general. This section provides further detail, especially with respect to features unique to PE.

21.4.1 Private Equity Management Fees and Carried Interest

At the heart of the difference between public and PE governance structures are the compensation structures that provide incentives for the managers and investors.

Management fees for PE depend on the size of the fund, generally ranging from 1.5% of committed capital for large funds to 2.5% for smaller funds. During the investment period, the management fee is generally assessed on the amount of committed capital, not invested capital. Once the investment period concludes, the management fee should be charged on invested capital, not committed capital. **Committed capital** is the cash investment that has been promised by an investor.

Consider the implications of this fee arrangement. The manager collects a management fee from the moment an investor signs a subscription agreement to invest capital in the fund, even though no capital has actually been contributed by the LP yet. Further, VC funds typically provide for capital calls. **Capital calls** are options for the manager to demand, according to the subscription agreement, that investors contribute additional capital. The potential for the manager to earn incentive fees on capital from capital calls may give the manager an incentive to call for capital, even when investment opportunities are not of the highest quality. Capital calls are typically made when each portfolio company investment is identified (and if the VC fund holds insufficient uninvested cash).

☞ APPLICATION 21.4.1A

A VC fund manager raises $100 million in committed capital for his VC fund. The management fee is 2.5%. To date, only $50 million of the raised capital has been called and invested in start-ups. What would be the annual management fee? The annual management fee that the manager collects is $2.5 million (2.5% × $100 million), even though not all of the capital has been invested.

General partners can earn a wide variety of fees from their portfolio companies, including director fees, buyout fees, financing fees, divestment fees, and so on, as detailed in the management services agreement between the GP and the portfolio company. There are considerable differences from one fund to the next regarding the level of fees and how those fees are attributed between the GP and the LP. These can have an impact on returns and often account for material differences between gross and net returns. LPs would prefer that all fees earned by the GP would offset the management fees due from the LPs.

The main upside incentive for GPs comes in the form of carried interest, typically 20% of the profits realized by the fund. Incentive fees are typically entitled carried interest in PE funds and can be calculated on either a fund-as-a-whole or a deal-by-deal basis, as detailed in Chapter 3. In recent years, LPs have been overwhelmingly rejecting deal-by-deal carry. But whether this approach is now really extinct or the pendulum will swing back toward more GP-friendly carried interest mechanisms remains to be seen.

21.4.2 Private Equity and Clawback Provisions

Most PE partnership agreements include a clawback provision. A clawback provision, introduced in Chapter 3, is a covenant that allows the LPs to receive back (or claw back) previously paid incentive fees. The previously paid incentive fees are returned if, at the end or liquidation of the venture fund, the LPs have returns below the annualized preferred return. There is often a **clawback escrow agreement**, in which a portion of the manager's incentive fees are held in a segregated account until the entire fund is liquidated. This ensures that the fund manager does not walk away with incentive fees unless the LPs earn a profit in excess of the hurdle rate or the preferred return. Only after every limited partner has earned a profit are the escrow proceeds released to the manager. Sometimes this covenant may stipulate that all management fees must also be recouped by the LPs before the manager can collect incentive fees.

Responsibility for payment of the clawback rests with the persons or entity that received the carried-interest distributions. In such a case, the GP is required to return some proceeds to make the investor whole. But clawback can also exist for LPs. In this case, it is triggered when, at the end of a fund's life, the GPs have received less than their share of the fund's profits. Such clawback is relevant in situations in which a portion of the committed capital has not been drawn, and LPs have received full repayment of their commitment plus hurdle before the GP has access to his or her carry.

The simplest and, from the viewpoint of an LP, most desirable solution is that GPs do not take carried interest until all invested, or sometimes even all committed, capital has been repaid to investors. In this scenario, however, the several years it could take for the fund's team to see any gains could lead to demotivation. Accordingly, carried interest is usually distributed to GPs as profits are realized. A clawback ensures that managers will not receive a greater share of the fund's distributions than they are entitled to.

21.4.3 Private Equity Carried Interest and Hurdle Rates

In the case of PE, carried interest can be subject to a hurdle rate, or preferred return, so that it begins to accrue only once investors have received their capital back and a minimum previously agreed-on rate of return. Once the preferred return has been attained, GPs typically receive 100% of returns to the point at which they have received the carried interest on the entire amount. This is called a catch-up and is synonymous with the soft hurdle concept used by hedge funds and detailed in Chapter 3. Exhibit 21.7 illustrates the effect of hurdle rates with a catch-up clause.

In Exhibit 21.7 the function that maps the value of the portfolio to the net asset value (NAV) contains three segments from left to right. In the hurdle zone, the LPs receive all the cash inflows. This is followed by the catch-up period, during which the

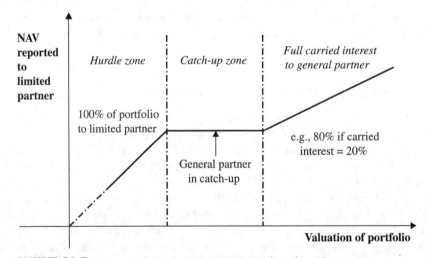

EXHIBIT 21.7 Impact of Catch-Up on NAV Attributed to LPs

EXHIBIT 21.8 Example of Waterfall Using a Hurdle Rate

	LPs	GP	Total
Original contribution	−€100 million		−€100 million
Sale of investment for €200 million			
Return of capital	€100 million		€100 million
Preferred return for limited partners	€8 million		€8 million
Catch-up for GP		€2 million	€2 million
80/20 split of residual amount	€72 million	€18 million	€90 million
Closing balance	€80 million	€20 million	€100 million

GP receives all or the major share of distributions. As discussed in the next section, these zones can cause unintended consequences. The catch-up period ends when the agreed-on carried-interest split, or stated share of the fund's profits to be received by the GP and the LPs, is reached. Thereafter, distributions are shared between the fund manager and investors in the proportion agreed to in the legal documentation, normally 20% for the GP and 80% for LPs.

These mechanisms for carried interest payments are not standardized (e.g., whether an interest rate such as a hurdle rate is compounded on a quarterly or on an annual basis). Sometimes there is a full catch-up, whereas other agreements may foresee only a partial catch-up or no catch-up at all. With a 100% catch-up, the LPs are effectively excluded from all new distributions until the GP has fully recovered the agreed-on GP share of the profit.

Exhibit 21.8 provides a numerical example that brings together many of the components of the cash waterfall that were introduced in Chapter 3. To simplify, assume a €100 million contribution by the LPs in the first year to fund an investment, an 8% hurdle rate, a 100% catch-up, an 80/20 carry split, and the sale of the investment by the fund in the second year for €200 million. In this case, the sales proceeds are distributed as shown in Exhibit 21.8. The €2 million catchup for the GP is found by ensuring that the GP gets 20% of the *total*, which is 25% of the LPs' payout. The 25% figure is found as: 20%/(1 − 20%) where 20% is the GP's share.

Note that simply splitting the profit of €100 million (the difference of €200 million in sales proceeds minus the €100 million purchase price) on an 80/20 basis would have given the same result. The reason for this is that the fund's return is above the catch-up zone, and therefore the hurdle is extinguished and does not make any difference.

☞ APPLICATION 21.4.3A

Assume a $200 million contribution by the LPs in the first year to fund an investment, a 6% hurdle rate, a 100% catch-up, an 80/20 carry split, and the sale of the investment by the fund in the third year for $300 million. What is the total cash flow to the LPs and the total cash flow to the GPs? For simplicity, assume that the hurdle rate is not compounded and ignore all other expenses such as management fees.

The preferred return to the LPs is $24 million ($200 million × 6% × 2), leaving $76 million after also returning the $200 million to the LPs. The 100% catch-up to the GPs for an 80%/20% split is $6 million ($24 million × 20%/(1 − 20%)). The residual is $70 million, found as $300 million − ($200 million + $24 million + $6 million), and is split 80%/20%.

	To LPs	To GPs	Total
Return of capital	$200 million		$200 million
Preferred return to LPs	$24 million		$24 million
Catch-up for GP		$6 million	$6 million
80/20 split of residual	$56 million	$14 million	$70 million
Total profit	$80 million	$20 million	$100 million

21.4.4 Private Equity Perverse Incentives from Fees

There are two potentially major perverse incentives generated by hurdle rates.

First, high hurdle rates can cause excessive risk taking. Managers of funds with overly high hurdle rates (or of struggling funds) can become unmotivated if it becomes unlikely that they will receive carried interest. When the GP's call-option-like incentive fee moves far out-of-the-money, the high hurdle rates may lead to desperate risk taking. The option-like payoffs to GPs may mean that the more risk a manager takes, the greater the upside potential, with little immediate downside impact from losses. This is why the GP's capital contribution (discussed in the next section) is so important.

There are also some timing issues with hurdle rates (preferred returns). GPs are faced with the dilemma of whether to realize an investment over a short period of time to optimize the spread of the IRR over the hurdle rate or to hold on to the investment and try to optimize the long-term multiple. For example, is it better to generate a 50% IRR for a period of three months, which yields a 1.11 × multiple on capital invested, or only a 10% IRR for a period of three years, leading to a 1.33 × multiple? The standard preferred return, being based on the IRR, gives incentive to the former. To the extent that GPs game the timing of the investment realizations based on the effect of the timing decision on the carried interest split, it is likely that the LPs suffer adverse consequences.

Investors need to read the limited partnership agreement carefully, as there is a potential for substantial conflicts of interest between the GP and the LP. If LPs don't understand the terms, the GPs may earn much larger fees than those that are clearly stated (such as 2 and 20 over 8%). There has been an increasing use of **subscription lines,** which are lines of credit used by the GP to make investments in portfolio companies. If subscription lines are used to delay capital calls and reduce the time that LPs are invested in the fund, the IRR of the fund may be higher than if capital calls were made at the time the investments were made in the portfolio company.

21.4.5 GP's Contribution to Initial Private Equity Fund Investment

Excessive risk taking can be reduced or eliminated if managers have a significant portion of their personal wealth in the fund. In this case the manager, being directly exposed to fund losses, has little or no incentive to take excessive risks, to work on non-fund-related activities, or to abandon ship once the prospects for generating carry and launching a follow-on fund become highly unlikely.

Typically, investors in PE funds see 1% of the fund's committed capital as a standard and acceptable contribution for GPs to make. The capital contribution by GPs, also known as **hurt money**, should be contributed in cash rather than through the waiver of management fees (or as surplus from the management company's budget). However, in the case of wealthy managers, 1% may at times be too low, as LPs prefer that the GP contribution be at a level that is a substantial portion, perhaps one-quarter to one-half, of the personal net worth of the top partners of the fund management company.

To better understand this relationship, it makes sense to look at the GP's and LPs' relative exposure. Typically, the GP's contribution to the fund is a significant share of his or her personal wealth, whereas the LPs' investment, although in absolute terms is far higher, represents an immaterial share of the institution's overall assets. It is a challenge to determine the appropriate contribution level for a GP: one that provides a reasonable incentive but is not excessively onerous. An analysis of profits earned from past investments, salaries, budget surpluses, and so forth may provide useful information for determining a contribution level that is appropriate for a particular GP.

21.4.6 Key-Person Provision

PE is to a large degree a people business. Depending on the size, experience, and depth of the team, the inability of one or several key persons to carry out their duties could have a substantial adverse effect on the partnership. Consequently, the **key-personnel clause** is a common and important clause in partnerships that allows LPs to take specified actions in the event that one or several of the named key persons depart the team, stop committing sufficient time to the management of the fund, or sell their interests in the management company.

The key-personnel (or key-person) clause (or provision) allows LPs to suspend investment and/or divestment activities until a replacement or replacements are found. The LPs may even be able to terminate the fund if they so choose. Key-person clauses may also be put in place in anticipation of the retirement of senior fund managers.

21.4.7 Termination and Divorce

LPs may include a **bad-leaver clause**, which is a for-cause removal of the GP that, if exercised (normally following a simple majority vote of the LPs), causes investments to be suspended until a new fund manager is elected or, in the extreme, the fund is liquidated. In practical terms, conditions leading to a for-cause removal are difficult to both define and determine. In PE, ultimately very little is legally enforced; issues are highly subjective, and taking matters to court carries high legal risk for an investor, as it is very difficult and lengthy to prove wrongdoing.

A **good-leaver clause** enables investors to cease additional funding of the partnership with a vote requiring a qualified majority (generally more than 75% of LPs). This "without-cause" clause provides a clear framework for shutting down a partnership that is not working, or when confidence is lost. The good-leaver clause sometimes provides for compensation amounting to six months to one year of management fees; the bad-leaver clause provides no such compensation and foresees no entitlement to carried interest.

In deciding whether to exercise one of these clauses, reputation considerations play a key role, as the market consists of a small number of players who repeatedly interact with one another. GPs who are removed with or without cause may subsequently be unable to raise funds or participate in investment syndicates with other partnerships. To avoid such disastrous outcomes, GPs tend to agree on a fund restructuring to prevent a forced removal.

21.4.8 Other Covenants

The terms of the partnership agreements of VC funds contain details regarding the partnership's funding, the distribution of cash, the operation of the fund, the investment practices of the fund, and various covenants.

Typically, the most important covenant is the size of an investment by the VC fund in any one start-up venture, usually expressed as a percentage of the capital committed to the VC fund. The purpose is to ensure that the manager does not commit too much capital to a single investment. In any VC fund there will be start-up ventures that fail to generate a return. By diversifying across several venture investments, this risk is mitigated.

Other covenants may include a restriction on the use of debt or leverage by the fund. VC investments are risky enough without the manager gearing up the fund through borrowing. *Gearing* is a term for increasing risk through leverage. In addition, there may be a restriction on co-investments (detailed in Level 2 of the CAIA curriculum) with prior or future funds controlled by the manager. Furthermore, there is usually a covenant regarding the distribution of profits. Investors find that it is optimal for them to receive the profits as they are realized. Distributed profits reduce the amount of committed capital in the venture fund, which in turn reduces the fees paid to the manager. It is in the VC fund manager's economic interest to retain profits.

Primary among restrictions on the general partner's activities is a limit on the amount of private investments the VC fund manager can make on its own in any of the firms funded by the VC fund. If the VC fund manager makes private investments in a select group of companies, these companies may receive more attention than the remaining portfolio of companies funded by the VC fund. GPs are often limited in their ability to sell their general partnership interests in the VC fund to a third party. Such a sale would be likely to reduce the general partner's incentive to monitor investments and produce an effective exit strategy for the VC fund's portfolio companies.

Two other covenants also relate to keeping the manager's focus on managing the fund. The first is a restriction on the amount of future fundraising. Fundraising is time-consuming and can detract from the manager's time spent managing the investments of the existing fund. Also, LPs typically demand that the general partner spend substantially all of the time managing the investments of the fund; outside interests are limited or restricted.

There are often additional covenants that keep VC fund managers focused on investing in those companies, industries, and transactions in which they have the greatest experience. For instance, there may be restrictions or prohibitions on investing in buyouts, other VC funds, foreign securities, or companies and industries outside the realm of the manager's expertise.

21.5 KEY DETERMINANTS OF VENTURE CAPITAL FUND RISKS AND RETURNS

VC funds require different management from most other investment funds and contain different risks. This section summarizes key issues.

21.5.1 Access as a Key to Enhanced Returns

The key to enhanced returns in VC investing by institutions is accessing the top-tier VC fund managers. There is substantial evidence that return performance is very persistent in the PE industry. The VC firms that are successful tend to form a series of VC funds through time. The VC managers that perform well in one VC fund tend to perform well in their next VC fund.

The likelihood of return persistence in VC is different from that of other asset classes, including large-cap public equities, in which the marketplace is much more liquid and competitive. Superior management teams of public equities are accessible to everyone; virtually anyone can purchase equity in such public firms. The result tends to be that the share price of public firms with highly successful management teams is bid up to a market price that reflects the likelihood that the management team will continue to be successful. In a competitive and efficient market, superior shareholder returns would not be likely to persist when managers continue to excel as expected. However, VC funds are not funded at market prices driven through competition.

Superior performance in a PE firm's most recent funds is usually viewed as a predictor that the firm's next fund will also generate superior performance. Quite a bit of this performance persistence can be explained by the reputation of the general partner managing the VC fund. The best VC firms attract the very best entrepreneurs, business plans, and investment opportunities. The most successful VC firms have an established track record of getting start-up companies to an initial public offering. Their track record allows them to attract investment capital from their LPs, as well as proprietary deal flow from start-up companies seeking VC. The general partner of a better-performing VC fund is more likely to raise a follow-on fund and to raise larger funds than a VC firm that performs poorly. GPs of the most successful PE funds can pick and choose among numerous investors desiring to participate in their next fund.

21.5.2 Three Dimensions to Diversifying Venture Capital Risk

Achieving diversification, especially vintage-year and industry diversification, is the key to reducing risk. Given the cyclical nature of the overall economy and of PE in particular, a deal's vintage year can be an important determinant of the deal's success. Institutions investing in PE funds often analyze their holdings with respect to vintage years. They may seek diversification of their fund holdings across vintage years, or they may seek higher returns by strategically allocating with respect to vintage years based on their market view. Kaplan and Schoar find evidence of a boom and bust cycle in which high PE returns encourage new investment, which leads to reduced subsequent returns.[3] Presumably, in vintage years when there were large investment amounts and greater competition for deals, the higher deal prices eventually led to lower returns. An institution that concentrates investments in a particular vintage year runs the risk that the vintage year will turn out few winning ventures. Accordingly, investors should diversify into PE funds of different vintage years.

Further dimensions over which investors should consider diversifying their VC portfolios include industry and geography.

21.5.3 Three Main Risks and the Required Risk Premiums for Venture Capital

Most venture capitalists are long-term investors who expect to earn a premium from VC that is about 400 to 800 basis points over the returns of the public stock market, depending on the VC stage of financing. This risk premium can be viewed as providing compensation for three main risks.

First, there is the business risk of a start-up company. Although some start-ups successfully make it to the initial public offering stage, many more do not succeed. Venture capitalists must anticipate earning a return that sufficiently compensates them for bearing the risk of potential corporate failure. Although public companies can also fail, VC is unique in that the investor takes on this business risk before a company has had the opportunity to fully implement its business plan.

Second, there is substantial liquidity risk. There is no liquid public market for trading VC interests. The secondary trading that does exist is generally limited to exchange among a small group of other PE investors. This is a fragmented and thus inefficient market. The tailored nature of a venture capitalist's holdings is unlikely to appeal to more than a very select group of potential buyers. Consequently, the sale of an interest in a VC fund is not an easy task. Further, another VC firm may not have the time or ability to perform as thorough a due diligence process as the initial investing firm. Thus, a secondary sale often requires a substantial pricing discount.

Third, there may be an idiosyncratic risk due to the lack of diversification associated with a VC portfolio. The capital asset pricing model (CAPM) shows that the only risk that investors should be compensated for is the risk of the general stock market, or systematic risk. This is because unsystematic or company-specific risk can theoretically be diversified away. However, the CAPM is predicated on securities being freely transferable and infinitely divisible, and portfolios being fully diversifiable. Since the lack of liquidity in VC severely impairs transferability, some venture capitalists are not well diversified, and they bear substantial idiosyncratic risk. In the case of numerous investors who are not highly diversified, the CAPM does not hold, and idiosyncratic risk may be rewarded.

VC firms have become increasingly specialized as a result of the intensive knowledge base required to invest in the technology, telecommunications, and biotechnology industries, and specialization has expanded further to include the stage of investment in the life cycle of a start-up company. Unfortunately, specialization leads to concentrated portfolios, the very anathema of reduced risk through diversification. This concentration leads to the need for higher risk premiums.

21.6 ROLES AND THREE KEY DISTINCTIONS OF VENTURE CAPITAL AND BUYOUT MANAGERS

Depending on the strategy, the roles of the PE managers can differ markedly.

The PE market is evolving. A few decades ago, the supply of PE capital came primarily through a limited number of large PE firms. These PE firms obtained much of their financing from creating PE funds and offering limited partnership investments to institutions and wealthy investors. The PE market emphasized relationships. PE firms invested capital in deals within a moderately inefficient market and a relatively less competitive environment. Established PE firms also obtained their external capital within a relatively less competitive environment, wherein institutions wishing to invest in PE faced concerns over whether they would have access to promising deals.

In buyout transactions, a greater proportion of time and manpower is spent analyzing specific investments and adjusting the business model. Buyout managers look to apply their expertise to turn around underperforming businesses, improve profitable businesses, or optimize the companies' balance sheets and financing. They typically engage in hiring new management teams or retooling strategies. In an operating company, it is easier to give guidance to a seasoned management team, whereas in early-stage investments, one often needs to build and coach the management team from the ground up.

The major distinctions between VC and buyout fund managers can be summarized as being driven by these three goals: (1) Venture capitalists look to launch new or emerging companies, whereas buyout managers focus on leveraging an established company's assets; (2) venture capitalists back entrepreneurs, whereas buyout managers deal with experienced managers; and (3) venture capitalists often play a more active role in the companies in which they invest, by either sitting on the board of directors or becoming involved in the day-to-day management of the company.

21.7 LEVERAGED BUYOUT FUNDS

The dominant type of buyout in terms of aggregate size is the LBO. This section provides details about LBOs and LBO funds.

21.7.1 LBO Fund Structures

Leveraged buyout (LBO) funds distinguish themselves by the size of the companies they take private. Generally, they classify themselves as investing in small-capitalization companies ($100 million to $1 billion in sales revenue), mid-capitalization companies ($1 billion to $5 billion in sales revenue), or large-capitalization companies ($5 billion and above in sales revenue). The large-cap category of LBOs also includes super-sized or mega LBOs.

Almost all LBO funds are structured as limited partnerships. This is very similar to the way that VC funds are established. LBO funds are run by a general partner, typically an LBO firm. All investment discretion and day-to-day operations vest with the general partner. LPs, as the name implies, have a very limited role in the management of the LBO fund. For the most part, LPs are passive investors who rely on the general partner to source, analyze, perform due diligence, and invest the committed capital of the fund.

The number of LPs in a PE fund is not fixed. Most PE funds have 20 to 50 LPs, but some have as few as five and others more than 50. PE funds have contractually set lifetimes—typically 10 years, with provisions to extend the limited partnership for one to two more years. Limited partners would prefer to not pay management fees after the stated life of the fund, such as 10 years, has passed. If LPs are not paying management fees during the extended life of the fund, GPs have an incentive to wrap up the fund more quickly. During the first five years of the partnership, deals are sourced and reviewed and partnership capital is invested. After companies are taken private, the investments are managed and eventually liquidated. As the portfolio companies are sold, taken public, or recapitalized, distributions are made to the LPs, usually in cash but sometimes in securities, as is often the case when an IPO is used to exit an investment.

21.7.2 Total Number, Size, and Implications of Buyout Fund Fees

LBO firms have numerous ways to make money. First, there are the annual management fees, which range from 1.25% to 3% of investor capital. Incentive fees, or carried interest, usually range from 20% to 30% of the fund's total profits.

For arranging and negotiating an LBO, an LBO firm may also charge fees of up to 1% of the total selling price to the corporation it is taking private. As an example, Kohlberg Kravis Roberts & Co. (KKR) earned $75 million for arranging the buyout of RJR Nabisco and $60 million for arranging the buyout of Safeway, Inc. Some LBO firms (i.e., GPs) keep all of these fees for themselves rather than sharing them with the limited partner investors. Other LBO firms split the transaction fees, with LPs receiving typically 25% to 75%. Still other LBO firms include all of these fees as part of the profits to be split up among the general partner and the LPs. Not only do LBO firms earn fees for arranging deals, but they can also earn breakup fees if a deal fails.

In addition to these fees, LBO firms may charge a divestiture fee for arranging the sale of a division of a private company after the buyout has been completed. Further, an LBO firm may charge directors' fees to a buyout company if managing partners of the LBO firm sit on the company's board of directors after the buyout has occurred. The debate over PE fees has intensified in recent years, especially because as buyout funds have grown in size, the management fees of the funds have not been adjusted downward as a percentage.

When the buyout industry started, the 1% to 2% management fee was necessary to pay the expenses of the PE general partner. This fee covered travel expenses, utility bills, and the salaries of the general partner's staff. In short, the management fee was originally used to keep the PE manager afloat until the incentive fee could be realized, which often took several years. Now, however, PE funds have grown to immense size; $10 billion funds are common. The PE manager now earns a considerable amount of profit from its management fees. This could blunt the incentive of the PE manager to seek only the most potentially profitable PE opportunities.

Let's take a simple example of typical fees. Assume a PE firm raises a $10 billion buyout fund and charges a management fee of 1.5%. This is a fee of $150 million during the investment period of the fund. Assuming a 10-year life for a fully invested fund and an 8% discount rate for the time value of money, the present value of just the management fees to the PE firm is $1.006 billion. With management fees like this, there could be a disincentive to take risks.

While managers of buyout funds generally offer their investors an 8% preferred return before they take a share of the profits for themselves, this is less common in the case of VC funds, at least in the United States. In this context, Fleischer puts forward an alternative explanation for the preferred return: It is more important as an incentive to properly screen the deal flow.[4] Without it, buyout fund managers could pursue a low-risk, low-return strategy, for example, by being inactive or by choosing companies that have little potential to generate large returns. A preferred return forces managers to make riskier investments to generate a return in line with the investor's targets. In the case of VC funds, however, investments are always risky, and the high-risk, high-reward strategy makes it meaningless to bother about preferred returns.

21.7.3 Agency Relationships and Costs

The objectives of the senior managers of listed corporations may be very different from those of the corporation's equity owners. For instance, management of public firms may be highly concerned with keeping their jobs and presiding over a large empire. Conversely, shareholders want value creation (i.e., share price maximization). In agency theory, senior corporate managers are the agents and shareholders are the principals. Shareholders, as the owners of the company, delegate day-to-day decision-making authority to management with the expectation or hope that management will act in the best interests of the shareholders. However, in a large company, equity ownership may be so widely dispersed that the shareholders of the company may not be able to fully align managerial objectives with shareholder objectives or otherwise control management's natural tendencies. Thus, the separation of ownership and control of the corporation results in conflicts of interest and agency costs.

Agency costs come in two forms. First, there is the cost to better align management's goals with the value-creation goal of shareholders. These costs include the costs of monitoring management, which may include audits of financial statements, shareholder review of management perquisites, and independent reviews of management's compensation structure. Better alignment is also sought via the compensation arrangements. Compensation arrangements that are designed to better align shareholder and management objectives include stock options, bonuses, and other performance-based compensation. Second, agency costs can include the erosion of shareholder value from agency conflicts that are too costly to resolve efficiently. These costs include the adverse effect on shareholders of managerial actions that are not in the best interests of shareholders. The optimal strategy regarding agency conflicts is to implement only those actions that have benefits that exceed their costs, not necessarily to minimize agency costs. Thus, conflicts of interest and agency costs are realities of doing business using structures that use agency relationships.

LBO firms replace a dispersed group of shareholders with a highly concentrated group of owners. The concentrated and private nature of the new shareholders helps incentivize the managers of the buyout firm to focus on maximizing shareholder wealth. Further, the management of the now private company is often given a substantial equity stake in the company that provides a strong alignment of interests between the management/agents of the company and its principals/shareholders. As the company's fortunes increase, so do the personal fortunes of the management team. The large incentives to an LBO's management team are often vital to the LBO's goal of unlocking value.

With a majority of the remaining equity of the once public, now private, company concentrated in the hands of the LBO firm, the interaction between equity owners and management becomes particularly important. After a company is taken private, LBO firms maintain an active role in guiding and monitoring the management of the company. After a transaction is complete, an LBO firm remains in continuous contact with company management. As the majority equity owner, the LBO firm has the right to monitor the progress of management, ask questions, and demand accountability.

21.7.4 LBO Auction Markets

In the past, LBO deals were sourced by a single PE firm without any competitive bidding from other PE firms. The traditional model of PE was one in which a single PE firm approached a stand-alone public company about going private or approached a parent company with respect to spinning off a subsidiary. In this model, the lone PE firm worked with the executive management of the public company or the parent company to develop a financing plan for taking the public company or a subsidiary private. Bringing this deal to fruition may have taken months or years, as the PE firm worked on building its relationship with the senior management of the company.

Whenever large sums of capital enter an informationally inefficient market, the inefficiencies begin to erode. An influx of investment in LBOs has led to the development of an auction market environment. Single-sourced deals are a thing of the past. Now, when a parent company decides to sell a subsidiary in an LBO format, it almost always hires an investment banker to establish an auction process. An **auction process** involves bidding among several PE firms, with the deal going to the highest bidder. This competitive bidding process can often involve several rounds and can result in less upside for the PE investor, yet it reflects the maturation of the PE industry.

21.7.5 LBOs, Club Deals, Benefits, and Concerns

Another development in the PE market is club deals. In the past, LBO firms worked on exclusive deals, one-on-one with the acquired company. However, the large inflow of capital into the PE market and the increasing market capitalization of firms targeted for LBOs have forced LBO firms to work together in so-called clubs. In a **club deal**, two or more LBO firms work together to share costs, present a business plan, and contribute capital to the deal. There is considerable debate about whether club deals add or detract value. Both sellers of target companies and potential buyers can initiate club deals.

Some have posited that club deals tend to increase the number of potential buyers by enabling firms that could not individually bid on a target company to do so through a club. A fund might not have sufficient capital to purchase a target alone because of either restrictions on investing more than a specified portion of its capital in a single deal or the large size of the target. For example, a common restriction found in many limited partnership agreements limits PE funds from investing more than 25% of their total capital in any one deal. For some of the very large buyouts, club deals are necessary.

Another benefit of club deals is that they allow PE firms to pool resources for pre-buyout due diligence research, which can often be quite costly. In addition, club deals allow one PE firm to get a second opinion about the value of a potential acquisition from another member of the club.

Some have expressed concern that club deals could depress acquisition prices by reducing the number of firms bidding on target companies, because there may be more competition from numerous individual bidders than from a few clubs of bidders. There is also concern that in a club deal it is less clear who will take the lead in the business plan, which PE firm will sit on the board of directors of the private company, who will be responsible for monitoring performance, and who will negotiate with outside lenders to provide the debt financing for the LBO.

21.7.6 Three Factors Driving Buyout Risks Relative to Venture Capital Risks

LBO funds have less risk than VC funds for three reasons.

First, LBO funds tend to purchase public companies that are established and mature. Typically, buyouts target successful but undervalued companies. These companies generally have long-term operating histories, generate a positive cash flow, and have established brand names and identities with consumers. Also, the management teams of the companies have an established track record. Therefore, assessment of key employees is easier than assessment of a new team in a VC deal. VC funds face the substantial business risks associated with start-up companies.

Second, LBO funds tend to be less specialized than VC funds. While LBO firms may concentrate on one sector from time to time, they tend to be more diversified in their choice of targets. Their target companies can range from movie theaters to grocery stores. Therefore, although they maintain smaller portfolios than traditional long-only managers, they tend to have greater diversification than their VC counterparts.

Third, the eventual exit strategy of a new IPO is much more likely for an LBO than for a VC deal. This is because the buyout company already had publicly traded stock outstanding. A prior history as a public company, demonstrable operating profits, and a proven management team make an IPO for a buyout firm much more feasible than an IPO for a start-up venture.

21.8 PRIVATE EQUITY LIQUID ALTERNATIVES

Liquid alternatives, or liquid alts, have emerged in a variety of alternative investment sectors, and PE is no exception. In the United States, business development companies serve as a prominent example of liquid access to PE.

21.8.1 Business Development Companies

Business development companies (BDCs) are publicly traded funds with underlying assets typically consisting of equity or equity-like positions in small private companies. BDCs use a closed-end structure and trade on major stock exchanges, especially the NASDAQ in the United States.

BDCs are investment companies with a primary purpose of pooling financial assets and issuing pro rata claims against those assets. The key to investment companies is that they can avoid the double taxation of corporate profits. Investment companies holding listed financial assets were authorized in the United States by the Investment Company Act of 1940. Legislation in the United States allowing BDCs to qualify as investment companies and enjoy a pass-through income tax status originated from amendments to the '40 Act in 1980. However, BDCs did not become popular until much later (approximately 2012).

To be classified as a BDC and enjoy the accompanying benefits, such as avoiding corporate income tax, a BDC must provide significant managerial assistance to the firms that it owns and must invest at least 70% of its investments in eligible assets, as specified by the Securities and Exchange Commission (SEC). BDCs must invest primarily in small firms, must maintain no more than moderate leverage, must distribute at least 90% of their income, and must meet diversification requirements to avoid corporate income taxes.

BDCs enable liquid ownership of pools of illiquid PE, just as REITs can be used to provide liquid access to illiquid private real estate. The shareholders are subject to income tax on the distributed profits. Any profits retained at the BDC level are subject to corporate income tax. Therefore, most BDCs distribute almost all profits to shareholders to avoid the income tax on retained earnings.

Recent figures indicate that there are more than 40 publicly traded BDCs in the United States, with over $10 billion of combined market value. A few of the largest BDCs fall into the mid-cap category in terms of total market capitalization. Over 90% of the BDCs fall into the small-cap category. BDCs are tracked by several indices and ETFs, including at least one ETF that is leveraged. The indices and ETFs use market weights or modified market weights and tend to cover virtually all listed U.S. BDCs. As discussed in the next section, the market prices of BDCs reflect their underlying closed-end fund structure.

21.8.2 Business Development Companies as Closed-End Funds

BDCs use a closed-end fund investment structure that transforms ownership of underlying fund assets into shares (tradable pro rata claims). A major attribute of a closed-end structure is that it facilitates liquid ownership of illiquid pools of assets much better than would an open-end structure. Closed-end funds are especially popular in facilitating ownership of municipal bonds, international stocks, and illiquid instruments.

An open-end mutual fund has serious flaws with regard to providing liquid access to investors when the fund holds large quantities of highly illiquid pools of assets. Open-end funds must redeem shares on a regular basis, which can be difficult when holding illiquid assets, such as those held by BDCs. The primary distinction of closed-end funds relative to open-end funds is that the closed-end investment company does not regularly create new shares or redeem old shares in order to meet the desire of investors to invest in the fund or divest from the fund. Therefore, closed-end funds avoid the problems caused in open-end funds by using inaccurate net asset values (NAVs), as measured by the investment company, to create and redeem shares. However, closed-end funds introduce another problem: When investors transact in the secondary market, the price per share that they receive from or pay to another investor may be highly subject to short-term supply and demand factors in the secondary market and can diverge from the fund's NAV.

When there is a surge in demand for closed-end fund shares from investors who wish to establish or expand positions in a particular closed-end fund, the market price of the closed-end fund must rise until the supply of shares meets the demand. The price rises to encourage increased supply of shares from sales by existing shareholders and to discourage demand for shares from prospective shareholders. Similarly, when there is a surge in supply of closed-end fund shares from investors who wish to exit their holdings, the market price must decrease to restore a balance between the supply and demand for the fund's shares in the secondary market.

Closed-end fund share prices are often viewed relative to the net asset value per share that is reported by the investment companies. For example, a closed-end fund that reports a net asset value of $20 per share is said to be selling at a 5% premium if the market price is $21. If the market price of the closed-end fund is $18.50, the closed-end fund shares would be said to be selling at a discount of 7.5%. The formula for the premium (or discount if negative) of a closed-end fund share price is shown in Equation 21.1:

$$\text{Premium (or Discount)} = (\text{Market Price}/\text{Net Asset Value}) - 1 \quad (21.1)$$

The left-hand side of Equation 21.1 is typically expressed as a percentage and is termed a discount if the value is negative.

☞ APPLICATION 21.8.2A

Shares of closed-end fund ABC were selling at a premium of 10% and then fell to $44 per share while ABC's net asset value held constant at $50 per share. What were the previous market price, subsequent discount, NAV-based return, and market-price return for ABC?

The previous market price was $55 (solved using Equation 21.1, with 0.10 on the left-hand side and $50 for the NAV). The subsequent discount (solved as −12% using Equation 21.1, with $44/$50 as the fraction inside the parentheses) was 12%. The NAV-based return was 0%, since the NAV was assumed unchanged, and the market-price return was −20% (−$11/$55), assuming no dividends or other distributions.

As illustrated in the example, large temporary changes in supply and demand can cause substantial dislocations of the market price of a closed-end fund. Investors with positions in closed-end funds bear the risk that they will need to liquidate their shares at a time when the market price of the shares has been substantially reduced by selling pressures. Thus, returns from investing in closed-end fund structures are driven both by the returns of the underlying assets and the premiums or discounts of the fund shares when positions are established and closed.

During periods of severe illiquidity caused by a financial crisis or another major event, closed-end fund discounts have been observed to reach extreme levels. Owners of closed-end fund shares needing to exit their investment in a liquidity crisis experience the double loss of selling not only when NAVs are down but also when the market price of the closed-end fund is at an extreme discount to its NAV. Thus, investors in BDCs are potentially exposed to especially large losses in the event of liquidations during periods of severe illiquidity. Note that an open-end mutual fund with listed equities as underlying assets would allow liquidation at NAVs based on market prices.

Finally, it should be noted that for many closed-end fund structures, the underlying assets are market traded, and the computation of the fund's NAV is straightforward. The premium or discount of such funds tends to be a simple and effective indicator of the attractiveness of the fund's market price. However, in the cases of BDCs, REITs, and other funds with unlisted underlying assets, the reported NAVs are based on non-market valuations, such as professional appraisals or accounting standards. Listed PE securities such as BDCs, closed-end funds, and publicly traded PE firms are much like REITs: They offer the liquidity of public trading with underlying assets that are illiquid and that when held directly are presumed to offer premiums for illiquidity. When the NAVs are based on subjective valuation methods rather than current market prices, the premiums or discounts of the closed-end fund shares may be poor indicators of the attractiveness of the fund's shares, because the NAVs themselves may be flawed indicators of the actual underlying values.

21.8.3 Extending Closed-End Fund Pricing to Illiquid Alternatives

As detailed in the previous section, the premiums and discounts of closed-end fund share prices are generally perceived as varying through time, based on both large purchases by entities attempting to enter positions and large sales by entities attempting to exit positions. The direct application of these supply and demand pressures to BDCs is straightforward, since BDCs use a closed-end fund structure. However, the principles may be even more applicable to the transaction prices of illiquid alternatives. For example, when the limited partner of a PE partnership or other illiquid alternative investment wants to exit an investment, how much of a "discount" might that seller be forced to offer in order to entice a prospective buyer to purchase the position?

Careful observation and understanding of the behavior of closed-end fund share prices provide indications of the effect of illiquidity on transaction prices. In the previous section, there was an example of a closed-end fund moving from trading at a 10% premium to a 12% discount. Although the transaction prices and underlying net asset values of private partnerships are usually not quoted on a daily basis, the concept of illiquid assets trading at premiums and discounts applies. Of course, privately traded PE may also be exchanged at depressed prices when there are numerous partners wishing to exit. Simply put, the realized returns of PE investors who must liquidate their positions may be low when liquidity is poor, whether or not the investment uses a closed-end structure.

21.8.4 Are Liquid Private Equity Pools Diversifiers?

Most PE is not directly listed or publicly traded. PE is often described as offering substantial diversification benefits. However, the lack of market prices on PE makes substantiation of such claims difficult. Prices for PE based on illiquid trading data or professional judgment can be argued to be smoothed, and therefore analysis based on those data should be expected to underestimate true volatilities and correlations.

However, listed BDCs provide an opportunity to observe market prices of PE. As in the case of real estate and REITs, the market data on liquid alternatives can be analyzed to provide evidence regarding the correlations and volatilities of the underlying illiquid assets. A critical underlying issue is how the returns of liquid PE (e.g., BDCs) compare to the returns of illiquid PE (e.g., private partnerships) when the underlying assets are similar.

As indicated in Exhibit 21.9, the BDCS ETF had high correlations of monthly returns with the monthly returns of both SPY and IWM. SPY is an ETF of large U.S. stocks and IWM is an ETF of small U.S. stocks. The correlation of the returns of BDCS with the small-cap index (IWM) was higher than the correlation with the large-cap index (SPY). As observed in numerous analyses of REITs, the liquid alternatives appear to take on correlations more closely with small-caps than with large-caps. The BDCS ETF had a volatility of monthly returns approximately midway between the volatilities of SPY and IWM. In theory, the volatility of the returns of BDCS should be driven by the volatilities and correlations of the returns of the small business ventures that underlie the BDCs being tracked by BDCS.

The results in Exhibit 21.9 are roughly analogous to the results for REITs, based on numerous studies involving a variety of time periods. Simply put, listed liquid alternative investment companies appear to exhibit return performance that is highly correlated with listed equities in general. In particular, performance is most highly correlated with equities of similar capitalization size. Exhibit 21.9 therefore provides evidence that BDCs do not serve as effective diversifiers relative to listed equities.

21.8.5 Are Liquid Private Equity Pools Return Enhancers?

Exhibit 21.9 lists the average annualized returns of the three ETFs: BDCS, SPY, and IWM. The returns indicate that BDCS underperformed the S&P 500 ETF and the Russell 2000 ETF. It should be pointed out that investors in BDCS incur two levels of

EXHIBIT 21.9 Return Analysis of BDCS, May 2011 to December 2018

	Mean Return	Volatility	Correlation to BDCS
BDCS	−3.3%	13.5%	1.00
SPY	8.8%	11.6%	0.64
IWM	7.3%	16.1%	0.78

fees. First, BDCS imposes fees at the ETF level and has an expense ratio substantially higher than the expense ratios of many large ETFs, such as SPY. Second, the portfolio companies (i.e., the underlying BDCs) also have potentially large expense ratios.

PE accessed through private limited partnerships is also subject to substantial management fees, including incentive fees. Perhaps the critical determinant of long-term PE performance is the quality of the management teams. Therefore, a key issue in determining whether liquid PE funds such as BDCs can provide return enhancement is whether the BDCs offer superior management teams that can successfully acquire and manage underlying business enterprises.

21.9   PRIVATE EQUITY FUNDS OF FUNDS

This section discusses PE funds of funds: private fund structures with underlying assets composed of private PE funds.

21.9.1   Private Equity Funds of Funds and Fees

Funds of funds are often seen as less efficient than single GP funds (i.e., direct fund investments) because of the additional layer of management fees and incentive fees. This double layer of fees is perceived to be one of the main disadvantages of this structure. However, given the resources required for an institutional investor to select, monitor, and manage a portfolio of PE funds internally, investing through a fund-of-funds structure might well prove more cost-efficient than a direct fund investing approach in the end.

The cost of outsourcing investment management, including the carried interest of the funds of funds, needs to be compared to performance-related incentives, if any, paid in a program managed internally. Whether an in-house program can work effectively without investment performance – related incentives is debatable.

According to Otterlei and Barrington,[5] the annual costs of an in-house team can be substantial compared to that of a typical fund of funds. Even with a 5% carried interest charged by the fund-of-funds manager, these authors find that the fees have an insignificant impact on the net returns of the investor.

21.9.2   Private Equity Funds of Funds and the Value of Information and Control

Information can be a valuable asset in an opaque environment such as PE. Funds of funds can provide the necessary resources and address the information gap for inexperienced PE investors through their expertise in due diligence, monitoring, and restructuring. Successful investing in PE funds requires: (1) a wide-reaching network of contacts in order to gain access to high-quality funds, (2) well-trained investment judgment, and (3) the ability to assemble balanced portfolios.

An institutional investor taking the fund-of-funds route (as opposed to taking a direct investment route) can lose access to information and control, essentially a cost in itself. Because PE programs follow a learning curve, inexperienced institutions may initially have little option other than to go through a fund-of-funds vehicle. Experience with the funds-of-funds approach may allow institutional investors new to PE to build knowledge and sophistication, eventually leading to building their own portfolios of funds.

Funds of funds can therefore be used as a first step into PE and may be worth the additional layer of fees in exchange for avoiding expensive learning-curve mistakes and for providing access to a broader selection of funds.

21.9.3 Private Equity Funds of Funds, Diversification, and Intermediation

Funds of funds can add value in several respects, especially in the case of investments in new technologies, new teams, or emerging markets. A fund of funds approach allows for reasonable downside protection through greater diversification than many investors can achieve through a direct program. It is important to diversify a PE investment program across vintage years, GPs, industry, stage of investment, and geography. Not surprisingly, various studies have shown that because of their diversification, funds of funds perform similarly to individual funds but with less pronounced extremes.[6] For larger institutions, investments in PE funds and especially VC funds may be too cost-intensive when the size of such investments is small compared to administrative expenses. A fund of funds can mediate these potential size issues by either scaling up through pooling of commitments of smaller investors and providing each of them with sufficient diversification, or scaling down through sharing administrative expenses and making such investments less cost-intensive by allowing larger commitment to the fund of funds.

21.9.4 Private Equity Funds of Funds, Access, Selection Skills, and Expertise

Funds-of-funds management may offer the advantage of being able to invest in top-performing funds, either by having access to successful invitation-only funds or by identifying the future stars among the young and lesser-known funds. Funds of funds managers focus their expertise on managing portfolio companies, and they are often more skilled and experienced in managing portfolio companies (than direct funds investors) such as in cases of restructuring failing funds. Finally, funds of funds may offer better access to top fund managers because those top managers may welcome funds-of-funds investors as a more stable and experienced source of pooled capital.

Liquidity management can also be quite challenging, as it demands a full-time team with insight and an industry network, adequate resources, and access to research databases and models, as well as skills and experience in due diligence, negotiation, and contract structuring. Depending on the overall market situation, access to quality funds can be highly competitive, and being a newcomer to the market can pose a significant barrier. Funds of funds are continuously involved in the PE space, speak the language, and understand the trade-offs in the industry.

21.10 PRIVATE INVESTMENTS IN PUBLIC EQUITY

Private investments in public equity (PIPE) transactions are privately issued equity or equity-linked securities that are placed outside of a public offering, are exempt from registration, and are used as vehicles for publicly traded companies to issue additional equity shares (or other securities) in their firms. Investors purchase the securities directly from a publicly traded company in a private transaction. In other words, the "public" part of the name reflects that they are vehicles for publicly traded companies to issue additional equity shares (or other securities) in their firms. The "private" part of the name reflects that the securities are sold directly to investors, who usually cannot trade them in secondary markets for a specified period of time, frequently three to six months. PIPEs are often used as a substitute for secondary offerings of shares that are immediately publicly traded. Since 2001, the proceeds of PIPEs and secondary equity offerings (SEOs) in the U.S. market are approximately equal.

21.10.1 Characteristics and Types of Securities Issued through PIPEs

In the United States, PIPE issuers can be anything from small companies listed in the over-the-counter market to large companies listed on the New York Stock Exchange (NYSE). Some PIPE transactions involve small, nascent corporations of the type that interest venture capitalists. They are also often issued by small to medium-size firms that may face difficulties, expenses, or delays in using public security offerings. The typical profile is a company with a market capitalization of under $500 million that seeks an equity infusion of between $10 million and $75 million. However, some PIPE transactions involve established public companies, the domain of the buyout market.

PIPE deals offer investors a variety of securities that can be issued including the following:

- PRIVATELY PLACED COMMON STOCK: The greater the illiquidity, the greater the discount on the PIPE's issue price.
- REGISTERED COMMON STOCK: The advantage to the investor is that it can acquire a block of stock at a discount to the public market price for the registered common stock. This is particularly appealing for PE firms that have large chunks of cash to commit to companies.
- CONVERTIBLE PREFERRED SHARES OR CONVERTIBLE DEBT: Conversion prices embedded in preferred stock and convertible debt tend to be lower than the conversion prices on publicly traded instruments. In addition, the issuer of the PIPE usually commits to register the equity securities within the next six months. This feature is particularly appealing for PE firms to the extent that they are able to purchase cheap equity with a ready-made exit strategy.
- EQUITY LINE OF CREDIT: An **equity line of credit** (ELC) is a contractual agreement between an issuer and an investor that enables the issuer to sell a formula-based quantity of stock at set intervals of time.

21.10.2 Buyer and Seller Motivations for PIPEs

The greatest advantages for the issuing company of a PIPE are: (1) that the company can quickly raise capital (a PIPE transaction can be completed in just a few weeks) without the need for a lengthy registration process (which can take up to nine months), and (2) larger companies view PIPEs as a cheaper process for raising capital quickly, especially from a friendly investor.

Further, the management of the issuing company does not need to be distracted with the prolonged road show that typically precedes a public offering of stock. Management can remain focused on the operations of the business while receiving an equity infusion that strengthens the balance sheet.

The documentation required for a PIPE is relatively simple, compared to a registration statement. Typically, all that is needed is an offering memorandum that summarizes the terms of the PIPE, the business of the issuer, and the intended uses of the PIPE proceeds.

Another reason PE firms are interested in PIPEs is that they allow the PE firm to gain a substantial stake in the company, even control, at a discount. This is very enticing to PE firms, which normally have to pay a premium for a large chunk of a company's equity.

21.10.3 Traditional PIPEs and Structured PIPEs

The biggest distinction between PIPEs is that of traditional PIPEs and structured PIPEs. The large majority of PIPE transactions are **traditional PIPEs,** in which investors can buy common stock at a fixed price. Most traditional PIPE transactions are initiated using convertible preferred stock or convertible debt with a fixed price at which the securities can be converted into common stock. The conversion price is the price per share at which the convertible security can be exchanged into shares of common stock, expressed in terms of the principal value of the convertible security. The conversion ratio is the number of shares of common stock into which each convertible security can be exchanged. The conversion ratio and the conversion price are inversely related measures of the same concept.

☞ **APPLICATION 21.10.3A**

A convertible preferred stock with a par or face value of $100 per share is convertible into four shares of common stock. What is the conversion ratio, and what is the conversion price? What would be the conversion ratio if the conversion price were $20?

The original example of the preferred stock has a conversion ratio of 4:1. The conversion option may be expressed as a conversion price of $25 (using the face value of the preferred stock to make the purchase). In the second example of a $20 conversion price, the conversion ratio would be 5:1.

Having a fixed conversion price or conversion ratio limits the amount of dilution to existing shareholders. Also, the convertible preferred stock or debt may provide the investor with dividends and other rights in a sale, merger, or liquidation of the company that are superior to the residual claims of the existing stockholders.

Structured PIPEs include more exotic securities, like floating-rate convertible preferred stock, convertible resets, and common stock resets. These PIPEs have a floating conversion price that can change depending on the price of the publicly traded common stock. They are sometimes referred to as floating convertibles because the conversion price of the convertible preferred stock or debt floats up or down with the company's common stock price.

21.10.4 Toxic PIPEs

In the past, structuring of PIPEs led to the creation of toxic PIPEs and so-called death spirals. A **toxic PIPE** is a PIPE somewhat popular years ago with adjustable conversion terms that can generate accelerating levels of shareholder dilution in the event of declining prices in the firm's common stock. Floating convertibles received a bad reputation because, unlike standard convertible bonds or preferred stocks, which get converted at a fixed conversion price, the conversion price for toxic PIPEs adjusts downward whenever the underlying common stock price declines. The drop in stock price leads to a drop in the conversion price, which can lead to a substantial dilution of shareholder value.

For example, under a structured PIPE, if the stock price of the issuer declines in value, the PIPE investor receives a greater number of shares upon converting the PIPE. Expressed differently, the conversion price of the PIPE declines commensurately with the underlying stock price. This can lead to a situation that is potentially poisonous to the issuing company's financial health. A toxic PIPE can generate the following sequence:

- A company with a weak balance sheet and uncertain cash flows cannot issue additional publicly traded shares of its common stock.
- PE investors agree to provide more capital in return for structured PIPEs that can be converted into stock at a floating conversion rate and at a discount to the common stock price.
- The stock price of the company falls. The price decline may be triggered by PE investors short selling the publicly traded stock of the company to hedge their purchase of the PIPE, by a decline in the company's profitability, or both. A large downward movement in the stock price is the catalyst that can turn a structured PIPE into a toxic PIPE.
- The downward pressure on the company's common stock price triggers larger and larger conversion ratios for the PIPE investors (i.e., lower conversion prices), resulting in greater and greater dilution of the common stock of the company as the PIPE investors are granted an ever-growing number of shares representing an ever-rising percentage ownership in the firm.
- Prospects for greater dilution of the company's stock drive the market price of the stock further downward. The lower stock price again forces the company to reduce the conversion price for the PIPEs into common stock at lower and lower prices.
- The process of lower conversion prices, greater dilution, and lower share prices repeats in a downward **death spiral**.
- Ultimately, the PIPE investors exercise their conversion rights at greatly depressed conversion prices and either sell their converted shares (obtained at a large discount) or take control of the company using the large number of new shares.

Although this scenario sounds improbable, some PIPE transactions led to poisonous results for the issuing company. Although structured PIPEs still exist, both investors and companies receiving PIPE financing have become much more sophisticated regarding the details and floating conversion rates in toxic PIPEs. The learning experiences of the late 1990s and early 2000s led to a PIPE market with more sensible deals and less likelihood of perverse incentives.

21.11 PRIVATE EQUITY SECONDARY MARKETS AND STRUCTURES

This final section on PE funds briefly covers four topics that involve the trading mechanisms and organizational structures of PE investment.

21.11.1 The Secondary Market for Private Equity Partnerships

This section discusses secondary trading of PE limited partnership interests. Many PE interests are organized as limited partnerships. The lack of registration and public trading makes the purchase and sale of LP interests less liquid than listed stock or other registered securities. Investors in PE are typically subject to a 10-year lockup period. Investors wishing to liquidate their investment before these exits will need to access the secondary market.

THREE PRIMARY REASONS TO SELL LIMITED PARTNERSHIP INTERESTS: Most investors considering the acquisition of an investment take into account its liquidity, which means the ability to sell the investment without needing to offer a substantial discount from the value that would be obtained in a liquid market. There are three primary reasons that a PE investor may need to sell part of a portfolio:

1. To raise cash for funding requirements: For example, a pension fund may need to generate cash to fund retirement benefits for pension recipients or meet capital calls.
2. To trim the risk of the investment portfolio: During the global financial crisis, many large investors decided that they needed to strategically adjust the risk profiles of their investment portfolios.
3. To rebalance the portfolio from time to time: This is a form of active portfolio management in which allocations to asset classes are changed resulting in a partial liquidation of an asset class.

These three reasons are about the motivation to sell secondary PE interests and not about the value of the underlying investment. Without a secondary market, these liquidity needs might be more difficult or expensive to meet, leading an institution to allocate less to PE or to demand higher expected returns in compensation. With an active secondary market, the institution not only can meet liquidity needs at lower costs but also can better understand and manage its risk exposure through the information and opportunities provided by the market and its prices.

THE ROLE OF GPs IN SECONDARY MARKET TRANSACTIONS: There are two potential problems other than unfavorable price execution with selling limited partnerships into the secondary market. First, the general partner's permission (sign on) may be necessary to consummate the exchange. Second, GPs usually do not like to see their investors sell their limited partnership interests to outside third parties and may be unlikely to invite that limited partner to join in future PE funds that the general partner sponsors.

BUYERS OF SECONDARY MARKET LIMITED PARTNERSHIP INTERESTS: From a buyer's perspective, there are several advantages to a secondary purchase of PE limited partnerships: (1) the investor might gain exposure to a portfolio of companies with a vintage year that is different from the investor's existing portfolio (facilitating vintage year diversification); (2) secondary interests typically represent an investment with a PE firm that is further along in the investment process than a new PE fund and may be closer to harvesting profits from the private portfolio; (3) purchasing the secondary interest of a limited partner who wishes to exit a PE fund may be a way for another investor to gain access to future funds offered by the general partner; and (4) the buyer may see greater potential for cash flows from the secondary portfolio than current primary investments. Simply stated, this is opportunistic buying, especially if the limited partnership interests are trading at substantial discounts.

21.11.2 Private Equity, Hedge Funds, and Six Fee Differences

Competition for capital and for deals is forcing changes in the PE and hedge fund industries. Particularly, there is an increasingly blurry line between hedge funds and PE firms. Hedge fund managers are now bidding for operating assets in open competition with PE firms.

Hedge funds are moving into PE for diversification and their desire to apply their skills to new areas. In particular, the issues are based on differing fee structures for hedge fund managers compared to PE fund managers. The following list summarizes the six major differences between typical hedge fund incentive fees and typical PE fund incentive fees:

1. Hedge fund incentive fees are front loaded. PE fund fees tend to be collected at the termination of deals.
2. Hedge fund incentive fees are based on changes in net asset value whether the gains are realized or unrealized. PE fund fees are based on realized values of exited positions.
3. Hedge fund incentive fees are collected on a regular basis, either quarterly or semiannually. PE fund incentive fees tend to be collected at the time of an event, such as exit.
4. Investor capital does not need to be returned first to collect incentive fees in a hedge fund. PE funds typically do not distribute incentive fees until the original investor capital has been repaid.
5. Hedge funds often have no provisions for the clawback of management or incentive fees. PE funds typically have clawback provisions requiring the return of fees on prior profits when subsequent losses are experienced.
6. Hedge funds rarely have a preferred rate (hurdle rate) of return (e.g., 6%) that must be exceeded before the hedge fund manager can collect an incentive fee. Most PE funds have a hurdle rate.

In sum, the deal terms for a hedge fund are much more favorable to managers than are those for PE fund managers. Another consideration is that hedge funds with hurdle rates tend to have lower hurdle rates than PE funds in the computation of incentive fees. Most PE funds target returns in the 20% range, whereas hedge funds aim to beat a cash index plus some premium (e.g., LIBOR plus 6%). This provides hedge fund managers with a competitive advantage against PE firms when bidding for operating assets, since lower hurdle rates provide hedge fund managers with an incentive to bid more aggressively than PE firms.

21.11.3 Publicly Traded Private Equity Firms and Their Governance

There are relatively few publicly traded PE strategies in the liquid alternative space. Those strategies that are available tend to use the closed-end fund format, as the relatively permanent capital of those structures matches the constrained liquidity of the underlying investments. However, **publicly traded PE firms** offer investors exposure to PE and earning carried interest from high returns to those firms generated from the underlying fund investments.

Publicly traded shares of PE asset management companies include major firms such as Apollo, Ares, Blackstone, Carlyle, KKR, and Oaktree. PE exposure to these firms and others can be achieved through ETFs such as the Invesco Global Listed PE. Exposure can also be achieved through open-end mutual funds and listed companies, such as Onex, that hold stakes in a large number of private companies.

Drury discusses the governance issues raised by publicly held PE firms in detail.[7] The following are among Drury's observations:

1. Listed PE firms tend to be organized as limited partnerships and LLCs rather than corporations, which, among other things, can be used to reduce personal liability for managers to LPs and be less friendly to the interests of the non-insiders.
2. The organizational structures used by listed PE firms tend to retain control of the firm by insiders (managers) as opposed to other shareholders.
3. The structures and jurisdictions selected by listed PE firms tend to reduce or even waive the management's fiduciary duties to its shareholders.
4. Listed PE firms tend to exclude normal corporate controls by shareholders through the board of directors and opt out of governance rules promulgated by stock exchanges.

As discussed in the next section, these governance issues can be argued to be attempts to preserve the strength of traditional PE firms: strong management that is highly incentivized to take risks in unlocking value. On the other hand, the governance structures used by listed PE firms may place non-inside shareholders at uncompensated peril.

21.11.4 The Battle between Private Equity Governance Structures

One or more legal structures—both private and public—can be inserted between PE investors and underlying private enterprises. On the private end of the private-public spectrum are the purely private PE firms such as Bain Capital. On the public end of the spectrum are ETFs that invest in listed PE firms that, in turn, invest directly in enterprises. But there are increasingly blurred lines, with private PE firms deciding to go public and with listed firms taking large private PE exposures through direct investments in private PE firms.

The PE landscape can be viewed as a competition or battle between public and private governance structures at various levels, with advantages and disadvantages to each. This section discusses three potentially important issues over which private and public access have varying strengths and weaknesses: diversification, liquidity (listing), and regulation.

DIVERSIFICATION AS A DOUBLE-EDGED SWORD: Diversification reduces risk. Well-diversified investors can require lower rates of return on capital, thereby offering a competitive advantage to firms with diversified investors. A top reason that PE firms seek capital through listing is to attract substantial capital at relatively low cost. However, one of the primary advantages to PE management is that the top managers are incentivized to focus their considerable strengths and energies into creating value *because* their wealth is disproportionately concentrated in the investments that they are overseeing. One reason that the private PE structure is so successful is the skill and devotion of its poorly diversified management teams (i.e., who have concentrated exposures to the investments).

LIQUIDITY (LISTING) AS A DOUBLE-EDGED SWORD: Liquidity in PE involves not only the ability to exit an investment quickly at a non-discounted price, it also means not having to meet capital calls on committed capital. Listed investments also offer investors the confidence that the market price is likely to be better protected on the downside due to the ability of short sellers to constrain listed securities from being overpriced. In other words, the presence of short sellers provides some level of confidence that market prices are deemed to be reasonable by at least some investment professionals. Prices of private deals do not offer this protection. However, public listing involves substantial fees and has been argued to cause the prices of listed PE to take on the volatility of the entire stock market during times of crisis, as evidenced by the contrast between the reactions of public REITs and private real estate during the global financial crisis. Public listing provides visibility, which can help enterprises market their products and signal positive reputations, perhaps even building loyalty from customers who are also shareholders. However, public listing invites scrutiny such as nuisance shareholder proposals and government intrusions.

REGULATION AS A DOUBLE-EDGED SWORD: On the one hand, strong regulations tend to generate better information revelation by the firm to the public and may provide some protection to investors against fraud and other abuses. On the other hand, regulations can be burdensome, expensive, and may constrain top managers from fully unlocking potential value.

REVIEW QUESTIONS

1. Fill in the blanks of the following sentence using the terms *PE fund*, *PE firm*, and *underlying business enterprises*: A _____ serves as the general partner to a _____ that invests its money in _____.
2. What two roles do PE firms play in a partnership and how do carried interest and management fees line up with those two roles?
3. What are the five stages of the life cycle of a VC fund?

4. What are the three phases in the relationship between LPs and GPs of PE funds?
5. Describe bad-leaver and good-leaver clauses in PE partnerships.
6. What is a club deal?
7. Discuss the following statement: Empirical evidence indicates that investors in listed BDCs are subject to greater return volatility and enjoy less diversification benefits than investors in PE that is not publicly traded.
8. Why might a PE fund of funds be especially appropriate for an investor new to PE?
9. What is the primary difference between a traditional PIPE and a toxic PIPE?
10. Describe six differences between typical PE and hedge fund fees.

NOTES

1. EVCA. 2013.
2. Josh Lerner and Antoinette Schoar, "The Illiquidity Puzzle: Theory and Evidence from Private Equity," *Journal of Financial Economics* 72, no. 1 (2004): 3–40.
3. Steven Kaplan and Antoinette Schoar, "Private Equity Performance: Returns, Persistence, and Capital Flow," *Journal of Finance* 60, no. 4 (2005): 1791–1823, doi:10.1111/j.1540-6261.2005.00780.x.
4. Victor Fleischer, "The Missing Preferred Return," UCLA School of Law, Law & Economics Working Paper 465 (February 22, 2005).
5. John Otterlei and Scott Barrington, "Alternative Assets—Private Equity Fund-of-Funds." Special Report (2003), Piper Jaffray Private Capital.
6. Tom Weidig and Pierre-Yves Mathonet, *The Risk Profiles of Private Equity* (Brussels: EVCA, 2004); Pierre-Yves Mathonet and Thomas Meyer, *J-Curve Exposure: Managing a Portfolio of Venture Capital and Private Equity Funds* (Chichester, UK: John Wiley & Sons, 2007).
7. Lloyd L. Drury III, "Publicly-Held PE Firms and the Rejection of Law as a Governance Device," 16 *University of Pennsylvania Journal of Business Law* 57 (2013).

CHAPTER 22

Private Credit and Distressed Debt

Four primary types of debt are detailed in this chapter: leveraged loans, direct lending, mezzanine debt, and distressed debt. While leveraged loans and direct lending are referred to as private *credit*, mezzanine and distressed debt instruments can be referred to as private *equity* due to their equity-like risks.

The private credit and distressed debt market grew from $200 billion at the end of 2007 to over $600 billion 10 years later. Some analysts believe that the global financial crisis and the subsequent regulations led directly to the growth of the private credit market.

During the global financial crisis of 2008, there were a number of bank bailouts in both the United States and Europe, leading to increased regulations, such as the Dodd-Frank Act in the United States and the Basel III framework in Europe. These new regulations require banks to comply with stress tests and capital adequacy requirements, making banks more accountable for the types of loans they make and for the types of risks that they take. As these regulations took effect, European banks reduced their balance sheets by EUR 600 billion, leading to five straight years of a decline in the amount of lending by banks to small and medium enterprises. If small companies aren't allowed to access bank credit, they need to have access to alternative lending or marketplace financing in order to run their firms, so as banks have largely backed off from making loans to small and medium enterprises in order to improve their risk-based capital requirements, hedge funds, private equity funds, and private credit funds have stepped in to make these loans.

Over $200 billion of the private debt investments are held in **dry powder**, which are investments pledged to private debt investment firms that have not yet been lent out to a borrower or capital that has been committed but not yet called or invested. An oversupply of dry powder may reduce credit spreads and weaken covenant protections. An undersupply of dry powder may mean that there could not be enough private credit available if there is a surge of buyout and merger activity, combined with a continued need for borrowings at small and medium enterprises.

22.1 TYPES OF FUND PRIVATE CREDIT VEHICLES

Because of the illiquid nature of private credit, there is only a limited opportunity to access these investments through funds containing mostly liquid assets such as open-end mutual funds. Private credit investments are made predominately through closed-end vehicles such as hedge funds, private equity funds, and business development companies (BDCs), described in Chapter 21, and the relatively new structure of interval funds discussed next. One of the downsides to investing in publicly traded BDCs is that they are subject to wide swings in their premium or discount to net asset value. As such, BDCs often exhibit high price volatility, especially compared to other vehicles evaluated simply using monthly NAVs.

22.1.1 Interval Funds

Interval funds are semi-liquid, semi-illiquid closed-end funds that do not trade on the secondary market but offer the opportunity for investors to redeem or exit their investments at regularly scheduled intervals. Investors can purchase these funds at a regular NAV, as frequently as on a daily or weekly basis, with a low minimum investment. Interval funds might have a five-to-seven-year stated life, a long holding period that allows the fund to invest in less liquid credits that are likely to have a higher yield than publicly traded bonds. Investors can access liquidity in interval funds, as the fund manager will offer to repurchase some of the outstanding shares of the fund at regular intervals. The redemption opportunities of interval funds offer a degree of liquidity to investors despite the fund's holding of illiquid assets.

For example, the fund may offer to purchase 5% of outstanding shares at the end of each calendar quarter. Any investor who wishes to exit the fund will be able to tender their shares at that repurchasing interval. If the manager offers to repurchase 5% and investors tender 5% or less of the total shares outstanding, all of those investors will be cashed out at the end of that interval. If there's an offer to repurchase 5% of the shares and investors tendered 10% of the outstanding shares, each investor would sell half of their shares to the fund that will be repurchased on a pro rata basis, leaving investors with half of their redemption request unfulfilled. Investors can tender those unsold shares at the next repurchase interval, at which time a new queue will form for the amount of shares the fund seeks to repurchase at that time.

22.1.2 Drawdown Funds

A **drawdown fund** is a type of private equity fund (that can be used for private credit) in which investor commitments are called as needed (e.g., to fund investments or meet expenses), in essence providing partnership-like liquidity features in a fund structure. These funds may have an indefinite term or a fixed life, such as three or five years or longer. They can purchase bank loans or bonds as well as underwrite new debt, which is when the private debt fund lends directly to a company after carefully reviewing their financials and negotiating with the borrower. Banks typically underwrite a loan based on the ability to repay, as investors in investment-grade debt simply seek to be repaid principal and interest as scheduled.

22.1.3 Funds with a Loan-to-Own Objective

Some private equity funds underwrite debt with a loan-to-own objective. A **loan-to-own investment** occurs when the investor focuses on the value of the borrower's assets and the value of the company that could be repossessed if the borrower was unable to service the loan, not necessarily evaluating the ability of the company to pay back the principal and interest as scheduled. In some cases, the lenders may prefer that the company default in order for the loan to turn into an ownership stake in the firm or its assets.

22.1.4 Fulcrum Securities and Reorganization

A private equity firm may seek to invest in a fulcrum security. A **fulcrum security** is the senior-most debt security in a reorganization process that is not paid in full with cash but rather is the security that is most likely to be repaid with equity in the reorganized firm. Some of the largest gains in private credit investing can occur from converting a debt security into an equity security. For example, if the fulcrum security is a second-lien debt issue that trades at 20% of par value, it might be converted into an equity stake in the new firm that is initially worth 30% of face value, but may appreciate over time, perhaps eventually exceeding the par value of the original borrowing.

The equity in the newly reorganized firm may be substantially undervalued during its first year, for several reasons. First, many investors, such as bond funds, banks, or insurance companies, may not be legally allowed to hold the equity recovered in the reorganization process. As such, they would quickly sell the equity holdings, which would initially depress the stock price. Outside investors may be slow to warm up to the new stock, as they are focused on the negative headlines of the recently completed bankruptcy process, and perhaps underestimate the reduced risk and increased cash flow of the firm that just reduced or eliminated its liabilities. After a few quarterly reports as a new company, the lower-risk and higher-return nature of the stock reveals itself, leading to enhanced profits for the long-term investor in the fulcrum security that morphed into a highly successful stock holding. Of course, not all newly reorganized companies play out this way, as some enter into bankruptcy a second time within a few years, so investors need to consider how the cash flow and risk of the new company will evolve over time.

While a private equity fund might have a longer-term investment in the equity of the firm, hedge funds might have a shorter-term trading-oriented view, where they can profit in the role of a liquidity provider. Consider a pension plan or an insurance company, where a governmental entity or the state insurance regulator prohibits more than a 5% allocation to non-investment-grade debt with an outright prohibition on the ownership of nonperforming or distressed debt. The result of these regulations might be that as soon as the firm has defaulted or been downgraded, the pension plan or the insurance company must immediately sell the debt held in their portfolio. As pension funds and insurance companies become forced sellers, the traditional buyers of debt, such as mutual funds, may not be interested in buying this debt. With the reduced demand for the debt, hedge funds may step in to meet supply (i.e., provide liquidity). If the prices of the downgraded debt issues fall substantially, the hedge funds may be the only large buyers and they make relatively low bids, resulting in low market prices that cause pension funds and insurance companies to realize large losses. For example, the hedge funds may offer to purchase a defaulted debt issue at 20% of its face value, which can lead to a large profit if that debt issue eventually receives a recovery value of, say, 40%.

22.2 FIXED-INCOME ANALYSIS

Much of the investment capital allocated to private credit and distressed debt is invested in unrated debt or debt that is rated as below investment grade. Given the prevalence of these lower-quality credits in the private debt space, it is important to understand the risks and rewards of this debt, which requires an understanding of appropriate credit spreads and the bankruptcy and recovery rate processes.

22.2.1 Three Key Differences between Bonds and Loans

Investment banks underwrite bond issues and sell the bonds to external investors. The borrowers receive capital today, and the lenders receive an annuity of coupons and a return of the face value at maturity. Loans are privately traded debt instruments that are underwritten by a bank. After the bank has made the loan, it can either retain that loan on its balance sheet or sell it to other investors. Syndicated loans involve multiple lenders for a single borrower, which gives borrowers access to larger loans, especially those used for buyout transactions. Loans are private placements that are not subject to the same regulatory oversight as securities issued in the public bond market, and are less liquid than publicly traded bonds.

Corporate bonds and loans have several key differences from an investment perspective.

1. LIQUIDITY: Bonds are publicly traded debt securities with relatively high liquidity, which leads to bonds generally offering higher prices and lower yields compared to some other instruments in the private loan market. Therefore, some investors may be attracted to loans, as they may earn an illiquidity premium that would increase the yield above that of a bond with similar credit quality and features.
2. DEFAULT RISK: Loans are typically the most senior debt instrument in the capital structure and are often secured by significant collateral. Bonds are typically more junior in the capital structure relative to loans and may be unsecured, meaning that loans might have higher recovery rates.
3. INTEREST RATE RISK: Most bonds are fixed-rate, meaning that the coupon rate set when the bond is issued will not change during the life of the bond. Most bonds are non-callable, at least for some time period, so the borrower cannot immediately refinance or repay the principal on the bonds before the maturity or call date. Many loans are callable, meaning they can be prepaid at any time without prepayment penalties. Loans are also likely to have floating rates, so the interest rate on the loan increases when the market level of interest rates rises. This means that bonds tend to have higher interest rate risk.

22.2.2 Implications of Floating Rates versus Fixed Rates on Interest Rate Risk

Fixed-rate debt declines in value as interest rates rise. This risk is measured by duration, which is introduced in Chapter 5 on financial economics and Chapter 17 on relative value funds. Duration in the case of a simple fixed-rate bond is the average time to receive the cash flows of a bond, and is closely related to the maturity of fixed-rate debt.

When interest rates rise, the price of debt with fixed-rate coupons falls because the present value of each cash flow is diminished. The effect of rising interest rates on the prices of seasoned bond issues can also be seen by considering the valuation of newly issued debt. Newly issued debt must be issued at higher yields when market interest rates rise. In order to issue the new debt at a price near par, the newly issued debts must offer relatively high coupons when market interest rates rise. Therefore, seasoned coupon bonds must decline in price (i.e., rise in yields) so that the yields of seasoned debt approximate the yields of newly issued debt, *ceteris paribus*.

For example, consider a seasoned 4% coupon bond in a 4% market that is priced at par (i.e., 100% of the bond's principal or maturity value). What happens when interest rates rise? When interest rates are 5%, newly issued bonds available in the market must offer a higher level of coupon income (i.e., 5%) to be issued at a price near its face value. For a seasoned 4% coupon bond to trade in equilibrium with a recently issued 5% coupon bond, the price of that 4% bond must decline until its yield approaches the new competitive level of 5%.

22.2.3 Implications of Floating Rates versus Fixed Rates on Duration

Floating-rate notes respond differently to interest rate shifts than fixed-rate notes do, as discussed in Chapter 5. Floating-rate coupons reset periodically to new market interest rates levels, thereby avoiding the level of interest rate risk inherent in fixed-rate notes. Therefore, floating-rate note prices are less volatile and have lower durations.

For example, consider a floating-rate note that resets semiannually to a new interest rate of 1% above LIBOR, which is a benchmark interest rate for many floating-rate notes trading at or near par. If the floating-rate note resets to this new interest rate level every six months, its price will move to par at each reset because the note at that point in time will be offering the market yield. In the time period between coupon resets, there's not a lot of time for the interest rate on the loan to move far away from the market level of interest rates. As detailed in Chapter 5, the duration of a floating-rate note is equal to its remaining time to reset. Therefore, a floating-rate note with a semiannual reset will have a duration that declines from roughly 0.5 years (immediately after each reset) to roughly zero as the time to the next reset declines from 0.5 years to zero.

☞ **APPLICATION 22.2.3A**

A fixed-rate bond and a floating-rate note each have a five-year maturity. The fixed-rate bond has a duration of 4.5 years. The floating-rate note will reset its coupon to market rates in 0.5 years. Approximating bond price changes as the product of duration and interest rate shifts (times minus one), if continuously compounded interest rates increase by 1.5%, how much will the price of the fixed-rate bond and floating-rate note decline? The price of the fixed-rate bond will drop by approximately 6.75% (4.5 duration × 1.5% rate rise). The price of the floating-rate note will drop by approximately 0.75% (0.5 duration × 1.5% rise).

In summary, with a semiannual reset, the worst thing that could happen from the perspective of an investor in that loan is that the market rate increases the day after the semiannual reset, which means that it will be earning a below-market interest rate for the next six months. However, six months from now, that interest rate is going to adjust to the now-higher level of market interest rates. Duration risk only exists during that length of time between now and the next reset date. Thus, floating-rate notes have a lower price risk relative to a change in interest rates than a fixed-rate note does. When interest rates rise, notes with shorter durations decline less in value than notes with longer durations. When interest rates fall, notes with longer durations rise more in value than notes with shorter durations. Fixed-rate bonds have longer durations and floating rate loans have shorter durations even if their maturities are the same (and it is prior to the last reset period). Note that, ignoring possible default risk, a floating-rate bond that resets continuously to short-term (overnight) market interest rates has the same interest rate risk profile as cash.

22.2.4 Implications of Compounding Conventions on Modified Duration

The discussion of duration in Chapter 5 (as well as the previous example) focused on bond price volatility based on shifts in *continuously compounded* interest rates. One reason for the focus on continuously compounded rates is that the duration of a bond (times negative one) equals its price elasticity *only* with respect to a shift in *continuously* compounded rates (as demonstrated in Equation 5.8).

In debt markets, interest rates are typically expressed based on *semiannual compounding*. **Modified duration** is an interest rate risk measure very similar to regular duration that adjusts duration for discrete compounding in order to reflect the differing effects of various compounding conventions on measuring interest rate risk. Modified duration is calculated as shown in Equation 22.1:

$$\text{Modified Duration} = \text{Duration} / [1 + (y/m)] \qquad (22.1)$$

where m is the number of compounding periods per year, y is the stated annual yield or interest rate, and (y/m) is the periodic non-annualized rate. For example, assume that the non-annualized yield or interest rate is 5% over a six-month period. First, note that $m = 2$, since there are two six-month periods in a year. Second, note that $y/m = 5\%$ (i.e., the periodic non-annualized rate, which is the stated annual rate divided by m). Third, the *stated* annual yield or rate (y) would simply be 10%. Note that the stated annual rate does not include the effects of interest compounded on interest. Finally, note that the *effective* annual rate would be 10.25% because effective annual rates reflect the effects of compounding (adding compounded interest of $5\% \times 5\%$ to the stated annual rate).

Equation 22.1 adjusts the measure of price volatility to reflect the compounding assumption. For example, consider a position with a regular duration that is exactly 10 and in which the stated annual interest rate or yield (y) is exactly 10%. In bond markets with stated annual rates of 10% that use semiannual compounding (i.e., $m = 2$), the modified duration would be 10.0/1.05 or 9.52. Using annual compounding (i.e., $m = 1$), the modified duration would be 10.0/1.10 or 9.09. Using continuous compounding (i.e., $m \to 0$), the modified duration would be 10.0/1.0 or 10. Note that if the stated annual interest rate is 10% in an example with continuous compounding, the effective annual rate would be 10.52%.

☞ APPLICATION 22.2.4A

A bond has a duration of exactly 5.0 and a stated annual yield of 4.00%. Calculate the bond's modified duration for each of the following cases: annual compounding, semi-annual compounding, and continuous compounding.

Based on Equation 22.1, the modified duration = $5.0/[1 + (.04/m)]$. Inserting values for m of 1, 2, and infinity solves for the cases of annual compounding, semi-annual compounding, and continuous compounding, respectively, as 4.81, 4.90 and 5.00.

The intuition of Equation 22.1 is best understood by starting with the case of continuous compounding. A 1% shift in continuously compounded rates has a relatively large effect on bond prices because effective annual rates (which include the effects of compounding) are more responsive to shifts in continuously compounded rates than to shifts in rates that are not compounded. Therefore, the modified duration of a bond with a 10-year duration is highest (10.0) when based on continuously compounded rates. When modified duration is reported based on annually compounded rates ($m = 1$), the modified duration is lesser (9.09), reflecting that, say, a 1% shift in a stated annual rate has a smaller effect on effective annual rates than a 1% shift in a continuously compounded rate.

Finally, note that while floating-rate debt has less interest rate risk than fixed-rate debt, the majority of floating-rate debt may be unrated or of lower credit quality. When moving from fixed-rate debt to floating-rate debt to reduce interest rate risk, investors have to understand that they may be increasing credit risk as a result of this reallocation. That is, investors may trade increased credit risk for reduced interest rate risk when moving from relatively higher-rated fixed-rate bonds to relatively lower-rated floating-rate loans.

22.3 CREDIT RISK ANALYSIS AND THE BANKRUPTCY PROCESS

Because much of the private credit market is below investment grade, it is imperative that investors understand how to value these loans, as well as the work that is necessary to recover and protect assets in the case of a bankruptcy filing.

22.3.1 Credit Ratings, Yields, and Financial Ratios

Moody's, S&P, Fitch, and other rating agencies are paid by borrowers to assign ratings to bond issues and large loans. Investors rely heavily on these ratings to understand the credit risk of issues and to assign credit spreads to loans and bonds. Debt rated as investment-grade (such as Moody's Baa and above, S&P BBB and above) is expected to have very low default rates, and therefore, lower credit spreads. With a sovereign debt yield of 4% and an investment-grade credit spread of 1%, an A-rated bond would have a yield of 5%, regardless of the coupon rate of the security. Debt rated as below-investment-grade is expected to have higher default rates and higher credit spreads. With a sovereign debt yield of 4% and a credit spread of 3%, a B-rated bond would have a yield of 7%, regardless of the coupon rate of the security.

Of course, most transactions in the private credit market, especially smaller loans with a single lender, are not rated by the credit ratings agencies. Investors can estimate the ratings that might be assigned by a rating agency by studying the balance sheet and income statement of the borrower. Once investors understand the credit risk, they can assign a credit spread to the unrated debt. As the debt gets more risky and more likely to default, the implied credit rating declines and the interest rate charged to the borrower increases. Most borrowers in the private credit market are unrated, but the implied credit rating methodology would classify many of these borrowers as having a credit rating of B.

Ratings agencies consider a number of variables when rating the credit quality of a borrower. Less-risky borrowers have higher profit margins, higher assets, lower debt, and lower interest expense. Businesses with lower revenue volatility and lower profit volatility are also regarded as less likely to default. Exhibit 22.1 illustrates the relations between ratings, credit risk, and two key financial ratios (interest coverage and leverage).

For example, the high-yield borrowers illustrated in Exhibit 22.1 typically have interest coverage ratios (such as EBITA/interest expense ratios) below 3.7, meaning that the annual cash flow of the company is less than 3.7 times the annual interest expense paid on all borrowings. In contrast, investment-grade borrowers may have interest coverage ratios of 6 to 12 times. Leverage ratios are also very important, as high-yield borrowers have average debt levels at least 3.7 times EBITDA, whereas investment-grade borrowers have leverage ratios closer to 2 to 3 times. A complete listing of 11 financial ratios, as excerpted in Exhibit 22.1, and their link to credit ratings is available online from Moody's Financial Metrics.[1] Private credit investments may have even wider credit spreads than found using this implied credit rating method, as the illiquidity of the investment and the value added to the borrower are greater than is found in the public bond market.

| | | Moody's | | |
Moody's	S&P's/Fitch	EBITA/Interest Expense	Debt/EBITDA	Low
Aaa	AAA	11.5	1.9	
Aa	AA	13.9	1.8	
A	A	10.7	2.3	
Baa	BBB	6.3	2.9	
Ba	BB	3.7	3.7	
B	B	1.9	5.2	
Caa	CCC	0.7	8.1	
Ca	CC			
C	C			
D	D			High

EXHIBIT 22.1 Leverage and Debt Coverage Ratios Vary by Credit Rating
Source: Moody's Financial Metrics.

22.3.2 Credit Spreads and Credit Risk

One of the ways to analyze the fixed-income market is by the size of the credit spread observed on a given debt issue, ranging from safer investment-grade debt to more risky non-investment-grade debt. A **credit spread** is the excess of the yield on a debt security with credit risk relative to the yield on a debt security of similar maturity but no credit risk.

An investment-grade credit spread is the amount of yield on an investment-grade debt security relative to a sovereign debt with comparable maturity demanded for investing in firms that have modest default risk. As investors move from the sovereign debt or risk-free level of interest rates into investment grade, they take on that additional amount of credit risk for which investors require compensation, which was around 100 basis points in the United States during 2018. The investment-grade market has relatively low interest rates because these issues have a low probability of default, as the debt is backed by a larger amount of assets and dependable cash flows compared to the debt load of the firm.

However, there is often a tremendous difference between the yields of investment-grade debt and non-investment-grade debt. This non-investment-grade debt is also termed high-yield, speculative, or junk bonds. A company with lesser assets or lesser cash flows or a greater volatility of financial results may be determined to be a speculative-grade issuer, meaning that they would pay the higher interest rates required of below-investment-grade issuers. Firms in the high-yield or speculative-grade category will be charged higher borrowing costs, as they have a significantly higher probability of default, meaning that they might not pay their principal and interest as scheduled. Sometimes the defaults are not driven by the failure to pay principal and interest, but rather by the failure to maintain covenants that might require the company to maintain a given level of cash flows or assets.

It's hard to estimate a yield curve for long-term high-yield debt, especially going out for very long maturities, because investors and borrowers may not want to contract for 30 years when the borrower (company) has a highly questionable ability to repay that loan due to concerns by lenders of high risk and concerns by borrowers of high costs. As a result, high-yield bonds tend to be issued with much shorter maturities. During 2018, the credit spread between U.S. Treasuries and high-yield bonds was over 3.5%, which means that investors could earn more than double the amount of interest on the high-yield bonds than they could on U.S. Treasury bonds. Of course, high-yield issuers don't have the same ability to make coupon and principal payments as a sovereign issuer, which justifies the higher interest rate sought by investors to compensate for the increased credit risk, as losses from defaults offset part of the higher interest rate.

Chapter 24 on credit derivatives discusses credit spreads in detail, including important models of credit spreads. Credit spreads depend on default probabilities, expected losses given default, and various potential risk premiums.

22.3.3 Credit Risk and the Probability of Default

A relatively low spread of 100 basis points between sovereign debt and investment-grade issuers may be explained by the relatively minimal defaults on investment-grade issues. This is the safest type of corporate debt, as even when the business cycle is getting rough, default rates on investment-grade debt don't reach 1%. Thus,

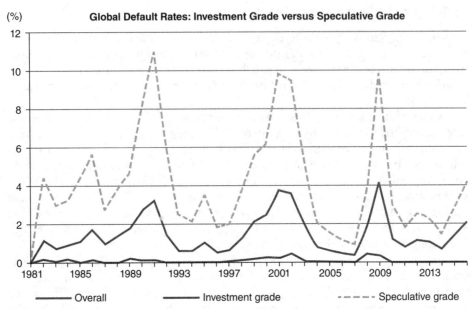

EXHIBIT 22.2 The Cyclicality of Global Default Rates
Source: S&P Global Fixed Income Research Ratings.

a credit spread of 100 basis points between sovereign debt and investment-grade debt is often viewed as sufficient to compensate investors for expected credit losses and systematic risk.

Exhibit 22.2 shows the cyclicality of these markets and how extreme the losses on the speculative-grade, high-yield, or junk bond issues can be. The default rate on high-yield bonds actually exceeded 9% three times in the past 30 years (around 1990, 2001, and 2008). A credit spread of 3 or 4% might not be sufficient to compensate for the losses at the bottom of the credit cycle. Default rates vary with the economy: The default rate can be very low for a long period of time when the economy is strong and very high during times of economic or financial crisis. The question is whether a credit spread of, say, 3.5% at the issue date of new debt will be sufficient to pay for expected default losses and increased risk over the life of the debt issue.

22.3.4 Covenants

Chapter 12's section on commercial mortgages introduces covenants and other terms regarding default risk analysis. Covenants are promises made by a debtor to the creditor that strengthen the perceived credit quality of the obligation. Loan covenants may be required by creditors to protect their interests, or they may be offered by debtors to negotiate better terms. The types of bond covenants have been known to affect credit risk. For example, a factor that has driven the size of the distressed market in the past has been the proportion of loans that are covenant-light (cov-lite) loans. **Covenant-lite loans** are loans that place minimal restrictions on the debtor in terms of loan covenants. In 2016, over half of European loans were covenant-lite, compared to just 5% in 2007, while more recently over three-quarters of U.S. loans were covenant-lite. As the strength of covenants declines, the likely default rates rise and the likely recovery rates decline. Wigglesworth (2018) quotes Moody's estimates of these declines in recovery rates given the demise of covenants, with the recovery rate on first-lien debt perhaps falling from an historical average of 77% to 43%, while second-lien recoveries could decline from 43% to 14%.

An **indenture** is the contract between the borrower and the lender that sets out the terms of the borrowing. These terms may include the interest rate, maturity date, face value, the schedule of payments, as well as covenants. **Affirmative covenants** are requirements for the borrower to comply with, such as to maintain a debt service coverage ratio that requires a minimum income relative to the size of the current year principal and interest payments. Ideally, investors would require that the cash flow of the company be at least twice what the firm owes in current-year debt payments, giving a cushion in order for the borrower to service their debt payments as well as to reinvest in their business. Under these affirmative covenants, the firm must disclose their financial results to prove compliance with covenants, such as the need to maintain a given level of assets relative to their debt burden or a specific level of cash flow or earnings before interest, taxes, depreciation, and amortization (EBITDA) relative to their annual interest expense. **Negative covenants,** or prohibitions on actions of the borrower, might prevent the company from increasing their debt load or issuing any new debt with seniority to the current first-lien debt issues.

When a borrower fails to maintain either the affirmative or the negative covenants, they can be in technical default on the loan. Upon that default, the creditors can step in and take action to accelerate the loan by requiring immediate repayment, restructure the loan at a higher borrowing cost, move to seize collateral, or force the borrower into bankruptcy proceedings.

Covenants are in the bond indenture in order to protect the lenders and/or lower the borrowing cost of the borrower. Covenants increase the security of a loan, requiring the company to meet certain financial targets and submit to oversight by the lender. As investment capital continues to flow into the increasingly competitive private credit market, there is an increasing amount of covenant-light issuance in both the high-yield bond market and the private debt market, transferring the balance of power toward the borrowers.

Another distinction between covenants is incurrence covenants versus maintenance covenants. **Incurrence covenants** typically require a borrower to take or not take a specific action once a specified event occurs. For instance, if an incurrence covenant states that the borrower must maintain a limit on total debt of five times EBITDA (earnings before interest, taxes, depreciation, and amortization), the borrower can take on more debt only as long as it is still within this constraint. A borrower that breaches this covenant by incurring additional debt is in default of the covenant and the loan. However, if the borrower found itself above the five times EBITDA limit simply because its earnings and cash flow had deteriorated (without having incurred additional debt), it would not be in violation of the incurrence covenant and would not be in default. Cov-lite loans have bond-like incurrence covenants, much like high-yield bonds.

Maintenance covenants are stricter than incurrence covenants in that they require that a standard be regularly met to avoid default. Returning to the previous example of a covenant wherein the debt is limited to five times EBITDA, in the case of a maintenance covenant, the borrower must pass this test each and every quarter, regardless of whether it added more debt or its earnings and cash flow deteriorated. Thus, the covenant would be triggered if the borrower's earnings and cash flows eroded, even if the firm did not issue new debt. Clearly, maintenance covenants are much stronger than incurrence covenants. Without maintenance covenants, lenders do not have the ability to step in at an early stage to reprice risk, restructure the loan, or shore up collateral provisions.

22.3.5 Five Ways Covenants Can Control Risk

Antczak, Lucas, and Fabozzi (2009) explain five ways in which covenants can control risk for lenders:

1. PRESERVATION OF COLLATERAL: Because the value of the collateral is key to both the quality of the loan and the eventual recovery rate upon distress, lenders can control risk by limiting the size of the loan relative to the value of the firm and the value of the collateral. In many cases, lenders may require a maximum loan-to-value ratio of 50% for inventory, 60% for property, plant, and equipment, and 80% for receivables. Senior secured loans should be of a limited size, perhaps half of the enterprise value of the firm. Finally, each asset should be pledged as collateral to only a single lender, which should go without saying.
2. APPROPRIATION OF EXCESS CASH FLOW: Lenders are protected when the uses of corporate cash are limited. Many lenders require the majority or the entirety of the value of asset sales and new debt to be paid to the debt holders rather than to the equity holders. Increasing the debt load while liquidating assets reduces the value of the firm, so paying the proceeds from those transactions to equity holders reduces the security of the debt and increases the risk of the debt.
3. CONTROL OF BUSINESS RISK: There is an inherent conflict between stockholders and bondholders. When the company prospers, the equity holders can experience large gains, whereas lenders earn principal and interest as contracted. When the company becomes distressed, the bondholders have a downside risk much larger than their upside return potential. Simply, the stockholders are long a call option on the firm's assets and the bondholders are therefore short a put option on the assets. This conflict leads to equity holders wishing to undertake risky projects when the firm is approaching distress, because the upside risk benefits the equity holders and hurts the bondholders. Therefore, it is in the best interest of the lenders to limit the types and sizes of investments, mergers, and debt that the firm can undertake.
4. PERFORMANCE REQUIREMENTS: Under negative covenants, the company must maintain strong ratios of assets and cash flow relative to the debt and interest burden of the firm. Capital expenditures may need to be limited in order to maintain compliance with the requested financial ratios.
5. REPORTING REQUIREMENTS: Under affirmative covenants, the company needs to report financial results to lenders, including other material information regarding projections of revenues and expenses, litigation, and regulatory issues.

Consider the case of the 2018 leveraged buyout by Refinitiv, which purchased the data division of Thomson Reuters. Some analysts noted that the high-leverage multiple and weak covenants in this deal made it especially likely for this company to become distressed and could mark the beginning of the end of a credit cycle with increasingly borrower-friendly terms. There were three especially concerning non-standard terms in this deal. First, the borrowers could prepay the unsecured bonds before the secured debt, meaning that cash flows are potentially going to the bottom of the capital structure when they are typically directed toward the top of the capital structure. Second, the company could be sold without the contractual requirement of paying off the debt, although typical transactions would require the buyer of a firm to secure financing of their own at terms that made sense at the time of the buyout. Third, and perhaps most concerning, is that there is not a limit on the cash that can be paid to equity holders, even when the borrower is not servicing their debt. It is certainly not a standard risk management practice to allow large dividends to be paid to the equity holders at the bottom of the capital stack when payments are delinquent to the debt holders at the top of the capital stack.

22.3.6 Capital Structure and Priority

The capital structure, or capital stack, shown in Exhibit 22.3, is the mix of equity and debt in any given firm. The riskier parts of the capital structure, such as equity, have a higher expected return, and the safest parts of an investment, such as secured and first-lien debt, should have a lower expected return. The lower-risk investments at the top of the capital structure may have a claim to a specific asset, such as a mortgage on a building, meaning that this loan has to be paid back before any other obligation of the firm.

Loans and secured borrowings typically have the highest credit quality, the highest claim or priority to assets in the case of a bankruptcy, and the lowest potential return. Next in line come bonds and unsecured debt with lower recovery rates and higher potential returns. Junior, mezzanine, subordinated, and convertible debt sit in the middle of the capital structure. These are debts of the firm, but each has a lesser

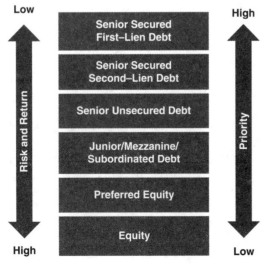

EXHIBIT 22.3 Priority of Claims in the Capital Structure

claim to cash flows and assets than seen in the senior secured and first-lien debt. These issues in the middle of the capital structure are riskier than the senior debt and are likely to have a higher interest rate. The amount of risk an investor takes should be commensurate with the yield the investor is going to earn. As one invests in riskier and riskier parts of a given company, or as one invests in riskier or riskier companies, one should have a higher level of return expectations.

Equity and preferred issues sit at the bottom of the capital stack. These investors have the lowest claim on assets of the distressed firm, but the highest potential return on investment when the firm performs well.

The capital structure of the firm can change over time, such as when there's a debt-equity swap, where the proceeds of a debt issue are paid to the equity holders through dividends or stock buybacks. Increasing borrowing and repurchasing stock changes the capital structure of the firm and increases the debt-to-equity ratio.

Historically, senior debt issues had lower interest rates and a higher place in the capital stack. If borrowers needed to access more debt capital than allowed in the senior debt market, they would need to turn to the subordinated debt market to access that extra debt capital at a much higher interest rate.

In recent years, there has been substantial growth in the **unitranche** debt market, in which a large piece of debt is issued that includes both senior and junior debt at a blended interest rate in a single debt issue. The unitranche structure could bring benefits for both borrowers and lenders. Borrowers have a less complex capital structure and may be willing to pay a higher interest rate on a unitranche borrowing for this convenience. Lenders may also prefer a less complex capital structure, as it avoids conflicts between creditors and makes workouts much easier, as the lender of the junior debt is also the lender of the senior debt. Unitranche debt has become so popular that it appears that mezzanine lending is declining due to the rise of direct lending and unitranche structures.

22.3.7 Recovery Rates

When a firm defaults, they may not be able to pay their principal and interest as scheduled or the firm may fail to comply with one or more of their covenants, in that their cash flow or asset value drops to a point where it appears that they're not able to service the debt. Our first concern is the default rate, which is the percentage of loans or bonds in our portfolio that have defaulted. Next, lenders are concerned about recovery rates.

The **recovery rate** is the portion of the face value of the debt that is paid back from the assets of the firm in a bankruptcy. In a liquidation bankruptcy, the lenders or the court have decided that this company is no longer a going concern. The business model of the company is not likely to earn cash flows that are sufficient to pay back the debt, even if that debt has been restructured. In a liquidation bankruptcy, the assets of the firm are distributed to creditors or sold with the proceeds being distributed. Firms are in default because their assets and cash flows are not sufficient to pay the liabilities of the firm.

A reorganization bankruptcy can make sense for a good company with a bad balance sheet. If the liabilities can be reduced or reorganized, the company could be profitable. If the firm simply had less debt, it would be able to be profitable going forward. In a reorganization bankruptcy, the firm can renegotiate any and all liabilities, such as union contracts, leases, pensions, and debt issues. With the assistance of the court, the borrower renegotiates all liabilities and seeks to change contracts in a way that allows the firm to continue its operations in a profitable manner.

First-lien term loans or secured bonds have the highest recovery rate, as those debt issues sit at the top of the capital structure as the safest investments likely recover the majority of the value of those assets in bankruptcy. Recovery rates have averaged 76% on first-lien loans, 56% on secured bonds, and 44% on senior unsecured bonds. Subordinated debt or junior debt will have lower recovery rates, often in the 20% to 30% range. In a reorganization, the senior debt holders often take a **haircut,** or a reduction in the amount owed, perhaps accepting new debt with a face value of 70% to 80% of the old debt, which is a haircut of 20% to 30% of the face value. Subordinated debt is often cancelled and converted into an equity stake in the newly reorganized firm, which hopefully is a going concern where the ongoing cash flows of the firm are no longer encumbered by the legacy liabilities.

At the bottom of the capital stack, the equity holders before bankruptcy typically lose their entire investment in a liquidation or a reorganization bankruptcy because the firm is in default and doesn't have the assets or the cash flow to pay their senior and junior debt in full. If the assets and the cash flow are insufficient to pay the senior debt and the junior debt, there are no assets left over for the equity holders. Equity is the riskiest part of the company's capital structure, where stockholders who expect to make the highest return also can experience the largest losses. In a reorganization or in a liquidation bankruptcy, equity holders typically earn a zero recovery or experience a 100% loss of their capital.

22.3.8 Distressed Debt and the Bankruptcy Process

Investing in below-investment-grade and distressed debt is inextricably linked with the bankruptcy process. Many distressed debt investors purchase the debt while the borrowing company is in the throes of bankruptcy. Other investors purchase the debt before a company enters into bankruptcy proceedings with the expectation of gaining control of the company through the bankruptcy proceedings. In either case, distressed investors need to be experts in bankruptcy procedures. This section illustrates issues involved in bankruptcy using U.S. bankruptcy law. Some countries only have laws that allow for liquidations as a result of a bankruptcy filing, as reorganizations are not supported by the legal structure in all domiciles.

There are two major forms of U.S. corporate bankruptcy: chapter 7 and chapter 11. **Chapter 7 bankruptcy** is when the assets of a firm are liquidated when a company is determined to no longer be a viable business. Essentially, the firm shuts down its operations and parcels out its assets to various claimants and creditors. The critical issue in chapter 7 bankruptcies is the priority of claims: who gets paid first, who gets paid most, and which obligations are never repaid.

Chapter 11 bankruptcy is a reorganization that attempts to maintain operations of a distressed corporation that may be viable as a going concern. It therefore affords a troubled company protection from its creditors while the company attempts to work through its operational and financial problems. Generally, under a chapter 11 bankruptcy, the debtor company proposes a plan of reorganization. A **plan of reorganization** is a business plan for emerging from bankruptcy protection as a viable concern, including operational changes. The plan includes how creditors and shareholders are to be treated under the new business plan. The claimants in each class of creditors are entitled to vote on the plan of reorganization. If all impaired classes of security holders vote in favor of the plan, the bankruptcy court conducts a confirmation hearing. If all requirements of the bankruptcy code are met, the plan is confirmed, and a newly reorganized company emerges from bankruptcy protection.

Thus, the sequence of events in a chapter 11 bankruptcy centers on a plan of reorganization. The skeleton of the process is as follows:

- The debtor company files for protection under chapter 11.
- The bankruptcy court automatically stays, or suspends, all default notices from lenders.
- The debtor company exclusively has 120 days to develop and file a plan of reorganization.
- The debtor company then has another 60 days to convince creditors to accept the plan.
- If half of the number and two-thirds of the value of each class of claimants accept the plan, then court approval is sought through a confirmation hearing.

During the first 180 days after filing for protection, no other party of interest may file a competing reorganization plan. By giving the debtor company 120 days to propose its reorganization plan and another 60 days to persuade creditors, the bankruptcy code puts the emphasis on reorganization over liquidation and puts the debtor in the driver's seat, at least initially. After the exclusive period ends, any claimant may file a reorganization plan with the bankruptcy court. At this point, the process can become very acrimonious.

There are numerous variations and contingencies of the process. The following items provide introductions to some of the most important concepts involved in bankruptcy proceedings:

- CLASSIFICATION OF CLAIMS: Under the bankruptcy code, a reorganization plan may place a claim in a particular class only if such claim is substantially similar to the other claims in that class. For instance, all issues of subordinated debt by a company may constitute one class of creditor under a bankruptcy plan. Similarly, all secured bank loans (usually the most senior of creditor claims) are usually grouped together as one class of creditor. Finally, at the bottom of the pile is common equity, the last class of claimants in a bankruptcy.
- PREPACKAGED BANKRUPTCY FILING: Sometimes a debtor company agrees in advance with its creditors on a plan of organization before it formally files for protection under chapter 11. Creditors usually agree to make concessions up front in return for equity in the reorganized company. The company then files with the bankruptcy court, submits a previously negotiated plan of reorganization, and quickly emerges with a new structure.
- BLOCKING POSITION: A **blocking position** exists when a creditor or group of creditors holds more than one-third of the dollar amount of any class of claimants and utilizes those holdings to prevent a plan of reorganization. Recall that acceptance of a plan is usually predicated on a vote of each class of security holders, which requires support of two-thirds of the dollar amount of the claims in each

class of creditors. Therefore, a single investor can obtain a blocking position by purchasing more than one-third of the debt in any class. A blocking position forces the other parties to negotiate with the blocking creditor.

- THE CRAMDOWN: The bankruptcy code provides that a reorganization plan may be confirmed over the objection of any impaired class that votes against it as long as the plan (1) does not unfairly discriminate against the members of that class and (2) is fair and equitable with respect to the members of that class. This process within a bankruptcy is called a **cramdown** when a bankruptcy court judge implements a plan of reorganization over the objections of an impaired class of security holders (the plan is "crammed down the throats" of the objecting claimants). Cramdowns are usually an option of last resort when the debtor and creditors cannot come to an agreement. Bankruptcy courts have considerable discretion to determine what constitutes unfair discrimination and fair and equitable treatment for members of a class. In practice, cramdown reorganizations are rare. Eventually, the debtor and creditors usually come to some resolution.

- ABSOLUTE PRIORITY: An **absolute priority rule** is a specification of which claims in a liquidation process are satisfied first, second, third, and so forth in receiving distributions. Payments to employees, payments for taxes, and accounts payable generally take priority over payments to security holders. Senior secured debt holders (typically bank loans) must be satisfied first among security holders. The company's bondholders come next. These may be split between senior and subordinated bondholders. The company's preferred and common shareholders get whatever remains. As the company pie is split up, it is usually the case that senior secured debt is made whole and that subordinated debt receives some payment less than its face value, while the remainder of the company's obligations is transformed into equity in the reorganized company. Last, the original equity holders often receive nothing. Their equity is replaced by the new equity converted from the old subordinated debt. The ability of the court in the bankruptcy process to wipe out the ownership of existing shareholders and to transform the debt of senior and subordinated creditors into the company's new equity class is a key factor in distressed debt investing.

- DEBTOR-IN-POSSESSION FINANCING: When secured lenders extend additional credit to the debtor company, it is commonly known as **debtor-in-possession financing** (DIP financing). The borrower's desire in seeking DIP financing is clear: Without additional credit, the borrower might not continue in business and would be forced to shut down. Creditors are often willing to grant DIP financing for a number of reasons. First, it keeps the debtor company afloat and gives it a chance to work out from under its debt load. Second, under bankruptcy law, DIP loans get priority over any forms of debt or financing incurred by the debtor before filing for bankruptcy under chapter 11.

22.4 LEVERAGED LOANS

Another asset class of fixed-income securities that private equity firms have moved into is leveraged loans, which are also referred to as senior loans or syndicated loans.

22.4.1 Leveraged Loan Basics

Leveraged loans are syndicated bank loans to non-investment-grade borrowers. The term **syndicated** refers to the use of a group of entities, often investment banks, in underwriting a security offering or, more generally, jointly engaging in other financial activities. Loans made by banks to corporations can be divided into two general classes: (1) those made to companies with investment-grade credit ratings (BBB or Baa and above), and (2) those made to companies with non-investment-grade credit ratings (BB or Ba and lower). This second class of loans refers to leveraged loans.

A leveraged loan is made to a corporate borrower that is leveraged—that is, a company that is not investment grade, often due to excess leverage on its balance sheet. Thus, the word *leveraged* refers to the use of leverage by the borrower. The loan has a second-lien interest after other senior secured loans. The second-lien loan market is often viewed synonymously with the leveraged loan market. Exact definitions of a leveraged loan vary. Generally, a loan is considered leveraged if (1) the borrower has outstanding debt that is rated below BBB by Standard & Poor's or lower than Baa by Moody's, or (2) the loan bears a coupon that is in excess of 125 to 200 basis points over the London Interbank Offered Rate (LIBOR).

A leveraged loan for a firm without a credit rating is identified by having a coupon that is in excess of LIBOR by a particular number of basis points, which varies through time and by source. The standard for that spread should be linked to the spreads observed in credit markets for loans rated BB (Ba) or lower. In other words, a leveraged loan for an unrated firm would have a credit spread similar to the credit spreads on bank loans of firms with non-investment-grade credit ratings.

In many respects, leveraged loans are similar to high-yield debt or junk bonds in terms of credit rating and corporate profile. Many non-investment-grade corporations have both high-yield bonds and leveraged loans outstanding. Since private equity firms are accustomed to dealing with banks and other fixed-income investors to finance their buyouts, leveraged loans provide a natural extension of their financing business.

22.4.2 Growth in Leveraged Loans

The growth of leveraged loans has been driven by the development and expansion of their secondary market. Secondary trading of leveraged loans improved substantially with the introduction of their credit ratings by recognized rating agencies. For example, Moody's began to assign credit ratings to bank loans in 1995 and has rated trillions of dollars of bank loans since. An active secondary market has encouraged banks to issue loans and has motivated institutions to invest in those loans. With the entry of institutional investors into this market through private equity vehicles, leveraged loans have become an accepted form of investing, and the rate of issuance of leveraged loans has surpassed that of high-yield bond financing.

Many large commercial banks have changed their business model from that of a traditional lender, in which the bank loans are kept on their balance sheets, to that of an originator and distributor of debt. These commercial banks are in the fee-generation business more than the asset-management business. Origination and distribution of bank loans allows these banks to both collect fees and manage their credit risk. In short, these commercial banks are capitalizing on their strengths:

lending money, collecting loan fees, and then divesting the loans into a secondary market. The subsequent management of the resulting assets (the leveraged loans) is left to institutional investors who acquire the loans through the secondary market.

22.4.3 Liquidity and the Demand for Leveraged Loans

Davies (2018a and 2018b) expresses concern for the leveraged loan market and its potential impact on liquidity, financing availability, and the outlook for future LBO activity. Although many loans have maturities of three to seven years, many corporate borrowers never fully retire their debt. With over 40% of leveraged loans being used to refinance existing debt, borrowers may not have the ability to pay off loans at maturity if and when credit conditions tighten and the refinancing window closes. In 2018, nearly 80% of newly issued leveraged loans were purchased by structured credit products such as collateralized loan obligations (CLOs) and open-end mutual funds. Should the demand for CLOs decline and mutual fund investors seek to redeem their holdings, the availability of affordable financing for buyouts and refinancing will become challenging. However, leveraged loans typically have high priority in corporate reorganizations when they are senior loans, a potential source of high recovery rates, which may keep investor demand for the loans high.

22.5 DIRECT LENDING

Direct lending (also called market-based lending, shadow banking, or nonbank lending) is a transaction in which investors extend credit to borrowers outside of the traditional banking system. In direct lending, borrowers do not go to banks for their lending; rather, they obtain funding from loans originated by private equity, private credit, and hedge fund lenders. Because the borrowers don't have access to funds through bank loans, they might pay higher interest rates, but there are other benefits for the borrowers besides access to credit. Nonbank lenders tend to have more flexible terms and offer faster loan processing than banks.

The underwriting process for traditional loans typically focuses on credit analysis, which considers whether the cash flow of the firm is sufficient to service the debt. A portion of the private credit market is focused on asset-based lending, where lenders consider the value of the collateral rather than the strength of the firm's cash flows. Some direct lending might be unsecured, but most direct lending is secured or senior in the capital structure of the corporation. Revolving lines of credit can be secured by the value of inventory or accounts receivables, while term loans may be secured by the value of property, plant, and equipment.

Successful investors in the private credit market need to have skills that go beyond traditional credit analysis. Given that the borrowers are typically below investment grade, private credit firms need expertise in workouts and restructurings, knowing how to work with a borrower to get the loan back on track or knowing how to work though the legal system to protect the value of their loan. Perhaps the most valuable skill in the private credit market is sourcing deals by finding companies in need of financing without having a number of lenders bidding down the rate on the loan.

One key advantage to investors in direct-lending strategies is that fees charged by fund managers are typically assessed on invested capital, rather than on committed capital as is common for many private equity funds. These lower fees and higher cash yields make it unlikely for direct-lending funds to experience a J-curve effect in which negative returns early in the life of the fund are followed by positive returns at the end of the fund when investments are exited.

Most of the direct-lending opportunity is to support middle-market corporations with revenues of up to $100 million and EBITDA of up to $10 million, with loans of up to $20 million to $50 million. Much of the origination activity is focused on first-lien and senior secured debt, placing the direct lender in control of a situation that moves toward distress. As the senior lender to a firm, investors can potentially seize the firm or specific assets, leaving equity holders and subordinated lenders with potentially large losses.

A growing subset of the direct-lending opportunity is peer-to-peer lending. **Peer-to-peer lending** is originating loans directly to consumers and is done by both institutional and retail investors who have an opportunity to originate consumer loans, often through an Internet-based underwriting and brokerage platform. Peer-to-peer (P2P) lending can reduce the interest rates that consumers pay when they refinance other consumer credit, such as credit cards and student loans, with lower-cost P2P loans. Investors can earn a higher yield than on other forms of similarly risky credit if the spread between risk-free debt and credit card rates is wide. While the P2P business started as individuals lending to individuals, disintermediating banks from both savings and lending products, over two-thirds of the lending was funded by institutional investors by 2014. It is notable that some of the leading Internet-based brokerage firms in the P2P lending space fund loans for only 10% of potential borrowers, as the lenders are highly focused on funding only the most highly qualified borrowers seeking loans on these platforms.

22.6 MEZZANINE DEBT

Mezzanine financing, by definition, defies generalization. Some investors, such as insurance companies, view mezzanine financing as a traditional form of debt. Insurance companies seek preservation of capital and consistency of cash flows, and they invest in mezzanine debt that tends to meet these priorities. Other investors, such as mezzanine limited partnerships, leveraged buyout (LBO) firms, and commercial banks, seek potential capital appreciation. Issuers often structure mezzanine debt so as to offer enough potential capital appreciation that it becomes equity-like.

22.6.1 Mezzanine Debt Structures

Mezzanine debt becomes equity-like when an equity kicker is attached to the debt. This equity kicker, introduced in Chapter 20, is usually in the form of equity warrants to purchase stock, with a strike price as low as $0.01 per share. A **warrant** is a call option issued by a corporation on its own stock. The number of warrants included in the equity kicker is inversely proportional to the coupon rate: The higher the coupon rate, the fewer warrants need to be issued. The investor receives both a coupon payment and participation in the upside of the company, should it achieve its growth potential. The equity component can be substantial, representing 5% to 20% of the outstanding equity of the company. For this reason, mezzanine debt is often viewed as an equity investment in the company as opposed to an unsecured lien on assets.

The idea that mezzanine debt becomes more equity-like when call options are attached is clarified through the application of option theory to the capital structure of a firm. Within Merton's view of the capital structure of a firm, discussed in Chapter 24, corporate debt may be seen as the combination of a long position in the firm's assets and a short position in a call option (written to the shareholders), with a strike price equal to the face value of the firm's debt (and a time to expiration equal to the maturity of the debt). Equation 22.2 illustrates this structural view of corporate debt:

$$\text{Corporate Debt} = \text{Firm's Assets} - \text{Call Option on Firm's Assets} \qquad (22.2)$$

When explicit long positions in equity kickers (i.e., call options) are attached to the corporate debt on the left side of Equation 22.2, the options hedge the debt holders' implicit short positions in call options on the right side of the equation. The net result is that the remaining exposure is the debt holders' implicit long position in the firm's assets. Thus, mezzanine debt with equity kickers can behave like an unlevered long position in the firm's underlying assets.

Mezzanine financing does not necessarily involve control of the company, in contrast to an LBO, and is therefore much more passive than an LBO. Mezzanine financing is an appropriate financing source for those companies that have a reliable cash flow. This is in contrast to venture capital (VC), in which the start-up company does not have sufficient cash flow to support debt.

There is no typical or standard mezzanine deal structure. Each financing consists of unique terms and conditions that depend on the preferences of the user and provider and that emerge from a highly negotiated process. The mezzanine piece can be structured as debt or equity, depending on how much capital the owner wants to obtain and how much control the owner is willing to cede to the mezzanine partner. The flexibility of mezzanine financing is what makes it so popular with borrowers and investors alike. Both sides can tailor the financing to fit their borrowing and investment criteria.

Mezzanine financing provides a higher risk profile to an investor than does senior debt because of its unsecured status, lower credit priority, and equity kicker. However, the return range sought for mezzanine debt is substantially below that for venture capital and leveraged buyouts. The reduced return reflects a lower risk profile than is found in other forms of private equity. Typically, the total return sought by investors in mezzanine financing is in the range of 15% to 20%. The largest piece of the total return is the coupon rate on the mezzanine security, usually 10% to 14%. The remainder of the upside comes from the equity kicker, either warrants or some other equity conversion. The equity kicker can provide an additional 5% to 10% return to the mezzanine finance provider.

The typical exit strategy for mezzanine debt occurs when the underlying company goes public or obtains capital through a large equity issuance. In addition, the mezzanine debt may be paid prior to maturity if the borrowing firm is acquired or recapitalized. When one of these events happens, the mezzanine debt provider gets back the face value of the mezzanine debt plus the sale of stock from the conversion rights or sale of warrants attached to the mezzanine debt.

With a mezzanine fund, the J-curve effect is not a factor. One of the distinct advantages of mezzanine financing is its immediate cash-on-cash return. Mezzanine debt bears a coupon that requires twice-yearly interest payments to investors. As a result, mezzanine financing funds can avoid the early negative returns associated with venture capital or leveraged buyout funds.

22.6.2 Stylized Example of Mezzanine Debt Advantage

The left-hand side of Exhibit 22.4 shows a simple capital structure for a company faced with a 60% bank loan–40% equity capital structure. Bank debt is assumed to be cheap, and equity is assumed to be expensive. Unfortunately, a bank may be willing to lend only up to 60% of the total capital structure of the company. Therefore, expensive equity capital might be used to fill the remaining capital gap if mezzanine debt is unavailable. The **weighted average cost of capital** for a firm is the sum of the products of the percentages of each type of capital used to finance a firm times its annual cost to the firm. Exhibit 22.4 illustrates a relatively high weighted average cost of capital (WACC) using only bank loans and equity. Without mezzanine debt, the weighted average cost of capital is 16.8%.

The right-hand side of Exhibit 22.4 lays out how mezzanine capital might lower the capital costs for a company. In this example, half of the equity capital is replaced with mezzanine debt at a coupon rate of 15%. This makes the equity riskier and therefore likely to increase its cost of capital, which is assumed to rise to 32%. At the bottom of the exhibit, the new weighted average cost of capital for the company is

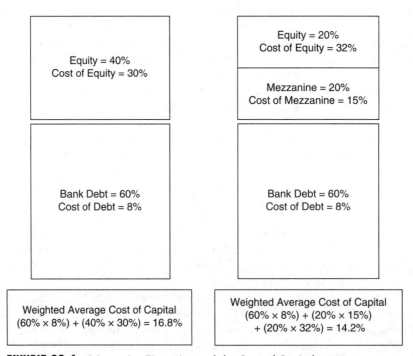

EXHIBIT 22.4   Mezzanine Financing and the Cost of Capital

calculated. When mezzanine debt is added to the capital structure, the WACC declines from 16.8% to 14.2%.

The reduced weighted average cost of capital is generated by replacing relatively expensive equity financing with less expensive mezzanine financing. The reduction in capital costs illustrated in Exhibit 22.4 demonstrates the motivation for a firm to use mezzanine financing.

This simplified example assumes that the required return on equity changes only slightly when half of the equity is replaced with mezzanine debt and the leverage is increased. In the case of very-well-functioning capital markets, it would usually be argued that sources of financing are efficiently priced and that different capital structures cannot be used to generate lower aggregate costs of capital (i.e., lower weighted average costs of capital). The justifications for advantages to mezzanine debt are based on inefficiencies and imperfections in the capital markets for the size of companies that tend to use mezzanine financing.

☞ APPLICATION 22.6.2A

Suppose that the structure on the right-hand side of Exhibit 22.4 is changed such that the mezzanine debt rises to being 30% of the capital structure, and the bank debt falls to being 50% of the capital structure. If the costs of bank debt and equity remain the same (8% and 32%, respectively), what must the new cost of mezzanine debt be such that the weighted average cost of capital would be 15.8%?

The answer is found by solving for x: $15.8\% = (0.20 \times 32\%) + (0.30x) + (0.50 \times 8\%)$. The solution is that the cost of mezzanine debt, x, is 18%.

22.6.3 Mezzanine Financing Compared with Other Forms of Financing

Generally, mezzanine financing occurs in amounts below $400 million. In other words, mezzanine financing is generally used by middle-market companies, which are the larger stocks within the small-cap classification. These firms do not usually have access to the large public debt markets as a relatively efficiently priced source of debt capital. High-yield debt issues tend to start at sizes of $400 million. The same is true for leveraged loans.

Mezzanine financing is highly negotiated and can be tailored to any company's situation. The flip side is that the level of tailoring makes mezzanine debt illiquid. Exiting mezzanine debt involves a lengthy negotiation process for the investor, either with the company that issued the mezzanine debt to buy back its securities or with a secondary private equity investor to purchase the position. In both cases, mezzanine debt is often sold at a large discount.

Mezzanine debt is typically held by mezzanine debt funds raised by private equity firms. Mezzanine financing stands behind senior debt and is usually analyzed on an earnings before interest, taxes, depreciation, and amortization (EBITDA) multiple basis. Bank loans and other senior loans generally require a loan-to-EBITDA multiple of no more than 2 to 2.5. In other words, a firm with EBITDA of $100 million per year would typically be allowed to borrow between $200 million and $250 million in senior loans. However, mezzanine debt typically allows for a higher loan-to-EBITDA multiple. Thus, with a multiple of 4 to 4.5, a firm with EBITDA of $100 million per year could expand its total debt to between $400 million and $450 million, including perhaps $225 million of senior debt and $200 million of mezzanine debt. As shown in Exhibit 22.5, debt multiples for buyout transactions have been increasing, with total debt loads now exceeding six times EBITDA.

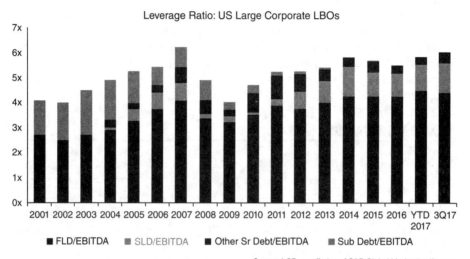

Source: LCD, an offering of S&P Global Market Intelligence

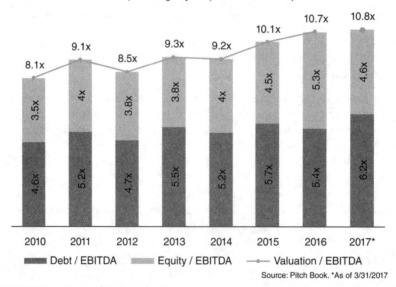

Source: Pitch Book. *As of 3/31/2017

EXHIBIT 22.5   Deal Multiples and Leverage Multiples Have Been Rising in Large U.S. LBOs
*As of March 31, 2017.
Source: LCD, An offering of S&P Global Market Intelligence; Pitchbook.

Because mezzanine debt is not backed by collateral, it carries a higher coupon payment than does senior debt. Mezzanine debt is generally medium-term money, usually with maturities from five to seven years. Typically, mezzanine financing requires only payment of interest until maturity; there is no amortization of the underlying debt. Mezzanine debt often includes a payment in kind (PIK) toggle. A **PIK toggle** allows the underlying company to choose whether it will make required coupon payments in the form of cash or in kind, meaning with more mezzanine bonds. Leveraged loans do not have such a provision.

Exhibit 22.6 compares mezzanine debt to leveraged loans and high-yield bonds. Notice that leveraged loans have the strictest debt covenants, which lead to greater protection from default but also to a lower return. Also, a credit rating is typically required before a bank will lend credit through a leveraged loan, whereas this is not necessary for mezzanine debt. In addition, leveraged loans typically have a floating interest rate tied to the London Interbank Offered Rate (LIBOR), whereas mezzanine debt has a fixed coupon.

The risk of bonds or loans can be differentiated even further based on whether a transaction is sponsored or unsponsored. Many private credit funds participate in **sponsored lending**, whereby the borrowing firm is backed by an investment from a private equity fund or buyout fund sponsor. Investing in the debt that's generated through an LBO transaction might be a bit safer because there's a private equity or a buyout fund that owns the equity and maybe some of the debt of the firm. When that

EXHIBIT 22.6   Comparison of Leveraged Loans, High-Yield Bonds, and Mezzanine Debt

	Leveraged Loans	High-Yield Bonds	Mezzanine Debt
Seniority	Most senior	Contractual and structural subordination	Lowest priority
Type of security	First lien on assets	Unsecured	Unsecured
Credit rating	Usually required	Required	Not required
Loan covenants	Extensive	Less comprehensive	Minimal: typically related only to payment of coupons
Term	5 years	7–10 years	4–6 years
Amortization	Installments	Bullet payment	Bullet payment
Coupon type	Cash/floating	Cash/fixed	Cash/PIK/fixed
Coupon rate	LIBOR + spread	5%–8%	8%–11%
Prepayment penalty	Usually none	High: usually the company must pay a call premium	Moderate: sometimes equity conversion is forced
Equity kicker	None	Sometimes	Almost always: usually equity warrants
Recovery if default	60%–100%	40%–50%	20%–30%
Liquidity	High	Low	Minimal

firm starts to experience distress, hopefully, the private equity or buyout manager will step in and inject additional capital, which might help to protect the value of their equity investment. A sponsored lending transaction may be therefore less risky than a nonsponsored lending transaction, because a nonsponsored transaction doesn't have that private equity manager who might be willing to come and invest additional equity in the firm when it becomes distressed.

One last point is that leveraged loans do not contain any type of equity kicker, so they do not share in any upside of the company. Mezzanine debt investors focus on the total return from mezzanine financing, including future equity participation through a convertible security or warrants attached to the mezzanine debt. This is distinctly different from bank loans, which focus exclusively on the cash yield. High-yield bonds fall somewhere between these two forms of financing.

22.6.4 Seven Basic Examples of Mezzanine Financing

As noted earlier, mezzanine financing can be viewed as filling either a gap in a company's financial structure or a gap in the supply of capital in the financial markets. This makes mezzanine financing extremely flexible. The diversity of transaction types that follow demonstrates this flexibility.

There are seven basic transactions to which mezzanine debt is applied: management buyouts, growth and expansion, acquisitions, recapitalizations, real estate financing, leveraged buyouts, and bridge financing.

1. MEZZANINE FINANCING FOR A MANAGEMENT BUYOUT (MBO): When the senior management team of a firm leads an MBO, mezzanine debt can fill the gap between senior debt claims and equity.
2. MEZZANINE FINANCING FOR GROWTH AND EXPANSION: A company pursuing growth that cannot raise traditional bank financing or public financing may seek mezzanine financing.
3. MEZZANINE FINANCING FOR AN ACQUISITION: A middle-market company seeking to purchase an even smaller company may seek mezzanine debt financing as part of the capital for the acquisition.
4. MEZZANINE FINANCING TO RECAPITALIZE A COMPANY: Mezzanine debt may be used as part of a new capital structure for a firm to create a new balance sheet, such as having a senior term loan, senior subordinated mezzanine debt, junior subordinated mezzanine debt, convertible preferred stock, and common equity.
5. MEZZANINE FINANCING IN COMMERCIAL REAL ESTATE: Mezzanine capital fills the gap between first-mortgage financing, which usually has a loan-to-value ratio of 40% to 75%, and the equity contributed to the project. Typical equity contributions for real estate are in the 10% to 15% range. It is in between bank loans and equity that mezzanine financing exists, historically supplying 10% to 40% of a project's capital structure.
6. MEZZANINE FINANCING IN A LEVERAGED BUYOUT: Mezzanine financing is an established component of many leveraged buyouts. An LBO requires a large amount of debt, and not all debt can be senior. A significant amount of the financing may come from mezzanine investors.

7. MEZZANINE FINANCING AS BRIDGE FINANCING: Often, a good portion of the initial debt in an LBO is raised as bridge financing. **Bridge financing** is a form of gap financing—a method of debt financing that is temporarily used to maintain liquidity while waiting for an anticipated and reasonably expected inflow of cash.

22.6.5 Investors in Mezzanine Debt

This section reviews four major types of investors in mezzanine debt:

1. MEZZANINE FUNDS: Mezzanine funds are organized like hedge funds, venture capital funds, and buyout funds. Investors in mezzanine funds are generally pension funds, endowments, and foundations. These institutional investors do not have the internal infrastructure or expertise to invest directly in the mezzanine market. Therefore, they enter this alternative investment strategy as limited partners through a mezzanine fund.

   Mezzanine funds tend to charge a fee structure similar to venture capital (VC) and LBO funds: a management fee in the 1% to 2% range and a profit-sharing fee of 20%. Like hedge funds, VC funds, and LBO funds, mezzanine funds are managed by a general partner who has full investment discretion. Many mezzanine funds are managed by merchant banks that have experience with gap financing or by mezzanine professionals who previously worked in the mezzanine departments of insurance companies and banks.

   There are two key distinctions between other private equity funds and mezzanine funds. The first lies in return expectations. Mezzanine funds seek total rates of return in the 15% to 20% range. Compare this to LBO funds, which seek returns in the 20% to 30% range, and VC funds, which seek returns in the 30% to 50% range. This puts mezzanine funds at the lower end of the private equity risk-return spectrum. However, contrasted to debt, mezzanine financing is the most expensive because it is the last to be repaid, ranking at the bottom of the creditor spectrum, just above equity. Second, mezzanine fund staff have different expertise than is typically found at a venture capital fund. Most VC funds have staff with heavy technology-related experience, including former senior executives of medical, software, semiconductor, and Internet companies. In contrast, mezzanine funds are inundated with financial engineers who are experienced at structuring and negotiating loans that incorporate the use of equity kickers and warrants.

   Mezzanine funds look for businesses that have a high potential for growth and earnings but do not have a sufficient cash flow to receive full funding from banks or other senior creditors. Banks may be unwilling to lend because of a short operating history or a high debt-to-equity ratio. Mezzanine funds look for companies that can repay the mezzanine debt over the next four to seven years through a debt refinancing, an initial equity offering, or being acquired. Mezzanine funds are considerably smaller than the huge ($20 billion plus) leveraged buyout funds. This reflects the fact that mezzanine financing is distinctly a middle-market phenomenon and cannot support megafunds of the type commonly associated with LBOs.

Mezzanine funds are risk lenders. This means that in a liquidation of the company, mezzanine investors expect little or no recovery of their principal. Mezzanine debt is rarely secured. As the last rung of the financing ladder, it is often viewed as a form of equity by the more senior lenders.

2. INSURANCE COMPANIES: Insurance companies are a major source of mezzanine financing. They are natural providers of mezzanine debt because the durations of their liabilities (life insurance policies and annuities) are best matched with longer-term debt instruments. These investors take more of a fixed-income approach and place a high value on the scheduled repayment of principal. Insurance companies are more concerned with a higher coupon payment than with the total return, including equity warrants. Therefore, insurance companies act more like traditional lenders than like equity investors. They provide mezzanine financing to higher-quality credit names and emphasize preservation versus appreciation of capital.

3. TRADITIONAL SENIOR LENDERS: Interestingly, banks and other providers of senior secured debt often participate in mezzanine financing. This financing takes the form of so-called **stretch financing**, where a bank lends more money than it believes would be prudent with traditional lending standards and traditional lending terms. This excess of debt beyond the collateral value of a company's business assets is the "stretch" part of the financing. Senior lenders may ask for an equity kicker, such as warrants, to compensate the institution for stretching financing beyond the assets available.

4. TRADITIONAL VENTURE CAPITAL FIRMS: When the economy softens, venture capital firms look for ways to maintain their stellar returns. In addition, times of large flows of capital into venture capital funds make it necessary for them to expand their investment horizons, resulting in a greater interest in mezzanine financing. Mezzanine financing and venture capital frequently go hand in hand, with mezzanine debt serving as the bridge. In this case, the bridge is the last round of private financing before a start-up company goes public. The lines between mezzanine financing and different forms of private equity can become blurred. With respect to pre–initial public offering (IPO) companies, it is difficult to distinguish where venture capital ends and mezzanine financing begins. Also, mezzanine financing can be used as the last leg in the capital structure of a start-up company before it goes public. This bridge financing allows the company to clean up its balance sheet before its IPO.

22.6.6 Eight Characteristics of Mezzanine Debt

Mezzanine debt has eight characteristics that help distinguish it from other sources of financing and types of investments:

1. BOARD REPRESENTATION: A subordinated lender generally expects to be considered an equity partner. In some cases, mezzanine lenders may request board observation rights; in other cases, mezzanine lenders may insist on a seat on the board of directors with full voting rights.

2. RESTRICTIONS ON THE BORROWER: Although mezzanine debt is typically unsecured, it may still come with restrictions on the borrower. The mezzanine lender may have the right to approve or disapprove of additional debt and require that

any new debt be subordinated to the original mezzanine debt. The lender may also enjoy final approval over any contemplated acquisitions, changes in the management team, or payment of dividends.

3. FLEXIBILITY: There are no set terms to mezzanine financing. The structure of mezzanine debt can be as flexible as needed to accommodate the parties involved. For example, mezzanine debt can be structured so that no interest payments begin for two to three years.

4. NEGOTIATIONS WITH SENIOR CREDITORS: The subordination of mezzanine debt is typically accomplished with an intercreditor agreement. An **intercreditor agreement** is an agreement with the company's existing creditors that places restrictions on both the senior creditor and the mezzanine investor. The intercreditor agreement may be negotiated separately between the senior creditors and the mezzanine investor, or it may be incorporated directly into the loan agreement between the mezzanine investor and the company. Intercreditor agreements usually restrict amendments to the credit facility so that the terms of the intercreditor agreement cannot be circumvented by new agreements between the individual lenders and the borrower.

5. SUBORDINATION: The subordination (lowered priority) may be either a blanket subordination or a springing subordination. A **blanket subordination** prevents any payment of principal or interest to the mezzanine investor until after the senior debt has been fully repaid. A **springing subordination** allows the mezzanine investor to receive interest payments while the senior debt is still outstanding. However, if a default occurs or a covenant is violated, the subordination springs up to stop all payments to the mezzanine investor until either the default is cured or the senior debt has been fully repaid.

6. ACCELERATION: The violation of any covenant may result in acceleration. **Acceleration** is a requirement that debt be repaid sooner than originally scheduled, such as when the senior lender can declare the senior debt due and payable immediately. This typically forces a default and allows the senior lender to enforce the collateral security.

7. ASSIGNMENT: Senior lenders typically restrict the rights of the mezzanine investor to assign, or sell, its interests to a third party. However, senior lenders generally allow an assignment, providing the assignee executes a new intercreditor agreement with the senior lender.

8. TAKEOUT PROVISIONS: A **takeout provision** allows the mezzanine investor to purchase the senior debt once it has been repaid to a specified level. This is one of the most important provisions in an intercreditor agreement and goes to the heart of mezzanine investing. By taking out the senior debt, the mezzanine investor becomes the most senior level of financing in the company and, in fact, can take control of the company. At this point, the mezzanine investor usually converts the debt into equity through either convertible bonds or warrants and becomes the largest shareholder of the company.

22.7 DISTRESSED DEBT

Distressed debt investing involves purchasing the debt of companies that are in or near default.

22.7.1 Describing Distressed Debt

Distressed debt is often defined as debt that has deteriorated in quality since issued and that has a market price less than half its principal value, yields 1,000 or more basis points over the riskless rate, or has a credit rating of CCC (Caa) or lower.

Distressed debt investors are usually equity investors "in debt's clothing." They are relatively unconcerned with coupon payments, debt service, and repayment schedules, being interested in distressed debt for the capital appreciation that can be achieved in various situations. They are sometimes viewed as vultures looking to swoop in, purchase cheap debt securities, convert them to stock, turn the company around, and reap the rewards of appreciation. As discussed in Chapter 20, the risks are large because the underlying company is in some form of distress. Consequently, distressed debt investors are exposed to event risk that the company will not be able to emerge from bankruptcy protection or will otherwise fail.

Within the risk spectrum, private equity distressed debt investors fall between LBO firms and venture capital. Like LBO firms, distressed debt investors purchase securities of companies that have established operating histories. In most cases, these companies have progressed far beyond their IPO stage. However, unlike LBO firms that target successful but stagnant companies, distressed investing targets troubled companies. These companies have declined and may already be in bankruptcy proceedings. Like venture capital and LBO funds, distressed debt investors assume considerable business risk. A company's current problems might be due to poor execution of an existing business plan, an obsolete business plan, excessive leverage, or simply poor cash management. These problems are more likely to be fixable than in the case of a start-up company with a nonviable product.

Mezzanine debt is made equity-like primarily through equity kickers. Distressed debt becomes equity-like through potential default risk. As in the case of mezzanine debt, the idea that debt can be equity-like can be clarified using Merton's view of the capital structure of a firm. In that framework, corporate debt can be seen as being equal to the combination of a long position in the firm's assets and a short position in a call option on the firm's assets. Equation 22.2 illustrated this option view of corporate debt.

If the value of the firm's assets falls near or below the face value of the debt, the debt holders' short position in the call option moves out-of-the-money and becomes a smaller and smaller value relative to the debt holders' long position in the firm's assets. The further out-of-the-money the call option moves, the closer the value of the call option on the right-hand side of Equation 22.2 moves toward zero. Thus, the corporation's debt behaves increasingly like an unlevered long position in the firm's assets as the value of the firm's assets falls below the face value of the firm's debt.

22.7.2 The Supply of Distressed Debt

Debt rarely becomes distressed because of some spectacular event that renders a company's products worthless overnight. Rather, a company's financial condition typically deteriorates over a period of time. The management of a company that was once established in the marketplace may become lacking in energy or rigid, unable or unwilling to cope with new market dynamics. This is where successful private equity managers earn superior returns. Revitalizing companies and implementing new business plans are their specialty. The adept distressed investor is able to spot these tired companies, identify their weaknesses, and bring a fresh approach to the table. By purchasing the debt of the company, the distressed debt investor creates a seat at the table and the opportunity to turn the company around.

Leveraged buyout firms are a major source for distressed debt, as the debt used to initiate the LBO often becomes distressed debt. There is a natural cycle between private equity and distressed debt investing. Since LBOs use a substantial amount of debt to take a company private, this debt burden sometimes becomes too much to bear, and the private company enters into a distressed situation. These so called leveraged fallouts occur frequently, leaving large amounts of distressed debt in their wake. However, this provides an opportunity for distressed debt buyers to jump in, purchase nonperforming bank loans and subordinated debt cheaply, eliminate the prior private equity investors, and assert their own private equity ownership.

22.7.3 The Demand for Distressed Debt

There is no standard model for successful distressed debt investing. Each distressed situation requires a unique approach and solution. Successful distressed debt investing entails selection of companies (credit risks) that are undervalued in the marketplace and intervention in the operations of the companies and in bankruptcy reorganizations to secure high returns.

One reason the distressed debt market is attractive to vulture and other investors is that it is an inefficient market. First, distressed debt is not publicly traded like stocks. Further, most distressed debt was originally issued in private offerings and sold directly to institutional investors seeking investment-grade debt. This debt lacked liquidity from the outset, and what little liquidity existed dried up when the company became distressed. This lack of liquidity can lead to bonds trading at steep discounts to their true value. Institutional investors uncomfortable with the increased risk of their positions in distressed bonds may need to sell their claims at depressed prices.

Sometimes investors use distressed debt as a way to gain an equity investment stake in a company. In these cases, the distressed debt owners agree to exchange their debt in return for stock in the company. At other times, distressed debt owners help the troubled company get back on its feet, thus earning a substantial return as their distressed debt recovers in value.

Finally, distressed debt is not always an entree into private equity; it can simply be an investment in an undervalued security. At these times, distressed debt buyers may serve as patient creditors. They buy the debt from anxious sellers at steep discounts and wait for the company to correct itself and for the value of the distressed debt to recover.

22.7.4 Expected Default Losses on Distressed Debt

The annual **default rate** is the annual portion of debt issues that default by failing to pay principal and interest as scheduled or that experience a technical default when a company is unable to comply with the covenants, or terms of the loan outside the payment of principal and interest. The annual **loan loss rate** is the annual default rate multiplied by the losses on the debt that aren't recovered through bankruptcy.

$$\text{Loan Loss Rate} = \text{Default Rate} \times \text{Loss Given Default}$$
$$= \text{Default Rate} \times (1 - \text{Recovery Rate}) \quad (22.3)$$

The loan loss rate in Equation 22.3 is the expected annual losses to the portfolio from default losses expressed as a percentage of the portfolio's total initial value.

☞ APPLICATION 22.7.4A

If 20% of the bonds in a portfolio default each year and if 60% of each defaulted bond's value is ultimately unrecoverable (i.e., 40% of the bond's cost is recovered), what would be the expected annual default losses as a percentage rate relative to the portfolio's value?

The total annual loss due to default is 12%, found from Equation 22.3: $[20\% \times (1 - 40\%)] = 12\%$.

Like LBO funds and venture capital funds, distressed debt funds tend to run concentrated portfolios of companies. However, distressed debt investors tend to invest across industries as opposed to concentrating in a single industry. This may lead to better diversification than is found in VC funds. Distressed debt portfolios may be viewed as suffering credit losses at rates that are more than offset by income and recoveries from firms that turn around. Equation 22.4 illustrates this minimum criterion based on a credit spread, an expected default rate, and an expected loss rate:

$$\text{Credit Spread} \geq \text{Loan Loss Rate} + \text{Required Risk Premiums} \quad (22.4)$$

Equation 22.4 illustrates the distressed investor's goal of receiving a credit spread (above the riskless rate) at least large enough to cover expected annual credit losses (the loan loss rate, which is the product of the default rate and the loss rate given default on the portfolio). Further, the investor likely requires a risk premium to compensate the investor for risks such as illiquidity and the uncertainty with regard to default rates (especially to the extent that default rates exhibit systematic risk).

☞ APPLICATION 22.7.4B

If the expected recovery rate is 50% and the annual default losses as a percentage rate relative to the portfolio's value is 9%, what would be the minimum credit spread that an investor would require if the investor seeks a 5% premium for bearing the risks associated with the portfolio's various risks?

> The total minimum credit spread is 14% found from Equation 22.4 (Credit Spread $\geq 9\% + 5\% = 14\%$). The recovery rate of 50% was already included in the annual default loss rate of 9%.

Credit spreads can be observed at a specific point in time, but spreads can change dramatically during times of rising defaults and increasing risk in financial markets. Credit spreads can exceed 6% during times of increasing default rates and declining recovery rates. Further, both credit spreads and loan losses are cyclical. Investors require being paid more on the loan credit spread than it eventually costs for the loan loss rate to receive compensation for associated risks. Jenkins and Thomas (2017) encourage investors to consider a strategy of having lower allocations to risky debt late in the credit cycle when spreads are tight, but increasing allocations quickly after spreads have widened, which often occurs during times of crisis when spreads and defaults are rising and investors are selling debt to reduce leverage.

22.7.5 Three Distressed Debt Investment Strategies

There are three broad strategic categories of investing in distressed debt securities.

The first approach is an active approach with the intent to obtain control of the company. These investors typically purchase distressed debt to gain control through a blocking position in the bankruptcy process with the goal of subsequent conversion into the equity of the reorganized company. This strategy of gaining control also seeks seats on the board of directors and even the chairmanship of the board. This is the riskiest and most time-intensive of the distressed investment strategies. Returns are expected in the 20% to 25% range, consistent with those for leveraged buyouts. Often, these investors purchase fulcrum securities.

The second general category of distressed debt investing seeks to play an active role in the bankruptcy and reorganization process but stops short of taking control of the company. Here, the principals may be willing to swap their debt for equity or for another form of restructured debt. An equity conversion is not required, because control of the company is not sought. These investors participate actively in the bankruptcy process, working with or against other creditors to ensure the most beneficial outcome for their debt. They may accept equity kickers such as warrants with their restructured debt. Their return target is in the 15% to 20% range, very similar to that of mezzanine debt investors.

Last, there are passive or opportunistic investors. These investors do not usually take an active role in the reorganization of the company and rarely seek to convert their debt into equity. These investors buy debt securities that no one else is eager to buy. These distressed debt buyers usually buy their positions from financial institutions that do not have the time or inclination to participate in the bankruptcy reorganization, from mutual funds that are restricted in their ability to hold distressed securities, and from investors with positions in high-yield bonds who do not want to convert a high cash yield into an equity position in the company.

22.7.6 Risks of Distressed Debt Investing

The main risk associated with distressed debt investing is business risk. Just because distressed debt investors can purchase the debt of a company at large discounts from face value does not mean it cannot go lower. This is the greatest risk to distressed debt investing: that a troubled company may ultimately prove to be worthless and unable to pay off its creditors. Although creditors often convert their debt into equity, the company may in the end not be viable as a going concern. If the company cannot develop a successful plan of reorganization, it simply continues its downward spiral. Purchasers of distressed debt must have long-term investment horizons. Workout and turnaround situations do not happen overnight; it may take several years for a troubled company to correct its course and appreciate in value.

It may seem strange, but traditional views of creditworthiness, such as probability of default, may not apply here. In other words, lack of creditworthiness is already established. Credit risk and other fixed-income-based views of risk are less relevant. The debt is already distressed and may already be in default. Consequently, failure to pay interest and debt service may have already occurred.

Instead, vulture investors consider the business risks of the company. They are concerned not with the short-term payment of interest and debt service but with the ability of the company to execute a viable business plan. From this perspective, it can be said that distressed debt investors are truly equity investors. They view the purchase of distressed debt as an equity-like investment in the company as opposed to a decision to become a fixed-income investor.

22.7.7 Five Observations on Vulture Investing

Schultze (2012) wrote an insightful and entertaining book describing the vulture investing process. Schultze's insights are summarized here.

First, while some vulture investors may resent the label, Schultze embraces it, specifically comparing his role in the economy to the role of the vulture in the natural world. Schultze notes that buzzards are good for the environment, cleaning up the toxic waste of dead and decaying animals. Analogously, **vulture investors** help the economy by cleaning up after bankruptcies, recycling bad debt and turning poorly run companies into new investments with greater potential profits and job growth. Vulture investors do dirty work, but it pays well, especially for those with the legal training and skill to understand and influence the bankruptcy process.

Second, Schultze describes a credit cycle as one of booms and busts exacerbated by government policy. The boom is inflated by loose monetary policy and cheap credit designed to clean up the last bust, but with the cheap credit actually encouraging the next boom. By patiently waiting for the point in the cycle when credit has fully deteriorated, Schultze contends that a vulture investor may be able to buy distressed debt at 20% of its face value and potentially earn a recovery value of 60% at the end of the bankruptcy process.

Third, Schultze claims that the most important skill is the identification of the fulcrum security, as the largest profits to vultures come through holding the post-bankruptcy equity (through recovery) and not from the cash recovery values of debt senior to the fulcrum security.

Fourth, while previously the fulcrum security was usually a subordinated debt issue, the increasing debt load of corporations worldwide has changed capital structures so dramatically that the fulcrum security is often now a senior secured bank loan.

Finally, Schultze notes that the negative perception of vulture investors does not come from their purchase of impaired debt in a fire sale, but rather from *originating* debt with a loan-to-own mentality. Traditional credit analysis focuses on the cash flows of the firm, seeking to determine that the cash flow is sufficient to service the debt until its maturity. In contrast, loan-to-own strategies don't underwrite the loan focused on the borrower's ability to pay, but on making senior secured loans that are likely to default where the underwriter seeks to control the firm or a specific asset that is deemed to be worth more than the value of the loan. That is, a lender in a loan-to-own strategy seeks out and structures deals that are likely to default, preferring to take control of a firm or its assets rather than to be paid principal and interest on the loan. Rather than thinking of this financing as a lending transaction, the vulture in the loan-to-own scenario considers the financing an acquisition due to its high probability of default.

22.8 PRIVATE CREDIT PERFORMANCE AND DIVERSIFICATION

As with any investment, investors should be concerned with how private credit and distressed investments will alter the risk and return of their portfolio. Specifically, it is imperative to understand how the asset allocation will change when new investments are made in alternative credit vehicles.

Munday et al. (2018) evaluated the risk and return characteristics of a variety of credit vehicles using data from the vintage years 2004 to 2016, which of course includes the global financial crisis of 2008 and 2009. The first observation is that reported valuations of mezzanine, distressed, and direct-lending strategies excluding mezzanine exhibited relatively low price volatility. However, this perception was due to the smoothing effects of a lack of liquidity on the valuations of these strategies, where either the loans were not regularly traded or were held to maturity by the originator of the loan. After adjusting for the smoothing of this illiquidity using autocorrelation techniques, the annual standard deviations of returns to mezzanine funds, direct-lending funds, and distressed funds were 5.1%, 6.7%, and 13.5%, respectively. In contrast, the standard deviations of the more liquid and highly traded high-yield funds, BDCs, and leveraged loans were 11.5%, 29.8%, and 11.0%, respectively. Volatility was also demonstrated in the degree of drawdowns in 2008 and 2009, with mezzanine losing 15% and BDCs experiencing a temporary loss of value of 50%.

The second observation is that there was a relatively high correlation of returns between distressed debt, BDCs, high-yield bonds, and leveraged loans, with most pairwise correlations varying between 0.8 and 0.9. In contrast, direct lending strategies ex-mezzanine had a much lower correlation of just 0.2 to 0.3 relative to the high yield, BDC, and leveraged loan strategies.

The third observation is that mezzanine, leveraged loan, and high-yield investments had lower levels of return, averaging 7.7%, 5.5%, and 8.2%, respectively, over this time period. Distressed and direct-lending ex-mezzanine investments had higher returns, averaging 8.9% and 11.8%, respectively, over the same time period.

While it appears that mezzanine, direct-lending ex-mezzanine, and distressed funds have lower risk, it is not accurate to compare the volatility and correlation of returns of these less liquid investments to the seemingly higher volatility and correlation of returns of the high-yield, BDC, and leveraged loan strategies. The role of illiquidity in understating asset price volatility is detailed in Level II of the CAIA curriculum. Nevertheless, it appears that over the given time period (which includes the global financial crisis), distressed and direct lending strategies, the most complex and illiquid investments in this sector, exhibit sustained outperformance relative to the more liquid fixed-income strategies.

In alternative credit strategies, it appears that illiquid strategies performed well. That is, investors who avoided being forced sellers and had the cash to buy at the bottom of the last credit cycle profited handsomely from this strategy, especially if they had the expertise to work through the bankruptcy process and hold equity assets at the end of the restructuring process. Hedge funds with shorter holding periods and less willingness to work through the restructuring process may be able to profit simply by buying from forced sellers such as pensions and insurance companies subject to regulations that prohibit the holding of distressed paper, open-end funds that have significant investor redemptions, and investors with too much leverage who are forced by a counterparty to quickly reduce their degree of leverage. Each scenario has, at times, led investors to sell more than half of their illiquid fixed income holdings in less than a month. History shows that it is much better to be a buyer than a seller at the bottom of a fire sale.

REVIEW QUESTIONS

1. What is a fulcrum security and how might it facilitate a private equity fund strategy?
2. Explain how and why an increase in the portion of loans that are covenant-lite will affect default rates and the magnitude of losses given default.
3. Briefly describe mezzanine financing.
4. Does mezzanine debt with an equity kicker exhibit the J-curve return pattern of private equity? Why or why not?
5. What would be the primary justification for believing that the use of mezzanine financing can lower a firm's weighted average cost of capital?
6. How does mezzanine debt tend to differ from high-yield bonds and leveraged loans in seniority, term, and liquidity?
7. By what standards or measures is distressed debt usually distinguished from nondistressed debt?
8. Provide two major sources of distressed debt.
9. What is the primary distinction between chapter 7 bankruptcy and chapter 11 bankruptcy in the United States?
10. Who is the initial investor in debtor-in-possession financing?

NOTE

1. Moody's Financial Metris Key Ratios by Rating and Industry for Global Non-Financial Corporates: December 2016.

REFERENCES

Antczak, Stephen J., Douglas J. Lucas, and Frank J. Fabozzi. 2009. *Leveraged Finance: Concepts, Methods, and Trading of High-Yield Bonds, Loans, and Derivatives.* Hoboken, NJ: John Wiley & Sons.

Davies, Paul J. 2018a. "The Big Weakness in the Buyout Funding Chain." *Wall Street Journal*, August 7.

————. 2018b. "The Unseen Risk in the Booming Loan Market." *Wall Street Journal*, August 6.

Jenkins, Mark, and Jason M. Thomas. 2017. "Capturing the Credit Risk Premium." Carlyle Group, July.

Munday, Shawn, Wendy Hu, Tobias True, and Jian Zhang. 2018. "Performance of Private Credit Funds: A First Look." *Journal of Alternative Investments*, July 2.

Schultze, George. 2012. *The Art of Vulture Investing: Adventures in Distressed Securities Management.* Hoboken, NJ: John Wiley & Sons.

Wigglesworth, Robin. 2018. "Investors Should Beware Leveraged Loan Delights That Risk Violent Ends." *Financial Times*, August 25.

Five

Structured Products

Structured products and the concept of structuring are central to finance and investments. The concept of structured claims is ancient, extending at least to early landowner–tenant agricultural relationships, in which landowner and tenants would have claims of different priority on receiving the benefits of the harvest.

Chapter 23 provides an introduction to structuring and to the structural modeling approach to credit risk. The chapter goes on to introduce an important sector of structured products that includes collateralized mortgage obligations and collateralized debt obligations. Chapter 24 discusses credit risk and credit derivatives, with an emphasis on interest rate derivatives and credit default swaps. These important derivatives facilitate the management and transfer of interest rate risk and credit risk, which facilitates, among other things, efficient diversification. The chapter also discusses the reduced-form modeling approach to credit risk. Chapter 25 provides a more detailed analysis of collateralized debt obligations. Chapter 26 discusses equity-linked structured products.

CHAPTER 23

Introduction to Structuring

In the context of alternative investments, **structuring** is the process of engineering unique financial opportunities from existing asset exposures. An example of a structured product is an investment specially designed to provide downside protection against losses while offering potential profits through exposure to increases in the value of an index or an underlying portfolio.

23.1 OVERVIEW OF FINANCIAL STRUCTURING

Financial structuring enables different investors to hold claims with different risk exposures (or other characteristics) from the same underlying assets. This section provides an overview. The most common major structuring of assets is the typical capital structure of the corporate form of business organization. This capital structure partitions the risks of the corporation's underlying assets into claims of relatively low risk (e.g., debt) and relatively high risk (equity), as illustrated in Exhibit 23.1.

The typical capital structuring of a business enterprise into debt and equity claims captures the most fundamental concepts and motivations to financial structuring: tailoring the risks of securities to the risk preferences of investors.

The capital structure of a traditional operating firm, illustrated in Exhibit 23.1, is a very common application of the concept of structuring for risk purposes. The risk purpose served by a firm's capital structure is that the risk of the firm's assets is partitioned among the firm's capital providers. Different security classes in the firm are primarily differentiated by their levels of risk. Structuring risk is the primary motivation to the structured products discussed in Chapters 23 to 26. Structuring may be used to differentiate ownership on attributes other than risk. Taxation can play an important role in structuring. The idea is to divvy up the claims to an asset, with cash flows being distributed based on aggregate tax minimization. In that scenario, highly taxed cash flows are distributed to tax-exempt investors or investors in low tax brackets, while tax-advantaged cash flows are distributed to investors in high tax brackets.

Structuring can also accommodate other preferences, such as those involving liquidity. Heterogeneous liquidity preferences are accommodated by structuring an asset into short-term claims for investors who place a high value on liquidity and long-term claims for investors less concerned about liquidity.

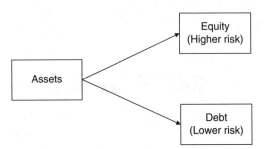

EXHIBIT 23.1 Capital Structure as Creating Structured Products

23.2 MAJOR TYPES OF STRUCTURING

As noted in the introduction and in Chapter 1, structured products are instruments created to exhibit particular return, risk, taxation, or other attributes. The key element of a structured product is that it offers an investor an altered exposure to one or more underlying assets. A collateralized debt obligation (CDO), detailed in Chapter 25, is a good example of a structured product because the tranches of a typical CDO provide substantially altered risk exposures to the pool of assets underlying the CDO. However, a forward contract on an equity index would not be commonly described as a structured product because most forward contracts do not provide a substantially altered exposure to the fundamental characteristics of the underlying asset.

Chapters 24 to 26 cover three topics related to structuring: credit derivatives, CDOs, and equity-linked structured products. The next three sections briefly overview these topics.

23.2.1 Hedging with Credit Derivatives

Chapter 24 discusses simple credit derivatives. Although simple credit derivatives, such as credit default swaps (CDS), are not usually referred to as structured products, they often serve similar roles. Credit default swaps allow for the cost-effective transfer of default risk.

Consider an investor who holds the bonds of XYZ Corporation but wishes to hedge the risk that the bonds of XYZ might default. The investor enters a CDS on the debt of XYZ Corporation with a major bank. In effect, the bank sells credit protection to the investor that functions much like an insurance contract. The CDS transfers the financial risk of XYZ's default from the credit protection buyer (the investor) to the credit protection seller (the bank). Now the investor is hedged. If the XYZ bonds that the investor holds experience default, the investor is made whole through the CDS. Of course, the bank receives compensation from the investor for providing the credit protection. CDSs help organizations manage their credit risk.

23.2.2 Structuring with Tranches

CDOs are structures that partition the risk of a portfolio into ownership claims called tranches which differ in seniority. More senior tranches tend to be the first to receive cash flows and the last to bear losses. The key point of a CDO, therefore, is to engineer the risk of a portfolio into a spectrum of risks tailored to meet the needs, preferences, or market views of various investors. The tranching of CDOs performs a function quite similar to the capital structure of an operating corporation.

For example, the sponsor of a highly simplified CDO structure might buy bonds of XYZ Corporation and place them into the portfolio of a CDO structure (typically along with other corporate bonds). The CDO structure has various tranches with claims to receiving the coupons and principal payments from those bonds. Investors can select a tranche that best meets their preferences for risk and return.

23.2.3 Creating Structured Products

The term *structured products* can be used as an umbrella term to describe a spectrum of innovative financial instruments, or it can be used more specifically to refer to specially tailored securities that are financially engineered to provide specific attributes, such as risk, that meet the preferences of one or more investors. An example of a structured product based on the equity of XYZ Corporation would be a security that paid an investor greater amounts of money if the value of XYZ equity performed poorly and lower amounts of money if XYZ performed well, but had a minimum value to the payout. The structured product might be ideal for an investor with a very large position in XYZ stock who is trying to avoid selling that position due to the potential tax liabilities from a sale. The investor desires downside protection while retaining some upside potential, so a major bank structures a product tailored to meet the investor's precise preferences with regard to size, timing, and payoff profiles.

23.3 THE PRIMARY ECONOMIC ROLE OF STRUCTURING

What economic roles do structured products serve? A structured product exists because both the issuer of the structured product and the investor in the structured product were driven by one or more economic motivations. The primary direct motivation of the issuer is usually to earn fees—either explicit fees or implicit fees. However, other motivations of the issuer and the investor exist and are discussed throughout these four chapters on structured products. The motivation to the buyer could be risk management, tax minimization, liquidity enhancement, or some other goal. From the perspective of a financial economist, the primary economic role of structured products is usually market completion.

23.3.1 Completing Markets as an Economic Role

One of the most central motivations to structured products is market completion. A **complete market** is a financial market in which enough different types of distinct securities exist to meet the needs and preferences of all participants.

For example, consider a world without any risk, uncertainty, taxes, or transaction costs. In such a world, the only difference between securities would be the timing of their cash flows. A complete market in this idealized example would exist when investors could assemble a portfolio that offered exactly the cash flows they desired on every possible date. Thus, a pension fund obligated to disperse cash on the first day of every month would be able to establish long and short positions in existing securities that generated cash on exactly those days that the cash was needed (i.e., the first day of every month).

In the United States, investors seeking riskless investments (in terms of U.S. dollars) tend to invest in U.S. Treasury bills, notes, and bonds. The market for Treasury securities contains many securities across a wide spectrum of maturity dates. But even ignoring the risk of a U.S. Treasury default, the Treasury market could not be described as being perfectly complete. The longest ordinary Treasury security is the 30-year Treasury bond, with an initial maturity of 30 years. What should an investor such as a pension fund do with liabilities requiring cash flows in perhaps 40 or 50 years? And there was a four-year period (2002 to 2006) when even the 30-year Treasury bond was no longer being issued. The U.S. Treasury began issuing the 30-year bond again based in part on the very function being discussed here—the benefits of completing a market by creating investment products that meet the needs of investors (in this case, mostly financial institutions with long-term time horizons).

In the idealized world of a complete market, individual investors could manage their wealth optimally because sufficient distinct securities would exist to allow any desired investment exposure. It should be noted that the financial market will never be fully completed. The term *completing the market* simply means that the market is being brought one step closer to completion by offering investors unique opportunities with which to manage their finances.

23.3.2 States of the World within Structured Products

In the real world of uncertainty and asymmetric information, markets are highly incomplete. Incomplete markets are understood in the context of "states of the world." A **state of the world**, or state of nature (or state), is a precisely defined and comprehensive description of an outcome of the economy that specifies the realized values of all economically important variables. For example, a particular state of the world might be briefly summarized as being when an equity market index closes at $X, a bond market index closes at $Y, the gross domestic product (GDP) of a particular nation reaches $Z, and so on. The concept is theoretical since it is impossible to fully describe the entire world or all states that could occur. However, the concept provides valuable insight into why many structured products exist.

To demonstrate, let's examine a highly simplified example in which an investor defines the states of the world on only three outcomes: her job, the level of the equity market, and the level of the debt market. One of the many states in this example might be an outcome in which global stock markets rise, interest rates fall, but the investor gets fired from her job. How can this investor prepare for this potential state of the world? One answer would be to purchase unemployment insurance—although it might be very expensive or impossible to get large amounts of insurance against the economic consequences of being fired. The reason, of course, is that the insurance company would be concerned about moral hazard: the possibility that the insured would intentionally perform poorly at work in order to collect insurance. The point is that markets will always be in a condition of having substantial and important incompleteness.

23.3.3 Structured Products as Market Completers

Although markets can never be complete, the primary role of structured products is to move them toward being more complete. For example, most investors would define the states of the world as including the condition of their physical properties. How can investors prepare for the potential that fire might destroy their real estate? The answer, of course, is to purchase fire insurance. Centuries ago, in a world with very incomplete markets, investors might not have been able to purchase fire insurance and so would have had to bear the very undesirable and highly diversifiable risk of losing substantial wealth due to fire. But in a complete market, investors could purchase fire insurance, a "security" that pays a substantial payoff in states in which the real estate burns and pays nothing in other states. This example illustrates that the primary economic role of insurance companies is to make the market more complete.

To summarize, people and organizations can be viewed as analyzing future scenarios of the world (i.e., states of the world) and estimating their probabilities. For risk management purposes, investors typically seek products that offer high payoffs in those states in which the investor's wealth would otherwise be low. For return enhancement purposes, investors might seek products that offer high payouts in states that the investor believes are unusually likely to occur. In both cases, the structuring of products serves the economic role of meeting the needs and preferences of these investors by completing the market. In other words, the structured products offer an otherwise unavailable combination of payoffs in various states that enables the investor to better manage risk and return.

In the context of alternative investments, financial institutions strive to meet the preferences of various investors by creating securities or products that move the market toward being more complete. As shown, insurance companies are an excellent example of a type of financial institution that addresses the deficiencies of incomplete markets. Major banks, insurance companies, and other financial institutions offer structured products that are tailored to the needs of individuals and institutions for risk management or risk enhancement purposes.

It should be noted that many simple financial derivatives, such as call options and put options, trade in the financial markets and can be used by market participants to manage basic risks of traditional assets, such as indices and individual securities. But when a market participant desires a product that is peculiar to individualized circumstances or preferences, structured products may be the solution that can be engineered to tailor a solution.

23.4 COLLATERALIZED MORTGAGE OBLIGATIONS

Collateralized mortgage obligations (CMOs) are an excellent example of a highly effective and somewhat simple use of structuring. CMOs assemble mortgage assets and finance those assets by issuing securities. CMOs divide the cash flows from assets such as mortgage pools or other mortgage-related products and distribute them with varying characteristics to different classes of security holders.

23.4.1 Prioritization of Claims within CMOs

The key distinguishing feature between CMOs and other investment pools, such as mutual funds or the mortgage-backed securities discussed in Chapter 12, is that CMOs use extensive structuring. Specifically, CMOs are financed with security classes or tranches that have substantially varied characteristics. A **tranche** is a distinct claim on assets that differs substantially from other claims in such aspects

Simplified CMO Structure

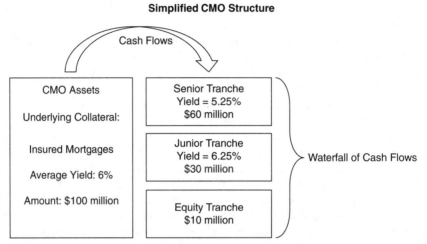

EXHIBIT 23.2 Simplified CMO Structure

as seniority, risk, and maturity. Each tranche is typically tradable in units that may differ in size.

A CMO issuer structures these tranches to have different seniorities to the cash flows from the underlying mortgages. Exhibit 23.2 illustrates a stylized CMO structure for insured mortgages with only three tranches. In practice, CMOs usually have numerous tranches.

The assets on the left side of Exhibit 23.2 are often referred to as the collateral pool. The assets generate the cash inflows that are structured and distributed to the various tranches. In the case of insured residential mortgages, the structuring of the cash flows focuses on maturity and cash flow timing, because lenders bear little or no risk of principal losses due to mortgage defaults. In the case of commercial mortgages and subprime residential mortgages, the focus of the structuring of the cash flows from the mortgage pool is more on the allocation of default losses, since these loans are generally not insured.

The issuer of the CMO receives the monthly mortgage payments (principal and interest payments) from the collateral pool, and after collecting its fees, the issuer passes the payments on to the various tranches, following the procedures and priorities defined in the CMO prospectus. Each tranche has a coupon that it is promised and a prespecified priority in receiving distributions of principal payments.

23.4.2 Structuring of Sequential-Pay CMOs

The **sequential-pay collateralized mortgage obligation** is the simplest form of CMO. In a sequential-pay CMO, each tranche receives a prespecified share of the interest payments based on each tranche's coupon and principal amount. Each tranche also potentially receives principal. When there is no default risk, it is the seniority to principal payments that is the focus of CMOs.

In the case of a sequential-pay CMO, the first-pay tranche (labeled as the senior tranche in Exhibit 23.2) receives all principal repayments until the tranche's face value has been fully repaid. As a tranche's principal is paid down, its receipt of coupon payments is proportionately reduced. A tranche matures once it has received repayment of its entire principal value. The next senior tranche then receives the entire principal payments until it, in turn, matures. There is a final tranche, typically called the Z-tranche, that receives any residual cash flows.

The purpose to the structuring offered by a CMO is that it provides investors with a spectrum of risk-and-return opportunities. For example, an investor seeking short-term, low-risk securities may purchase a highly senior tranche, while a longer-term investor might seek a tranche with a longer maturity, higher yield, and greater uncertainty of cash flow timing.

The structuring of the cash flows from the underlying mortgage collateral pools divides the prepayment risks (and, in other cases, default risks) of the pool into tranches that have low risk and tranches that have high risk. The higher-risk tranches can have extreme sensitivity to unexpected changes in prepayment rates (and, in some cases, default rates). Accordingly, the analysis and modeling of prepayment risks and default risks become even more crucial in the case of highly structured products.

In the case of insured residential mortgages, the exposure of each tranche to prepayment risk depends on the seniority of that tranche. The most senior tranches are virtually certain to mature quickly, regardless of prepayment rates. The tranches with the lowest seniority for receiving principal payments can have maturities that are extremely sensitive to prepayment rates. If interest rates increase, then prepayments by homeowners are likely to fall.

23.4.3 Longevity Characteristics of CMO Tranches

Fluctuations in interest rates and other factors that drive mortgage prepayments cause a phenomenon known as extension risk. **Extension risk** is dispersion in economic outcomes caused by uncertainty in the longevity—especially increased longevity—of cash flow streams. For example, when interest rates rise, prepayment rates usually fall, and the life of most tranches, especially the more junior tranches, is extended, thereby increasing or extending the expected life of the tranche further than originally expected. In most CMO tranches, extension lowers the value. This reflects the general tendency of fixed-income instruments to fall in value when interest rates rise. However, some tranches can benefit from extension. These types of tranches might fall in value due to contraction when anticipated longevity declines. **Contraction risk** is dispersion in economic outcomes caused by uncertainty in the longevity—especially decreased longevity—of cash flow streams.

23.4.4 Estimating Cash Flows through a CMO Structure

Consider a CMO with an underlying collateral pool of mortgages that generates $1,620,000 of cash flow in its first month (after fees): $1,500,000 in interest fees (9% annualized) and $120,000 in principal repayments. A stylized sequential-pay two-tranche CMO structure is presented in Exhibit 23.3. Payments are made first to Tranche A and then to Tranche B.

Exhibit 23.3 illustrates that, in month 1, both Tranche A and Tranche B receive their corresponding interest payments of $1,062,500 ($150,000,000 × 8.5%/12) for Tranche A and $437,500 ($50,000,000 × 10.5%/12) for Tranche B, for a total of $1,500,000 in interest payments. In this simplified example, the interest payments

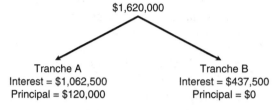

START OF MONTH VALUES

Tranche A	Tranche B
Principal = $150,000,000	Principal = $50,000,000
Coupon = 8.50%	Coupon = 10.50%

TOTAL CASH FLOW FROM POOL
$1,620,000

Tranche A	Tranche B
Interest = $1,062,500	Interest = $437,500
Principal = $120,000	Principal = $0

END-OF-MONTH VALUES

Tranche A	Tranche B
Principal = $149,880,000	Principal = $50,000,000

EXHIBIT 23.3   Stylized Example of $1,620,000 Cash Flow to a Sequential-Pay CMO with Two Tranches

received equal the interest payments owed to the two tranches, and there is no residual tranche. The remaining cash flow of $120,000 is a principal repayment received from the underlying collateral, and it is used only to pay principal to Tranche A. The reason is that this is a sequential-pay two-tranche CMO, in which principal payments are made to Tranche A until the principal of Tranche A has been fully paid off, after which payments are made to Tranche B. Therefore, at the end of month 1, the principal balance for Tranche A is reduced to $149,880,000 ($150,000,000 − $120,000), and the principal balance of Tranche B remains at the initial $50,000,000, since Tranche B received no principal payment.

The mechanics of the payments in the following months will be similar. In the case of Tranche A, however, the interest payments due in the second month will decline because the total principal is decreasing with each principal repayment. For example, in the second month, Tranche A would be entitled to interest payments of only $1,061,650 ($149,880,000 principal at 8.5%/12 interest).

The principal for Tranche B will start to be paid off only after the principal for Tranche A has been fully paid. If the prepayment rates of the mortgages underlying the CMO increase, Tranche A would be paid off faster and Tranche B would start to be amortized earlier. Conversely, if unscheduled principal repayments slow, the anticipated longevity of Tranche A will extend, but perhaps only modestly, as scheduled principal payments would presumably continue (i.e., extension risk would likely be minimal). However, the anticipated term of Tranche B could extend substantially. In this simplified example, Tranche B would continue until the last underlying mortgage made its final payment, and therefore, depending on prevailing rates and anticipated reinvestment opportunities, would likely be positively exposed to extension risk.

In actual CMO structures, there is typically an accrual tranche, or Z-bond, that receives no promised interest or coupon payments. Rather, the tranche serves as a residual, equity-like claimant, with rights to cash flows that remain after all fixed-income tranches have been satisfied.

23.4.5 Other CMO Structures and Tranches

Numerous variations can be structured within a CMO issue other than the sequential-pay structure introduced in the previous section. This section highlights an important aspect of structuring: There is often an evolution that occurs in structured products wherein relatively simply structured products, if successful, evolve into increasingly complex and sophisticated products.

Here are several of the more popular types of CMOs.

PLANNED AMORTIZATION CLASS TRANCHES: **Planned amortization class (PAC) tranches** receive principal payments in a more complex manner than do sequential pay CMOs. Investors in some PAC tranches have high priority for receiving principal payments as long as the prepayment rates are within a prespecified range (the planned prepayment levels). When prepayments diverge from what was originally projected, the relative priorities of tranches can shift. In a sequential-pay structure, the relation between tranche longevity and prepayment rates is somewhat linear, meaning that each tranche's longevity to changes in prepayment speeds is somewhat stable at various levels of prepayment. But with PAC tranches, it is possible that a tranche will contract in longevity as prepayment rates accelerate to a certain point but then extend in longevity beyond that point. In other words, a tranche might have high priority to receiving principal payments in one range of prepayment speed and low priority if other prepayment speeds occur. Thus, PAC tranches can be riskier and more complex to analyze.

TARGETED AMORTIZATION CLASS TRANCHES: **Targeted amortization class (TAC) tranches** receive principal payments in a manner similar to PAC tranches but generally with an even narrower and more complex set of ranges. The amortization procedures tend to identify narrower ranges of prepayment speeds within which tranches have particular priorities for receiving principal payments and interest. These prepayment ranges can be viewed more as targeted outcomes than as planned outcomes. TAC tranches can be especially complex and risky. A sensitive TAC tranche can quickly switch from being quickly paid off to receiving no principal payments (and vice versa), even when prepayment speeds change by only a small amount.

PRINCIPAL-ONLY TRANCHES AND INTEREST-ONLY TRANCHES: **Principal-only (PO) tranches** receive only principal payments from the collateral pool, whereas **interest-only (IO) tranches** receive only interest payments from the collateral pool. Both tranches are therefore created by dividing cash flows from the mortgage collateral into the portion that is principal repayment and the portion that is interest. The principal repayment cash flows are distributed to one bond, the PO, and the interest cash flows are distributed to a second bond, the IO.

Investors in PO bonds are ultimately paid the face value of their bonds as borrowers eventually make the principal payments on their mortgages. The logic behind a PO is that investors buy these bonds at a discount from face value and eventually receive the face value through the scheduled principal repayments and prepayments received from the mortgages. PO tranches are positively exposed to extension risk in that their values decline when prepayments slow, since they receive no coupons.

An IO bond has a notional principal used to compute each interest payment. The cash flows received by investors in IOs decline as the principal is paid down. IO tranches are positively exposed to contraction risk in that their values decline when prepayments accelerate, since their payments are only interest because the notional principal is not repaid.

Prepayment sensitivity tends to be severe for POs and IOs, with one generally profiting when the other suffers. For example, in the case of POs on fixed-rate mortgages, when interest rates decline, the speed of prepayments typically accelerates. This contraction in longevity reduces the life of both the IO and the PO. PO tranches benefit from quicker receipt of their only cash flows: principal repayments in the fixed amount of the PO's face value. IO tranches suffer from principal reductions, since their only cash flows (interest payments) are proportionately reduced. On the other hand, when interest rates increase, the speed of prepayments declines, and the PO investor is paid the face value further in the future, lowering its effective return, while the IO receives a longer annuity of interest payments. Both tranches can be issued with adjustable- and fixed-rate underlying mortgages.

FLOATING-RATE TRANCHES: **Floating-rate tranches** earn interest rates that are linked to an interest rate index, such as the London Interbank Offered Rate (LIBOR), and are usually used to finance collateral pools of adjustable-rate mortgages. A collateral pool of adjustable-rate mortgages provides a stream of variable interest rate payments that can flow through to floating-rate tranches, which also have floating coupons. Floating-rate tranches can be structured to have rates that move more than the underlying index (e.g., twice the floating rate) or even in the opposite direction, which is known as an inverse floater tranche. An **inverse floater tranche** offers a coupon that increases when interest rates fall and decreases when interest rates rise. Floating-rate tranches can have specified upper and lower limits to their adjustable coupons.

23.4.6 Motivations of Structured Mortgage Products

The primary motivations driving the demand for CMOs in the case of insured mortgages are summarized in Exhibit 23.4. Mortgages offer up to 30 years of coupons and principal payments, with high uncertainty regarding the level of unscheduled prepayments. Some investors prefer to take slices from this maturity range rather than invest in the entire range. Tranches permit investors to select securities that match their preferred exposures in terms of longevity and sensitivity to unscheduled prepayments.

As depicted in Exhibit 23.4, these preferences are driven by two primary motivations: risk and return. Investors can lower their risk by selecting tranches with durations that match the duration of their liability stream. Cash flow matching is one of many risk-reducing strategies that can be facilitated by the structuring of claims.

Some investors have a market view of future interest rates or prepayment speeds. An investor can select tranches of CMOs that offer enhanced returns to the extent that the investor's market view is superior.

In the cases of both motivations in Exhibit 23.4, the overall role being served by the CMOs is completion of the market. CMOs create numerous otherwise

---

1. *Risk management: Investors may be better able to manage risk through structured products.*
2. *Return enhancement: Investors may be better able to establish positions that will enhance returns if the investor's market view is superior.*

EXHIBIT 23.4 Investor Motivations for Structured Products

unavailable investment opportunities (i.e., tranches) from a pool of previously existing collateral. When the structuring is formulated in response to market demand, the enhanced set of opportunities facilitates improved portfolios from the perspective of the market participants.

23.4.7 Valuing Default-Free CMOs

Chapter 12 discusses unscheduled mortgage principal payments (i.e., prepayments). Prepayment decisions are made by property owners based on idiosyncratic events to the homeowners (e.g., job-related relocations) and macroeconomic factors, such as interest rates and housing prices. Chapter 12 discusses the role of these unscheduled prepayment rates in driving the risks, returns, and values of residential mortgage pools.

The effect of prepayment speeds on the valuation of CMO tranches can be even more critical than the effects on the overall mortgage pools. The reason is that structuring creates tranches with varying risks. Suppose that overall mortgage values drop by 1% due to increased interest rates. Whereas collateral pools will tend to drop by 1%, the losses to various tranches will vary based on the sensitivity of each tranche to interest rates. Long-term, highly sensitive tranches might drop by 5% or more, while very short-term tranches may be virtually unaffected. Some tranches, such as IO tranches, might even gain in value.

TAC, IO, and PO tranches can be especially sensitive to interest rates and prepayment speeds. Valuation of tranches requires careful and sophisticated analysis using advanced models of interest rates and prepayment speeds. The complexity of many CMOs creates both opportunities and threats. The sophistication of the models used to evaluate tranches creates the potential for analysts with superior skills to locate tranches of CMOs that are mispriced. However, the complexity of the products and models also carries the danger that analysts with inferior skills will be induced into consistently making trading decisions that generate negative net present values. Highly complex tranches with innovative characteristics can appear to be attractively priced when they are actually overpriced; thus, the importance of due diligence cannot be overstated.

23.4.8 Systemic Risk and the History of Structured Mortgage Products

There was a U.S. financial crisis involving CMOs on insured residential mortgages in 1994. Interest rates rose dramatically, causing most CMO tranches to extend in maturity as prepayment rates fell. The combination of extended maturities and higher interest rates caused market values of most tranches to fall, some quite severely. As investors and institutions suffered large losses, market liquidity eroded, and CMO tranches began to trade at prices reflecting even more conservative prepayment rate forecasts, further exacerbating the crisis.

Perhaps the worst case involved inverse-floating TAC tranches. Some of these tranches offered high coupons and were expected to mature within months at the end of 1993, due to high prepayment rates in the underlying mortgage pool and low interest rates. Therefore, these high-coupon and presumably short-term tranches traded at premium prices to their principal values and appeared to have little risk exposure to small or moderate interest rate changes. However, as part of a TAC structure, the tranches could experience dramatic shifts in seniority to principal payments if prepayment rates deviated from target ranges. In early 1994, prepayment speeds dropped such that the anticipated maturities of some of the TAC tranches extended from several months to many years, and switched from being the most senior to being the least senior tranches. Further, in the case of inverse floaters, the coupons on the tranches fell from high coupons to zero coupons as interest rates such as LIBOR skyrocketed.

The result was that some of the tranches, previously viewed by some market participants as having very low risk, fell from trading at premiums to trading at as little as 20% of face value by the summer of 1994. This incredible drop in value occurred on tranche securities even though there was never a doubt that the principal value of the tranche would ultimately be recovered, since the underlying mortgage pool was insured by U.S. government agencies. Many institutions suffered huge losses, some firms collapsed, and the crisis widened until interest rates reversed their climb in the fall of 1994.

The prevalence and power of the structuring of mortgage products is often cited as causing or exacerbating both the financial crisis of 1994 and the financial crisis that began in 2007. In the most recent financial crisis, the financial losses in mortgage-backed structured products centered on default risk. In both cases, structured products contributed to increased systemic risk, substantially harming or even bankrupting major financial institutions and increasing uncertainty throughout financial markets.

Despite the past problems with structured mortgage products, the power of structured products has generated tremendous benefits. The long maturity and substantial prepayment risk of insured residential mortgages make unstructured ownership of mortgages undesirable to most market participants. Mortgages offer cash flows that range in maturity from 1 month to 360 months and offer uncertainty as to the size of each cash flow due to the prepayment options held by the borrowers. Relatively few market participants find mortgages to be attractive direct investments because of their range of scheduled cash flows and their exposure to prepayment rates and interest rates.

However, structured mortgage products allow market participants to select longevities and risk exposures that more closely align with their preferences. Thus, shorter-term fixed-income money managers can purchase short-term senior tranches, and longer-term managers, such as pension funds, can focus on longer-term tranches of insured mortgages. The emergence of structured mortgage products in the past several decades coincides with substantially reduced mortgage rate spreads, suggesting that structured products have enabled hundreds of millions of homeowners to enjoy substantially lower financing costs.

23.4.9 Commercial CMOs and Default Risk

The previous sections discussed prepayment risk and extension risk. For CMOs with underlying portfolios of commercial mortgages or subprime residential mortgages, the primary risk is usually default risk. In CMO structures with substantial default risk, the primary result of the structuring of the cash flows is to vary the level of exposure of each tranche to default risk. The most senior tranches have the first right to scheduled and unscheduled principal payments and are last to bear losses from defaults. Conversely, the more junior tranches are highly subject to default losses from the underlying mortgage portfolio. The exposure of most CMO tranches to default risk is indicated by credit ratings assigned to each tranche.

As would be expected, credit ratings tend to differ quite considerably between the different tranches of a commercial mortgage-backed security (CMBS) because each tranche has different risk profiles, maturities, and subordination. Due to their subordination, more junior tranches have lower credit ratings. Conversely, senior tranches are often rated AAA because they have a high-priority claim on the cash flows and enjoy the extra security embedded by having initial default losses absorbed by the junior tranches.

The most junior tranches, often referred to as first-loss tranches, are often rated at non-investment-grade levels. This dispersion in credit risk exposure and credit ratings has the advantage of broadening the pool of appropriate investors. The senior, investment-grade-rated tranches are generally viewed as fixed-income securities, since they have limited expected exposure to default risk and are therefore primarily analyzed in the context of interest rate risk. In contrast, the most junior tranches are generally viewed and analyzed as risky securities substantially influenced by the risks of the underlying real estate rather than being influenced primarily by interest rate risks. Even a single large default can have a considerable impact on the performance of these junior securities. Therefore, in the case of CMBSs, junior tranches generally have higher coupons than senior tranches in the same structure. Particular attention is placed on the credit quality and other risk characteristics of the underlying mortgage pool, which is the collateral for the structure.

Default-risk CMO models focus on the expected rates of default, the correlation between defaults, and the losses on each defaulted issue. The idea is to forecast the probabilities of various cash flow streams from the underlying mortgage pool and to project the likelihood of payoffs to each of the tranches.

23.5 STRUCTURAL MODEL APPROACH TO CREDIT RISK

A key approach to understanding and analyzing credit risk uses structural models. **Structural credit risk models** use option theory to explicitly take into account credit risk and the various underlying factors that drive the default process, such as (1) the behavior of the underlying assets, and (2) the structuring of the cash flows (i.e., debt levels). Typically, structural models directly relate valuation of debt securities to financial characteristics of the economic entity that has issued the credit security. These factors include firm-level variables, such as the debt-to-equity ratio and the volatility of asset values or cash flows. The key is that credit risk is understood through analysis and observation of the entity's underlying assets and its financial structure.

23.5.1 The Intuition of Merton's Structural Model

Robert Merton pioneered the understanding of the option-like aspects of capital structure.[1] The key to Merton's approach is to recognize the option-like characteristics of structured cash flows, especially the option-like characteristics of credit risk that are inherent in the simplified capital structure of a traditional operating firm.

For simplicity, assume that a levered operating firm has only two securities: a single issue of zero-coupon debt and a single class of equity. Perhaps the most intuitive way of seeing the option-like nature of traditional corporate securities is based on call options. The **call option view of capital structure** views the equity of a levered firm as a call option on the assets of the firm. The call option implicit in equity has a strike price equal to the face value of the debt and an expiration date equal to the maturity date of the debt. If the firm does well, the firm pays its debt holders fully when the debt matures, and the assets of the firm belong to the shareholders. If the firm does poorly, the shareholders can declare bankruptcy and walk away from the firm, leaving the assets to the debt holders. The situation is highly analogous to a traditional call option, in which the owner of the call either pays the strike price of the option to claim the underlying asset or lets the option expire worthless. Equity holders are like the owner of a call option who enjoys unlimited upside potential from gains in the underlying asset but has limited loss exposure to declines in the underlying asset, since the option can be allowed to expire. This situation is depicted in Equation 23.1:

$$\text{Equity of Levered Firm} = \text{Call Option on Firm's Assets} \qquad (23.1)$$

The view of the equity of a corporation as a call option also leads to an option-based view of the corporation's debt. Specifically, if the value of the assets of the firm equals the sum of the liabilities plus equity, and if equity is a call option, then owning debt is equivalent to owning the assets and writing a call option. In other words, owning debt is equivalent to owning a covered call, meaning being long assets and short a call option on those assets.

An analogous application of options theory can be performed using put options rather than call options. Note that due to put-call parity (see Chapter 6), a call option can be viewed as a long position in a put option and the underlying assets financed with a riskless bond. By inserting these positions in place of the call options from the call option view of capital structure, the relationship is changed to the put option view of capital structure. The **put option view of capital structure** views the equity holders of a levered firm as owning the firm's assets through riskless financing and having a put option to deliver those assets to the debt holders. As depicted in Equation 23.2, the risky debt of a levered firm can be viewed as being equivalent to owning a riskless bond and writing a put option that allows the stockholders to put the assets of the firm to the debt holders without further liability (i.e., in exchange for the debt).

$$\text{Debt of Levered Firm} = \text{Riskless Bond} - \text{Put Option on Firm's Assets} \quad (23.2)$$

In Equation 23.2, the put option reflects the ability of equity owners to declare bankruptcy and enjoy limited liability. If the assets fall sufficiently, the debt holders suffer losses because they must pay a strike price to the stockholders that equals the face value of the riskless bond. In default, debt holders receive only the depleted value of the underlying assets rather than the face value of their debt, a risk that is captured by the short put position that debt holders have in the put option view of capital structure (part of which is shown in Equation 23.2).

Within either the call option view or the put option view of the levered firm, the value of the securities of a firm can be viewed in terms of the values of the underlying assets and the options on those assets. Accordingly, arbitrage-free option pricing models such as the Black-Scholes option pricing model (discussed in Chapter 6) may be used to analyze credit instruments. The analyst implementing the structural approach examines market prices to find reasonable values of the model's parameters, such as asset volatility and interest rate levels, and inserts those parameters into the structural model to generate prices for assets with credit risk.

23.5.2 The Conflict of Interest Regarding Risk in Structuring

There is an inherent conflict between the stockholders and the bondholders with regard to the optimal level of risk for a firm's assets. The equity holders, with their long position in a call option, prefer higher levels of risk, especially when the value of the firm's assets is near or below the face value of the debt. This is because the value of the equity at the maturity of the debt is the maximum of zero and the difference between the value of the firm's assets and the face value of the debt. As long as there is time before the debt matures and volatility in the value of the underlying assets, the implicit call option of the equity has time value. Importantly, the time value of the equity as a call option monotonically increases with higher asset volatilities (everything else being equal). Especially when the credit risk of the debt is high, equity holders may have a strong incentive to encourage managers to invest in risky projects, because if the projects fail, the bondholders are the losers, whereas the shareholders gain more when the projects succeed. Conversely, bondholders prefer safer projects and reduced asset volatility, as seen through their short position in a put option. The conflict of interest may be viewed as a zero-sum game in which managers can transfer wealth from bondholders to stockholders by increasing the risk of the firm's assets (or vice versa).

The conflict of interest between stockholders and bondholders in the capital structure of a firm is similar to the case of structured products with multiple tranches. The manager of the collateral pool can cause wealth transfers between tranches by altering the risk of the assets. In most structures, high levels of asset risk benefit junior tranche holders at the expense of senior tranche holders.

23.5.3 The Mechanics of Merton's Structural Model

This section takes a more precise look at Merton's application of option theory to credit risk. Throughout this discussion, it is assumed that the firm has a simple capital structure consisting of a single issue of debt in the form of a zero-coupon bond and a single issue of equity. The structural model view of the firm's capital structure expresses the firm's debt and equity in terms of a hypothetical call option and put option on the firm's assets, with a strike price equal to the face value of the zero coupon bond and an expiration date equal to the maturity of the bond.

Inserting the call option view of the equity of a firm and the put option view of the debt into the fundamental relationship that the value of the firm equals the sum of the value of the equity and the debt produces the relation in Equation 23.3:

$$\text{Assets} = [\text{Call}] + [\text{Riskless Bond} - \text{Put}] \tag{23.3}$$

The term in the first bracket on the right-hand side of Equation 23.3 represents the equity, and the terms in the second bracket represent the firm's risky debt. Note that the value of the risky debt is equal to the value of an otherwise identical riskless bond reduced by the value of the put. The reduction in the value of the debt by the value of the put option is the market's price for bearing the credit risk of the firm.

☞ APPLICATION 23.5.3A

Consider a firm with $50 million in assets and $25 million in equity value. The firm has one debt issue: a zero-coupon bond maturing in one year with a face value of $30 million. A riskless zero-coupon bond of the same maturity sells for 90% of its face value. What is the value of the firm's debt? What is the value of a one-year put option on the firm's assets with a strike price of $30 million?

Since the assets are worth $50 million and the equity is worth $25 million, the firm's risky debt must be worth $25 million, since Assets = Equity + Risky Debt. Since the riskless bond in Equation 23.3 is worth $27 million, the put option must be worth $2 million.

Equation 23.3 illustrates the conflict of interest between stockholders and bondholders. Consider a change in the anticipated volatility of the firm's assets that leaves the current value of the firm's assets unchanged. Perhaps the firm embarked on a risky venture with a net present value of zero. Equation 23.3 indicates that the equity is a long position in a call option on the underlying assets of a levered firm. Thus, the value of the equity, like any call option, will rise when the volatility of the underlying assets increases (everything else being equal). Equation 23.3 indicates that for every dollar that the equity increases in value, the firm's risky debt must fall in value by $1. The decline in the value of the firm's debt is captured in Equation 23.3 as an increase in the value of the put option. Equity's increase when volatility increases is due to its long vega exposure, while the decline in the value of the debt is due to its short vega exposure.

23.5.4 Valuing Risky Debt with Black-Scholes Option Pricing

The Black-Scholes option pricing model can be used along with Equation 23.3 to derive estimates of the value of debt that contains credit risk. In other words, fixed-income analysts can value risky debt using option pricing models. For example, a credit analyst wishes to value the risk of Firm XYZ's only issue of debt. The analyst follows a four-step process, which involves estimating the volatility of the firm's assets and using the estimated volatility to price the debt:

1. Estimating the volatility of Firm XYZ's equity: This estimate may be derived through analysis of XYZ's historical stock volatility, through the implied volatility of options on XYZ's stock, or through a combination of the two approaches.
2. Unlevering XYZ's estimated equity volatility (from step 1) based on XYZ's capital structure: XYZ's estimated asset volatility, σ_{assets}, can be approximated as

XYZ's estimated equity volatility, σ_{equity}, times the ratio of the value of XYZ's equity to the value of the firm's assets, as illustrated in Equation 23.4 (assuming that the debt is riskless for simplicity).

$$\sigma_{assets} \approx \sigma_{equity} \times (\text{Equity}/\text{Assets}) \tag{23.4}$$

3. Solving for the price of a call and put on the firm's assets: The estimated asset volatility can be inserted into the Black-Scholes option pricing model along with observable parameters to generate call and put prices.
4. Using the call price as the value of XYZ's stock, and subtracting the put price from the price of a riskless bond to value XYZ's debt.

☞ APPLICATION 23.5.4A

Consider a firm with $100 million in assets and $60 million in equity value. The firm's debt has a face value of $50 million and a maturity of one year. The volatility of the firm's equity is estimated at 40%. How would an analyst estimate the value of the firm's equity if the volatility of the firm's assets doubled?

Step 2 is based on Equation 23.4 and unlevers the current equity volatility from 40% to an asset volatility of 24% through multiplying the equity volatility (40%) by the ratio of the value of the equity to the value of the assets ($60 million/$100 million, or 0.60). A doubling in the asset volatility increases the asset volatility to 48%. The value of the firm's equity can be found using an option pricing model for a call option, with an underlying asset value of $100 million, an underlying asset volatility of 48%, a strike price of $50 million, a time to expiration of one year, and the prevailing riskless rate.

Note that the accuracy of estimated option values may be reduced to the extent that the assumptions of the model are violated. Three assumptions are particularly troublesome: (1) that the percentage changes in the values of the firm's underlying assets through time are lognormally distributed, (2) that the volatility of the firm's assets can be accurately estimated, and (3) that there is a single issue of debt with no coupon. Nevertheless, option pricing models can be especially useful in providing normative guidance of relative yields within the same firm or between similar firms.

23.5.5 Binomial Trees and Structured Product Valuation

The application of the structural model is not limited to the use of the Black-Scholes option pricing model. Chapter 9 discussed the application of binomial option pricing to real options—that is, options regarding real assets. As introduced in Chapter 5, binomial tree models are extremely flexible and valuable tools for analyzing assets with embedded options. In the case of credit instruments, binomial tree models allow analysts to estimate prices based on volatilities and observable parameters using the principles of risk-neutral pricing.

For example, the value of credit-risky securities in a capital structure or a structured product can often be well estimated using two underlying binomial trees: one for the value of the assets, and one for interest rates. The analyst simply estimates future cash flows contingent on the asset values and then prices the securities through backward induction. Whereas the Black-Scholes option pricing model is often used in simple option analysis, it is the binomial tree approach that serves as the primary valuation tool in the case of most structured products with complex optionalities.

23.5.6 Advantages and Disadvantages of Structural Model Applications

Merton's structural model and its extensions have two major potential advantages:

1. The structural approach tends to rely on data from equity markets, such as observed stock price volatilities or implied stock price volatilities backed out of option prices. Since equity markets are generally more liquid and transparent than corporate bond markets, some argue that equity markets provide more reliable information than credit markets provide.
2. Structural models are well suited for handling different securities of the same issuer, including bonds of various seniorities and convertible bonds. The different securities or tranches rely on the same assets with the same asset parameters.

The structural model has three major disadvantages as well:

1. If equity prices are highly unreliable, then estimates of asset volatility and values are also highly unreliable. For example, private equity or real estate equity valuations may be unreliable sources to the extent that the valuations are not based on liquid markets.
2. Current data on a firm's or structure's liabilities may be unreliable and, in the case of sovereign issuers, may be unworkable.
3. The valuations generated by simple structural models are sometimes unreasonable, especially for short-term, very high-quality debt and for debt that is very near default.

23.6 INTEREST RATE OPTIONS

In this section, we describe and value interest rate caps and floors—two important types of interest rate derivatives. The interest rate derivatives market is the largest derivative market in the world.

23.6.1 Interest Rate Caps

In an interest rate cap, one party agrees to pay the other when a specified reference rate is above a predetermined rate (known as the cap rate, which is similar to the strike price of a European call option). A **caplet** is an interest rate cap guaranteed for only one specific date. A **cap** is a series of caplets, and its price is equal to the sum of the prices of the caplets, which, in turn, can be valued using various term-structure models and a procedure similar to the Black-Scholes option pricing model. Issuers of floating-rate debt can buy these options contracts to hedge against the possibility of increases in short-term interest rates (i.e., against variable or floating interest rate risk). Caps, also known as ceilings, work as insurance, a service for which purchasers of these contracts pay sellers a premium. Equation 23.5 denotes the periodic payment for a cap based on m periods per year:

Cap Payment = Max[(Reference Rate − Strike Rate), 0] × Notional Value$/m$

$$(23.5)$$

To illustrate, consider a three-year interest rate cap. Party A buys the interest rate cap from party B with the following terms: The contract is for three years, the strike rate is 3%, the reference rate is three-month LIBOR, settlement is every three months, and the notional value is $10 million. Thus, every three months for the next three years, B will pay A if three-month LIBOR exceeds the strike rate of 3% at settlement. For example, suppose that the three-month LIBOR (i.e., the reference rate) is 4% on a settlement date. In this case, B will pay A $25,000, which is given by (4% − 3%) × $10,000,000/4 = $25,000. Suppose instead that three-month LIBOR is 2% on a settlement date. In this case, B will not make any payment to A. The maximum amount that A can lose from entering into this options contract is the up-front premium that A paid for the option.

☞ APPLICATION 23.6.1A

Firm XYZ buys an interest rate cap from Bank DEF. The cap is for five years, has a strike rate of 5%, is settled quarterly, and has a notional value of $50 million. What are the payments, if any, from Bank DEF to Firm XYZ in the first four quarters, if the reference rates for those quarters are, respectively, 4%, 5%, 6%, and 7%?

The solution is found using Equation 23.5, with $m = 4$ and the strike rate equal to 5%. For the third quarter, the formula is (6% − 5%) × $50,000,000/4, which is equal to $125,000. The four answers are $0, $0, $125,000, and $250,000. Note that the formula for a cap generates no payment when the strike rate equals or exceeds the reference rate.

23.6.2 Interest Rate Floors

In an **interest rate floor**, one party agrees to pay the other when a specified reference rate is below a predetermined rate (known as the floor rate, which is analogous to the strike price of a European put option). A **floorlet** is an interest rate floor guaranteed for only one specific date. A **floor** is a series of floorlets, and its price is equal to the sum of the prices of the floorlets. Similar to caps, floors can be valued using derivative pricing models like the Black-Scholes option pricing model. These options contracts can be purchased by lenders in floating-rate debt to hedge against the possibility of declining short-term interest rates. A seller in an interest rate floor is compensated for guaranteeing the interest rate. Equation 23.6 denotes the periodic payment for a cap based on m periods per year:

Floor Payment = Max[(Strike Rate − Reference Rate), 0] × Notional Value$/m$

$$(23.6)$$

To illustrate, consider a four-year interest rate floor. Party A buys the interest rate floor from party B with the following terms: The contract is for four years, the strike rate is 3%, the reference rate is three-month LIBOR, settlement is every three months, and the notional value is $20 million. Thus, every three months for the next four years B will pay A if three-month LIBOR is less than the strike rate of 3% at settlement. For example, suppose that the three-month LIBOR (i.e., the reference rate) is 1% on a settlement date. In this case, B will pay A $100,000, which is given by (3% − 1%) × $20,000,000/4 = $100,000. Suppose instead that three-month LIBOR is 4% on a settlement date. In this case, B will not make any payment to A. The maximum amount that A can lose from entering into this options contract is the up-front premium that A paid for the option.

☞ APPLICATION 23.6.2A

Firm XYZ buys an interest rate floor from Bank DEF. The floor is for three years, has a strike rate of 7%, is settled quarterly, and has a notional value of $10 million. What are the payments, if any, from Bank DEF to Firm XYZ in the first four quarters if the reference rates for those quarters are, respectively, 4%, 6%, 8%, and 10%?

The solution is found using Equation 23.6, with $m = 4$ and the strike rate equal to 7%. For the first quarter, the formula is (7% − 4%) × $10,000,000/4, which is equal to $75,000. The four answers are $75,000, $25,000, $0, and $0. Note that the formula for a floor generates no payment when the strike rate is equal to or less than the reference rate.

23.6.3   Interest Rate Options and Counterparty Risk

The parties to caps or floors are exposed to interest rate risk, which can be used to hedge the risk present in an existing position. However, since caps and floors are not typically exchange-traded instruments, there will be some exposure to counterparty risk. With either instrument, the buyers are exposed to counterparty risk because the potential payoffs are paid by long options writers. However, because the options writers are paid up front, the writers have no exposure to the credit risk of the buyer.

23.7   INTRODUCTION TO COLLATERALIZED DEBT OBLIGATIONS

This section introduces the concept of a collateralized debt obligation. A **collateralized debt obligation** (CDO) applies the concept of structuring to cash flows from a portfolio of debt securities into multiple claims; these claims are securities and are referred to as tranches.

Of course, in practice, traditional operating corporations and other applications of structuring are usually financed with numerous classes of securities. Major corporations usually have multiple types of debt (accounts payable, short-term credit facilities, senior bonds, junior bonds) or preferred stock. Some corporations even have multiple types of equity, which may differ in terms of voting rights or liquidity. The concept of multiple security types also extends beyond the traditional operating firm to such applications as multiple commercial mortgages on a single property, multiple types of securities as sources of capital for closed-end funds, and multiple bond issues for various levels of government.

The use of structuring to create multiple security types in alternative investing centers on CDOs. The concept of a CDO is relatively new, but in just a few decades, CDOs have become an important part of financial institutions, markets, and activities. As previously illustrated in the case of mortgages, the structures are quite simple. In its simplest form, a CDO is a collection or portfolio of assets financed with multiple securities (or tranches) that differ in regard to their seniority. This section provides an introduction to the structuring of cash flows for default risk. Chapter 25 provides a more detailed discussion of various types of CDO structures, purposes for their establishment, and their common applications.

23.7.1 A Stylized CDO

Exhibit 23.5 illustrates the concept of a CDO that is being used to structure the cash flows and default risk from a portfolio of high-yield bonds. There are $100 million of high-yield bonds on the left-hand side of Exhibit 23.5 that serve as the assets or collateral portfolio (or pool) for the structure. These bonds generate cash flows in the form of coupon payments and principal payments. The bond portfolio can also generate losses from events such as defaults in the bonds and from profits or losses from trading activity. On the right-hand side of the structure are the various classes of securities (or tranches) that provided the financing for the portfolio and that have claims of varying seniorities to receive cash inflows.

The cash flows from the collateral pool of assets are distributed using a waterfall approach somewhat analogous to that discussed in Chapter 2 for limited

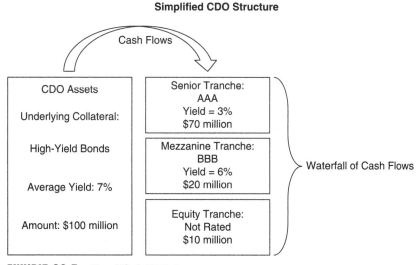

EXHIBIT 23.5 Simplified CDO Structure

partnerships. Without any defaults, the assets should generate $7 million in coupon income, found as the product of the asset size ($100 million) and the average coupon of the assets (7%). The first priority of the cash flows is to meet direct expenses and fees for the operation and management of the CDO. For simplicity, this example ignores the expenses and fees.

After expenses and fees, the cash flows are distributed to the various tranches in order of their seniority. The **senior tranche** is a tranche with the first or highest priority to cash flows in the structured product. In this case, the senior tranche is owed the first $2.1 million per year in coupon income, found as the product of its size ($70 million) and the coupon rate (3%). A **mezzanine tranche** is a tranche with a moderate priority to cash flows in the structured product and with lower priority than the senior tranche. In this case, the mezzanine tranche is owed $1.2 million per year after the senior tranche has been paid. The **equity tranche** has lowest priority and serves as the residual claimant. In this case, the equity tranche has claim to the remaining $3.7 million.

☞ APPLICATION 23.7.1A

Suppose that the CDO depicted in Exhibit 23.5 alters its portfolio such that the average coupon on the assets is 6%. Ignoring defaults, fees, and expenses, how much annual income should be available to the equity tranche?

The answer is that $3.3 million would go to the senior and mezzanine tranches, and $2.7 million would be available for the equity tranche.

23.7.2 Default Risk and CDO Cash Flows

The previous numerical example ignored defaults in the bond portfolio. However, this CDO contains bonds subject to substantial credit risk, since they are below investment grade (i.e., are rated BB or lower), and therefore it is reasonable to expect defaults. When collateral assets default, the order of the waterfall reverses relative to the order for receiving cash flows, such that the lowest seniority tranches experience the losses first. The losses from asset defaults are posted against the lowest remaining tranche until that tranche is wiped out, at which point the losses are posted against the next lowest seniority tranche. For example, if $11 million of assets completely defaulted (i.e., experienced no recovery), the equity tranche would be wiped out, and the notional principal of the mezzanine tranche would be reduced from $20 million to $19 million. If $11 million of assets defaulted with 60% recovery, the assets would drop by only $4.4 million, causing loss only to the equity tranche.

Note that defaults in the CDO's collateral portfolio reduce both the left and right sides of Exhibit 23.5. The assets are reduced in size and in annual income. The aggregated tranches are reduced in size by reducing the tranches, starting with the lowest-seniority tranche. As the debt tranches are reduced in notional principal, their claim to coupon income is reduced. Thus, if the mezzanine tranche in the example is reduced from $20 million to $19 million, the annual coupons owed to the mezzanine tranche holders would fall from $1.20 million to $1.14 million.

APPLICATION 23.7.2A

Suppose that the CDO depicted in Exhibit 23.5 experiences defaults in $50 million of the assets with 30% recovery. What will happen to the tranches?

First, note that the 30% recovery reduces the losses to 70% of $50 million ($35 million). After the equity tranche is eliminated due to the first $10 million in defaults, the mezzanine tranche is eliminated due to the next $20 million in defaults. The remaining $5 million of defaults will bring down the notional value of the senior tranche from $70 million to $65 million. The senior tranche has first priority to the recovered value of the bonds ($15 million), which may be distributed to the senior tranche, further reducing its notional value to $50 million.

23.7.3 Attachment Points, Detachment Points, Calls, and Puts

Note that the 20% of the structure in Exhibit 23.5 that is represented by the mezzanine debt tranche lies between the 70% financed by senior debt and the 10% financed by the most junior tranche (the equity tranche). As losses to the collateral pool are experienced due to defaults in the portfolio of bonds, the first 10% of the losses are applied against the equity tranche, and the last 70% are applied against the senior tranche. Thus, the losses to the mezzanine tranche begin when 10% of the collateral assets have been lost to default and end when 30% of the collateral assets have been lost to default and the mezzanine tranche is eliminated.

The first percentage loss in the collateral pool that begins to cause reduction in a tranche is known as the **lower attachment point**, or simply the **attachment point**. The higher percentage loss point at which the given tranche is completely wiped out is known as the **upper attachment point**, or the **detachment point**. Thus, the mezzanine tranche in the simplified example has a lower attachment point of 10% and an upper attachment point of 30%. Each tranche is often identified using these points, such that the mezzanine tranche in the example might be described as being a 10%/30% mezzanine tranche.

The risks and payoffs to the most senior and most junior tranches in a CDO can be viewed using positions in either a call or a put. Similarly, the structural credit risk model discussed earlier in this chapter expressed the positions of equity holders and debt holders in the traditional capital structure of an operating firm as being synonymous with call options or put options. The senior debt tranche in the example illustrated in Exhibit 23.5 may be viewed in the structural model as either a covered call or a riskless bond with a short put position on the assets. Similarly, the equity tranche can be viewed in the structural model as either a long position in a call option or a financed long position in the assets with a long put position.

23.7.4 Option Collars Are Similar to a Mezzanine Tranche

The economic essence of the 10%/30% mezzanine tranche in the previous section was that the mezzanine tranche benefits from investment success in the collateral pool within the range of the assets retaining 70% of their value to 90% of their value. If the assets fall below 70% of their original value, the mezzanine tranche is wiped out, and the senior tranche begins bearing losses. If the assets retain 90% or more of their value, the value in excess of 90% benefits the equity tranche. Whereas the most senior and most junior tranches can be viewed with single positions in options, mezzanine tranches can be viewed with option strategies involving two options. There are three theoretically equivalent option strategies that mimic a mezzanine tranche, each involving two options: a collar position, a bull call spread, and a bull put spread.

Let's begin with viewing a mezzanine tranche as a collar position. As detailed in Chapter 6, a collar combines a long position in an asset with a short position in a call option and a long position in a put option. In this example, the long position in the asset is 70% financed. Both options are on the same asset and have the same expiration date, but the call option has a higher strike price than the put option. Owning a mezzanine tranche is like owning the collateral asset, owning a put option that places a floor on losses when the assets are below a particular amount (70% in the example), and writing a call option that places a cap on profits when the assets remain at or above a particular amount (90% in the example).

Thus, the mezzanine tranche in Exhibit 23.5 may be described as a collar with a financed position in the collateral pool, a long position in a put at the lower attachment point, and a short position in a call at the upper attachment point. The mezzanine tranche is net long between $70 million and $90 million in assets, with profits limited at and above $90 million in assets, and losses limited at and below $70 million in assets.

23.7.5 Mezzanine Tranches and Option Spreads

As noted in Chapter 6, a collar position has the same payout as a bull option spread; thus, a mezzanine tranche may be mimicked with a bull option spread. A bull spread combines a long and short position in either calls or puts, which differ only with regard to strike prices. A bull spread involves a long position in the option with the lower strike price and a short position in the option with the higher strike price. The bull spread offers positively correlated performance between the strike prices, places a cap on profits at the higher strike price, and places a floor on losses at the lower strike price. The top left panel in Exhibit 6.7 illustrates the profit and loss diagram of a bull spread (as well as a collar position).

Bull spreads may be formed with two calls or two puts. A **bull call spread** has two calls that differ only by strike price, in which the long position is in the lower strike price and the short position is in the higher strike price. A **bull put spread** has two puts that differ only by strike price, in which the long position is in the lower strike price and the short position is in the higher strike price. Bear spreads are the mirror positions. The underlying assets to the options are the collateral pool.

A bull call spread that mimics the 10%/30% mezzanine tranche in the example contains a long call option with a strike price of $70 million and a short call option with a strike price of $90 million. The bull call spread, like the mezzanine tranche, benefits from increases in the collateral pool between $70 million and $90 million. The analogous bull spread with put options (i.e., a bear call spread) is long a put option with a strike price of $70 million and short a put option with a strike price of $90 million. In summary, a mezzanine tranche can be viewed as a bull call spread or a bull put spread on the CDO's portfolio.

It may appear counterintuitive that a bull option spread has a long position in the option with the lower strike price and a short position in the option with the higher strike price regardless of whether the spread uses calls or puts. However, note that in the previous example, when the structure's assets (i.e., the collateral pool) are worth $80 million, the bull call spread has only one option that is in-the money (a long call), and the bull put spread has only one option that is in-the-money (a short put). Both a long call and a short put are bullish positions.

REVIEW QUESTIONS

1. What is the similarity between a structured product and the capital structure of an operating firm?
2. What is the primary role of structuring in an economy?
3. How could a financial market become less complete?
4. From an investor's viewpoint, what is the difference between owning a tranche in a sequential-pay CMO and owning a tranche in a TAC CMO in a rising interest rate environment?
5. What is the extension risk and contraction risk of a PO tranche to a CMO?
6. What are the two major types of investor motivations to investing in a tranche of a CMO rather than investing directly in mortgages similar to the mortgages of the CMO's collateral pool?
7. Name two prominent time periods when structured mortgage products are believed to have increased systemic risk and led to a financial crisis. What is the major difference between the underlying economic events that led to the losses in these two crises?
8. In Merton's structural model, how is debt with default risk viewed as having exposure to a put option?
9. In Merton's structural model, what is the conflict of interest between stockholders and debt holders with regard to asset risk, and how does this conflict relate to structured products?
10. What are three major option strategies that resemble the ownership of a mezzanine tranche?

NOTE

1. Robert C. Merton, "On the Pricing of Corporate Debt: The Risk Structure of Interest Rates," *Journal of Finance* 29, no. 2 (1974): 449–70.

Credit Risk and Credit Derivatives

Credit risk is dispersion in financial outcomes associated with the failure or potential failure of a counterparty to fulfill its financial obligations. In contrast to equity-related risk, which tends to have somewhat symmetrical payoff distributions, credit risk generally leads to payoff distributions that are substantially skewed to the left. In other words, the upside performance of a traditional position exposed to credit risk is limited to the recovery of the original investment plus the promised yield, whereas the downside performance could lead to the loss of the entire investment.

> ✔ **FOUNDATION CHECK**
>
> The material in this chapter assumes familiarity with credit ratings, credit spreads, and credit rating migration.

24.1 AN OVERVIEW OF CREDIT RISK

Default risk is the risk that the issuer of a bond or the debtor on a loan will not repay the interest and principal payments of the outstanding debt in full. A debtor is deemed to be in default when it fails to make a scheduled payment on its outstanding obligations. Default risk can be complete, in that no amount of the bond or loan will be repaid, or it can be partial, in that some portion of the original debt will be recovered.

Credit risk is influenced by both macroeconomic events and company-specific events. For instance, credit risk typically increases during recessions or slowdowns in the economy. In an economic contraction, revenues and earnings decline across a broad swath of industries, reducing the interest coverage with respect to loans and outstanding bonds for many companies caught in the slowdown. Additionally, credit risk can be affected by a liquidity crisis when investors seek the haven of liquid U.S. government securities. This was demonstrated clearly in the global financial crisis of 2007 to 2009.

Idiosyncratic or company-specific events are unrelated to the business cycle and affect a single company at a time. These events could be due to a deteriorating client base, an obsolete business plan, noncompetitive products, outstanding litigation, fraud, or any other reason that shrinks the revenues, assets, and earnings of a particular company.

As a company's credit quality deteriorates, a larger credit risk premium is demanded to compensate investors for the risk of default. In fact, the non–U.S. Treasury fixed-income market is often referred to as the spread product market. This is because all other U.S.-dollar-denominated fixed-income products (e.g., bank loans, high-yield bonds, investment-grade corporate bonds, and emerging markets debt) trade at a credit spread relative to U.S. Treasury securities. Similarly, risky debt denominated in other currencies trades at a credit spread over the bonds of the dominant sovereign issuer in that currency.

24.2 REDUCED-FORM MODELING OF CREDIT RISK

Credit risk emanates from the structuring of cash flows. Cash flows are promised but are backed by an uncertain ability to meet those contractual obligations. Financial institutions and investors who have substantial exposure to credit risk look for effective ways to measure and manage their credit exposures consistently and accurately. This has led to a growing body of knowledge regarding credit models. Hedge funds and other institutions that take on credit exposure to enhance the risk-return profiles of their portfolios employ these models to implement various relative value and arbitrage strategies. Credit models are also employed to price illiquid securities that do not have reliable market prices and to calculate hedge ratios.

24.2.1 Intuition of Reduced-Form Credit Risk Models

Speaking broadly, credit models can be divided into two groups: structural models and reduced-form models. Structural models, discussed in Chapter 25, explicitly take into account underlying factors that drive the default process, such as the volatility of the underlying assets and the structuring of the cash flows (i.e., debt levels). Structural models directly relate the valuation of debt securities to the financial characteristics of the economic entity that has issued the credit security. These factors usually include firm-level variables, such as the debt-to-equity ratio and the volatility of asset values or cash flows. The key is that structural credit models describe credit risk in terms of the risks of the underlying assets and the financial structures that have claims to the underlying assets (i.e., degree of leverage).

Reduced-form credit models, in contrast, do not attempt to look at the structural reasons for default risk. Therefore, reduced-form credit models do not rely extensively on asset volatility or underlying structural details, such as the degree of leverage, to analyze credit risk. Instead, **reduced-form credit models** focus on default probabilities based on observations of market data of similar-risk securities. In other words, reduced-form approaches typically model the observed relationships among yield spreads, default rates, recovery rates, and frequencies of rating changes throughout the market. The key feature of reduced-form credit models is that credit risk is understood through analysis and observation of market data from similar credit risks rather than through the underlying structural details of the entities, such as the amount of leverage.

24.2.2 Expected Loss Due to Credit Risk

In general, the expected credit loss of a credit exposure can be determined by three factors:

1. **Probability of default** (PD), which specifies the probability that the counterparty fails to meet its obligations
2. **Exposure at default** (EAD), which specifies the nominal value of the position that is exposed to default at the time of default
3. **Loss given default** (LGD), which specifies the economic loss in case of default[1]

The converse of LGD is the economic proceeds given default—that is, the recovery rate (RR). The recovery rate is the percentage of the credit exposure that the lender ultimately receives through the bankruptcy process and all available remedies. Therefore, $LGD = (1 - RR)$, and $RR = (1 - LGD)$.

Given these three factors, and expressing the loss given default through the recovery rate, the expected credit loss can be expressed as follows:

$$\text{Expected Credit Loss} = PD \times EAD \times (1 - RR) \qquad (24.1)$$

☞ APPLICATION 24.2.2A

A bank has extended a $50 million one-year loan at an interest rate of 14% to a client with a BBB credit rating. Suppose that historical data indicate that the one-year probability of default for firms with a BBB rating is 5% and that investors are typically able to recover 40% of the notional value of an unsecured loan to such firms. What is the expected credit loss?

The expected credit loss of the bank is as follows:

PD = 5%
EAD = $50 million × (1 + 0.14) = $57 million
RR = 0.40 so that LGD = 0.60
Expected Credit Loss = 0.05 × $57 million × (1 − 0.40) = $1.71 million

Note that this calculation is an estimate of the average loss. If a default actually occurs, then the loss in this example is 60% × $57 million = $34.2 million.

The expected loss of a portfolio of credit exposures is simply the sum of the expected credit losses of the individual exposures. In addition to expected loss exposures, analysts are generally concerned with understanding the variation in potential credit losses. Note that the variation of the potential credit losses in a portfolio of credit exposures is generally less than the sum of the variations of the individual exposures due to diversification (imperfect correlation of the individual losses).

24.2.3 Two Key Characteristics of the Risk-Neutral Modeling Approach

The previous section provided a framework and terminology with which expected losses can be modeled. This section describes a risk-neutral approach to pricing a bond with credit risk. A **risk-neutral approach** models financial characteristics, such as asset prices, within a framework that assumes that investors are risk neutral. A **risk-neutral investor** is an investor that requires the same rate of return on all investments, regardless of levels and types of risk because the investor is indifferent with regard to how much risk is borne. Economic theory associates investor risk neutrality with investors whose utility or happiness is a linear function of their wealth.

Few, if any, investors are risk neutral with regard to substantial financial decisions. Although the assumption of risk neutrality by investors is unrealistic, the power of risk-neutral modeling emanates from two key characteristics: (1) the risk-neutral modeling approach provides highly simplified and easily tractable modeling, and (2) in some cases, it can be shown that the prices generated by risk-neutral modeling must be the same as the prices in an economy where investors are risk averse.

Let's look further at each key characteristic. One reason that the risk-neutral approach is so important to finance in general and to derivative pricing in particular is that risk-neutral price modeling is greatly simplified by not having to either differentiate between systematic and idiosyncratic risks or estimate the risk premium required to bear systematic risk. The other major reason that the risk-neutral approach to asset pricing is so essential to investments is that, as mentioned in the previous paragraph, under specific conditions, the prices obtained in a risk-neutral framework can be theoretically proven to be the same as the prices that would exist in a world of risk-averse investors. When applicable, risk-neutral pricing provides extremely simplified frameworks to price assets in a risk-averse world.

24.2.4 Pricing Risky Bonds with a Risk-Neutral Approach

Consider a risky zero-coupon, one-period debt with the face value of K (i.e., promising a cash flow of K at maturity in one period). Given the expected recovery for this bond in case of default, RR, the bond has an expected payoff of $K \times RR$ in default with the probability λ (the probability of default) and, of course, a payoff of K in the absence of default with the probability of $(1 - \lambda)$.

Given the bond's forecasted cash flows, the current value (time 0) of the one-period bond, $B(0,1)$, can be expressed in a risk-neutral model as the sum of the probability-weighted and discounted cash flows, as shown in Equation 24.2:

$$B(0, 1) = \lambda \times \frac{K \times RR}{(1 + r)} + (1 - \lambda) \times \frac{K}{(1 + r)}$$
$$= \frac{K}{(1 + r)}(RR \times \lambda + [1 - \lambda]) \tag{24.2}$$

The first line of Equation 24.2 uses λ, a probability of default, to probability weight the cash flows associated with the two outcomes (default and no default). Careful inspection of Equation 24.2 reveals that both potential cash flows (the cash flow in the event of default and the cash flow in the absence of default) are discounted at the riskless interest rate, r. Why would risky cash flows be discounted at a riskless rate? The answer is that it is due to the assumption of risk neutrality and that it is a technique used in risk-neutral arbitrage-free modeling.

Equation 24.2 is derived under the assumption of risk neutrality: that investors do not require a premium for bearing risk. In risk-neutral modeling, every discount rate is equal to the riskless rate. In a risk-neutral model, the probability of default, λ, is known as a risk-neutral probability. A risk-neutral probability is a probability-like value that adjusts the statistical probability of default to account for risk premiums. A risk-neutral probability is equal to the statistical probability of default only when investors are risk neutral; it should not be interpreted as the probability of default that would occur if investors were risk averse. Of course, investors are not risk neutral, and they demand a premium for investing in risky investments. To account for the risk premium, risk-neutral probabilities can be used rather than statistical probabilities. Other approaches to risk adjustment include use of higher discount rates and reduction of expected cash flows (the certainty-equivalent approach).

The second line of Equation 24.2 rearranges the first line, emphasizing the view that the price of the risky bond is equal to the price of an otherwise risk-free bond [i.e., $K/(1+r)$] times an adjustment factor that accounts for the probability of default and expected recovery, or $(RR \times \lambda + [1 - \lambda])$. Clearly, the price of the risky debt declines as the probability of default, λ, increases, or the expected recovery rate, RR, declines. Risk-neutral models use a value of λ greater than the true default probability in order to reduce the values of risky cash flows relative to safe cash flows.

24.2.5 Credit Spreads

In bond markets, a bond price is often described as being determined by its credit spread, s. Equation 24.3 expresses the current price (time zero) of this debt due in one year, $B(0,1)$, using a credit spread:

$$B(0,1) = K/(1 + r + s) \tag{24.3}$$

In Equation 24.3, the risk premium required to hold a risky bond is expressed through the use of a higher discount rate: the addition of the credit spread, s, to the riskless rate, r.

Equations 24.2 and 24.3 express two approaches to pricing a risky bond. Equation 24.2 calculates the price of the risky bond by adjusting its default probability (and its expected payoff), whereas Equation 24.3 obtains the price by increasing the discount rate. If done properly, both should give the same price. By setting the two equations equal to each other, the risk-neutral default probability can be related to the credit spread, as is precisely shown in Equation 24.4 and simplified into an approximation in Equation 24.5:

$$\lambda = \frac{1}{1 - RR}\left(\frac{s}{1 + r + s}\right) \tag{24.4}$$

$$\lambda \approx \frac{s}{(1 - RR)} \tag{24.5}$$

Equation 24.5 is an important and useful approximation. If the short-term rate and the spread are not very large, then the well-known result displayed in Equation 24.5 approximately holds. That is, the risk-neutral probability of default is equal to the credit spread divided by the expected loss given default, or $(1 - RR)$. In the simple case of a risk-neutral world and a bond with no recovery $(RR = 0)$, the credit spread of a bond will equal its annual probability of default!

☞ APPLICATION 24.2.5A

Suppose that the risk-free rate is 5% per year and that a one-year, zero-coupon corporate bond yields 6% per year. What are the precise and approximate risk neutral probabilities of default?

Assuming a recovery rate of 80% on the corporate bond, the precise risk-neutral probability of default can be estimated as shown in Equation 24.4:

$$\lambda = \frac{1}{1 - 0.80} \left(\frac{0.01}{1 + 0.05 + 0.01} \right) = 4.7\%$$

If the approximation formula (the approximation in Equation 24.5) is used, the risk-neutral probability of default would be 5%, found as 0.01/0.20.

Equation 24.6 factors the approximation in Equation 24.5 to express the credit spread as depending on the probability of default and the recovery rate:

$$s \approx \lambda \times (1 - RR) \tag{24.6}$$

There is substantial logic and intuition to Equation 24.6. It indicates that s, the credit spread (the excess of a risky bond's yield above the riskless yield), is equal to the expected percentage loss of the one-year bond over the remaining year under the assumption of risk neutrality. The expected annual loss is the product of the risk-neutral probability of default (λ) and the proportion of loss given default $(1 - RR)$.

This result makes perfect sense. In a risk-neutral world, bondholders demand a yield premium on a risky bond (i.e., a spread) that compensates them for the expected losses on the bond due to default. For example, if bonds of a particular rating class tend to default at a rate of 1% per year, and if 55% of the typical bond's nominal value can eventually be recovered, then a portfolio of such bonds tends to lose 0.45% per year due to default. A risk-neutral investor would therefore require that such bonds offer a yield that is at least 0.45% higher (approximately) than the riskless bond yield to offset these expected losses.

☞ APPLICATION 24.2.5B

Suppose that the risk-neutral probability of default for a bond is 5% per year and that the recovery rate of the bond is 70%. What is the approximate spread by which the bond should trade relative to the yield of a riskless bond?

The approximate credit spread (from Equation 24.6) is $5\% \times (1 - 0.70)$, or 1.5%.

24.2.6 Applying the Reduced-Form Models Using Risk Neutrality

Equation 24.4 should not be interpreted as predicting an actual probability of default (i.e., a true statistical probability that would exist in an economy in which investors require a premium for bearing risk). Rather, λ should be viewed as a modeling tool. The actual probability of default will be less than λ to the extent that investors demand a risk premium.

Nevertheless, the risk-neutral probability of default (λ) provides a valuable pricing tool. Risk-neutral modeling and risk-neutral probabilities can have tremendous value. The risk-neutral probability implied by one bond, presumably a highly liquid publicly traded bond, can be used as a tool for pricing other bonds. The reduced-form credit model approach utilizes riskless interest rates as discount rates much like arbitrage-free option pricing models use riskless rates rather than discount rates that contain a risk premium. That is the essence of the reduced-form modeling approach.

Consider an example in which a bond that trades in a highly efficient and liquid market has a 1% credit spread (*s*) and an estimated 80% recovery rate. The risk-neutral default probability of 4.7% is found using Equation 24.4 (or 5% using the approximation formula in Equation 24.5).

The reduced-form approach generally uses pricing information obtained from more liquid segments of the market to price bonds that are less liquid. In other words, information implicit in bond prices that are observed in highly competitive markets is used to calibrate a model that is then used to price bonds that are less liquid. To **calibrate a model** means to establish values for the key parameters in a model, such as a default probability or an asset volatility, typically using an analysis of market prices of highly liquid assets. For example, the volatility of short-term interest rates might be calibrated in a model by using the implied volatility of highly liquid options on short-term bonds.

A key application of the reduced-form model is to price alternative debt securities in the same structure, such as both senior and junior debt. Note that debt securities within the same capital structure have the same underlying assets and the same probabilities of default (either the corporation defaults or it does not). The primary difference is simply the recovery rates. Senior debt should generally be expected to have higher recovery rates than junior debt, since senior debt generally has higher priority for liquidating cash flows in the bankruptcy process. Reduced-form models relate credit spreads to recovery rates, and therefore reduced-form models can be used to determine relative prices of securities in the same structure that differ in seniority.

☞ APPLICATION 24.2.6A

Suppose that the junior debt of XYZ Corporation is frequently traded and currently trades at a credit spread of 2.50% over riskless bonds of comparable maturity. The senior debt of the firm has not been regularly traded because it was primarily held by a few institutions, and a new issue of debt that is subordinated to all other debt has been rated as speculative. The expected recovery rate of the senior debt is 80%, the old junior debt is 50%, and the recently issued speculative debt is 20%. Using approximation formulas, what arbitrage-free credit spreads should be expected on the senior and speculative debt issues?

The 2.50% credit spread and 50% recovery rate of the junior debt implies a risk-neutral default probability of 5.0% using Equation 24.5. The same risk-neutral default probability (in this case, 5%) is then used with recovery rates of 80% and 20% to find credit spreads on the other debt using Equation 24.6. That process generates a credit spread of 1.0% on the senior debt and 4.0% on the speculative debt.

Reduced-form models are also used to price illiquid securities based on information from liquid securities with different issuers. The credit spreads observed in competitively traded debt markets can be used to calibrate a reduced-form model and generate relatively reliable estimates of risk-neutral default probabilities. The estimated risk-neutral default probabilities can then be used to determine appropriate credit spreads for bonds of similar total risk that are not frequently traded.

The examples of the previous sections discussed single-period models with simple zero-coupon bonds. In reality, a fixed-income debt instrument represents a basket of risks: the risk from changes in the term structure of interest rates that differ in size and shape; the risk that the issuer will prepay the debt issue (call risk); liquidity risks; and the risk of defaults, downgrades, and widening credit spreads (credit risk). Sophisticated reduced-form models use the prices and, in some cases, the volatilities of riskless bonds to incorporate their effects on the prices of risky bonds.

24.2.7 Advantages and Disadvantages of Reduced-Form Models

Reduced-form models have two advantages:

1. They can be calibrated using derivatives such as credit default swap spreads, which are highly liquid. (Credit default swaps are discussed later in the chapter.)
2. They are extremely tractable and are well suited for pricing derivatives and portfolio products. The models can rapidly incorporate credit rating changes and can be used in the absence of balance sheet information (e.g., for sovereign issuers).

Reduced-form models have four disadvantages:

1. There may be limited reliable market data with which to calibrate a model.
2. They can be sensitive to assumptions, particularly those regarding the recovery rate.
3. Information on actual historical default rates can be problematic. That is, few observations are available for defaults by major firms or sovereign states.
4. Historical default rates on classes of borrowers (e.g., borrowers of a particular ratings class) may have limited value in the prediction of future default rates to the extent that economies undergo major fundamental changes.

Finally, it should be noted that **hazard rate** is a term often used in the context of reduced-form models to denote the default rate. The number is usually annualized and may be based on historical analysis of similar bonds or on expectations. Thus, an asset with a hazard rate of 2% is believed to have a 2% actual (i.e., statistical rather than risk-neutral) probability of default on an annual basis.

24.2.8 Distinguishing between Structural and Reduced-Form Credit Models

Reduced-form credit models focus on metrics, such as yields and yield spreads. These models observe, measure, and approximate the relationship between those metrics and the characteristics of the securities being analyzed, such as differences in recovery rates. The underlying motivation is to use known information (such as yield spreads) on securities in highly liquid markets to infer corresponding information (yield spreads) for other securities, while adjusting for factors such as recovery rates.

Common inputs to reduced-form credit model approaches include bond yields, yield spreads, and bond ratings, as well as historical or anticipated recovery rates and hazard rates (i.e., default rates).

Structural credit models focus on valuing securities based on option pricing models. Structural models estimate underlying asset values, degrees of leverage, and the partitioning of the assets' cash flows to debt and equity claimants.

Common inputs to structural credit models include the value of the underlying assets and equity of a structure, the face value of the debt, and estimates of the volatility of the underlying assets or equity. Like reduced-form credit models, structural credit models use riskless rates and the time to maturity of the debt.

24.3 CREDIT DERIVATIVES MARKETS

Derivatives are cost-effective vehicles for the transfer of risk, with values driven by an underlying asset. **Credit derivatives** transfer credit risk from one party to another such that both parties view themselves as having an improved position as a result of the derivative. Roughly, most credit derivative transactions transfer the risk of default from a buyer of credit protection to a seller of credit protection.

24.3.1 Three Economic Roles of Credit Derivatives

The primary way that credit derivatives contribute to the economy and its participants is by facilitating risk management in general and diversification in particular. Consider the challenge faced by a major bank that has established a long-term relationship with a traditional operating firm. The bank provides many services to its clients, including payment services and credit. If the client is very large, the credit risk exposure of the bank to the firm through its loans to the firm may become substantial relative to the size of the bank. However, the bank may wish to be the sole direct creditor of the firm for several reasons. Perhaps the bank may view meeting all of the client's loan needs as increasing the chances that the bank will remain the firm's sole supplier of other services. Alternatively, the bank may wish to avoid the potential conflicts of interest and legal complexities of making loans to a firm alongside other creditors. As the sole creditor, the bank may be better able to pursue its self-interest. Credit derivatives can provide the bank with a cost-effective solution: The bank can make large loans to the firm and transfer as much risk as the bank desires to other market participants through credit derivatives. At the same time, other banks can transfer the credit risk of their portfolios to other market participants through credit derivatives. Through this process, banks and other institutions may be able to hold relatively well-diversified portfolios of credit risks while maintaining efficient and effective relationships with key clients.

Second, credit derivatives can provide liquidity to the market in times of credit stress. The availability and use of credit derivatives has soared in recent decades, with the result that credit risk has gradually changed from an illiquid risk that was not considered suitable for trading to a risk that can be traded like other sources of risk (e.g., equity, interest rates, and currencies).

Third, highly liquid markets for credit derivatives provide ongoing and reliable price revelation. **Price revelation,** or price discovery, is the process of observing prices being used or offered by informed buyers and sellers. Prices are the mechanism through which values of resources are communicated in a large economy. Ongoing and reliable price revelation regarding the credit risk of major firms serves as a highly valuable tool for decision making and enhances overall economic efficiency.

24.3.2 Three Groupings of Credit Derivatives

Credit derivatives can differ in many ways. Following are three major methods for grouping credit derivatives.

SINGLE-NAME VERSUS MULTI-NAME INSTRUMENTS: **Single-name credit derivatives** transfer the credit risk associated with a single entity. This is the most common type of credit derivative and can be used to build more complex credit derivatives. Most single-name credit derivatives are credit default swaps (CDSs), which are the most popular way to allow one party to buy credit protection from another party.

   Multi-name instruments, in contrast to single-name instruments, make payoffs that are contingent on one or more credit events (e.g., defaults) affecting two or more reference entities. Credit indices are examples of multi-name credit instruments. CDSs on baskets of credit risk offer specified payouts based on specified numbers of defaults in the underlying credit risks. In the most common form of a basket CDS, a first-to-default CDS, the protection seller compensates the buyer for losses associated with the first entity in the basket to default, after which the swap terminates and provides no further protection.

UNFUNDED VERSUS FUNDED INSTRUMENTS: **Unfunded credit derivatives** involve exchanges of payments that are tied to a notional amount, but the notional amount does not change hands until a default occurs. An unfunded credit derivative is similar to an interest rate swap in which there is no initial cash purchase of a promise to receive principal but rather an agreement to exchange future cash flows. The most common unfunded credit derivative is the CDS. As discussed later in this chapter, unfunded instruments expose at least one party to counterparty risk. Unfunded instruments can be for a single name or for multiple names.

Funded credit derivatives require cash outlays and create exposures similar to those gained from traditional investing in corporate bonds through the cash market. Credit-linked notes, discussed later in this chapter, are a common type of funded instrument. They can be thought of as a riskless debt instrument with an embedded credit derivative.

SOVEREIGN VERSUS NONSOVEREIGN ENTITIES: The reference entities of credit derivatives can be sovereign nations or corporate entities. Credit derivatives on sovereign nations tend to be more complex because their analysis has to consider not only the possible inability of the entity to meet its obligations but also the potential unwillingness of the nation to meet its obligations. The modeling of the credit risk associated with sovereign risk involves political and macroeconomic risks that are normally not present in modeling corporate credit risk. Finally, the market for credit derivatives on sovereign nations is smaller than the market for other credit derivatives.

24.3.3 Stages of Credit Derivative Activity

Both Smithson and Mengle have observed four stages in the evolution of credit derivatives activity.[2] The first, or defensive, stage, which started in the late 1980s and ended in the early 1990s, was characterized by ad hoc attempts by banks to lay off some of their credit exposures.

The second stage, which began about 1991 and lasted through the mid- to late 1990s, was the emergence of an intermediated market in which dealers applied derivatives technology to the transfer of credit risk, and investors entered the market to seek exposure to credit risk.[3] An example of dealer applications of derivatives technology is the total return swap, which is detailed later in this chapter. Another innovation during this phase was the synthetic securitization structure. Synthetic securitization represents the extension of credit derivatives to structured finance products, such as CDOs, in which the CDOs take credit risks through selling CDSs rather than through purchasing bonds.

The third stage was maturing from a new product into one resembling other forms of derivatives. Major financial regulators issued guidance for the regulatory capital treatment of credit derivatives, and this guidance served to clarify the constraints under which the emerging market would operate. Further, in 1999, the International Swaps and Derivatives Association (ISDA) issued a set of standard definitions for credit derivatives to be used in connection with the ISDA master agreement, as discussed in more detail later in the chapter. Finally, dealers began warehousing risks and running hedged and diversified portfolios of credit derivatives. During this stage, the market encountered a series of challenges, ranging from credit events associated with restructuring to renegotiation of emerging market debts.

The fourth stage centered on the development of a liquid market. With new ISDA credit derivative definitions in place in 2003, dealers began to trade according to standardized practices (e.g., standard settlement dates) that went beyond those adopted for other over-the-counter (OTC) derivatives. Further, substantial index trading began in 2004 and grew rapidly, and hedge funds entered the market on a large scale as both buyers and sellers.

The development of all these activities served to increase liquidity, price discovery, and efficiency in the market. And now, in the United States and elsewhere, legislation may require some credit derivatives to be exchange traded and backed by a clearinghouse; similar changes are likely to emanate from the European Union. This could take credit derivative activity into a fifth stage, from its OTC origins to the domain of the futures and derivatives exchanges.

24.4 INTEREST RATE SWAPS

A **swap** is a contract between two parties to exchange cash flows at specified dates in the future, according to prearranged rules.

24.4.1 Simple Interest Rate Swaps

The simplest interest swap is often referred to as a "plain vanilla" interest rate swap. In a plain vanilla **interest rate swap**, party A agrees to pay party B cash flows based on a fixed interest rate in exchange for receiving from B cash flows in accordance with a specified floating interest rate. Both payments are based on a notional principal and a specified number of years, which typically range from two to 15 years.

24.4.2 Payers and Receivers of Interest Rate Swaps

The payer in a vanilla swap is the party that agrees to pay a fixed rate in exchange for receiving a floating rate. The receiver (i.e., the buyer of the fixed rate) is the party that agrees to pay a floating rate in exchange for receiving a fixed rate. Interest rate swaps are subject to interest rate risk and credit risk (counterparty risk). Ignoring the counterparty risk, the payer in a vanilla swap will benefit from a rise in interest rates and will be hurt by a decline in interest rates. As a result, these instruments can be used to speculate, hedge, and manage interest rate risk. However, the most common motivation offered to explain the rationale of an interest rate swap is the comparative advantage argument.

For example, a firm may have a comparative advantage borrowing in the floating rate market but a desire to borrow at the fixed rate. The firm then issues debt at the floating rate and, by entering into a swap contract with another party, is able to convert the floating-rate loan into a fixed-rate loan. Given the borrower's comparative advantage, the net fixed interest rate paid is lower after the swap transaction than would have been available by borrowing directly at the fixed rate. An interest rate swap can also be used to convert a liability from a fixed to a floating rate. It can also be used to convert an investment from a fixed to a floating rate, or from a floating to a fixed rate.

24.4.3 Use of Interest Rate Swaps by Pensions

In recent years, pension funds have become active users of interest rate swaps. Pension fund assets are managed to support liabilities that represent promises made to future retirees. In many countries, pension funds are expected to calculate the present value of these liabilities in order to determine the funding status of the fund. If the present value of liabilities exceeds the value of the pension fund's assets, then the fund may be considered to be underfunded. As a result, everything else being the same, a decline in interest rates will increase the present value of a fund's liabilities, increasing the gap between its assets and its liabilities. Pension funds have two broad options in managing this risk.

First, they could reduce the interest rate risk by investing in long-term bonds. In this case, a decline in interest rates will increase the values of both their assets and liabilities, reducing the volatility in the gap between assets and liabilities. This strategy requires a pension fund to commit capital to the strategy, and therefore allocations to other asset classes have to be reduced.

Second, a pension fund may decide to invest its funds in asset classes that are expected to generate higher returns (e.g., private equity, hedge funds, or public equities) and then use an interest rate swap to manage its interest rate risk. In this case, the pension fund would agree to receive fixed payments in exchange for making floating payments. Should interest rates decline, the pension fund would benefit from a decline in the value of the future floating payments that it is expected to make.

24.4.4 The Mechanics of Interest Rate Swaps

Exhibit 24.1 illustrates the mechanics of an interest rate swap. Suppose that pension fund A has entered into an agreement to pay six-month LIBOR in exchange for receiving (from bank B) a fixed interest rate of 4% per annum every six months for four years, on a notional principal of $100 million. The exhibit shows the resulting cash flows from the point of view of the pension fund, assuming the six-month LIBOR rates depicted in the second column of the table (expressed as rates per year with semiannual compounding).[4]

On April 3 of year 1, the six-month LIBOR rate is 3.20%. This is the rate that would be applied to the floating payment made six months later, on October 3. Therefore, the first floating cash flow paid by the pension fund is equal to $1,600,000. This payment is calculated as follows: $(3.20\%/2) \times \$100,000,000 = \$1,600,000$. The same procedure can be followed to find the floating rate payments that will be made in subsequent periods. The net cash flow to the pension fund is equal to the difference between the fixed cash flow to be received and the floating cash flow to be paid. The

EXHIBIT 24.1 Interest Rate Swap Example

Date	Six-Month LIBOR	Floating Cash Flow	Fixed Cash Flow	Net Cash Flow
April 3, year 1	3.20%			
October 3, year 1	3.50%	−$1,600,000	$2,000,000	$400,000
April 3, year 2	4.00%	−$1,750,000	$2,000,000	$250,000
October 3, year 2	4.50%	−$2,000,000	$2,000,000	$ 0
April 3, year 3	4.60%	−$2,250,000	$2,000,000	−$250,000
October 3, year 3	4.10%	−$2,300,000	$2,000,000	−$300,000
April 3, year 4	3.90%	−$2,050,000	$2,000,000	−$ 50,000
October 3, year 4	3.70%	−$1,950,000	$2,000,000	$ 50,000
April 3, year 5		−$1,850,000	$2,000,000	$150,000

principal in a swap contract (known as notional principal) is not exchanged at the end of the life of the swap; it is used only for the computation of interest payments. In practice, only the net cash flows, or the difference between the fixed and floating rate payments, are exchanged.

The fixed rate of an interest rate swap is referred to as the **swap rate**. Initially, the swap rate is set so that the present value of expected floating payments is equal to the present value of expected fixed payments. Ignoring counterparty risks, the expected fixed payments are known with certainty and the expected floating payments can be estimated from the currently available interest rate futures prices. Then, using all available information, the swap rate is set so that the present values of fixed and floating payments are equal. An example later in this section will demonstrate this procedure.

Similar to other fixed-income instruments, swaps of different maturities carry different swap rates. By the same token, the **swap rate curve** displays the relationship between swap rates and the maturities of their corresponding contracts, having a concept analogous to that of the yield curve. The swap rate curve is an important benchmark for interest rates in the United States. It is also frequently used in Europe as the benchmark for all European government bonds. Worldwide, in terms of size and volume, interest rate swaps represent one of the most important interest rate derivative contracts.

24.4.5 Initial Valuation of an Interest Rate Swap

Interest rate swaps are worth zero when the two parties agree to the transaction. Once the contract is entered into, payments from the floating-rate party or leg of the agreement will change as market interest rates change.

An interest rate swap is equivalent to a bond transaction in which the fixed-rate payer issues a fixed-coupon bond and invests the proceeds in a floating-rate bond with the same payment dates and maturity. Then, on each payment date, the floating-rate payment is received and the fixed-coupon payment is made. Thus, the swap can be valued as the difference between the market value of the fixed-coupon bond and the market value of the floating-rate bond. It is important to bear in mind that interest payments are netted in the actual swap, and that the contract does not require principal payments. The procedure of estimating the market values of fixed- and floating-rate bonds is simply an artifice that facilitates the calculation of the value of the swap. The valuation of an interest rate swap will be explained using an example.[5]

☞ APPLICATION 24.4.5A

On January 1, ABC pension fund enters a one-year swap, agreeing to pay 4.3464% fixed rate on a notional amount of $10 million and receive a floating payment based on three-month LIBOR. Both the fixed and the floating payments will be made on a quarterly basis. The three-month LIBOR rate on

January 1 is observed to be 4%. In addition, the interest rate futures market indicates the following rates for the next three quarters: 4.20%, 4.40%, and 4.80%. Calculate the expected payments for the swap.

The expected payments for both fixed and floating payments are displayed in Exhibit 24.2.[6]

A question that arises from the previous example is why the swap rate is set equal to 4.3464%. As discussed, given all available information, this is the rate that sets the present value of future fixed payments equal to the present value of future floating payments. In other words, 4.3464% is the swap rate that sets the net value of the swap to zero. After the swap agreement has been made, market interest rates will change and the swap's value will vary. The next example demonstrates the nonzero valuation of the swap agreement after interest rates have shifted.

EXHIBIT 24.2   Fixed and Floating Payments

(1)	(2)	(3)	(4)	(5)	(6)	(7) = (6) × 10M	(8) = 4.3464% × (3)/360 × 10M
Quarter Starts	Quarter Ends	Number of Days in Quarter	Current LIBOR	Future LIBOR Rates Start of Quarter	Quarterly Future LIBOR Start of Quarter	Floating Payment End of Quarter	Fixed Payment End of Quarter
January 1	March 31	90	4.00%		1.00%	100,000	108,660
April 1	June 30	90		4.20%	1.05%	105,000	108,660
July 1	September 30	90		4.40%	1.10%	110,000	108,660
October 1	December 31	90		4.80%	1.20%	120,000	108,660

Notice that floating payments are made at the end of each quarter based on the three-month LIBOR rate observed at the beginning or the same quarter. For instance,

$$100,000 = \frac{90}{360} \times 4.0\% \times 10,000,000$$

$$105,000 = \frac{90}{360} \times 4.2\% \times 10,000,000$$

Similarly, the fixed payments are calculated using the swap rate of 4.3464%. For instance,

$$108,660 = \frac{90}{360} \times 4.3464\% \times 10,000,000$$

☞ **APPLICATION 24.4.5B**

Given the cash flows and interest rates from Exhibit 24.2, calculate the value of the swap as the discounted values of the expected cash flows. To value the expected future cash flows of the swap, it is necessary to specify the discount rate that needs to be applied to future cash flows. It turns out that the interest rates obtained from the futures contracts can provide us with the information needed to calculate these present values. Exhibit 24.2 is based on the figures displayed in Exhibit 24.1, but three new columns have been added and columns 3–5 have been removed because of space concerns. The exhibit displays all the information needed to calculate the present values of the two streams of cash flows.

Note that the sum of the present values of the floating payments in column 10 is equal to the sum of the present values of the fixed payments in column 11. This demonstrates that the swap has an initial value of zero. Note that a twelfth column of the netted expected cash flows could be formed and used to calculate the same net value. The keys to our calculations are the forward discounts that appear in column 9. They are based on the quarterly three-month LIBOR rates that appear in column 6. For instance,

$$0.990099 = \frac{1}{(1 + 1.00\%)}$$
$$0.979811 = \frac{1}{(1 + 1.00\%) \times (1 + 1.05\%)}$$

In other words, the denominator of each discount factor is compounded using the current and previous three-month LIBOR rates. The present values of the two streams are calculated using these discount rates. It can be seen that when using 4.3464% as the swap rate, the present values of the two streams are equal when the swap contract is initiated.

24.4.6 Valuation of an Existing Swap

Suppose that after the first quarterly payments interest rates increase, changing the current and remaining three-month LIBOR rates to 4.4%, 4.8%, and 5.0%, respectively. What is the gain by the fixed-rate payer? Exhibit 24.4 and Exhibit 24.5 duplicate the calculations displayed in Exhibit 24.2 and Exhibit 24.3 using the new three-month LIBOR rates, taking into account that the first payments have already been made.

It can be seen that while the fixed payments remain the same, the floating payments have increased, benefiting the party that pays the fixed rate. Given the new structure of the three-month LIBOR rates, we can calculate the present values of the two streams.

The present value of the remaining floating payments will be higher than the present value of the remaining fixed payments, benefiting the fixed-rate payer. In other words, while the net present value (NPV) of the swap was zero

EXHIBIT 24.3   Present Values of Fixed and Floating Payments

(1)	(2)	(6)	(7)	(8)	(9)	(10) = (7) × (9)	(11) = (8) × (9)
Quarter Starts	Quarter Ends	Quarterly Future LIBOR Start of Quarter	Floating Payment End of Quarter	Fixed Payment End of Quarter	Forward Discount	PV of Floating Payments	PV of Fixed Payments
January 1	March 31	1.00%	100,000	108,660	0.990099	99,010	107,584
April 1	June 30	1.05%	105,000	108,660	0.979811	102,880	106,466
July 1	September 30	1.10%	110,000	108,660	0.969150	106,607	105,307
October 1	December 31	1.20%	120,000	108,660	0.957658	114,919	104,059
Total						423,416	423,416

Note: There is a slight rounding error in the last column of this exhibit.

EXHIBIT 24.4   Interest Rate Swap Payments after a Change in Three-Month LIBOR

(1)	(2)	(3)	(4)	(5)	(6)	(7)	(8)
Quarter Starts	Quarter Ends	Number of Days in Quarter	Current LIBOR	Future LIBOR Rates Start of Quarter	Quarterly Future LIBOR Start of Quarter	Floating Payment End of Quarter	Fixed Payment End of Quarter
April 1	June 30	90	4.40%		1.10%	110,000	108,660
July 1	September 30	90		4.80%	1.20%	120,000	108,660
October 1	December 31	90		5.00%	1.25%	125,000	108,660

EXHIBIT 24.5   Present Values of Fixed and Floating Payments

(1)	(2)	(6)	(7)	(8)	(9)	(10)	(11)
Quarter Starts	Quarter Ends	Quarterly Future LIBOR Start of Quarter	Floating Payment End of Quarter	Fixed Payment End of Quarter	Forward Discount	PV of Floating Payments	PV of Fixed Payments
April 1	June 30	1.10%	110,000	108,660	0.989120	108,803	107,478
July 1	September 30	1.20%	120,000	108,660	0.977391	117,287	106,203
October 1	December 31	1.25%	125,000	108,660	0.965324	120,666	104,892
Total						346,756	318,573

when it was initiated, the NPV became positive for the fixed-rate payer (i.e., $28,183 = $346,756 − $318,573), and negative (i.e., − $28,183) for the floating-rate payer after interest rates increased.

24.4.7 Risks Associated with Interest Rate Swaps

In this section, we briefly discuss the main risks to which interest rate swaps are subject—namely, credit risk and interest rate risk. Furthermore, the events of 2007–2009 showed that it is no longer acceptable to assume that top-tier banks could never default. As a consequence, LIBOR rates should not be regarded as risk-free rates, a problem that in turn affects the valuation of interest rate swaps.

Credit risk on a two-leg swap exists when one of the parties to the contract is in-the-money, because that leg of the contract will face the possibility of default by the other party. On the other hand, when a swap is agreed upon through an intermediary (i.e., a financial institution), typically the intermediary will bear the default risk in exchange for a fixed percentage of the value of the contract in the form of a bid-ask spread.

The credit risk of an interest rate swap can be managed according to two dimensions:

1. Contractual provisions, documentation, collateral, and contingencies
2. Diversification of the swap book across industry and market sectors[7]

The risk exposure of a swap due to unanticipated interest rate changes is another potentially important risk. For example, Ferrara and Ali (2013) simulate many forward yield curves (using an arbitrage-free interest rate model), and evaluate the potential exposure of vanilla interest rate swaps under the most familiar yield curve shapes and under different volatility assumptions.[8] The authors highlight that unanticipated changing interest rates can, on one hand, create substantial mark-to-market (MTM) or counterparty exposure, which may cause significant MTM losses and require substantial collateral posting. On the other hand, they also find that unanticipated changing interest rates can generate considerable MTM gains, which can lead to counterparty exposure if the swap contract is not collateralized.

Credit risk and interest rate risk interact in fine ways. These interactions can be examined by estimating the MTM value of swaps for a range of term-structure scenarios and credit-risk assumptions. These estimations can be performed using Monte Carlo simulation or other techniques.

24.4.8 The Global Financial Crisis of 2007–2009

The two key assumptions under which the traditional approach to pricing and valuing standard interest rate swaps is based are that LIBOR discount factors are (1) reasonable proxies for the credit quality of the counterparty when the contract is uncollateralized, and (2) suitable measures for the risk-free term structure when the contract is collateralized.

Smith (2012) argues that the financial crisis of 2007 defied the second assumption.[9] This is because collateralization is now usual in the swap market, and the existence of considerable and persistent differences between LIBOR and other proxies for risk-free rates implies that LIBOR discount factors can no longer be regarded as risk-free rates. Because of this, fixed rates on overnight indexed swaps are now considered more appropriate for valuing collateralized contracts. The spread can arise in two ways—first, as a liquidity premium to compensate for liquidity risk, and second, as a credit spread.

Prior to the 2007–2009 global financial crisis, most swap market participants ignored the counterparty risk associated with large global banks. The reason was that most assumed that these institutions would never default on their obligations. The global financial crisis changed all of that, and as a result, a credit spread reflecting the counterparty risk is now incorporated into swap spreads.

In 2004, interest rates were historically low. Harvard University entered into a series of interest rate swaps in anticipation of the future funding needs for construction projects. According to Ferrara and Ali (2013), Harvard had entered these swaps as payer of the fixed leg.[10] A subsequent drop in interest rates caused the values of these interest rate swaps to negatively affect Harvard's financial position. Harvard's problems with its interest rate swaps were compounded by the fact that the swaps required the university to deliver collateral (in cash) proportional to the magnitude of the NPV on its interest rate swaps, which in this case had become negative. As Harvard's NPV became increasingly negative, the amount of cash it had to post as collateral increased, thus creating an illiquidity problem for the university. These difficulties explain, at least partially, Harvard's decision to pay almost $500 million in fiscal year 2009 to terminate a subset of its portfolio of interest rate swaps that had a total notional value of $1.1 billion.

24.5 CREDIT DEFAULT SWAPS

By far the most important development for credit derivatives is the credit default swap. A **credit default swap (CDS)** is an insurance-like bilateral contract in which the buyer pays a periodic fee (analogous to an insurance premium) to the seller in exchange for a contingent payment from the seller if a credit event occurs with respect to an underlying credit-risky asset. A CDS may be negotiated on any of a variety of credit-risky investments, primarily corporate bonds.

24.5.1 Credit Default Swaps and Total Return Swaps

There are two primary types of swaps involving credit risk. The first type, by far the more predominant, is the CDS. In a CDS, the **credit protection buyer** pays a periodic premium on a predetermined amount (the notional amount) in exchange for a contingent payment from the credit protection seller if a specified credit event occurs. The credit protection buyer typically uses the payment to hedge losses suffered from the specified credit event. The **credit protection seller** receives a periodic premium in exchange for delivering a contingent payment to the credit protection buyer if a specified credit event occurs.[11]

Exhibit 24.6 demonstrates a CDS. In this illustration, the credit protection buyer is assumed to hold a cash position in a credit-risky asset and is using a CDS to purchase credit protection. In Exhibit 24.6, the credit risk of the underlying risky asset is transferred from the credit protection buyer to the credit protection seller. The credit

EXHIBIT 24.6 Credit Default Swap

protection seller may be interested in bearing the credit risk for the potential rewards or may hedge the credit risk away, using, for example, another credit derivative. Subsequent sections discuss CDSs in detail.

A variation on the CDS is a total return swap with a credit-risky reference asset. In a **total return swap**, the credit protection buyer, typically the owner of the credit risky asset, passes on the total return of the asset to the credit protection seller in return for a certain payment. Thus, the credit protection buyer gives up the uncertain returns of the credit-risky asset in return for a certain payment from the credit protection seller. The credit protection seller now receives both the upside and the downside of the return associated with the credit-risky asset. The credit protection seller takes on all of the economic risk of the underlying asset, just as if that asset were on the balance sheet or in the investment portfolio. Exhibit 24.7 demonstrates this total return swap.

The left sides of both Exhibits 24.6 and 24.7 are the same and illustrate the idea that the credit protection buyer is assumed in these examples to own the underlying asset that contains the credit risk (e.g., a risky corporate bond). Comparison of the two exhibits illustrates the essential differences between a CDS and a total return swap on the same credit risk. In the case of a CDS, the credit protection buyer makes fixed payments, known as the swap premium, to the credit protection seller. If the credit experiences a trigger event (e.g., a default), the credit protection buyer receives cash from the credit protection seller. In the case of a total return swap, the credit protection buyer makes payments to the credit protection seller based on the total market return of the underlying asset. The total market return is composed of any coupon payments and any change in the underlying bond's market price. The credit protection buyer receives a payment from the credit protection seller that may vary with interest rates but does not vary based on the performance of the same credit risk.

CDSs and total return swaps on credit-risky assets are used to transfer risk. For example, a bank may use a CDS to hedge the credit exposure on its balance sheet, such as its exposure to a particular corporate borrower or to an industry that the bank believes is geared for difficult times. The bank can reduce its exposure to the credit risk of one or more of its customers, in most cases without the knowledge or consent of the customers.

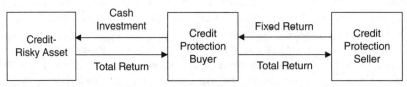

EXHIBIT 24.7 Total Return Swap on a Risky Asset

CDSs are very flexible. For instance, a CDS may state in its contract the exact amount of insurance payment in the event of a credit event. Alternatively, a CDS may be structured so that the amount of the swap payment by the credit protection seller is determined after the credit event. Usually, the payment by the credit protection seller in the event of a credit event is determined by the market value of the referenced asset after the credit event has occurred. In total return swaps, there is no need to specify the events that lead to payments, since payments are driven by market values.

24.5.2 Mechanics of a Credit Default Swap

The CDS market is contract driven. This means that each CDS is a privately negotiated transaction between the credit protection buyer and the credit protection seller. Fortunately, the ISDA, the primary industry body for derivatives documentation, has established standardized terms for CDSs. These terms are not mandated for use but are available to market participants and are used as a framework for negotiating a deal. This section provides some detail regarding the standard ISDA agreement. The **standard ISDA agreement** serves as a template to negotiated credit agreements that contains provisions commonly used by market participants. The standard ISDA agreement provides specifications relating to the following five aspects of the deal:

1. CDS SPREAD: The **CDS spread** or **CDS premium** is paid by the credit protection buyer to the credit protection seller and is quoted in basis points per annum on the notional value of the CDS. The CDS spread is not a credit yield spread but a price or rate quote for buying credit insurance. Typically, the price of this credit insurance is paid quarterly by the protection buyer.
2. CONTRACT SIZE: ISDA does not impose any limits on size or length of term of a CDS; this is up to the negotiation of the parties involved. The notional value of most CDSs falls in the range of $20 million to $200 million, with a tenor (term) of three to five years.
3. TRIGGER EVENTS: This is the heart of every CDS transaction. Trigger events determine when the credit protection seller must make a payment to the credit protection buyer. Both sides to a CDS negotiate these terms intensely. The broader the definition of a trigger event, the more likely cash will flow from the protection seller to the protection buyer and the higher the appropriate spread will be. The ISDA agreement provides for seven kinds of potential trigger events; the parties to a CDS are welcome to add more, although the seven events identified by ISDA cover virtually all types of credit events:
   1. *Bankruptcy.* A filing for bankruptcy is typically associated with a company's inability to pay its debt.
   2. *Failure to pay.* Although a company may not be in bankruptcy yet, it may not be able to meet its debt obligations as they come due.
   3. *Restructuring.* This is any form of debt restructuring that is disadvantageous to a holder of the referenced credit. Restructuring is a fuzzy term, and ISDA attempts to clarify this part of the standard contract by offering the following four options for the parties to consider: no restructuring, full restructuring, modified restructuring (which limits resulting obligations to bonds maturing in less than 30 months), and modified-modified restructuring (which is less

strict than modified restructuring because resulting bonds can have maturities of up to 60 months).

4. *Obligation acceleration.* All bond and loan covenants contain provisions that accelerate the repayment of the loan or bond if the credit quality of the borrower begins to deteriorate due to a number of events, such as a failure to pay, a bankruptcy (which ISDA covers independently), or a ratings downgrade.

5. *Obligation default.* This is any failure to meet a condition in the bond or loan covenant that would put the borrower in breach of the covenant. It could be something like the failure to maintain a sufficient current ratio or a minimum interest earnings coverage ratio.

6. *Repudiation/moratorium.* This is most frequently associated with sovereign or emerging markets debt. It is simply a refusal by the sovereign government to repay its debt as it comes due or even an outright rejection of its debt obligations.

7. *Government intervention.* A government's action or announcement reduces required payments or reduces the priority of making payments.

4. SETTLEMENT: If a credit event occurs, settlement can be made either with a cash payment or with a physical settlement. In a **cash settlement**, the credit protection seller makes the credit protection buyer whole by transferring to the buyer an amount of cash based on the contract. The settlement price can sometimes be the present value of the contractual cash flows over its remaining life, or it may be determined through auction processes. Cash settlement does not occur as frequently as one might expect, because it is difficult to agree on a good market-based measure of the loss. Therefore, most CDSs use physical settlement upon the occurrence of a credit event. Under **physical settlement**, the credit protection seller purchases the impaired loan or bond from the credit protection buyer at par value. The credit-risky asset is physically transferred to the credit protection seller's balance sheet, and the face or par value of the bond is transferred to the protection buyer from the protection seller.

5. DELIVERY: Within particular limits, the credit protection buyer has a choice of assets that can be delivered for physical settlement. This raises the issue of which of those assets is cheapest to deliver. The concept of multiple deliverable assets is common throughout derivatives and provides an option to the holder of the short option position that should be reflected in the contract's price or terms. Deliverables can include direct obligations of the referenced entity, such as corporate bonds or bank loans; obligations of a subsidiary of the referenced entity if the subsidiary is at least 50% owned by the referenced entity (sometimes referred to as qualifying affiliate guarantees); and obligations of a third party that the referenced entity may have guaranteed (known as qualifying guarantees). Note that physical settlement can create problems if there is an insufficient supply of assets to deliver, possibly because the notional value of an outstanding CDS exceeds the principal value of the underlying bonds.

Keep in mind that although ISDA provides standard terms, the parties to a CDS can negotiate any and all terms, plus add their own if they both wish. The main point is that the standardization of CDS terms has provided the infrastructure for the huge growth of the credit derivatives market.

☞ APPLICATION 24.5.2A

In this example, a hypothetical transaction takes place between a hedge fund (the Fund) as a credit protection seller and a commercial bank (the Bank) as a credit protection buyer. The referenced entity is an airline company (the Firm). The referenced asset is $20 million of face value debt. The term of the transaction is seven years. In exchange for the protection provided over the next seven years, the Fund receives 2% of the notional amount per year, payable quarterly. The contract will be settled physically. This means that if a credit event takes place, the Bank will deliver $20 million in face value of any qualifying senior unsecured paper issued by the Firm in return for a $20 million payment by the Fund. Further, the contract will be terminated, and no further payments will be made by the Bank. Let's assume that default takes place after exactly three years. What cash flows and exchanges take place?

Each quarter for 12 quarters, the Bank pays the Fund $100,000. This value is found by multiplying the notional amount ($20 million) by the quarterly rate of 0.5% (i.e., 2%/4). When the default occurs, the Bank delivers $20 million in face value of the referenced bond to the Fund in exchange for $20 million in cash. The CDS terminates immediately after these exchanges.

As this example shows, four major terms define a CDS:

1. CREDIT REFERENCE: CDS contracts specify a referenced asset. The **referenced asset** (also called the *referenced bond, referenced obligation,* or *referenced credit*) is the underlying security on which the credit protection is provided. Following a credit event, particular qualifying bonds are deliverable. Typically, a senior unsecured bond is the reference entity, but bonds at other levels of the capital structure may be referenced.
2. NOTIONAL AMOUNT: CDS contracts specify the amount of credit risk being transferred. This amount, agreed on by both the protection buyer and the protection seller, is analogous to the principal value of a cash bond.
3. CDS SPREAD: This is the annual payment rate, quoted in basis points. Payments are paid quarterly and accrue on an actual/360-day basis. The spread is also called the *fixed rate, coupon, premium,* or *price.*
4. CDS MATURITY: Typically, CDS contracts expire on the 20th of March, June, September, or December. The five-year contract is usually the most common and most liquid.

The economics of the CDS in the previous example can be viewed from the perspective of the bank. Suppose that the bank owned $20 million in face value of the referenced credit (bond). What yield would that bond be expected to offer relative to the riskless rate, given that a CDS was available at a spread of 2%? The answer is that the yield on the risky debt must exceed the yield on riskless debt of similar maturity by approximately the same rate as the CDS spread, 2%. Thus, in the example, the bank earns 2% more than the riskless rate (i.e., earns the credit spread) by holding the risky bond, then lays off all that risk by paying a 2% CDS spread.

The bank as a protection buyer hedges the credit risk and earns a return equal to the riskless rate. In practice, the CDS spread can differ from the yield spread due to factors such as the counterparty risk of the CDS.

24.5.3 Valuing CDS Contracts

Generally, CDSs and other swaps are entered into without immediate cash payments from either side and are viewed as having near zero market values to each side at inception. This is because the present value of the expected premiums paid by the CDS buyer should be approximately equal to the present value of the expected payments to be made by the CDS seller. As time passes, the risk of the referenced asset may change, general credit conditions may change, and market prices and yields may change. Thus, the value of a CDS should be expected to change through time.

The process of altering the value of a CDS in the accounting and financial systems of the CDS parties is known as a **mark-to-market adjustment**. Investors perform a mark-to-market (MTM) adjustment to the value of CDS contracts for three primary reasons: financial reporting, realizing economic gains or losses, and managing collateral.

If the market premium moves wider than the contract premium, a protection buyer experiences an MTM gain because the protection was bought more cheaply than is currently available in the market. But if the market premium tightens, the protection seller experiences an MTM gain (and the protection buyer experiences an MTM loss). Calculating a CDS MTM adjustment is essentially the same as calculating the cost of entering into an offsetting transaction.

Suppose an investor bought five-year protection through a CDS at a spread of 100 basis points (bps) per year. One year later, the spread for the same protection (with four remaining years) has widened to 120 bps. The investor would then have an MTM gain, since the protection, for which the investor is paying 100 bps per year, now has a market value of 120 bps per year. To calculate this MTM amount, one can assume a hypothetical offsetting trade in which the investor sells identical protection at 120 bps for four years to hedge the position. This would leave a fixed residual cash flow of 20 bps per year for up to four years in favor of the investor. However, this hypothetical annuity would terminate prior to four years if a triggering credit event occurred. The present value of this annuity, adjusted for the possibility of termination prior to four years, is the MTM amount.

24.5.4 Unwinding a CDS Transaction

A party to an OTC derivative that decides to unwind a position (perhaps to monetize the gains or losses or because the credit exposure of the CDS is no longer desired) typically has three alternatives. First, the party can enter into an offsetting transaction. Second, the party can enter into a novation, also known as an assignment. A **novation** or an **assignment** is when one party to a contract reaches an agreement with a third party to take over all rights and obligations to a contract. Third, the parties to the OTC contract can agree to terminate the contract (with or without a payment from one party to the other). Details of each of these alternatives follow:

1. ENTERING AN OFFSETTING POSITION: The CDS exposure can be offset with a position either in another CDS contract or in one of the underlying deliverable obligations. If the offset is in the underlying bonds, the investor has to separately

hedge out the residual interest rate risk. If the offset is with another CDS contract, it most likely results in counterparty risk and a spread differential reflecting changes in the market spread since the first CDS position was established.

2. ASSIGNING THE CONTRACT: Investors may be able to locate a dealer or another entity that will take over the rights and obligations of the contract with or without a cash payment from one party to the other. If so, the investor can assign (i.e., novate) the contract. The original counterparty must give permission for assignment because of the counterparty risk present in any CDS contract. The ISDA master agreement requires a transferrer to obtain prior written consent from the remaining party before a novation takes place. Due to potential exposures of CDS parties to the credit risk of the other party, assignments typically occur only when the non-dealer in the contract is replaced by a dealer.

3. TERMINATING THE CONTRACT: The CDS contract can be terminated with mutual consent if necessary by having one of the counterparties pay the other counterparty any lost value from discontinuing the swap. (The valuation of an existing CDS is discussed in a previous section.)

24.5.5 Participants in Credit Derivatives Markets

Credit derivatives in general and CDSs in particular have been adopted by virtually all types of financial institutions to take on credit risk, reduce credit risk, or otherwise manage credit risk, or to implement various investment strategies. Although banks remain important players in credit derivatives markets, trends indicate that asset managers are likely to be the major force behind the future growth of these markets. Participants use CDSs for various reasons and follow different trading strategies to hedge risk, increase return, make markets, and reduce funding costs. The following are the main strategies adopted by market participants.[12]

- BANK TRADING ACTIVITIES: Major banks serve as market makers in credit derivatives markets and were historically constrained in their ability to provide liquidity because of limits on the amount of credit exposure they could have in one company or sector. The use of more efficient hedging strategies, including credit derivatives, has helped market makers trade more efficiently and employ less capital. Also, CDSs allow market makers to hold their inventory of bonds during a downturn in the credit cycle while remaining neutral in terms of credit risk.

- BANK LOAN PORTFOLIOS: Banks were once the primary participants in credit derivatives markets. They developed the CDS market to reduce their risk exposure to companies to which they lent money or became exposed through other transactions, thus reducing the amount of capital needed to satisfy regulatory requirements. Banks continue to use credit derivatives for hedging both single-name and broad market credit exposure.

- HEDGE FUNDS: Since their early participation in credit derivatives markets, hedge funds have continued to increase their presence and the variety of trading strategies in the markets. Whereas the activity of hedge funds was once primarily driven by convertible bond arbitrage, many funds now use CDSs as the most efficient method to buy and sell credit risk. Additionally, hedge funds have been the primary users of relative value trading opportunities and new products that facilitate the trading of credit spread volatility, correlation, and recovery rates.

- OTHER ASSET MANAGERS: Asset managers use credit derivatives markets because they provide opportunities that the managers cannot find in the bond market, such as a particular credit risk with a particular maturity. In addition, credit derivatives markets provide a relatively easy method for avoiding cash sales or overcoming difficulties of short selling. For example, an asset manager might purchase three-year protection to hedge a 10-year bond position whose credit-worthiness is under stress but expected to improve if it can survive the next three years. Finally, the emergence of a liquid CDS index market has provided asset managers with a vehicle to efficiently express macro views on the credit markets.
- INSURANCE COMPANIES: The participation of insurance companies in credit derivatives markets can be separated into two distinct groups: (1) life insurers and property-casualty companies, and (2) monolines and reinsurers. Life insurers and property-casualty companies typically use CDSs to sell credit protection to enhance the return on their asset portfolios. Monolines (providers of bond guarantees) and reinsurers often sell credit protection as a source of additional premiums and to diversify their portfolios to include credit risk.
- CORPORATIONS: Operating firms use credit derivatives markets to manage credit exposure to third parties (e.g., accounts receivable). In some cases, the greater liquidity, transparency of pricing, and structural flexibility of the CDS market make it an appealing alternative to credit insurance or factoring arrangements. Some corporations invest in CDS indices and structured credit products as a way to increase expected returns on pension assets or balance sheet cash positions. Finally, corporations are focused on minimizing their funding costs; to this end, many corporate treasurers monitor their own CDS spreads as a benchmark for pricing new bank and bond deals.

24.5.6 Five Motivations for Credit Default Swaps

The following are five motivations for entering into CDSs:

1. RISK DECOMPOSITION: Credit derivatives provide an efficient way to decompose and separate risks embedded in complex securities. CDS spreads reflect the price to bear pure credit risk. A corporate bond represents a bundle of risks, including interest rate risk, potential callability risk, potential currency risk, credit risk (constituting both the risk of default and the risk of volatility in credit spreads), and liquidity risk. Before the advent of CDSs, the primary way for a bond investor to adjust a credit risk position was to buy or sell that bond, consequently affecting the investor's positions across the entire bundle of risks. Credit derivatives provide a way to manage default risk independently of interest rate risks. Arbitrage strategies can be efficiently implemented using these instruments. For example, convertible arbitrage managers can use CDSs to hedge the credit risk of their convertible positions without affecting the interest rate risk of the portfolio.

2. SYNTHETIC SHORTS: Credit derivatives provide an efficient way to hedge credit risk through shorting credit (i.e., taking a position with a value that varies inversely with default). The credit risk exposure of a corporate bond portfolio might be manageable by selling or shorting the bonds. However, bank loans and other credit instruments may turn out to be impossible or at least very costly to

short. CDS contracts can be constructed based on those credit risks. Thus, CDSs can allow investors to establish synthetic short positions to hedge or manage specific credit risks or a broad index of credit risks.

3. SYNTHETIC CASH POSITIONS: Credit derivatives offer ways to synthetically create loan or bond substitutes through tailor-made credit products. Credit derivatives are OTC instruments that can be tailored to provide investors with various choices for customizing their risk exposures. For example, investors can select maturities to express views about the timing of future credit events. CDS contracts often refer to a senior unsecured bond, but some CDS contracts refer to senior secured and syndicated secured loans. Having CDSs on several components of the same capital structure allows investors to express views on the relative values within a company's capital structure. Credit derivatives can even be used as an alternative to equity derivatives to express a directional view on a firm.

4. MARKET LINKING: The high liquidity of credit derivatives can serve as a source of information that links structurally separate markets. The CDS market often reacts first and facilitates a reflection of revised prices in less liquid markets, such as bond or loan markets. For example, investors buying newly issued convertible debt are exposed to the credit risk in the bond component of the convertible instrument and may seek to hedge this risk using CDSs. As the buyers of convertible bonds purchase protection, the spreads in the CDS market widen. The spread change may occur before the pricing implications of the convertible debt are reflected in bond market spreads. However, the change in CDS spreads may cause bond spreads to widen as investors seek to maintain the value relationship between bonds and CDSs. Thus, the CDS market can serve as an information conduit and as a link between structurally separate markets.

5. LIQUIDITY DURING STRESS: Credit derivatives provide liquidity in times of turbulence in the credit markets. Before the CDS market, a holder of a distressed or defaulted bond often had difficulty selling the bond, even at reduced prices, because cash bond desks are typically long credit risk due to owning an inventory of bonds. As a result, they are often unwilling to purchase bonds and assume more risk in times of market stress. In contrast, credit derivatives desks typically hold an inventory of protection (short credit risk), having bought protection through CDSs. In distressed markets, investors can reduce long credit risk positions by purchasing credit protection through credit derivatives desks, which may be better positioned to sell credit protection and change their inventory position from being short credit risk to being neutral.

24.6 OTHER CREDIT DERIVATIVES

Generally, CDSs are not viewed as options, because in many ways they do not fit the classic view of options: They do not tend to require a single up-front premium, and they do not offer the buyer a right to initiate a transaction. However, in some ways CDSs are option-like. They tend to offer an asymmetric payout stream, much like an option: If no default or other trigger event occurs, then there is no related payment; and if there is an event, then there is a potentially large payment from the protection seller to the protection buyer. However, another key distinction between CDSs and classic options is that in most cases the decision to exercise a classic option and receive a potentially large payment is initiated at the discretion of the option buyer. In CDSs, payments are automatically triggered by specified events; there is no discretion on the part of the credit protection buyer as to whether the protection is provided or when it is provided. In summary, in credit derivatives, there can be a fine line between options and other derivatives.

The next three sections focus on credit options: credit derivatives that more closely resemble classic options. Like CDSs, credit options may be used for transferring or accumulating credit exposure. Whereas CDSs involve a series of payments from the protection buyer to the protection seller, credit options involve a single payment from the credit protection buyer to the credit protection seller that leads to an asymmetric payout (i.e., a potentially large payment from the credit protection seller to the credit protection buyer). The decision to exercise the option may be governed by the discretion of the option buyer, or it may be automatically generated by the terms of the contract and the specification of a trigger event. Thus, not all credit options give an option buyer the right but not an obligation to exercise the option.

24.6.1 Term of Credit Options

A credit call option allows the holder to "buy" a credit-risky price or rate, whereas a credit put option allows the holder to "sell" a credit-risky price or rate. "Buy" and "sell" are in quotation marks here to reflect that the option may be on a rate, rather than a price, and that rates are generally not viewed as being bought or sold. Typically, the underlying asset is a credit-risky bond, and so a credit put option is the right to sell a credit-risky bond at a prespecified price. However, the underlying asset can also be a credit spread. For example, a credit call option can be the right to buy a credit spread at a prespecified level.

Since prices and spreads move inversely, a call option on a price is the opposite directional bet as a call option on a rate. Thus, while either a call or a put can reference a rate or a price, an entity wishing to purchase credit protection can establish a long position in a put option on a bond price or a call option on a credit spread. The two positions both purchase credit protection because prices and credit spreads move inversely. Credit options may trade on a stand-alone basis or may be a component of a security or a contract.

Binary options (sometimes termed digital options) offer only two possible payouts, usually zero and some other fixed value. Thus, binary options do not offer the payout structure of a classic option: limited downside risk with large upside potential. Accordingly, binary credit options offer a fixed payout if exercised or triggered; traditional options offer a payout based on prevailing market conditions, such as the difference between the market price of a credit-risky asset and the strike price of the option. In a binary option, there is little or no discretion regarding exercise of the option; the binary option's contract specifies the basis on which the final payout will or will not be made. As with other options, **European credit options** are credit options exercisable only at expiration, and **American credit options** are credit options that can be exercised prior to or at expiration.

24.6.2 Credit Put Option on a Bond Price

Consider an American credit put option on a bond that pays the holder of the option the excess, if any, of the strike price of the option over the market value of the bond.

The option is typically exercised if the bond experiences a credit event, such as a default. In OTC options, the contract specifies whether the exercise of the option is triggered by specified events or by the discretion of the option buyer. This option may be described as paying:

$$\text{Max}[0, X - B(t)] \text{ in default, and } 0 \text{ otherwise} \qquad (24.7)$$

where X is the strike price of the put option and $B(t)$ is the market value of the bond at default.

This option may be combined with the underlying credit risk to provide a hedged position. The combination of the underlying bond and the credit put option offers full repayment of the bond's principal if no credit event occurs, and payment of the option's strike price if a credit event does occur. Note that the option is not a binary option, which pays a fixed amount when a credit event occurs.

24.6.3 Call Option on a CDS

Consider an American call option on a CDS. A long position in the option is established by paying a premium. The call option allows the holder of the call option to enter a CDS at the rate (strike) specified in the option contract. Suppose that a bank holds a credit-risky asset and seeks credit protection using a call option on a CDS on the risky asset. If the credit-worthiness of the bond issuer deteriorates or if overall credit market conditions deteriorate, the credit-risky asset's price falls and its credit spread widens. After the credit spread widens, the call option holder may choose to enter a CDS at the prespecified spread by exercising the option.

The combination of a call option on a CDS and the underlying bond offers a different payout than the combination of a CDS and the underlying bond. With the call option, the bondholder can benefit from improvements in credit; the bond price rises, and the option goes out-of-the-money. If credit conditions deteriorate, the call option can be exercised to purchase credit protection using a CDS at a prespecified rate. The combination of a credit-risky bond and a CDS is hedged such that the value is protected from loss but also prevented from benefiting if credit conditions improve. Of course, the option buyer pays a premium for this ability to benefit from bond price increases while being protected from bond price declines.

24.6.4 Credit-Linked Notes

Credit-linked notes (CLNs) are bonds issued by one entity with an embedded credit option on one or more other entities. Typically, these notes can be issued with reference to the credit risk of a single corporation or to a basket of credit risks. A CLN with an embedded credit option on Firm XYZ is not issued by Firm XYZ. The CLN is like a CDS in that it is engineered to have payoffs related to the credit risk of Firm XYZ while being legally distinct from Firm XYZ.

The holder of the CLN is paid a periodic coupon and then the par value of the note at maturity if there is no default on the underlying referenced corporation or basket of credits. However, if there is some default, downgrade, or other adverse credit event, the holder of the CLN receives a lower coupon payment or only a partial redemption of the CLN principal value. Note that the cash flows received by the holder of the CLN are not delivered by the underlying referenced corporation.

Thus, the long position in a CLN bears credit risk of the referenced entity or entities without being a direct part of any bankruptcy. By agreeing to bear some of the credit risk associated with a corporation or basket of other credits, the holder of the CLN receives a higher yield on the CLN than would be received on a riskless note. In effect, the holder of the CLN has sold some credit insurance (i.e., served as a credit protection seller) to the issuer of the note (i.e., the credit protection buyer). If a credit event occurs, the CLN holder must forgo some of the coupon or principal value to make the seller of the note whole. If there is no credit event, the holder of the CLN collects an insurance premium in the form of a higher yield.

CLNs appeal to investors who wish to take on more credit risk but are either wary of stand-alone credit derivatives such as swaps and options or limited in their ability to access credit derivatives directly. A CLN is a coupon-paying note. Unlike traditional derivatives, they are on-balance-sheet debt instruments that virtually any investor can purchase. Furthermore, they can be tailored to achieve the specific credit risk profile that the CLN holder wishes to target.

24.7 CDS INDEX PRODUCTS

CDS indices are indices or portfolios of single-name CDSs. They are tradable products that allow investors to create long or short positions in baskets of credits and have now been developed globally under the CDX (North America and emerging markets) and iTraxx (Europe and Asia) banners. The CDX and iTraxx indices now encompass all the major corporate bond markets in the world.

CDS indices reflect the performance of a basket of assets—namely, a basket of single-name CDSs. For instance, CDX and iTraxx indices consist of 125 credit names. CDS indices have a fixed composition and fixed maturities. Equal weight is given to each underlying credit in the CDX and iTraxx portfolios. If there is a credit event in an underlying CDS, the credit is effectively removed from the indices.

As time passes, the maturity term of an index decreases, making it substantially shorter than the benchmark's term. A new series of indices is established periodically, with a new underlying portfolio and maturity date to reflect changes in the credit market and to help investors maintain a relatively constant duration, if they so choose. The latest series of the index represents the current on-the-run index. Markets have continued to trade previous series of indices, albeit with somewhat less liquidity.

The indices roll every six months. Investors who were holding an existing (i.e., on-the-run) index may decide to roll into the new index by selling the old index contract and buying the new one. The new index has a longer maturity and therefore a higher market value because the credit spread curve tends to be upward sloping. The composition of the new index is likely to be different from that of the old one. For example, some of the old credit names may have been downgraded since the first index was created.

The market for CDS indices is highly liquid, meaning that the spread on a CDS index is likely to contain a smaller liquidity premium than the premium embedded in a single-name CDS. In a rapidly changing market, the index tends to move more quickly than the underlying credits, because in buying and selling, index investors can express positive and negative views about the broader credit market in a single trade. This creates greater liquidity in the indices than with the individual credits. As a result, the basis to theoretical valuations for the indices tends to increase in magnitude in volatile markets. In addition, CDX and iTraxx products are increasingly used to hedge and manage structured credit products.

Just as in the case of a single-name CDS, the credit protection buyer of a CDS index pays a fixed premium (such as 4% per year of notional value), typically on a quarterly basis. But in the case of a CDS index, the notional value of the index is based on the combined notional values of 100 or more credit risks rather than on a single credit risk. Since the referenced asset is a portfolio of credit risks, the credit protection seller must make settlement payments for credit events on each and every credit risk in the index. Each credit event in a CDS index causes a payment and then lowers the notional value of the index.

For example, consider a CDS index on 125 investment-grade U.S. corporate bonds. Suppose that an institution with a $1 billion portfolio of such bonds wishes to temporarily hedge part ($100 million) of the portfolio's risk. The institution enters a position with $100 million of notional value in the CDS index as a credit protection buyer. The credit protection buyer pays a fixed coupon on a quarterly basis to the protection seller. Suppose that during the first year, one of the 125 bonds underlying the index defaults and there is no recovery; that is, there are no proceeds to bondholders from the liquidation of the firm. The credit protection buyer would receive $800,000 from the credit protection seller, and the notional value of the CDS index would drop by $800,000. Note that the credit protection buyer and seller do not directly gain or lose when the notional value of the CDS index falls; the size of the notional value simply serves to scale the size of future payments. The CDS index functions much like a portfolio of 125 separate single-name CDSs.

24.8 FIVE KEY RISKS OF CREDIT DERIVATIVES

Although credit derivatives offer investors alternative strategies to access credit-risky assets, they come with specialized risks. These risks apply both to credit options and to credit swaps.

1. EXCESSIVE RISK TAKING: First, there is the risk that traders or portfolio managers may use CDSs to obtain excessive and imprudent leverage, either by design or by chance. Since these are off-balance-sheet contractual agreements, excessive credit exposures can be achieved without appearing on an investor's balance sheet (although it should be discernible elsewhere in the accounts, such as in footnotes). As with all investments, proper accounting systems and other back office operations should be utilized.

2. PRICING RISK: OTC credit derivatives can involve pricing risk, including risk from valuation subjectivity. As the derivative markets have matured, the mathematical models used to price derivative contracts have become increasingly complex. These models are dependent on assumptions regarding underlying economic parameters. Consequently, the pricing of credit derivatives is sensitive to the assumptions of the models and the specification of the parameters. Accounting and control procedures can be hampered by the lack of market prices.

3. LIQUIDITY RISK: Another source of risk is liquidity risk. Credit derivatives that are OTC contractual agreements between two parties can be illiquid. A party to

a custom-tailored credit derivative contract may not be able to obtain the fair value of the contract in exiting the position. Further, the legal documentation associated with a CDS usually prevents one party from selling its share of the CDS without the other party's consent. For a standardized CDS, there are likely to be market makers providing liquidity.

4. COUNTERPARTY RISK: Most OTC credit derivatives contain counterparty risk. Exchange-traded derivatives are backed not only by the parties on the other side of the contracts but also by institutions, such as brokerage firms and clearing-houses.

   In the case of OTC options, there is only one side of a transaction that can be at counterparty risk: the long position. The reason that the long side faces counterparty risk is that if the option writer defaults, the option becomes worth-less. Note that the credit protection buyer only suffers a counterparty loss when all three of the following conditions occur: the referenced entity experiences a credit event, the counterparty to the derivative defaults, and there is insufficient collateral posted to cover the loss.

   The reason that the short side does not face counterparty risk is that once the option has been purchased, there is no loss to the option writer from the buyer's insolvency. However, in the case of a swap, both sides of the derivative can face counterparty risk. After a swap is initiated, it is possible for market prices to move such that one side of the contract has a positive market value and the other side has a negative market value. The side with the positive market value clearly has counterparty risk. The side with the negative market value has counterparty risk to the extent that it is possible that the market value may become positive.

   The primary counterparty risk created by a CDS is to the credit protection buyer. Losses to the credit protection buyer due to counterparty risk may be manifested in two ways. First, if there is a credit event on the underlying credit risky asset that triggers the CDS and the credit protection seller defaults on its obligations to the credit protection buyer, then the credit protection buyer can lose the entire amount due under the CDS. However, even if a trigger event has not occurred, the true value of the CDS to the credit protection buyer varies directly with the financial health of the credit protection seller. This is because reduction in the credit-worthiness of the credit protection seller decreases the probability that the seller will be able to fulfill its commitments to the buyer that are contained in the CDS.

   Note that the probability that the credit protection seller will default at the same time that the referenced asset of the CDS experiences a trigger event can be relatively high if both events are driven by the same macroeconomic factors. In other words, a major credit crisis can cause CDS trigger events at a time when both the seller experiences distress and the buyer most needs the protection. It is ironic that a credit protection buyer with a goal of reducing credit risk can introduce a new form of credit risk, known as counterparty risk, into a portfolio from the purchase of a CDS.

   Prior to the financial crisis that began in 2007, counterparty risk was consid-ered a relatively small risk in credit derivative documentation. However, coun-terparty risk wreaked havoc on firms when Lehman Brothers, a huge financial institution, declared bankruptcy in September 2008. Even though many partici-pants in the market had agreements with Lehman Brothers that required Lehman to post collateral, the bankruptcy of Lehman froze much of that collateral; years later, many counterparties to Lehman were still waiting for their collateral to be released through the bankruptcy process.

5. BASIS RISK: Finally, credit derivatives may be viewed as having basis risk. In this context, basis risk is risk due to imperfect correlation between the values of the CDS and the asset being hedged by the protection buyer. The protection buyer takes on basis risk to the extent that the reference entity specified in the CDS does not precisely match the asset being hedged. A bank hedging a loan, for example, might buy protection on a bond issued by the borrower instead of negotiating a more customized, and potentially less liquid, CDS linked directly to the loan. If the value of the loan and the value of the bond are not perfectly correlated, there is basis risk. Another example is a bank using a CDS with a five-year maturity to hedge a loan with four years to maturity. The reason for doing so is potentially higher liquidity in CDSs with five years to maturity. However, the protection buyer takes on basis risk to the extent that the four- and five-year loan values experience different price movements.

REVIEW QUESTIONS

1. Why is the market for fixed-income securities other than riskless bonds often termed the spread product market?
2. What are the three factors that determine the expected credit loss of a credit exposure?
3. What is the relationship between the recovery rate and the loss given default?
4. List the two key characteristics that can make risk-neutral modeling a powerful tool for pricing financial derivatives.
5. List the four stages in the evolution of credit derivative activity.
6. What is the primary difference between a total return swap on an asset with credit risk and a CDS on that same asset?
7. List the seven kinds of potential trigger events in the standard ISDA agreement.
8. How can one party to a CDS terminate credit exposure (other than counterparty risk) to a CDS without the consent of the counterparty to the CDS?
9. If a speculator believes that the financial condition of XYZ Corporation will substantially deteriorate relative to expectations reflected in market prices, should the speculator purchase a credit call option on a spread or on a price?
10. What CDS product should an investor consider when attempting to hedge the credit risk of a very large portfolio of credit risks rather than hedge a few issues?

NOTES

1. Philippe Jorion, *Financial Risk Manager Handbook* (Hoboken, NJ: John Wiley & Sons, 2010).
2. Charles Smithson, *Credit Portfolio Management* (Hoboken, NJ: John Wiley & Sons, 2003); David Mengle, "Credit Derivatives: An Overview," Federal Reserve Bank of Atlanta, *Economic Review* 92, no. 4 (2007): 1–24.
3. Karen Spinner, "Building the Credit Derivatives Infrastructure," *Derivatives Strategy* (Credit Derivatives Supplement), June 1997.

4. Throughout this section, we ignore the precise day count that takes place in practice. In other words, it is assumed that there are 90 days in each quarter, 180 days in each six months, and 360 days in each year.
5. Alternatively, interest rate swaps can be valued as a portfolio of forward rate agreements (FRAs).
6. As stated, to keep the calculations simple, it is assumed that there are 90 days in each quarter.
7. Sundaresan, S. 2002. *Fixed Income Markets and Their Derivatives*. 2nd ed. Cincinnati, OH: South-Western.
8. Ferrara, P., and S. Ali. 2013. "Interest Rate Swaps: An Exposure Analysis." Society of Actuaries, July.
9. Smith, D. 2012. "A Teaching Note on Pricing and Valuing Interest Rate Swaps Using LIBOR and OIS Discounting." Boston University School of Management, June.
10. Ferrara, Ibid.
11. In dealing with credit derivatives, practitioners often shorten the terms *credit protection buyer* and *credit protection seller* to protection buyer and protection seller, or even simply buyer and seller. This chapter transitions from the longer terms to the shorter terms as the reader is assumed to be developing better familiarity with the terminology and concepts.
12. JPMorgan, *Credit Derivatives Handbook* (New York: Corporate Quantitative Research, 2006); Bank of America, *Credit Default Swap Primer* (San Francisco: Banc of America Securities, 2008).

CHAPTER 25

CDO Structuring of Credit Risk

The basic collateralized debt obligation (CDO) structure was introduced in Chapter 23. This chapter takes a close look at CDO structures with a focus on CDOs that structure credit risk.

25.1 OVERVIEW OF CDO VARIATIONS

The CDO structure can be used to partition or distribute cash flows from the structure's assets and other positions to various tranches. The CDO structure has several variations, including the balance sheet CDO, the arbitrage CDO, and the market value CDO. All of these CDO structures share the feature that the entire risk of the portfolio is gathered within a special purpose vehicle (SPV) and then distributed to investors through various CDO securities or tranches. Chapter 23 illustrated the CDO structure with stylized CDOs. In those simplified illustrations, there were only three tranches and very limited discussion of details and terms. This chapter explores CDOs in greater detail.

25.1.1 Credit-Related Motivations for CDOs

The CDO structure was born in the late 1980s. One of the first major uses of the structure was to place a portfolio of high-yield (i.e., speculative or non-investment-grade) bonds into a CDO structure to serve as its collateral and to issue securities (tranches) against that collateral. The portfolio of non-investment-grade bonds inside the CDO offers diversification benefits, and the remaining risks can be partially reduced through credit enhancements, which are discussed later. The risks of the portfolio are then distributed to various tranches. The tranches vary in the degree to which they bear credit risk, from junior tranches that bear the brunt of the risk to senior tranches that bear risk only from the most extreme levels of losses.

The key to the use of the CDO structure in the case of credit risk is that a large portion of the financing of the CDO (i.e., the security tranches) can be in the form of senior tranches, which contain relatively little credit risk compared to the CDO's underlying collateral portfolio. Thus, a large portion of a capital structure financing high-yield debt (or other credit-risky assets) can be rated as investment grade by the rating agencies. Many institutions, such as insurance companies and banks, are restricted from directly holding non-investment-grade debt. The use of CDO structuring can transform undesirable securities (high-yield debt) into desirable securities (highly rated senior tranches).

---

1. Risk management: Investors may be better able to manage risk through structured products.
2. Return enhancement: Investors may be better able to establish positions that will enhance returns if the investor's market view is superior.
3. *Diversification: Investors may be better able to achieve diversification through structured products.*
4. *Relaxing regulatory constraints: Investors may be able to use CDO structures to circumvent restrictions from regulations.*
5. *Access to superior management: Investors may obtain efficient access to any superior investment skills of the manager of the CDO.*
6. *Liquidity enhancement: Tranches of CDOs can be more liquid than the underlying collateral pool.*

EXHIBIT 25.1 Investor Motivations for Structured Products

The high credit ratings given to senior tranches when the underlying collateral pool consists of non-investment-grade bonds are based on three primary justifications: (1) the senior position; (2) the diversification inherent in the collateral portfolio; and (3) credit enhancements that were structured into the deal, such as a major bank providing additional safety features.

25.1.2 Investor Motivations for Structured Products

Exhibit 25.1 adds to the list of two economic motivations for structured products begun in Exhibit 23.4 of Chapter 23. The first two additional economic motivations in Exhibit 25.1, #3 and #4, relate to the CDO structuring of non-investment-grade debt just discussed. CDOs provide diversified investment opportunities to investors by assembling highly diversified collateral pools. Further, the CDOs allow financial institutions restricted from substantial investments in high-yield debt to obtain indirect exposure without violating regulations. Strong arguments can be made that using CDOs to circumvent regulations on high-yield debt offerings does not interfere with the goals of the regulations. It is reasonable to believe that financial institutions investing in a senior position of a CDO holding a highly diversified and credit-enhanced portfolio of high-yield debt are taking less risk than are financial institutions that concentrate their portfolios in the investment-grade bond market. In other words, in this situation, the regulations interfere with diversification, and CDO structuring enables institutions to achieve the benefits of better diversification.

Originally, these deals focused on bonds and were called collateralized bond obligations (CBOs). Following on the heels of CBOs, banks began to realize that they had assets on their balance sheets (e.g., leveraged loans) that could be repackaged into a collateral pool and sold to investors. Hence, collateralized loan obligations (CLOs) were born in the early 1990s. From these two streams of asset-backed securities, CDOs were born. A CDO can be a security that is backed by a portfolio of bonds and loans together. However, the term *CDO* is often used broadly to refer to any CLO or CBO structure. CDOs are usually designed to repackage and transfer risk, typically credit risk. But CDOs can also be used to transfer the uncertainty of insured mortgages with regard to the timing and size of prepayments. Often, CDOs of mortgages are called collateralized mortgage obligations (CMOs).

25.1.3 General Structure of CDOs

In most CDOs, there is a three-period life cycle. First, there is the **ramp-up period**, during which the CDO trust issues securities (tranches) and uses the proceeds from the CDO note sale to acquire the initial collateral pool (the assets). The CDO's trust documents govern what type of assets may be purchased. The second phase is normally called the **revolving period**, during which the manager of the CDO trust may actively manage the collateral pool for the CDO, potentially buying and selling securities and reinvesting the excess cash flows received from the CDO collateral pool. The last phase is the amortization period. During the **amortization period**, the manager of the CDO stops reinvesting excess cash flows and begins to wind down the CDO by repaying the CDO's debt securities. As the CDO collateral matures, the manager uses these proceeds to redeem the CDO's outstanding notes.

A major bank usually serves as the sponsor for the trust. The **sponsor of the trust** establishes the trust and bears the associated administrative and legal costs. At the center of every CDO structure is a special purpose vehicle. A special purpose vehicle (SPV) is a legal entity at the heart of a CDO structure that is established to accomplish a specific transaction, such as holding the collateral portfolio. In the United States, an SPV is usually set up as either a Delaware or a Massachusetts business trust or as a special purpose corporation (SPC), typically Delaware based. The SPV owns the collateral placed in the trust, and issues notes and equity (tranches) against the collateral it owns.

SPVs are often referred to as being bankruptcy remote. **Bankruptcy remote** means that if the sponsoring bank or money manager goes bankrupt, the CDO trust is not affected. In other words, the trust assets remain secure from any financial difficulties suffered by the sponsoring entity so that investors in the CDO tranches have a direct claim on the collateral. In structured products and elsewhere, investments that are bankruptcy remote provide enhanced liquidity by lowering the probability that an investment will become tied up in a bankruptcy process.

Each tranche of a CDO structure may have its own credit rating. Typically, most of the tranches of notes issued by the CDO receive an investment-grade rating by a nationally recognized statistical rating organization (NRSRO), with the exception of highly subordinated fixed-income tranches or the equity tranche. The equity tranche is the first-loss tranche. It is the last tranche to receive any cash flows from the CDO collateral and the first tranche on the hook for any defaults or lost value of the CDO collateral. Often, the issuer of the trust holds the equity tranche.

25.1.4 Terms and Details of CDOs

The underlying portfolio or pool of assets (and/or derivatives) held in the SPV within the CDO structure is also known as the collateral or **reference portfolio**. Every CDO active manager must balance risk and return. The risk and return of credit-risky collateral assets are often described using three major terms: weighted average rating factor, weighted average spread, and diversity score.

Risk is typically measured with the weighted average rating factor of the underlying collateral pool and its diversity score. The weighted average rating factor measures the average credit rating of the underlying collateral contained in the CDO trust. Return is typically measured as the weighted average return spread over LIBOR.

The **weighted average rating factor (WARF)**, as described by Moody's Investors Service, is a numerical scale ranging from 1 (for AAA-rated credit risks) to 10,000 (for the worst credit risks) that reflects the estimated probability of default. The rating factor increases nonlinearly, with small numerical differences between the higher ratings and large numerical differences between the lower ratings. The WARF of a portfolio is an average of those numbers across the securities weighted by market values. The CDO indentures contain covenants as to the average rating factor of the collateral pool.

A **diversity score** is a numerical estimation of the extent to which a portfolio is diversified. Portfolios of 100 securities can have substantially different levels of diversification, depending on the extent to which the securities are correlated. The diversity score is designed to indicate the number of uncorrelated securities in a hypothetical portfolio that would have the same probabilities of losses as the portfolio for which the diversity score is being computed. For example, if all 100 of the securities in a portfolio were perfectly correlated, the portfolio would behave as if it contained only one large position in one security and would have a diversity score of 1. If all 100 of the securities were uncorrelated, the diversity score would be 100. Values between these two extremes are computed using estimates of correlations.

The CDO indentures often have a weighted average spread over LIBOR that they are required to maintain. The **weighted average spread (WAS)** of a portfolio is a weighted average of the return spreads of the portfolio's securities in which the weights are based on market values. The spread of each security is computed as the excess of the security's yield over a specified reference rate, such as LIBOR, with a specified maturity. Historically, there is a very strong positive relation between rating factors and credit spreads. An active manager of a CDO can increase the WARF to get more yield (WAS). Conversely, the manager may increase the creditworthiness of the CDO collateral pool (lower the level of WARF), but only at the expense of yield (a lower WAS).

The **tranche width** is the percentage of the CDO's capital structure that is attributable to a particular tranche. Chapter 23 discussed attachment and detachment points. The tranche width is a positive percentage that is computed as the distance between those two points. Thus, a 10%/25% tranche would have a tranche width of 15% (i.e., 25% − 10%). The process of structuring a CDO typically involves altering the risk of the structure's assets and the widths of various tranches in an attempt to earn credit ratings for the more senior tranches that allow those tranches to be sold to investors at attractive financing rates.

25.2 BALANCE SHEET CDOs AND ARBITRAGE CDOs

The distinction between balance sheet and arbitrage CDOs focuses on the purposes for the creation of the structure. **Balance sheet CDOs** are created to assist a financial institution in divesting assets from its balance sheet. **Arbitrage CDOs** are created to attempt to exploit perceived opportunities to earn superior profits through money management.

25.2.1 Three Goals for Issuing Balance Sheet CDOs

Banks and insurance companies are the primary sources of balance sheet CDOs. Issuers have the economic motivation to use balance sheet CDOs to manage the

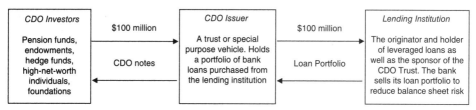

EXHIBIT 25.2   A Balance Sheet CDO

assets on their balance sheets. In a balance sheet CDO, the seller of the assets, a financial institution, seeks to remove a portion of its loan portfolio or other assets from its balance sheet. The bank constructs an SPV to dispose of some of its balance sheet assets into the CDO structure. The CDO's asset manager is often the selling bank, which is hired under a separate agreement to manage the portfolio of loans that it sold to the CDO trust. In addition, the CDO trust will have a trustee whose job it is to protect the interests of the CDO tranche investors. This is usually not the bank or an affiliate due to conflict-of-interest provisions. The financial institution using a balance sheet CDO to divest assets may be looking to achieve one or more of three goals: (1) to reduce its credit exposure to a particular client or industry by transferring those risks to the CDO, (2) to get a much-needed capital infusion, or (3) to reduce its regulatory capital charges. By selling a portion of its loan or bond portfolio to a CDO, the institution can free up regulatory capital required to support those credit-risky assets.

25.2.2   The Balance Sheet CDO Structure

Many balance sheet CDOs are self-liquidating. All interest and principal payments from the commercial loans are passed through to the CDO investors rather than reinvested in new assets. Other balance sheet CDOs provide for the reinvestment of loan payments into additional commercial loans to be purchased by the CDO trust. After any reinvestment period, the CDO trust enters into an amortization period, during which the loan proceeds are used to pay down the principal of the outstanding CDO tranches. Exhibit 25.2 shows schematically the transactions between CDO investors (who, in this example, put up $100 million in cash), the CDO issuer, and the lending institution.

25.2.3   Arbitrage CDO Structures

Whereas balance sheet CDOs are motivated by the desire of an institution such as a bank to divest assets, arbitrage CDOs are primarily motivated by a goal of successful selection and management of the CDO's collateral pool. A sponsor, such as a money management firm, establishes a CDO and takes an equity stake to earn a direct profit from the CDO. Arbitrage CDOs are designed to make a profit by capturing a spread for the equity investors in the CDO and by earning fees for money management services. The spread is captured as the excess of the higher-yielding securities that the CDO contains in its collateral portfolio and the yield that it must pay out on its fixed-income tranches issued to CDO investors. Put differently, an arbitrage profit is earned if the CDO trust can issue its tranches at a yield substantially lower than the yield earned on the bond collateral contained in the trust, such that the equity tranche of the trust receives expected residual income disproportionate to its risk. Further, money management firms earn fees on the amount of assets under management. By creating an arbitrage CDO, an investment management firm can increase both its assets under management and its income.

Another way to view the profit motive of an arbitrage CDO is in terms of market values rather than spreads and yields. The profit is earned by selling (issuing) securities (tranches) to outside investors at an aggregated price that is higher than that paid for all of the assets placed into the CLO/CBO structure as collateral. Thus, the value of the equity tranche to the issuer could be greater than the money the sponsor invested in the equity tranche.

25.3 MECHANICS OF AND MOTIVATIONS FOR AN ARBITRAGE CDO

This section begins with a simplified example of an arbitrage CDO.

25.3.1 Example of an Arbitrage CDO

Assume a money manager establishes an arbitrage CDO to invest in high-yield bonds. The trust has a life of five years and raises $500 million by selling (issuing) tranches of securities. For simplicity, assume that there are only three tranches, although in practice there can be numerous tranches. The security tranches issued by the trust are divided by credit rating. The most senior tranche, Tranche A, is a fixed-income tranche that is issued with the highest priority against the trust collateral. This highly rated debt will have a lower coupon, lower yield, lower expected return, and lower volatility than the collateral pool.

The second, or mezzanine, tranche, Tranche B, has lower seniority than Tranche A but enjoys the subordination of the equity tranche that will bear first losses. The credit rating of Tranche B may be only slightly higher than or roughly similar to the average high-yield bond owned by the CDO trust. The final tranche, Tranche C, is subordinated to the other two CDO tranches. For this tranche, the risk is the highest. This equity tranche also collects any residual income generated by the CDO collateral.

Exhibit 25.3 illustrates this arbitrage CDO trust. The money manager assembles a $450 million portfolio of high-yield bonds, with credit ratings of the underlying issuers equal to BB. The bonds pay an average annual coupon of 9% and have a face value of $500 million and a current market value of $450 million. In addition, the money manager charges an annual management fee of 50 basis points for managing the market value of the trust's assets: 50 basis points × $500 million = $2.5 million. Last, suppose there are annual expenses totaling $1.5 million that include such fees as $250,000 for the trustee to oversee the indenture clauses of the CDO notes. As illustrated in Exhibit 25.3, the CDO trust also buys a $50 million five-year U.S. Treasury note at an annual coupon rate of 6%.

25.3.2 Three Tranches and Their Priorities

The Treasury note is used to provide credit protection to Tranche A and helps allow for an AA credit rating to the senior tranche, along with the diversification and the

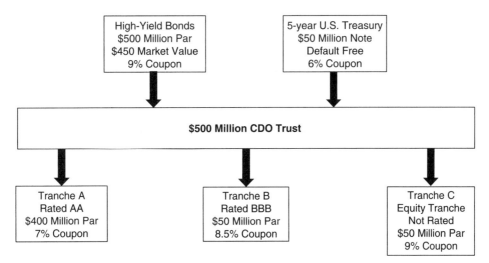

EXHIBIT 25.3   An Arbitrage CDO Structure

subordination of the other tranches. Tranche A has a $400 million face value and a coupon of 7%, and, as an AA-rated security, it is easily sold to institutions seeking securities with investment grade ratings. The investors in Tranche A receive a higher yield than that given by U.S. Treasuries because the CDO has credit risk and perhaps merits a complexity premium.

The second tranche has a face value of $50 million and a stated coupon of 8.5% and is rated BBB. This tranche has a higher rating than the underlying high-yield bonds because of the Treasury notes in the portfolio and because it has first-loss protection from the subordination of the equity tranche. The first-loss protection of this mezzanine tranche covers only the first $50 million worth of defaulted bonds. After the equity tranche is wiped out, Tranche B will lose dollar for dollar from defaulted bonds in the CDO collateral pool. Therefore, this tranche does not have the same principal protection as Tranche A and consequently receives a lower credit rating.

Tranche C is the equity tranche. It does not receive cash until and unless Tranches A and B receive their coupon payments. Consequently, this tranche bears the residual risk of the CDO trust, just as stockholders bear the residual risk in a corporation. This tranche has more risk than the collateral pool. The explanation is simple: The risk of the collateral pool is transferred to the tranches, with the senior tranche receiving lower risk than the pool; therefore, the most junior tranche must receive higher risk than the pool. The $50 million equity pool has a stated coupon of 9% and is not rated.

25.3.3   The Waterfall of an Arbitrage CDO

The collateral assets in Exhibit 25.3 generate $48 million in annual income, assuming no defaults. The Treasury note generates $3 million ($50 million with a coupon of 6%), and the high-yield bonds generate $45 million ($500 million in face value with a coupon rate of 9%). The first priority for the cash flows from the collateral pool is to pay the expenses and fees of the trust, including the money manager's annual fee of $2.5 million and total annual expenses of $1.5 million. Thus, $44 million of cash is available to the tranches in the absence of defaults in the collateral pool.

The coupon payments due to the senior tranche (Tranche A) and mezzanine tranche (Tranche B) total $32.25 million, which is composed of $28 million due to Tranche A ($400 million at 7%) and $4.25 million due to Tranche B ($50 million at 8.5%). The remaining cash is the residual cash flow of $11.75 million, assuming no defaults. This cash represents the spread, after fees and expenses, between the coupons collected from the CDO collateral pool of high-yield bonds and the Treasury note, and the coupon payments it must pay out to the CDO note holders. This residual income accrues to the equity tranche and results from the difference between the receipt of income from the high-yield bonds and the payments required to the CDO note holders. The $11.75 million of residual cash flow is more than the $4.5 million needed to pay the 9% coupon on the $50 million equity tranche. Without defaults, the residual cash flow would represent a 23.5% return on the equity tranche.

However, the equity tranche is the first to suffer default losses from the collateral pool. Default losses lower both the value of the collateral assets and the flow of coupon income. For example, a 3% default rate in the CDO's high-yield collateral in the first year would lower coupon income by $1.35 million (3% × $500 million × 9%). The value of the collateral assets would drop by $13.5 million (3% × $450 million). Although some of the defaulted funds may be recovered, the loss number ($13.5 million) illustrates the rate at which the collateral assets can be depleted relative to the original size of the equity tranche ($50 million). If the collateral pool experiences low default rates, the equity tranche can earn exceptional returns. If the collateral pool experiences high default rates, the equity tranche can be quickly wiped out, and the mezzanine tranche and perhaps even the senior tranche can be invaded.

25.3.4 Motivation of an Arbitrage CDO

There can be three direct financial motivations for a manager of an arbitrage CDO. First, the money manager can earn a transaction fee for selling its high-yield portfolio to the CDO trust. Second, the CDO sponsor is usually also the manager of the CDO trust and can therefore earn management fees for its money management expertise. Third, as an equity investor in the CDO trust, the money manager can earn the spread or arbitrage income from the CDO trust between the CDO collateral income and the payouts on the CDO notes. Earning a higher expected return from bearing credit risk should not be termed *arbitrage* in the strict sense of the term. However, if tranche note holders accept sufficiently low coupons on highly rated tranches (due, for example, to regulatory restrictions on directly holding non-investment-grade securities), it can be argued that arbitrage CDOs may at times truly offer arbitrage profits.

Finally, investors can be motivated to select arbitrage CDOs based on the belief that superior portfolio management within the CDO structure will provide enhanced income to the CDO that will then strengthen the credit-worthiness of the tranches. This economic motivation is included in Exhibit 25.1.

25.4 CASH-FUNDED CDOs VERSUS SYNTHETIC CDOs

In addition to balance sheet versus arbitrage CDOs, another major distinction between CDOs is that of cash-funded versus synthetic. This distinction focuses on

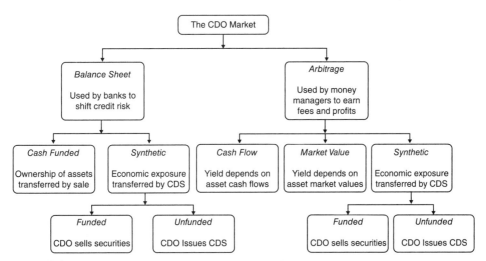

EXHIBIT 25.4 Overview of Collateralized Debt Obligations

whether the SPV obtains the risk of the portfolio using actual (cash) holdings of assets or through derivative positions.

Synthetic balance sheet CDOs differ from the cash-funded variety in several important ways. First, cash-funded CDOs are constructed with an actual sale and transfer of the loans or assets to the CDO trust. Ownership of the assets is transferred from the bank or other seller to the CDO trust in return for cash. In a synthetic CDO, however, the sponsoring bank or other institution transfers the risks and returns of a designated basket of loans or other assets via a credit derivative transaction, usually a credit default swap (CDS) or a total return swap. Therefore, the institution transfers the risk profile associated with its assets but does not give up the legal ownership of the assets and does not receive cash from selling assets. Exhibit 25.4 presents an overview of CDOs based on all of the distinctions detailed in this chapter.

25.4.1 Cash-Funded CDOs and Regulatory Capital

A **cash-funded CDO** involves the actual purchase of the portfolio of securities serving as the collateral for the trust and to be held in the trust. In other words, physical ownership of the assets is acquired by the CDO. As is discussed in the next section, an analogous result can be obtained through derivatives in the case of a synthetic CDO. However, one advantage of a cash-funded CDO to a bank is that it can be used to completely replace risky assets with cash on the bank's balance sheet, rather than synthetically removing only the risk through derivatives.

There are several potential advantages to the financial institution in divesting risky assets using a cash-funded balance sheet CDO. Banks are required by regulators to maintain a particular level of capital, depending on the risk of their assets. Higher-risk assets require higher quantities of regulatory capital. Banks maintain regulatory capital by obtaining financing through common stock and other sources of financing that are considered to be more expensive than sources of capital that do not serve as regulatory capital, such as deposits. Reducing risk-based/regulatory capital is the most important motivation for a bank to form a CDO trust. Most major banks are required to maintain risk-based capital, such as 8% of the outstanding balance of commercial loans. Using a CDO trust to securitize and sell a portfolio of commercial loans can free up regulatory capital that must be committed to support the loan portfolio.

☞ APPLICATION 25.4.1A

Consider a bank with a $500 million loan portfolio that it wishes to sell. It must hold risk-based capital equal to 8% to support these loans. If the bank sponsors a CDO trust in which the trust purchases the $500 million loan portfolio from the bank for cash, how much reduction in risk-based capital will the bank receive if it finds outside investors to purchase all of the CDO securities?

Since the bank no longer has any exposure to the basket of commercial loans, it has now freed $40 million of regulatory capital (8% × $500 million = $40 million) from needing to be held to support these loans.

Sometimes the equity tranche of the CDO trust is unappealing to outside investors and cannot be sold. In this circumstance, the sponsoring bank may have to retain an equity or first-loss position in the CDO trust. If this is the case, the regulatory capital standards require the bank to maintain risk-based capital equal to its first-loss position. Thus, the bank needs to maintain $1 in regulatory capital for each $1 of ownership in an equity tranche.

☞ APPLICATION 25.4.1B

Consider a bank with a $400 million loan portfolio that it wishes to sell. It must hold risk-based capital equal to 8% to support these loans. If the sponsoring bank has to retain a $10 million equity piece in the CDO trust to attract other investors, how much reduction in regulatory capital will result?

Since the bank must take a one-for-one regulatory capital charge ($10 million) for this first-loss position, only $22 million ($32 million − $10 million) of regulatory capital is freed by the CDO trust.

There are numerous economic motivations to banks for issuing cash-funded balance sheet CDOs. By selling existing loans into a CDO trust, a lending institution receives cash proceeds from the sale of its loans to the CDO trust that can be used to originate additional commercial loans or to strengthen its balance sheet. With its cash in hand, the bank can reduce its overall balance sheet by paying down its liabilities. Additionally, the selling bank may be able to reduce its credit exposure to one industry or group of borrowers if the bank deems that its exposures are too high. The bank can preserve a relationship with a particular client by lending to a higher credit exposure than it would otherwise wish in order to maintain its relationship with its borrower, and then reduce its exposure through divesting some of the loans into a CDO.

25.4.2 Mechanics of Synthetic CDOs

In a **synthetic CDO**, the CDO obtains risk exposure for the collateral pool through the use of a credit derivative, such as a total return swap or a CDS. Physical ownership of the underlying basket of securities is not transferred to the CDO, only the economic exposure. In effect, the CDO trust sells credit protection on a referenced basket of assets. For this protection and in the case of a CDS, the CDO receives income in the form of CDS payments from the credit protection buyer. The credit protection payments are then divided up among the CDO's investors into tranches, based on the seniority of the securities issued by the CDO.

In most cases, the CDO trust collects cash from the sale of the tranche securities and earns interest by investing the cash in low-risk collateral. Typically, the CDO invests the proceeds from issuing tranches in assets such as Treasury securities. The interest from the collateral combines with the CDS payments from the credit protection buyer to form a total return that should approximate the total return that would be received from physical ownership of the reference assets.

Synthetic CDOs are not limited to balance sheet CDOs. Synthetic arbitrage CDOs use derivatives to obtain desired risk exposure to reference assets similar to the exposure that could be attained through the cash purchase of the reference assets and avoid the need for any change in the legal ownership of the assets. Most synthetic balance sheet CDOs are constructed with a CDS. The CDO receives periodic payments from the credit protection buyer and must make a payment only if a trigger event such as a default occurs.

Synthetic arbitrage CDOs are used by asset management companies, insurance companies, and other investment shops with the intent of exploiting a mismatch between the higher income earned on the collateral and the lower cost of financing using the CDO tranches. Synthetic CDO structures are less administratively burdensome than cash-funded structures, particularly for attempting to transfer only a portion of a credit risk.

25.4.3 Comparison of Synthetic and Cash-Funded CDOs

There are three major potential advantages to synthetic CDOs over cash-funded CDOs. First, a synthetic CDO is less burdensome than the transfer of assets required for a cash-funded CDO. Commercial loans may require borrower notification and consent before being transferred to the CDO trust. This can take time, increase administration costs, and lead to dissatisfaction on the part of the bank's loan customers. These problems are avoided if the risk is transferred by a CDS or a total return swap. Second, synthetic CDO trusts can be used to provide economic exposure to credit-risky assets that may be relatively scarce and difficult to acquire in the cash market. Last, synthetic CDO trusts can employ leverage by using derivatives to sell credit protection on assets of a size that is greater than the level of assets in the collateral pool.

Two difficulties posed by synthetic CDOs relative to cash-funded CDOs are potential exposure to counterparty risk and reduction in bankruptcy remoteness. First, consider the difference between a cash-funded CDO that purchases bonds from Bank XYZ and a synthetic CDO that enters a credit derivative with Bank XYZ. The exposure to counterparty risk emanates from the use of a credit derivative to obtain risk exposure rather than from the actual purchase of collateral assets with risk exposures. The CDO is exposed to the risk of bankruptcy by counterparties to the credit derivatives at the same time that the credit derivatives have positive market values. Second, a major advantage of CDOs is that their bankruptcy remoteness enhances the safety of tranches by reducing the chances that payments to tranche holders will be bogged down by the financial distress of one of the entities providing the collateral assets. When the CDO has direct ownership and physical possession of the credit risky collateral assets (cash funded), there are reduced potential legal entanglements than when the CDO has a relationship with an entity through one or more credit derivatives (synthetic).

25.5 CASH FLOW CDOs VERSUS MARKET VALUE CDOs

Under the arbitrage CDO structure, there can be a further subdivision between cash flow CDOs and market value CDOs. The primary distinctions relate to the extent to which the assets are selected to match the maturities of the liabilities or the extent to which assets are selected in an attempt to earn superior rates of return. Under a balance sheet CDO, the assets are selected according to the preferences of the financial institution wishing to divest the assets.

In a **cash flow CDO**, the proceeds of the issuance and sale of securities (tranches) are used to purchase a portfolio of underlying credit-risky assets, with attention paid to matching the maturities of the assets and liabilities. Typically, there is a fixed tenor (maturity) for a cash flow CDO's liabilities that coincides with the maturity of the underlying CDO portfolio assets. Cash inflows are anticipated to be received in time to meet the cash outflows required by the tranche holders. Thus, the CDO portfolio is managed to wind down and pay off the CDO's liabilities through the collection of interest and principal on the underlying CDO portfolio. The CDO manager should focus on maintaining sufficient credit quality for the underlying portfolio such that the portfolio can redeem the liabilities issued by the CDO.

In some cases, the cash flow arbitrage CDO is static. This means that the collateral held by the CDO trust does not change, remaining static throughout the life of the trust. There is no active buying or selling of securities once the CDO trust is established. For static CDOs, the key is minimizing the default risk of the underlying assets, because it is the return of principal from the underlying CDO portfolio securities that is used to pay back the CDO investors. However, most arbitrage CDOs are actively managed. This means that after the initial CDO portfolio is constructed, the manager of the CDO trust can buy and sell bonds that meet the CDO trust's criteria to enhance the yield to the CDO investors and reduce the risk of loss through default.

In a **market value CDO**, the underlying portfolio is actively traded without a focus on cash flow matching of assets and liabilities. The liabilities of the CDO are paid off through the trading and sale of the underlying portfolio. In a market value CDO, the portfolio manager is most concerned with the market value of the assets and the volatility of those market values, because precipitous declines in the CDO's portfolio reduce the CDO's ability to redeem its liabilities. In market value CDO structures, the return earned by investors is linked to the market value of the underlying collateral contained in the CDO trust.

Consider the example of a CDO trust that buys high-yield bonds. It is unlikely that the trust will be able to issue tranches that perfectly match the maturity of the high-yield bonds held as collateral. The cash flows associated with a market value arbitrage CDO come not only from the interest payments received on the collateral bonds but also from the potential sale of these bonds to make the principal payments on the CDO securities. Therefore, the performance of the CDO securities is dependent on the market value of the high-yield bonds at the time of resale. Given this dependency on market prices, market value arbitrage CDOs use the total rate of return as a measure of performance. The total rate of return takes into account the interest received from the high-yield bonds as well as their appreciation or depreciation in value.

25.6 CREDIT ENHANCEMENTS

The measurement and analysis of credit risk are central aspects in the study of CDOs involving credit risk. Understanding the credit risk of the CDO's collateral portfolio is essential to understanding the risks of the tranches. This section discusses the measurement of that risk and the potential effects of risk changes on the values of the tranches.

One widely used method of modifying the risk of the various CDO tranches is to alter the securities in the collateral portfolio. However, other methods fall under the category of credit enhancements. Most CDO structures contain some form of credit enhancement to ensure that the majority of the securities issued to investors will receive an investment-grade credit rating. These enhancements can be internal or external. An **internal credit enhancement** is a mechanism that protects tranche investors and is made or exists within the CDO structure, such as a large cash position. Generally, credit enhancements are made at the expense of lower coupon rates paid on the CDO securities.

25.6.1 Subordination

Subordination is the most common form of credit enhancement in a CDO transaction, and it flows from the structure of the CDO trust. It is an internal credit enhancement. Subordination is the process of protecting a given security (i.e., tranche) by issuing other securities that have a lower seniority to cash flows.

For instance, CDO trusts typically issue several classes or tranches of securities. The lower-rated, or subordinated, tranches provide credit support for the higher rated tranches. The equity tranche in a CDO trust is the first-loss position and therefore provides credit enhancement for every class of CDO securities above it. Junior tranches of a CDO are rated lower than senior tranches; however, they receive a higher coupon rate commensurate with their subordinated status and therefore greater credit risk.

CDO structures can also be used for collateral assets with little or no credit risk, such as insured mortgages. In these cases, subordination affects the timing of payments to the various tranches rather than the credit risk of those payments. In a traditional sequential-pay CDO, the principal of the senior tranches must be paid in full before any principal is paid to the junior tranches. This sequential payment structure is often referred to as a waterfall. As interest and principal payments are received from the underlying collateral, they flow down the waterfall: first to the senior tranches of the CDO trust and then to the lower-rated tranches. Subordinated tranches must wait for sufficient interest and principal payments to flow down the tranche structure before they can receive a payment.

25.6.2 Overcollateralization

Overcollateralization refers to the excess of assets over a given liability or group of liabilities. Overcollateralization of a senior tranche occurs when there are subordinated tranches in a CDO. For example, consider a CDO trust with a market value of collateral trust assets of $100 million. The CDO trust issues three tranches: Tranche A is the senior tranche and consists of $70 million of securities; Tranche B consists of $20 million of subordinated fixed-income securities and is paid after the senior tranche is paid in full; finally, there is a $10 million equity tranche with the lowest seniority.

The level of overcollateralization is the ratio of the assets available to meet an obligation to the size of the obligation and all other obligations senior to that obligation. The overcollateralization rate for the senior tranche in this example is $100/$70 = 143%. The numerator is the millions of dollars of assets. The denominator is the millions of dollars of value that would be necessary to pay off that obligation, as well as any other obligation of equal or greater seniority.

The funds used to purchase the excess collateral come from both of the subordinated tranches, Tranche B plus the equity tranche. The level of overcollateralization of Tranche B is $100/$90 = 111%. The equity tranche provides the overcollateralization to Tranche B. Overcollateralization is an internal credit enhancement.

25.6.3 Spread Enhancement

Another internal enhancement can be excess spread of the loans contained in the CDO collateral portfolio compared to the interest, or coupons, promised on the CDO tranche securities. In other words, the average coupon on the assets may exceed the average coupon on the tranches such that in the absence of default, the CDO should be able to receive more cash than it is required to distribute. This excess interest may be retained and serve to enhance the credit-worthiness of the outstanding tranches. The excess spread may arise because the assets of the CDO trust earn a premium for illiquidity or because the assets are of lower credit quality than the CDO securities and therefore yield a higher interest rate than the rate paid on the CDO securities. A higher yield on the trust assets may also result from a sloped term structure and mismatched assets and liabilities. This excess spread may be used to cover losses associated with the CDO portfolio. If there are no losses on the loan portfolio, the excess spread accrues to the equity tranche of the CLO trust.

25.6.4 Cash Collateral or Reserve Account

A **reserve account** holds excess cash in highly rated instruments, such as U.S. Treasury securities or high-grade commercial paper, to provide security to the debt holders of the CDO trust. Cash reserves are often used in the initial phase of a cash flow transaction. During this phase, cash proceeds received by the trust from the sale of its securities are used to purchase the underlying collateral and fund the reserve account. It is sometimes argued that cash reserves are not the most efficient form of internal credit enhancement because they generally earn a lower rate of return than that required to fund the CDO securities.

25.6.5 External Credit Enhancement

An **external credit enhancement** is a protection to tranche investors that is provided by an outside third party, such as a form of insurance against defaults in the loan portfolio. This insurance may be a straightforward insurance contract, the purchase of a put option by the CDO, or the negotiation of a CDS to protect the downside from any loan losses. The effect is to transfer the credit risks associated with the CDO trust collateral from the holders of the CDO trust securities to an outside company. These external credit enhancements from a third party guarantee timely payment of interest and principal on the CDO securities up to a specified amount and thereby enhance the credit ratings of the tranches.

25.7 OTHER TYPES OF CDOs

CDO structures can be used with various underlying assets including distressed debt, hedge funds, commodity exposures, and private equity, as well as being structured with single tranches.

25.7.1 Distressed Debt CDOs

Default rates on debt increased in the United States during 2000 and 2001 and again beginning in 2008. This increase in default rates led to an increased availability of and interest in distressed debt, which in turn led to the development of distressed debt CDOs. The emergence of distressed debt CDOs followed the pattern of using the CDO structure to facilitate investments in diversified portfolios of credit-risky assets.

As its name implies, a **distressed debt CDO** uses the CDO structure to securitize and structure the risks and returns of a portfolio of distressed debt securities, in which the primary collateral component is distressed debt. Distressed debt CDOs usually have a combination of defaulted securities, distressed but unimpaired securities, and nondistressed securities. The appeal of the CDO structure is the ability to provide a series of tranches of collateralized securities that can have an investment-grade credit rating, even though the underlying collateral in the CDO is mostly distressed debt. The CDO securities can receive a higher investment rating than the underlying distressed collateral through diversification, subordination, and one or several of the other credit enhancements described previously in this chapter. Investors are then able to diversify into the distressed debt market and to do so more effectively by choosing a distressed debt CDO tranche that matches their level of risk aversion.

Historically, the main suppliers of assets for distressed debt CDOs have been banks, which use the CDOs to manage the credit exposure on their balance sheets. Assets for a CDO are purchased at market value. When a bank sells a distressed loan or bond to a distressed debt CDO, it usually takes a loss because it issued the loan or purchased the bond at par value. It was after the issuance of the loan or bond purchase that the asset became distressed, resulting in a decline in market value. Banks are willing to provide the collateral to distressed debt CDOs for several reasons. First, it improves the bank's balance sheet by removing distressed loans and reducing its nonperforming assets. The divestiture of distressed debt also allows the bank to obtain regulatory capital relief by reducing the amount of regulatory capital it is required to maintain. Finally, the divestiture provides cash, or liquidity, to the bank.

25.7.2 Hedge Fund CDOs

Another new application of the CDO structure has been the extension of CDOs to hedge funds. A **collateralized fund obligation (CFO)** applies the CDO structure concept to the ownership of hedge funds as the collateral pool. This innovation came as a result of the tremendous amount of capital pouring into the hedge fund market prior to the financial crisis that began in 2007. The CDOs of hedge funds facilitate diversification and allow investors to have professional management and reduced difficulties due to minimum investment sizes. Because CFOs are structured, they can offer access to hedge funds with a spectrum of risks and returns.

25.7.3 Single-Tranche CDOs

Single-tranche CDOs provide a highly targeted structure of credit risk exposure. In a **single-tranche CDO**, the CDO may have multiple tranches, but the sponsor issues (sells) only one tranche from the capital structure to an outside investor. In a single tranche CDO, the sponsor could sell just one of these tranches and potentially keep the rest for its balance sheet. A single-tranche CDO uses a CDS, just like a regular synthetic CDO. The main difference is that in a single-tranche CDO, only a specific slice of the portfolio risk is transferred to the investors, rather than the entire portfolio risk.

Single-tranche CDOs allow even more customization for an investor, such as collateral composition, maturity of the single-tranche note, and weighted average credit rating. As a result, single-tranche CDOs are the most fine-tuned of any structure. For this reason, single-tranche CDOs are sometimes referred to as bespoke CDOs, or CDOs on demand.

25.8 RISKS OF CDOs

The risks associated with CDO trusts are considerable. The meltdown in the subprime mortgage market that began in 2007 and spilled over into the CDO marketplace with a vengeance illustrated these risks. By the end of 2008, large financial institutions such as Citigroup, UBS, and Merrill Lynch had written down more than $160 billion of CDOs linked to the mortgage market. These are complicated instruments, and the risks are not always apparent. This section reviews the major risks associated with CDOs.

25.8.1 Risk from the Underlying Collateral

The risk of the underlying collateral is the single greatest driver of risk associated with an investment in a CDO structure. This chapter and the previous two chapters on structured products have focused on credit risk. But the CDO structure can also be used to engineer commodity price risk, private equity risk, hedge fund risk, and interest rate risk, such as risks inherent with unscheduled principal payments.

Note that a CDO structure does not change the risk of the assets in the underlying portfolio. Instead, the structure merely distributes the risks of the collateral pool to the various tranche holders of the CDO. The risks of the collateral portfolio can change due to either changes in market conditions or changes in the composition of the portfolio itself, and CDO investors bear the risk that the true nature of the collateral will differ from the previously understood nature. In other words, the nature of the actual portfolio may stray from the intended nature of the portfolio. Further, in times of stress, CDO managers may be slow or reluctant to write down or write off the poorly performing investments contained in the CDO trust. The investor may need to perform an independent analysis to determine accurate values and risks of the actual portfolio.

Default rates are a key driver of returns to collateral portfolios exposed to credit risk. Further, collateral portfolio value is driven by the level of losses given default (i.e., the proportion of the underlying credit risk that is not recovered in the event of default). Low recovery rates can combine with high default rates to generate high credit losses.

25.8.2 Financial Engineering Risk

The massive losses beginning in 2008 on CDO investments that had the highest possible credit rating (AAA) illustrate just how wrong financially engineered products can go. Financial engineering involves powerful tools that can generate enormous benefits. For example, the securitization and structuring of residential mortgages have been estimated to have substantially reduced the costs of financing homes for more than three decades. However, financial engineering can also be used, intentionally or unintentionally, to allocate risks in highly complex manners that are not well understood. **Financial engineering risk** is potential loss attributable to securitization, structuring of cash flows, option exposures, and other applications of innovative financing devices.

The financial engineering of insured residential mortgages in the 1990s facilitated a cost-effective supply of mortgage financing. CMOs played an important role in facilitating efficient mortgage financing, developing more and more sophisticated and complex structuring of tranches. By 1994, the complexities of CMO structures had soared to the point that many CMO tranches contained enormous interest-rate-related risks, even though the underlying collateral assets were virtually free of default risk. In 1994, a CMO crisis was triggered by rising interest rates; several large entities failed, and many others suffered enormous unanticipated losses. Interest rates reversed their course by the end of 1994, and further damage was averted.

Despite the grave lessons that should have been learned from the 1994 CMO crisis, a larger and more serious crisis emerged in 2007, primarily due to the default risk of subprime mortgages. At the heart of the subprime debacle were mortgage loan borrowers with substantially greater default risk than prime-grade borrowers. Small banks and mortgage lenders made these loans and then sold them into pools that were eventually financed by mortgage-backed securities (MBSs). Large investment banks purchased these MBSs and repackaged them yet again into a second pool, a CDO trust. The structures were used to slice and dice the risks of the subprime MBSs. When the underlying subprime mortgages began to default at much faster rates than previously experienced, the whole financial structure collapsed, bringing down Fannie Mae, Freddie Mac, and several major investment banks.

The lesson that was apparently not fully learned in 1994, and that was again taught in 2008, is that financial engineering is powerful and complicated. All market participants are directly or indirectly exposed to risks from the use of financially engineered products. Therefore, market participants should be aware of financial engineering risk and participate directly in engineered products with care and concern.

25.8.3 Correlation Risk

CDOs are often called *correlation products* because the collateral pool of a CDO can reference numerous assets and because the correlations of the returns of those assets drive the aggregate risks of the portfolio. Higher correlation increases aggregate risk. Investors in a CDO are therefore exposed to correlation risk. The major risk of large losses comes from numerous defaults occurring at or near the same time. Thus, large losses occur when defaults are correlated. If defaults are uncorrelated, then the risk is diversified, and default rates tend to be steady. The safety of more senior tranches is maximized when correlation risk is minimized. That is, the senior tranche holders do not want numerous defaults to occur at the same time such that all subordinated tranches are wiped out. Rather, senior tranche holders want default risk diversified such that default losses do not reach the magnitude necessary to wipe out mezzanine tranches and more.

25.8.4 Risk Shifting

Risk shifting is the process of altering the risk of an asset or a portfolio in a manner that differentially affects the risks and values of related securities and the investors who own those securities. A potential conflict of interest exists between the issuer of the CDO and the investors in the CDO tranches. The issuer may have an incentive to divest or otherwise place assets into the collateral pool that contain worse credit quality than is recognized by the investors. Also, the managers of the assets of a CDO may take on increasing risk or greater risk than initially indicated. Or, the manager may fail to take risk-reducing actions when the risks of the portfolio change due to market conditions. To reduce moral hazard, sometimes the equity tranche is held by the issuer. The idea is that equity tranche holders are then first in line to bear losses from asset defaults and have an incentive to lessen the default risks. However, as shown in the next section, ownership of junior tranches can actually encourage risk taking.

25.8.5 The Effects of Risk Shifting and Correlation on Tranches

At first glance, it may appear that if higher-risk assets are placed into the collateral asset pool and/or if those assets are poorly diversified due to high return correlations, the higher risk will make all tranches less desirable. However, risk shifting in CDOs can have very different effects on different tranches. As discussed earlier, an equity tranche position in a CDO may be viewed as a call option. As a call option, equity tranches, and to a lesser extent other highly subordinated tranches, can actually benefit from increases in the risk of the collateral pool. The potential for equity holders to benefit from upward shifts in asset risks is detailed in the structural model approach in Chapter 23.

The relations between the level of risk of the collateral assets of a CDO and the values of the CDO's various tranches is interesting. Let's assume that the risks of a CDO's assets can be altered substantially without having an immediate impact on the value of the assets. Generally, the sum of the values of all of the tranches, including the equity tranche of a CDO, should tend to equal the value of the collateral pool. However, a large change in the risks of the assets (e.g., an increase in the WARF) can have immediate effects on the relative values of the tranches. Specifically, increases in the risks of the CDO's assets tend to transfer wealth from the holders of more senior tranches to the holders of less senior tranches.

It is intuitively obvious that senior tranches become less valuable as the volatility of the CDO's assets rise (with asset values held constant). The senior tranches have less probability of being fully paid while the coupons remain fixed. It is less obvious why the junior tranches might gain in value. However, if the value of the assets remains constant and if the value of the senior tranches declines, then the value of the junior tranches should rise. This effect is also consistent with the structural model's view of equity as a call option and the well-known result of option theory that call option values increase when the volatility of the underlying assets increases. The most junior tranche may be viewed as a long call option on the collateral assets. The most senior tranche may be viewed as a long riskless bond and short an out-of-the-money put option on the collateral assets. Higher volatility of the collateral pool helps the tranches that are long options (i.e., long vega) at the expense of the tranches that are short options.

Finally, note that higher risk in the collateral asset pool can occur both from higher-risk assets and from higher return correlations among the assets (i.e., reduced diversification). Thus, a lower diversity score can shift wealth from senior tranches to junior tranches even when the WARF is held constant. Note that a very well diversified portfolio will generate a low but constant default rate. A low but constant default rate will spare senior tranches from losses, as all of the losses will be absorbed by the junior tranches. A very poorly diversified portfolio gives senior tranche holders an increased chance of losses (when the assets experience very large losses) and junior tranche holders an increased chance of bearing few or no losses (when assets experience minimal losses).

25.8.6 Other CDO Risks

The successful risk management of a CDO's portfolio requires understanding numerous potential risks. This section briefly surveys these risks.

A risk due to the difference in payment dates arises from a mismatch between the dates on which payments are received on the underlying trust collateral and the dates on which the trust securities must be paid. This risk can be compounded when payments on different assets are received with different frequencies, known as periodicity. This problem is often solved through the use of a swap agreement with an outside party, in which the trust swaps the payments on the underlying collateral in return for interest payments that are synchronized with those of the trust securities.

A type of basis risk occurs when the index used for the determination of interest earned on the CDO trust collateral is different from the index used to calculate the interest to be paid on the CDO trust securities. For instance, the interest paid on most bank loans is calculated on LIBOR plus a spread, but other assets may be based on certificate of deposit rates in the United States. The risk in this case is when a mismatch occurs and the indices underlying cash income from the collateral assets differ from the indices underlying payments to the tranche holders.

CDO tranches suffer when the collateral pool performs poorly. Collateral assets may perform poorly for several reasons. The market prices of collateral assets respond immediately to shifts in the levels, slope, or curvature of the yield curve of riskless rates. Yield curve shifts can cause the value of the collateral assets to change and can affect the cash flows available from reinvestment of cash flows from existing assets. Spread compression, when credit spreads decline or compress over time, reduces interest rate receipts from the CDO's collateral and may cause the CDO to face cash shortfalls even in the absence of defaults. A steeply upward-sloping yield curve can magnify the negative carry between the interest earned on the CDO's cash reserve accounts and the coupon rates of the CDO's tranches.

25.8.7 Modeling Credit Risk in CDOs

Initially, it may appear that modeling credit risk should not be that different from modeling other risks, such as equity, interest rate, currency, and commodity risks. For instance, in theory (such as in the CAPM), it could be argued that one should be able to calculate the beta of the CDO collateral portfolio and use that beta to estimate the beta of the various tranches. However, credit risk displays a number of properties that are not shared by these other sources of risk; thus, a different type of model is required. First, default is a relatively rare event. Most corporations currently in existence have never defaulted. Therefore, there are limited observations available with which to estimate various statistics through historical analysis. Second, many defaults occur due to systematic factors, such as changes in macroeconomic conditions, rather than idiosyncratic factors, such as mismanagement at the firm level. Third, many of the financial institutions that invest in credit products are not able to hold diversified portfolios of credit products to eliminate the idiosyncratic risks of these securities. Fourth, in some cases (e.g., sovereign debt), credit risk may arise not just because of the inability of the counterparty to pay but also because of its unwillingness to do so.

The drivers of losses to a CDO of underlying credit risks are the default rate and loss rate given default. The default rate refers to the percentage of the collateral assets experiencing default. The loss rate given default, as discussed in Chapter 24, is the percentage of the defaulted security values that cannot be ultimately recovered. The primary method for ascertaining the risks of tranches due to default risk in the CDO portfolio uses a copula approach.

A **copula approach** to analyzing the credit risk of a CDO may be viewed like a simulation analysis of the effects of possible default rates on the cash flows to the CDO's tranches and the values of the CDO's tranches. The idea behind the copula model of CDO default risk is that defaults are generated by two normally distributed factors: an idiosyncratic factor and a market factor. The idiosyncratic factor takes on a different value for each credit risk (i.e., bond) and generates hypothetical defaults whenever the factor's value for that particular bond is sufficiently high. The market factor is common to all credit risks in the CDO portfolio and reflects the tendency of defaults to occur in unison.

A parameter set by the user of the copula model determines the relative weights of the two factors (i.e., idiosyncratic versus market). Taken together, along with a user-specified expected default rate, the model allows simulation of the probabilities of various default levels for the collateral pool. The estimated probabilities of various default levels are then combined with a user-supplied loss rate given default (i.e., 1 – recovery rate) to estimate the probabilities of losses to each of the tranches in the CDO structure. Rating agencies have used the copula model to estimate return distributions for CDO tranches involving credit risk—both corporate bonds and uninsured mortgages. The copula model has been maligned as an important cause of the credit crisis that began in 2007. Specifically, the model was criticized for underestimating the risk of the most senior mortgage tranches from mortgage defaults. However, there is debate as to whether the difficulties, including apparently erroneous credit ratings, were caused by misunderstandings of the model, misspecification of the model, or misestimation of the model's parameters.

CDOs and other structured products are very powerful tools for engineering risk and other attributes. Those tools have been at the center of the 1994 CMO crisis as well as the financial crisis of 2007 to 2009. Whenever the next financial crisis occurs, highly engineered products will undoubtedly be involved, as a transmitter of risk or even as a contributor to risk. Accordingly, these powerful tools need to be well understood by their users.

REVIEW QUESTIONS

1. How would the exposure to credit risk of the most senior and most junior tranches of a CDO tend to compare to the average credit risk of the collateral pool?
2. List two major economic motivations to the CDO structuring of non-investment-grade debt.
3. What is the WARF of a portfolio?
4. What is the primary difference between the motivations for creating a balance sheet CDO and the motivations for creating an arbitrage CDO?
5. What is the primary difference between a cash-funded CDO and a synthetic CDO?
6. Is subordination an internal or an external credit enhancement?
7. How many tranches can be in a single-tranche CDO?
8. Suppose that the total value of the collateral pool of a CDO remains constant but the riskiness of the pool increases. If the value of the most senior tranches decreases, what should happen to the combined value of the other tranches?
9. What is the explanation, based on option theory, as to why the most junior tranche of a CDO would fall in value when the collateral pool of assets becomes more diversified?
10. What is the primary purpose of using a copula approach to analyze a CDO?

CHAPTER 26

Equity-Linked Structured Products

Financial institutions throughout the world are offering investors innovative structured products with complex payouts based on one or more market values, such as the returns of an equity index. One example might be an insurance-related product that guarantees to protect the investor against losses while offering upside returns based on the returns of the FTSE 100 index up to a certain limit. Large institutions offer these structured products using trademarked names along with descriptions of the potential attractiveness of each product in various market environments. This chapter refers to these products as equity-linked structured products, even though some of them have returns driven by market values other than equity values, such as interest rates or commodity prices. The chapter introduces and provides an overview of this large and growing sector of alternative investment opportunities.

26.1 STRUCTURED PRODUCTS AND SIX TYPES OF WRAPPERS

Most of the structured products discussed in Chapters 23 to 25 emphasize the goal of transferring relatively simple risk exposures related to an asset or a portfolio from one party to another. Often this transfer serves the dual purpose of meeting the risk preferences of both the issuer and the investor.

Equity-linked structured products, as defined in this chapter, are distinguished from the structured products in Chapters 23 to 25 by one or more of the following three aspects: (1) They are tailored to meet the preferences of the investors and to generate fee revenue for the issuer; (2) they are not usually collateralized with risky assets; and (3) they rarely serve as a pass-through or simple tranching of the risks of a long-only exposure to an asset, such as a risky bond or a loan portfolio.

The primary distinction of these equity-linked structured products is that while the issuers of the products may hedge their exposures by issuing the products, the main purpose for the transactions from the perspective of the issuer is fee generation, not risk management.

The structured products in this chapter represent a large and growing sector of investments. Estimates of the global market for structured products range from just over one trillion dollars to several trillion dollars, with annual issuances exceeding $100 billion.

Structured products are often placed inside wrappers. A **wrapper** is the legal vehicle or construct within which an investment product is offered. As an example, for more than 30 years U.S. banks have issued insured certificates of deposit (CDs) that offer a low guaranteed minimum interest rate with the potential for higher interest based on the growth of a pre-specified index, such as the S&P 500 Equity Index. These CDs are commonly referred to as market-linked, equity-linked, or indexed CDs. The wrapper in this example is a bank deposit. By using a bank deposit wrapper, U.S. investors can enjoy government protection against the counterparty risk of a bank default on the principal and any guaranteed interest.

The wrapper that is used to offer an investment typically has regulatory and tax consequences. BNP Paribas provides the following six examples of structured product wrappers in its *Equities and Derivatives Handbook*:[1]

1. OVER-THE-COUNTER (OTC) CONTRACTS: Private contracts negotiated between the investor and the issuing institution. Like credit default swaps (CDSs), they are usually formed under an International Swaps and Derivatives Association (ISDA) framework (as discussed in Chapter 24).
2. MEDIUM-TERM NOTES/CERTIFICATES/WARRANTS: Low-cost securities that can be public or private. Many such securities are traded on major stock exchanges.
3. FUNDS: A pooled investment vehicle with an objective of replicating a structured product. Funds may be public and may offer tax advantages.
4. LIFE INSURANCE POLICIES: Life insurance policies embedded within structured products. The products are subject to investment restrictions but may offer tax advantages.
5. STRUCTURED DEPOSITS: Offered through deposits at a financial institution, as illustrated in the previous CD example.
6. ISLAMIC WRAPPERS: Legal envelopes that are Shari'a compliant. Common interpretations of this compliance include the avoidance of interest and speculation (or excessive interest and speculation), and the avoidance of investing in prohibited underlying activities.

A key aspect of wrappers can be to give investors access to underlying investment opportunities that would otherwise not be available or would be less cost-effectively accessed through other means. For example, an investor may be able to invest in a portfolio of hedge funds through an insurance wrapper, thereby circumventing minimum subscription requirements. Or a mutual fund might invest in commodities through a gold-linked note, thereby circumventing regulatory restrictions on direct holdings of illiquid assets.

26.2 FOUR POTENTIAL TAX EFFECTS OF WRAPPERS

Different wrappers can offer different taxability of cash flows from investment products. The pre-tax internal rate of return, r, of an investment prior to consideration of taxes is found as the rate that discounts the anticipated inflows to being equal to the cost of acquiring the asset. The after-tax rate of return, $r*$, is the analogous rate computed on after-tax cash flows.

This section examines the relationship between pre-tax and after-tax returns for four tax scenarios. In some cases, marginal income tax rates are assumed constant through time for an investor and are denoted as T. In other cases, two tax rates are considered, T_0 as the initial tax rate and T_N as the terminal tax rate. All returns arc expressed as annualized and annually compounded rates.

26.2.1   Tax Effects of Tax-Free Wrappers

A tax-free wrapper takes an investment that would ordinarily be subject to income tax and allows tax-free accrual and distribution of income and capital gains. Roth individual retirement accounts (IRAs) in the United States and individual savings accounts (ISAs) in the United Kingdom are examples of these wrappers. The mathematics of these accounts is simplified because the after-tax return, $r*$, equals the pre-tax return, r. Thus, investors using either a Roth IRA or an ISA in a fund that generates a pre-tax return of 10% can expect the after-tax value of their investment to grow at 10%.

Tax-free wrappers do not generally offer tax deductibility of investment contributions. Although a tax-free return can be very attractive, as noted in the following text, the benefits of tax-deductible contributions to investors in high-income tax brackets may exceed the advantages of tax-free wrappers.

26.2.2   Tax Effects of Fully Taxed Wrappers

Fully taxed investments refer to products for which income and gains are taxable in the year in which they accrue or are distributed. The after-tax return on a fully taxed investment is shown in Equation 26.1:

$$r^* = r(1 - T) \tag{26.1}$$

Thus, an investor in a 40% tax bracket earning a pre-tax return of 10% experiences an after-tax return of only 6%.

☞ APPLICATION 26.2.2A

An investor in a 40% tax bracket earns an after-tax return of 9%. What must be the investor's pre-tax return?

Rearranging Equation 26.1 generates an answer of 15%, found as 9% divided by 0.6.

It should be noted that in most jurisdictions, some components of investment returns are tax-free or partially taxed. For example, capital gains are often taxed at a proportion (e.g., 50%) of the rate of fully taxed income items, especially in the taxation of long-term investments. When components of investment income are taxed differently, the after-tax return of the investment can be estimated as a weighted average of the after-tax return of each component by applying Equation 26.1 to each component.

APPLICATION 26.2.2B

An investor in a 40% tax bracket on ordinary income invests in a product that earns a pre-tax return of 10%. Sixty percent of the income is distributed as a capital gain that is taxed at 40% of the ordinary income tax rate. What is the investor's total after-tax return?

The investor's total after-tax return is the weighted average of the after-tax returns of the return components. Sixty percent of the total return (i.e, 6%) is taxed at a capital gains rate of 16% (found as 40% × 40%), leaving an after-tax capital gain return of 5.04%. Forty percent of the total return (i.e., 4%) is taxed at the ordinary rate of 40%, leaving an after-tax ordinary income return of 2.40%. The total weighted average is 7.44%, found as the sum of the two components (5.04% + 2.40%). This can also be found as the pre-tax return of 10% reduced by the weighted average tax rate of 25.6%. The average tax rate of 25.6% reflects the weighted average of 60% of the income being taxed as capital gains at 16%, and 40% of the income being taxed at the ordinary rate of 40%.

26.2.3 Tax Effects of Tax-Deferral Wrappers

Tax deferral refers to the delay between when income or gains on an investment occur and when they are taxed. Without wrappers, income is usually taxed when distributed, and gains are usually taxed when recognized (e.g., when a position is closed). Wrappers often defer taxation until funds are distributed from the wrapped product to the investor.

Consider the case of a product that defers all income and gains until the funds are fully distributed at a termination date N years later. The after-tax return on this investment is a function of r, T, and N:

$$r^* = \{1 + [(1 + r)^N - 1](1 - T)\}^{1/N} - 1 \tag{26.2}$$

 APPLICATION 26.2.3A

Consider an investor with a current and anticipated tax rate of 30% who anticipates withdrawing funds in 20 years. If the investor places money into a wrapper that offers tax deferment, how much will the after-tax annual rate of return improve through the use of the wrapper if the pre-tax rate is 8% and the time horizon is 20 years?

The answer is found as follows: $(1 + r)^N$ is the pre-tax future value, 4.661, which generates a taxable income of $4.661 - 1 = 3.661$. The 3.661 is taxed at 30%, leaving 2.563. Re-adding the principal (1.0) gives an after-tax future value of 3.563 (the value inside the outermost brackets). The 20th root of 3.563 generates 1.0656, from which 1 is subtracted to yield 0.0656. The answer

(6.56% interest) improves by 0.96% the 5.60% after-tax return found using the same inputted values in Equation 26.1.

26.2.4 Tax Effects of Tax-Deferral and Tax-Deduction Wrappers

An especially powerful wrapper for tax purposes is one that allows both immediate tax deduction of contributions and full deferral of taxes on income and gains until funds are withdrawn. **Tax deduction** of an item is the ability of a taxpayer to reduce taxable income by the value of the item. Retirement investment wrappers often offer these tax benefits, as do some insurance products (when contributions are classified as deductible premiums). The benefits can be astounding when the tax rate at withdrawal, T_N, is substantially less than the tax rate at contribution, T_0:

$$r^* = \{(1 + r)^N[(1 - T_N)/(1 - T_0)]\}^{1/N} - 1 \tag{26.3}$$

Brackets have been placed around the terms involving the two tax rates, T_N and T_0. Note that when tax rates do not change, a tax-deductible and tax-deferred investment wrapper enables investors to receive an after-tax rate of return equal to the pre-tax rate of return. When tax rates decline between contribution and withdrawal ($T_N < T_0$), the after-tax rate of return exceeds the pre-tax rate of return. The intuition of this fascinating result is that the tax savings from the deductibility of contributions serve as an interest-free loan.

☞ APPLICATION 26.2.4A

Consider an investor in a current tax rate of 35% who anticipates a reduced tax rate of 20% in 10 years (after retirement). If the investor places money into a wrapper that offers tax deduction and tax deferment, what will the investor's after-tax rate of annual return be if the pre-tax rate is 6% and the time horizon is 10 years?

The future value (1.791) is multiplied by the after-tax ratio $(1 - 0.20)/(1 - 0.35) = 1.231$ to generate 2.2041. The 10th root of 2.2041 followed with the subtraction of 1 generates the answer that the after-tax rate is 8.22%. Note the dramatic magnitude of the after-tax yield (8.22%), which exceeds the pre-tax yield (6%).

26.3 STRUCTURED PRODUCTS WITH EXOTIC OPTION FEATURES

The first example of a structured product in this chapter was the case of an insured CD that offered upside potential based on the performance of an equity index. Structured products have evolved to include highly creative and potentially highly complex investments. Many of these products use complex optionalities and often have highly sophisticated underlying valuation models.

For example, consider the following stylized description of a retail structured product that illustrates the complexity of some of these products.

This structured product provides five years of exposure to a basket of 10 underlying equities. Semiannually, the return of the best-performing equity is locked in (subject to a cap) and removed from the basket. At termination, the product pays the average of the locked-in returns of the 10 equities (subject to a floor).

What is the motivation of an investor in this product? How can an investor determine an appropriate value for the product? How can the issuer manage the risk of providing this product?

The spectrum of potential products is vast, varying on such dimensions as the number of underliers, the observation dates, floors, caps, and principal protections. Some products are sufficiently complex that their valuations depend on myriad parameters and the use of highly sophisticated Monte Carlo simulation techniques.

The starting point for understanding many complex structured products is to understand exotic options. Chapter 6 provides an introduction to options that emphasizes simple European-style call options and put options. A **simple option** has (1) payoffs based only on the value of a single underlying asset observed at the expiration date, and (2) linear payoffs to the long position of the calls and puts based on the distance between the option's strike price and the value of the underlying asset. These simple options, detailed in Chapter 6, are sometimes called "plain-vanilla" or "non-exotic" options. This material uses the term *simple options*.

Although there is no universally accepted definition of an exotic option, a useful definition is that an **exotic option** is an option that has one or more features that prevent it from being classified as a simple option, including payoffs based on values prior to the expiration date, and/or payoffs that are nonlinear or discontinuous functions of the underlying asset. This analysis of structured products makes the following distinction: A **structured product without exotic options** has a payoff diagram defined exclusively in terms of the payoff to the value of a single underlier at termination and is (1) a continuous relationship, (2) a one-to-one relationship, and (3) a relationship composed entirely of two linear segments. Thus, a structured product based on exotic options violates one or more of the three properties.

The structured products described in this chapter are generally engineered to the preferences of the investor. Examples are provided as a general guide to common practices in the industry. It should be noted, however, that details regarding the structured products are stylized into general conventions in this chapter and the illustrations provided in this chapter are not necessarily those found in actual products.

26.3.1 Structured Products with No Exotic Options

Exhibit 26.1a is representative of a structured product that does not have exotic option features. The payout in Exhibit 26.1a is a simple example of a popular investment known as a principal-protected structured product. A **principal-protected structured product** is an investment that is engineered to provide a minimum payout guaranteed by the product's issuer (counterparty). For example, a major bank may

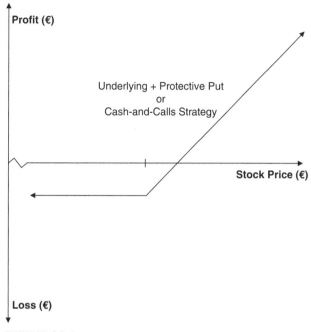

EXHIBIT 26.1a Equivalence of Two Strategies

offer a structured product with a term of five years that has a payout that increases if an underlying index increases but also a minimum guaranteed payout regardless of any declines in the underlying index. Of course, the payout is subject to the counterparty risk of the issuer. Thus, in the context of structured products, principal protection is the promise by the issuer to guarantee the return of most or all of the investor's principal.

Another important feature of many structured products is the participation rate. The **participation rate** indicates the ratio of the product's payout to the value of the underlying asset. A structured product with a participation rate of 100% has a payout that increases by the same percentage that the underlying asset's value increases. A participation rate of 50% indicates half the risk exposure, whereas a participation rate above 100% indicates leveraged exposure of the structured product to the value of the underlying asset.

Note that principal protection and participation rates are not exotic option features. Simple call options and put options can easily be combined to provide principal protection (e.g., long a put option) and participation rates not equal to 100% (e.g., having option exposures with notional amounts above or below the principal amount of the structured product).

The diagram in Exhibit 26.1a can be constructed with a long exposure to an underlying asset and a protective put. The structured product in Exhibit 26.1a is easy to understand and easy to value since valuation of simple options is quite easy.

The exposure illustrated in Exhibit 26.1a can also be viewed as a cash-and-call strategy. A **cash-and-call strategy** is a long position in cash, or a zero-coupon bond, combined with a long position in a call option. The identity between a protective put strategy and a cash-and-call strategy is a straightforward implication of put-call parity, as discussed in Chapter 6. Thus, prices of the components of a structured product may often be related based on the put-call parity relationship.

☞ APPLICATION 26.3.1A

Consider a five-year zero-coupon cash-and-call position on the S&P 500 Index that has an initial cost of $1,000 and offers $1,000 principal protection (ignoring counterparty risk). The product's payout will be the greater of $1,000 and $1,000 × (1 + r), where r is the total return (non-annualized) of the underlying index over the five-year life of the product. If the riskless market interest is 5% (compounded annually), what is the value of the call option and the cash that replicates this product as a cash-and-call strategy (ignoring dividends)?

Assuming that the position is efficiently priced and that the riskless market interest rate is 5% (compounded annually), the present value of the minimum $1,000 payout is $783.53. Thus, the cash position at the start of the investment is $783.53. The remaining value of the structured product ($216.47) is attributable to the call option with a strike price of $1,000.

The structured product depicted in Exhibit 26.1a may be viewed and valued quite simply using simple options. However, the payoffs in Exhibits 26.1b and 26.1c contain exotic options, some of which may be very difficult to price.

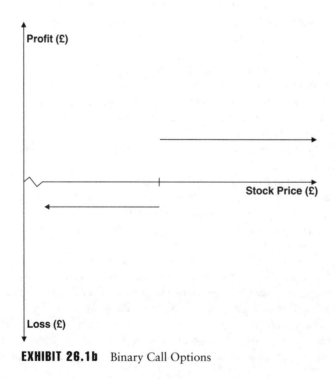

EXHIBIT 26.1b   Binary Call Options

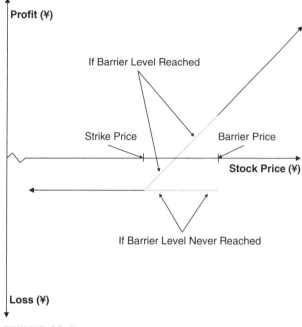

EXHIBIT 26.1c   Up-and-In Barrier Call Option

26.3.2   Structured Products and Asian Options

Some options have payoffs that depend on market values at multiple points in time. An **Asian option** is an option with a payoff that depends on the average price of an underlying asset through time.

Consider an Asian call option on oil prices that pays the greater of $X - K$ or zero, where X is the average market price of the underlying asset observed monthly over a one-year period and K is the strike price. A firm that uses oil every month can purchase this single option and, in so doing, can cap its average oil costs over the 12 months. The purchase of one Asian option is less expensive than the purchase of 12 monthly European options because it offers less protection. However, the protection offered by the Asian option might better fit the firm's desire to lock in a maximum average annual price of the oil purchases.

A **path-dependent option** is any option with a payoff that depends on the value of the underlying asset at points prior to the option's expiration date. An American option is a path-dependent option because the payoff from the option writer to the option holder can be affected by the values of the underlying asset prior to the option's expiration.

There are other options discussed in later sections, such as path-dependent options, that are more complex than Asian options. Note that just because an option has an average price as an underlier does not necessarily mean that the option should be characterized as an Asian option. The averaging process in an Asian option should be based on averaging prices through time. An option on the average price of two or more underlying assets at the same point in time does not typically qualify as an

Asian option. For example, an option on the average (non-annualized) return of 10 securities is not an Asian option; it is an option on a portfolio.

26.3.3   Structured Products and Binary Options

Binary options were introduced in Chapter 24 in the context of credit derivatives. In the case of credit options, a binary option provides two payoffs, contingent on whether a specified credit event occurs at any point in time over the life of the option.

The binary options in the structured products in this chapter are European options and are a little different. A binary option in a structured product has two potential payoffs, based on whether the value of the underlying asset is above or below the binary option's strike price at the option's expiration (i.e., at the termination of the structured product).

Exhibit 26.1b illustrates the upward jump in the payoff of a binary call option that occurs when the underlying asset's price exceeds the call option's strike price at the termination of the product. The diagram is discontinuous and is based solely on the final price of the underlier, as illustrated in Exhibit 26.1b. The discontinuous jump in the option price relative to the price of the underlying asset at the termination of the product is the key feature of a binary option. Other types of structured products or options, discussed later, offer large price jumps, but they do so either with multiple payoff levels or based on prices other than the price of the underlier at the termination of the product.

26.3.4   Structured Products and Barrier Options

Barrier options are a type of path-dependent option. Structured products often include barrier options. A **barrier option** is an option in which a change in the payoff is triggered if the underlying asset reaches a prespecified level during a prespecified time period. For example, a structured product that permanently loses principal protection if the underlying asset reaches a specified loss level contains a barrier option.

Barrier option features are either knock-in options or knock-out options. A **knock-in option** is an option that becomes active if and only if the underlying asset reaches a prespecified barrier. An **active option** in a barrier option is an option for which the underlying asset has reached the barrier and is therefore triggered as being in effect. Once a barrier option has become an active option, the option can affect the payoff without further need for the underlying asset to reach the barrier again. If the underlying asset price never reaches the barrier, then the option remains inactive and expires worthless. Knock-in options can be calls or puts, depending on whether it is a call or put that becomes active.

For example, consider a knock-in call option on an asset with a current price of $100 and a barrier of $110. If the underlying asset moves up and reaches the barrier ($110), the option becomes a simple active call option. Further, suppose that the option's strike price is $105. If the price of the underlying asset never reaches the barrier ($110), the option expires worthless. Thus, even if the underlying asset reaches $109 prior to expiration, the option holder receives no payoff if the $110 level was never reached. Once the barrier has been reached, the option will behave like a simple option with a payoff that is determined solely by the relationship between the price of the underlying asset and the strike price.

EXHIBIT 26.2 Barrier Calls and Puts

	Barrier > Underlier	Barrier < Underlier
Knock-in	Up-and-in call or put	Down-and-in call or put
Knock-out	Up-and-out call or put	Down-and-out call or put

26.3.5 Characteristics of In versus Out and Up versus Down Barrier Options

The option described in the preceding section is a type of knock-in option known as an up-and-in call option. It is an "up" option because the price of the underlying asset is less than the barrier price at inception, and therefore the underlying asset must move up in price for the option to have value. It is an "in" option because the option becomes active if the barrier is reached. It is a call option because the option that can become active is a call option.

A **knock-out option** is an option that becomes inactive (i.e., terminates) if and only if the underlying asset reaches a prespecified barrier. If the underlying asset price never reaches the barrier, then the option remains active and can be exercised at expiration. Knock-out options can be calls or puts and be issued as up or down options.

Exhibit 26.2 depicts eight types of options differentiated by being up/down, in/out, or call/put. The up-and-in call option is depicted in the upper left corner.

In the lower right corner of Exhibit 26.2 is a type of knock-out option known as a down-and-out put. A down-and-out put becomes inactive if the price of the underlying asset falls to the barrier. Thus, the payoff of the put is limited to the excess of the strike price (K) above the barrier (H). It is a "down" option because the price of the underlying asset is greater than the barrier price at inception, and, therefore, the underlying asset must move down in price to reach the barrier. It is an "out" option because the option becomes inactive if the barrier is reached. It is a put option because the option that can become inactive is a put option.

Note that a down-and-out put is not the same as a simple put option spread that is long a put with a strike price of K and short a put with a strike price of H (with $K > H$). The reason is that at expiration, the put spread will pay the greater of $K - H$ or zero. However, the down-and-out put will pay $K - H$ only if the barrier is never reached. If the barrier is reached at any time prior to expiration of the knock-out feature, the barrier put pays nothing.

Note that barrier options should always have values equal to or less than simple options of the same maturity and strike price, as barrier options can have the potential for an earlier expiration and lower payoff.

☞ **APPLICATION 26.3.5A**

An asset sells for $100. A European knock-in call option on that asset has a strike price of $110 and a barrier of $90. Describe the option using the terms in Exhibit 26.2 and describe that payoff under each of the folllowing scenarios:

(a) the asset moves monotonically to $120; (b) the asset declines monotonically to $89 before rising monotonically to $110 at expiration.

Answer: The option is a down-and-in call option. It pays nothing under scenario (a) because the option never knocks in; it pays nothing under scenario (b) because although the option becomes active, it does not finish in-the-money.

Exhibit 26.1c illustrates the payoff diagram of a barrier option. Notice that the payoff is no longer purely a function of the value of the underlier at option expiration. Over some of the range, the payoff to the option can take on one of two values depending on the path that the underlier took. Specifically, one path is based on the underlier not having reached the barrier, and the other is based on the underlier having reached the barrier.

Structured products with path-dependent options tend to have complex payout diagrams that capture the paths through multiple payout lines based on conditions related to the paths, as shown in Exhibit 26.1c.

26.3.6 Structured Products and Spread Options

A **spread option** has a payoff that depends on the difference between two prices or two rates, such as the price (or rate) of asset #1 minus the price (or rate) of asset #2. The option's payoff is the greater of zero and the underlying spread less the option's strike price (or strike rate) at expiration. *Note:* A spread option should not be confused with option spreads, discussed in Chapter 6, which are portfolios with multiple call or put positions.

Consider, for example, a one-year European spread call option with a strike price (or strike rate) of 2% on the difference of the percentage return of a large-cap equity index over the percentage return of a small-cap equity index. Assume that at the end of the year, the large-cap index has risen 10% and the small-cap index has risen 4%. Accordingly, the spread between the returns is +6%. A spread call with a strike price of 2% would pay 4% (of the option's notional value) to its holder. A call spread option pays its holder when the spread exceeds the strike, whereas a put spread option pays its holder when the spread is less than the strike. A spread put with a strike price of 2% in this example would expire worthless.

Note that the spread between two assets may be represented as either asset #1 minus asset #2 or the reverse, asset #2 minus asset #1. A call spread with a strike of K is identical to a put spread with a strike of $-K$ if the definition of the spread on the put is the reverse of the definition of the spread on the call.

☞ **APPLICATION 26.3.6A**

Consider two indices: a gold index and a copper index. Consider a European option that pays 0% if the gold index has performance equal to or better than −2% relative to the copper index. For each percentage point that the gold index return is worse than 2% below the copper index, the option pays 1% of its notional value. Describe the type of option and its strike price in terms of both calls and puts

Answer: The option is a spread option. In the case of a spread put, the strike price of the put is −2%, and the spread is defined as the performance of the gold index less the performance of the copper index. In the case of a spread call, the strike price of the call is +2%, and the spread is defined as the performance of the copper index less the performance of the gold index.

26.3.7 Structured Products and Look-Back Options

Another type of path-dependent option is a look-back option. A **look-back option** has a payoff based on a minimum or maximum price that occurs over a specified period of time (the look-back period). Typically, the look-back period is the entire life of the option. An in-the-money look-back call pays the maximum price over the look-back period minus the strike price. An in-the-money look-back put pays the strike price minus the minimum price over the look-back period.

26.3.8 Quantos and Other Structured Products

The spectrum of structured products provided by issuers throughout the world to meet investor preferences is astounding. An example of a very specialized option is a quanto. A **quanto option** is an option with a payoff based in one currency using the numerical value of the underlying asset expressed in a different currency. For example, the Nikkei 225 is a yen-based index of Japanese stock prices. Consider a U.S. dollar–based quanto call option on the Nikkei with a strike price of 17,000 issued when the Nikkei 225 was at 16,000. This quanto call option on the Nikkei 225 would pay $1 for every point by which the Nikkei 225 exceeded 17,000 at the option's expiration.

The preceding discussions have covered some of the major categories of exotic options used in structured products, but other option-driven products exist. For example, some advanced structured products have payouts that depend on the prices of a set of underlying assets. The payouts to these structured products can involve valuations at a variety of points in time (e.g., quarterly over the product's life), resulting in payouts related to some of the underlying asset values being capped or frozen at each valuation point, and payouts related to the remaining underlying assets being allowed to continue to vary until the option's expiration.

26.4 POPULAR STRUCTURED PRODUCT TYPES

A popular class of structured products offers payouts based on absolute returns. An **absolute return structured product** offers payouts over some or all underlying asset returns that are equal to the absolute value of the underlying asset's returns. Thus, whether the underlier rises 2% or declines 2%, the structured product pays +2%.

The core concept of an absolute return structured product is easily replicated in the options market with an at-the-money straddle (see Chapter 6). In the case of a long option straddle, the option buyer pays a price or premium to establish the straddle, makes money if the underlying asset makes a large directional move, and loses money if the underlying asset does not move substantially. In the case of a structured product based on absolute returns, the benefit to the investor of gaining from large moves in either direction must be offset by features that benefit the issuer.

A **principal protected absolute return barrier note** offers to pay absolute returns to the investor if the underlying asset stays within both an upper barrier and a lower barrier over the life of the product. If the underlying asset reaches either barrier, the payout is equal to the principal of the product. Note that as a path-dependent option, the underlying asset may lie inside the barriers at the termination of the structured product but fail to produce absolute returns if its path reached a barrier.

If the barriers are placed 5% from the initial value of the underlier, the principal protected absolute return barrier note would pay the absolute return of the underlier if the barrier was not reached, or 0% if the barrier was reached. This structured product can be replicated as a long straddle position in exotic options (knock-out options):

$$\text{Product} = +\text{At-the-Money Up-and-Out Call}$$
$$+ \text{At-the-Money Down-and-Out Put}$$

By placing this product into an individual savings account, many UK investors can enjoy tax-free distributions of any profits.

Many structured products are listed and are therefore liquid alternatives. For example, in the United States, there are numerous structured products issued by major institutions that trade on the New York Stock Exchange.

A disadvantage of a liquid structured product is that it must be standardized in terms of maturity, participation rates, principal protection, and so forth, in order to attract numerous investors; however, some investors may prefer a structured product that is tailored to their individual preferences. The advantage of a liquid structured product to an investor is not only that the product can be sold through the listing market but also that its price and its price volatility can be observed through time.

Interestingly, although many structured products in the United States continue to be registered with the SEC, the proportion of these products actually being listed has diminished in recent years. Apparently the benefits of listing are not perceived as being worth the costs, yet the products are standardized and registered so that they can be marketed to a wider audience.

26.5 THE EUSIPA CLASSIFICATION

Structured products include a wide spectrum of offerings throughout the world that are difficult to categorize precisely. However, the EUSIPA has developed a valuable categorization that is partly summarized in this section. The **EUSIPA** (European Structured Investment Products Association) was founded in 2009 as a nonprofit association "to promote the interests of the structured retail investment products market." The EUSIPA publishes the **EUSIPA Derivative Map,** which categorizes structured products with two major classifications: investment products and leverage products. The **Investment Products in the EUSIPA Derivative Map** includes three major sub-categories: capital protection products, yield enhancement products, and participation products. The next four subsections of this chapter briefly overview the three investment products' sub-categories and the leverage products category.

26.5.1 Capital Protection Structured Products

The EUSIPA Derivative Map (May 2016) has five capital protection structured products, four of which are illustrated in Exhibit 26.3. In each diagram, the payoff of the structured product (the thicker, kinked line) is overlaid on the payoff of the product's underlying asset (the thinner, straight line). The underlying asset is often an equity index. **Capital protection structured products** tend to offer long call-option-like payoffs: downside protection, upside potential, and below-market interest income.

Note that the uncapped capital protection product offers great downside protection but has a less attractive upside potential than the equity index. Specifically, investors in this product gain only a portion of any profits generated by the underlying asset (i.e., they have a participation rate of less than 100%). The exchangeable certificates offer downside protection and a 100% participation rate for profits, but the participation in profits does not take effect until there has been a prespecified increase in the value of the underlying index. The capped capital protection and

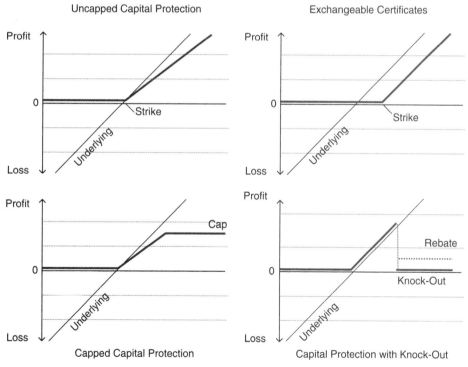

EXHIBIT 26.3 Four Capital Protection Structured Products
Source: EUSIPA Derivative Map (May 2016).

capital protection structured products with a knock-out shown on the bottom of Exhibit 26.3 also offer only a portion of any upside profits generated by the underlying asset.

The full downside protection (principal protection) and the partial upside participation are the two key attributes to the four capital structured products in Exhibit 26.3 and form an important concept discussed in greater detail at the end of the chapter: Issuers of these types of structured products cannot earn competitive rates of return by offering products that guarantee investors uniformly superior payoffs, such as full upside participation with no downside risk. Some structured products, such as collateralized loan obligations in which the issuing institution (e.g., a bank) is gaining advantages such as freeing up regulatory capital, may be willing to offer attractive returns to investors who purchase the loans. The equity-linked structured products discussed in this chapter are issued to provide compensation to the issuer for creating products that investors perceive as enhancing their expected utility.

In essence, capital protection structured products are similar to long call options. The buyer usually compensates the issuer for this call option by accepting little or no interest income on the buyer's investment. To varying extents, investing in these products is similar to purchasing call options through the sacrifice of current income.

26.5.2 Two Yield Enhancement Structured Products

The EUSIPA Derivative Map (May 2016) has seven yield enhancement structured products, two of which are illustrated in Exhibit 26.4. **Yield enhancement structured products** tend to offer short put-option-like payoffs with full downside exposure, capped upside potential, and above-market interest income (i.e., yield enhancement).

Note that the discount certificate payoff diagram is identical to a short put option. However, the barrier discount certificate has a range that contains two potential payoffs: one in the case that a barrier is reached (the horizontal solid line) and one in the case that the barrier is not reached (the dotted line). Barrier options are a common component of complex structured products.

26.5.3 Two Participation Structured Products

The EUSIPA Derivative Map (May 2016) has five participation structured products, two of which are illustrated in Exhibit 26.5. **Participation structured products** tend to

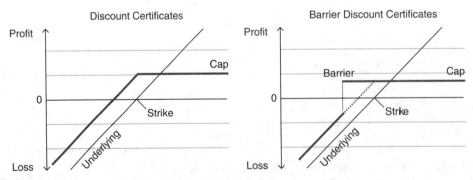

EXHIBIT 26.4 Two Yield Enhancement Structured Products
Source: EUSIPA Derivative Map (May 2016).

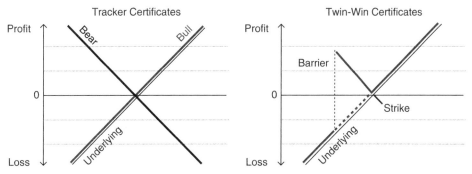

EXHIBIT 26.5 Participation Structured Products
Source: EUSIPA Derivative Map (May 2016).

offer exposures (bull or bear) to the underlying index (or assets) that are not capped in terms of potential profits or losses (i.e., in either the bull or bear scenarios). Therefore, participation structured products differ from capital protection products (that tend to be long call options) or yield enhancement products (that tend to be short put options).

The tracker certificates depicted on the left side of Exhibit 26.5 offer full exposures—bull or bear—to the underlier. The purpose for a buyer to use this tracker product rather than simply establish a long or short position directly in the cash market for the index may be to obtain the exposures inside one of the various wrappers discussed earlier in this chapter.

The twin-win certificates on the right side of Exhibit 26.5 offer absolute return exposures over a limited range similar to a long position in an option straddle. As with many other long-option-like structured products, the cost of the long option will be embedded in the product through reduced income.

26.5.4 Four Leverage Structured Products

The EUSIPA Derivative Map (May 2016) has seven leverage structured products, four of which are illustrated in Exhibit 26.6. **Leverage structured products** have three subcategories: leverage without knock-outs, leverage with knock-outs, and constant leverage. They tend to offer exotic exposures that do not fit neatly in the map's investment structured product categories.

The top two products in Exhibit 26.6 use knock-outs to create limits to profits and losses, thereby providing targeted exposures over limited ranges of the underlier. The leverage product in the lower left corner depicts offerings of bull spreads and bear spreads, whereas the bottom right corner product depicts pure leveraged products that offer participation rates (bull or bear) in excess of 100%.

This brief survey of types of structured products demonstrates the tremendous variety of exposures available. It should be noted that actual products are often far more complex than the exposures discussed in this section. The structured products focused on the retail market are designed by issuers to meet the preferences, predictions—and, some would argue, behavioral biases—of non-institutional investors. With the tremendous spectrum of risk exposures available, and perhaps with the high degree of complexity, at least some of the products would appear to be attractive to any investor with a "market view." Unfortunately, that market view may

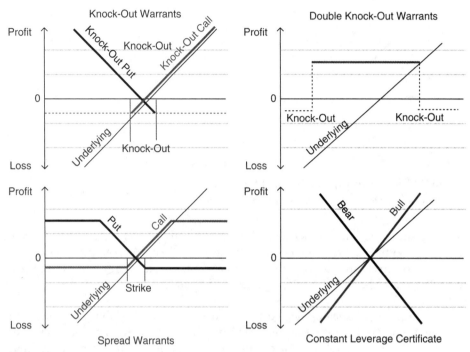

EXHIBIT 26.6 Leverage Structured Products
Source: EUSIPA Derivative Map (May 2016).

emanate more from an emotional reaction to the casual observation of recent market performance than from sound economic reasoning and sound analysis of long-term historical data.

26.6 GLOBAL STRUCTURED PRODUCT CASES

This section describes three stylized products abstracted from descriptions of actual products that have been offered throughout the world. The descriptions are not intended to be precise specifications of the actual products issued by a particular institution but simplified illustrations of the spectrum of structured products available. Also, the geographic location attributed to each product is not intended to suggest that the particular product is more highly available in that jurisdiction or not available in the other jurisdictions. Rather, the cases are presented to indicate the diversity of regions and types of structured products. Generally, most structured products are issued in and available within most jurisdictions.

26.6.1 A U.S.-Based Structured Product with Multiple Kinks

This product is a hypothetical example based on some of the properties of a product offered by MetLife, a major U.S. insurance company. The product has an annuity wrapper from an insurance company. An investor can choose an underlying asset from a set of indices, including a broad U.S. equity index, a small-cap index, an international equity index, and a commodity index. The investor also selects a maturity term of one, three, or six years. The payout to the contract depends on the performance of the index over the contract term. The distinguishing feature of the structuring is that the payout diagram has kinks at up to three price levels, based on a cap and a floor that can be selected by the investor from a set of available values. A kink may be viewed as the location in a payoff diagram where the slope changes.

The investor may be viewed as first selecting a partial floor of $x\%$. The floor is termed here as "partial" because the issuer covers only the first $x\%$ of losses if the index experiences a decline at the end of the term. For losses beyond $x\%$, the investor is at risk (unless the investor selects $x\% = 100\%$ protection). Thus, if $x\% = 10\%$, the investor breaks even if the index has losses smaller than 10%. If the index declines by more than 10%, say 35%, the investor loses the excess of the losses beyond 10% (in this instance, 25%).

Based on the investor's other choices and market conditions, the issuer will impose a cap on profits. For example, a product on the S&P 500 Index with a partial loss floor of 10% and a term of three years might offer a cap of 20%. The cap determines the maximum possible payout. Suppose that at the end of the three-year term, the S&P 500 has experienced a capital gain or loss of $r\%$. Here is the payout of the hypothetical product with a partial loss floor of 10% and a cap of 20%:

$$-100\% < r \leq -10\% \qquad \text{Return payout} = r + 10\%$$
$$-10\% < r \leq 0\% \qquad \text{Return payout} = 0\%$$
$$0\% < r \leq 20\% \qquad \text{Return payout} = r$$
$$r > 20\% \qquad \text{Return payout} = 20\%$$

The product offers investors an ability to tailor their investment as a trade-off between loss protection (the partial floor) and limited profit potential (the cap). The product can be replicated in theory with European options and therefore, despite its complexity, it does not contain exotic options:

Product = Underlying Asset + Bear Put Spread − Out-of-the-Money Call

By placing this product in an insurance wrapper, U.S. residents are able to enjoy tax deferral of any gains until the investor receives distributions from the insurance plan.

26.6.2 A German-Based Structured Product with Leverage

The product discussed in this section is a hypothetical example based on some of the properties of a similar product offered in Germany. According to Deutsche Bank Research, certificates are wrappers that offer low trading costs, liquidity, versatile structures, and permanent bid and offer quotes by issuers.[2]

The spectrum of products offered in Germany rivals those of other jurisdictions. As an example, a Sprint product combines a long position in an underlying asset with a long call option position at a relatively low strike price that provides upside leverage (e.g., a double participation rate of 200%). The product's double upside protection is capped via short call positions at a relatively high strike price. The result is a somewhat collar-like payoff diagram that offers leveraged participation over a prespecified range but with limited profit potential at very high values:

$$\text{Product} = \text{Underlying Asset} + \text{Bull Spread}$$

By placing this product in a certificate wrapper, investors may be able to enjoy a substantial degree of liquidity and low trading costs.

26.6.3 A Japan-Based Structured Product Based on Multiple Currencies

Japan's Nomura Securities is part of the Nomura Group, which includes world-class investment and banking activities. Major world financial services firms, including Nomura Securities, offer structured products based on foreign exchange rates and interest rate differentials between currencies.

Consider a power reverse dual-currency note. At its core, in a **power reverse dual-currency note** (PRDC), an investor pays a fixed interest rate in one currency in exchange for receiving a payment based on a fixed interest rate in another currency. However, the payment that the investor receives is increased or decreased proportionately as the exchange rate between the two currencies changes. For example, if the exchange rate during the life of the note rises to 1.25 from an exchange rate of 1.00 at the inception of the note, the cash payments received by the investor will be changed by the same proportion (25%). Typically, the deal includes various option features, such as caps and floors. For example, the issuer may structure the deal so that any net cash flow of payments from the investor to the issuer is limited.

From the perspective of the investor, the structured product allows for a leveraged carry trade in which the investor attempts to benefit from receiving higher coupon payments than the investor is paying. The product would, therefore, be attractive to an observer of interest rate differentials between nations who believes they will persist and thus generate benefits that will not be offset by changes in exchange rates.

26.7 STRUCTURED PRODUCT VALUATION

This section begins by describing three methods of valuing structured products. The approaches to the estimation of structured product values follow the approaches used to value many complex derivatives.

26.7.1 Valuing Structured Products Using Dynamic Hedging

Structured products are often valued using the dynamic hedging approach. In the dynamic hedging approach, a portfolio consisting of the structured product and its underlying asset is created. **Dynamic hedging** alters the portfolio weights through time to maintain a desired risk exposure, such as zero risk. The dynamics of this risk-free portfolio are often represented by partial differential equations; therefore, this approach is also referred to as the partial differential equation approach. The **partial differential equation approach (PDE approach)** finds the value to a financial derivative based on the assumption that the underlying asset follows a specified stochastic process and that a hedged portfolio can be constructed using a combination of the derivative and its underlying asset(s).

An example of a dynamically hedged portfolio is a long position in a stock that is initially hedged by a short position in four units of the call options on that stock when the delta of the call option is 0.25. As the delta of the call option continuously changes through time, the number of short calls must be continuously changed to maintain the hedge. Thus, if the delta fell to 0.20 or rose to 0.50, the option hedge would be adjusted to being short five calls or short two calls, respectively.

The PDE approach can be illustrated through a simple example. Consider a riskless security in a world of fixed and certain interest rates. The riskless security is a zero-coupon bond that pays F at time T. The first step is to express the change in the value of the riskless security. Since it is riskless, the change in price would be equal to the value of the security (P) times the periodic interest rate, which can be factored to produce the following ordinary differential equation:

$$dP/dt = rP$$

The fact that the value of the bond must be F at time T is a boundary condition. A **boundary condition** of a derivative is a known relationship regarding the value of that derivative at some future point in time that can be used to generate a solution to the derivative's current value. The boundary condition combined with the mathematics of ordinary differential equations generates the following solution to the price of the bond, P, at time t:

$$P = Fe^{-r(T-t)}$$

In a similar fashion, the PDE approach uses one or more boundary values and a differential equation to generate a price model. There are two major differences between the actual PDE approach and the previous simple example: (1) The PDE approach uses partial differential equations that are based on changes in two factors, time and the price of the underlying asset; and (2) the PDE approach requires construction of a riskless portfolio. Note that in the simplified example, the bond itself was riskless, and hence there was no need to construct a riskless hedge.

Partial differential equations are based on continuous-time mathematics. By specifying the relationship between the changes in two or more variables through time, one can derive a functional relationship between their levels. The PDE approach (1) relates the stochastic process followed by an option to the process followed by its underlying asset, (2) constructs a riskless portfolio by combining the derivative and its underlying asset, and (3) solves for the price of the derivative by setting the return of the riskless portfolio to r and imposing boundary conditions.[3]

In the case of a simple European option, Black and Scholes derived an analytic solution in the form of the well-known Black-Scholes option pricing model, in which the option price is a simple function of five underlying variables. The boundary conditions are that the call price is zero when S (the price of the underlying stock) is zero; the call price approaches infinity as S approaches infinity; and the value of the call option at expiration is max$\{S - K, 0\}$, where K is the strike price. The solution is **analytical** because the model can be exactly solved using a finite set of common mathematical operations. In the case of the Black-Scholes option pricing model, the solution is analytical because the option's price is a relatively simple function of five underlying variables.

Complex options and complex structured products often lack an analytical solution. Cases involving complex underlying stochastic processes or numerous boundary conditions often require solutions through numerical methods. **Numerical methods for derivative pricing** are potentially complex sets of procedures to approximate derivative values when analytical solutions are unavailable. Numerical methods can be difficult. Solutions to derivative values are often estimated using the methods discussed in the following two sections: simulation and building blocks.

26.7.2 Valuing Structured Products with Simulation

A powerful and popular approach to valuing complex financial positions is Monte Carlo simulation, introduced and discussed in Chapter 7. Consider a complex structured product with possible payouts that depend on the values of two or more underlying assets at various points in time through the product's life.

A solution to the value of such a complex product using the PDE approach may be intractable. However, it is relatively easy to estimate the product's value if the potential paths of the underlying assets can be reasonably estimated.

As a simplified example, a very large number of projected paths for the value of an asset could be formed under the assumption that its price followed a particular stochastic process. The assumed process is simulated under the assumption that investors are risk neutral. For example, while simulating the behavior of a common stock, the mean return of the process is set equal to the risk-free rate. The payoffs of a derivative on that asset could then be projected for each path. The discounted values of the derivative payoffs for each path could then be averaged to form an estimate of the current value for the derivative. Since the underlying asset is simulated under risk neutrality, the structured product's average payoff is discounted using the risk-free rate. The simulation approach can be a conceptually simple method of estimating the value of complex derivatives and complex structured products when analytical solutions are unavailable and numerical methods are complex.

26.7.3 Valuing Structured Products with Building Blocks

The **building blocks approach** (i.e., portfolio approach) models a structured product or other derivatives by replicating the investment as the sum of two or more simplified assets, such as underlying cash-market securities and simple options. The value of the structured product is simply the sum of the values of its building blocks. The value of each building block is in turn estimated through observation of market prices or well-known derivative pricing equations (e.g., option pricing models).

The primary distinction between the building blocks approach and the dynamic hedging approach (PDE approach) is that the portfolio weights are regularly and dynamically adjusted to maintain the desired risk exposure in PDE.

In the building blocks approach, portfolios are formed using a static hedge. A **static hedge** is when the positions in the portfolio do not need to be adjusted through time in response to stochastic price changes to maintain a hedge. For example, a static hedge approach can be used to value a European put option using a portfolio of three assets: the underlying asset, a European call option with the same maturity and strike price as the put that is being valued, and a riskless bond. As indicated in previous chapters, put-call parity establishes that a short position in the stock, a long position in the call option, and a long position in a riskless bond will replicate the return from holding the put option. Note that the key to the building block approach is that the value of the portfolio at some horizon point (e.g., expiration of the options) will be equal to the value of the derivative that is being analyzed regardless of what happens to the values of the securities used to create the static hedge.

In practice, the building block positions necessary to replicate a complex structured product perfectly may not be available or may not be trading at informationally efficient values.

26.7.4 Two Principles from Payoff Diagram Shapes and Levels

Exhibit 26.1 illustrates a few of the many different payoff shapes that structured products offer. The **payoff diagram** *shape* indicates the risk exposure of a product relative to an underlier. The shape of the payoff diagram can be analyzed by investors to ascertain the extent to which the product's payoffs align with the investor's risk preferences or the investor's market view of the return distribution of the underlying asset.

Exhibit 26.1 does not indicate the *level* of the payoff diagram relative to the cost of the product.[4] The **payoff diagram level** determines the amount of money or the percentage return that an investor can anticipate in exchange for paying the price of the product. Thus, the investor can use the level of the payoff diagram relative to the cost of the product to estimate whether the product is attractively or unattractively priced.

Principle 1 is that any payoff diagram shape can be constructed given a sufficient availability of options. In other words, any relationship between a portfolio of options and a related asset can be engineered if there are sufficient derivatives with which to manage the exposure. Slopes can be mimicked using calls and puts; discontinuous jumps can be mimicked using binary options.

Principle 2 is that it is the level of the payoff diagram that dictates whether the product is overpriced, underpriced, or appropriately priced. In other words, the vertical level of the payoff diagram drives the relative magnitudes of the profits and losses; therefore, it is the level of the payoffs that determines the attractiveness of an exposure in terms of prospective returns.

The enormous spectrum of structured products available enables investors to locate products that best meet their preferences regarding risk (the shape of the payoff diagram). If an investor's market view turns out to be correct, then the variety of structured products serves the purpose of enabling the investor to better achieve attractive returns or other financial goals.

However, the enormous spectrum of structured products available can also play into the investor's behavioral biases. In other words, an investor analyzing a very large number of diverse structured products may substantially overestimate the value of some products and underestimate the value of other products. The spectrum of available products may lead an investor with behavioral biases into taking otherwise undesirable risks if the investor falsely believes that a particular product is underpriced. For example, investors subject to the behavioral trait known as overconfidence bias will tend to overweight structured products that appear underpriced based on the investor's market view even when those products are overpriced due to high fees. An **overconfidence bias** is a tendency to overestimate the true accuracy of one's beliefs and predictions.

26.7.5 Evidence on Structured Product Prices

A key issue in complex structured products is whether the prices at which the investments are issued are fair. In other words, how do the actual prices of the products compare with the estimated prices of the products using market-based valuation methods? The high degree of complexity in some structured products makes valuation challenging and subject to discretion.

Deng and others examine the issue price of principal protected absolute return barrier notes (ARBNs) and find that the fair price of ARBNs "is approximately 4.5% below the actual issue price on average."[5]

A white paper by McCann and Luo estimates that "between 15% and 20% of the premium paid by investors in equity-linked annuities is a transfer of wealth from unsophisticated investors to insurance companies and their sales forces."[6]

Some industry sources point to lower fees for some products than those indicated by the previously cited empirical analyses of particular products. For example, in the Bank of Scotland's *A Guide to Structured Products*, the "total fees & expenses" component (i.e., building block) of its structured products is listed as representing 2% to 3% of the product's price.[7]

26.8 MOTIVATIONS OF STRUCTURED PRODUCTS

Chapters 23 and 25 listed a total of six investor motivations for structured products. Those six motivations are repeated in Exhibit 26.7, followed by two additional motivations.

The seventh motivation in Exhibit 26.7 involves the investor's income taxes. As discussed earlier in this chapter, investment wrappers can have an effect on after-tax returns. In many jurisdictions, capital gain investment income is taxed at a lower rate than are other forms of income and in some jurisdictions long-term capital gains are not taxed at all for individual investors. Structured products can reduce the effective tax rates (i.e., increase the tax efficiency of the investment) in many circumstances by structuring cash flows such that the investor's income is directed toward preferred classifications and away from undesirable classifications.

Some jurisdictions impose taxes on transactions. For example, in the United Kingdom, there is a Stamp Duty Reserve Tax (SDRT) imposed on share transactions at a rate of 0.5%, which is paid by both residents and nonresidents. Structured products can be designed to mitigate some transaction taxes, the eighth motivation in Exhibit 26.7.

1. Risk management: Investors may be better able to manage risk through structured products.
2. Return enhancement: Investors may be better able to establish positions that will enhance returns if the investor's market view is superior.
3. Diversification: Investors may be better able to achieve diversification through structured products.
4. Relaxing regulatory constraints: Investors may be able to use CDO structures to circumvent restrictions from regulations.
5. Access to superior management: Investors may obtain efficient access to any superior investment skills of the manager of the CDO.
6. Liquidity enhancement: Tranches of CDOs can be more liquid than the underlying collateral pool.
7. Income tax efficiency.
8. Transaction tax efficiency.

EXHIBIT 26.7 Investor Motivations for Structured Products

A primary investor motivation of the structured products discussed in this chapter is the ability of structuring to make additional investment opportunities available to an investor. Chapter 23 details the ability of structured products to complete the market, or more precisely, to reduce the level of market incompleteness. Equity-linked structured products enable investors to achieve otherwise unavailable combinations of risk and return.

This investor motivation to structured products enables efficient access of investors to otherwise unavailable exposures. For example, structured products can be engineered to help investors tailor their exposures to match their market views.

Up to this point, the discussion of motivations has generally focused on the motivations of investors in structured products. The motivations of the issuers of structured products tend to focus on fee revenue and profitability. However, other motivations exist. Some issuers can issue uncollateralized structured products as a source of financing. To some issuers, structured products may offer lower financing costs, preferable risk exposures, or preferable maturities. For example, Chapter 25 on CDOs details the benefits of balance sheet CDOs, through which institutions can divest assets to free regulatory capital.[8]

REVIEW QUESTIONS

1. List the six primary types of structured product wrappers.
2. What can cause the after-tax rate of return of a product with tax deferral and tax deduction to be higher than the after-tax rate of return of an otherwise identical product with tax deferral only?
3. What does a participation rate indicate in a structured product?
4. How does a long position in an up-and-in call differ from a short position in a down-and-out put?
5. What is the name of an option that offers a payoff in a currency based on the numerical value of an underlying asset with a price that is expressed in another currency?

6. What simple option portfolio mimics the payoff to an absolute return structured product?
7. List the three major approaches to estimating the value of a highly complex structured product.
8. Describe the difference between an analytical solution and a solution estimated with numerical methods.
9. In an informationally efficient market, can a structured product be engineered to offer both any payoff diagram shape and any payoff diagram level?
10. Briefly summarize the evidence on whether the offering prices of structured products are overpriced or underpriced relative to the values of similar exposures composed of market-traded products.

NOTES

1. BNP Paribas, *BNP Paribas Equities & Derivatives Structured Products Handbook*, London 2010.
2. Deutsche Bank Research, "Retail Certificates: A German Success Story," *EU Monitor* 43 (March 19, 2007).
3. Candidates wishing to explore the PDE approach further may be interested in the following material: To value a derivative, V, using the PDE approach, the underlying asset, S, is often assumed to be a stochastic process with instantaneous returns subject to a normally distributed random process. Ito's formula is used to derive a stochastic process for V, knowing that V is a function of S. A risk-free portfolio containing the derivative and the underlying asset is formed, and its return can be set equal to the riskless rate, r:

$$d(v + \Delta s)/dt = r \times (V + \Delta S)$$

This equation indicates that a portfolio consisting of one unit of the derivative and delta (Δ) units of the underlying asset earns the riskless return, r, on the investment required $(V + \Delta S)$. Relating the evolution of V to the process followed by S creates the following PDE, which can lead to a solution for the value of the derivative, V, once appropriate boundary conditions are imposed.

$$\frac{\partial V}{\partial t} + rS\frac{\partial V}{\partial S} + \frac{\sigma^2}{2}\frac{\partial^2 V}{\partial S^2} - rV = 0$$

4. The diagrams do not indicate the option price (cost) relative to the strike price.
5. Geng Deng, Ilan Guedj, Craig J. McCann, and Joshua Mallett, "The Anatomy of Principal Protected Absolute Return Notes," *Journal of Derivatives* 19, no. 2 (2011): 61–70.
6. Craig J. McCann and Dengpan Luo, "An Overview of Equity-Indexed Annuities," Securities Litigation & Consulting Group, June 2006.
7. Bank of Scotland, "A Guide to Structured Products," January 2012, https://www.bankofscotland.co.uk/sharedealing/filestore/BoS_Guide_to_Structured_Products.pdf.
8. The CAIA Association deeply appreciates comments and suggestions from Paolo Piccitto that were used in the revision of this chapter.

Index

Bold page numbers indicate keyword definitions or explanations.